The
LEGAL
ENVIRONMENT
of BUSINESS

TEXT AND CASES

Eleventh Edition

Frank B. Cross

Herbert D. Kelleher
Centennial Professor in Business Law
University of Texas at Austin

Roger LeRoy Miller

Institute for University Studies
Arlington, Texas

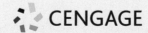 CENGAGE

Australia • Brazil • Mexico • Singapore • United Kingdom • United States

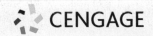

The Legal Environment of Business
Text and Cases, Eleventh Edition
Frank B. Cross
Roger LeRoy Miller

Senior Vice President, Higher Education Product Management: Erin Joyner

Vice President, Product Management: Mike Schenk

Senior Product Team Manager: Joe Sabatino

Senior Product Managers: Vicky True-Baker, Michael Giffen

Senior Content Managers: Martha Conway, Julia Chase

Learning Designers: Sarah Huber, Courtney Wolstoncroft

Subject Matter Expert: Lisa Elliott

Digital Delivery Leads: Jennifer Chinn, Stephen McMillian

Product Assistants: Christian Wood, Nick Perez

Marketing Director: Kimberly Kanakes

Marketing Manager: Andrew Stock

Marketing Coordinator: Rachel Treinen

Project Manager: Ann Borman

Manufacturing Planner: Kevin Kluck

Inventory Analyst: Alister Santos

Senior IP Director: Julie Geagan-Chavez

IP Analyst: Ashley Maynard

IP Project Manager: Carly Belcher

Art Director: Creative Studio

Cover Designer: Chris Doughman

Interior Designer: Harasymczuk Design

Design Elements: Linen texture: Lisa-Blue/iStockphoto; justice scales: imagedb.com/Shutterstock

For product information and technology assistance, contact us at
Cengage Customer & Sales Support, 1-800-354-9706
or **support.cengage.com.**

For permission to use material from this text or product, submit all requests online at **www.cengage.com/permissions.**

Library of Congress Control Number: 2019910524

Hardcover Edition:
ISBN: 978-0-357-12976-0

Loose-leaf Edition:
ISBN: 978-0-357-12983-8

Cengage
200 Pier 4 Boulevard
Boston, MA 02210
USA

Cengage is a leading provider of customized learning solutions with employees residing in nearly 40 different countries and sales in more than 125 countries around the world. Find your local representative at: **www.cengage.com.**

Cengage products are represented in Canada by Nelson Education, Ltd.

To learn more about Cengage platforms and services, register or access your online learning solution, or purchase materials for your course, visit **www.cengage.com.**

Printed in the United States of America
Print Number: 01   Print Year: 2019

Brief Contents

Appendices

Contents

Concept Summaries

Exhibits

Preface

The study of the legal environment of business has universal applicability. A student entering any field of business must have at least a passing understanding of the legal environment in order to function in the real world. *The Legal Environment of Business,* Eleventh Edition, provides the information that students need in an interesting and contemporary way.

Additionally, students preparing for a career in accounting, government and political science, economics, and even medicine can use much of the information they learn in a legal environment course. In fact, every individual throughout his or her lifetime can benefit from knowledge of contracts, employment law, intellectual property rights, real property, and other legal environment topics. Consequently, we have fashioned this text as a useful "tool for living" for all of your students (including those taking the CPA exam).

The Eleventh Edition of this text is more modern, exciting, and visually appealing than ever before. We have added new features, cases, concept summaries, and exhibits. The text also contains hundreds of highlighted and numbered *Cases in Point* and *Examples,* as well as new case problems and unit-ending *Task-Based Simulations.* Special pedagogical elements within the text focus on legal, ethical, global, and corporate issues while addressing core curriculum requirements.

Highlights of the Eleventh Edition

Instructors have come to rely on the coverage, accuracy, and applicability of *The Legal Environment of Business.* To make sure that our text engages your students, solidifies their understanding of legal concepts, and provides the best teaching tools available, we offer the following.

The IDDR Approach: A New Emphasis on Ethics

The ability of businesspersons to reason through ethical issues is now more important than ever. For the Eleventh Edition of *The Legal Environment of Business,* we have created a completely new framework for helping students

(and businesspersons) make ethical decisions. We present **The IDDR Approach** in Chapter 3 (Ethics in Business). This systematic approach provides students with a clear step-by-step process to analyze the legal and ethical implications of decisions that arise in everyday business operations.

The new IDDR Approach uses four logical steps:
- **STEP 1: Inquiry**
- **STEP 2: Discussion**
- **STEP 3: Decision**
- **STEP 4: Review**

Students can remember the first letter of each step easily by using the phrase: "I Desire to Do Right."

Completely Revised Chapter 3 on Ethics in Business A newly revised Chapter 3 details each IDDR step's goals and then provides a Sample Scenario to help students apply this new approach to ethical decision making. In addition to introducing the IDDR Approach, we have made Chapter 3 more current and more practical, and reduced the amount of theoretical ethical principles it presents. The chapter now focuses on real-life application of ethical principles.

New *A Question of Ethics* Case Problems throughout Text After Chapter 3, to reinforce the application of the IDDR Approach, students are asked to use its various steps when answering each chapter's *A Question of Ethics.* To challenge students in analyzing the ethical angles in today's business legal environment, we have replaced every *A Question of Ethics* problem throughout the text to be based on a 2017, 2018, or 2019 case.

A Variety of Exciting Features

The Eleventh Edition of *The Legal Environment of Business* is filled with numerous features specifically designed to cover current legal topics of high interest.

Each feature is related to a topic discussed in the text and ends with *Critical Thinking* or *Business Questions.* Suggested answers to all of the *Critical Thinking* and *Business Questions* are included in the *Answers Manual* for this text.

1. ***Ethics Today.*** These features focus on the ethical aspects of a topic discussed in the text to emphasize that ethics is an integral part of a legal environment of business course. Examples include the following:

   - Applying the IDDR Framework (Chapter 3)
   - Is It Ethical (and Legal) to Brew "Imported" Beer Brands Domestically? (Chapter 11)
   - Should There Be More Relief for Student Loan Defaults? (Chapter 15)
   - Is It Fair to Classify Uber and Lyft Drivers as Independent Contractors? (Chapter 19)

2. ***Global Insight.*** These features illustrate how other nations deal with specific legal concepts to give students a sense of the global legal environment. Subjects include the following:

   - Aleve versus Flanax—Same Pain Killer, but in Different Countries (Chapter 8)
   - Does Cloud Computing Have a Nationality? (Chapter 18)
   - Islamic Law and *Respondeat Superior* (Chapter 19)
   - Can a River Be a Legal Person? (Chapter 25)

3. ***Digital Update.*** These features are designed to examine cutting-edge cyberlaw topics, such as the following:

   - Does Everyone Have a Constitutional Right to Use Social Media? (Chapter 2)
   - Should Employees Have a "Right of Disconnecting"? (Chapter 3)
   - Revenge Porn and Invasion of Privacy (Chapter 6)
   - Riot Games, Inc., Protects Its Online Video Game Copyrights (Chapter 9)
   - Hiring Discrimination Based on Social Media Posts (Chapter 21)

4. ***Managerial Strategy.*** These features emphasize the management aspects of business law and the legal environment. Topics include the following:

   - Should You Consent to Have Your Business Case Decided by a U.S. Magistrate Judge? (Chapter 4)
   - When Is a Warning Legally Bulletproof? (Chapter 7)
   - The Criminalization of American Business (Chapter 10)
   - Commercial Use of Drones (Chapter 14)
   - The SEC's Pay-Ratio Disclosure Rule (Chapter 28)

Entire Chapter on Internet Law, Social Media, and Privacy

The Eleventh Edition again includes a whole chapter (Chapter 9) on *Internet Law, Social Media, and Privacy.*

Social media have entered the mainstream and become a part of everyday life for many businesspersons. In this special chapter, we give particular emphasis to the legal issues surrounding the Internet, social media, and privacy. We also recognize this trend throughout the text by incorporating the Internet and social media as they relate to the topics under discussion.

Coverage of Topics on the Revised CPA Exam

In 2016, the American Institute of CPAs (AICPA) issued its final report on "Maintaining the Relevance of the Uniform CPA Exam." In addition to more focus on critical thinking, authentic applications, and problem solving, the content of the exam has changed to some extent.

The Eleventh Edition of *The Legal Environment of Business* incorporates information on the new topics on the CPA exam, specifically addressing the following:

- Agency law (worker classification and duties of principals and agents)
- Employment law (Affordable Care Act)
- Business organizations (corporate governance issues, including Sarbanes-Oxley compliance and criminal liability for organizations and management)

In addition, the Eleventh Edition continues to cover topics that are essential to new CPAs who are working with sophisticated business clients, regardless of whether the CPA exam covers these topics.

We recognize that today's business leaders must often think "outside the box" when making business decisions. For this reason, we strongly emphasize business and critical thinking elements throughout the text. We have carefully chosen cases, features, and problems that are relevant to business operations. Almost all of the features and cases conclude with some type of critical thinking question. For those teaching future CPAs, this is consistent with the new CPA exam's focus on higher-order skills, such as critical thinking and problem solving.

Highlighted and Numbered *Examples* and *Case in Point* Illustrations

Many instructors use cases and examples to illustrate how the law applies to business. Students understand legal concepts better in the context of their real-world application. Therefore, for this edition of *The Legal Environment of Business*, we have expanded the number of highlighted numbered *Examples* and *Cases in Point* in every chapter.

Examples illustrate how the law applies in a specific situation. *Cases in Point* present the facts and issues of an actual case and then describe the court's decision and rationale. These two features are uniquely designed and consecutively numbered throughout each chapter for easy reference. The *Examples* and *Cases in Point* are integrated throughout the text to help students better understand how courts apply legal principles in the real world.

Task-Based Simulations: A New Unit-Ending Feature

A new *Task-Based Simulation* feature concludes each of the five units in the Eleventh Edition. This feature presents a hypothetical business situation and then asks a series of questions about how the law applies to various actions taken by the firm. To answer the questions, the students must apply the laws discussed throughout the unit.

In addition, each unit ends with an *Application and Ethics* feature that provides additional analysis on a topic related to that unit and explores its ethics ramifications. Each of the features ends with two questions—a *Critical Thinking* question and an *Ethics Question*. Some topics covered include the following:

- One of the Biggest Data Breaches Ever (Unit 2)
- Nondisclosure Agreements (Unit 3)
- Health Insurance and Small Business (Unit 4)
- Climate Change (Unit 5)

Suggested answers to the questions in the new *Task-Based Simulation* features (and the *Application and Ethics* features) are included in the *Answers Manual* for this text.

New Cases and Case Problems

For the Eleventh Edition of *The Legal Environment of Business*, we have added thirty-one new cases, thirty-five new regular case problems, and twenty-eight new *A Question of Ethics* case problems from 2017, 2018, and 2019. The new cases and problems have been carefully selected to illustrate important points of law and to be of high interest to students and instructors. We have made it a point to find recent cases that enhance learning and are relatively easy to understand.

1. **Spotlight Cases and Classic Cases.** Certain cases and case problems that are exceptionally good teaching cases are labeled as *Spotlight Cases* and *Spotlight Case Problems*. Examples include *Spotlight on Beer Labels, Spotlight on Gucci, Spotlight on Nike, Spotlight on the Seattle Mariners* and *Spotlight on Verizon*. Instructors will find these *Spotlight*

Cases and *Spotlight Case Problems* useful to illustrate the legal concepts under discussion, and students will enjoy studying the cases because they involve interesting and memorable facts. Other cases have been chosen as *Classic Cases* because they establish a legal precedent in a particular area of law.

2. **Critical Thinking Section.** Each case concludes with a *Critical Thinking* section, which normally includes two questions. The questions may address *Legal Environment, E-Commerce, Economic, Environmental, Ethical, Global, Political,* or *Technological* issues, or they may ask *What If the Facts Were Different?* Each *Classic Case* ends with an *Impact of This Case on Today's Law* discussion and a *Critical Thinking* question.

3. **Longer Excerpts for Case Analysis.** We have also included one longer case excerpt in many chapters—labeled *Case Analysis*—followed by three *Legal Reasoning Questions*. The questions are designed to guide students' analysis of the case and build their legal reasoning skills. These *Case Analysis* features may be used for case-briefing assignments.

Suggested answers to all case-ending questions and case problems are included in the *Answers Manual* for this text.

Business Case Problem with Sample Answer

In response to those instructors who would like students to have sample answers available for some of the questions and case problems, we include a *Business Case Problem with Sample Answer* in each chapter. The *Business Case Problem with Sample Answer* is based on an actual case, and students can find a sample answer in Appendix C at the end of this text.

Exhibits and Concept Summaries

We have spent considerable effort developing and designing all of the exhibits and concept summaries in this text to achieve better clarity and more visual appeal.

Practice and Review

In the Eleventh Edition of *The Legal Environment of Business*, we offer a *Practice and Review* feature at the end of every chapter to help solidify students' understanding of the chapter materials. Each *Practice and Review* feature presents a hypothetical scenario and then asks a series of questions that require students to identify the issues and apply the legal concepts discussed in the chapter.

These features are designed to help students review the chapter topics in a simple and interesting way and see how the legal principles discussed in the chapter affect the world in which they live. An instructor can use these features as the basis for in-class discussion or encourage students to use them for self-study prior to completing homework assignments. Suggested answers to the questions posed in the *Practice and Review* features can be found in the *Answers Manual* for this text.

Issue Spotters

At the conclusion of each chapter, we have included a special section with two *Issue Spotters* related to the chapter's topics. These questions facilitate student learning and review of the chapter materials. Sample answers to the *Issue Spotters* in every chapter are provided in Appendix B and in the *Answers Manual* for this text.

Time-Limited Group Assignment

For instructors who want their students to engage in group projects, each chapter of the Eleventh Edition includes a special *Time-Limited Group Assignment*. Each activity begins by describing a business scenario and then poses several questions pertaining to the scenario. Each question is to be answered by a different group of students based on the information in the chapter. These projects may be used in class to spur discussion or as homework assignments. Suggested answers to the *Time-Limited Group Assignments* are included in the *Answers Manual* for this text.

Supplements/Digital Learning Systems

The Legal Environment of Business, Eleventh Edition, provides a comprehensive supplements package designed to make the tasks of teaching and learning more enjoyable and efficient. The following supplements and digital products are offered in conjunction with the text.

MindTap for The Legal Environment of Business

MindTap™ for *The Legal Environment of Business*, Eleventh Edition, is a fully online, highly personalized learning experience built upon Cengage Learning content. By combining readings, multimedia, activities, and assessments into a singular Learning Path, *MindTap* guides students through their course with ease and engagement.

Instructors can personalize the experience by customizing Cengage Learning resources and adding their own content via apps that integrate into the *MindTap* framework seamlessly with Learning Management Systems (LMS).

The *MindTap* product provides a four-step Learning Path, Case Repository, Adaptive Test Prep, and an Interactive eBook designed to meet instructors' needs while also allowing instructors to measure skills and outcomes with ease. Each item is assignable and gradable. This gives instructors knowledge of class standings and students' mastery of concepts that may be difficult. Additionally, students gain knowledge about where they stand—both individually and compared to the highest performers in class.

Cengage Testing Powered by Cognero

Cengage Testing Powered by Cognero is a flexible, online system that allows you to do the following:

- Author, edit, and manage *Test Bank* content from multiple Cengage Learning solutions.
- Create multiple test versions in an instant.
- Deliver tests from your LMS, your classroom, or wherever you want.

Start Right Away! *Cengage Testing Powered by Cognero* works on any operating system or browser.

- Use your standard browser; no special installs or downloads are needed.
- Create tests from school, home, the coffee shop—anywhere with Internet access.

What Will You Find?
- *Simplicity at every step.* A desktop-inspired interface features drop-down menus and familiar intuitive tools that take you through content creation and management with ease.
- *Full-featured test generator.* Create ideal assessments with your choice of fifteen question types—including true/false, multiple choice, opinion scale/Likert, and essay. Multi-language support, an equation editor, and unlimited metadata help ensure your tests are complete and compliant.
- *Cross-compatible capability.* Import and export content to and from other systems.

Instructor's Companion Website

The Instructor's Companion Website for the Eleventh Edition of *The Legal Environment of Business* contains the following supplements:

- **Instructor's Manual.** Includes sections entitled "Additional Cases Addressing This Issue" at the end of selected case synopses.
- **Answers Manual.** Provides answers to all questions presented in the text, including the questions in each case and feature, the *Practice and Review*, the *Issue Spotters*, the *Business Scenarios and Case Problems*, and the unit-ending *Task-Based Simulation* and *Application and Ethics* features.
- **Test Bank.** A comprehensive test bank that contains multiple-choice, true/false, and short essay questions.
- **Case-Problem Cases.**
- **Case Printouts.**
- **PowerPoint Slides.**
- **Lecture Outlines.**
- **MindTap Integrated Syllabus.**

For Users of the Previous Edition

First of all, we want to thank you for helping make *The Legal Environment of Business* one of the best-selling legal environment texts in America today. Second, we want to make you aware of the numerous additions and changes that we have made in this edition—many in response to comments from reviewers.

Every chapter of the Eleventh Edition has been revised as necessary to incorporate new developments in the law or to streamline the presentations. Other major changes and additions for this edition include the following:

- Chapter 2 (Business and the Constitution)—The chapter has been revised and updated to be more business oriented. It has a new case, two new case problems, and a new *Digital Update* feature on a United States Supreme Court decision concerning whether everyone has a constitutional right to use social media.
- Chapter 3 (Ethics in Business)—The chapter contents have been revised and updated to be more practical for businesspersons. A new section introduces a systematic approach to resolving ethical issues called the IDDR Approach. ("I Desire to Do Right" is a useful mnemonic device for remembering the individual steps:

Inquiry, Discussion, Decision, and Review.) There is a new Exhibit and a new *Ethics Today* feature that illustrates how to apply the IDDR framework. The step-by-step IDDR Approach is then reiterated in the problems labeled *A Question of Ethics* that appear in every subsequent chapter. There are five new *Cases in Point*, seven new *Examples*, a new case, and four new case problems in the chapter. A *Digital Update* feature explores whether employees have a right to disconnect from their electronic devices after work hours. The chapter concludes with a new *Time-Limited Group Assignment* on corporate social responsibility.

- Chapter 8 (Intellectual Property Rights)—The materials on intellectual property rights have been thoroughly revised and updated to reflect the most current laws and trends. A new *Global Insight* feature discusses confusion in the context of trademark infringement. There is a new case, a new *Example*, and two new case problems.
- Chapter 9 (Internet Law, Social Media, and Privacy)— This chapter, which covers legal issues that are unique to the Internet, has been thoroughly revised and updated for the Eleventh Edition. It includes a new case, four new *Cases in Point*, and a new *Digital Update* feature on how copyright law applies to video games.
- Chapter 11 (International and Space Law)—The chapter now includes a section on space law—international and domestic. There are two new cases presented, as well as an updated discussion of NAFTA (now called USMCA) and of a United States Supreme Court decision concerning the Alien Tort Statute. The chapter also includes an updated *Ethics Today* feature on the domestic brewing of imported beer brands.
- Chapter 14 (Sales and Lease Contracts)—We have streamlined and simplified our coverage of the Uniform Commercial Code and added a new case, a new *Example*, six new *Cases in Point*, and one new case problem.
- Chapter 20 (Employment Law), Chapter 21 (Employment Discrimination), and Chapter 22 (Immigration and Labor Law)—These three chapters covering employment law have been thoroughly updated to include discussions of legal issues facing employers today. Chapter 20 a new case, three new *Cases in Point*, one new *Example*, and two new case problems. It also includes an *Ethics Today* feature on whether employees should receive paid bathroom breaks.

Chapter 21 has a new case, five new *Cases in Point*, a new concept summary, and two new case problems. A revised *Digital Update* feature discusses hiring discrimination based on social media posts. Chapter 22 includes a new case and a *Managerial Strategy* feature on union organizing using company e-mail systems. We discuss relevant United States Supreme Court decisions affecting employment issues throughout these chapters.

• Chapter 24 (Consumer Protection)—The chapter has been revised and updated and includes a new subsection on state laws concerning false

advertising. It has a new case, three new *Cases in Point,* and three new case problems.

• Chapter 28 (Investor Protection and Corporate Governance)—The contents of this chapter have been thoroughly revised and updated in light of the amendments to Regulation A (Regulation A+). There is a new *Digital Update* feature titled Investment Crowdfunding—Regulations and Restrictions, as well as a new example and a new exhibit on this topic. In addition, there is a new subsection, a new case, three new *Cases in Point,* and two new case problems.

Acknowledgments for Previous Editions

Since we began this project many years ago, a sizable number of legal environment of business professors and others have helped us in revising the book, including the following:

Peter W. Allan
Victor Valley College, California

William Dennis Ames
Indiana University of Pennsylvania

Thomas M. Apke
California State University, Fullerton

Linda Axelrod
Metropolitan State University, Minnesota

Jane Bennett
Orange Coast College, California

Robert C. Bird
University of Connecticut

Dean Bredeson
University of Texas at Austin

Sam Cassidy
University of Denver, Colorado

Thomas D. Cavenagh
North Central College, Illinois

Angela Cerino
Villanova University, Pennsylvania

Corey Ciocchetti
University of Denver, Colorado

David Cooper
Fullerton College, California

Steven R. Donley
Cypress College, California

Paul F. Dwyer
Siena College, New York

Nena Ellison
Florida Atlantic University

Joan Gabel
Florida State University

Gamewell Gant
Idaho State University

Jacqueline Hagerott
Franklin University, Ohio

Arlene M. Hibschweiler
State University of New York at Fredonia

Barbara W. Kincaid
Southern Methodist University, Texas

Marty P. Ludlum
Oklahoma City Community College

Diane May
Winona State University, Minnesota

Marty Salley McGee
South Carolina State University

Robert Mitchum
Arkansas State University Beebe

Melanie Morris
Raritan Valley Community College, New Jersey

Kathleen A. Phillips
University of Houston, Texas

David Redle
University of Akron, Ohio

Larry A. Strate
University of Nevada, Las Vegas

Dawn Swink
Minnesota State University

Brian Terry
Johnson and Wales University, Rhode Island

John Theis
Colorado Mesa University

William H. Volz
Wayne State University, Michigan

Michael G. Walsh
Villanova University, Pennsylvania

Glynda White
College of Southern Nevada

LeVon E. Wilson
Western Carolina University, North Carolina

John A. Wrieden
Florida International University

Eric D. Yordy
Northern Arizona University

Mary-Kathryn Zachary
State University of West Georgia

As in all past editions, we owe a debt of extreme gratitude to the numerous individuals who worked directly with us or at Cengage. In particular, we wish to thank Vicky True-Baker and Michael Giffen, senior product managers; Joe Sabatino, product director; Martha Conway and Julia Chase, senior content managers; and Lisa Elliot, Cengage subject matter expert. We also thank Sarah Huber and Courtney Wolstoncroft, learning designers; Jennifer Chinn and Stephen McMillian, digital delivery leads; Christian Wood and Nick Perez, product assistants; Chris Doughman, designer; Carly Belcher, intellectual property project manager; and Ashley Maynard, intellectual property analyst. We are indebted as well to the staff at SPi Global, our compositor, as well as Ann Borman, project manager, for accurately generating pages for this text and making it possible for us to meet our ambitious schedule for print and digital products.

We especially wish to thank Katherine Marie Silsbee for her management of the entire project, as well as for the application of her superb research and editorial skills. We also wish to thank William Eric Hollowell, who coauthored the *Instructor's Manual* and the *Test Bank*, for his excellent research efforts. We were fortunate enough to have the copyediting of Jeanne Yost and the proofreading of Kristi Wiswell. We are grateful for the many efforts of Vickie Reierson, Roxanna Lee, and Suzanne Jasin, which helped to ensure an error-free text.

Through the years, we have enjoyed an ongoing correspondence with many of you who have found points on which you wish to comment. We continue to welcome all comments and promise to respond promptly. By incorporating your ideas, we can continue to write a legal environment text that is best for you and best for your students.

F.B.C.
R.L.M.

To my parents and sisters.
F.B.C.

For Vicky,
We've had so many years
working together, and they
have been wonderful,
productive, and exciting.
I have always valued
your professionalism.

R.L.M.

The Foundations

Chapter 1

Law and Legal Reasoning

One of the most important functions of law in any society is to provide stability, predictability, and continuity so that people can know how to order their affairs. If any society is to survive, its citizens must be able to determine what is legally right and legally wrong. They must know what sanctions will be imposed on them if they commit wrongful acts. If they suffer harm as a result of others' wrongful acts, they must know how they can seek compensation. By setting forth the rights, obligations, and privileges of citizens, the law enables individuals to go about their business with confidence and a certain degree of predictability.

Although law has various definitions, they all are based on the general observation that **law** consists of *enforceable rules governing relationships among individuals and between individuals and their society*. In some societies, these enforceable rules may consist of unwritten principles of behavior. In other societies, they are set forth in ancient or contemporary law codes. In the United States, our rules consist of written laws and court decisions created by modern legislative and judicial bodies. Regardless of how such rules are created, they all have one feature in common: they establish rights, duties, and privileges that are consistent with the values and beliefs of their society or its ruling group.

In this introductory chapter, we look at how business law and the legal environment affect business decisions. For instance, suppose that Hellix Communications, Inc., wants to buy a competing cellular company. It also wants to offer unlimited data plans once it has acquired this competitor. Management fears that if the company does not expand, one of its bigger rivals will put it out of business. But Hellix Communications cannot simply buy its rivals. Nor can it just offer a low-cost cell-phone plan to its customers. It has to follow the laws pertaining to its proposed actions. Some of these laws (or regulations) depend on interpretations by those running various regulatory agencies. The rules that control Hellix Communications' actions reflect past and current thinking about how large telecommunications companies should and should not act.

1–1 Business Activities and the Legal Environment

Laws and government regulations affect almost all business activities—from hiring and firing decisions to workplace safety, the manufacturing and marketing of products, business financing, and more. To make good business decisions, a basic knowledge of the laws and regulations governing these activities is beneficial—if not essential.

Realize also that, in today's business world, knowing what conduct can lead to legal **liability** is not enough. Businesspersons must develop critical thinking and legal reasoning skills so that they can evaluate how various laws might apply to a given situation and determine the best course of action.

Our goal in this text is not only to teach you about specific laws, but also to teach you how to think about the law and the legal environment and to develop your critical-thinking and legal-reasoning skills. The laws may change, but the ability to analyze and evaluate the legal (and ethical) ramifications of situations as they arise is an invaluable and lasting skill.

1–1a Many Different Laws May Affect a Single Business Decision

As you will note, each chapter in this text covers specific areas of the law and shows how the legal rules in each area affect business activities. Although compartmentalizing the law in this fashion promotes conceptual clarity, it does not indicate the extent to which a number of different laws may apply to just one decision. Exhibit 1–1 illustrates the various areas of the law that may influence business decision making.

■ **Example 1.1** When Mark Zuckerberg, as a Harvard student, first launched Facebook, others claimed that Zuckerberg had stolen their ideas for a social networking

Exhibit 1–1   Areas of the Law That Can Affect Business Decision Making

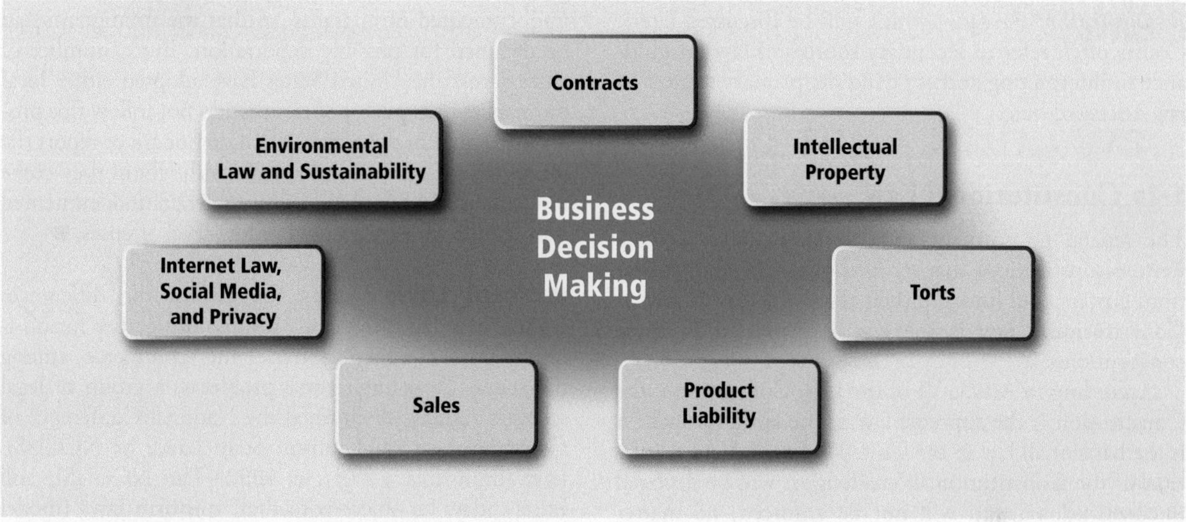

site. They filed a lawsuit against him alleging theft of intellectual property, fraudulent misrepresentation, and violations of partnership law and securities law. Facebook ultimately paid $65 million to settle those claims out of court. Since then, Facebook has been sued repeatedly for violating users' privacy (and federal laws) by tracking their website usage and by scanning private messages for purposes of data mining and user profiling. Facebook's business decisions have also come under scrutiny by federal regulators, such as the Federal Trade Commission (FTC), and by international authorities, such as the European Union. The company settled a complaint filed by the FTC alleging that Facebook had failed to keep "friends" lists and other user information private. ∎

1–1b Ethics and Business Decision Making

Merely knowing the areas of law that may affect a business decision is not sufficient in today's business world. Today, business decision makers need to consider not just whether a decision is legal, but also whether it is ethical.

Ethics generally is defined as the principles governing what constitutes right or wrong behavior. Often, as in several of the claims against Facebook just discussed, disputes arise in business because one party feels that he or she has been treated unfairly. Thus, the underlying reason for bringing some lawsuits is a breach of ethical duties (such as when a partner or employee attempts to secretly take advantage of a business opportunity).

Throughout this text, you will learn about the relationship between the law and ethics, as well as about some of the types of ethical questions that arise in business. For instance, all of the unit-ending *Application and Ethics* features include an *Ethical Connection* section that explores the ethical dimensions of a topic treated within the unit. We have also included *Ethical Questions* for each unit, as well as within many of the cases presented in this text. *Ethics Today* features, which focus on ethical considerations in today's business climate, appear in selected chapters, including this chapter. *A Question of Ethics* case problem is included at the end of every chapter to introduce you to the ethical aspects of specific cases involving real-life situations.

1–2 Sources of American Law

American law has numerous sources. Often, these sources of law are classified as either primary or secondary.

Primary sources of law, or sources that establish the law, include the following:

1. The U.S. Constitution and the constitutions of the various states.
2. Statutory law—including laws passed by Congress, state legislatures, or local governing bodies.
3. Regulations created by administrative agencies, such as the Federal Trade Commission.
4. Case law and common law doctrines.

Next, we will describe each of these important sources of law.

Secondary sources of law are books and articles that summarize and clarify the primary sources of law.

Examples include legal encyclopedias, treatises, articles in law reviews, and compilations of law, such as the *Restatements of the Law* (which will be discussed later). Courts often refer to secondary sources of law for guidance in interpreting and applying the primary sources of law discussed here.

1–2a Constitutional Law

The federal government and the states have separate written constitutions that set forth the general organization, powers, and limits of their respective governments. **Constitutional law** is the law as expressed in these constitutions.

According to Article VI of the U.S. Constitution, the Constitution is the supreme law of the land. As such, it is the basis of all law in the United States. A law in violation of the Constitution, if challenged, will be declared unconstitutional and will not be enforced, no matter what its source.

The Tenth Amendment to the U.S. Constitution reserves to the states all powers not granted to the federal government. Each state in the union has its own constitution. Unless it conflicts with the U.S. Constitution or a federal law, a state constitution is supreme within the state's borders.

1–2b Statutory Law

Laws enacted by legislative bodies at any level of government, such as statutes passed by Congress or by state legislatures, make up the body of law known as **statutory law.** When a legislature passes a statute, that statute ultimately is included in the federal code of laws or the relevant state code of laws.

Statutory law also includes local **ordinances**—regulations passed by municipal or county governing units to deal with matters not covered by federal or state law. Ordinances commonly have to do with city or county land use (zoning ordinances), building and safety codes, and other matters affecting the local community.

A federal statute, of course, applies to all states. A state statute, in contrast, applies only within the state's borders. State laws thus may vary from state to state. No federal statute may violate the U.S. Constitution, and no state statute or local ordinance may violate the U.S. Constitution or the relevant state constitution.

Statutory Conflicts Tension may sometimes arise between federal, state, and local laws. ■ **Example 1.2** This tension is evident in the national debate over so-called sanctuary cities—cities that limit their cooperation with federal immigration authorities. Normally, local law enforcement officials are supposed to alert federal immigration authorities when they come into contact with undocumented immigrants, so that the immigrants can be detained for possible deportation. But a number of cities across the United States have adopted either local ordinances or explicit policies that do not follow this procedure. Police in these cities often do not ask or report the immigration status of individuals with whom they come into contact. Other places refuse to detain undocumented immigrants who are accused of low-level offenses. ■

Uniform Laws During the 1800s, the differences among state laws frequently created difficulties for businesspersons conducting trade and commerce among the states. To counter these problems, a group of legal scholars and lawyers formed the National Conference of Commissioners on Uniform State Laws, or NCCUSL (www.uniformlaws.org), in 1892. The NCCUSL still exists today. Its object is to draft **uniform laws** (model statutes) for the states to consider adopting.

Each state has the option of adopting or rejecting a uniform law. *Only if a state legislature adopts a uniform law does that law become part of the statutory law of that state.* Note that a state legislature may adopt all or part of a uniform law as it is written, or the legislature may rewrite the law however the legislature wishes. Hence, even though many states may have adopted a uniform law, those states' laws may not be entirely "uniform."

The earliest uniform law, the Uniform Negotiable Instruments Law, was completed by 1896 and adopted in every state by the 1920s (although not all states used exactly the same wording). Over the following decades, other acts were drawn up in a similar manner. In all, more than two hundred uniform acts have been issued by the NCCUSL since its inception. The most ambitious uniform act of all, however, was the Uniform Commercial Code.

The Uniform Commercial Code One of the most important uniform acts is the Uniform Commercial Code (UCC), which was created through the joint efforts of the NCCUSL and the American Law Institute.[1] The UCC was first issued in 1952 and has been adopted in all fifty states,[2] the District of Columbia, and the Virgin Islands.

The UCC facilitates commerce among the states by providing a uniform, yet flexible, set of rules governing commercial transactions. Because of its importance in the area of commercial law, we cite the UCC frequently in this text.

---

1. This institute was formed in the 1920s and consists of practicing attorneys, legal scholars, and judges.
2. Louisiana has not adopted Articles 2 and 2A (covering contracts for the sale and lease of goods), however.

1–2c Administrative Law

Another important source of American law is **administrative law,** which consists of the rules, orders, and decisions of administrative agencies. An **administrative agency** is a federal, state, or local government agency established to perform a specific function. Administrative law and procedures constitute a dominant element in the regulatory environment of business.

Rules issued by various administrative agencies now affect almost every aspect of a business's operations. Regulations govern a business's capital structure and financing, its hiring and firing procedures, its relations with employees and unions, and the way it manufactures and markets its products. Regulations enacted to protect the environment also often play a significant role in business operations.

Federal Agencies At the national level, the cabinet departments of the executive branch include numerous **executive agencies.** The U.S. Food and Drug Administration, for instance, is an agency within the U.S. Department of Health and Human Services. Executive agencies are subject to the authority of the president, who has the power to appoint and remove their officers.

There are also major **independent regulatory agencies** at the federal level, such as the Federal Trade Commission, the Securities and Exchange Commission, and the Federal Communications Commission. The president's power is less pronounced in regard to independent agencies, whose officers serve for fixed terms and cannot be removed without just cause.

State and Local Agencies There are administrative agencies at the state and local levels as well. Commonly, a state agency (such as a state pollution-control agency) is created as a parallel to a federal agency (such as the Environmental Protection Agency). Just as federal statutes take precedence over conflicting state statutes, federal agency regulations take precedence over conflicting state regulations.

1–2d Case Law and Common Law Doctrines

The rules of law announced in court decisions constitute another basic source of American law. These rules include interpretations of constitutional provisions, of statutes enacted by legislatures, and of regulations created by administrative agencies.

Today, this body of judge-made law is referred to as **case law.** Case law—the doctrines and principles announced in cases—governs all areas not covered by statutory law or administrative law and is part of our common law tradition. We look at the origins and characteristics of the common law tradition in some detail in the pages that follow.

See Concept Summary 1.1 for a review of the sources of American law.

Concept Summary 1.1

Sources of American Law

Constitutional Law	• Law as expressed in the U.S. Constitution or state constitutions. • The U.S. Constitution is the supreme law of the land. • State constitutions are supreme within state borders to the extent that they do not conflict with the U.S. Constitution.
Statutory Law	• Statutes (including uniform laws) and ordinances enacted by federal, state, and local legislatures. • Federal statutes may not violate the U.S. Constitution. • State statutes and local ordinances may not violate the U.S. Constitution or the relevant state constitution.
Administrative Law	• The rules, orders, and decisions of federal, state, and local administrative agencies.
Case Law and Common Law Doctrines	• Judge-made law, including interpretations of constitutional provisions, of statutes enacted by legislatures, and of regulations created by administrative agencies.

1–3 The Common Law Tradition

Because of our colonial heritage, much of American law is based on the English legal system. Knowledge of this tradition is crucial to understanding our legal system today because judges in the United States still apply common law principles when deciding cases.

1–3a Early English Courts

After the Normans conquered England in 1066, William the Conqueror and his successors began the process of unifying the country under their rule. One of the means they used to do this was the establishment of the king's courts, or *curiae regis*.

Before the Norman Conquest, disputes had been settled according to the local legal customs and traditions in various regions of the country. The king's courts sought to establish a uniform set of customs for the country as a whole. What evolved in these courts was the beginning of the **common law**—a body of general rules that applied throughout the entire English realm. Eventually, the common law tradition became part of the heritage of all nations that were once British colonies, including the United States.

Courts of Law and Remedies at Law The early English king's courts could grant only very limited kinds of **remedies** (the legal means to enforce a right or redress a wrong). If one person wronged another in some way, the king's courts could award as compensation one or more of the following: (1) land, (2) items of value, or (3) money.

The courts that awarded this compensation became known as **courts of law,** and the three remedies were called **remedies at law.** (Today, the remedy at law normally takes the form of monetary **damages**—an amount given to a party whose legal interests have been injured.) This system made the procedure for settling disputes more uniform. When a complaining party wanted a remedy other than economic compensation, however, the courts of law could do nothing, so "no remedy, no right."

Courts of Equity When individuals could not obtain an adequate remedy in a court of law, they petitioned the king for relief. Most of these petitions were decided by an adviser to the king, called a *chancellor*, who had the power to grant new and unique remedies. Eventually, formal chancery courts, or **courts of equity,** were established. *Equity* is a branch of law—founded on notions of justice and fair dealing—that seeks to supply a remedy when no adequate remedy at law is available.

Remedies in Equity The remedies granted by the equity courts became known as **remedies in equity,** or equitable remedies. These remedies include specific performance, injunction, and rescission. *Specific performance* involves ordering a party to perform an agreement as promised. An *injunction* is an order to a party to cease engaging in a specific activity or to undo some wrong or injury. *Rescission* is the cancellation of a contractual obligation. We will discuss these and other equitable remedies in more detail in later chapters.

As a general rule, today's courts, like the early English courts, will not grant equitable remedies unless the remedy at law—monetary damages—is inadequate. ■ **Example 1.3** Ted forms a contract (a legally binding agreement) to purchase a parcel of land that he thinks will be perfect for his future home. The seller **breaches** (fails to fulfill) this agreement. Ted could sue the seller for the return of any deposits or down payment he might have made on the land, but this is not the remedy he really wants. What Ted wants is to have a court order the seller to perform the contract. In other words, Ted will seek the equitable remedy of specific performance because monetary damages are inadequate in this situation. ■

Equitable Maxims In fashioning appropriate remedies, judges often were (and continue to be) guided by so-called **equitable maxims**—propositions or general statements of equitable rules. Exhibit 1–2 lists some important equitable maxims.

The last maxim listed in the exhibit—"Equity aids the vigilant, not those who rest on their rights"—merits special attention. It has become known as the equitable doctrine of **laches** (a term derived from the Latin *laxus*, meaning "lax" or "negligent"), and it can be used as a defense. A **defense** is an argument raised by the **defendant** (the party being sued) indicating why the **plaintiff** (the suing party) should not obtain the remedy sought. (Note that in equity proceedings, the party bringing a lawsuit is called the **petitioner,** and the party being sued is referred to as the **respondent.**)

The doctrine of laches arose to encourage people to bring lawsuits while the evidence was fresh. What constitutes a reasonable time, of course, varies according to the circumstances of the case. Time periods for different types of cases are now usually fixed by **statutes of limitations.** After the time allowed under a statute of limitations has

Exhibit 1–2 Equitable Maxims

1. *Whoever seeks equity must do equity.* (Anyone who wishes to be treated fairly must treat others fairly.)

2. *Where there is equal equity, the law must prevail.* (The law will determine the outcome of a controversy in which the merits of both sides are equal.)

3. *One seeking the aid of an equity court must come to the court with clean hands.* (The plaintiff must have acted fairly and honestly.)

4. *Equity will not suffer a wrong to be without a remedy.* (Equitable relief will be awarded when there is a right to relief and there is no adequate remedy at law.)

5. *Equity regards substance rather than form.* (Equity is more concerned with fairness and justice than with legal technicalities.)

6. *Equity aids the vigilant, not those who rest on their rights.* (Equity will not help those who neglect their rights for an unreasonable period of time.)

expired, no action (lawsuit) can be brought, no matter how strong the case was originally.

1–3b Legal and Equitable Remedies Today

The establishment of courts of equity in medieval England resulted in two distinct court systems: courts of law and courts of equity. The courts had different sets of judges and granted different types of remedies. During the nineteenth century, however, most states in the United States adopted rules of procedure that resulted in the combining of courts of law and equity. A party now may request both legal and equitable remedies in the same action, and the trial court judge may grant either or both forms of relief.

The distinction between legal and equitable remedies remains relevant to students of business law, however, because these remedies differ. To seek the proper remedy for a wrong, you must know what remedies are available. Additionally, certain vestiges of the procedures used when there were separate courts of law and equity still exist. For instance, a party has the right to demand a jury trial in an action at law, but not in an action in equity. Exhibit 1–3 summarizes the procedural differences (applicable in most states) between an action at law and an action in equity.

1–3c The Doctrine of *Stare Decisis*

One of the unique features of the common law is that it is *judge-made* law. The body of principles and doctrines that form the common law emerged over time as judges decided legal controversies.

Case Precedents and Case Reporters When possible, judges attempted to be consistent and to base their decisions on the principles suggested by earlier cases. They sought to decide similar cases in a similar way, and they considered new cases with care because they knew that their decisions would make new law. Each interpretation became part of the law on the subject and thus served as a legal **precedent.** A precedent is a decision that furnishes an example or authority for deciding subsequent cases involving identical or similar legal principles or facts.

In the early years of the common law, there was no single place or publication where court opinions, or written decisions, could be found. By the fourteenth century, portions of the most important decisions from each year were being gathered together and recorded in *Year Books*, which became useful references for lawyers and judges. In the sixteenth century, the *Year Books* were discontinued,

Exhibit 1–3 Procedural Differences between an Action at Law and an Action in Equity

Procedure	Action at Law	Action in Equity
Initiation of lawsuit	By filing a complaint	By filing a petition
Decision	By jury or judge	By judge (no jury)
Result	Judgment	Decree
Remedy	Monetary damages or property	Injunction, specific performance, or rescission

and other forms of case publication became available. Today, cases are published, or "reported," in volumes called **reporters,** or *reports*—and are also posted online. We describe today's case reporting system in detail later in this chapter.

Stare Decisis and the Common Law Tradition

The practice of deciding new cases with reference to former decisions, or precedents, became a cornerstone of the English and American judicial systems. The practice formed a doctrine known as ***stare decisis***,[3] a Latin phrase meaning "to stand on decided cases."

Under the doctrine of *stare decisis*, judges are obligated to follow the precedents established within their jurisdictions. The term *jurisdiction* refers to a geographic area in which a court or courts have the power to apply the law. Once a court has set forth a principle of law as being applicable to a certain set of facts, that court must apply the principle in future cases involving similar facts. Courts of lower rank (within the same jurisdiction) must do likewise. Thus, *stare decisis* has two aspects:

1. A court should not overturn its own precedents unless there is a compelling reason to do so.
2. Decisions made by a higher court are binding on lower courts.

Controlling Precedents Precedents that must be followed within a jurisdiction are called *controlling precedents*. Controlling precedents are a type of binding authority. A **binding authority** is any source of law that a court must follow when deciding a case. Binding authorities include constitutions, statutes, and regulations that govern the issue being decided, as well as court decisions that are controlling precedents within the jurisdiction. United States Supreme Court case decisions, no matter how old, remain controlling until they are overruled by a subsequent decision of the Supreme Court or changed by further legislation or a constitutional amendment.

Stare Decisis and Legal Stability The doctrine of *stare decisis* helps the courts to be more efficient because, if other courts have analyzed a similar case, their legal reasoning and opinions can serve as guides. *Stare decisis* also makes the law more stable and predictable. If the law on a subject is well settled, someone bringing a case can usually rely on the court to rule based on what the law has been in the past. See this chapter's *Ethics Today*

feature for a discussion of how courts often defer to case precedent even when they disagree with the reasoning in the case.

Although courts are obligated to follow precedents, sometimes a court will depart from the rule of precedent if it decides that the precedent should no longer be followed. If a court decides that a ruling precedent is simply incorrect or that technological or social changes have rendered the precedent inapplicable, the court might rule contrary to the precedent. Cases that overturn precedent often receive a great deal of publicity.

■ **Case in Point 1.4**   The United States Supreme Court expressly overturned precedent in the case of *Brown v. Board of Education of Topeka*.[4] The Court concluded that separate educational facilities for whites and blacks, which it had previously upheld as constitutional,[5] were inherently unequal. The Supreme Court's departure from precedent in this case received a tremendous amount of publicity as people began to realize the ramifications of this change in the law. ■

Note that a lower court will sometimes avoid applying a precedent set by a higher court in its jurisdiction by distinguishing the two cases based on their facts. When this happens, the lower court's ruling stands unless it is appealed to a higher court and that court overturns the decision.

When There Is No Precedent   Occasionally, courts must decide cases for which no precedents exist, called *cases of first impression*. For instance, as you will read throughout this text, the Internet and certain other technologies have presented many new and challenging issues for the courts to decide.

In deciding cases of first impression, courts often look at **persuasive authorities**—legal authorities that a court may consult for guidance but that are not binding on the court. A court may consider precedents from other jurisdictions, for instance, although those precedents are not binding. A court may also consider legal principles and policies underlying previous court decisions or existing statutes. Additionally, a court might look at issues of fairness, social values and customs, and public policy (governmental policy based on widely held societal values). Today, federal courts can also look at unpublished opinions (those not intended for publication in a printed legal reporter) as sources of persuasive authority.[6]

---

unced *stahr-ee dih-si-sis*.

4. 347 U.S. 483, 74 S.Ct. 686, 98 L.Ed. 873 (1954).
5. See *Plessy v. Ferguson*, 163 U.S. 537, 16 S.Ct. 1138, 41 L.Ed. 256 (1896).
6. See Rule 32.1 of the Federal Rules of Appellate Procedure.

Ethics Today

Stare Decisis versus Spider-Man

Supreme Court Justice Elena Kagan, in a recent decision involving Marvel Comics' Spider-Man, ruled that, "What we can decide, we can undecide. But *stare decisis* teaches that we should exercise that authority sparingly." Citing a Spider-Man comic book, she went on to say that "in this world, with great power there must also come—great responsibility."[a] In its decision in the case—*Kimble v. Marvel Entertainment, LLC*—the Supreme Court applied *stare decisis* and ruled against Stephen Kimble, the creator of a toy related to the Spider-Man figure.[b]

Can a Patent Involving Spider-Man Last Super Long?

A patent is an exclusive right granted to the creator of an invention. Under U.S. law, patent owners generally possess that right for twenty years. Patent holders can license the use of their patents as they see fit during that period. In other words, they can allow others (called *licensees*) to use their invention in return for a fee (called *royalties*).

More than fifty years ago, the Supreme Court ruled in its *Brulotte* decision that a licensee cannot be forced to pay royalties to a patent holder after the patent has expired.[c] So if a licensee signs a contract to continue to pay royalties after the patent has expired, the contract is invalid and thus unenforceable.

At issue in the *Kimble* case was a contract signed between Marvel Entertainment and Kimble, who had invented a toy made up of a glove equipped with a valve and a canister of pressurized foam. The patented toy allowed people to shoot fake webs intended to look like Spider-Man's. In 1990, Kimble tried to cut a deal with Marvel Entertainment concerning his toy, but he was unsuccessful. Then Marvel started selling its own version of the toy.

a. Lee, S., *Spider-Man: Amazing Fantasy*, No. 15 (New York: Marvel Comics, 1962).
b. 576 U.S. ___,135 S.Ct. 2401, 192 L.Ed.2d 463 (2015). Also see *Nautilus, Inc. v. ICON Health & Fitness, Inc.*, 304 F.Supp.3d 552 (W.D.Texas—San Antonio 2018).
c. *Brulotte v. Thys Co.*, 379 U.S. 29, 85 S.Ct. 176 (1964).

When Kimble sued Marvel for patent infringement, he won. The result was a settlement that involved a licensing agreement between Kimble and Marvel with a lump-sum payment plus a royalty to Kimble of 3 percent of all sales of the toy. The agreement did not specify an end date for royalty payments to Kimble, and Marvel later sued to have the payments stop after the patent expired, consistent with the Court's earlier *Brulotte* decision.

A majority of the Supreme Court justices agreed with Marvel. As Justice Kagan said in the opinion, "Patents endow their holders with certain super powers, but only for a limited time." The court further noted that the fifty-year-old *Brulotte* decision was perhaps based on what today is an outmoded understanding of economics. That decision, according to some, may even hinder competition and innovation. But "respecting *stare decisis* means sticking to some wrong decisions."

The Ethical Side

In a dissenting opinion, Supreme Court Justice Samuel A. Alito, Jr., said, "The decision interferes with the ability of parties to negotiate licensing agreements that reflect the true value of a patent, and it disrupts contractual expectations. *Stare decisis* does not require us to retain this baseless and damaging precedent. . . . *Stare decisis* is important to the rule of law, but so are correct judicial decisions."

In other words, *stare decisis* holds that courts should adhere to precedent in order to promote predictability and consistency. But in the business world, shouldn't parties to contracts be able to, for example, allow a patent licensee to make smaller royalty payments that exceed the life of the patent? Isn't that a way to reduce the yearly costs to the licensee? After all, the licensee may be cash-strapped in its initial use of the patent. Shouldn't the parties to a contract be the ones to decide how long the contract should last?

Critical Thinking *When is the Supreme Court justified in not following the doctrine of* stare decisis?

1–3d *Stare Decisis* and Legal Reasoning

In deciding what law applies to a given dispute and then applying that law to the facts or circumstances of the case, judges rely on the process of **legal reasoning.** Through the use of legal reasoning, judges harmonize their decisions with those that have been made before, as the doctrine of *stare decisis* requires.

Students of business law and the legal environment also engage in legal reasoning. You may be asked to provide answers for some of the case problems that appear at the end of every chapter in this text. Each problem describes the facts of a particular dispute and the legal question at issue. If you are assigned a case problem, you will be asked to determine how a court would answer that question, and why. In other words, you will need to give legal reasons for whatever conclusion you reach. We look next at the basic steps involved in legal reasoning and then describe some forms of reasoning commonly used by the courts in making their decisions.

Basic Steps in Legal Reasoning At times, the legal arguments set forth in court opinions are relatively simple and brief. At other times, the arguments are complex and lengthy. Regardless of the length of a legal argument, however, the basic steps of the legal reasoning process remain the same. These steps, which you can also follow when analyzing cases and case problems, form what is commonly referred to as the *IRAC method* of legal reasoning. IRAC is an acronym formed from the first letters of the words *Issue, Rule, Application*, and *Conclusion*. To apply the IRAC method, you ask the following questions:

1. **Issue—What are the key facts and issues?** Suppose that a plaintiff comes before the court claiming *assault* (words or acts that wrongfully and intentionally make another person fearful of immediate physical harm). The plaintiff claims that the defendant threatened her while she was sleeping. Although the plaintiff was unaware that she was being threatened, her roommate heard the defendant make the threat. The legal issue is whether the defendant's action constitutes the tort of assault, given that the plaintiff was unaware of that action at the time it occurred. (A tort is a wrongful act. As you will see later, torts fall under the governance of civil law rather than criminal law.)
2. **Rule—What rule of law applies to the case?** A rule of law may be a rule stated by the courts in previous decisions, a state or federal statute, or a state or federal administrative agency regulation. In our hypothetical case, the plaintiff **alleges** (claims) that the defendant committed a tort. Therefore, the applicable law is the common law of torts—specifically, tort law governing assault. Case precedents involving similar facts and issues thus would be relevant. Often, more than one rule of law will be applicable to a case.
3. **Application—How does the rule of law apply to the particular facts and circumstances of this case?** This step is often the most difficult because each case presents a unique set of facts, circumstances, and parties. Although cases may be similar, no two cases

are ever identical in all respects. Normally, judges (and lawyers and law students) try to find **cases on point**—previously decided cases that are as similar as possible to the one under consideration.
4. **Conclusion—What conclusion should be drawn?** This step normally presents few problems. Usually, the conclusion is evident if the previous three steps have been followed carefully.

There Is No One "Right" Answer Many people believe that there is one "right" answer to every legal question. In most legal controversies, however, there is no single correct result. Good arguments can usually be made to support either side of a legal controversy. Quite often, a case does not involve a "good" person suing a "bad" person. In many cases, both parties have acted in good faith in some measure or in bad faith to some degree. Additionally, each judge has her or his own personal beliefs and philosophy. At least to some extent, these personal factors shape the legal reasoning process. In short, the outcome of a particular lawsuit before a court cannot be predicted with certainty.

1–3e The Common Law Today

Today, the common law derived from judicial decisions continues to be applied throughout the United States. Common law doctrines and principles, however, govern only areas *not* covered by statutory or administrative law. In a dispute concerning a particular employment practice, for instance, if a statute regulates that practice, the statute will apply rather than the common law doctrine that applied before the statute was enacted. The common law tradition and its application are reviewed in Concept Summary 1.2.

Courts Interpret Statutes Even in areas governed by statutory law, judge-made law continues to be important because there is a significant interplay between statutory law and the common law. For instance, many statutes essentially codify existing common law rules, and regulations issued by various administrative agencies usually are based, at least in part, on common law principles. Additionally, the courts, in interpreting statutory law, often rely on the common law as a guide to what the legislators intended. Frequently, the applicability of a newly enacted statute does not become clear until a body of case law develops to clarify how, when, and to whom the statute applies.

Clearly, a judge's function is not to *make* the laws—that is the function of the legislative branch of government—but to interpret and apply them. From a

Concept Summary 1.2

The Common Law Tradition

Origins of Common Law	The American legal system is based on the common law tradition, which originated in medieval England.
Legal and Equitable Remedies	Remedies at law (land, items of value, or money) and remedies in equity (including specific performance, injunction, and rescission of a contractual obligation) originated in the early English courts of law and courts of equity, respectively.
Case Precedents and the Doctrine of *Stare Decisis*	In the king's courts, judges attempted to make their decisions consistent with previous decisions, called precedents. This practice gave rise to the doctrine of *stare decisis*. This doctrine, which became a cornerstone of the common law tradition, obligates judges to abide by precedents established in their jurisdictions.
Common Law Today	The common law governs all areas not covered by statutory law or administrative laws. Courts interpret statutes and regulations.

practical point of view, however, the courts play a significant role in defining the laws enacted by legislative bodies, which tend to be expressed in general terms. Judges thus have some flexibility in interpreting and applying the law. It is because of this flexibility that different courts can, and often do, arrive at different conclusions in cases that involve nearly identical issues, facts, and applicable laws.

Restatements of the Law Clarify and Illustrate the Common Law   The American Law Institute (ALI) has published compilations of the common law called *Restatements of the Law*, which generally summarize the common law rules followed by most states. There are *Restatements of the Law* in the areas of contracts, torts, agency, trusts, property, restitution, security, judgments, and conflict of laws. The *Restatements,* like other secondary sources of law, do not in themselves have the force of law, but they are an important source of legal analysis and opinion. Hence, judges often rely on them in making decisions.

Many of the *Restatements* are now in their second, third, or fourth editions. We refer to the *Restatements* frequently in subsequent chapters of this text, indicating in parentheses the edition to which we are referring. For instance, we refer to the third edition of the *Restatement of the Law of Contracts* as simply the *Restatement (Third) of Contracts.*

1–4 Schools of Legal Thought

How judges apply the law to specific cases, including disputes relating to the business world, depends in part on their philosophical approaches to law. Thus, the study of law, or **jurisprudence,** involves learning about different schools of legal thought and how the approaches to law characteristic of each school can affect judicial decision making.

1–4a The Natural Law School

An age-old question about the nature of law has to do with the finality of a nation's laws. What if a particular law is deemed to be a "bad" law by a substantial number of the nation's citizens? Must they obey that law? According to the **natural law** theory, a higher, or universal, law exists that applies to all human beings. Each written law should reflect the principles inherent in natural law. If it does not, then it loses its legitimacy and need not be obeyed.

The natural law tradition is one of the oldest and most significant schools of jurisprudence. It dates back to the days of the Greek philosopher Aristotle (384–322 B.C.E.), who distinguished between natural law and the laws governing a particular nation. According to Aristotle, natural law applies universally to all humankind.

The notion that people have "natural rights" stems from the natural law tradition. Those who claim that a specific foreign government is depriving certain citizens of their human rights, for instance, are implicitly appealing to a higher law that has universal applicability.

The question of the universality of basic human rights also comes into play in the context of international business operations. U.S. companies that have operations abroad often hire foreign workers as employees. Should the same laws that protect U.S. employees apply to these foreign employees? This question is rooted implicitly in a concept of universal rights that has its origins in the natural law tradition.

1-4b The Positivist School

Positive law, or national law, is the written law of a given society at a particular time. In contrast to natural law, it applies only to the citizens of that nation or society. Those who adhere to **legal positivism** believe that there can be no higher law than a nation's positive law.

According to the positivist school, there are no "natural rights." Rather, human rights exist solely because of laws. If the laws are not enforced, anarchy will result. Thus, whether a law is "bad" or "good" is irrelevant. The law is the law and must be obeyed until it is changed—in an orderly manner through a legitimate lawmaking process. A judge who takes this view will probably be more inclined to defer to an existing law than would a judge who adheres to the natural law tradition.

1-4c The Historical School

The **historical school** of legal thought emphasizes the evolutionary process of law by concentrating on the origin and history of the legal system. This school looks to the past to discover what the principles of contemporary law should be. The legal doctrines that have withstood the passage of time—those that have worked in the past—are deemed best suited for shaping present laws. Hence, law derives its legitimacy and authority from adhering to the standards that historical development has shown to be workable. Followers of the historical school are more likely than those of other schools to strictly follow decisions made in past cases.

1-4d Legal Realism

In the 1920s and 1930s, a number of jurists and scholars, known as *legal realists*, rebelled against the historical approach to law. **Legal realism** is based on the idea that law is just one of many institutions in society and that it is shaped by social forces and needs. Because the law is a human enterprise, this school reasons that judges should take social and economic realities into account when deciding cases.

Legal realists also believe that the law can never be applied with total uniformity. Given that judges are human beings with unique personalities, value systems, and intellects, different judges will obviously bring different reasoning processes to the same case. Female judges, for instance, might be more inclined than male judges to consider whether a decision might have a negative impact on the employment of women or minorities.

Legal realism strongly influenced the growth of what is sometimes called the **sociological school,** which views law as a tool for promoting justice in society. In the 1960s, for instance, the justices of the United States Supreme Court helped advance the civil rights movement by upholding long-neglected laws calling for equal treatment for all Americans, including African Americans and other minorities. Generally, jurists who adhere to this philosophy of law are more likely to depart from past decisions than are jurists who adhere to other schools of legal thought.

Concept Summary 1.3 reviews the schools of jurisprudential thought.

1-5 Classifications of Law

The law may be broken down according to several classification systems. One system, for instance, divides law into substantive law and procedural law. **Substantive law** consists of all laws that define, describe, regulate, and create legal rights and obligations. **Procedural law** consists of all laws that outline the methods of enforcing the rights established by substantive law.

Note that many statutes contain both substantive and procedural provisions. ■ **Example 1.5** A state law that provides employees with the right to *workers' compensation benefits* for on-the-job injuries is a substantive law because it creates legal rights. Procedural laws establish the method by which an employee must notify the employer about an on-the-job injury, prove the injury, and periodically submit additional proof to continue receiving workers' compensation benefits. ■

Other classification systems divide law into federal law and state law, private law (dealing with relationships between private entities) and public law (addressing the relationship between persons and their governments), and national law and international law. Here we look at still another classification system, which divides law into civil law and criminal law. We also explain what is meant by the term *cyberlaw*.

Concept Summary 1.3

Schools of Jurisprudential Thought

Natural Law School	One of the oldest and most significant schools of legal thought. Those who believe in natural law hold that there is a universal law applicable to all human beings.
Positivist School	A school of legal thought centered on the assumption that there is no law higher than the laws created by the government.
Historical School	A school of legal thought that stresses the evolutionary nature of law and looks to doctrines that have withstood the passage of time for guidance in shaping present laws.
Legal Realism	A school of legal thought that advocates a less abstract and more realistic and pragmatic approach to the law, taking into account customary practices and the circumstances surrounding the particular transaction.

1–5a Civil Law and Criminal Law

Civil law spells out the rights and duties that exist between persons and between persons and their governments, as well as the relief available when a person's rights are violated. Typically, in a civil case, a private party sues another private party who has failed to comply with a duty. (Note that the government can also sue a party for a civil law violation.) Much of the law that we discuss in this text is civil law, including contract law and tort law.

Criminal law, in contrast, is concerned with wrongs committed *against the public as a whole.* Criminal acts are defined and prohibited by local, state, or federal government statutes. Criminal defendants are thus prosecuted by public officials, such as a district attorney (D.A.), on behalf of the state, not by their victims or other private parties. Some statutes, such as those protecting the environment or investors, have both civil and criminal provisions.

1–5b Cyberlaw

The use of the Internet to conduct business has led to new types of legal issues. In response, courts have had to adapt traditional laws to unique situations. Additionally, legislatures at both the federal and the state levels have created laws to deal specifically with such issues.

Frequently, people use the term **cyberlaw** to refer to the emerging body of law that governs transactions conducted via the Internet. Cyberlaw is not really a classification of law, though, nor is it a new *type* of law. Rather, it is an informal term used to refer to both new laws and

modifications of traditional laws that relate to the online environment. Throughout this book, you will read how the law in a given area is evolving to govern specific legal issues that arise in the online context.

1–6 How to Find Primary Sources of Law

This text includes numerous references, or *citations,* to primary sources of law—federal and state statutes, the U.S. Constitution and state constitutions, regulations issued by administrative agencies, and court cases. A **citation** identifies the publication in which a legal authority—such as a statute or a court decision or other source—can be found. In this section, we explain how you can use citations to find primary sources of law. Note that in addition to being published in sets of books, as described next, most federal and state laws and case decisions are available online.

1–6a Finding Statutory and Administrative Law

When Congress passes laws, they are collected in a publication titled *United States Statutes at Large.* When state legislatures pass laws, they are collected in similar state publications. Most frequently, however, laws are referred to in their codified form—that is, the form in which they appear in the federal and state codes. In these codes, laws are compiled by subject.

United States Code The *United States Code* (U.S.C.) arranges all existing federal laws by broad subject. Each of the fifty-two subjects is given a title and a title number. For instance, laws relating to commerce and trade are collected in Title 15, "Commerce and Trade." Each title is subdivided by sections. A citation to the U.S.C. includes both title and section numbers. Thus, a reference to "15 U.S.C. Section 1" means that the statute can be found in Section 1 of Title 15. ("Section" may be designated by the symbol §, and "Sections," by §§.)

In addition to the print publication, the federal government provides a searchable online database at www.gpo.gov. It includes the *United States Code,* the U.S. Constitution, and many other federal resources.

Commercial publications of federal laws and regulations are also available. For instance, Thomson Reuters publishes the *United States Code Annotated* (U.S.C.A.). The U.S.C.A. contains the official text of the U.S.C., plus notes (annotations) on court decisions that interpret and apply specific sections of the statutes. The U.S.C.A. also includes additional research aids, such as cross-references to related statutes, historical notes, and library references. A citation to the U.S.C.A. is similar to a citation to the U.S.C.: "15 U.S.C.A. Section 1."

State Codes State codes follow the U.S.C. pattern of arranging law by subject. They may be called codes, revisions, compilations, consolidations, general statutes, or statutes, depending on the preferences of the states.

In some codes, subjects are designated by number. In others, they are designated by name. ■ **Example 1.6** "13 Pennsylvania Consolidated Statutes Section 1101" means that the statute can be found in Title 13, Section 1101, of the Pennsylvania code. "California Commercial Code Section 1101" means that the statute can be found under the subject heading "Commercial Code" of the California code in Section 1101. Abbreviations are often used. For instance, "13 Pennsylvania Consolidated Statutes Section 1101" is abbreviated "13 Pa. C.S. § 1101," and "California Commercial Code Section 1101" is abbreviated "Cal. Com. Code § 1101." ■

Administrative Rules Rules and regulations adopted by federal administrative agencies are initially published in the *Federal Register,* a daily publication of the U.S. government. Later, they are incorporated into the *Code of Federal Regulations* (C.F.R.). The C.F.R. is available online on the government database (www.gpo.gov).

Like the U.S.C., the C.F.R. is divided into titles. Rules within each title are assigned section numbers. A full citation to the C.F.R. includes title and section numbers. ■ **Example 1.7** A reference to "17 C.F.R.

Section 230.504" means that the rule can be found in Section 230.504 of Title 17. ■

1–6b Finding Case Law

Before discussing the case reporting system, we need to look briefly at the court system. There are two types of courts in the United States, federal courts and state courts. Both systems consist of several levels, or tiers, of courts. *Trial courts,* in which evidence is presented and testimony given, are on the bottom tier. Decisions from a trial court can be appealed to a higher court, which commonly is an intermediate *court of appeals,* or *appellate court.* Decisions from these intermediate courts of appeals may be appealed to an even higher court, such as a state supreme court or the United States Supreme Court.

State Court Decisions Most state trial court decisions are not published in books (except in New York and a few other states, which publish selected trial court opinions). Decisions from state trial courts are typically filed in the office of the clerk of the court, where the decisions are available for public inspection. (Increasingly, they can be found online as well.)

Written decisions of the appellate, or reviewing, courts, however, are published and distributed (in print and online). Many of the state court cases presented in this textbook are from state appellate courts. The reported appellate court decisions are published in volumes called *reports* or *reporters,* which are numbered consecutively. State appellate court decisions are found in the state reporters of that particular state. Official reports are published by the state, whereas unofficial reports are published by nongovernment entities.

Regional Reporters. State court opinions appear in regional units of the West's National Reporter System, published by Thomson Reuters. Most lawyers and libraries have these reporters because they report cases more quickly and are distributed more widely than the state-published reporters. In fact, many states have eliminated their own reporters in favor of the National Reporter System.

The National Reporter System divides the states into the following geographic areas: *Atlantic* (A., A.2d, or A.3d), *North Eastern* (N.E., N.E.2d, or N.E.3d), *North Western* (N.W. or N.W.2d), *Pacific* (P., P.2d, or P.3d), *South Eastern* (S.E. or S.E.2d), *South Western* (S.W., S.W.2d, or S.W.3d), and *Southern* (So., So.2d, or So.3d). (The *2d* and *3d* in the preceding abbreviations refer to *Second Series* and *Third Series,* respectively.) The states included in each of these regional divisions are indicated in Exhibit 1–4, which illustrates the National Reporter System.

Exhibit 1–4 National Reporter System—Regional/Federal

Regional Reporters	Coverage Beginning	Coverage
Atlantic Reporter (A., A.2d, or A.3d)	1885	Connecticut, Delaware, District of Columbia, Maine, Maryland, New Hampshire, New Jersey, Pennsylvania, Rhode Island, and Vermont.
North Eastern Reporter (N.E., N.E.2d, or N.E.3d)	1885	Illinois, Indiana, Massachusetts, New York, and Ohio.
North Western Reporter (N.W. or N.W.2d)	1879	Iowa, Michigan, Minnesota, Nebraska, North Dakota, South Dakota, and Wisconsin.
Pacific Reporter (P., P.2d, or P.3d)	1883	Alaska, Arizona, California, Colorado, Hawaii, Idaho, Kansas, Montana, Nevada, New Mexico, Oklahoma, Oregon, Utah, Washington, and Wyoming.
South Eastern Reporter (S.E. or S.E.2d)	1887	Georgia, North Carolina, South Carolina, Virginia, and West Virginia.
South Western Reporter (S.W., S.W.2d, or S.W.3d)	1886	Arkansas, Kentucky, Missouri, Tennessee, and Texas.
Southern Reporter (So., So.2d, or So.3d)	1887	Alabama, Florida, Louisiana, and Mississippi.

Federal Reporters		
Federal Reporter (F., F.2d, or F.3d)	1880	U.S. Circuit Courts from 1880 to 1912; U.S. Commerce Court from 1911 to 1913; U.S. District Courts from 1880 to 1932; U.S. Court of Claims (now called U.S. Court of Federal Claims) from 1929 to 1932 and since 1960; U.S. Courts of Appeals since 1891; U.S. Court of Customs and Patent Appeals since 1929; U.S. Emergency Court of Appeals since 1943.
Federal Supplement (F.Supp., F.Supp.2d, or F.Supp.3d)	1932	U.S. Court of Claims from 1932 to 1960; U.S. District Courts since 1932; U.S. Customs Court since 1956.
Federal Rules Decisions (F.R.D.)	1939	U.S. District Courts involving the Federal Rules of Civil Procedure since 1939 and Federal Rules of Criminal Procedure since 1946.
Supreme Court Reporter (S.Ct.)	1882	United States Supreme Court since the October term of 1882.
Bankruptcy Reporter (Bankr.)	1980	Bankruptcy decisions of U.S. Bankruptcy Courts, U.S. District Courts, U.S. Courts of Appeals, and the United States Supreme Court.
Military Justice Reporter (M.J.)	1978	U.S. Court of Military Appeals and Courts of Military Review for the Army, Navy, Air Force, and Coast Guard.

NATIONAL REPORTER SYSTEM MAP

Case Citations. After appellate decisions have been published, they are normally referred to (cited) by the name of the case and the volume, name, and page number of the reporter(s) in which the opinion can be found. The citation first lists the state's official reporter (if different from the National Reporter System), then the National Reporter, and then any other selected reporter. (Citing a reporter by volume number, name, and page number, in that order, is common to all citations. The year that the decision was issued is often included at the end in parentheses.) When more than one reporter is cited for the same case, each reference is called a *parallel citation.*

Note that some states have adopted a "public domain citation system" that uses a somewhat different format for the citation. For instance, in Wisconsin, a Wisconsin Supreme Court decision might be designated "2019 WI 6," meaning that the case was decided in the year 2019 by the Wisconsin Supreme Court and was the sixth decision issued by that court during that year. Parallel citations to the *Wisconsin Reports* and the *North Western Reporter* are still included after the public domain citation.

■ **Example 1.8** Consider the following case citation: *Simms v. Friel,* 302 Neb. 1, 921 N.W.2d 369 (2019). We see that the opinion in this case can be found in Volume 302 of the official *Nebraska Reports,* on page 1. The parallel citation is to Volume 921 of the *North Western Reporter, Second Series,* page 369. ■

When we present opinions in this text, in addition to the reporter, we give the name of the court hearing the case and the year of the court's decision. Sample citations to state court decisions are explained in Exhibit 1–5.

Federal Court Decisions Federal district (trial) court decisions are published unofficially in the *Federal Supplement* (F.Supp., F.Supp.2d, or F.Supp.3d), and opinions from the circuit courts of appeals (reviewing courts) are reported unofficially in the *Federal Reporter* (F., F.2d, or F.3d). Cases concerning federal bankruptcy law are published unofficially in the *Bankruptcy Reporter* (Bankr. or B.R.).

The official edition of the United States Supreme Court decisions is the *United States Reports* (U.S.), which is published by the federal government. Unofficial editions of Supreme Court cases include the *Supreme Court Reporter* (S.Ct.) and the *Lawyers' Edition of the Supreme Court Reports* (L.Ed. or L.Ed.2d). Sample citations for federal court decisions are also listed and explained in Exhibit 1–5.

Unpublished Opinions Many court opinions that are not yet published or that are not intended for publication can be accessed through Thomson Reuters Westlaw® (abbreviated in citations as "WL"), an online legal database. When no citation to a published reporter is available for cases cited in this text, we give the WL citation (such as 2019 WL 325268, which means it was case number 325268 decided in the year 2019). In addition, federal appellate court decisions that are designated as unpublished may appear in the *Federal Appendix* (Fed.Appx.) of the National Reporter System.

Sometimes, both in this text and in other legal sources, you will see blank lines left in a citation. This occurs when the decision will be published, but the particular volume number and page number are not yet available.

Old Case Law On a few occasions, this text cites opinions from old, classic cases dating to the nineteenth century or earlier. Some of these are from the English courts. The citations to these cases may not conform to the descriptions just presented because the reporters in which they were originally published were often known by the names of the persons who compiled the reporters.

1–7 How to Read and Understand Case Law

The decisions made by the courts establish the boundaries of the law as it applies to almost all business relationships. It thus is essential that businesspersons know how to read and understand case law.

The cases that we present in this text have been condensed from the full text of the courts' opinions and are presented in a special format. In approximately two-thirds of the cases (including the cases designated as *Classic* and *Spotlight*), we have summarized the background and facts, as well as the court's decision and remedy, in our own words. In those cases, we have included only selected excerpts from the court's opinion ("In the Language of the Court"). In the remaining one-third of the cases (labeled "Case Analysis"), we have provided a longer excerpt from the court's opinion without summarizing the background and facts or decision and remedy.

Exhibit 1–5 How to Read Citations

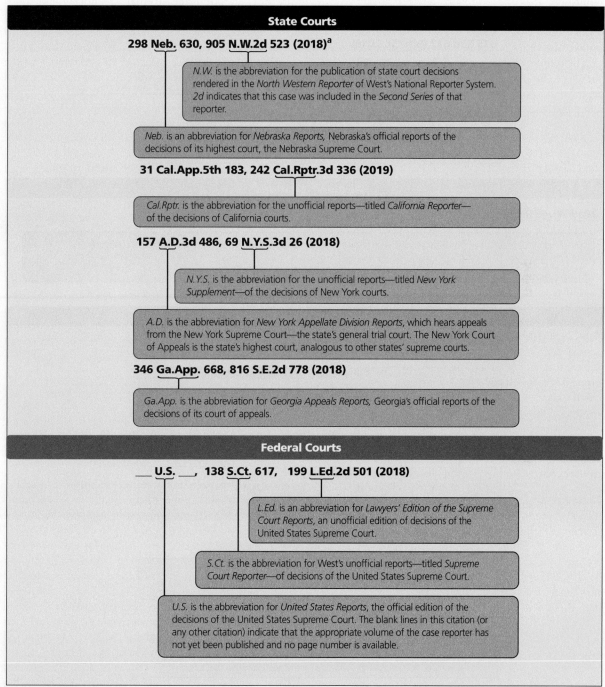

State Courts

298 Neb. 630, 905 N.W.2d 523 (2018)ᵃ

N.W. is the abbreviation for the publication of state court decisions rendered in the *North Western Reporter* of West's National Reporter System. *2d* indicates that this case was included in the *Second Series* of that reporter.

Neb. is an abbreviation for *Nebraska Reports,* Nebraska's official reports of the decisions of its highest court, the Nebraska Supreme Court.

31 Cal.App.5th 183, 242 Cal.Rptr.3d 336 (2019)

Cal.Rptr. is the abbreviation for the unofficial reports—titled *California Reporter*—of the decisions of California courts.

157 A.D.3d 486, 69 N.Y.S.3d 26 (2018)

N.Y.S. is the abbreviation for the unofficial reports—titled *New York Supplement*—of the decisions of New York courts.

A.D. is the abbreviation for *New York Appellate Division Reports,* which hears appeals from the New York Supreme Court—the state's general trial court. The New York Court of Appeals is the state's highest court, analogous to other states' supreme courts.

346 Ga.App. 668, 816 S.E.2d 778 (2018)

Ga.App. is the abbreviation for *Georgia Appeals Reports,* Georgia's official reports of the decisions of its court of appeals.

Federal Courts

___ U.S. ___, 138 S.Ct. 617,   199 L.Ed.2d 501 (2018)

L.Ed. is an abbreviation for *Lawyers' Edition of the Supreme Court Reports,* an unofficial edition of decisions of the United States Supreme Court.

S.Ct. is the abbreviation for West's unofficial reports—titled *Supreme Court Reporter*—of decisions of the United States Supreme Court.

U.S. is the abbreviation for *United States Reports*, the official edition of the decisions of the United States Supreme Court. The blank lines in this citation (or any other citation) indicate that the appropriate volume of the case reporter has not yet been published and no page number is available.

a. The case names have been deleted from these citations to emphasize the publications. It should be kept in mind, however, that the name of a case is as important as the specific page numbers in the volumes in which it is found. If a citation is incorrect, the correct citation may be found in a publication's index of case names. In addition to providing a check on errors in citations, the date of a case is important because the value of a recent case as an authority is likely to be greater than that of older cases from the same court.

Continued

Exhibit 1–5   How to Read Citations—Continued

Federal Courts (Continued)

915 F.3d 617 (9th Cir. 2019)

> *9th Cir.* is an abbreviation denoting that this case was decided in the U.S. Court of Appeals for the Ninth Circuit.

324 F.Supp.3d 1172 (D.Nev. 2018)

> *D.Nev.* is an abbreviation indicating that the U.S. District Court for the District of Nevada decided this case.

Westlaw® Citations[b]

2019 WL 491862

> *WL* is an abbreviation for Westlaw. The number 2019 is the year of the document that can be found with this citation in the Westlaw database. The number 491862 is a number assigned to a specific document. A higher number indicates that a document was added to the Westlaw database later in the year.

Statutory and Other Citations

18 U.S.C. Section 1961(1)(A)

> *U.S.C.* denotes *United States Code*, the codification of *United States Statutes at Large*. The number 18 refers to the statute's U.S.C. title number and 1961 to its section number within that title. The number 1 in parentheses refers to a subsection within the section, and the letter A in parentheses to a subsection within the subsection.

UCC 2–206(1)(b)

> *UCC* is an abbreviation for *Uniform Commercial Code*. The first number 2 is a reference to an article of the UCC, and 206 to a section within that article. The number 1 in parentheses refers to a subsection within the section, and the letter b in parentheses to a subsection within the subsection.

Restatement (Third) of Torts, Section 6

> *Restatement (Third) of Torts* refers to the third edition of the American Law Institute's *Restatement of the Law of Torts*. The number 6 refers to a specific section.

17 C.F.R. Section 230.505

> *C.F.R.* is an abbreviation for *Code of Federal Regulations*, a compilation of federal administrative regulations. The number 17 designates the regulation's title number, and 230.505 designates a specific section within that title.

b. Many court decisions that are not yet published or that are not intended for publication can be accessed through Westlaw, an online legal database.

The following sections provide useful insights into how to read and understand case law.

1–7a Case Titles and Terminology

The title of a case, such as *Adams v. Jones*, indicates the names of the parties to the lawsuit. The *v.* in the case title stands for *versus*, which means "against." In the trial court, Adams was the plaintiff—the person who filed the suit. Jones was the defendant.

If the case is appealed, however, the appellate court will sometimes place the name of the party appealing the decision first, so the case may be called *Jones v. Adams* if Jones appealed. Because some appellate courts retain the trial court order of names, it is often impossible to distinguish the plaintiff from the defendant in the title of a reported appellate court decision. You must carefully read the facts of each case to identify the parties.

The following terms, phrases, and abbreviations are frequently encountered in court opinions and legal publications.

Parties to Lawsuits The party initiating a lawsuit is referred to as the *plaintiff* or *petitioner*, depending on the nature of the action. The party against whom a lawsuit is brought is the *defendant* or *respondent*. Lawsuits frequently involve more than one plaintiff and/or defendant.

When a case is appealed from the original court or jurisdiction to another court or jurisdiction, the party appealing the case is called the **appellant.** The **appellee** is the party against whom the appeal is taken. (In some appellate courts, the party appealing a case is referred to as the *petitioner*, and the party against whom the suit is brought or appealed is called the *respondent*.)

Judges and Justices The terms *judge* and *justice* are usually synonymous and represent two designations given to judges in various courts. All members of the United States Supreme Court, for instance, are referred to as justices. Justice is the formal title often given to judges of appellate courts, although this is not always true. In New York, a justice is a judge of the trial court (called the Supreme Court), and a member of the Court of Appeals (the state's highest court) is called a judge.

The term *justice* is commonly abbreviated to J., and *justices*, to JJ. A United States Supreme Court case might refer to Justice Sotomayor as Sotomayor, J., or to Chief Justice Roberts as Roberts, C.J.

Decisions and Opinions Most decisions reached by reviewing, or appellate, courts are explained in written **opinions.** The opinion contains the court's reasons for its decision, the rules of law that apply, and the judgment. You may encounter several types of opinions as you read appellate cases, including the following:

- When all the judges (or justices) agree, a *unanimous opinion* is written for the entire court.
- When there is not unanimous agreement, a **majority opinion** is generally written. It outlines the views of the majority of the judges deciding the case.
- A judge who agrees (concurs) with the majority opinion as to the result but not as to the legal reasoning often writes a **concurring opinion.** In it, the judge sets out the reasoning that he or she considers correct.
- A **dissenting opinion** presents the views of one or more judges who disagree with the majority view.
- Sometimes, no single position is fully supported by a majority of the judges deciding a case. In this situation, we may have a **plurality opinion.** This is the opinion that has the support of the largest number of judges, but the group in agreement is less than a majority.
- Finally, a court occasionally issues a *per curiam* **opinion** (*per curiam* is Latin for "of the court"), which does not indicate which judge wrote the opinion.

1–7b Sample Court Case

To illustrate the various elements contained in a court opinion, we present an annotated court opinion in Exhibit 1–6. The opinion is from an actual case that the United States Court of Appeals for the Tenth Circuit decided in 2018.

Editorial Practice You will note that triple asterisks (* * *) and quadruple asterisks (* * * *) frequently appear in the opinion. The triple asterisks indicate that we have deleted a few words or sentences from the opinion for the sake of readability or brevity. Quadruple asterisks mean that an entire paragraph (or more) has been omitted.

Additionally, when the opinion cites another case or legal source, the citation to the case or source has been omitted, again for the sake of readability and brevity. These editorial practices are continued in the other court opinions presented in this book. In addition, whenever

Exhibit 1–6 A Sample Court Case

This section contains the citation— the name of the case, the name of the court that heard the case, the reporters in which the court's opinion can be found, and the year of the decision.	**YEASIN V. DURHAM**
	United States Court of Appeals, Tenth Circuit,
	719 Fed.Appx. 844 (2018).
This line provides the name of the judge (or justice) who authored the court's opinion.	Gregory A. *PHILLIPS*, Circuit Judge.
	* * * *
The court divides the opinion into sections, each headed by an explanatory heading. The first section summarizes the facts of the case.	**BACKGROUND**
	* * * *

[Navid] Yeasin and A.W. [were students at the University of Kansas when they] dated from the fall of 2012 through June 2013. On June 28, 2013, Yeasin physically restrained A.W. in his car, took her phone from her, threatened to commit suicide if she broke up with him, threatened to spread rumors about her, and threatened to make the University of Kansas's "campus environment so hostile, that she would not attend any university in the state of Kansas."

Battery is an unexcused and harmful or offensive physical contact intentionally performed.

For this conduct, Kansas charged Yeasin with * * * **battery** * * * . A.W. * * * obtained a **protection order** against Yeasin.

A *protection order* is an order issued by a court that protects a person by requiring another person to do, or not to do, something. The order can protect someone from being physically or sexually threatened or harassed.

* * * A.W. filed a complaint against Yeasin with the university's Office of Institutional Opportunity and Access (IOA). * * * The IOA * * * issued * * * a

A *no-contact order* prohibits a person from being in contact with another person.

no-contact order * * * [that] "prohibited [Yeasin] from initiating, or contributing through third-parties, to any physical, verbal, electronic, or written communication with A.W., her family, her friends or her associates."

A *hearing* is a proceeding that takes place before a decision-making body. Testimony and other evidence can be presented to help determine the issue.

[Despite the order,] Yeasin posted more than a dozen tweets about A.W., including disparaging comments about her body.

To *adjudicate* is to hear evidence and arguments in order to determine and resolve a dispute.

[The university held a **hearing** to **adjudicate** A.W.'s complaint against Yeasin.] Both parties testified. The hearing panel submitted the **record** to Dr. Tammara Durham, the university's vice provost for student affairs, for a decision regarding

A *record* is a written account of proceedings.

whether and how to sanction Yeasin's conduct.]

Exhibit 1–6 A Sample Court Case—Continued

> *Sexual harassment* can consist of language or conduct that is so offensive it creates a hostile environment.

* * * Durham found that Yeasin's June 28, 2013 conduct and his tweets were "so severe, pervasive and objectively offensive that it interfered with A.W.'s academic performance and equal opportunity to participate in or benefit from University programs or activities." She found that his tweets violated the [university's] **sexual-harassment** policy because they were "unwelcome comments about A.W.'s body." And she found that his conduct "threatened the physical health, safety and welfare of A.W., making the conduct a violation of * * * the [university's Student] Code."

* * * Durham * * * expelled Yeasin from the university and banned him from campus.

* * * *

> *First Amendment rights* include the freedom of speech, which is the right to express oneself without government interference. This right is guaranteed under the First Amendment to the U.S. Constitution.

Yeasin contested his expulsion in a Kansas state court. The court set aside Yeasin's expulsion, reasoning that * * * "KU and Dr. Durham erroneously interpreted the Student Code of Conduct by applying it to off-campus conduct."

* * * *

> *Moved to dismiss* means that a party filed a motion (applied to the court to obtain an order) to dismiss a claim on the ground that it had no basis in law.

Yeasin then brought this suit in federal court, claiming that Dr. Durham had violated his **First Amendment rights** by expelling him for * * * off-campus speech. * * * Dr. Durham **moved to dismiss** * * * Yeasin's claim * * *. The * * * court granted the motion after concluding that Dr. Durham hadn't violated Yeasin's clearly established rights.

> To *appeal* is to request an appellate court to review the decision of a lower court.

[Yeasin **appealed** to the U.S. Court of Appeals for the Tenth Circuit.]

> The second major section of the opinion responds to the party's appeal.

DISCUSSION

* * * *

Yeasin's case presents interesting questions regarding the tension between some students' free-speech rights and other students' * * * rights to receive an education absent * * * sexual harassment.

Continued

Exhibit 1–6   A Sample Court Case—Continued

An *enclave* is a distinct group within a larger community.

To *circumscribe* is to restrict.

Here, *establish* means to settle firmly.

Judges are obligated to follow the precedents established in prior court decisions. A *precedent* is a decision that stands as authority for deciding a subsequent case involving identical or similar facts. Otherwise, the decision may be persuasive, but it is not controlling.

A *reasonable belief* exists when there is a reasonable basis to believe that a crime or other violation is being or has been committed.

A *doctrine* is a rule, principle, or tenet of the law.

Colleges and universities are not **enclaves** immune from the sweep of the First Amendment. * * * The [courts] permit schools to **circumscribe** students' free-speech rights in certain contexts [particularly in secondary public schools].

* * * *

Yeasin argues that [three United States Supreme Court cases—*Papish v. Board of Curators of the University of Missouri, Healy v. James,* and *Widmar v. Vincent*] clearly **establish** * * * that universities may not restrict university-student speech in the same way secondary public school officials may restrict secondary-school student speech. * * * Yeasin argues these cases clearly establish his right to tweet about A.W. without the university being able to place restrictions on, or discipline him for, * * * his tweets.

But **none of the** * * * **cases present circumstances similar to his own**. *Papish, Healy,* and *Widmar* don't concern university-student conduct that interferes with the rights of other students or risks disrupting campus order.

* * * *

* * * In those cases no student had been charged with a crime against another student and followed that up with sexually-harassing comments affecting her ability to feel safe while attending classes. Dr. Durham had a **reasonable belief** based on the June 28, 2013 incident and on Yeasin's tweets that his continued enrollment at the university threatened to disrupt A.W.'s education and interfere with her rights.

At the intersection of university speech and social media, First Amendment **doctrine** is unsettled. Compare *Keefe v. Adams* [in which a federal appellate court concluded] that a college's removal of a student from school based on off-campus statements on his social media page didn't violate his First Amendment free-speech rights, with *J.S. v. Blue Mountain School District* [in which a different federal appellate court held] that a school district violated the First Amendment rights of a plaintiff when it suspended her for creating a private social media profile mocking the school principal.

Exhibit 1–6 A Sample Court Case—Continued

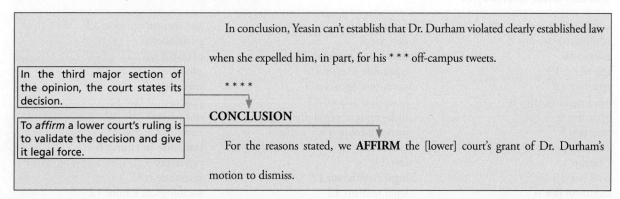

In conclusion, Yeasin can't establish that Dr. Durham violated clearly established law when she expelled him, in part, for his * * * off-campus tweets.

In the third major section of the opinion, the court states its decision.

* * * *

CONCLUSION

To *affirm* a lower court's ruling is to validate the decision and give it legal force.

For the reasons stated, we **AFFIRM** the [lower] court's grant of Dr. Durham's motion to dismiss.

---

we present a court opinion that includes a term or phrase that may not be readily understandable, a bracketed definition or paraphrase has been added.

Briefing Cases Knowing how to read and understand court opinions and the legal reasoning used by the courts is an essential step in undertaking accurate legal research. A further step is "briefing," or summarizing, the case.

Legal researchers routinely brief cases by reducing the texts of the opinions to their essential elements.

Generally, when you brief a case, you first summarize the background and facts of the case, as the authors have done for most of the cases presented in this text. You then indicate the issue (or issues) before the court. An important element in the case brief is, of course, the court's decision on the issue and the legal reasoning used by the court in reaching that decision.

Detailed instructions on how to brief a case are given in Appendix A, which also includes a briefed version of the sample court case presented in Exhibit 1–6.

Practice and Review: Law and Legal Reasoning

Suppose that the California legislature passes a law that severely restricts carbon dioxide emissions from automobiles in that state. A group of automobile manufacturers files suit against the state of California to prevent the enforcement of the law. The automakers claim that a federal law already sets fuel economy standards nationwide and that fuel economy standards are essentially the same as carbon dioxide emission standards. According to the automobile manufacturers, it is unfair to allow California to impose more stringent regulations than those set by the federal law. Using the information presented in the chapter, answer the following questions.

1. Who are the parties (the plaintiffs and the defendant) in this lawsuit?
2. Are the plaintiffs seeking a legal remedy or an equitable remedy?
3. What is the primary source of the law that is at issue here?
4. Where would you look to find the relevant California and federal laws?

> **Debate This** . . .   *Under the doctrine of stare decisis, courts are obligated to follow the precedents established in their jurisdiction unless there is a compelling reason not to. Should U.S. courts continue to adhere to this common law principle, given that our government now regulates so many areas by statute?*

Terms and Concepts

<table>
<tr><td>administrative agency 5</td><td>defendant 6</td><td>per curiam opinion 19</td></tr>
<tr><td>administrative law 5</td><td>defense 6</td><td>petitioner 6</td></tr>
<tr><td>alleges 10</td><td>dissenting opinion 19</td><td>plaintiff 6</td></tr>
<tr><td>appellant 19</td><td>equitable maxims 6</td><td>plurality opinion 19</td></tr>
<tr><td>appellee 19</td><td>executive agencies 5</td><td>precedent 7</td></tr>
<tr><td>binding authority 8</td><td>historical school 12</td><td>procedural law 12</td></tr>
<tr><td>breaches 6</td><td>independent regulatory agencies 5</td><td>remedies 6</td></tr>
<tr><td>case law 5</td><td>jurisprudence 11</td><td>remedies at law 6</td></tr>
<tr><td>cases on point 10</td><td>laches 6</td><td>remedies in equity 6</td></tr>
<tr><td>citation 13</td><td>law 2</td><td>reporters 8</td></tr>
<tr><td>civil law 13</td><td>legal positivism 12</td><td>respondent 6</td></tr>
<tr><td>common law 6</td><td>legal realism 12</td><td>sociological school 12</td></tr>
<tr><td>concurring opinion 19</td><td>legal reasoning 9</td><td>stare decisis 8</td></tr>
<tr><td>constitutional law 4</td><td>liability 2</td><td>statutes of limitations 6</td></tr>
<tr><td>courts of equity 6</td><td>majority opinion 19</td><td>statutory law 4</td></tr>
<tr><td>courts of law 6</td><td>natural law 11</td><td>substantive law 12</td></tr>
<tr><td>criminal law 13</td><td>opinions 19</td><td>uniform laws 4</td></tr>
<tr><td>cyberlaw 13</td><td>ordinances 4</td><td></td></tr>
<tr><td>damages 6</td><td>persuasive authorities 8</td><td></td></tr>
</table>

Issue Spotters

1. Under what circumstances might a judge rely on case law to determine the intent and purpose of a statute? (See *Sources of American Law*.)

2. After World War II, several Nazis were convicted of "crimes against humanity" by an international court. Assuming that these convicted war criminals had not disobeyed any law of their country and had merely been following their government's orders, what law had they violated? Explain. (See *Schools of Legal Thought*.)

• **Check your answers to the Issue Spotters against the answers provided in Appendix B at the end of this text.**

Business Scenarios and Case Problems

1–1. Binding versus Persuasive Authority. A county court in Illinois is deciding a case involving an issue that has never been addressed before in that state's courts. The Iowa Supreme Court, however, recently decided a case involving a very similar fact pattern. Is the Illinois court obligated to follow the Iowa Supreme Court's decision on the issue? If the United States Supreme Court had decided a similar case, would that decision be binding on the Illinois court? Explain. (See *The Common Law Tradition*.)

1–2. Sources of Law. This chapter discussed a number of sources of American law. Which source of law takes priority in the following situations, and why? (See *Sources of American Law*.)

(a) A federal statute conflicts with the U.S. Constitution.

(b) A federal statute conflicts with a state constitutional provision.

(c) A state statute conflicts with the common law of that state.

(d) A state constitutional amendment conflicts with the U.S. Constitution.

1–3. Stare Decisis. In this chapter, we stated that the doctrine of *stare decisis* "became a cornerstone of the English and American judicial systems." What does *stare decisis* mean, and why has this doctrine been so fundamental to the development of our legal tradition? (See *The Common Law Tradition*.)

1–4. Spotlight on AOL—Common Law. AOL, LLC, mistakenly made public the personal information of 650,000 of its members. The members filed a suit, alleging violations of California law. AOL asked the court to dismiss the suit on the basis of a "forum-selection clause" in its member agreement that designates Virginia courts as the place where member disputes will be tried. Under a decision of the United States Supreme Court, a forum-selection clause is unenforceable "if enforcement would contravene a strong public policy of the forum in which suit is brought." California courts have declared in other cases that the AOL clause contravenes a strong public policy. If the court applies the doctrine of *stare decisis*, will it dismiss the suit? Explain. [*Doe 1 v. AOL LLC*, 552 F.3d 1077 (9th Cir. 2009)] (See *The Common Law Tradition*.)

1–5. Business Case Problem with Sample Answer—Reading Citations. Assume that you want to read the entire court opinion in the case of *Ryan Data Exchange, Ltd. v. Graco, Inc.*, 913 F.3d 726 (8th Cir. 2019). Refer to the subsection entitled "Finding Case Law" in this chapter, and then explain specifically where you would find the court's opinion. (See *How to Find Primary Sources of Law*.)

• For a sample answer to Problem 1–5, go to Appendix C at the end of this text.

1–6. A Question of Ethics—The Doctrine of Precedent. *Sandra White operated a travel agency. To obtain lower airline fares for her nonmilitary clients, she booked military-rate travel by forwarding fake military identification cards to the airlines. The government charged White with identity theft, which requires the "use" of another's identification. The trial court cited two cases that represented precedents.*

In the first case, David Miller obtained a loan to buy land by representing that certain investors had approved the loan when, in fact, they had not. Miller's conviction for identity theft was overturned because he had merely said that the investors had done something when they had not. According to the court, this was not the "use" of another's identification.

In the second case, Kathy Medlock, an ambulance service operator, had transported patients when there was no medical necessity to do so. To obtain payment, Medlock had forged a physician's signature. The court concluded that this was "use" of another person's identity. [United States v. White, 846 F.3d 170 (6th Cir. 2017)] (See Sources of American Law.*)*

(a) Which precedent—the *Miller* case or the *Medlock* case—is similar to White's situation, and why?

(b) In the two cases cited by the court, were there any ethical differences in the actions of the parties? Explain your answer.

Time-Limited Group Assignment

1–7. Court Opinions. Read through the subsection in this chapter entitled "Decisions and Opinions." (See *How to Read and Understand Case Law*.)

(a) One group will explain the difference between a concurring opinion and a majority opinion.

(b) Another group will outline the difference between a concurring opinion and a dissenting opinion.

(c) A third group will explain why judges and justices write concurring and dissenting opinions, given that these opinions will not affect the outcome of the case at hand, which has already been decided by majority vote.

Chapter 2

Business and the Constitution

Laws that govern business have their origin in the lawmaking authority granted by the U.S. Constitution, which is the supreme law in this country. Neither Congress nor any state may pass a law that is in conflict with the Constitution.

Disputes over constitutional rights frequently come before the courts. Consider Norman's, Inc., a family-owned pharmacy in Olympia, Washington. The owners of Norman's have religious objections to the use of Plan B emergency contraception ("the morning-after pill"). Washington state, however, requires every pharmacy to stock an assortment of drugs approved by the Food and Drug Administration (FDA). In addition, state administrative rules effectively prevent pharmacies from refusing to provide FDA-approved devices or drugs (such as Plan B contraception) to patients for religious reasons.

Norman's owners believe that these state administrative rules violate their constitutional rights to freedom of religion and equal protection, and they file a suit against the Washington State Department of Health. Do these rules violate the free exercise clause? Do they violate the equal protection clause? In this chapter, we examine these and other constitutional issues that businesses and courts must deal with in today's world.

2–1 The Constitutional Powers of Government

Following the Revolutionary War, the states adopted the Articles of Confederation. The Articles created a *confederal form of government* in which the states had the authority to govern themselves and the national government could exercise only limited powers. Problems soon arose because the nation was facing an economic crisis and state laws interfered with the free flow of commerce. A national convention was called, and the delegates drafted the U.S. Constitution. This document, after its ratification by the states in 1789, became the basis for an entirely new form of government.

2–1a A Federal Form of Government

The new government created by the U.S. Constitution reflected a series of compromises made by the convention delegates on various issues. Some delegates wanted sovereign power to remain with the states. Others wanted the national government alone to exercise sovereign power. The end result was a compromise—a **federal form of government** in which the national government and the states *share* sovereign power.

Federal Powers The Constitution sets forth specific powers that can be exercised by the national (federal) government. It further provides that the national government has the implied power to undertake actions necessary to carry out its expressly designated powers (or *enumerated powers*). All other powers are expressly "reserved" to the states under the Tenth Amendment to the U.S. Constitution.

Regulatory Powers of the States As part of their inherent **sovereignty** (power to govern themselves), state governments have the authority to regulate certain affairs within their borders. As mentioned, this authority stems, in part, from the Tenth Amendment, which reserves all powers not delegated to the national government to the states or to the people.

State regulatory powers are often referred to as **police powers**. The term encompasses more than just the enforcement of criminal laws. Police powers also give state governments broad rights to regulate private activities to protect or promote the public order, health, safety, morals, and general welfare. Fire and building codes, antidiscrimination laws, parking regulations, zoning restrictions, licensing requirements, and thousands of other state statutes have been enacted pursuant to states' police powers. Local governments, such as cities, also exercise police powers.[1] Generally, state laws enacted pursuant to a state's police powers carry a strong presumption of validity.

2–1b Relations among the States

The U.S. Constitution also includes provisions concerning relations among the states in our federal system. Particularly important are the *privileges and immunities clause* and the *full faith and credit clause.*

The Privileges and Immunities Clause Article IV, Section 2, of the Constitution provides that the "Citizens of each State shall be entitled to all Privileges and Immunities of Citizens in the several States." This clause is often referred to as the interstate **privileges and immunities clause**. It prevents a state from imposing unreasonable burdens on citizens of another state—particularly with regard to means of livelihood or doing business.

When a citizen of one state engages in basic and essential activities in another state (the "foreign state"), the foreign state must have a *substantial reason* for treating the nonresident differently than its own residents. Basic activities include transferring property, seeking employment, and accessing the court system. The foreign state must also establish that its reason for the discrimination is *substantially related* to the state's ultimate purpose in adopting the legislation or regulating the activity.[2]

The Full Faith and Credit Clause Article IV, Section 1, of the U.S. Constitution provides that "Full Faith and Credit shall be given in each State to the public Acts, Records, and judicial Proceedings of every other State." This clause, which is referred to as the **full faith and credit clause,** applies only to civil matters. It ensures that rights established under deeds, wills, contracts, and similar instruments in one state will be honored by other states. It also ensures that any judicial decision with respect to such property rights will be honored and enforced in all states.

The full faith and credit clause has contributed to the unity of American citizens because it protects their legal rights as they move about from state to state. It also

protects the rights of those to whom they owe obligations, such as persons who have been awarded monetary damages by courts. The ability to enforce such rights is extremely important for the conduct of business in a country with a very mobile citizenry.

2–1c The Separation of Powers

To make it more difficult for the national government to use its power arbitrarily, the Constitution provided for three branches of government. The legislative branch makes the laws, the executive branch enforces the laws, and the judicial branch interprets the laws. Each branch performs a separate function, and no branch may exercise the authority of another branch.

Additionally, a system of **checks and balances** allows each branch to limit the actions of the other two branches, thus preventing any one branch from exercising too much power. Some examples of these checks and balances include the following:

1. The legislative branch (Congress) can enact a law, but the executive branch (the president) has the constitutional authority to veto that law.
2. The executive branch is responsible for foreign affairs, but treaties with foreign governments require the advice and consent of the Senate.
3. Congress determines the jurisdiction of the federal courts, and the president appoints federal judges, with the advice and consent of the Senate. The judicial branch has the power to hold actions of the other two branches unconstitutional.[3]

2–1d The Commerce Clause

To prevent states from establishing laws and regulations that would interfere with trade and commerce among the states, the Constitution expressly delegated to the national government the power to regulate interstate commerce. Article I, Section 8, of the U.S. Constitution explicitly permits Congress "[t]o regulate Commerce with foreign Nations, and among the several States, and with the Indian Tribes." This clause, referred to as the **commerce clause,** has had a greater impact on business than any other provision in the Constitution. The commerce clause provides the basis for the national government's extensive regulation of state and even local affairs.

---

1. Local governments derive their authority to regulate their communities from the state, because they are creatures of the state. In other words, they cannot come into existence unless authorized by the state to do so.
2. This test was first announced in *Supreme Court of New Hampshire v. Piper,* 470 U.S. 274, 105 S.Ct. 1272, 84 L.Ed.2d 205 (1985). For another example, see *Lee v. Miner,* 369 F.Supp.2d 527 (D.Del. 2005).

3. The power of judicial review was established by the United States Supreme Court in *Marbury v. Madison,* 5 U.S. (1 Cranch) 137, 2 L.Ed. 60 (1803).

Initially, the courts interpreted the commerce clause to apply only to commerce between the states (*interstate* commerce) and not commerce within the states (*intrastate* commerce). That changed in 1824, however, when the United States Supreme Court decided the landmark case of *Gibbons v. Ogden*.[4] The Court held that commerce within the states could also be regulated by the national government as long as the commerce *substantially affected* commerce involving more than one state.

The Expansion of National Powers under the Commerce Clause
As the nation grew and faced new kinds of problems, the commerce clause became a vehicle for the additional expansion of the national government's

regulatory powers. Even activities that seemed purely local in nature came under the regulatory reach of the national government if those activities were deemed to substantially affect interstate commerce.

■ **Case in Point 2.1** In a classic case from 1942, the Supreme Court held that wheat production by an individual farmer intended wholly for consumption on his own farm was subject to federal regulation. The Court reasoned that the home consumption of wheat reduced the market demand for wheat and thus could have a substantial effect on interstate commerce.[5] ■

The following *Classic Case* involved a challenge to the scope of the national government's constitutional authority to regulate local activities.

---

4. 22 U.S. (9 Wheat.) 1, 6 L.Ed. 23 (1824).

5. *Wickard v. Filburn*, 317 U.S. 111, 63 S.Ct. 82, 87 L.Ed. 122 (1942).

Classic Case 2.1

Heart of Atlanta Motel v. United States
Supreme Court of the United States, 379 U.S. 241, 85 S.Ct. 348, 13 L.Ed.2d 258 (1964).

Background and Facts In the 1950s, the United States Supreme Court ruled that racial segregation imposed by the states in school systems and other public facilities violated the Constitution. Privately owned facilities were not affected until Congress passed the Civil Rights Act in 1964, which prohibited racial discrimination in "establishments affecting interstate commerce."

The owner of the Heart of Atlanta Motel, in violation of the Civil Rights Act, refused to rent rooms to African Americans. The motel owner brought an action in a federal district court to have the Civil Rights Act declared unconstitutional on the ground that Congress had exceeded its constitutional authority to regulate commerce by enacting the statute.

The owner argued that his motel was not engaged in interstate commerce but was "of a purely local character." The motel, however, was accessible to state and interstate highways. The owner advertised nationally, maintained billboards throughout the state, and accepted convention trade from outside the state (75 percent of the guests were residents of other states).

The district court ruled that the act did not violate the Constitution and enjoined (prohibited) the owner from discriminating on the basis of race. The motel owner appealed. The case ultimately went to the United States Supreme Court.

In the Language of the Court
Mr. Justice *CLARK* delivered the opinion of the Court.
* * * *

While the Act as adopted carried no congressional findings, the record of its passage through each house is replete with evidence of the burdens that discrimination by race or color places upon interstate commerce * * * . This testimony included the fact that our people have become increasingly mobile with millions of all races traveling from State to State; that Negroes in particular have been the subject of discrimination in transient accommodations, having to travel great distances to secure the same; that often they have been unable to obtain accommodations and have had to call upon friends to put them up overnight. * * * These exclusionary practices were found to be nationwide, the Under Secretary of Commerce testifying that there is "no question that this discrimination in the North still exists to a large degree" and in the West and Midwest as well * * * . This testimony indicated a qualitative as well as quantitative effect on interstate travel by Negroes. The former was the obvious impairment of the Negro

traveler's pleasure and convenience that resulted when he continually was uncertain of finding lodging. As for the latter, there was evidence that this uncertainty stemming from racial discrimination had the effect of discouraging travel on the part of a substantial portion of the Negro community * * * . We shall not burden this opinion with further details since the voluminous testimony presents overwhelming evidence that discrimination by hotels and motels impedes interstate travel.
    * * * *

    It is said that the operation of the motel here is of a purely local character. But, assuming this to be true, "if it is interstate commerce that feels the pinch, it does not matter how local the operation that applies the squeeze." * * * *Thus the power of Congress to promote interstate commerce also includes the power to regulate the local incidents thereof, including local activities in both the States of origin and [the States of] destination, which might have a substantial and harmful effect upon that commerce.* [Emphasis added.]

Decision and Remedy *The United States Supreme Court upheld the constitutionality of the Civil Rights Act of 1964. The power of Congress to regulate interstate commerce permitted the enactment of legislation that could halt local discriminatory practices.*

Critical Thinking
- **What If the Facts Were Different?** *If this case had involved a small, private retail business that did not advertise nationally, would the result have been the same? Why or why not?*
- **Impact of This Case on Today's Law** *If the United States Supreme Court had invalidated the Civil Rights Act of 1964, the legal landscape of the United States would be much different today. The act prohibits discrimination based on race, color, national origin, religion, or gender in all "public accommodations," including hotels and restaurants.*
    The act also prohibits discrimination in employment based on these criteria. Although state laws now prohibit many of these forms of discrimination as well, the protections available vary from state to state—and it is not certain whether such laws would have been passed had the outcome in this case been different.

The Commerce Clause Today Today, at least theoretically, the power over commerce authorizes the national government to regulate almost every commercial enterprise in the United States. The breadth of the commerce clause permits the national government to legislate in areas in which Congress has not explicitly been granted power. Only occasionally has the Supreme Court curbed the national government's regulatory authority under the commerce clause.

The Supreme Court has, for instance, allowed the federal government to regulate noncommercial activities relating to medical marijuana that take place wholly within a state's borders. ■ **Case in Point 2.2** California was one of the first states to allow the use of medical marijuana. Marijuana possession, however, is illegal under the federal Controlled Substances Act (CSA).[6] After the federal government seized the marijuana that two seriously ill California women were using on the advice of their physicians, the women filed a lawsuit.

They argued that it was unconstitutional for the federal statute to prohibit them from using marijuana for medical purposes that were legal within the state.

The Supreme Court, though, held that Congress has the authority to prohibit the *intrastate* possession and noncommercial cultivation of marijuana as part of a larger regulatory scheme (the CSA).[7] In other words, the federal government may still prosecute individuals for possession of marijuana regardless of whether they reside in a state that allows the use of marijuana. ■

The "Dormant" Commerce Clause The Supreme Court has interpreted the commerce clause to mean that the national government has the *exclusive* authority to regulate commerce that substantially affects trade and commerce among the states. This express grant of authority to the national government is often referred to as the "positive" aspect of the commerce clause. But this positive aspect also implies a negative aspect—that the states do

---

6. 21 U.S.C. Sections 801 *et seq.*

7. *Gonzales v. Raich*, 545 U.S. 1, 125 S.Ct. 2195, 162 L.Ed.2d 1 (2005).

not have the authority to regulate interstate commerce. This negative aspect of the commerce clause is often referred to as the "dormant" (implied) commerce clause.

The dormant commerce clause comes into play when state regulations affect interstate commerce. In this situation, the courts weigh the state's interest in regulating a certain matter against the burden that the state's regulation places on interstate commerce. Because courts balance the interests involved, predicting the outcome in a particular case can be difficult. State laws that alter conditions of competition to favor in-state interests over out-of-state competitors in a market are usually invalidated, however.

■ **Case in Point 2.3** Maryland imposed personal income taxes on its residents at the state level and the county level. Maryland residents who paid income tax in another state were allowed a credit against the *state* portion of their Maryland taxes, but not the *county* portion. Several Maryland residents who had earned profits in and paid taxes to other states but had not received a credit against their county tax liability sued. They claimed that Maryland's system discriminated against intrastate commerce because those who earned income in other states paid more taxes than residents whose only income came from within Maryland. When the case reached the United States Supreme Court, the Court held that Maryland's personal income tax scheme violated the dormant commerce clause.[8] ■

2–1e The Supremacy Clause and Federal Preemption

Article VI of the U.S. Constitution, commonly referred to as the **supremacy clause,** provides that the Constitution, laws, and treaties of the United States are "the supreme Law of the Land." When there is a direct conflict between a federal law and a state law, the state law is rendered invalid. Because some powers are *concurrent* (shared by the federal government and the states), however, it is necessary to determine which law governs in a particular circumstance.

Preemption When Congress chooses to act exclusively in a concurrent area, **preemption** occurs. In this circumstance, a valid federal statute or regulation will take precedence over a conflicting state or local law or regulation on the same general subject.

Congressional Intent Often, it is not clear whether Congress, in passing a law, intended to preempt an entire subject area. In these situations, the courts determine whether Congress intended to exercise exclusive power.

No single factor is decisive as to whether a court will find preemption. Generally, though, congressional intent to preempt will be found if a federal law regulating an activity is so pervasive, comprehensive, or detailed that the states have little or no room to regulate in that area. In addition, when a federal statute creates an agency to enforce the law, matters that may come within the agency's jurisdiction will likely preempt state laws.

■ **Case in Point 2.4** A man who alleged that he had been injured by a faulty medical device sued the manufacturer. The case ultimately came before the United States Supreme Court. The Court noted that the relevant federal law (the Medical Device Amendments of 1976) had included a preemption provision. Furthermore, the device had passed the U.S. Food and Drug Administration's rigorous premarket approval process. Therefore, the Court ruled that the federal regulation of medical devices preempted the man's state law claims.[9] ■

2–1f The Taxing and Spending Powers

Article I, Section 8, of the U.S. Constitution provides that Congress has the "Power to lay and collect Taxes, Duties, Imposts, and Excises." Section 8 further requires uniformity in taxation among the states, and thus Congress may not tax some states while exempting others.

In the distant past, if Congress attempted to regulate indirectly, by taxation, an area over which it had no authority, the courts would invalidate the tax. Today, however, if a tax measure is reasonable, it generally is held to be within the national taxing power. Moreover, the expansive interpretation of the commerce clause almost always provides a basis for sustaining a federal tax.

Article I, Section 8, also gives Congress its spending power—the power "to pay the Debts and provide for the common Defence and general Welfare of the United States." Through the use of its spending power, Congress can require states to comply with specified conditions of particular federal programs before a state is qualified to receive federal funds. The spending power necessarily involves policy choices, with which taxpayers (and politicians) may disagree.

2–2 Business and the Bill of Rights

The importance of a written declaration of the rights of individuals caused the first Congress of the United States to submit twelve amendments to the U.S. Constitution to the states for approval. Ten of these amendments, known

---

8. *Comptroller of Treasury of Maryland v. Wynne*, ___ U.S. ___, 135 S.Ct. 1787, 191 L.Ed.2d 813 (2015).

9. *Riegel v. Medtronic, Inc.*, 552 U.S. 312, 128 S.Ct. 999, 169 L.Ed.2d 892 (2008); see also *Mink v. Smith & Nephew, Inc.*, 860 F.3d 1319 (11th Cir. 2017).

as the **Bill of Rights,** were adopted in 1791 and embody a series of protections for the individual against various types of interference by the federal government.[10]

The protections guaranteed by these ten amendments are summarized in Exhibit 2–1. Some of these constitutional protections apply to business entities as well as individuals. For instance, corporations exist as separate legal entities, or *legal persons*, and enjoy many of the same rights and privileges as *natural persons* do.

2–2a Limits on Federal and State Governmental Actions

As originally intended, the Bill of Rights limited only the powers of the national government. Over time, however, the United States Supreme Court "incorporated" most of these rights into the protections against state actions afforded by the Fourteenth Amendment to the Constitution.

The Fourteenth Amendment The Fourteenth Amendment, passed in 1868 after the Civil War, provides,

in part, that "[n]o State shall . . . deprive any person of life, liberty, or property, without due process of law." Starting in 1925, the Supreme Court began to define various rights and liberties guaranteed in the U.S. Constitution as constituting "due process of law," which was required of state governments under that amendment.

Today, most of the rights and liberties set forth in the Bill of Rights apply to state governments as well as the national government. In other words, neither the federal government nor state governments can deprive persons of those rights and liberties.

Judicial Interpretation The rights secured by the Bill of Rights are not absolute. Many of the rights guaranteed by the first ten amendments are set forth in very general terms. The Second Amendment for instance, states that people have a right to keep and bear arms, but it does not describe the extent of this right. As the Supreme Court has noted, this right does not mean that people can "keep and carry any weapon whatsoever in any manner whatsoever and for whatever purpose."[11] Legislatures can prohibit the carrying of concealed weapons or certain types of weapons, such as machine guns.

---

10. Another of these proposed amendments was ratified more than two hundred years later (in 1992) and became the Twenty-seventh Amendment to the Constitution.

11. *District of Columbia v. Heller*, 554 U.S. 570, 128 S.Ct. 2783, 171 L.Ed.2d 637 (2008).

Exhibit 2–1 Protections Guaranteed by the Bill of Rights

First Amendment:	Guarantees the freedoms of religion, speech, and the press and the rights to assemble peaceably and to petition the government.
Second Amendment:	States that the right of the people to keep and bear arms shall not be infringed.
Third Amendment:	Prohibits, in peacetime, the lodging of soldiers in any house without the owner's consent.
Fourth Amendment:	Prohibits unreasonable searches and seizures of persons or property.
Fifth Amendment:	Guarantees the rights to *indictment* (formal accusation) by a grand jury, to due process of law, and to fair payment when private property is taken for public use. The Fifth Amendment also prohibits compulsory self-incrimination and double jeopardy (trial for the same crime twice).
Sixth Amendment:	Guarantees the accused in a criminal case the right to a speedy and public trial by an impartial jury and with counsel. The accused has the right to cross-examine witnesses against him or her and to solicit testimony from witnesses in his or her favor.
Seventh Amendment:	Guarantees the right to a trial by jury in a civil case involving at least twenty dollars.
Eighth Amendment:	Prohibits excessive bail and fines, as well as cruel and unusual punishment.
Ninth Amendment:	Establishes that the people have rights in addition to those specified in the Constitution.
Tenth Amendment:	Establishes that those powers neither delegated to the federal government nor denied to the states are reserved to the states and to the people.

Ultimately, the United States Supreme Court, as the final interpreter of the Constitution, gives meaning to these rights and determines their boundaries. Changing public views on controversial topics, such as gun rights, privacy, and the rights of gay men and lesbians, can affect the way the Supreme Court decides a case.

2–2b Freedom of Speech

A democratic form of government cannot survive unless people can freely voice their political opinions and criticize government actions or policies. Freedom of speech, particularly political speech, is thus a prized right, and traditionally the courts have protected this right to the fullest extent possible.

Symbolic speech—gestures, movements, articles of clothing, and other forms of expressive conduct—is also given substantial protection by the courts. The Supreme Court has held that the burning of the American flag as part of a peaceful protest is a constitutionally protected form of expression.[12] Similarly, wearing a T-shirt with a

---

12. *Texas v. Johnson*, 491 U.S. 397, 109 S.Ct. 2533, 105 L.Ed.2d 342 (1989).

photo of a presidential candidate is constitutionally protected. ■ **Example 2.5** As a form of expression, Nate has gang signs tattooed on his torso, arms, neck, and legs. If a reasonable person would interpret this conduct as conveying a message, then it might be a protected form of symbolic speech. ■

Reasonable Restrictions A balance must be struck between a government's obligation to protect its citizens and those citizens' exercise of their rights. Expression—oral, written, or symbolized by conduct—is therefore subject to reasonable restrictions. Reasonableness is analyzed on a case-by-case basis.

(See this chapter's *Digital Update* feature for a discussion of how the United States Supreme Court balanced the government's obligation against the rights of a convicted sex offender.)

Content-Neutral Laws. Laws that regulate the time, manner, and place, but not the content, of speech receive less scrutiny by the courts than do laws that restrict the content of expression. If a restriction imposed by the government is content neutral, then a court may allow it.

Digital Update   Does Everyone Have a Constitutional Right to Use Social Media?

Social media have become the predominant means by which many Americans communicate, obtain news updates, and discover what is "trending." At least one state, though, legislated a ban on the use of social media by convicted sex offenders. One of them chose to challenge the law.

North Carolina and the Use of Social Media

North Carolina's legislature passed the "Protect Children from Sexual Predators Act" in an attempt to prevent predators from finding potential victims on the Internet. Part of that act was codified as North Carolina General Statute 14-202.5. About a thousand sex offenders had been prosecuted for violating this law.

A Long Road through the Courts

When convicted sex offender Lester Packingham, Jr., wrote a Facebook post about a traffic ticket, a police officer saw the post and reported it, and Packingham was convicted of violating a criminal statute. He fought his conviction, and on appeal, it was overturned.

The state then appealed, and the North Carolina Supreme Court ruled in the state's favor.[a]

Packingham appealed to the United States Supreme Court, where he prevailed. The Court pointed out that prohibiting sex offenders from accessing all social media violates their First Amendment rights to free speech. Further, this prohibition "bars access to what for many are the principle sources of knowing current events, checking ads for employment, speaking and listening in a modern public square, and otherwise exploring the vast realms of human thought and knowledge."[b]

Critical Thinking *The Court said in its opinion that "specific criminal acts are not protected speech even if speech is the means for their commission." What use of social media and the Internet might therefore still be unlawful (and not protected free speech) for registered sex offenders?*

---

a. *State of North Carolina v. Packingham*, 368 N.C. 380, 777 S.E.2d 738 (2015).
b. *Packingham v. State of North Carolina*, ___ U.S. ___, 137 S.Ct. 1730, 198 L.Ed.2d 273 (2017).

To be content neutral, the restriction must be aimed at combatting some societal problem, such as crime or drug abuse, and not be aimed at suppressing the expressive conduct or its message.

Courts have often protected nude dancing as a form of symbolic expression but typically allow content-neutral laws that ban all public nudity. ■ **Case in Point 2.6** Ria Ora was charged with dancing nude at an annual "anti-Christmas" protest in Harvard Square in Cambridge, Massachusetts, under a statute banning public displays of open and gross lewdness. Ora argued that the statute was overbroad and unconstitutional, and a trial court agreed. On appeal, however, a state appellate court upheld the statute as constitutional in situations in which there was an unsuspecting or unwilling audience.[13] ■

Laws That Restrict the Content of Speech. Any law that regulates the content of expression must serve a compelling state interest and must be narrowly written to achieve that interest. Under the **compelling government interest** test, the government's interest is balanced against the

individual's constitutional right to free expression. For the statute to be valid, there must be a compelling government interest that can be furthered only by the law in question.

The United States Supreme Court has held that schools may restrict students' speech at school events. ■ **Case in Point 2.7** Some high school students held up a banner saying "Bong Hits 4 Jesus" at an off-campus but school-sanctioned event. The Supreme Court ruled that the school did not violate the students' free speech rights when school officials confiscated the banner and suspended the students for ten days. Because the banner could reasonably be interpreted as promoting drugs, the Court concluded that the school's actions were justified. Several justices disagreed, however, noting that the majority's holding creates an exception that will allow schools to censor any student speech that mentions drugs.[14] ■

In the following case, the issue before the court was whether a restriction on the making of audio and video recordings of an agricultural production facility could meet the "narrow tailoring requirement."

---

13. *Commonwealth of Massachusetts v. Ora*, 451 Mass. 125, 883 N.E.2d 1217 (2008).

14. *Morse v. Frederick*, 551 U.S. 393, 127 S.Ct. 2618, 168 L.Ed.2d 290 (2007).

Case 2.2

Animal Legal Defense Fund v. Wasden
United States Court of Appeals, Ninth Circuit, 878 F.3d 1184 (2018).

Background and Facts An animal rights activist who worked at an Idaho dairy farm secretly filmed ongoing animal abuse. After being posted online, the film attracted national attention. The dairy owner fired the abusive employees, established a code of conduct, and undertook an animal welfare audit of the farm. Meanwhile, the Idaho state legislature enacted the Interference with Agricultural Production statute, which was targeted at undercover investigation of agricultural operations. The statute's "Recordings Clause" criminalized making audio and video recordings of an agricultural production facility without the owner's consent.

The Animal Legal Defense Fund filed a suit in a federal district court against Lawrence Wasden, the Idaho attorney general, alleging that the statute's Recordings Clause violated the First Amendment of the U.S. Constitution. The court issued an injunction against its enforcement. The state appealed this order to the U.S. Court of Appeals for the Ninth Circuit.

In the Language of the Court
McKEOWN, Circuit Judge:
* * * *

* * * The Recordings Clause regulates speech protected by the First Amendment and is a classic example of a content-based restriction that cannot survive strict scrutiny.

We easily dispose of Idaho's claim that the act of creating an audiovisual recording is not speech protected by the First Amendment. This argument is akin to saying that even though a book is protected by the First Amendment, the process of writing the book is not. *Audiovisual recordings are protected by the*

Case 2.2 Continues

Case 2.2 Continued

First Amendment as recognized organs of public opinion and as a significant medium for the communication of ideas. [Emphasis added.]

* * * *

The Recordings Clause prohibits the recording of a defined topic—"the conduct of an agricultural production facility's operations." * * * A regulation is content-based when it draws a distinction on its face regarding the message the speaker conveys or when the purpose and justification for the law are content based. The Recordings Clause checks both boxes. * * * A videographer could record an after-hours birthday party among co-workers, a farmer's antique car collection, or a historic maple tree but not the animal abuse, feedlot operation, or slaughterhouse conditions.

* * * *

As a content-based regulation, the Recordings Clause is constitutional only if it * * * is necessary to serve a compelling state interest and is narrowly drawn to achieve that end. * * * Idaho asserts that the Recordings Clause protects both property and privacy interests. *Even assuming a compelling government interest, Idaho has not satisfied the narrow tailoring requirement because the statute is both under-inclusive and over-inclusive.* [Emphasis added.]

[For example,] prohibiting only "audio or video recordings," but saying nothing about photographs, is suspiciously under-inclusive. Why the making of audio and video recordings of operations would implicate property or privacy harms, but photographs of the same content would not, is a mystery.

* * * *

The Recordings Clause is also over-inclusive and suppresses more speech than necessary to further Idaho's stated goals of protecting property and privacy. Because there are various other laws at Idaho's disposal that would allow it to achieve its stated interests while burdening little or no speech, the law is not narrowly tailored. For example, agricultural production facility owners can vindicate their rights through tort laws against theft of trade secrets, * * * invasion of privacy, [and] defamation.

Decision and Remedy *The U.S. Court of Appeals for the Ninth Circuit affirmed the lower court's order preventing the enforcement of the statute. A law that concerns rights under the First Amendment must be narrowly tailored to accomplish its objective. The federal appellate court concluded that Idaho's Recordings Clause could not "survive First Amendment scrutiny" and was unconstitutional.*

Critical Thinking

- **Legal Environment** *How does the making of "audio and video recordings of an agricultural production facility" fall under the protection of the First Amendment?*
- **What If the Facts Were Different?** *Suppose that instead of banning recordings of an agricultural production facility's operations, the state had criminalized misrepresentations by journalists to gain access to such a facility. Would the result have been different? Explain.*

Corporate Political Speech Political speech by corporations also falls within the protection of the First Amendment. Many years ago, the United States Supreme Court struck down as unconstitutional a Massachusetts statute that prohibited corporations from making political contributions or expenditures that individuals were permitted to make.[15] The Court has also held that a law forbidding a corporation from including inserts with its bills to express its views on controversial issues violates the First Amendment.[16]

Corporate political speech continues to receive significant protection under the First Amendment. ■ **Case in Point 2.8** In *Citizens United v. Federal Election Commission*,[17] the Supreme Court issued a landmark decision that overturned a twenty-year-old precedent on campaign financing. The case involved Citizens United, a nonprofit corporation.

Citizens United had produced a film called *Hillary: The Movie* that was critical of Hillary Clinton, who was seeking the Democratic nomination for the presidency. Campaign-finance law restricted Citizens United from broadcasting the movie. The Court ruled that these

---

15. *First National Bank of Boston v. Bellotti*, 435 U.S. 765, 98 S.Ct. 1407, 55 L.Ed.2d 707 (1978).

16. *Consolidated Edison Co. v. Public Service Commission*, 447 U.S. 530, 100 S.Ct. 2326, 65 L.Ed.2d 319 (1980).

17. 558 U.S. 310, 130 S.Ct. 876, 175 L.Ed.2d 753 (2010).

restrictions were unconstitutional and that the First Amendment prevents limits from being placed on independent political expenditures by corporations. ∎

Commercial Speech The courts also give substantial protection to *commercial speech*, which consists of communications—primarily advertising and marketing—made by business firms that involve only their commercial interests. The protection given to commercial speech under the First Amendment is less extensive than that afforded to noncommercial speech, however.

A state may restrict certain kinds of advertising, for instance, in the interest of preventing consumers from being misled. States also have a legitimate interest in roadside beautification and therefore may impose restraints on billboard advertising. ∎ **Example 2.9** Café Erotica, a nude dancing establishment, sues the state after being

denied a permit to erect a billboard along an interstate highway in Florida. Because the law directly advances a substantial government interest in highway beautification and safety, a court will likely find that it is not an unconstitutional restraint on commercial speech. ∎

Generally, a restriction on commercial speech will be considered valid as long as it meets three criteria:

1. It must seek to implement a substantial government interest.
2. It must directly advance that interest.
3. It must go no further than necessary to accomplish its objective.

At issue in the following case was whether a government agency had unconstitutionally restricted commercial speech when it prohibited the inclusion of a certain illustration on beer labels.

Spotlight on Beer Labels

Case 2.3 Bad Frog Brewery, Inc. v. New York State Liquor Authority
United States Court of Appeals, Second Circuit, 134 F.3d 87 (1998).

Background and Facts Bad Frog Brewery, Inc., makes and sells alcoholic beverages. Some of the beverages feature labels that display a drawing of a frog making the gesture generally known as "giving the finger." Bad Frog's authorized New York distributor, Renaissance Beer Company, applied to the New York State Liquor Authority (NYSLA) for brand label approval, as required by state law before the beer could be sold in New York.

The NYSLA denied the application, in part, because "the label could appear in grocery and convenience stores, with obvious exposure on the shelf to children of tender age." Bad Frog filed a suit in a federal district court against the NYSLA, asking for, among other things, an injunction against the denial of the application. The court granted summary judgment in favor of the NYSLA. Bad Frog appealed to the U.S. Court of Appeals for the Second Circuit.

In the Language of the Court
Jon O. NEWMAN, Circuit Judge:
* * * *

* * * To support its asserted power to ban Bad Frog's labels [NYSLA advances] * * * the State's interest in "protecting children from vulgar and profane advertising" * * * .

[This interest is] substantial * * * . *States have a compelling interest in protecting the physical and psychological wellbeing of minors* * * * . [Emphasis added.]
* * * *

* * * NYSLA endeavors to advance the state interest in preventing exposure of children to vulgar displays by taking only the limited step of barring such displays from the labels of alcoholic beverages. *In view of the wide currency of vulgar displays throughout contemporary society, including comic books targeted directly at children, barring such displays from labels for alcoholic beverages cannot realistically be expected to reduce children's exposure to such displays to any significant degree.* [Emphasis added.]

* * * If New York decides to make a substantial effort to insulate children from vulgar displays in some significant sphere of activity, at least with respect to materials likely to be seen by children,

Case 2.3 Continues

Case 2.3 Continued NYSLA's label prohibition might well be found to make a justifiable contribution to the material advancement of such an effort, but its currently isolated response to the perceived problem, applicable only to labels on a product that children cannot purchase, does not suffice. * * * A state must demonstrate that its commercial speech limitation is part of a substantial effort to advance a valid state interest, not merely the removal of a few grains of offensive sand from a beach of vulgarity.

* * * *

* * * Even if we were to assume that the state materially advances its asserted interest by shielding children from viewing the Bad Frog labels, it is plainly excessive to prohibit the labels from all use, including placement on bottles displayed in bars and taverns where parental supervision of children is to be expected. Moreover, to whatever extent NYSLA is concerned that children will be harmfully exposed to the Bad Frog labels when wandering without parental supervision around grocery and convenience stores where beer is sold, that concern could be less intrusively dealt with by placing restrictions on the permissible locations where the appellant's products may be displayed within such stores.

Decision and Remedy *The U.S. Court of Appeals for the Second Circuit reversed the judgment of the district court and remanded the case for the entry of a judgment in favor of Bad Frog. The NYSLA's ban on the use of the labels lacked a "reasonable fit" with the state's interest in shielding minors from vulgarity. In addition, the NYSLA had not adequately considered alternatives to the ban.*

Critical Thinking
- **What If the Facts Were Different?** *If Bad Frog had sought to use the offensive label to market toys instead of beer, would the court's ruling likely have been the same? Why or why not?*
- **Legal Environment** *Whose interests are advanced by the banning of certain types of advertising?*

Unprotected Speech The United States Supreme Court has made it clear that certain types of speech will not be protected under the First Amendment. Unprotected speech includes fighting words, or words that are likely to incite others to respond violently. It also includes speech that harms the good reputation of another, or defamatory speech. In addition, speech that violates criminal laws is not constitutionally protected. Speech that violates criminal laws includes threatening speech and certain types of obscene speech, such as that involving child pornography.

Threatening Speech. In the case of threatening speech, the speaker must have posed a "true threat"—that is, must have meant to communicate a serious intent to commit an unlawful, violent act against a particular person or group. ■ **Case in Point 2.10** After Anthony Elonis's wife, Tara, left him and took their two children, Elonis was upset and experienced problems at work. A coworker filed five sexual harassment reports against him. When Elonis posted a photograph of himself in a Halloween costume holding a toy knife to the coworker's neck, he was fired from his job. Elonis then began posting violent statements on his Facebook page, mostly focusing on his former wife and talking about killing her.

Elonis continued to post statements about killing his wife and eventually was arrested and prosecuted for his online posts. Elonis was convicted by a jury of violating a statute and ordered to serve time in prison. He appealed to the United States Supreme Court, which held that it is not enough that a reasonable person might view the defendant's Facebook posts as threats. Elonis must have intended to issue threats or known that his statements would be viewed as threats to be convicted of a crime. The Court reversed Elonis's conviction and remanded the case back to the lower court to determine if there was sufficient evidence of intent.[18] ■

Obscene Speech. The First Amendment, as interpreted by the Supreme Court, does not protect obscene speech. Numerous state and federal statutes make it a crime to disseminate and possess obscene materials, including child pornography. Objectively defining obscene speech has proved difficult, however. It is even more difficult to prohibit the dissemination of obscenity and pornography online.

Most of Congress's attempts to pass legislation protecting minors from pornographic materials on the Internet have been struck down on First Amendment grounds when challenged in court. One exception is a law that requires public schools and libraries to install **filtering software** on computers to keep children from accessing

---

18. *Elonis v. United States,* ___ U.S. ___, 135 S.Ct. 2001, 192 L.Ed.2d 1 (2015).

adult content.[19] Such software is designed to prevent persons from viewing certain websites based on a site's Internet address or its **meta tags**, or key words. The Supreme Court held that the act does not unconstitutionally burden free speech because it is flexible and libraries can disable the filters for any patrons who ask.[20]

Another exception is a law that makes it a crime to intentionally distribute *virtual child pornography*—which uses computer-generated images, not actual people— without indicating that it is computer-generated.[21] In a case challenging the law's constitutionality, the Supreme Court held that the statute is valid because it does not prohibit a substantial amount of protected speech.[22] Nevertheless, because of the difficulties of policing the Internet, as well as the constitutional complexities of prohibiting obscenity through legislation, online obscenity remains a legal issue.

2–2c Freedom of Religion

The First Amendment states that the government may neither establish any religion nor prohibit the free exercise of religious practices. The first part of this constitutional provision is referred to as the **establishment clause,** and the second part is known as the **free exercise clause**. Government action, both federal and state, must be consistent with this constitutional mandate.

The Establishment Clause The establishment clause prohibits the government from establishing a state-sponsored religion, as well as from passing laws that promote (aid or endorse) religion or show a preference for one religion over another. Although the establishment clause involves the separation of church and state, it does not require a complete separation.

Applicable Standard. Establishment clause cases often involve such issues as the legality of allowing or requiring school prayers, using state-issued vouchers to pay tuition at religious schools, and teaching creation theories versus evolution. Federal or state laws that do not promote or place a significant burden on religion are constitutional even if they have some impact on religion. For a government law or policy to be constitutional, it must not have the primary effect of promoting or inhibiting religion.

Religious Displays. Religious displays on public property have often been challenged as violating the establishment clause. The United States Supreme Court has ruled on a number of such cases, often focusing on the proximity of the religious display to nonreligious symbols or on the balance of symbols from different religions. The Supreme Court eventually decided that public displays having historical, as well as religious, significance do not necessarily violate the establishment clause.

■ **Case in Point 2.11** Mount Soledad is a prominent hill near San Diego. There has been a forty-foot cross on top of Mount Soledad since 1913. In the 1990s, a war memorial with six walls listing the names of veterans was constructed next to the cross. The site was privately owned until 2006, when Congress authorized the property's transfer to the federal government "to preserve a historically significant war memorial."

Steve Trunk and the Jewish War Veterans filed lawsuits claiming that the cross violated the establishment clause because it endorsed the Christian religion. A federal appellate court agreed, finding that the primary effect of the memorial as a whole sent a strong message of endorsement of Christianity and exclusion of non-Christian veterans. The court noted that although not all cross displays at war memorials violate the establishment clause, the cross in this case physically dominated the site. Additionally, it was originally dedicated to religious purposes, had a long history of religious use, and was the only portion visible to drivers on the freeway below.[23] ■

The Free Exercise Clause The free exercise clause guarantees that people can hold any religious beliefs they want or can hold no religious beliefs. The constitutional guarantee of personal freedom restricts only the actions of the government, however, and not those of individuals or private businesses.

Restrictions Must Be Necessary. The government must have a compelling state interest for restricting the free exercise of religion, and the restriction must be the only way to further that interest. ■ **Case in Point 2.12** Gregory Holt, an inmate in an Arkansas state prison, was a devout Muslim who wished to grow a beard in accord with his religious beliefs. The Arkansas Department of Correction prohibited inmates from growing beards (except for medical reasons). Holt asked for an exemption to grow a half-inch beard on religious grounds, and prison officials denied his request. Holt filed a suit in a federal district court against Ray Hobbs, the director of the department, and others.

---

19. Children's Internet Protection Act (CIPA), 17 U.S.C. Sections 1701–1741.
20. *United States v. American Library Association*, 539 U.S. 194, 123 S.Ct. 2297, 156 L.Ed.2d 221 (2003).
21. The Prosecutorial Remedies and Other Tools to End the Exploitation of Children Today Act (Protect Act), 18 U.S.C. Section 2252A(a)(5)(B).
22. *United States v. Williams*, 553 U.S. 285, 128 S.Ct. 1830, 170 L.Ed.2d 650 (2008).

23. *Trunk v. City of San Diego*, 629 F.3d 1099 (9th Cir. 2011).

A federal statute prohibits the government from taking any action that substantially burdens the religious exercise of an institutionalized person unless the action constitutes the least restrictive means of furthering a compelling governmental interest. The defendants argued that beards compromise prison safety—a compelling government interest—because contraband can be hidden in them and because an inmate can quickly shave his beard to disguise his identity. The case ultimately reached the United States Supreme Court. The Court noted that "an item of contraband would have to be very small indeed to be concealed by a 1/2–inch beard." Moreover, the Court reasoned that the department could satisfy its security concerns by simply searching the beard, the way it already searches prisoners' hair and clothing. The Court concluded that the department's grooming policy, which prevented Holt from growing a half-inch beard, violated his right to exercise his religious beliefs.[24] ∎

Restrictions Must Not Be a Substantial Burden. To comply with the free exercise clause, a government action must not place a substantial burden on religious practices. A burden is substantial if it pressures an individual to modify his or her behavior and to violate his or her beliefs.

Public Welfare Exception. When religious *practices* work against public policy and the public welfare, the government can act. For instance, the government can require that a child receive certain types of vaccinations or medical treatment if his or her life is in danger—regardless of the child's or parent's religious beliefs. When public safety is an issue, an individual's religious beliefs often have to give way to the government's interest in protecting the public.

∎ **Example 2.13** A woman of the Muslim faith may choose not to appear in public without a scarf, known as a *hijab*, over her head. Nevertheless, due to public safety concerns, many courts today do not allow the wearing of any headgear (hats or scarves) in courtrooms. ∎

2–2d Searches and Seizures

The Fourth Amendment protects the "right of the people to be secure in their persons, houses, papers, and effects." Before searching or seizing private property, law enforcement officers must usually obtain a **search warrant**—an order from a judge or other public official authorizing the search or seizure. Because of the strong government interest in protecting the public, however, a warrant normally is not required for seizures of spoiled or contaminated food. Nor are warrants required for searches of

businesses in such highly regulated industries as liquor, guns, and strip mining.

To obtain a search warrant, law enforcement officers must convince a judge that they have reasonable grounds, or **probable cause,** to believe a search will reveal evidence of a specific illegality. To establish probable cause, the officers must have trustworthy evidence that would convince a reasonable person that the proposed search or seizure is more likely justified than not.

∎ **Case in Point 2.14** Citlalli Flores was driving across the border into the United States from Tijuana, Mexico, when a border protection officer became suspicious because she was acting nervous and looking around inside her car. On further inspection, the officer found thirty-six pounds of marijuana hidden in the car's quarter panels. Flores claimed that she had not known about the marijuana.

Flores was arrested for importing marijuana into the United States. She then made two jail-recorded phone calls in which she asked her cousin to delete whatever he felt needed to be removed from Flores's Facebook page. The government got a warrant to search Flores's Facebook messages, where they found references to her "carrying" or "bringing" marijuana into the United States that day. Flores's Facebook posts were later used as evidence against her at trial, and she was convicted.

On appeal, the court held that the phone calls had given the officers probable cause to support a warrant to search Flores's social networking site for incriminating statements. Her conviction was affirmed.[25] ∎

2–2e Self-Incrimination

The Fifth Amendment guarantees that no person "shall be compelled in any criminal case to be a witness against himself." Thus, in any court proceeding, an accused person cannot be forced to give testimony that might subject him or her to any criminal prosecution. The guarantee applies to both federal and state proceedings because the due process clause of the Fourteenth Amendment (discussed shortly) extends the protection to state courts.

The Fifth Amendment's guarantee against self-incrimination extends only to natural persons. Neither corporations nor partnerships receive Fifth Amendment protection. When a partnership is required to produce business records, it must therefore do so even if the information provided incriminates the individual partners of the firm. In contrast, sole proprietors and sole practitioners (those who individually own their businesses) cannot be compelled to produce their business records. These individuals have full protection against self-incrimination because there is no separate business entity.

---

24. *Holt v. Hobbs*, ___ U.S. ___, 135 S.Ct. 853, 190 L.Ed.2d 747 (2015).

25. *United States v. Flores*, 802 F.3d 1028 (9th Cir. 2015).

2–3 Due Process and Equal Protection

Other constitutional guarantees of great significance to Americans are mandated by the *due process clauses* of the Fifth and Fourteenth Amendments and the *equal protection clause* of the Fourteenth Amendment.

2–3a Due Process

Both the Fifth and Fourteenth Amendments provide that no person shall be deprived "of life, liberty, or property, without due process of law." The **due process clause** of these constitutional amendments has two aspects—procedural and substantive. Note that the due process clause applies to "legal persons" (that is, corporations), as well as to individuals.

Procedural Due Process *Procedural* due process requires that any government decision to take life, liberty, or property must be made equitably. In other words, the government must give a person proper notice and an opportunity to be heard. Fair procedures must be used in determining whether a person will be subjected to punishment or have some burden imposed on her or him.

Fair procedure has been interpreted as requiring that the person have at least an opportunity to object to a proposed action before an impartial, neutral decision maker (who need not be a judge). ■ **Example 2.15** Doyle Burns, a nursing student in Kansas, poses for a photograph standing next to a placenta used as a lab specimen. Although she quickly deletes the photo from her library, it ends up on Facebook. When the director of nursing sees the photo, Burns is expelled. She sues for reinstatement and wins. The school violated Burns's due process rights by expelling her from the nursing program for taking a photo without giving her an opportunity to present her side to school authorities. ■

Substantive Due Process *Substantive* due process focuses on the content of legislation rather than the fairness of procedures. Substantive due process limits what the government may do in its legislative and executive capacities. Legislation must be fair and reasonable in content and must further a legitimate governmental objective.

If a law or other governmental action limits a fundamental right, the state must have a legitimate and compelling interest to justify its action. Fundamental rights include interstate travel, privacy, voting, marriage

and family, and all First Amendment rights. Thus, for instance, a state must have a substantial reason for taking any action that infringes on a person's free speech rights.

In situations not involving fundamental rights, a law or action does not violate substantive due process if it rationally relates to any legitimate government purpose. It is almost impossible for a law or action to fail this test.

2–3b Equal Protection

Under the Fourteenth Amendment, a state may not "deny to any person within its jurisdiction the equal protection of the laws." The United States Supreme Court has interpreted the due process clause of the Fifth Amendment to make the **equal protection clause** applicable to the federal government as well. Equal protection means that the government cannot enact laws that treat similarly situated individuals differently.

Equal protection, like substantive due process, relates to the substance of a law or other governmental action. When a law or action limits the liberty of *all* persons, it may violate substantive due process. When a law or action limits the liberty of *some* persons but not others, it may violate the equal protection clause. ■ **Example 2.16** If a law prohibits all advertising on the sides of trucks, it raises a substantive due process question. If the law makes an exception to allow truck owners to advertise their own businesses, it raises an equal protection issue. ■

In an equal protection inquiry, when a law or action distinguishes between or among individuals, the basis for the distinction—that is, the classification—is examined. Depending on the classification, the courts apply different levels of scrutiny, or "tests," to determine whether the law or action violates the equal protection clause. The courts use one of three standards: strict scrutiny, intermediate scrutiny, or the "rational basis" test.

Strict Scrutiny If a law or action prohibits or inhibits some persons from exercising a fundamental right, the law or action will be subject to "strict scrutiny" by the courts. Under this standard, the classification must be necessary to promote a *compelling state interest*.

Compelling state interests include remedying past unconstitutional or illegal discrimination but do not include correcting the general effects of "society's discrimination." ■ **Example 2.17** For a city to give preference to minority applicants in awarding construction contracts, it normally must identify past unconstitutional or illegal discrimination against minority construction firms. Because the policy is based on suspect traits (race and national origin), it will violate the equal protection clause *unless* it is necessary to promote a compelling state interest. ■ Generally, few laws or actions survive strict-scrutiny analysis by the courts.

Intermediate Scrutiny Another standard, that of *intermediate scrutiny*, is applied in cases involving discrimination based on gender or legitimacy (children born out of wedlock). Laws using these classifications must be *substantially related to important government objectives*. ■ **Example 2.18** An important government objective is preventing illegitimate teenage pregnancies. Males and females are not similarly situated in this regard because only females can become pregnant. Therefore, a law that punishes men but not women for statutory rape will be upheld even though it treats men and women unequally. ■

The state also has an important objective in establishing time limits (called *statutes of limitation*) for how long after an event a particular type of action can be brought. Nevertheless, the limitation period must be substantially related to the important objective of preventing fraudulent or outdated claims. ■ **Example 2.19** A state law requires illegitimate children to bring paternity suits within six years of their births in order to seek support from their fathers. A court will strike down this law if legitimate children are allowed to seek support from their parents at any time. Distinguishing between support claims on the basis of legitimacy is not related to the important government objective of preventing fraudulent or outdated claims. ■

The "Rational Basis" Test In matters of economic or social welfare, a classification will be considered valid if there is any conceivable *rational basis* on which the classification might relate to a legitimate government interest. It is almost impossible for a law or action to fail the rational basis test. ■ **Case in Point 2.20** A Kentucky statute prohibits businesses that sell substantial amounts of staple groceries or gasoline from applying for a license to sell wine and liquor. A local grocer (Maxwell's Pic-Pac) filed a lawsuit against the state, alleging that the statute and the regulation were unconstitutional under the equal protection clause. The court applied the rational basis test and ruled that the statute and regulation were rationally related to a legitimate government interest in reducing access to products with high alcohol content.

The court cited the problems caused by alcohol, including drunk driving, and noted that the state's interest in limiting access to such products extends to the general public. Grocery stores and gas stations pose a greater risk of exposing members of the public to alcohol. For these and other reasons, the state can restrict these places from selling wine and liquor.[26] ■

2–4 Privacy Rights

The U.S. Constitution does not explicitly mention a general right to privacy. In a 1928 Supreme Court case, *Olmstead v. United States*,[27] Justice Louis Brandeis stated in his dissent that the right to privacy is "the most comprehensive of rights and the right most valued by civilized men." The majority of the justices at that time, however, did not agree with Brandeis.

It was not until the 1960s that the Supreme Court endorsed the view that the Constitution protects individual privacy rights. In a landmark 1965 case, *Griswold v. Connecticut*,[28] the Supreme Court held that a constitutional right to privacy was implied by the First, Third, Fourth, Fifth, and Ninth Amendments.

Today, privacy rights receive protection under various federal statutes as well as the U.S. Constitution. State constitutions and statutes also secure individuals' privacy rights, often to a significant degree. Privacy rights are also protected to an extent under tort law, consumer law, and employment law.

2–4a Federal Privacy Legislation

In the last several decades, Congress has enacted a number of statutes that protect the privacy of individuals in various areas of concern. Most of these statutes deal with personal information collected by governments or private businesses.

In the 1960s, Americans were sufficiently alarmed by the accumulation of personal information in government files that they pressured Congress to pass laws permitting individuals to access their files. Congress responded by passing the Freedom of Information Act, which allows persons to request copies of any information on them contained in federal government files. Congress later enacted the Privacy Act, which also gives persons the right to access such information.

In the 1990s, responding to the growing need to protect the privacy of individuals' health records—particularly computerized records—Congress passed the Health Insurance Portability and Accountability Act (HIPAA).[29] This act defines and limits the circumstances in which an individual's "protected health information" may be used or disclosed by health-care providers, health-care plans, and others. These and other major federal laws protecting privacy rights are listed and briefly described in Exhibit 2–2.

---

26. *Maxwell's Pic-Pac, Inc. v. Dehner*, 739 F.3d 936 (6th Cir. 2014).

27. 277 U.S. 438, 48 S.Ct. 564, 72 L.Ed. 944 (1928). The majority's decision was later overruled in *Katz v. United States*, 389 U.S. 347, 88 S.Ct. 507, 19 L.Ed.2d 576 (1967).
28. 381 U.S. 479, 85 S.Ct. 1678, 14 L.Ed.2d 510 (1965).
29. HIPAA was enacted as Pub. L. No. 104-191, 110 Stat. 1936 (1996) and is codified in 29 U.S.C.A. Sections 1181 *et seq.*

Exhibit 2–2 Federal Legislation Relating to Privacy

Freedom of Information Act (1966)	Provides that individuals have a right to obtain access to information about them collected in government files.
Privacy Act (1974)	Protects the privacy of individuals about whom the federal government has information. Regulates agencies' use and disclosure of data, and gives individuals access to and a means to correct inaccuracies.
Electronic Communications Privacy Act (1986)	Prohibits the interception of information communicated by electronic means.
Health Insurance Portability and Accountability Act (1996)	Requires health-care providers and health-care plans to inform patients of their privacy rights and of how their personal medical information may be used. States that medical records may not be used for purposes unrelated to health care or disclosed without permission.
Financial Services Modernization Act (Gramm-Leach-Bliley Act) (1999)	Prohibits the disclosure of nonpublic personal information about a consumer to an unaffiliated third party unless strict disclosure and opt-out requirements are met.

2–4b The USA Patriot Act

The USA Patriot Act was passed by Congress in the wake of the terrorist attacks of September 11, 2001, and then reauthorized twice.[30] The Patriot Act has given government officials increased authority to monitor Internet activities (such as e-mail and website visits) and to gain access to personal financial information and student information. Law enforcement officials can track the telephone and e-mail communications of one party to find out the identity of the other party or parties. Privacy advocates argue that this law adversely affects the constitutional rights of all Americans, and it has been widely criticized in the media.

---

30. The Uniting and Strengthening America by Providing Appropriate Tools Required to Intercept and Obstruct Terrorism Act of 2001, also known as the USA Patriot Act, was enacted as Pub. L. No. 107-56, 115 Stat. 272 (2001) and last amended and reauthorized in 2015.

Practice and Review: Business and the Constitution

A state legislature enacted a statute that required any motorcycle operator or passenger on the state's highways to wear a protective helmet. Jim Alderman, a licensed motorcycle operator, sued the state to block enforcement of the law. Alderman asserted that the statute violated the equal protection clause because it placed requirements on motorcyclists that were not imposed on other motorists. Using the information presented in the chapter, answer the following questions.

1. Why does this statute raise equal protection issues instead of substantive due process concerns?
2. What are the three levels of scrutiny that the courts use in determining whether a law violates the equal protection clause?
3. Which standard of scrutiny, or test, would apply to this situation? Why?
4. Applying this standard, is the helmet statute constitutional? Why or why not?

Debate This . . . *Legislation aimed at "protecting people from themselves" concerns the individual as well as the public in general. Protective helmet laws are just one example of such legislation. Should individuals be allowed to engage in unsafe activities if they choose to do so?*

Terms and Concepts

Bill of Rights 31	federal form of government 26	privileges and immunities clause 27
checks and balances 27	filtering software 36	probable cause 38
commerce clause 27	free exercise clause 37	search warrant 38
compelling government interest 33	full faith and credit clause 27	sovereignty 26
due process clause 39	meta tags 37	supremacy clause 30
equal protection clause 39	police powers 26	symbolic speech 32
establishment clause 37	preemption 30	

Issue Spotters

1. South Dakota wants its citizens to conserve energy. To help reduce consumer consumption of electricity, the state passes a law that bans all advertising by power utilities within the state. What argument could the power utilities use as a defense to the enforcement of this state law? (See *Business and the Bill of Rights.*)

2. Suppose that a state imposes a higher tax on out-of-state companies doing business in the state than it imposes on in-state companies. Is this a violation of equal protection if the only reason for the tax is to protect the local firms from out-of-state competition? Explain. (See *The Constitutional Powers of Government.*)

• Check your answers to the Issue Spotters against the answers provided in Appendix B at the end of this text.

Business Scenarios and Case Problems

2–1. Commerce Clause. A Georgia state law requires the use of contoured rear-fender mudguards on trucks and trailers operating within Georgia state lines. The statute further makes it illegal for trucks and trailers to use straight mudguards. In approximately thirty-five other states, straight mudguards are legal. Moreover, in Florida, straight mudguards are explicitly required by law. There is some evidence suggesting that contoured mudguards might be a little safer than straight mudguards. Discuss whether this Georgia statute violates any constitutional provisions. (See *The Constitutional Powers of Government.*)

2–2. Equal Protection. With the objectives of preventing crime, maintaining property values, and preserving the quality of urban life, New York City enacted an ordinance to regulate the locations of adult entertainment establishments. The ordinance expressly applied to female, but not male, topless entertainment. Adele Buzzetti owned the Cozy Cabin, a New York City cabaret that featured female topless dancers. Buzzetti and an anonymous dancer filed a suit in a federal district court against the city, asking the court to block the enforcement of the ordinance. The plaintiffs argued, in part, that the ordinance violated the equal protection clause. Under the equal protection clause, what standard applies to the court's consideration of this ordinance? Under this test, how should the court rule? Why? (See *Due Process and Equal Protection.*)

2–3. Business Case Problem with Sample Answer— Freedom of Speech. Mark Wooden sent an e-mail to an alderwoman for the city of St. Louis. Attached was a nineteen-minute audio file that compared her to the biblical character Jezebel. The audio said she was a "bitch in the Sixth Ward," spending too much time with the rich and powerful and too little time with the poor. In a menacing, maniacal tone, Wooden said that he was "dusting off a sawed-off shotgun," called himself a "domestic terrorist," and referred to the assassination of President John Kennedy, the murder of federal judge John Roll, and the shooting of Representative Gabrielle Giffords. Feeling threatened, the alderwoman called the police. Wooden was convicted of harassment under a state criminal statute. Was this conviction unconstitutional under the First Amendment? Discuss. [*State of Missouri v. Wooden*, 388 S.W.3d 522 (Mo. 2013)] (See *Business and the Bill of Rights.*)

• For a sample answer to Problem 2–3, go to Appendix C at the end of this text.

2–4. Equal Protection. Abbott Laboratories licensed SmithKline Beecham Corp. to market an Abbott human immunodeficiency virus (HIV) drug in conjunction with one of SmithKline's drugs. Abbott then increased the price of its drug fourfold, forcing SmithKline to increase its prices and thereby driving business to Abbott's own combination drug. SmithKline filed a suit in a federal district court against Abbott. During jury selection, Abbott struck the only self-identified gay person among the potential jurors. (The pricing of HIV drugs is of considerable concern in the gay community.) Could the equal protection clause be applied to prohibit discrimination based on sexual orientation in jury selection?

Discuss. [*SmithKline Beecham Corp. v. Abbott Laboratories*, 740 F.3d 471 (9th Cir. 2014)] (See *Due Process and Equal Protection*.)

2–5. Procedural Due Process. Robert Brown applied for admission to the University of Kansas School of Law. Brown answered "no" to questions on the application asking if he had a criminal history and acknowledged that a false answer constituted "cause for . . . dismissal." In fact, Brown had criminal convictions for domestic battery and driving under the influence. He was accepted for admission to the school. When school officials discovered his history, however, he was notified of their intent to dismiss him and given an opportunity to respond in writing. He demanded a hearing. The officials refused to grant Brown a hearing and then expelled him. Did the school's actions deny Brown due process? Discuss. [*Brown v. University of Kansas*, 599 Fed.Appx. 833 (10th Cir. 2015)] (See *Due Process and Equal Protection*.)

2–6. The Commerce Clause. Regency Transportation, Inc., operates a freight business throughout the eastern United States. Regency maintains its corporate headquarters, four warehouses, and a maintenance facility and terminal location for repairing and storing vehicles in Massachusetts. All of the vehicles in Regency's fleet were bought in other states. Massachusetts imposes a use tax on all taxpayers subject to its jurisdiction, including those that do business in interstate commerce, as Regency does. When Massachusetts imposed the tax on the purchase price of each tractor and trailer in Regency's fleet, the trucking firm challenged the assessment as discriminatory under the commerce clause. What is the chief consideration under the commerce clause when a state law affects interstate commerce? Is Massachusetts's use tax valid? Explain. [*Regency Transportation, Inc. v. Commissioner of Revenue*, 473 Mass. 459, 42 N.E.3d 1133 (2016)] (See *The Constitutional Powers of Government*.)

2–7. Freedom of Speech. Wandering Dago, Inc. (WD), operates a food truck in Albany, New York. WD brands itself and the food it sells with language generally viewed as ethnic slurs. Owners Andrea Loguidice and Brandon Snooks, however, view the branding as giving a "nod to their Italian heritage" and "weakening the derogatory force of the slur." Twice, WD applied to participate as a vendor in a summer lunch program in a state-owned plaza. Both times, the New York State Office of General Services (OGS) denied the application because of WD's branding. WD filed a suit in a federal district court against RoAnn Destito, the commissioner of OGS, contending that the agency had violated WD's right to free speech. What principles apply to the government's regulation of the content of speech? How do those principles apply in WD's case? Explain. [*Wandering Dago, Inc. v. Destito*, 879 F.3d 20 (2d Cir. 2018)] (See *Business and the Bill of Rights*.)

2–8. A Question of Ethics—Free Speech. *Michael Mayfield, the president of Mendo Mill and Lumber Co., in California, received a "notice of a legal claim" from Edward Starski. The "claim" alleged that a stack of lumber had fallen on a customer as a result of a Mendo employee's "incompetence." The "notice" presented a settlement offer on the customer's behalf in exchange for a release of liability for Mendo. In a follow-up phone conversation with Mayfield, Starski said that he was an attorney—which, in fact, he was not. Starski was arrested and charged with violating a state criminal statute that prohibited the unauthorized practice of law.* [People v. Starski, 7 Cal.App.5th 215, 212 Cal.Rptr.3d 622 (1 Dist. Div. 2 2017)] *(See* Business and the Bill of Rights.*)*

(a) Starski argued that "creating an illusion" that he was an attorney was protected by the First Amendment. Is Starski correct? Explain.

(b) Identify, discuss, and resolve the conflict between the right to free speech and the government's regulation of the practice of law.

Time-Limited Group Assignment

2–9. Free Speech and Equal Protection. For many years, New York City has had to deal with the vandalism and defacement of public property caused by unauthorized graffiti. In an effort to stop the damage, the city banned the sale of aerosol spray-paint cans and broad-tipped indelible markers to persons under twenty-one years of age. The new rules also prohibited people from possessing these items on property other than their own. Within a year, five people under age twenty-one were cited for violations of these regulations, and 871 individuals were arrested for actually making graffiti.

Lindsey Vincenty and other artists wished to create graffiti on legal surfaces, such as canvas, wood, and clothing. Unable to buy supplies in the city or to carry them into the city from elsewhere, Vincenty and others filed a lawsuit on behalf of themselves and other young artists against Michael Bloomberg,

the city's mayor at the time, and others. The plaintiffs claimed that, among other things, the rules violated their right to freedom of speech.

(a) One group will argue in favor of the plaintiffs and provide several reasons why the court should hold that the city's rules violate the plaintiffs' freedom of speech. (See *Business and the Bill of Rights*.)

(b) Another group will develop a counterargument that outlines the reasons why the rules do not violate free speech rights. (See *Business and the Bill of Rights*.)

(c) A third group will argue that the city's ban violates the equal protection clause because it applies only to persons under age twenty-one. (See *Due Process and Equal Protection*.)

Chapter 3

Ethics in Business

One of the most complex issues businesspersons and corporations face is ethics. Ethics is not as well defined as the law, and yet it can have substantial impacts on a firm's finances and reputation, especially when the firm is involved in a well-publicized scandal. Some scandals arise from activities that are legal but ethically questionable. Other scandals arise from conduct that is both illegal and unethical.

Suppose, for instance, that graduate student Shannon Clayborn develops a new chemical compound that delays the deterioration of human cells. Clayborn finds investors and starts a company, called Vital, Inc., to develop the compound into anti-aging products. Vital successfully markets and sells the products to millions of consumers for nearly six years—until it is discovered that the products cause birth defects. Numerous consumers and government agencies file lawsuits against Clayborn and Vital. Clayborn's profitable company now faces an uncertain future. Should Clayborn have performed more research on possible side effects before marketing her products to protect the products' potential users? Would that have been the ethical thing to do?

The goal of business ethics is not to stifle innovation. There is nothing unethical about a company selling an idea or technology that is still being developed. In fact, that is exactly what many successful start-ups do—take a promising idea and develop it into a reality. But businesspersons also need to consider what will happen if new technologies or products end up not working or causing unintended consequences. Should they go ahead with production and sales? What are the ethical problems with putting a product on the market that does not perform as advertised or is unsafe? To be sure, there is not always one clear answer to an ethical question. What is clear is that rushing to production and not thinking through the ethical ramifications of decisions can be disastrous for a business.

3–1 Ethics and the Role of Business

At the most basic level, the study of **ethics** is the study of what constitutes right or wrong behavior. It is a branch of philosophy focusing on morality and the way moral principles are derived and implemented. Ethics has to do with the fairness, justness, rightness, or wrongness of an action.

The study of **business ethics** typically looks at the decisions businesses make or have to make and whether those decisions are right or wrong. It has to do with how businesspersons apply moral and ethical principles in making their decisions. Those who study business ethics also evaluate what duties and responsibilities exist or should exist for businesses.

In this book, we cover ethical issues in *Ethics Today* features that appear in selected chapters. We also provide an ethics-based case problem, called *A Question of Ethics*, at the end of every chapter. Finally, we include an *Application and Ethics* feature at the end of each unit to expand on the concepts of business ethics discussed in that unit.

3–1a The Relationship of Law and Ethics

The government has institutionalized some ethical rights and duties through the passage of laws and regulations. Many laws are designed to prevent fraudulent (misleading, deceptive) conduct in various contexts, including contracts, health care, financial reporting, mortgages, and sales. ■ **Example 3.1** The Fraud Reduction and Data Analytics Act was passed by Congress in 2016 to identify and assess fraud risks in federal government agencies. The purpose of the law is to prevent, detect, and respond to fraud (including improper payments) in federal programs. ■

Sometimes, major legislation is passed after well-publicized ethical transgressions by industries or companies result in harm to the public. ■ **Example 3.2** After alleged ethical lapses on Wall Street contributed to a financial crisis, Congress passed the Dodd-Frank Wall Street Reform and Consumer Protection Act.[1] Dodd-Frank made

---

1. Pub. L. No. 111–203, 124 Stat. 1376, July 21, 2010, 12 U.S.C. Sections 5301 *et seq.*

sweeping changes to the United States' financial regulatory environment in an attempt to promote financial stability and protect consumers from abusive financial services practices.

Similarly, Congress enacted the Sarbanes-Oxley Act[2] (SOX) after Enron, a major energy company, engaged in risky financial maneuvers that resulted in the loss of billions of dollars to shareholders. SOX was designed to help reduce corporate fraud and unethical management decisions by setting up accountability measures for publicly traded companies. Company heads must verify that they have read quarterly and annual reports and vouch for their accuracy. SOX also requires companies to set up confidential systems so that employees and others can "raise red flags" about suspected illegal or unethical auditing and accounting practices.[3] ■

Gray Areas in the Law Laws cannot codify all ethical requirements. For a number of reasons, laws may sometimes be difficult to interpret and apply. When legislatures draft laws, they typically use broad language so that the provisions will apply in a variety of circumstances. It can be hard to determine how such broad provisions apply to specific situations. In addition, laws intended to address one situation may apply to other situations as well. And the legislative body that passes a law may not give clear guidance on the purpose of the law or the definition of terms in the law.

Other issues arise because laws are created through the political process. They therefore often involve compromises among competing interests and industries. As a result, a law's provisions may be ambiguous, may be weaker than intended by the original drafters, or may lack a means of enforcement. In short, the law is not always clear, and these "gray areas" in the law make it difficult to predict with certainty how a court will apply a given law to a particular action.

The Moral Minimum Compliance with the law is sometimes called the **moral minimum.** If people and entities merely comply with the law, they are acting at the lowest ethical level that society will tolerate.

Failure to meet the moral minimum can have significant consequences, especially in the context of litigation. A businessperson who fails to respond to a lawsuit filed against him or her can be held liable. ■ **Case in Point 3.3** Rick Scott deposited $2 million into an escrow account

maintained by a company owned by Salvatore Carpanzano. Immediately after the deposit was made, the funds were withdrawn in violation of the escrow agreement. When Scott was unable to recover his money, he filed a suit against Salvatore Carpanzano and others, including Salvatore's daughter, Carmela. In the complaint, Scott made no allegations of acts or knowledge on Carmela's part. (The complaint claimed only that she had received a $46,600 Land Rover Range Rover purchased with the funds.)

Salvatore failed to cooperate with discovery and did not respond to attempts to contact him by certified mail, regular mail, and e-mail. He also refused to make an appearance in court and did not finalize a settlement negotiated between the parties' attorneys. Carmela denied that she was involved in her father's business or the Scott transaction. The court found that the defendants had intentionally failed to respond to the litigation and issued a judgment for more than $6 million in Scott's favor. On appeal, a federal appellate court affirmed the district court's judgment against Salvatore but reversed the judgment against Carmela. The court reasoned that there was no evidence that Carmela was willfully involved in her father's wrongdoing.[4] ■

Although the moral minimum is important, the study of ethics goes well beyond these legal requirements to evaluate what is right for society. *Businesspersons must remember that an action that is legal is not necessarily ethical.* For instance, a company can legally refuse to negotiate liability claims for injuries allegedly caused by a faulty product. But if the company's refusal is meant to increase the injured party's legal costs and force the party to drop a legitimate claim, the company is not acting ethically.

Private Company Codes of Ethics Most companies attempt to link ethics and law through the creation of internal codes of ethics. (We present the code of ethics of Costco Wholesale Corporation as an example in the appendix following this chapter.) Company codes are not laws. Instead, they are rules that the company sets forth and that it can enforce (by terminating an employee who does not follow them, for instance). Codes of conduct typically outline the company's policies on particular issues and indicate how employees are expected to act.

■ **Example 3.4** Google's code of conduct starts with the motto "Don't be evil." The code then makes general statements about how Google promotes integrity, mutual respect, and the highest standard of ethical business

2. 15 U.S.C. Sections 7201 *et seq.*

3. In one such system, employees can click on an on-screen icon that anonymously links them with NAVEX Global to report suspicious accounting practices, sexual harassment, and other possibly unethical behavior.

4. *Scott v. Carpanzano*, 556 Fed.Appx. 288 (5th Cir. 2014).

conduct. Google's code also provides specific rules on a number of issues, such as privacy, drugs and alcohol, conflicts of interest, co-worker relationships, and confidentiality—it even includes a dog policy. The company takes a stand against employment discrimination that goes further than the law requires. It prohibits discrimination based on sexual orientation, gender identity or expression, and veteran status. ■

Industry Ethical Codes Numerous industries have also developed codes of ethics. The American Institute of Certified Public Accountants (AICPA) has a comprehensive Code of Professional Conduct for the ethical practicing of accounting. The American Bar Association (ABA) has model rules of professional conduct for attorneys, and the American Nurses Association (ANA) has a code of ethics that applies to nurses. These codes can give guidance to decision makers facing ethical questions. Violation of a code may result in the discipline of an employee or sanctions against a company from the industry organization. Remember, though, that these internal codes are not laws, so their effectiveness is determined by the commitment of the industry or company leadership to enforcing the codes.

3–1b The Role of Business in Society

Over the last two hundred years, public perception has moved toward expecting corporations to participate in society as corporate citizens. Originally, though, the only perceived duty of a corporation was to maximize profits and generate revenues for its owners. Although many people today may view this idea as greedy or ruthless, the rationale for the profit-maximization theory is still valid.

Business as a Pure Profit Maximizer In theory, if all firms strictly adhere to the goal of maximizing profits, resources flow to where they are most highly valued by society. Corporations can focus on their strengths. Other entities that are better suited to deal with social problems and perform charitable acts can specialize in those activities. The government, through taxes and other financial allocations, can shift resources to those other entities to perform public services. Thus, profit maximization can lead to the most efficient allocation of scarce resources.

Even when profit maximization is the goal, companies benefit by ethical behavior. For instance, customer satisfaction with a company is key to its profitability. Repeat customers are good for business. When customers are happy, word gets around, and it generates more business for the firm. Unsatisfied customers go elsewhere for the goods or services that the firm provides. When a business behaves badly, customers quickly report this online by posting bad reviews on such sites as Angie's List, Yelp, and TripAdvisor. Bad reviews obviously hurt a business's profits, while good reviews lead to higher profits.

Business as a Corporate Citizen Over the years, many people became dissatisfied with profit-maximization theory. Investors and others began to look beyond profits and dividends and to consider the **triple bottom line**—a corporation's profits, its impact on people, and its impact on the planet. Magazines and websites began to rank companies based on their environmental impacts and their ethical decisions. Corporations came to be viewed as "citizens" that were expected to participate in bettering communities and society.

A Four-Part Analysis Whether one believes in profit-maximization theory or corporate citizenship, ethics is important in business decision making. When making decisions, a business should evaluate each of the following:

1. The legal implications of each decision.
2. The public relations impact.
3. The safety risks for consumers and employees.
4. The financial implications.

This four-part analysis will assist the firm in making decisions that not only maximize profits but also reflect good corporate citizenship.

3–1c Ethical Issues in Business

Ethical issues can arise in numerous aspects of doing business. A fundamental ethical issue for business is developing integrity and trust. Businesspersons should exhibit integrity in their dealings with other people in the company, other businesses, clients, and the community. Companies that are honest and treat others fairly earn trust.

Businesses should also ensure that the workplace respects diversity and enforces equal opportunity employment and civil rights laws. In addition, businesses must comply with a host of federal and state laws and regulations, including those pertaining to the environment, financial reporting, and safety standards. Compliance with these rules can involve ethical issues. See this chapter's *Digital Update* feature for a discussion of an ethical issue that has arisen from employees' work-related use of digital technology after work hours.

The most difficult aspect of ethics that businesses face is in decision making. Businesspersons must learn to recognize ethical issues, get the pertinent facts, evaluate the alternatives, and then make a decision. Decision makers should also test and reflect on the outcome of their decisions. We focus here on this aspect of ethics.

Should Employees Have a "Right of Disconnecting"?

Almost all jobs today involve digital technology, whether it be e-mails, Internet access, or smartphone use. Most employees, when interviewed, say that digital technology increases their productivity and flexibility. The downside is what some call an "electronic leash"—employees are constantly connected and therefore end up working when they are not "at work." Over one-third of full-time workers, for example, say that they frequently check e-mails outside normal working hours.

Do Workers Have the Right to Disconnect?

Because the boundaries between being "at work" and being "at leisure" can be so hazy, some labor unions in other countries have attempted to pass rules that allow employees to disconnect from e-mail and other work-related digital communication during nonworking hours. For example, a French labor union representing high-tech workers signed an agreement with a large business association recognizing a "right of disconnecting."

In Germany, Volkswagen and BMW no longer forward e-mail to staff from company servers after the end of the working day. Other German firms have declared that workers are not expected to check e-mail on weekends and holidays. The government is considering legislating such restrictions nationwide.

The Thorny Issue of Overtime and the Fair Labor Standards Act

In the United States, payment for overtime work is strictly regulated under the Fair Labor Standards Act (FLSA), as amended.[a] An employee is normally entitled to compensation for off-duty work if such work is an "integral and indispensible part of [employees'] activities."[b] For example, a court ruled that Hormel Foods Corporation had to pay its factory workers for the time it took them to change into and out of the required white clothes before and after their shifts.[c] In contrast, a federal court held that a group of warehouse employees at Amazon.com were not entitled under the FLSA to be paid for the time spent passing through a metal detector at the ends of their shifts.[d]

Today's modern digital connectivity raises issues about the definition of *work*. Employees at several major companies, including Black & Decker, T-Mobile, and Verizon, have sued for unpaid overtime related to smartphone use. In another case, a police sergeant sued the city of Chicago, claiming that he should have been paid overtime for hours spent using his personal digital assistant (PDA). The police department had issued PDAs to officers and required them to respond to work-related communications even while off duty. The court agreed that some of the officers' off-duty PDA activities were compensable. Nevertheless, it ruled in favor of the city because the officers had failed to follow proper procedures for filing overtime claims.[e]

Critical Thinking *From an ethical point of view, is there any difference between calling subordinates during off hours for work-related questions and sending them e-mails or text messages?.*

a. The courts have broad authority to interpret the FLSA's definition of *work*. 29 U.S.C. Section 251(a). See *Integrity Staffing Solutions, Inc. v. Busk*, ___ U.S. ___, 135 S.Ct. 513, 190 L.Ed.2d 410 (2014).

b. *Steiner v. Mitchell*, 350 U.S. 247, 76 S.Ct. 330, 100 L.Ed. 267 (1956).
c. *United Food & Commercial Workers Union, Local 1473 v. Hormel Foods Corp.*, 367 Wis.2d 131, 876 N.W.2d 99 (2016).
d. *In re Amazon.com, Inc. Fulfillment Center Fair Labor Standards Act (FLSA) and Wage and Hour Litigation*, 905 F.3d 387 (6th Cir. 2018).
e. *Allen v. City of Chicago*, 2015 WL 8493996 (N.D.Ill. 2015).

3–1d The Importance of Ethical Leadership

In ethics, as in other areas, employees take their cues from management. Talking about ethical business decision making is meaningless if management does not set standards. Furthermore, managers must apply the same standards to themselves as they do to the company's employees. This duty starts with top management.

Attitude of Top Management One of the most important ways to create and maintain an ethical workplace is for top management to demonstrate its commitment to ethical decision making. A manager who is not totally committed to an ethical workplace will rarely succeed in creating one. More than anything else, top management's behavior sets the ethical tone of a firm.

Managers have found that discharging even one employee for ethical reasons has a tremendous impact as a deterrent to unethical behavior in the workplace. This is true even if the company has a written code of ethics. If management does not enforce the company code, the code essentially does not exist.

The administration of a university may have had this concept in mind in the following case when it applied the school's professionalism standard to a student who had engaged in serious misconduct.

Al-Dabagh v. Case Western Reserve University

United States Court of Appeals, Sixth Circuit, 777 F.3d 355 (2015).

Background and Facts   The curriculum at Case Western Reserve University School of Medicine identifies nine "core competencies." At the top of the list is professionalism, which includes "ethical, honest, responsible and reliable behavior." The university's Committee on Students determines whether a student has met the professionalism requirements.

Amir Al-Dabagh enrolled at the school and did well academically. But he sexually harassed fellow students, often asked an instructor not to mark him late for class, received complaints from hospital staff about his demeanor, and was convicted of driving while intoxicated. The Committee on Students unanimously refused to certify him for graduation and dismissed him from the university.

He filed a suit in a federal district court against Case Western, alleging a breach of good faith and fair dealing. The court ordered the school to issue a diploma. Case Western appealed.

In the Language of the Court

SUTTON, Circuit Judge.

* * * *

* * * Case Western's student handbook * * * makes clear that the only thing standing between Al-Dabagh and a diploma is the Committee on Students's finding that he lacks professionalism. Unhappily for Al-Dabagh, that is an academic judgment. And *we can no more substitute our personal views for the Committee's when it comes to an academic judgment than the Committee can substitute its views for ours when it comes to a judicial decision.* [Emphasis added.]

* * * *

* * * *The Committee's professionalism determination is an academic judgment. That conclusion all but resolves this case. We may overturn the Committee only if it substantially departed from accepted academic norms when it refused to approve Al-Dabagh for graduation.* And given Al-Dabagh's track record—one member of the Committee does not recall encountering another student with Al-Dabagh's "repeated professionalism issues" in his quarter century of experience—we cannot see how it did. [Emphasis added.]

To the contrary, Al-Dabagh insists: The Committee's decision was a "punitive disciplinary measure" that had nothing to do with academics. * * * His argument fails to wrestle with the prominent place of professionalism in the university's academic curriculum—which itself is an academic decision courts may not lightly disturb.

Even if professionalism is an academic criterion, Al-Dabagh persists that the university defined it too broadly. As he sees it, the only professional lapses that matter are the ones linked to academic performance. That is not how we see it or for that matter how the medical school sees it. That many professionalism-related cases involve classroom incidents does not establish that only classroom incidents are relevant to the professionalism inquiry * * * . Our own standards indicate that professionalism does not end at the courtroom door. Why should hospitals operate any differently?

As for the danger that an expansive view of professionalism might forgive, or provide a cloak for, arbitrary or discriminatory behavior, we see no such problem here. Nothing in the record suggests that the university had impermissible motives or acted in bad faith in this instance. And nothing in our deferential standard prevents us from invalidating genuinely objectionable actions when they occur.

Decision and Remedy   The federal appellate court reversed the lower court's order to issue a diploma to Al-Dabagh. The court found nothing to indicate that Case Western had "impermissible motives," acted in bad faith, or dealt unfairly with Al-Dabagh.

Critical Thinking

- **What If the Facts Were Different?**   *Suppose that Case Western had tolerated Al-Dabagh's conduct and awarded him a diploma. What impact might that have had on other students at the school? Why?*

Unrealistic Goals for Employees Certain types of behavior on the part of managers and owners contribute to unethical behavior among employees. Managers who set unrealistic production or sales goals increase the probability that employees will act unethically. If a sales quota can be met only through high-pressure, unethical sales tactics, employees will try to act "in the best interest of the company" and behave unethically. A manager who looks the other way when she or he knows about an employee's unethical behavior also sets an example—one indicating that ethical transgressions will be accepted.

Note that even when large companies have policies against sales incentives, individual branches may still promote them. ■ **Case in Point 3.5** The financial firm Morgan Stanley Smith Barney, LLC, has an internal policy barring sales contests. Nevertheless, Morgan Stanley branches in Massachusetts and Rhode Island held a sales contest in which brokers were given cash incentives of up to $5,000 for selling securities-based loans, or SBLs (loans that allow clients to borrow against their investments). Thirty financial advisers participated in the sales contest for almost a year until Morgan Stanley's compliance office noticed and halted the practice. One regional branch reportedly tripled its loans as a result of the contest. The state of Massachusetts ultimately sued Morgan Stanley, claiming that the practice violated state securities rules.[5] ■

Fostering of Unethical Conduct Business owners and managers sometimes take more active roles in fostering unethical and illegal conduct, with negative consequences for their businesses. ■ **Case in Point 3.6** Dr. Rajendra Gandhi and his wife were devout Hindus who wanted to redecorate their entire home with high-quality custom designer furniture and draperies. They hired Sonal Furniture and Custom Draperies, LLC, because Sonal's owner, Shyam Garg, represented himself to be culturally and religiously like-minded. Garg told the Gandhis that he would use only the highest-quality materials in their home, and Dr. Gandhi gave Garg a $20,000 deposit. Garg later showed up at the couple's home unannounced with four trucks full of furniture. The Gandhis paid Garg $190,000 (for a total of $210,000).

Within weeks, the Gandhis began noticing that the items provided were of inferior quality. Nearly every piece was damaged in some way. Eventually, Dr. Gandhi demanded a full refund from Garg. Garg threatened to pursue criminal action against Dr. Gandhi, among other things. The Gandhis sued Sonal Furniture and Garg. An expert testified that the furniture was "not actually intended for functional use, almost like movie set furniture," and "would be very difficult to repair." The court ruled in favor of the Gandhis and awarded a full refund of the price, plus $100,000 in damages. The court found that Garg had misrepresented the quality of the furniture and had preyed on the Ghandis' cultural and religious heritage, using outrageous threats, coercion, and extortion. The judgment was affirmed on appeal.[6] ■

3–2 Ethical Principles and Philosophies

How do business decision makers decide whether a given action is the "right" one for their firms? What ethical standards should be applied? Broadly speaking, **ethical reasoning**—the application of morals and ethics to a situation—applies to businesses just as it does to individuals. As businesses make decisions, they must analyze their alternatives in a variety of ways, one of which is the ethical implications of each alternative.

Generally, the study of ethics identifies two major categories—duty-based ethics and outcome-based ethics. **Duty-based ethics** is rooted in the idea that every person has certain duties to others, including both humans and the planet. **Outcome-based ethics** focuses on the impacts of a decision on society or on key *stakeholders*.

3–2a Duty-Based Ethics

Duty-based ethics focuses on the obligations of the corporation. It deals with standards for behavior that traditionally were derived from revealed truths, religious authorities, or philosophical reasoning. These standards involve concepts of right and wrong, duties owed, and rights to be protected. Corporations today often describe these values or duties in their mission statements or strategic plans. Some companies base their statements on a nonreligious rationale, while others derive their values from religious doctrine.

Religious Ethical Principles Nearly every religion has principles or beliefs about how one should treat others. In the Judeo-Christian tradition, which is the dominant religious tradition in the United States, the Ten Commandments of the Old Testament establish these fundamental rules for moral action. The principles of the Muslim faith are set out in the Qur'an, and Hindus find their principles in the four Vedas.

5. *In re Morgan Stanley Smith Barney, LLC*, Docket No. E-2016-0055. *www.sec.state.ma.us.* 3 Oct. 2016. Web.

6. *Gandhi v. Sonal Furniture and Custom Draperies, LLC*, 192 So.3d 783 (La.App. 2015).

Religious rules generally are absolute with respect to the behavior of their adherents. ■ **Example 3.7** The commandment "Thou shalt not steal" is an absolute mandate for a person who believes that the Ten Commandments reflect revealed truth. Even a benevolent motive for stealing (such as Robin Hood's) cannot justify the act because the act itself is inherently immoral and thus wrong. ■

For businesses, religious principles can be a unifying force for employees or a rallying point to increase employee motivation. They can also present problems, however, because different owners, suppliers, employees, and customers may have different religious backgrounds. Taking an action based on religious principles, especially when those principles address socially or politically controversial topics, can lead to negative publicity and even to protests or boycotts.

Principles of Rights Another view of duty-based ethics focuses on basic rights. The principle that human beings have certain fundamental rights (to life, freedom, and the pursuit of happiness, for instance) is deeply embedded in Western culture.

Those who adhere to this **principle of rights,** or "rights theory," believe that a key factor in determining whether a business decision is ethical is how that decision affects the rights of others. These others include the firm's owners, its employees, the consumers of its products or services, its suppliers, the community in which it does business, and society as a whole.

Conflicting Rights. A potential dilemma for those who support rights theory is that they may disagree on which rights are most important. When considering all those affected by a business decision to downsize a firm, for example, how much weight should be given to employees relative to shareholders? Which employees should be laid off first—those with the highest salaries or those who have less seniority (have worked there for the shortest time)? How should the firm weigh the rights of customers relative to the community, or employees relative to society as a whole?

Resolving Conflicts. In general, rights theorists believe that whichever right is stronger in a particular circumstance takes precedence. ■ **Example 3.8** Murray Chemical Corporation has to decide whether to keep a chemical plant in Utah open, thereby saving the jobs of a hundred and fifty workers, or shut it down. Closing the plant will avoid contaminating a river with pollutants that might endanger the health of tens of thousands of people. In this situation, a rights theorist can easily choose which group to favor because the value of the right to health and well-being is obviously stronger than a right to work. Not all choices are so clear-cut, however. ■

Kantian Ethical Principles Duty-based ethical standards may also be derived solely from philosophical reasoning. The German philosopher Immanuel Kant (1724–1804) identified some general guiding principles for moral behavior based on what he thought to be the fundamental nature of human beings. Kant believed that human beings are qualitatively different from other physical objects and are endowed with moral integrity and the capacity to reason and conduct their affairs rationally.

People Are Not a Means to an End. Based on this view of human beings, Kant said that when people are treated merely as a means to an end, they are being treated as the equivalent of objects and are being denied their basic humanity. For instance, a manager who treats subordinates as mere profit-making tools is not treating them with the respect they deserve as human beings. Such a manager is less less likely to retain motivated and loyal employees than a manager who respects employees. Management research has shown that, in fact, employees who feel empowered to share their thoughts, opinions, and solutions to problems are happier and more productive.

Categorical Imperative. When a business makes unethical decisions, it often rationalizes its action by saying that the company is "just one small part" of the problem or that its decision has had "only a small impact." A central theme in Kantian ethics is that individuals should evaluate their actions in light of the consequences that would follow if everyone in society acted in the same way. This **categorical imperative** can be applied to any action.

■ **Example 3.9** CHS Fertilizer is deciding whether to invest in expensive equipment that will decrease profits but will also reduce pollution from its factories. If CHS has adopted Kant's categorical imperative, the decision makers will consider the consequences if every company invested in the equipment (or if no company did so). If the result would make the world a better place (less polluted), CHS's decision would be clear. ■

3–2b Outcome-Based Ethics: Utilitarianism

In contrast to duty-based ethics, outcome-based ethics focuses on the consequences of an action, not on the nature of the action itself or on any set of preestablished moral values or religious beliefs. Outcome-based ethics looks at the impacts of a decision in an attempt to maximize benefits and minimize harms.

The premier philosophical theory for outcome-based decision making is **utilitarianism,** a philosophical theory developed by Jeremy Bentham (1748–1832) and modified by John Stuart Mill (1806–1873)—both British philosophers. "The greatest good for the greatest number" is a paraphrase of the major premise of the utilitarian approach to ethics.

Cost-Benefit Analysis Under a utilitarian model of ethics, an action is morally correct, or "right," when, among the people it affects, it produces the greatest amount of good for the greatest number or creates the least amount of harm for the fewest people. When an action affects the majority adversely, it is morally wrong. Applying the utilitarian theory thus requires the following steps:

1. A determination of which individuals will be affected by the action in question.
2. A **cost-benefit analysis,** which involves an assessment of the negative and positive effects of alternative actions on these individuals.
3. A choice among alternative actions that will produce maximum societal utility (the greatest positive net benefits for the greatest number of individuals).

For instance, assume that expanding a factory would provide hundreds of jobs but generate pollution that could endanger the lives of thousands of people. A utilitarian analysis would find that saving the lives of thousands creates greater good than providing jobs for hundreds.

Problems with the Utilitarian Approach There are problems with a strict utilitarian analysis. In some situations, an action that produces the greatest good for the most people may not seem to be the most ethical.
■ **Example 3.10** Phazim Company is producing a drug that will cure a disease in 99 percent of patients, but the other 1 percent will experience agonizing side effects and a horrible, painful death. A quick utilitarian analysis would suggest that the drug should be produced and marketed because the majority of patients will benefit. Many people, however, have significant concerns about manufacturing a drug that will cause such harm to anyone. ■

3–2c Corporate Social Responsibility

In pairing duty-based concepts with outcome-based concepts, strategists and theorists developed the idea of the corporate citizen. **Corporate social responsibility (CSR)** combines a commitment to good citizenship with a commitment to making ethical decisions, improving society, and minimizing environmental impact.

CSR is a relatively new concept in the history of business, but a concept that becomes more important every year. Although CSR is not imposed on corporations by law, it does involve a commitment to self-regulation in a way that attends to the text and intent of the law as well as to ethical norms and global standards. A survey of U.S. executives undertaken by the Boston College Center for Corporate Citizenship found that more than 70 percent of those polled agreed that corporate citizenship must be treated as a priority. More than 60 percent said that good corporate citizenship added to their companies' profits.

CSR can be a successful strategy for companies, but corporate decision makers must not lose track of the two descriptors in the title: *corporate* and *social*. The company must link the responsibility of citizenship with the strategy and key principles of the business. Incorporating both the social and the corporate components of CSR and making ethical decisions can help companies grow and prosper.

CSR is most successful when a company undertakes activities that are significant and related to its business operations. Some types of activities that businesses are engaging in today include the following:

1. Environmental efforts.
2. Ethical labor practices.
3. Charitable donations.
4. Volunteer work.

The Corporate Aspects of CSR Arguably, any socially responsible activity will benefit a corporation. A corporation may see an increase in goodwill from the local community for creating a park, for instance. A corporation that is viewed as a good citizen may see an increase in sales.

At times, the benefit may not be immediate. Constructing a new plant that meets high energy and environmental standards may cost more initially. Nevertheless, over the life of the building, the savings in maintenance and utilities may more than make up for the extra cost of construction.

Surveys of college students about to enter the job market confirm that young people are looking for socially responsible employers. Socially responsible activities may thus cost a corporation now, but may lead to more impressive and more committed employees. Corporations that engage in meaningful social activities retain workers longer, particularly younger ones.

■ **Example 3.11** Google's focus on social responsibility attracts many young workers. Google has worked to reduce its carbon footprint and to make its products and services better for the environment. The company promotes green commuting, recycling, and reducing energy consumption at its data centers. ■

The Social Aspects of CSR Because business controls so much of the wealth and power in this country, business has a responsibility to use that wealth and power in socially beneficial ways. Thus, the social aspects of CSR require corporations to demonstrate that they are promoting goals that society deems worthwhile and are moving toward solutions to social problems. Companies may be judged on how much they donate to social causes, as well as how they conduct their operations with respect to employment discrimination, human rights, environmental concerns, and similar issues.

Some corporations publish annual social responsibility reports, which may also be called sustainability or citizenship reports. ■ **Example 3.12** The multinational technology company Cisco Systems, Inc., issues corporate responsibility reports to demonstrate its focus on people, society, and the planet. In a recent report, Cisco outlined its commitment to developing its employees' skills, ethical conduct, and charitable donations (including matching employee contributions and giving employees time off for volunteer work). Cisco also reported on the global impact of its business in the areas of human rights, labor, privacy and data security, and responsible manufacturing. The report indicated that Cisco had completed more than a hundred energy-efficient projects and was on track to meet its goals of reducing emissions from its worldwide operations by 40 percent. ■

Stakeholders and CSR One view of CSR stresses that corporations have a duty not just to shareholders, but also to other groups affected by corporate decision making, called **stakeholders.** The rationale for this "stakeholder view" is that, in some circumstances, one or more of these groups may have a greater stake in company decisions than the shareholders do.

A corporation's stakeholders include its employees, customers, creditors, suppliers, and the community in which it operates. Advocacy groups, such as environmental groups and animal rights groups, may also be stakeholders. Under the stakeholder approach, a corporation considers the impact of its decision on these stakeholders, which helps it to avoid making a decision that may appear unethical and may result in negative publicity.

The most difficult aspect of the stakeholder analysis is determining which group's interests should receive greater weight if the interests conflict. For instance, companies that are struggling financially sometimes lay off workers to reduce labor costs. But some corporations have found ways to avoid slashing their workforces and to prioritize their employees' interests. Companies finding alternatives to layoffs include Dell (extended unpaid holidays), Cisco (four-day end-of-year shutdowns), Motorola (salary cuts), and Honda (voluntary unpaid vacation time). These alternatives benefit not only the employees who get to keep their jobs, but also the community as a whole. Working people can afford to go out to local restaurants and shops and use local service providers. Thus, other businesses in the community benefit.

3–3 Sources of Ethical Issues in Business Decisions

A key to avoiding unethical conduct is to recognize how certain situations may lead individuals to act unethically. In this section, we first consider some specific areas in which ethical decisions may often arise. We then discuss some additional problems in making ethical business decisions.

3–3a Short-Term Profit Maximization

Businesspersons often commit ethical violations because they are too focused on one issue or one needed result, such as increasing profits or outperforming the competition. Some studies indicate that top-performing companies may actually be more likely to behave unethically than less successful companies, because employees feel they are expected to continue performing at a high level. Thus, abnormally high profits and stock prices may lead to unethical behavior.

In attempting to maximize profits, corporate executives and employees have to distinguish between *short-run* and *long-run* profit maximization. In the short run, a company may increase its profits by continuing to sell a product even though it knows that the product is defective. In the long run, though, because of lawsuits, large settlements, and bad publicity, such unethical conduct will cause profits to suffer. An overemphasis on short-run profit maximization is perhaps the most common reason that ethical problems occur in business.

■ **Case in Point 3.13** Volkswagen's corporate executives were accused of cheating on the pollution emissions tests of millions of vehicles that were sold in the United States. Volkswagen (VW) eventually admitted that it had installed "defeat device" software in its diesel models. The software detected when the car was being tested and changed its performance to improve the test outcome. As a result, the diesel cars showed low emissions— a feature that made the cars more attractive to today's consumers.

Ultimately, Volkswagen agreed to plead guilty to criminal charges and pay $2.8 billion in fines. The company also agreed to pay $1.5 billion to the Environmental Protection Agency to settle the federal investigation into its "clean diesel" emissions fraud. Overall, the scandal cost

VW nearly $15 billion (in fines and to compensate consumers or buy back their vehicles). Six top executives at VW were charged with criminal wire fraud, conspiracy, and violations of the Clean Air Act. In the end, the company's focus on maximizing profits in the short run (with increased sales) led to unethical conduct that hurt profits in the long run.[7] ■

In the following case, a drug manufacturer was accused of fabricating "average wholesale prices" for its drugs to maximize its profits and receive overpayments from Medicaid.

---

7. *In re Volkswagen "Clean Diesel" Marketing, Sales Practices, and Product Liability Litigation*, 229 F.Supp.3d 1052 and 2017 WL 66281 (N.D.Cal. 2017).

Case 3.2

Watson Laboratories, Inc. v. State of Mississippi

Supreme Court of Mississippi, 241 So.3d 573 (2018).

Background and Facts Watson Laboratories, Inc., makes generic drugs, which are provided by pharmacies to Medicaid patients. In the state of Mississippi, a claim is submitted for the cost of the drug to Mississippi Medicaid. The claim is paid according to a percentage of the drug's average wholesale price (AWP). Like other drug makers, Watson published its products' AWPs. But for more than a dozen years, Watson set each AWP to meet the requirements to obtain a generic designation for the drug, without regard to the actual price.

When Mississippi Medicaid learned that the actual prices were much lower than the published AWPs, the state filed a lawsuit in a Mississippi state court against Watson, alleging fraud. The court concluded that Watson had caused the state to overpay for the drugs and ordered the payment of more than $30 million in penalties, damages, and interest. Watson appealed.

In the Language of the Court

CHAMBERLIN, Justice, for the court:

* * * *

* * * The elements of an intentional * * * fraudulent representation are:

(1) a representation, (2) its falsity, (3) its materiality, (4) the speaker's knowledge of its falsity or ignorance of its truth, (5) his intent that it should be acted on by the hearer and in the manner reasonably contemplated, (6) the hearer's ignorance of its falsity, (7) his reliance on its truth, (8) his right to rely thereon, and (9) his consequent and proximate injury.

* * * *

* * * *The numbers [published] by Watson * * * were not "suggested wholesale prices" or "list prices." They were fabricated numbers tied to nothing more than a ceiling amount it was necessary to stay under in order to obtain a generic designation.* [Emphasis added.]

* * * Thus, Watson did make a false representation.

* * * *

* * * Watson knew that Mississippi Medicaid would rely on its false statements and benefitted from this reliance. It is evident that Watson intended to deceive Mississippi Medicaid.

* * * *

Mississippi Medicaid had every right to rely on AWP [average wholesale price] as a "starting point" or "benchmark" for determining appropriate reimbursement rates. They were held out as a "suggested wholesale price."

Case 3.2 Continues

Case 3.2 Continued   * * * *

Evidence in the record is sufficient to show the overpayment for the drugs in question. The extent of the damages, through just and reasonable inference, has been supported by the evidence. [Emphasis added.]
* * * *

In sum, * * * Watson defrauded the State. For years, Watson intentionally published its AWPs * * * with the knowledge and intent that Mississippi Medicaid would rely on the figures for its reimbursement formulas. * * * Mississippi Medicaid did not know that the AWPs had no relation to the actual prices paid for the drugs. As such, Mississippi Medicaid continued to reasonably rely on the AWPs * * * . All the while, Watson * * * exploited Mississippi Medicaid's lack of knowledge at the expense of the taxpayers of the State of Mississippi.

Decision and Remedy The Supreme Court of Mississippi affirmed the lower court's order. Watson falsely represented its AWPs. Furthermore, "Watson knew that Mississippi Medicaid would rely on its false statements and benefitted from this reliance."

Critical Thinking
- **Economic** *What marketing tool did Watson gain by inflating its AWPs?*
- **What If the Facts Were Different?** *Watson argued that AWP was a specialized term in the pharmaceutical industry that meant "suggested price." Suppose that the court had accepted this argument. What might have been the effect of this decision?*

3–3b Social Media

Advancements in technology have created various new ethical issues for companies. Here, we focus on those involving social media. Most people think of social media—Facebook, Flickr, Instagram, Snapchat, Tumblr, Twitter, Pinterest, WhatsApp, LinkedIn, and the like—as simply ways to communicate rapidly. But everyone knows that they can quickly encounter ethical and legal disputes for posting statements that others interpret as harassing, inappropriate, insulting, or racist. Businesses often face ethical issues with respect to these social media platforms.

The Use of Social Media to Make Hiring Decisions In the past, to learn about a prospective employee, an employer would ask the candidate's former employers for references. Today, employers are likely to also conduct Internet searches to discover what job candidates have posted on their Facebook pages, blogs, and tweets.

On the one hand, job candidates may be judged by what they post on social media. On the other hand, though, they may be judged because they *do not participate* in social media. Given that the vast majority of younger people use social media, some employers have decided that the failure to do so raises a red flag. In either case, many people believe that judging a job candidate based on what she or he does outside the work environment is unethical.

The Use of Social Media to Discuss Work-Related Issues Because so many Americans use social media daily, they often discuss work-related issues there. Numerous companies have strict guidelines about what is appropriate and inappropriate for employees to say when posting on their own or others' social media accounts. A number of companies have fired employees for such activities as criticizing other employees or managers through social media outlets. Until recently, such disciplinary measures were considered ethical and legal.

The Responsibility of Employers. A ruling by the National Labor Relations Board (NLRB—the federal agency that investigates unfair labor practices) has changed the legality of such actions. ■ **Example 3.14** At one time, Costco's social media policy specified that its employees should not make statements that would damage the company, harm another person's reputation, or violate the company's policies. Employees who violated these rules were subject to discipline and could be fired.

The NLRB ruled that Costco's social media policy violated federal labor law, which protects employees' right to engage in "concerted activities." Employees can freely associate with each other and have conversations about common workplace issues without employer interference. This right extends to social media posts. Therefore, an employer cannot broadly prohibit its employees from criticizing the company or co-workers, supervisors, or managers via social media. ■

The Responsibility of Employees. While most of the discussion in this chapter concerns the ethics of business management, employee ethics is also an important issue. For instance, is it ethical for employees to make negative posts in social media about other employees or, more commonly, about managers? After all, negative comments about managers reflect badly on those managers, who often are reluctant to respond via social media to such criticism. Disgruntled employees may exaggerate the negative qualities of managers whom they do not like.

Some may consider the decision by the National Labor Relations Board outlined in *Example 3.14* to be too lenient toward employees and too stringent toward management. There is likely to be an ongoing debate about how to balance employees' right to free expression against employers' right to prevent the spreading of inaccurate negative statements online.

3–3c Awareness

Regardless of the context in which a decision is called for, sometimes businesspersons are not even aware that the decision has ethical implications. Perhaps they are focused on something else, for instance, or perhaps they do not take the time to think through their actions.

■ **Case in Point 3.15** Japanese airbag maker Takata Corporation manufactured some airbags that used an ammonium nitrate-based propellant without a chemical drying agent. It was later discovered that these airbags tended to deploy explosively, especially in higher temperatures, higher humidity, and older vehicles. When the airbags deployed, metal inflator cartridges inside them sometimes ruptured, sending metal shards into the passenger cabin.

The defective airbags caused a number of deaths and injuries in the United States, and the federal government ordered recalls of the devices in nearly 42 million vehicles nationwide. Takata executives likely did not intend to hurt consumers and may not even have considered the ethics of their decision. Takata, however, continued to produce airbags with this defect for years. A class-action lawsuit was filed against the company, which later sought bankruptcy protection.[8] ■

3–3d Rationalization

Sometimes, businesspersons make decisions that benefit them or their company knowing that the decisions are ethically questionable. Afterward, they rationalize their bad behavior. For instance, an employee might rationalize that it is acceptable to take company property for personal use or to lie to a client just this one time, because she or

he normally does not act in this way. An executive might rationalize that unethical conduct directed against a certain competitor is acceptable because that company deserves it. Individuals might rationalize that their conduct is not unethical because it is simply a part of doing business.

One suggestion that is useful in counteracting rationalization is for businesspersons to *first decide the right thing to do on an ethical level before making a business decision*. Then they can figure out how to mitigate the costs of doing the right thing. This works much better to prevent unethical conduct than making decisions based solely on a financial or business basis and then trying to make that result seem ethical (by rationalizing).

3–3e Uncertainty

One common denominator identified by businesspersons who have faced ethical problems is the feeling of uncertainty. They may be uncertain as to what they should do, what they should have done, or (as mentioned) whether there was even an ethical issue or ethical breach involved. Such uncertainty is practically unavoidable, but it should be treated as an indicator of a potential ethical problem.

When employees or executives express uncertainty about a particular decision, it is best to treat the situation as involving an ethical issue. Decision makers should try to identify what the ethical dilemma is and why the individual or group is feeling uneasy. They should also take the time to think through the decision completely and discuss various options. They might want to consider whether the company would be pleased if the decision were reported to its clients or to the public. Building a process that supports and assists those facing ethical dilemmas can be key to avoiding unethical business practices (and any corresponding negative publicity).

3–4 Making Ethical Business Decisions

Even if officers, directors, and others in a company want to make ethical decisions, it is not always clear what is ethical in a given situation. Sometimes, there is no "good" answer to the questions that arise. Therefore, it is important to have tools to help in the decision-making process and a framework for organizing those tools.

Several frameworks exist to help businesspersons make ethical decisions. Some frameworks, for instance, focus more on legal than ethical implications. This approach tends to be primarily outcome-based and, as such, may not be appropriate for a company that is values driven

---

8. *In re Takata Airbag Products Liability Litigation*, 84 F.Supp.3d 1371 (2015).

or committed to corporate social responsibility (or has a consumer or investor base that is focused on CSR). Other models, such as the Business Process Pragmatism™ procedure developed by ethics consultant Leonard H. Bucklin, set out a series of steps to follow. In this text, we present a modified version of this system that we call IDDR. ("I Desire to Do Right" is a useful mnemonic device for remembering the name.)

3–4a A Systematic Approach: IDDR ("I Desire to Do Right")

Using the IDDR approach involves organizing the issues and approaching them systematically. This process can help eliminate various alternatives and identify the strengths and weaknesses of the remaining alternatives. Often, the best approach is for a group (rather than an individual) to carry out the process. Thus, if an individual employee is facing an ethical issue, she or he should talk with her or his supervisor, and then they should perform the following steps together.

Step 1: Inquiry The first step in making an ethical decision is to understand the problem. If an employee feels uneasy about a particular decision, decision makers should pay attention and ask questions. People generally know when something does not "feel" right, and this is often a good indicator that there may be an ethical problem. The decision makers must identify the ethical problem and all the parties involved—the stakeholders. It is important that they *not* frame the issue in a way that gives them the answer they might prefer. After gathering the relevant facts, the decision makers can also consider which ethical theories can help them analyze the problem thoroughly. Making a list of the ethical principles that will guide the decision may be helpful at this point.

Step 2: Discussion Once the ethical problem or problems have been clarified, a list of possible actions can be compiled. In discussing these alternatives, the decision makers should take time to think through each alternative completely and analyze its potential impact on various groups of stakeholders. They must evaluate the strengths and weaknesses of each option, along with its ethical and legal consequences. It is helpful to discuss with management the ultimate goals for the decision. At this point, too, the decision makers need to consider what they *should* do (what is the most ethical) before considering what they can or will do.

Step 3: Decision With all the relevant facts collected and the alternatives thoroughly analyzed and discussed,

it's time to make a decision. Those participating in the decision-making process now work together to craft a consensus decision or plan of action for the company. Once the decision has been made, the decision makers should use the analysis from the discussion step to articulate the reasons they arrived at the decision. This results in documentation that can be shared with stakeholders to explain why the course of action is an ethical solution to the problem.

Step 4: Review After the decision has been made and implemented, it is important for the decision makers to review the outcome to determine whether the solution was effective. Did the action solve the ethical problem? Were the stakeholders satisfied with the result? Could anything have been handled better? The results of this evaluation can be used in making future decisions. Successful decision makers learn from their mistakes and continue to improve.

3–4b Applying the IDDR Approach—A Sample Scenario

To really understand the IDDR approach, it is helpful to work through the process by analyzing an ethical problem. Here, as a sample, we present a scenario that is based on a real story but contains fictional elements as well. The conversations and analyses included in the scenario are fictional. Because any discussions that may have taken place in the real situation took place behind closed doors, we cannot know if any ethical analysis occurred.

■ **Example 3.16** Assume that you are an intern working on a social media campaign for Duane Reade, a New York pharmacy chain. As part of your internship, you follow several celebrity gossip Web pages and do regular Internet searches looking for any picture or mention of the stores. In the course of these searches, you find a picture of Katherine Heigl leaving a Duane Reade store carrying bags imprinted with the company logo. (Katherine Heigl is a recognizable actress from television's *Grey's Anatomy* and several major movies.) You can easily copy the picture to the company's Twitter account and add a caption about her shopping at one of the stores. Having customers or potential customers see this well-known person carrying Duane Reade bags and leaving the store could increase store visits and sales.

The question is this: Is it appropriate to use Heigl's photo without her permission as part of an advertising campaign? Use the IDDR approach to analyze what you should do. Assume that you, your supervisor, and a few other members of the marketing department engage in this analysis. ■

Step 1: Inquiry To begin, clarify the nature of the problem. You want to use a picture of Heigl from a celebrity gossip Web page to potentially increase profits for the company. The problem could be phrased in this way: "Is it ethical to use a picture of a famous person to try to improve sales without contacting her or the photographer first?" Note that the way you frame the question will affect how you answer it. For instance, if the question was phrased, "Should we steal this picture?" the answer would be obvious. Remember *not* to frame the issue in a way that gives you the answer you might want.

You also need to identify the stakeholders. Here, the stakeholders include Heigl, the photographer who took the picture, Heigl's fans, and the potential customers of Duane Reade. Other stakeholders include your boss (who will get credit if sales increase due to the marketing campaign), Duane Reade stockholders, and store employees (who might see an increase in customers).

When gathering the facts, determine whether there are any legal issues. Given these facts, there may be state and federal laws that would guide a decision. For instance, reproducing a photograph without the owner's permission might violate federal copyright laws. In addition, most states have laws (sometimes called *right to publicity* laws) that protect a person's name, voice, or likeness (image or picture) from being used for advertising without the person's consent.

You can also consider which ethical theories can help you analyze the problem. The ethical theories may include religious values, rights theory, the categorical imperative, and utilitarianism. Ask yourself whether it is right, or ethical, to use Heigl's name or face without her permission as part of an advertising campaign.

Step 2: Discussion Several actions could be taken in this sample situation. Each action should be thoroughly analyzed using the various ethical approaches identified by the decision makers. The ultimate goals for the decision are to increase sales and do the least amount of harm to the business and its reputation without compromising the values of the business. In this step, it is best for decision makers to brainstorm and find as many options as possible. Here, though, we analyze only three alternatives. Exhibit 3–1 shows how these alternatives could be analyzed.

Exhibit 3–1 An Analysis of Ethical Approaches to the Sample Dilemma

Alternative	Legal Implications	Religious Values	Categorical Imperative	Rights Theory	Utilitarianism
1. Use the Picture without Permission	How does this alternative comply with copyright law? Are there any exceptions to copyright law that would allow this use?	Is this stealing? If so, it violates religious principles. Is it stealing to use a picture taken on a public street?	If everyone did this, then the images and names of famous people would often be used to promote products. Is this a good thing or not?	Using the picture may negatively impact the Web page or Heigl's ability to make money using her image. It also may violate some right to privacy.	If we use the picture, we may see an increase in sales and an improvement in reputation. We may, however, be sued for using her image without permission.
2. Contact the Web Page and/ or Heigl for Permission	Are there any laws that would make this alternative illegal? Are there any precautions we should take when asking for permission to avoid any appearance of threat or intimidation?	This alternative clearly is not stealing and thus would align with religious principles.	If everyone asked for permission, then such material would not be used without permission. This would seem to make the world a better place.	Getting permission would not seem to violate anyone's rights. In fact, giving someone the opportunity to decide might enhance that person's rights.	If we contact the parties for permission, we may be able to use the image, make more money, and improve our reputation. But the parties might refuse to give permission or demand payment, which would cost the company money.
3. Do Not Use the Picture	There are no legal implications to not using the picture.	This alternative clearly is not stealing and thus would align with religious principles.	If companies never used public, candid images of famous people, then all advertising would be staged. This might not make the world a better place.	Not using the picture may damage the stockholders' right to maximum income or the company's right to advertise as it sees fit.	If we do not use the picture, we avoid potential lawsuits. Alternatively, we won't have the potential increase in sales associated with the use of the famous face.

It is important to note that different ethical perspectives will be more or less helpful in different situations. In the sample scenario, a strong argument can be made that Heigl's rights to privacy and to control her image are very important. Under other circumstances, however, the right to privacy might be outweighed by some other right, such as another person's right to safety. Using multiple theories will help ensure that the decision makers can work through the analytical process and find a result.

Step 3: Decision After a lively discussion concerning Heigl's rights to privacy and to compensation for the use of her image, you and your fellow decision makers come to a consensus. Given the potential for increased income, you decide to use the picture. It will be posted on the company's Twitter account with a caption that reads, "Love a quick #DuaneReade run? Even @KatieHeigl can't resist shopping #NYC's favorite drugstore."

Make sure to articulate the reasons you arrived at the decision to serve as documentation explaining why the plan of action was ethical. In this meeting, the persuasive evidence was the projection for increased revenue balanced by the minimal harm to Heigl. Because the picture was taken on a public street, the people in the room did not feel that it involved a violation of any privacy right. The company would not have paid Heigl to do an advertisement. Also, because only people who followed Duane Reade on Twitter could view the tweet, the group felt the likelihood of any damage to Heigl was small. Most people felt that the worst that could happen would be that Heigl would ask them to remove the picture.

Step 4: Review You and the other decision makers at Duane Reade need to review the effectiveness of your decision. Assume that after the picture and caption are posted on Twitter, Heigl sees it and sues Duane Reade for "no less than $6 million." She argues that the company violated her rights by falsely claiming that she had endorsed its stores and that it misappropriated her name and likeness for a profit. The case is settled out of court, with Duane Reade paying an undisclosed amount to a foundation that Heigl created.

Here, the decision did not solve the ethical problem and, in fact, led to liability. You and the other decision makers need to determine what you could have done better. Perhaps the company should change its practices and obtain legal counsel for the marketing department—or at least hire a legal consultant when ethical issues arise. Perhaps it should establish an internal process for getting permission to use pictures from social media or other sources. In any event, the company likely should change some of its policies and practices related to social media marketing.

The decision-making process is not easy or precise. It may entail repeating steps as decision makers recognize new alternatives or as unforeseen stakeholders appear. Sometimes, the analysis will lead to a clear decision, and other times it will not. Even if it does not, though, the process will allow decision makers to enter the public phase of the decision (action) with a better idea of what consequences to expect.

For more on the IDDR approach to ethical decision making, see the *Ethics Today* feature.

3–5 Business Ethics on a Global Level

Just as individual religions have different moral codes, individual countries and regions have different ethical expectations and priorities. Some of these differences are based on religious values, whereas others are cultural in nature. Such differences can make it even more difficult to determine what is ethical in a particular situation.

3–5a World Religions, Cultural Norms, and Ethics

Global businesses need to be conscious of the impact of different religious principles and cultural norms on ethics. For instance, in certain countries the consumption of alcohol is forbidden for religious reasons. It would be considered unethical for a U.S. business to produce alcohol in those countries and employ local workers to assist in alcohol production.

In other countries, women may not be treated as equals because of cultural norms or religion. In contrast, discrimination against employees on the basis of sex (or race, national origin, age, or disability) is prohibited in the United States. The varying roles of women can give rise to ethical issues regarding how women working for a U.S. company should dress or behave in certain regions of the world. Should female executives have to cover their heads? Should they avoid involvement in certain business transactions? How will various stakeholders react to whatever decisions companies make in these situations?

How far should companies go to cater to business partners in other nations? Going too far to please clients in another country can alienate a firm's employees and domestic customers and generate bad press. Decision makers in charge of global business operations should consider these ethical issues and make some determinations from the outset.

Ethics Today

Applying the IDDR Framework

Pfizer, Inc., developed a new antibiotic called Trovan (trovafloxacin mesylate). Tests in animals showed that Trovan had life-threatening side effects, including joint disease, abnormal cartilage growth, liver damage, and a degenerative bone condition. Pfizer was seeking approval from the Food and Drug Administration (FDA) to market Trovan for use in the United States when an epidemic of bacterial meningitis swept across Nigeria.

Pfizer sent three U.S. physicians to test Trovan on children who were patients in Nigeria's Infectious Disease Hospital. Pfizer's representatives obtained all necessary approvals from the Nigerian government and had Nigerian nurses explain the details of the study to parents and inform them that participation was voluntary. They did not, however, alert the parents or patients about the serious risks involved, or tell them about an effective conventional treatment that Doctors without Borders was providing at the same site.

The results of the study showed that Trovan had a success rate of 94.4 percent in treating the children's condition. Nevertheless, eleven children died in the experiment, and others were left blind, deaf, paralyzed, or brain damaged. Rabi Abdullahi and other Nigerian children filed a suit in a U.S. federal court against Pfizer, alleging a violation of a customary international law norm prohibiting involuntary medical experimentation on humans.

Analysis

Pfizer could have applied the IDDR approach to review the ethical conflicts in a test of Trovan. (1) In the inquiry step, decision makers ask questions to understand the ethical dilemma, identify the stakeholders, gather relevant facts, and articulate the ethical principles at issue. (2) In the discussion step, the decision makers further explore potential actions and their effects. (3) The next step is to come to a consensus decision as to what to do. This consensus should withstand moral scrutiny and fulfill corporate, community, and individual values. (4) The last step is to review the outcome to determine whether it was effective and what the company could do better. In this instance, for example, fully informing the patients and their parents about the risks of the treatment would have been a better course of action.

Result and Reasoning

It seems unlikely that a proposed Trovan test on children, based on the facts described here, would have survived an IDDR analysis, under either a duty-based or an outcome-based ethical standard. It also would appear that Pfizer was rushing to test and market Trovan as soon as possible. This focus on short-run profit maximization took precedence over any ethical considerations. It is often easier to see ethical lapses in retrospect than it is to identify potential ethical problems in advance, however.

Critical Thinking *What might Pfizer have done differently to avert the consequences?*

3–5b Outsourcing

Outsourcing is the practice by which a company hires an outside firm or individual to perform work rather than hiring employees to do it. Ethical problems involving outsourcing most often arise when global companies outsource work to other countries in an attempt to save on labor costs. This type of outsourcing elicits an almost automatic negative reaction in the U.S. public. Some people feel that companies should protect American jobs above all else. Furthermore, ethical questions often arise as to the employment practices of the foreign companies to which the work is outsourced.

Outsourcing covers a wide spectrum of ethical gray areas and is not always clearly unethical. Outsourcing domestically, for instance—such as when companies hire outside firms to transport goods—generally does not raise ethical issues. Nonetheless, companies involved in global operations need to be careful when outsourcing to make sure that employees in other nations are being treated fairly.

3–5c Avoiding Corruption

Another ethical problem in global business dealings has to do with corruption in foreign governments. Under the Foreign Corrupt Practices Act,[9] U.S. businesses are prohibited from making payments to (bribing) foreign officials to secure beneficial contracts, with certain exceptions. If such payments are lawful within the foreign country, then they are permitted. It is also acceptable to pay small amounts to minor officials to facilitate or speed

---

9. 15 U.S.C. Sections 78dd-1 *et seq.* This act will be discussed in more detail in the context of criminal law.

up the performance of administrative services (such as approval of construction). Payments to private foreign companies or other third parties are also permissible.

Corruption is widespread in some nations, however, and it can be the norm in dealing with both government and private businesses in certain locations. Global companies must take special care when doing business in countries where corruption is common. Decision makers should discuss potential ethical problems with employees in advance and again when situations arise. The company's goal should be to ensure that it supports management and employees in doing the right thing and following the firm's anticorruption policies.

3–5d Monitoring the Employment Practices of Foreign Suppliers

Many businesses contract with companies in developing nations to produce goods, such as shoes and clothing, because the wage rates in those nations are significantly lower than those in the United States. But what if one of those contractors hires women and children at below-minimum-wage rates or requires its employees to work long hours in a workplace full of health hazards? What if the company's supervisors routinely engage in workplace conduct that is offensive to women? What if factories located abroad routinely violate U.S. labor and environmental standards?

Wages and Working Conditions Allegations that a business allows its suppliers to engage in unethical practices hurt the firm's reputation. ■ **Example 3.17** Noi Supalai, a garment worker in Thailand, came forward with reports about how harshly she and other workers had

been treated at Eagle Speed factory, which produced apparel for Nike Corporation. Because the workers did not produce all of the "Just Do the Right Thing" line of products by a set deadline, Nike fined the factory and barred it from paying its workers. The factory then forced some two thousand employees to work sixteen-hour days or longer, and to take turns going home to shower. Workers eventually formed a union and named Supalai as president, but they were unsuccessful in getting the conditions improved. A meeting was set up between Supalai and a Nike representative, but Nike did not even show up. Supalai later learned that Nike chose to use other suppliers. ■

Corporate Watch Groups Given today's global communications network, few companies can assume that their actions in other nations will go unnoticed by "corporate watch" groups that discover and publicize unethical corporate behavior. As a result, U.S. businesses today usually take steps to avoid such adverse publicity—either by refusing to deal with certain suppliers or by arranging to monitor their suppliers' workplaces to make sure that employees are not being mistreated.

■ **Example 3.18** A Chinese factory supplied parts for certain Apple products. After Apple discovered that the factory had violated labor and environmental standards, it began evaluating the practices at all the companies in its supply chain. Apple's audits revealed numerous violations, such as withholding worker pay as a disciplinary measure, falsifying pay records, and forcing workers to use unsafe machines. Apple terminated its relationship with one foreign supplier and turned over its findings to the Fair Labor Association, a nonprofit organization that promotes adherence to national and international labor laws, for further inquiry. ■

Practice and Review: Ethics in Business

James Stilton is the chief executive officer (CEO) of RightLiving, Inc., a company that buys life insurance policies at a discount from terminally ill persons and sells the policies to investors. RightLiving pays the terminally ill patients a percentage of the future death benefit (usually 65 percent) and then sells the policies to investors for 85 percent of the value of the future benefit. The patients receive the cash to use for medical and other expenses. The investors are "guaranteed" a positive return on their investment, and RightLiving profits on the difference between the purchase and sale prices.

Stilton is aware that some sick patients might obtain insurance policies through fraud (by not revealing the illness on the insurance application). Insurance companies that discover this will cancel the policy and refuse to pay. Stilton believes that most of the policies he has purchased are legitimate, but he knows that some probably are not. Using the information presented in this chapter, answer the following questions.

1. Would a person who adheres to the principle of rights consider it ethical for Stilton not to disclose the potential risk of cancellation to investors? Why or why not?
2. Using Immanuel Kant's categorical imperative, are the actions of RightLiving, Inc., ethical? Why or why not?
3. Under utilitarianism, are Stilton's actions ethical? Why or why not? If most of the policies are, in fact, legitimate, does this make a difference in your analysis?
4. Using the IDDR approach, discuss the decision process Stilton should use in deciding whether to disclose the risk of fraudulent policies to potential investors.

Debate This . . . *Executives in large corporations are ultimately rewarded if their companies do well, particularly as evidenced by rising stock prices. Consequently, should we let those who run corporations decide what level of negative side effects of their goods or services is "acceptable"?*

Terms and Concepts

business ethics 44	duty-based ethics 49	outsourcing 59
categorical imperative 50	ethical reasoning 49	principle of rights 50
corporate social responsibility (CSR) 51	ethics 44	stakeholders 52
	moral minimum 45	triple bottom line 46
cost-benefit analysis 51	outcome-based ethics 49	utilitarianism 51

Issue Spotters

1. Acme Corporation decides to respond to what it sees as a moral obligation to correct for past discrimination by adjusting pay differences among its employees. Does this raise an ethical conflict between Acme and its employees? Between Acme and its shareholders? Explain your answers. (See *Ethical Principles and Philosophies*.)
2. Delta Tools, Inc., markets a product that under some circumstances is capable of seriously injuring consumers. Does

Delta have an ethical duty to remove this product from the market, even if the injuries result only from misuse? Why or why not? (See *Making Ethical Business Decisions*.)

• **Check your answers to the Issue Spotters against the answers provided in Appendix B at the end of this text.**

Business Scenarios and Case Problems

3–1. Business Ethics. Jason Trevor owns a commercial bakery in Blakely, Georgia, that produces a variety of goods sold in grocery stores. Trevor is required by law to perform internal tests on food produced at his plant to check for contamination. On three occasions, the tests of food products containing peanut butter were positive for salmonella contamination. Trevor was not required to report the results to U.S. Food and Drug Administration officials, however, so he did not. Instead, Trevor instructed his employees to simply repeat the tests until the results were negative. Meanwhile, the products that had originally tested positive for salmonella were eventually shipped out to retailers.

Five people who ate Trevor's baked goods that year became seriously ill, and one person died from a salmonella infection.

Even though Trevor's conduct was legal, was it unethical for him to sell goods that had once tested positive for salmonella? Why or why not? (See *Ethics and the Role of Business*.)

3–2. Ethical Conduct. Internet giant Zoidle, a U.S. company, generated sales of £2.5 billion in the United Kingdom (UK) in one year (roughly $4 billion in U.S. dollars). The UK corporate tax rate is usually between 20 percent and 24 percent, but Zoidle paid only 3 percent (£6 million). At a press conference, company officials touted how the company took advantage of tax loopholes and sheltered profits to avoid paying the full corporate income tax. They justified their practices as ethical, declaring that it would be verging on illegal to tell shareholders that the company paid more taxes than it should.

Zoidle receives significant benefits for doing business in the UK, including large sales tax exemptions and some property tax breaks. The UK relies on the corporate income tax to provide services to the poor and to help run the agency that regulates corporations. Is it ethical for Zoidle to avoid paying taxes? Why or why not? (See *Ethics and the Role of Business*.)

3–3. Consumer Rights. Best Buy, a national electronics retailer, offered a credit card that allowed users to earn "reward points" that could be redeemed for discounts on Best Buy goods. After reading a newspaper advertisement for the card, Gary Davis applied for, and was given, a credit card. As part of the application process, he visited a Web page containing Frequently Asked Questions as well as terms and conditions for the card. He clicked on a button affirming that he understood the terms and conditions. When Davis received his card, it came with seven brochures about the card and the reward point program. As he read the brochures, he discovered that a $59 annual fee would be charged for the card. Davis went back to the Web pages he had visited and found a statement that the card "may" have an annual fee. Davis sued, claiming that the company did not adequately disclose the fee. Is it unethical for companies to put terms and conditions, especially terms that may cost the consumer money, in an electronic document that is too long to read on one screen? Why or why not? Assuming that the Best Buy credit-card materials were legally sufficient, discuss the ethical aspects of businesses strictly following the language of the law as opposed to following the intent of the law. [*Davis v. HSBC Bank Nevada, N.A.*, 691 F.3d 1152 (9th Cir. 2012)] (See *Ethics and the Role of Business*.)

3–4. Business Ethics. Mark Ramun worked as a manager for Allied Erecting and Dismantling Co., where he had a tense relationship with his father, who was Allied's president. After more than ten years, Mark left Allied, taking 15,000 pages of Allied's documents on DVDs and CDs, which constituted trade secrets. Later, he joined Genesis Equipment & Manufacturing, Inc., a competitor. Genesis soon developed a piece of equipment that incorporated elements of Allied equipment. How might business ethics have been violated in these circumstances? Discuss. [*Allied Erecting and Dismantling Co. v. Genesis Equipment & Manufacturing, Inc.*, 511 Fed.Appx. 398 (6th Cir. 2013)] (See *Making Ethical Business Decisions*.)

3–5. Ethical Principles. Stephen Glass made himself infamous as a dishonest journalist by fabricating material for more than forty articles for *The New Republic* magazine and other publications. He also fabricated supporting materials to delude *The New Republic's* fact checkers. At the time, he was a law student at Georgetown University. Once suspicions were aroused, Glass tried to avoid detection. Later, Glass applied for admission to the California bar. The California Supreme Court denied his application, citing "numerous instances of dishonesty and disingenuousness" during his "rehabilitation" following the exposure of his misdeeds. How do these circumstances underscore the importance of ethics? Discuss. [*In re Glass*, 58 Cal.4th 500, 316 P.3d 1199 (2014)] (See *Ethical Principles and Philosophies*.)

3–6. Business Case Problem with Sample Answer— Business Ethics. Operating out of an apartment in Secane, Pennsylvania, Hratch Ilanjian convinced Vicken Setrakian, the president of Kenset Corp., that he was an international businessman who could help Kenset turn around its business in the Middle East. At Ilanjian's insistence, Setrakian provided confidential business documents. Claiming that they had an agreement, Ilanjian demanded full, immediate payment and threatened to disclose the confidential information to a Kenset supplier if payment was not forthcoming. Kenset denied that they had a contract and filed a suit in a federal district court against Ilanjian, seeking return of the documents. During discovery, Ilanjian was uncooperative. Who behaved unethically in these circumstances? Explain. [*Kenset Corp. v. Ilanjian*, 600 Fed.Appx. 827 (3rd Cir. 2015)] (See *Making Ethical Business Decisions*.)

- For a sample answer to Problem 3–6, go to Appendix C at the end of this text.

3–7. Spotlight on Bed Bath & Beyond—Ethics and the Role of Business. Bed Bath & Beyond Inc. sold a ceramic pot, called the "FireBurners" Pot, with a stainless steel fuel reservoir at its center and a bottle of gelled fuel called "FireGel." A red sticker on the fire pot warned, "DON'T REFILL UNTIL FLAME IS OUT & CUP IS COOL." "CARE AND USE INSTRUCTIONS" with the product cautioned, in a "WARNINGS" section, "Do not add fuel when lit and never pour gel on an open fire or hot surface." The label on the back of the fuel gel bottle instructed, "NEVER add fuel to a burning fire," and under a bold "WARNING" stated, "DANGER, FLAMMABLE LIQUID & VAPOR." M.H., a minor, was injured when a fire pot in one of the products—bought from Bed Bath & Beyond—was refueled with the gel and an explosion occurred. Safer alternatives for the design of the fire pot existed, but its manufacturer chose not to use them. In these circumstances, is Bed Bath & Beyond ethically responsible for the injury to M.H.? Discuss. [*M.H. v. Bed, Bath & Beyond, Inc.*, 156 A.D.3d 33, 64 N.Y.S.3d 205 (1 Dept. 2017)] (See *Ethics and the Role of Business*.)

3–8. Ethical Leadership. Mark Clapp and Albert DiBrito worked for the Public Safety Department (PSD) in St. Joseph, Michigan. Clapp was the director, and DiBrito was the deputy director. They were under the supervision of the city manager. One day, Clapp told Tom Vaught, a PSD employee, that the previous city manager had hired DiBrito only because DiBrito had been investigating the city manager for possible wrongdoing. Clapp said that DiBrito had dropped his investigation in exchange for the deputy director position. DiBrito learned of Clapp's statement and filed a formal complaint against him on another matter with Richard Lewis, the current city manager. The investigation that followed revealed management problems within the PSD. A consultant hired by the city concluded that Clapp's remarks about DiBrito had been "inappropriate statements for a commanding officer to make regarding a second in charge." However, the consultant also identified issues regarding DiBrito's "honesty, inappropriate statements to subordinates regarding a commanding officer, favoritism, and retaliation." How do a manager's attitudes and actions affect a workplace? What steps do you think Lewis could take to prevent future ethical misconduct? [*DiBrito v. City of St. Joseph*, 675 Fed.Appx. 593 (6th Cir. 2017)] (See *Ethics and the Role of Business.*)

3–9. A Question of Ethics—Applying the IDDR Framework.

Priscilla Dickman worked as a medical technologist at the University of Connecticut Health Center for twenty-eight years. Early in her career at the Health Center, Dickman sustained a back injury while at work. The condition eventually worsened, causing her significant back pain and disability. Her physician ordered restrictions on her work duties for several years. Then Dickman's supervisor received complaints that Dickman was getting personal phone calls and was frequently absent from her work area. Based on e-mails and other documents found on her work computer, it appeared that she had been running two side businesses (selling jewelry and providing travel agent services) while at work. The state investigated, and she was convicted of a civil ethics violation for engaging in "personal business for financial gain on state time utilizing state resources." Separate investigations resulted in criminal convictions for forgery and the filing of an unrelated fraudulent insurance claim.

Dickman "retired" from her job (after she obtained approval for disability retirement) and filed a claim with the state of Connecticut against the health center. She alleged that her former employer had initiated the investigations to harass her and force her to quit. She claimed that the Health Center was unlawfully retaliating against her for being disabled and being put on workplace restrictions. [Dickman v. University of Connecticut Health Center, *162 Conn.App. 441, 132 A.3d 739 (2016)]* (See Making Ethical Business Decisions.)

(a) Assume that you are Dickman's supervisor and have been informed that she is frequently away from her desk and often makes personal phone calls. The first step of using the IDDR method is *inquiry*, so you start asking questions. Several people tell you that that Dickman has offered to sell them jewelry. Others say she has offered to make travel arrangements for them. You have not spoken to Dickman directly about the complaints and are not sure if you should. You also know that the Health Center would need more evidence of wrongdoing to justify firing Dickman but are uncertain as to whether you can search her computer. Should you report your findings to management? Is there any ethical problem involved in investigating and possibly firing a long-term employee? Is it fair to terminate an employee who is under disability restrictions? How would you frame the ethical dilemma that the Health Center faced in this case, and who are the stakeholders? What ethical theories would you use to guide your decision?

(b) Now suppose that you are Dickman. You have been a medical technologist for a long time but now experience severe back pain while at your desk at the Health Center. You find that you have less pain if you get up and move around during the day, rather than just sitting. That is why you are often away from your desk. You know that you will not be able to do this job much longer, and that is why you recently started a jewelry business and began providing travel services. Sure, you have made a few personal phone calls related to those businesses while at the Health Center, but other employees make personal calls, and they have not been fired. You feel that the Health Center's investigation was intended to force you to quit because you are disabled and cannot perform the tasks that you used to perform. Using the inquiry portion of the IDDR method, how might you frame the ethical issue you face, and who are the stakeholders? What ethical principles can help you analyze the problem thoroughly?

Time-Limited Group Assignment

3–10. Corporate Social Responsibility.

Methamphetamine (meth) is an addictive drug made chiefly in small toxic labs (STLs) in homes, tents, barns, and hotel rooms. The manufacturing process is dangerous, often resulting in explosions, burns, and toxic fumes. Government entities spend time and resources to find and destroy STLs, imprison meth dealers and users, treat addicts, and provide services for affected families.

Meth cannot be made without ingredients that are also used in cold and allergy medications. Arkansas has one of the highest numbers of STLs in the United States. To recoup the costs of fighting the meth epidemic, twenty counties in Arkansas filed a suit against Pfizer, Inc., which makes cold and allergy medications. They argued that it was Pfizer's ethical responsibility to either stop using the ingredients in their cold and allergy medications that can be used to make meth or to compensate the government for the amount it spends closing down meth labs. (See *Ethics and the Role of Business, Ethical Principles and Philosophies,* and *Making Ethical Business Decisions.*)

(a) The first group will outline Pfizer's ethical responsibility under the corporate social responsibility doctrine. To whom does Pfizer owe duties?

(b) The second group will formulate an argument on behalf of Pfizer that the company has not breached any of its ethical responsibilities.

(c) The third group will assume that they work for Pfizer and that the company is trying to determine the best course of action to prevent its medications from being used to make meth. The group will apply the IDDR approach and explain the steps in the reasoning used.

(d) The fourth group will adopt a utilitarian point of view and perform a cost-benefit analysis to determine what the company should do. Specifically, should the company pay compensation to the state, or should it stop using certain ingredients in its medications?

COSTCO

CODE OF ETHICS

By Jim Sinegal

OBEY THE LAW

The law is irrefutable! Absent a moral imperative to challenge a law, we must conduct our business in total compliance with the laws of every community where we do business.

- Comply with all statutes.
- Cooperate with authorities.
- Respect all public officials and their positions.
- Avoid all conflict of interest issues with public officials.
- Comply with all disclosure and reporting requirements.
- Comply with safety and security standards for all products sold.
- Exceed ecological standards required in every community where we do business.
- Comply with all applicable wage and hour laws.
- Comply with all applicable anti-trust laws.
- Protect "inside information" that has not been released to the general public.

TAKE CARE OF OUR MEMBERS

The member is our key to success. If we don't keep our members happy, little else that we do will make a difference.

- Provide top-quality products at the best prices in the market.
- Provide a safe shopping environment in our warehouses.
- Provide only products that meet applicable safety and health standards.
- Sell only products from manufacturers who comply with "truth in advertising/packaging" standards.
- Provide our members with a 100% satisfaction guaranteed warranty on every product and service we sell, including their membership fee.
- Assure our members that every product we sell is authentic in make and in representation of performance.
- Make our shopping environment a pleasant experience by making our members feel welcome as our guests.
- Provide products to our members that will be ecologically sensitive.

Our member is our reason for being. If they fail to show up, we cannot survive. Our members have extended a "trust" to Costco by virtue of paying a fee to shop with us. We can't let them down or they will simply go away. We must always operate in the following manner when dealing with our members:

Rule #1 – The member is always right.

Rule #2 – In the event the member is ever wrong, refer to rule #1.

There are plenty of shopping alternatives for our members. We will succeed only if we do not violate the trust they have extended to us. We must be committed at every level of our company, with every ounce of energy and grain of creativity we have, to constantly strive to "bring goods to market at a lower price."

If we do these four things throughout our organization, we will realize our ultimate goal, which is to
REWARD OUR SHAREHOLDERS.

TAKE CARE OF OUR EMPLOYEES

To claim "people are our most important asset" is true and an understatement. Each employee has been hired for a very important job. Jobs such as stocking the shelves, ringing members' orders, buying products, and paying our bills are jobs we would all choose to perform because of their importance. The employees hired to perform these jobs are performing as management's "alter egos." Every employee, whether they are in a Costco warehouse, or whether they work in the regional or corporate offices, is a Costco ambassador trained to give our members professional, courteous treatment.

Today we have warehouse managers who were once stockers and callers, and vice presidents who were once in clerical positions for Costco. We believe that Costco's future executive officers are currently working in our warehouses, depots, buying offices, and accounting departments, as well as in our home offices.

To that end, we are committed to these principles:

- Provide a safe work environment.
- Pay a fair wage.
- Make every job challenging, but make it fun!
- Consider the loss of any employee as a failure on the part of the company and a loss to the organization.
- Teach our people how to do their jobs and how to improve personally and professionally.
- Promote from within the company to achieve the goal of a minimum of 80% of management positions being filled by current employees.
- Create an "open door" attitude at all levels of the company that is dedicated to "fairness and listening."

RESPECT OUR VENDORS

Our vendors are our partners in business and for us to prosper as a company, they must prosper with us. It is important that our vendors understand that we will be tough negotiators, but fair in our treatment of them.

- Treat all vendors and their representatives as you would expect to be treated if visiting their places of business.
- Pay all bills within the allocated time frame.
- Honor all commitments.
- Protect all vendor property assigned to Costco as though it were our own.
- Always be thoughtful and candid in negotiations.
- Provide a careful review process with at least two levels of authorization before terminating business with an existing vendor of more than two years.
- Do not accept gratuities of any kind from a vendor.

These guidelines are exactly that - guidelines, some common sense rules for the conduct of our business. Intended to simplify our jobs, not complicate our lives, these guidelines will not answer every question or solve every problem. At the core of our philosophy as a company must be the implicit understanding that not one of us is required to lie or cheat on behalf of PriceCostco. In fact, dishonest conduct will not be tolerated. To do any less would be unfair to the overwhelming majority of our employees who support and respect Costco's commitment to ethical business conduct.

If you are ever in doubt as to what course of action to take on a business matter that is open to varying ethical interpretations, take the high road and do what is right.

If you want our help, we are always available for advice and counsel. That's our job and we welcome your questions or comments.

Our continued success depends on you. We thank each of you for your contribution to our past success and for the high standards you have insisted upon in our company.

Chapter 4

Courts and Alternative Dispute Resolution

The United States has fifty-two court systems—one for each of the fifty states, one for the District of Columbia, and a federal system. Keep in mind that the federal courts are not superior to the state courts. They are simply an independent system of courts, which derives its authority from Article III, Section 2, of the U.S. Constitution. By the power given to it under the U.S. Constitution, Congress has extended the federal court system to U.S. territories such as Guam, Puerto Rico, and the Virgin Islands.[1]

Although an understanding of our nation's court systems is beneficial for anyone, it is particularly crucial in the business world—almost every businessperson will face a lawsuit at some time. Anyone involved in business should thus be familiar with the basic requirements that must be met to bring a lawsuit before a particular court, as well as the various methods of dispute resolution available outside the courts.

Assume that Evan Heron is a top executive at Des Moines Semiconductor Manufacturing Company, Inc. (DSMC), and that DSMC is one of the largest U.S. makers of mobile phone processors. Heron negotiates some of its most lucrative contracts, under which DSMC provides companies like Apple, Inc., with the chips they use in smartphones.

A dispute arises between DSMC and one of its customers, a Canadian smartphone company, concerning the price the Canadian company was charged for chips. The Canadian firm threatens litigation, but Heron convinces his colleagues at DSMC to agree to arbitrate, rather than litigate, the dispute. The arbitration panel ends up deciding that DSMC overcharged for the chips and awards the Canadian company $800 million. Heron and DSMC are dissatisfied with the result. Is the panel's decision binding? Can DSMC appeal the arbitration award to a court? These are a few of the concerns discussed in this chapter.

---

1. In Guam and the Virgin Islands, territorial courts serve as both federal courts and state courts. In Puerto Rico, they serve only as federal courts.

4–1 The Judiciary's Role in American Government

The body of American law includes the federal and state constitutions, statutes passed by legislative bodies, administrative law, and the case decisions and legal principles that form the common law. These laws would be meaningless, however, without the courts to interpret and apply them. The essential role of the judiciary—the courts—in the American governmental system is to interpret the laws and apply them to specific situations.

4–1a Judicial Review

As the branch of government entrusted with interpreting the laws, the judiciary can decide, among other things, whether the laws or actions of the other two branches are constitutional. The process for making such a determination is known as **judicial review.** The power of judicial review enables the judicial branch to act as a check on the other two branches of government, in line with the system of checks and balances established by the U.S. Constitution.

4–1b The Origins of Judicial Review in the United States

The power of judicial review is not mentioned in the U.S. Constitution (although many constitutional scholars believe that the founders intended the judiciary to have this power). The United States Supreme Court explicitly established this power in 1803 in the case *Marbury v. Madison.*[2] In that decision, the Court stated, "It is emphatically the province [authority] and duty of the Judicial Department to say what the law is. . . . If two laws conflict with each other, the courts must decide on the operation of each. . . . [I]f both [a] law and the Constitution apply to a particular

---

2. 5 U.S. (1 Cranch) 137, 2 L.Ed. 60 (1803).

case, . . . the Court must determine which of these conflicting rules governs the case. This is of the very essence of judicial duty." Since the *Marbury v. Madison* decision, the power of judicial review has remained unchallenged. Today, this power is exercised by both federal and state courts. (Indeed, many other constitutional democracies, including Canada, France, and Germany, have adopted some form of judicial review.)

4–2 Basic Judicial Requirements

Before a lawsuit can be brought before a court, certain requirements must be met. These requirements relate to jurisdiction, venue, and standing to sue. We examine each of these important concepts here.

4–2a Jurisdiction

In Latin, *juris* means "law," and *diction* means "to speak." Thus, "the power to speak the law" is the literal meaning of the term **jurisdiction.** Before any court can hear a case, it must have jurisdiction over the person (or company) against whom the suit is brought (the defendant) or over the property involved in the suit. The court must also have jurisdiction over the subject matter of the dispute.

Jurisdiction over Persons or Property Generally, a particular court can exercise *in personam* **jurisdiction** (personal jurisdiction) over any person or business that resides in a certain geographic area. A state trial court, for instance, normally has jurisdictional authority over residents (including businesses) of a particular area of the state, such as a county or district. A state's highest court (often called the state supreme court[3]) has jurisdictional authority over all residents within the state.

A court can also exercise jurisdiction over property that is located within its boundaries. This kind of jurisdiction is known as *in rem* **jurisdiction,** or "jurisdiction over the thing." ■ **Example 4.1** A dispute arises over the ownership of a boat in dry dock in Fort Lauderdale, Florida. The boat is owned by an Ohio resident, over whom a Florida court normally cannot exercise personal jurisdiction. The other party to the dispute is a resident of Nebraska. In this situation, a lawsuit concerning the boat could be brought in a Florida state court on the basis of the court's *in rem* jurisdiction. ■

Long Arm Statutes and Minimum Contacts. Under the authority of a state **long arm statute,** a court can exercise personal jurisdiction over certain out-of-state defendants based on activities that took place within the state. Before a court can exercise jurisdiction, though, it must be demonstrated that the defendant had sufficient contacts, or *minimum contacts*, with the state to justify the jurisdiction.[4] Generally, the minimum-contacts requirement means that the defendant must have sufficient connection to the state for the judge to conclude that it is fair for the state to exercise power over the defendant.

If an out-of-state defendant caused an automobile accident within the state or sold defective goods within the state, for instance, a court will usually find that minimum contacts exist to exercise jurisdiction over that defendant. ■ **Case in Point 4.2** An Xbox game system caught fire in Bonnie Broquet's home in Texas and caused substantial personal injuries. Broquet filed a lawsuit in a Texas court against Ji-Haw Industrial Company, a nonresident company that made the Xbox components. Broquet alleged that Ji-Haw's components were defective and had caused the fire. Ji-Haw argued that the Texas court lacked jurisdiction over it, but a state appellate court held that the Texas long arm statute authorized the exercise of jurisdiction over the out-of-state defendant.[5] ■

Corporate Contacts. A corporation normally is subject to personal jurisdiction in the state in which it is incorporated, has its principal office, and/or is doing business. Courts apply the minimum-contacts test to determine if they can exercise jurisdiction over out-of-state corporations.

In the past, corporations were usually subject to jurisdiction in any state in which they were doing business, such as advertising or selling products. The United States Supreme Court has now clarified that large corporations that do business in many states are not automatically subject to jurisdiction in all of them. A corporation is subject to jurisdiction only in states where it does such substantial business that it is "at home" in that state.[6] The courts look at the amount of business the corporation does within the state relative to the amount it does elsewhere.

■ **Case in Point 4.3** Norfolk Southern Railway Company is a Virginia corporation. Russell Parker, a resident of

---

3. As will be discussed shortly, a state's highest court is often referred to as the state supreme court, but there are exceptions. For instance, in New York the supreme court is a trial court.

4. The minimum-contacts standard was first established in *International Shoe Co. v. State of Washington*, 326 U.S. 310, 66 S.Ct. 154, 90 L.Ed. 95 (1945).
5. *Ji-Haw Industrial Co. v. Broquet*, 2008 WL 441822 (Tex.App.—San Antonio 2008).
6. *Daimler AG v. Bauman*, 571 U.S. 117, 134 S.Ct. 746, 187 L.Ed. 624 (2014).

Indiana and a former employee of Norfolk, filed a lawsuit against the railroad in Missouri. Parker claimed that while working for Norfolk in Indiana he had sustained a cumulative injury. Norfolk argued that Missouri courts did not have jurisdiction over the company. The Supreme Court of Missouri agreed. Simply having train tracks running through Missouri was not enough to meet the minimum-contacts requirement. Norfolk also had tracks and operations in twenty-one other states. The plaintiff worked and was allegedly injured in Indiana, not Missouri. Even though Norfolk did register its corporation in Missouri, the amount of business that it did in Missouri was not so substantial that it was "at home" in that state.[7] ∎

Jurisdiction over Subject Matter Jurisdiction over subject matter is a limitation on the types of cases a court can hear. In both the federal and the state court systems, there are courts of *general* (unlimited) *jurisdiction* and courts of *limited jurisdiction*. An example of a court of general jurisdiction is a state trial court or a federal district court. An example of a state court of limited jurisdiction is a probate court. **Probate courts** are state courts that handle only matters relating to the transfer of a person's assets and obligations after that person's death, including matters relating to the custody and guardianship of children. An example of a federal court of limited subject-matter jurisdiction is a bankruptcy court. **Bankruptcy courts** handle only bankruptcy proceedings, which are governed by federal bankruptcy law.

A court's jurisdiction over subject matter is usually defined in the statute or constitution creating the court. In both the federal and the state court systems, a court's subject-matter jurisdiction can be limited by any of the following:

1. The subject of the lawsuit.
2. The sum in controversy.
3. Whether the case involves a felony (a more serious type of crime) or a misdemeanor (a less serious type of crime).
4. Whether the proceeding is a trial or an appeal.

Original and Appellate Jurisdiction The distinction between courts of original jurisdiction and courts of appellate jurisdiction normally lies in whether the case is being heard for the first time. Courts having original jurisdiction are courts of the first instance, or trial courts. These are courts in which lawsuits begin, trials take place, and evidence is presented. In the federal court system, the

district courts are trial courts. In the various state court systems, the trial courts are known by various names, as will be discussed shortly.

The key point here is that any court having original jurisdiction normally serves as a trial court. Courts having appellate jurisdiction act as reviewing, or appellate, courts. In general, cases can be brought before appellate courts only on appeal from an order or a judgment of a trial court or other lower courts.

Jurisdiction of the Federal Courts Because the federal government is a government of limited powers, the jurisdiction of the federal courts is limited. Federal courts have subject-matter jurisdiction in two situations: when a federal question is involved and when there is diversity of citizenship.

Federal Questions. Article III of the U.S. Constitution establishes the boundaries of federal judicial power. Section 2 of Article III states that "the judicial Power shall extend to all Cases, in Law and Equity, arising under this Constitution, the Laws of the United States, and Treaties made, or which shall be made, under their Authority."

In effect, this clause means that whenever a plaintiff's cause of action is based, at least in part, on the U.S. Constitution, a treaty, or a federal law, a **federal question** arises. Any lawsuit involving a federal question, such as a person's rights under the U.S. Constitution, can originate in a federal court. Note that in a case based on a federal question, a federal court will apply federal law.

Diversity of Citizenship. Federal district courts can also exercise original jurisdiction over cases involving **diversity of citizenship.** The most common type of diversity jurisdiction[8] requires *both* of the following:

1. The plaintiff and defendant must be residents of different states.
2. The dollar amount in controversy must exceed $75,000.

For purposes of diversity jurisdiction, a corporation is a citizen of both the state in which it is incorporated and the state in which its principal place of business is located.

A case involving diversity of citizenship can be filed in the appropriate federal district court. If the case starts in a state court, it can sometimes be transferred, or "removed," to a federal court. As already noted, a federal court will apply federal law in cases involving federal questions.

---

7. *State ex rel. Norfolk Southern Railway Co. v. Dolan*, 512 S.W.3d 41 (Sup.Ct. Mo. 2017).

8. Diversity jurisdiction also exists in cases between (1) a foreign country and citizens of a state or of different states and (2) citizens of a state and citizens or subjects of a foreign country. Cases based on these types of diversity jurisdiction occur infrequently.

In a case based on diversity of citizenship, in contrast, a federal court will apply the relevant state law (which is often the law of the state in which the court sits).

The following case focused on whether diversity jurisdiction existed. A boat owner was severely burned when his boat exploded after being overfilled with fuel at a marina in the U.S. Virgin Islands. The owner filed a suit in a federal district court against the marina and sought a jury trial. The defendant argued that a plaintiff in an admiralty, or maritime, case (a case based on something that happened at sea) does not have a right to a jury trial unless the court has diversity jurisdiction. The defendant claimed that because both parties were citizens of the Virgin Islands, the court had no such jurisdiction.

Case Analysis 4.1

Mala v. Crown Bay Marina, Inc.

United States Court of Appeals, Third Circuit, 704 F.3d 239 (2013).

In the Language of the Court

SMITH, Circuit Judge.
* * * *

Kelley Mala is a citizen of the United States Virgin Islands. * * * He went for a cruise in his powerboat near St. Thomas, Virgin Islands. When his boat ran low on gas, he entered Crown Bay Marina to refuel. Mala tied the boat to one of Crown Bay's eight fueling stations and began filling his tank with an automatic gas pump. Before walking to the cash register to buy oil, Mala asked a Crown Bay attendant to watch his boat.

By the time Mala returned, the boat's tank was overflowing and fuel was spilling into the boat and into the water. The attendant manually shut off the pump and acknowledged that the pump had been malfunctioning in recent days. Mala began cleaning up the fuel, and at some point, the attendant provided soap and water. Mala eventually departed the marina, but as he did so, the engine caught fire and exploded. Mala was thrown into the water and was severely burned. His boat was unsalvageable.

* * * Mala sued Crown Bay in the District Court of the Virgin Islands. Mala's * * * complaint asserted * * * that Crown Bay negligently maintained its gas pump. [*Negligence* is the failure to exercise the standard of care that a reasonable person would exercise in similar circumstances. Negligence can form the basis for a legal claim.] The complaint also alleged that the District Court had admiralty and diversity jurisdiction over the case, and it requested a jury trial.

* * * *
* * * Crown Bay filed a motion to strike Mala's jury demand. Crown Bay argued that plaintiffs generally do not have a jury-trial right in admiralty cases—only when the court also has diversity jurisdiction. And Crown Bay asserted that the parties were not diverse in this case * * *. In response to this motion, the District Court ruled that both Mala and Crown Bay were citizens of the Virgin Islands. The court therefore struck Mala's jury demand, but nevertheless opted to empanel an advisory jury. [The court could accept or reject the advisory jury's verdict.]

* * * At the end of the trial, the advisory jury returned a verdict of $460,000 for Mala—$400,000 for pain and suffering and $60,000 in compensatory damages. It concluded that Mala was 25 percent at fault and that Crown Bay was 75 percent at fault. The District Court ultimately rejected the verdict and entered judgment for Crown Bay.

* * * *
This appeal followed.
* * * *

Mala * * * argues that the District Court improperly refused to conduct a jury trial. This claim ultimately depends on whether the District Court had diversity jurisdiction.

The Seventh Amendment [to the U.S. Constitution] creates a right to civil jury trials in federal court: "In Suits at common law * * * the right of trial by jury shall be preserved." Admiralty suits are not "Suits at common law," which means that when a district court has only admiralty jurisdiction the plaintiff does not have a jury-trial right. But [a federal statute] allows plaintiffs to pursue state claims in admiralty cases as long as the district court also has diversity jurisdiction. In such cases [the statute] preserves whatever jury-trial right exists with respect to the underlying state claims.

Mala argues that the District Court had both admiralty and diversity jurisdiction. As a preliminary matter, the court certainly had admiralty jurisdiction. The alleged tort occurred on navigable water and bore a substantial connection to maritime activity.

The grounds for diversity jurisdiction are less certain. *District courts have jurisdiction only if the parties are completely diverse. This means that no plaintiff may have the same state or territorial citizenship as any defendant.* The parties agree that Mala was a citizen of the Virgin Islands. [Emphasis added.]

Unfortunately for Mala, the District Court concluded that Crown Bay also was a citizen of the Virgin Islands. Mala rejects this conclusion.

Mala bears the burden of proving that the District Court had diversity jurisdiction. Mala failed to meet that burden because he did not offer evidence that Crown Bay was anything other than a citizen of the Virgin Islands. Mala contends that Crown Bay admitted to being a citizen of Florida, but Crown Bay actually denied Mala's allegation.

Absent evidence that the parties were diverse, we are left with Mala's allegations. *Allegations are insufficient at trial. And they are especially insufficient on appeal*, where we review the District Court's underlying factual findings for clear error. Under this standard, we will not reverse unless we are left with the definite and firm conviction that Crown Bay was in fact a citizen of Florida. Mala has not presented any credible evidence that Crown Bay was a citizen of Florida—much less evidence that would leave us with the requisite firm conviction. [Emphasis added.]

* * * Accordingly, the parties were not diverse and Mala does not have a jury-trial right.

* * * *

* * * For these reasons we will affirm the District Court's judgment.

Legal Reasoning Questions

1. What is "diversity of citizenship"?
2. How does the presence—or lack—of diversity of citizenship affect a lawsuit?
3. What did the court conclude with respect to the parties' diversity of citizenship in this case?

Exclusive versus Concurrent Jurisdiction When both federal and state courts have the power to hear a case, as is true in lawsuits involving diversity of citizenship, **concurrent jurisdiction** exists. When cases can be tried only in federal courts or only in state courts, **exclusive jurisdiction** exists.

Federal courts have exclusive jurisdiction in cases involving federal crimes, bankruptcy, most patent and copyright claims, suits against the United States, and some areas of admiralty law. State courts also have exclusive jurisdiction over certain subjects—for instance, divorce and adoption.

When concurrent jurisdiction exists, a party may choose to bring a suit in either a federal court or a state court. Many factors can affect a party's decision to litigate in a federal versus a state court. Examples include the availability of different remedies, the distance to the respective courthouses, or the experience or reputation of a particular judge. For instance, a plaintiff might choose to litigate in a state court if the court has a reputation for awarding substantial amounts of damages or if the judge is perceived as being pro-plaintiff. The concepts of exclusive and concurrent jurisdiction are illustrated in Exhibit 4–1.

Jurisdiction in Cyberspace The Internet's capacity to bypass political and geographic boundaries undercuts the traditional basis on which courts assert personal jurisdiction. As discussed, for a court to compel a defendant to come before it, the defendant must have a sufficient connection— that is, minimum contacts—with the state. When a defendant's only contacts with the state are through a website, however, it can be difficult to determine whether these contacts are sufficient for a court to exercise jurisdiction.

The "Sliding-Scale" Standard. The courts have developed a "sliding-scale" standard to determine when they can exercise personal jurisdiction over an out-of-state defendant based on the defendant's Web activities. The sliding-scale standard identifies three types of Internet business contacts and outlines the following rules for jurisdiction:

1. When the defendant conducts substantial business over the Internet (such as contracts and sales), jurisdiction is proper.
2. When there is some interactivity through a website, jurisdiction may be proper, depending on the circumstances. It is up to the courts to decide how much online interactivity is enough to satisfy the minimum-contacts requirement. ■ **Case in Point 4.4** Dr. Arthur Delahoussaye, a Louisiana resident, bought a special racing bicycle on eBay from Frederick Boelter, who lived in Wisconsin. Later, while Delahoussaye was riding the bike, the front wheel disconnected, pushing the forks of the bicycle into the ground and propelling him over the handlebars and onto the pavement. Delahoussaye suffered serious injuries. He sued Boelter in a Louisiana court, alleging that Boelter had negligently removed the retention devices designed to prevent the detachment of the front wheel.

   The Louisiana court ruled that the state did not have jurisdiction over Boelter, and a state appellate court affirmed. Boelter did not have any prior relationship with Delahoussaye, did not initiate communications with Delahoussaye, and discussed the transaction with Delahoussaye only over the Internet. Payment was made through an intermediary, PayPal, and Boelter shipped the bicycle to Louisiana. The sale of a single bicycle to Delahoussaye on eBay was not enough to give Louisiana state jurisdiction over Boelter, so the plaintiff's case was dismissed.[9] ■
3. When a defendant merely engages in passive advertising on the Web, jurisdiction is never proper.[10]

---

9. *Delahoussaye v. Boelter*, 199 So.3d 633 (La.App. 2016).
10. For a leading case on this issue, see *Zippo Manufacturing Co. v. Zippo Dot Com, Inc.*, 952 F.Supp. 1119 (W.D.Pa. 1997).

Exhibit 4–1 Exclusive and Concurrent Jurisdiction

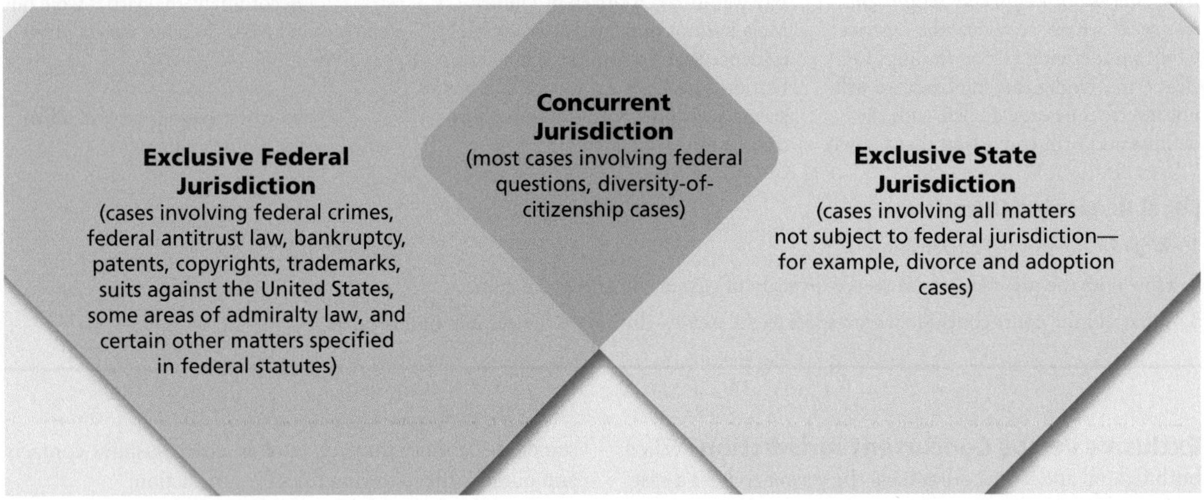

Exclusive Federal Jurisdiction
(cases involving federal crimes, federal antitrust law, bankruptcy, patents, copyrights, trademarks, suits against the United States, some areas of admiralty law, and certain other matters specified in federal statutes)

Concurrent Jurisdiction
(most cases involving federal questions, diversity-of-citizenship cases)

Exclusive State Jurisdiction
(cases involving all matters not subject to federal jurisdiction— for example, divorce and adoption cases)

International Jurisdictional Issues. Because the Internet is international in scope, it obviously raises international jurisdictional issues. The world's courts seem to be developing a standard that echoes the requirement of minimum contacts applied by the U.S. courts.

Most courts are indicating that minimum contacts— doing business within the jurisdiction, for instance—are enough to compel a defendant to appear. The effect of this standard is that a business firm has to comply with the laws in any jurisdiction in which it targets customers for its products. This situation is complicated by the fact that many countries' laws on particular issues— free speech, for instance—are very different from U.S. laws.

The following case illustrates how federal courts apply a sliding-scale standard to determine if they can exercise jurisdiction over a foreign defendant whose only contact with the United States is through a website.

Spotlight on Gucci

Case 4.2 Gucci America, Inc. v. Wang Huoqing

United States District Court, Northern District of California, 2011 WL 30972 (2011).

Background and Facts Gucci America, Inc., a New York corporation headquartered in New York City, is part of Gucci Group, a global fashion firm with offices in China, France, Great Britain, Italy, and Japan. In connection with its products, Gucci uses twenty-one federally registered trademarks. Gucci also operates a number of boutiques, some of which are located in California.

Wang Huoqing, a resident of the People's Republic of China, operates numerous websites. When Gucci discovered that Wang Huoqing's websites offered for sale counterfeit goods—products bearing Gucci's trademarks but not genuine Gucci articles—it hired a private investigator in San Jose, California, to buy goods from the websites. The investigator purchased a wallet that was labeled Gucci but was counterfeit.

Gucci filed a trademark infringement lawsuit against Wang Huoqing in a federal district court in California seeking damages and an injunction to prevent further infringement. Wang Huoqing was notified of the lawsuit via e-mail but did not appear in court. Gucci asked the court to enter a default judgment—that is, a judgment entered when the defendant fails to appear. First, however, the court had to determine whether it had personal jurisdiction over Wang Huoqing based on the Internet sales.

In the Language of the Court
Joseph C. *SPERO*, United States Magistrate Judge.
* * * *

* * * Under California's long-arm statute, federal courts in California may exercise jurisdiction to the extent permitted by the Due Process Clause of the Constitution. The Due Process Clause allows federal courts to exercise jurisdiction where * * * the defendant has had sufficient minimum contacts with the forum to subject him or her to the specific jurisdiction of the court. The courts apply a three-part test to determine whether specific jurisdiction exists:

(1) The nonresident defendant must do some act or consummate some transaction with the forum or perform some act by which he purposefully avails himself of the privilege of conducting activities in the forum, thereby invoking the benefits and protections of its laws; (2) the claim must be one which arises out of or results from the defendant's forum-related activities; and (3) exercise of jurisdiction must be reasonable.

* * * *

In order to satisfy the first prong of the test for specific jurisdiction, a defendant must have either purposefully availed itself of the privilege of conducting business activities within the forum or purposefully directed activities toward the forum. *Purposeful availment typically consists of action taking place in the forum that invokes the benefits and protections of the laws of the forum, such as executing or performing a contract within the forum.* To show purposeful availment, a plaintiff must show that the defendant "engage[d] in some form of affirmative conduct allowing or promoting the transaction of business within the forum state." [Emphasis added.]

"In the Internet context, the Ninth Circuit utilizes a sliding scale analysis under which 'passive' websites do not create sufficient contacts to establish purposeful availment, whereas interactive websites may create sufficient contacts, depending on how interactive the website is." * * * *Personal jurisdiction is appropriate where an entity is conducting business over the Internet and has offered for sale and sold its products to forum [California] residents.* [Emphasis added.]

Here, the allegations and evidence presented by Plaintiffs in support of the Motion are sufficient to show purposeful availment on the part of Defendant Wang Huoqing. Plaintiffs have alleged that Defendant operates "fully interactive Internet websites operating under the Subject Domain Names" and have presented evidence in the form of copies of web pages showing that the websites are, in fact, interactive. * * * Additionally, Plaintiffs allege Defendant is conducting counterfeiting and infringing activities within this Judicial District and has advertised and sold his counterfeit goods in the State of California. * * * Plaintiffs have also presented evidence of one actual sale within this district, made by investigator Robert Holmes from the website bag2do.cn.* * * Finally, Plaintiffs have presented evidence that Defendant Wang Huoqing owns or controls the twenty-eight websites listed in the Motion for Default Judgment. * * * Such commercial activity in the forum amounts to purposeful availment of the privilege of conducting activities within the forum, thus invoking the benefits and protections of its laws. Accordingly, the Court concludes that Defendant's contacts with California are sufficient to show purposeful availment.

Decision and Remedy *The U.S. District Court for the Northern District of California held that it had personal jurisdiction over the foreign defendant, Wang Huoqing. The court entered a default judgment against Wang Huoqing and granted Gucci an injunction.*

Critical Thinking
- **What If the Facts Were Different?** *Suppose that Gucci had not presented evidence that Wang Huoqing had made one actual sale through his website to a resident of the court's district (the private investigator). Would the court still have found that it had personal jurisdiction over Wang Huoqing? Why or why not?*
- **Legal Environment** *Is it relevant to the analysis of jurisdiction that Gucci America's principal place of business is in New York rather than California? Explain.*

Jurisdiction Summarized In summary, jurisdiction has to do with whether a court has authority to hear a case involving specific persons, property, or subject matter. To review the various types of jurisdiction discussed in this section, see Concept Summary 4.1.

4–2b Venue

Venue[11] is concerned with the most appropriate location for a trial. For instance, two state courts (or two federal courts) may have the authority to exercise jurisdiction

11. Pronounced *ven*-yoo.

over a case. Nonetheless, it may be more appropriate or convenient to hear the case in one court than in the other.

The concept of venue reflects the policy that a court trying a case should be in the geographic neighborhood (usually the county) where the incident occurred or where the parties reside. Venue in a civil case typically is where the defendant resides or does business, whereas venue in a criminal case normally is where the crime occurred.

In some cases, pretrial publicity or other factors may require a change of venue to another community, especially in criminal cases in which the defendant's right to a fair and impartial jury has been impaired. Note, though, that

Concept Summary 4.1

Jurisdiction

Personal	Exists when a defendant: • Is located in the court's territorial boundaries. • Qualifies under state long arm statutes. • Is a corporation doing business within the state. • Advertises, sells, or places goods into commerce within the state.
Property	Exists when the property that is subject to a lawsuit is located within the court's territorial boundaries.
Subject Matter	Limits the court's jurisdictional authority to particular types of cases. • *General jurisdiction*—Exists when a court can hear cases involving a broad array of issues. • *Limited jurisdiction*—Exists when a court is limited to a specific subject matter, such as probate or divorce.
Original	Exists with courts that have the authority to hear a case for the first time (trial courts, district courts).
Appellate	Exists with courts of appeal and review. Generally, appellate courts do not have original jurisdiction.
Federal	A federal court can exercise jurisdiction: • When the plaintiff's cause of action involves a federal question (is based at least in part on the U.S. Constitution, a treaty, or a federal law). • In cases between citizens of different states (or cases involving U.S. citizens and foreign countries or their citizens) when the amount in controversy exceeds $75,000 (diversity-of-citizenship jurisdiction).
Concurrent	Exists when both federal and state courts have authority to hear the same case.
Exclusive	Exists when only state courts or only federal courts have authority to hear a case.
Cyberspace	The courts have developed a sliding-scale standard to use in determining when jurisdiction over a website owner or operator in another state is proper.

venue has lost some significance in today's world because of the Internet and 24/7 news reporting. Courts now rarely grant requests for a change of venue. Because everyone has instant access to the same information about a purported crime, courts reason that no community is more or less informed or prejudiced for or against a defendant.

4–2c Standing to Sue

Before a party can bring a lawsuit to court, that party must have **standing to sue,** or a sufficient stake in a matter to justify seeking relief through the court system. Standing means that the party that filed the action in court has a legally protected interest at stake in the litigation. At times, a person can have standing to sue on behalf of another person, such as a minor (child) or a mentally incompetent person.

Standing can be broken down into three elements:

1. *Harm.* The party bringing the action must have suffered harm—an invasion of a legally protected interest—or must face imminent harm. The controversy must be real and substantial rather than hypothetical.
2. *Causation.* There must be a causal connection between the conduct complained of and the injury.
3. *Remedy.* It must be likely, as opposed to merely speculative, that a favorable court decision will remedy the injury suffered.

■ **Case in Point 4.5** Harold Wagner obtained a loan through M.S.T. Mortgage Group to buy a house in Texas. After the sale, M.S.T. transferred its interest in the loan to another lender, which, in turn, assigned it to another lender (a common practice in the mortgage industry). Eventually, when Wagner failed to make the loan payments, CitiMortgage, Inc., notified him that it was going to foreclose on the property and sell the house.

Wagner filed a lawsuit, claiming that the lenders had improperly assigned the mortgage loan. A federal district court ruled that Wagner lacked standing to contest the assignment. Under Texas law, only the parties directly involved in an assignment can challenge its validity. In this case, the assignment was between two lenders and did not directly involve Wagner.[12] ■

4–3 The State and Federal Court Systems

Each state has its own court system. Additionally, there is a system of federal courts. The right-hand side of Exhibit 4–2 illustrates the basic organizational framework characteristic of the court systems in many states. The exhibit also shows how the federal court system is structured. We turn now to an examination of these court systems, beginning with the state courts.

4–3a The State Court Systems

No two state court systems are exactly the same. Typically, though, a state court system includes several levels, or tiers, of courts, as shown in Exhibit 4–2. State courts may include (1) trial courts of limited jurisdiction, (2) trial courts of general jurisdiction, (3) appellate courts (intermediate appellate courts), and (4) the state's highest court (often called the state supreme court).

---

12. *Wagner v. CitiMortgage, Inc.*, 995 F.Supp.2d 621 (N.D.Tex. 2014).

Exhibit 4–2 The State and Federal Court Systems

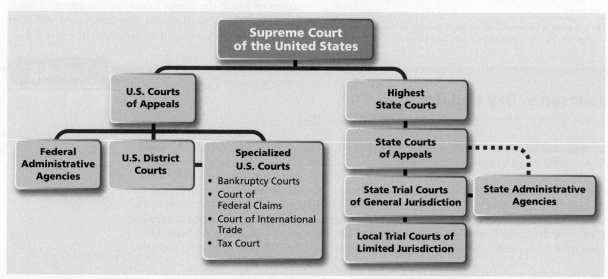

Generally, any person who is a party to a lawsuit has the opportunity to plead the case before a trial court and then, if he or she loses, before at least one level of appellate court. If the case involves a federal statute or a federal constitutional issue, the decision of the state supreme court may be further appealed to the United States Supreme Court.

The states use various methods to select judges for their courts. Usually, voters elect judges, but in some states judges are appointed. For instance, in Iowa, the governor appoints judges, and then the general population decides whether to confirm their appointment in the next general election. The states usually specify the number of years that judges will serve.

Trial Courts Trial courts are exactly what their name implies—courts in which trials are held and testimony is taken. State trial courts have either general or limited jurisdiction, as defined earlier.

General Jurisdiction. Trial courts that have general jurisdiction as to subject matter may be called county, district, superior, or circuit courts.[13] State trial courts of general jurisdiction have jurisdiction over a wide variety of subjects, including both civil disputes and criminal prosecutions. In some states, trial courts of general jurisdiction may hear appeals from courts of limited jurisdiction.

Limited Jurisdiction. Courts of limited jurisdiction as to subject matter are generally inferior trial courts or minor judiciary courts. Limited jurisdiction courts might include local municipal courts (which could include separate traffic courts and drug courts) and domestic relations courts (which handle divorce and child-custody disputes). **Small claims courts** are inferior trial courts that hear only civil cases involving claims of less than a certain amount, such as $5,000 (the amount varies from state

13. The name in Ohio and Pennsylvania is Court of Common Pleas. The name in New York is Supreme Court, Trial Division.

to state). Procedures in small claims courts are generally informal, and lawyers are not required (in a few states, lawyers are not even allowed). Decisions of small claims courts and municipal courts may sometimes be appealed to a state trial court of general jurisdiction.

Appellate, or Reviewing, Courts Every state has at least one court of appeals (appellate court, or reviewing court), which may be an intermediate appellate court or the state's highest court. About three-fourths of the states have intermediate appellate courts.

Generally, courts of appeals do not conduct new trials, in which evidence is submitted to the court and witnesses are examined. Rather, an appellate court panel of three or more judges reviews the record of the case on appeal, which includes a transcript of the trial proceedings. The appellate court hears arguments from attorneys and determines whether the trial court committed an error.

Reviewing courts focus on questions of law, not questions of fact. A **question of fact** deals with what really happened in regard to the dispute being tried—such as whether a party actually burned a flag. A **question of law** concerns the application or interpretation of the law—such as whether flag-burning is a form of speech protected by the First Amendment to the U.S. Constitution. Only a judge, not a jury, can rule on questions of law.

Appellate courts normally defer (give significant weight) to the trial court's findings on questions of fact because the trial court judge and jury were in a better position to evaluate testimony. The trial court judge and jury can directly observe witnesses' gestures, demeanor, and other nonverbal behavior during the trial. An appellate court cannot.

In the following case, neither the administrative agency that initially ruled on the dispute nor the trial court to which the agency's decision was appealed made a finding on a crucial question of fact. Faced with that circumstance, what should a state appellate court do?

Case 4.3

Johnson v. Oxy USA, Inc.

Court of Appeals of Texas—Houston, 14th District, 533 S.W.3d 395 (2016).

Background and Facts Jennifer Johnson was working as a finance analyst for Oxy USA, Inc., when Oxy changed the job's requirements. To meet the new standards, Johnson took courses to become a certified public accountant. Oxy's "Educational Assistance Policy" was to reimburse employees for the cost of such courses. Johnson further agreed that Oxy could withhold the reimbursed amount from her final paycheck if she quit Oxy within a year. When she resigned less than a year later, Oxy withheld that amount from her last check. Johnson filed a claim for the amount with the Texas Workforce Commission (TWC). The TWC ruled that she was not entitled to the unpaid wages. She filed a suit in a Texas state court against Oxy, alleging breach of contract. The court affirmed the TWC's ruling. Johnson appealed.

In the Language of the Court

Ken *WISE*, Justice
* * * *

* * * The trial court * * * held that Johnson's [claim for breach of contract was] barred by *res judicata* ["a matter judged"]. In a court of law, a claimant typically cannot pursue one remedy to an unfavorable outcome and then seek the same remedy in another proceeding before the same or a different tribunal. Res judicata *bars the relitigation of claims that have been finally adjudicated or that could have been litigated in the prior action.* [Emphasis added.]

Johnson argues that *res judicata* does not apply here because the TWC did not render a final judgment on the merits of her claim that Oxy misinterpreted its Educational Assistance Policy. Specifically, Johnson claims she was "denied the right of full adjudication of her claim because the TWC refused to consider her arguments at the administrative level as beyond its jurisdiction." To support this contention, Johnson points to the following excerpt from the * * * decision:

* * * The TWC does not interpret contracts between employers and employee but only enforces the Texas Payday Law [the Texas state law that governs the timing of employees' paychecks]. * * * The question of whether the employer properly interpreted their policy on reimbursed educational expenses versus a business expense is a question for a different forum.

According to Johnson, this language shows that the TWC refused to consider the merits of the issue she raised as "beyond its reach." In contrast, the defendants contend that Johnson's claims are barred by *res judicata* because they are based on claims previously decided by the TWC.
* * * *

In Johnson's case, however, the TWC did not decide the key question of fact in dispute—whether Oxy violated its own Educational Assistance Policy when it withheld Johnson's final wages as reimbursement for the CPA courses. In fact, the TWC explicitly refused to do so, stating that the agency "does not interpret contracts between employers and employee." * * * Because this question goes to the heart of Johnson's breach of contract * * * claim, we hold that *res judicata* does not bar [that] claim. [Emphasis added.]

The defendants argue that because Johnson seeks to recover the same wages in this suit as she did in her claim with the TWC, *res judicata* must bar her common law cause of action. However, * * * *res judicata* would only bar a claim if TWC's order is considered final. * * * Here, the order in Johnson's case made no such findings with regard to the Educational Assistance Policy. The order expressly declined to address that issue. Therefore, * * * *res judicata* will not bar Johnson's breach of contract * * * claim.

Decision and Remedy *A state intermediate appellate court reversed the lower court's decision. "The TWC did not decide the key question of fact in dispute—whether Oxy violated its own Educational Assistance Policy when it withheld Johnson's final wages. In fact, the TWC explicitly refused to do so, stating that the agency 'does not interpret contracts between employers and employee.'" The appellate court remanded the case for a trial on the merits.*

Critical Thinking
- **Legal Environment** *Who can decide questions of fact? Who can rule on questions of law? Why?*
- **Global** *In some cases, a court may be asked to determine and interpret the law of a foreign country. Some states consider the issue of what the law of a foreign country requires to be a question of fact. Federal rules of procedure provide that this issue is a question of law. Which position seems more appropriate? Why?*

Highest State Courts The highest appellate court in a state is usually called the supreme court but may be designated by some other name. For instance, in both New York and Maryland, the highest state court is called the Court of Appeals. The highest state court in Maine and Massachusetts is the Supreme Judicial Court. In West Virginia, it is the Supreme Court of Appeals.

The decisions of each state's highest court on all questions of state law are final. Only when issues of federal law are involved can the United States Supreme Court overrule a decision made by a state's highest court. ■ **Example 4.6** A city enacts an ordinance that prohibits citizens from engaging in door-to-door advocacy without first registering with the mayor's office and receiving a permit. A religious group then sues the city, arguing that the law violates the freedoms of speech and religion guaranteed by the First Amendment. If the state supreme court upholds the law, the group could appeal the decision to the United States Supreme Court, because a constitutional (federal) issue is involved. ∎

4–3b The Federal Court System

The federal court system is basically a three-tiered model consisting of (1) U.S. district courts (trial courts of general jurisdiction) and various courts of limited jurisdiction, (2) U.S. courts of appeals (intermediate courts of appeals), and (3) the United States Supreme Court.

Unlike state court judges, who are usually elected, federal court judges—including the justices of the Supreme Court—are appointed by the president of the United States, subject to confirmation by the U.S. Senate. Federal judges receive lifetime appointments under Article III of the U.S. Constitution, which states that federal judges "hold their offices during good Behaviour." In the entire history of the United States, only a handful of federal judges have been removed from office through impeachment proceedings.

Certain federal court officers are not chosen in the way just described. This chapter's *Managerial Strategy* feature describes how U.S. magistrate judges are selected.

Managerial Strategy

Should You Consent to Have Your Business Case Decided by a U.S. Magistrate Judge?

You have a strong case in a contract dispute with one of your business's suppliers. The supplier is located in another state. Your attorney did everything necessary to obtain your "day in court." The court in question is a federal district court. But you have just found out that your case may not be heard for several years—or even longer. Your attorney tells you that the case can be heard in just a few months if you consent to place it in the hands of a U.S. magistrate judge.[a] Should you consent?

A Short History of U.S. Magistrate Judges

Congress authorized the creation of a new federal judicial officer, the U.S. magistrate, in 1968 to help reduce delays in the U.S. district courts.[b] These junior federal officers were to conduct a wide range of judicial proceedings as set out by statute and as assigned by the district judges under whom they served. In 1979, Congress gave U.S. magistrates consent jurisdiction, which authorized them to conduct all civil trials as long as the parties consent.[c] Currently, magistrate judges dispose of over 1 million civil and criminal district court matters, which include motions and hearings.

The Selection and Quality of Magistrate Judges

As mentioned, federal district judges are nominated by the president, confirmed by the Senate, and appointed for life. In contrast, U.S. magistrate judges are selected by federal district court judges based on the recommendations of a merit screening committee. They serve an eight-year term (which can be renewed).

By statute, magistrate judges must be chosen through a merit selection process. Applicants are interviewed by a screening committee of lawyers and others from the district in which the position will be filled.[d] Political party affiliation plays no part in the process.

A variety of experienced attorneys, administrative law judges, state court judges, and others apply for magistrate judge positions. A typical opening receives about a hundred applicants. The merit selection panel selects the five most qualified, who are then voted on by federal district court judges.

Because the selection process for a magistrate judge is not the same as for a district judge, some critics have expressed concerns about the quality of magistrate judges. Some groups, such as People for the American Way, are not in favor of allowing magistrate judges the power to decide cases. These critics believe that because of their limited terms, they are not completely immune from outside pressure.

Business Questions

1. *If you were facing an especially complex legal dispute—one involving many facets and several different types of law—would you consent to allowing a U.S. magistrate judge to decide the case? Why or why not?*

2. *If you had to decide whether to allow a U.S. magistrate judge to hear your case, what information might you ask your attorney to provide concerning that individual?*

---

a. 28 U.S.C. Sec 636(c); see also *Coleman v. Labor and Industry Review Commission of Wisconsin*, 860 F.3d 461 (7th Cir. 2017).
b. Federal Magistrates Act, 82 Stat. 1107, October 17, 1968.
c. U.S.C. Section 636(c)(1).

d. 28 U.S.C. Section 631(b)(5).

U.S. District Courts At the federal level, the equivalent of a state trial court of general jurisdiction is the district court. U.S. district courts have original jurisdiction in matters involving a federal question and concurrent jurisdiction with state courts when diversity jurisdiction exists. Federal cases typically originate in district courts. There are other federal courts with original, but special (or limited), jurisdiction, such as the federal bankruptcy courts and tax courts.

Every state has at least one federal district court. The number of judicial districts can vary over time, primarily owing to population changes and corresponding changes in caseloads. Today, there are ninety-four federal judicial districts. Exhibit 4–3 shows the boundaries of both the U.S. district courts and the U.S. courts of appeals.

U.S. Courts of Appeals In the federal court system, there are thirteen U.S. courts of appeals—referred to as U.S. circuit courts of appeals. Twelve of these courts (including the Court of Appeals for the D.C. Circuit) hear appeals from the federal district courts located within their respective judicial circuits (shown in Exhibit 4–3).[14]

14. Historically, judges were required to "ride the circuit" and hear appeals in different courts around the country, which is how the name "circuit court" came about.

The Court of Appeals for the Thirteenth Circuit, called the Federal Circuit, has national appellate jurisdiction over certain types of cases, including those involving patent law and those in which the U.S. government is a defendant.

The decisions of a circuit court of appeals are binding on all courts within the circuit court's jurisdiction. These decisions are final in most cases, but appeal to the United States Supreme Court is possible.

The United States Supreme Court The highest level of the three-tiered federal court system is the United States Supreme Court. According to the U.S. Constitution, there is only one national Supreme Court. All other courts in the federal system are considered "inferior." Congress is empowered to create inferior courts as it deems necessary. The inferior courts that Congress has created include the second tier in our model—the U.S. circuit courts of appeals—as well as the district courts and the various federal courts of limited, or specialized, jurisdiction.

The United States Supreme Court consists of nine justices. Although the Supreme Court has original, or trial, jurisdiction in rare instances (set forth in Article III, Sections 1 and 2), most of its work is as an appeals

Exhibit 4–3 Geographic Boundaries of the U.S. Courts of Appeals and U.S. District Courts

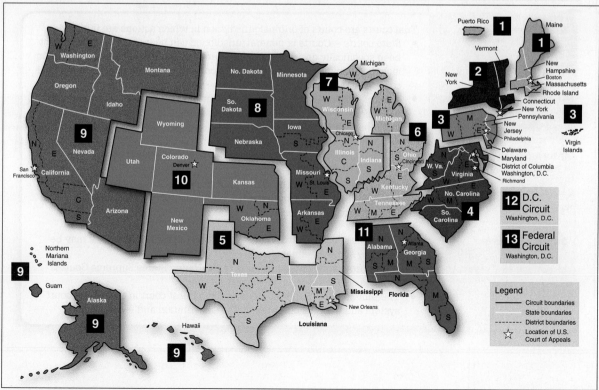

Source: Administrative Office of the United States Courts.

court. The Supreme Court can review any case decided by any of the federal courts of appeals. It also has appellate authority over cases involving federal questions that have been decided in the state courts. The Supreme Court is the final authority on the Constitution and federal law.

Appeals to the Supreme Court. To bring a case before the Supreme Court, a party requests the Court to issue a writ of *certiorari*.[15] A **writ of *certiorari*** is an order issued by the Supreme Court to a lower court requiring the latter to send it the record of the case for review. The Court will not issue a writ unless at least four of the nine justices approve of it. This is called the **rule of four.**

Whether the Court will issue a writ of *certiorari* is entirely within its discretion, and most petitions for writs are denied. (Although thousands of cases are filed with the Supreme Court each year, it hears, on average, fewer

than one hundred of these cases.)[16] A denial of the request to issue a writ of *certiorari* is not a decision on the merits of the case, nor does it indicate agreement with the lower court's opinion. Also, denial of the writ has no value as a precedent. Denial simply means that the lower court's decision remains the law in that jurisdiction.

Petitions Granted by the Court. Typically, the Court grants petitions when cases raise important constitutional questions or when the lower courts have issued conflicting decisions on a significant issue. The justices, however, never explain their reasons for hearing certain cases and not others, so it is difficult to predict which type of case the Court might select.

Concept Summary 4.2 reviews the courts in the federal and state court systems.

---

15. Pronounced sur-shee-uh-*rah*-ree.

16. From the mid-1950s through the early 1990s, the Supreme Court reviewed more cases per year than it has since then. In the Court's 1982–1983 term, for example, the Court issued written opinions in 151 cases. In contrast, during the last fifteen years, on average, the Court has issued written opinions in only about 70 cases.

Concept Summary 4.2

Types of Courts

Trial Courts	Trial courts are courts of original jurisdiction in which actions are initiated. • *State courts* —Courts of general jurisdiction can hear any case that has not been specifically designated for another court. Courts of limited jurisdiction include, among others, domestic relations courts, probate courts, municipal courts, and small claims courts. • *Federal courts* —The federal district court is the equivalent of the state trial court. Federal courts of limited jurisdiction include the bankruptcy courts and others shown in Exhibit 4–2.
Intermediate Appellate Courts	Courts of appeals are reviewing courts. Generally, appellate courts do not have original jurisdiction. • About three-fourths of the states have intermediate appellate courts. • In the federal court system, the U.S. circuit courts of appeals are the intermediate appellate courts.
Supreme Courts	• The highest state court is that state's supreme court, although it may be called by some other name. • Appeal from state supreme courts to the United States Supreme Court is possible only if a federal question is involved. • The United States Supreme Court is the highest court in the federal court system and the final authority on the Constitution and federal law.

4-4 Alternative Dispute Resolution

Litigation—the process of resolving a dispute through the court system—is expensive and time consuming. Litigating even the simplest complaint is costly, and because of the backlog of cases pending in many courts, several years may pass before a case is actually tried. For these and other reasons, more and more businesspersons are turning to **alternative dispute resolution (ADR)** as a means of settling their disputes.

The great advantage of ADR is its flexibility. Methods of ADR range from the parties sitting down together and attempting to work out their differences to multinational corporations agreeing to resolve a dispute through a formal hearing before a panel of experts. Normally, the parties themselves can control how they will attempt to settle their dispute. They can decide what procedures will be used, whether a neutral third party will be present or make a decision, and whether that decision will be legally binding or nonbinding. ADR also offers more privacy than court proceedings and allows disputes to be resolved relatively quickly.

Today, more than 90 percent of civil lawsuits are settled before trial using some form of ADR. Indeed, most states either require or encourage parties to undertake ADR prior to trial. Many federal courts have instituted ADR programs as well. Several forms of ADR have been developed.

4-4a Negotiation

The simplest form of ADR is **negotiation,** a process in which the parties attempt to settle their dispute informally, with or without attorneys to represent them. Attorneys frequently advise their clients to negotiate a settlement voluntarily before they proceed to trial. Parties may even try to negotiate a settlement during a trial or after the trial but before an appeal. Negotiation usually involves just the parties themselves and (typically) their attorneys.

4-4b Mediation

In **mediation,** a neutral third party acts as a mediator and works with both sides in the dispute to facilitate a resolution. The mediator, who need not be a lawyer, usually charges a fee for his or her services (which can be split between the parties). States that require parties to undergo ADR before trial often offer mediation as one of the ADR options or (as in Florida) the only option.

During mediation, the mediator normally talks with the parties separately as well as jointly, emphasizes their points of agreement, and helps them to evaluate their options. Although the mediator may propose a solution (called a mediator's proposal), he or she does not make a decision resolving the matter.

One of the biggest advantages of mediation is that it is less adversarial than litigation. In mediation, the mediator takes an active role and attempts to bring the parties together so that they can come to a mutually satisfactory resolution. The mediation process tends to reduce the antagonism between the disputants, allowing them to resume their former relationship while minimizing hostility. For this reason, mediation is often the preferred form of ADR for disputes between business partners, employers and employees, or other parties involved in long-term relationships.

4-4c Arbitration

A more formal method of ADR is **arbitration,** in which an arbitrator (a neutral third party or a panel of experts) hears a dispute and imposes a resolution on the parties. Arbitration differs from other forms of ADR in that the third party hearing the dispute makes a decision for the parties. Exhibit 4–4 outlines the basic differences among the three traditional forms of ADR.

Usually, the parties in arbitration agree that the third party's decision will be *legally binding*, although the parties can also agree to *nonbinding* arbitration. In nonbinding arbitration, the parties can go forward with a lawsuit if they do not agree with the arbitrator's decision. Arbitration that is mandated by the courts often is not binding on the parties.

In some respects, formal arbitration resembles a trial, although usually the procedural rules are much less restrictive than those governing litigation. In a typical arbitration, the parties present opening arguments and ask for specific remedies. Both sides present evidence and may call and examine witnesses. The arbitrator then renders a decision.

The Arbitrator's Decision The arbitrator's decision is called an **award.** It is usually the final word on the matter. Although the parties may appeal an arbitrator's decision, a court's review of the decision will be much more restricted in scope than an appellate court's review of a trial court's decision. The general view is that because the parties were free to frame the issues and set the powers of the arbitrator at the outset, they cannot complain

Exhibit 4–4   Basic Differences in the Traditional Forms of ADR

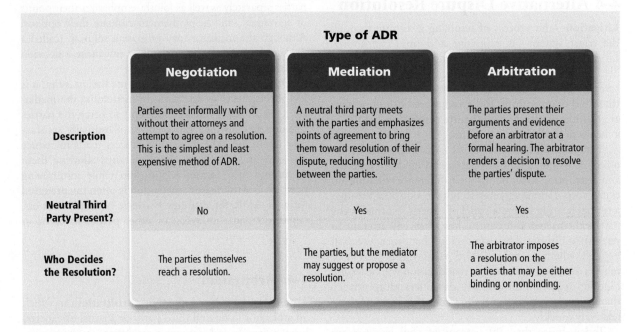

	Type of ADR		
	Negotiation	**Mediation**	**Arbitration**
Description	Parties meet informally with or without their attorneys and attempt to agree on a resolution. This is the simplest and least expensive method of ADR.	A neutral third party meets with the parties and emphasizes points of agreement to bring them toward resolution of their dispute, reducing hostility between the parties.	The parties present their arguments and evidence before an arbitrator at a formal hearing. The arbitrator renders a decision to resolve the parties' dispute.
Neutral Third Party Present?	No	Yes	Yes
Who Decides the Resolution?	The parties themselves reach a resolution.	The parties, but the mediator may suggest or propose a resolution.	The arbitrator imposes a resolution on the parties that may be either binding or nonbinding.

about the results. A court will set aside an award only in the event of one of the following:

1. The arbitrator's conduct or "bad faith" substantially prejudiced the rights of one of the parties.
2. The award violates an established public policy.
3. The arbitrator exceeded her or his powers—that is, arbitrated issues that the parties did not agree to submit to arbitration.

Arbitration Clauses Almost any commercial matter can be submitted to arbitration. Frequently, parties include an **arbitration clause** in a contract specifying that any dispute arising under the contract will be resolved through arbitration rather than through the court system. Parties can also agree to arbitrate a dispute *after* it arises.

Arbitration Statutes Most states have statutes (often based, in part, on the Uniform Arbitration Act) under which arbitration clauses will be enforced. Some state statutes compel arbitration of certain types of disputes, such as those involving public employees.

At the federal level, the Federal Arbitration Act (FAA), enacted in 1925, enforces arbitration clauses in contracts involving maritime activity and interstate commerce. The courts have defined *interstate commerce* broadly, and so arbitration agreements involving transactions only slightly connected to the flow of interstate commerce may fall under the FAA. The FAA established a national policy favoring arbitration that the United States Supreme Court has continued to reinforce.[17]

■ **Case in Point 4.7** Cable subscribers sued Cox Communications, Inc., in federal court. They claimed that Cox violated antitrust law by tying premium cable service to the rental of set-top cable boxes. Cox filed a motion to compel arbitration based on an agreement it had sent to its subscribers. A district court granted the motion to compel, and the subscribers appealed. A federal appellate court affirmed, based on the Federal Arbitration Act. The subscribers' antitrust claims fell within the scope of the arbitration agreement.[18] ■

The Issue of Arbitrability The terms of an arbitration agreement can limit the types of disputes that the parties agree to arbitrate. Disputes can arise, however, when the parties do not specify limits or when the parties disagree on whether a particular matter is covered by their arbitration agreement.

When one party files a lawsuit to compel arbitration, it is up to the court to resolve the issue of *arbitrability*. That is, the court must decide whether the matter is one

---

17. See, for example, *AT&T Mobility, LLC v. Concepcion*, 563 U.S. 333, 131 S.Ct. 1740, 179 L.Ed.2d 742 (2010).
18. *In re Cox Enterprises, Inc. Set-top Cable Television Box Antitrust Litigation*, 835 F.3d 1195 (10th Cir. 2016).

that must be resolved through arbitration. If the court finds that the subject matter in controversy is covered by the agreement to arbitrate, then it may compel arbitration.

Usually, a court will allow a claim to be arbitrated if the court finds that the relevant statute (the state arbitration statute or the FAA) does not exclude such claims. No party, however, will be ordered to submit a particular dispute to arbitration unless the court is convinced that the party has consented to do so. Additionally, the courts will not compel arbitration if it is clear that the arbitration rules and procedures are inherently unfair to one of the parties.

Mandatory Arbitration in the Employment Context A significant question for businesspersons has concerned mandatory arbitration clauses in employment contracts. Many employees claim they are at a disadvantage when they are forced, as a condition of being hired, to agree to arbitrate all disputes and thus waive their rights under statutes designed to protect employees.

The United States Supreme Court, however, has held that mandatory arbitration clauses in employment contracts are generally enforceable. ■ **Case in Point 4.8** In a landmark decision, *Gilmer v. Interstate Johnson Lane Corp.*,[19] the Supreme Court held that a claim brought under a federal statute prohibiting age discrimination could be subject to arbitration. The Court concluded that the employee had waived his right to sue when he agreed, as part of a required application to be a securities representative, to arbitrate "any dispute, claim, or controversy" relating to his employment. ■

4–4d Other Types of ADR

The three forms of ADR just discussed are the oldest and traditionally the most commonly used forms. In addition, a variety of newer types of ADR have emerged, including those described here.

1. In **early neutral case evaluation,** the parties select a neutral third party (generally an expert in the subject matter of the dispute) and explain their respective positions to that person. The case evaluator assesses the strengths and weaknesses of each party's claims.
2. In a **mini-trial,** each party's attorney briefly argues the party's case before the other party and a panel of representatives from each side who have the authority to settle the dispute. Typically, a neutral third party (usually an expert in the area being disputed) acts as an adviser. If the parties fail to reach an agreement, the adviser renders an opinion as to how a court would likely decide the issue.

3. Numerous federal courts hold **summary jury trials,** in which the parties present their arguments and evidence and the jury renders a verdict. The jury's verdict is not binding, but it does act as a guide to both sides in reaching an agreement during the mandatory negotiations that immediately follow the trial.
4. Other alternatives being employed by the courts include *summary proceedings,* which dispense with some formal court procedures, and the appointment of *special masters* to assist judges in deciding complex issues.

4–4e Providers of ADR Services

ADR services are provided by both government agencies and private organizations. A major provider of ADR services is the American Arbitration Association (AAA), which handles more than 200,000 claims a year in its numerous offices worldwide. Most of the largest U.S. law firms are members of this nonprofit association.

Cases brought before the AAA are heard by an expert or a panel of experts in the area relating to the dispute and are usually settled quickly. Generally, about half of the panel members are lawyers. To cover its costs, the AAA charges a fee, paid by the party filing the claim. In addition, each party to the dispute pays a specified amount for each hearing day, as well as a special additional fee in cases involving personal injuries or property loss.

Hundreds of for-profit firms around the country also provide dispute-resolution services. Typically, these firms hire retired judges to conduct arbitration hearings or otherwise assist parties in settling their disputes. The judges follow procedures similar to those of the federal courts and use similar rules. Usually, each party to the dispute pays a filing fee and a designated fee for a hearing session or conference.

4–4f Online Dispute Resolution

An increasing number of companies and organizations are offering dispute-resolution services using the Internet. The settlement of disputes in these forums is known as **online dispute resolution (ODR).** The disputes resolved have most commonly involved rights to domain names (website addresses) or the quality of goods sold via the Internet, including goods sold through Internet auction sites.

Rules being developed in online forums may ultimately become a code of conduct for everyone who does business in cyberspace. Most online forums do not automatically apply the law of any specific jurisdiction. Instead, results are often based on general, universal legal

19. 500 U.S. 20, 111 S.Ct. 1647, 114 L.Ed.2d 26 (1991).

principles. As with most offline methods of dispute resolution, any party may appeal to a court at any time.

ODR may be best for resolving small to medium-sized business liability claims, which may not be worth the expense of litigation or traditional ADR methods. In addition, some cities use ODR as a means of resolving claims against them. ■ **Example 4.9** New York City uses Cybersettle.com to resolve auto accident, sidewalk, and other personal-injury claims made against the city. Parties with complaints submit their demands, and the city submits its offers confidentially online. If an offer exceeds a demand, the claimant keeps half the difference as a bonus, plus the original claim. ■

4–5 International Dispute Resolution

Businesspersons who engage in international business transactions normally take special precautions to protect themselves in the event that a party in another country with whom they are dealing breaches an agreement. Often, parties to international contracts include special clauses in their contracts providing for how disputes arising under the contracts will be resolved. Sometimes, international treaties (formal agreements among several nations) even require parties to arbitrate any disputes.

4–5a Forum-Selection and Choice-of-Law Clauses

Parties to international transactions often include forum-selection and choice-of-law clauses in their contracts. These clauses designate the jurisdiction (court or country) where any dispute arising under the contract will be litigated and which nation's law will be applied.

When an international contract does not include such clauses, any legal proceedings arising under the contract will be more complex and attended by much more uncertainty. For instance, litigation may take place in two or more countries, with each country applying its own national law to the particular transactions.

Furthermore, even if a plaintiff wins a favorable judgment in a lawsuit litigated in the plaintiff's country, the defendant's country could refuse to enforce the court's judgment. The judgment may be enforced in the defendant's country for reasons of courtesy. The United States, for instance, will generally enforce a foreign court's decision if it is consistent with U.S. national law and policy. Other nations, however, may not be as accommodating as the United States, and the plaintiff may be left empty-handed.

4–5b Arbitration Clauses

International contracts also often include arbitration clauses that require a neutral third party to decide any contract disputes. Many of the institutions that offer arbitration, such as the International Chamber of Commerce and the Hong Kong International Arbitration Centre, have formulated model clauses for parties to use. In international arbitration proceedings, the third party may be a neutral entity, a panel of individuals representing both parties' interests, or some other group or organization.

The United Nations Convention on the Recognition and Enforcement of Foreign Arbitral Awards[20] has been implemented in more than 145 countries, including the United States. This convention assists in the enforcement of arbitration clauses, as do provisions in specific treaties among nations. The American Arbitration Association provides arbitration services for international as well as domestic disputes.

---

20. June 10, 1958, 21 U.S.T. 2517, T.I.A.S. No. 6997 (the "New York Convention").

Practice and Review: Courts and Alternative Dispute Resolution

Stan Garner resides in Illinois and promotes boxing matches for SuperSports, Inc., an Illinois corporation. Garner created the concept of "Ages" promotion—a three-fight series of boxing matches pitting an older fighter (George Foreman) against a younger fighter. The concept had titles for each of the three fights, including "Battle of the Ages." Garner contacted Foreman and his manager, who both reside in Texas, to sell the idea, and they arranged a meeting in Las Vegas, Nevada. During negotiations, Foreman's manager signed a nondisclosure agreement prohibiting him from disclosing Garner's promotional concepts unless the parties signed a contract. Nevertheless, after negotiations fell through, Foreman used Garner's "Battle of the Ages" concept to promote a subsequent fight. Garner filed a suit against

Foreman and his manager in a federal district court located in Illinois, alleging breach of contract. Using the information presented in the chapter, answer the following questions.

1. On what basis might the federal district court in Illinois exercise jurisdiction in this case?
2. Does the federal district court have original or appellate jurisdiction?
3. Suppose that Garner had filed his action in an Illinois state court. Could an Illinois state court have exercised personal jurisdiction over Foreman or his manager? Why or why not?
4. Now suppose that Garner had filed his action in a Nevada state court. Would that court have had personal jurisdiction over Foreman or his manager? Explain.

Debate This . . .   *In this age of the Internet, when people communicate via e-mail, texts, tweets, Facebook, and Skype, is the concept of jurisdiction losing its meaning?*

Terms and Concepts

alternative dispute resolution (ADR) 79
arbitration 79
arbitration clause 80
award 79
bankruptcy courts 67
concurrent jurisdiction 69
diversity of citizenship 67
early neutral case evaluation 81
exclusive jurisdiction 69

federal question 67
in personam jurisdiction 66
in rem jurisdiction 66
judicial review 65
jurisdiction 66
litigation 79
long arm statute 66
mediation 79
mini-trial 81
negotiation 79

online dispute resolution (ODR) 81
probate courts 67
question of fact 74
question of law 74
rule of four 78
small claims courts 74
standing to sue 73
summary jury trials 81
venue 72
writ of *certiorari* 78

Issue Spotters

1. Sue uses her smartphone to purchase a video security system for her architectural firm from Tipton, Inc., a company located in a different state. The system arrives a month after the projected delivery date, is of poor quality, and does not function as advertised. Sue files a suit against Tipton in a state court. Does the court in Sue's state have jurisdiction over Tipton? What factors will the court consider in determining jurisdiction? (See *Basic Judicial Requirements*.)

2. The state in which Sue resides requires that her dispute with Tipton be submitted to mediation or nonbinding arbitration. If the dispute is not resolved, or if either party disagrees with the decision of the mediator or arbitrator, will a court hear the case? Explain. (See *Alternative Dispute Resolution*.)

• Check your answers to the Issue Spotters against the answers provided in Appendix B at the end of this text.

Business Scenarios and Case Problems

4–1. Standing. Jack and Maggie Turton bought a house in Jefferson County, Idaho, located directly across the street from a gravel pit. A few years later, the county converted the pit to a landfill. The landfill accepted many kinds of trash that cause harm to the environment, including major appliances, animal carcasses, containers with hazardous content warnings, leaking car batteries, and waste oil. The Turtons complained to the county, but the county did nothing. The Turtons then filed a lawsuit against the county alleging violations of federal environmental laws pertaining to groundwater contamination and other pollution. Do the Turtons have standing to sue? Why or why not? (See *Basic Judicial Requirements*.)

4–2. Venue. Brandy Austin used powdered infant formula manufactured by Nestlé USA, Inc., to feed her infant daughter. Austin claimed that a can of the formula was contaminated with *Enterobacter sakazakii* bacteria, causing severe injury to the infant. The bacteria can cause infections of the bloodstream and central nervous system—in particular, meningitis (inflammation of the tissue surrounding the brain or spinal cord). Austin filed an action against Nestlé in Hennepin County District Court in Minnesota. Nestlé argued for a change of venue because the alleged harm had occurred in South Carolina. Austin is a South Carolina resident and had given birth to her daughter in that state. Should the case be transferred to a South Carolina venue? Why or why not? [*Austin v. Nestlé USA, Inc.*, 677 F.Supp.2d 1134 (D.Minn. 2009)] (See *Basic Judicial Requirements.*)

4–3. Arbitration.   PRM Energy Systems owned patents licensed to Primenergy to use in the United States. Their contract stated that "all disputes" would be settled by arbitration. Kobe Steel of Japan was interested in using the technology represented by PRM's patents. Primenergy agreed to let Kobe use the technology in Japan without telling PRM. When PRM learned about the secret deal, the firm filed a suit against Primenergy for fraud and theft. Does this dispute go to arbitration or to trial? Why? [*PRM Energy Systems v. Primenergy*, 592 F.3d 830 (8th Cir. 2010)] (See *Alternative Dispute Resolution.*)

4–4. Spotlight on the National Football League— Arbitration.   Bruce Matthews played football for the Tennessee Titans. As part of his contract, he agreed to submit any dispute to arbitration. He also agreed that Tennessee law would determine all matters related to workers' compensation. After Matthews retired, he filed a workers' compensation claim in California. The arbitrator ruled that Matthews could pursue his claim in California but only under Tennessee law. Should this award be set aside? Explain. [*National Football League Players Association v. National Football League Management Council*, 2011 WL 1137334 (S.D.Cal. 2011)] (See *Alternative Dispute Resolution.*)

4–5. Minimum Contacts.   Seal Polymer Industries sold two freight containers of latex gloves to Med-Express, Inc., a company based in North Carolina. When Med-Express failed to pay the $104,000 owed for the gloves, Seal Polymer sued in an Illinois court and obtained a judgment against Med-Express. Med-Express argued that it did not have minimum contacts with Illinois because it was incorporated under North Carolina law and had its principal place of business in North Carolina. Therefore, the Illinois judgment based on personal jurisdiction was invalid. Was this argument alone sufficient to prevent the Illinois judgment from being collected against Med-Express in North Carolina? Why or why not? [*Seal Polymer Industries v. Med-Express, Inc.*, 218 N.C.App. 447, 725 S.E.2d 5 (2012)] (See *Basic Judicial Requirements.*)

4–6. Arbitration.   Horton Automatics and the Industrial Division of the Communications Workers of America, the union that represented Horton's workers, negotiated a collective bargaining agreement. If an employee's discharge for a workplace-rule violation was submitted to arbitration, the agreement limited the arbitrator to determining whether the rule was reasonable and whether the employee had violated it. When Horton discharged employee Ruben de la Garza, the union appealed to arbitration. The arbitrator found that de la Garza had violated a reasonable safety rule, but "was not totally convinced" that Horton should have treated the violation more seriously than other rule violations. The arbitrator ordered de la Garza reinstated. Can a court set aside this order? Explain. [*Horton Automatics v. The Industrial Division of the Communications Workers of America, AFL-CIO*, 506 Fed.Appx. 253 (5th Cir. 2013)] (See *Alternative Dispute Resolution.*)

4–7. Business Case Problem with Sample Answer— Corporate Contacts.   LG Electronics, Inc., a South Korean company, and nineteen other foreign companies participated in the global market for cathode ray tube (CRT) products. CRTs were integrated as components in consumer goods, including television sets, and were sold for many years in high volume in the United States, including the state of Washington. The state filed a suit in a Washington state court against LG and the others, alleging a conspiracy to raise prices and set production levels in the market for CRTs in violation of a state consumer protection statute. The defendants filed a motion to dismiss the suit for lack of personal jurisdiction. Should this motion be granted? Explain. [*State of Washington v. LG Electronics, Inc.*, 185 Wash.App. 394, 341 P.3d 346 (Div. 1 2015)] (See *Basic Judicial Requirements.*)

- For a sample answer to Problem 4–7, go to Appendix C at the end of this text.

4–8. Appellate, or Reviewing, Courts.   Angelica Westbrook was employed as a collector for Franklin Collection Service, Inc. During a collection call, Westbrook told a debtor that a $15 processing fee was an "interest" charge. This violated company policy. Westbrook was fired. She filed a claim for unemployment benefits, which the Mississippi Department of Employment Security (MDES) approved. Franklin objected. At an MDES hearing, a Franklin supervisor testified that she had heard Westbrook make the false statement, although she admitted that there had been no similar incidents with Westbrook. Westbrook denied making the statement, but added that if she had said it, she did not remember it. The agency found that Franklin's reason for terminating Westbrook did not amount to the misconduct required to disqualify her for benefits and upheld the approval. Franklin appealed to a state intermediate appellate court. Is the court likely to uphold the agency's findings of fact? Explain. [*Franklin Collection Service, Inc. v. Mississippi Department of Employment Security*, 184 So.3d 330 (Miss.App. 2016)] (See *The State and Federal Court Systems.*)

4–9. A Question of Ethics—The IDDR Approach and Arbitration.   *John McAdams is a tenured professor of political science at Marquette University. McAdams posted a comment on his blog criticizing Cheryl Abbate, a philosophy instructor, for her interchange with a student in her Theory of Ethics class. Lynn Turner, also a member of the faculty, expressed a negative* *opinion of McAdams's comment in a letter to the* Marquette Tribune. *Meanwhile, on Abbate's complaint, the university convened the Faculty Hearing Committee (FHC)—which consists entirely of faculty members, including Turner—to consider the case. Acting on the FHC's recommendation, Marquette suspended McAdams for a semester without pay and ordered him to apologize to Abbate. He refused and filed a suit in a Wisconsin state court against Marquette.* [McAdams v. Marquette University, 383 Wis.2d

358, 914 N.W.2d 708 (2018)] *(See* Alternative Dispute Resolution.*)*

(a) Apply the IDDR approach to consider the ethics of Marquette's convening of the FHC in McAdams's case.

(b) From a legal perspective, was the university's disciplinary procedure the functional equivalent of arbitration, limiting McAdams's right to litigate his claim in court? Explain.

Time-Limited Group Assignment

4–10. Access to Courts. Assume that a statute in your state requires that all civil lawsuits involving damages of less than $50,000 be arbitrated. Such a case can be tried in court only if a party is dissatisfied with the arbitrator's decision. The statute also provides that if a trial does not result in an improvement of more than 10 percent in the position of the party who demanded the trial, that party must pay the entire cost of the arbitration proceeding. (See *Alternative Dispute Resolution.*)

(a) One group will argue that the state statute violates litigants' rights of access to the courts and trial by jury.

(b) Another group will argue that the statute does not violate litigants' right of access to the courts.

(c) A third group will evaluate how the determination on right of access would be changed if the statute was part of a pilot program that affected only a few judicial districts in the state.

Chapter 5

Court Procedures

American and English courts follow the *adversarial system of justice*. Although parties are allowed to represent themselves in court (called *pro se* representation), most parties do not, because they lack the legal expertise and knowledge of court procedures that lawyers possess. Typically, the parties to lawsuits hire attorneys to represent them. Each lawyer acts as his or her client's advocate. Each lawyer presents his or her client's version of the facts in such a way as to convince the judge (or the judge and jury, in a jury trial) that this version is correct. Most of the judicial procedures that you will read about are rooted in the adversarial framework of the American legal system.

5–1 Procedural Rules

The parties to a lawsuit must comply with the procedural rules of the court in which the lawsuit is filed. Although people often think that substantive law determines the outcome of a case, procedural law can have a significant impact on a person's ability to pursue a legal claim. Procedural rules provide a framework for every dispute and specify what must be done at each stage of the litigation process.

Procedural rules are complex, and they vary from court to court and from state to state. There is a set of federal rules of procedure as well as various sets of rules for state courts. Additionally, the applicable procedures will depend on whether the case is a civil or criminal proceeding. All civil trials held in federal district courts are governed by the **Federal Rules of Civil Procedure (FRCP).**[1]

5–1a Stages of Litigation

Broadly speaking, the litigation process has three phases: pretrial, trial, and posttrial. Each phase involves specific procedures, as discussed throughout this chapter. Although civil lawsuits may vary greatly in terms of complexity, cost, and detail, they typically progress through the stages charted in Exhibit 5–1.

To illustrate the procedures involved in a civil lawsuit, we will use a simple hypothetical case. The case arose from an automobile accident, which occurred when a car driven by Antonio Carvello, a resident of New Jersey, collided with a car driven by Jill Kirby, a resident of New York. The accident took place at an intersection in New York City. Kirby suffered personal injuries, which caused her to incur medical and hospital expenses as well as lost wages for four months. In all, she calculated that the cost to her of the accident was $500,000.[2] Carvello and Kirby have been unable to agree on a settlement, and Kirby now must decide whether to sue Carvello for the $500,000 compensation she feels she deserves.

5–1b Hire an Attorney

As mentioned, rules of procedure often affect the outcome of a dispute—a fact that highlights the importance of obtaining the advice of counsel. The first step taken by almost anyone contemplating a lawsuit is to seek the guidance of a licensed attorney.

In the hypothetical Kirby-Carvello case, assume that Kirby consults with a lawyer. The attorney will advise her regarding what she can expect in a lawsuit, her probability of success at trial, and the procedures that will be involved. If more than one court would have jurisdiction over the matter, the attorney will also discuss the advantages and disadvantages of filing in a particular court. In addition, the attorney will indicate how long it will take

---

1. The United States Supreme Court has authority to establish these rules, as spelled out in 28 U.S.C. Sections 2071–2077. Generally, though, the federal judiciary appoints committees that make recommendations to the Supreme Court. The Court then publishes any proposed changes in the rules and allows for public comment before finalizing the rules.

2. For simplicity, we are ignoring damages for pain and suffering and for permanent disabilities, which plaintiffs in personal-injury cases often seek.

Exhibit 5–1 Stages in a Typical Lawsuit

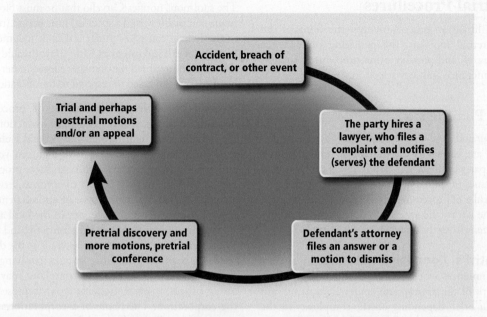

to resolve the dispute through litigation in a particular court and provide an estimate of the costs involved.

The attorney will also inform Kirby of the legal fees that she will have to pay in her attempt to collect damages from the defendant, Carvello. Attorneys base their fees on such factors as the difficulty of the matter at issue, the attorney's experience and skill, and the amount of time involved. In the United States, legal fees range from $200 to $700 per hour or even higher (the average fee is between $200 and $450 per hour). The client normally must also pay various expenses related to the case (called "out-of-pocket" costs), such as court filing fees, travel expenses, and the costs of expert witnesses and investigators.

Types of Attorneys' Fees For a particular legal matter, an attorney may charge one type of fee or a combination of several types.

1. *Fixed fees* may be charged for the performance of such services as drafting a simple will.
2. *Hourly fees* may be charged for matters that will involve an indeterminate period of time. The amount of time required to bring a case to trial, for instance, probably cannot be precisely estimated in advance.
3. *Contingency fees* are fixed as a percentage (usually 33 percent) of a client's recovery in certain types of lawsuits, such as a personal-injury lawsuit.[3] If the

---

3. Contingency-fee arrangements are typically prohibited in criminal cases, divorce cases, and cases involving the distribution of assets after death.

lawsuit is unsuccessful, the attorney receives no fee, but the client will have to reimburse the attorney for all out-of-pocket costs incurred.

Because Kirby's claim involves a personal injury, her lawyer will likely take the case on a contingency-fee basis. In some cases, the winning party may be able to recover at least some portion of her or his attorneys' fees from the losing party.

Settlement Considerations Once an attorney has been retained, the attorney is required to pursue a resolution of the matter on the client's behalf. Nevertheless, the amount of resources an attorney will spend on a given case is affected by the time and funds the client wishes to devote to the process.

If the client is willing to pay for a lengthy trial and one or more appeals, the attorney may pursue those actions. Often, however, after learning of the substantial costs that litigation entails, a client may decide to pursue a settlement of the claim. Attempts to settle the case may be ongoing throughout the litigation process.

Another important consideration in deciding whether to pursue litigation is the defendant's ability to pay the damages sought. Even if Kirby is awarded damages, it may be difficult to enforce the court's judgment if the amount exceeds the limits of Carvello's automobile insurance policy. (We will discuss the problems involved in enforcing a judgment later in this chapter.)

5–2 Pretrial Procedures

The pretrial litigation process involves the filing of the *pleadings*, pretrial motions, the gathering of evidence (called *discovery*), and possibly other procedures, such as a pretrial conference and jury selection.

5–2a The Pleadings

The *complaint* and *answer* (and other legal documents discussed here) are known as the **pleadings.** The pleadings inform each party of the other's claims, reveal the facts, and specify the issues (disputed questions) involved in the case. Because the rules of procedure vary depending on the jurisdiction of the court, the style and form of the pleadings may be different from those shown in this chapter.

The Plaintiff's Complaint Kirby's action against Carvello commences when her lawyer files a **complaint**[4] with the clerk of the appropriate court. Complaints can be lengthy or brief, depending on the complexity of the case and the rules of the jurisdiction. The complaint contains statements or allegations concerning the following:

1. *Jurisdiction.* Facts showing that the particular court has subject-matter and personal jurisdiction.
2. *Legal theory.* The facts establishing the plaintiff's claim and basis for relief.
3. *Remedy.* The remedy (such as an amount of damages) that the plaintiff is seeking.

Exhibit 5–2 illustrates how a complaint in the Kirby-Carvello case might appear. The complaint asserts facts indicating that the federal district court has subject-matter jurisdiction because of diversity of citizenship. It then gives a brief statement of the facts of the accident and alleges that Carvello negligently drove his vehicle through a red light, striking Kirby's car. The complaint alleges that Carvello's actions caused Kirby serious personal injury and property damage. The complaint goes on to state that Kirby is seeking $500,000 in damages. (In some state civil actions, the plaintiff need not specify the amount of damages sought.)

Service of Process. Before the court can exercise personal jurisdiction over the defendant (Carvello)—in effect, before the lawsuit can begin—the court must have proof that the defendant was notified of the lawsuit. Formally notifying the defendant of a lawsuit is called **service of process.**

The plaintiff must deliver, or serve, a copy of the complaint and a **summons** (a notice requiring the defendant to

appear in court and answer the complaint) to the defendant. The summons notifies Carvello that he must file an answer to the complaint within a specified time period (twenty days in the federal courts) or suffer a default judgment against him. A **default judgment** in Kirby's favor would mean that she would be awarded the damages alleged in her complaint because Carvello failed to respond to the allegations.

Method of Service. How service of process occurs depends on the rules of the court or jurisdiction in which the lawsuit is brought. Under the Federal Rules of Civil Procedure, anyone who is at least eighteen years of age and is not a party to the lawsuit can serve process in federal court cases. In state courts, the process server is often a county sheriff or an employee of an independent company that provides process service in the local area.

Usually, the server hands the summons and complaint to the defendant personally or leaves it at the defendant's residence or place of business. In cases involving corporate defendants, the summons and complaint may be served on an officer or on a *registered agent* (representative) of the corporation. The name of a corporation's registered agent can usually be obtained from the secretary of state's office in the state where the company incorporated its business. When the defendant cannot be reached, special rules provide for alternative means of service, such as publishing a notice in the local newspaper.

In some situations, courts allow service of process via e-mail, as long as it is reasonably calculated to provide notice and an opportunity to respond. ■ **Case in Point 5.1** A county in New York filed a petition to remove a minor child, J.T., from his mother's care due to neglect. The child's father had been deported to Jordan, and the county sought to terminate the father's parental rights. Although the father's exact whereabouts were unknown, the county caseworker had been in contact with him via e-mail. The court allowed the father to be served via e-mail because it was reasonably calculated to inform him of the proceedings and allow him an opportunity to respond.[5] ■

Today, some judges have even allowed defendants to be served legal documents via social media, as discussed in this chapter's *Digital Update* feature.

Waiver of Formal Service of Process. In many instances, the defendant is already aware that a lawsuit is being filed and is willing to waive (give up) her or his right to be served personally. The Federal Rules of Civil Procedure (FRCP) and many states' rules allow defendants to waive formal service of process, provided that certain procedures are followed.

In the Kirby case, for example, Kirby's attorney could mail to defendant Carvello a copy of the complaint,

---

4. Sometimes, the document filed with the court is called a *petition* or a *declaration* instead of a complaint.

5. *In re J.T.*, 53 Misc.3d 888, 37 N.Y.S.3d 846 (2016).

Exhibit 5-2 A Typical Complaint

IN THE UNITED STATES DISTRICT COURT
FOR THE SOUTHERN DISTRICT OF NEW YORK

CIVIL NO. 9-1047

JILL KIRBY

                    Plaintiff,

v.   COMPLAINT

ANTONIO CARVELLO

                    Defendant.

    The plaintiff brings this cause of action against the defendant, alleging as follows:

1. This action is between the plaintiff, who is a resident of the State of New York, and the defendant, who is a resident of the State of New Jersey. There is diversity of citizenship between the parties.
2. The amount in controversy, exclusive of interest and costs, exceeds the sum of $75,000.
3. On September 10th, 2025, the plaintiff, Jill Kirby, was exercising good driving habits and reasonable care in driving her car through the intersection of Boardwalk and Pennsylvania Avenue, New York City, New York, when the defendant, Antonio Carvello, negligently drove his vehicle through a red light at the intersection and collided with the plaintiff's vehicle.
4. As a result of the collision, the plaintiff suffered severe physical injury, which prevented her from working, and property damage to her car.

    WHEREFORE, the plaintiff demands judgment against the defendant for the sum of $500,000 plus interest at the maximum legal rate and the costs of this action.

By _____Joseph Roe_____

Joseph Roe
Attorney for Plaintiff
100 Main Street
New York, New York

1/3/26

along with "Waiver of Service of Summons" forms for Carvello to sign. If Carvello signs and returns the forms within thirty days, formal service of process is waived.

Moreover, under the FRCP, defendants who agree to waive formal service of process receive additional time to respond to the complaint (sixty days, instead of twenty days). Some states provide similar incentives to encourage defendants to waive formal service of process and thereby reduce associated costs and foster cooperation between the parties.

The Defendant's Response Typically, the defendant's response to the complaint takes the form of an **answer.** In an answer, the defendant either admits or denies each of the allegations in the plaintiff's complaint and may also set forth defenses to those allegations.

Under the federal rules, any allegations that are not denied by the defendant will be deemed by the court to have been admitted. If Carvello admits to all of Kirby's allegations in his answer, a judgment will be entered for Kirby. If Carvello denies Kirby's allegations, the matter will proceed further.

Using Social Media for Service of Process

Historically, when process servers failed to reach a defendant at home, they attempted to serve process at the defendant's workplace, by mail, or by publication. In our digital age, does publication via social media qualify as legitimate service of process?

Facebook has billions of active users. Assume that a man has a Facebook account and so does his spouse. He has moved out and is intentionally avoiding service of a divorce summons. Even a private investigator has not been able to deliver that summons. What to do? According to some courts today, the woman's lawyer can serve the divorce summons through a private message from her Facebook account.

An Increasing Use of Social Media for Service of Process

More and more courts are allowing service of process via Facebook and other social media. One New York City family court judge ruled that a divorced man could serve his ex-wife through her active Facebook account. She had moved out of the house and provided no for-warding address. A U.S. district court in Virginia allowed a plaintiff in a trademark case to serve a defen-dant residing in Turkey using Facebook, LinkedIn, and e-mail.[a] A federal judge in San Francisco permitted a plaintiff to use Twitter accounts to serve several

defendants located in Kuwait who had allegedly financed terrorism using their Twitter accounts.[b]

The key requirement appears to be that the plaintiff has diligently and reasonably attempted to serve pro-cess by traditional means. Once the plaintiff has exhausted the usual means to effect service, then a court is likely to allow service via social media.[c]

Not All Courts Agree, Though

In spite of these examples, the courts have not uni-formly approved of using social media to serve process. After all, it is relatively simple to create a fake Facebook account and nearly impossible to verify the true owner of that account. Some judges have voiced concerns that serving process via Facebook and other social media raises significant questions of whether that ser-vice comports with due process.[d]

Critical Thinking *In our connected world, is there any way a defendant could avoid service of process via social media?*

a. *WhosHere, Inc. v. Orun*, 2014 WL 670817 (E.D.Va. 2014).

b. *St. Francis Assisi v. Kuwait Finance House*, 2016 WL 5725002 (N.D.Cal. 2016).
c. *MetroPCS v. Devor*, 256 F.Supp.3d 807 (N.D.Ill. 2017).
d. *Federal Trade Commission v. PCCare247, Inc.*, 2013 WL 841037 (S.D.N.Y. 2013); and *In re Adoption of K.P.M.A.*, 341 P.3d 38 (Sup.Ct.Okla. 2014).

Affirmative Defenses. Carvello can also admit the truth of Kirby's complaint but raise new facts to show that he should not be held liable for Kirby's damages. This is called raising an **affirmative defense.** Defendants in both civil and criminal cases can raise affirmative defenses.

For instance, Carvello could assert Kirby's own neg-ligence as a defense by alleging that Kirby was driving negligently at the time of the accident. In some states, a plaintiff's contributory negligence operates as a complete defense. In most states, however, the plaintiff's own neg-ligence constitutes only a partial defense.

Counterclaims. Carvello could also deny Kirby's alle-gations and set forth his own claim that the accident occurred as a result of Kirby's negligence and that she therefore should pay for the damage to his car. This is appropriately called a **counterclaim.** If Carvello files a counterclaim, Kirby will have to submit an answer to the counterclaim.

5–2b Dismissals and Judgments before Trial

Many actions for which pleadings have been filed never come to trial. The parties may, for instance, negotiate a settlement of the dispute at any stage of the litigation process. There are also numerous procedural avenues for disposing of a case without a trial. Many of them involve one or the other party's attempts to get the case dismissed through the use of various motions.

A **motion** is a procedural request submitted to the court by an attorney on behalf of her or his client. When a motion is filed with the court, the filing party must also provide the opposing party with a *notice of motion*. The notice of motion informs the opposing party that the motion has been filed. **Pretrial motions** include the motion to dismiss, the motion for judgment on the pleadings, and the motion for summary judg-ment, as well as the other motions listed in Exhibit 5–3.

Exhibit 5–3 Pretrial Motions

Motion to Dismiss	A motion (normally filed by the defendant) that asks the court to dismiss the case for a specified reason, such as lack of personal jurisdiction or failure to state a claim
Motion to Strike	A defendant's motion asking the court to strike (delete or remove) certain paragraphs from the complaint to better clarify the issues in dispute
Motion to Make More Definite or Certain	A motion by the defendant when the complaint is vague that asks the court to compel the plaintiff to clarify the cause of action
Motion for Judgment on the Pleadings	A motion by either party asking the court to enter judgment in his or her favor based on the pleadings because there are no facts in dispute
Motion to Compel Discovery	A motion asking the court to force the nonmoving party to comply with a discovery request
Motion for Summary Judgment	A motion asking the court to enter a judgment in his or her favor without a trial

Motion to Dismiss Either party can file a **motion to dismiss** asking the court to dismiss the case for the reasons stated in the motion. Normally, though, it is the defendant who requests dismissal.

A defendant can file a motion to dismiss if the plaintiff's complaint fails to state a claim for which relief (a remedy) can be granted. Such a motion asserts that even if the facts alleged in the complaint are true, they do not give rise to any legal claim against the defendant. For example, if the allegations in Kirby's complaint do not constitute negligence on Carvello's part, Carvello can move to dismiss the case for failure to state a claim. Defendant Carvello could also file a motion to dismiss on the grounds that he was not properly served, that

the court lacked jurisdiction, or that the venue was improper.

If the judge grants the motion to dismiss, the plaintiff generally is given time to file an amended complaint. If the judge denies the motion, the suit will go forward, and the defendant must then file an answer. Note that if Carvello wishes to discontinue the suit because, for instance, an out-of-court settlement has been reached, he can likewise move for dismissal. The court can also dismiss a case on its own motion. In the following case, one party filed a complaint against two others, alleging a breach of contract. The defendants filed a motion to dismiss on the ground that the venue was improper. The court denied the motion, and the defendants appealed.

Case Analysis 5.1

Espresso Disposition Corp. 1 v. Santana Sales & Marketing Group, Inc.

Florida Court of Appeal, Third District, 105 So.3d 592 (2013).

In the Language of the Court
CORTIÑAS, J. [Judge]
* * * *

Espresso Disposition Corporation 1 and Rowland Coffee Roasters, Inc. (collectively "Appellants") seek review of the trial court's order denying their motions to dismiss [Santana Sales & Marketing Group,

Inc.'s ("Appellee's")] third amended complaint. Appellants claim that the trial court erred in denying their motions to dismiss because the plain and unambiguous language in the parties' * * * agreement contains a mandatory forum selection clause [a provision in a contract designating the court,

jurisdiction, or tribunal that will decide any disputes arising under the contract] requiring that all lawsuits brought under the agreement shall be in Illinois.

Espresso Disposition Corporation 1 and Santana and Associates entered into the * * * agreement in 2002. The agreement provides for a mandatory forum

Case 5.1 Continues

selection clause in paragraph 8. The provision states:

> The venue with respect to any action pertaining to this Agreement shall be the State of Illinois. The laws of the State of Illinois shall govern the application and interpretation of this Agreement.

However, Appellee filed a lawsuit against Appellants alleging a breach of the agreement in Miami–Dade County, Florida. In fact, Appellee filed four subsequent complaints—an initial complaint, amended complaint, second amended complaint, and third amended complaint—after each and every previous pleading's dismissal was based upon venue as provided for in the agreement's mandatory forum selection clause. Appellee's third amended complaint alleges the forum selection clause was a mistake that was made at the time the agreement was drafted. Additionally, Appellee attached an affidavit [a sworn statement] which states that, in drafting the agreement, Appellee * * * copied a form version of an agreement between different parties, and by mistake, forgot to change the venue provision from Illinois to Florida. In response, Appellants filed their motions to dismiss the third amended complaint, which the trial court denied.

Florida appellate courts interpret a contractual forum selection clause under a *de novo* standard of review. [The courts review the issue anew, as if the lower courts had not ruled on the issue.] Likewise, as the trial court's order denying appellant's motion to dismiss is based on the interpretation of the contractual forum selection clause, this court's

standard of review is *de novo*. Therefore, the narrow issue before this court is whether the * * * agreement provides for a mandatory forum selection clause that is enforceable under Florida law.

Florida courts have long recognized that forum selection clauses such as the one at issue here are presumptively valid. *This is because forum selection clauses provide a degree of certainty to business contracts by obviating [preventing] jurisdictional struggles and by allowing parties to tailor the dispute resolution mechanism to their particular situation. Moreover, forum selection clauses reduce litigation over venue, thereby conserving judicial resources, reducing business expenses, and lowering consumer prices.* [Emphasis added.]

Because Florida law presumes that forum selection clauses are valid and enforceable, the party seeking to avoid enforcement of such a clause must establish that enforcement would be unjust or unreasonable. Under Florida law, the clause is only considered unjust or unreasonable if the party seeking avoidance establishes that enforcement would result in no forum at all. There is absolutely no set of facts that Appellee could plead and prove to demonstrate that Illinois state courts do not exist. Illinois became the twenty-first state in 1818, and has since established an extensive system of state trial and appellate courts. Clearly, Appellee failed to establish that enforcement would be unreasonable since the designated forum—Illinois—does not result in Appellee's having "no forum at all."

Further, as we have said on a number of occasions, if a forum selection clause unambiguously mandates that litigation be subject to an agreed upon forum, then it is error for the trial court

to ignore the clause. Generally, the clause is mandatory where the plain language used by the parties indicates exclusivity. Importantly, if the forum selection clause states or clearly indicates that any litigation must or shall be initiated in a specified forum, then it is mandatory. Here, the agreement's plain language provides that the venue for any action relating to a controversy under the agreement * * * "shall be the State of Illinois." The clear language unequivocally renders the forum selection clause mandatory.

Appellee would have us create an exception to our jurisprudence on mandatory forum selection clauses based on their error in cutting and pasting the clause from another agreement. Of course, the origin of "cutting and pasting" comes from the traditional practice of manuscript-editing whereby writers used to cut paragraphs from a page with editing scissors, that had blades long enough to cut an 8½ inch-wide page, and then physically pasted them onto another page. Today, the cut, copy, and paste functions contained in word processing software render unnecessary the use of scissors or glue. However, what has not been eliminated is the need to actually read and analyze the text being pasted, especially where it is to have legal significance. Thus, in reviewing the mandatory selection clause which Appellant seeks to enforce, we apply the legal maxim "be careful what you ask for" and enforce the pasted forum.

Accordingly, we reverse [the] trial court's denial of the motions to dismiss Appellee's third amended complaint on the basis of improper venue, and remand for entry of an order of dismissal.

Legal Reasoning Questions

1. Compare and contrast a motion to dismiss with other pretrial motions. Identify their chief differences.

2. Why did the appellants in this case file a motion to dismiss?

3. What is the effect of granting a motion to dismiss?

Motion for Judgment on the Pleadings At the close of the pleadings, either party may make a **motion for judgment on the pleadings.** This motion asks the court to decide the issue solely on the pleadings without proceeding to trial.

The judge will grant the motion only when there is no dispute over the facts of the case and the sole issue to be resolved is a question of law. For instance, in the Kirby-Carvello case, if Carvello had admitted to all of Kirby's allegations in his answer and had raised no affirmative defenses, Kirby could file a motion for judgment on the pleadings.

In deciding a motion for judgment on the pleadings, the judge may consider only the evidence contained in the pleadings. In contrast, in a motion for summary judgment, discussed next, the court may consider evidence outside the pleadings.

Motion for Summary Judgment Like a motion for judgment on the pleadings, a **motion for summary judgment** asks the court to grant a judgment without a trial. The motion can be made by either party before or during the trial. As with a motion for judgment on the pleadings, a court will grant a motion for summary judgment only if no facts are in dispute and the only question is how the law applies to the facts.

As mentioned, however, a motion for summary judgment differs from a motion for judgment on the pleadings in that the party filing the motion can submit evidence obtained at any point before the trial that refutes the other party's factual claim. The evidence may consist of **affidavits** (sworn statements by parties or witnesses) or copies of documents, such as contracts, e-mails, and letters obtained during discovery (discussed next). Of course, the evidence must be *admissible* evidence—that is, evidence that the court would allow to be presented during the trial.

On appeal of a court's grant or denial of a motion for summary judgment, the appellate court engages in *de novo* review—that is, it reviews the issue anew, as if the lower court had not ruled on the issue. In the following case, an appellate court took a fresh look at the evidence that had been presented with a motion for summary judgment granted by the lower court.

Case 5.2

Lewis v. Twenty-First Century Bean Processing

United States Court of Appeals, Tenth Circuit, 638 Fed.Appx. 701 (2016).

Background and Facts Twenty-First Century Bean Processing hired Anthony Lewis, a forty-seven-year-old African American male, for a warehouse position, subject to a thirty-day probationary period. At the end of the period, Twenty-First Century evaluated Lewis's performance to determine whether he would remain an employee. The employer decided not to retain Lewis, who then filed a suit in a federal district court against Twenty-First Century. Lewis alleged discrimination on the basis of race and age in violation of Title VII of the Civil Rights Act and the Age Discrimination in Employment Act. Twenty-First Century filed a motion for summary judgment. As evidence, the employer presented proof concerning Lewis's job performance during the probationary period. The court granted the motion. Lewis appealed.

In the Language of the Court
Robert E. *BACHARACH,* Circuit Judge.
   * * * *

   When a plaintiff alleges discrimination but offers no direct evidence of discrimination, the plaintiff bears the initial burden to establish a prima facie *case of discrimination.* [This requires showing that (1) the plaintiff is a member of a protected class—a person defined by certain criteria, including race or age; (2) the plaintiff applied and was qualified for the job at issue; (3) the plaintiff was rejected by the employer; and (4) the employer filled the position with someone not in a protected class.] *If a plaintiff establishes a* prima facie *case, the burden shifts to the defendant to articulate a* * * * *nondiscriminatory reason for its actions.* If the defendant satisfies that burden, the employee would bear the burden to prove the defendant's actions were discriminatory, which the employee could do by showing defendant's proffered reason is a pretext for illegal discrimination. [Emphasis added.]

Case 5.2 Continues

* * * *

Mr. Lewis alleges age discrimination under the Age Discrimination in Employment Act. * * *
Mr. Lewis had not presented any direct evidence of discrimination [and] the court determined
that Mr. Lewis had not established a *prima facie* case because he had failed to provide evidence that his
work was satisfactory. In our view, that conclusion was proper. Therefore, we affirm the district court's
grant of summary judgment to Twenty-First Century on the age discrimination claim.

* * * *

Mr. Lewis also alleges race discrimination under Title VII of the Civil Rights Act. Again finding no
direct evidence of discrimination, * * * the court assumed without deciding that Mr. Lewis had established a *prima facie* case of race discrimination. Thus, the burden shifted to Twenty-First Century to
show a nondiscriminatory reason for terminating Mr. Lewis.

As evidence of a nondiscriminatory purpose, Twenty-First Century pointed out that Mr. Lewis had
missed too many work days, slept at work, used his personal cellphone at work, and reacted argumenta-
tively when warned about his cellphone usage. After finding that any one of these policy violations could
serve as a nondiscriminatory reason for the firing, the court placed the burden on Mr. Lewis to show
* * * that Twenty-First Century's explanation was pretextual [not legitimate]. The district court concluded that Mr. Lewis was unable to meet this burden, and we agree.

Decision and Remedy *The U.S. Court of Appeals for the Tenth Circuit affirmed the lower court's summary judgment. Of the twenty-five work days in the probationary period, Lewis was absent for four days,
found sleeping twice, and seen several times texting and talking on his personal phone. When informed
that this use of a phone was against company policy, Lewis argued with his superior.*

Critical Thinking
- **Legal Environment** *Should motions for summary judgment and other pretrial motions be abolished so
that all lawsuits proceed to trial? Why or why not?*
- **What If the Facts Were Different?** *Suppose that at this stage of the litigation, Twenty-First Century
had not been able to provide evidence in support of its asserted reason for Lewis's firing. What would have
been the result? Why?*

5–2c Discovery

Before a trial begins, the parties can use a number of procedural devices to obtain information and gather evidence
about the case. Kirby, for example, will want to know
how fast Carvello was driving. She will also want to learn
whether he had been drinking, was under the influence of medication, and was wearing corrective lenses if
required by law to do so while driving.

The process of obtaining information from the opposing party or from witnesses prior to trial is known as
discovery. Discovery includes gaining access to witnesses,
documents, records, and other types of evidence. In federal courts, the parties are required to make initial disclosures of relevant evidence to the opposing party. A court
can impose sanctions on a party who fails to respond to
discovery requests.

Discovery prevents surprises at trial by giving both
parties access to evidence that might otherwise be hidden. This allows the litigants to learn as much as they

can about what to expect at a trial before they reach the
courtroom. Discovery also serves to narrow the issues so
that trial time is spent on the main questions in the case.

Discovery Rules The FRCP and similar state rules
set forth the guidelines for discovery activity. Generally,
discovery is allowed regarding any matter that is relevant
to the claim or defense of any party. Discovery rules also
attempt to protect witnesses and parties from undue
harassment, and to prevent privileged or confidential
material from being disclosed. Only information that is
relevant to the case at hand—or likely to lead to the discovery of relevant information—is discoverable.

If a discovery request involves privileged or confidential business information, a court can deny the request and
can limit the scope of discovery in a number of ways. For
instance, a court can require the party to submit the materials to the judge in a sealed envelope so that the judge can
decide if they should be disclosed to the opposing party.

Depositions Discovery can involve the use of depositions. A **deposition** is sworn testimony by a party to the lawsuit or by any witness, recorded by an authorized court official. The person deposed gives testimony and answers questions asked by the attorneys from both sides. The questions and answers are recorded, sworn to, and signed. These answers, of course, will help the attorneys prepare their cases.

Depositions also give attorneys the opportunity to ask immediate follow-up questions and to evaluate how their witnesses will conduct themselves at trial. In addition, depositions can be employed in court to **impeach** (challenge the credibility of) a party or a witness who changes his or her testimony at the trial. Finally, a deposition can be used as testimony if the witness is not available at trial.

Interrogatories Discovery can also involve **interrogatories**—written questions for which written answers are prepared and then signed under oath. The main difference between interrogatories and written depositions is that interrogatories are directed to a party to the lawsuit (the plaintiff or the defendant), not to a witness. The party usually has thirty days to prepare answers.

The party's attorney often drafts the answers to interrogatories in a manner calculated to give away as little information as possible. Whereas depositions elicit candid answers not prepared in advance, interrogatories are designed to obtain accurate information about specific topics, such as how many contracts were signed and when. The scope of interrogatories is also broader because parties are obligated to answer questions, even if that means disclosing information from their records and files. As with discovery requests, a court can impose sanctions on a party who fails to answer interrogatories.

■ **Case in Point 5.2** Ronald J. Hass (doing business as Valley Corp. and R. J. Hass Corp.) was a contractor who built a home for Ty and Karen Levine. Probuilders Specialty Insurance Co. provided commercial liability insurance for the contractor. Later, when the Levines sued Hass and his company for shoddy and incomplete work, Hass blamed the subcontractors. Probuilders provided Hass with legal representation, but the Levines won a judgment for more than $2 million. Then Probuilders sued Hass and his company, claiming that he had made misrepresentations to them regarding the facts of the case and seeking to avoid paying the judgment. Hass filed a counterclaim against Probuilders.

During discovery, Hass refused to respond fully to interrogatories and other discovery requests, and refused to give a deposition. Probuilders filed a motion to compel, and the court ordered Hass to respond to the discovery requests. Although Probuilders sent letters specifying what was needed, Hass continued to be evasive.

The court imposed sanctions on Hass more than once. Ultimately, the court found that Hass had acted willfully and in bad faith, and recommended that his answers and counterclaim against Probuilders be dismissed.[6] ■

Requests for Admissions One party can serve the other party with a written request for an admission of the truth of matters relating to the trial. Any fact admitted under such a request is conclusively established as true for the trial. For instance, Kirby can ask Carvello to admit that his driver's license was suspended at the time of the accident. A request for admission shortens the trial because the parties will not have to spend time proving facts on which they already agree.

Requests for Documents, Objects, and Entry upon Land A party can gain access to documents and other items not in her or his possession in order to inspect and examine them. Carvello, for instance, can gain permission to inspect and copy Kirby's car repair bills. Likewise, a party can gain "entry upon land" to inspect the premises.

Requests for Examinations When the physical or mental condition of one party is in question, the opposing party can ask the court to order a physical or mental examination by an independent examiner. If the court agrees to make the order, the opposing party can obtain the results of the examination. Note that the court will make such an order only when the need for the information outweighs the right to privacy of the person to be examined.

Electronic Discovery Any relevant material, including information stored electronically, can be the object of a discovery request. The federal rules and most state rules (as well as court decisions) specifically allow individuals to obtain discovery of electronic "data compilations." Electronic evidence, or **e-evidence,** consists of all computer-generated or electronically recorded information, such as e-mail, voice mail, tweets, blogs, social media posts, spreadsheets, documents, and other data stored electronically.

E-evidence can reveal significant facts that are not discoverable by other means. Computers, smartphones, cameras, and other devices automatically record certain file information on their hard drives—such as who created the file and when, and who accessed, modified, or transmitted it. This information is called **metadata,** which can be thought of as "data about data." Metadata can be

---

6. *Probuilders Specialty Insurance Co. v. Valley Corp.*, 2012 WL 6045753 (N.D.Cal. 2012).

obtained only from the file in its electronic format—not from printed-out versions.

■ **Example 5.3** John McAfee, the programmer responsible for creating McAfee antivirus software, was wanted for questioning in the murder of his neighbor in Belize. McAfee left Belize and was on the run from police, but he allowed a journalist to come with him and photograph him. When the journalist posted photos of McAfee online, some metadata were attached to a photo. The police used the metadata to pinpoint the latitude and longitude of the image and subsequently arrested McAfee in Guatemala. ■

E-Discovery Procedures. The Federal Rules of Civil Procedure deal specifically with the preservation, retrieval, and production of electronic data. Although traditional interrogatories and depositions are still used to find out whether e-evidence exists, a party usually must hire an expert to retrieve the evidence in its electronic format. The expert uses software to reconstruct e-mail, text, and other exchanges to establish who knew what and when they knew it. The expert can even recover computer files that the user thought had been deleted.

Advantages and Disadvantages. Electronic discovery has significant advantages over paper discovery. Electronic versions of documents, e-mail, and text messages can provide useful—and often quite damaging—information about how a particular matter progressed over several weeks or months. E-discovery can uncover the proverbial smoking gun that will win the lawsuit. But it is also time consuming and expensive, especially when lawsuits involve large firms with multiple offices. Many companies have found it challenging to fulfill their duty to preserve electronic evidence from a vast number of sources. Failure to do so, however, can lead to sanctions and even force companies to agree to settlements that are not in their best interests.

A failure to provide e-evidence in response to a discovery request does not always arise from an unintentional failure to preserve documents and e-mail. The following case involved a litigant that delayed a response to gain time to intentionally alter and destroy data. At issue were the sanctions imposed for this spoliation. (*Spoliation of evidence* occurs when a document or information that is required for discovery is destroyed or altered significantly.)

Case 5.3

Klipsch Group, Inc. v. ePRO E-Commerce Limited

United States Court of Appeals, Second Circuit, 880 F.3d 620 (2018).

Background and Facts Klipsch Group, Inc., makes sound equipment, including headphones. Klipsch filed a suit in a federal district court against ePRO E-Commerce Limited, a Chinese corporation. Klipsch alleged that ePRO had sold $5 million in counterfeit Klipsch products. ePRO claimed that the sales of relevant products amounted to less than $8,000 worldwide. In response to discovery requests, ePRO failed to timely disclose the majority of the requested documents in its possession. In addition, ePRO restricted Klipsch's access to ePRO's e-data. The court directed ePRO to hold the relevant data to preserve evidence, but the defendant failed to do so. This led to the deletion of thousands of documents and significant quantities of data. To determine what data had been blocked or lost, and what might and might not be recovered, Klipsch spent $2.7 million on a forensic examination.

The federal district court concluded that ePRO had willingly engaged in spoliation of e-evidence. For this misconduct, the court imposed sanctions, including an order to pay Klipsch the entire $2.7 million for its restorative discovery efforts. ePRO appealed, contending that the sanctions were "disproportionate."

In the Language of the Court
Gerard E. *LYNCH*, Circuit Judge:
* * * *

ePRO argues that the monetary sanctions imposed against it are so out of proportion to the value of the evidence uncovered by Klipsch's efforts or to the likely ultimate value of the case as to be impermissibly punitive and a violation of due process. That position, although superficially sympathetic given the amount of the sanction, overlooks the fact that ePRO caused Klipsch to accrue those costs by failing to comply with its discovery obligations. *Such compliance is not optional or negotiable; rather, the integrity of our civil litigation process requires that the parties before us, although adversarial to one another, carry out their duties to maintain and disclose the relevant information in their possession in good faith.* [Emphasis added.]

The extremely broad discovery permitted by the Federal Rules depends on the parties' voluntary participation. The system functions because, in the vast majority of cases, we can rely on each side to preserve evidence and to disclose relevant information when asked (and sometimes even before then) without being forced to proceed at the point of a court order. The courts are ill-equipped to address parties that do not voluntarily comply: we do not have our own investigatory powers, and even if we did, the spoliation of evidence would frequently be extremely difficult for any outsider to detect.

Moreover, noncompliance vastly increases the cost of litigation * * * . Accordingly, we have held that discovery sanctions are proper * * * , because an alternative rule would encourage dilatory [delaying] tactics, and compliance with discovery orders would come only when the backs of counsel and the litigants were against the wall.

When we apply those principles to the case at hand, it is clear that the district court did not abuse its discretion by imposing monetary sanctions calculated to make Klipsch whole for the extra cost and efforts it reasonably undertook in response to ePRO's recalcitrance.
* * * *

In sum, we see nothing in ePRO's proportionality arguments compelling us to conclude that the district court abused its discretion by awarding full compensation for efforts that were * * * a reasonable response to ePRO's own evasive conduct. The proportionality that matters here is that the amount of the sanctions was plainly proportionate—indeed, it was exactly equivalent—to the costs ePRO inflicted on Klipsch in its reasonable efforts to remedy ePRO's misconduct.

Decision and Remedy *The U.S. Court of Appeals for the Second Circuit affirmed the sanctions. "The district court's award properly reflects the additional costs ePRO imposed on its opponent by refusing to comply with its discovery obligations."*

Critical Thinking
- **Economic** *Should the cost of corrective discovery efforts be imposed on an uncooperative party if those efforts turn up nothing of real value to the case? Explain.*
- **Legal Environment** *Should it be inferred from a business's failure to keep backup copies of its database that the business must therefore have destroyed the data? Discuss.*

5–2d Pretrial Conference

After discovery has taken place and before the trial begins, the attorneys may meet with the trial judge in a *pretrial conference*, or hearing. Usually, the conference consists of an informal discussion between the judge and the opposing attorneys after discovery has taken place. The purpose is to explore the possibility of a settlement without trial and, if this is not possible, to identify the matters in dispute and to plan the course of the trial. In particular, the parties may attempt to establish ground rules to restrict the number of expert witnesses or discuss the admissibility or costs of certain types of evidence.

5–2e The Right to a Jury Trial

The Seventh Amendment to the U.S. Constitution guarantees the right to a jury trial for cases at law in *federal* courts when the amount in controversy exceeds $20. Most states have similar guarantees in their own constitutions (although the threshold dollar amount is higher than $20).

The right to a trial by jury need not be exercised, and many cases are tried without a jury. In most states and in federal courts, one of the parties must request a jury, or the judge presumes the parties waive this right. If there is no jury, the judge determines the truth of the facts alleged in the case.

5–2f Jury Selection

Before a jury trial commences, a panel of jurors must be selected. Although some types of trials require twelve-person juries, most civil matters can be heard by six-person juries. The jury selection process is known as **voir dire**.[7] In most jurisdictions, attorneys for the plaintiff and the defendant ask prospective jurors oral questions to determine whether they are biased or have any connection with a party to the action or with a prospective witness. In some jurisdictions,

the judge may do all or part of the questioning based on written questions submitted by counsel for the parties.

During *voir dire*, a party may challenge a certain number of prospective jurors *peremptorily*—that is, ask that an individual not be sworn in as a juror without providing any reason. Alternatively, a party may challenge a prospective juror *for cause*—that is, provide a reason why an individual should not be sworn in as a juror. If the judge grants the challenge, the individual is asked to step down. A prospective juror, however, may not be excluded by the use of discriminatory challenges, such as those based on racial criteria or gender.

See Concept Summary 5.1 for a review of pretrial procedures.

---

7. Pronounced *vwahr deehr*. These verbs, based on Old French, mean "to speak the truth." In legal language, the phrase refers to the process of questioning jurors to learn about their backgrounds, attitudes, and similar attributes.

Concept Summary 5.1

Pretrial Procedures

The Pleadings	• *The plaintiff's complaint*—The plaintiff's statement of the cause of action and the parties involved, filed with the court by the plaintiff's attorney. After the filing, the defendant is notified of the suit through service of process. • *The defendant's response*—The defendant's response to the plaintiff's complaint may take the form of an answer, in which the defendant admits or denies the plaintiff's allegations. The defendant may also raise an affirmative defense and/or assert a counterclaim.
Pretrial Motions	• *Motion to dismiss*—See Exhibit 5–3. • *Motion for judgment on the pleadings*—May be made by either party and will be granted only if no facts are in dispute and only questions of law are at issue. • *Motion for summary judgment*—See Exhibit 5–3.
Discovery	The process of gathering evidence concerning the case, which may involve the following: • *Depositions* (sworn testimony by either party or any witness). • *Interrogatories* (in which parties to the action write answers to questions with the aid of their attorneys). • Requests for admissions, documents, examinations, or other information relating to the case. • Requests for electronically recorded information, such as e-mail, text messages, voice mail, and other data.
Pretrial Conference	A pretrial hearing, at the request of either party or the court, to identify the matters in dispute after discovery has taken place and to explore the possibility of settling the dispute without a trial. If no settlement is possible, the parties plan the course of the trial.
Jury Selection	In a jury trial, the selection of members of the jury from a pool of prospective jurors. During a process known as *voir dire*, the attorneys for both sides may challenge prospective jurors either for cause or peremptorily (for no cause).

5–3 The Trial

Various rules and procedures govern the trial phase of the litigation process. There are rules governing what kind of evidence will or will not be admitted during the trial, as well as specific procedures that the participants in the lawsuit must follow. For instance, a trial judge may instruct jurors not to communicate with anyone about the case or order reporters not to use social media to comment on the case while in the courtroom.

5–3a Opening Statements

At the beginning of the trial, both attorneys are allowed to make **opening statements** setting forth the facts that they expect to prove during the trial. The opening statement provides an opportunity for each lawyer to give a brief version of the facts and the supporting evidence that will be used during the trial. Then the plaintiff's case is presented. In our hypothetical case, Kirby's lawyer would introduce evidence (relevant documents, exhibits, and the testimony of witnesses) to support Kirby's position.

5–3b Rules of Evidence

Whether evidence will be admitted in court is determined by the **rules of evidence.** These are a series of rules that the courts have created to ensure that any evidence presented during a trial is fair and reliable. The Federal Rules of Evidence govern the admissibility of evidence in federal courts.

Evidence Must Be Relevant to the Issues

Evidence will not be admitted in court unless it is relevant to the matter in question. **Relevant evidence** is evidence that tends to prove or disprove a fact in question or to establish the degree of probability of a fact or action. For instance, evidence that the defendant was in another person's home when the victim was shot would be relevant, because it would tend to prove that the defendant was not the shooter.

Hearsay Evidence Is Not Admissible

Generally, hearsay is not admissible as evidence. **Hearsay** is testimony someone gives in court about a statement made by someone else who was not under oath at the time. Literally, it is what someone heard someone else say. If a witness in the Kirby-Carvello case testified in court concerning what he or she heard another observer say about the accident, for example, that testimony would be hearsay. Admitting hearsay into evidence carries many risks because, even though it may be relevant, there is no way to test its reliability.

5–3c Examination of Witnesses and Potential Motions

Because Kirby is the plaintiff, she has the burden of proving that her allegations are true. Her attorney begins the presentation of Kirby's case by calling the first witness for the plaintiff and examining, or questioning, the witness. (For both attorneys, the types of questions and the manner of asking them are governed by the rules of evidence.) This questioning is called **direct examination.**

After Kirby's attorney is finished, the witness is subject to **cross-examination** by Carvello's attorney. Then Kirby's attorney has another opportunity to question the witness in *redirect examination*, and Carvello's attorney may follow the redirect examination with a *recross-examination*. When both attorneys have finished with the first witness, Kirby's attorney calls the succeeding witnesses in the plaintiff's case. Each witness is subject to examination by the attorneys in the manner just described.

Expert Witnesses As part of their cases, both the plaintiff and the defendant may present testimony from one or more expert witnesses, such as forensic scientists, physicians, and psychologists. An *expert witness* is a person who, by virtue of education, training, skill, or experience, has scientific, technical, or other specialized knowledge in a particular area beyond that of an average person. In Kirby's case, her attorney might hire an accident reconstruction specialist to establish Carvello's negligence or a physician to testify to the extent of Kirby's injuries.

Normally, witnesses can testify only about the facts of a case—that is, what they personally observed. When witnesses are qualified as experts in a particular field, however, they can offer their opinions and conclusions about the evidence in that field. Because numerous experts are available for hire and expert testimony is powerful and effective with juries, there is tremendous potential for abuse. Therefore, judges act as gatekeepers to ensure that the experts are qualified. If a party believes that the opponent's expert witness is not a qualified expert in the relevant field, that party can make a motion to prevent the witness from testifying.[8]

---

8. See Edward J. Imwinkelried, *The Methods of Attacking Scientific Evidence*, 5th ed. (2014).

■ **Case in Point 5.4**   Yvette Downey bought a children's bedroom set from Bob's Discount Furniture Holdings, Inc. She later discovered that it was infested with bed bugs, which had spread throughout her home. Downey spoke with Edward Gordinier, a licensed and experienced exterminator, who identified the bedroom set as the source of the problem. Although Bob's retrieved the bedroom set and refunded the purchase price, it refused to pay for the costs of extermination or any other damages. Downey sued.

Before the trial, Downey's attorney named Gordinier as a witness but did not submit a written report describing his anticipated testimony or specifying his qualifications. The defendants filed a motion to prevent his testimony. The district court refused to allow Gordinier to testify, but that decision was reversed on appeal. The appellate court concluded that Gordinier was not the type of expert who regularly was hired by plaintiffs to testify in court, in which case a report would have been required. Gordinier was simply an expert on bugs, and he was allowed to give his opinion on the infestation.[9] ■

Possible Motion and Judgment   At the conclusion of the plaintiff's case, the defendant's attorney may ask the judge to direct a verdict for the defendant on the ground that the plaintiff has presented no evidence to support her or his claim. This is called a **motion for a judgment as a matter of law** (or a **motion for a directed verdict** in state courts). In considering the motion, the judge looks at the evidence in the light most favorable to the plaintiff and grants the motion only if there is insufficient evidence to raise an issue of fact. (Motions for directed verdicts at this stage of a trial are seldom granted.)

Defendant's Evidence   The defendant's attorney then presents the evidence and witnesses for the defendant's case. Witnesses are called and examined by the defendant's attorney. The plaintiff's attorney has the right to cross-examine them, and there may be a redirect examination and possibly a recross-examination.

At the end of the defendant's case, either attorney can move for a directed verdict. Again, the test is whether the jury can, through any reasonable interpretation of the evidence, find for the party against whom the motion has been made. After the defendant's attorney has finished introducing evidence, the plaintiff's attorney can present a **rebuttal** by offering additional evidence that refutes the defendant's case. The defendant's attorney can, in turn, refute that evidence in a **rejoinder.**

5–3d Closing Arguments, Jury Instructions, and Verdict

After both sides have rested their cases, each attorney presents a **closing argument.** In the closing argument, each attorney summarizes the facts and evidence presented during the trial and indicates why the facts and evidence support his or her client's claim. In addition to generally urging a verdict in favor of the client, the closing argument typically reveals the shortcomings of the points made by the opposing party during the trial.

Jury Instructions   Attorneys usually present closing arguments whether or not the trial was heard by a jury. If it was a jury trial, the attorneys will have met with the judge before the closing arguments to determine how the jury will be instructed on the law. The attorneys can refer to these instructions in their closing arguments. After closing arguments are completed, the judge instructs the jury in the law that applies to the case (these instructions are often called *charges*). The jury then retires to the jury room to deliberate a verdict.

Juries are instructed on the standard of proof they must apply to the case. In most civil cases, the standard of proof is a *preponderance of the evidence*.[10] In other words, the plaintiff (Kirby, in our hypothetical case) need only show that her factual claim is more likely to be true than the defendant's. In a criminal trial, the prosecution has a higher standard of proof to meet—it must prove its case *beyond a reasonable doubt.*

Verdict   Once the jury has reached a decision, it issues a **verdict** in favor of one party. The verdict specifies the jury's factual findings. In some cases, the jury also decides on the amount of the *award* (the compensation to be paid to the prevailing party). After the announcement of the verdict, which marks the end of the trial itself, the jurors are dismissed.

See Concept Summary 5.2 for a review of trial procedures.

---

9. *Downey v. Bob's Discount Furniture Holdings, Inc.*, 633 F.3d 1 (1st Cir. 2011). See also *Deere & Company v. FIMCO, Inc.*, 239 F.Supp.3d 964 (W.D.Ky. 2017).

10. Note that some civil claims must be proved by "clear and convincing evidence," meaning that the evidence must show that the truth of the party's claim is *highly* probable. This standard is often applied in situations that present a particular danger of deception, such as allegations of fraud.

Concept Summary 5.2

Trial Procedure

Opening Statements	Each party's attorney is allowed to present an opening statement indicating what the attorney will attempt to prove during the course of the trial.
Examination of Witnesses	• Plaintiff's introduction and direct examination of witnesses, cross-examination by defendant's attorney, possible redirect examination by plaintiff's attorney, and possible recross-examination by defendant's attorney. • Both the plaintiff and the defendant may present testimony from one or more expert witnesses. • At the close of the plaintiff's case, the defendant may make a motion for a directed verdict (or for judgment as a matter of law). If granted by the court, this motion will end the trial before the defendant presents witnesses. • Defendant's introduction and direct examination of witnesses, cross-examination by plaintiff's attorney, possible redirect examination by defendant's attorney, and possible recross-examination by plaintiff's attorney. • Possible rebuttal of defendant's argument by plaintiff's attorney, who presents more evidence. • Possible rejoinder by defendant's attorney to meet that evidence.
Closing Arguments, Jury Instructions, and Verdict	• Each party's attorney argues in favor of a verdict for his or her client. • The judge instructs (or charges) the jury as to how the law applies to the issue, and the jury retires to deliberate. • When the jury renders its verdict, the trial comes to an end.

5–4 Posttrial Motions

After the jury has rendered its verdict, either party may make a posttrial motion. The prevailing party usually requests that the court enter a judgment in accordance with the verdict. The nonprevailing party frequently files one of the motions discussed next.

5–4a Motion for a New Trial

At the end of the trial, the losing party may make a motion to set aside the adverse verdict and any judgment and to hold a new trial. After looking at all the evidence, the judge will grant the **motion for a new trial** only if she or he believes that the jury was in error and that it is not appropriate to grant judgment for the other side.

Usually, a new trial is granted only when the jury verdict is obviously the result of a misapplication of the law or a misunderstanding of the evidence presented at

trial. A new trial can also be granted on the grounds of newly discovered evidence, misconduct by the participants during the trial (such as when a juror has made prejudicial and inflammatory remarks), or an error by the judge.

5–4b Motion for Judgment *N.O.V.*

If Kirby wins and if Carvello's attorney has previously moved for a judgment as a matter of law, then Carvello's attorney can make a second motion for a judgment as a matter of law (the terminology used in federal courts).

In many state courts, if the defendant's attorney moved earlier for a directed verdict, he or she may now make a **motion for judgment *n.o.v.***—from the Latin *non obstante veredicto*, meaning "notwithstanding the verdict." Such a motion will be granted only if the jury's verdict was unreasonable and erroneous.

If the judge grants the motion, then the jury's verdict will be set aside, and a judgment will be entered in favor of the opposing party (Carvello). If the motion is denied, Carvello may then appeal the case. Kirby may also appeal the case, even though she won at trial. She might appeal, for instance, if she received a smaller monetary award than she had sought.

5–5 The Appeal

Either party may appeal not only the jury's verdict, but also the judge's ruling on any pretrial or posttrial motion. Many of the appellate court cases that appear in this text involve appeals of motions for summary judgment or other motions that were denied by trial court judges.

Note that a party must have legitimate grounds to file an appeal (some legal error) and that few trial court decisions are reversed on appeal. Moreover, the expenses associated with an appeal can be considerable.

5–5a Filing the Appeal

If Carvello decides to appeal the verdict in Kirby's favor, then his attorney must file a *notice of appeal* with the clerk of the trial court within a prescribed period of time. Carvello then becomes the *appellant* or *petitioner*. The clerk of the trial court sends to the reviewing court (usually an intermediate court of appeals) the *record on appeal*. The record contains all the pleadings, motions, and other documents filed with the court and a complete written transcript of the proceedings, including testimony, arguments, jury instructions, and judicial rulings.

Carvello's attorney will file an appellate **brief** with the reviewing court. The brief is a formal legal document outlining the facts and issues of the case, the judge's rulings or jury's findings that should be reversed or modified, the applicable law, and arguments on Carvello's behalf (citing applicable statutes and relevant cases as precedents). The attorney for the *appellee* (Kirby, in our hypothetical case) usually files an answering brief. Carvello's attorney can file a reply, although it is not required. The reviewing court then considers the case.

5–5b Appellate Review

A court of appeals does not hear any evidence. Rather, it reviews the record for errors of law. Its decision concerning a case is based on the record on appeal and the briefs and arguments. The attorneys present oral arguments, after which the case is taken under advisement. The court then issues a written opinion. In general, appellate courts do not reverse findings of fact unless the findings are unsupported or contradicted by the evidence.

An appellate court has the following options after reviewing a case:

1. The court can *affirm* the trial court's decision. (Most decisions are affirmed.)
2. The court can *reverse* the trial court's judgment if it concludes that the trial court erred or that the jury did not receive proper instructions.
3. The appellate court can *remand* (send back) the case to the trial court for further proceedings consistent with its opinion on the matter.
4. The court might also affirm or reverse a decision *in part*. For example, the court might affirm the jury's finding that Carvello was negligent but remand the case for further proceedings on another issue (such as the extent of Kirby's damages).
5. An appellate court can also *modify* a lower court's decision. If the appellate court decides that the jury awarded an excessive amount in damages, for example, the court might reduce the award to a more appropriate, or fairer, amount.

5–5c Higher Appellate Courts

If the reviewing court is an intermediate appellate court, the losing party may decide to appeal the decision to the state's highest court, usually called its supreme court. Although the losing party has a right to ask (petition) a higher court to review the case, the party does not have a right to have the case heard by the higher appellate court. Appellate courts normally have discretionary power and can accept or reject an appeal. Like the United States Supreme Court, state supreme courts generally deny most petitions for appeal.

If the petition for review is granted, new briefs must be filed before the state supreme court, and the attorneys may be allowed or requested to present oral arguments. Like the intermediate appellate courts, the state supreme court can reverse or affirm the lower appellate court's decision or remand the case. At this point, the case typically has reached its end (unless a federal question is at issue and one of the parties has legitimate grounds to seek review by a federal appellate court).

Concept Summary 5.3 reviews the options that the parties may pursue after the trial.

Concept Summary 5.3

Posttrial Options

Posttrial Motions	• *Motion for a new trial*—If the judge believes that the jury was in error but is not convinced that the losing party should have won, the motion normally is granted. It can also be granted on the basis of newly discovered evidence, misconduct by the participants during the trial, or error by the judge. • *Motion for judgment n.o.v.* ("*notwithstanding the verdict*")—The party making the motion must have filed a motion for a directed verdict at the close of the presentation of evidence during the trial. The motion will be granted if the judge is convinced that the jury was in error.
The Appeal	Either party can appeal the trial court's judgment to an appropriate court of appeals. • *Filing the appeal*—The appealing party must file a notice of appeal with the clerk of the trial court, who forwards the record on appeal to the appellate court. Attorneys file appellate briefs. • *Appellate review*—The appellate court does not hear evidence but bases its opinion, which it issues in writing, on the record on appeal and the attorneys' briefs and oral arguments. The court may affirm or reverse all (or part) of the trial court's judgment and/or remand the case for further proceedings consistent with its opinion. Most decisions are affirmed on appeal. • *Further review*—In some cases, further review may be sought from a higher appellate court, such as a state supreme court. If a federal question is involved, the case may ultimately be appealed to the United States Supreme Court.

5–6 Enforcing the Judgment

The uncertainties of the litigation process are compounded by the lack of guarantees that any judgment will be enforceable. Even if the jury awards Kirby the full amount of damages requested ($500,000), for example, Carvello's auto insurance coverage might have lapsed. If so, the company would not pay any of the damages. Alternatively, Carvello's insurance policy might be limited to $250,000, meaning that Carvello personally would have to pay the remaining $250,000.

5–6a Requesting Court Assistance in Collecting the Judgment

If the defendant does not have the funds available to pay the judgment, the plaintiff can go back to the court and request that the court issue a writ of execution. A **writ of execution** is an order directing the sheriff to seize and sell the defendant's nonexempt assets, or property

(certain assets are exempted by law from such actions). The proceeds of the sale are then used to pay the damages owed, and any excess proceeds are returned to the defendant. Alternatively, the nonexempt property itself could be transferred to the plaintiff in lieu of an outright payment. (Creditors' remedies, discussed elsewhere in this text, may also be available.)

5–6b Availability of Assets

The problem of collecting a judgment is less pronounced when a party is seeking to satisfy a judgment against a defendant with substantial assets that can be easily located, such as a major corporation. Usually, one of the factors considered by the plaintiff and his or her attorney before a lawsuit is initiated is whether the defendant has sufficient assets to cover the amount of damages sought. In addition, during the discovery process, attorneys routinely seek information about the location of the defendant's assets that might potentially be used to satisfy a judgment.

Practice and Review: Court Procedures

Ronald Metzgar placed his fifteen-month-old son, Matthew, awake and healthy, in his playpen. Ronald left the room for five minutes and on his return found Matthew lifeless. A toy block had lodged in the boy's throat, causing him to choke to death. Ronald called 911, but efforts to revive Matthew were to no avail. There was no warning of a choking hazard on the box containing the block. Matthew's parents hired an attorney and sued Playskool, Inc., the manufacturer of the block, alleging that the manufacturer had been negligent in failing to warn of the block's hazard. Playskool filed a motion for summary judgment, arguing that the danger of a young child's choking on a small block was obvious. Using the information presented in the chapter, answer the following questions.

1. Suppose that the attorney the Metzgars hired agreed to represent them on a contingency-fee basis. What does that mean?
2. How would the Metzgars' attorney likely have served process (the summons and complaint) on Playskool, Inc.?
3. Should Playskool's request for summary judgment be granted? Why or why not?
4. Suppose that the judge denied Playskool's motion and the case proceeded to trial. After hearing all the evidence, the jury found in favor of the defendant. What options do the plaintiffs have at this point if they are not satisfied with the verdict?

Debate This . . .   *Some consumer advocates argue that attorneys' high contingency fees—sometimes reaching 40 percent—unfairly deprive winning plaintiffs of too much of their awards. Should the government cap contingency fees at, say, 20 percent of the award? Why or why not?*

Terms and Concepts

affidavits 93	hearsay 99	pleadings 88
affirmative defense 90	impeach 95	pretrial motions 90
answer 89	interrogatories 95	rebuttal 100
brief 102	metadata 95	rejoinder 100
closing argument 100	motion 90	relevant evidence 99
complaint 88	motion for a directed verdict 100	rules of evidence 99
counterclaim 90	motion for a judgment as a matter	service of process 88
cross-examination 99	of law 100	summons 88
default judgment 88	motion for a new trial 101	verdict 100
deposition 95	motion for judgment *n.o.v.* 101	*voir dire* 98
direct examination 99	motion for judgment on the	writ of execution 103
discovery 94	pleadings 93	
e-evidence 95	motion for summary judgment 93	
Federal Rules of Civil Procedure	motion to dismiss 91	
(FRCP) 86	opening statements 99	

Issue Spotters

1. At the trial, after Sue calls her witnesses, offers her evidence, and otherwise presents her side of the case, Tom has at least two choices between courses of actions. Tom can call his first witness. What else might he do? (See *The Trial.*)
2. After the trial, the judge issues a judgment that includes a grant of relief for Sue, but the relief is less than Sue wanted. Neither Sue nor Tom is satisfied with this result. Who can appeal to a higher court? (See *The Appeal.*)

• **Check your answers to the Issue Spotters against the answers provided in Appendix B at the end of this text.**

Business Scenarios and Case Problems

5–1. Discovery Rules. In the past, the rules of discovery were very restrictive, and trials often turned on elements of surprise. For example, a plaintiff would not necessarily know until the trial what the defendant's defense was going to be. In the last several decades, however, new rules of discovery have substantially changed this situation. Now each attorney can access practically all of the evidence that the other side intends to present at trial, with the exception of certain information—namely, the opposing attorney's work product. Work product is not a precise concept. Basically, it includes all of the attorney's thoughts on the case. Can you see any reason why such information should not be made available to the opposing attorney? Discuss fully. (See *Pretrial Procedures*.)

5–2. Motions. When and for what purpose is each of the following motions made? Which of them would be appropriate if a defendant claimed that the only issue between the parties was a question of law and that the law was favorable to the defendant's position? (See *Pretrial Procedures*.)

(a) A motion for judgment on the pleadings.

(b) A motion for a directed verdict.

(c) A motion for summary judgment.

(d) A motion for judgment *n.o.v.*

5–3. Motion for a New Trial. Washoe Medical Center, Inc., admitted Shirley Swisher for the treatment of a fractured pelvis. During her stay, Swisher suffered a fatal fall from her hospital bed. Gerald Parodi, the administrator of her estate, and others filed an action against Washoe seeking damages for the alleged lack of care in treating Swisher. During *voir dire*, when the plaintiffs' attorney returned a few minutes late from a break, the trial judge led the prospective jurors in a standing ovation. The judge joked with one of the prospective jurors, whom he had known in college, about his fitness to serve as a judge and personally endorsed another prospective juror's business. After the trial, the jury returned a verdict in favor of Washoe. The plaintiffs moved for a new trial, but the judge denied the motion. The plaintiffs then appealed, arguing that the tone set by the judge during *voir dire* prejudiced their right to a fair trial. Should the appellate court agree? Why or why not? (See *Posttrial Motions*.)

5–4. Discovery. Advance Technology Consultants, Inc. (ATC), contracted with RoadTrac, LLC, to provide software and client software systems for the products of global positioning satellite (GPS) technology being developed by RoadTrac. RoadTrac agreed to provide ATC with hardware with which ATC's software would interface. Problems soon arose, however. ATC claimed that RoadTrac's hardware was defective, making it difficult to develop the software. RoadTrac contended that its hardware was fully functional and that ATC had simply failed to provide supporting software.

ATC told RoadTrac that it considered their contract terminated. RoadTrac filed a suit in a Georgia state court against ATC alleging breach of contract. During discovery, RoadTrac requested ATC's customer lists and marketing procedures. ATC objected to providing this information because RoadTrac and ATC had become competitors in the GPS industry. Should a party to a lawsuit have to hand over its confidential business secrets as part of a discovery request? Why or why not? What limitations might a court consider imposing before requiring ATC to produce this material? (See *Pretrial Procedures*.)

5–5. Service of Process. Dr. Kevin Bardwell owns Northfield Urgent Care, LLC, a Minnesota medical clinic. Northfield ordered flu vaccine from Clint Pharmaceuticals, a licensed distributer of flu vaccine located in Tennessee. The parties signed a credit agreement that specified that any disputes would be litigated in the Tennessee state courts. When Northfield failed to pay what it owed for the vaccine, Clint Pharmaceuticals filed a lawsuit in Tennessee and served process on the clinic via registered mail to Dr. Bardwell, the registered agent of Northfield.

Bardwell's wife, who worked as a receptionist at the clinic and handled inquiries on the clinic's Facebook site, signed for the letter. Bardwell did not appear on the trial date, however, and the Tennessee court entered a default judgment against Northfield. When Clint Pharmaceuticals attempted to collect on the judgment in Minnesota, Bardwell claimed that the judgment was unenforceable. He asserted that he had not been properly served because his wife was not a registered agent. Should the Minnesota court invalidate the Tennessee judgment? Was service of process proper, given that the notice was mailed to the defendant medical clinic and the wife of the physician who owned the clinic opened the letter? Explain. [*Clint Pharmaceuticals v. Northfield Urgent Care, LLC*, 2012 WL 3792546 (Minn.App. 2012).] (See *Pretrial Procedures*.)

5–6. Business Case Problem with Sample Answer—Discovery. Jessica Lester died from injuries suffered in an auto accident caused by the driver of a truck owned by Allied Concrete Co. Jessica's widower, Isaiah, filed a suit against Allied for damages. The defendant requested copies of all of Isaiah's Facebook photos and other postings. Before responding, Isaiah "cleaned up" his Facebook page. Allied suspected that some items had been deleted, including a photo of Isaiah holding a beer can while wearing a T-shirt that declared "I [heart] hotmoms." Can this material be recovered? If so, how? What effect might Isaiah's "postings" have on the result in this case? Discuss. [*Allied Concrete Co. v. Lester*, 285 Va. 295, 736 S.E.2d 699 (2013)] (See *Pretrial Procedures*.)

- **For a sample answer to Problem 5–6, go to Appendix C at the end of this text.**

5–7. Motion for Summary Judgment. Rebecca Nichols drove a truck for Tri-National Logistics, Inc. (TNI). On a delivery trip, Nichols's fellow driver, James Paris, made unwelcome sexual advances. Paris continued to make advances during a subsequent mandatory layover. Nichols reported this behavior to their employer. TNI nevertheless left her with Paris in

Pharr, Texas, for another seven days with no alternative form of transportation before sending a driver to pick her up. She filed a suit in a federal district court against TNI, alleging discrimination on the basis of sex in violation of Title VII of the Civil Rights Act. Disputed facts included whether Nichols subjectively felt abused by Paris and whether their employer was aware of his conduct and failed to take appropriate action. Could TNI successfully file a motion for summary judgment at this point? Explain. [*Nichols v. Tri-National Logistics, Inc.*, 809 F.3d 981 (8th Cir. 2016)] (See *Pretrial Procedures*.)

5–8. Service of Process. Bentley Bay Retail, LLC, filed a suit in a Florida state court against Soho Bay Restaurant, LLC, and against its corporate officers, Luiz and Karine Queiroz, in their individual capacities. Bentley Bay claimed that the Queirozes had breached their personal guaranty for Soho Bay's debt to Bentley Bay. The plaintiff filed notices with the court to depose the Queirozes, who resided in Brazil. The Queirozes argued that they could not be deposed in Brazil. The court ordered them to appear in Florida to provide depositions in their *corporate* capacity. Witnesses appearing in court outside the jurisdiction of their residence are immune from service of process while in court. On the Queirozes' appearance in Florida, can they be served with process in their *individual* capacities? Explain. [*Queiroz v. Bentley Bay Retail, LLC*, 43 Fla.L.Weekly D85, 237 So.3d 1108 (3 Dist. 2018)] (See *Pretrial Procedures*.)

5–9. A Question of Ethics—The IDDR Approach and Complaints. *John Verble worked as a financial adviser for Morgan Stanley Smith Barney, LLC. After nearly seven years, Verble was fired. He filed a suit in a federal district court against his ex-employer. In his complaint, Verble alleged that he had learned of illegal activity by Morgan Stanley and its clients. He claimed that he had reported the activity to the Federal Bureau of Investigation, and that he was fired in retaliation. His complaint contained no additional facts.* [Verble v. Morgan Stanley Smith Barney LLC, 676 Fed.Appx. 421 (6th Cir. 2017)] (See Pretrial Procedures.)

(a) To avoid a dismissal of his suit, does Verble have a *legal* obligation to support his claims with more facts? Explain.

(b) Does Verble owe an *ethical* duty to back up his claims with more facts? Use the IDDR approach to express your answer.

Time-Limited Group Assignment

5–10. Court Procedures. Bento Cuisine is a lunch-cart business. It occupies a street corner in Texarkana, a city that straddles the border of Arkansas and Texas. Across the street—and across the state line, which runs down the middle of the street—is Rico's Tacos. The two businesses compete for customers. Recently, Bento has begun to suspect that Rico's is engaging in competitive behavior that is illegal. Bento's manager overheard several of Rico's employees discussing these competitive tactics while on a break at a nearby Starbucks. Bento files a lawsuit against Rico's in a federal court based on diversity jurisdiction. (See *Pretrial Procedures*.)

(a) The first group will discuss whether Rico's could file a motion claiming that the federal court lacks jurisdiction over this dispute.

(b) The second group will assume that the case goes to trial. Bento's manager believes that Bento's has both the law and the facts on its side. Nevertheless, at the end of the trial, the jury decides against Bento, and the judge issues a ruling in favor of Rico's. If Bento is unwilling to accept this result, what are its options?

(c) As discussed in this chapter, hearsay is literally what a witness says he or she heard another person say. A third group will decide whether Bento's manager can testify about what he heard some of Rico's employees say to one another while at a coffee shop. This group will also discuss what makes the admissibility of hearsay evidence potentially unethical.

Joan owns and operates an antique furniture store in Eugene, Oregon. Initially, Joan's customers were from Eugene and nearby towns in Oregon. Today, through her website, she also sells furniture to buyers around the country.

1. **Jurisdiction.** Joan contracts with a furniture manufacturer in Maine to purchase five replicas of an early American dresser from the "federal period" for a price of $1,000 each. The manufacturer promises her that they will be delivered to her store in Oregon by March 1. Joan has already contracted with three customers to sell them dressers, promising delivery close to March 1. The dressers are never delivered, despite the manufacturer's continuing promises that they will be shipped "soon." Where can Joan file a lawsuit against the manufacturer?

2. **Service of Process.** One of Joan's customers, Don, in Kansas, ordered an antique hutch via Joan's website. After Don receives the hutch, he calls Joan to complain that she misrepresented the hutch's quality on her website. Joan contends that she did not make any misrepresentations and that Don has no claim. Don sues Joan in a Kansas state court, alleging that Joan is a liar and that she caused him emotional suffering during their conversations about the hutch. How can Don serve the summons and complaint on Joan to notify her of the lawsuit?

3. **Arbitration.** Rather than litigate, Don and Joan decide to arbitrate their dispute. The arbitrator subsequently determines that Joan misrepresented the quality of the hutch on her website and enters an award of damages in favor of Don. If Joan doesn't agree with the arbitrator's award, can she subsequently challenge it in court?

"Arbitration, No Class Actions"

It is nearly impossible to apply for credit, obtain phone or Internet service, or buy goods online without agreeing to submit any claim arising from the deal to arbitration. This is also true with respect to employment—job applicants are generally informed by a potential employer that "any controversy or claim arising out of or relating to this employment application shall be settled by arbitration."[1]

By including arbitration clauses in consumer and employment contracts, businesses can prevent customers and employees from getting their day in court. Claims removed from consideration by the courts in favor of arbitration have involved theft, fraud, sexual harassment, employment discrimination, and other serious issues.

Class Action

A *class action* is a suit in which a large number of plaintiffs file a complaint as a group. A class action can increase the efficiency of the legal process and lower the costs to the parties. It can be an important method by which plaintiffs with similar claims seek relief. More importantly, a class action may be the best means by which the costs of wrongdoing can be imposed on a wrongdoer.

Best Means to Stop a Bad Practice In some circumstances, a class-action suit may be the only practical method for a group of individuals to stop an allegedly harmful business practice. For example, suppose a business pads all of its customers' bills with an unexpected fee—adding up to millions in profit for the business. An individual customer may find it too costly to bring suit against the business or even to engage in arbitration to contest the charge. But a number of customers together could afford to fight the charge.

Groundless Claims and High Fees The phrase "Arbitration, No Class Actions" comes from the terms of use for Budget Rent a Car System, Inc.[2] Everyone who rents a car from Budget must agree to these terms. Businesses, such as Budget, assert that class-action suits are fomented by lawyers, who make millions of dollars in fees. Businesses claim that they have no choice but to settle such claims, even those that are groundless. Arbitration, they argue, can prevent these consequences.

Arbitration

Arbitration is a method of alternative dispute resolution in which a dispute is submitted to a third party (an arbitrator), who listens to the parties, reviews the evidence, and renders a decision. Arbitration clauses can be mandatory or voluntary. A dispute that is subject to mandatory

---

1. American Arbitration Association, *Drafting Dispute Resolution Clauses: A Practical Guide*, www.adr.org.
2. Budget Rent a Car System, Inc., *Terms of Use*, www.budget.com.

arbitration must be resolved through arbitration. The parties give up their right to sue in court, participate in a class action, or appeal the arbitration decision.

Professional and Unbiased Businesses argue that class-action suits are unnecessary because individuals can more easily resolve their complaints through arbitration. With arbitration, disputes can be resolved quickly without complicated procedures, the limits of judicial rules, or the time constraints of a crowded court's schedule.

Proponents of arbitration also contend that arbitrators can act professionally and without bias. The American Arbitration Association and JAMS, the two largest arbitration firms, claim to ensure a professional and unbiased process. These organizations require an arbitrator to disclose any conflict of interest before taking a case, for instance.

Biased and Unprofessional Opponents of arbitration emphasize that a party's right to appeal an arbitrator's handling of a case and its outcome is limited. Questions about a witness's testimony, a party's handling of the evidence, an arbitrator's potential conflict of interest, and many other issues are not grounds for appeal to a court.

Arbitrators often depend for their business on a company against whom a customer or employee may have a grievance. An arbitrator may handle many cases involving the same company and may therefore consider the company his or her client. For this reason, critics argue that an arbitrator is more likely to rule in favor of the business, regardless of the merits of a claim against it.

What Do the Courts Say?

Most plaintiffs who are blocked from pursuing their claim as a group drop their case. For instance, in one two-year period, judges remanded to arbitration four out of five of the class actions filed. During the same period, only about five hundred consumers went to arbitration over a dispute of $2,500 or less. Among those contesting a credit-card fee or loan fee, two-thirds received no award of money in arbitration.

In other words, individual consumers whose only recourse against a company is arbitration do not normally prevail in their claims. Despite this history, decisions by the United States Supreme Court consistently uphold the use of arbitration clauses in consumer and merchant contracts to prohibit class-action suits.

Class Actions Interfere with Arbitration Vincent and Liza Concepcion, along with other consumers, filed a class action in a California state court against AT&T Mobility, LLC, alleging that the company had promised them a free phone if they agreed to service but actually charged them $30.22 for the phone. AT&T responded that a class-action ban in an arbitration clause in the customers' contracts barred the suit. The court ruled that the ban was unconscionable.

AT&T appealed to the United States Supreme Court, which reasoned that "requiring the availability of class-wide arbitration interferes with fundamental attributes of arbitration." The main purpose of the federal law that applied in this case—the Federal Arbitration Act—"is to ensure the enforcement of arbitration agreements according to their terms." This conclusion relegated *state* law on this issue, including California's ruling, to the sidelines.[3]

Continues

---

3. *AT&T Mobility, LLC v. Concepcion*, 563 U.S. 333, 131 S.Ct. 1740, 179 L.Ed.2d 742 (2011).

Arbitration Clauses Trump Class Actions Meanwhile, Alan Carlson, the owner of the restaurant Italian Colors, pursued a suit against American Express Company over the fee that the company assessed merchants to process American Express credit-card charges. Carlson argued that a class-action ban in an arbitration clause in the company's merchant contract prevented merchants from exercising their *federal* right to fight a monopoly. None of the merchants could afford to fight the charge individually.

On appeal, the Supreme Court ruled in favor of American Express. The Court stated that federal antitrust "laws do not guarantee an affordable procedural path to the vindication of every claim."[4] Under this decision, an arbitration clause can outlaw a class action even if it is the only realistic, practical way to bring a case.

More recently, the U.S. Court of Appeals for the Fifth Circuit concluded that employers who require prospective employees to sign mandatory arbitration agreements do not violate the National Labor Relations Act.[5]

Ethical Connection

Some persons would contend that a business's principal ethical obligation is to make a profit for its owners. Others might propose that a business take a number of stakeholders' perspectives into account when deciding on a course of action. Still others might insist that a business has a responsibility to act chiefly in the best interests of society. And there may be some who would impose a different ethical standard—religious, philosophical, or political.

Whichever standard is applied, a business has an interest in staying in business. Sometimes, a class action may be based on a groundless claim and brought for the sole purpose of generating a fee for the lawyer who brings it. There is no ethical requirement for a business to exhaust its assets to litigate or settle such a case.

Other times, though, a class action may be the best means of curbing a bad business practice. In that circumstance, engaging in harmful conduct and then cutting off an important means of redress for those harmed by the conduct cannot be seen as ethical.

Ethics Question *Is it unethical for a business to include an arbitration clause with a class-action ban in its contracts with customers, employees, and other businesses? Discuss.*

Critical Thinking *Many businesses include opt-out provisions in their arbitration clauses, but few consumers and employees take advantage of them. Why?*

---

4. *American Express Co. v. Italian Colors Restaurant*, 570 U.S. 228, 133 S.Ct. 2304, 186 L.Ed.2d 417 (2013).
5. *Murphy Oil USA, Inc. v. National Labor Relations Board*, 808 F.3d 1013 (5th Cir. 2015).

The Public and International Environment

LEGAL ENVIRONMENT

CROSS · MILLER

Chapter 6

Tort Law

P art of doing business today—and, indeed, part of everyday life—is the risk of being involved in a lawsuit. The list of circumstances in which businesspersons can be sued is long and varied. A customer who is injured by a security guard at a business establishment, for instance, may sue the business owner, claiming that the security guard's conduct was intentionally wrongful. A person who slips and falls at a retail store may sue the company for negligence.

Any time that one party's allegedly wrongful conduct causes injury to another, an action may arise under the law of *torts* (the word *tort* is French for "wrong"). Through tort law, society compensates those who have suffered injuries as a result of the wrongful conduct of others. Many of the lawsuits brought by or against business firms are based on various tort theories.

6–1 The Basis of Tort Law

Two notions serve as the basis of all **torts**: wrongs and compensation. Tort law is designed to compensate those who have suffered a loss or injury due to another person's wrongful act. In a tort action, one person or group brings a lawsuit against another person or group to obtain compensation (monetary damages) or other relief for the harm suffered.

6–1a The Purpose of Tort Law

Generally, the purpose of tort law is to provide remedies for the violation of various *protected interests*. Society recognizes an interest in personal physical safety. Thus, tort law provides remedies for acts that cause physical injury or that interfere with physical security and freedom of movement. Society also recognizes an interest in protecting property, and tort law provides remedies for acts that cause destruction of or damage to property.

6–1b Damages Available in Tort Actions

Plaintiffs seek various remedies, or damages, in tort actions. Note that legal usage distinguishes between the terms *damage* and *damages*. *Damage* refers to harm or injury to persons or property, while **damages** refers to monetary compensation for such harm or injury.

Compensatory Damages A plaintiff is awarded **compensatory damages** to compensate or reimburse the plaintiff for actual losses. Thus, the goal is to make the plaintiff whole and put her or him in the same position that she or he would have been in had the tort not occurred. Compensatory damages awards are often broken down into *special damages* and *general damages*.

Special damages compensate the plaintiff for quantifiable monetary losses, such as medical expenses and lost wages and benefits (now and in the future). Special damages might also be awarded to compensate for extra costs, the loss of irreplaceable items, and the costs of repairing or replacing damaged property.

■ **Case in Point 6.1** Seaway Marine Transport operates the *Enterprise*, a large cargo ship, which has twenty-two hatches for storing coal. When the *Enterprise* positioned itself to receive a load of coal on the shores of Lake Erie, in Ohio, it struck a land-based coal-loading machine operated by Bessemer & Lake Erie Railroad Company. A federal court found Seaway liable and awarded $522,000 in special damages to compensate Bessemer for the cost of repairing the damage to the loading boom.[1] ■

General damages compensate individuals (not companies) for the nonmonetary aspects of the harm suffered, such as pain and suffering. A court might award general damages for physical or emotional pain and suffering, loss of companionship, loss of consortium

---

1. *Bessemer & Lake Erie Railroad Co. v. Seaway Marine Transport*, 596 F.3d 357 (6th Cir. 2010).

(losing the emotional and physical benefits of a spousal relationship), disfigurement, loss of reputation, or loss or impairment of mental or physical capacity.

Punitive Damages Occasionally, the courts also award **punitive damages** in tort cases to punish the wrongdoer and deter others from similar wrongdoing. Punitive damages are appropriate only when the defendant's conduct was particularly egregious (outrageous) or reprehensible (shameful).

Usually, this means that punitive damages are available in *intentional* tort actions and only rarely in negligence lawsuits (negligence actions will be discussed later in this chapter). They may be awarded, however, in suits involving *gross negligence*. Gross negligence can be defined as an intentional failure to perform a manifest duty in reckless disregard of the consequences of such a failure for the life or property of another.

Courts exercise great restraint in granting punitive damages to plaintiffs in tort actions because punitive damages are subject to limitations under the due process clause of the U.S. Constitution. The United States Supreme Court has held that to the extent that an award of punitive damages is grossly excessive, it furthers no legitimate purpose and violates due process requirements.[2] Consequently, an appellate court will sometimes reduce the amount of punitive damages awarded to a plaintiff on the ground that it is excessive.

Legislative Caps on Damages State laws may limit the amount of damages—both punitive and general—that can be awarded to the plaintiff. More than half of the states have placed caps ranging from $250,000 to $750,000 on noneconomic general damages (such as for pain and suffering), especially in medical malpractice suits. More than thirty states have limited punitive damages, with some imposing outright bans.

6–1c Classification of Torts

There are two broad classifications of torts: *intentional torts* and *unintentional torts* (torts involving negligence). The classification of a particular tort depends largely on how the tort occurs (intentionally or negligently) and the surrounding circumstances. Intentional torts result from the intentional violation of person or property (fault plus intent). Negligence results from the breach of a duty to act reasonably (fault without intent).

---

2. *State Farm Mutual Automobile Insurance Co. v. Campbell*, 538 U.S. 408, 123 S.Ct. 1513, 155 L.Ed.2d 585 (2003).

6–1d Defenses

Even if a plaintiff proves all the elements of a tort, the defendant can raise a number of legally recognized *defenses* (reasons why the plaintiff should not obtain damages). A successful defense releases the defendant from partial or full liability for the tortious act.

The defenses available may vary depending on the specific tort involved. A common defense to intentional torts against persons, for instance, is *consent*. When a person consents to the act that damages her or him, there is generally no liability. The most widely used defense in negligence actions is *comparative negligence*.

In addition, most states have a *statute of limitations* that establishes the time limit (often two years from the date of discovering the harm) within which a particular type of lawsuit can be filed. After that time period has run, the plaintiff can no longer file a claim.

6–2 Intentional Torts against Persons

An **intentional tort,** as the term implies, requires intent. The **tortfeasor** (the one committing the tort) must intend to commit an act, the consequences of which interfere with another's personal or business interests in a way not permitted by law. An evil or harmful motive is not required—in fact, the person committing the action may even have a beneficial motive for doing what turns out to be a tortious act.

In tort law, *intent* means only that the person intended the consequences of his or her act or knew with substantial certainty that specific consequences would result from the act. The law generally assumes that individuals intend the *normal* consequences of their actions. Thus, forcefully pushing another—even if done in jest—is an intentional tort (if injury results), because the object of a strong push can ordinarily be expected to fall down.

In addition, intent can be transferred when a defendant intends to harm one individual, but unintentionally harms a second person. This is called **transferred intent.** ■ **Example 6.2** Alex swings a bat intending to hit Blake but misses and hits Carson instead. Carson can sue Alex for the tort of battery (discussed shortly) because Alex's intent to harm Blake can be transferred to Carson. ■

6–2a Assault

An **assault** is any intentional and unexcused threat of immediate harmful or offensive contact—words or acts that create a reasonably believable threat. An assault can occur even if there is no actual contact with the plaintiff, provided that the defendant's conduct creates a reasonable apprehension of imminent harm in the plaintiff. Tort law aims to protect individuals from having to expect harmful or offensive contact.

6–2b Battery

If the act that created the apprehension is *completed* and results in harm to the plaintiff, it is a **battery**—an unexcused and harmful or offensive physical contact *intentionally* performed. ■ **Example 6.3** Ivan threatens Jean with a gun and then shoots her. The pointing of the gun at Jean is an assault. The firing of the gun (if the bullet hits Jean) is a battery. ■

The contact can be harmful, or it can be merely offensive (such as an unwelcome kiss). Physical injury need not occur. The contact can involve any part of the body or anything attached to it—for instance, a hat, a purse, or a jacket. The contact can be made by the defendant or by some force set in motion by the defendant, such as a rock thrown by the defendant. Whether the contact is offensive is determined by the *reasonable person standard*.[3]

If the plaintiff shows that there was contact, and the jury (or judge, if there is no jury) agrees that the contact was offensive, then the plaintiff has a right to compensation. A plaintiff may be compensated for the emotional harm or loss of reputation resulting from a battery, as well as for physical harm. A defendant may assert self-defense or defense of others in an attempt to justify his or her conduct.

6–2c False Imprisonment

False imprisonment is the intentional confinement or restraint of another person's activities without justification. False imprisonment interferes with the freedom to move without restraint. The confinement can be accomplished through the use of physical barriers, physical restraint, or threats of physical force. Moral pressure does not constitute false imprisonment. It is essential that the person being restrained does not wish to be restrained. (The plaintiff's consent to the restraint bars any liability.)

Businesspersons often face suits for false imprisonment after they have attempted to confine a suspected shoplifter for questioning. Under the "privilege to detain" granted to merchants in most states, a merchant can use *reasonable force* to detain or delay persons suspected of shoplifting

and hold them for the police. Although laws pertaining to this privilege vary from state to state, generally any detention must be conducted in a *reasonable* manner and for only a *reasonable* length of time. Undue force or unreasonable detention can lead to liability for the business.

■ **Case in Point 6.4** Justin Mills was playing blackjack at the Maryland Live! Casino when two casino employees approached him, grabbed his arm, and led him into a back hallway. The employees accused Mills of counting cards (which is not illegal in Maryland) and demanded his identification. They detained Mills and told him that they would not release him unless he produced his ID so that the casino could ban him from the premises.

Mills gave the employees his passport and was eventually allowed to leave, but he secretly recorded the interaction using the smartphone in his pocket. Mills later filed a lawsuit alleging, in part, false imprisonment. A federal district court granted Mills a summary judgment on the false imprisonment claim because the casino personnel had no legal justification for detaining him.[4] ■ Cities and counties may also face lawsuits for false imprisonment if they detain individuals without reason.

6–2d Intentional Infliction of Emotional Distress

The tort of *intentional infliction of emotional distress* involves an intentional act that amounts to extreme and outrageous conduct resulting in severe emotional distress to another. To be **actionable** (capable of serving as the ground for a lawsuit), the act must be extreme and outrageous to the point that it exceeds the bounds of decency accepted by society.

Outrageous Conduct Courts in most jurisdictions are wary of emotional distress claims and confine them to situations involving truly outrageous behavior. Generally, repeated annoyances (such as those experienced by a person who is being stalked), coupled with threats, are enough. Acts that cause indignity or annoyance alone usually are not sufficient.

■ **Example 6.5** A father attacks a man who has had consensual sexual relations with the father's nineteen-year-old daughter. The father handcuffs the man to a steel pole and threatens to kill him unless he leaves town immediately. The father's conduct may be sufficiently extreme and outrageous to be actionable as an intentional infliction of emotional distress. ■

---

3. The *reasonable person standard* is an "objective" test of how a reasonable person would have acted under the same circumstances. See "The Duty of Care and Its Breach" later in this chapter.

4. *Mills v. PPE Casino Resorts Maryland, LLC*, 2017 WL 2930460 (D.Md. 2017).

Limited by the First Amendment When the outrageous conduct consists of speech about a public figure, the First Amendment's guarantee of freedom of speech also limits emotional distress claims.

■ **Case in Point 6.6** *Hustler* magazine once printed a false advertisement that showed a picture of the late Reverend Jerry Falwell and described him as having lost his virginity to his mother in an outhouse while he was drunk. Falwell sued the magazine for intentional infliction of emotional distress and won, but the United States Supreme Court overturned the decision. The Court held that parodies of public figures are protected under the First Amendment from intentional infliction of emotional distress claims. (The Court uses the same standards that apply to public figures in defamation lawsuits, discussed next.)[5] ■

6–2e Defamation

The freedom of speech guaranteed by the First Amendment is not absolute. The courts are required to balance

5. *Hustler Magazine, Inc. v. Falwell*, 485 U.S. 46, 108 S.Ct. 876, 99 L.Ed.2d 41 (1988). For another example of how the courts protect parody, see *Busch v. Viacom International, Inc.*, 477 F.Supp.2d 764 (N.D.Tex. 2007), involving a false endorsement of televangelist Pat Robertson's diet shake.

the vital guarantee of free speech against other pervasive and strong social interests, including society's interest in preventing and redressing attacks on reputation.

Defamation of character involves wrongfully hurting a person's good reputation. The law imposes a general duty on all persons to refrain from making false, defamatory *statements of fact* about others. Breaching this duty in writing or other permanent form (such as a digital recording) involves the tort of **libel.** Breaching this duty orally involves the tort of **slander.** The tort of defamation also arises when a false statement of fact is made about a person's product, business, or legal ownership rights to property.

Establishing defamation involves proving the following elements:

1. The defendant made a false statement of fact.
2. The statement was understood as being about the plaintiff and tended to harm the plaintiff's reputation.
3. The statement was published to at least one person other than the plaintiff.
4. If the plaintiff is a public figure, she or he must also prove *actual malice*, discussed later in the chapter.

The following case involved the application of free speech guarantees to online reviews of professional services.

Blake v. Giustibelli

District Court of Appeal of Florida, Fourth District, 41 Fla.L.Weekly D122, 182 So.3d 881 (2016).

In the Language of the Court
CIKLIN, C.J. [Chief Judge]

* * * *

[Ann-Marie] Giustibelli represented Copia Blake in a dissolution of marriage proceeding brought against Peter Birzon. After a breakdown in the attorney-client relationship between Giustibelli and her client[,] Blake, and oddly, Birzon as well, took to the Internet to post defamatory reviews of Giustibelli. In response, Giustibelli brought suit [in a Florida state court against Blake and Birzon], pleading a count for libel.

Blake's and Birzon's posted Internet reviews contained the following statements:

This lawyer represented me in my divorce. She was combative and

explosive and took my divorce to a level of anger which caused major suffering of my minor children. She insisted I was an emotionally abused wife who couldn't make rational decisions which caused my case to drag on in the system for a year and a half so her FEES would continue to multiply!! She misrepresented her fees with regards to the contract I initially signed. The contract she submitted to the courts for her fees were 4 times her original quote and pages of the original had been exchanged to support her claims, only the signature page was the same. Shame on me that I did not have an original copy, but like an idiot * * * I trusted my lawyer. Don't mistake sincerity for honesty because I assure you, that in this attorney's case, they are NOT the same thing. She absolutely perpetuates

the horrible image of attorneys who are only out for the money and themselves. Although I know this isn't the case and there are some very good honest lawyers out there, Mrs. Giustibelli is simply not one of the "good ones." Horrible horrible experience. Use anyone else, it would have to be a better result.

* * * *

No integrity. Will say one thing and do another. Her fees outweigh the truth. Altered her charges to 4 times the original quote with no explanation. Do not use her. Don't mistake sincerity for honesty. In her case, they're not at all the same. Will literally lie to your face if it means more money for her. Get someone else. * * * Anyone else would do a superior effort for you.

Case 6.1 Continues

Case 6.1 Continued

* * * *

I accepted an initial VERY fair offer from my ex. Mrs. Giustibelli convinced me to "crush" him and that I could have permanent etc. Spent over a year (and 4 times her original estimate) to arrive at the same place we started at. Caused unnecessary chaos and fear with my kids, convinced me that my ex cheated (which he didn't), that he was hiding money (which he wasn't), and was mad at ME when I realized her fee circus had gone on long enough and finally said "stop." Altered her fee structures, actually replaced original documents with others to support her charges and generally gave the kind of poor service you only hear about. I'm not a disgruntled ex-wife. I'm just the foolish person who believes that a person's word should be

backed by integrity. Not even remotely true in this case. I've had 2 prior attorneys and never ever have I seen ego and monies be so blatantly out of control.

Both Blake and Birzon admitted to posting the reviews on various Internet sites. The evidence showed that Blake had agreed to pay her attorney the amount reflected on the written retainer agreement—$300 an hour. Blake and Birzon both admitted at trial that Giustibelli had not charged Blake four times more than what was quoted in the agreement. The court entered judgment in favor of Giustibelli and awarded punitive damages of $350,000.

On appeal, Blake and Birzon argue that their Internet reviews constituted statements of opinion and thus were

protected by the First Amendment and not actionable as defamation. We disagree. *An action for libel will lie for a false and unprivileged publication by letter, or otherwise, which exposes a person to distrust, hatred, contempt, ridicule or obloquy [censure or disgrace] or which causes such person to be avoided, or which has a tendency to injure such person in their office, occupation, business or employment.* [Emphasis added.]

Here, all the reviews contained allegations that Giustibelli lied to Blake regarding the attorney's fee. Two of the reviews contained the allegation that Giustibelli falsified a contract. These are factual allegations, and the evidence showed they were false.

* * * *

Affirmed.

Legal Reasoning Questions

1. What is the standard for the protection of free speech guaranteed by the First Amendment?

2. How did this standard apply to the statements posted online by Blake and Birzon?

3. The First Amendment normally protects statements of opinion, and this can be an effective defense against a charge of defamation. Does it seem reasonable to disregard this defense if *any* assertion of fact within a statement of opinion is false? Discuss.

Statement-of-Fact Requirement Often at issue in defamation lawsuits (including online defamation) is whether the defendant made a statement of fact or a *statement of opinion*. Statements of opinion normally are not actionable, because they are protected under the First Amendment.

In other words, making a negative statement about another person is not defamation unless the statement is false and represents something as a fact rather than a personal opinion. ■ **Example 6.7** The statement "Lane cheats on his taxes," if false, can lead to liability for defamation. The statement "Lane is a jerk" cannot constitute defamation because it is clearly an opinion. ■

The Publication Requirement The basis of the tort of defamation is the publication of a statement or statements that hold an individual up to contempt, ridicule, or hatred. *Publication* here means that the defamatory

statements are communicated (either intentionally or accidentally) to persons other than the defamed party.

The courts have generally held that even dictating a letter to a secretary constitutes publication (although the publication may be privileged, a concept that will be explained shortly). Moreover, if a third party merely overhears defamatory statements by chance, the courts usually hold that this also constitutes publication. Defamatory statements made via the Internet are actionable as well. Note also that any individual who repeats or republishes defamatory statements normally is liable even if that person reveals the source of the statements.

■ **Case in Point 6.8** Eddy Ramirez, a meat cutter at Costco Wholesale Corporation, was involved in a workplace incident with a co-worker, and Costco gave him a notice of suspension. After an investigation in which co-workers were interviewed, Costco fired Ramirez. Ramirez sued, claiming that the suspension notice was defamatory. The court ruled in Costco's favor. Ramirez could not establish defamation, because he had not shown that the suspension notice was published to any third parties. Costco did nothing beyond what was necessary to investigate the events that led to Ramirez's termination.[6] ■

Damages for Libel Once a defendant's liability for libel is established, general damages are presumed as a matter of law. General damages are designed to compensate the plaintiff for nonspecific harms such as disgrace or dishonor in the eyes of the community, humiliation, injured reputation, and emotional distress—harms that are difficult to measure. In other words, to recover damages, the plaintiff need not prove that he or she was actually harmed in any specific way as a result of the libelous statement.

Damages for Slander In contrast to cases alleging libel, in a case alleging slander, the plaintiff must prove *special damages* to establish the defendant's liability. The plaintiff must show that the slanderous statement caused her or him to suffer actual economic or monetary losses.

Unless this initial hurdle of proving special damages is overcome, a plaintiff alleging slander normally cannot go forward with the suit and recover any damages. This requirement is imposed in slander cases because oral statements have a temporary quality. In contrast, a libelous (written) statement has the quality of permanence and can be circulated widely, especially through tweets and blogs. Also, libel usually results from some degree of deliberation by the author.

Slander *Per Se* Exceptions to the burden of proving special damages in cases alleging slander are made for certain types of slanderous statements. If a false statement constitutes "slander *per se*," it is actionable with no proof of special damages required. In most states, the following four types of declarations are considered to be slander *per se:*

1. A statement that another has a "loathsome" disease (such as a sexually transmitted disease).
2. A statement that another has committed improprieties while engaging in a profession or trade.
3. A statement that another has committed or has been imprisoned for a serious crime.

4. A statement that a person is unchaste or has engaged in serious sexual misconduct. (This usually applies only to unmarried persons and sometimes only to women.)

Defenses to Defamation Truth is normally an absolute defense against a defamation charge. In other words, if a defendant in a defamation case can prove that the allegedly defamatory statements of fact were true, normally no tort has been committed.

■ **Case in Point 6.9** David McKee, a neurologist, went to examine a patient who had been transferred from the intensive care unit (ICU) to a private room. In the room were family members of the patient, including his son. The patient's son later made the following post on a "rate your doctor" website: "[Dr. McKee] seemed upset that my father had been moved [into a private room]. Never having met my father or his family, Dr. McKee said 'When you weren't in ICU, I had to spend time finding out if you transferred or died.' When we gaped at him, he said 'Well, 44 percent of hemorrhagic strokes die within 30 days. I guess this is the better option.'"

McKee filed suit for defamation but lost. The court found that all the statements made by the son were essentially true, and truth is a complete defense to a defamation action.[7] ■ In other words, true statements are not actionable no matter how disparaging. Even the presence of minor inaccuracies of expression or detail does not render basically true statements false.

Other defenses to defamation may exist if the speech is privileged or if it concerns a public figure. We discuss these defenses next. Note that the majority of defamation actions are filed in state courts, and state laws differ somewhat in the defenses they allow.

Privileged Communications. In some circumstances, a person will not be liable for defamatory statements because she or he enjoys a **privilege,** or immunity. Privileged communications are of two types: absolute and qualified.[8] Only in judicial proceedings and certain government proceedings is an *absolute privilege* granted. Thus, statements made by attorneys and judges in the courtroom during a trial are absolutely privileged, as are statements made by government officials during legislative debate.

---

6. *Ramirez v. Costco Wholesale Corp.*, 2014 WL 2696737 (Conn.Super.Ct. 2014).

7. *McKee v. Laurion*, 825 N.W.2d 725 (Minn. 2013).
8. Note that the term *privileged communication* in this context is not the same as privileged communication between a professional, such as an attorney, and his or her client.

In other situations, a person will not be liable for defamatory statements because he or she has a *qualified,* or *conditional, privilege.* An employer's statements in written evaluations of employees, for instance, are protected by a qualified privilege. Generally, if the statements are made in good faith and the publication is limited to those who have a legitimate interest in the communication, the statements fall within the area of qualified privilege.

■ **Example 6.10** Jorge has worked at Google for five years and is being considered for a management position. His supervisor, Lydia, writes a memo about Jorge's performance to those evaluating him for the position. The memo contains certain negative statements, which Lydia honestly believes are true. If Lydia limits the disclosure of the memo to company representatives, her statements will likely be protected by a qualified privilege. ■

Public Figures. Politicians, entertainers, professional athletes, and others in the public eye are considered **public figures.** Public figures are regarded as "fair game." False and defamatory statements about public figures that are published in the media will not constitute defamation unless the statements are made with **actual malice.**[9] To be made with actual malice, a statement must be made *with either knowledge of its falsity or a reckless disregard of the truth.*

Statements made about public figures, especially when they are communicated via a public medium, usually relate to matters of general interest. They are made about people who substantially affect all of us. Furthermore, public figures generally have some access to a public medium for answering belittling falsehoods about themselves. For these reasons, public figures have a greater burden of proof in defamation cases—to show actual malice—than do private individuals.

■ **Case in Point 6.11** *In Touch Weekly* magazine published a story about a former call girl who claimed to have slept with legendary soccer player David Beckham more than once. Beckham sued *In Touch* for libel, seeking $25 million in damages. He said that he had never met the woman, had not cheated on his wife with her, and had not paid her for sex. After months of litigation, a federal district court dismissed the case because Beckham could not show that the magazine had acted with actual malice. Whether or not the statements in the article were accurate, there was no evidence that the defendants had made the statements with knowledge of their falsity or reckless disregard for the truth.[10] ■

---

9. See the landmark case *New York Times Co. v. Sullivan,* 376 U.S. 254, 84 S.Ct. 710, 11 L.Ed.2d 686 (1964).

10. *Beckham v. Bauer Publishing Co., L.P.,* 2011 WL 977570 (C.D.Cal. 2011).

6–2f Invasion of Privacy

A person has a right to solitude and freedom from prying public eyes—in other words, to privacy. The courts have held that certain amendments to the U.S. Constitution imply a right to privacy. Some state constitutions explicitly provide for privacy rights, as do a number of federal and state statutes.

Tort law also safeguards these rights through the tort of *invasion of privacy.* Generally, to sue successfully for an invasion of privacy, a person must have a reasonable expectation of privacy, and the invasion must be highly offensive. (See this chapter's *Digital Update* feature for a discussion of how invasion of privacy claims can arise when someone posts pictures or videos taken with digital devices.)

Invasion of Privacy under the Common Law
The following four acts qualify as invasions of privacy under the common law:

1. *Intrusion into an individual's affairs or seclusion.* Invading someone's home or searching someone's briefcase or laptop without authorization is an invasion of privacy. This tort has been held to extend to eavesdropping by wiretap, unauthorized scanning of a bank account, compulsory blood testing, and window peeping. ■ **Example 6.12** A female sports reporter for ESPN is digitally videoed through the peephole in the door of her hotel room while naked. She probably will win a lawsuit against the man who took the video and posted it on the Internet. ■

2. *False light.* Publication of information that places a person in a false light is also an invasion of privacy. For instance, writing a story that attributes to a person ideas and opinions not held by that person is an invasion of privacy. (Publishing such a story could involve the tort of defamation as well.) ■ **Example 6.13** An Iowa newspaper prints an article saying that nineteen-year-old Yassine Alam is part of the terrorist organization Islamic State of Iraq and Syria (ISIS). Next to the article is a photo of Yassine's brother, Salaheddin. Salaheddin can sue the paper for putting him in a false light by using his photo. If the report is not true, and Yassine is not involved with ISIS, Yassine can sue the paper for defamation. ■

3. *Public disclosure of private facts.* This type of invasion of privacy occurs when a person publicly discloses private facts about an individual that an ordinary person would find objectionable or embarrassing. A newspaper account of a private citizen's sex life or financial affairs could be an actionable invasion of privacy.

Digital Update	Revenge Porn and Invasion of Privacy

Digital Update — Revenge Porn and Invasion of Privacy

Nearly every digital device today takes photos and videos at virtually no cost. Software allows the recording of conversations via Skype. Many couples immortalize their "private moments" using such digital devices. One partner may take a racy selfie and send it as an attachment to a text message or via Instagram to the other partner, for instance.

Occasionally, after a relationship ends, one partner seeks digital revenge. The result, called *revenge porn*, involves the online distribution of sexually explicit images of a nonconsenting individual with the intent to humiliate that person.

State Statutes

Thirty-five states have enacted statutes that make revenge porn a crime. But each state's law is different. (In some states, it is a misdemeanor with less serious consequences, and in other states, it is a felony with more serious penalties.) In addition, most of these criminal statutes do not provide victims with a right to obtain damages. Therefore, victims have sued in civil courts on the basis of (1) invasion of privacy, (2) public disclosure of private facts, and (3) intentional infliction of emotional distress.

A Case Example

Nadia Hussain had dated Akhil Patel on and off for seven years since high school. After they broke up, Patel hounded her with offensive and threatening phone calls, texts, and e-mails—often twenty to thirty per day. He did this for several years. He even came to her workplace a few times. Hussain filed police reports and changed her phone number multiple times, but the harassment continued. Patel also hacked or attempted to hack into her accounts.

Eventually, Patel posted secretly recorded sexual videos of Hussain on the Internet. (He had recorded, without her consent, a Skype conversation they once had in which Hussain had undressed and

masturbated.) Hussain sued Patel claiming invasion of privacy, public disclosure of private facts, and intentional infliction of emotional distress. A jury found in her favor and awarded $500,000 in damages for mental anguish and damage to her reputation. An appellate court affirmed but reduced the damages to $345,000 (because the intentional infliction of emotional distress claim was not supported by the evidence).[a]

It Is More Than Just Pictures and Videos

Perhaps the worst form of revenge porn occurs when the perpetrator provides detailed information about the victim. The information posted online may include the victim's name, Facebook page, address, and phone number, as well as the victim's photos and videos. Many of the hosting websites have been shut down, but others are still active.

Perpetrators also use social media sites, such as Facebook, Twitter, Instagram, and Reddit, to disseminate revenge porn. Even though Facebook and other companies have explicit policies against pornography and will take content down once it is reported, users often hide it within restricted or closed groups. For example, the Senate Armed Services Committee held hearings on a private Facebook group called Marines United. Marines United circulated nude photos of women (including fellow marines, ex-girlfriends, and strangers) without their consent. The group was closed down after one member reported it to the Marine Corps. At least one member was court-martialed.

Critical Thinking *Why might the appellate court have decided that the evidence did not support Nadia Hussain's intentional infliction of emotional distress claim?*

---

a. *Patel v. Hussain*, 485 S.W.3d 153 (Tex.App.—Houston 2016); see also *Doe v. Doe*, 2017 WL 3025885 (S.D.N.Y. 2017).

This is so even if the information revealed is true, because it should not be a matter of public concern.

4. *Appropriation of identity.* Using a person's name, picture, likeness, or other identifiable characteristic for commercial purposes without permission is also an invasion of privacy. An individual's right to privacy normally includes the right to the exclusive use of

her or his identity. ■ **Example 6.14** An advertising agency asks a singer with a distinctive voice and stage presence to take part in a marketing campaign for a new automobile. The singer rejects the offer. If the agency then uses someone who imitates the singer's voice and dance moves in the ad, it will be actionable as an appropriation of identity. ■

Appropriation Statutes Most states today have codified the common law tort of appropriation of identity in statutes that establish the distinct tort of appropriation, or right of publicity. States differ as to the degree of likeness that is required to impose liability for appropriation, however. Some courts have held that even when an animated character in a video or a video game is made to look like an actual person, there are not enough similarities to constitute appropriation.

■ **Case in Point 6.15** Robert Burck is a street entertainer in New York City who has become famous as "The Naked Cowboy." Burck performs wearing only a white cowboy hat, white cowboy boots, and white underwear. He carries a guitar strategically placed to give the illusion of nudity. Burck sued Mars, Inc., the maker of M&Ms candy, over a video it showed on billboards in Times Square that depicted a blue M&M dressed exactly like The Naked Cowboy. The court, however, held that the use of Burck's signature costume did not amount to appropriation.[11] ■

6–2g Fraudulent Misrepresentation

A misrepresentation leads another to believe in a condition that is different from the condition that actually exists. Although persons sometimes make misrepresentations accidentally because they are unaware of the existing facts, the tort of **fraudulent misrepresentation (fraud)**, involves *intentional* deceit for personal gain. The tort includes several elements:

1. A misrepresentation of material facts or conditions with knowledge that they are false or with reckless disregard for the truth.
2. An intent to induce another party to rely on the misrepresentation.
3. A justifiable reliance on the misrepresentation by the deceived party.
4. Damages suffered as a result of that reliance.
5. A causal connection between the misrepresentation and the injury suffered.

For fraud to occur, more than mere **puffery,** or *seller's talk*, must be involved. Fraud exists only when a person represents as a fact something he or she knows is untrue. For instance, it is fraud to claim that the roof of a building does not leak when one knows that it does. Facts are objectively ascertainable, whereas seller's talk (such as "I am the best accountant in town") is not, because the use of the word *best* is subjective.

■ **Case in Point 6.16** Joseph Guido bought nine rental houses in Stillwater, New York. The houses shared a waste disposal system that was not functioning. Guido hired someone to design and install a new system. When town officials later discovered sewage on the property, Guido had the system partially replaced. He then represented to prospective buyers of the property, including Danny Revell, that the "septic system [was] totally new—each field totally replaced." In response to a questionnaire from the buyers' bank, Guido denied any knowledge of environmental problems.

A month after the sale of the houses, the septic system failed and required substantial repairs. The buyers sued Guido for fraud. A jury found in favor of the plaintiffs and awarded damages. A state intermediate appellate court affirmed the judgment on appeal. Guido knew that the septic system was not totally new and that sewage had been released on the property (an environmental problem). He had misrepresented these facts to the buyers. The buyers' reliance on Guido's statements was justifiable because a visual inspection of the property did not reveal any problems.[12] ■

Statement of Fact versus Opinion Normally, the tort of fraudulent misrepresentation occurs only when there is reliance on a *statement of fact*. Sometimes, however, reliance on a *statement of opinion* may involve the tort of fraudulent misrepresentation if the individual making the statement of opinion has superior knowledge of the subject matter. For instance, when a lawyer makes a statement of opinion about the law in a state in which the lawyer is licensed to practice, a court might treat it as a statement of fact.

Negligent Misrepresentation Sometimes, a tort action can arise from misrepresentations that are made negligently rather than intentionally. The key difference between intentional and negligent misrepresentation is whether the person making the misrepresentation had actual knowledge of its falsity. Negligent misrepresentation requires only that the person making the statement or omission did not have a reasonable basis for believing its truthfulness.

Liability for negligent misrepresentation usually arises when the defendant who made the misrepresentation owed a duty of care to the plaintiff to supply correct information. (We discuss the duty of care in more detail later in the chapter.) Statements or omissions made by attorneys and accountants to their clients, for instance, can lead to liability for negligent misrepresentation.

---

11. *Burck v. Mars, Inc.*, 571 F.Supp.2d 446 (S.D.N.Y. 2008).

12. *Revell v. Guido*, 124 A.D.3d 1006, 2 N.Y.S.3d 252 (3 Dept. 2015).

6–2h Abusive or Frivolous Litigation

Tort law recognizes that people have a right not to be sued without a legally just and proper reason, and therefore it protects individuals from the misuse of litigation. Torts related to abusive litigation include malicious prosecution and abuse of process. If a party initiates a lawsuit out of malice and without a legitimate legal reason, and ends up losing the suit, that party can be sued for *malicious prosecution. Abuse of process* can apply to any person using a legal process against another in an improper manner or to accomplish a purpose for which the process was not designed.

The key difference between the torts of abuse of process and malicious prosecution is the level of proof. Unlike malicious prosecution, abuse of process is not limited to prior litigation and does not require the plaintiff to prove malice. It can be based on the wrongful use of subpoenas, court orders to attach or seize real property, or other types of formal legal process.

Concept Summary 6.1 reviews intentional torts against persons.

6–2i Business Torts

The torts known as *business torts* generally involve wrongful interference with another's business rights. Public policy favors free competition, and these torts protect against tortious interference with legitimate business. Business torts involving wrongful interference generally fall into two categories: interference with a contractual relationship and interference with a business relationship.

Wrongful Interference with a Contractual Relationship Three elements are necessary for wrongful interference with a contractual relationship to occur:

1. A valid, enforceable contract must exist between two parties.
2. A third party must know that this contract exists.
3. This third party must *intentionally induce* a party to the contract to breach the contract.

■ **Case in Point 6.17** A landmark case in this area involved an opera singer, Joanna Wagner, who was under contract to sing for a man named Lumley for a specified

Concept Summary 6.1

Intentional Torts against Persons

Assault and Battery	Any unexcused and intentional act that causes another person to be apprehensive of immediate harm is an assault. An assault resulting in physical contact is a battery.
False Imprisonment	An intentional confinement or restraint of another person's movement without justification.
Intentional Infliction of Emotional Distress	An intentional act that amounts to extreme and outrageous conduct resulting in severe emotional distress to another.
Defamation (Libel or Slander)	A false statement of fact, not made under privilege, that is communicated to a third person and that causes damage to a person's reputation. For public figures, the plaintiff must also prove that the statement was made with actual malice.
Invasion of Privacy	Publishing or otherwise making known or using information relating to a person's private life and affairs, with which the public has no legitimate concern, without that person's permission or approval.
Fraudulent Misrepresentation (Fraud)	A false representation made by one party, through misstatement of facts or through conduct, with the intention of deceiving another and on which the other reasonably relies to his or her detriment.
Abusive or Frivolous Litigation	The filing of a lawsuit without legitimate grounds and with malice. Alternatively, the use of a legal process in an improper manner.

period of years. A man named Gye, who knew of this contract, nonetheless "enticed" Wagner to refuse to carry out the agreement, and Wagner began to sing for Gye. Gye's action constituted a tort because it interfered with the contractual relationship between Wagner and Lumley. (Wagner's refusal to carry out the agreement also entitled Lumley to sue Wagner for breach of contract.)[13] ■

The body of tort law relating to wrongful interference with a contractual relationship has increased greatly in recent years. In principle, any lawful contract can be the basis for an action of this type. The contract could be between a firm and its employees or a firm and its customers. Sometimes, a competitor of a firm lures away one of the firm's key employees. In this situation, the original employer can recover damages from the competitor only if it can be shown that the competitor knew of the contract's existence and intentionally induced the breach.

Wrongful Interference with a Business Relationship Businesspersons devise countless schemes to attract customers. They are prohibited, however, from unreasonably interfering with another's business in their attempts to gain a greater share of the market.

There is a difference between *competitive practices* and *predatory behavior*—actions undertaken with the intention of unlawfully driving competitors completely out of the market. Attempting to attract customers in general is a legitimate business practice, whereas specifically targeting the customers of a competitor is more likely to be predatory. A plaintiff claiming predatory behavior must show that the defendant used predatory methods to intentionally harm an established business relationship or gain a prospective economic advantage.

■ **Example 6.18** A shopping mall contains two athletic shoe stores: Joe's and Ultimate Sport. Joe's cannot station an employee at the entrance of Ultimate Sport to divert customers to Joe's by telling them that Joe's will beat Ultimate Sport's prices. This type of activity constitutes the tort of wrongful interference with a business relationship, which is commonly considered to be an unfair trade practice. If this activity were permitted, Joe's would reap the benefits of Ultimate Sport's advertising. ■

Defenses to Wrongful Interference A person will not be liable for the tort of wrongful interference with a contractual or business relationship if it can be shown that the interference was justified or permissible. Bona fide competitive behavior—such as marketing and advertising strategies—is a permissible interference even if it results in the breaking of a contract.

---

13. *Lumley v. Gye*, 118 Eng.Rep. 749 (1853).

■ **Example 6.19** Taylor Meats advertises so effectively that it induces Sam's Restaurant to break its contract with Burke's Meat Company. In that situation, Burke's Meat Company will be unable to recover against Taylor Meats on a wrongful interference theory. The public policy that favors free competition through advertising outweighs any possible instability that such competitive activity might cause in contractual relations. ■

6–3 Intentional Torts against Property

Intentional torts against property include trespass to land, trespass to personal property, conversion, and disparagement of property. These torts are wrongful actions that interfere with individuals' legally recognized rights with regard to their property.

The law distinguishes real property from personal property. *Real property* is land and things permanently attached to the land, such as a house. *Personal property* consists of all other items, including cash and securities (such as stocks and bonds).

6–3a Trespass to Land

A **trespass to land** occurs when a person, without permission, does any of the following:

1. Enters onto, above, or below the surface of land that is owned by another.
2. Causes anything to enter onto land owned by another.
3. Remains on land owned by another or permits anything to remain on it.

Actual harm to the land is not an essential element of this tort, because the tort is designed to protect the right of an owner to exclusive possession.

Common types of trespass to land include walking or driving on another's land, shooting a gun over another's land, and throwing rocks at a building that belongs to someone else. Another common form of trespass involves constructing a building so that part of it extends onto an adjoining landowner's property.

Establishing Trespass Before a person can be a trespasser, the real property owner (or another person in actual and exclusive possession of the property, such as a renter) must establish that person as a trespasser. For instance, "posted" trespass signs expressly establish as a trespasser a person who ignores these signs and enters onto the property. Any person who enters onto another's property to commit an illegal act (such as a thief entering a lumberyard at night to steal lumber) is impliedly a trespasser, with or without posted signs.

Liability for Harm At common law, a trespasser is liable for any damage caused to the property and generally cannot hold the owner liable for injuries that the trespasser sustains on the premises. This common law rule is being modified in many jurisdictions, however, in favor of a *reasonable duty of care* rule that varies depending on the status of the parties.

For instance, a landowner may have a duty to post a notice that guard dogs patrol the property. Also, if young children are attracted to the property by some object, such a swimming pool or a sand pile, and are injured, the landowner may be held liable (under the *attractive nuisance doctrine*). Still, an owner can normally use reasonable force to remove a trespasser from the premises or detain the trespasser for a reasonable time without liability for damages.

Defenses against Trespass to Land One defense to a claim of trespass is to show that the trespass was warranted, such as when a trespasser enters a building to assist someone in danger. Another defense exists when the trespasser can show that she or he had a *license* to come onto the land.

A **licensee** is one who is invited (or allowed to enter) onto the property of another for the licensee's benefit. A person who enters another's property to read an electric meter, for instance, is a licensee. Another type of licensee is someone who is camping on another person's land with the owner's permission but without paying for the privilege.

Note that licenses to enter onto another's property are *revocable* by the property owner. If a property owner asks a meter reader to leave and she or he refuses to do so, the meter reader at that point becomes a trespasser.

6–3b Trespass to Personal Property

Whenever any individual wrongfully takes or harms the personal property of another or otherwise interferes with the lawful owner's possession and enjoyment of personal property, **trespass to personal property** occurs. This tort may also be called *trespass to chattels* or *trespass to personalty*.[14] In this context, harm means not only destruction of the property, but also anything that diminishes its value, condition, or quality.

Trespass to personal property involves intentional meddling with a possessory interest (one arising from possession), including barring an owner's access to personal property. ■ **Example 6.20** Kelly takes Ryan's business law book as a practical joke and hides it so that Ryan is unable to find it for several days before the final examination. Here, Kelly has engaged in a trespass to personal property (and also *conversion*, the tort discussed next). ■

If it can be shown that trespass to personal property was warranted, then a complete defense exists. Most states, for instance, allow automobile repair shops to hold a customer's car (under what is called an *artisan's lien*) when the customer refuses to pay for repairs already completed.

6–3c Conversion

Any act that deprives an owner of personal property or of the use of that property without the owner's permission and without just cause can constitute **conversion.** Even the taking of electronic records and data may form the basis of a conversion claim. Often, when conversion occurs, a trespass to personal property also occurs. The original taking of the personal property from the owner was a trespass. Wrongfully retaining the property is conversion.

Failure to Return Goods Conversion is the civil side of crimes related to theft, but it is not limited to theft. Even when the rightful owner consented to the initial taking of the property, so no theft or trespass occurred, a failure to return the property may still be conversion. ■ **Example 6.21** Chen borrows Mark's iPad mini to use while traveling home from school for the holidays. When Chen returns to school, Mark asks for his iPad back, but Chen says that he gave it to his little brother for Christmas. In this situation, Mark can sue Chen for conversion, and Chen will have to either return the iPad or pay damages equal to its replacement value. ■

Intention Conversion can occur even when a person mistakenly believed that she or he was entitled to the goods. In other words, good intentions are not a defense against conversion. Someone who buys stolen goods, for instance, may be sued for conversion even if he or she did not know the goods were stolen. If the true owner of the goods sues the buyer, the buyer must either return the property to the owner or pay the owner the full value of the property.

---

14. Pronounced *per-sun-ul-tee.*

Conversion can also occur from an employee's unauthorized use of a credit card. ■ **Case in Point 6.22** Nicholas Mora worked for Welco Electronics, Inc., but had also established his own company, AQM Supplies. Mora used Welco's credit card without permission and deposited more than $375,000 into AQM's account, which he then transferred to his personal account. Welco sued. A California court held that Mora was liable for conversion. The court reasoned that when Mora misappropriated Welco's credit card and used it, he took part of Welco's credit balance with the credit-card company.[15] ■

6–3d Disparagement of Property

Disparagement of property occurs when economically injurious falsehoods are made about another's product or property rather than about another's reputation (as in the tort of defamation). *Disparagement of property* is a general term for torts that can be more specifically referred to as *slander of quality* or *slander of title.*

Slander of Quality The publication of false information about another's product, alleging that it is not what its seller claims, constitutes the tort of **slander of quality, or trade libel.** To establish trade libel, the plaintiff must prove that the improper publication caused a third person to refrain from dealing with the plaintiff and that the

plaintiff sustained economic damages (such as lost profits) as a result.

An improper publication may be both a slander of quality and a defamation of character. For instance, a statement that disparages the quality of a product may also, by implication, disparage the character of a person who would sell such a product.

Slander of Title When a publication falsely denies or casts doubt on another's legal ownership of property, resulting in financial loss to the property's owner, the tort of **slander of title** occurs. Usually, this is an intentional tort in which someone knowingly publishes an untrue statement about another's ownership of certain property with the intent of discouraging a third person from dealing with the person slandered. For instance, it would be difficult for a car dealer to attract customers after competitors published a notice that the dealer's stock consisted of stolen automobiles.

See Concept Summary 6.2 for a review of intentional torts against property.

6–4 Unintentional Torts— Negligence

The tort of **negligence** occurs when someone suffers injury because of another's failure to live up to a required *duty of care.* In contrast to intentional torts, in

---

15. *Welco Electronics, Inc. v. Mora,* 223 Cal.App.4th 202, 166 Cal.Rptr.3d 877 (2014).

Concept Summary 6.2

Intentional Torts against Property

Trespass to Land	The invasion of another's real property without consent or privilege. Once a person is expressly or impliedly established as a trespasser, the property owner has specific rights, which may include the right to detain or remove the trespasser.
Trespass to Personal Property	The intentional interference with an owner's right to use, possess, or enjoy his or her personal property without the owner's consent.
Conversion	The wrongful possession or use of another person's personal property without just cause.
Disparagement of Property	Any economically injurious falsehood that is made about another's product or property; an inclusive term for the torts of *slander of quality* and *slander of title.*

torts involving negligence, the tortfeasor neither wishes to bring about the consequences of the act nor believes that they will occur. The person's conduct merely creates a risk of such consequences. If no risk is created, there is no negligence.

Moreover, the risk must be foreseeable. In other words, it must be such that a reasonable person engaging in the same activity would anticipate the risk and guard against it. In determining what is reasonable conduct, courts consider the nature of the possible harm.

Many of the actions giving rise to the intentional torts discussed earlier in the chapter constitute negligence if the element of intent is missing (or cannot be proved). ■ **Example 6.23** Juan walks up to Maya and intentionally shoves her. Maya falls and breaks her arm as a result. In this situation, Juan is liable for the intentional tort of battery. If Juan carelessly bumps into Maya, however, and she falls and breaks her arm as a result, Juan's action constitutes negligence. In either situation, Juan has committed a tort. ■

To succeed in a negligence action, the plaintiff must prove each of the following:

1. *Duty.* The defendant owed a duty of care to the plaintiff.
2. *Breach.* The defendant breached that duty.
3. *Causation.* The defendant's breach caused the plaintiff's injury.
4. *Damages.* The plaintiff suffered a legally recognizable injury.

6–4a The Duty of Care and Its Breach

Central to the tort of negligence is the concept of a **duty of care.** The basic principle underlying the duty of care is that people are free to act as they please so long as their actions do not infringe on the interests of others. When someone fails to comply with the duty to exercise reasonable care, a potentially tortious act may have been committed.

Failure to live up to a standard of care may be an act (accidentally setting fire to a building) or an omission (neglecting to put out a campfire). It may be a careless act or a carefully performed but nevertheless dangerous act that results in injury. In determining whether the duty of care has been breached, courts consider several factors:

1. The nature of the act (whether it is outrageous or commonplace).
2. The manner in which the act was performed (cautiously versus heedlessly).
3. The nature of the injury (whether it is serious or slight).

Creating even a very slight risk of a dangerous explosion might be unreasonable, whereas creating a distinct possibility of someone's burning his or her fingers on a stove might be reasonable.

The question in the following case was whether a fraternity's local chapter and its officers owed a duty of care to their pledges.

Case 6.2

Bogenberger v. Pi Kappa Alpha Corporation, Inc.
Supreme Court of Illinois, 2018 IL 120951, 104 N.E.3d 1110 (2018).

Background and Facts David Bogenberger attended a pledge event at the Pi Kappa Alpha fraternity house at Northern Illinois University (NIU). The NIU chapter officers planned an evening of hazing, during which the pledges were required to consume vodka provided by the members. By the end of the night, David's blood alcohol level was more than five times the legal limit. He lost consciousness. The chapter officers failed to seek medical attention. David died during the night. His father, Gary, filed a complaint in an Illinois state court against the NIU chapter and its officers, on a theory of negligence. The plaintiff alleged that the defendants required the pledges, including David, to participate in the pledge event and to consume excessive and dangerous amounts of alcohol in violation of the state's hazing statute. The court dismissed the complaint. A state intermediate appellate court reversed the dismissal. The defendants appealed to the Illinois Supreme Court.

In the Language of the Court
Justice FREEMAN delivered the judgment of the court, with opinion.
* * * *

* * * Every person owes a duty of ordinary care to all others to guard against injuries which naturally flow as a reasonably probable and foreseeable consequence of an act * * * . *Where an individual's course*

Case 6.2 Continues

of action creates a foreseeable risk of injury, the individual has a duty to protect others from such injury. [Emphasis added.]

* * * *

To determine whether the NIU Chapter and officers owed a duty to the pledges, *we look to the reasonable foreseeability of the injury, the likelihood of the injury, the magnitude of the burden of guarding against the injury, and the consequences of placing that burden on the defendant.* In deciding reasonable foreseeability, an injury is not reasonably foreseeable where it results from freakish, bizarre, or fantastic circumstances. Regarding the first two factors, we cannot say that * * * an injury resulting from hazing is freakish, bizarre, or occurs under fantastic circumstances. The existence of hazing statutes across the country, including the [national Pi Kappa Alpha organization's] written policy against hazing as well as Illinois's hazing statute, indicates that injury due to hazing is reasonably foreseeable. We also find that injuries resulting from hazing events, especially those involving the consumption of large amounts of alcohol, are likely to occur. When pledges are required to consume large quantities of alcohol in short periods of time, their risk of injury is great—not only physical injury due to their inebriated condition but injury or death resulting from alcohol poisoning. [Emphasis added.]

Regarding the last two factors, we find that the magnitude of the burden of guarding against injury is small and the consequences of placing that burden on the NIU Chapter and officers are reasonable. To require the NIU Chapter and officers to guard against hazing injuries is infinitesimal. Hazing is not only against the law in Illinois, it is against the university's rules as well as the Pi Kappa Alpha fraternity's rules. There can be no real burden to require the NIU Chapter and officers to comply with the law and the university's and fraternity's rules. And it seems quite reasonable to place that burden on the very people who are in charge of planning and carrying out the pledge event. We find that the NIU Chapter and the officers owed a duty to the pledges, including David, and plaintiff has sufficiently alleged a claim for negligence against them.

Decision and Remedy *The Illinois Supreme Court affirmed the intermediate appellate court's reversal of the trial court's dismissal. The plaintiff's "complaint . . . may proceed against the NIU Chapter [and] its officers."*

Critical Thinking
- **Legal Environment** *The NIU chapter invited nonmember sorority women to participate in the hazing event by filling the pledges' cups with vodka and directing them to drink it. Did these women owe a duty of care to the pledges? Discuss.*
- **What If the Facts Were Different?** *Suppose that the pledges' attendance at the hazing event had been optional, and the NIU chapter had furnished alcohol but not required its consumption. Would the result have been different? Explain.*

The Reasonable Person Standard Tort law measures duty by the **reasonable person standard.** In determining whether a duty of care has been breached, the courts ask how a reasonable person would have acted in the same circumstances. The reasonable person standard is said to be objective. It is not necessarily how a particular person *would* act. It is society's judgment of how an ordinarily prudent person *should* act. If the so-called reasonable person existed, he or she would be careful, conscientious, even-tempered, and honest.

The degree of care to be exercised varies, depending on the defendant's occupation or profession, her or his relationship with the plaintiff, and other factors. Generally, whether an action constitutes a breach of the duty of care is determined on a case-by-case basis. The outcome depends on how the judge (or jury) decides that a reasonable person in the position of the defendant would have acted in the particular circumstances of the case.

Note that the courts frequently use the reasonable person standard in other areas of law as well as in negligence cases. Indeed, the principle that individuals are required to exercise a reasonable standard of care in their activities is a pervasive concept in business law.

The Duty of Landowners Landowners are expected to exercise reasonable care to protect individuals coming onto their property from harm. In some jurisdictions, landowners may even have a duty to protect trespassers against certain risks. Landowners who rent or lease premises to tenants are expected to exercise reasonable care to ensure that the tenants and their guests are not harmed in common areas, such as stairways, entryways, and laundry rooms.

The Duty to Warn Business Invitees of Risks. Retailers and other business operators who explicitly or implicitly invite persons to come onto their premises have a duty to exercise reasonable care to protect these **business invitees.** The duty normally requires storeowners to warn business invitees of foreseeable risks, such as construction zones or wet floors, about which the owners knew or *should have known.*

■ **Example 6.24** Liz enters Kwan's neighborhood market, slips on a wet floor, and sustains injuries as a result. If there was no sign or other warning that the floor was wet at the time Liz slipped, the owner, Kwan, would be liable for damages. A court would hold that Kwan was negligent because he failed to exercise a reasonable degree of care to protect customers against foreseeable risks about which he knew or should have known. That a patron might slip on the wet floor and be injured was a foreseeable risk, and Kwan should have taken care to avoid this risk or warn the customer of it. ■

A business owner also has a duty to discover and remove any hidden dangers that might injure a customer or other invitee. Hidden dangers might include uneven surfaces or defects in the pavement of a parking lot or a walkway, or merchandise that has fallen off shelves in a store.

Obvious Risks Provide an Exception. Some risks are so obvious that an owner need not warn of them. For instance, a business owner does not need to warn customers to open a door before attempting to walk through it. Other risks, however, even though they may seem obvious to a business owner, may not be so in the eyes of another, such as a child. In addition, even if a risk is obvious, a business owner is not necessarily excused from the duty to protect customers from foreseeable harm from that risk.

The Duty of Professionals Persons who possess superior knowledge, skill, or training are held to a higher standard of care than others. Professionals—including physicians, dentists, architects, engineers, accountants, and lawyers, among others—are required to have a standard minimum level of special knowledge and ability. In determining what constitutes reasonable care in the case of professionals, the law takes their training and expertise into account. Thus, an accountant's conduct is judged not by the reasonable person standard, but by the reasonable accountant standard.

If a professional violates his or her duty of care toward a client, the client may bring a suit against the professional, alleging **malpractice,** which is essentially professional negligence. For instance, a patient might sue a physician for *medical malpractice.* A client might sue an attorney for *legal malpractice.*

6–4b Causation

Another element necessary to a negligence action is *causation.* If a person breaches a duty of care and someone suffers injury, the person's act must have caused the harm for it to constitute the tort of negligence.

Courts Ask Two Questions In deciding whether the requirement of causation is met, the court must address two questions:

1. *Is there causation in fact?* Did the injury occur because of the defendant's act, or would it have occurred anyway? If the injury would not have occurred without the defendant's act, then there is causation in fact.

   Causation in fact usually can be determined by use of the *but for* test: "but for" the wrongful act, the injury would not have occurred. This test seeks to determine whether there was a cause-and-effect relationship between the act and the injury suffered. In theory, causation in fact is limitless. One could claim, for instance, that "but for" the creation of the world, a particular injury would not have occurred. Thus, as a practical matter, the law has to establish limits, and it does so through the concept of proximate cause.

2. *Was the act the proximate, or legal, cause of the injury?* **Proximate cause,** or *legal cause,* exists when the connection between an act and an injury is strong enough to justify imposing liability. Proximate cause asks whether the injuries sustained were foreseeable or were too remotely connected to the incident to trigger liability. Judges use proximate cause to limit the scope of the defendant's liability to a subset of the total number of potential plaintiffs that might have been harmed by the defendant's actions.

   ■ **Example 6.25** Ackerman carelessly leaves a campfire burning. The fire not only burns down the forest but also sets off an explosion in a nearby chemical plant that spills chemicals into a river, killing all the fish for twenty miles downstream and ruining the economy of a tourist resort. Should Ackerman be liable to the resort owners? To the tourists whose vacations were ruined? These are questions of proximate cause that a court must decide. ∎

Both of these causation questions must be answered in the affirmative for liability in tort to arise. If there is causation in fact but a court decides that the defendant's action is not the proximate cause of the plaintiff's injury, the causation requirement has not been met. Therefore, the defendant normally will not be liable to the plaintiff.

Foreseeability Questions of proximate cause are linked to the concept of foreseeability because it would be unfair to impose liability on a defendant unless the defendant's actions created a foreseeable risk of injury. Generally, if the victim or the consequences of a harm done were unforeseeable, there is no proximate cause.

Probably the most cited case on the concept of foreseeability and proximate cause is the *Palsgraf* case, which established foreseeability as the test for proximate cause. ∎ **Case in Point 6.26** Helen Palsgraf was waiting for a train on a station platform. A man carrying a package was rushing to catch a train that was moving away from a platform across the tracks from Palsgraf. As the man attempted to jump aboard the moving train, he seemed unsteady and about to fall. A railroad guard on the car reached forward to grab him, and another guard on the platform pushed him from behind to help him board the train.

In the process, the man's package, which (unknown to the railroad guards) contained fireworks, fell on the railroad tracks and exploded. There was nothing about the package to indicate its contents. The repercussions of the explosion caused weighing scales at the other end of the train platform to fall on Palsgraf, causing injuries for which she sued the railroad company. At the trial, the jury found that the railroad guards had been negligent in their conduct. The railroad company appealed. New York's highest state court held that the railroad company was not liable to Palsgraf. The railroad had not been negligent toward her, because injury to her was not foreseeable.[16] ∎

6–4c The Injury Requirement and Damages

For tort liability to arise, the plaintiff must have suffered a *legally recognizable* injury. To recover damages, the plaintiff must have suffered some loss, harm, wrong, or invasion of a protected interest. Essentially, the purpose of tort law is to compensate for legally recognized harms and injuries resulting from wrongful acts. If no harm or injury results from a given negligent action, there is nothing to compensate, and no tort exists.

For instance, if you carelessly bump into a passerby, who stumbles and falls as a result, you may be liable in tort if the passerby is injured in the fall. If the person is unharmed, however, there normally can be no lawsuit for damages, because no injury was suffered.

Compensatory damages are the norm in negligence cases. A court will award punitive damages only if the defendant's conduct was grossly negligent, reflecting an intentional failure to perform a duty with reckless disregard of the consequences to others.

6–4d Good Samaritan Statutes

Most states now have what are called **Good Samaritan statutes**.[17] Under these statutes, someone who is aided voluntarily by another cannot turn around and sue the "Good Samaritan" for negligence. These laws were passed largely to protect physicians and medical personnel who volunteer their services in emergency situations to those in need, such as individuals hurt in car accidents.

6–4e Dram Shop Acts

Many states have also passed **dram shop acts**,[18] under which a bar's owner or a bartender may be held liable for injuries caused by a person who became intoxicated while drinking at the bar. The owner or bartender may also be held responsible for continuing to serve a person who was already intoxicated.

Some states' statutes also impose liability on *social hosts* (persons hosting parties) for injuries caused by guests who became intoxicated at the hosts' homes. Under these statutes, it is unnecessary to prove that the social host was negligent. ∎ **Example 6.27** Jane hosts a Super Bowl party at which Brett, a minor, sneaks alcoholic drinks. Jane is potentially liable for damages resulting from Brett's drunk driving after the party. ∎

6–5 Defenses to Negligence

Defendants often defend against negligence claims by asserting that the plaintiffs have failed to prove the existence of one or more of the required elements for

---

16. *Palsgraf v. Long Island Railroad Co.*, 248 N.Y. 339, 162 N.E. 99 (1928).

17. These laws derive their name from the Good Samaritan story in the Bible. In the story, a traveler who had been robbed and beaten lay along the roadside, ignored by those passing by. Eventually, a man from the region of Samaria (the "Good Samaritan") stopped to render assistance to the injured person.

18. A dram is a small unit of liquid, and distilled spirits were historically sold in drams. Thus, a dram shop was a place where liquor was sold in drams.

negligence. Additionally, there are three basic *affirmative* defenses in negligence cases (defenses that a defendant can use to avoid liability even if the facts are as the plaintiff states): *assumption of risk, superseding cause*, and *contributory and comparative negligence.*

6–5a Assumption of Risk

A plaintiff who voluntarily enters into a risky situation, knowing the risk involved, will not be allowed to recover. This is the defense of **assumption of risk,** which requires two elements:

1. Knowledge of the risk.
2. Voluntary assumption of the risk.

The defense of assumption of risk is frequently asserted when the plaintiff was injured during a recreational activity that involves known risk, such as skiing or skydiving.

Assumption of risk can apply not only to participants in sporting events, but also to spectators and bystanders who are injured while attending those events. In the following *Spotlight Case*, the issue was whether a spectator at a baseball game voluntarily assumed the risk of being hit by an errant ball thrown while the players were warming up before the game.

Spotlight on the Seattle Mariners

Case 6.3 Taylor v. Baseball Club of Seattle, LP

Court of Appeals of Washington, 132 Wash.App. 32, 130 P.3d 835 (2006).

Background and Facts Delinda Taylor went to a Seattle Mariners baseball game at Safeco Field with her boyfriend and her two minor sons. Their seats were four rows up from the field along the right field foul line. They arrived more than an hour before the game so that they could see the players warm up and get their autographs. When she walked in, Taylor saw that a Mariners pitcher, Freddy Garcia, was throwing a ball back and forth with José Mesa right in front of their seats.

As Taylor stood in front of her seat, she looked away from the field, and a ball thrown by Mesa got past Garcia and struck her in the face, causing serious injuries. Taylor sued the Mariners for the allegedly negligent warm-up throw. The Mariners filed a motion for summary judgment in which they argued that Taylor, a longtime Mariners fan, was familiar with baseball and the inherent risk of balls entering the stands. Thus, the motion asserted, Taylor had assumed the risk of her injury. The trial court granted the motion and dismissed Taylor's case. Taylor appealed.

In the Language of the Court

DWYER, J. [Judge]

* * * *

* * * For many decades, courts have required baseball stadiums to screen some seats—generally those behind home plate—to provide protection to spectators who choose it.

A sport spectator's assumption of risk and a defendant sports team's duty of care are accordingly discerned under the doctrine of primary assumption of risk. * * * "Implied *primary* assumption of risk arises where a plaintiff has impliedly consented (often in advance of any negligence by defendant) to relieve defendant of a duty to plaintiff regarding specific *known* and appreciated risks."

* * * *

Under this implied primary assumption of risk, defendant must show that plaintiff had full subjective understanding of the specific risk, both its nature and presence, and that he or she voluntarily chose to encounter the risk.

* * * It is undisputed that the warm-up is part of the sport, that spectators such as Taylor purposely attend that portion of the event, and that the Mariners permit ticket-holders to view the warm-up.

* * * We find the fact that Taylor was injured during warm-up is not legally significant because that portion of the event is necessarily incident to the game.

* * * *

Case 6.3 Continues

Case 6.3 Continued   Here, there is no evidence that the circumstances leading to Taylor's injury constituted an unusual danger. It is undisputed that it is the normal, every-day practice at all levels of baseball for pitchers to warm up in the manner that led to this incident. *The risk of injuries such as Taylor's are within the normal comprehension of a spectator who is familiar with the game.* Indeed, the possibility of an errant ball entering the stands is part of the game's attraction for many spectators. [Emphasis added.]

* * * The record contains substantial evidence regarding Taylor's familiarity with the game. She attended many of her sons' baseball games, she witnessed balls entering the stands, she had watched Mariners' games both at the Kingdome and on television, and she knew that there was no screen protecting her seats, which were close to the field. In fact, as she walked to her seat she saw the players warming up and was excited about being in an unscreened area where her party might get autographs from the players and catch balls.

Decision and Remedy   *The state intermediate appellate court affirmed the lower court's judgment. As a spectator who chose to sit in an unprotected area of seats, Taylor voluntarily undertook the risk associated with being hit by an errant baseball thrown during the warm-up before the game.*

Critical Thinking

- **What If the Facts Were Different?** *Would the result in this case have been different if it had been Taylor's minor son, rather than Taylor herself, who had been struck by the ball? Should courts apply the doctrine of assumption of risk to children? Discuss.*
- **Legal Environment** *What is the basis underlying the defense of assumption of risk? How does that basis support the court's decision in this case?*

6–5b Superseding Cause

An unforeseeable intervening event may break the causal connection between a wrongful act and an injury to another. If so, the intervening event acts as a **superseding cause**—that is, it relieves the defendant of liability for injuries caused by the intervening event.

■ **Example 6.28** While riding his bicycle, Derrick negligently runs into Julie, who is walking on the sidewalk. As a result of the impact, Julie falls and fractures her hip. While she is waiting for help to arrive, a small aircraft crashes nearby and explodes, and some of the fiery debris hits her, causing her to sustain severe burns. Derrick will be liable for the damages related to Julie's fractured hip, because the risk of injuring her with his bicycle was foreseeable. Normally, though, Derrick will not be liable for the burns caused by the plane crash, because he could not have foreseen the risk that a plane would crash nearby and injure Julie. ■

6–5c Contributory Negligence

All individuals are expected to exercise a reasonable degree of care in looking out for themselves. In the past, under the common law doctrine of **contributory negligence,** a plaintiff who was also negligent (who failed to exercise a reasonable degree of care) could not recover anything from the defendant. Under this rule, no matter how insignificant the plaintiff's negligence was relative to the defendant's negligence, the plaintiff would be precluded from recovering any damages. Today, only a few jurisdictions still follow this doctrine.

6–5d Comparative Negligence

In most states, the doctrine of contributory negligence has been replaced by a **comparative negligence** standard. Under this standard, both the plaintiff's and the defendant's negligence are computed, and the liability for damages is distributed accordingly.

Some jurisdictions have adopted a "pure" form of comparative negligence that allows the plaintiff to recover, even if the extent of his or her fault was greater than that of the defendant. Under pure comparative negligence, if the plaintiff was 80 percent at fault and the defendant 20 percent at fault, the plaintiff can recover 20 percent of his or her damages.

Many states' comparative negligence statutes, however, contain a "50 percent" rule that prevents the plaintiff from recovering any damages if she or he was more than 50 percent at fault. Under this rule, a plaintiff who was 35 percent at fault can recover 65 percent of his or her damages, but a plaintiff who was 65 percent at fault can recover nothing.

Practice and Review: Tort Law

Elaine Sweeney went to Ragged Mountain Ski Resort in New Hampshire with a friend. Elaine went snow tubing down a run designed exclusively for snow tubers. There were no Ragged Mountain employees present in the snow-tube area to instruct Elaine on the proper use of a snow tube. On her fourth run down the trail, Elaine crossed over the center line between snow-tube lanes, collided with another snow tuber, and was injured. Elaine filed a negligence action against Ragged Mountain seeking compensation for the injuries that she sustained. Two years earlier, the New Hampshire state legislature had enacted a statute that prohibited a person who participates in the sport of skiing from suing a ski-area operator for injuries caused by the risks inherent in skiing. Using the information presented in the chapter, answer the following questions.

1. What defense will Ragged Mountain probably assert?
2. The central question in this case is whether the state statute establishing that skiers assume the risks inherent in the sport bars Elaine's suit. What would your decision be on this issue? Why?
3. Suppose that the court concludes that the statute applies only to skiing and not to snow tubing. Will Elaine's lawsuit be successful? Explain.
4. Now suppose that the jury concludes that Elaine was partly at fault for the accident. Under what theory might her damages be reduced in proportion to the degree to which her actions contributed to the accident and her resulting injuries?

Debate This . . . *Each time a state legislature enacts a law that applies the assumption of risk doctrine to a particular sport, participants in that sport suffer.*

Terms and Concepts

actionable 114	dram shop acts 128	puffery 120
actual malice 118	duty of care 125	punitive damages 113
assault 113	fraudulent misrepresentation	reasonable person standard 126
assumption of risk 129	(fraud) 120	slander 115
battery 114	general damages 112	slander of quality 124
business invitees 127	Good Samaritan statutes 128	slander of title 124
causation in fact 127	intentional tort 113	special damages 112
comparative negligence 130	libel 115	superseding cause 130
compensatory damages 112	licensee 123	tortfeasor 113
contributory negligence 130	malpractice 127	torts 112
conversion 123	negligence 124	trade libel 124
damages 112	privilege 117	transferred intent 113
defamation 115	proximate cause 127	trespass to land 122
disparagement of property 124	public figures 118	trespass to personal property 123

Issue Spotters

1. Jana leaves her truck's motor running while she enters a Kwik-Pik Store. The truck's transmission engages, and the vehicle crashes into a gas pump, starting a fire that spreads to a warehouse on the next block. The warehouse collapses, causing its billboard to fall and injure Lou, a bystander. Can Lou recover from Jana? Why or why not? (See *Unintentional Torts—Negligence*.)

2. A water pipe bursts, flooding a Metal Fabrication Company utility room and tripping the circuit breakers on a panel in the room. Metal Fabrication contacts Nouri, a licensed electrician with five years' experience, to check the damage and turn the breakers back on. Without testing for short circuits, which Nouri knows that he should do, he tries to switch on a breaker. He is electrocuted,

and his wife sues Metal Fabrication for damages, alleging negligence. What might the firm successfully claim in defense? (See *Defenses to Negligence*.)

- **Check your answers to the Issue Spotters against the answers provided in Appendix B at the end of this text.**

Business Scenarios and Case Problems

6–1. Defamation. Richard is an employee of the Dun Construction Corp. While delivering materials to a construction site, he carelessly backs Dun's truck into a passenger vehicle driven by Green. This is Richard's second accident in six months. When the company owner, Dun, learns of this latest accident, a heated discussion ensues, and Dun fires Richard. Dun is so angry that he immediately writes a letter to the union of which Richard is a member and to all other construction companies in the community, stating that Richard is the "worst driver in the city" and that "anyone who hires him is asking for legal liability." Richard files a suit against Dun, alleging libel on the basis of the statements made in the letters. Discuss the results. (See *Intentional Torts against Persons*.)

6–2. Spotlight on Intentional Torts—Defamation. Sharon Yeagle was an assistant to the vice president of student affairs at Virginia Polytechnic Institute and State University (Virginia Tech). As part of her duties, Yeagle helped students participate in the Governor's Fellows Program. *Collegiate Times*, Virginia Tech's student newspaper, published an article about the university's success in placing students in the program. The article's text surrounded a block quotation attributed to Yeagle with the phrase "Director of Butt Licking" under her name. Yeagle sued *Collegiate Times* for defamation. She argued that the phrase implied the commission of sodomy and was therefore actionable. What is *Collegiate Times'* defense to this claim? [*Yeagle v. Collegiate Times*, 255 Va. 293, 497 S.E.2d 136 (1998)] (See *Intentional Torts against Persons*.)

6–3. Intentional Infliction of Emotional Distress. While living in her home country of Tanzania, Sophia Kiwanuka signed an employment contract with Anne Margareth Bakilana, a Tanzanian living in Washington, D.C. Kiwanuka traveled to the United States to work as a babysitter and maid in Bakilana's house. When Kiwanuka arrived, Bakilana confiscated her passport, held her in isolation, and forced her to work long hours under threat of having her deported. Kiwanuka worked seven days a week without breaks and was subjected to regular verbal and psychological abuse by Bakilana. Kiwanuka filed a complaint against Bakilana for intentional infliction of emotional distress, among other claims. Bakilana argued that Kiwanuka's complaint should be dismissed because the allegations were insufficient to show outrageous intentional conduct that resulted in severe emotional distress. If you were the judge, in whose favor would you rule? Why? [*Kiwanuka v. Bakilana*, 844 F.Supp.2d 107 (D.D.C. 2012)] (See *Intentional Torts against Persons*.)

6–4. Business Case Problem with Sample Answer—Negligence. At the Weatherford Hotel in Flagstaff, Arizona, in Room 59, a balcony extends across thirty inches of the room's only window, leaving a twelve-inch gap with a three-story drop to the concrete below. A sign prohibits smoking in the room but invites guests to "step out onto the balcony" to smoke. Toni Lucario was a guest in Room 59 when she climbed out of the window and fell to her death. Patrick McMurtry, her estate's personal representative, filed a suit against the Weatherford. Did the hotel breach a duty of care to Lucario? What might the Weatherford assert in its defense? Explain. [*McMurtry v. Weatherford Hotel, Inc.*, 231 Ariz. 244, 293 P.3d 520 (2013)] (See *Unintentional Torts—Negligence*.)

- **For a sample answer to Problem 6–4, go to Appendix C at the end of this text.**

6–5. Negligence. Ronald Rawls and Zabian Bailey were in an auto accident in Bridgeport, Connecticut. Bailey rear-ended Rawls at a stoplight. Evidence showed it was more likely than not that Bailey failed to apply his brakes in time to avoid the collision, failed to turn his vehicle to avoid the collision, failed to keep his vehicle under control, and was inattentive to his surroundings. Rawls filed a suit in a Connecticut state court against his insurance company, Progressive Northern Insurance Company, to obtain benefits under an underinsured motorist clause, alleging that Bailey had been negligent. Could Rawls collect? Discuss. [*Rawls v. Progressive Northern Insurance Co.*, 310 Conn. 768, 83 A.3d 576 (2014)] (See *Unintentional Torts—Negligence*.)

6–6. Negligence. Charles Robison, an employee of West Star Transportation, Inc., was ordered to cover an unevenly loaded flatbed trailer with a 150-pound tarpaulin (a waterproof cloth). The load included uncrated equipment and pallet crates of different heights, about thirteen feet off the ground at its highest point. While standing on the load, manipulating the tarpaulin without safety equipment or assistance, Robison fell and sustained a traumatic head injury. He filed a suit against West Star to recover for his injury. Was West Star "negligent in failing to provide a reasonably safe place to work," as Robison claimed? Explain. [*West Star Transportation, Inc. v. Robison*, 457 S.W.3d 178 (Tex.App.—Amarillo 2015)] (See *Unintentional Torts—Negligence*.)

6–7. Negligence. DSC Industrial Supply and Road Rider Supply are located in North Kitsap Business Park in Seattle, Washington. Both firms are owned by Paul and Suzanne Marshall. The Marshalls had outstanding commercial loans from Frontier Bank. The bank dispatched one of its employees,

Suzette Gould, to North Kitsap to "spread Christmas cheer" to the Marshalls as an expression of appreciation for their business. Approaching the entry to Road Rider, Gould tripped over a concrete "wheel stop" and fell, suffering a broken arm and a dislocated elbow. The stop was not clearly visible, it had not been painted a contrasting color, and it was not marked with a sign. Gould had not been aware of the stop before she tripped over it. Is North Kitsap liable to Gould for negligence? Explain. [*Gould v. North Kitsap Business Park Management, LLC*, 192 Wash.App. 1021 (2016)] (See *Unintentional Torts—Negligence.*)

6–8. Defamation. Jonathan Martin, an offensive lineman with the Miami Dolphins, abruptly quit the team and checked himself into a hospital seeking psychological treatment. Later, he explained that he left because of persistent taunting from other Dolphins players. The National Football League hired attorney Theodore Wells to investigate Martin's allegations of bullying. After receiving Wells's report, the Dolphins fired their offensive line coach, James Turner. Turner was a prominent person on the Dolphins, and during his career, he chose to thrust himself further into the public arena. He was the subject of articles discussing his coaching philosophy and the focus of one season of HBO's "Hard Knocks," showcasing his coaching style. Turner filed a suit in a federal district court against Wells, alleging defamation. He charged that Wells failed to properly analyze certain information. Is Turner likely to succeed on his claim? Explain. [*Turner v. Wells*, 879 F.3d 1254 (11th Cir. 2018)] (See *Intentional Torts against Persons.*)

6–9. A Question of Ethics—The IDDR Approach and Wrongful Interference. *Julie Whitchurch was an employee of Vizant Technologies, LLC. After she was fired, she created a website falsely accusing Vizant of fraud and mismanagement to discourage others from doing business with the company. Vizant filed a suit in a federal district court against her, alleging wrongful interference with a business relationship. The court concluded that Whitchurch's online criticism of Vizant adversely affected its employees and operations, forced it to accept reduced compensation to obtain business, and deterred outside investment. The court ordered Whitchurch to stop her online efforts to discourage others from doing business with Vizant. [Vizant Technologies, LLC v. Whitchurch, 675 Fed.Appx. 201 (3d Cir. 2017)] (See* Intentional Torts against Persons.*)*

(a) How does the motivation for Whitchurch's conduct differ from other cases that involve wrongful interference? What does this suggest about the ethics in this situation? Discuss.

(b) Using the IDDR approach, analyze and evaluate Vizant's decision to file a suit against Whitchurch.

Time-Limited Group Assignment

6–10. Negligence. Donald and Gloria Bowden hosted a cookout at their home in South Carolina, inviting mostly business acquaintances. Justin Parks, who was nineteen years old, attended the party. Alcoholic beverages were available to all of the guests, even those who, like Parks, were between the ages of eighteen and twenty-one. Parks consumed alcohol at the party and left with other guests. One of these guests detained Parks at the guest's home to give Parks time to "sober up." Parks then drove himself from this guest's home and was killed in a one-car accident. At the time of death, he had a blood alcohol content of 0.291 percent, which exceeded the state's limit for driving a motor vehicle. Linda Marcum, Parks's mother, filed a suit in a South Carolina state court against the Bowdens and others, alleging that they were negligent. (See *Unintentional Torts—Negligence.*)

(a) The first group will present arguments in favor of holding the social hosts liable in this situation.

(b) The second group will formulate arguments against holding the social hosts liable based on principles in this chapter.

(c) The third group will determine the reasons why some courts do not treat social hosts the same as parents who serve alcoholic beverages to their underage children.

Chapter 7

Strict Liability and Product Liability

In this chapter, we look at a category of tort called **strict liability,** or *liability without fault.* Under the doctrine of strict liability, a person who engages in certain activities can be held responsible for any harm that results to others, even if the person used the utmost care.

We then look at an area of tort law of particular importance to businesspersons—product liability. The manufacturers and sellers of products may incur **product liability** when product defects cause injury or property damage to consumers, users, or bystanders.

For instance, suppose that one night, before going to bed, Braden plugs in his laptop to charge the battery. While he is asleep, it explodes into flames and sets the apartment on fire. The fire seriously injures Braden and his roommate (a bystander). Under product liability laws, Braden can sue the maker of the laptop for the injuries and damages. Braden's roommate can also sue the manufacturer for product liability, even though he was not the person who purchased the laptop.

Although multimillion-dollar product liability claims often involve big automakers, pharmaceutical companies, or tobacco companies, many businesses face potential liability. In fact, even small retailers may be sued when products they sell turn out to be defective. Product liability lawsuits also reach across international borders, as when a manufacturer or supplier of a defective product is located outside the United States.

7-1 Strict Liability

The modern concept of strict liability traces its origins, in part, to an English case decided in 1868. ■ **Case in Point 7.1** In the coal-mining area of Lancashire, England, the Rylands, who were mill owners, had constructed a reservoir on their land. Water from the reservoir broke through a filled-in shaft of an abandoned coal mine nearby and flooded the connecting passageways in an active coal mine owned by Fletcher.

Fletcher sued the Rylands, and the court held that the Rylands were liable, even though the circumstances did not fit within existing tort liability theories. The court held that a "person who for his own purposes brings on his land and collects and keeps there anything likely to do mischief if it escapes . . . is *prima facie*[1] answerable for all the damage which is the natural consequence of its escape."[2] ■

British courts liberally applied the doctrine that emerged from the case. Initially, though, few U.S. courts accepted the doctrine, presumably because the courts were worried about its effect on the expansion of American business. Today, however, the doctrine of strict liability is the norm rather than the exception.

7-1a Abnormally Dangerous Activities

Strict liability for damages proximately caused by an abnormally dangerous, or ultrahazardous, activity is one application of strict liability. Courts apply the doctrine of strict liability in these situations because of the extreme risk of the activity. Abnormally dangerous activities are those that involve a high risk of serious harm to persons or property that cannot be completely guarded against by the exercise of reasonable care.

An activity such as blasting or storing explosives qualifies as abnormally dangerous, for instance. Even if blasting with dynamite is performed with all reasonable care, there is still a risk of injury. Considering the potential for harm, it seems reasonable to ask the person engaged in the activity to pay for injuries caused by that activity. Although there is no fault, there is still responsibility because of the dangerous nature of the undertaking.

---

1. *Prima facie* is Latin for "at first sight." Legally, it refers to a fact that is presumed to be true unless contradicted by evidence.
2. *Rylands v. Fletcher*, 3 L.R.–E & I App. [Law Reports, English & Irish Appeal Cases] (H.L. [House of Lords] 1868).

Similarly, persons who keep wild animals are strictly liable for any harm inflicted by the animals. The basis for applying strict liability is that wild animals, should they escape from confinement, pose a serious risk of harm to people in the vicinity. Even an owner of domestic animals (such as dogs or horses) may be strictly liable for harm caused by those animals if the owner knew, or should have known, that the animals were dangerous or had a propensity to harm others.

7–1b Application of Strict Liability to Product Liability

A significant application of strict liability is in the area of product liability—liability of manufacturers and sellers for harmful or defective products. Liability here is a matter of social policy and is based on two factors:

1. The manufacturer can better bear the cost of injury because it can spread the cost throughout society by increasing the prices of its goods.
2. The manufacturer is making a profit from its activities and therefore should bear the cost of injury as an operating expense.

We discuss product liability in detail next. Strict liability is also applied in certain types of *bailments* (a bailment exists when goods are transferred temporarily into the care of another).

7–2 Product Liability

Those who make, sell, or lease goods can be held liable for physical harm or property damage caused by those goods to a consumer, user, or bystander. This is called *product liability*. Product liability may be based on the tort theories of negligence, misrepresentation, strict liability, and breach of warranty. Multiple theories of liability can be, and often are, asserted in the same case. We look here at product liability based on negligence and on misrepresentation.

7–2a Based on Negligence

Negligence is the failure to exercise the degree of care that a reasonable, prudent person would have exercised under the circumstances. If a manufacturer fails to exercise "due care" to make a product safe, a person who is injured by the product may sue the manufacturer for negligence.

Due Care Must Be Exercised Manufacturers must use due care in all of the following areas:

1. Designing the product.
2. Selecting the materials.
3. Using the appropriate production process.
4. Assembling and testing the product.
5. Placing adequate warnings on the label to inform the user of dangers of which an ordinary person might not be aware.
6. Inspecting and testing any purchased components used in the product.

Privity of Contract Not Required A product liability action based on negligence does not require *privity of contract* between the injured plaintiff and the defendant-manufacturer. **Privity of contract** refers to the relationship that exists between the parties to a contract. Privity is the reason that normally only the parties to a contract can enforce that contract.

In the context of product liability law, though, privity is not required. A person who is injured by a defective product may bring a negligence suit even though he or she was not the one who actually purchased the product—and thus is not in privity. A manufacturer, seller, or lessor is liable for failure to exercise due care to *any person* who sustains an injury proximately caused by a negligently made (defective) product.

A 1916 landmark decision established this exception to the privity requirement. ■ **Case in Point 7.2** Donald MacPherson suffered injuries while riding in a Buick automobile that suddenly collapsed because one of the wheels was made of defective wood. The spokes crumbled into fragments, throwing MacPherson out of the vehicle and injuring him.

MacPherson had purchased the car from a Buick dealer, but he brought a lawsuit against the manufacturer, Buick Motor Company, alleging negligence. Buick itself had not made the wheel but had bought it from another manufacturer. There was evidence, though, that the defects could have been discovered by a reasonable inspection by Buick and that no such inspection had taken place. The primary issue was whether Buick owed a duty of care to anyone except the immediate purchaser of the car—that is, the Buick dealer. Although Buick itself had not manufactured the wheel, New York's highest state court held that Buick had a duty to inspect the wheels and that Buick "was responsible for the finished product." Therefore, Buick was liable to MacPherson for the injuries he sustained.[3] ■

---

3. *MacPherson v. Buick Motor Co.*, 217 N.Y. 382, 111 N.E. 1050 (1916).

"Cause in Fact" and Proximate Cause In a product liability suit based on negligence, as in any action alleging that the defendant was negligent, the plaintiff must show that the defendant's conduct was the "cause in fact" of an injury. "Cause in fact" requires showing that "but for" the defendant's action, the injury would not have occurred.

It must also be determined that the defendant's act was the *proximate cause* of the injury. This determination focuses on the foreseeability of the consequences of the act. For proximate cause to become a relevant issue, however, a plaintiff first must establish cause in fact. The cause of a serious accident was at issue in the following case.

Schwarck v. Arctic Cat, Inc.
Court of Appeals of Michigan, 2016 WL 191992 (2016).

In the Language of the Court
PER CURIAM. [By the Whole Court]

* * * *

* * * Karen Schwarck * * * was operating an Arctic Cat [660 snowmobile] near Mackinac Island's Grand Hotel [in Michigan] with her sister, Edith Bonno, as passenger. The sisters met their demise when the Arctic Cat went, in reverse, backward through a wooden fence and over the West Bluff of the Island.

[Donald Schwarck and Joshua Bonno] the spouses of decedents, as their personal representatives, filed this action [in a Michigan state court] against defendant Arctic Cat [the manufacturer of the 660]. Plaintiffs alleged that the Arctic Cat 660 was negligently designed * * * without a backup alarm that operated throughout all the reverse travel positions and as a result proximately caused decedents' injuries.

Defendant filed a motion for summary [judgment]. Defendant denied the existence of a "silent reverse zone," but argued that even if such a zone existed, it was not a cause of the accident because the alarm was intended as a warning to bystanders and not as an indicator of shift position for operators.

* * * *

* * * The court issued its decision and order in favor of defendant. [The plaintiffs appealed.]

* * * *

There is no dispute that on the day of the accident decedent Schwarck was driving the Arctic Cat 660 * * * and that she attempted to execute a three-point or

K-turn * * * . To make the turn decedent Schwarck had to turn left to face north, stop, reverse south, stop, and then complete the turn to drive east. * * * Plaintiffs argue that after decedent Schwarck reversed, she stopped a second time and shifted forward, and not hearing the reverse alarm, believed she was in forward, and accelerated. As a result, the craft went in reverse through the fence and off the bluff.

The trial court determined that there were no material questions of fact on * * * the operability of the reverse alarm. * * * It was undisputed that an inspection of the Arctic Cat post-accident showed the reverse alarm to be operable.

* * * *

* * * [But] the court's conclusion that the reverse alarm was working at the time of the accident does not determine whether its operational process constituted a product defect. Plaintiffs' claim was that the reverse alarm was defective because it did not sound during the entire time the vehicle was in reverse. Plaintiffs' causation theory was that the Arctic Cat's reverse alarm caused decedent Schwarck to be confused about whether she was in forward or reverse gear and that the confusion led to the accident that caused decedents' deaths.

[Plaintiffs' expert John Frackelton, an accident reconstructionist and snowmobile mechanic,] observed that the shift lever traveled from full reverse to full forward in a distance of four inches. Frackelton's testing revealed that when

the lever was shifted all the way down and pressed against the reverse buffer switch, the switch sounded a chime and the snowmobile was in full reverse mode. Frackelton experimented with the lever, shifting it up toward forward gear, an inch at a time. For the next two inches of shift travel forward, the reverse alarm did not sound, but the snowmobile was still in reverse. Frackelton observed that it was only in the last or fourth inch of shift travel that the snowmobile was in full forward.

* * * Frackelton observed that the transition from full reverse to full forward was smooth and accomplished with little pressure. He opined that an operator could "become accustomed to the highly repeatable return performance." On two occasions, however, Frackelton pushed the gearshift forward and the Arctic Cat did not return to forward gear as expected.

* * * Frackelton's opinion * * * creates a material question of fact as to whether the alarm failed to sound at all times when the gear was in reverse. Defendant argues that the alarm served its intended purpose which is to notify bystanders and not operators that the snowmobile is in reverse and that it was unreasonable for decedent Schwarck to rely on the alarm to determine the gear of the snowmobile. *The fact that the manufacturer's intended purpose for the alarm was to warn third parties is not dispositive of the issue of whether decedent Schwarck relied on the alarm to determine her gear or whether that reliance was reasonable or a*

foreseeable misuse of the alarm and snow-mobile. Decedent Schwarck is assumed to have acted with due care for her own safety. Her widower averred that, based upon his observations, decedent Schwarck had a practice and routine of relying upon the sounding of the alarm as a signal that she was in reverse. Evidence from Frackelton's test runs also demonstrate that despite manual control of the shift lever, the lever could stop just short of the forward position and prevent the snowmobile from going into drive. [Emphasis added.]

Reasonable minds could differ as to whether a reverse alarm that does not sound throughout the reverse trajectory or only operates in a partial manner is defective.

* * * *

Legal cause becomes a relevant issue after cause in fact has been established. * * * *To establish legal cause, the plaintiff must show that it was foreseeable that the* *defendant's conduct may create a risk of harm to the victim, and* * * * *that the result of that conduct and intervening causes were foreseeable.* * * * It is foreseeable that an operator of the Arctic Cat may rely on the sound of the reverse alarm to indicate when the snowmobile is no longer in reverse and experience unexpected travel backward because the alarm does not sound during the entire reverse gear. It is further foreseeable that unanticipated reverse travel may cause a risk of harm to the operator. * * * Frackelton's tests regarding speed velocity without aggressive throttle demonstrate how the Arctic Cat can travel almost thirty feet in just 5.4 seconds. Not only can an operator of the Arctic Cat find him or herself unexpectedly travelling in reverse, but also doing so quickly. Plaintiffs' other expert [Lila Laux, a psychologist and engineer] testified * * * that time is * * * required for the operator to determine how to respond to the unexpected stimuli,

to engage the brake, and for the brake to activate. [Emphasis added.]

A jury could infer that traveling backward when one thought he or she would go forward is an unexpected stimulus. It is also a reasonable inference, from the opinions of both plaintiffs' experts, that it was foreseeable that the operator would be surprised by the rearward motion. Given the evidence, reasonable minds may differ as to whether decedent Schwarck did not or could not correct the snowmobile's rearward direction in the time allotted.

Based on the whole record, there is evidence that warrants submission of this case to a jury to determine whether the reverse alarm was defective and whether that defect caused decedent Schwarck and Bonno's deaths.

* * * *

[The trial court's judgment is] vacated and remanded for proceedings consistent with this opinion.

Legal Reasoning Questions

1. According to the plaintiffs, what was the product defect at the center of this case? According to the defendant, why was this not a defect?
2. How did the plaintiffs use evidence to support their claim?
3. Why did the court conclude that this case should be submitted to a jury? Explain.

7–2b Based on Misrepresentation

When a user or consumer is injured as a result of a manufacturer's or seller's fraudulent misrepresentation, the basis of liability may be the tort of fraud. In this situation, the misrepresentation must have been made knowingly or with reckless disregard for the facts. The intentional mislabeling of packaged cosmetics, for instance, or the intentional concealment of a product's defects constitute fraudulent misrepresentation.

In addition, the misrepresentation must be of a material fact, and the seller must have intended to induce the buyer's reliance on the misrepresentation. Misrepresentation on a label or advertisement is enough to show an intent to induce the reliance of anyone who may use

the product. Finally, the buyer must have relied on the misrepresentation.

7–3 Strict Product Liability

We turn now to the application of strict liability in the area of product liability. Recall that, under the doctrine of strict liability, people may be liable for the results of their acts regardless of their intentions or their exercise of reasonable care. In addition, liability does not depend on privity of contract. In the 1960s, courts applied the doctrine of strict liability in several landmark cases involving manufactured goods, and it has since become a common method of holding manufacturers liable.

7–3a Strict Product Liability and Public Policy

The law imposes strict product liability as a matter of public policy, which may be expressed in a statute or in the common law. This public policy rests on a threefold assumption:

1. Consumers should be protected against unsafe products.
2. Manufacturers and distributors should not escape liability for faulty products simply because they are not in privity of contract with the ultimate user of those products.
3. Manufacturers and distributors can better bear the costs associated with injuries caused by their products, because they can ultimately pass the costs on to all consumers in the form of higher prices.

California was the first state to impose strict product liability in tort on manufacturers. ■ **Case in Point 7.3** William Greenman was injured when his Shopsmith combination power tool threw off a piece of wood that struck him in the head. He sued the manufacturer, claiming that he had followed the manufacturer's instructions and that the product must be defective. In a landmark decision, *Greenman v. Yuba Power Products, Inc.*,[4] the California Supreme Court set out the reason for applying tort law rather than contract law (including laws governing warranties) in cases involving consumers who were injured by defective products.

According to the *Greenman* court, the "purpose of such liability is to [e]nsure that the costs of injuries resulting from defective products are borne by the manufacturers . . . rather than by the injured persons who are powerless to protect themselves." ■ Today, the majority of states recognize strict product liability, although some state courts limit its application to situations involving personal injuries (rather than property damage).

7–3b The Requirements for Strict Product Liability

After the *Restatement (Second) of Torts* was issued in 1964, Section 402A became a widely accepted statement of how the doctrine of strict liability should be applied to sellers of goods (including manufacturers, processors, assemblers, packagers, bottlers, wholesalers, distributors,

retailers, and lessors). The bases for an action in strict liability that are set forth in Section 402A can be summarized as a set of six requirements.

1. The product must be in a *defective condition* when the defendant sells it.
2. The defendant must normally be engaged in the *business of selling* (or otherwise distributing) that product.
3. The product must be *unreasonably dangerous* to the user or consumer because of its defective condition (in most states).
4. The plaintiff must incur *physical harm* to self or property by use or consumption of the product.
5. The defective condition must be the *proximate cause* of the injury or damage.
6. The *goods must not have been substantially changed* from the time the product was sold to the time the injury was sustained.

Depending on the jurisdiction, if these requirements are met, a manufacturer's liability to an injured party can be almost unlimited.

Proving a Defective Condition Under these requirements, in any action against a manufacturer, seller, or lessor, the plaintiff need not show why or in what manner the product became defective. The plaintiff does, however, have to prove that the product was defective at the time it left the hands of the seller or lessor. The plaintiff must also show that this defective condition made the product "unreasonably dangerous" to the user or consumer.

Unless evidence can be presented to support the conclusion that the product was defective when it was sold or leased, the plaintiff will not succeed. If the product was delivered in a safe condition and subsequent mishandling made it harmful to the user, the seller or lessor normally is not strictly liable.

Unreasonably Dangerous Products The *Restatement* recognizes that many products cannot be made entirely safe for all uses. Thus, sellers or lessors are liable only for products that are *unreasonably* dangerous. A court could consider a product so defective as to be an **unreasonably dangerous product** in either of the following situations:

1. The product was dangerous beyond the expectation of the ordinary consumer.
2. A less dangerous alternative was *economically* feasible for the manufacturer, but the manufacturer failed to produce it.

A product may be unreasonably dangerous due to the defects discussed next.

---

4. 59 Cal.2d 57, 377 P.2d 897, 27 Cal.Rptr. 697 (1962).

7–3c Product Defects

The *Restatement (Third) of Torts: Products Liability* defines three types of product defects that have traditionally been recognized in product liability law—manufacturing defects, design defects, and inadequate warnings.

Manufacturing Defects According to Section 2(a) of the *Restatement (Third) of Torts*, a product "contains a manufacturing defect when the product departs from its intended design even though all possible care was exercised in the preparation and marketing of the product." Basically, a manufacturing defect is a departure from a product unit's design specifications that results in products that are physically flawed, damaged, or incorrectly assembled. A glass bottle that is made too thin and explodes in a consumer's face is an example of a product with a manufacturing defect.

Quality Control. Usually, manufacturing defects occur when a manufacturer fails to assemble, test, or check the quality of a product adequately. Liability is imposed on the manufacturer (and on the wholesaler and retailer) regardless of whether the manufacturer's quality control efforts were "reasonable." The idea behind holding defendants strictly liable for manufacturing defects is to encourage greater investment in product safety and stringent quality control standards.

Expert Testimony. Cases involving allegations of a manufacturing defect are often decided based on the opinions and testimony of experts. ■ **Case in Point 7.4** Kevin Schmude purchased an eight-foot stepladder and used it to install radio-frequency shielding in a hospital room. While Schmude was standing on the ladder, it collapsed, and he was seriously injured. He filed a lawsuit against the ladder's maker, Tricam Industries, Inc., based on a manufacturing defect.

Experts testified that the preexisting holes in the ladder's top cap did not properly line up with the holes in the rear right rail and backing plate. As a result of the misalignment, the rear legs of the ladder were not securely fastened in place, causing the ladder to fail. A jury concluded that this manufacturing defect made the ladder unreasonably dangerous and awarded Schmude more than $677,000 in damages.[5] ■

Design Defects Unlike a product with a manufacturing defect, a product with a design defect is made in conformity with the manufacturer's design specifications.

Nevertheless, the product results in injury to the user because the design itself was faulty. A product "is defective in design when the foreseeable risks of harm posed by the product could have been reduced or avoided by the adoption of a reasonable alternative design by the seller or other distributor, or a predecessor in the commercial chain of distribution, and the omission of the alternative design renders the product not reasonably safe."[6]

Test for Design Defects. To successfully assert a design defect, a plaintiff has to show that:

1. A reasonable alternative design was available.
2. As a result of the defendant's failure to adopt the alternative design, the product was not reasonably safe.

In other words, a manufacturer or other defendant is liable only when the harm was reasonably preventable.

Factors to Be Considered. According to the *Restatement*, a court can consider a broad range of factors in deciding claims of design defects. These include the magnitude and probability of the foreseeable risks, as well as the relative advantages and disadvantages of the product as it was designed and as it could have been designed.

Risk-Utility Analysis. Most courts engage in a risk-utility analysis to determine whether the risk of harm from the product as designed outweighs its utility to the user and to the public. ■ **Case in Point 7.5** Benjamin Riley, the county sheriff, was driving his Ford F-150 pickup truck near Ehrhardt, South Carolina, when it collided with another vehicle. The impact caused Riley's truck to leave the road and roll over. The driver's door of the truck opened in the collision, and Riley was ejected and killed.

Riley's widow, Laura, as the representative of his estate, filed a product liability suit against Ford Motor Company. She alleged that the design of the door-latch system of the truck allowed the door to open in the collision. A state court awarded the estate $900,000 in damages "because of the stature of Riley and what he's done in life, what he's contributed to his family."

Ford appealed, but the court found that a reasonable alternative design was available for the door-latch system. Evidence showed that Ford was aware of the safety problems presented by the current system (a rod-linkage system). After conducting a risk-utility analysis of a different system (a cable-linkage system), Ford had concluded that the alternative system was feasible and perhaps superior. The state's highest court affirmed the damages award.[7] ■

---

5. *Schmude v. Tricam Industries, Inc.*, 550 F.Supp.2d 846 (E.D.Wis. 2008).

6. *Restatement (Third) of Torts: Products Liability*, Section 2(b).
7. *Riley v. Ford Motor Co.*, 414 S.C. 185, 777 S.E.2d 824 (2015).

Consumer-Expectation Test. Other courts apply the consumer-expectation test to determine whether a product's design was defective. Under this test, a product is unreasonably dangerous when it fails to perform in the manner that would reasonably be expected by an ordinary consumer.

■ **Case in Point 7.6** A representative from Wilson Sporting Goods Company gave Edwin Hickox an umpire's mask that was designed to be safer than other such masks. The mask had a newly designed throat guard that angled forward instead of extending straight down. Hickox was wearing the mask while working as an umpire at a game when he was struck by a ball and injured. He suffered a concussion and damage to his inner ear, which caused permanent hearing loss.

Hickox and his wife sued Wilson for product liability based on a defective design and won. Wilson appealed. The reviewing court affirmed the jury's verdict. The design was defective because "an ordinary consumer would have expected the mask to perform more safely than it did." The evidence presented to the jury had

shown that Wilson's mask was more dangerous than comparable masks sold at the time.[8] ■

Inadequate Warnings A product may also be deemed defective because of inadequate instructions or warnings. A product will be considered defective "when the foreseeable risks of harm posed by the product could have been reduced or avoided by the provision of reasonable instructions or warnings by the seller or other distributor . . . and the omission of the instructions or warnings renders the product not reasonably safe."[9] Generally, a seller must also warn consumers of harm that can result from the *foreseeable misuse* of its product.

Note that the plaintiff must show that the inadequate warning was the proximate cause of the injuries that she or he sustained. In the following case, a drug manufacturer argued that an injured plaintiff had failed to prove that an inadequate warning was the cause of his injuries.

---

8. *Wilson Sporting Goods Co. v. Hickox*, 59 A.3d 1267 (D.C.App. 2013).
9. *Restatement (Third) of Torts: Products Liability*, Section 2(c).

Case 7.2

Stange v. Janssen Pharmaceuticals, Inc.

Superior Court of Pennsylvania, 2018 PA Super 4, 179 A.3d 45 (2018).

Background and Facts Timothy Stange was twelve years old when his doctor prescribed Risperdal, an antipsychotic drug, to treat his Tourette's syndrome. Stange subsequently developed female breasts, a condition known as gynecomastia. Surgery successfully removed Stange's breasts, but left him with permanent scars and pain. Risperdal is made by Janssen Pharmaceuticals, Inc. Janssen knew that gynecomastia was a frequent adverse event in children and adolescents who took Risperdal. But its label significantly downplayed the risk, stating, for example, that the disorder's occurrence was "rare."

Stange filed a suit in a Pennsylvania state court against Janssen, alleging that the maker had negligently failed to adequately warn of the risk of gynecomastia associated with Risperdal use. The court entered a judgment in favor of the plaintiff for more than $500,000. Janssen appealed to a state intermediate appellate court.

In the Language of the Court

Opinion by *FORD ELLIOTT*, P.J.E. [Presiding Judge Emeritus]

* * * *

* * * Janssen argues that Stange failed to prove proximate cause, *i.e.*, that an inadequate warning was the cause of Stange's injuries. * * * Janssen argues that it was entitled to [a judgment notwithstanding the verdict (JNOV) because] Stange failed to prove that additional risk information would have changed Dr. Kovnar's prescribing decision.

To support his claim of negligence, Stange must establish that Janssen breached its duty to warn, and that the breach caused his injuries.

A plaintiff who has established both a duty and a failure to warn must also establish causation by showing that, if properly warned, he or she would have altered behavior and avoided injury. * * * Absent proof that a more complete or explicit warning would have prevented Stange's use of Risperdal, he cannot establish that Janssen's alleged failure to warn was the proximate cause of his injuries. [Emphasis added.]

In cases involving the failure to warn of risks associated with prescription drugs, * * * a manufacturer will be held liable only where it fails to exercise reasonable care to inform a physician of the facts which make the drug likely to be dangerous. The manufacturer has the duty to disclose risks to the physician, as opposed to the patient, because it is the duty of the prescribing physician to be fully aware of (1) the characteristics of the drug he is prescribing, (2) the amount of the drug which can be safely administered, and (3) the different medications the patient is taking. It is also the duty of the prescribing physician to advise the patient of any dangers or side effects associated with the use of the drug as well as how and when to take the drug.

* * * There was substantial evidence that Janssen intentionally downplayed the risk of gynecomastia for adolescent boys using Risperdal. * * * The * * * label * * * reported that gynecomastia occurred in less than 1% of adult patients and less than 5% of pediatric patients treated with Risperdal. Both of these warnings were inaccurate based on the scientific evidence that the Defendants possessed [which] indicated that gynecomastia was a frequent adverse event, not "rare." * * * These warnings were not accurate, strong, or clear. Instead, the warnings, to the extent they warned at all, were inaccurate and misleading about the risks of gynecomastia.

Furthermore, Dr. Kovnar, Stange's pediatric neurologist, testified that * * * he would not have prescribed Risperdal to Stange had he been aware of the increased risk.

* * * The trial court did not err in refusing to grant JNOV.

Decision and Remedy *The appellate court affirmed the judgment in favor of Stange. "Due to Janssen's inadequate labeling and failure to warn, Dr. Kovnar was unaware of the specific heightened risks associated with the use of Risperdal." Otherwise, he would have prescribed a different drug for Stange.*

Critical Thinking
- **Economic** *Why did Janssen downplay the risks of Risperdal in the warnings to physicians? Discuss.*
- **What If the Facts Were Different?** *Suppose that instead of suffering harm through a prescription drug's legitimate use, the plaintiff had been injured by a drug's illegal abuse. Would the result have been different? Explain.*

Content of Warnings. Important factors for a court to consider include the risks of a product, the "content and comprehensibility" and "intensity of expression" of warnings and instructions, and the "characteristics of expected user groups."[10] Courts apply a "reasonableness" test to determine if the warnings adequately alert consumers to the product's risks. For instance, children will likely respond readily to bright, bold, simple warning labels, whereas educated adults might need more detailed information. For more on tips on making sure a product's warnings are adequate, see this chapter's *Managerial Strategy* feature.

■ **Case in Point 7.7** Jeffrey Johnson went to an emergency room for an episode of atrial fibrillation, a heart rhythm disorder. Dr. David Hahn used a defibrillator manufactured by Medtronic, Inc., to deliver electric shocks to Johnson's heart. The defibrillator had synchronous and asynchronous modes, and it reverted to the asynchronous mode after each use. Hahn intended to deliver synchronized shocks, which would have required

him to select the synchronous mode for each shock. But Hahn did not read the device's instructions, which Medtronic had provided both in a manual and on the device itself. As a result, the physician delivered one synchronized shock, followed by twelve asynchronous shocks that endangered Johnson's life.

Johnson and his wife filed a product liability suit against Medtronic, asserting that Medtronic had provided inadequate warnings about the defibrillator and that the device had a design defect. A Missouri appellate court held that the Johnsons could not pursue a claim based on the inadequacy of Medtronic's warnings, but they could pursue a claim alleging a design defect. The court reasoned that, in some cases, "a manufacturer may be held liable where it chooses to warn of the danger . . . rather than preclude the danger by design."[11] ■

Obvious Risks. There is no duty to warn about risks that are obvious or commonly known. Warnings about such risks do not add to the safety of a product and could

---

10. *Restatement (Third) of Torts: Products Liability*, Section 2, Comment h.

11. *Johnson v. Medtronic, Inc.*, 365 S.W.3d 226 (Mo.App. 2012).

Managerial Strategy

When Is a Warning Legally Bulletproof?

A company can sell a perfectly manufactured and designed product, yet still face product liability lawsuits for failure to provide appropriate warnings. According to the *Restatement (Third) of Torts*, a product may be deemed defective because of inadequate instructions or warnings when the foreseeable risks of harm posed by the product could have been reduced by reasonable warnings offered by the seller or other distributor.

Manufacturers and distributors have a duty to warn users of any hidden dangers of their products. Additionally, they have a duty to instruct users in how to use the product to avoid any dangers. Warnings generally must be clear and specific. They must also be conspicuous.

When No Warning Is Required

Not all products have to provide warnings. People are expected to know that knives can cut fingers, for example, so a seller need not place a bright orange label on each knife sold reminding consumers of this danger. Most household products are generally safe when used as intended.

In a New Jersey case, an appeals court reviewed a product liability case against the manufacturer of a Razor A–type kick scooter. A ten-year-old boy was injured when he fell and struck his face on the scooter's handlebars. The padded end caps on the handlebars had deteriorated, and the boy's mother had thrown them away, exposing the metal ends.

The boy and his mother sued, claiming that the manufacturer was required to provide a warning to prevent injuries of this type. The appellate court noted, however, that the plaintiffs were not able to claim that the Razor A was defective. "Lacking evidence that Razor A's end-cap design was defective, plaintiffs cannot show

that Razor A had a duty to warn of such a defect, and therefore cannot make out their failure to warn claim."[a]

Warnings on Medications

In a case involving a prescription medication, a woman suffered neurological disorders after taking a generic drug to treat her gastroesophageal reflux disease. Part of her complaint asserted strict liability for failure to warn. The plaintiff claimed that the manufacturer had not updated its label to indicate that usage should not exceed twelve weeks. The reviewing court reasoned that "The adequacy of the instructions . . . made no difference to the outcome . . . because [the plaintiff alleges that her prescribing physician] did not read those materials."[b]

In contrast, in a Pennsylvania case, a family was awarded over $10 million in a lawsuit against Johnson & Johnson for defective warnings on bottles of children's Motrin. A three-year-old girl suffered burns over 84 percent of her skin, experienced brain damage, and went blind after suffering a reaction to the drug. The drug did have a specific warning label that instructed consumers to stop taking the medication and contact a physician in the event of an allergic reaction. Nonetheless, Johnson & Johnson was found liable for failing to warn about the known risk of severe side effects.[c]

Business Questions

1. *To protect themselves, manufacturers have been forced to include lengthy safety warnings for their products. What might be the downside of such warnings?*

2. *Does a manufacturer have to create safety warnings for every product? Why or why not?*

a. *Vann v. Toys R Us*, 2014 WL 3537937 (N.J.Super.Ct. A.D. 2014).
b. *Brinkley v. Pfizer, Inc.*, 772 F.3d 1133 (8th Cir. 2014).
c. *Maya v. Johnson & Johnson*, 2014 PA Super 152, 97 A.3d 1203 (2014).

even detract from it by making other warnings seem less significant. As will be discussed later in the chapter, the obviousness of a risk and a user's decision to proceed in the face of that risk may be a defense in a product liability suit based on an inadequate warning.

■ **Example 7.8** Sixteen-year-old Lana White attempts to do a back flip on a trampoline and fails. She is paralyzed as a result. There are nine warning labels affixed to the trampoline, an instruction manual with safety

warnings, and a placard at the entrance advising users not to do flips. If White sues the manufacturer for inadequate warnings in this situation, she is likely to lose. The warning labels are probably sufficient to make the risks obvious and insulate the manufacturer from liability for her injuries. ■

Risks that may seem obvious to some users, though, will not be obvious to all users, especially when the users are likely to be children. A young child may not be able to read or understand warning labels or comprehend the risk of certain activities. To avoid liability, the manufacturer would have to prove that the warnings it provided were adequate to make the risk of injury obvious to a young child.[12]

State Laws and Constitutionality. An action alleging that a product is defective due to an inadequate label can be based on state law, but that law must not violate the U.S. Constitution. ■ **Case in Point 7.9** California once enacted a law imposing restrictions and a labeling requirement on the sale or rental of "violent video games" to minors. Although the video game industry had adopted a voluntary rating system for games, the legislators deemed those labels inadequate.

The Video Software Dealers Association and the Entertainment Software Association immediately filed a suit in federal court to invalidate the law, and the law was struck down. The state appealed to the United States Supreme Court. The Court found that the definition of a violent video game in California's law was unconstitutionally vague and violated the First Amendment's guarantee of freedom of speech.[13] ■

7–3d Market-Share Liability

Ordinarily, in all product liability claims, a plaintiff must prove that the defective product that caused his or her injury was the product of a specific defendant. In a few situations, however, courts have dropped this requirement when plaintiffs could not prove which of many distributors of a harmful product supplied the particular product that caused the injuries. Under a theory of **market-share liability,** a court can hold each manufacturer responsible for a percentage of the plaintiff's damages that is equal to the percentage of its market share.

■ **Case in Point 7.10** Suffolk County Water Authority (SCWA) is a municipal water supplier in New York. SCWA discovered the presence of a toxic chemical—perchloroethylene (PCE), which is used by dry cleaners and others—in its local water. SCWA filed a product liability lawsuit against Dow Chemical Corporation and other companies that manufactured and distributed PCE. Dow filed a motion to dismiss the case for failure to state a claim, because SCWA could not identify each

defendant whose allegedly defective product caused the water contamination. A state trial court refused to dismiss the action, holding that SCWA's allegations were sufficient to invoke market-share liability.[14] ■

Many jurisdictions do not recognize the market-share theory of liability because they believe that it deviates too significantly from traditional legal principles. Jurisdictions that do recognize market-share liability apply it only when it is difficult to determine which company made a particular product.

7–3e Other Applications of Strict Product Liability

Almost all courts extend the strict liability of manufacturers and other sellers to injured bystanders. Thus, if a defective forklift that will not go into reverse injures a passerby, that individual can sue the manufacturer for product liability (and possibly also sue the forklift operator for negligence).

Strict product liability also applies to suppliers of component parts. ■ **Example 7.11** Toyota buys brake pads from a subcontractor and puts them in Corollas without changing their composition. If those pads are defective, both the supplier of the brake pads and Toyota will be held strictly liable for the injuries caused by the defects. ■

7–4 Defenses to Product Liability

Defendants in product liability suits can raise a number of defenses. One defense, of course, is to show that there is no basis for the plaintiff's claim. Thus, for instance, in an action based on negligence, if a defendant can show that the plaintiff has *not* met the requirements for such an action (such as causation), then generally the defendant will not be liable.

Similarly, in a case involving strict product liability, a defendant can claim that the plaintiff failed to meet one of the requirements. For instance, if the defendant shows that the goods were altered after they were sold, normally the defendant will not be held liable.

In the following case, a product's safety switch had been disabled before the plaintiff used the product.

12. See, for example, *Bunch v. Hoffinger Industries, Inc.*, 123 Cal.App.4th 1278, 20 Cal.Rptr.3d 780 (2004).

13. *Video Software Dealers Association v. Schwarzenegger*, 556 F.3d 950 (9th Cir. 2009); *Brown v. Entertainment Merchants Association*, 564 U.S. 786, 131 S.Ct. 2729, 180 L.Ed.2d 708 (2011).

14. *Suffolk County Water Authority v. Dow Chemical Co.*, 44 Misc.3d 569, 987 N.Y.S.2d 819 (2014).

VeRost v. Mitsubishi Caterpillar Forklift America, Inc.

New York Supreme Court, Appellate Division, Fourth Department, 124 A.D.3d 1219, 1 N.Y.S.3d 589 (2015).

Background and Facts Drew VeRost was employed at a manufacturing facility in Buffalo, New York, owned by Nuttall Gear, LLC. While operating a forklift at Nuttall's facility, VeRost climbed out of the seat and attempted to engage a lever on the vehicle. As he stood on the front of the forklift and reached for the lever with his hand, he inadvertently stepped on the vehicle's gearshift. The activated gears caused part of the forklift to move backward, injuring him. He filed a suit in a New York state court against the forklift's maker, Mitsubishi Caterpillar Forklift America, Inc., and others, asserting claims in product liability.

The defendants established that the vehicle had been manufactured with a safety switch that would have prevented the accident had it not been disabled after delivery to Nuttall. The court issued a summary judgment in the defendants' favor. VeRost appealed.

In the Language of the Court

MEMORANDUM:

* * * *

The forklift in question was manufactured by defendant Mitsubishi Caterpillar Forklift America, Inc. (MCFA), and sold new to Nuttall Gear by defendants Buffalo Lift Trucks, Inc. (Buffalo Lift) and Mullen Industrial Handling Corp. (Mullen). The forklift as manufactured was equipped with a seat safety switch that would render the forklift inoperable if the operator was not in the driver's seat. At the time of the accident, however, someone had intentionally disabled the safety switch by installing a "jumper wire" under the seat of the forklift. As a result, the forklift still had power when the operator was not in the driver's seat. Of the 10 forklifts owned by Nuttall Gear, seven had "jumper wires" installed that disabled the safety switches.

The complaint asserts causes of action against MCFA, Buffalo Lift and Mullen sounding in strict products liability, alleging, *inter alia* ["among other things"], that the forklift was defectively designed and that those defendants failed to provide adequate "warnings for the safe operation, maintenance repair and servicing of the forklift." * * * Following discovery, the * * * defendants * * * each moved for summary judgment dismissing the complaint against them, contending that the forklift was safe when it was manufactured and delivered to Nuttall Gear, and that it was thereafter rendered unsafe by a third party who deactivated the safety switch. * * * [The] Supreme Court [of New York] granted the motions and dismissed the complaint in its entirety, and this appeal ensued.

We conclude that the court properly granted the motions of the * * * defendants. * * * *A manufacturer, who has designed and produced a safe product, will not be liable for injuries resulting from substantial alterations or modifications of the product by a third party which render the product defective or otherwise unsafe.* Here, the * * * defendants established as a matter of law that the forklift was not defectively designed by establishing that, when it was manufactured and delivered to Nuttall Gear, it had a safety switch that would have prevented plaintiff's accident, and a third party thereafter made a substantial modification to the forklift by disabling the safety switch. [Emphasis added.]

Decision and Remedy *The state intermediate appellate court affirmed the lower court's judgment in Mitsubishi's favor. To succeed in an action based on product liability, the goods at issue must not have been substantially changed from the time the product was sold to the time the injury was sustained. VeRost could not meet this requirement.*

Critical Thinking

- **Legal Environment** *Could VeRost succeed in an action against Nuttall, alleging that the company's failure to maintain the forklift in a safe condition constituted negligence? Discuss.*

7–4a Preemption

A defense that has been successfully raised by defendants in recent years is preemption—that government regulations preempt claims for product liability. An injured party may not be able to sue the manufacturer of defective products that are subject to comprehensive federal regulatory schemes.

■ **Case in Point 7.12** Medical devices are subject to extensive government regulation and undergo a rigorous premarket approval process. The United States Supreme Court decided in *Riegel v. Medtronic, Inc.*,[15] that a man who was injured by an approved medical device (a balloon catheter) could not sue its maker for product liability. The Court reasoned that Congress had created a comprehensive scheme of federal safety oversight for medical devices. The U.S. Food and Drug Administration is required to review the design, labeling, and manufacturing of medical devices before they are marketed to make sure that they are safe and effective. Because premarket approval is a "rigorous process," it preempts all common law claims challenging the safety or effectiveness of a medical device that has been approved. ■

Since the *Medtronic* decision, some courts have extended the preemption defense to other product liability actions. Other courts have been unwilling to deny an injured party relief simply because the federal government was supposed to ensure a product's safety.[16] Even the United States Supreme Court refused to extend the preemption defense to preclude a drug maker's liability in one subsequent case.[17]

7–4b Assumption of Risk

Assumption of risk can sometimes be used as a defense in a product liability action. To establish assumption of risk, the defendant must show the following:

1. The plaintiff knew and appreciated the risk created by the product defect.
2. The plaintiff voluntarily assumed the risk—by express agreement or by words or conduct—even though it was unreasonable to do so.

Some states do not allow the defense of assumption of risk in strict product liability claims, however. ■ **Case in Point 7.13** When Savannah Boles became a customer of Executive Tans, she signed a contract. One part of the contract stated that signers used the company's tanning booths at their own risk. It also released the manufacturer and others from liability for any injuries.

Later, Boles's fingers were partially amputated when they came into contact with a tanning booth's fan. Boles sued the manufacturer for strict product liability. The Colorado Supreme Court held that assumption of risk was not applicable because strict product liability is driven by public-policy considerations. The theory focuses on the nature of the product rather than the conduct of either the manufacturer or the person injured.[18] ■

7–4c Product Misuse

Similar to the defense of voluntary assumption of risk is that of **product misuse,** which occurs when a product is used for a purpose for which it was not intended. The courts have severely limited this defense, and it is now recognized as a defense *only when the particular use was not foreseeable.* If the misuse is reasonably foreseeable, the seller must take measures to guard against it.

■ **Case in Point 7.14** David Stults developed bronchiolitis obliterans ("popcorn lung") from consuming multiple bags of microwave popcorn daily for several years. When Stults filed a lawsuit against the popcorn manufacturers, they asked the court for a summary judgment in their favor. The court denied the defendants' motion and found that a manufacturer has a duty to warn of dangers associated with reasonably foreseeable misuses of a product. If it is foreseeable that a person might consume several bags of microwave popcorn a day, then the manufacturer might have to warn users about the potential health risks associated with doing so.[19] ■

7–4d Comparative Negligence (Fault)

Comparative negligence, or fault, can also affect strict liability claims. Today, courts in many jurisdictions consider the negligent or intentional actions of both the plaintiff and the defendant when apportioning liability

---

15. 552 U.S. 312, 128 S.Ct. 999, 169 L.Ed.2d 892 (2008). For another case in which the Court found preemption, see *Bruesewitz v. Wyeth, LLC,* 562 U.S. 223, 131 S.Ct. 1068, 179 L.Ed.2d 1 (2011).
16. See, for example, *Fortner v. Bristol-Myers Squibb Co.,* 2017 WL 3193928 (S.D.N.Y. 2017).
17. *Wyeth v. Levine,* 555 U.S. 555, 129 S.Ct. 1187, 173 L.Ed.2d 51 (2009).

18. *Boles v. Sun Ergoline, Inc.,* 223 P.3d 724 (Colo. 2010).
19. *Stults v. International Flavors and Fragrances, Inc.,* 31 F.Supp.3d 1015 (N.D. Iowa 2014).

and damages. A defendant may be able to limit some of its liability if it can show that the plaintiff's misuse of the product contributed to his or her injuries.

When proved, comparative negligence differs from other defenses in that it does not completely absolve the defendant of liability. It can, however, reduce the total amount of damages that will be awarded to the plaintiff. Note that some jurisdictions allow only intentional conduct to affect a plaintiff's recovery, whereas other states allow ordinary negligence to be used as a defense to product liability.

7–4e Commonly Known Dangers

The dangers associated with certain products (such as matches and sharp knives) are so commonly known that, as mentioned, manufacturers need not warn users of those dangers. If a defendant succeeds in convincing the court that a plaintiff's injury resulted from a *commonly known danger*, the defendant will not be liable.

■ **Case in Point 7.15** In a classic example, Marguerite Jamieson was injured when an elastic exercise rope slipped off her foot and struck her in the eye, causing a detachment of the retina. Jamieson claimed that the manufacturer should be liable because it had failed to warn users that the exerciser might slip off a foot in such a manner.

The court stated that to hold the manufacturer liable in these circumstances "would go beyond the reasonable dictates of justice in fixing the liabilities of manufacturers." After all, stated the court, "almost every physical object can be inherently dangerous or potentially dangerous in a sense. . . . A manufacturer cannot manufacture a knife that will not cut or a hammer that will not mash a thumb or a stove that will not burn a finger. The law does not require [manufacturers] to warn of such common dangers."[20] ■

7–4f Knowledgeable User

A related defense is the *knowledgeable user* defense. If a particular danger (such as electrical shock) is or should be commonly known by particular users of a product (such as electricians), the manufacturer need not warn these users of the danger.

■ **Case in Point 7.16** The parents of teenagers who had become overweight and developed health problems filed a product liability suit against McDonald's. The plaintiffs claimed that the fast-food chain had failed to warn customers of the adverse health effects of eating its food. The court rejected this claim, however, based on the knowledgeable user defense.

The court found that it is well known that the food at McDonald's contains high levels of cholesterol, fat, salt, and sugar and is therefore unhealthful. The court stated, "If consumers know (or reasonably should know) the potential ill health effects of eating at McDonald's, they cannot blame McDonald's if they, nonetheless, choose to satiate their appetite with a surfeit [excess] of supersized McDonald's products."[21] ■

7–4g Statutes of Limitations and Repose

Statutes of limitations restrict the time within which an action may be brought. The statute of limitations for product liability cases varies according to state law. Usually, the injured party must bring a product liability claim within two to four years. Often, the running of the prescribed period is **tolled** (that is, suspended) until the party suffering an injury has discovered it or should have discovered it.

To ensure that sellers and manufacturers will not be left vulnerable to lawsuits indefinitely, many states have passed **statutes of repose,** which place *outer* time limits on product liability actions. For instance, a statute of repose may require that claims be brought within twelve years from the date of sale or manufacture of the defective product. If the plaintiff does not bring an action before the prescribed period expires, the seller cannot be held liable.

Concept Summary 7.1 reviews the possible defenses in product liability actions.

20. *Jamieson v. Woodward & Lothrop*, 247 F.2d 23 (D.C.Cir. 1957).

21. *Pelman v. McDonald's Corp.*, 237 F.Supp.2d 512 (S.D.N.Y. 2003).

Concept Summary 7.1

Defenses to Product Liability

Preemption	If the product is subject to comprehensive federal safety regulations
Assumption of Risk	When the user or consumer knew the risk and voluntarily assumed it
Product Misuse	If the consumer misused the product in an unforeseeable way
Comparative Negligence	Apportions liability if the defendant was also negligent
Commonly Known Dangers	If the product was commonly known to be dangerous
Knowledgeable User	If the particular danger is commonly known by particular users of the product
Statutory Time Periods	If the statute of limitations or statute of repose period has expired

---

Practice and Review: Strict Liability and Product Liability

Shalene Kolchek bought a Great Lakes Spa from Val Porter, a dealer who was selling spas at the state fair. Kolchek signed an installment contract. Porter then handed her the manufacturer's paperwork and arranged for the spa to be delivered and installed for her. Three months later, Kolchek left her six-year-old daughter, Litisha, alone in the spa. While exploring the spa's hydromassage jets, Litisha stuck her index finger into one of the jet holes and was unable to remove her finger from the jet.

Litisha yanked hard, injuring her finger, then panicked and screamed for help. Kolchek was unable to remove Litisha's finger, and the local police and rescue team were called to assist. After a three-hour operation that included draining the spa, sawing out a section of the spa's plastic molding, and slicing the jet casing, Litisha's finger was freed. Following this procedure, the spa was no longer functional. Litisha was taken to the local emergency room, where she was told that a bone in her finger was broken in two places. Using the information presented in the chapter, answer the following questions.

1. Under which theories of product liability can Kolchek sue Porter to recover for Litisha's injuries?
2. Would privity of contract be required for Kolchek to succeed in a product liability action against Great Lakes? Explain.
3. For an action in strict product liability against Great Lakes, what six requirements must Kolchek meet?
4. What defenses to product liability might Porter or Great Lakes be able to assert?

Debate This . . .   *All liability suits against tobacco companies for lung cancer should be thrown out of court now and forever.*

Terms and Concepts

market-share liability 143	product misuse 145	tolled 146
privity of contract 135	statutes of repose 146	unreasonably dangerous
product liability 134	strict liability 134	product 138

Issue Spotters

1. Rim Corporation makes tire rims that it sells to Superior Vehicles, Inc., which installs them on cars. One set of rims is defective, which an inspection would reveal. Superior does not inspect the rims. The car with the defective rims is sold to Town Auto Sales, which sells the car to Uri. Soon, the car is in an accident caused by the defective rims, and Uri is injured. Is Superior Vehicles liable? Explain your answer. (See *Strict Product Liability*.)

2. Bensing Company manufactures generic drugs for the treatment of heart disease. A federal law requires generic drug makers to use labels that are identical to the labels on brand-name versions of the drugs. Hunter Rothfus purchased Bensing's generic drugs in Ohio and wants to sue Bensing for defective labeling based on its failure to comply with Ohio state common law (rather than the federal labeling requirements). What defense might Bensing assert to avoid liability under state law? (See *Defenses to Product Liability*.)

• **Check your answers to the Issue Spotters against the answers provided in Appendix B at the end of this text.**

Business Scenarios and Case Problems

7–1. Strict Liability. Danny and Marion Klein were injured when part of a fireworks display went astray and exploded near them. They sued Pyrodyne Corp., the pyrotechnic company that was hired to set up and discharge the fireworks. The Kleins alleged, among other things, that the company should be strictly liable for damages caused by the fireworks display. Will the court agree with the Kleins? What factors will the court consider in making its decision? Discuss fully. (See *Strict Liability*.)

7–2. Product Liability. Jason Clark, an experienced hunter, bought a paintball gun. Clark practiced with the gun and knew how to screw in the carbon dioxide cartridge, pump the gun, and use its safety and trigger. Although Clark was aware that he could purchase protective eyewear, he chose not to buy it. Clark had taken gun safety courses and understood that it was "common sense" not to shoot anyone in the face. Clark's friend, Chris Wright, also owned a paintball gun and was similarly familiar with the gun's use and its risks.

Clark, Wright, and their friends played a game that involved shooting paintballs at cars whose occupants also had the guns. One night, while Clark and Wright were cruising with their guns, Wright shot at Clark's car, but hit Clark in the eye. Clark filed a product liability lawsuit against the manufacturer of Wright's paintball gun to recover for the injury. Clark claimed that the gun was defectively designed. During the trial, Wright testified that his gun "never malfunctioned." In whose favor should the court rule? Why? (See *Product Liability*.)

7–3. Strict Product Liability. David Dobrovolny bought a new Ford F-350 pickup truck. A year later, the truck spontaneously caught fire in Dobrovolny's driveway. The truck was destroyed, but no other property was damaged, and no one was injured. Dobrovolny filed a suit in a Nebraska state court against Ford Motor Company on a theory of strict product liability to recover the cost of the truck. Nebraska limits the application of strict product liability to situations involving personal injuries. Is Dobrovolny's claim likely to succeed? Why or why not? Is there another basis for liability on which he might recover? Explain. [*Dobrovolny v. Ford Motor Co.*, 281 Neb. 86, 793 N.W.2d 445 (2011)] (See *Strict Product Liability*.)

7–4. Product Misuse. Five-year-old Cheyenne Stark was riding in the backseat of her parents' Ford Taurus. Cheyenne was not sitting in a booster seat. Instead, she was using a seatbelt designed by Ford but was wearing the shoulder belt behind her back. The car was involved in a collision. As a result, Cheyenne suffered a spinal cord injury and was paralyzed from the waist down. The family filed a suit against Ford Motor Co., alleging that the seatbelt was defectively designed. Could Ford successfully claim that Cheyenne had misused the seatbelt? Why or why not? [*Stark v. Ford Motor Co.*, 365 N.C. 468, 723 S.E.2d 753 (2012)] (See *Defenses to Product Liability*.)

7–5. Business Case Problem with Sample Answer— Product Liability. While driving on Interstate 40 in North Carolina, Carroll Jett became distracted by a texting system in the cab of his tractor-trailer truck. He smashed into several vehicles that were slowed or stopped in front of him, injuring Barbara and Michael Durkee and others. The injured motorists filed a suit in a federal district court against Geologic Solutions, Inc., the maker of the texting system, alleging product liability. Was the accident caused by Jett's inattention or the texting device? Should a manufacturer be required to design a product that is incapable of distracting a driver?

Discuss. [*Durkee v. Geologic Solutions, Inc.*, 502 Fed.Appx. 326 (4th Cir. 2013)] (See *Product Liability*.)

- For a sample answer to Problem 7–5, go to Appendix C at the end of this text.

7–6. Strict Product Liability. Duval Ford, LLC, sold a new Ford F-250 pick-up truck to David Sweat. Before taking delivery, Sweat ordered a lift kit to be installed on the truck by a Duval subcontractor. Sweat also replaced the tires and modified the suspension system to increase the towing capacity. Later, through Burkins Chevrolet, Sweat sold the truck to Shaun Lesnick. Sweat had had no problems with the truck's steering or suspension, but Lesnick did. He had the steering repaired and made additional changes, including installing a steering stabilizer and replacing the tires. Two months later, Lesnick was driving the truck when the steering and suspension suddenly failed, and the truck flipped over, causing Lesnick severe injuries. Could Lesnick successfully claim that Duval and Burkins had failed to warn him of the risk of a lifted truck? Explain. [*Lesnick v. Duval Ford, LLC*, 41 Fla.L.Weekly D281, 185 So.3d 577 (1 Dist. 2016)] (See *Strict Product Liability*.)

7–7. Spotlight on Pfizer, Inc.—Defenses to Product Liability. Prescription drugs in the United States must be approved by the Food and Drug Administration (FDA) before they can be sold. A drug maker whose product is approved through the FDA's "abbreviated new drug application" (ANDA) process cannot later change the label without FDA approval. Pfizer, Inc., makes and sells Depo-T, a testosterone replacement drug classified as an ANDA-approved drug. Rodney Guilbeau filed a claim in a federal district court against Pfizer, alleging that he had suffered a "cardiovascular event" after taking Depo-T. He sought recovery based on a state-law product liability theory, arguing that Pfizer had failed to warn patients adequately about the risks. He claimed that after the drug's approval, its maker had become aware of a higher incidence of heart attacks, strokes, and other cardiovascular events among those who took it but had not added a warning to its label. What is Pfizer's best defense to this claim? Explain. [*Guilbeau v. Pfizer, Inc.*, 880 F.3d 304 (7th Cir. 2018)] (See *Defenses to Product Liability*.)

7–8. A Question of Ethics—The IDDR Approach and Product Liability. *While replacing screws in a gutter, John Baugh fell off a ladder and landed headfirst on his concrete driveway. He sustained a severe brain injury, which permanently limited his ability to perform routine physical and intellectual functions. He filed a suit in a federal district court against Cuprum S.A. de C.V., the company that designed and made the ladder, alleging a design defect under product liability theories. Baugh weighed nearly 200 pounds, which was the stated weight limit on this ladder. Kevin Smith, a mechanical engineer, testified on Baugh's behalf that the gusset (bracket) on the ladder's right front side was too short to support Baugh's weight. This caused the ladder's leg to fail and Baugh to fall. In Smith's opinion, a longer gusset would have prevented the accident. Cuprum argued that the accident occurred because Baugh climbed too high on the ladder and stood on its fourth step and pail shelf, neither of which were intended for the purpose. No other person witnessed Baugh using the ladder prior to his fall, however, so there was no evidence to support Cuprum's argument. [Baugh v. Cuprum S.A. de C.V., 845 F.3d 838 (7th Cir. 2017)] (See Strict Product Liability.)*

(a) What is a manufacturer's legal and ethical duty when designing and making products for consumers? Did Cuprum meet this standard? Discuss.

(b) Did the mechanical engineer's testimony establish that a reasonable alternative design was available for Cuprum's ladder? Explain.

Time-Limited Group Assignment

7–9. Product Liability. Bret D'Auguste was an experienced skier when he rented equipment to ski at Hunter Mountain Ski Bowl in New York. When D'Auguste entered an extremely difficult trail, he noticed immediately that the surface consisted of ice with almost no snow. He tried to exit the steeply declining trail by making a sharp right turn, but in the attempt, his left ski snapped off. D'Auguste lost his balance, fell, and slid down the mountain, striking his face and head against a fence along the trail. According to a report by a rental shop employee, one of the bindings on D'Auguste's skis had a "cracked heel housing." D'Auguste filed a lawsuit against the bindings' manufacturer on a theory of strict product liability. The manufacturer filed a motion for summary judgment. (See *Product Liability*.)

(a) The first group will take the position of the manufacturer and develop an argument for why the court should *grant* the summary judgment motion and dismiss the strict product liability claim.

(b) The second group will take the position of D'Auguste and formulate a basis for why the court should *deny* the motion and allow the strict product liability claim.

(c) The third group will evaluate whether D'Auguste assumed the risk of this type of injury.

(d) The fourth group will analyze whether the manufacturer could claim that D'Auguste's negligence (under the comparative negligence doctrine) contributed to his injury.

Chapter 8

Intellectual Property Rights

ntellectual property is any property that results from intellectual, creative processes—the products of an individual's mind. Although it is an abstract term for an abstract concept, intellectual property is nonetheless familiar to almost everyone. The apps for your iPhone, iPad, or Samsung Galaxy, the movies you see, and the music you listen to are all forms of intellectual property.

More than two hundred years ago, the framers of the U.S. Constitution recognized the importance of protecting creative works in Article I, Section 8. Statutory protection of these rights began in the 1940s and continues to evolve to meet the needs of modern society.

Suppose that JD Beverage Company makes and sells a line of flavored vodkas called "Hot Lips Vodka." The name Hot Lips Vodka, along with an image of puckered lips, appears on the label of each bottle. The color of the lips logo depends on the vodka's flavor—red for chili pepper, green for apple, and so on. JD Beverage has registered trademarks for the name Hot Lips Vodka and the puckered lips logo, and the company heavily markets the vodka using hot lips as a theme. Sales of Hot Lips Vodka are at an all-time high.

Now another alcoholic beverage company begins to distribute a line of flavored vodkas called "Kiss Vodka." Like the Hot Lips label, the new vodka's label features the product's name and a puckered lips logo, and the company uses the lips in its marketing. JD Beverage believes that Kiss Vodka's use of the lips logo is diminishing the value of its Hot Lips brand and cutting into its sales. What can JD Beverage do? The answer lies in intellectual property law.

8–1 Trademarks and Related Property

A **trademark** is a distinctive mark, motto, device, or implement that a manufacturer stamps, prints, or otherwise affixes to the goods it produces so that they can be identified on the market and their origins made known. In other words, a trademark is a source indicator. At common law, the person who used a symbol or mark to identify a business or product was protected in the use of that trademark. Clearly, by using another's trademark, a business could lead consumers to believe that its goods were made by the other business. The law seeks to avoid this kind of confusion.

In the following *Classic Case*, the defendants argued that the Coca-Cola trademark was entitled to no protection under the law because the term did not accurately represent the product.

Classic Case 8.1

The Coca-Cola Co. v. The Koke Co. of America
Supreme Court of the United States, 254 U.S. 143, 41 S.Ct. 113, 65 L.Ed. 189 (1920).

Background and Facts John Pemberton, an Atlanta pharmacist, invented a caramel-colored, carbonated soft drink in 1886. His bookkeeper, Frank Robinson, named the beverage Coca-Cola after two of the ingredients, coca leaves and kola nuts. Asa Candler bought the Coca-Cola Company in 1891, and within seven years, he had made the soft drink available throughout the United States, as well as in parts of Canada and Mexico. Candler continued to sell Coke aggressively and to open up new markets, reaching Europe before 1910. In doing so, however, he attracted numerous competitors, some of which tried to capitalize directly on the Coke name.

The Coca-Cola Company sought to enjoin (prevent) the Koke Company of America and other beverage companies from, among other things, using the word *Koke* for their products. The Koke Company of America and other beverage companies contended that the Coca-Cola trademark was a fraudulent representation and that Coca-Cola was therefore not entitled to any help from the courts. The Koke Company and the other defendants alleged that the Coca-Cola Company, by its use of the Coca-Cola name, represented that the beverage contained cocaine (from coca leaves), which it no longer did. The trial court granted the injunction against the Koke Company, but the appellate court reversed the lower court's ruling. Coca-Cola then appealed to the United States Supreme Court.

In the Language of the Court
Mr. Justice *HOLMES* delivered the opinion of the Court.
* * * *

* * * Before 1900 the beginning of [Coca-Cola's] good will was more or less helped by the presence of cocaine, a drug that, like alcohol or caffeine or opium, may be described as a deadly poison or as a valuable [pharmaceutical item, depending on the speaker's purposes]. The amount seems to have been very small,[a] but it may have been enough to begin a bad habit and after the Food and Drug Act of June 30, 1906, if not earlier, long before this suit was brought, it was eliminated from the plaintiff's compound.

* * * Since 1900 the sales have increased at a very great rate corresponding to a like increase in advertising. The name now characterizes a beverage to be had at almost any soda fountain. It means a single thing coming from a single source, and well known to the community. It hardly would be too much to say that the drink characterizes the name as much as the name the drink. In other words *Coca-Cola probably means to most persons the plaintiff's familiar product to be had everywhere rather than a compound of particular substances.* * * * Before this suit was brought the plaintiff had advertised to the public that it must not expect and would not find cocaine, and had eliminated everything tending to suggest cocaine effects except the name and the picture of [coca] leaves and nuts, which probably conveyed little or nothing to most who saw it. It appears to us that it would be going too far to deny the plaintiff relief against a palpable [readily evident] fraud because possibly here and there an ignorant person might call for the drink with the hope for incipient cocaine intoxication. The plaintiff's position must be judged by the facts as they were when the suit was begun, not by the facts of a different condition and an earlier time. [Emphasis added.]

Decision and Remedy *The district court's injunction was allowed to stand. The competing beverage companies were enjoined from calling their products Koke.*

Critical Thinking
- **What If the Facts Were Different?** *Suppose that Coca-Cola had been trying to make the public believe that its product contained cocaine. Would the result in this case likely have been different? Why or why not?*
- **Impact of This Case on Today's Law** *In this early case, the United States Supreme Court made it clear that trademarks and trade names (and nicknames for those marks and names, such as the nickname "Coke" for "Coca-Cola") that are in common use receive protection under the common law. This holding is historically significant because it is the predecessor to the federal statute later passed to protect trademark rights—the Lanham Act of 1946. In many ways, this act represented a codification of common law principles governing trademarks.*

a. In reality, until 1903 the amount of active cocaine in each bottle of Coke was equivalent to one "line" of cocaine.

8–1a Statutory Protection of Trademarks

Statutory protection of trademarks and related property is provided at the federal level by the Lanham Act of 1946.[1] The Lanham Act was enacted, in part, to protect manufacturers from losing business to rival companies that used confusingly similar trademarks. The act incorporates the common law of trademarks and provides remedies for owners of trademarks who wish to enforce their claims in federal court. Many states also have trademark statutes.

Trademark Dilution   In 1995, Congress amended the Lanham Act by passing the Federal Trademark Dilution Act,[2] which allowed trademark owners to bring suits in federal court for trademark **dilution.** In 2006, Congress further amended the law on trademark dilution by passing the Trademark Dilution Revision Act (TDRA).[3]

---

1. 15 U.S.C. Sections 1051–1128.
2. 15 U.S.C. Section 1125.
3. Pub. L. No. 103-312, 120 Stat. 1730 (2006).

Under the TDRA, to state a claim for trademark dilution, a plaintiff must prove the following:

1. The plaintiff owns a famous mark that is distinctive.
2. The defendant has begun using a mark in commerce that allegedly is diluting the famous mark.
3. The similarity between the defendant's mark and the famous mark gives rise to an *association* between the marks.
4. The association is likely to impair the distinctiveness of the famous mark or harm its reputation.

Trademark dilution laws protect "distinctive" or "famous" trademarks (such as Rolls Royce, McDonald's, Starbucks, and Apple) from certain unauthorized uses. Such a mark is protected even when the use is on noncompeting goods or is unlikely to cause confusion. More than half of the states have also enacted trademark dilution laws.

The following case involved an alleged violation of a state trademark law. The parties disputed whether the plaintiff had used the allegedly infringed mark in commerce in the state.

Case 8.2

Headspace International, LLC v. Podworks Corp.

Court of Appeals of Washington, Division 1, 5 Wash.App.2d 883, 428 P.3d 1260 (2018).

Background and Facts   Headspace International, LLC, creates and develops highly refined essential plant oils, including cannabis concentrate, along with other products and services. Headspace uses the trademark "THE CLEAR" for its products and services. The company, which is based in California, licensed the mark to X-Tracted Laboratories 502, Inc., which sells marijuana-related products, including cannabis concentrate, in the state of Washington. The licensing agreement contained terms that provided Headspace with quality assurances related to X-Tracted's use of the trademark.

On learning that another company, Podworks Corporation, was also using "THE CLEAR" to sell cannabis concentrate in Washington, Headspace filed a suit in a Washington state court against Podworks, alleging trademark infringement under state law. The defendant filed a motion to dismiss the complaint on the ground that the plaintiff had failed to allege use of "THE CLEAR" in the ordinary course of trade in Washington and therefore had no rights in the mark in the state. The court granted the motion. Headspace appealed to a state appellate court.

In the Language of the Court

DWYER, J. [Judge]

* * * *

* * * Our state legislature * * * explicitly instructed Washington courts to construe the language of our trademark statute in accordance with federal decisions interpreting the Lanham Act.

Our Supreme Court has employed just such an approach. * * * Thus, consistent with the direction provided by both the legislature and our Supreme Court, we turn to federal court interpretations of the Lanham Act to guide our interpretation of the requirements of our state trademark statute.

Both the Lanham Act and Washington's trademark statute require that a mark be used before it will receive trademark protection. Federal law requires lawful use in commerce, and Washington's statute contains an analogous provision requiring that a mark be placed in the ordinary course of trade in

Washington. *Although Washington's statute does not explicitly state that such placement must be lawful, such a requirement is clearly implied.* [Emphasis added.]

* * * *

Headspace asserts that it alleged use of its mark in the ordinary course of trade in Washington when it alleged X-Tracted's use of the mark on cannabis products X-Tracted produced and sold in Washington. In response, Podworks avers that such indirect placement of the mark in the ordinary course of trade in Washington does not satisfy the requirements of the statute. We disagree. *It does not matter if the use of the mark is direct or indirect. Either can be sufficient to satisfy the requirements of the statute.* [Emphasis added.]

* * * Common law principles and federal court interpretations of the Lanham Act support the view that indirect placement can be sufficient. It is an established principle of the common law of trademark that indirect use of a protected mark by a licensee inures to the benefit of [benefits] the owner of the mark when the owner has sufficient control over the quality of the goods or services provided to customers under the licensed mark.

Similarly, *federal courts have opined that the licensing of trademarked marks is permissible under the Lanham Act when the trademark owner has sufficient control over the quality of goods or services produced by the licensee.* [Emphasis added.]

Here, Headspace's * * * license agreement with X-Tracted included terms that provided Headspace sufficient quality assurances. * * * Because either the * * * quality control terms in the license agreement or Headspace's * * * reliance on X-Tracted's quality control measures would satisfy the applicable test for quality control, we hold that Headspace has made the necessary showing that it alleged use of its mark "THE CLEAR" in the ordinary course of trade in Washington.

Decision and Remedy *The state appellate court reversed the lower court's dismissal of the suit. Headspace used its mark in Washington when it licensed the mark to X-Tracted, subject to terms of quality assurance, and X-Tracted placed the mark on cannabis concentrate in the ordinary course of trade in the state.*

Critical Thinking

• **Legal Environment** *Under Washington state law, an out-of-state company cannot obtain a license to produce, process, or sell marijuana products in Washington. In addition, a Washington-based business that obtains a license to produce, process, or sell marijuana products cannot permit any other entity to participate in the process. Is Headspace in violation of these provisions? Explain.*

• **Social** *Although Washington's statute does not explicitly state that the placement of a mark in commerce must be lawful, why does the court reason that "such a requirement is clearly implied"? Discuss.*

Marks Need Not Be Identical Note that a famous mark may be diluted by the use of an *identical* mark or by the use of a *similar* mark.[4] A similar mark is more likely to lessen the value of a famous mark when the companies using the marks provide related goods or compete against each other in the same market.

■ **Case in Point 8.1** Samantha Lundberg opened a coffee shop under the name "Sambuck's Coffee" in Astoria, Oregon, even though she knew that "Starbucks" was one of the largest coffee chains in the nation. Starbucks Corporation filed a dilution lawsuit, and a federal court ruled that use of the "Sambuck's" mark constituted trademark dilution. Not only was there a "high degree" of similarity between the marks, but also

both companies provided coffee-related services and marketed their services through stand-alone retail stores. Therefore, the use of the similar mark (Sambuck's) reduced the value of the famous mark (Starbucks).[5] ■

8–1b Trademark Registration

Trademarks may be registered with the state or with the federal government. To register for protection under federal trademark law, a person must file an application with the U.S. Patent and Trademark Office in Washington, D.C. Under current law, a mark can be registered (1) if it is currently in commerce or (2) if the applicant intends to put it into commerce within six months.

---

4. See *Moseley v. V Secret Catalogue, Inc.*, 537 U.S. 418, 123 S.Ct. 1115, 155 L.Ed.2d 1 (2003).

5. *Starbucks Corp. v. Lundberg*, 2005 WL 3183858 (D.Or. 2005).

In special circumstances, the six-month period can be extended by thirty months. Thus, the applicant would have a total of three years from the date of notice of trademark approval to make use of the mark and file the required use statement. Registration is postponed until the mark is actually used. During this waiting period, any applicant can legally protect his or her trademark against a third party who previously has neither used the mark nor filed an application for it.

Registration is renewable between the fifth and sixth years after the initial registration and every ten years thereafter (every twenty years for trademarks registered before 1990).

8–1c Trademark Infringement

Registration of a trademark with the U.S. Patent and Trademark Office gives notice on a nationwide basis that the trademark belongs exclusively to the registrant. The registrant is also allowed to use the symbol® to indicate that the mark has been registered. Whenever that trademark is copied to a substantial degree or used in its entirety by another, intentionally or unintentionally, the trademark has been *infringed* (used without authorization).

When a trademark has been infringed, the owner of the mark has a cause of action against the infringer. To succeed in a trademark infringement action, the owner must show that the defendant's use of the mark created a likelihood of confusion about the origin of the defendant's goods or services. (See this chapter's *Global Insight* feature for a discussion of how confusion can arise from product packaging.) The owner need not prove that the infringer acted intentionally or that the trademark was registered (although registration does provide proof of the date of inception of the trademark's use).

Global Insight   ALEVE versus FLANAX—Same Pain Killer, But in Different Countries

How many U.S. residents have not heard of the pain relief drug Aleve? Not many, because the product is so heavily advertised. The same could be said about the painkiller Flanax in Mexico. In fact, Aleve and Flanax are the same drug, owned by the same company, Bayer AG. Bayer has been selling Flanax in Mexico and Latin America since the 1970s.

Trademark Rights versus the Lanham Act

Traditionally, trademark rights have been territorial. Consequently, Bayer did not register the Flanax brand name in the United States. After all, Bayer never sold or marketed any products under the Flanax name in this country. Here, it chose to use the name Aleve.

Taking advantage of this lack of trademark registration in the United States, a small pharmaceutical company named Belmora applied for and obtained a U.S. trademark registration for Flanax. Belmora also used packaging identical to that used for Bayer's Flanax in Mexico, including color schemes and type style. Within the United States, it targeted the Mexican American community with such advertising copy as "Flanax products have been used [for] many, many years in Mexico [and are] now being produced in the United States by Belmora." Clearly, such practices make it difficult, if not impossible, for consumers to distinguish between Bayer's Mexican product and the product offered by Belmora. Bayer petitioned the U.S. Patent and Trademark Office to cancel Belmora's Flanax trademark registration under the provisions of the Lanham Act.[a]

Cancelling a Registered Trademark

The Trademark Trial and Appeal Board cancelled Belmora's trademark registration, citing obvious misuse of the Flanax mark. A Virginia district court reversed the trademark registration cancellation, and Bayer appealed.

The U.S. Court of Appeals for the Fourth Circuit held that Bayer had standing under Section 43(a) of the Lanham Act, which did not require that Bayer hold a U.S. trademark registration. Bayer was clearly damaged by Belmora's activities in the United States, and that was sufficient under the plain language of the statute. Bayer's claim came "within the zone of interest in a suit for false advertising."[b] This case established that the owner of a non-U.S. trademark can bring an action under the Lanham Act for the unauthorized use of a brand that the owner never marketed in this country.

Critical Thinking The federal district court in Virginia, in upholding Belmora's registered trademark, held that "Bayer could not have an economic loss for a mark it did not use in U.S. commerce." Why did the appellate court not accept this reasoning?

---

a. 15 U.S.C. Section 1064.
b. *Belmora, LLC v. Bayer Consumer Care, A.G.*, 819 F.3d 697 (4th Cir. 2016), *cert.* denied, 137 S.Ct. 1202, 197 L.Ed.2d 246 (2017).

The most commonly granted remedy for trademark infringement is an *injunction* to prevent further infringement. Under the Lanham Act, a trademark owner that successfully proves infringement can recover actual damages, plus the profits that the infringer wrongfully received from the unauthorized use of the mark. A court can also order the destruction of any goods bearing the unauthorized trademark. In some situations, the trademark owner may also be able to recover attorneys' fees.

8–1d Distinctiveness of the Mark

A trademark must be sufficiently distinctive to enable consumers to identify the manufacturer of the goods easily and to distinguish between those goods and competing products.

Strong Marks Fanciful, arbitrary, or suggestive trademarks are generally considered to be the most distinctive (strongest) trademarks. These marks receive automatic protection because they serve to identify a particular product's source, as opposed to describing the product itself.

Fanciful and Arbitrary Trademarks Fanciful trademarks use invented words, such as "Xerox" for one manufacturer's copiers and "Google" for a search engine. Arbitrary trademarks use common words in an uncommon way that is not descriptive of the product, such as "Dutch Boy" as a name for paint.

Even a single letter used in a particular style can be an arbitrary trademark. ■ **Case in Point 8.2** Sports entertainment company ESPN sued Quiksilver, Inc., a maker of youth-oriented clothing, alleging trademark infringement. ESPN claimed that Quiksilver's clothing used the stylized "X" mark that ESPN uses in connection with the "X Games" ("extreme" sports competitions).

Quiksilver filed counterclaims for trademark infringement and dilution, arguing that it had a long history of using the stylized X on its products. ESPN asked the court to dismiss Quiksilver's counterclaims, but the court refused, holding that the X on Quiksilver's clothing is clearly an arbitrary mark. The court found that the two Xs are "similar enough that a consumer might well confuse them." Therefore, Quiksilver could continue its claim for trademark infringement.[6] ■

Suggestive Trademarks Suggestive trademarks indicate something about a product's nature, quality, or characteristics, without describing the product directly. These marks require imagination on the part of the consumer to identify the characteristic. "Dairy Queen," for instance, suggests an association between its products and milk, but it does not directly describe ice cream. A suggestive mark can be transformed into a strong mark if it achieves a high degree of marketplace recognition, such as through substantial advertising.

Secondary Meaning Descriptive terms, geographic terms, and personal names are not inherently distinctive and do not receive protection under the law until they acquire a secondary meaning. A secondary meaning may arise when customers begin to associate a specific term or phrase (such as *Calvin Klein*) with specific trademarked items (designer clothing and goods) made by a particular company. Whether a secondary meaning becomes attached to a name usually depends on how extensively the product is advertised, the market for the product, the number of sales, and other factors.

Once a secondary meaning is attached to a term or name, the trademark is considered distinctive and is protected. Even a color can qualify for trademark protection, as did the color schemes used by some state university sports teams, including The Ohio State University and Louisiana State University.[7]

■ **Case in Point 8.3** Federal Express Corporation (FedEx) provides transportation and delivery services worldwide using the logo FedEx in a specific color combination. FedEx sued a competitor, JetEx Management Services, Inc., for using the same color combination and a similar name and logo. JetEx also mimicked FedEx's trademarked slogan ("The World on Time" for FedEx, and "Keeping the World on Time" for JetEx). FedEx alleged trademark infringement and dilution, among other claims. A federal district court in New York granted a permanent injunction to block JetEx from using the infringing mark in FedEx colors. When JetEx (now called JetEx Air Express) continued to use the infringing mark on its vehicles, FedEx went back to court to enforce the injunction and was awarded attorneys' fees and costs.[8] ■

Generic Terms Generic terms that refer to an entire class of products, such as *bicycle* and *computer*, receive no protection, even if they acquire secondary meanings. A particularly thorny problem arises when a trademark acquires generic use. For instance, *aspirin* and *thermos* were originally the names of trademarked products, but today the words are used generically. Other trademarks that have acquired generic use are *escalator, trampoline, raisin bran, dry ice, lanolin, linoleum, nylon*, and *cornflakes*.

---

6. *ESPN, Inc. v. Quiksilver, Inc.*, 586 F.Supp.2d 219 (S.D.N.Y. 2008).

7. *Board of Supervisors of Louisiana State University v. Smack Apparel Co.*, 438 F.Supp.2d 653 (E.D.La. 2006). See also *Abraham v. Alpha Chi Omega*, 781 F.Supp.2d 396 (N.D.Tex. 2011).

8. *Federal Express Corp. v. JetEx Air Express, Inc.*, 2017 WL 816479 (E.D.N.Y. 2017).

A trademark does not become generic simply because it is commonly used, however. ■ **Case in Point 8.4** David Elliot and Chris Gillespie sought to register numerous domain names (Internet addresses), including "google-disney.com" and "googlenewstvs.com." They were unable to register the names because all of them used the word *google*, a trademark of Google, Inc.

Elliot and Gillespie brought an action in federal court to have the Google trademark cancelled because it had become a generic term. They argued that because most people now use *google* as a verb ("to google") when referring to searching the Internet with any search engine (not just Google), the term should no longer be protected. The court held that even if people do use the word *google* as a verb, it is still a protected trademark if consumers associate the noun with one company. The court concluded that "the primary significance of the word *google* to a majority of the public who utilize Internet search engines is a designation of the Google search engine."[9] ■

8–1e Service, Certification, and Collective Marks

A **service mark** is essentially a trademark that is used to distinguish the *services* (rather than the products) of one person or company from those of another. For instance, each airline has a particular mark or symbol associated with its name. Titles and character names used in radio and television are frequently registered as service marks.

Other marks protected by law include certification marks and collective marks. A **certification mark** is used by one or more persons, other than the owner, to certify the region, materials, mode of manufacture, quality, or other characteristic of specific goods or services. Certification marks include "Good Housekeeping Seal of Approval" and "UL Tested."

When used by members of a cooperative, association, or other organization, a certification mark is referred to as a **collective mark.** ■ **Example 8.5** Collective marks appear at the ends of motion picture credits to indicate the various associations and organizations that participated in the making of the films. The union marks found on the tags of certain products are also collective marks. ■

8–1f Trade Dress

The term **trade dress** refers to the image and overall appearance of a product. Trade dress is a broad concept that can include either all or part of the total image or overall impression created by a product or its packaging.

■ **Example 8.6** The distinctive decor, menu, layout, and style of service of a Vinny's restaurant may be regarded as trade dress. Trade dress can also include the layout and appearance of a catalogue, the use of a lighthouse as part of the design of a golf hole, the fish shape of a cracker, or the G-shaped design of a Gucci watch. ■

Basically, trade dress is subject to the same protection as trademarks. In cases involving trade dress infringement, as in trademark infringement cases, a major consideration is whether consumers are likely to be confused by the allegedly infringing use.

■ **Example 8.7** Converse makes Chuck Taylor All-Star shoes. Nike, Inc., owns Converse. Nike sued thirty-one companies, including Ralph Lauren, for manufacturing shoes very similar to All-Stars. The knockoffs used the same white rubber soles, rubber caps on the toes, canvas tops, and conspicuous stitching as the All-Star shoes. Nike claimed the similarity was likely to confuse consumers. Ralph Lauren ultimately agreed to settle its dispute with Nike by destroying all remaining shoes in its line and paying Nike an undisclosed sum. ■

8–1g Counterfeit Goods

Counterfeit goods copy or otherwise imitate trademarked goods, but they are not the genuine trademarked goods. The importation of goods that bear counterfeit (fake) trademarks poses a growing problem for U.S. businesses, consumers, and law enforcement. In addition to the negative financial effects on legitimate businesses, certain counterfeit goods, such as pharmaceuticals and nutritional supplements, can present serious public health risks.

The Stop Counterfeiting in Manufactured Goods Act The Stop Counterfeiting in Manufactured Goods Act[10] (SCMGA) was enacted to combat counterfeit goods. The act makes it a crime to traffic intentionally in or attempt to traffic in counterfeit goods or services, or to knowingly use a counterfeit mark on or in connection with goods or services.

Before this act, the law did not prohibit the creation or shipment of counterfeit labels that were not attached to any product. Therefore, counterfeiters would make labels and packaging bearing another's trademark, ship the labels to another location, and then affix them to an inferior product to deceive buyers. The SCMGA closed this loophole by making it a crime to knowingly traffic in counterfeit labels, stickers, packaging, and the like, regardless of whether the items are attached to any goods.

---

9. *Elliot v. Google, Inc.*, 45 F.Supp.3d 1156 (D.Ariz. 2014).

10. Pub. L. No. 109-181, 120 Stat. 285 (2006), which amended 18 U.S.C. Sections 2318–2320.

Penalties for Counterfeiting Persons found guilty of violating the SCMGA may be fined up to $2 million or imprisoned for up to ten years (or more if they are repeat offenders). If a court finds that the statute was violated, it must order the defendant to forfeit the counterfeit products (which are then destroyed), as well as any property used in the commission of the crime. The defendant must also pay restitution (compensation) to the trademark holder or victim in an amount equal to the victim's actual loss.

■ **Case in Point 8.8** Charles Anthony Jones pleaded guilty to trafficking in counterfeit prescription erectile dysfunction drugs. The court sentenced Jones to thirty-seven months in prison and ordered him to pay $633,019 in restitution. Jones appealed, arguing that the amount awarded was more than the pharmaceutical companies' actual losses. The court agreed. The pharmaceutical companies were entitled only to their lost net profits rather than the retail price of the genuine drugs.[11] ■

Combating Foreign Counterfeiters Although Congress has enacted statutes against counterfeit goods, the United States cannot prosecute foreign counterfeiters because our national laws do not apply to them. One effective tool that U.S. officials have used to combat online sales of counterfeit goods is to obtain a court order to close down the domain names of websites that sell such goods. For instance, U.S. agents have shut down hundreds of domain names on the Monday after Thanksgiving ("Cyber Monday"). Shutting down the websites, particularly on key shopping days, prevents some counterfeit goods from entering the United States. Europol, an international organization, has also used this tactic.

8-1h Trade Names

Trademarks apply to *products*. A **trade name** indicates part or all of a business's name, whether the business is a sole proprietorship, a partnership, or a corporation. Generally, a trade name is directly related to a business and its goodwill.

A trade name may be protected as a trademark if the trade name is also the name of the company's trademarked product—for instance, Coca-Cola. Unless it is also used as a trademark or service mark, a trade name cannot be registered with the federal government. Trade names are protected under the common law, but only if they are unusual or fancifully used. The word *Safeway*, for instance, was sufficiently fanciful to obtain protection as a trade name for a grocery chain.

8-1i Licensing

One way to avoid litigation and still make use of another's trademark or other form of intellectual property is to obtain a license to do so. A **license** in this context is an agreement, or contract, permitting the use of a trademark, copyright, patent, or trade secret for certain purposes. The party that owns the intellectual property rights and issues the license is the *licensor*, and the party obtaining the license is the *licensee*. The licensee generally pays fees, or *royalties*, for the privilege of using the intellectual property.

A license grants only the rights expressly described in the license agreement. A licensor might, for instance, allow the licensee to use the trademark as part of its company or domain name, but not otherwise use the mark on any products or services. Disputes frequently arise over licensing agreements, particularly when the license involves Internet uses.

■ **Case in Point 8.9** George V Restauration S.A. and others owned and operated the Buddha Bar Paris, a restaurant with an Asian theme in Paris, France. One of the owners allowed Little Rest Twelve, Inc., to use the Buddha Bar trademark and its associated concept in New York City under the name *Buddha Bar NYC*. Little Rest paid royalties for its use of the Buddha Bar mark and advertised Buddha Bar NYC's affiliation with Buddha Bar Paris. This connection was also noted on its website and in the media.

When a dispute arose, the owners of Buddha Bar Paris withdrew their permission for Buddha Bar NYC's use of their mark, but Little Rest continued to use it. The owners of the mark filed a suit in a New York state court against Little Rest. The court granted an injunction to prevent Little Rest from using the mark.[12] ■

8-2 Patents

A **patent** is a grant from the government that gives an inventor the exclusive right to make, use, or sell his or her invention for a period of twenty years. Patents for designs, as opposed to those for inventions, are given for a fourteen-year period.

For many years, U.S. patent law differed from the laws of many other countries because the first person to invent a product obtained the patent rights rather than the first person to file for a patent. It was often difficult to prove who invented an item first, however, which prompted

---

11. *United States v. Jones*, 616 Fed.Appx. 726 (5th Cir. 2015).

12. *George V Restauration S.A. v. Little Rest Twelve, Inc.*, 58 A.D.3d 428, 871 N.Y.S.2d 65 (2009).

Congress to change the system in 2011 by passing the America Invents Act.[13] Now the first person to file an application for a patent on a product or process will receive patent protection. In addition, the new law established a nine-month limit for challenging a patent on any ground.

The period of patent protection begins on the date the patent application is filed, rather than when the patent is issued, which may sometimes be years later. After the patent period ends (either fourteen or twenty years later), the product or process enters the public domain, and anyone can make, sell, or use the invention without paying the patent holder.

8–2a Searchable Patent Databases

A significant development relating to patents is the availability online of the world's patent databases. The website of the U.S. Patent and Trademark Office (www.uspto.gov) provides searchable databases covering U.S. patents granted since 1976. The website of the European Patent Office (www.epo.org) provides online access to 100 million patent documents in more than seventy nations through a searchable network of databases.

Businesses use these searchable databases in many ways. Companies may conduct patent searches to list or inventory their patents, which are valuable assets. Patent searches may also be conducted to study trends and patterns in a specific technology or to gather information about competitors in the industry.

8–2b What Is Patentable?

Under federal law, "[w]hoever invents or discovers any new and useful process, machine, manufacture, or composition of matter, or any new and useful improvement thereof, may obtain a patent therefor, subject to the conditions and requirements of this title."[14] Thus, to be patentable, the applicant must prove that the invention, discovery, process, or design is *novel, useful,* and *not obvious* in light of current technology.

In sum, almost anything is patentable, except the laws of nature, natural phenomena, and abstract ideas (including algorithms[15]). Even artistic methods and works of art, certain business processes, and the structures of storylines are patentable, provided that they are novel and not obvious.[16]

Plants that are reproduced asexually (by means other than from seed), such as hybrid or genetically engineered plants, are patentable in the United States, as are genetically engineered (or cloned) microorganisms and animals. ■ **Case in Point 8.10** Monsanto, Inc., sells its patented genetically modified (GM) seeds to farmers to help them achieve higher yields from crops using fewer pesticides. It requires farmers who buy GM seeds to sign licensing agreements promising to plant the seeds for only one crop and to pay a technology fee for each acre planted. To ensure compliance, Monsanto has many full time employees whose job is to investigate and prosecute farmers who use the GM seeds illegally. Monsanto has filed hundreds of lawsuits against farmers in the United States and has been awarded millions of dollars in damages (not including out-of-court settlement amounts).[17] ■

8–2c Patent Infringement

If a firm makes, uses, or sells another's patented design, product, or process without the patent owner's permission, that firm commits the tort of patent infringement. Patent infringement may occur even though the patent owner has not put the patented product into commerce. Patent infringement may also occur even though not all features or parts of a product are copied. (To infringe the patent on a process, however, all steps or their equivalent must be copied.)

Patent Infringement Lawsuits and High-Tech Companies Obviously, companies that specialize in developing new technology stand to lose significant profits if someone "makes, uses, or sells" devices that incorporate their patented inventions. Because these firms are the holders of numerous patents, they are frequently involved in patent infringement lawsuits (as well as other types of intellectual property disputes).

■ **Case in Point 8.11** Apple sued Samsung in federal court alleging that Samsung's Galaxy smartphones and tablets that use Google's HTC Android operating system infringe on Apple's patents. Apple has design patents that cover its devices' graphical user interface (the display of icons on the home screen), shell, and screen and button

---

13. The full title of this law is the Leahy-Smith America Invents Act, Pub. L. No. 112-29, 125 Stat. 284 (2011), which amended 35 U.S.C. Sections 1, 41, and 321 of the Patent Act.

14. 35 U.S.C. Section 101.

15. An *algorithm* is a step-by-step procedure, formula, or set of instructions for accomplishing a specific task. An example is the set of rules used by a search engine to rank the listings contained within its index in response to a query.

16. For a United States Supreme Court case discussing the obviousness requirement, see *KSR International Co. v. Teleflex, Inc.*, 550 U.S. 398, 127 S.Ct. 1727, 167 L.Ed.2d 705 (2007).

17. See, for example, *Monsanto Co. v. Bowman*, 657 F.3d 1341 (Fed. Cir. 2011); and *Monsanto Co. v. Scruggs*, 345 Fed.Appx. 552 (Fed. Cir. 2009).

design. Apple has also patented the way information is displayed on iPhones and other devices, the way windows pop open, and the way information is scaled and rotated.

A jury found that Samsung had willfully infringed five of Apple's patents and awarded damages. The parties appealed. A judge later reduced the amount of damages awarded on the patent claims, but litigation continued. In 2015, a federal appellate court held that elements of the physical design of these two manufacturers' mobile devices and their on-screen icons were not protected under the Lanham Act. The United States Supreme Court reversed and remanded. The Court explained that the Patent Act provision governing damages for design patent infringement encompasses both a product sold to a consumer and a component of that product. Therefore, components of the infringing smartphones could be considered relevant to damages, even though the consumers could not purchase those components separately from the smartphones.[18] ■

Patent Infringement and Foreign Sales Many companies that make and sell electronics and computer software and hardware are based in foreign nations (for instance, Samsung Electronics Company is a Korean firm). Foreign firms can apply for and obtain U.S. patent protection on items that they sell within the United States. Similarly, U.S. firms can obtain protection in foreign nations where they sell goods.

In the United States, the Supreme Court has narrowly construed patent infringement as it applies to exported software, however. As a general rule, under U.S. law, no patent infringement occurs when a patented product is made and sold in another country. ■ **Case in Point 8.12** AT&T Corporation holds a patent on a device used to digitally encode, compress, and process recorded speech. AT&T brought an infringement case against Microsoft Corporation, which admitted that its Windows operating system incorporated software code that infringed on AT&T's patent.

The United States Supreme Court held that Microsoft was liable only for infringement in the United States and not for the Windows-based computers produced in foreign locations. The Court reasoned that Microsoft had not "supplied" the software for the computers but had only electronically transmitted a master copy, which the foreign manufacturers copied and loaded onto the computers.[19] ■

8–2d Remedies for Patent Infringement

If a patent is infringed, the patent holder may sue for relief in federal court. The patent holder can seek an injunction against the infringer and can also request damages for royalties and lost profits. In some cases, the court may grant the winning party reimbursement for attorneys' fees and costs. If the court determines that the infringement was willful, the court can triple the amount of damages awarded (treble damages).

In the past, permanent injunctions were routinely granted to prevent future infringement. Today, however, according to the United States Supreme Court, a patent holder must prove that it has suffered irreparable injury and that the public interest would not be *disserved* by a permanent injunction.[20] Thus, courts have discretion to decide what is equitable in the circumstances and to consider what is in the public interest rather than just the interests of the parties.

■ **Case in Point 8.13** Cordance Corporation developed some of the technology and software that automates Internet communications. Cordance sued Amazon.com, Inc., for patent infringement, claiming that Amazon's one-click purchasing interface infringed on one of Cordance's patents. After a jury found Amazon guilty of infringement, Cordance requested the court to issue a permanent injunction against Amazon's infringement or, alternatively, to order Amazon to pay Cordance an ongoing royalty.

The court refused to issue a permanent injunction because Cordance had not proved that it would otherwise suffer irreparable harm. Cordance and Amazon were not direct competitors in the relevant market. Cordance had never sold or licensed the technology infringed by Amazon's one-click purchasing interface and had presented no market data or evidence to show how the infringement negatively affected Cordance. The court also refused to impose an ongoing royalty on Amazon.[21] ■

8–3 Copyrights

A **copyright** is an intangible property right granted by federal statute to the author or originator of a literary or artistic production of a specified type. The Copyright Act of 1976,[22] as amended, governs copyrights. Works created after January 1, 1978, are automatically given statutory copyright protection for the life of the author plus 70 years. For copyrights owned by publishing houses, the

18. *Apple, Inc. v. Samsung Electronics Co., Ltd.*, 678 Fed.Appx. 1012 (Fed. Cir. 2017); *Samsung Electronics Co., Ltd. v. Apple, Inc.*, __ U.S. __, 137 S.Ct. 429, 196 L.Ed.2d 363 (2016).
19. *Microsoft Corp. v. AT&T Corp.*, 550 U.S. 437, 127 S.Ct. 1746, 167 L.Ed.2d 737 (2007).
20. *eBay, Inc. v. MercExchange, LLC*, 547 U.S. 388, 126 S.Ct. 1837, 164 L.Ed.2d 641 (2006).
21. *Cordance Corp. v. Amazon.com, Inc.*, 730 F.Supp.2d 333 (D.Del. 2010).
22. 17 U.S.C. Sections 101 *et seq.*

copyright expires 95 years from the date of publication or 120 years from the date of creation, whichever comes first. For works by more than one author, the copyright expires 70 years after the death of the last surviving author.[23]

When copyright protection ends, works enter into the *public domain.* Intellectual property, such as songs and other published works, that have entered into the public domain belong to everyone and are not protected by copyright or patent laws.

■ **Case in Point 8.14** The popular character Sherlock Holmes originated in stories written by Arthur Conan Doyle and published from 1887 through 1927. Over the years, elements of the characters and stories created by Doyle have appeared in books, movies, and television series, including *Elementary* on CBS and *Sherlock* on BBC.

Before 2013, those who wished to use the copyrighted Sherlock material had to pay a licensing fee to Doyle's estate. Then, in 2013, the editors of a book of Holmes-related stories filed a lawsuit in federal court claiming that the basic Sherlock Holmes story elements introduced before 1923 should no longer be protected. The court agreed and ruled that these elements have entered the public domain—that is, the copyright has expired, and they can be used without permission.[24] ■

8–3a Registration

Copyrights can be registered with the U.S. Copyright Office (www.copyright.gov) in Washington, D.C. Registration is not required, however. A copyright owner no longer needs to place the symbol © or the term *Copr.* or *Copyright* on the work to have the work protected against infringement. Chances are that if somebody created it, somebody owns it.

Generally, copyright owners are protected against the following:

1. Reproduction of the work.
2. Development of derivative works.
3. Distribution of the work.
4. Public display of the work.

8–3b What Is Protected Expression?

Works that are copyrightable include books, records, films, artworks, architectural plans, menus, music videos, product packaging, and computer software. To be

---

23. These time periods reflect the extensions of the length of copyright protection enacted by Congress in the Copyright Term Extension Act of 1998, 17 U.S.C. Section 302. The United States Supreme Court upheld the constitutionality of the act in 2003. See *Eldred v. Ashcroft*, 537 U.S. 186, 123 S.Ct. 769, 154 L.Ed.2d 683 (2003).
24. *Klinger v. Conan Doyle Estate, Ltd.*, 988 F.Supp.2d 879 (N.D.Ill. 2013).

protected, a work must be "fixed in a durable medium" from which it can be perceived, reproduced, or communicated. As noted, protection is automatic, and registration is not required.

Section 102 of the Copyright Act explicitly states that it protects original works that fall into one of the following categories:

1. Literary works (including newspaper and magazine articles, computer and training manuals, catalogues, brochures, and print advertisements).
2. Musical works and accompanying words (including advertising jingles).
3. Dramatic works and accompanying music.
4. Pantomimes and choreographic works (including ballets and other forms of dance).
5. Pictorial, graphic, and sculptural works (including cartoons, maps, posters, statues, and even stuffed animals).
6. Motion pictures and other audiovisual works (including multimedia works).
7. Sound recordings.
8. Architectural works.

Section 102 Exclusions Generally, anything that is not an original expression will not qualify for copyright protection. Facts widely known to the public are not copyrightable. Page numbers are not copyrightable because they follow a sequence known to everyone. Mathematical calculations are not copyrightable.

Furthermore, it is not possible to copyright an *idea.* Section 102 of the Copyright Act specifically excludes copyright protection for any "idea, procedure, process, system, method of operation, concept, principle, or discovery, regardless of the form in which it is described, explained, illustrated, or embodied." Thus, anyone can freely use the underlying ideas or principles embodied in a work.

What is copyrightable is the particular way in which an idea is *expressed.* Whenever an idea and an expression are inseparable, the expression cannot be copyrighted. An idea and its expression, then, must be separable to be copyrightable. Thus, for the design of a useful item to be copyrightable, the way it looks must be separate from its utilitarian (functional) purpose.

■ **Case in Point 8.15** Inhale, Inc., registered a copyright on a hookah—a device for smoking tobacco by filtering the smoke through water held in a container at the base. Starbuzz Tobacco, Inc., sold hookahs with water containers shaped exactly like the Inhale containers.

Inhale filed a suit in a federal district court against Starbuzz for copyright infringement. The court determined that the shape of the water container on Inhale's hookahs was not copyrightable. The U.S. Court of Appeals for the Ninth Circuit affirmed the judgment. "The shape of a container is not independent of the container's utilitarian function—to hold the contents within its shape—because the shape accomplishes the function."[25] ■

Compilations of Facts Unlike ideas, *compilations* of facts are copyrightable. Under Section 103 of the Copyright Act, a compilation is "a work formed by the collection and assembling of preexisting materials or data that are selected, coordinated, or arranged in such a way that the resulting work as a whole constitutes an original work of authorship."

The key requirement in the copyrightability of a compilation is originality. If the facts are selected, coordinated,

---

25. *Inhale, Inc. v. Starbuzz Tobacco, Inc.*, 755 F.3d 1038 (9th Cir. 2014).

or arranged in an original way, they can qualify for copyright protection.

8–3c Copyright Infringement

Whenever the form or expression of an idea is copied, an infringement of copyright has occurred. The reproduction does not have to be exactly the same as the original, nor does it have to reproduce the original in its entirety. If a substantial part of the original is reproduced, the copyright has been infringed.

In the following case, rapper Curtis Jackson—better known as "50 Cent"—was the defendant in a suit that claimed his album *Before I Self-Destruct*, and the film of the same name, infringed the copyright of Shadrach Winstead's book *The Preacher's Son—But the Streets Turned Me into a Gangster.*

Case Analysis 8.3

Winstead v. Jackson
United States Court of Appeals, Third Circuit, 509 Fed.Appx. 139 (2013).

In the Language of the Court
PER CURIAM. [By the Whole Court]
* * * *

* * * Winstead filed his * * * complaint in the United States District Court for the District of New Jersey, claiming that Jackson's album/CD and film derived their contents from, and infringed the copyright of, his book.
* * * *

* * * The District Court dismissed Winstead's * * * complaint * * *, concluding that Jackson * * * did not improperly copy protected aspects of Winstead's book.
* * * *

Winstead appeals.
* * * *

Here, it is not disputed that Winstead is the owner of the copyrighted property * * *. However, *not all copying is copyright infringement, so even if actual copying is proven, the court must decide, by comparing the allegedly infringing work with the original work, whether the copying was unlawful. Copying may be proved inferentially by showing that the allegedly*

infringing work is substantially similar to the copyrighted work. A court compares the allegedly infringing work with the original work, and considers whether a "lay-observer" would believe that the copying was of protectable aspects of the copyrighted work. The inquiry involves distinguishing between the author's expression and the idea or theme that he or she seeks to convey or explore, because the former is protected and the latter is not. The court must determine whether the allegedly infringing work is similar because it appropriates the unique expressions of the original work, or merely because it contains elements that would be expected when two works express the same idea or explore the same theme. [Emphasis added.]

* * * A lay observer would not believe that Jackson's album/CD and film copied protectable aspects of Winstead's book. Jackson's album/CD is comprised of 16 individual songs, which explore drug-dealing, guns and money, vengeance, and other similar clichés of hip hop gangsterism. Jackson's fictional film

is the story of a young man who turns to violence when his mother is killed in a drive-by shooting. The young man takes revenge by killing the man who killed his mother, and then gets rich by becoming an "enforcer" for a powerful criminal. He takes up with a woman who eventually betrays him, and is shot to death by her boyfriend, who has just been released from prison. The movie ends with his younger brother vowing to seek vengeance. Winstead's book purports to be autobiographical and tells the story of a young man whose beloved father was a Bishop in the church. The protagonist was angry as a child because his stepmother abused him, but he found acceptance and self-esteem on the streets of Newark because he was physically powerful. He earned money robbing and beating people, went to jail, returned to crime upon his release, and then made even more money. The protagonist discusses his time at Rahway State Prison in great and compelling detail. The story ends when the protagonist learns that his father has passed away; he conveys

Case 8.3 Continues

Case 8.3 Continued

his belief that this tragedy has led to his redemption, and he hopes that others might learn from his mistakes.

* * * Although Winstead's book and Jackson's works share similar themes and setting, the story of an angry and wronged protagonist who turns to a life of violence and crime has long been a part of the public domain [and is therefore not protected by copyright law]. Winstead argues * * * that a protagonist asking for God's help when his father dies, cutting drugs with mixing agents to maximize profits, and complaining about relatives who are addicts and steal the product, are protectable, but these things are not unique. To the extent that Jackson's works contain these elements, they are to be expected when two works express the same idea about "the streets" or explore the same theme. Winstead argues that not every protagonist whose story concerns guns, drugs, and violence in an urban setting winds up in prison or loses a parent, but this argument only serves to illustrate an important difference between his book and Jackson's film. Jackson's protagonist never spends

any time in prison, whereas Winstead's protagonist devotes a considerable part of his story to his incarcerations.

In addition, Winstead's book and Jackson's works are different with respect to character, plot, mood, and sequence of events. Winstead's protagonist embarks on a life of crime at a very young age, but is redeemed by the death of his beloved father. Jackson's protagonist turns to crime when he is much older and only after his mother is murdered. He winds up dead at a young age, unredeemed. Winstead's book is hopeful; Jackson's film is characterized * * * by moral apathy. It is true that both works involve the loss of a parent and the protagonist's recognition of the parent's importance in his life, but nowhere does Jackson appropriate anything unique about Winstead's expression of this generic topic.

Winstead contends that direct phrases from his book appear in Jackson's film. * * * He emphasizes these phrases: "Yo, where is my money at," "I would never have done no shit like that to you," "my father, my strength

was gone," "he was everything to me," and "I did not know what to do," but, like the phrases "putting the work in," "get the dope, cut the dope," "let's keep it popping," and "the strong take from the weak but the smart take from everybody," they are either common in general or common with respect to hip hop culture, and do not enjoy copyright protection. The average person reading or listening to these phrases in the context of an overall story or song would not regard them as unique and protectable. Moreover, words and short phrases do not enjoy copyright protection. The similarity between Winstead's book and the lyrics to Jackson's songs on the album/CD is even more tenuous. "Stretching the dope" and "bloodshot red eyes" are common phrases that do not enjoy copyright protection. A side-by-side comparison of Winstead's book and the lyrics from Jackson's album/CD do not support a claim of copyright infringement.

For the foregoing reasons, we will affirm the order of the District Court dismissing [Winstead's] complaint.

Legal Reasoning Questions

1. Which expressions of an original work are protected by copyright law?

2. Is all copying copyright infringement? If not, what is the test for determining whether a creative work has been unlawfully copied?

3. How did the court in this case determine whether the defendant's work infringed on the plaintiff's copyright?

Remedies for Copyright Infringement Those who infringe copyrights may be liable for damages or criminal penalties. These range from actual damages or statutory damages, imposed at the court's discretion, to criminal proceedings for willful violations.

Actual damages are based on the harm caused to the copyright holder by the infringement, while statutory damages, not to exceed $150,000, are provided for under the Copyright Act. Criminal proceedings may result in fines and/or imprisonment. A court can also issue a permanent injunction against a defendant when the court deems it necessary to prevent future copyright infringement.

■ **Case in Point 8.16** Rusty Carroll operated an online term paper business, R2C2, Inc., that offered up to 300,000 research papers for sale at nine websites. Individuals whose

work was posted on these websites without their permission filed a lawsuit against Carroll for copyright infringement. Because Carroll had repeatedly failed to comply with court orders regarding discovery, the court found that the copyright infringement was likely to continue unless an injunction was issued. The court therefore issued a permanent injunction prohibiting Carroll and R2C2 from selling any term paper without sworn documentary evidence that the paper's author had given permission.[26] ■

The "Fair Use" Exception An exception to liability for copyright infringement is made under the "fair use" doctrine. In certain circumstances, a person or organization

---

26. *Weidner v. Carroll*, 2010 WL 310310 (S.D.Ill. 2010).

can reproduce copyrighted material without paying royalties. Section 107 of the Copyright Act provides as follows:

> [T]he fair use of a copyrighted work, including such use by reproduction in copies or phonorecords or by any other means specified by [Section 106 of the Copyright Act], for purposes such as criticism, comment, news reporting, teaching (including multiple copies for classroom use), scholarship, or research, is not an infringement of copyright. In determining whether the use made of a work in any particular case is a fair use the factors to be considered shall include—
>
> (1) the purpose and character of the use, including whether such use is of a commercial nature or is for nonprofit educational purposes;
> (2) the nature of the copyrighted work;
> (3) the amount and substantiality of the portion used in relation to the copyrighted work as a whole; and
> (4) the effect of the use upon the potential market for or value of the copyrighted work.

What Is Fair Use? Because these guidelines are very broad, the courts determine whether a particular use is fair on a case-by-case basis. Thus, anyone who reproduces copyrighted material may be committing a violation. In determining whether a use is fair, courts have often considered the fourth factor to be the most important.

■ **Case in Point 8.17** A number of research universities, in partnership with Google, Inc., agreed to digitize books from their libraries and create a repository for them. Eighty member institutions (including many colleges and universities) contributed more than 10 million works into the HathiTrust Digital Library. Some authors complained that this book scanning violated their rights and sued the HathiTrust and several associated entities for copyright infringement.

The court, however, sided with the defendants and held that making digital copies for the purposes of online search was a fair use. The library's searchable database enabled researchers to find terms of interest in the digital volumes—but not to read the volumes online. Therefore, the court concluded that the digitization did not provide a substitute that damaged the market for the original works.[27] ■

The First Sale Doctrine Section 109(a) of the Copyright Act provides that the owner of a particular item that is copyrighted can, without the authority of the copyright owner, sell or otherwise dispose of it. This rule is known as the first sale doctrine.

Under this doctrine, once a copyright owner sells or gives away a particular copy of a work, the copyright owner no longer has the right to control the distribution of that copy. Thus, for instance, a person who buys a copyrighted book can sell it to someone else.

■ **Case in Point 8.18** Supap Kirtsaeng, a citizen of Thailand, was a graduate student at the University of Southern California. He enlisted friends and family in Thailand to buy copies of textbooks there and ship them to him in the United States. Kirtsaeng resold the textbooks on eBay, where he eventually made about $100,000.

John Wiley & Sons, Inc., had printed eight of those textbooks in Asia. Wiley sued Kirtsaeng in federal district court for copyright infringement. Kirtsaeng argued that Section 109(a) of the Copyright Act allows the first purchaser-owner of a book to sell it without the copyright owner's permission. The trial court held in favor of Wiley, and that decision was affirmed on appeal. Kirtsaeng then appealed to the United States Supreme Court, which ruled in Kirtsaeng's favor. The first sale doctrine applies even to goods purchased abroad and resold in the United States.[28] ■

8–3d Copyright Protection for Software

The Computer Software Copyright Act amended the Copyright Act to include computer programs in the list of creative works protected by federal copyright law.[29] Generally, copyright protection extends to those parts of a computer program that can be read by humans, such as the "high-level" language of a source code. Protection also extends to the binary-language object code, which is readable only by the computer, and to such elements as the overall structure, sequence, and organization of a program.

Not all aspects of software are protected. Courts typically have not extended copyright protection to the "look and feel"—the general appearance, command structure, video images, menus, windows, and other screen displays—of computer programs. (Note, however, that copying the "look and feel" of another's product may be a violation of trade dress or trademark laws.) Sometimes it can be difficult for courts to decide which particular aspects of software are protected.

■ **Case in Point 8.19** Oracle America, Inc., is a software company that owns numerous application programming interfaces, or API packages. Oracle grants licenses to others to use these API packages to write applications in the Java programming language. Java is open and free for anyone to use, but using it requires an interface. When Google began using some of Oracle's API packages to run

---

27. *Authors Guild, Inc., v. HathiTrust*, 755 F.3d 87 (2d Cir. 2014).

28. *Kirtsaeng v. John Wiley & Sons, Inc.*, 568 U.S. 519, 133 S.Ct. 1351, 185 L.Ed.2d 392 (2013).
29. Pub. L. No. 96-517, 94 Stat. 3015 (1980), amending 17 U.S.C. Sections 101, 117.

Java on its Android mobile devices, Oracle sued for copyright infringement. Google argued that the software packages were command structure and, as such, not protected under copyright law. Ultimately, a federal appellate court concluded that the API packages were source code and were entitled to copyright protection.[30] ■

8–4 Trade Secrets

The law of trade secrets protects some business processes and information that are not, or cannot be, patented, copyrighted, or trademarked. A **trade secret** is basically information of commercial value, such as customer lists, plans, and research and development. Trade secrets may also include pricing information, marketing methods, production techniques, and generally anything that makes an individual company unique and that would have value to a competitor.

Unlike copyright and trademark protection, protection of trade secrets extends to both ideas and their expression. For this reason, and because there are no registration or filing requirements for trade secrets, trade secret protection may be well suited for software.

Of course, a company's trade secrets must be disclosed to some persons, particularly to key employees. Businesses generally attempt to protect their trade secrets by having all employees who use a protected process or information agree in their contracts, or in confidentiality agreements, never to divulge it.

8–4a State and Federal Law on Trade Secrets

Under Section 757 of the *Restatement of Torts*, those who disclose or use another's trade secret, without authorization, are liable to that other party if either of the following is true:

1. They discovered the secret by improper means.
2. Their disclosure or use constitutes a breach of a duty owed to the other party.

Stealing confidential business data by industrial espionage, such as by tapping into a competitor's computer, is a theft of trade secrets without any contractual violation and is actionable in itself.

Trade secrets have long been protected under the common law. Today, nearly every state has enacted trade secret laws based on the Uniform Trade Secrets Act.[31]

Additionally, the Economic Espionage Act[32] makes the theft of trade secrets a federal crime.

8–4b Trade Secrets in Cyberspace

Computer technology is undercutting many business firms' ability to protect their confidential information, including trade secrets. For example, a dishonest employee could e-mail trade secrets in a company's computer to a competitor or a future employer. If e-mail is not an option, the employee might walk out with the information on a flash drive.

Misusing a company's social media account is yet another way in which employees may appropriate trade secrets. ■ **Case in Point 8.20** Noah Kravitz worked for a company called PhoneDog for four years as a product reviewer and video blogger. PhoneDog provided him with the Twitter account "@PhoneDog_Noah." Kravitz's popularity grew, and he had approximately 17,000 followers by the time he quit. PhoneDog requested that Kravitz stop using the Twitter account. Although Kravitz changed his handle to "@noahkravitz," he continued to use the account. PhoneDog subsequently sued Kravitz for misappropriation of trade secrets, among other things. Kravitz moved for a dismissal, but the court found that the complaint adequately stated a cause of action for misappropriation of trade secrets and allowed the suit to continue.[33] ■

Exhibit 8–1 outlines trade secrets and other forms of intellectual property discussed in this chapter.

8–5 International Protection for Intellectual Property

For many years, the United States has been a party to various international agreements relating to intellectual property rights. For instance, the Paris Convention of 1883, to which almost 180 countries are signatory, allows parties in one country to file for patent and trademark protection in any of the other member countries. Other international agreements in this area include the Berne Convention, the Trade-Related Aspects of Intellectual Property Rights (known as the TRIPS agreement), the Madrid Protocol, and the Anti-Counterfeiting Trade Agreement.

30. *Oracle America, Inc. v. Google Inc.*, 750 F.3d 1339 (Fed. Cir. 2014).
31. The Uniform Trade Secrets Act, as drafted by the National Conference of Commissioners on Uniform State Laws (NCCUSL), can be found at uniformlaws.org.
32. 18 U.S.C. Sections 1831–1839.
33. *PhoneDog v. Kravitz*, 2011 WL 5415612 (N.D.Cal. 2011). See also *Mintel Learning Technology, Inc. v. Ambrow Education Holding Ltd.*, 2012 WL 762126 (N.D.Cal. 2012).

Exhibit 8-1 Forms of Intellectual Property

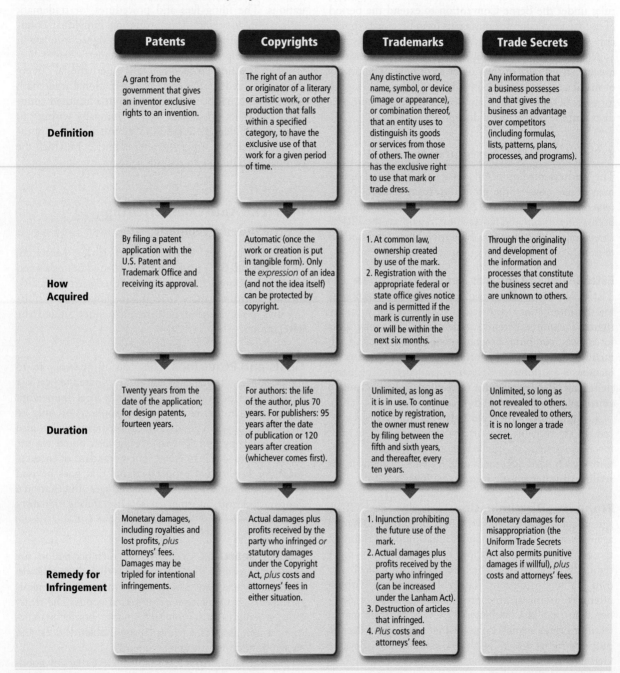

	Patents	Copyrights	Trademarks	Trade Secrets
Definition	A grant from the government that gives an inventor exclusive rights to an invention.	The right of an author or originator of a literary or artistic work, or other production that falls within a specified category, to have the exclusive use of that work for a given period of time.	Any distinctive word, name, symbol, or device (image or appearance), or combination thereof, that an entity uses to distinguish its goods or services from those of others. The owner has the exclusive right to use that mark or trade dress.	Any information that a business possesses and that gives the business an advantage over competitors (including formulas, lists, patterns, plans, processes, and programs).
How Acquired	By filing a patent application with the U.S. Patent and Trademark Office and receiving its approval.	Automatic (once the work or creation is put in tangible form). Only the *expression* of an idea (and not the idea itself) can be protected by copyright.	1. At common law, ownership created by use of the mark. 2. Registration with the appropriate federal or state office gives notice and is permitted if the mark is currently in use or will be within the next six months.	Through the originality and development of the information and processes that constitute the business secret and are unknown to others.
Duration	Twenty years from the date of the application; for design patents, fourteen years.	For authors: the life of the author, plus 70 years. For publishers: 95 years after the date of publication or 120 years after creation (whichever comes first).	Unlimited, as long as it is in use. To continue notice by registration, the owner must renew by filing between the fifth and sixth years, and thereafter, every ten years.	Unlimited, so long as not revealed to others. Once revealed to others, it is no longer a trade secret.
Remedy for Infringement	Monetary damages, including royalties and lost profits, *plus* attorneys' fees. Damages may be tripled for intentional infringements.	Actual damages plus profits received by the party who infringed *or* statutory damages under the Copyright Act, *plus* costs and attorneys' fees in either situation.	1. Injunction prohibiting the future use of the mark. 2. Actual damages plus profits received by the party who infringed (can be increased under the Lanham Act). 3. Destruction of articles that infringed. 4. *Plus* costs and attorneys' fees.	Monetary damages for misappropriation (the Uniform Trade Secrets Act also permits punitive damages if willful), *plus* costs and attorneys' fees.

8-5a The Berne Convention

Under the Berne Convention, if a U.S. citizen writes a book, every country that has signed the convention must recognize the U.S. author's copyright in the book. Also, if a citizen of a country that has not signed the convention first publishes a book in one of the 176 countries that have signed, all other countries that have signed the convention must recognize that author's copyright. Copyright notice is not needed to gain protection under the Berne Convention for works published after March 1, 1989.

In 2011, the European Union altered its copyright rules under the Berne Convention to extend the period of royalty protection for musicians from fifty years to seventy years. This decision aids major record labels as well as performers and musicians who previously faced losing royalties from sales of their older recordings. The profits of musicians and record companies have been shrinking for years because of the sharp decline in sales of compact discs and the rise in illegal downloads.

8–5b The TRIPS Agreement

The Berne Convention and other international agreements have given some protection to intellectual property on a worldwide level. None of them, however, has been as significant and far reaching in scope as the TRIPS agreement. Representatives from more than one hundred nations signed the TRIPS agreement in 1994.

Establishes Standards and Procedures The TRIPS agreement established, for the first time, standards for the international protection of intellectual property rights, including patents, trademarks, and copyrights for movies, computer programs, books, and music. Each member country of the World Trade Organization must include in its domestic laws broad intellectual property rights and effective remedies (including civil and criminal penalties) for violations of those rights.

Each member nation must also ensure that legal procedures are available for parties who wish to bring actions for infringement of intellectual property rights. Additionally, a related document established a mechanism for settling disputes among member nations.

Prohibits Discrimination Generally, the TRIPS agreement forbids member nations from discriminating against foreign owners of intellectual property rights in the administration, regulation, or adjudication of those rights. In other words, a member nation cannot give its own nationals (citizens) favorable treatment without offering the same treatment to nationals of all other member countries. ■ **Example 8.21** A U.S. software manufacturer brings a suit for the infringement of intellectual property rights under Germany's national laws. Because Germany is a member of the TRIPS agreement, the U.S. manufacturer is entitled to receive the same treatment as a German manufacturer. ■

8–5c The Madrid Protocol

In the past, one of the difficulties in protecting U.S. trademarks internationally was the time and expense required to apply for trademark registration in foreign nations. The filing fees and procedures for trademark registration vary significantly among individual countries. The Madrid Protocol, which was signed into law in 2003, may help to resolve these problems.

The Madrid Protocol is an international treaty designed to reduce the costs of international trademark protection. It has been signed by about a hundred countries. Under its provisions, a U.S. company wishing to register its trademark abroad can submit a single application and designate other member countries in which the company would like to register its mark.

8–5d The Anti-Counterfeiting Trade Agreement

In 2011, Australia, Canada, Japan, Korea, Morocco, New Zealand, Singapore, and the United States signed the Anti-Counterfeiting Trade Agreement (ACTA), an international treaty to combat global counterfeiting and piracy. Other nations have since signed the agreement.

Goals and Provisions The goals of the treaty are to increase international cooperation, facilitate the best law enforcement practices, and provide a legal framework to combat counterfeiting. ACTA applies not only to counterfeit physical goods, such as medications, but also to pirated copyrighted works being distributed via the Internet. The idea is to create a new standard of enforcement for intellectual property rights that goes beyond the TRIPS agreement and encourages international cooperation and information sharing among signatory countries.

Border Searches Under ACTA, member nations are required to establish border measures that allow officials, on their own initiative, to search commercial shipments of imports and exports for counterfeit goods. The treaty neither requires nor prohibits random border searches of electronic devices, such as laptops, tablet devices, and smartphones, for infringing content.

If border authorities reasonably believe that any goods in transit are counterfeit, the treaty allows them to keep the suspect goods unless the owner proves that the items are authentic and noninfringing. The treaty allows member nations, in accordance with their own laws, to order online service providers to furnish information about suspected trademark and copyright infringers, including their identities.

Practice and Review: Intellectual Property Rights

Two computer science majors, Trent and Xavier, have an idea for a new video game, which they propose to call Hallowed. They form a business and begin developing their idea. Several months later, Trent and Xavier run into a problem with their design and consult a friend, Brad, who is an expert in designing computer source codes. After the software is completed but before Hallowed is marketed, a video game called Halo 2 is released for the Xbox and Playstation systems. Halo 2 uses source codes similar to those of Hallowed and imitates Hallowed's overall look and feel, although not all the features are alike. Using the information presented in the chapter, answer the following questions.

1. Would the name *Hallowed* receive protection as a trademark or as trade dress? Explain.
2. If Trent and Xavier had obtained a patent on Hallowed, would the release of Halo 2 have infringed on their patent? Why or why not?
3. Based only on the facts described above, could Trent and Xavier sue the makers of Halo 2 for copyright infringement? Why or why not?
4. Suppose that Trent and Xavier discover that Brad took the idea of Hallowed and sold it to the company that produced Halo 2. Which type of intellectual property issue does this raise?

Debate This . . .   *Congress has amended copyright law several times so that copyright holders now have protection for many decades. Was Congress right in extending these copyright time periods?*

Terms and Concepts

certification mark 156	intellectual property 150	trade dress 156
collective mark 156	license 157	trademark 150
copyright 159	patent 157	trade name 157
dilution 152	service mark 156	trade secret 164

Issue Spotters

1. Roslyn, a food buyer for Organic Cornucopia Food Company, decides to go into business for herself as Roslyn's Kitchen. She contacts Organic's suppliers, offering to buy their entire harvest for the next year. She also contacts Organic's customers, offering to sell her products at prices lower than Organic's prices. Has Roslyn violated any of the intellectual property rights discussed in this chapter? Explain. (See *Trade Secrets.*)

2. Global Products develops, patents, and markets software. World Copies, Inc., sells Global's software without the maker's permission. Is this patent infringement? If so, how might Global save the cost of suing World for infringement and at the same time profit from World's sales? (See *Patents.*)

- **Check your answers to the Issue Spotters against the answers provided in Appendix B at the end of this text.**

Business Scenarios and Case Problems

8–1. Fair Use. Professor Wise is teaching a summer seminar in business torts at State University. Several times during the course, he makes copies of relevant sections from business law texts and distributes them to his students. Wise does not realize that the daughter of one of the textbook authors is a member of his seminar. She tells her father about Wise's copying activities, which have taken place without her father's or

his publisher's permission. Her father sues Wise for copyright infringement. Wise claims protection under the fair use doctrine. Who will prevail? Explain. (See *Copyrights.*)

8–2. Patent Infringement. John and Andrew Doney invented a hard-bearing device for balancing rotors. Although they obtained a patent for their invention from the U.S. Patent and Trademark Office, it was never used as an automobile wheel balancer. Some time later, Exetron Corp. produced an automobile wheel balancer that used a hard-bearing device with a support plate similar to that of the Doneys' device. Given that the Doneys had not used their device for automobile wheel balancing, does Exetron's use of a similar device infringe on the Doneys' patent? Why or why not? (See *Patents*.)

8–3. Spotlight on Macy's—Copyright Infringement. United Fabrics International, Inc., bought a fabric design from an Italian designer and registered a copyright to it with the U.S. Copyright Office. When Macy's, Inc., began selling garments with a similar design, United filed a copyright infringement suit against Macy's. Macy's argued that United did not own a valid copyright to the design and so could not claim infringement. Does United have to prove that the copyright is valid to establish infringement? Explain. [*United Fabrics International, Inc. v. C&J Wear, Inc.*, 630 F.3d 1255 (9th Cir. 2011)] (See *Copyrights*.)

8–4. Theft of Trade Secrets. Hanjuan Jin, a citizen of China, worked as a software engineer for Motorola for many years in a division that created proprietary standards for cellular communications. Contrary to Motorola's policies, Jin also secretly began working as a consultant for Lemko Corp., as well as with Sun Kaisens, a Chinese software company, and with the Chinese military. She started corresponding with Sun Kaisens's management about a possible full-time job in China. Jin took several medical leaves of absence from Motorola to return to Beijing and work with Sun Kaisens and the military.

After one of these medical leaves, Jin returned to Motorola. Over a period of several days, Jin accessed and downloaded thousands of documents on her personal laptop and on pen drives. When, later, she attempted to board a flight to China from Chicago, she was randomly searched by U.S. Customs and Border Protection officials at the airport. U.S. officials discovered the downloaded Motorola documents. Are there any circumstances under which Jin could avoid being prosecuted for theft of trade secrets? If so, what are these circumstances? Discuss fully. [*United States v. Hanjuan Jin*, 833 F.Supp.2d 977 (N.D.Ill. 2012)] (See *Trade Secrets*.)

8–5. Copyright Infringement. SilverEdge Systems Software hired Catherine Conrad to perform a singing telegram. SilverEdge arranged for James Bendewald to record Conrad's performance of her copyrighted song to post on its website. Conrad agreed to wear a microphone to assist in the recording, told Bendewald what to film, and asked for an additional fee only if SilverEdge used the video for a commercial purpose. Later, the company chose to post a video of a different performer's singing telegram instead. Conrad filed a suit in a federal district court against SilverEdge and Bendewald for copyright infringement. Are the defendants liable? Explain. [*Conrad v. Bendewald*, 500 Fed.Appx. 526 (7th Cir. 2013)] (See *Copyrights*.)

8–6. Business Case Problem with Sample Answer—Patents. The U.S. Patent and Trademark Office (PTO) denied Raymond Gianelli's application for a patent for a "Rowing Machine"—an exercise machine on which a user *pulls* on handles to perform a rowing motion against a selected resistance. The PTO considered the device obvious in light of a previously patented "Chest Press Apparatus for Exercising Regions of the Upper Body"—an exercise machine on which a user *pushes* on handles to overcome a selected resistance. On what ground might this result be reversed on appeal? Discuss. [*In re Gianelli*, 739 F.3d 1375 (Fed. Cir. 2014)] (See *Patents*.)

• For a sample answer to Problem 8–6, go to Appendix C at the end of this text.

8–7. Patents. Rodney Klassen was employed by the U.S. Department of Agriculture (USDA). Without the USDA's authorization, Klassen gave Jim Ludy, a grape grower, plant material for two unreleased varieties of grapes. For almost two years, most of Ludy's plantings bore no usable fruit, none of the grapes were sold, and no plant material was given to any other person. The plantings were visible from publicly accessible roads, but none of the vines were labeled, and the variety could not be identified by simply viewing the vines. Under patent law, an applicant may not obtain a patent for an invention that is in public use for more than one year before the date of the application. Could the USDA successfully apply for patents on the two varieties given to Ludy? Explain. [*Delano Farms Co. v. California Table Grape Commission*, 778 F.3d 1243 (Fed. Cir. 2015)] (See *Patents*.)

8–8. Copyright Infringement. Savant Homes, Inc., is a custom home designer and builder. Using what it called the "Anders Plan," Savant built a model house in Windsor, Colorado. This was a ranch house with two bedrooms on one side and a master suite on the other, separated by a combined family room, dining room, and kitchen. Ron and Tammie Wagner toured the Savant house. The same month, the Wagners hired builder Douglas Collins and his firm, Douglas Consulting, LLC, to build a house for them in Windsor. After it was built, Savant filed a suit in a federal district court against Collins for copyright infringement, alleging that the builder had copied the Anders Plan in the design and construction of the Wagner house. Collins showed that the Anders Plan consisted of standard elements and standard arrangements of elements. In these circumstances, has infringement occurred? Explain. [*Savant Homes, Inc. v. Collins*, 809 F.3d 1133 (10th Cir. 2016)] (See *Copyrights*.)

8–9. Patent Infringement. Finjan, Inc., owns a patent— U.S. Patent No. 7,418,731, or "the '731 patent"—for a system and method that provide computer security from malicious software embedded in websites on the Internet. The system consists of a gateway that compares security profiles associated with requested files with the security policies of requesting users. The method includes scanning an incoming file to create the profile, which comprises a list of computer commands the file is programmed to perform. The '731 patent required "a list of computer commands." Blue Coat Systems, Inc., sold a competing product. Blue Coat's product scanned an incoming file for certain commands and created a new file called Cookie2 that contained a field showing whether, and how often, those commands appeared.

Finjan filed a suit against Blue Coat, alleging patent infringement. Blue Coat argued that its profiles did not contain the '731 patent's required "list of computer commands." Did Blue Coat's product infringe Finjan's patent? Explain. [*Finjan, Inc. v. Blue Coat Systems, Inc.*, 879 F.3d 1299 (Fed. Cir. 2018)] (See *Patents.*)

8–10. A Question of Ethics—The IDDR Approach and Copyright Infringement. *Usenet is an online bulletin board network. A user gains access to Usenet posts through a commercial service. One such service is Giganews, Inc. Although Giganews deletes or blocks posts that contain child pornography, it does not otherwise monitor content. Perfect 10, Inc., owns the copyrights*

to tens of thousands of images, many of which have been illegally posted on Usenet through Giganews. When Perfect 10 notified Giganews of posts that contained infringing images, the service took them down. Despite these efforts, illegal posting continued. Perfect 10 filed a suit in a federal district court against Giganews, alleging copyright infringement. [Perfect 10, Inc. v. Giganews, Inc., 847 F.3d 657 (9th Cir. 2017)] (See Copyrights.*)*

(a) Is Giganews liable for copyright infringement? Do Internet service providers have an ethical duty to do more to prevent infringement? Why or why not?

(b) Using the IDDR approach, decide whether a copyright owner has an ethical duty to protect against infringement.

Time-Limited Group Assignment

8–11. Patents. After years of research, your company develops a product that might revolutionize the green (environmentally conscious) building industry. The product is made from relatively inexpensive and widely available materials combined in a unique way that can substantially lower the heating and cooling costs of residential and commercial buildings. The company has registered the trademark it intends to use on the product and has filed a patent application with the U.S. Patent and Trademark Office. (See *Patents.*)

(a) One group will provide three reasons why this product does or does not qualify for patent protection.

(b) A second group will develop a four-step procedure for how the company can best protect its intellectual property rights (trademark, trade secret, and patent) and prevent domestic and foreign competitors from producing counterfeit goods or cheap knockoffs.

(c) A third group will list and explain three ways in which the company can utilize licensing.

Chapter 9

Internet Law, Social Media, and Privacy

The Internet has changed our lives and our laws. Technology has put the world at our fingertips and now allows even the smallest business to reach customers around the globe. At the same time, the Internet presents a variety of challenges for the law.

Courts are often in uncharted waters when deciding disputes that involve the Internet, social media, and online privacy. Judges may have no common law precedents to rely on. Long-standing principles of justice may be inapplicable. New rules are evolving, but often not as quickly as technology.

For instance, Facebook is confronting numerous class-action lawsuits concerning its user privacy policy. In response to complaints about the policy, Facebook has changed it several times to satisfy critics and ward off potential government investigations. Other companies, including mobile app developers, have also changed their privacy policies to provide more information to consumers. Consequently, it is frequently the companies, rather than courts or legislatures, that are defining the privacy rights of their online users.

9–1 Internet Law

A number of laws specifically address issues that arise only on the Internet. Three such issues are unsolicited e-mail, domain names, and cybersquatting, as we discuss here. We also discuss how the law is dealing with problems of trademark infringement and dilution online.

9–1a Spam

Businesses and individuals alike are targets of **spam**.[1] Spam is the unsolicited "junk e-mail" that floods virtual mailboxes with advertisements, solicitations, and other messages. Considered relatively harmless in the early days of the Internet, spam has become a serious problem and accounts for roughly 75 percent of all e-mails.

State Regulation of Spam In an attempt to combat spam, thirty-seven states have enacted laws that prohibit or regulate its use. Many state laws that regulate spam require the senders of e-mail ads to instruct the recipients on how they can "opt out" of further e-mail ads from the same sources. For instance, in some states, an unsolicited e-mail must include a toll-free phone number or return e-mail address that the recipient can use to ask the sender to stop forwarding unsolicited e-mails.

The Federal CAN-SPAM Act In 2003, Congress enacted the Controlling the Assault of Non-Solicited Pornography and Marketing (CAN-SPAM) Act.[2] The legislation applies to any "commercial electronic mail messages" that are sent to promote a commercial product or service. Significantly, the statute preempts state antispam laws except for those provisions in state laws that prohibit false and deceptive e-mailing practices.

Generally, the act permits the sending of unsolicited commercial e-mail but prohibits certain types of spamming activities. Prohibited activities include the use of a false return address and the use of false, misleading, or deceptive information when sending e-mail. The statute also prohibits the use of "dictionary attacks"—sending messages to randomly generated e-mail addresses— and the "harvesting" of e-mail addresses from websites through the use of specialized software.

■ **Example 9.1** Sanford Wallace, known as the "Spam King," is considered to be one of the world's most prolific spammers. He operated several businesses over the years that used *botnets* (automated spamming networks) to send out hundreds of millions of unwanted e-mails. Wallace also infected computers with spyware and then

---

1. The term *spam* is said to come from the lyrics of a Monty Python song that repeats the word *spam* over and over.

2. 15 U.S.C. Sections 7701 *et seq.*

sold consumers the software to fix it. He infiltrated Facebook accounts to spam 27 million of its users.

As a result, Wallace was sued by the Federal Trade Commission and Facebook, and ordered to pay millions of dollars in fines. The Federal Bureau of Investigation ultimately arrested Wallace, and he pleaded guilty to fraud, spam, and violating a court order not to access Facebook. ■ Arresting prolific spammers, however, has done little to curb spam, which continues to flow at a rate of many billions of messages per day.

The U.S. Safe Web Act After the CAN-SPAM Act prohibited false and deceptive e-mails originating in the United States, spamming from servers located in other nations increased. These cross-border spammers generally were able to escape detection and legal sanctions because the Federal Trade Commission (FTC) lacked the authority to investigate foreign spamming.

Congress sought to rectify the situation by enacting the U.S. Safe Web Act (also known as the Undertaking Spam, Spyware, and Fraud Enforcement with Enforcers Beyond Borders Act).[3] The act allows the FTC to cooperate and share information with foreign agencies in investigating and prosecuting those involved in spamming, spyware, and various Internet frauds and deceptions.

The Safe Web Act also provides a "safe harbor" for **Internet service providers (ISPs)**—organizations that provide access to the Internet. The safe harbor gives ISPs immunity from liability for supplying information to the FTC concerning possible unfair or deceptive conduct in foreign jurisdictions.

9–1b Domain Names

As e-commerce expanded worldwide, one issue that emerged involved the rights of a trademark owner to use the mark as part of a domain name. A **domain name** is part of an Internet address, such as "cengage.com."

Structure of Domain Names Every domain name ends with a top-level domain (TLD), which is the part of the name to the right of the period. The TLD often indicates the type of entity that operates the site. For instance, com is an abbreviation for commercial, and edu is short for education.

The second-level domain (SLD)—the part of the name to the left of the period—is chosen by the business entity or individual registering the domain name. Competition for SLDs among firms with similar names

and products has led to numerous disputes. By using an identical or similar domain name, parties have attempted to profit from a competitor's **goodwill** (the nontangible value of a business).

Distribution System The Internet Corporation for Assigned Names and Numbers (ICANN), a nonprofit corporation, oversees the distribution of domain names and operates an online arbitration system. Due to numerous complaints, ICANN overhauled the domain name distribution system in 2012.

ICANN started selling new generic top-level domain names (gTLDs) for an initial price of $185,000 plus an annual fee of $25,000. Whereas the older TLDs were limited to only a few terms (such as com, net, and org), gTLDs can take any form. Many companies and corporations acquire gTLDs based on their brands, such as aol, bmw, canon, target, and walmart. Some companies have numerous gTLDs. Google's gTLDs, for instance, include android, bing, chrome, gmail, goog, and YouTube.

Because gTLDs have greatly increased the potential number of domain names, domain name registrars have proliferated. Registrar companies charge a fee to businesses and individuals to register new names and to renew annual registrations (often through automated software). Many of these companies also buy and sell expired domain names.

9–1c Cybersquatting

One of the goals of the new gTLD system was to address the problem of *cybersquatting*. **Cybersquatting** occurs when a person registers a domain name that is the same as, or confusingly similar to, the trademark of another and then offers to sell the domain name back to the trademark owner.

■ **Case in Point 9.2** Apple, Inc., has repeatedly sued cybersquatters that registered domain names similar to the names of its products, such as ipods.com. Apple won a judgment in litigation at the World Intellectual Property Organization against a company that was squatting on the domain name iPhone6s.com.[4] ■

Anticybersquatting Legislation Because cybersquatting has led to so much litigation, Congress enacted the Anticybersquatting Consumer Protection Act (ACPA),[5] which amended the Lanham Act—the federal

---

3. Pub. L. No. 109-455, 120 Stat. 3372 (2006), codified in various sections of 15 U.S.C. and 12 U.S.C. Section 3412.

4. World Intellectual Property Organization Case No. D2012-0951.
5. 15 U.S.C. Section 8131.

law protecting trademarks. The ACPA makes cybersquatting illegal when both of the following are true:

1. The domain name is identical or confusingly similar to the trademark of another.
2. The one registering, trafficking in, or using the domain name has a "bad faith intent" to profit from that trademark.

■ **Case in Point 9.3** CrossFit, Inc., is a Delaware corporation that provides personal fitness services and products. CrossFit is well known in the fitness industry and licenses affiliates to operate individual CrossFit-branded programs. CrossFit granted a license to Andres Del Cueto Davalos to operate a location in Mexico and allowed him to use the domain name "CrossFitAlfa." Davalos later registered the domain name CrossFitBeta without CrossFit's permission and then used both of these domain names to redirect website visitors to a third website, www.woodbox.com. Davalos was attempting to siphon off CrossFit customers to another business that he co-owned, Woodbox Training Centers, which operated in twenty-five locations across Mexico. CrossFit sued under the ACPA. Because of Davalos's bad faith intent, the court awarded CrossFit the maximum amount of statutory damages available ($100,000 for each domain name), plus costs and attorneys' fees.[6] ■

Frequent Changes in Domain Name Ownership Facilitate Cybersquatting Despite the ACPA, cybersquatting continues to present a problem for businesses. All domain name registrars are supposed to relay information about their transactions to ICANN and other companies that keep a master list of domain names, but this does not always occur. The speed at which domain names change hands and the difficulty in tracking mass automated registrations have created an environment in which cybersquatting can flourish.

Typosquatting Typosquatting is registering a name that is a misspelling of a popular brand, such as googl.com or appple.com. Because many Internet users are not perfect typists, Web pages using these misspelled names receive a lot of traffic. More traffic generally means increased profit (advertisers often pay websites based on the number of unique visits, or hits).

■ **Case in Point 9.4** Counter Balance Enterprises, Ltd., registered and used domain names that misspelled Facebook, such as "facebobk.com" and "facemonk.com." Facebook, Inc., filed a suit in a California federal court under the ACPA against Counter Balance (and ten other

defendants, including Banana Ads, LLC) for typosquatting. The defendants failed to appear, and the court entered a default judgment in favor of Facebook. The court permanently enjoined the defendants from using the infringing domain names and awarded Facebook a total of $2.8 million in damages (ranging from $5,000 to $1.3 million per individual defendant).[7] ■

Typosquatting may sometimes fall beyond the reach of the ACPA. If the misspelling is significant, the trademark owner may have difficulty proving that the name is identical or confusingly similar to the trademark of another, as the ACPA requires.

Typosquatting adds costs for businesses seeking to protect their domain name rights. Companies must attempt to register not only legitimate variations of their domain names but also potential misspellings. Large corporations may have to register thousands of domain names across the globe just to protect their basic brands and trademarks.

Applicability and Sanctions of the ACPA The ACPA applies to all domain name registrations of trademarks. Successful plaintiffs in suits brought under the act can collect actual damages and profits, or they can elect to receive statutory damages ranging from $1,000 to $100,000.

Although some companies have successfully sued under the ACPA, there are roadblocks to pursuing such lawsuits. Some domain name registrars offer privacy services that hide the true owners of websites, making it difficult for trademark owners to identify cybersquatters. Thus, before bringing a suit, a trademark owner has to ask the court for a subpoena to discover the identity of the owner of the infringing website. Because of the high costs of court proceedings, discovery, and even arbitration, many disputes over cybersquatting are settled out of court.

To facilitate dispute resolution, ICANN offers two dispute resolution forums: the Uniform Domain-Name Dispute Resolution Policy (UDRP) and the Uniform Rapid Suspension (URS) system. More disputes are resolved through the UDRP, which allows common law trademark claims and has fewer procedural requirements. The URS system can be used only by registered trademark holders with clear-cut infringement claims.

9–1d Meta Tags

Meta tags are key words that give Internet browsers specific information about a Web page. Meta tags can be used to increase the likelihood that a site will be included

---

6. *CrossFit, Inc. v. Davalos*, 2017 WL 733213 (N.D.Cal. 2017).

7. *Facebook, Inc. v. Banana Ads, LLC*, 2013 WL 1873289 (N.D.Cal. 2013).

in search engine results, even if the site has nothing to do with the key words. In effect, one site can appropriate the key words of other sites with more frequent hits so that the appropriating site will appear in the same search engine results as the more popular sites.

Using another's trademark in a meta tag without the owner's permission normally constitutes trademark infringement. Some uses of another's trademark as a meta tag may be permissible, however, if the use is reasonably necessary and does not suggest that the owner authorized or sponsored the use.

■ **Case in Point 9.5** Farzad and Lisa Tabari are auto brokers—the personal shoppers of the automotive world. They contact authorized dealers, solicit bids, and arrange for customers to buy from the dealer offering the best combination of location, availability, and price. The Tabaris offered this service at the websites buy-a-lexus.com and buyorleaselexus.com.

Toyota Motor Sales U.S.A., Inc., the exclusive distributor of Lexus vehicles and the owner of the Lexus mark, objected to the Tabaris' practices. The Tabaris removed Toyota's photographs and logo from their site and added a disclaimer in large type at the top, but they refused to give up their domain names. Toyota sued for infringement. The court forced the Tabaris to stop using any "domain name, service mark, trademark, trade name, meta tag or other commercial indication of origin that includes the mark LEXUS."[8] ■

9–1e Trademark Dilution in the Online World

Trademark dilution occurs when a trademark is used, without authorization, in a way that diminishes the distinctive quality of the mark. Unlike trademark infringement, a claim of dilution does not require proof that consumers are likely to be confused by a connection between the unauthorized use and the mark. For this reason, the products involved need not be similar, as the following *Spotlight Case* illustrates.

---

8. *Toyota Motor Sales, U.S.A., Inc. v. Tabari*, 610 F.3d 1171 (9th Cir. 2010).

Spotlight on Internet Porn

Case 9.1 Hasbro, Inc. v. Internet Entertainment Group, Ltd.

United States District Court, Western District of Washington, 1996 WL 84853 (1996).

Background and Facts In 1949, Hasbro, Inc.—then known as the Milton Bradley Company—published its first version of Candy Land, a children's board game. Hasbro is the owner of the trademark "Candy Land," which has been registered with the U.S. Patent and Trademark Office since 1951. Over the years, Hasbro has produced several versions of the game, including Candy Land puzzles, a travel version, a computer game, and a handheld electronic version. In the mid-1990s, Brian Cartmell and his employer, the Internet Entertainment Group, Ltd., used the term *candyland.com* as a domain name for a sexually explicit Internet site. Anyone who performed an online search using the word *candyland* was directed to this adult website. Hasbro filed a trademark dilution claim in a federal court, seeking a permanent injunction to prevent the defendants from using the Candy Land trademark.

In the Language of the Court
DWYER, U.S. District Judge
 * * * *

2. Hasbro has demonstrated a probability of proving that defendants Internet Entertainment Group, Ltd., Brian Cartmell and Internet Entertainment Group, Inc. (collectively referred to as "defendants") have been diluting the value of Hasbro's CANDY LAND mark by using the name CANDYLAND to identify a sexually explicit Internet site, and by using the name string "candyland.com" as an Internet domain name which, when typed into an Internet-connected computer, provides Internet users with access to that site.
 * * * *

4. Hasbro has shown that defendants' use of the CANDY LAND name and the domain name candyland.com in connection with their Internet site is causing irreparable injury to Hasbro.

Case 9.1 Continues

5. *The probable harm to Hasbro from defendants' conduct outweighs any inconvenience that defendants will experience if they are required to stop using the CANDYLAND name.* [Emphasis added.]
* * * *

THEREFORE, IT IS HEREBY ORDERED that Hasbro's motion for preliminary injunction is granted.

Decision and Remedy *The federal district court granted Hasbro an injunction against the defendants, agreeing that the domain name* candyland *was "causing irreparable injury to Hasbro." The judge ordered the defendants to immediately remove all content from the* candyland.com *website and to stop using the Candy Land mark.*

Critical Thinking
- **Economic** *How can companies protect themselves from others who create websites that have similar domain names, and what limits each company's ability to be fully protected?*
- **What If the Facts Were Different?** *Suppose that the site using* candyland.com *had not been sexually explicit but had sold candy. Would the result have been the same? Explain.*

9–1f Licensing in the Online World

A company may permit another party to use a trademark (or other intellectual property) under a license. A licensor might grant a license allowing its trademark to be used as part of a domain name, for instance.

Another type of license involves the use of a product such as software. This sort of licensing is ubiquitous in the online world. When you download an application on your smartphone, tablet, or other mobile device, for instance, you are typically entering into a license agreement. You are obtaining only a *license* to use that app and not ownership rights in it. Apps published on Google Play, for instance, may use its licensing service to prompt users to agree to a license at the time of installation and use.

Licensing agreements frequently include restrictions that prohibit licensees from sharing the file and using it to create similar software applications. The license may also limit the use of the application to a specific device or give permission to the user for a certain time period.

9–2 Copyrights in Digital Information

Copyright law is probably the most important form of intellectual property protection on the Internet. This is because much of the material on the Internet (including software and database information) is copyrighted, and in order for that material to be transferred online,

it must be "copied." Generally, whenever a party downloads software or music into a computer's random access memory, or RAM, without authorization, a copyright is infringed.

Initially, criminal penalties for copyright violations could be imposed only if unauthorized copies were exchanged for financial gain. Then, Congress amended the law and extended criminal liability for the piracy of copyrighted materials to persons who exchange unauthorized copies of copyrighted works without realizing a profit. See this chapter's *Digital Update* feature for a discussion of copyright law in the context of video games.

9–2a Digital Millennium Copyright Act

The Digital Millennium Copyright Act (DMCA)[9] gave significant protection to owners of copyrights in digital information. Among other things, the act established civil and criminal penalties for anyone who circumvents (bypasses) encryption software or other technological antipiracy protection. Also prohibited are the manufacture, import, sale, and distribution of devices or services for circumvention.

Allows Fair Use The DMCA provides for exceptions to fit the needs of libraries, scientists, universities, and others. In general, the law does not restrict the "fair use"

---

9. 17 U.S.C. Sections 512, 1201–1205, 1301–1332; and 28 U.S.C. Section 4001.

Digital Update — Riot Games, Inc., Protects Its Online Video Game Copyrights

The acronym *LoL* generally means "laugh out loud." But when it comes to the popular online video game *League of Legends* owned by Riot Games, Inc., *LoL* means something much different. More than 100 million people use this free multiplayer video game online each month.

Taking on a Chinese Competitor

To protect its *LoL* copyrights, U.S.-based Riot Games filed a lawsuit against a Chinese company, Shanghai MoBai Computer Technology (Moby). Riot Games alleges that Moby "blatantly and slavishly copied *LoL* in [Moby's online video game called] Arena of Battle."[a] In particular, Moby's copycat game features nearly sixty champions with names, sound effects, icons, and abilities similar to those used in *LoL*. Moby marketed *Arena of Battle* through the Apple App Store as well as Google Play, and it used alternative titles and aliases in order to sell its game.

Note that copyright law does not protect video gameplay. *Gameplay* describes how players interact with a video game, such as through its plot and its rules. Specific expressions of that gameplay, however— as measured by look, settings, stories, characters, and sound—are protected.

The Mobile Game Market in China

While *LoL* has been China's top computer desktop game for years, millions of Chinese online game players use only mobile platforms, such as smartphones or tablets. As a result, Tencent, the parent company of Riot Games, created a mobile version of *LoL* called *King of Glory*. It is almost an exact copy of *LoL*. *King of Glory* is one of China's top-grossing Apple mobile games. Of course, there are no copyright issues with *King of Glory* because Tencent can copy its own video game.

Taking on a Cheating Software Developer

In addition to suing Moby, as mentioned earlier, Riot Games accused the makers of LeagueSharp of violating the Digital Millennium Copyright Act.[b] The plaintiff claimed that the defendants violated the act by circumventing *LoL*'s anti-cheating software. Customers paid a monthly fee to use LeagueSharp. Among other things, the service enabled them to see hidden information, automate gameplay to perform with enhanced accuracy, and accumulate certain rewards at a rate not possible for a normal human player.

The obvious question is why anybody would want to pay for LeagueSharp services—recall that *LoL* is a free online game. The reason is the advantage the cheating players gained over ordinary players. They could, for instance, more quickly and easily win "swords," which they could use to buy new characters with which to play. LeagueSharp's makers ultimately agreed to pay $10 million to Riot Games.[c]

Critical Thinking *If LoL is free to players, why would a Chinese company want to copy it?*

---

a. *Riot Games, Inc., v. Shanghai MoBai Computer Technology Co., Ltd. et al.*, Case No. 3:17-CV-00331 (N.D.Cal. 2017).

b. *Riot Games, Inc. v. Argote*, Case No. 2:16-CV-5871 (C.D.Cal. 2017).

c. Andy Chalk, "Riot awarded $10 million in Leaguesharp lawsuit settlement." pcgamer.com, March 3, 2017.

---

of circumvention methods for educational and other noncommercial purposes. For instance, circumvention is allowed to test computer security, to conduct encryption research, to protect personal privacy, and to enable parents to monitor their children's use of the Internet.

The fair use doctrine has been applied in other situations as well. ■ **Case in Point 9.6** Stephanie Lenz posted a short video on YouTube of her toddler son dancing with the Prince song "Let's Go Crazy" playing in the background. Universal Music Group (UMG) sent YouTube a take-down notice that stated the video violated copyright law under the DMCA. YouTube removed the "dancing baby" video and notified Lenz of the allegations of copyright infringement, warning her that repeated incidents of infringement could lead it to delete her account.

Lenz filed a lawsuit against UMG claiming that accusing her of infringement constituted a material misrepresentation (fraud) because UMG knew that Lenz's video was a fair use of the song. The district court held that UMG should have considered the fair use doctrine before sending the take-down notice. UMG appealed, and the U.S. Court of Appeals for the Ninth Circuit affirmed. Lenz was allowed to pursue nominal damages from UMG for sending the notice without considering whether her use was fair.[10] ■

---

10. *Lenz v. Universal Music Corp.*, 815 F.3d 1145 (9th Cir. 2016).

Limits Liability of Internet Service Providers

The DMCA also limits the liability of Internet service providers (ISPs). Under the act, an ISP is not liable for copyright infringement by its customer *unless* the ISP is aware of the subscriber's violation. An ISP may be held liable only if it fails to take action to shut down the subscriber after learning of the violation. A copyright holder must act promptly, however, by pursuing a claim in court, or the subscriber has the right to be restored to online access.

9–2b File-Sharing Technology

Soon after the Internet became popular, a few enterprising programmers created software to compress large data files, particularly those associated with music. The best-known compression and decompression system is MP3, which enables music fans to download songs or entire CDs onto their computers or onto portable listening devices, such as smartphones and tablets. The MP3 system also made it possible for music fans to access other fans' files by engaging in file-sharing via the Internet.

Methods of File-Sharing File-sharing is accomplished through **peer-to-peer (P2P) networking.** The concept is simple. Rather than going through a central Web server, P2P networking uses numerous computers that are connected to one another, often via the Internet. Individuals on the same network can access files stored on one another's computers through a **distributed network.** Parts of the network may be distributed all over the country or the world, which offers an unlimited number of uses.

A newer method of sharing files via the Internet is **cloud computing,** which is essentially a subscription-based or pay-per-use service that extends a computer's software or storage capabilities. Cloud computing can deliver a single application through a browser to multiple users. Alternatively, cloud computing might provide data storage and virtual servers that can be accessed on demand. Amazon, Facebook, Google, IBM, and Sun Microsystems are using and developing more cloud-computing services.

Sharing Stored Music and Movies When file-sharing is used to download others' stored music files, copyright issues arise. Recording artists and their labels stand to lose large amounts of royalties and revenues if relatively few digital downloads or CDs are purchased and then made available for free on distributed networks. These concerns have prompted recording companies to pursue not only companies involved in file-sharing but also individuals who have file-shared copyrighted works.

In the following case, the owner of copyrights in musical compositions sought to recover from an Internet service provider, some of whose subscribers used a P2P network to share the owner's copyrighted compositions without permission.

Case 9.2

BMG Rights Management (US), LLC v. Cox Communications, Inc.

United States Court of Appeals, Fourth Circuit, 881 F.3d 293 (2018).

Background and Facts Cox Communications, Inc., is an Internet service provider (ISP) with 4.5 million subscribers. Some of Cox's subscribers used BitTorrent to share copyrighted files, including music files, without the copyright owners' permission. (BitTorrent is a peer-to-peer file transfer protocol for sharing large amounts of data online.) Cox's stated policy is to suspend or terminate subscribers who use the service to "infringe the . . . copyrights . . . of any party." Despite this policy, Cox failed to terminate infringing subscribers.

BMG Rights Management (US), LLC, owned copyrights in some of the music shared by the subscribers. BMG sent millions of notices to Cox to alert the ISP to the infringing activity. Cox deleted the notices without acting on them. BMG filed a suit in a federal district court against Cox, seeking to hold the ISP liable under the Digital Millennium Copyright Act (DMCA) for its subscribers' infringement of BMG's copyrights. Cox claimed a "safe harbor" under the act. The court issued a judgment in BMG's favor. Cox appealed to the U.S. Court of Appeals for the Fourth Circuit.

In the Language of the Court

Diana Gribbon *MOTZ*, Circuit Judge:

* * * *

[The Digital Millennium Copyright Act (DMCA)] requires that, to obtain the benefit of the * * * safe harbor, Cox must have reasonably implemented "a policy that provides for the termination in appropriate circumstances" of its subscribers who repeatedly infringe copyrights. * * * Cox formally adopted a repeat infringer "policy," but * * * made every effort to avoid reasonably implementing that policy. Indeed, * * * Cox very clearly determined *not* to terminate subscribers who in fact repeatedly violated the policy.

The words of Cox's own employees confirm this conclusion. In [an] email, Jason Zabek, the executive managing the Abuse Group, a team tasked with addressing subscribers' violations of Cox's policies, explained to his team that "if a customer is terminated for DMCA, you are able to reactivate them." * * * This would allow Cox to "collect a few extra weeks of payments for their account." * * * As a result of this practice, * * * Cox *never* terminated a subscriber for infringement without reactivating them.

Cox nonetheless contends that it lacked "actual knowledge" of its subscribers' infringement and therefore did not have to terminate them. That argument misses the mark. The evidence shows that Cox *always* reactivated subscribers after termination, regardless of its knowledge of the subscriber's infringement. * * * *An ISP cannot claim the protections of the DMCA safe harbor provisions merely by terminating customers as a symbolic gesture before indiscriminately reactivating them within a short timeframe.* [Emphasis added.]

* * * *

Moreover, Cox dispensed with terminating subscribers who repeatedly infringed BMG's copyrights in particular when it decided to delete automatically all infringement notices received from [BMG]. As a result, Cox received none of the millions of infringement notices that [BMG] sent to Cox.

* * * *

* * * Cox suggests that because the DMCA merely requires termination of repeat infringers in "appropriate circumstances," Cox decided not to terminate certain subscribers only when "appropriate circumstances" were lacking. But Cox failed to provide evidence that a determination of "appropriate circumstances" played *any* role in its decisions to terminate (or not to terminate). * * * Instead, the evidence shows that Cox's decisions not to terminate * * * were based on one goal: not losing revenue from paying subscribers.

Decision and Remedy   *The federal appellate court affirmed the judgment of the lower court. To qualify for the DMCA safe-harbor defense, an ISP must implement a repeat-infringer policy. The court stated, "Cox failed to qualify . . . because it failed to implement its policy."*

Critical Thinking
- **Technology**   *Should an ISP be liable for copyright infringement by its subscribers regardless of whether the ISP is aware of the violation? Why or why not?*
- **Legal Environment**   *Could Cox legitimately claim that it had no knowledge of subscribers who infringed BMG's copyrights, since the ISP was deleting all of BMG's infringement notices? Explain.*

Pirated Movies and Television   File-sharing also creates problems for the motion picture and television industries, which lose significant amounts of revenue annually as a result of piracy. Numerous websites offer software that facilitates the illegal copying of movies and television programs. BitTorrent, for instance, is a P2P protocol that enables users to download and transfer high-quality files from the Internet. Popcorn Time is a BitTorrent site that offers streaming services that enable users to watch pirated movies and television shows without downloading them.

■ **Case in Point 9.7**   Malibu Media, LLC, produces and distributes erotic films through its website X-Art. com. Customers pay a monthly or yearly subscription fee to access an online library of copyrighted pornographic content. Malibu hires investigators to identify individuals who use BitTorrent to illegally download, reproduce, and distribute content from its website. After investigators named Jonathan Gonzales as a suspect, Malibu filed a copyright infringement action against him. A federal district court in Texas ruled in favor of Malibu Media. Gonzales had infringed on fifteen of

Malibu's copyrighted films. Thus, Malibu was entitled to damages and to an injunction prohibiting Gonzales from future infringement. [11] ■

9-3 Social Media

Social media provide a means by which people can create and exchange ideas and comments via the Internet. Facebook and YouTube are the biggest social media sites. Additional social media platforms include WhatsApp, Pinterest, and Twitter, along with many others used by hundreds of millions of people worldwide.

9-3a Legal Issues

The emergence of Facebook and other social networking sites has created a number of legal and ethical issues for businesses. For instance, a firm's rights in valuable intellectual property may be infringed if users post trademarked images or copyrighted materials on these sites without permission. The content of social media may play a role in various parts of the legal process, as discussed next. Employers' social media policies may also be at issue.

Impact on Litigation Social media posts are routinely included in discovery in litigation because they can provide damaging information that establishes a person's intent or what she or he knew at a particular time. Like e-mail, posts on social networks can be the smoking gun that leads to liability.

Tweets and other social media posts can also be used to reduce damages awards. ■ **Example 9.8** Jill Daniels sued for injuries she sustained in a car accident, claiming that her injuries made it impossible for her to continue working as a hairstylist. The jury initially determined that her damages were $237,000, but when the jurors saw tweets and photographs of Daniels partying in New Orleans and vacationing on the beach, they reduced the final award to $142,000. ■

Impact on Settlement Agreements Social media posts have been used to invalidate settlement agreements that contain confidentiality clauses. ■ **Case in Point 9.9** Patrick Snay was the headmaster of Gulliver Preparatory School in Florida. When Gulliver did not renew Snay's employment contract, Snay sued the school for age discrimination. During mediation, Snay agreed to settle the case for $80,000 and signed a confidentiality clause that required him and his wife not to disclose the "terms and existence" of the agreement. Nevertheless, Snay and his wife told their daughter, Dana, that the dispute had been settled and that they were happy with the results.

Dana, a college student, had recently graduated from Gulliver and, according to Snay, had suffered retaliation at the school. Dana posted a Facebook comment that said "Mama and Papa Snay won the case against Gulliver. Gulliver is now officially paying for my vacation to Europe this summer. SUCK IT." The comment went out to 1,200 of Dana's Facebook friends, many of whom were Gulliver students, and school officials soon learned of it. The school immediately notified Snay that he had breached the confidentiality clause and refused to pay the settlement amount. Ultimately, a state intermediate appellate court held that Snay had breached the confidentiality clause and therefore could not enforce the settlement agreement.[12] ■

Criminal Investigations Law enforcement uses social media to detect and prosecute criminals. A surprising number of criminals boast about their illegal activities on social media. ■ **Example 9.10** A nineteen-year-old posts a message on Facebook bragging about how drunk he was on New Year's Eve and apologizing to the owner of the parked car that he hit. The next day, police officers arrest him for drunk driving and leaving the scene of an accident. ■

Some police departments authorize officers to go undercover on social media sites. ■ **Example 9.11** As part of Operation Crew Cut, New York Police Department (NYPD) officers routinely pretend to be young women in order to "friend" suspects on Facebook. Using these fake identities, officers are able to avoid the social media site's privacy settings and gain valuable information about illegal activities. ■

Administrative Agency Investigations Federal regulators also use social media posts in their investigations into illegal activities. ■ **Example 9.12** Reed Hastings, the top executive of Netflix, stated on Facebook that Netflix subscribers had watched a billion hours of video the previous month. As a result, Netflix's stock price rose, which prompted a federal agency investigation. Under securities laws, such a statement is considered to be material information to investors. Thus, it must be disclosed

---

11. *Malibu Media, LLC v. Gonzales*, 2017 WL 2985641 (S.D.Tex.—Houston 2017).

12. *Gulliver Schools, Inc. v. Snay*, 39 Fla.L.Weekly D457, 137 So.3d 1045 (2014).

to all investors, not just a select group, such as those who had access to Hastings's Facebook post.

The agency ultimately concluded that it could not hold Hastings responsible for any wrongdoing because the agency's policy on social media use was not clear. The agency then issued new guidelines that allow companies to disclose material information through social media if investors have been notified in advance. ■

In addition, an administrative law judge can base her or his decision on the content of social media posts. ■ **Case in Point 9.13** Jennifer O'Brien was a tenured teacher at a public school in New Jersey when she posted two messages on her Facebook page: "I'm not a teacher—I'm a warden for future criminals!" and "They had a scared straight program in school—why couldn't I bring first graders?" Not surprisingly, outraged parents protested. The deputy superintendent of schools filed a complaint against O'Brien with the state's commissioner of education, charging her with conduct unbecoming a teacher.

After a hearing, an administrative law judge ordered that O'Brien be removed from her teaching position. O'Brien appealed to a state court, claiming that her Facebook postings were protected by the First Amendment and could not be used by the school district to discipline or discharge her. The court found that O'Brien had failed to establish that her Facebook postings were protected speech and that the seriousness of O'Brien's conduct warranted removal from her position.[13] ■

Employers' Social Media Policies Many large corporations have established specific guidelines on using social media in the workplace. Employees who use social media in a way that violates their employer's stated policies may be disciplined or fired from their jobs. Courts and administrative agencies usually uphold an employer's right to terminate a person based on his or her violation of a social media policy.

■ **Case in Point 9.14** Virginia Rodriquez had worked for Walmart Stores, Inc., for almost twenty years and had been promoted to management. Then she was disciplined for violating the company's policies by having a fellow employee use Rodriquez's password to alter the price of an item that she purchased. Under Walmart's rules, another violation within a year would mean termination.

Nine months later, on Facebook, Rodriquez publicly chastised employees under her supervision for calling in sick to go to a party. The posting violated Walmart's "Social Media Policy," which was "to avoid public comment

that adversely affects employees." Walmart terminated Rodriquez. She filed a lawsuit, alleging discrimination, but the court issued a summary judgment in Walmart's favor.[14] ■

9–3b The Electronic Communications Privacy Act

The Electronic Communications Privacy Act (ECPA)[15] amended federal wiretapping law to cover electronic forms of communications. Although Congress enacted the ECPA many years before social media networks existed, it nevertheless applies to communications through social media.

The ECPA prohibits the intentional interception of any wire, oral, or electronic communication. It also prohibits the intentional disclosure or use of the information obtained through the interception.

Exclusions for Employers Excluded from the ECPA's coverage are any electronic communications through devices that an employer provides for an employee to use "in the ordinary course of its business." Consequently, if a company provides an employee with a cell phone, laptop, or tablet for ordinary business use, the company is not prohibited from intercepting business communications made on it. This "business-extension exception" permits employers to monitor employees' electronic communications made in the ordinary course of business. It does not, however, permit employers to monitor employees' personal communications.

Another exception to the ECPA allows an employer to avoid liability under the act if the employees consent to having their electronic communications monitored by the employer.

Stored Communications Part of the ECPA is known as the Stored Communications Act (SCA).[16] The SCA prohibits intentional and unauthorized access to *stored* electronic communications and sets forth criminal and civil sanctions for violators. A person can violate the SCA by intentionally accessing a stored electronic communication. The SCA also prevents "providers" of communication services (such as cell phone companies and social media networks) from divulging private communications to certain entities and individuals.

■ **Case in Point 9.15** As part of an investigation into disability fraud, the New York County District Attorney's Office sought from Facebook the data and stored

---

13. *In re O'Brien*, 2013 WL 132508 (N.J.Super.Ct. App.Div. 2013).

14. *Rodriquez v. Wal-Mart Stores, Inc.*, 2013 WL 102674 (N.D.Tex. 2013).
15. 18 U.S.C. Sections 2510–2521.
16. 18 U.S.C. Sections 2701–2711.

communications of 381 retired police officers and fire-fighters. The government suspected that these individuals had faked illness after 9/11 in order to obtain disability.

Facebook challenged the warrants in court, arguing that they were unconstitutional because they were overly broad. The court ruled against Facebook and ordered it to comply. It also ordered the company not to notify the users that it was disclosing their data to government investigators. Facebook complied but appealed the decision. The reviewing court held that only the individuals, not Facebook, could challenge the warrants as violations of privacy. Thus, the government was allowed to seize all of Facebook's digital data pertaining to these users.[17] ■

9–3c Protection of Social Media Passwords

Employees and applicants for jobs or colleges have sometimes been asked to divulge their social media passwords. An employer or school may look at an individual's Facebook or other account to see if it includes controversial postings such as racially discriminatory remarks or photos of drug parties. Such postings can have a negative effect on a person's prospects even if they were made years earlier or are taken out of context.

A majority of the states have enacted legislation to protect individuals from having to disclose their social media passwords. Each state's law is slightly different. Some states, such as Michigan, prohibit employers from taking adverse action against an employee or job applicant based on what the person has posted online. Michigan's law also applies to e-mail and cloud storage accounts.

Legislation will not completely prevent employers and others from taking actions against a person based on his or her social network postings, though. Management and human resources personnel are unlikely to admit that they looked at someone's Facebook page and that it influenced their decision. They may not even have to admit to looking at the Facebook page if they use private browsing, which enables people to keep their Web browsing activities confidential. How, then, would a rejected job applicant be able to prove that she or he was rejected because the employer accessed social media postings?

9–3d Company-wide Social Media Networks

Many companies, including Dell, Inc., and Nikon Instruments, form their own internal social media networks.

Software companies offer a variety of systems, including Salesforce.com's Chatter, Microsoft's Yammer, and Cisco Systems' WebEx Social. Posts on these internal networks, or *intranets*, are quite different from the typical posts on Facebook, LinkedIn, and Twitter. Employees use these intranets to exchange messages about topics related to their work, such as deals that are closing, new products, production flaws, how a team is solving a problem, and the details of customer orders. Thus, the tone is businesslike.

Protection of Trade Secrets An important advantage to using an internal system for employee communications is that the company can better protect its trade secrets. The company usually decides which employees can see particular intranet files and which employees will belong to each specific "social" group within the company. Companies providing internal social media networks often keep the resulting data on their own servers in secure clouds.

Other Advantages Internal social media systems also offer additional benefits. They provide real-time information about important issues, such as production glitches. Additionally, posts can include tips on how to best sell new products or deal with difficult customers, as well as information about competitors' products and services. Another major benefit is a significant reduction in e-mail. Rather than wasting fellow employees' time reading mass e-mailings, workers can post messages or collaborate on presentations via the company's social network.

9–4 Online Defamation

Cyber torts are torts that arise from online conduct. One of the most prevalent cyber torts is online defamation. Defamation involves wrongfully hurting a person's reputation by communicating false statements about that person to others. Because the Internet enables individuals to communicate with large numbers of people simultaneously (via a blog or tweet, for instance), online defamation has become a problem in today's legal environment.

■ **Example 9.16** Singer-songwriter Courtney Love was sued for defamation based on remarks she posted about fashion designer Dawn Simorangkir on Twitter. Love claimed that her statements were statements of opinion (rather than statements of fact, as required) and therefore were not actionable as defamation. Nevertheless,

---

17. *In re 381 Search Warrants Directed to Facebook, Inc.*, 29 N.Y.S.3d 231, 55 N.Y.S.3d 696, 78 N.E.3d 141 (2017).

Love ended up paying $430,000 to settle the case out of court. ■

9–4a Identifying the Author of Online Defamation

An initial issue raised by online defamation is simply discovering who is committing it. In the real world, identifying the author of a defamatory remark generally is an easy matter. It is more difficult if a business firm discovers that defamatory statements about its policies and products are being posted in an online forum, because the postings are anonymous. Therefore, a threshold barrier to anyone who seeks to bring an action for online defamation is discovering the identity of the person who posted the defamatory message.

An Internet service provider (ISP) can disclose personal information about its customers only when ordered to do so by a court. Consequently, businesses and individuals are increasingly bringing lawsuits against "John Does." (John Doe, Jane Doe, and the like are fictitious names used in lawsuits when the identity of a party is not known or when a party wishes to conceal his or her name for privacy reasons.) Then, using the authority of the courts, the plaintiffs can obtain from the ISPs the identity of the persons responsible for the defamatory website.

9–4b Liability of Internet Service Providers

Recall that under tort law those who repeat or otherwise republish a defamatory statement are normally subject to liability. Thus, newspapers, magazines, and television and radio stations are subject to liability for defamatory content that they publish or broadcast, even though the content was prepared or created by others. Applying this rule to cyberspace, however, raises an important issue: Should ISPs be regarded as publishers and therefore be held liable for defamatory messages that are posted by their users?

General Rule The Communications Decency Act (CDA) states that "[n]o provider or user of an interactive computer service shall be treated as the publisher or speaker of any information provided by another information content provider."[18] Thus, under the CDA, ISPs

usually are treated differently from publishers in print and other media and are not liable for publishing defamatory statements that come from a third party.

Exceptions Although the courts generally have construed the CDA as providing a broad shield to protect ISPs from liability for third party content, some courts have started establishing limits to this immunity. ■ **Case in Point 9.17** Roommate.com, LLC, operated an online roommate-matching website that helped individuals find roommates based on their descriptions of themselves and their roommate preferences. Users responded to a series of online questions, choosing from answers in drop-down and select-a-box menus.

Some of the questions asked users to disclose their sex, family status, and sexual orientation—which is not permitted under the federal Fair Housing Act. When a nonprofit housing organization sued Roommate.com, the company claimed it was immune from liability under the CDA. A federal appellate court disagreed and ruled that Roommate.com was not immune from liability. By creating the website and the questionnaire and answer choices, Roommate.com prompted users to express discriminatory preferences and matched users based on these preferences in violation of federal law.[19] ■

9–5 Other Actions Involving Online Posts

Online conduct can give rise to a wide variety of legal actions. E-mails, tweets, posts, and every sort of online communication can form the basis for almost any type of tort. For instance, in addition to defamation, suits relating to online conduct may involve allegations of wrongful interference or infliction of emotional distress.

Besides actions grounded in the common law, online conduct may give rise to a cause of action directed expressly at online communications by a statute. In the following case, the court was asked to issue an injunction to prohibit speech that was alleged to constitute *cyberstalking*. The applicable statute defined this term to require, in part, "substantial emotional distress."

---

18. 47 U.S.C. Section 230.

19. *Fair Housing Council of San Fernando Valley v. Roommate.com, LLC*, 666 F.3d 1216 (9th Cir. 2012).

David v. Textor

District Court of Appeal of Florida, Fourth District, 41 Fla.L.Weekly D131,189 So.3d 871(2016).

In the Language of the Court

WARNER, J. [Judge].

* * * *

[Alkiviades] David and [John] Textor both have companies which produce holograms used in the music industry. * * * Shortly before the Billboard Music Awards show, it was announced that Textor's company, Pulse Entertainment, would show a Michael Jackson hologram performance. Immediately thereafter, David's company, Hologram USA, Inc., * * * filed suit for patent infringement against Pulse in the U.S. District Court in Nevada * * * . Pulse countered by filing a business tort suit against David in California.

[One month later,] Textor filed a petition [in a Florida state court against David under Florida Statutes] Sections 784.046 and 784.0485, which concern cyberstalking.

The alleged acts of cyberstalking were (1) a * * * text from David to Textor, demanding that Textor give credit to David's company at the Billboard Awards show for the hologram, for which David would drop his patent infringement suit; otherwise, he threatened to increase damages in that suit and stated, "You will be ruined I promise you"; (2) an e-mail from David to business associates (other than Textor) that he had more information about Textor that would be released soon, but not specifying what that information was; (3) an online article from July 2014 on Entrepreneur.com, in which David was quoted as saying that he "would have killed [Textor] if he could"; and (4) articles about Textor that David posted and reposted in various online outlets.

* * * *

The trial court [issued an injunction] prohibiting David from communicating with Textor or posting any information about him online, and ordering that

he remove any materials he already had posted.

David * * * moved to dissolve the * * * injunction. * * * The court denied the motion to dissolve and amended its order to prohibit David from communicating with Textor either through electronic means, in person, or through third parties. The amended order also provided:

> Respondent David shall immediately cease and desist from sending any text messages, e-mails, posting any tweets (including the re-tweeting or forwarding), posting any images or other forms of communication directed at John Textor without a legitimate purpose. Threats or warnings of physical or emotional harm or attempts to extort Textor or any entity associated with Textor by Respondent David, personally or through his agents, directed to John Textor, directly or by other means, are prohibited.

From this order, David appeals.

David claims that none of the allegations in the petition constitute cyberstalking, but are merely heated rhetoric over a business dispute. Further, he claims that the injunction constitutes a prior restraint on speech, which violates the First Amendment.

[Florida Statutes] Section 784.0485 allows an injunction against * * * cyberstalking. * * * Section 784.048 defines * * * cyberstalking:

> * * * "Cyberstalk" means to engage in a course of conduct to communicate, or to cause to be communicated, words, images, or language by or through the use of electronic mail or electronic communication, directed at a specific person, causing substantial emotional distress to that person and serving no legitimate purpose.

*Whether a communication causes substantial emotional distress * * * is governed*

by the reasonable person standard. * * * Whether a communication serves a legitimate purpose * * * will cover a wide variety of conduct. * * * Where comments are made on an electronic medium to be read by others, they cannot be said to be directed to a particular person. [Emphasis added.]

In this case, Textor alleged that two communications came directly from David to him, both of which were demands that Textor drop his lawsuit. In neither of them did David make any threat to Textor's safety. From the full e-mail, David's threats that Textor would be "sorry" if he didn't settle must be taken in the context of the lawsuit and its potential cost to Textor. Because of the existence of the various lawsuits and the heated controversy over the hologram patents, these e-mails had a legitimate purpose in trying to get Textor to drop what David considered a spurious lawsuit. Moreover, nothing in the e-mails should have caused substantial emotional distress to Textor, himself a sophisticated businessman. Indeed, that they did not is reflected in Textor's refusal to settle or adhere to their terms.

The postings online are also not communications which would cause substantial emotional distress. Most of them are simply re-tweets of articles or headlines involving Textor. That they may be embarrassing to Textor is not at all the same as causing him substantial emotional distress sufficient to obtain an injunction.

Even the alleged physical threat made by David in an online interview, that David would have killed Textor if he could have, would not cause a reasonable person substantial emotional distress. In the online article the author stated that "David joked" when stating that he would have killed Textor. Spoken to a journalist for publication, it hardly amounts to an actual and credible threat of violence to Textor.

In sum, none of the allegations in Textor's petition show acts constituting cyberstalking, in that a reasonable person would not suffer substantial emotional distress over them. Those communications made directly to Textor served a legitimate purpose.

An injunction in this case would also violate [the freedom of speech under the U.S. Constitution's First Amendment.

An] injunction directed to speech is a classic example of prior restraint on speech triggering First Amendment concerns. * * * *Prior restraints on speech and publication are the most serious and the least tolerable infringement on First Amendment rights.* [Florida Statutes] Section 784.048 itself recognizes the First Amendment rights of individuals by concluding that a "course of conduct" for purposes of the statute does not include protected speech. [Emphasis added.]

Here, the online postings simply provide information, gleaned from other sources, regarding Textor and the many lawsuits against him. The injunction prevents not only communications *to* Textor, but also communications *about* Textor. Such prohibition by prior restraint violates the Constitution.

For the foregoing reasons, we reverse the * * * injunction and remand with directions to dismiss the petition.

Legal Reasoning Questions

1. How is *cyberstalking* defined by the statute in this case, and what conduct by the defendant allegedly fit this definition?

2. What standard determines whether certain conduct meets the requirements of the cyberstalking statute? What law or legal principle limits an injunction that is directed at speech?

3. Why did the court in this case "reverse the . . . injunction and remand with directions to dismiss the petition"? Explain.

9–6 Privacy

Facebook, Google, and Yahoo have all been accused of violating users' privacy rights. The right to privacy is guaranteed implicitly by the Supreme Court's interpretation of the Bill of Rights and explicitly by some state constitutions. To maintain a suit for the invasion of privacy, though, a person must have a reasonable expectation of privacy in the particular situation.

9–6a Reasonable Expectation of Privacy

People clearly have a reasonable expectation of privacy when they enter their personal banking or credit-card information online. They also have a reasonable expectation that online companies will follow their own privacy policies. But it is probably not reasonable to expect privacy in statements made on Twitter—or photos posted on Twitter, Flickr, or Instagram, for that matter.

Sometimes, to be sure, people mistakenly believe that they are making statements or posting photos in a private forum. ■ **Example 9.18** Randi Zuckerberg, the older sister of Mark Zuckerberg (the founder of Facebook), used a mobile app called Poke to post a "private" photo on Facebook of their family gathering during the holidays. Poke allows the sender to decide how long the photo can be seen by others. Facebook allows users to configure their

privacy settings to limit access to photos, which Randi thought she had done. Nonetheless, the photo showed up in the Facebook feed of Callie Schweitzer, who then put it on Twitter, where it eventually "went viral." Schweitzer apologized and removed the photo, but it had already gone public for the world to see. ■

9–6b Data Collection and Cookies

Whenever a consumer purchases items online from a retailer, such as Amazon.com or Best Buy, the retailer collects information about the consumer. **Cookies** are invisible files that computers create to track a user's Web browsing activities. Cookies provide detailed information to marketers about an individual's online behavior and preferences, which is then used to personalize online services.

Over time, a retailer can amass considerable data about a person's shopping habits. Does collecting this information violate a consumer's right to privacy? Should retailers be able to pass on the data they have collected to their affiliates? Should they be able to use the information to predict what a consumer might want and then create online "coupons" customized to fit the person's buying history?

■ **Example 9.19** Facebook, Inc., once used a targeted advertising technique called "Sponsored Stories." An ad would display a Facebook friend's name and profile picture, along with a statement that the friend "likes" the company sponsoring the advertisement. A group of plaintiffs filed suit, claiming that Facebook had used their pictures for advertising without their permission. When a federal court refused to dismiss the case, Facebook agreed to settle. ■

9–6c Internet Companies' Privacy Policies

The Federal Trade Commission (FTC) investigates consumer complaints of privacy violations. The FTC has forced many companies, including Google, Facebook, and Twitter, to enter consent decrees that give the FTC broad power to review their privacy and data practices. It can then sue companies that violate the terms of the decrees.

■ **Example 9.20** Google settled a suit brought by the FTC alleging that it had misused data from Apple's Safari users and had used cookies to trick the Safari browser on iPhones and iPads. The FTC claimed that this practice allowed Google to monitor users who had blocked such tracking, in violation of the company's prior consent decree with the FTC. Google agreed to pay $22.5 million to settle the suit without admitting liability. ■

Practice and Review: Internet Law, Social Media, and Privacy

While he was in high school, Joel Gibb downloaded numerous songs to his smartphone from an unlicensed file-sharing service. He used portions of the copyrighted songs when he recorded his own band and posted videos on YouTube and Facebook. Gibb also used BitTorrent to download several movies from the Internet. Now he has applied to Boston University. The admissions office has requested access to his Facebook password, and he has complied. Using the information presented in the chapter, answer the following questions.

1. What laws, if any, did Gibb violate by downloading the music and videos from the Internet?
2. Was Gibb's use of portions of copyrighted songs in his own music illegal? Explain.
3. Can individuals legally post copyrighted content on their Facebook pages? Why or why not?
4. Did Boston University violate any laws when it asked Joel to provide his Facebook password? Explain.

Debate This . . . *Internet service providers should be subject to the same defamation laws as newspapers, magazines, and television and radio stations.*

Terms and Concepts

cloud computing 176	distributed network 176	peer-to-peer (P2P) networking 176
cookies 183	domain name 171	social media 178
cybersquatting 171	goodwill 171	spam 170
cyber torts 180	Internet service providers (ISPs) 171	typosquatting 172

Issue Spotters

1. Karl self-publishes a cookbook titled *Hole Foods*, in which he sets out recipes for donuts, Bundt cakes, tortellini, and other foods with holes. To publicize the book, Karl designs the website holefoods.com. Karl appropriates the key words of other cooking and cookbook sites with more frequent hits so that holefoods.com will appear in the same search engine results as the more popular sites. Has Karl done anything wrong? Explain. (See *Internet Law.*)

2. Eagle Corporation began marketing software under the mark "Eagle." Ten years later, Eagle.com, Inc., a different company selling different products, begins to use *eagle* as part of its URL and registers it as a domain name. Can Eagle Corporation stop this use of *eagle*? If so, what must the company show? (See *Internet Law.*)

• **Check your answers to the Issue Spotters against the answers provided in Appendix B at the end of this text.**

Business Scenarios and Case Problems

9–1. Internet Service Providers. CyberConnect, Inc., is an Internet service provider (ISP). Pepper is a CyberConnect subscriber. Market Reach, Inc., is an online advertising company. Using sophisticated software, Market Reach directs its ads to those users most likely to be interested in a particular product. When Pepper receives one of the ads, she objects to the content. Further, she claims that CyberConnect should pay damages for "publishing" the ad. Is the ISP regarded as a publisher and therefore liable for the content of Market Reach's ad? Why or why not? (See *Online Defamation*.)

9–2. Privacy. SeeYou, Inc., is an online social network. SeeYou's members develop personalized profiles to interact and share information—photos, videos, stories, activity updates, and other items—with other members. Members post the information that they want to share and decide with whom they want to share it. SeeYou launched a program to allow members to share what they do elsewhere online. For example, if a member rents a movie through Netflix, SeeYou will broadcast that information to everyone in the member's online network. How can SeeYou avoid complaints that this program violates its members' privacy? (See *Privacy*.)

9–3. Privacy. Using special software, South Dakota law enforcement officers found a person who appeared to possess child pornography at a specific Internet address. The officers subpoenaed Midcontinent Communications, the service that assigned the address, for the personal information of its subscriber. With this information, the officers obtained a search warrant for the residence of John Rolfe, where they found a laptop that contained child pornography. Rolfe argued that the subpoenas violated his "expectation of privacy." Did Rolfe have a privacy interest in the information obtained by the subpoenas issued to Midcontinent? Discuss. [*State of South Dakota v. Rolfe*, 825 N.W.2d 901 (S.Dak. 2013)] (See *Privacy*.)

9–4. File-Sharing. Dartmouth College professor M. Eric Johnson, in collaboration with Tiversa, Inc., a company that monitors peer-to-peer networks to provide security services, wrote an article titled "Data Hemorrhages in the Health-Care Sector." In preparing the article, Johnson and Tiversa searched the networks for data that could be used to commit medical or financial identity theft. They found a document that contained the Social Security numbers, insurance information, and treatment codes for patients of LabMD, Inc. Tiversa notified LabMD of the find in order to solicit its business. Instead of hiring Tiversa, however, LabMD filed a suit in a federal district court against the company, alleging trespass, conversion, and violations of federal statutes. What do these facts indicate about the security of private information? Explain. How should the court rule? [*LabMD, Inc. v. Tiversa, Inc.*, 509 Fed.Appx. 842 (11th Cir. 2013)] (See *Copyrights in Digital Information*.)

9–5. Business Case Problem with Sample Answer—Social Media. Mohammad Omar Aly Hassan and nine others were indicted in a federal district court on charges of conspiring to advance violent jihad (holy war against enemies of Islam) and other offenses related to terrorism. The evidence at Hassan's trial included postings he had made on Facebook concerning his adherence to violent jihadist ideology. Convicted, Hassan appealed, contending that the Facebook items had not been properly authenticated (established as his own comments). How might the government show the connection between postings on Facebook and those who post them? Discuss. [*United States v. Hassan*, 742 F.3d 104 (4th Cir. 2014)] (See *Social Media*.)

- **For a sample answer to Problem 9–5, go to Appendix C at the end of this text.**

9–6. Social Media. Kenneth Wheeler was angry at certain police officers in Grand Junction, Colorado, because of a driving-under-the-influence arrest that he viewed as unjust. While in Italy, Wheeler posted a statement to his Facebook page urging his "religious followers" to "kill cops, drown them in the blood of their children, hunt them down and kill their entire bloodlines" and provided names. Later, Wheeler added a post to "commit a massacre in the Stepping Stones preschool and day care, just walk in and kill everybody." Could a reasonable person conclude that Wheeler's posts were true threats? How might law enforcement officers use Wheeler's posts? Explain. [*United States v. Wheeler*, 776 F.3d 736 (10th Cir. 2015)] (See *Social Media*.)

9–7. Social Media. Irvin Smith was charged in a Georgia state court with burglary and theft. Before the trial, during the selection of the jury, the state prosecutor asked the prospective jurors whether they knew Smith. No one responded affirmatively. Jurors were chosen and sworn in, without objection. After the trial, during deliberations, the jurors indicated to the court that they were deadlocked. The court charged them to try again. Meanwhile, the prosecutor learned that "Juror 4" appeared as a friend on the defendant's Facebook page and filed a motion to dismiss her. The court replaced Juror 4 with an alternate. Was this an appropriate action, or was it an "abuse of discretion"? Should the court have admitted evidence that Facebook friends do not always actually know each other? Discuss. [*Smith v. State of Georgia*, 335 Ga.App. 497, 782 S.E.2d 305 (2016)] (See *Social Media*.)

9–8. Internet Law. Jason Smathers, an employee of America Online (AOL), misappropriated an AOL customer list with 92 million screen names. He sold the list for $28,000 to Sean Dunaway, who sold it to Braden Bournival. Bournival used it to send AOL customers more than 3 billion unsolicited, deceptive e-mail ads. AOL estimated its cost of processing the ads to be at least $300,000. Convicted of conspiring to relay deceptive e-mail in violation of federal law, Smathers was ordered to pay AOL restitution of $84,000 (treble the amount for which he had sold the AOL customer list). Smathers appealed, seeking to reduce the amount. He cited a judgment in a civil suit for a different offense against

Bournival and others for which AOL had collected $95,000. Smathers also argued that his obligation should be reduced by restitution payments made by Dunaway. Which federal law did Smathers violate? Should the amount of his restitution be reduced? Explain. [*United States v. Smathers*, 879 F.3d 453 (2d Cir. 2018)] (See *Internet Law.*)

9–9. A Question of Ethics—The IDDR Approach and Social Media. *One August morning, around 6:30 A.M., a fire occurred at Ray and Christine Nixon's home in West Monroe, Louisiana, while the Nixons were inside the home. The Nixons told Detective Gary Gilley of the Ouachita Parish Sheriff's Department that they believed the fire had been deliberately set by Matthew Alexander, a former employee of Ray's company. Ray gave Alexander's phone number to Gilley, who contacted the number's service provider, Verizon Wireless Services, LLC. Gilley said that he was investigating a house fire and that he wanted to know where the number's subscriber had been that day. He did not present a warrant, but he did certify that Verizon's response would be considered an "emergency disclosure." [Alexander v. Verizon Wireless Services, LLC, 875 F.3d 243 (5th Cir. 2017)] (See Social Media.)*

(a) Using the *Inquiry* and *Discussion* steps in the IDDR approach, identify the ethical dilemma that Verizon faced in this situation and actions that the company might have taken to resolve that issue.

(b) Suppose that Verizon gave Gilley the requested information and that later Alexander filed a suit against the provider, alleging a violation of the Stored Communications Act. Could Verizon successfully plead "good faith" in its defense?

Time-Limited Group Assignment

9–10. File-Sharing. James, Chang, and Sixta are roommates. They are music fans and frequently listen to the same artists and songs. They regularly exchange MP3 music files that contain songs from their favorite artists. (See *Copyrights in Digital Information.*)

(a) One group of students will decide whether the fact that the roommates are transferring files among themselves for no monetary benefit precludes them from being subject to copyright law.

(b) A second group will consider the situation in which each roommate bought music on CDs, downloaded it to their computers, and then gave the CDs to the other roommates to do the same. Does this violate copyright law? Is it the same as file-sharing digital music? Explain.

(c) A third group will consider streaming music services. If one roommate subscribes to a streaming service and the other roommates use the service for free, would this violate copyright law? Why or why not?

Chapter 10

Criminal Law and Cyber Crime

Criminal law is an important part of the legal environment of business. Society imposes a variety of sanctions to protect businesses from harm so that they can compete and flourish. These sanctions include damages for various types of tortious conduct, damages for breach of contract, and various equitable remedies. Additional sanctions are imposed under criminal law.

Many statutes regulating business provide for criminal as well as civil sanctions. For instance, federal statutes that protect the environment often include criminal sanctions. Large companies that violate environmental laws may face criminal penalties that include millions of dollars in fines.

In this chapter, after explaining some essential differences between criminal law and civil law, we look at how crimes are classified and at the elements that must be present for criminal liability to exist. We then examine the various categories of crimes, the defenses that can be raised to avoid criminal liability, and the rules of criminal procedure.

10-1 Civil Law and Criminal Law

Civil law pertains to the duties that exist between persons or between persons and their governments. Criminal law, in contrast, has to do with crime. A **crime** can be defined as a wrong against society set forth in a statute and punishable by a fine and/or imprisonment—or, in some cases, death.

10-1a Key Differences between Civil Law and Criminal Law

Criminal law differs in a number of ways from civil law, including the parties who bring suit, the burden of proof, and the remedies. Exhibit 10–1 summarizes these important differences.

Prosecuted by the State In civil cases, those who have suffered harm from a wrongful act bring lawsuits against those who caused the harm. In contrast, because crimes are *offenses against society as a whole* and violate statutes, they are prosecuted by a public official, such as a district attorney (D.A.) or an attorney general (A.G.), not by the victims. Once a crime has been reported, the D.A.'s office decides whether to file criminal charges and to what extent to pursue the prosecution or carry out additional investigation.

Burden of Proof In a civil case, the plaintiff usually must prove his or her case by a *preponderance of the evidence.* Under this standard, the plaintiff must convince the court that based on the evidence presented by both parties, it is more likely than not that the plaintiff's allegation is true.

Exhibit 10–1 Key Differences between Civil Law and Criminal Law

Issue	Civil Law	Criminal Law
Party who brings suit	The person who suffered harm.	The state.
Wrongful act	Causing harm to a person or to a person's property.	Violating a statute that prohibits some type of activity.
Burden of proof	Preponderance of the evidence.	Beyond a reasonable doubt.
Verdict	Three-fourths majority (typically).	Unanimous (almost always).
Remedy	Damages to compensate for the harm or a decree to achieve an equitable result.	Punishment (fine, imprisonment, or death).

In a criminal case, in contrast, the government must prove its case **beyond a reasonable doubt.** If the jury views the evidence in the case as reasonably permitting either a guilty or a not guilty verdict, then the jury's verdict must be not guilty. In other words, the government (prosecutor) must prove beyond a reasonable doubt that the defendant has committed every essential element of the offense with which she or he is charged.

Note also that in a criminal case, the jury's verdict normally must be unanimous—agreed to by all members of the jury—to convict the defendant.[1] (In a civil trial by jury, in contrast, typically only three-fourths of the jurors need to agree.)

Criminal Sanctions The sanctions imposed on criminal wrongdoers are normally harsher than those applied in civil cases. Remember that the purpose of tort law is to enable a person harmed by a wrongful act to obtain compensation (damages) from the wrongdoer, rather than to punish the wrongdoer. In contrast, criminal sanctions are designed to punish those who commit crimes and to deter others from committing similar acts in the future.

---

1. Two states, Louisiana and Oregon, allow jury verdicts that are not unanimous.

Criminal sanctions include fines as well as the much stiffer penalty of the loss of liberty by incarceration in a jail or prison. Most criminal sanctions also involve probation and sometimes require performance of community service, completion of an educational or treatment program, or payment of restitution. The harshest criminal sanction is, of course, the death penalty.

10–1b Civil Liability for Criminal Acts

Some torts, such as assault and battery, provide a basis for a criminal prosecution as well as a civil action in tort. ■ **Example 10.1** Jonas is walking down the street, minding his own business, when a person attacks him. In the ensuing struggle, the attacker stabs Jonas several times, seriously injuring him. A police officer restrains and arrests the assailant. In this situation, the attacker may be subject both to criminal prosecution by the state and to a tort lawsuit brought by Jonas to obtain compensation for his injuries. ■

Exhibit 10–2 illustrates how the same wrongful act can result in both a civil (tort) action and a criminal action against the wrongdoer.

Exhibit 10–2 Civil (Tort) Lawsuit and Criminal Prosecution for the Same Act

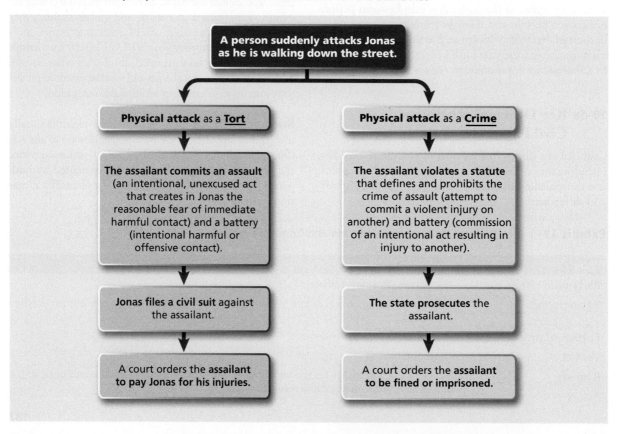

10–1c Classification of Crimes

Depending on their degree of seriousness, crimes are classified as felonies or misdemeanors. **Felonies** are serious crimes punishable by death or by imprisonment for more than one year.[2] Many states also define different degrees of felony offenses and vary the punishment according to the degree.[3] For instance, most jurisdictions punish a burglary that involves forced entry into a home at night more harshly than a burglary that involves breaking into a nonresidential building during the day.

Misdemeanors are less serious crimes, punishable by a fine or by confinement for up to a year. **Petty offenses** are minor violations, such as jaywalking or violations of building codes, considered to be a subset of misdemeanors. Even for petty offenses, however, a guilty party can be put in jail for a few days, fined, or both, depending on state or local law. Whether a crime is a felony or a misdemeanor can determine in which court the case is tried and, in some states, whether the defendant has a right to a jury trial.

---

2. Federal law and most state laws use this definition, but there is some variation among states as to the length of imprisonment associated with a felony conviction.
3. The American Law Institute issued the Model Penal Code in 1962 to help states standardize their penal laws. Note, however, that the Model Penal Code is not a uniform code and each state has developed its own set of laws governing criminal acts. Thus, types of crimes and prescribed punishments may differ from one jurisdiction to another.

10–2 Criminal Liability

The following two elements normally must exist *simultaneously* for a person to be convicted of a crime:

1. The performance of a prohibited act *(actus reus)*.
2. A specified state of mind, or intent, on the part of the actor *(mens rea)*.

10–2a The Criminal Act

Every criminal statute prohibits certain behavior. Most crimes require an act of *commission*—that is, a person must *do* something in order to be accused of a crime. In criminal law, a prohibited act is referred to as the **actus reus**,[4] or guilty act. In some instances, an act of omission can be a crime, but only when a person has a legal duty to perform the omitted act, such as filing a tax return.

The guilty act requirement is based on one of the premises of criminal law—that a person should be punished for harm done to society. For a crime to exist, the guilty act must thus cause some harm to a person or to property. Thinking about killing someone or about stealing a car may be morally wrong, but the thoughts do no harm until they are translated into action. (See this chapter's *Digital Update* feature for an illustration of how a person can commit a crime by sending a flashing video via Twitter to an epileptic.)

---

4. Pronounced *ak*-tuhs *ray*-uhs.

Digital Update   Using Twitter to Cause Seizures—A Crime?

Vanity Fair contributing editor and *Newsweek* senior writer Kurt Eichenwald has epilepsy, and he writes about his battle with the disease on occasion. For many suffering from this illness, strobe lights can spark seizures. For instance, a *Pokémon* episode once apparently sent hundreds of Japanese children to the hospital because of the flashing lights.

Using Twitter to Create a Seizure

John Rayne Rivello did not like Eichenwald's political views. He therefore created a strobe-light image within a tweet he sent to Eichenwald. In that tweet, Rivello said, "You deserve a seizure for your posts." When Eichenwald clicked on the embedded .gif file, the resulting epileptogenic flashing images did, in fact, cause a seizure in the tweet's intended victim.

Arrested for Cyberstalking

Rivello was arrested by the Federal Bureau of Investigation at his residence in Salisbury, Maryland, on the charge of cyberstalking. The federal cyberstalking law criminalizes the intentional use of electronic communications systems to place another in reasonable fear of death or serious bodily injury.[a] This was the first known criminal arrest for using electronic communications to create a seizure in a recipient.

Critical Thinking *What other types of cyberstalking crimes might involve the use of tweets?*

---

a. 18 U.S.C. Section 875.

Of course, a person can be punished for *attempting* murder or robbery, but normally only if he or she has taken substantial steps toward the criminal objective. Additionally, the person must have specifically intended to commit the crime to be convicted of an attempt.

10–2b State of Mind

Mens rea,[5] or wrongful mental state, also is typically required to establish criminal liability. The required mental state, or intent, is indicated in the applicable statute or law. Murder, for instance, involves the guilty act of killing another human being, and the guilty mental state is

---
5. Pronounced *mehns ray*-uh.

---

the desire, or intent, to take another's life. For theft, the guilty act is the taking of another person's property. The mental state involves both the awareness that the property belongs to another and the desire to deprive the owner of it. A court can also find that the required mental state is present when the defendant acts recklessly or is criminally negligent.

A criminal conspiracy exists when two or more people agree to commit an unlawful act and then take some action toward its completion. The required mental state involves both the intent to agree and the intent to commit the underlying crime. In the following case, the issue was whether the evidence was sufficient to prove that the defendant had "knowingly and voluntarily" participated in a conspiracy to commit health-care fraud.

Case **10.1**

United States v. Crabtree
United States Court of Appeals, Eleventh Circuit, 878 F.3d 1274 (2018).

Background and Facts Health Care Solutions Network, Inc. (HCSN), operated mental health centers to provide psychiatric therapy. HCSN organized its business around procuring, retaining, and readmitting patients to maximize billing potential, without respect to their health needs. It ensured that patient files complied with strict Medicare requirements by editing intake information, fabricating treatment plans, and falsifying therapy and treatment notes. The scheme spanned seven years and amounted to more than $63 million in fraudulent Medicare claims.

At one of HCSN's facilities, Doris Crabtree was responsible for patient therapy notes. The notes were systematically altered and falsified to support Medicare claims. Convicted in a federal district court of conspiracy to commit health-care fraud, Crabtree appealed to the U.S. Court of Appeals for the Eleventh Circuit. She argued that she had been only negligent and careless.

In the Language of the Court
WILSON, Circuit Judge:
* * * *

* * * According to Crabtree, * * * the evidence against [her] was primarily circumstantial and * * * did not show that [she] knowingly and voluntarily joined a conspiracy to defraud Medicare.
* * * *

* * * The very nature of conspiracy frequently requires that the existence of an agreement be proved by inferences from the conduct of the alleged participants or from circumstantial evidence of a scheme. *The government need only prove that the defendant knew of the essential nature of the conspiracy, and we will affirm a conspiracy conviction when the circumstances surrounding a person's presence at the scene of conspiratorial activity are so obvious that knowledge of its character can fairly be attributed to [her].* The government can show that a defendant voluntarily joined a conspiracy through proof of surrounding circumstances such as acts committed by the defendant which furthered the purpose of the conspiracy. [Emphasis added.]
* * * *

The government put forth considerable evidence that Crabtree [was] directly aware of the essential nature of the conspiracy and that the circumstances at HCSN were so obvious that knowledge of the fraud's character can fairly be attributed to [her]. Multiple former-employees testified that Crabtree * * * complied with their requests to doctor patient notes so that they would pass Medicare review.

* * * Numerous witnesses spoke of the overwhelming evidence that patients were unqualified for * * * treatment [at HCSN]: that it was obvious, and widely observed, that patients at HCSN suffered from Alzheimer's, dementia, autism, and forms of mental retardation that rendered treatment ineffective; that this was evidenced, for example, by patients * * * who were unable to engage in group therapy sessions; and that Crabtree [was] involved in multiple conversations about the unsuitability of [the] patients for * * * treatment [at HCSN]. One former-employee put it simply: "everybody was aware of the fraud."

Likewise, a reasonable jury could have found that Crabtree * * * voluntarily joined the conspiracy, given the substantial evidence of [her] role in furthering the fraud. The government put forth evidence that Crabtree * * * complied with requests to alter and fabricate notes for billing and Medicare auditing purposes; * * * and that [she] misrepresented the therapy that patients received when, for example, they * * * were * * * absent but notes indicated that they participated fully.

Decision and Remedy *The federal appellate court affirmed Crabtree's conviction. The court concluded that Crabtree "had knowledge of the conspiracy at HCSN" and that she had "voluntarily joined the conspiracy, given the substantial evidence of [her] role in furthering the fraud."*

Critical Thinking
- **Legal Environment** *Could Crabtree have successfully avoided her conviction by arguing that her only "crime" was naively trusting her co-workers? Why or why not?*
- **Ethical** *It seems reasonable to assume that one of the purposes of any business is to maximize billing potential. When does conduct to accomplish that purpose become unethical?*

Recklessness A defendant is *criminally reckless* if he or she consciously disregards a substantial and unjustifiable risk. ■ **Example 10.2** A fourteen-year-old New Jersey girl posts a Facebook message saying that she is going to launch a terrorist attack on her high school and asking if anyone wants to help. The police arrest the girl for the crime of making a terrorist threat. The statute requires the intent to commit an act of violence with "the intent to terrorize" or "in reckless disregard of the risk of causing" terror or inconvenience. Although the girl argues that she did not intend to cause harm, the police can prosecute her under the "reckless disregard" part of the statute. ■

Criminal Negligence *Criminal negligence* involves the mental state in which the defendant takes an unjustified, substantial, and foreseeable risk that results in harm. A defendant can be negligent even if she or he was not actually aware of the risk but *should have been aware* of it.[6]

A homicide is classified as *involuntary manslaughter* when it results from an act of criminal negligence and there is no intent to kill. ■ **Example 10.3** Dr. Conrad Murray, the personal physician of pop star Michael Jackson, was convicted of involuntary manslaughter for prescribing the drug that led to Jackson's sudden death.

Murray had given Jackson propofol, a powerful anesthetic normally used in surgery, as a sleep aid on the night of his death, even though he knew that Jackson had already taken other sedatives. ■

Strict Liability and Overcriminalization An increasing number of laws and regulations impose criminal sanctions for strict liability crimes. *Strict liability crimes are offenses that do not require a wrongful mental state to establish criminal liability.*

Proponents of strict liability criminal laws argue that they are necessary to protect the public and the environment. Critics say laws that criminalize conduct without requiring intent have led to *overcriminalization*. They argue that when the requirement of intent is removed, people are more likely to commit crimes unknowingly— and perhaps even innocently. When an honest mistake can lead to a criminal conviction, the idea that crimes are wrongs against society is undermined.

Federal Crimes. The federal criminal code lists more than four thousand criminal offenses, many of which do not require a specific mental state. In addition, many of these rules do not require intent. See this chapter's *Managerial Strategy* feature for a discussion of how these laws and rules affect American businesspersons.

---

6. Model Penal Code Section 2.02(2)(d).

Managerial Strategy — The Criminalization of American Business

What do Bank of America, Citigroup, JPMorgan Chase, and Goldman Sachs have in common? All paid hefty fines for purportedly misleading investors about mortgage-backed securities. In fact, these companies paid the government a total of $50 billion in fines. The payments were made in lieu of criminal prosecutions.

Today, several hundred thousand federal rules that apply to businesses carry some form of criminal penalty. That is in addition to more than four thousand federal laws, many of which carry criminal sanctions for their violation. Each year, scores of business firms are charged with violating federal statutes or rules.

Criminal Convictions

The first successful criminal conviction in a federal court against a company—the New York Central & Hudson River Railroad—was upheld by the Supreme Court in 1909 (the violation: cutting prices).[a] Many other successful convictions followed.

One landmark case developed the *aggregation test,* now called the collective knowledge doctrine.[b] This test aggregates the omissions and acts of two or more persons in a corporation, thereby constructing an *actus reus* and a *mens rea* out of the conduct and knowledge of several individuals.

Not all government attempts to apply criminal law to corporations survive. Courts sometimes find the evidence insufficient to show that a company acted with specific intent to commit a particular offense.[c] Often, however, companies choose to reach settlement agreements with the government rather than fight criminal indictments.

Many Pay Substantial Fines in Lieu of Prosecution

Settlement agreements—also called non-prosecution agreements—between business firms and the government typically involve multimillion- or multibillion-dollar fines. In addition to the amounts paid in settlements, companies pay expensive fines to the Environmental Protection Agency or to the Fish and Wildlife Service.

According to law professors Margaret Lemos and Max Minzner, "Public enforcers often seek large monetary awards for self-interested reasons divorced from the public interest and deterrents. The incentives are strongest when enforcement agencies are permitted to retain all or some of the proceeds of enforcement."[d]

Business Questions

1. *Why might a corporation's managers agree to pay a large fine rather than be indicted and proceed to trial?*
2. *How does a manager determine the optimal amount of legal research to undertake to prevent her or his company from violating the many thousands of federal regulations?*

a. *New York Central & Hudson River Railroad v. United States*, 212 U.S. 481, 29 S.Ct. 304, 53 L.Ed 613 (1909).
b. *United States v. Bank of New England, N.A.*, 821 F.2d 844 (1st Cir. 1987).
c. See, for example, *McGee v. Sentinel Offender Services, LLC,* 719 F.3d 1236 (11th Cir. 2013); and *United States ex rel. Salters v. American Family Care, Inc.*, 262 F.Supp.3d 1266 (N.D.Ala. 2017).
d. Margaret Lemos and Max Minzner, "For-Profit Public Enforcement," *Harvard Law Review,* Vol. 127, January 17, 2014.

■ **Example 10.4** Eddie Leroy Anderson, a retired logger and former science teacher, went digging for arrowheads with his son near a campground in Idaho. They did not realize that they were on federal land and that it is a felony to remove artifacts from federal land without a permit. Although the crime carries a penalty of as much as two years in prison, the father and son pleaded guilty, and each received a sentence of probation and a $1,500 fine. ■

Strict liability crimes are particularly common in environmental laws, laws aimed at combatting illegal drugs, and other laws affecting public health, safety, and welfare. Under federal law, for instance, tenants can be evicted from public housing if one of their relatives or a guest used illegal drugs—regardless of whether the tenant knew about the drug activity.

State Crimes. Many states have also enacted laws that punish behavior as criminal without the need to show criminal intent. ■ **Example 10.5** In Arizona, a hunter who shoots an elk outside the area specified by the hunting permit has committed a crime. The hunter can be convicted of the crime regardless of her or his intent or knowledge of the law. ■

10–2c Corporate Criminal Liability

A corporation is a legal entity created under the laws of a state. At one time, it was thought that a corporation could not incur criminal liability because, although a corporation is a legal person, it can act only through its agents (corporate directors, officers, and employees). Therefore, the corporate entity itself could not "intend" to commit a crime. Over time, this view has changed. Obviously, corporations cannot be imprisoned, but they can be fined or denied certain legal privileges (such as necessary licenses).

Liability of the Corporate Entity Today, corporations normally are liable for the crimes committed by their agents and employees within the course and scope of their employment.[7] For liability to be imposed, the prosecutor generally must show that the corporation could have prevented the act or that a supervisor authorized or had knowledge of the act. In addition, corporations can be criminally liable for failing to perform specific duties imposed by law (such as duties under environmental laws or securities laws).

■ **Case in Point 10.6** A prostitution ring, the Gold Club, was operating out of some motels in West Virginia. A motel manager, who was also a corporate officer, gave discounted rates to Gold Club prostitutes, and they paid him in cash. The corporation received a portion of the funds generated by the Gold Club's illegal operations. A jury found that the corporation was criminally liable because a supervisor within the corporation—the motel manager—had knowledge of the prostitution activities and the corporation had allowed the crimes to continue.[8] ■

Liability of Corporate Officers and Directors Corporate directors and officers are personally liable for the crimes they commit, regardless of whether the crimes were committed for their private benefit or on the corporation's behalf. Additionally, corporate directors and officers may be held liable for the actions of employees under their supervision. Under the *responsible corporate officer* doctrine, a court may impose criminal liability on a corporate officer who participated in, directed, or merely knew about a given criminal violation.

■ **Case in Point 10.7** Austin DeCoster owned and controlled Quality Egg, LLC, an egg production and processing company with facilities across Iowa. His son Peter DeCoster was the chief operating officer. Due to unsanitary conditions in some of its facilities, Quality shipped and sold eggs that contained salmonella bacteria, which sickened thousands of people across the United States.

The federal government prosecuted the DeCosters under the responsible corporate officer doctrine based, in part, on Quality's failure to comply with regulations on egg production facilities. The DeCosters ultimately pleaded guilty to violating three criminal statutes. But when they were ordered to serve three months in jail, the DeCosters challenged the sentence as unconstitutional. The court held that the sentence of incarceration was appropriate because the evidence suggested that the defendants knew about the unsanitary conditions in their processing plants.[9] ■

10–3 Types of Crimes

Federal, state, and local laws provide for the classification and punishment of hundreds of thousands of different criminal acts. Generally, though, criminal acts fall into five broad categories: violent crime (crimes against persons), property crime, public order crime, white-collar crime, and organized crime. In addition, when crimes are committed in cyberspace rather than in the physical world, we often refer to them as cyber crimes.

10–3a Violent Crime

Certain crimes are called *violent crimes*, or crimes against persons, because they cause others to suffer harm or death. Murder is a violent crime. So is sexual assault, or rape. **Robbery**—defined as the taking of money, personal property, or any other article of value from a person by means of force or fear—is also a violent crime. Typically, states have more severe penalties for *aggravated robbery*—robbery with the use of a deadly weapon.

Assault and battery, which are torts, are also classified as violent crimes. ■ **Example 10.8** The song "Look at Me" by XXXTentacion (whose real name was Jahseh Onfroy) became a hit while the rapper was serving time in jail for aggravated battery of a pregnant victim. After Onfroy was killed following his release from jail, the prosecutor uncovered a secret recording in which he confessed to multiple acts of abuse and violence towards this woman that would substantiate additional criminal convictions. ■

Each violent crime is further classified by degree, depending on the circumstances surrounding the criminal act. These circumstances include the intent of the person committing the crime and whether a weapon was used. For crimes other than murder, the level of pain and suffering experienced by the victim is also a factor.

---

7. See Model Penal Code Section 2.07.
8. As a result of the convictions, the motel manager was sentenced to fifteen months in prison, and the corporation was ordered to forfeit the motel property. *United States v. Singh*, 518 F.3d 236 (4th Cir. 2008).
9. *United States v. Quality Egg, LLC*, 99 F.Supp.3d 920 (N.D. Iowa 2015).

10–3b Property Crime

The most common type of criminal activity is property crime, in which the goal of the offender is some form of economic gain or the damaging of property. Robbery is a form of property crime, as well as a violent crime, because the offender seeks to gain the property of another.

Burglary Traditionally, **burglary** was defined as breaking and entering the dwelling of another at night with the intent to commit a felony. This definition was aimed at protecting an individual's home and its occupants.

Most state statutes have eliminated some of the requirements found in the common law definition. The time of day at which the breaking and entering occurs, for instance, is usually immaterial. State statutes frequently omit the element of breaking, and some states do not require that the building be a dwelling. When a deadly weapon is used in a burglary, the perpetrator can be charged with *aggravated burglary* and punished more severely.

Larceny Under the common law, the crime of **larceny** involved the unlawful taking and carrying away of someone else's personal property with the intent to permanently deprive the owner of possession. Put simply, larceny is stealing, or theft. Whereas robbery involves force or fear, larceny does not. Therefore, picking pockets is larceny, not robbery. Similarly, an employee taking company products and supplies home for personal use without permission is committing larceny.

Most states have expanded the definition of property that is subject to larceny statutes. Stealing computer programs may constitute larceny even though the "property" is not physical (see the discussion of computer crime later in this chapter). The theft of natural gas, Internet access, or television cable service can also constitute larceny.

Obtaining Goods by False Pretenses Obtaining goods by means of false pretenses is a form of theft that involves trickery or fraud, such as using someone else's credit-card number without permission. Statutes dealing with such illegal activities vary widely from state to state. They often apply not only to property, but also to services and cash.

■ **Case in Point 10.9** While Matthew Steffes was incarcerated, he started a scheme to make free collect calls from prison. (A *collect call* is a telephone call in which the calling party places a call at the called party's expense.) Steffes had his friends and family members set up new phone number accounts by giving false information to AT&T. This information included fictitious business names, as well as

personal identifying information stolen from a health-care clinic. Once a new phone number was working, Steffes made unlimited collect calls to it without paying the bill until AT&T eventually shut down the account. For nearly two years, Steffes used sixty fraudulently obtained phone numbers to make hundreds of collect calls. The loss to AT&T was more than $28,000.

Steffes was convicted in a state court of theft by fraud of property in excess of $10,000. He appealed, arguing that he had not made false representations to AT&T. The Wisconsin Supreme Court affirmed his conviction. The court held that Steffes had made false representations to AT&T by providing fictitious business names and stolen personal identifying information to the phone company. He made these false representations so that he could make phone calls without paying for them, which deprived the company of its "property"—meaning the electricity used to power its network.[10] ■

Theft Sometimes, state statutes consolidate the crime of obtaining goods by false pretenses with other property offenses, such as larceny and embezzlement (discussed shortly), into a single crime called simply "theft." Under such a statute, it is not necessary for a defendant to be charged specifically with larceny or obtaining goods by false pretenses. *Petty theft* is the theft of a small quantity of cash or low-value goods. *Grand theft* is the theft of a larger amount of cash or higher-value property.

Receiving Stolen Goods It is a crime to receive goods that a person knows or should have known were stolen or illegally obtained. To be convicted, the recipient of such goods need not know the true identity of the owner or the thief, and need not have paid for the goods. All that is necessary is that the recipient knows or should know that the goods are stolen, which implies an intent to deprive the true owner of those goods.

Arson The willful and malicious burning of a building (or, in some states, a vehicle or other item of personal property) is the crime of **arson.** At common law, arson applied only to burning down another person's house. The law was designed to protect human life. Today, arson statutes have been extended to cover the destruction of any building, regardless of ownership, by fire or explosion.

Every state has a special statute that covers the act of burning a building for the purpose of collecting insurance. (Of course, the insurer need not pay the claim when insurance fraud is proved.)

---

10. *State of Wisconsin v. Steffes*, 347 Wis.2d 683, 832 N.W.2d 101 (2013).

Forgery The fraudulent making or altering of any writing (including an electronic record) in a way that changes the legal rights and liabilities of another is **forgery**.
■ **Example 10.10** Without authorization, Severson signs Bennett's name to the back of a check made out to Bennett and attempts to cash it. Severson is committing forgery. ■ Forgery also includes changing trademarks, falsifying public records, counterfeiting, and altering a legal document.

10–3c Public Order Crime

Historically, societies have always outlawed activities that are considered contrary to public values and morals. Today, the most common public order crimes include public drunkenness, prostitution, gambling, and illegal drug use. These crimes are sometimes referred to as *victimless crimes* because they normally harm only the offender. From a broader perspective, however, they are deemed detrimental to society as a whole because they may create an environment that gives rise to property and violent crimes.
■ **Example 10.11** A flight attendant observes a man and woman engaging in sex acts while on a flight to Las Vegas. A criminal complaint is filed, and the two defendants plead guilty in federal court to misdemeanor disorderly conduct. ■

10–3d White-Collar Crime

Crimes occurring in the business context are popularly referred to as *white-collar crimes*, although this is not an official legal term. Ordinarily, **white-collar crime** involves an illegal act or series of acts committed by an individual or business entity using some nonviolent means to obtain a personal or business advantage.

White-collar crime usually takes place in the course of a legitimate business occupation. Corporate crimes fall into this category. Certain property crimes, such as larceny and forgery, may also be white-collar crimes if they occur within the business context. The crimes discussed next normally occur only in the business context.

Embezzlement When a person who is entrusted with another person's property fraudulently appropriates it, **embezzlement** occurs. Embezzlement is not larceny, because the wrongdoer does not *physically* take the property from another's possession, and it is not robbery, because no force or fear is used.

Typically, embezzlement is carried out by an employee who steals funds a small amount at a time over a long period. Banks are particularly prone to this problem, but embezzlement can occur in any firm. In a number of businesses, corporate officers or accountants have fraudulently converted funds for their own benefit and then "fixed" the books to cover up their crimes.

Embezzlement occurs whether the embezzler takes the funds directly from the victim or from a third person. If the financial officer of a large corporation pockets checks from third parties that were given to her to deposit into the corporate account, she is embezzling.

The intent to return embezzled property—or its actual return—is not a defense to the crime of embezzlement, as the following *Spotlight Case* illustrates.

Spotlight on White-Collar Crime

Case 10.2 People v. Sisuphan
Court of Appeal of California, First District, 181 Cal.App.4th 800, 104 Cal.Rptr.3d 654 (2010).

Background and Facts Lou Sisuphan was the director of finance at a Toyota dealership. His responsibilities included managing the financing contracts for vehicle sales and working with lenders to obtain payments. Sisuphan complained repeatedly to management about the performance and attitude of one of the finance managers, Ian McClelland. The general manager, Michael Christian, would not terminate McClelland "because he brought a lot of money into the dealership."

One day, McClelland accepted $22,600 in cash and two checks totaling $7,275.51 from a customer in payment for a car. McClelland placed the cash, the checks, and a copy of the receipt in a large envelope. As he tried to drop the envelope into the safe through a mechanism at its top, the envelope became stuck. While McClelland went for assistance, Sisuphan wiggled the envelope free and kept it. On McClelland's return, Sisuphan told him that the envelope had dropped into the safe. When the payment turned up missing, Christian told all the managers he would not bring criminal charges if the payment was returned within twenty-four hours.

Case 10.2 Continues

After the twenty-four-hour period had lapsed, Sisuphan told Christian that he had taken the envelope, and he returned the cash and checks to Christian. Sisuphan claimed that he had no intention of stealing the payment but had taken it to get McClelland fired. Christian fired Sisuphan the next day, and the district attorney later charged Sisuphan with embezzlement.

After a jury trial, Sisuphan was found guilty. Sisuphan appealed, arguing that the trial court had erred by excluding evidence that he had returned the payment. The trial court had concluded that the evidence was not relevant because return of the property is not a defense to embezzlement.

In the Language of the Court
JENKINS, J. [Judge]
* * * *

Fraudulent intent is an essential element of embezzlement. Although restoration of the property is not a defense, evidence of repayment may be relevant to the extent it shows that a defendant's intent at the time of the taking was not fraudulent. Such evidence is admissible "only when [a] defendant shows a relevant and probative [confirming] link in his subsequent actions from which it might be inferred his original intent was innocent." The question before us, therefore, is whether evidence that Sisuphan returned the money reasonably tends to prove he lacked the requisite intent at the time of the taking. [Emphasis added.]

Section 508 [of the California Penal Code], which sets out the offense of which Sisuphan was convicted, provides: "Every clerk, agent, or servant of any person who fraudulently appropriates to his own use, or secretes with a fraudulent intent to appropriate to his own use, any property of another which has come into his control or care by virtue of his employment * * * is guilty of embezzlement." Sisuphan denies he ever intended "to use the [money] to financially better himself, even temporarily" and contends the evidence he sought to introduce showed "he returned the [money] without having appropriated it to his own use in any way." He argues that this evidence negates fraudulent intent because it supports his claim that he took the money to get McClelland fired and acted "to help his company by drawing attention to the inadequacy and incompetency of an employee." We reject these contentions.

In determining whether Sisuphan's intent was fraudulent at the time of the taking, the issue is not whether he intended to spend the money, but whether he intended to use it for a purpose other than that for which the dealership entrusted it to him. *The offense of embezzlement contemplates a principal's entrustment of property to an agent for certain purposes and the agent's breach of that trust by acting outside his authority in his use of the property.* * * * Sisuphan's undisputed purpose—to get McClelland fired—was beyond the scope of his responsibility and therefore outside the trust afforded him by the dealership. Accordingly, even if the proffered evidence shows he took the money for this purpose, it does not tend to prove he lacked fraudulent intent, and the trial court properly excluded this evidence. [Emphasis added.]

Decision and Remedy   *The California appellate court affirmed the trial court's decision. The fact that Sisuphan had returned the payment was irrelevant. He was guilty of embezzlement.*

Critical Thinking
- **Legal Environment**   *Why was Sisuphan convicted of embezzlement instead of larceny? What is the difference between these two crimes?*
- **Ethical**   *Given that Sisuphan returned the cash and checks, was it fair of the dealership's general manager to terminate Sisuphan's employment? Why or why not?*

Mail and Wire Fraud   Among the most potent weapons against white-collar criminals are the federal laws that prohibit mail fraud[11] and wire fraud.[12] These laws make it a federal crime to devise any scheme that uses U.S. mail, commercial carriers (FedEx, UPS), or wire (telegraph, telephone, television, the Internet, e-mail) with the intent to defraud the public. These laws are often applied when persons send out advertisements or e-mails with the intent to obtain cash or property by false pretenses.

---

11. The Mail Fraud Act, 18 U.S.C. Sections 1341–1342.
12. 18 U.S.C. Section 1343.

■ **Case in Point 10.12** Cisco Systems, Inc., offers a warranty program to authorized resellers of Cisco parts. Iheanyi Frank Chinasa and Robert Kendrick Chambliss devised a scheme to intentionally defraud Cisco with respect to this program and to obtain replacement parts to which they were not entitled. The two men sent numerous e-mails and Internet service requests to Cisco to convince the company to ship them new parts via commercial carriers. Ultimately, Chinasa and Chambliss were convicted of mail and wire fraud and of conspiracy to commit mail and wire fraud.[13] ■

The maximum penalty under these statutes is substantial. Persons convicted of mail, wire, and Internet fraud may be imprisoned for up to twenty years and/or fined. If the violation affects a financial institution or involves fraud in connection with emergency disaster-relief funds, the violator may be fined up to $1 million, imprisoned for up to thirty years, or both.

Bribery The crime of bribery involves offering to give something of value to a person in an attempt to influence that person in a way that serves a private interest. Three types of bribery are considered crimes: bribery of public officials, commercial bribery, and bribery of foreign officials.

The bribe itself can be anything the recipient considers to be valuable, but the defendant must have intended it as a bribe. Realize that the *crime of bribery occurs when the bribe is offered*—it is not required that the bribe be accepted. *Accepting a bribe* is a separate crime.

Commercial bribery involves corrupt dealings between private persons or businesses. Typically, people make commercial bribes to obtain proprietary information, cover up an inferior product, or secure new business. Industrial espionage sometimes involves commercial bribes. ■ **Example 10.13** Kent Peterson works at the firm of Jacoby & Meyers. He offers to pay Laurel, an employee in a competing firm, to give him that firm's trade secrets and pricing schedules. Peterson has committed commercial bribery. ■ So-called kickbacks, or payoffs for special favors or services, are a form of commercial bribery in some situations.

The Foreign Corrupt Practices Act In many foreign countries, government officials make the decisions on most major construction and manufacturing contracts because of extensive government regulation and control over trade and industry. Side payments to government officials in exchange for favorable business contracts are not unusual in such countries. The Foreign Corrupt

Practices Act[14] (FCPA) prohibits U.S. businesspersons from bribing foreign officials to secure beneficial contracts. Firms that violate the FCPA can be fined up to $2 million. Individuals can be fined up to $100,000 and imprisoned for up to five years.

Prohibition against the Bribery of Foreign Officials. The first part of the FCPA applies to all U.S. companies and their directors, officers, shareholders, employees, and agents. This part of the act prohibits the bribery of most officials of foreign governments if the purpose of the payment is to motivate the official to act in his or her official capacity to provide business opportunities.

The FCPA does not prohibit payments made to minor officials whose duties are ministerial. A ministerial action is a routine activity, such as the processing of paperwork, that involves little or no discretion. These payments are often referred to as "grease," or facilitating payments. They are meant to accelerate the performance of administrative services that might otherwise be carried out at a slow pace. Thus, for instance, if a firm makes a payment to a minor official to speed up an import licensing process, the firm has not violated the FCPA.

Generally, the act permits payments to foreign officials if such payments are lawful within the foreign country. Payments to private foreign companies or other third parties are permissible—unless the U.S. firm knows that the payments will be passed on to a foreign government in violation of the FCPA.

Accounting Requirements. In the past, bribes were often concealed in corporate financial records. Thus, the second part of the FCPA is directed toward accountants. All companies must keep detailed records that "accurately and fairly" reflect their financial activities. Their accounting systems must provide "reasonable assurance" that all transactions entered into by the companies are accounted for and legal. These requirements assist in detecting illegal bribes. The FCPA prohibits any person from making false statements to accountants or false entries in any record or account.

■ **Case in Point 10.14** Noble Corporation operated some drilling rigs offshore in Nigeria. Mark Jackson and James Ruehlen were officers at Noble. The U.S. government accused Noble of bribing Nigerian government officials and charged Jackson and Ruehlen individually with violating the FCPA's accounting provisions. Jackson and Ruehlen allegedly approved numerous "special handling" and "procurement" payments to the Nigerian government, knowing that those payments were actually bribes. By allowing illegal payments to be listed on the

13. *United States v. Chinasa*, 789 F.Supp.2d 691 (E.D.Va. 2011).

14. 15 U.S.C. Sections 78dd-1, *et seq.*

books as legitimate operating expenses, they violated the FCPA.[15] ∎

Bankruptcy Fraud Federal bankruptcy law allows individuals and businesses to be relieved of oppressive debt through bankruptcy proceedings. Numerous white-collar crimes may be committed during the many phases of a bankruptcy action. A creditor may file a false claim against the debtor, which is a crime. Also, a debtor may fraudulently transfer assets to favored parties before or after the bankruptcy is filed. For instance, a company-owned automobile may be "sold" at a bargain price to a trusted friend or relative. Closely related to the crime of fraudulent transfer of property is the crime of fraudulent concealment of property, such as the hiding of gold coins.

Insider Trading An individual who obtains "inside information" about the plans of a publicly listed corporation can often make stock-trading profits by purchasing or selling corporate securities based on this information. *Insider trading* is a violation of securities law. Basically, a person who possesses inside information and has a duty not to disclose it to outsiders may not trade on that information. A person may not profit from the purchase or sale of securities based on inside information until the information is made available to the public.

Theft of Trade Secrets and Other Intellectual Property The Economic Espionage Act[16] makes the theft of trade secrets a federal crime. The act also makes it a federal crime to buy or possess another person's trade secrets, knowing that the trade secrets were stolen or otherwise acquired without the owner's authorization.

Violations of the Economic Espionage Act can result in steep penalties: imprisonment for up to ten years and a fine of up to $500,000. A corporation or other organization can be fined up to $5 million. Additionally, any property acquired as a result of the violation, such as airplanes and automobiles, is subject to criminal forfeiture, or seizure by the government. Similarly, any property used in the commission of the violation is subject to forfeiture.

10–3e Organized Crime

White-collar crime takes place within the confines of the legitimate business world. *Organized crime*, in contrast, operates *illegitimately* by, among other things, providing illegal goods and services. Traditionally, organized crime has been involved in gambling, prostitution, illegal narcotics, counterfeiting, and loan sharking (lending funds at higher-than-legal interest rates), along with more recent ventures into credit-card scams and cyber crime.

Money Laundering The profits from organized crime and illegal activities amount to billions of dollars a year. These profits come from illegal drug transactions and, to a lesser extent, from racketeering, prostitution, and gambling. Under federal law, banks, savings and loan associations, and other financial institutions are required to report currency transactions involving more than $10,000. Consequently, those who engage in illegal activities face difficulties in depositing their cash profits from illegal transactions.

As an alternative to storing the cash from illegal transactions in a safe-deposit box, wrongdoers and racketeers often launder "dirty" money through legitimate businesses to make it "clean." **Money laundering** is engaging in financial transactions to conceal the identity, source, or destination of illegally gained funds.

∎ **Example 10.15** Leo Harris, a successful drug dealer, becomes a partner with a restaurateur. Little by little, the restaurant shows increasing profits. As a partner in the restaurant, Harris is able to report the "profits" of the restaurant as legitimate income on which he pays federal and state taxes. He can then spend those funds without worrying that his lifestyle may exceed the level possible with his reported income. ∎

Racketeering To curb the entry of organized crime into the legitimate business world, Congress enacted the Racketeer Influenced and Corrupt Organizations Act (RICO).[17] The statute makes it a federal crime to:

1. Use income obtained from racketeering activity to purchase any interest in an enterprise.
2. Acquire or maintain an interest in an enterprise through racketeering activity.
3. Conduct or participate in the affairs of an enterprise through racketeering activity.
4. Conspire to do any of the preceding activities.

Broad Application of RICO. The broad language of RICO has allowed it to be applied in cases that have little or nothing to do with organized crime. RICO incorporates by reference thirty-five separate types of federal and state crimes.[18] If a person commits two of these offenses, he or she is guilty of "racketeering activity."

---

15. *Securities and Exchange Commission v. Jackson*, 908 F.Supp.2d 834 (S.D.Tex.—Houston 2012).
16. 18 U.S.C. Sections 1831–1839.
17. 18 U.S.C. Sections 1961–1968.
18. See 18 U.S.C. Section 1961(1)(A). The crimes listed in this section include murder, kidnapping, gambling, arson, robbery, bribery, extortion, money laundering, securities fraud, counterfeiting, dealing in obscene matter, dealing in controlled substances (illegal drugs), and a number of others.

Under the criminal provisions of RICO, any individual found guilty is subject to a fine of up to $25,000 per violation, imprisonment for up to twenty years, or both. Additionally, any assets (property or cash) that were acquired as a result of the illegal activity or that were "involved in" or an "instrumentality of" the activity are subject to government forfeiture.

Civil Liability. In the event of a RICO violation, the government can seek not only criminal penalties but also civil penalties. The government can, for instance, seek the divestiture of a defendant's interest in a business or the dissolution of the business. (Divestiture refers to forfeiture of the defendant's interest and its subsequent sale.)

Moreover, in some cases, the statute allows private individuals to sue violators and potentially recover three times their actual losses (treble damages), plus attorneys' fees, for business injuries caused by a RICO violation. This is perhaps the most controversial aspect of RICO and one that continues to cause debate in the nation's federal courts. The prospect of receiving treble damages in civil RICO lawsuits has given plaintiffs a financial incentive to pursue businesses and employers for violations.

See Concept Summary 10.1 for a review of the different types of crimes just discussed.

10–4 Defenses to Criminal Liability

Persons charged with crimes may be relieved of criminal liability if they can show that their criminal actions were justified under the circumstances. In certain situations, the law may also allow a person to be excused from criminal liability because she or he lacks the required mental state. We look at several defenses to criminal liability here.

Note that procedural violations (such as obtaining evidence without a valid search warrant) may also operate as defenses. Evidence obtained in violation of a defendant's constitutional rights may not be admitted in court. If the evidence is suppressed, then there may be no basis for prosecuting the defendant.

10–4a Justifiable Use of Force

Probably the best-known defense to criminal liability is **self-defense.** Other situations, however, also justify the use of force: the defense of one's dwelling, the defense of other property, and the prevention of a crime. In all of these situations, it is important to distinguish between deadly and nondeadly force. *Deadly force* is likely to result in death or serious bodily harm. *Nondeadly force* is force

Concept Summary 10.1

Types of Crimes

Violent Crime	Crimes that cause others to suffer harm or death, such as murder, assault and battery, and robbery.
Property Crime	Crimes in which the goal of the offender is some form of economic gain or the damaging of property. Property crime includes theft-related offenses such as burglary, larceny, and forgery.
Public Order Crime	Crimes that are contrary to public values and morals, such as public drunkenness and prostitution.
White-Collar Crime	An illegal act or series of acts committed by an individual or business entity using some nonviolent means to obtain a personal or business advantage. These crimes are usually committed in the course of a legitimate occupation. Examples include embezzlement, bribery, and fraud.
Organized Crime	Crime conducted by groups operating illegitimately to provide illegal goods and services, such as narcotics. Organized crime may also include money laundering and racketeering.

that reasonably appears necessary to prevent the imminent use of criminal force.

Generally speaking, people can use the amount of nondeadly force that seems necessary to protect themselves, their dwellings, or other property, or to prevent the commission of a crime. Deadly force can be used in self-defense only when the defender *reasonably believes* that imminent death or grievous bodily harm will otherwise result. In addition, normally the attacker must be using unlawful force, and the defender must not have initiated or provoked the attack.

Many states are expanding the situations in which the use of deadly force can be justified. Florida, for instance, allows the use of deadly force to prevent the commission of a "forcible felony," including robbery, carjacking, and sexual battery.

10-4b Necessity

Sometimes, criminal defendants can be relieved of liability by showing **necessity**—that a criminal act was necessary to prevent an even greater harm. ■ **Example 10.16** Jake Trevor is a convicted felon and, as such, is legally prohibited from possessing a firearm. While he and his wife are in a convenience store, a man draws a gun, points it at the cashier, and demands all the cash in the register. Afraid that the man will start shooting, Trevor grabs the gun and holds onto it until police arrive. In this situation, if Trevor is charged with possession of a firearm, he can assert the defense of necessity. ■

10-4c Insanity

A person who suffers from a mental illness may be incapable of the state of mind required to commit a crime. Thus, insanity may be a defense to a criminal charge. Note that an insanity defense does not enable a person to avoid imprisonment. It simply means that if the defendant successfully proves insanity, she or he will be placed in a mental institution. ■ **Example 10.17** James Holmes opened fire with an automatic weapon in a crowded Colorado movie theater during a screening of *The Dark Knight Rises*, killing twelve people and injuring seventy. Holmes had been a graduate student but had suffered from mental health problems and had left school. Before the incident, he had no criminal history. Holmes's attorneys asserted the defense of insanity to try to avoid a possible death sentence. Although a jury ultimately rejected the defense and convicted Holmes of multiple counts of murder, he was sentenced to life in prison rather than death. If the insanity defense had been successful, Holmes would have been confined to a mental institution, not a prison. ■

10-4d Mistake

Everyone has heard the saying "Ignorance of the law is no excuse." Ordinarily, ignorance of the law or a mistaken idea about what the law requires is not a valid defense. A *mistake of fact*, however, as opposed to a *mistake of law*, can normally excuse criminal responsibility if it negates the mental state necessary to commit a crime.

■ **Example 10.18** Oliver Wheaton mistakenly walks off with Julie Tyson's briefcase. If Wheaton genuinely thought that the case was his, there is no theft. Theft requires knowledge that the property belongs to another. (If Wheaton's act causes Tyson to incur damages, however, she may sue him in a civil tort action for trespass to personal property or conversion.) ■

10-4e Duress

Duress exists when the *wrongful threat* of one person induces another person to perform an act that he or she would not otherwise have performed. In such a situation, duress is said to negate the mental state necessary to commit a crime because the defendant was forced or compelled to commit the act.

Duress can be used as a defense to most crimes except murder. Both the definition of duress and the types of crimes that it can excuse vary among the states, however. Generally, to successfully assert duress as a defense, the defendant must reasonably have believed that he or she was in immediate danger, and the jury (or judge) must conclude that the defendant's belief was reasonable.

10-4f Entrapment

Entrapment is a defense designed to prevent police officers or other government agents from enticing persons to commit crimes in order to later prosecute them for those crimes. In the typical entrapment case, an undercover agent *suggests* that a crime be committed and somehow pressures or induces an individual to commit it. The agent then arrests the individual for the crime.

For entrapment to be considered a defense, both the suggestion and the inducement must take place. The defense is not intended to prevent law enforcement agents from setting a trap for an unwary criminal. Rather, its purpose is to prevent them from pushing the individual into a criminal act. The crucial issue is whether the person who committed a crime was predisposed to commit the illegal act or did so only because the agent induced it.

10–4g Statute of Limitations

With some exceptions, such as the crime of murder, statutes of limitations apply to crimes just as they do to civil wrongs. In other words, the government must initiate criminal prosecution within a certain number of years. If a criminal action is brought after the statutory time period has expired, the accused person can raise the statute of limitations as a defense.

The running of the time period in a statute of limitations may be *tolled*—that is, suspended or stopped temporarily—if the defendant is a minor or is not in the jurisdiction. When the defendant reaches the age of majority or returns to the jurisdiction, the statutory time period begins to run again.

10–4h Immunity

Accused persons are understandably reluctant to give information if it will be used to prosecute them, and they cannot be forced to do so. The privilege against **self-incrimination** is guaranteed by a clause in the Fifth Amendment to the U.S. Constitution. The clause reads "nor shall [any person] be compelled in any criminal case to be a witness against himself."

When the state wishes to obtain information from a person accused of a crime, the state can grant *immunity* from prosecution. Alternatively, the state can agree to prosecute the accused for a less serious offense in exchange for the information. Once immunity is given, the person has an absolute privilege against self-incrimination and therefore can no longer refuse to testify on Fifth Amendment grounds.

Often, a grant of immunity from prosecution for a serious crime is part of the **plea bargaining** between the defending and prosecuting attorneys. The defendant may be convicted of a lesser offense, while the state uses the defendant's testimony to prosecute accomplices for serious crimes carrying heavy penalties.

10–5 Criminal Procedures

Criminal law brings the force of the state, with all of its resources, to bear against the individual. Criminal procedures are designed to protect the constitutional rights of individuals and to prevent the arbitrary use of power on the part of the government.

The U.S. Constitution provides specific safeguards for those accused of crimes. The United States Supreme Court has ruled that most of these safeguards apply not only in federal court but also in state courts by virtue of

the due process clause of the Fourteenth Amendment. These protections include the following:

1. The Fourth Amendment protection from unreasonable searches and seizures.
2. The Fourth Amendment requirement that no warrant for a search or an arrest be issued without probable cause.
3. The Fifth Amendment requirement that no one be deprived of "life, liberty, or property without due process of law."
4. The Fifth Amendment prohibition against **double jeopardy** (trying someone twice for the same criminal offense).[19]
5. The Fifth Amendment requirement that no person be required to be a witness against (incriminate) himself or herself.
6. The Sixth Amendment guarantees of a speedy trial, a trial by jury, a public trial, the right to confront witnesses, and the right to a lawyer at various stages in some proceedings.
7. The Eighth Amendment prohibitions against excessive bail and fines and against cruel and unusual punishment.

10–5a Fourth Amendment Protections

The Fourth Amendment protects the "right of the people to be secure in their persons, houses, papers, and effects." Before searching or seizing private property, normally law enforcement officers must obtain a **search warrant**—an order from a judge or other public official authorizing the search or seizure.

Advances in technology allow the authorities to track phone calls and vehicle movements with greater ease and precision. The use of such technology can constitute a search within the meaning of the Fourth Amendment. ■ **Case in Point 10.19** Antoine Jones owned and operated a nightclub in the District of Columbia. Government agents suspected that he was also trafficking in narcotics. As part of their investigation, agents obtained a warrant to attach a global positioning system (GPS) device to Jones's wife's car, which Jones regularly used. The warrant authorized installation in the District of Columbia within ten days, but agents installed the device on the eleventh day in Maryland.

The agents then tracked the vehicle's movement for about a month, eventually arresting Jones for possession

---

19. The prohibition against double jeopardy does not preclude the crime victim from bringing a *civil* suit against that same person to recover damages, however. Additionally, a state's prosecution of a crime may not prevent a separate federal prosecution of the same crime, and vice versa.

of and intent to distribute cocaine. Jones was convicted. He appealed, arguing that the government did not have a valid warrant for the GPS tracking. The United States Supreme Court held that the attachment of a GPS tracking device to a suspect's vehicle does constitute a Fourth Amendment search. The Court did not rule on whether the search in this case was unreasonable, however, and allowed Jones's conviction to stand.[20] ■

Probable Cause To obtain a search warrant, law enforcement officers must convince a judge that they have reasonable grounds, or **probable cause,** to believe a search will reveal a specific illegality. Probable cause requires the officers to have trustworthy evidence that would convince a reasonable person that the proposed search or seizure is more likely justified than not.

■ **Case in Point 10.20** Based on a tip that Oscar Gutierrez was involved in drug trafficking, law enforcement officers went to his home with a drug-sniffing dog. The dog alerted officers to the scent of narcotics at the home's front door. Officers knocked for fifteen minutes, but no one answered. Eventually, they entered and secured the men inside the home. They then obtained a search warrant based on the dog's positive alert. Officers found eleven pounds of methamphetamine in the search, and Gutierrez was convicted. The evidence of the drug-sniffing dog's positive alert for the presence of drugs established probable cause for the warrant.[21] ■

Scope of Warrant The Fourth Amendment prohibits general warrants. It requires a specific description of what is to be searched or seized. General searches through a person's belongings are impermissible. The search cannot extend beyond what is described in the warrant.

Reasonable Expectation of Privacy The Fourth Amendment protects only against searches that violate a person's *reasonable expectation of privacy*. A reasonable expectation of privacy exists if (1) the individual actually expects privacy and (2) the person's expectation is one that society as a whole would consider legitimate.

■ **Case in Point 10.21** Angela Marcum was the drug court coordinator responsible for collecting money for the District Court of Pittsburg County, Oklahoma. She was romantically involved with James Miller, an assistant district attorney. The state charged Marcum with obstructing an investigation of suspected embezzlement and offered in evidence text messages sent and received by her and Miller. The state had obtained a search warrant

and collected the records of the messages from U.S. Cellular, Miller's phone company.

Marcum filed a motion to suppress the messages, which the court granted. The state appealed. A state intermediate appellate court reversed the lower court's judgment. Marcum had no reasonable expectation of privacy in U.S. Cellular's records of her text messages in Miller's account. "Once the messages were both transmitted and received, the expectation of privacy was lost."[22] ■

10–5b The Exclusionary Rule

Under what is known as the **exclusionary rule,** any evidence obtained in violation of the constitutional rights spelled out in the Fourth, Fifth, and Sixth Amendments generally is not admissible at trial. All evidence derived from the illegally obtained evidence is known as the "fruit of the poisonous tree," and it normally must also be excluded from the trial proceedings. For instance, if a confession is obtained after an illegal arrest, the arrest is the "poisonous tree," and the confession, if "tainted" by the arrest, is the "fruit."

The purpose of the exclusionary rule is to deter police from conducting warrantless searches and engaging in other misconduct. The rule can sometimes lead to injustice, however. If evidence of a defendant's guilt was obtained improperly (without a valid search warrant, for instance), it normally cannot be used against the defendant in court.

10–5c The *Miranda* Rule

In *Miranda v. Arizona*,[23] a landmark case decided in 1966, the United States Supreme Court established the rule that individuals who are arrested must be informed of certain constitutional rights. Suspects must be informed of their Fifth Amendment right to remain silent and their Sixth Amendment right to counsel. If the arresting officers fail to inform a criminal suspect of these constitutional rights, any statements the suspect makes normally will not be admissible in court.

Although the Supreme Court's decision in the *Miranda* case was controversial, it has survived several attempts by Congress to overrule it. Over time, however, the Court has made a number of exceptions to the *Miranda* ruling. For instance, the Court has recognized a "public safety" exception that allows certain statements to be admitted into evidence even if the defendant was not given *Miranda* warnings. A defendant's

20. *United States v. Jones*, 565 U.S. 400, 132 S.Ct. 945, 181 L.Ed.2d 911 (2012).
21. *United States v. Gutierrez*, 760 F.3d 750 (7th Cir. 2014).
22. *State of Oklahoma v. Marcum*, 319 P.3d 681 (Okla. Crim.App. 2014).
23. 384 U.S. 436, 86 S.Ct. 1602, 16 L.Ed.2d 694 (1966).

statements that reveal the location of a weapon would be admissible under this exception.

Additionally, a suspect must unequivocally and assertively ask to exercise her or his right to counsel in order to stop police questioning. Saying "Maybe I should talk to a lawyer" during an interrogation after being taken into custody is not enough.

10-5d Criminal Process

A criminal prosecution differs significantly from a civil case in several respects. These differences reflect the desire to safeguard the rights of the individual against the state. Exhibit 10–3 summarizes the major steps in processing a criminal case, several of which we discuss here.

Exhibit 10–3 Major Procedural Steps in a Criminal Case

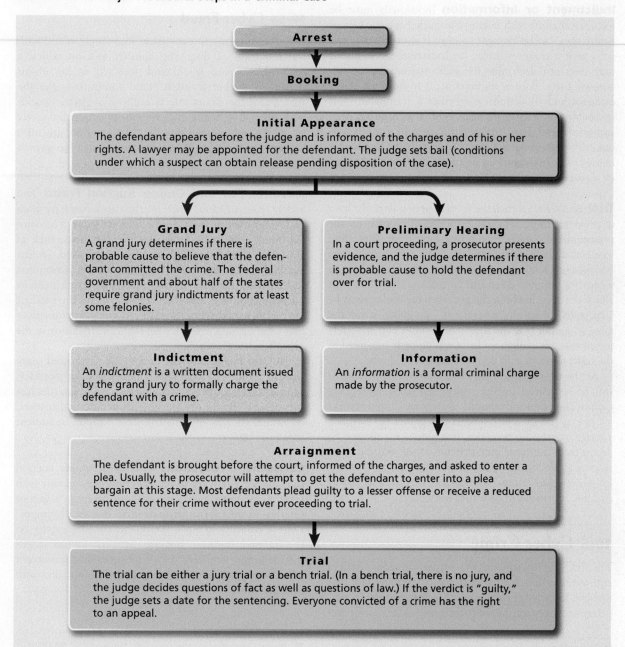

Arrest

Booking

Initial Appearance
The defendant appears before the judge and is informed of the charges and of his or her rights. A lawyer may be appointed for the defendant. The judge sets bail (conditions under which a suspect can obtain release pending disposition of the case).

Grand Jury
A grand jury determines if there is probable cause to believe that the defendant committed the crime. The federal government and about half of the states require grand jury indictments for at least some felonies.

Preliminary Hearing
In a court proceeding, a prosecutor presents evidence, and the judge determines if there is probable cause to hold the defendant over for trial.

Indictment
An *indictment* is a written document issued by the grand jury to formally charge the defendant with a crime.

Information
An *information* is a formal criminal charge made by the prosecutor.

Arraignment
The defendant is brought before the court, informed of the charges, and asked to enter a plea. Usually, the prosecutor will attempt to get the defendant to enter into a plea bargain at this stage. Most defendants plead guilty to a lesser offense or receive a reduced sentence for their crime without ever proceeding to trial.

Trial
The trial can be either a jury trial or a bench trial. (In a bench trial, there is no jury, and the judge decides questions of fact as well as questions of law.) If the verdict is "guilty," the judge sets a date for the sentencing. Everyone convicted of a crime has the right to an appeal.

Arrest Before a warrant for arrest can be issued, there must be probable cause to believe that the individual in question has committed a crime. Note that probable cause involves a substantial likelihood that the person has committed a crime, not just a possibility. Arrests can be made without a warrant if there is no time to obtain one, but the action of the arresting officer is still judged by the standard of probable cause.

Indictment or Information Individuals must be formally charged with having committed specific crimes before they can be brought to trial. If issued by a grand jury, such a charge is called an **indictment.**[24] A **grand jury** does not determine the guilt or innocence of an accused party. Rather, its function is to hear the state's evidence and to determine whether a reasonable basis (probable cause) exists for believing that a crime has been committed and that a trial ought to be held. For less serious crimes, an individual may be formally charged with a crime by an **information,** or criminal complaint, issued by a government prosecutor.

Trial At a criminal trial, the accused person does not have to prove anything. The entire burden of proof is on the prosecutor (the state). The prosecution must show that, based on all the evidence, the defendant's guilt is established *beyond a reasonable doubt.* If there is reasonable doubt as to whether a criminal defendant committed the crime with which she or he has been charged, then the verdict must be "not guilty." Returning a verdict of "not guilty" is not the same as stating that the defendant is innocent. It merely means that not enough evidence was properly presented to the court to prove guilt beyond a reasonable doubt.

At the conclusion of the trial, a convicted defendant will be sentenced by the court. The U.S. Sentencing Commission performs the task of standardizing sentences for *federal* crimes. The commission's guidelines establish a range of possible penalties, but judges are allowed to depart from the guidelines if circumstances warrant. Sentencing guidelines also provide for enhanced punishment for white-collar crimes, violations of the Sarbanes-Oxley Act, and violations of securities laws.

10–6 Cyber Crime

The U.S. Department of Justice broadly defines **computer crime** as any violation of criminal law that involves knowledge of computer technology for its perpetration, investigation, or prosecution. Many computer crimes fall under the broad label of **cyber crime,** which describes any criminal activity occurring via a computer in the virtual community of the Internet.

Most cyber crimes are simply existing crimes, such as fraud and theft, in which the Internet is the instrument of wrongdoing. Here, we look at several types of activities that constitute cyber crimes against persons or property.

10–6a Cyber Fraud

Fraud is any misrepresentation knowingly made with the intention of deceiving another and on which a reasonable person would and does rely to her or his detriment. **Cyber fraud** is fraud committed over the Internet. Cyber fraud affects millions of people worldwide every day. Scams that were once conducted solely by mail or phone can now be found online, and new technology has led to increasingly more creative ways to commit fraud.

Advance Fee and Online Auction Fraud Two widely reported forms of cyber crime are *advance fee fraud* and *online auction fraud.* In the simplest form of advance fee fraud, consumers order and pay for items, such as automobiles or antiques, that are never delivered. Online auction fraud is also fairly straightforward. A person lists an expensive item for auction, on either a legitimate or a fake auction site, and then refuses to send the product after receiving payment. Or, as a variation, the wrongdoer may send the purchaser an item that is worth less than the one offered in the auction.

■ **Case in Point 10.22** Jeremy Jaynes grossed more than $750,000 per week selling nonexistent or worthless products such as "penny stock pickers" and "Internet history erasers." By the time he was arrested, he had amassed an estimated $24 million from his various fraudulent schemes.[25] ■

Consumer Protections The larger online auction sites, such as eBay, try to protect consumers against such schemes by providing warnings about deceptive sellers or offering various forms of insurance. It is nearly impossible to completely block fraudulent auction activity on the Internet, however. Because users can assume multiple identities, it is very difficult to pinpoint fraudulent sellers—they will simply change their screen names with each auction.

---

24. Pronounced in-*dyte*-ment.

25. *Jaynes v. Commonwealth of Virginia,* 276 Va. 443, 666 S.E.2d 303 (2008).

10–6b Cyber Theft

In cyberspace, thieves are not subject to the physical limitations of the "real" world. A thief can steal data stored in a networked computer with Internet access from anywhere on the globe. Only the speed of the connection and the thief's computer equipment limit the quantity of data that can be stolen.

Identity Theft **Identity theft** occurs when the wrongdoer steals a form of identification—such as a name, date of birth, or Social Security number—and uses the information to access the victim's financial resources. Millions of Americans are victims of identity theft each year.

More than half of identity thefts involve the misappropriation of existing credit-card accounts. In most situations, the legitimate holders of credit cards are not held responsible for the costs of purchases made with a stolen number. The loss is borne by the businesses and banks.

The Internet has provided relatively easy access to private data that includes credit-card numbers and more. Frequent Web surfers surrender a wealth of information about themselves. Websites use "cookies" to collect data on those who visit their sites and make purchases. Often, sites store information such as the consumers' names, e-mail addresses, and credit-card numbers. Identity thieves may be able to steal this information by fooling a website into thinking that they are the true account holders.

In addition, people often enter important personal information, such as their birthdays, hometowns, or employers, on social media sites. Identity thieves can use such information to convince a third party to reveal someone's Social Security or bank account number.

Identity theft can be committed in the course of pursuing other criminal objectives. In the following case, for instance, the defendant was charged with identity theft in connection with the filing of five thousand false income tax returns to obtain refunds. He challenged his conviction on these charges and sought a new trial.

Case Analysis 10.3

United States v. Warner

United States Court of Appeals, Eleventh Circuit, 638 Fed.Appx. 961 (2016).

In the Language of the Court
PER CURIAM [By the Whole Court]:
* * * *

A [federal district court] jury convicted Mauricio Warner on all 50 counts of an indictment that charged him with obtaining individuals' identities and using such identities to file over 5,000 false income tax returns resulting in millions of dollars in refunds that were deposited in bank accounts Warner controlled. [The court sentenced Warner to prison for a total of 240 months.] He now appeals his convictions. He seeks the vacation of his convictions and a new trial on the grounds that the District Court abused its discretion (1) in refusing to permit a polygraph examiner to testify to the results of a polygraph examination he administered to Warner; (2) admitting into evidence government Exhibits 500 and 500A, spreadsheets of fraudulently submitted tax returns, as business records; and (3) permitting each juror to have a copy of the indictment throughout trial.

* * * *

A district court's decision to admit or exclude expert testimony under Federal Rule of Evidence 702 is reviewed for abuse of discretion, which is the standard we apply in reviewing evidentiary rulings in general. *A district court abuses its discretion when it applies the wrong law, follows the wrong procedure, bases its decision on clearly erroneous facts, or commits a clear error in judgment.* [Emphasis added.]

Federal Rule of Evidence 702 provides that an expert witness may testify in the form of an opinion if the expert's specialized knowledge will assist the trier of fact to understand the evidence or to determine a fact at issue.

The results of a polygraph examination are not inadmissible *per se*. The trial judge in the exercise of discretion may admit the results of such examination to impeach or corroborate witness testimony.

The District Court did not abuse its discretion in concluding that the polygraph examination was inadmissible

under Rule 702. The question posed by the examiner addressed an issue that was to be decided by the jury, that is, whether Warner knowingly filed tax returns without the individuals' authority or knowing that they were not entitled to the refund requested. Since Warner took the stand and answered the same questions, the jury was capable of determining his credibility without the aid of an expert.

* * * *

Federal Rule of Evidence 1006 authorizes the admission into evidence of a summary of voluminous business records but only where the originals or duplicates of those originals are available for examination or copying by the other party.

The business record exception to the hearsay rule under Federal Rule of Evidence 803(6) states, in relevant part, that a record will be admitted if:

(A) the record was made at or near the time by—or from information transmitted by—someone with knowledge;

Case 10.3 Continues

Case 10.3 Continued

(B) the record was kept in the course of a regularly conducted activity of a business, organization, occupation, or calling, whether or not for profit;

(C) making the record was a regular practice of that activity;

(D) all these conditions are shown by the testimony of the custodian or another qualified witness * * *;

(E) the opponent does not show that the source of information or the method of circumstances of preparation indicate a lack of trustworthiness.

Rule 803(6) requires that both the underlying records and the report summarizing those records be prepared and maintained for business purposes in the ordinary course of business and not for purposes of litigation. * * * *The touchstone of admissibility under Rule 803(6) is reliability, and a trial judge has broad discretion to determine the admissibility of such evidence.* [Emphasis added.]

Computer-generated business records are admissible under the following circumstances: (1) the records must be kept pursuant to some routine procedure designed to assure their accuracy, (2) they must be created for motives that would tend to assure accuracy (preparation for litigation, for example, is not such a motive), and (3) they must not themselves be mere accumulations of hearsay or uninformed opinion.

* * * A typed summary of handwritten business records created solely for litigation [is] inadmissible hearsay evidence. [This is] distinguishable from * * * records [that consist of] electronically stored information and the summary [is] simply a printout of that information.

* * * *

* * * Airline check-in and reservation records and flight manifests that [are] kept in the ordinary course of business and printed at the government's request [for a trial are admissible]. Computer data compiled and presented in computer printouts prepared specifically for trial is admissible under Rule 803(6), even though the printouts themselves are not kept in the ordinary course of business.

We find no abuse of discretion in admitting government Exhibits 500 and 500A under Rule 803(6). Although the spreadsheets were formatted to be easier to understand and printed for litigation, the underlying records were kept in the ordinary course of business and the data was not modified or combined when entered into the spreadsheet.

* * * *

The decision to provide the jury with a copy of an indictment is committed to the district court's sound discretion.

As a general rule, a trial court may, in the exercise of discretion, allow the indictment to be taken into the jury room. Likewise, a court may provide the jury copies of the indictment before trial, provided that the court gives specific instructions that the indictment is not evidence.

There was no abuse of discretion here. The court specifically instructed the jurors on two separate occasions that the indictment was not evidence or proof of any guilt. Even if the court's lack of contemporaneous instructions was error, it was harmless.

For the foregoing reasons, Warner's convictions are
AFFIRMED.

Legal Reasoning Questions

1. What three reasons did the defendant assert to support a request for a new trial?

2. What standard applies to an appellate court's consideration of a contention that a trial court's evidentiary ruling was in error?

3. What were the appellate court's conclusions with respect to the trial court's rulings in this case? What reasons support these conclusions?

Password Theft The more personal information a cyber criminal obtains, the easier it is for him or her to find a victim's online user name at a particular website. Once the online user name has been compromised, it is easier to steal the victim's password, which is often the last line of defense to financial information.

Numerous software programs aid identity thieves in illegally obtaining passwords. A technique called *keystroke logging*, for instance, relies on software that embeds itself in a victim's computer and records every keystroke made on that computer. User names and passwords are then recorded and sold to the highest bidder. Internet users should also be wary of any links contained within e-mails sent from unknown sources. These links can sometimes be used to illegally obtain personal information.

Phishing A form of identity theft known as **phishing** has added a different wrinkle to the practice. In a phishing attack, the perpetrator "fishes" for financial data and passwords from consumers by posing as a legitimate business, such as a bank or credit-card company. The "phisher" sends an e-mail asking the recipient to update or confirm vital information. Often, the e-mail includes a threat that an account or some other service will be discontinued if the information is not provided. Once the unsuspecting individual enters the information, the phisher can sell it or use it to masquerade as that person or to drain his or her bank or credit account.

■ **Example 10.23** Customers of Wells Fargo Bank receive official-looking e-mails telling them to type in personal information in an online form to complete a mandatory installation of a new Internet security certificate. But the website is bogus. When the customers complete the forms, their computers are infected and funnel their data to a computer server. The cyber criminals then sell the data. ■ Phishing scams can also take place in text messaging and social networking sites.

10–6c Hacking

A **hacker** is someone who uses one computer to break into another. The danger posed by hackers is significantly increased by **botnets,** or networks of computers that have been appropriated by hackers without the knowledge of their owners. A hacker may secretly install a program on thousands, even millions, of personal computer "robots," or "bots." The program, in turn, allows the hacker to forward transmissions to an even larger number of systems.

Malware Botnets are only one form of **malware,** a term that refers to any program that is harmful to a computer or, by extension, a computer user. Malware can be programmed to perform a number of functions, such as prompting host computers to continually "crash" and reboot or otherwise infecting the systems.

Another type of malware is a **worm**—a software program that is capable of reproducing itself as it spreads from one computer to the next. The Conficker worm, for instance, spread to more than a million computers around the world within a three-week period. It was transmitted to some computers through the use of Facebook and Twitter.

A **virus,** yet another form of malware, is also able to reproduce itself but must be attached to an "infested" host file to travel from one computer network to another. For instance, hackers can corrupt banner ads that use Adobe's Flash Player or send bogus Flash Player updates. When an Internet user clicks on the banner ad, a virus is installed.

■ **Example 10.24** During one holiday season, a group of Eastern European hackers gained access to Target's computer system. Once "inside," the hackers infected the in-store devices that Target customers use to swipe their credit and debit cards with "memory scraper" malware nicknamed Kaptoxa. Over the course of several weeks, the malware was used to steal the credit- and debit-card data of as many as 40 million Target customers and the personal data of roughly 70 million more customers. ■

Service-Based Hacking Many companies offer "software as a service." Instead of buying software to install on a computer, the user connects to Web-based software to perform various tasks.

Cyber criminals have adapted this method to provide "crimeware as a service." A would-be thief no longer has to be a computer hacker to create a botnet or steal banking information and credit-card numbers. He or she can rent the online services of cyber criminals to do the work for a small price. Fake security software (also known as scareware) is a common example. Another example is ransom malware, or ransomware, which prevents users from accessing their system or personal files and demands a ransom payment in order to regain access. Criminals using ransomware services frequently target U.S. cities and hospitals.

Cyberterrorism Cyberterrorists, as well as hackers, may target businesses. The goals of a hacking operation might include a wholesale theft of data, such as a merchant's customer files, or the monitoring of a computer to discover a business firm's plans and transactions. A cyberterrorist might also want to insert false codes or data. For instance, the processing control system of a food manufacturer could be changed to alter the levels of ingredients so that consumers of the food would become ill.

A cyberterrorist attack on a major financial institution, such as the New York Stock Exchange or a large bank, could leave securities or money markets in flux. Such an attack could seriously affect U.S. citizens, business operations, and national security.

10–6d Prosecuting Cyber Crime

Cyber crime raises new issues in the investigation of crimes and the prosecution of offenders. Determining the "location" of a cyber crime and identifying a criminal in cyberspace present significant challenges for law enforcement.

Jurisdiction and Identification Challenges A threshold issue is, of course, jurisdiction. Each state and nation has jurisdiction, or authority, over crimes committed within its boundaries. But geographic boundaries simply do not apply in cyberspace. A person who commits an act against a business in California, where the act is a cyber crime, might never have set foot in California. Instead, the perpetrator might reside in another state, or even another nation, where the act may not be a crime. Indeed, many cyber crimes emanate from Russia and China.

Identifying the wrongdoer can also be difficult. Cyber criminals do not leave physical traces, such as fingerprints or DNA samples, as evidence of their crimes. Even electronic "footprints" can be hard to find and follow. For instance, cyber criminals may employ software to mask their IP addresses (codes that identify individual computers) and the IP addresses of those with whom they communicate. Law enforcement has to hire computer forensic experts to bypass the software and track down the criminal. For these reasons, laws written to protect physical property are often difficult to apply in cyberspace.

The Computer Fraud and Abuse Act   Perhaps the most significant federal statute specifically addressing cyber crime is the Counterfeit Access Device and Computer Fraud and Abuse Act.[26] This act is commonly known as the Computer Fraud and Abuse Act (CFAA).

Among other things, the CFAA provides that a person who accesses a computer online, without authority, to obtain classified, restricted, or protected data (or attempts to do so) is subject to criminal prosecution. Such data may include financial and credit records, medical records, legal files, military and national security files, and other confidential information. The data can be located in government or private computers. The crime has two elements: accessing a computer without authority and taking data.

The theft is a felony if it is committed for a commercial purpose or for private financial gain, or if the value of the stolen data (or computer time) exceeds $5,000. Penalties include fines and imprisonment for up to twenty years. A person who violates the CFAA can also be sued in a civil action for damages.

---

26. 18 U.S.C. Section 1030.

Practice and Review: Criminal Law and Cyber Crime

Edward Hanousek worked for Pacific & Arctic Railway and Navigation Company (P&A) as a roadmaster of the White Pass & Yukon Railroad in Alaska. Hanousek was responsible "for every detail of the safe and efficient maintenance and construction of track, structures and marine facilities of the entire railroad," including special projects. One project was a rock quarry, known as "6-mile," above the Skagway River. Next to the quarry, and just beneath the surface, ran a high-pressure oil pipeline owned by Pacific & Arctic Pipeline, Inc., P&A's sister company. When the quarry's backhoe operator punctured the pipeline, an estimated 1,000 to 5,000 gallons of oil were discharged into the river. Hanousek was charged with negligently discharging a harmful quantity of oil into a navigable water of the United States in violation of the criminal provisions of the Clean Water Act (CWA). Using the information presented in the chapter, answer the following questions.

1. Did Hanousek have the required mental state *(mens rea)* to be convicted of a crime? Why or why not?
2. Which theory discussed in the chapter would enable a court to hold Hanousek criminally liable for violating the statute if he participated in, directed, or merely knew about the specific violation?
3. Could the backhoe operator who punctured the pipeline also be charged with a crime in this situation? Explain.
4. Suppose that at trial, Hanousek argued that he should not be convicted because he was not aware of the requirements of the CWA. Would this defense be successful? Why or why not?

Debate This . . .   *Because of overcriminalization, particularly by the federal government, Americans may be breaking the law regularly without knowing it. Should Congress rescind many of the more than four thousand federal crimes now on the books?*

Terms and Concepts

actus reus 189	beyond a reasonable doubt 188	burglary 194
arson 194	botnets 207	computer crime 204

Issue Spotters

1. Dana takes her roommate's credit card without permission, intending to charge expenses that she incurs on a vacation. Her first stop is a gas station, where she uses the card to pay for gas. With respect to the gas station, has she committed a crime? If so, what is it? (See *Types of Crimes*.)

2. Without permission, Ben downloads consumer credit files from a computer belonging to Consumer Credit Agency. He then sells the data to Dawn. Has Ben committed a crime? If so, what is it? (See *Cyber Crime*.)

• **Check your answers to the Issue Spotters against the answers provided in Appendix B at the end of this text.**

Business Scenarios and Case Problems

10–1. Types of Cyber Crimes. The following situations are similar, but each represents a variation of a particular crime. Identify the crime involved in each of the following situations. (See *Cyber Crime*.)

(a) Chen, posing fraudulently as being from Centell, the provider of Emily's security software, sends an e-mail to Emily, stating that the company has observed suspicious activity in her account and on her network. The e-mail asks Emily to call Chen immediately to provide a new credit-card number and password to update her security software and reopen the account.

(b) Claiming falsely to be Big Buy Retail Finance Company, Conner sends an e-mail to Dino, asking him to confirm or update his personal security information to prevent his Big Buy account from being discontinued.

10–2. Cyber Scam. Kayla, a student at Learnwell University, owes $20,000 in unpaid tuition. If Kayla does not pay the tuition, Learnwell will not allow her to graduate. To obtain the funds to pay the debt, she sends e-mails to people that she does not personally know asking for financial help to send Milo, her disabled child, to a special school. In reality, Kayla has no children. Is this a crime? If so, which one? (See *Cyber Crime*.)

10–3. Criminal Liability. During the morning rush hour, David Green threw bottles and plates from a twenty-sixth floor hotel balcony overlooking Seventh Avenue in New York City. A video of the incident also showed him doing cartwheels while holding a beer bottle and sprinting toward the balcony while holding a glass steadily in his hand. When he saw police

on the street below and on the roof of the building across the street, he suspended his antics but resumed tossing objects off the balcony after the police left. He later admitted that he could recall what he had done, but claimed to have been intoxicated and said his only purpose was to amuse himself and his friends. Did Green have the mental state required to establish criminal liability? Discuss. [*State of New York v. Green*, 104 A.D.3d 126, 958 N.Y.S.2d 138 (1 Dept. 2013)] (See *Criminal Liability*.)

10–4. Business Case Problem with Sample Answer— White-Collar Crime. Matthew Simpson and others created and operated a series of corporate entities to defraud telecommunications companies, creditors, credit reporting agencies, and others. Through these entities, Simpson and his confederates used routing codes and spoofing services to make long-distance calls appear to be local. They stole other firms' network capacity and diverted payments to themselves. They leased goods and services without paying for them. To hide their association with their corporate entities and with each other, they used false identities, addresses, and credit histories, and issued false bills, invoices, financial statements, and credit references. Did these acts constitute mail and wire fraud? Discuss. [*United States v. Simpson*, 741 F.3d 539 (5th Cir. 2014)] (See *Types of Crimes*.)

• **For a sample answer to Problem 10–4, go to Appendix C at the end of this text.**

10–5. Defenses to Criminal Liability. George Castro told Ambrosio Medrano that a bribe to a certain corrupt Los Angeles County official would buy a contract with the county hospitals.

To share in the deal, Medrano recruited Gustavo Buenrostro. In turn, Buenrostro contacted his friend James Barta, the owner of Sav-Rx, which provides prescription benefit management services. Barta was asked to pay a "finder's fee" to Castro. He did not pay, even after frequent e-mails and calls with deadlines and ultimatums delivered over a period of months. Eventually, Barta wrote Castro a Sav-Rx check for $6,500, saying that it was to help his friend Buenrostro. Castro was an FBI agent, and the county official and contract were fictional. Barta was charged with conspiracy to commit bribery. At trial, the government conceded that Barta was not predisposed to commit the crime. Could he be absolved of the charge on a defense of entrapment? Explain. [*United States v. Barta*, 776 F.3d 931 (7th Cir. 2015)] (See *Defenses to Criminal Liability.*)

10–6. Criminal Process. Gary Peters fraudulently told an undocumented immigrant that Peters could help him obtain lawful status. Peters said that he knew immigration officials and asked for money to aid in the process. The victim paid Peters at least $25,000 in wire transfers and checks. Peters had others call the victim, falsely represent that they were agents with the U.S. Department of Homeland Security, and induce continued payments. He threatened to contact authorities to detain or deport the victim and his wife. Peters was charged with wire fraud and convicted in a federal district court. Peters's attorney argued that his client's criminal history was partially due to "difficult personal times" caused by divorce, illness, and job loss. Despite this claim, Peters was sentenced to forty-eight months imprisonment, which exceeded the federal sentencing guidelines but was less than the statutory maximum of twenty years. Was this sentence too harsh? Was it too lenient? Discuss. [*United States v. Peters*, 597 Fed.Appx. 1033 (11th Cir. 2015)] (See *Criminal Procedures.*)

10–7. Criminal Procedures. Federal officers obtained a warrant to arrest Kateena Norman on charges of credit-card fraud and identity theft. Evidence of the crime included videos, photos, and a fingerprint on a fraudulent check. A previous search of Norman's house had uncovered credit cards, new merchandise, and identifying information for other persons. An Internet account registered to the address had been used to apply for fraudulent credit cards, and a fraudulently obtained rental car was parked on the property. As the officers arrested Norman outside her house, they saw another woman and a caged pit bull inside. They further believed that Norman's boyfriend, who had a criminal record and was also suspected of identify theft, could be there. In less than a minute, the officers searched only those areas within the house in which a person could hide. Would it be reasonable to admit evidence revealed in this "protective sweep" during Norman's trial on the arrest charges? Discuss. [*United States v. Norman*, 638 Fed. Appx. 934 (11th Cir. 2016)] (See *Criminal Procedures.*)

10–8. Types of Crimes. In Texas, Chigger Ridge Ranch, LP, operated a 700-acre commercial hunting area called Coyote Crossing Ranch (CCR). Chigger Ridge leased CCR and its assets for twelve months to George Briscoe's company, VPW Management, LLC. The lease identified all of the vehicles and equipment that belonged to Chigger Ridge, which VPW could use in the course of business, but the lease did not convey any ownership interest. During the lease term, however, Briscoe told his employees to sell some of the vehicles and equipment. Briscoe did nothing to correct the buyers' false impression that he owned the property and was authorized to sell it. The buyers paid with checks, which were deposited into an account to which only Briscoe and his spouse had access. Which crime, if any, did Briscoe commit? Explain. [*Briscoe v. State of Texas*, 542 S.W.3d 100 (Tex.App.—Texarkana 2018)] (See *Types of Crimes.*)

10–9. A Question of Ethics—The IDDR Approach and Identity Theft. *Heesham Broussard obtained counterfeit money instruments. To distribute them, he used account information and numbers on compromised FedEx accounts procured from hackers. Text messages from Broussard indicated that he had participated previously in a similar scam and that he knew the packages would be delivered only if the FedEx accounts were "good." For his use of the accounts, Broussard was charged with identity theft. In defense, he argued that the government could not prove he knew the misappropriated accounts belonged to real persons or businesses.* [United States v. Broussard, *675 Fed.Appx. 454 (5th Cir. 2017)] (See* Cyber Crime.*)*

(a) Does the evidence support Broussard's assertion? From an ethical perspective, does it matter whether he knew that the accounts belonged to real customers? Why or why not?

(b) Assuming that FedEx knew its customers' account information had been compromised, use the IDDR approach to consider whether the company had an ethical obligation to take steps to protect those customers from theft.

Time-Limited Group Assignment

10–10. Cyber Crime. Cyber crime costs consumers billions of dollars per year, and it costs businesses, including banks and other credit-card issuers, even more. Nonetheless, when cyber criminals are caught and convicted, they are rarely ordered to pay restitution or sentenced to long prison terms. (See *Cyber Crime.*)

(a) One group will formulate an argument that stiffer sentences would reduce the amount of cyber crime.

(b) A second group will determine how businesspersons might best protect themselves from cyber crime and avoid the associated costs.

(c) A third group will decide how and when a court should order a cyber criminal to pay restitution to his or her victims. Should victims whose computers have been infected with worms or viruses be entitled to restitution, or only victims of theft who have experienced financial loss? What should the measure of restitution be? Should large companies that are victims of cyber crime be entitled to the same restitution as individuals?

Chapter 11

International and Space Law

Commerce has always crossed national borders. But technology has fueled dramatic growth in world trade and the emergence of a global business community. Exchanges of goods, services, and intellectual property on a global level are now routine. Therefore, students of business law and the legal environment should be familiar with the laws pertaining to international business transactions.

Laws affecting the international legal environment of business include both international law and national law. **International law** can be defined as a body of law—formed as a result of international customs, treaties, and organizations—that governs relations among or between nations. International law may be created when individual nations agree to comply with certain standards (such as by signing a treaty). It may also be created when industries or nations establish international standards for private transactions that cross national borders (such as a law that prohibits importation of genetically modified organisms).

National law is the law of a particular nation, such as Brazil, Germany, Japan, or the United States. In some ways, national laws that involve property rights, border searches, regulations, and taxes effectively become international law when they are applied at a nation's borders.

An emerging area of global importance is space law, which governs humans' activities in outer space. Space law also has both international and national components.

11–1 International Law

The major difference between international law and national law is that government authorities can enforce national law. What government, however, can enforce international law?

By definition, a *nation* is a sovereign entity—which means that there is no higher authority to which that nation must submit. If a nation violates an international law and persuasive tactics fail, other countries or international organizations have no recourse except to take coercive actions. Coercive actions might include economic sanctions, severance of diplomatic relations, boycotts, and, as a last resort, war against the violating nation.

■ **Example 11.1** Russia sent troops into the neighboring nation of Ukraine in 2014 and supported an election that allowed Crimea (part of Ukraine) to secede from Ukraine. Because Russia's actions violated Ukraine's independent sovereignty, the United States and the European Union imposed economic sanctions on Russia. Nevertheless, Russia continued to support military action in Eastern Ukraine. ■

In essence, international law attempts to reconcile each country's need to be the final authority over its own affairs with the desire of nations to benefit economically from trade and harmonious relations with one another. Sovereign nations can, and do, voluntarily agree to be governed in certain respects by international law, usually for the purpose of facilitating international trade and commerce. As a result, a body of international law has evolved.

11–1a Sources of International Law

Basically, there are three sources of international law: international customs, treaties and international agreements, and international organizations. We look at each of these sources here.

International Customs One important source of international law consists of the international customs that have evolved among nations in their relations with one another. Article 38(1) of the Statute of the International Court of Justice refers to an international custom as "evidence of a general practice accepted as law." The legal principles and doctrines that you will read about shortly are rooted in international customs and traditions that have evolved over time in the international arena.

Treaties and International Agreements Treaties and other explicit agreements between or among foreign nations provide another important source of international law. A **treaty** is an agreement or contract between two or more nations that must be authorized and ratified by the supreme power of each nation. Under Article II, Section 2, of the U.S. Constitution, the president has the power "by and with the Advice and Consent of the Senate, to make Treaties, provided two-thirds of the Senators present concur."

A *bilateral* agreement, as the term implies, is an agreement formed by two nations to govern their commercial exchanges or other relations with one another. A *multilateral* agreement is formed by several nations. For instance, regional trade associations such as the Andean Community, the Association of Southeast Asian Nations, and the European Union are the result of multilateral trade agreements.

International Organizations The term **international organization** generally refers to an organization composed mainly of officials of member nations and usually established by treaty. The United States is a member of more than one hundred multilateral and bilateral organizations, including at least twenty through the United Nations.

Adopt Resolutions. International organizations adopt resolutions, declarations, and other types of standards that often require nations to behave in a particular manner. The General Assembly of the United Nations, for instance, has adopted numerous nonbinding resolutions and declarations that embody principles of international law. Disputes with respect to these resolutions and declarations may be brought before the International Court of Justice. That court, however, normally has authority to settle legal disputes only when nations voluntarily submit to its jurisdiction.

Create Uniform Rules. The United Nations Commission on International Trade Law has made considerable progress in establishing uniformity in international law as it relates to trade and commerce. One of the commission's most significant creations to date is the 1980 Convention on Contracts for the International Sale of Goods (CISG).

The CISG is similar to Article 2 of the Uniform Commercial Code in that it is designed to settle disputes between parties to sales contracts. It spells out the duties of international buyers and sellers that will apply if the parties have not agreed otherwise in their contracts. The CISG governs only sales contracts between trading partners in nations that have ratified the CISG.

11–1b Common Law and Civil Law Systems

Companies operating in foreign nations are subject not only to international agreements but also to the laws of the nations in which they operate. In addition, international disputes are often resolved through the court systems of individual nations. Therefore, businesspersons should have some familiarity with these nations' legal systems.

Generally, legal systems around the globe are divided into *common law* and *civil law* systems. Exhibit 11–1 lists some of the nations that use common law systems and some that use civil law systems.

Common Law Systems Recall that in a common law system, such as the United States, the courts independently develop the rules governing certain areas of law, such as torts and contracts. These common law rules apply to all areas not covered by statutory law. Although the common law doctrine of *stare decisis* obligates judges to follow precedential decisions in their jurisdictions, courts may modify or even overturn precedents when deemed necessary.

Civil Law Systems In contrast to common law countries, most European nations, as well as nations in Latin America, Africa, and Asia, base their legal systems on Roman civil law, or "code law." The term *civil law*, as used here, refers not to civil as opposed to criminal law but to *codified* law—an ordered grouping of legal principles enacted into law by a legislature or other governing body.

In a **civil law system**, the primary source of law is a statutory code. Courts interpret the code and apply the rules to individual cases, but courts may not depart from the code and develop their own laws. Judicial precedents are not binding, as they are in a common law system. In theory, the law code sets forth all of the principles needed for the legal system. Trial procedures also differ in civil law systems. Unlike judges in common law systems, judges in civil systems often actively question witnesses.

Islamic Legal Systems A third, less prevalent, legal system is common in Islamic countries, where the law is often influenced by *sharia*, the religious law of Islam. *Sharia* is a comprehensive code of principles that governs both the public and the private lives of persons of the

Exhibit 11–1 The Legal Systems of Selected Nations

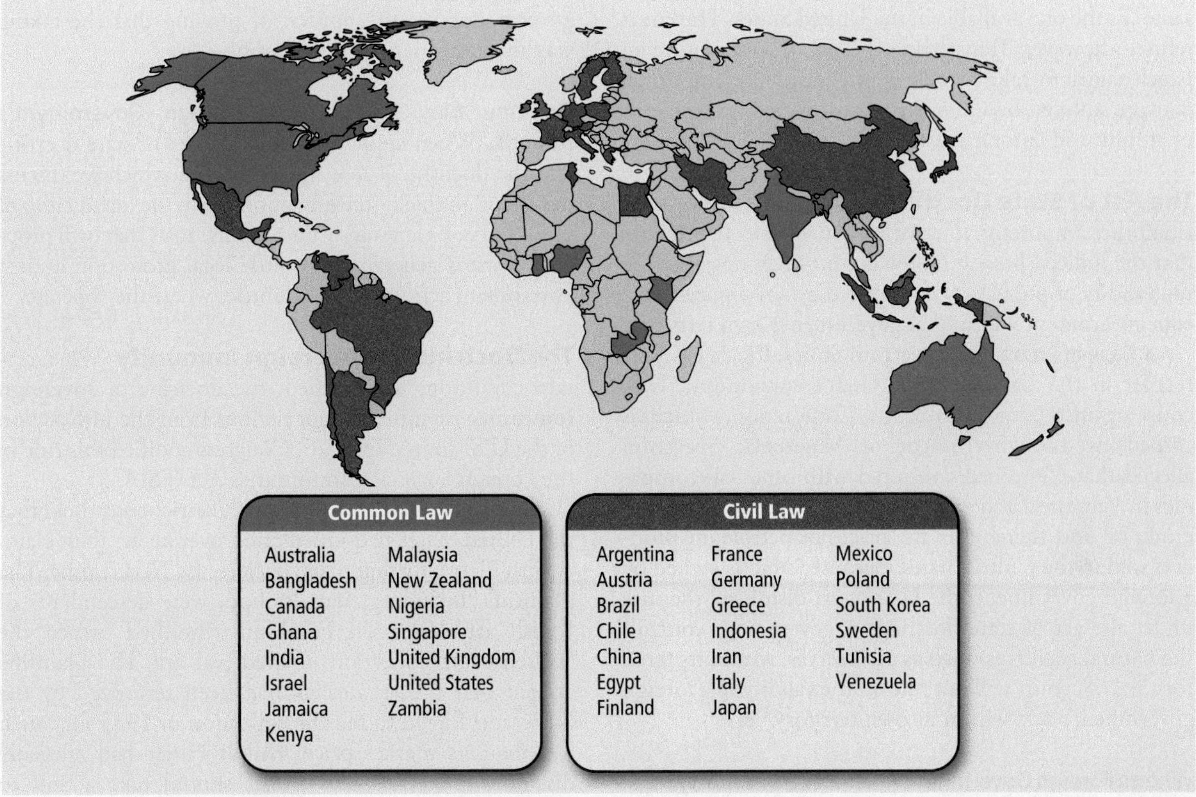

Common Law		Civil Law		
Australia	Malaysia	Argentina	France	Mexico
Bangladesh	New Zealand	Austria	Germany	Poland
Canada	Nigeria	Brazil	Greece	South Korea
Ghana	Singapore	Chile	Indonesia	Sweden
India	United Kingdom	China	Iran	Tunisia
Israel	United States	Egypt	Italy	Venezuela
Jamaica	Zambia	Finland	Japan	
Kenya				

Islamic faith. *Sharia* directs many aspects of day-to-day life, including politics, economics, banking, business law, contract law, and social issues.

Although *sharia* affects the legal codes of many Muslim countries, the extent of its impact, as well as its interpretation, vary widely. In some Middle Eastern nations, aspects of *sharia* have been codified and are enforced by national judicial systems.

11–1c International Principles and Doctrines

Over time, a number of legal principles and doctrines have evolved in the international context. These principles and doctrines are employed—to a greater or lesser extent—by the courts of various nations to resolve or reduce conflicts that involve a foreign element. The three important legal principles discussed next are based primarily on courtesy and respect, and are applied in the interests of maintaining harmonious relations among nations.

The Principle of Comity The principle of **comity** basically refers to legal reciprocity. One nation will defer and give effect to the executive, legislative, and judicial acts of another country, as long as the acts are consistent with the law and public policy of the accommodating nation. For instance, a U.S. court ordinarily will recognize and enforce a default judgment from an Australian court because the legal procedures in Australia are compatible with those in the United States. Nearly all nations recognize the validity of marriage decrees (at least, those between a man and a woman) issued in another country.

■ **Case in Point 11.2** Karen Goldberg's husband was killed in a terrorist bombing in Israel. She filed a lawsuit in a federal court in New York against UBS AG, a Switzerland-based global financial services company with many offices in the United States. Goldberg claimed that UBS was liable under the U.S. Anti-Terrorism Act for aiding and abetting in the murder of her husband. She argued that UBS was liable because it provided financial services to the international terrorist organizations responsible for his murder.

UBS requested that the case be transferred to a court in Israel, which would offer a remedy "substantially the same" as the one available in the United States. The court refused, however. Transferring the case would require an Israeli court to take evidence and judge the emotional damage suffered by Goldberg, "raising distinct concerns of comity and enforceability."[1] ■

The Act of State Doctrine

The **act of state doctrine** is another important international doctrine. It provides that the judicial branch of one country will not examine the validity of public acts committed by a recognized foreign government within that government's own territory.

■ **Case in Point 11.3** Spectrum Stores, Inc., a gasoline retailer in the United States, filed a lawsuit in a U.S. court against Citgo Petroleum Corporation, which is owned by the government of Venezuela. Spectrum alleged that Citgo had conspired with other oil companies in Venezuela and Saudi Arabia to limit production of crude oil and thereby fix the prices of petroleum products sold in the United States. Because Citgo is owned by a foreign government, the U.S. court dismissed the case under the act of state doctrine. A government controls the natural resources, such as oil reserves, within its territory. A U.S. court will not rule on the validity of a foreign government's acts within its own territory.[2] ■

When a Foreign Government Takes Private Property. The act of state doctrine can have important consequences for individuals and firms doing business with, and investing in, other countries. This doctrine is frequently employed in cases involving expropriation or confiscation.

Expropriation occurs when a government seizes a privately owned business or privately owned goods for a proper public purpose and awards just compensation. When a government seizes private property for an illegal purpose and without just compensation, the taking is referred to as a **confiscation.** The line between these two forms of taking is sometimes blurred because of differing interpretations of what is illegal and what constitutes just compensation.

■ **Example 11.4** Flaherty, Inc., a U.S. company, owns a mine in Brazil. The government of Brazil seizes the mine for public use and claims that the profits Flaherty has already realized from the mine constitute just compensation. Flaherty disagrees, but the act of state doctrine may prevent the company's recovery in a U.S. court. ■

Note that in a case alleging that a foreign government has wrongfully taken the plaintiff's property, the defendant government has the burden of proving that the taking was an expropriation, not a confiscation.

Doctrine May Immunize a Foreign Government's Actions. When applicable, both the act of state doctrine and the doctrine of *sovereign immunity*, which we discuss next, tend to shield foreign nations from the jurisdiction of U.S. courts. As a result, firms or individuals that own property overseas generally have little legal protection against government actions in the countries where they operate.

The Doctrine of Sovereign Immunity

When certain conditions are satisfied, the doctrine of **sovereign immunity** exempts foreign nations from the jurisdiction of the U.S. courts. In 1976, Congress codified this rule in the Foreign Sovereign Immunities Act (FSIA).[3]

■ **Case in Point 11.5** A federal district court held that the United States had jurisdiction over an art theft claim against Germany that dated back to the Nazi regime. The plaintiffs, including Alan Philipp, were descendants of Jewish art dealers in Frankfurt who had owned the Welfenschatz collection of medieval art. The plaintiffs argued that the art dealers had been terrorized by the Nazis and forced to sell the collection in 1935 for much less than its market price. (Adolf Hitler had allegedly discussed in letters how Nazis should take action to "save the Welfenschatz.") Germany claimed immunity under the FSIA, but the federal judge disagreed. The court was convinced by the plaintiffs that Germany was not entitled to sovereign immunity in this case.[4] ■

The FSIA exclusively governs the circumstances in which an action may be brought in the United States against a foreign nation, including attempts to attach a foreign nation's property. Because the law is jurisdictional in nature, a plaintiff generally has the burden of showing that a defendant is not entitled to sovereign immunity.

When a Foreign State Will Not Be Immune. Section 1605 of the FSIA sets forth the major exceptions to the jurisdictional immunity of a foreign state. A foreign state is not immune from the jurisdiction of U.S. courts in the following situations:

1. When the foreign state has waived its immunity either explicitly or by implication.
2. When the foreign state has engaged in commercial activity within the United States or in commercial activity

---

1. *Goldberg v. UBS AG*, 690 F.Supp.2d 92 (E.D.N.Y. 2010). For another case on the financing of terrorism and the Anti-Terrorism Act, see *Linde v. Arab Bank, PLC*, 706 F.3d 92 (2d Cir. 2013).
2. *Spectrum Stores, Inc. v. Citgo Petroleum Corp.*, 632 F.3d 938 (5th Cir. 2011).

3. 28 U.S.C. Sections 1602–1611.
4. *Philipp v. Federal Republic of Germany*, 248 F.Supp.3d 59 (D.D.C. 2017).

outside the United States that has "a direct effect in the United States."

3. When the foreign state has committed a tort in the United States or has violated certain international laws.

4. When a foreign state that has been designated "a state sponsor of terrorism" is sued under the FSIA for "personal injury or death that was caused by an act of torture" or a related act of terrorism.

The following case involved an action against the property of a foreign state that had been held liable for the results of acts of terrorism. At issue was whether the property was immune from the action.

Case 11.1

Rubin v. Islamic Republic of Iran

Supreme Court of the United States, __ U.S. __, 138 S.Ct. 816, __ L.Ed.2d __ (2018).

Background and Facts Hamas, a terrorist organization sponsored by the Islamic Republic of Iran, carried out three suicide bombings in Jerusalem, causing the deaths of five people and injuring nearly two hundred others. Jenny Rubin and other U.S. citizens who were injured or related to those injured obtained a judgment under Section 1605A of the Foreign Sovereign Immunities Act (FSIA) against Iran for $71.5 million in damages.

To collect on the judgment, the plaintiffs sued Iran in a federal district court under Section 1610(g) of the FSIA. The plaintiffs sought to attach and execute against a collection of ancient art owned by Iran that was being housed at the University of Chicago. Attachment and execution is the legal process of seizing property to ensure payment of a debt. The property of a foreign sovereign is typically immune to attachment and execution, and the court explained that Section 1610(g), in and of itself, provided no basis for bypassing this immunity. The court ruled in the defendant's favor, and the plaintiffs appealed. The U.S. Court of Appeals for the Seventh Circuit affirmed. The plaintiffs then petitioned the United States Supreme Court.

In the Language of the Court

Justice *SOTOMAYOR* delivered the opinion of the Court.

* * * *

* * * Section 1610(g) provides: * * * "The property of a foreign state against which a judgment is entered under Section 1605A * * * is subject to attachment in aid of execution, and execution, upon that judgment as provided in this section."

* * * The issue at hand is whether Section 1610(g) * * * allows a Section 1605A judgment holder to attach and execute against *any* property of the foreign state.

* * * *

* * * The most natural reading is that "this section" refers to Section 1610 as a whole, so that Section 1610(g) will govern the attachment and execution of property that is exempted from the grant of immunity as provided elsewhere in Section 1610.

Other provisions of Section 1610 unambiguously revoke the immunity of property of a foreign state, including specifically where a plaintiff holds a judgment under Section 1605A, provided certain express conditions are satisfied. For example, [Section 1610(a)] provides that "property in the United States * * * used for a commercial activity in the United States * * * shall not be immune" from attachment and execution in seven enumerated circumstances * * * . [Section 1610(b), (d), (e), and (f)] similarly set out circumstances in which certain property of a foreign state "shall not be immune."

Section 1610(g) conspicuously lacks the textual markers, "shall not be immune" or "notwithstanding any other provision of law," that would have shown that it serves as an independent avenue for abrogation [abolition] *of immunity.* In fact, its use of the phrase "as provided in this section" signals the opposite: A judgment holder seeking to take advantage of Section 1610(g) must identify a basis under one of Section 1610's express immunity-abrogating provisions to attach and execute against a relevant property. [Emphasis added.]

* * * *

Case 11.1 Continues

Throughout the FSIA, special avenues of relief to victims of terrorism exist * * * . Where the FSIA goes so far as to divest a foreign state or property of immunity in relation to terrorism-related judgments, however, it does so expressly. Out of respect for the delicate balance that Congress struck in enacting the FSIA, we decline to read into the statute a blanket abrogation of attachment and execution immunity for Section 1605A judgment holders absent a clearer indication of Congress's intent.

Decision and Remedy *The United States Supreme Court concluded that Section 1610(g) does not provide "a freestanding basis for parties holding a judgment under Section 1605A to attach and execute against the property of a foreign state, where the immunity of the property is not otherwise rescinded under a separate provision within Section 1610." The Court affirmed the judgment of the federal appellate court.*

Critical Thinking
- **Legal Environment** *Is the Court's interpretation of Section 1610(g) consistent with the purpose of the FSIA? Explain.*
- **Economic** *What practical lesson might be learned from the decision and result in the* Rubin *case? Discuss.*

Application of the Act. When courts apply the FSIA, questions frequently arise as to whether an entity is a "foreign state" and what constitutes a "commercial activity." Under Section 1603 of the FSIA, a *foreign state* includes both a political subdivision of a foreign state and an instrumentality of a foreign state. An *instrumentality* includes any department or agency of any branch of a government.

Section 1603 broadly defines a *commercial activity* as a regular course of commercial conduct, a transaction, or an act that is carried out by a foreign state within the United States. Section 1603, however, does not describe the particulars of what constitutes a commercial activity. Thus, the courts are left to decide whether a particular activity is governmental or commercial in nature.

See Exhibit 11–2 for a graphic illustration of the three principles of international law just discussed.

Exhibit 11–2 Examples of International Principles and Doctrines

The Principle of Comity	The Act of State Doctrine	The Doctrine of Sovereign Immunity
Nations will defer to and give effect to the laws and judicial decrees of other nations when those laws are consistent with their own.	U.S. courts will avoid passing judgment on the validity of public acts committed by a recognized foreign government within its own territory.	Foreign nations are immune from U.S. jurisdiction under the Foreign Sovereign Immunities Act when certain circumstances are satisfied. Some major exceptions apply, however.
Example: A U.S. court will most likely uphold the validity of a contract created in England, because England's legal procedures are compatible with those of the United States.	*Example:* A U.S. gas company files a lawsuit against a Saudi Arabian petroleum company, claiming a price-fixing conspiracy. A U.S. court will dismiss the case under the act of state doctrine because Saudi Arabia controls its own natural resources.	*Example:* A German governmental agency engages in commercial activity in New York. If a party in New York files a lawsuit against the agency, the foreign state is not immune from U.S. jurisdiction.

11–2 Doing Business Internationally

A U.S. domestic firm can engage in international business transactions in a number of ways. The simplest way is for U.S. firms to **export** their goods and services to foreign markets. Alternatively, a U.S. firm can establish foreign production facilities to be closer to the foreign market or markets in which its products are sold. The advantages may include lower labor costs, fewer government regulations, and lower taxes and trade barriers. A domestic firm can also obtain revenues by licensing its technology to an existing foreign company or by selling franchises to overseas entities. (In some situations, domestic companies have profited by marketing goods, such as beer, as "imported" when they are not, as discussed in this chapter's *Ethics Today* feature.)

11–2a Exporting

Exporting can take two forms: direct exporting and indirect exporting. Companies that export indirectly can make use of agency relationships or distributorships.

Direct versus Indirect Exporting In *direct exporting*, a U.S. company signs a sales contract with a foreign purchaser that provides for the conditions of shipment and payment for the goods.

If sufficient business develops in a foreign country, a U.S. company may establish a specialized marketing organization there by appointing a foreign agent or a foreign distributor. This is called *indirect exporting.*

Agency Relationships versus Distributorships When a U.S. firm engaged in indirect exporting wishes to limit its involvement in an international market, it will typically establish an *agency relationship* with a foreign firm. The foreign firm then acts as the U.S. firm's agent and can enter contracts in the foreign location on behalf of the principal (the U.S. company).

When a foreign country represents a substantial market, a U.S. firm may wish to appoint a distributor located in that country. The U.S. firm and the distributor enter into a **distribution agreement**. This is a contract setting out the terms and conditions of the distributorship, such as price, currency of payment, guarantee of supply availability, and method of payment. Disputes concerning distribution agreements may involve jurisdictional or other issues, as well as contract law.

11–2b Manufacturing Abroad

An alternative to direct or indirect exporting is the establishment of foreign manufacturing facilities. Typically, U.S. firms establish manufacturing plants abroad when they believe that by doing so they will reduce costs. Costs for labor, shipping, and raw materials may be lower in foreign nations, which can enable the business to compete more effectively in foreign markets.

Foreign firms have done the same in the United States. Sony, Nissan, and other Japanese manufacturers, for instance, have established U.S. plants to avoid import duties that the U.S. Congress may impose on Japanese products entering this country.

There are several ways in which an American firm can manufacture in other countries. They include licensing and franchising, as well as investing in a wholly owned subsidiary or a joint venture.

Licensing A U.S. firm may license a foreign manufacturing company to use its copyrighted, patented, or trademarked intellectual property or trade secrets. Basically, licensing allows the foreign firm to use an established brand name for a fee. A licensing agreement with a foreign-based firm is much the same as any other licensing agreement. Its terms require a payment of royalties on some basis—such as so many cents per unit produced or a certain percentage of profits from units sold in a particular geographic territory.

■ **Example 11.6** The Coca-Cola Bottling Company licenses firms worldwide to use (and keep confidential) its secret formula for the syrup in its soft drink. In return, the company receives a percentage of the income earned from the sale of Coca-Cola by those firms. ■

The firm that receives the license can take advantage of an established reputation for quality. The firm that grants the license receives income from the foreign sales of its products and also establishes a global reputation. Once a firm's trademark is known worldwide, the demand for other products manufactured or sold by that firm may increase—obviously, an important consideration.

Franchising Franchising is a well-known form of licensing worldwide. The owner of a trademark, trade name, or copyright (the franchisor) licenses another (the franchisee) to use the mark, name, or copyright, under certain conditions, in the selling of goods or services. Franchising allows the franchisor to maintain greater control over the business operation than is possible with most other licensing agreements. In return, the franchisee pays a fee, usually based on a monthly percentage of gross or net sales. Examples of international franchises include Holiday Inn and Hertz.

Wholly Owned Subsidiaries Another way to expand into a foreign market is to establish a wholly owned subsidiary firm in a foreign country. In many European countries, a subsidiary would likely take the form of a *société anonyme* (S.A.), which is similar to a U.S. corporation. In German-speaking nations, it would be called an *aktiengesellschaft* (A.G.). When a wholly owned subsidiary is established, the parent company remains in the United States. The parent maintains complete ownership of all of the facilities in the foreign country, as well as total authority and control over all phases of the operation.

Joint Ventures A U.S. firm can also expand into international markets through a *joint venture.* In a joint venture, the U.S. company owns only part of the operation. The rest is owned either by local owners in the foreign country or by another foreign entity. All of the firms involved in a joint venture share responsibilities, as well as profits and liabilities.

11–3 Regulation of Specific Business Activities

International business relationships can affect the economies, foreign policies, domestic politics, and other national interests of the countries involved. For this reason, nations impose laws to restrict or facilitate international business. Controls may also be imposed by international agreements.

11–3a Investment Protections

Firms that invest in foreign nations face the risk that the foreign government may expropriate the investment property. Expropriation, as mentioned earlier, occurs when property is taken and the owner is paid just compensation. This practice generally does not violate accepted principles of international law.

Confiscating property without compensation (or without adequate compensation), in contrast, normally violates international law. Few remedies are available for confiscation of property by a foreign government. Claims are often resolved by lump-sum settlements after negotiations between the United States and the taking nation.

Because the possibility of confiscation may deter potential investors, many countries guarantee compensation to foreign investors if their property is taken. A guaranty can be in the form of national constitutional or statutory laws or provisions in international treaties. As further protection for foreign investments, some countries provide insurance for their citizens' investments abroad.

11–3b Export Controls

Article I, Section 9, of the U.S. Constitution provides that "No Tax or Duty shall be laid on Articles exported from any State." Thus, Congress cannot impose any export taxes.

Congress can, however, use a variety of other devices to restrict or encourage exports, including the following:

1. *Export quotas.* Congress sets export **quotas,** or limits, on various items, such as grain being sold abroad.
2. *Restrictions on technology exports.* Under the Export Administration Act,[5] the flow of technologically advanced products and technical data can be restricted.
3. *Incentives and subsidies.* The United States (along with other nations) also uses incentives and subsidies

to stimulate exports and thereby aid domestic businesses. ■ **Example 11.7** The Export Trading Company Act[6] encourages U.S. banks to invest in export trading companies, which are formed when exporting firms join together to export a line of goods. The Export-Import Bank of the United States provides financial assistance, primarily in the form of credit guaranties given to commercial banks, which in turn lend funds to U.S. exporting companies. ■

11–3c Import Controls

All nations have restrictions on imports, and the United States is no exception. Restrictions include strict prohibitions, quotas, and tariffs (including antidumping duties).

Prohibitions Under the Trading with the Enemy Act,[7] no goods may be imported from nations that have been designated enemies of the United States. Other laws prohibit the importation of illegal drugs, of agricultural products that pose dangers to domestic crops or animals, and of goods that infringe on U.S. patents. The International Trade Commission is the government agency that investigates allegations that imported goods infringe U.S. patents and imposes penalties if necessary.

Quotas and Tariffs Limits on the amounts of goods that can be imported are known as import quotas. At one time, the United States had legal quotas on the number of automobiles that could be imported from Japan. Today, Japan "voluntarily" restricts the number of automobiles exported to the United States.

Tariffs are taxes on imports. A tariff is usually a percentage of the value of the import, but it can be a flat rate per unit (such as per barrel of oil). Tariffs raise the prices of imported goods, causing some consumers to purchase domestically manufactured goods instead of imports.

Antidumping Duties The United States has laws specifically directed at what it sees as unfair international trade practices. **Dumping,** for instance, is the sale of imported goods at "less than fair value." Foreign firms that engage in dumping in the United States hope to undersell U.S. businesses and obtain a larger share of the U.S. market. To prevent this, an extra tariff—known as an *antidumping duty*—may be assessed on the imports.

Two U.S. government agencies are instrumental in imposing antidumping duties: the International Trade

---

5. 50 U.S.C. Sections 2401–2420.

6. 15 U.S.C. Sections 4001, 4003.
7. 50 U.S.C. Section 4303 *et seq.*

Commission (ITC) and the International Trade Administration (ITA). The ITC assesses the effects of dumping on domestic businesses and then makes recommendations to the president concerning temporary import restrictions. The ITA, which is part of the Department of Commerce, decides whether imports were sold at less than fair value.

Fair value is usually determined by the domestic price of the goods in the exporting country. The ITA's determination of fair value establishes the amount of the antidumping duties. These duties are set to equal the difference between the price charged in the United States and the price charged in the exporting country. A duty may be retroactive to cover past dumping.

In the following case, a Chinese producer challenged the ITC's determination that the import of its products into the United States materially injured the domestic industry.

Case 11.2

Changzhou Trina Solar Energy Co., Ltd. v. United States International Trade Commission

United States Court of Appeals, Federal Circuit, 879 F.3d 1377 (2018).

Background and Facts Changzhou Trina Solar Energy Company, a Chinese firm, makes crystalline silicon photovoltaic (CSPV) cells and related products. Trina Solar (U.S.), Inc., imported Changzhou's CSPV products into the United States. The U.S. Department of Commerce found that the imports were subsidized by the Chinese government and sold in the United States at less than fair value. The International Trade Commission (ITC) determined that the domestic CSPV industry was materially injured by the imports from China. Changzhou and Trina challenged this determination in the U.S. Court of International Trade. The court rejected the challenge and sustained the ITC's determination. Changzhou and Trina appealed this decision to the U.S. Court of Appeals for the Federal Circuit.

In the Language of the Court

TARANTO, Circuit Judge.
* * * *

In this case, [Changzhou and Trina] * * * argue * * * that the Commission failed to make findings, supported by substantial evidence, that the domestic industry would have been materially better off * * * if the subject imports had not been introduced into the market.
* * * *

[Changzhou and Trina] argue that * * * the domestic industry would have been materially as badly off * * * even had there been no unfairly priced and subsidized subject imports. * * * *The question is whether the Commission found, with adequate reasons and substantial-evidence support, that the difference between the state of the domestic industry as it actually was * * * and the state of the domestic industry as it would have been without the subject imports was more than inconsequential, immaterial, or unimportant.* [Emphasis added.]
* * * The Commission's summary * * * rested on detailed findings about demand conditions and the business cycle in the domestic market, the roles of conventional and renewable sources of electricity, government incentives and regulations at federal, state, and local levels, domestic consumption trends, market segments, who was supplying the domestic market, what happened to prices and market shares * * * , and the ways in which the domestic industry's financial performance was very poor and deteriorating. The findings rested on various types of evidence, including the answers to questionnaires addressed to market participants such as purchasers.
* * * *

* * * The Commission recognized "there may have been additional factors exerting downward pricing pressure on CSPV products," but it found "that subject imports were a significant cause of the decline in prices.

" * * * In sum, the significant and growing volume of low-priced subject imports from China competed directly with the domestic like product, was sold in the same channels of distribution to the same segments of the U.S. market, and undersold the domestic like product at significant margins, causing domestic producers to lose revenue and market share and leading to significant depression and suppression of the domestic industry's prices."

Decision and Remedy *The U.S. Court of Appeals for the Federal Circuit affirmed the decision of the lower court. The reviewing court agreed that the imposition of antidumping duties was appropriate because the ITC's explanation for the determination that the imported products unfairly impacted the domestic industry relied on concrete evidence.*

Critical Thinking
- **Economic** *How does the* Changzhou *case illustrate that dumping is an unfair international trade practice? Discuss.*
- **What If the Facts Were Different?** *Suppose that the ITC had not issued detailed findings supported by a variety of evidence, but had only released a statement that the subject imports seemed to have a negative effect on the domestic industry. Would the result have been different? Explain.*

11–3d Minimizing Trade Barriers

Restrictions on imports are also known as *trade barriers.* The elimination of trade barriers is sometimes seen as essential to the world's economic well-being. Various regional trade agreements and associations also help to minimize trade barriers between nations.

The World Trade Organization Most of the world's leading trading nations are members of the World Trade Organization (WTO). To minimize trade barriers among nations, each member country is required to grant **normal trade relations (NTR) status** to other member countries. This means that each member must treat other members at least as well as it treats the country that receives its most favorable treatment with regard to imports or exports.

The European Union (EU) The European Union (EU) arose out of the 1957 Treaty of Rome. The treaty created the Common Market, a free trade zone comprising the nations of Belgium, France, Italy, Luxembourg, the Netherlands, and West Germany. Today, the EU is a single integrated trading unit made up of a number of European nations.

The EU has gone a long way toward creating a new body of law to govern all of the member nations. Its governing authorities issue regulations, or directives, that define EU law in various areas, such as environmental law, product liability, anticompetitive practices, and corporations. The directives normally are binding on all member countries. Nevertheless, some of the EU's efforts to create uniform laws have been confounded by nationalism. For instance, in 2016 Great Britain voted to withdraw from the EU—an event known as "Brexit."

The United States–Mexico–Canada Agreement (USMCA) The United States–Mexico–Canada Agreement (USMCA) was formerly known as the North American Free Trade Agreement (NAFTA). NAFTA created a regional trading unit consisting of Canada, Mexico, and the United States. The goal was to eliminate tariffs among these three nations on substantially all goods by reducing the tariffs incrementally over a period of time. NAFTA gave the three countries a competitive advantage by retaining tariffs on goods imported from countries outside the NAFTA trading unit. It also eliminated barriers that prevented the cross-border movement of services, such as financial and transportation services.

Despite these benefits, U.S. critics pointed to weaknesses in NAFTA, including a trade deficit between the United States and Mexico that favored Mexico. In an effort to address these problems, the administration of President Donald Trump convinced Canada and Mexico to renegotiate NAFTA, which was renamed the USMCA. The new agreement altered NAFTA's provisions in several ways, including the following:

1. Automakers can qualify for zero tariffs if they manufacture at least 75 percent of their cars' components in Canada, Mexico, and the United States (up from 62 percent under NAFTA). In addition, 70 percent of the steel and aluminum used in vehicles must come from the United States, Canada, and Mexico.
2. Eventually, 40 percent of vehicle production must be performed by workers earning an average wage of at least $16 per hour (equivalent to about three times the pay of the average Mexican autoworker at the time of the agreement).
3. Canada will ease its restrictions and open its dairy market to U.S. farmers, allowing American farmers to export about $560 million worth of dairy products.
4. The USMCA provides more protection for intellectual property rights than NAFTA did and allows law

enforcement to stop suspected counterfeit or pirated goods in any of the three countries.[8]

5. U.S. drug companies can sell products in Canada for ten years before facing competition from generics. (It was eight years under NAFTA.)

Trade disputes will continue to be decided by a panel of representatives from all three nations. The USMCA will be reviewed every six years starting in 2026. It could expire in 2036 or be extended until 2052.

The Central America–Dominican Republic–United States Free Trade Agreement (CAFTA-DR)

The Central America–Dominican Republic–United States Free Trade Agreement (CAFTA-DR) was formed by Costa Rica, the Dominican Republic, El Salvador, Guatemala, Honduras, Nicaragua, and the United States. Its purpose is to reduce trade tariffs and improve market access among all of the signatory nations. Legislatures from all seven countries have approved the CAFTA-DR, despite significant opposition in certain nations.

The Republic of Korea–United States Free Trade Agreement (KORUS FTA)

The Republic of Korea–United States Free Trade Agreement (KORUS FTA) was aimed at eliminating 95 percent of each nation's tariffs on industrial and consumer exports from the other nation. KORUS was expected to boost U.S. exports and benefit U.S. automakers, farmers, ranchers, and manufacturers by enabling them to compete in new markets. To date, however, exports have not increased as much as predicted.

Other Free Trade Agreements

Congress has also ratified free trade agreements with Colombia and Panama. The Colombian trade agreement includes a provision requiring an exchange of tax information, and the Panama bill incorporates assurances on labor rights.

11–4 International Dispute Resolution

Contractual disputes arise in international business relationships, just as they do in domestic ones. International contracts often include terms to indicate how disputes will be resolved.

11–4a The New York Convention

International contracts frequently include arbitration clauses. By means of such clauses, the parties agree in advance to be bound by the decision of a specified third party in the event of a dispute.

The United Nations Convention on the Recognition and Enforcement of Foreign Arbitral Awards (often referred to as the New York Convention) assists in the enforcement of arbitration clauses. (Specific treaties among nations may also include such provisions.) Basically, the convention requires courts in nations that have signed it to honor private agreements to arbitrate and recognize arbitration awards made in other contracting states. The New York Convention has been implemented in nearly one hundred countries, including the United States.

Under the New York Convention, a court will compel the parties to arbitrate their dispute if all of the following are true:

1. There is a written (or recorded) agreement to arbitrate the matter.
2. The agreement provides for arbitration in a convention signatory nation.
3. The agreement arises out of a commercial legal relationship.
4. One party to the agreement is not a U.S. citizen. In other words, both parties cannot be U.S. citizens.

■ **Case in Point 11.8** Juridica Investments, Ltd. (JIL), entered into a financing contract with S & T Oil Equipment & Machinery, Ltd., a U.S. company. The contract was signed and performed in Guernsey, which is a British Crown dependency in the English Channel. It included an arbitration clause. When a dispute arose between the parties, JIL initiated arbitration in Guernsey, and S & T filed a suit in a U.S. court. JIL filed a motion to dismiss in favor of arbitration, which the court granted. S & T appealed. A federal appellate court affirmed and compelled arbitration under the New York Convention.[9] ■

11–4b Effect of Choice-of-Law and Forum-Selection Clauses

If a sales contract does not include an arbitration clause, litigation may occur. When the contract contains forum-selection and choice-of-law clauses, the lawsuit will be heard by a court in the specified forum and decided according to that forum's law.

As you may recall, a *forum-selection clause* indicates what court, jurisdiction, or tribunal will decide any disputes arising under the contract. A *choice-of-law clause*

---

8. The USMCA's intellectual property protections essentially adopted many provisions from the Trans-Pacific Partnership, an agreement from which the Trump administration withdrew.

9. *S & T Oil Equipment & Machinery, Ltd. v. Juridica Investments, Ltd.*, 456 Fed.Appx. 481 (5th Cir. 2012).

designates the applicable law. Both are useful additions to international contracts.

11–5 U.S. Laws in a Global Context

The globalization of business raises questions about the extraterritorial application of a nation's laws—that is, the effect of the country's laws outside its boundaries. To what extent do U.S. domestic laws apply to other nations' businesses? To what extent do U.S. domestic laws apply to U.S. firms doing business abroad? Here, we discuss the extraterritorial application of certain U.S. laws, including antitrust laws, tort laws, and laws prohibiting employment discrimination.

11–5a U.S. Antitrust Laws

U.S. antitrust laws have a wide application. They may *subject* firms in foreign nations to their provisions, as well as *protect* foreign consumers and competitors from violations committed by U.S. citizens. Section 1 of the Sherman Act—the most important U.S. antitrust law—provides for the extraterritorial effect of the U.S. antitrust laws.

Any conspiracy that has a *substantial effect* on U.S. commerce is within the reach of the Sherman Act. The law applies even if the violation occurs outside the United States, and foreign governments as well as businesses can be sued for violations. Before U.S. courts will exercise jurisdiction and apply antitrust laws, however, it must be shown that the alleged violation had a substantial effect on U.S. commerce.

■ **Example 11.9** An investigation by the U.S. government revealed that a Tokyo-based auto-parts supplier, Furukawa Electric Company, and its executives had conspired with competitors in an international price-fixing agreement. The agreement lasted more than ten years and resulted in automobile manufacturers' paying noncompetitive, higher prices for parts in cars sold to U.S. consumers. Because the conspiracy had a substantial effect on U.S. commerce, the United States had jurisdiction to prosecute the case. Furukawa agreed to plead guilty and pay a $200 million fine. The Furukawa executives from Japan also agreed to serve up to eighteen months in a U.S. prison and to cooperate fully with the ongoing investigation. ■

11–5b International Tort Claims

The international application of tort liability is growing in significance and controversy. An increasing number of U.S. plaintiffs are suing foreign (or U.S.) entities for torts that these entities have allegedly committed overseas. Often, these cases involve human rights violations by foreign governments.

The Alien Tort Statute (ATS)[10] allows foreign citizens to bring civil suits in U.S. courts for injuries caused by violations of the law of nations or a treaty of the United States. As a result, foreign plaintiffs increasingly used this act to bring actions against companies operating in nations such as Colombia, Ecuador, Egypt, Guatemala, India, Indonesia, Nigeria, and Saudi Arabia. Critics argued that such suits extended the application of the ATS too far. The United States Supreme Court apparently agreed when it held that foreign corporations could no longer be defendants in suits brought under the ATS.[11]

In the following *Spotlight Case*, the United States Supreme Court considered the parameters of the ATS. The question was whether the statute allows U.S. courts to exercise jurisdiction over a cause of action based on conduct that occurred outside the United States.

---

10. 28 U.S.C. Section 1350.
11. *Jesner v. Arab Bank, PLC*, __ U.S. __, 138 S.Ct. 1396, 200 L.Ed.2d 612 (2018).

Spotlight on International Torts

Case 11.3 Daimler AG[a] v. Bauman
Supreme Court of the United States, 571 U.S. 117 , 134 S.Ct. 746 , 187 L.Ed.2d 624 (2014).

Background and Facts Barbara Bauman and twenty-one other residents of Argentina filed a suit in a federal district court in California against Daimler AG, a German company. They alleged that Mercedes-Benz (MB) Argentina, a subsidiary of Daimler, had collaborated with state security forces to kidnap, detain, torture, and kill certain MB Argentina workers. These workers included the plaintiffs and some of their relatives. Their claims were asserted under the Alien Tort Statute.

---

a. The initials *A.G.* stand for *aktiengesellschaft*, which is a similar to the U.S. corporate form of business in Germany, Austria, and Switzerland.

Case 11.3 Continues

Personal jurisdiction was based on the California contacts of Mercedes-Benz USA (MBUSA), a Daimler subsidiary incorporated in Delaware with its principal place of business in New Jersey. MBUSA distributes Daimler-made vehicles to dealerships throughout the United States, including California. The district court dismissed the suit for lack of jurisdiction. The U.S. Court of Appeals for the Ninth Circuit reversed this ruling. Daimler appealed to the United States Supreme Court.

In the Language of the Court
Justice *GINSBURG* delivered the opinion of the Court.
* * * *

Even if we were to assume that MBUSA is at home in California, and further to assume MBUSA's contacts are imputable [attributable] to Daimler, there would still be no basis to subject Daimler to general jurisdiction in California, for Daimler's slim contacts with the State hardly render it at home there.

* * * Only a limited set of affiliations with a forum will render a defendant amenable to all-purpose jurisdiction there. For an individual, the paradigm forum [the typical forum] for the exercise of general jurisdiction is the individual's domicile; for a corporation, it is an equivalent place, one in which the corporation is fairly regarded as at home. *With respect to a corporation, the place of incorporation and principal place of business are paradigm * * * bases for general jurisdiction.* Those affiliations have the virtue of being unique—that is, each ordinarily indicates only one place—as well as easily ascertainable. These bases afford plaintiffs recourse to at least one clear and certain forum in which a corporate defendant may be sued on any and all claims. [Emphasis added.]

[This does not mean] that a corporation may be subject to general jurisdiction *only* in a forum where it is incorporated or has its principal place of business * * * . [But] plaintiffs would have us look beyond the exemplar bases identified [above] and approve the exercise of general jurisdiction in every State in which a corporation engages in a substantial, continuous, and systematic course of business. That formulation, we hold, is unacceptably grasping.

* * * The inquiry * * * is not whether a foreign corporation's in-forum contacts can be said to be in some sense continuous and systematic; it is whether that corporation's affiliations with the State are so continuous and systematic as to render it essentially at home in the forum State.

Here, neither Daimler nor MBUSA is incorporated in California, nor does either entity have its principal place of business there. If Daimler's California activities sufficed to allow adjudication of this Argentina-rooted case in California, the same global reach would presumably be available in every other State in which MBUSA's sales are sizable. Such exorbitant exercises of all-purpose jurisdiction would scarcely permit out-of-state defendants to structure their primary conduct with some minimum assurance as to where that conduct will and will not render them liable to suit.

It was therefore [an] error for the Ninth Circuit to conclude that Daimler, even with MBUSA's contacts attributed to it, was at home in California, and hence subject to suit there on claims by foreign plaintiffs having nothing to do with anything that occurred or had its principal impact in California.

Decision and Remedy *The United States Supreme Court reversed the decision of the lower court. A federal district court in California could not exercise jurisdiction over Daimler in this case, given the absence of any California connection to the atrocities, perpetrators, or victims described in the complaint.*

Critical Thinking
- **Legal Environment** *What are the consequences for Daimler of the decision in this case?*
- **Global** *If the Court had adopted the plaintiffs' argument, how might U.S. citizens have been affected?*

11–5c Antidiscrimination Laws

As you probably know, federal laws in the United States prohibit discrimination on the basis of race, color, national origin, religion, sex, age, and disability. These laws, as they affect employment relationships, generally apply extraterritorially.

Thus, employees from the United States who are working abroad for U.S. employers are protected under the

Age Discrimination in Employment Act. Similarly, the Americans with Disabilities Act, which requires employers to accommodate the needs of workers with disabilities, applies to U.S. nationals working abroad for U.S. firms.

In addition, the major U.S. law regulating employment discrimination—Title VII of the Civil Rights Act—applies extraterritorially to all U.S. employees working for U.S. employers abroad. Generally, U.S. employers must abide by U.S. discrimination laws unless to do so would violate the laws of the country where their workplaces are located. This "foreign laws exception" allows employers to avoid being subjected to conflicting laws.

11-6 Space Law

Space law consists of the international and national laws that govern activities in outer space. For the first fifty years of space exploration, national governments conducted most of those activities. Thus, space law was directed primarily at governments and government activities. More recently, private companies have been preparing to undertake some space-related activities and open outer space to the rest of us. Space law, accordingly, faces new challenges.

11-6a International Space Law

International space law consists of international treaties—primarily negotiated by the United Nations (U.N.)—and U.N. resolutions. These sources recognize fundamentally that activities conducted in outer space and the benefits derived from those activities should improve the welfare of all nations and all humanity.

The major space law treaties were concluded by the U.N. Committee on the Peaceful Uses of Outer Space (COPUOS). COPUOS also administers the treaties and advises the international community on space policy matters.

Exploration and Exploitation The foundation of international space law is the U.N. Treaty on Principles Governing the Activities of States in the Exploration and Use of Outer Space, including the Moon and Other Celestial Bodies.[12] This treaty—generally referred to as the Outer Space Treaty—established the framework for later international agreements and U.N. resolutions.

The Outer Space Treaty expresses general principles that have been expanded and applied in subsequent treaties. In Article I and Article II, outer space is declared to

be free for the exploration and use of all nations. The moon, the planets, asteroids, and other celestial bodies are not subject to the appropriation of any single nation.[13] In addition, space objects are to be used exclusively for peaceful purposes. No weapons of mass destruction are permitted in outer space under Article IV.[14]

According to Article VI, each nation is responsible for its activities in outer space, whether they are conducted by the government or by a private entity. In fact, the activities of private entities require authorization and supervision by a government. Article VIII provides that each nation retains jurisdiction and control over its space objects and the personnel on them. Article VII imposes on each nation liability for damage caused by its space objects. Finally, Article IX requires that space exploration be conducted so as to avoid "harmful contamination."[15]

Astronauts and Space Objects The Outer Space Treaty was followed by several other agreements:

- The Agreement on the Rescue of Astronauts, the Return of Astronauts and the Return of Objects Launched into Outer Space (the Rescue Agreement).[16]
- The Convention on International Liability for Damage Caused by Space Objects (the Liability Convention).[17]
- The Convention on Registration of Objects Launched into Outer Space (the Registration Convention).[18]

The Rescue Agreement expands on Articles V and VIII of the Outer Space Treaty. It provides that each nation will undertake to rescue and assist astronauts in distress and return them to their "launching State." All nations are to assist in recovering space objects that return to earth outside the territory of the launching state.

The Liability Convention elaborates on Article VII of the Outer Space Treaty. This agreement provides that a launching state is absolutely liable for personal injury and property damage caused by its space objects on the surface of the earth or to aircraft in flight. Liability for injury or damage in space is subject to a determination of fault. The convention also prescribes procedures for the settlement of claims for damages.

The Registration Convention provides for the mandatory registration of objects launched into outer space. Each launching state is to maintain a registry of the

---

12. 18 U.S.T. 2410, T.I.A.S. 6347, 610 U.N.T.S. 205.

13. After the treaty entered into force, the United States and Russia conducted joint space activities.
14. Establishing military bases, testing weapons, and conducting military maneuvers are prohibited.
15. Other articles promote further international cooperation in the exploration and use of space.
16. 19 U.S.T. 7570, T.I.A.S. 6599, 672 U.N.T.S. 119.
17. 24 U.S.T. 2389, T.I.A.S. 7762, 961 U.N.T.S. 187.
18. 28 U.S.T. 695, T.I.A.S. 8480, 1023 U.N.T.S. 15.

objects that it launches into space. The intent is to assist in the objects' identification.

Space Debris An estimated 650,000 objects made by humans are in orbit around the earth. Most of these objects are no longer under any party's control and are classified as *space debris*. In 2009, two orbiting satellites collided for the first time, causing total destruction of both and generating a significant amount of space debris. Several other satellite collisions have occurred since then, with similar results. As noted previously, the Liability Convention sets out principles of liability to apply in instances of injury or damage in space.

The U.N. has endorsed guidelines to reduce space debris.[19] The guidelines, which reflect the practices of a number of national and international organizations, apply to the planning, design, manufacture, and operational phases of spacecraft. Among other points, the guidelines suggest that systems should be designed not to release debris during normal operations. They also recognize that some objects no longer in operation should be removed from orbit if this can be accomplished in a controlled manner.

11–6b U.S. Space Law

In the United States, each government agency that operates or authorizes spacecraft is responsible for complying with U.S. law and international treaties. Federal law, state law, and more than half a century of common practices in space-related industries also affect government and private space activities.

Commercial Spaceflight The Federal Aviation Administration (FAA) regulates private spaceports and the launch and reentry of private spacecraft under the Commercial Space Launch Act.[20]

The FAA is working to establish licensing and safety criteria for private spacecraft. Some states, including Florida, New Mexico, Texas, and Virginia, limit the

liability of space tourism providers under state tort law. But state legislatures and, ultimately, courts will need to consider other issues in this context, including insurance requirements and the enforceability of liability waivers.

In 2015, Congress enacted landmark legislation called the U.S. Commercial Space Launch Competitiveness Act.[21] The act, aimed at encouraging commercial spaceflight companies, streamlines regulatory processes and promotes safety standards. In addition, it provides that if a U.S. citizen or company retrieves minerals or other resources from an asteroid or other space location, that person or company owns them.

Exports of Space Technology Under U.S. regulations, all spacecraft are classified as "defense articles." The defense classification restricts the transfer of space technology and related information to any foreign person or nation under the U.S. Department of State's International Traffic in Arms Regulations.[22] This restriction makes it difficult for U.S. space companies to compete in global space markets.

Property Rights to Space Resources Article II of the Outer Space Treaty bans the national appropriation of territory in space. If the United States cannot appropriate territory in space, then it cannot give U.S. citizens title to property associated with this territory. Under U.S. law, the government must have sovereignty over territory before it can confer title to associated property to its citizens.

Article VIII, however, provides that a state party to the treaty retains jurisdiction over objects on its space registry that are launched into space. In addition, Article IX prohibits interference with space activities. In effect, these provisions confer the protections associated with property rights on private space activities.

The U.S. Commercial Space Launch Competitiveness Act changed the law somewhat by granting private citizens property rights over asteroid resources that they obtain from space. The act specifically recognizes that the United States is not attempting to assert sovereignty or exclusive right or jurisdiction over any celestial body.

---

19. Space Debris Mitigation Guidelines of the Committee on the Peaceful Uses of Outer Space, G.A. Res. 62/217, U.N. GAOR, 50th Sess., U.N.Doc. A/62/20 (Dec. 22, 2007).
20. 51 U.S.C. Sections 50901 *et seq.*

21. Pub. L. No. 114-90, 129 Stat. 704 (2015).
22. 22 C.F.R. Sections 120.1 *et seq.*

Practice and Review: International and Space Law

Robco, Inc., was a Florida arms dealer. The armed forces of Honduras contracted to purchase weapons from Robco over a six-year period. After the government was replaced and a democracy installed, the Honduran government sought to reduce the size of its military, and its relationship with Robco deteriorated. Honduras refused to honor the contract and purchase the inventory of arms, which Robco could sell only at a much lower price. Robco filed a suit in a federal district court in the United States to recover damages for this breach of contract by the government of Honduras. Using the information presented in the chapter, answer the following questions.

1. Should the Foreign Sovereign Immunities Act (FSIA) preclude this lawsuit? Why or why not?
2. Does the act of state doctrine bar Robco from seeking to enforce the contract? Explain.
3. Suppose that prior to this lawsuit, the new government of Honduras had enacted a law making it illegal to purchase weapons from foreign arms dealers. What doctrine of deference might lead a U.S. court to dismiss Robco's case in that situation?
4. Now suppose that the U.S. court hears the case and awards damages to Robco. The government of Honduras, however, has no assets in the United States that can be used to satisfy the judgment. Under which doctrine might Robco be able to collect the damages by asking another nation's court to enforce the U.S. judgment?

Debate This ... *The U.S. federal courts are accepting too many lawsuits initiated by foreigners that concern matters not relevant to this country.*

Terms and Concepts

act of state doctrine 214
civil law system 212
comity 213
confiscation 214
distribution agreement 218
dumping 219
export 217

expropriation 214
international law 211
international organization 212
national law 211
normal trade relations (NTR)
   status 221
quotas 219

sovereign immunity 214
space law 225
tariffs 219
treaty 212

Issue Spotters

1. Café Rojo, Ltd., an Ecuadoran firm, agrees to sell coffee beans to Dark Roast Coffee Company, a U.S. firm. Dark Roast accepts the beans but refuses to pay. Café Rojo sues Dark Roast in an Ecuadoran court and is awarded damages, but Dark Roast's assets are in the United States. Under what circumstances would a U.S. court enforce the judgment of the Ecuadoran court? (See *International Law*.)

2. Gems International, Ltd., is a foreign firm that has a 12 percent share of the U.S. market for diamonds. To capture a larger share, Gems offers its products at a below-cost discount to U.S. buyers (and inflates the prices in its own country to make up the difference). How can this attempt to undersell U.S. businesses be defeated? (See *Regulation of Specific Business Activities*.)

• **Check your answers to the Issue Spotters against the answers provided in Appendix B at the end of this text.**

Business Scenarios and Case Problems

11–1. Doing Business Internationally. Macrotech, Inc., develops an innovative computer chip and obtains a patent on it. The firm markets the chip under the trademarked brand name "Flash." Macrotech wants to sell the chip to Nitron, Ltd., in Pacifica, a foreign country. Macrotech is concerned, however, that after an initial purchase, Nitron will duplicate the chip, pirate it, and sell the pirated version to computer manufacturers in Pacifica. To avoid this possibility, Macrotech could establish its own manufacturing facility in Pacifica, but it does not want to do this. How can Macrotech, without establishing a manufacturing facility in Pacifica, protect Flash from being pirated by Nitron? (See *Doing Business Internationally*.)

11–2. Dumping. The U.S. pineapple industry alleged that producers of canned pineapple from the Philippines were selling their canned pineapple in the United States for less than its fair market value (dumping). In addition to canned pineapple, the Philippine producers exported other products, such as pineapple juice and juice concentrate. These products used separate parts of the same fresh pineapple used for the canned pineapple. All these products shared raw material costs with the canned fruit, according to the producers' own financial records. To determine fair value and antidumping duties, the pineapple industry argued that a court should calculate the Philippine producers' cost of production and allocate a portion of the shared fruit costs to the canned fruit. The result of this allocation showed that more than 90 percent of the canned fruit sales were below the cost of production. Is this a reasonable approach to determining the production costs and fair market value of canned pineapple in the United States? Why or why not? (See *Regulation of Specific Business Activities*.)

11–3. Sovereign Immunity. Taconic Plastics, Ltd., is a manufacturer incorporated in Ireland with its principal place of business in New York. Taconic enters into a contract with a German firm, Werner Voss Architects and Engineers, acting as an agent for the government of Saudi Arabia. The contract calls for Taconic to supply special material for tents designed to shelter religious pilgrims visiting holy sites in Saudi Arabia. Most of the material is made in, and shipped from, New York. The German company does not pay Taconic and files for bankruptcy. Taconic files a suit in a U.S. Court against the government of Saudi Arabia, seeking to collect $3 million. The defendant files a motion to dismiss the suit based on the doctrine of sovereign immunity. Under what circumstances does this doctrine apply? What are its exceptions? Should this suit be dismissed? Explain. (See *International Law*.)

11–4. Sovereign Immunity. In 1954, the government of Bolivia began expropriating land from Francisco Loza for public projects, including an international airport. The government directed the payment of compensation in exchange for at least some of his land. But the government never paid the full amount. Decades later, his heirs, Genoveva and Marcel Loza Santivanez, who were both U.S. citizens, filed a suit in a federal district court in the United States against the government of Bolivia. The Santivanezes sought damages for the taking. Can the court exercise jurisdiction? Explain. [*Santivanez v. Estado Plurinacional de Bolivia*, 512 Fed.Appx. 887 (11th Cir. 2013)] (See *International Law*.)

11–5. Business Case Problem with Sample Answer— Import Controls. The Wind Tower Trade Coalition is an association of domestic manufacturers of utility-scale wind towers. The coalition filed a suit in the U.S. Court of International Trade against the U.S. Department of Commerce. It challenged the Commerce Department's decision to impose only *prospective* antidumping duties, rather than *retrospective* (retroactive) duties, on imports of utility-scale wind towers from China and Vietnam. The department had found that the domestic industry had not suffered any "material injury"

or "threat of material injury" from such imports. It had further found that the industry would be protected by a prospective assessment. Can an antidumping duty be assessed retrospectively? If so, should it be assessed here? Discuss. [*Wind Tower Trade Coalition v. United States*, 741 F.3d 89 (Fed. Cir. 2014)] (See *Regulation of Specific Business Activities*.)

- For a sample answer to Problem 11–5, go to Appendix C at the end of this text.

11–6. The Principle of Comity. Holocaust survivors and the heirs of Holocaust victims filed a suit in a U.S. federal district court against the Hungarian national railway, the Hungarian national bank, and several private Hungarian banks. The plaintiffs alleged that the defendants had participated in expropriating the property of Hungarian Jews who were victims of the Holocaust. The claims arose from events in Hungary seventy years earlier. The plaintiffs, however, had not exhausted remedies available through Hungarian courts. Indeed, they had not even attempted to seek remedies in Hungarian courts, and they did not provide a legally compelling reason for their failure to do so. The defendants asked the court to dismiss the suit. Does the principle of comity support the defendants' request? Explain. [*Fischer v. Magyar Államvasutak Zrt.*, 777 F.3d 847 (7th Cir. 2015)] (See *International Law*.)

11–7. International Law. For fifty years, the Soviet Union made and sold Stolichnaya vodka. At the time, VVO-SPI, a Soviet state enterprise, licensed the Stolichnaya trademark in the United States. When the Soviet Union collapsed, VVO-SPI was purportedly privatized and fell under the control of Spirits International B.V. (SPI). In 2000, a Russian court held that VVO-SPI had not been validly privatized under Russian law. Thus, ownership of the Stolichnaya mark remained with the Soviet Union's successor, the Russian Federation. The Russian Federation assigned the mark to Federal Treasury Enterprise Sojuzplodoimport (FTE). FTE then filed a suit in a U.S. federal district court against SPI, asserting unlawful misappropriation and commercial exploitation of the mark in violation of the Lanham Act. Is the validity of the assignment of the mark to FTE a question to be determined by the court? Why or why not? [*Federal Treasury Enterprise Sojuzplodoimport v. Spirits International B.V.*, 809 F.3d 737 (2d Cir. 2016)] (See *International Law*.)

11–8. Import Controls. Goods exported to a foreign country for repair or alteration can qualify for tariff-free or reduced-tariff treatment when they re-enter the United States. But the goods do not qualify for favorable import-duty treatment if, in the foreign country, they are transformed into commercially different goods. Daimler-Chrysler Sprinter vans are marketed in the United States as cargo vans. Pleasure–Way Industries, Inc., bought 144 Sprinter vans and exported them to Canada for conversion into motor homes. This included the installation of fully plumbed and furnished kitchens, bathrooms, and sleeping quarters. After the conversion, Pleasure–Way sought to import the vehicles back into the United States to market the motor homes under new model names as upscale leisure vehicles at prices double or triple the price for Sprinter vans. Do the converted vans qualify for favorable import-tariff treatment? Discuss. [*Pleasure–Way Industries, Inc. v. United States*, 878 F.3d 1348 (Fed. Cir. 2018)] (See *Regulation of Specific Business Activities*.)

11–9. A Question of Ethics—The IDDR Approach and Foreign Jurisdiction. *Incorporated under Venezuelan law, a subsidiary of U.S.-based Helmerich & Payne International Drilling Company supplied oil-drilling rigs to entities that were part of the government of Venezuela. The government fell behind in payment on contracts for the use of the rigs. When the overdue amounts topped $100 million, the government nationalized the rigs and took possession. Helmerich filed a suit in a U.S. federal district court against Venezuela, claiming expropriation of* property *in violation of international law. Helmerich asserted that the U.S. court had jurisdiction under the Foreign Sovereign Immunities Act (FSIA).* [*Bolivarian Republic of Venezuela v. Helmerich & Payne International Drilling Co.,* ___ *U.S.* ___, *137 S.Ct. 1312, 197 L.Ed.2d 663 (2017)] (See* International Law.*)*

(a) Venezuela argued that the FSIA did not apply because Helmerich did not have rights in the rigs, which were the subsidiary's property. Does that fact make Helmerich's claim frivolous and unethical? Explain.

(b) Using the IDDR approach, determine whether a company is ethically obligated to become familiar with the political situation before doing business in another country.

Time-Limited Group Assignment

11–10. Expanding Abroad.   Assume that you are manufacturing iPad accessories and that your business is becoming more successful. You are now considering expanding operations into another country. (See *Doing Business Internationally*.)

(a) One group will explore the costs and benefits of advertising on the Internet.

(b) Another group will consider whether to take in a partner from a foreign nation and will explain the benefits and risks of having a foreign partner.

(c) A third group will discuss what problems may arise if a business chooses to manufacture in a foreign location.

CompTac, Inc., which is headquartered in San Francisco, California, is one of the leading software manufacturers in the United States. The company invests millions of dollars to research and develop new software applications and computer games, which are sold worldwide. It also has a large service department and takes great pains to offer its customers excellent support services.

1. **Negligence.** A customer at one of CompTac's retail stores stumbles over a crate in the parking lot and breaks her leg. Just moments earlier, the crate had fallen off a CompTac truck that was delivering goods from a CompTac warehouse to the store. The customer sues CompTac, alleging negligence. Will she succeed in her suit? Why or why not?

2. **Wrongful Interference.** Roban Electronics, a software manufacturer and one of CompTac's major competitors, has been trying to convince one of CompTac's key employees, Jim Baxter, to come to work for Roban. Roban knows that Baxter has a written employment contract with CompTac, which Baxter would breach if he left CompTac before the contract expired. Baxter goes to work for Roban, and the departure of a key employee causes CompTac to suffer substantial losses due to delays in completing new software. Can CompTac sue Roban to recoup some of these losses? If so, on what ground?

3. **Cyber Crime.** One of CompTac's employees in its accounting division, Alan Green, has a gambling problem. To repay a gambling debt of $10,000, Green decides to "borrow" from CompTac to cover the debt. Using his knowledge of CompTac account numbers, Green electronically transfers $10,000 from a CompTac account into his personal checking account. A week later, he is luckier at gambling and uses the same electronic procedures to transfer funds from his personal checking account back to the CompTac account. Has Green committed any crimes? If so, what are they?

4. **Intellectual Property.** CompTac wants to sell one of its best-selling software programs to An Phat Company, a firm located in Ho Chi Minh City, Vietnam. CompTac is concerned, however, that after an initial purchase, An Phat will duplicate the software without permission (in violation of U.S. copyright laws) and sell the illegal software to other firms in Vietnam. How can CompTac protect its software from being pirated by An Phat Company?

5. **Privacy and Social Media.** CompTac seeks to hire fourteen new employees. Its human resources (HR) department asks all candidates during their interview to disclose their social media passwords so that the company can access their social media accounts. Is it legal for employers to ask prospective employees for their social media passwords? Explain. If CompTac does not ask for passwords, can it legally look at a person's online posts when evaluating whether to hire or fire the person?

6. **International Law.** To offer goods at low prices, CompTac software reduces its costs by obtaining products made, distributed, and shipped by companies located in other countries. Because of developments affecting the global economy, the prices that CompTac's sources charge the U.S. retailer are increasing. CompTac wants to take steps to reduce those expenses. Also, as the economies in other nations grow, CompTac is interested in expanding its retail operations into those markets. What are CompTac's options for attaining these goals? What are the characteristics of each of these choices?

One of the Biggest Data Breaches Ever

For almost ten years, a group of hackers in Russia and Ukraine attacked the computer systems of U.S. companies, including 7-Eleven, Inc., JetBlue Airways Corporation, and J.C. Penney Company. The systems of firms based in other countries, including Visa Jordan and French retailer Carrefour SA, came under attack as well. The hackers stole more than 160 million credit- and debit-card numbers and breached 800,000 bank accounts.[1] Among incidents of unauthorized outside access to company systems, this was one of the biggest data breaches ever.

Businesses collect, process, and store confidential information on computer systems and transmit that data across networks to other computer systems. Data compromised by hackers affects all of these systems, and us as individuals, in ways that range from inconvenient to devastating. As the number of users and networks increases, the opportunities for breaches multiply.

Data Breaches

A *data breach* is an event in which sensitive, protected, or confidential data are copied, transmitted, viewed, stolen, or used by an individual unauthorized to do so. The data may include individuals' personal health information or personal identity information, such as birth dates and addresses, or a company's intellectual property, including patents, copyrights, and trade secrets.

Most breaches reported in the media involve individuals' private information, such as credit-card numbers. Loss of a business's data often goes unreported, unless there is a potential for harm to private individuals, because the publicity can do more damage to the business than the loss of the data.

How Do They Do It? Hackers break into computer systems by exploiting vulnerabilities in software code. A hacker may spend days, weeks, or longer setting up a position within the system, creating escape routes, and stealing information. Data may be stolen through phishing or spoofing, or with the help of malware.

Users of a system themselves may unwittingly facilitate attacks by downloading files or software, opening e-mail attachments, clicking on ads, or visiting fraudulent sites. In fact, individuals within an organization may cause as many as 37 percent of all data breaches.

Why Do They Do It? Normally, the focus of a hacker's attack is to steal data and sell the information.[2] With stolen personal information obtained from a hacker, a criminal can buy goods, empty bank accounts, or obtain funds in a number of ways. Intellectual property theft is a leading cause of financial losses to businesses. Hackers often steal trade secrets and other intellectual property for competing businesses.

Cyber Security

Cyber security consists of steps that can be taken to protect computers, networks, software, and confidential data from unauthorized access, alteration, or destruction. As the number and

---

1. A total loss for all of the victims was not determined, but three of the companies estimated their combined loss was more than $300 million.
2. The hackers who committed this data breach sold U.S. citizens' stolen credit-card numbers for $10 apiece.

sophistication of attacks increases, ongoing attention to security is required to protect sensitive business and personal information.

Prevent Attacks Being vigilant in protecting information is an important way to prevent attacks. A business can encrypt data, install firewalls, and train employees to take appropriate steps to guard customers' personal information and company trade secrets.

Notify Authorities and Victims If an attack does occur, a business should respond appropriately. Forty-seven states, the District of Columbia, Guam, Puerto Rico, and the Virgin Islands require businesses (and other entities) to notify individuals of data breaches involving their personal information.[3] Businesses should also notify the appropriate authorities.

A breached business may offer to cover the cost of credit monitoring and identity-theft protection for those whose personal information was stolen. In any event, individuals who are the victims of identity theft should inform their banks of the theft, place fraud alerts on their credit files, and review their credit reports.

Prosecute Hackers Hackers who can be identified can be charged with computer crimes. That happened to the hackers who committed the massive data breach described at the beginning of this feature. Five defendants were charged in a federal district court with unauthorized access of protected computers, wire fraud, and conspiracy to commit those crimes.[4] One of the five, Vladimir Drinkman, pleaded guilty. Drinkman and two of the others, Alexandr Kalinin and Mikhail Rytikov, were charged in connection with other data breaches as well.

Recover Losses Traditional insurance policies for businesses typically exclude the risk of a data breach. *Cyber security insurance* is designed to protect against losses from a variety of online incidents, including data breaches. The protection may cover costs arising from the destruction or theft of data, hacking, or denial of service attacks, as well as any related liability for privacy violations. Some policies limit coverage to $100 million.

Avoid Sanctions Earlier, we mentioned the importance of protecting data by preventing attacks. Attack prevention can have the added benefit of helping the business to avoid government sanctions.

A lack of security that allows hackers to steal customers' personal data from a business's computer system can be the ground for a suit by the Federal Trade Commission (FTC). The business may be liable for any resulting fraudulent charges to the customers' accounts. The FTC may also impose a fine and oversee the company's data protection for up to twenty years.

"A company does not act equitably when it publishes a privacy policy to attract customers who are concerned about data privacy, fails to make good on that promise by investing inadequate resources in cybersecurity, exposes its unsuspecting customers to substantial financial injury, and retains the profits of their business."[5]

---

3. See, for example, California Civil Code Sections 1798.29 and 1798.80 *et seq.*
4. These charges represent violations of the Computer Fraud and Abuse Act, 18 U.S.C. Section 1030; the Mail Fraud Act, 18 U.S.C. Sections 1343 and 1349; and 18 U.S.C. Section 371 ("Conspiracy to Commit Offense or to Defraud the United States").
5. *Federal Trade Commission v. Wyndham Worldwide Corp.*, 799 F.3d 236 (3d Cir. 2015).

Ethical Connection

Does a business have an ethical duty to prevent potential harm to its customers' credit that may result from a data breach? Some courts have held that consumers whose data have been stolen from a business's computer system can base a suit against the business on injuries consisting of lost time and money.[6]

The idea is that consumers whose data are stolen must spend time and money to resolve fraudulent charges and to protect against future identity theft and fraud. These individuals, after all, trusted the business with their information. They must now cancel or replace credit or debit cards and monitor credit reports, even if actual fraud has not yet occurred.

As mentioned earlier, a business may offer credit monitoring and identity-theft protection after a breach. This offer indicates that the business recognizes a continuing risk of harm from the breach. It also supports the existence of an ethical duty on the part of the business to prevent this harm.

Ethics Question *What is the extent of a business's ethical obligation to protect the personal information of its customers and employees? Discuss.*

Critical Thinking *Most likely, hackers will always exist, attempting to breach computer systems using the most up-to-date technology. What can businesses do to prevent breaches to their systems?*

---

6. See, for example, *Remijas v. Neiman Marcus Group, LLC,* 794 F.3d 688 (7th Cir. 2015). Some courts disagree—for example, see *Beck v. McDonald,* 848 F.3d 262 (4th Cir. 2017) and *Reilly v. Ceridian Corp.,* 664 F.3d 38 (3d Cir. 2011).

The Commercial Environment

Chapter 12

Formation of Traditional and E-Contracts

No aspect of modern life is entirely free of contractual relationships. You acquire rights and obligations, for instance, when you borrow funds, buy or lease a house, obtain insurance, and purchase goods or services. Contract law is designed to provide stability and predictability, as well as certainty, in the marketplace.

Contract law deals with, among other things, the formation and keeping of promises. A **promise** is a declaration by a person (the *promisor*) to do or not to do a certain act. As a result, the person to whom the promise is made (the *promisee*) has a right to expect or demand that something either will or will not happen in the future.

Like other types of law, contract law reflects our social values, interests, and expectations at a given point in time. It shows, for instance, to what extent our society allows people to make promises or commitments that are legally binding. It distinguishes between promises that create only *moral* obligations (such as a promise to take a friend to lunch) and promises that are legally binding (such as a promise to pay for items ordered online).

Contract law also demonstrates which excuses our society accepts for breaking certain types of promises. In addition, it indicates which promises are considered to be contrary to public policy—against the interests of society as a whole—and therefore legally invalid. When the person making a promise is a child or is mentally incompetent, for instance, a question will arise as to whether the promise should be enforced. Resolving such questions is the essence of contract law.

12–1 An Overview of Contract Law

Before we look at the numerous rules that courts use to determine whether a particular promise will be enforced, it is necessary to understand some fundamental concepts of contract law. In this section, we describe the sources and general function of contract law and introduce the objective theory of contracts.

12–1a Sources of Contract Law

The common law governs all contracts except when it has been modified or replaced by statutory law, such as the Uniform Commercial Code (UCC), or by administrative agency regulations. Contracts relating to services, real estate, employment, and insurance, for instance, generally are governed by the common law of contracts.

Contracts for the sale and lease of goods, however, are governed by the UCC—to the extent that the UCC has modified general contract law. In the discussion of general contract law that follows, we indicate in footnotes the areas in which the UCC has significantly altered common law contract principles.

12–1b The Definition of a Contract

A **contract** is "a promise or a set of promises for the breach of which the law gives a remedy, or the performance of which the law in some way recognizes as a duty."[1] Put simply, a contract is an agreement that can be enforced in court. It is formed by two or more parties who agree to perform or to refrain from performing some act now or in the future.

Generally, contract disputes arise when there is a promise of future performance. If the contractual promise is not fulfilled, the party who made it is subject to the sanctions of a court. That party may be required to pay damages for failing to perform the contractual promise. In a few instances, the party may be required to perform the promised act.

12–1c The Objective Theory of Contracts

In determining whether a contract has been formed, the element of intent is of prime importance. In contract law, intent is determined by what is called the

---

1. *Restatement (Second) of Contracts*, Section 1.

objective theory of contracts, not by the personal or subjective intent, or belief, of a party.

The theory is that a party's intention to enter into a legally binding agreement, or contract, is judged by outward, objective facts. The facts are as interpreted by a *reasonable* person, rather than by the party's own secret, subjective intentions. Objective facts may include:

1. What the party said when entering into the contract.
2. How the party acted or appeared (intent may be manifested by conduct as well as by oral or written words).
3. The circumstances surrounding the transaction.

■ **Case in Point 12.1** Cornell University in New York offered Leslie Weston an associate professorship for an initial term of five years. The offer letter described the position as being "with tenure," but it stated that the offer of tenure would have to be confirmed by the university's review process after she was hired. For a variety of reasons, Weston delayed her tenure submission for five years and, when she finally submitted it, she was not awarded tenure.

Cornell gave Weston a two-year extension, this time as an "associate professor without tenure," to allow her an opportunity to improve and resubmit her tenure package. Although she resubmitted her tenure request, it was again denied, resulting in her eventual termination. Weston sued Cornell for breach of contract, and lost. The court held that Cornell's two-year extension of Weston's position had clearly modified the original contract by stating that she was working as an associate professor "without tenure." Weston's subjective beliefs and unsupported arguments regarding the modification of her employment agreement were irrelevant.[2] ■

12–1d Requirements of a Valid Contract

The following list briefly describes the four requirements that must be met before a valid contract exists. If any of these elements is lacking, no contract will have been formed. (Each requirement will be explained more fully later in this chapter.)

1. *Agreement.* An agreement to form a contract includes an *offer* and an *acceptance*. One party must offer to enter into a legal agreement, and another party must accept the terms of the offer.
2. *Consideration.* Any promises made by the parties to the contract must be supported by legally sufficient

and bargained-for *consideration* (something of value received or promised, such as money, to convince a person to make a deal).
3. *Contractual capacity.* Both parties entering into the contract must have the contractual *capacity* to do so. The law must recognize them as possessing characteristics that qualify them as competent parties.
4. *Legality.* The contract's purpose must be to accomplish some goal that is legal and not against public policy.

12–1e Defenses to the Enforceability of a Contract

Even if all of the four requirements of a valid contract are satisfied, a contract may be unenforceable if the following requirements are not met. These requirements typically are raised as *defenses* to the enforceability of an otherwise valid contract.

1. *Voluntary consent.* The consent of both parties must be voluntary. For instance, if a contract was formed as a result of fraud, undue influence, mistake, or duress, the contract may not be enforceable.
2. *Form.* The contract must be in whatever form the law requires. Some contracts must be in writing to be enforceable.

12–1f Types of Contracts

There are many types of contracts. They are categorized based on legal distinctions as to their formation, performance, and enforceability.

Bilateral versus Unilateral Contracts Every contract involves at least two parties. The **offeror** is the party making the offer. The **offeree** is the party to whom the offer is made. Whether the contract is classified as *bilateral* or *unilateral* depends on what the offeree must do to accept the offer and bind the offeror to a contract.

If the offeree can accept simply by promising to perform, the contract is a **bilateral contract.** Hence, a bilateral contract is a "promise for a promise." No performance, such as payment of funds or delivery of goods, needs to take place for a bilateral contract to be formed. The contract comes into existence at the moment the promises are exchanged.

If the offer is phrased so that the offeree can accept the offer only by completing the contract performance, the contract is a **unilateral contract.** Hence, a unilateral contract is a "promise for an act." In other words, a unilateral

---

2. *Weston v. Cornell University*, 136 A.D.3d 1094, 24 N.Y.S.3d 448 (2016).

contract is formed not at the moment when promises are exchanged but at the moment when the contract is *performed*.

■ **Example 12.2** Reese says to Celia, "If you drive my car from New York to Los Angeles, I'll give you $1,000." Only on Celia's completion of the act—bringing the car to Los Angeles—does she fully accept Reese's offer to pay $1,000. If she chooses not to accept the offer to drive the car to Los Angeles, there are no legal consequences. ■

Formal versus Informal Contracts **Formal contracts** are contracts that require a special form or method of creation (formation) to be enforceable.[3] One example is *negotiable instruments*, which include checks, drafts, promissory notes, bills of exchange, and certificates of deposit. Negotiable instruments are formal contracts because the Uniform Commercial Code (UCC) requires a special language to create them. *Letters of credit*, which are frequently used in international sales contracts, are another type of formal contract.

Informal contracts (also called *simple contracts*) include all other contracts. No special form is required (except for certain types of contracts that must be in writing), as the contracts are usually based on their substance rather than their form. Typically, businesspersons put their contracts in writing (including electronic records) to establish proof of a contract's existence should disputes arise.

Express versus Implied Contracts Contracts may also be categorized as *express* or *implied*. In an **express contract,** the terms of the agreement are fully and explicitly stated in words, oral or written. A signed lease for an apartment or a house is an express written contract. If one classmate calls another on the phone and agrees to buy her textbooks from last semester for $200, an express oral contract has been made.

A contract that is implied from the conduct of the parties is called an **implied contract** (or sometimes an *implied-in-fact contract*). This type of contract differs from an express contract in that the conduct of the parties, rather than their words, creates and defines the terms of the contract.

Requirements for Implied Contracts. For an implied contract to arise, certain requirements must be met. Normally, if the following conditions exist, a court will hold that an implied contract was formed:

1. The plaintiff furnished some service or property.

2. The plaintiff expected to be paid for that service or property, and the defendant knew or should have known that payment was expected.
3. The defendant had a chance to reject the services or property and did not.

■ **Example 12.3** Alex, a small-business owner, needs an accountant to complete his tax return. He drops by a local accountant's office, explains his situation to the accountant, and learns what fees she charges. The next day, he returns and gives the receptionist all of the necessary documents to complete his return. Then he walks out without saying anything further to the accountant. In this situation, Alex has entered into an implied contract to pay the accountant the usual fees for her services. The contract is implied because of Alex's conduct and hers. She expects to be paid for completing the tax return, and by bringing in the records she will need to do the job, Alex has implied an intent to pay her. ■

Mixed Contracts with Express and Implied Terms. Note that a contract may be a mixture of an express contract and an implied contract. In other words, a contract may contain some express terms and some implied terms. During the construction of a home, for instance, the homeowner often asks the builder to make changes in the original specifications.

■ **Case in Point 12.4** Lamar Hopkins hired Uhrhahn Construction & Design, Inc., for several projects in building his home. For each project, the parties signed a written contract that was based on a cost estimate and specifications and that required changes to the agreement to be in writing. While the work was in progress, however, Hopkins repeatedly asked Uhrhahn to deviate from the contract specifications, which Uhrhahn did. None of these requests was made in writing.

One day, Hopkins asked Uhrhahn to use Durisol blocks instead of the cinder blocks specified in the original contract, indicating that the cost would be the same. Uhrhahn used the Durisol blocks but demanded extra payment when it became clear that the Durisol blocks were more complicated to install. Although Hopkins had paid for the other deviations from the contract that he had orally requested, he refused to pay Uhrhahn for the substitution of the Durisol blocks. Uhrhahn sued for breach of contract. The court found that Hopkins, through his conduct, had waived the provision requiring written contract modification and created an implied contract to pay the extra cost of installing the Durisol blocks.[4] ■

---

3. See *Restatement (Second) of Contracts*, Section 6, which explains that formal contracts include (1) contracts under seal, (2) recognizances, (3) negotiable instruments, and (4) letters of credit.

4. *Uhrhahn Construction & Design, Inc. v. Hopkins*, 2008 UT App 41, 179 P.3d 808 (2008).

Executed versus Executory Contracts Contracts are also classified according to the degree to which they have been performed. A contract that has been fully performed on both sides is called an **executed contract.** A contract that has not been fully performed by the parties is called an **executory contract.** If one party has fully performed but the other has not, the contract is said to be executed on the one side and executory on the other, but the contract is still classified as executory.

■ **Example 12.5** Jackson, Inc., agrees to buy ten tons of coal from the Northern Coal Company. Northern delivers the coal to Jackson's steel mill, where it is being burned. At this point, the contract is executed on the part of Northern and executory on Jackson's part. After Jackson pays Northern, the contract will be executed on both sides. ■

Enforceable versus Unenforceable Contracts A **valid contract** has the necessary elements to entitle at least one of the parties to enforce it in court. Those elements, as mentioned earlier, consist of (1) an agreement (offer and acceptance), (2) supported by legally sufficient consideration, (3) made by parties who have the legal capacity to enter into the contract, and (4) a legal purpose.

Valid contracts may be enforceable or unenforceable. An **unenforceable contract** is one that cannot be enforced because of certain legal defenses against it. It is not unenforceable because a party failed to satisfy a legal requirement of the contract. Rather, it is a valid contract rendered unenforceable by some statute or law. For instance, certain contracts must be in writing, and if they are not, they will not be enforceable except in certain exceptional circumstances.

Voidable Contracts. A **voidable contract** is a valid contract but one that can be avoided at the option of one or both of the parties. The party having the option can elect either to avoid any duty to perform or to *ratify* (make valid) the contract. If the contract is avoided, both parties are released from it. If it is ratified, both parties must fully perform their respective legal obligations. For instance, contracts made by minors generally are voidable at the option of the minor (with certain exceptions). Contracts made by mentally incompetent persons and intoxicated persons may also be voidable.

Void Contracts. A **void contract** is no contract at all. None of the parties have any legal obligations if a contract is void. A contract can be void because one of the parties was determined by a court to be mentally incompetent, for instance, or because the purpose of the contract was illegal.

To review the various types of contracts, see Concept Summary 12.1.

Concept Summary 12.1

Types of Contracts

Formation	• *Bilateral*—A promise for a promise. • *Unilateral*—A promise for an act—that is, acceptance is the completed performance of the act. • *Formal*—Requires a special form for creation. • *Informal*—Requires no special form for creation. • *Express*—Formed by words, such as oral, written, or a combination. • *Implied*—Formed by the conduct of the parties.
Performance	• *Executed*—A fully performed contract. • *Executory*—A contract not fully performed.
Enforceability	• *Valid*—The contract has the necessary contractual elements: agreement (offer and acceptance), consideration, legal capacity of the parties, and legal purpose. • *Unenforceable*—A contract exists, but it cannot be enforced because of a legal defense. • *Voidable*—One party has the option of avoiding or enforcing the contractual obligation. • *Void*—No contract exists, or there is a contract without legal obligations.

12–2 Agreement

One of the four essential elements for contract formation is **agreement**—the parties must agree on the terms of the contract and manifest to each other their *mutual assent* (agreement) to the same bargain. Ordinarily, agreement is evidenced by two events: an *offer* and an *acceptance*. One party offers a certain bargain to another party, who then accepts that bargain. Once an agreement is reached, if the other elements of a contract (consideration, capacity, and legality) are present, a valid contract is formed.

12–2a Requirements of the Offer

An **offer** is a promise or commitment to do or refrain from doing some specified action in the future. The party making an offer is called the *offeror*, and the party to whom the offer is made is called the *offeree*. Under the common law, three elements are necessary for an offer to be effective:

1. The offeror must have a serious intention to become bound by the offer.

2. The terms of the offer must be reasonably certain, or definite, so that the parties and the court can ascertain the terms of the contract.
3. The offer must be communicated to the offeree.

Once an effective offer has been made, the offeree's acceptance of that offer creates a legally binding contract (providing the other essential elements for a valid and enforceable contract are present).

Intention The first requirement for an effective offer is a serious intent on the part of the offeror. Serious intent is not determined by the subjective intentions, beliefs, and assumptions of the offeror. Rather, it is determined by what a reasonable person in the offeree's position would conclude that the offeror's words and actions meant.

Offers made in obvious anger, jest, or undue excitement do not meet the serious-and-objective-intent test. A reasonable person would realize that such offers were not made seriously. Because these offers are not effective, an offeree's acceptance does not create an agreement.

In the classic case presented next, the court considered whether an offer made "after a few drinks" met the serious-and-objective-intent requirement.

Classic Case 12.1

Lucy v. Zehmer

Supreme Court of Appeals of Virginia, 196 Va. 493, 84 S.E.2d 516 (1954).

Background and Facts W. O. Lucy, the plaintiff, filed a suit against A. H. and Ida Zehmer, the defendants, to compel the Zehmers to transfer title of their property, known as the Ferguson Farm, to the Lucys (W. O. and his wife) for $50,000, as the Zehmers had allegedly agreed to do. Lucy had known A. H. Zehmer for fifteen or twenty years and for the last eight years or so had been anxious to buy the Ferguson Farm from him. One night, Lucy stopped to visit the Zehmers in the combination restaurant, filling station, and motor court they operated. While there, Lucy tried to buy the Ferguson Farm once again. This time he tried a new approach. According to the trial court transcript, Lucy said to Zehmer, "I bet you wouldn't take $50,000 for that place." Zehmer replied, "Yes, I would too; you wouldn't give fifty." Throughout the evening, the conversation returned to the sale of the Ferguson Farm for $50,000. All the while, the men continued to drink whiskey and engage in light conversation.

Eventually, Lucy enticed Zehmer to write up an agreement to the effect that the Zehmers would sell the Ferguson Farm to Lucy for $50,000. Later, Lucy sued Zehmer to compel him to go through with the sale. Zehmer argued that he had been drunk and that the offer had been made in jest and hence was unenforceable. The trial court agreed with Zehmer, and Lucy appealed.

In the Language of the Court

BUCHANAN, J. [Justice] delivered the opinion of the court.
* * * *

In his testimony, Zehmer claimed that he "was high as a Georgia pine," and that the transaction "was just a bunch of two doggoned drunks bluffing to see who could talk the biggest and say the most." That claim is inconsistent with his attempt to testify in great detail as to what was said and what was done.

* * * *

The appearance of the contract, the fact that it was under discussion for forty minutes or more before it was signed; Lucy's objection to the first draft because it was written in the singular, and he wanted Mrs. Zehmer to sign it also; the rewriting to meet that objection and the signing by Mrs. Zehmer; the discussion of what was to be included in the sale, the provision for the examination of the title, the completeness of the instrument that was executed, the taking possession of it by Lucy with no request or suggestion by either of the defendants that he give it back, are facts which furnish persuasive evidence that the execution of the contract was a serious business transaction rather than a casual, jesting matter as defendants now contend.

* * * *

In the field of contracts, as generally elsewhere, *we must look to the outward expression of a person as manifesting his intention rather than to his secret and unexpressed intention.* The law imputes to a person an intention corresponding to the reasonable meaning of his words and acts. [Emphasis added.]

* * * *

Whether the writing signed by the defendants and now sought to be enforced by the complainants was the result of a serious offer by Lucy and a serious acceptance by the defendants, or was a serious offer by Lucy and an acceptance in secret jest by the defendants, in either event it constituted a binding contract of sale between the parties.

Decision and Remedy   *The Supreme Court of Appeals of Virginia determined that the writing was an enforceable contract and reversed the ruling of the lower court. The Zehmers were required by court order to follow through with the sale of the Ferguson Farm to the Lucys.*

Critical Thinking

- **What If the Facts Were Different?**   *Suppose that the day after Lucy signed the purchase agreement, he decided that he did not want the farm after all, and Zehmer sued Lucy to perform the contract. Would this change in the facts alter the court's decision that Lucy and Zehmer had created an enforceable contract? Why or why not?*
- **Impact of This Case on Today's Law**   *This is a classic case in contract law because it illustrates so clearly the objective theory of contracts with respect to determining whether a serious offer was intended. Today, the courts continue to apply the objective theory of contracts and routinely cite* Lucy v. Zehmer *as a significant precedent in this area.*

Situations in Which Intent May Be Lacking   The concept of intention can be further clarified by looking at statements that are *not* offers and situations in which the parties' intent to be bound might be questionable.

1. *Expressions of opinion.* An expression of opinion is not an offer. It does not indicate an intention to enter into a binding agreement.
2. *Statements of future intent.* A statement of an intention to do something in the future (such as "I plan to sell my Verizon stock") is not an offer.
3. *Preliminary negotiations.* A request or invitation to negotiate is not an offer. It only expresses a willingness to discuss the possibility of entering into a contract. Statements such as "Will you sell your farm?" or "I wouldn't sell my car for less than $8,000" are examples.
4. *Invitations to bid.* When a government entity or private firm needs to have construction work done, contractors are invited to submit bids. The invitation to submit bids is not an offer. The bids that contractors submit are offers, however, and the government entity or private firm can bind the contractor by accepting the bid.
5. *Advertisements and price lists.* In general, representations made in advertisements and price lists are treated not as offers to contract but as invitations to negotiate.[5]
6. *Live and online auctions.* In a live auction, a seller "offers" goods for sale through an auctioneer, but this is not an offer to form a contract. Rather, it is an invitation asking bidders to submit offers. In the context of an auction, a bidder is the offeror, and the auctioneer is the offeree. The offer is accepted when the auctioneer strikes the hammer.

---

5. *Restatement (Second) of Contracts,* Section 26, Comment b.

The most familiar type of auction today takes place online through websites like eBay and eBid. "Offers" to sell an item on these sites generally are treated as invitations to negotiate.

Agreements to Agree. Traditionally, *agreements to agree*—that is, agreements to agree to the material terms of a contract at some future date—were not considered to be binding contracts. The modern view, however, is that agreements to agree may be enforceable agreements (contracts) if it is clear that the parties intended to be bound by the agreements. In other words, under the modern view the emphasis is on the parties' intent rather than on form.

Preliminary Agreements. A *preliminary agreement* can constitute a binding contract if the parties have agreed on all essential terms and no disputed issues remain to be resolved. ■ **Case in Point 12.6** Basis Technology Corporation created software and provided technical services for a Japanese-language website belonging to Amazon.com, Inc. The agreement between the two companies allowed for separately negotiated contracts for additional services that Basis might provide to Amazon.

Later, a dispute arose and Basis sued Amazon for various claims involving these contracts and for failure to pay for services performed by Basis. During the trial, the two parties appeared to reach an agreement to settle out of court via a series of e-mail exchanges outlining the settlement. When Amazon reneged, Basis served a motion to enforce the proposed settlement. The trial judge entered a judgment against Amazon, which appealed. The reviewing court affirmed the trial court's finding that Amazon intended to be bound by the terms of the e-mail exchange, which contained a complete and unambiguous statement of the parties' settlement terms.[6] ■

In contrast, if the parties agree on certain major terms but leave other terms open for further negotiation, a preliminary agreement is not binding. The parties are bound only in the sense that they have committed themselves to negotiate the undecided terms in good faith in an effort to reach a final agreement.

Definiteness of Terms The second requirement for an effective offer involves the definiteness of its terms. An offer must have reasonably definite terms so that a court can determine if a breach has occurred and give an appropriate remedy.[7] The specific terms required depend, of course, on the type of contract. Generally, a contract must include the following terms, either expressed in the contract or capable of being reasonably inferred from it:

1. The identification of the parties.
2. The identification of the object or subject matter of the contract (also the quantity, when appropriate), including the work to be performed, with specific identification of such items as goods, services, and land.
3. The consideration to be paid.
4. The time of payment, delivery, or performance.

An offer may invite an acceptance to be worded in such specific terms that the contract is made definite. ■ **Example 12.7** Nintendo of America, Inc., contacts a Play 2 Win Games store and offers to sell "from one to twenty-five Nintendo 3DS.XL gaming systems for $75 each. State number desired in acceptance." The store manager agrees to buy twenty systems. Because the quantity is specified in the acceptance, the terms are definite, and the contract is enforceable. ■

When the parties have clearly manifested their intent to form a contract, courts sometimes are willing to supply a missing term in a contract, especially a sales contract.[8] But a court will not rewrite a contract if the parties' expression of intent is too vague or uncertain to be given any precise meaning.

Communication The third requirement for an effective offer is communication—the offer must be communicated to the offeree. Ordinarily, one cannot agree to a bargain without knowing that it exists. ■ **Case in Point 12.8** Adwoa Gyabaah was hit by a bus owned by Rivlab Transportation Corporation. Gyabaah filed a suit in a New York state court against the bus company. Rivlab's insurer offered to tender the company's policy limit of $1 million in full settlement of Gyabaah's claims. On the advice of her attorney, Jeffrey Aronsky, Gyabaah signed a *release* (a contract forfeiting the right to pursue a legal claim) to obtain the settlement funds.

The release, however, was not sent to Rivlab or its insurer, National Casualty. Moreover, Gyabaah claimed that she had not decided whether to settle. Two months later, Gyabaah changed lawyers and changed her mind about signing the release. Her former attorney, Aronsky, filed a motion to enforce the release so that he could obtain his fees from the settlement funds. The court denied the motion, and Aronsky appealed. The reviewing court held that there was no binding settlement agreement. The release was never delivered to Rivlab

6. *Basis Technology Corp. v. Amazon.com, Inc.*, 71 Mass.App.Ct. 29, 878 N.E.2d 952 (2008).
7. *Restatement (Second) of Contracts*, Section 33.

8. See UCC 2–204. Article 2 of the UCC modifies general contract law by requiring *less* specificity, or definiteness of terms, in sales and lease contracts.

or its insurer nor was acceptance of the settlement offer otherwise communicated to them.[9] ■

12–2b Termination of the Offer

The communication of an effective offer to an offeree gives the offeree the power to transform the offer into a binding, legal obligation (a contract) by an acceptance. This power of acceptance does not continue forever, though. It can be terminated either by action of the parties or by operation of law.

Termination by Action of the Offeror The offeror's act of revoking, or withdrawing, an offer is known as **revocation.** Unless an offer is irrevocable, the offeror usually can revoke the offer, as long as the revocation is communicated to the offeree before the offeree accepts. Revocation may be accomplished by either of the following:

1. Express repudiation of the offer (such as "I withdraw my previous offer of October 17").
2. Performance of acts that are inconsistent with the existence of the offer and are made known to the offeree (for instance, selling the offered property to another person in the offeree's presence).

In most states, a revocation becomes effective when the offeree or the offeree's *agent* (a person acting on behalf of the offeree) actually receives it. Therefore, a revocation sent via FedEx on April 1 and delivered at the offeree's residence or place of business on April 3 becomes effective on April 3.

Although most offers are revocable, some can be made irrevocable—that is, they cannot be revoked. One form of irrevocable offer is an **option contract.** An option contract is created when an offeror promises to hold an offer open for a specified period of time in return for a payment (consideration) given by the offeree. An option contract takes away the offeror's power to revoke the offer for the period of time specified in the option.

Option contracts are frequently used in conjunction with the sale or lease of real estate. ■ **Example 12.9** Tyler agrees to lease a house from Jackson, the property owner. The lease contract includes a clause stating that Tyler is paying an additional $15,000 for an option to purchase the property within a specified period of time. If Tyler decides not to purchase the house after the specified period has lapsed, he loses the $15,000, and Jackson is free to sell the property to another buyer. ■

Termination by Action of the Offeree If the offeree rejects the offer—by words or by conduct—the offer is terminated. Any subsequent attempt by the offeree to accept will be construed as a new offer, giving the original offeror (now the offeree) the power of acceptance.

Like a revocation, a rejection of an offer is effective only when it is actually received by the offeror or the offeror's agent. ■ **Example 12.10** Goldfinch Farms offers to sell specialty Maitake mushrooms to a Japanese buyer, Kinoko Foods. If Kinoko rejects the offer by sending a letter via U.S. mail, the rejection will not be effective (and the offer will not be terminated) until Goldfinch receives the letter. ■

Inquiries about an Offer. Merely inquiring about the "firmness" of an offer does not constitute rejection. ■ **Example 12.11** Raymond offers to buy Francie's digital pen for $25. She responds, "Is that your best offer?" A reasonable person would conclude that Francie has not rejected the offer but has merely made an inquiry. Francie could still accept and bind Raymond to the $25 price. ■

Counteroffer. A **counteroffer** is a rejection of the original offer and the simultaneous making of a new offer. ■ **Example 12.12** Burke offers to sell his home to Lang for $270,000. Lang responds, "Your price is too high. I'll offer to purchase your house for $250,000." Lang's response is a counteroffer because it rejects Burke's offer to sell at $270,000 and creates a new offer by Lang to purchase the home for $250,000. ■

At common law, the **mirror image rule** requires the offeree's acceptance to match the offeror's offer exactly—to mirror the offer. Any change in, or addition to, the terms of the original offer automatically terminates that offer and substitutes the counteroffer. The counteroffer, of course, need not be accepted, but if the original offeror does accept the terms of the counteroffer, a valid contract is created.[10]

Termination by Operation of Law The power of the offeree to transform the offer into a binding, legal obligation can be terminated by operation of law through the occurrence of any of the following events:

1. Lapse of time.
2. Destruction of the specific subject matter of the offer.
3. Death or incompetence of the offeror or the offeree.
4. Supervening illegality of the proposed contract.

---

9. *Gyabaah v. Rivlab Transportation Corp.*, 102 A.D.3d 451, 958 N.Y.S.2d 109 (1 Dept. 2013).

10. The mirror image rule has been greatly modified in regard to sales contracts. Section 2–207 of the UCC provides that a contract is formed if the offeree makes a definite expression of acceptance (such as signing a form in the appropriate location), even though the terms of the acceptance modify or add to the terms of the original offer.

Lapse of Time. An offer terminates automatically by law when the period of time *specified in the offer* has passed. If the offer states that it will be left open until a particular date, then the offer will terminate at midnight on that day. If the offer states that it will be open for a number of days, this time period normally begins to run when the offeree *receives* the offer (not when it is formed or sent).

If the offer does not specify a time for acceptance, the offer terminates at the end of a *reasonable* period of time. What constitutes a reasonable period of time depends on the subject matter of the contract, business and market conditions, and other relevant circumstances. An offer to sell farm produce, for instance, will terminate sooner than an offer to sell farm equipment. Farm produce is perishable and is also subject to greater fluctuations in market value.

Destruction, Death, or Incompetence. An offer is automatically terminated if the specific subject matter of the offer (such as a smartphone or a house) is destroyed before the offer is accepted.[11] Notice of the destruction is not required for the offer to terminate. An offeree's power of acceptance is also terminated when the offeror or offeree dies or is legally incapacitated—*unless the offer is irrevocable.*

Supervening Illegality. A statute or court decision that makes an offer illegal automatically terminates the offer. ■ **Example 12.13** Shane Lee offers to lend Sue Kim $10,000 at an annual interest rate of 15 percent. Before Kim can accept the offer, a law is enacted that prohibits interest rates higher than 8 percent. Lee's offer is automatically terminated. (If the statute is enacted after Kim

11. *Restatement (Second) of Contracts*, Section 36.

accepts the offer, a valid contract is formed, but the contract may still be unenforceable.) ■

Concept Summary 12.2 reviews the ways in which an offer can be terminated.

12–2c Acceptance

Acceptance is a voluntary act by the offeree that shows assent (agreement) to the terms of an offer. The offeree's act may consist of words or conduct. The acceptance must be unequivocal and must be communicated to the offeror. Generally, only the person to whom the offer is made or that person's agent can accept the offer and create a binding contract.

Unequivocal Acceptance To exercise the power of acceptance effectively, the offeree must accept unequivocally. This is the *mirror image rule* previously discussed. An acceptance may be unequivocal even though the offeree expresses dissatisfaction with the contract. For instance, "I accept the offer, but can you give me a better price?" is an effective acceptance.

An acceptance cannot impose new conditions or change the terms of the original offer. If it does, the acceptance may be considered a counteroffer, which is a rejection of the original offer. For instance, the statement "I accept the offer but only if I can pay on ninety days' credit" is a counteroffer and not an unequivocal acceptance.

Note that even when the additional terms are construed as a counteroffer, the other party can accept the terms by words or by conduct. ■ **Case in Point 12.14** Lagrange Development is a nonprofit corporation in Ohio that acquires and rehabilitates real property. Sonja Brown presented Lagrange with a written offer to buy a

Concept Summary 12.2

Methods by Which an Offer Can Be Terminated

By Action of the Parties	• Revocation • Rejection • Counteroffer
By Operation of Law	• Lapse of time • Destruction of the subject matter • Death or incompetence of the offeror or offeree • Supervening illegality

particular house for $79,900. Lagrange's executive director, Terry Glazer, penciled in modifications to the offer—an increased purchase price of $84,200 and a later date for acceptance. Glazer initialed the changes and signed the document.

Brown initialed the date change but not the price increase, and did not sign the revised document. Nevertheless, Brown went through with the sale and received ownership of the property. When a dispute later arose as to the purchase price, a court found that Glazer's modification of the terms had constituted a counteroffer, which Brown had accepted by performance. Therefore, the contract was enforceable for the modified price of $84,200.[12] ∎

Silence as Acceptance Ordinarily, silence cannot constitute acceptance, even if the offeror states, "By your silence and inaction, you will be deemed to have accepted this offer." An offeree should not be obligated to act affirmatively to reject an offer when no consideration (nothing of value) has passed to the offeree to impose such a duty.

In some instances, however, the offeree does have a duty to speak, and her or his silence or inaction will

operate as an acceptance. Silence can constitute an acceptance when the offeree has had prior dealings with the offeror. ∎ **Example 12.15** Marabel's restaurant routinely receives shipments of produce from a certain supplier. That supplier notifies Marabel's that it is raising its prices because its crops were damaged by a late freeze. If the restaurant does not respond in any way, the silence may operate as an acceptance, and the supplier will be justified in continuing regular shipments. ∎

Communication of Acceptance Whether the offeror must be notified of the acceptance depends on the nature of the contract. In a unilateral contract, the full performance of some act is called for. Acceptance is usually evident, and notification is therefore unnecessary (unless the law requires it or the offeror asks for it). In a bilateral contract, in contrast, communication of acceptance is necessary, because acceptance is in the form of a promise. The bilateral contract is formed when the promise is made rather than when the act is performed.

At issue in the following case was the validity and enforceability of a waiver of liability on the back page of a gym's membership agreement. In this case, the court had to determine whether the circumstances indicated that the offeree's acceptance of the agreement was unequivocal and clearly communicated.

---

12. *Brown v. Lagrange Development Corp.*, 2015 WL 223877 (Ohio Ct. App. 2015).

Case Analysis 12.2

Hinkal v. Pardoe
Superior Court of Pennsylvania, 2016 PA Super 11, 133 A.3d 738 (2016).

In the Language of the Court
Opinion by *STABILE*, J. [Judge]
* * * *

[Melinda Hinkal filed a suit in a Pennsylvania state court against personal trainer Gavin Pardoe and Gold's Gym, Inc., alleging that] she sustained a serious neck injury while using a piece of exercise equipment under * * * Pardoe's direction [at Gold's Gym. Hinkal] alleges that she suffered a rupture of the C5 disc in her neck requiring two separate surgeries. [Gold's and Pardoe] filed a Motion for Summary Judgment [asserting] that as a member of Gold's Gym [Hinkal] signed * * * a Membership Agreement [that] contains legally valid "waiver of liability" provisions, which in turn, bar [her] claims.

The trial court concluded that the waiver language set forth in Gold's Membership Agreement was valid and enforceable.

[Hinkal] filed a timely appeal to this [state intermediate appellate] Court.
* * * *

* * * Appellant [Hinkal] questions whether the waiver on the back page of her membership agreement is valid and enforceable. The language on the back page of the agreement reads in pertinent part as follows:

WAIVER OF LIABILITY; ASSUMPTION OF RISK: Member acknowledges that the use of Gold's Gym's facilities, equipment, services and programs involves an inherent risk of personal injury to Member. * * * Member

voluntarily agrees to assume all risks of personal injury to Member * * * and waives any and all claims or actions that Member may have against Gold's Gym * * * and any * * * employees * * * for * * * injuries arising from use of any exercise equipment * * * in supervised or unsupervised activities.

The Gold's Gym Membership Agreement signed by Appellant further instructs:

Do not sign this Agreement until you have read both sides. The terms on each side of this form are a part of this Agreement. * * * By signing this Agreement, Member acknowledges that This Agreement is a contract that will become legally binding upon its acceptance.

Case 12.2 Continues

Case 12.2 Continued

The signature line follows immediately and the words "Notice: See other side for important information" appear in bold typeface below the signature line.
* * * *

* * * Appellant * * * asserts that her claim is not barred by the "exclusion clause" on the back of the membership agreement. * * * Appellant contends the waiver is invalid because the waiver language appeared on the back of the agreement, she never read or was told to read the back of the agreement, and the clause was not "brought home" to her in a way that could suggest she was aware of the clause and its contents. However, * * * Appellant admitted she did not read the agreement prior to signing it. * * * Her failure to read her agreement does not render it either invalid or unenforceable. *The law of Pennsylvania is clear. One who is about to sign a contract has a duty to read that contract first.* * * * It is well established that, in the absence of fraud,

the failure to read a contract before signing it is an unavailing excuse or defense and cannot justify an avoidance, modification or nullification of the contract. [Emphasis added.]

[To support her claim, Appellant cites *Beck-Hummel v. Ski Shawnee, Inc.*, a previous case before this court, but] the signed Gold's Gym membership agreement cannot be compared in any way to the unread and unsigned disclaimer on a ski facility ticket in [*Beck-Hummel.*]
* * * *

* * * In [*Beck-Hummel,*] the release provision was contained on the face of an entry ticket purchased for use of a ski facility. The ticket did not require a signature or an express acknowledgment that its terms were read and accepted before using the facility. Nothing about the ticket ensured that a purchaser would be aware of its release provision. The purchasers were mere recipients of the document. In short, there was not sufficient

evidence to find conclusively that there was a meeting of the minds that part of the consideration for use of the facility was acceptance of a release provision. In stark contrast, here there is a written, signed and acknowledged agreement between the parties.
* * * *

Here, without reading it, Appellant signed the membership agreement, which included an unambiguous directive not to sign before reading both sides, a clear pronouncement that the terms on both sides of the form are part of the agreement, and a straightforward statement that the agreement constitutes the entire agreement between the parties. * * * We find no genuine issue as to any material fact or any error in the lower court's determination that the waiver was valid and enforceable. Appellant is not entitled to relief based on [this] issue.
* * * *

Order affirmed.

Legal Reasoning Questions

1. What indicated that the terms in the agreement at issue in this case were accepted?

2. What were the appellant's arguments in support of her claim? Which of those contentions did the court imply was irrelevant? Why?

3. How did the court distinguish its conclusion in this case from its decision in *Beck-Hummel*?

Mode and Timeliness of Acceptance
In bilateral contracts, acceptance must be timely. The general rule is that acceptance in a bilateral contract is timely if it is made before the offer is terminated. Problems may arise, though, when the parties involved are not dealing face to face. In such situations, the offeree should use an authorized mode of communication.

The Mailbox Rule. Acceptance takes effect, thus completing formation of the contract, at the time the offeree sends or delivers the communication via the mode expressly or impliedly authorized by the offeror. This is the so-called **mailbox rule**, also called the *deposited acceptance rule*, which the majority of courts follow. Under this rule, if the authorized mode of communication is the mail, then an acceptance becomes valid when it is dispatched (placed in the control of the U.S. Postal Service)—*not* when it is received by the offeror. (Note, however, that if the offer

stipulates when acceptance will be effective, then the offer will not be effective until the time specified.)

The mailbox rule does not apply to instantaneous forms of communication, such as when the parties are dealing face to face, by telephone, by fax, and (usually) by e-mail. Under the Uniform Electronic Transactions Act (discussed shortly), e-mail is considered sent when it either leaves the control of the sender or is received by the recipient. This rule takes the place of the mailbox rule when the parties have agreed to conduct transactions electronically and allows an e-mail acceptance to become effective when sent.

Authorized Means of Acceptance. A means of communicating acceptance can be expressly authorized by the offeror or impliedly authorized by the facts and circumstances of the situation. An acceptance sent by means not expressly or impliedly authorized normally is not effective until it is received by the offeror.

When an offeror specifies how acceptance should be made (for instance, by overnight delivery), *express authorization* is said to exist. The contract is not formed unless the offeree uses that specified mode of acceptance. Moreover, both offeror and offeree are bound in contract the moment this means of acceptance is employed.

If the offeror does not expressly authorize a certain mode of acceptance, then acceptance can be made by *any reasonable means*. Courts look at the prevailing business usages and the surrounding circumstances to determine whether the mode of acceptance used was reasonable. Usually, the offeror's choice of a particular means in making the offer implies that the offeree can use the *same or a faster means* for acceptance.

Substitute Method of Acceptance. Sometimes, the offeror authorizes a particular method of acceptance, but the offeree accepts by a different means. In that situation, the acceptance may still be effective if the substituted method serves the same purpose as the authorized means.

Acceptance by a substitute method is not effective on dispatch, however. No contract will be formed until the acceptance is received by the offeror. ■ **Example 12.16** Bennion's offer to Morgan specifies acceptance via FedEx overnight delivery, but Morgan (the offeree) accepts instead by overnight delivery from UPS. The substitute method of acceptance will still be effective, but not until Bennion (the offeror) receives Morgan's acceptance from UPS. ■

12–3 E-Contracts

Numerous contracts are formed online. Electronic contracts, or **e-contracts,** must meet the same basic requirements (agreement, consideration, contractual capacity, and legality) as paper contracts. Disputes concerning e-contracts, however, tend to center on contract terms and whether the parties voluntarily agreed to those terms.

Online contracts may be formed not only for the sale of goods and services but also for *licensing.* The "sale" of software generally involves a license, or a right to use the software, rather than the passage of title (ownership rights) from the seller to the buyer. When you download an app on your smartphone, for instance, you normally must agree to the terms of use in a licensing agreement before using it.

Although we typically refer to the offeror and the offeree as a *seller* and a *buyer,* in many online transactions these parties would be more accurately described as a *licensor* and a *licensee.*

12–3a Online Offers

Sellers doing business via the Internet can protect themselves against contract disputes and legal liability by creating offers that clearly spell out the terms that will govern their transactions if the offers are accepted. All important terms should be conspicuous and easy to view.

The seller's website should include a hypertext link to a page containing the full contract so that potential buyers are made aware of the terms to which they are assenting. The contract generally must be displayed online in a readable format, such as a twelve-point typeface. All provisions should be reasonably clear.

Provisions to Include An important point to keep in mind is that the offeror (the seller) controls the offer and thus the resulting contract. The seller should therefore anticipate the terms he or she wants to include in a contract and provide for them in the offer. In some instances, a standardized contract form may suffice.

At a minimum, an online offer should include the following provisions:

1. *Acceptance of terms.* A clause that clearly indicates what constitutes the buyer's agreement to the terms of the offer, such as a box containing the words "I accept" that the buyer can click.
2. *Payment.* A provision specifying how payment for the goods (including any applicable taxes) must be made.
3. *Return policy.* A statement of the seller's refund and return policies.
4. *Disclaimer.* Disclaimers of liability for certain uses of the goods. For instance, an online seller of business forms may add a disclaimer that the seller does not accept responsibility for the buyer's reliance on the forms rather than on an attorney's advice.
5. *Limitation on remedies.* A provision specifying the remedies available to the buyer if the goods are found to be defective or if the contract is otherwise breached. Any limitation of remedies should be clearly spelled out.
6. *Privacy policy.* A statement indicating how the seller will use the information gathered about the buyer.
7. *Dispute resolution.* Provisions relating to dispute settlement, which we examine more closely in the following section.

Dispute-Settlement Provisions Online offers frequently include provisions relating to dispute settlement. For instance, an offer might include an arbitration clause specifying that any dispute arising under the contract will be arbitrated in a designated forum. The parties might also select the forum and the law that will govern any disputes.

The same contract may include arbitration, forum-selection, and choice-of-law clauses. ■ **Case in Point 12.17** Xlibris Publishing provides a variety of editing, publishing, and marketing services online to authors who wish to self-publish their work. Avis Smith, a New York resident, had previously submitted his manuscript to Xlibris. Smith received an e-mail from Xlibris offering to sell him a service package at half price. Smith agreed and entered into a contract to purchase the package for $7,500 to be paid over three months.

A clause in the contract stated that any disputes between the parties would be arbitrated in Indianapolis, under the laws of Indiana. Communications between Smith and Xlibris deteriorated, and Smith ultimately sued the company in a federal court in New York. Xlibris asked the court to compel arbitration in Indiana. The court ruled that Smith had consented to the arbitration, forum-selection, and choice-of-law clauses, which were enforceable. Smith was required to arbitrate the dispute in Indiana.[13] ■

12–3b Online Acceptances

The *Restatement (Second) of Contracts*, which is a compilation of common law contract principles, states that parties may agree to a contract "by written or spoken words or by other action or by failure to act."[14] The Uniform Commercial Code (UCC), which governs sales contracts, has a similar provision. Section 2–204 of the UCC states that any contract for the sale of goods "may be made in any manner sufficient to show agreement, including conduct by both parties which recognizes the existence of such a contract." The courts have used these provisions in determining what constitutes an online acceptance.

Click-On Agreements The courts have concluded that the act of clicking on a box labeled "I accept" or "I agree" can indicate acceptance of an online offer. The agreement resulting from such an acceptance is often called a **click-on agreement** (sometimes referred to as a *click-on license* or *click-wrap agreement*).

Generally, the law does not require that the parties have read all of the terms in a contract for it to be effective. Therefore, clicking on a box that states "I agree" to certain terms can be enough. The terms may be contained on a website through which the buyer is obtaining goods or services. They may also appear on a screen when software is downloaded from the Internet.

■ **Case in Point 12.18** Any person who agrees to work as an Uber driver must enter into a services agreement and driver addendum contract with Uber Technologies, Inc. The contracts include an arbitration provision. New drivers must click the "Yes, I agree" button to use the Uber app and to start picking up passengers.

A group of Chinese-speaking Uber drivers filed a breach-of-contract suit against the company. Uber responded with a motion to compel arbitration, which a federal district court granted. The plaintiffs had downloaded the Chinese version of the Uber app and could read the arbitration provision in their native language. Each had clicked on the button and agreed to arbitrate any disputes (whether or not they had actually read the clause). Thus, the arbitration clause was enforceable, and the lawsuit was dismissed.[15] ■

Shrink-Wrap Agreements With a **shrink-wrap agreement** (or *shrink-wrap license*), the terms are expressed inside the box in which the goods are packaged. (The term *shrink-wrap* refers to the plastic that covers the box.) Usually, the party who opens the box is told that she or he agrees to the terms by keeping whatever is in the box. Similarly, when a purchaser opens a software package, he or she agrees to abide by the terms of the limited license agreement.

In most instances, a shrink-wrap agreement is not between a retailer and a buyer, but is between the manufacturer of the hardware or software and the ultimate buyer-user of the product. The terms generally concern warranties, remedies, and other issues associated with the use of the product.

Shrink-Wrap Agreements and Enforceable Contract Terms. In some cases, the courts have enforced the terms of shrink-wrap agreements in the same way as the terms of other contracts. These courts have reasoned that by including the terms with the product, the seller proposed a contract. The buyer could accept this contract by using the product after having an opportunity to read the terms. Thus, a buyer's failure to object to terms contained within a shrink-wrapped software package may constitute an acceptance of the terms by conduct.

Shrink-Wrap Terms That May Not Be Enforced. Sometimes, however, the courts have refused to enforce certain terms included in shrink-wrap agreements because the buyer did not expressly consent to them. An important factor is when the parties formed their contract.

---

13. *Smith v. Xlibris Publishing*, 2016 WL 5678566 (E.D.N.Y. 2016).
14. *Restatement (Second) of Contracts*, Section 19.

15. *Kai Peng v. Uber Technologies, Inc.*, 237 F.Supp.3d 36 (E.D.N.Y. 2017).

If a buyer orders a product over the telephone, for instance, and is not informed of an arbitration clause or a forum-selection clause at that time, the buyer clearly has not expressly agreed to these terms. If the buyer discovers the clauses *after* the parties have entered into a contract, a court may conclude that those terms were proposals for additional terms and were not part of the contract.

■ **Case in Point 12.19** David Noble purchased a Samsung Smartwatch from an AT&T store after seeing ads saying that its battery life was twenty-four to forty-eight hours with typical use. But Noble's Smartwatch battery lasted only about four hours, so he returned the Smartwatch and received a new one. The second Smartwatch suffered from the same battery problem. Noble again went to the AT&T store and, this time, was directed to ship the Smartwatch to Samsung. Samsung sent Noble a third Smartwatch with equally poor battery life. Noble then filed a suit against Samsung in a federal district court. Samsung filed a motion to compel arbitration, which the district court denied. Samsung appealed.

Inside each of the Smartwatch boxes that Noble received was a tiny booklet titled "Health and Safety and Warranty Guide" that included a standard limited warranty. On page ninety-seven of the guide, a boldfaced question read, "What is the procedure for resolving disputes?" Under that was a statement saying that any disputes would be resolved exclusively through binding arbitration. The court held that this language "tucked away in a brochure" was not sufficient to show that Noble had agreed to arbitration. Because consumers were not given reasonable notice of the arbitration clause (on the outside of the guide or somewhere obvious in the packaging), it was unenforceable.[16] ■

Browse-Wrap Terms. Like the terms of a click-on agreement, **browse-wrap terms** can appear in a transaction conducted over the Internet. Unlike a click-on agreement, however, browse-wrap terms do not require the buyer or user to assent to the terms before, say, downloading or using certain software. ■ **Case in Point 12.20** James McCants bought dietary supplements over the Internet that allegedly seriously damaged his liver. When he sued the seller, Vitacost.com, Inc., the company moved for arbitration based on a clause in the browse-wrap terms. To see the arbitration clause, a purchaser would have had to scroll to the bottom of the seller's Web page and click on a hyperlink labeled "Terms and Conditions." The trial court denied the motion to compel arbitration, and Vitacost.com appealed. The reviewing court held that these browse-wrap terms were not part of the sales agreement and were thus unenforceable.[17] ■

12–3c Federal Law on E-Signatures and E-Documents

An **e-signature** has been defined as "an electronic sound, symbol, or process attached to or logically associated with a record and executed or adopted by a person with the intent to sign the record."[18] Thus, e-signatures can include encrypted digital signatures, names (intended as signatures) at the ends of e-mail messages, and "clicks" on a Web page if the clicks include some means of identification.

Congress enacted the Electronic Signatures in Global and National Commerce Act (E-SIGN Act) in 2000.[19] The E-SIGN Act provides that no contract, record, or signature may be "denied legal effect" solely because it is in electronic form. In other words, under this law, an electronic signature is as valid as a signature on paper, and an e-document can be as enforceable as a paper one. For an e-signature to be enforceable, the contracting parties must have agreed to use electronic signatures. For an electronic document to be valid, it must be in a form that can be retained and accurately reproduced.

The E-SIGN Act does not apply to all types of documents. Documents that are exempt include court papers, divorce decrees, evictions, foreclosures, health-insurance terminations, prenuptial agreements, and wills. Also, the only agreements governed by the UCC that fall under this law are those covered by Articles 2 and 2A (sales and lease contracts) and UCC 1–107 and 1–206.

12–3d The Uniform Electronic Transactions Act

States have their own laws governing electronic transactions, which are frequently based on the Uniform Electronic Transactions Act (UETA). Among other things, the UETA declares that a signature may not be denied legal effect or enforceability solely because it is in electronic form.

The primary purpose of the UETA was to remove barriers to e-commerce by giving the same legal effect to electronic records and signatures as is given to paper documents and signatures. In addition to its broad definition of an e-signature, the UETA defines a **record** as

---

16. *Noble v. Samsung Electronics Company, Inc.*, 682 Fed.Appx. 113 (3d Cir. 2017).

17. *Vitacost.com, Inc. v. McCants*, 42 Fla.L.Weekly D394, 210 So.3d 761 (3 Dist. 2017).

18. This definition is from Section 102(8) of the Uniform Electronic Transactions Act.

19. 15 U.S.C. Sections 7001 *et seq.*

"information that is inscribed on a tangible medium or that is stored in an electronic or other medium and is retrievable in perceivable [visual] form."[20] Under UETA provisions, records, signatures, and contracts may not be denied enforceability solely due to their electronic form.

The UETA does not apply to all writings and signatures. It covers only electronic records and electronic signatures *relating to a transaction.* A *transaction* is defined as an interaction between two or more people relating to business, commercial, or governmental activities. The act specifically does not apply to wills or testamentary trusts or to transactions governed by the UCC (other than those covered by Articles 2 and 2A). In addition, the provisions of the UETA allow the states to exclude its application to other areas of law.

The UETA does not apply to a transaction unless each of the parties has previously agreed to conduct transactions by electronic means. The agreement may be explicit, or it may be implied by the conduct of the parties and the surrounding circumstances. It may sometimes be reasonable to infer that a person who gives out a business card with an e-mail address on it has consented to transact business electronically, for instance. Agreement may also be inferred from an e-mail or even a verbal communication between the parties.

12–4 Consideration

The second element of a valid contract is *consideration.* The fact that a promise has been made does not mean the promise can or will be enforced. Under the common law, a primary basis for the enforcement of promises is consideration. **Consideration** usually is defined as the value given in return for a promise (in a bilateral contract) or in return for a performance (in a unilateral contract). It is the inducement, price, or motive that causes a party to enter into an agreement. As long as consideration is present, the courts generally do not interfere with contracts based on the amount of consideration paid.

Often, consideration is broken down into two parts: (1) something of *legally sufficient value* must be given in exchange for the promise, and (2) there must be a *bargained-for exchange.*

12–4a Legally Sufficient Value

To be legally sufficient, consideration must be something of value in the eyes of the law and may consist of the following:

20. UETA 102(15).

1. A promise to do something that one has no prior legal duty to do.
2. The performance of an action that one is otherwise not obligated to undertake.
3. The refraining from an action that one has a legal right to undertake (called a **forbearance**).

Consideration in bilateral contracts normally consists of a promise in return for a promise. In a contract for the sale of goods, for instance, the seller promises to ship specific goods to the buyer, and the buyer promises to pay for those goods. Each of these promises constitutes consideration for the contract.

In contrast, unilateral contracts involve a promise in return for a performance (an action). ■ **Example 12.21** Anita says to her neighbor, "When you finish painting the garage, I will pay you $800." Anita's neighbor paints the garage. The act of painting the garage is the consideration that creates Anita's contractual obligation to pay her neighbor $800. ■

12–4b Bargained-for Exchange

The second element of consideration is that it must provide the basis for the bargain struck between the contracting parties. That is, the item of value must be given or promised by the promisor (offeror) in return for the promisee's promise, performance, or promise of performance.

This element of bargained-for exchange distinguishes contracts from gifts. ■ **Case in Point 12.22** USS–POSCO Industries (UPI) hired Floyd Case as an entry-level laborer and side trim operator. Because UPI faced a shortage of skilled maintenance technical electrical (MTE) workers, it decided to implement an educational program for its existing employees. UPI would cover the costs ($46,000) of a program that required 135 weeks of instruction, 90 weeks of on-the-job training, and 45 weeks of classroom work.

Case applied for and was accepted into the program. UPI paid his wages, benefits, and training expenses, but it did not guarantee him a position as an MTE worker. Case signed a reimbursement agreement to participate, stating that if he voluntarily left UPI within 30 months after completing the program, he would (absent a compelling hardship) refund $30,000 to UPI. Two months after completing the program and starting work as an MTE worker, Case left UPI for a position with another employer as an electrician. He refused to refund $30,000 to UPI, and UPI sued for breach.

Case argued that the reimbursement agreement lacked consideration because UPI had no obligation to keep

Case employed, and thus there was no bargained-for exchange. The court disagreed. "The exchange, frankly, is obvious: Case got continued wages and fronted education costs, and UPI got Case's agreement to repay those costs if he both completed the training and left the company before it could benefit from the investment." The court enforced the agreement and ordered Case to refund $30,000 to UPI.[21] ∎

12–4c Agreements That Lack Consideration

Sometimes, one of the parties (or both parties) to an agreement may think that consideration has been exchanged when in fact it has not. Here, we look at some situations in which the parties' promises or actions do not qualify as contractual consideration.

Preexisting Duty Under most circumstances, a promise to do what one already has a legal duty to do does not constitute legally sufficient consideration. The preexisting legal duty may be imposed by law or may arise out of a previous contract.

If a party is already bound by contract to perform a certain duty, that duty cannot serve as consideration for a second contract. ∎ **Example 12.23** Ajax Contractors begins construction on a seven-story office building and after three months demands an extra $75,000 on its contract. If the extra $75,000 is not paid, the contractor will stop working. The owner of the land, finding no one else to complete the construction, agrees to pay the extra $75,000. The agreement is unenforceable because it is not supported by legally sufficient consideration. Ajax Contractors had a preexisting contractual duty to complete the building. ∎

Unforeseen Difficulties. The rule regarding preexisting duty is meant to prevent extortion and the so-called holdup game. Nonetheless, if, during performance of a contract, extraordinary difficulties arise that were totally unforeseen at the time the contract was formed, a court may allow an exception to the rule. The key is whether the court finds that the modification is fair and equitable in view of circumstances not anticipated by the parties when the contract was made.

Suppose that in *Example 12.23*, Ajax Contractors had asked for the extra $75,000 because it encountered a rock formation that no one knew existed. If the landowner agrees to pay the extra $75,000 to excavate the rock and the court finds that it is fair to do so, Ajax Contractors

can enforce the agreement. If rock formations are common in the area, however, the court may determine that the contractor should have known of the risk. In that situation, the court may choose to apply the preexisting duty rule and prevent Ajax Contractors from obtaining the extra $75,000.

Rescission and New Contract. The law recognizes that two parties can mutually agree to rescind, or cancel, their contract, at least to the extent that it is *executory* (still to be carried out). **Rescission**[22] is the unmaking of a contract so as to return the parties to the positions they occupied before the contract was made.

Sometimes, parties rescind a contract and make a new contract at the same time. When this occurs, it is often difficult to determine whether there was consideration for the new contract, or whether the parties had a preexisting duty under the previous contract. If a court finds there was a preexisting duty, then the new contract will be invalid because there was no consideration.

Past Consideration Promises made in return for actions or events that have already taken place are unenforceable. These promises lack consideration in that the element of bargained-for exchange is missing. In short, you can bargain for something to take place now or in the future but not for something that has already taken place. Therefore, **past consideration** is no consideration.

∎ **Case in Point 12.24** Jamil Blackmon became friends with Allen Iverson when Iverson was a high school student who showed tremendous promise as an athlete. One evening, Blackmon suggested that Iverson use "The Answer" as a nickname in the summer league basketball tournaments. Blackmon said that Iverson would be "The Answer" to all of the National Basketball Association's woes. Later that night, Iverson said that he would give Blackmon 25 percent of any proceeds from the merchandising of products that used "The Answer" as a logo or a slogan. Because Iverson's promise was made in return for past consideration, it was unenforceable. In effect, Iverson stated his intention to give Blackmon a gift.[23] ∎

In a variety of situations, an employer will often ask a new employee to sign a *noncompete agreement*, also called a *covenant not to compete*. Under such an agreement, the employee agrees not to compete with the employer for a certain period of time after the employment relationship ends. When a current employee is required to sign a noncompete agreement, his or her employment is not sufficient consideration for the agreement, because the

---

21. *USS–POSCO Industries v. Case*, 244 Cal.App.4th 197, 197 Cal.Rptr.3d 791 (Div. 1 2016).

22. Pronounced reh-*sih*-zhen.
23. *Blackmon v. Iverson*, 324 F.Supp.2d 602 (E.D.Pa. 2003).

individual is already employed. To be valid, the agreement requires new consideration.

Illusory Promises If the terms of the contract express such uncertainty of performance that the promisor has not definitely promised to do anything, the promise is said to be *illusory*—without consideration and unenforceable. A promise is illusory when it fails to bind the promisor.

■ **Example 12.25** The president of Tuscan Corporation says to her employees, "If profits continue to be high, everyone will get a 10 percent bonus at the end of the year—if management agrees." This is an *illusory promise*, or no promise at all, because performance depends solely on the discretion of management. There is no bargained-for consideration. The statement indicates only that management may or may not do something in the future. Therefore, even though the employees work hard and profits remain high, the company is not obligated to pay the bonus now or later. ■

Exhibit 12–1 illustrates some common situations in which promises or actions do not constitute contractual consideration.

12-4d Settlement of Claims

Businesspersons and others often enter into contracts to settle legal claims. It is important to understand the nature of consideration given in these kinds of settlement agreements, or contracts. A claim may be settled through an *accord and satisfaction*, a *release*, or a *covenant not to sue*.

Accord and Satisfaction In an **accord and satisfaction**, a debtor offers to pay, and a creditor accepts, a lesser amount than the creditor originally claimed was owed. The *accord* is the agreement. In the accord, one party undertakes to give or perform, and the other to accept, in satisfaction of a claim, something other than that on which the parties originally agreed. *Satisfaction* is the performance (usually payment) that takes place after the accord is executed.

A basic rule is that there can be no satisfaction unless there is first an accord. In addition, for accord and satisfaction to occur, the amount of the debt *must be in dispute.*

Liquidated Debts. If a debt is *liquidated*, accord and satisfaction cannot take place. A **liquidated debt** is one whose amount has been ascertained, fixed, agreed on, settled, or exactly determined.

In most states, a creditor's acceptance of a lesser sum than the entire amount of a liquidated debt is *not* satisfaction, and the balance of the debt is still legally owed. The reason for this rule is that the debtor has given no consideration to satisfy the obligation of paying the balance to the creditor. The debtor had a preexisting legal obligation to pay the entire debt. (Creditors do, of course, sometimes settle with debtors for less than the amount owed or even write off certain liquidated debts as uncollectible.)

Unliquidated Debts. An **unliquidated debt** is the opposite of a liquidated debt. The amount of the debt is *not* settled, fixed, agreed on, ascertained, or determined, and

Exhibit 12–1 Examples of Agreements That Lack Consideration

Preexisting Duty	**Past Consideration**	**Illusory Promises**
When a person already has a legal duty to perform an action, there is no legally sufficient consideration.	When a person makes a promise in return for actions or events that have already taken place, there is no consideration.	When a person expresses contract terms with such uncertainty that the terms are not definite, the promise is illusory.
Example: A firefighter cannot receive a cash reward from a business owner for putting out a fire in a downtown commercial district. As a city employee, the firefighter had a duty to extinguish the fire.	*Example:* A real estate agent sells a friend's house without charging a commission, and in return, the friend promises to give the agent $1,000. The friend's promise is simply an intention to give a gift.	*Example:* A storeowner promises a $500 bonus to each employee who works Christmas Day, as long as the owner feels that they did their jobs well. The owner's promise is just a statement of something she may or may not do in the future.

reasonable persons may differ over the amount owed. In these circumstances, acceptance of a lesser sum operates as satisfaction, or discharge, of the debt because there is valid consideration. The parties give up a legal right to contest the amount in dispute.

Release A **release** is a contract in which one party forfeits the right to pursue a legal claim against the other party. It bars any further recovery beyond the terms stated in the release.

A release generally will be binding if it meets the following requirements:

1. The agreement is made in good faith (honestly).
2. The release contract is in a signed writing (required in many states).
3. The contract is accompanied by consideration.

Clearly, an individual is better off knowing the extent of his or her injuries or damages before signing a release.

■ Example 12.26 Lupe's car is damaged in an automobile accident caused by Dexter's negligence. Dexter offers to give her $3,000 if she will release him from further liability resulting from the accident. Lupe agrees and signs the release. If Lupe later discovers that it will cost $4,200 to repair her car, she normally cannot recover the additional amount from Dexter. ■

Covenant Not to Sue Unlike a release, a **covenant not to sue** does not always bar further recovery. The parties simply substitute a contractual obligation for some other type of legal action based on a valid claim. Suppose that, in *Example 12.26*, Lupe agrees with Dexter not to sue for damages in a tort action if he will pay for the damage to her car. If Dexter fails to pay for the repairs, Lupe can bring an action against him for breach of contract.

As the following case illustrates, a covenant not to sue can form the basis for a dismissal of the claims of either party to the covenant.

Spotlight on Nike

Case 12.3 Already, LLC v. Nike, Inc.
Supreme Court of the United States, 568 U.S. 85, 133 S.Ct. 721, 184 L.Ed.2d 553 (2013).

Background and Facts Nike, Inc., designs, makes, and sells athletic footwear, including a line of shoes known as "Air Force 1." Already, LLC, also designs and markets athletic footwear, including the "Sugar" and "Soulja Boy" lines. Nike filed a suit in a federal district court against Already, alleging that Soulja Boys and Sugars infringed the Air Force 1 trademark. Already filed a counterclaim, contending that the Air Force 1 trademark was invalid.

While the suit was pending, Nike issued a covenant not to sue. Nike promised not to raise any trademark claims against Already or any affiliated entity based on Already's existing footwear designs or any future Already designs that constituted a "colorable imitation" of Already's current products. Nike then filed a motion to dismiss its own claims and to dismiss Already's counterclaim. Already opposed the dismissal of its counterclaim, but the court granted Nike's motion. The U.S. Court of Appeals for the Second Circuit affirmed. Already appealed to the United States Supreme Court.

In the Language of the Court
Chief Justice *ROBERTS* delivered the opinion of the Court.
* * * *

* * * A defendant cannot automatically moot a case simply by ending its unlawful conduct once sued. [A matter is *moot* if it involves no actual controversy for the court to decide, and federal courts will dismiss moot cases.] Otherwise, a defendant could engage in unlawful conduct, stop when sued to have the case declared moot, then pick up where he left off, repeating this cycle until he achieves all his unlawful ends. Given this concern, * * * *a defendant claiming that its voluntary compliance moots a case bears the formidable burden of showing that it is absolutely clear the allegedly wrongful behavior could not reasonably be expected to recur.* [This is the voluntary cessation test. Emphasis added.]
* * * *

Case 12.3 Continues

Case 12.3 Continued

We begin our analysis with the terms of the covenant:

> [Nike] unconditionally and irrevocably covenants to refrain from making *any* claim(s) or demand(s) * * * against Already or *any* of its * * * related business entities * * * [including] distributors * * * and employees of such entities and *all* customers * * * on account of any *possible* cause of action based on or involving trademark infringement * * * relating to the NIKE Mark based on the appearance of *any* of Already's current and/or previous footwear product designs, and *any* colorable imitations thereof, regardless of whether that footwear is produced * * * or otherwise used in commerce.

The breadth of this covenant suffices to meet the burden imposed by the voluntary cessation test.

In addition, Nike originally argued that the Sugars and Soulja Boys infringed its trademark; in other words, Nike believed those shoes were "colorable imitations" of the Air Force 1s. Nike's covenant now allows Already to produce all of its existing footwear designs—including the Sugar and Soulja Boy—and any "colorable imitation" of those designs. * * * It is hard to imagine a scenario that would potentially infringe Nike's trademark and yet not fall under the covenant. Nike, having taken the position in court that there is no prospect of such a shoe, would be hard pressed to assert the contrary down the road. If such a shoe exists, the parties have not pointed to it, there is no evidence that Already has dreamt of it, and we cannot conceive of it. It sits, as far as we can tell, on a shelf between Dorothy's ruby slippers and Perseus's winged sandals.

* * * *

* * * Given the covenant's broad language, and given that Already has asserted no concrete plans to engage in conduct not covered by the covenant, we can conclude the case is moot because the challenged conduct cannot reasonably be expected to recur.

Decision and Remedy *The United States Supreme Court affirmed the judgment of the lower court. Under the covenant not to sue, Nike could not file a claim for trademark infringement against Already, and Already could not assert that Nike's trademark was invalid.*

Critical Thinking

- **Economic** *Why would any party agree to a covenant not to sue?*
- **Legal Environment** *Which types of contracts are similar to covenants not to sue? Explain.*

12–4e Promissory Estoppel

Sometimes, individuals rely on promises to their detriment, and their reliance may form a basis for a court to infer contract rights and duties. Under the doctrine of **promissory estoppel** (also called *detrimental reliance*), a person who has reasonably and substantially relied on the promise of another may be able to obtain some measure of recovery.

Promissory estoppel is applied in a wide variety of contexts in which a promise is otherwise unenforceable, such as when a promise is made *without consideration*. Under this doctrine, a court may enforce an otherwise unenforceable promise to avoid the injustice that would otherwise result. For the promissory estoppel doctrine to be applied, the following elements are required:

1. There must be a clear and definite promise.
2. The promisor should have expected that the promisee would rely on the promise.
3. The promisee reasonably relied on the promise by acting or refraining from some act.

4. The promisee's reliance was definite and resulted in substantial detriment.
5. Enforcement of the promise is necessary to avoid injustice.

If these requirements are met, a promise may be enforced even though it is not supported by consideration.[24] In essence, the promisor will be **estopped** (prevented) from asserting the lack of consideration as a defense.

12–5 Contractual Capacity

In addition to agreement and consideration, for a contract to be deemed valid, the parties to the contract must have **contractual capacity**—the legal ability to enter into a contractual relationship. Courts generally presume the existence of contractual capacity, but in some situations, as when a person is young or mentally incompetent, capacity may be lacking or questionable.

---

24. *Restatement (Second) of Contracts*, Section 90.

12–5a Minors

In almost all states, the *age of majority* (when a person is no longer a minor) for contractual purposes is eighteen years.[25] In addition, some states provide for the termination of minority on marriage. Minority status may also be terminated by a minor's *emancipation*, which occurs when a child's parent or legal guardian relinquishes the legal right to exercise control over the child. Normally, minors who leave home to support themselves are considered emancipated.

The general rule is that a minor can enter into any contract that an adult can, except contracts prohibited by law for minors (for instance, the purchase of tobacco or alcoholic beverages). A contract entered into by a minor, however, is voidable at the option of that minor, subject to certain exceptions.

The legal avoidance, or setting aside, of a contractual obligation is referred to as **disaffirmance.** To disaffirm, a minor must express his or her intent, through words or conduct, not to be bound to the contract.

■ **Case in Point 12.27** S.L. was a female sixteen-year-old minor who worked at a KFC Restaurant operated by PAK Foods Houston, LLC. PAK Foods' policy was to resolve any dispute with an employee through arbitration. At the employer's request, S.L. signed an acknowledgment of this policy. S.L. was injured on the job and subsequently terminated her employment. S.L.'s mother, Marissa Garcia, filed a suit on S.L.'s behalf in a Texas state court against PAK Foods to recover the medical expenses for the injury. PAK Foods filed a motion to compel arbitration. The court denied the motion, and PAK Foods appealed. A state intermediate appellate court affirmed the decision. A minor may disaffirm a contract at his or her option. The court concluded that S.L. opted to disaffirm the agreement to arbitrate by terminating her employment and filing the lawsuit.[26] ■

Note that an adult who enters into a contract with a minor cannot avoid his or her contractual duties on the ground that the minor can do so. Unless the minor exercises the option to disaffirm the contract, the adult party normally is bound by it.

12–5b Intoxication

Intoxication is a condition in which a person's normal capacity to act or think is inhibited by alcohol or some other drug. A contract entered into by an intoxicated person can be either voidable or valid (and thus enforceable).

If the person was sufficiently intoxicated to lack mental capacity, then the agreement may be voidable even if the intoxication was purely voluntary. If a contract is voidable because one party was intoxicated, that person has the option of disaffirming it while intoxicated and for a reasonable time after becoming sober. If, despite intoxication, the person understood the legal consequences of the agreement, the contract will be enforceable.

Courts look at objective indications of the intoxicated person's condition to determine if he or she possessed or lacked the required capacity. It is difficult to prove that a person's judgment was so severely impaired that he or she could not comprehend the legal consequences of entering into a contract. Therefore, courts rarely permit contracts to be avoided due to intoxication.

12–5c Mental Incompetence

Contracts made by mentally incompetent persons can be void, voidable, or valid. If a court has previously determined that a person is mentally incompetent, any contract made by that person is *void*—no contract exists. Only a guardian appointed by the court to represent a mentally incompetent person can enter into binding legal obligations on that person's behalf.

If a court has not previously judged a person to be mentally incompetent but the person was incompetent at the time the contract was formed, the contract may be voidable.[27] A contract is *voidable* if the person did not know he or she was entering into the contract or lacked the mental capacity to comprehend its nature, purpose, and consequences.

■ **Case in Point 12.28** Annabelle Duffie was mildly mentally retarded and suffering from dementia. She had lived with her brother, Jerome, for her entire life. When Jerome died, he left Annabelle his property, including 180 acres near Hope, Arkansas, valued at more than $400,000. Less than three months later, Annabelle signed a deed granting her interest in the land to Charles and Joanne Black for $150,000.

Later, when Annabelle's nephew, Jack, was appointed to be her legal guardian, he filed a lawsuit against the Blacks seeking to void the land deal because of Annabelle's lack of mental competence. The trial court ordered the Blacks to return the property to Annabelle, and a state appellate court affirmed. The evidence showed that Annabelle had been incompetent her entire life. She lacked the cognitive ability to make the complex

---

25. The age of majority may still be twenty-one for other purposes, such as the purchase and consumption of alcohol.
26. *PAK Foods Houston, LLC v. Garcia,* 433 S.W.3d 171 (Tex.App.—Houston 2014).
27. This is the rule in the majority of states. See, for example, *Hernandez v. Banks,* 65 A.3d 59 (D.C. 2013).

financial decisions involved in selling property. There-fore, the contract was voidable.[28] ∎

A contract entered into by a mentally incompetent person (not previously declared incompetent) may also be *valid* if the person had capacity *at the time the contract was formed.* Some people who are incompetent due to age or illness have *lucid intervals*—temporary periods of sufficient intelligence, judgment, and will. During such intervals, they will be considered to have legal capacity to enter into contracts.

12–6 Legality

The final requirement for a contract to be valid and enforceable is that it must be formed for a legal purpose. A contract to do something that is prohibited by federal or state statutory law is illegal and, as such, void from the outset and thus unenforceable. Additionally, a contract to commit a tortious act (such as an agreement to engage in fraud) is contrary to public policy and therefore illegal and unenforceable.

12–6a Contracts Contrary to Statute

Statutes often set forth rules specifying which terms and clauses may be included in contracts and which are pro-hibited. We now examine several ways in which contracts may be contrary to statute and thus illegal.

Contracts to Commit a Crime Any contract to commit a crime is in violation of a statute. Thus, a con-tract to sell illegal drugs in violation of criminal laws is unenforceable, as is a contract to cover up a corporation's violation of an environmental or other law.

Sometimes, the object or performance of a contract is rendered illegal by a statute *after* the parties entered into the contract. In that situation, the contract is considered to be discharged by law.

Usury Almost every state has a statute that sets the max-imum rate of interest that can be charged for different types of transactions, including ordinary loans. A lender who makes a loan at an interest rate above the lawful max-imum commits **usury.**

Although usurious contracts are illegal, most states simply limit the interest that the lender may collect on the contract to the lawful maximum interest rate in that state. In a few states, the lender can recover the principal

amount of the loan but no interest. In addition, states can make exceptions to facilitate business transactions. For instance, nearly all states allow higher-interest-rate loans for borrowers who could not otherwise obtain funds because of the risk being assumed by the lenders.

Gambling Gambling is the creation of risk for the pur-pose of assuming it. Any scheme that involves the distri-bution of property by chance among persons who have paid valuable consideration for the opportunity (chance) to receive the property is gambling.

Traditionally, the states deemed gambling contracts illegal and thus void. Today, many states allow (and reg-ulate) certain forms of gambling, such as horse racing, video poker machines, and charity-sponsored bingo. In addition, nearly all states allow state-operated lotteries and gambling on Native American reservations. Even in states that permit certain types of gambling, though, courts often find that gambling contracts are illegal.

Licensing Statutes All states require members of certain professions—including physicians, lawyers, real estate brokers, accountants, architects, electricians, and stockbrokers—to have licenses. Some licenses are obtained only after extensive schooling and examinations, which indicate to the public that a special skill has been acquired. Others require only that the applicant be of good moral character and pay a fee.

Whether a contract with an unlicensed person is legal and enforceable depends on the purpose of the licens-ing statute. If the statute's purpose is to protect the pub-lic from unauthorized practitioners (such as unlicensed architects, attorneys, and electricians), then a contract involving an unlicensed practitioner is generally illegal and unenforceable. If the statute's purpose is merely to raise government revenues, however, a court may enforce the contract and fine the unlicensed person.

12–6b Contracts Contrary to Public Policy

Although contracts involve private parties, some are not enforceable because of the negative impact they would have on society. These contracts are said to be *contrary to public policy.* Examples include a contract to commit an immoral act, such as selling a child, and a contract that prohibits marriage. Business contracts that may be against public policy include contracts in restraint of trade and unconscionable contracts or clauses.

Contracts in Restraint of Trade The United States has a strong public policy favoring competition in the econ-omy. Thus, contracts in restraint of trade (anticompetitive

---

28. *Black v. Duffie,* 2016 Ark.App. 584, 508 S.W.3d 40 (2016).

agreements) generally are unenforceable because they are contrary to public policy. Typically, such contracts also violate one or more federal or state antitrust statutes.

An exception is recognized when the restraint is reasonable and is contained in an ancillary (secondary or subordinate) clause in a contract. Such restraints often are included in contracts for the sale of an ongoing business and in employment contracts.

Covenants Not to Compete and the Sale of an Ongoing Business. Many contracts involve a type of restraint called a **covenant not to compete,** or a restrictive covenant (promise). A covenant not to compete may be created when a merchant who sells a store agrees not to open a new store in a certain geographic area surrounding the old business. Such an agreement enables the seller to sell, and the purchaser to buy, the goodwill and reputation of an ongoing business without having to worry that the seller will open a competing business a block away. Provided the restrictive covenant is reasonable and is an ancillary part of the sale of an ongoing business, it is enforceable.

Covenants Not to Compete in Employment Contracts. Sometimes, agreements not to compete (also referred to as *noncompete agreements*) are included in employment contracts. People in middle- or upper-level management positions commonly agree not to work for competitors or not to start competing businesses for a specified period of time after termination of employment.

Noncompete agreements are legal in most states so long as the specified period of time (of restraint) is not excessive in duration and the geographic restriction is reasonable. What constitutes a reasonable time period may be shorter in the online environment than in conventional employment contracts. Because the geographical restrictions apply worldwide, the time restrictions may be shorter.

A restraint that is found to be overly broad will not be enforced. ■ **Case in Point 12.29** An insurance firm in New York City, Brown & Brown, Inc., hired Theresa Johnson to perform actuarial analysis. On her first day of work, Johnson was asked to sign a nonsolicitation covenant. The covenant prohibited her from soliciting or servicing any of Brown's clients for two years after the termination of her employment.

Less than five years later, when Johnson's employment with Brown was terminated, she went to work for Lawley Benefits Group, LLC. Brown sued to enforce the covenant. A state appellate court ultimately ruled that the covenant was overly broad and unenforceable. The court noted that the employer had required all of its employees, regardless of position, to sign nonsolicitation covenants as a condition of employment. This evidence undercut Brown's argument that the covenant was necessary to protect legitimate business interests.[29] ■

Enforcement Issues. The laws governing the enforceability of covenants not to compete vary significantly from state to state. California prohibits the enforcement of covenants not to compete altogether. In some states, including Texas, such a covenant will not be enforced unless the employee has received some benefit in return for signing the noncompete agreement. This is true even if the covenant is reasonable as to time and area. If the employee receives no benefit, the covenant will be deemed void.

Occasionally, depending on the jurisdiction, courts will *reform* covenants not to compete. If a covenant is found to be unreasonable in time or geographic area, the court may convert the terms into reasonable ones and then enforce the reformed covenant. Such court actions present a problem, though, in that the judge implicitly becomes a party to the contract. Consequently, courts usually resort to contract **reformation** only when necessary to prevent undue burdens or hardships.

In the following case, the court reformed a noncompete agreement by adding the words "current location." Was this modification reasonable, given the facts of the case?

29. *Brown & Brown, Inc. v. Johnson*, 158 A.D.3d 1148, 71 N.Y.S.3d 255 (4 Dept. 2018).

Case 12.4

Kennedy v. Shave Barber Co.
Court of Appeals of Georgia, 348 Ga.App. 298, 822 S.E.2d 606 (2018).

Background and Facts Patricia Kennedy worked as a master barber for The Shave, a barbershop in the Virginia-Highland neighborhood of Atlanta, Georgia. Under the terms of her employment contract, Kennedy agreed that, after leaving her employment, she would not work in the men's grooming industry within a three-mile radius of The Shave for two years and would not solicit customers of The Shave for one year.

Case 12.4 Continues

Case 12.4 Continued

Less than a month after quitting her position, Kennedy opened a new salon, "PK Does Hair," two miles from The Shave. She solicited customers through social media accounts on which she posted photos that had been originally posted on social media by The Shave. The photos were taken at The Shave and were of various Shave customers, whom she tagged in the posts.

The Shave filed a suit in a Georgia state court against Kennedy, alleging a breach of the noncompete provision of her employment contract. Kennedy claimed, among other things, that the geographic restriction in the agreement was "unreasonable and uncertain." The court limited the geographic scope of the provision to a three-mile radius of The Shave's current location and issued an injunction in The Shave's favor. Kennedy appealed.

In the Language of the Court

GOBEIL, Judge.

* * * *

Kennedy argues that * * * the non-compete provision * * * contained an unreasonable and uncertain geographic restriction.

* * * *

* * * Most of The Shave's customers live and work within three miles of its Virginia-Highland location. * * * The Shave lost customers and * * * its business suffered when two former employees of The Shave opened competing barbershops within three miles of The Shave. Based on the limited territorial restriction involved in the non-compete covenant, and the demonstrated harm if the covenant is not enforced, we find the geographic limitation in this case to be reasonable and that Kennedy had fair notice of this restriction. Further, although The Shave currently operates only one location and has no immediate plans to open other locations, the trial court eliminated any uncertainty in the geographic scope of the non-compete by limiting the restricted area to a three-mile radius surrounding The Shave's current location.

Kennedy argues that The Shave failed to show that it had a legitimate business interest justifying the extent of the non-compete provision. We disagree.

* * * *

* * * *The Shave's non-compete provision was supported by legitimate business interests in that it had devoted considerable resources to developing its name recognition and customer base. * * * The Shave had a legitimate business interest in protecting itself from the risk that Kennedy might appropriate customers by taking advantage of the contacts developed while she worked at The Shave.* [Emphasis added.]

* * * *

* * * Kennedy * * * asserts that "using her social media accounts to post pictures of her work" and "tagging The Shave's customers in pictures" posted to her social media accounts does not constitute solicitation.

* * * *

* * * Many of Kennedy's social media posts constituted customer solicitation. * * * Kennedy was attempting to solicit clients with whom she had material contact during her employment with The Shave and that she met * * * as a direct result of her employment with The Shave. * * * *These targeted posts and tags constituted solicitation.* [Emphasis added.]

Decision and Remedy *A state intermediate appellate court affirmed the lower court's order in favor of The Shave. "Kennedy is in violation of several of the restrictive covenants which were specifically designed to protect The Shave from competition from its former employees and loss of its client base." The trial court's modification of the noncompete agreement to prohibit a former employee from operating a business within a three-mile radius was not unreasonable. "Therefore, the trial court did not err in finding the noncompete enforceable against Kennedy and in granting [an injunction] on this ground."*

Critical Thinking

- **Legal Environment** *What "legitimate business interests" justify the enforcement of a noncompete provision?*
- **Economic** *What sort of harm, particularly in Kennedy's situation, would support a court's refusal to enforce an employment contract's noncompete provision?*

Unconscionable Contracts or Clauses A court ordinarily does not look at the fairness or equity of a contract (or inquire into the adequacy of consideration). Persons are assumed to be reasonably intelligent, and the courts will not come to their aid just because they have made unwise or foolish bargains.

In certain circumstances, however, bargains are so oppressive that the courts relieve innocent parties of part or all of their duties. Such bargains are deemed **unconscionable**[30] because they are so unscrupulous or grossly unfair as to be "void of conscience." The Uniform Commercial Code (UCC) incorporates the concept of unconscionability in its provisions regarding the sale and lease of goods.[31]

A contract can be unconscionable on either procedural or substantive grounds. *Procedural* unconscionability often involves inconspicuous print, unintelligible language ("legalese"), or the lack of an opportunity to read the contract or ask questions about its meaning. This type of unconscionability typically arises when a party's lack of knowledge or understanding of the contract terms deprived him or her of any meaningful choice. *Substantive* unconscionability occurs when contracts, or portions of contracts, are oppressive or overly harsh. Courts generally focus on provisions that deprive one party of the benefits of the agreement or leave that party without a remedy for nonperformance by the other.

Exculpatory Clauses Often closely related to the concept of unconscionability are **exculpatory clauses,** which release a party from liability in the event of monetary or physical injury *no matter who is at fault.* Indeed, courts sometimes refuse to enforce such clauses on the ground that they are unconscionable.

Violation of Public Policy. Most courts view exculpatory clauses with disfavor. Exculpatory clauses found in rental agreements for commercial property are frequently held to be contrary to public policy, and such clauses are almost always unenforceable in residential property leases. Courts also usually hold that exculpatory clauses are against public policy in the employment context.

Court Enforcement of Exculpatory Clauses. Courts do enforce exculpatory clauses if they are reasonable, do not violate public policy, and do not protect parties from liability for intentional misconduct. The language used must not be ambiguous, and the parties must have been in relatively equal bargaining positions.

Businesses such as health clubs, racetracks, amusement parks, skiing facilities, horse-rental operations, golf-cart concessions, and skydiving organizations frequently use exculpatory clauses to limit their liability for patrons' injuries. ■ **Case in Point 12.30** Colleen Holmes participated in the Susan G. Komen Race for the Cure in St. Louis, Missouri. Her signed entry form included an exculpatory clause under which Holmes agreed to release the event sponsors from liability "for any injury or damages I might suffer in connection with my participation in this Event."

During the race, Holmes sustained injuries when she tripped and fell over an audiovisual box left on the ground by one of the sponsors. She filed a negligence suit against the sponsor whose employees had placed the box on the ground without barricades or warnings of its presence. The court held that the language used in the exculpatory clause clearly released all sponsors and their agents and employees from liability for future negligence. Holmes could not sue for the injuries she sustained during the race.[32] ■

Courts also may enforce reasonable exculpatory clauses in loan documents, real estate contracts, and trust agreements. See this chapter's *Managerial Strategy* feature for more about exculpatory clauses that will not be considered unconscionable.

Discriminatory Contracts Contracts in which a party promises to discriminate on the basis of race, color, national origin, religion, gender, age, or disability are contrary to both statute and public policy. They are also unenforceable.[33] For instance, if a property owner promises in a contract not to sell the property to a member of a particular race, the contract is unenforceable. The public policy underlying these prohibitions is very strong, and the courts are quick to invalidate discriminatory contracts.

12–7 Form—The Writing Requirement

A contract that is otherwise valid may still be unenforceable if it is not in the proper form. Certain types of contracts are required to be in writing or evidenced by a memorandum or electronic record. The writing requirement does not mean that an agreement must be a formal written contract. An exchange of e-mails that evidences the parties' agreement usually is sufficient, provided that they are "signed," or agreed to, by the party against whom enforcement is sought.

---

30. Pronounced un-*kon*-shun-uh-bul.
31. See UCC 2–302 and 2A–719.
32. *Holmes v. Multimedia KSDK, Inc.*, 395 S.W.3d 557 (Mo.Ct.App. 2013).
33. The major federal statute prohibiting discrimination is the Civil Rights Act of 1964, 42 U.S.C. Sections 2000e–2000e-17.

Managerial Strategy — Creating Liability Waivers That Are Not Unconscionable

Blanket liability waivers that absolve a business from virtually every event, even those caused by the business's own negligence, usually are unenforceable because they are unconscionable. Exculpatory waivers are common, nonetheless. We observe such waivers in gym memberships, on ski lift tickets, on admissions tickets to sporting events, and in simple contracts for the use of campgrounds.

Normally, courts view liability waivers as voluntarily bargained for whether or not they have been read. Thus, a waiver included in the fine print on the back of an admission ticket or on an entry sign to a stadium may be upheld. In general, if such waivers are unambiguous and conspicuous, the assumption is that patrons have had a chance to read them and have accepted their terms.

Activities with Inherent Risks

Cases challenging liability waivers have been brought against skydiving operations, skiing operations, bobsledding operations, white-water rafting companies, and health clubs. For example, in *Bergin v. Wild Mountain, Inc.,*[a] an appellate court in Minnesota upheld a ski resort's liability waiver. In that case, the plaintiff hit a snowmaking mound, which was "an inherent risk of skiing." Before the accident, the plaintiff had stated that he knew "that an inherent risk of serious injury in downhill skiing was hitting snowmaking mounds." Furthermore, he had not rejected the season pass that contained the resort's exculpatory clause. Thus, the ski resort prevailed.

In a similar case, Teresa Brigance fell and broke her leg when her ski boot caught on a chairlift as she was attempting to get off the lift. She sued the lift's owner, Vail Summit Resorts, Inc., for her injuries. Brigance had signed a liability waiver before taking ski lessons at the resort, however. The waiver stated that she understood the inherent dangers and risks of skiing, and it specifically mentioned lift loading and unloading. The court

found that the waiver was valid and enforceable, and therefore dismissed Brigance's suit against Vail Summit. Brigance appealed, but a federal appellate court affirmed the lower court's dismissal.[b]

Overly Broad Waivers

While most liability waivers have survived legal challenges, some have not. In *Bagley v. Mt. Bachelor, Inc.,*[c] the Supreme Court of Oregon ruled against a ski resort's "very broad" liability waiver. The case involved an eighteen-year-old, Myles Bagley, who was paralyzed from the waist down after a snowboarding accident at Mt. Bachelor ski resort. The season pass that Bagley had signed included a liability waiver. The waiver stated that the signer agreed not to sue the resort for injury even if "caused by negligence."

Bagley argued that the resort had created a dangerous condition because of the way it had set up a particular ski jump. He sued for $21.5 million and eventually won the right to go forward with his lawsuit. The Oregon Supreme Court found that, for various reasons, enforcement of the release would have been unconscionable. "Because the release is unenforceable, genuine issues of fact exist that preclude summary judgment in defendant's favor."

Business Questions

1. *If you were operating a business, why would you opt to include overly broad waivers in your contracts with customers?*
2. *Under what circumstances would you, as a business owner, choose to aggressively defend your business against a customer's liability lawsuit?*

a. 2014 WL 996788 (Minn.Ct.App. 2014).

b. *Brigance v. Vail Summit Resorts, Inc.*, 883 F.3d 1243 (10th Cir. 2018). See also, *Johnson v. Gold's Gym Rockies, LLC*, 2019 WL 1112374 (D.Colo. 2019).

c. 356 Or. 543, 340 P.3d 27 (2014).

Every state has a statute that stipulates what types of contracts must be in writing, often referred to as the **Statute of Frauds.** The actual name of the Statute of Frauds is misleading because the statute does not apply to fraud. Rather, it denies enforceability to certain contracts that do not comply with its writing requirements.

The following types of contracts are generally required to be in writing or evidenced by a written memorandum or electronic record:

1. Contracts involving interests in land.
2. Contracts that cannot *by their terms* be performed within *one year from the day after* the date of formation.
3. Collateral, or secondary, contracts, such as promises to answer for the debt or duty of another and promises by the administrator or executor of an estate to pay a debt of the estate personally—that is, out of her or his own pocket.
4. Promises made in consideration of marriage.
5. Under the Uniform Commercial Code, contracts for the sale of goods priced at $500 or more.

A contract that is oral when it is required to be evidenced by a writing or an electronic record is voidable by a party who does not wish to follow through with the agreement.

12–8 Third Party Rights

Once it has been determined that a valid and legally enforceable contract exists, attention can turn to the rights and duties of the parties to the contract. A contract is a private agreement between the parties who have entered into it, and traditionally these parties alone have rights and liabilities under the contract. This principle is referred to as **privity of contract.** A *third party*—one who is not a direct party to a particular contract—normally does not have rights under that contract.

There are exceptions to the rule of privity of contract. One exception allows a party to a contract to transfer the rights or duties arising from the contract to another person through an *assignment* (of rights) or a *delegation* (of duties). Another exception involves a *third party beneficiary contract*—a contract in which the parties to the contract intend that the contract benefit a third party.

In a bilateral contract, one party has a *right* to require the other to perform some task, and the other has a *duty* to perform it. The transfer of contractual *rights* to a third party is known as an **assignment.** The transfer of contractual *duties* to a third party is known as a **delegation.** An assignment or a delegation occurs *after* the original contract was made.

12–8a Assignments

In an assignment, the party assigning the rights to a third party is known as the *assignor*,[34] and the party receiving the rights is the *assignee*.[35] When rights under a contract are assigned unconditionally, the rights of the assignor are extinguished. The third party (the assignee) has a right to demand performance from the other original party to the contract. The assignee takes only those rights that the assignor originally had, however.

Assignments are important because they are used in many types of business financing. Banks, for instance, frequently assign their rights to receive payments under their loan contracts to other firms, which pay for those rights.

As a general rule, all rights can be assigned. Exceptions are made, however, under certain circumstances, including the following:

1. The assignment is prohibited by statute.
2. The contract is personal.

3. The assignment significantly changes the risk or duties of the *obligor* (the person contractually obligated to perform).
4. The contract prohibits assignment.

12–8b Delegations

Just as a party can transfer rights through an assignment, a party can also transfer duties. Duties are not assigned, however, they are *delegated*. The party delegating the duties is the *delegator*, and the party to whom the duties are delegated is the *delegatee*. Normally, a delegation of duties does not relieve the delegator of the obligation to perform in the event that the delegatee fails to do so.

No special form is required to create a valid delegation of duties. As long as the delegator expresses an intention to make the delegation, it is effective. The delegator need not even use the word *delegate*.

As a general rule, any duty can be delegated. There are, however, some circumstances in which delegation is prohibited:

1. When special trust has been placed in the *obligor*.
2. When performance depends on the personal skill or talents of the obligor.
3. When performance by a third party will vary materially from that expected by the *obligee* (the person to whom an obligation is owed) under the contract.
4. When the contract expressly prohibits delegation by including an *antidelegation clause*.

If a delegation of duties is enforceable, the obligee must accept performance from the delegatee. As noted, a valid delegation of duties does not relieve the delegator of obligations under the contract. Although there are many exceptions, the general rule today is that the obligee can sue both the delegatee and the delegator if the duties are not performed.

12–8c Third Party Beneficiaries

Another exception to the doctrine of privity of contract arises when the contract is intended to benefit a third party. When the original parties to the contract agree that the contract performance should be rendered to or directly benefit a third person, the third person becomes an *intended* **third party beneficiary** of the contract. As the **intended beneficiary** of the contract, the third party has legal rights and can sue the promisor directly for breach of the contract.

■ **Case in Point 12.31** The classic case that gave third party beneficiaries the right to bring a suit directly against a promisor was decided in 1859. The case involved three parties—Holly, Lawrence, and Fox. Holly had

---

34. Pronounced uh-*sye*-nore.
35. Pronounced uh-*sye*-nee.

borrowed $300 from Lawrence. Shortly thereafter, Holly loaned $300 to Fox, who in return promised Holly that he would pay Holly's debt to Lawrence on the following day. When Lawrence failed to obtain the $300 from Fox, he sued Fox to recover the funds. The court had to decide whether Lawrence could sue Fox directly (rather than suing Holly). The court held that when "a promise [is] made for the benefit of another, he for whose benefit it is made may bring an action for its breach."[36] ∎

The law distinguishes between *intended* beneficiaries and *incidental* beneficiaries. An *incidental beneficiary* is a third person who receives a benefit from a contract even though that person's benefit is not the reason the contract was made. Because the benefit is unintentional, an incidental beneficiary cannot sue to enforce the contract. Only intended beneficiaries acquire legal rights in a contract.

---

36. *Lawrence v. Fox*, 20 N.Y. 268 (1859).

Practice and Review: Formation of Traditional and E-Contracts

Shane Durbin wanted to have a recording studio custom-built in his home. He sent invitations to a number of local contractors to submit bids on the project. Rory Amstel submitted the lowest bid, which was $20,000 less than any of the other bids Durbin received. Durbin called Amstel to ascertain the type and quality of the materials that were included in the bid and to find out if he could substitute a superior brand of acoustic tiles for the same bid price. Amstel said he would have to check into the price difference. The parties also discussed a possible start date for construction. Two weeks later, Durbin changed his mind and decided not to go forward with his plan to build a recording studio. Amstel filed a suit against Durbin for breach of contract. Using the information presented in the chapter, answer the following questions.

1. Did Amstel's bid meet the requirements of an offer? Explain.
2. Was there an acceptance of the offer? Why or why not?
3. How is an offer terminated? Assuming that Durbin did not inform Amstel that he was rejecting the offer, was the offer terminated at any time described here? Explain.

Debate This ...   *The terms and conditions in click-on agreements are so long and detailed that no one ever reads the agreements. Therefore, the act of clicking on "I agree" is not really an acceptance.*

Terms and Concepts

acceptance 244	executed contract 239	promissory estoppel 254
accord and satisfaction 252	executory contract 239	record 249
agreement 240	express contract 238	reformation 257
assignment 261	forbearance 250	release 253
bilateral contract 237	formal contracts 238	rescission 251
browse-wrap terms 249	implied contract 238	revocation 243
click-on agreement 248	informal contracts 238	shrink-wrap agreement 248
consideration 250	intended beneficiary 261	Statute of Frauds 260
contract 236	liquidated debt 252	third party beneficiary 261
contractual capacity 254	mailbox rule 246	unconscionable 259
counteroffer 243	mirror image rule 243	unenforceable contract 239
covenant not to compete 257	objective theory of contracts 237	unilateral contract 237
covenant not to sue 253	offer 240	unliquidated debt 252
delegation 261	offeree 237	usury 256
disaffirmance 255	offeror 237	valid contract 239
e-contracts 247	option contract 243	void contract 239
e-signature 249	past consideration 251	voidable contract 239
estopped 254	privity of contract 261	
exculpatory clause 259	promise 236	

Issue Spotters

1. Applied Products, Inc., does business with Beltway Distributors, Inc., online. Under the Uniform Electronic Transactions Act, what determines the effect of the electronic documents evidencing the parties' deal? Is a party's "signature" necessary? Explain. (See *E-Contracts*.)

2. Before Maria starts her first year of college, Fred promises to give her $5,000 when she graduates. She goes to college, borrowing and spending far more than $5,000. At the beginning of the spring semester of her senior year, she reminds Fred of the promise. Fred sends her a note that says, "I revoke the promise." Is Fred's promise binding? Explain. (See *Consideration*.)

- **Check your answers to the Issue Spotters against the answers provided in Appendix B at the end of this text.**

Business Scenarios and Case Problems

12–1. Unilateral Contract. Rocky Mountain Races, Inc., sponsors the "Pioneer Trail Ultramarathon," with an advertised first prize of $10,000. The rules require the competitors to run one hundred miles from the floor of Blackwater Canyon to the top of Pinnacle Mountain. The rules also provide that Rocky reserves the right to change the terms of the race at any time. Monica enters the race and is declared the winner. Rocky offers her a prize of $1,000 instead of $10,000. Did Rocky and Monica have a contract? Explain. (See *An Overview of Contract Law*.)

12–2. Preexisting Duty. Tabor is a buyer of file cabinets manufactured by Martin. Martin's contract with Tabor calls for delivery of fifty file cabinets at $40 per cabinet in five equal installments. After delivery of two installments (twenty cabinets), Martin informs Tabor that because of inflation, Martin is losing money. Martin will promise to deliver the remaining thirty cabinets only if Tabor will pay $50 per cabinet. Tabor agrees in writing to do so. Discuss whether Martin can legally collect the additional $100 on delivery to Tabor of the next installment of ten cabinets. (See *Consideration*.)

12–3. Business Case Problem with Sample Answer—Requirements of the Offer. Technical Consumer Products, Inc. (TCP), makes and distributes energy-efficient lighting products. Emily Bahr was TCP's district sales manager in Minnesota, North Dakota, and South Dakota when the company announced the details of a bonus plan. A district sales manager who achieved 100 percent year-over-year sales growth and a 42 percent gross margin would earn 200 percent of his or her base salary as a bonus. TCP retained absolute discretion to modify the plan. Bahr's base salary was $42,500. Her final sales results for the year showed 113 percent year-over-year sales growth and a 42 percent gross margin. She anticipated a bonus of $85,945, but TCP could not afford to pay the bonuses as planned, and Bahr received only $34,229. In response to Bahr's claim for breach of contract, TCP argued that the bonus plan was too indefinite to be an offer. Is TCP correct? Explain. [*Bahr v. Technical Consumer Products, Inc.*, 601 Fed.Appx. 359 (6th Cir. 2015)] (See *Agreement*.)

- **For a sample answer to Problem 12–3, go to Appendix C at the end of this text.**

12–4. Acceptance. Altisource Portfolio Solutions, Inc., is a global corporation that provides real property owners with a variety of services, including property preservation—repairs, debris removal, and so on. Lucas Contracting, Inc., is a small trade contractor in Carrollton, Ohio. On behalf of Altisource, Berghorst Enterprises, LLC, hired Lucas to perform preservation work on certain foreclosed properties in eastern Ohio. When Berghorst did not pay for the work, Lucas filed a suit in an Ohio state court against Altisource. Before the trial, Lucas e-mailed the terms of a settlement. The same day, Altisource e-mailed a response that did not challenge or contradict Lucas's proposal and indicated agreement to it. Two days later, however, Altisource forwarded a settlement document that contained additional terms. Which proposal most likely satisfies the element of agreement to establish a contract? Explain. [*Lucas Contracting, Inc. v. Altisource Portfolio Solutions, Inc.*, 2016 -Ohio- 474 (5 Dist. 2016)] (See *Agreement*.)

12–5. Agreements That Lack Consideration. Arkansas-Missouri Forest Products, LLC (Ark-Mo), sells supplies to make wood pallets. Blue Chip Manufacturing (BCM) makes pallets. Mark Garnett, an owner of Ark-Mo, and Stuart Lerner, an owner of BCM, went into business together. Garnett and Lerner agreed that Ark-Mo would have a 30-percent ownership interest in their future projects. When Lerner formed Blue Chip Recycling, LLC (BCR), to manage a pallet repair facility in California, however, he allocated only a 5-percent interest to Ark-Mo. Garnett objected. In a "Telephone Deal," Lerner then promised Garnett that Ark-Mo would receive a 30-percent interest in their future projects in the Midwest, and Garnett agreed to forgo an ownership interest in BCR. But when Blue Chip III, LLC (BC III), was formed to operate a repair facility in the Midwest, Lerner told Garnett that he "was not getting anything." Ark-Mo filed a suit in a Missouri state court against Lerner, alleging breach of contract. Was there consideration to support the Telephone Deal? Explain. [*Arkansas-Missouri Forest Products, LLC v. Lerner*, 486 S.W.3d 438 (Mo.App.E.D. 2016)] (See *Consideration*.)

12–6. Legality. Sue Ann Apolinar hired a guide through Arkansas Valley Adventures, LLC, for a rafting excursion on the Arkansas River. At the outfitter's office, Apolinar signed a release that detailed potential hazards and risks, including "overturning," "unpredictable currents," "obstacles" in the water, and "drowning." The release clearly stated that her signature discharged Arkansas Valley from liability for all claims arising in connection with the trip. On the river, while attempting to maneuver around a rapid, the raft capsized. The current swept Apolinar into a logjam where, despite efforts to save her, she drowned. Her son, Jesus Espinoza, Jr., filed a suit in a federal district court against the rafting company, alleging negligence. What are the arguments for and against enforcing the release that Apolinar signed? Discuss. [*Espinoza v. Arkansas Valley Adventures, LLC*, 809 F.3d 1150 (10th Cir. 2016)] (See *Legality.*)

12–7. Online Acceptances. Airbnb, Inc., maintains a website that lists, advertises, and takes fees or commissions for property rentals posted on the site. To offer or book accommodations on the site, a party must register and create an account. The sign-up screen states, "By clicking 'Sign Up' . . . you confirm that you accept the Terms of Service" (TOS). The TOS, which are hyperlinked, include a mandatory arbitration provision. Francesco Plazza registered with Airbnb and created an account but did not read the TOS. Later, Plazza filed a suit in a federal district court against Airbnb, alleging that the defendant was acting as an unlicensed real estate broker and committing deceptive trade practices in violation of New York state law. Airbnb filed a motion to compel arbitration, pursuant to the TOS. Can Plazza avoid arbitration? Explain. [*Plazza v. Airbnb, Inc.*, 289 F.Supp.3d 537 (S.D.N.Y. 2018)] (See *E-Contracts.*)

12–8. Contracts Contrary to Public Policy. P.M. and C.M. (the "Ms") are married and live in Iowa. Unable to conceive their own child, they signed a contract with T.B., who, in exchange for $13,000 and medical expenses, agreed to be impregnated with embryos fertilized with P.M.'s sperm and the ova of an anonymous donor. T.B. agreed to carry the pregnancy to term, and she and her spouse, D.B., (the "Bs") promised to hand over the baby at birth to the Ms. During the pregnancy, the relations between the parties deteriorated. When the baby was born, T.B. refused to honor the agreement to give up the child. Meanwhile, genetic testing excluded T.B. and D.B. as the biological parents and established P.M. as the father. Iowa exempts "surrogacy" from a state criminal statute that prohibits selling babies. There is no other state law on point. Is the contract between the Ms and the Bs enforceable? Discuss. [*P.M. v. T.B.*, 907 N.W.2d 522 (Iowa 2018)] (See *Legality.*)

12–9. A Question of Ethics—The IDDR Approach and Minors. *Sky High Sports Nashville Operations, LLC, operated a trampoline park in Nashville, Tennessee. At the park, during a dodgeball tournament, Jacob Blackwell, a minor, suffered a torn tendon and a broken tibia. His mother, Crystal, filed a suit on his behalf in a Tennessee state court against Sky High, alleging negligence and seeking $500,000 to cover medical and other expenses. Sky High asserted that the claim was barred by a waiver of liability in a contract between the parties, which the defendant asked the court to enforce. The waiver released Sky High from liability for any "negligent acts or omissions."* [Blackwell v. Sky High Sports Nashville Operations, LLC, *523 S.W.3d 624 (Tenn.Ct.App. 2017)*] (See Contractual Capacity.)

(a) Should Sky High offer a defense to the suit? What might Sky High argue as a reason for enforcing the waiver? Use the IDDR approach to answer these questions.

(b) Would it be unethical to allow Jacob to recover damages? Apply the IDDR approach to explain.

Time-Limited Group Assignment

12–10. Preexisting Duty. Melissa Faraj owns a lot and wants to build a house according to a particular set of plans and specifications. She solicits bids from building contractors and receives three bids: one from Carlton for $160,000, one from Feldberg for $158,000, and one from Siegel for $153,000. She accepts Siegel's bid. One month after beginning construction of the house, Siegel contacts Faraj and tells her that because of inflation and a recent price hike for materials, his costs have gone up. He says he will not finish the house unless Faraj agrees to pay an extra $13,000. Faraj reluctantly agrees to pay the additional sum. (See *Consideration.*)

(a) One group will discuss whether a contractor can ever raise the price of completing construction because of inflation and the rising cost of materials.

(b) A second group will assume that after the house is finished, Faraj refuses to pay the extra $13,000. The group will decide whether Faraj is legally required to pay this additional amount.

(c) A third group will discuss the types of extraordinary difficulties that could arise during construction that would justify a contractor's charging more than the original bid.

Chapter 13

Contract Performance, Breach, and Remedies

In a perfect world, every party who signs a contract would perform his or her duties completely and in a timely fashion, thereby discharging the contract. The real world is more complicated. Events often occur that affect our performance or our ability to perform contractual duties.

In addition, the duty to perform under a contract is not always *absolute*. It may instead be *conditioned* on the occurrence or nonoccurrence of a certain event. The legal environment of business requires the identification of some point at which the parties can reasonably know that their duties have ended.

When one party breaches a contract, the other party—the nonbreaching party—can choose one or more of several remedies. A *remedy* is the relief provided for an innocent party when the other party has breached the contract. It is the means employed to enforce a right or to redress an injury. Remedies may include *damages, rescission* and *restitution, specific performance,* and *reformation.*

13–1 Voluntary Consent

An otherwise valid contract may still be unenforceable if the parties have not genuinely agreed to its terms. A lack of **voluntary consent** (assent) can be used as a defense to the contract's enforceability.

Voluntary consent may be lacking because of a mistake, misrepresentation, undue influence, or duress—in other words, because there is no true "meeting of the minds." Generally, a party who demonstrates that he or she did not truly agree to the terms of a contract has a choice. That party can choose either to carry out the contract or to rescind (cancel) it and thus avoid the entire transaction.

13–1a Mistakes

We all make mistakes, so it is not surprising that mistakes are made when contracts are formed. In certain circumstances, contract law allows a contract to be avoided on the basis of mistake.

It is important to distinguish between *mistakes of fact* and *mistakes of value or quality.* Only a mistake of fact makes a contract voidable. Also, the mistake must involve some *material fact*—a fact that a reasonable person would consider important when determining his or her course of action.

Mistakes of fact occur in two forms—*bilateral* and *unilateral.* A unilateral mistake is made by only *one* of the contracting parties. A bilateral, or mutual, mistake is made by *both* of the parties. We look next at these two types of mistakes and illustrate them graphically in Exhibit 13–1.

Unilateral Mistakes of Fact A **unilateral mistake** is made by only one of the parties. In general, a unilateral mistake does not give the mistaken party any right to relief from the contract. Normally, the contract is enforceable.

■ **Example 13.1** Elena intends to sell her jet ski for $2,500. When she learns that Chin is interested in buying a used jet ski, she sends him an e-mail offering to sell the jet ski to him. When typing the e-mail, however, she mistakenly keys in the price of $1,500. Chin immediately sends Elena an e-mail reply accepting her offer. Even though Elena intended to sell her personal jet ski for $2,500, she has made a unilateral mistake and is bound by the contract to sell it to Chin for $1,500. ■

This general rule has at least two exceptions.[1] The contract may not be enforceable if:

1. The *other* party to the contract knows or should have known that a mistake of fact was made.

---

1. The *Restatement (Second) of Contracts,* Section 153, liberalizes the general rule to take into account the modern trend of allowing avoidance even though only one party has been mistaken.

265

Exhibit 13–1 Mistakes of Fact

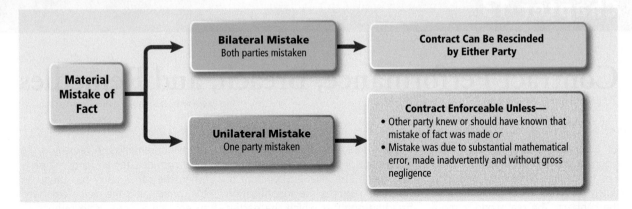

2. The error was due to a *substantial* mathematical mistake in addition, subtraction, division, or multiplication and was made inadvertently and without gross (extreme) negligence. If, for instance, a contractor's bid was significantly low because he or she made a mistake in addition when totaling the estimated costs, any contract resulting from the bid normally may be rescinded.

Of course, in both situations, the mistake must still involve some material fact.

Bilateral (Mutual) Mistakes of Fact A **bilateral mistake** is a "mutual misunderstanding concerning a basic assumption on which the contract was made."[2] Note that, as with unilateral mistakes, the mistake must be about a material fact.

When both parties are mistaken about the same material fact, the contract can be rescinded by either party. ■ **Case in Point 13.2** Coleman Holdings, LP, bought a parcel of real estate subject to setback restrictions imposed in a document entitled "Partial Release of Restrictions." The restrictions effectively precluded building a structure on the property. Lance and Joanne Eklund offered to buy the parcel from Coleman, intending to combine it with an adjacent parcel and build a home. Coleman gave the Eklunds a title report that referred to the "Partial Release of Restrictions," but they were not given a copy of the release.

Mistakenly believing that the document released restrictions on the property, the Eklunds did not investigate further. Meanwhile, Coleman also mistakenly believed that the setback restrictions had been removed.

After buying the property and discovering the restrictions, the Eklunds filed a suit in a Nevada state court against Coleman, seeking rescission of the sale. The court ordered the deal rescinded. The Nevada Supreme Court affirmed the order. "The parties made a mutual mistake in their mutual belief that the parcel had no setback restrictions."[3] ■

A word or term in a contract may be subject to more than one reasonable interpretation. If the parties to the contract attach materially different meanings to the term, a court may allow the contract to be rescinded because there has been no true "meeting of the minds."

Mistakes of Value If a mistake concerns the future market value or quality of the object of the contract, the mistake is one of *value*, and the contract normally is enforceable. ■ **Example 13.3** Phil Sung buys a violin from Bev Lee for $250. Although the violin is very old, neither party believes that it is valuable. Later, however, an antiques dealer informs the parties that the violin is rare and worth thousands of dollars. Here, both parties were mistaken, but the mistake is a mistake of *value* rather than a mistake of *fact*. Because mistakes of value do not warrant contract rescission, Lee normally cannot rescind the contract. ■

The reason that mistakes of value do not affect the enforceability of contracts is that value is variable. Depending on the time, place, and other circumstances, the same item may be worth considerably different amounts. When parties form a contract, their agreement establishes the value of the object of their transaction—for the moment.

---

2. *Restatement (Second) of Contracts*, Section 152.

3. *Coleman Holdings, L.P. v. Eklund*, 2015 WL 428567 (Nev. 2015).

Each party is considered to have assumed the risk that the value will change in the future or prove to be different from what he or she thought. Without this rule, almost any party who did not receive what she or he considered a fair bargain could argue mistake.

13–1b Fraudulent Misrepresentation

Although fraud is a tort, the presence of fraud also affects the authenticity of the innocent party's consent to the contract. When an innocent party is fraudulently induced to enter into a contract, the contract usually can be avoided, because that party has not *voluntarily* consented to its terms.[4] The innocent party can either rescind the contract and be restored to her or his original position or enforce the contract and seek damages for any harms resulting from the fraud.

Generally, fraudulent misrepresentation refers only to misrepresentation that is consciously false and is intended to mislead another. The person making the fraudulent misrepresentation knows or believes that the assertion is false or knows that she or he does not have a basis (stated or implied) for the assertion.[5]

---

4. *Restatement (Second) of Contracts*, Sections 163 and 164.
5. *Restatement (Second) of Contracts*, Section 162.

Typically, fraudulent misrepresentation consists of the following elements:

1. A misrepresentation of a material fact must occur.
2. There must be an intent to deceive.
3. The innocent party must justifiably rely on the misrepresentation.
4. To collect damages, the innocent party must have been harmed as a result of the misrepresentation.

Misrepresentation Has Occurred The first element of proving fraud is to show that misrepresentation of a material fact has occurred. This misrepresentation can occur by words or actions. For instance, the statement "This sculpture was created by Michelangelo" is a misrepresentation of fact if another artist sculpted the statue. Similarly, if a customer asks to see only paintings by Jasper Johns and the gallery owner immediately leads the customer to paintings that were not done by Johns, the owner's actions may be a misrepresentation.

The following case concerns the effect of a merger clause on an allegation of fraud. A *merger clause* is a contract clause stating that the contract embodies the entire agreement between the parties. In other words, no separate agreements between the parties are to be considered in interpreting the contract.

Case 13.1

McCullough v. Allstate Property and Casualty Insurance Co.

Alabama Court of Civil Appeals, 256 So.3d 103 (2018).

Background and Facts Allstate Property and Casualty Insurance Company issued a policy to Jerry McCullough, insuring his pickup truck. McCullough loaned the truck to an acquaintance who returned it damaged. McCullough filed a claim on the policy. Allstate treated the claim as involving multiple different claims (each with a $250 deductible) and reported these claims to Verisk Analytics Automobile Property Loss Underwriting Service (A-PLUS).[a]

Contending that the damage had resulted from only one claim, McCullough filed a suit in a federal district court against Allstate. The insurer agreed to settle the suit for $8,000. McCullough agreed to this amount, but only if Allstate corrected the report to reflect that he was making only one insurance claim and that Allstate paid nothing on that claim. (McCullough felt that the $8,000 settlement was not a payment for the damage to his truck.) Allstate's lawyer sent McCullough an e-mail agreeing to these terms, but the promise was not included in the release and settlement agreement that the parties signed. The release had a merger clause saying that there were no other agreements, verbal or otherwise, between the parties except as set forth in the contract.

---

a. A-PLUS reports information received from insurance companies regarding claims. The reports can affect a claimant's insurance costs.

Case 13.1 Continues

Case 13.1 Continued

Later, McCullough learned that Allstate had reported to A-PLUS that it had paid $8,000 to him on his claim. He filed a suit in an Alabama state court against Allstate, seeking damages for fraud. Both parties filed motions for summary judgment. The court granted Allstate's motion and denied McCullough's. McCullough appealed.

In the Language of the Court
MOORE, Judge.
* * * *

On appeal, McCullough argues that the trial court erred in granting Allstate's motion for a summary judgment * * *. Allstate simply argued that McCullough's claim was barred by * * * the release. McCullough argues, though, that he should be permitted to present * * * evidence to prove that the release was procured by fraud.

*The law in this state renders [a] merger clause ineffective to bar * * * evidence of fraud in the inducement or procurement of a contract. * * * Such a holding is required. To hold otherwise is to encourage deliberate fraud.* [Emphasis added.]

* * * Allstate was incorrect in its argument that McCullough's claim * * * was barred * * * by the language of the release. * * * Therefore, Allstate's summary-judgment motion was due to be denied.
* * * *

McCullough also argues that the trial court erred in denying his motion for * * * summary judgment on his claim.

According to McCullough, he informed Allstate, through its attorney, that he would not settle the federal lawsuit unless Allstate reported no payment on the claim. McCullough averred [declared] that Allstate's attorney * * * informed McCullough that Allstate had reported * * * that it had paid nothing on the claim. According to McCullough, that fact * * * led McCullough to settle the federal lawsuit because he believed that no reported payment on the claim would be on record; however, Allstate subsequently reported the $8,000 payment to * * * A-PLUS.

Although McCullough presented evidence of fraud, the release contained a merger clause * * *. Considering that the release did not specify that Allstate must report that nothing was paid on the claim, coupled with * * * the merger clause, we conclude that *there is a genuine issue of material fact as to whether Allstate, willfully to deceive, or recklessly without knowledge, agreed to report an amount of $0 on the claim and whether McCullough reasonably relied on any representation outside those contained in the release.* [Emphasis added.]

Based on the foregoing, McCullough's motion for * * * summary judgment on his claim * * * was properly denied.

Decision and Remedy *A state intermediate appellate court reversed the lower court's summary judgment in favor of Allstate, affirmed the court's denial of McCullough's motion for summary judgment, and remanded the case. Genuine issues of material fact precluded summary judgment on McCullough's claim for fraudulent misrepresentation.*

Critical Thinking
- **Legal Environment** *In most cases involving the interpretation and application of a contract, a party is not allowed to present evidence outside the "four corners" of the parties' expression of their agreement. Why not?*
- **What If the Facts Were Different?** *Suppose that under the law, a merger clause barred evidence of fraud in the inducement of a contract. How would this affect contract negotiations? Would the result in this case have been different? Discuss.*

Misrepresentation by Conduct. Misrepresentation also occurs when a party takes specific action to conceal a fact that is material to the contract.[6] Therefore, if a seller, by her or his actions, prevents a buyer from learning of some fact that is material to the contract, such behavior constitutes misrepresentation by conduct.

■ **Case in Point 13.4** Actor Tom Selleck contracted to purchase a horse named Zorro for his daughter from

---
6. *Restatement (Second) of Contracts,* Section 160.

Dolores Cuenca. Cuenca acted as though Zorro were fit to ride in competitions, when in reality the horse was unfit for this use because of a medical condition. Selleck filed a lawsuit against Cuenca for wrongfully concealing the horse's condition and won. A jury awarded Selleck more than $187,000 for Cuenca's misrepresentation by conduct.[7] ■

Statements of Opinion. Statements of opinion and representations of future facts (predictions) generally are not subject to claims of fraud. Statements such as "This land will be worth twice as much next year" and "This car will last for years and years" are statements of opinion, not fact. A fact is objective and verifiable, whereas an opinion is usually subject to debate. Contracting parties should know the difference and should not rely on statements of opinion. Nevertheless, in certain situations, such as when a naïve purchaser relies on an opinion from an expert, the innocent party may be entitled to rescission or reformation. (*Reformation* occurs when a court alters the terms of a contract to prevent undue hardships or burdens.)

Intent to Deceive The second element of fraud is knowledge on the part of the misrepresenting party that facts have been falsely represented. This element, normally called *scienter*,[8] or "guilty knowledge," signifies that there was an *intent to deceive*.

Scienter clearly exists if a party knows that a fact is not as stated. ■ **Example 13.5** Richard Wright applies for a position as a business law professor two weeks after his release from prison. On his résumé, he lies and says that he was a corporate president for fourteen years and taught business law at another college. After he is hired, his probation officer alerts the school to Wright's criminal history. The school immediately fires him. If Wright sues the school for breach of his employment contract, he is unlikely to succeed. Because Wright clearly exhibited an intent to deceive the college by not disclosing his history, the school can rescind his employment contract without incurring liability. ■ *Scienter* also exists if a party makes a statement that he or she believes is not true or makes a statement recklessly, without regard to whether it is true or false.

Justifiable Reliance on the Misrepresentation The third element of fraud is reasonably *justifiable reliance* on the misrepresentation of fact. The deceived party must have a justifiable reason for relying on the misrepresentation. Also, the misrepresentation must be an important

factor (but not necessarily the sole factor) in inducing the deceived party to enter into the contract. Reliance is not justified if the innocent party knows the true facts or relies on obviously extravagant statements (such as, "this pickup truck will get fifty miles to the gallon").

Injury to the Innocent Party Most courts do not require a showing of injury in an action to rescind a contract. These courts hold that because rescission returns the parties to the positions they held before the contract was made, a showing of injury to the innocent party is unnecessary.

In contrast, to recover damages caused by fraud, proof of harm is universally required. The measure of damages is ordinarily equal to the property's value had it been delivered as represented, less the actual price paid for the property. Because fraud actions necessarily involve wrongful conduct, courts may also sometimes award punitive damages, which are not ordinarily available in contract actions. The potential for punitive damages awards leads many plaintiffs to assert fraudulent misrepresentation claims in their contract disputes.

13–1c Undue Influence

Undue influence arises from relationships in which one party can greatly influence another party, thus overcoming that party's free will. A contract entered into under excessive or undue influence lacks voluntary consent and is therefore voidable.[9]

In various types of relationships, one party may have the opportunity to dominate and unfairly influence another party. Minors and elderly people, for instance, are often under the influence of guardians (persons who are legally responsible for them). If a guardian induces a young or elderly ward (a person whom the guardian looks after) to enter into a contract that benefits the guardian, the guardian may have exerted undue influence. Undue influence can arise from a number of fiduciary relationships, such as physician-patient, parent-child, husband-wife, or guardian-ward situations.

The essential feature of undue influence is that the party being taken advantage of does not exercise free will in entering into a contract. It is not enough that a person is elderly or suffers from some physical or mental impairment. There must be clear and convincing evidence that the person did not act out of her or his free will. Similarly, the existence of a fiduciary relationship alone is insufficient to prove undue influence.

---

7. *Selleck v. Cuenca*, Case No. GIN056909, North County of San Diego, California, decided September 9, 2009.
8. Pronounced sy-*en*-ter.

9. *Restatement (Second) of Contracts*, Section 177.

When the dominant party in a fiduciary relationship benefits from that relationship, a presumption of undue influence arises. The dominant party must exercise the utmost good faith in dealing with the other party. When a contract enriches the dominant party, the court will often *presume* that the contract was made under undue influence.

13–1d Duress

Agreement to the terms of a contract is not voluntary if one of the parties is *forced* into the agreement. The use of threats to force a party to enter into a contract constitutes **duress.** Similarly, the use of blackmail or extortion to induce consent to a contract is duress. Duress is both a defense to the enforcement of a contract and a ground for the rescission of a contract.

To establish duress, there must be proof of a threat to do something that the threatening party has no right to do. Generally, for duress to occur, the threatened act must be wrongful or illegal. It also must render the person who is threatened incapable of exercising free will. A threat to exercise a legal right, such as the right to sue someone, ordinarily does not constitute duress.

13–2 Performance and Discharge

The most common way to **discharge,** or terminate, contractual duties is by the **performance** of those duties. For instance, a buyer and seller enter into an agreement via e-mail for the sale of a Lexus RX for $48,000. This contract will be discharged by performance when the buyer pays $48,000 to the seller and the seller transfers possession of the Lexus to the buyer.

13–2a Conditions

In most contracts, promises of performance are not expressly conditioned or qualified. Instead, they are *absolute promises.* They must be performed, or the parties promising the acts will be in breach of contract.

In some situations, however, performance is *conditioned.* A **condition** is a qualification in a contract based on a possible future event. The occurrence or nonoccurrence of the event will trigger the performance of a legal obligation or terminate an existing legal obligation.[10] If the condition is not satisfied, the obligations of the parties are discharged. A condition that must be fulfilled

before a party's performance can be required is called a **condition precedent.** The condition precedes the absolute duty to perform.

A contract to lease university housing, for instance, may be conditioned on the person's being a student at the university. ■ **Case in Point 13.6** James Maciel leased an apartment in a university-owned housing facility for Regent University (RU) students in Virginia. The lease ran until the end of the fall semester. Maciel had an option to renew the lease semester by semester as long as he maintained his status as an RU student.

When Maciel told RU that he intended to withdraw, the university told him that he had to move out of the apartment by May 31, the final day of the semester. Maciel asked for two additional weeks, but the university denied the request. On June 1, RU changed the locks on the apartment. Maciel entered through a window and e-mailed the university that he planned to stay "for another one or two weeks." He was convicted of trespassing. He appealed, arguing that he had "legal authority" to occupy the apartment. The reviewing court affirmed his conviction. The court found that being enrolled as a student in RU was a condition precedent to living in its student housing.[11] ■

13–2b Discharge by Performance

The great majority of contracts, as noted earlier, are discharged by performance. The contract comes to an end when both parties fulfill their respective duties by performing the acts they have promised.

Performance can also be accomplished by *tender.* **Tender** is an unconditional offer to perform by a person who is ready, willing, and able to do so. Therefore, a seller who places goods at the disposal of a buyer has tendered delivery and can demand payment. A buyer who offers to pay for goods has tendered payment and can demand delivery of the goods.

Once performance has been tendered, the party making the tender has done everything possible to carry out the terms of the contract. If the other party then refuses to perform, the party making the tender can sue for breach of contract. There are two basic types of performance— *complete performance* and *substantial performance.*

Complete Performance When a party performs exactly as agreed, the party's performance is said to be complete. Normally, conditions expressly stated in a contract must fully occur in all respects for complete

---

10. The *Restatement (Second) of Contracts,* Section 224, defines a condition as "an event, not certain to occur, which must occur, unless its nonoccurrence is excused, before performance under a contract becomes due."

11. *Maciel v. Commonwealth of Virginia,* 2011 WL 65942 (Va.App. 2011).

performance (strict performance) of the contract to take place. Any deviation breaches the contract and discharges the other party's obligation to perform.

Most construction contracts, for instance, require the builder to meet certain specifications. If the specifications are conditions, complete performance is required to avoid material breach (*material breach* will be discussed shortly). If the conditions are met, the other party to the contract must then fulfill her or his obligation to pay the builder.

If the parties to the contract did not expressly make the specifications a condition, however, and the builder fails to meet the specifications, performance is not complete. What effect does such a failure have on the other party's obligation to pay? The answer is part of the doctrine of *substantial performance.*

Substantial Performance
A party who in good faith performs substantially all of the terms of a contract can enforce the contract against the other party under the doctrine of substantial performance. The basic requirements for performance to qualify as substantial are as follows:

1. The party must have performed in good faith. Intentional failure to comply with the contract terms is a breach of the contract.
2. The performance must not vary greatly from the performance promised in the contract. An omission, variance, or defect in performance is considered minor if it can easily be remedied by compensation (monetary damages).
3. The performance must create substantially the same benefits as those promised in the contract.

Courts Must Decide.
Courts decide whether the performance was substantial on a case-by-case basis, examining all of the facts of the particular situation. ■ **Case in Point 13.7** Angele and Borjius Guient hired Sterling Doucette and Doucette & Associated Contractors, Inc., to construct a new home for them in New

Orleans. The original contract price was $177,000. The Guients paid Doucette a total of $159,300 for the work. They withheld the final $17,700 payment because of alleged deficiencies in the work, delays in construction, and Doucette's failure to complete the home.

Doucette filed a breach-of-contract action, seeking to recover the $17,700 balance. A state appellate court held that Doucette was not entitled to recover the balance. When the Guients took possession of the home from Doucette, it failed to pass inspections, and before they could move in, they had to hire other subcontractors to complete the work. Therefore, Doucette could not claim substantial performance.[12] ■

Effect on Duty to Perform. If one party's performance is substantial, the other party's duty to perform remains absolute. In other words, the parties must continue performing under the contract. For instance, the party that substantially performed is entitled to payment. If performance is not substantial, there is a material breach (to be discussed shortly), and the nonbreaching party is excused from further performance.

Measure of Damages. Because substantial performance is not perfect, the other party is entitled to damages to compensate for the failure to comply with the contract. The measure of the damages is the cost to bring the object of the contract into compliance with its terms, if that cost is reasonable under the circumstances.

What if the cost is unreasonable? Then the measure of damages is the difference in value between the performance rendered and the performance that would have been rendered if the contract had been performed completely.

The following case is a classic illustration that there is no exact formula for deciding when a contract has been substantially performed. ■

---

12. *Doucette v. Guient*, 208 So.3d 444 (La.App. 4 Cir. 2016).

Classic Case 13.2

Jacob & Youngs v. Kent
Court of Appeals of New York, 230 N.Y. 239, 129 N.E. 889 (1921).

Background and Facts The plaintiff, Jacob & Youngs, Inc., was a builder that had contracted with George Kent to construct a country residence for him. A specification in the building contract required that "all wrought-iron pipe must be well galvanized, lap welded pipe of the grade known as 'standard pipe' of Reading manufacture." Jacob & Youngs installed substantially similar pipe that was not of Reading manufacture. When Kent became aware of the difference, he ordered the builder to remove

Case 13.2 Continues

Case 13.2 Continued

all of the plumbing and replace it with the Reading type. To do so would have required removing finished walls that encased the plumbing—an expensive and difficult task. The builder explained that the plumbing was of the same quality, appearance, value, and cost as Reading pipe. When Kent nevertheless refused to pay the $3,483.46 still owed for the work, Jacob & Youngs sued to compel payment. The trial court ruled in favor of Kent. The plaintiff appealed, and the appellate court reversed the trial court's decision. Kent then appealed to the Court of Appeals of New York, the state's highest court.

In the Language of the Court

CARDOZO, Justice.

* * * *

* * * The courts never say that one who makes a contract fills the measure of his duty by less than full performance. They do say, however, that *an omission, both trivial and innocent, will sometimes be atoned [compensated] for by allowance of the resulting damage, and will not always be the breach of a condition[.]* [Emphasis added.]

* * * Where the line is to be drawn between the important and the trivial cannot be settled by a formula. * * * *We must weigh the purpose to be served, the desire to be gratified, the excuse for deviation from the letter, [and] the cruelty of enforced adherence. Then only can we tell whether literal fulfillment is to be implied by law as a condition.* [Emphasis added.]

* * * We think the measure of the allowance is not the cost of replacement, which would be great, but the difference in value, which would be either nominal or nothing. * * * The owner is entitled to the money which will permit him to complete, unless the cost of completion is grossly and unfairly out of proportion to the good to be attained.

Decision and Remedy   *New York's highest court affirmed the appellate court's decision, holding that Jacob & Youngs had substantially performed the contract.*

Critical Thinking

- **Legal Environment**   *The New York Court of Appeals found that Jacob & Youngs had substantially performed the contract. To what, if any, remedy was Kent entitled?*
- **Impact of This Case on Today's Law**   *At the time of the* Jacob & Youngs *case, some courts did not apply the doctrine of substantial performance to disputes involving breaches of contract. This landmark decision contributed to a developing trend toward equity and fairness in those circumstances. Today, an unintentional and trivial deviation from the terms of a contract will not prevent its enforcement but will permit an adjustment in the value of its performance.*

Performance to the Satisfaction of Another

Contracts often state that completed work must personally satisfy one of the parties or a third person. When the subject matter of the contract is *personal*, the obligation is conditional, and performance must actually satisfy the party specified in the contract. For instance, contracts for portraits, works of art, and tailoring are considered personal because they involve matters of personal taste. Therefore, only the personal satisfaction of the party fulfills the condition. (An exception exists, of course, if a court finds that the party is expressing dissatisfaction simply to avoid payment or otherwise is not acting in good faith.)

Most other contracts need to be performed only to the satisfaction of a reasonable person unless they *expressly state otherwise.* When the subject matter of the contract is mechanical, courts are more likely to find that the performing party has performed satisfactorily if a reasonable person would be satisfied with what was done.

■ **Example 13.8**   Mason signs a contract with Jen to mount a new heat pump on a concrete platform to her satisfaction. Such a contract normally need only be performed to the satisfaction of a reasonable person. ■

When contracts require performance to the satisfaction of a third party with superior knowledge or training in the subject matter—such as a supervising engineer—the courts are divided. A majority of courts require the work to be satisfactory to a reasonable person, but some courts require the personal satisfaction of the third party designated in the contract. (Again, the personal judgment must be made honestly, or the condition will be excused.)

Material Breach of Contract A **breach of contract** is the nonperformance of a contractual duty. The breach is *material* when performance is not at least substantial. As mentioned earlier, when there is a material breach, the nonbreaching party is excused from the performance of contractual duties. That party can also sue the breaching party for damages resulting from the breach.

■ **Example 13.9** When country singer Garth Brooks's mother died, he donated $500,000 to a hospital in his hometown in Oklahoma to build a new women's health center named after his mother. After several years passed and the health center was not built, Brooks demanded a refund. The hospital refused, claiming that while it had promised to honor his mother in some way, it had not promised to build a women's health center. Brooks sued for breach of contract. A jury determined that the hospital's failure to build a women's health center and name it after Brooks's mother was a material breach of the contract. The jury awarded Brooks $1 million in damages. ■

If the breach is *minor* (not material), the nonbreaching party's duty to perform is not entirely excused, but it can sometimes be suspended until the breach has been remedied. Once the minor breach has been cured, the nonbreaching party must resume performance of the contractual obligations.

Note that any breach entitles the nonbreaching party to sue for damages, but only a material breach discharges the nonbreaching party from the contract. The policy underlying these rules allows a contract to go forward when only minor problems occur but allows it to be terminated if major difficulties arise. Exhibit 13–2 reviews how performance can discharge a contract.

Anticipatory Repudiation Before either party to a contract has a duty to perform, one of the parties may refuse to carry out his or her contractual obligations. This is called **anticipatory repudiation**[13] of the contract.

When an anticipatory repudiation occurs, it is treated as a material breach of the contract, and the nonbreaching party is permitted to bring an action for damages immediately. The nonbreaching party can file a suit even if the scheduled time for performance under the contract is still in the future. Until the nonbreaching party treats an early repudiation as a breach, however, the repudiating party can retract the anticipatory repudiation by proper notice and restore the parties to their original obligations.[14]

An anticipatory repudiation is treated as a present, material breach for two reasons. First, the nonbreaching party should not be required to remain ready and willing to perform when the other party has already repudiated the contract. Second, the nonbreaching party should have the opportunity to seek a similar contract elsewhere and may have a duty to do so to minimize his or her loss.

---

13. *Restatement (Second) of Contracts*, Section 253; Section 2–610 of the Uniform Commercial Code (UCC).
14. See UCC 2–611.

Exhibit 13–2 Discharge by Performance

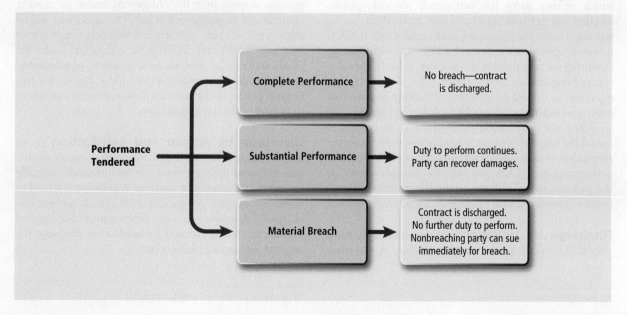

Time for Performance If no time for performance is stated in a contract, a *reasonable time* is implied.[15] If a specific time is stated, the parties usually must perform by that time. Unless time is expressly stated to be vital, though, a delay in performance will not destroy the performing party's right to payment.

When time is expressly stated to be "of the essence," or vital, the parties normally must perform within the stated time period, because the time element becomes a condition. Even when the contract states that time is of the essence, however, a court may find that a party who fails to complain about the other party's delay has waived the breach of the time provision (*waiver* will be discussed later in this chapter).

13–2c Discharge by Agreement of the Parties

Any contract can be discharged by agreement of the parties. The agreement can be contained in the original contract, or the parties can form a new contract for the express purpose of discharging the original contract.

Discharge by Mutual Rescission *Rescission* is the process by which a contract is canceled or terminated and the parties are returned to the positions they occupied prior to forming it. For **mutual rescission** to take place, the parties must make another agreement that also satisfies the legal requirements for a contract. There must be an *offer*, an *acceptance*, and *consideration*. Ordinarily, if the parties agree to rescind the original contract, their promises not to perform the acts stipulated in the original contract will be legal consideration for the second contract (the rescission).

Agreements to rescind most executory contracts (in which neither party has performed) are enforceable, whether the original agreement was made orally or in writing. Under the Uniform Commercial Code (UCC), however, agreements to rescind a sales contract must be in writing (or contained in an electronic record) when the contract requires a written rescission [UCC 2–209(2), (4)]. Agreements to rescind contracts involving transfers of realty also must be evidenced by a writing or record.

When one party has fully performed, an agreement to cancel the original contract normally will *not* be enforceable unless there is additional consideration. Because the performing party has received no consideration for the promise to call off the original bargain, additional consideration is necessary to support a rescission contract.

Discharge by Novation A contractual obligation may also be discharged through novation. A **novation** occurs when both of the parties to a contract agree to substitute a third party for one of the original parties. The requirements of a novation are as follows:

1. A previous valid obligation.
2. An agreement by all parties to a new contract.
3. The extinguishing of the old obligation (discharge of the prior party).
4. A new contract that is valid.

■ **Example 13.10** Union Corporation contracts to sell its pharmaceutical division to British Pharmaceuticals, Ltd. Before the transfer is completed, Union, British Pharmaceuticals, and a third company, Otis Chemicals, execute a new agreement to transfer all of British Pharmaceuticals' rights and duties in the transaction to Otis Chemicals. As long as the new contract is supported by consideration, the novation will discharge the original contract (between Union and British Pharmaceuticals) and replace it with the new contract (between Union and Otis Chemicals). ■

A novation expressly or impliedly revokes and discharges a prior contract. The parties involved may expressly state in the new contract that the old contract is now discharged. If the parties do not expressly discharge the old contract, it will be impliedly discharged if the new contract's terms are inconsistent with the old contract's terms. It is this immediate discharge of the prior contract that distinguishes a novation from both an accord and satisfaction, discussed shortly, and an assignment of all rights.

Discharge by Settlement Agreement A compromise, or settlement agreement, that arises out of a genuine dispute over the obligations under an existing contract will be recognized at law. The agreement will be substituted as a new contract and will either expressly or impliedly revoke and discharge the obligations under the prior contract. In contrast to a novation, a substituted agreement does not involve a third party. Rather, the two original parties to the contract form a different agreement to substitute for the original one.

Discharge by Accord and Satisfaction In an accord and satisfaction, the parties agree to accept performance that is different from the performance originally promised. An *accord* is a contract to perform some act to satisfy an existing contractual duty that is not yet discharged.[16] A *satisfaction* is the performance of the accord agreement. An accord and its satisfaction discharge the original contractual obligation.

---

15. See UCC 2–204.

16. *Restatement (Second) of Contracts*, Section 281.

Once the accord has been made, the original obligation is merely suspended until the accord agreement is fully performed (a satisfaction). If it is not performed, the obligee (the one to whom performance is owed) can file a lawsuit based on either the original obligation or the accord. ■ **Example 13.11** Fahreed has a judgment against Ling for $8,000. Later, both parties agree that the judgment can be satisfied by Ling's transfer of his automobile to Fahreed. This agreement to accept the auto in lieu of $8,000 in cash is the accord. If Ling transfers the car to Fahreed, the accord is fully performed (satisfied), and the debt is discharged. If Ling refuses to transfer the car, the accord is breached. Because the original obligation was merely suspended, Fahreed can sue Ling to enforce the original judgment for $8,000 in cash or bring an action for breach of the accord. ■

13–2d Discharge by Operation of Law

Under specified circumstances, contractual duties may be discharged by operation of law. These circumstances include material alteration of the contract, the running of the statute of limitations, bankruptcy, and the impossibility or impracticability of performance.

Material Alteration of the Contract To discourage parties from altering written contracts, the law allows an innocent party to be discharged when the other party has materially altered a written contract without consent. For instance, suppose that a party alters a material term of a contract, such as the stated quantity or price, without the knowledge or consent of the other party. In this situation, the party who was unaware of the alteration can treat the contract as discharged.

Statutes of Limitations As mentioned earlier in this text, statutes of limitations restrict the period during which a party can sue on a particular cause of action. After the applicable limitations period has passed, a suit can no longer be brought. The limitations period for bringing suits for breach of oral contracts usually is two to three years, and for written contracts, four to five years. Parties generally have ten to twenty years to file for recovery of amounts awarded in judgments, depending on state law.

Lawsuits for breach of a contract for the sale of goods typically must be brought within four years after the cause of action has accrued [UCC 2–725]. A cause of action for a sales contract accrues when the breach occurs, even if the aggrieved party is not aware of the breach. A breach of warranty normally occurs when the seller delivers the goods to the buyer. In their original

contract, the parties can agree to reduce this four-year period to not less than one year, but they cannot agree to extend it.

Bankruptcy A proceeding in bankruptcy attempts to allocate the debtor's assets to the creditors in a fair and equitable fashion. Once the assets have been allocated, the debtor receives a **discharge in bankruptcy.** A discharge in bankruptcy ordinarily prevents the creditors from enforcing most of the debtor's contracts. Partial payment of a debt *after* discharge in bankruptcy will not revive the debt.

Impossibility of Performance After a contract has been made, supervening events (such as a fire) may make performance impossible in an objective sense. This is known as **impossibility of performance** and can discharge a contract.[17] The doctrine of impossibility of performance applies only when the parties could not have reasonably foreseen, at the time the contract was formed, the event that rendered performance impossible.

Objective impossibility ("It can't be done") must be distinguished from *subjective impossibility* ("I'm sorry, I simply can't do it"). An example of subjective impossibility occurs when a party cannot deliver goods on time because of freight car shortages or cannot make payment on time because the bank is closed. In effect, in each of these situations the party is saying, "It is impossible for *me* to perform," not "It is impossible for *anyone* to perform." Accordingly, such excuses do not discharge a contract, and the nonperforming party is normally held in breach of contract.

When Performance Is Impossible. Three basic types of situations may qualify as grounds for the discharge of contractual obligations based on impossibility of performance:[18]

1. *When one of the parties to a personal contract dies or becomes incapacitated prior to performance.* ■ **Example 13.12** Frederic, a famous dancer, contracts with Ethereal Dancing Guild to play a leading role in its new ballet. Before the ballet can be performed, Frederic becomes ill and dies. His personal performance was essential to the completion of the contract. Thus, his death discharges the contract and his estate's liability for his nonperformance. ■
2. *When the specific subject matter of the contract is destroyed.* ■ **Example 13.13** A-1 Farm Equipment agrees to sell Gunther the green tractor on its lot and

---

17. *Restatement (Second) of Contracts*, Section 261.
18. *Restatement (Second) of Contracts*, Sections 262–266; UCC 2–615.

promises to have the tractor ready for Gunther to pick up on Saturday. On Friday night, however, a truck veers off the nearby highway and smashes into the tractor, destroying it beyond repair. Because the contract was for this specific tractor, A-1's performance is rendered impossible owing to the accident. ■

3. *When a change in law renders performance illegal.*
   ■ **Example 13.14** Hopper contracts with Playlist, Inc., to create a website through which users can post and share movies, music, and other forms of digital entertainment. Hopper begins working on the new website. Before the site is operational, however, Congress passes the No Online Piracy in Entertainment (NOPE) Act. The NOPE Act makes it illegal to operate a website on which copyrighted works are posted without the copyright owners' consent. In this situation, the contract is discharged by operation of law. The purpose of the contract has been rendered illegal, and contract performance is objectively impossible. ■

Temporary Impossibility. An occurrence or event that makes performance temporarily impossible operates to suspend performance until the impossibility ceases. Once the temporary event ends, the parties ordinarily must perform the contract as originally planned. ■ **Case in Point 13.15** Keefe Hurwitz contracted to sell his home in Louisiana to Wesley and Gwendolyn Payne for $241,500. Four days later, Hurricane Katrina made

landfall and caused extensive damage to the house. The cost of repairs was estimated at $60,000. Hurwitz refused to spend $60,000 for the repairs and still sell the property to the Paynes for the previously agreed-on price of $241,500. The Paynes filed a lawsuit to enforce the contract.

Hurwitz argued that Hurricane Katrina had made it impossible for him to perform and had discharged his duties under the contract. The court, however, ruled that Hurricane Katrina had caused only a temporary impossibility. Hurwitz was required to pay for the necessary repairs and to perform the contract as written. He could not obtain a higher purchase price to offset the cost of the repairs.[19] ■

Sometimes, the lapse of time and the change in circumstances surrounding the contract make it substantially more burdensome for the parties to perform the promised acts. In that situation, the contract is discharged.

It can be difficult to predict how a court will—or should—rule on whether performance is impossible in a particular situation, as discussed in this chapter's *Ethics Today* feature.

Commercial Impracticability Courts may also excuse parties from their performance when it becomes much more difficult or expensive than the parties

---

19. *Payne v. Hurwitz,* 978 So.2d 1000 (La.App. 1 Cir. 2008).

Ethics Today	**When Is Impossibility of Performance a Valid Defense?**

The doctrine of impossibility of performance is applied only when the parties could not have reasonably foreseen, at the time the contract was formed, the event or events that rendered performance impossible. In some cases, the courts may seem to go too far in holding that the parties should have foreseen certain events or conditions. Such a holding means that the parties cannot avoid their contractual obligations under the doctrine of impossibility of performance.

Actually, courts today are more likely to allow parties to raise this defense than courts in the past, which rarely excused parties from performance under the impossibility doctrine. Indeed, until the latter part of the nineteenth century, courts were reluctant to

discharge a contract even when performance appeared to be impossible.

Generally, the courts must balance the freedom of parties to contract (and thereby assume the risks involved) against the injustice that may result when certain contractual obligations are enforced. If the courts allowed parties to raise impossibility of performance as a defense to contractual obligations more often, freedom of contract would suffer.

Critical Thinking *Why might those entering into contracts be worse off in the long run if the courts increasingly accepted impossibility of performance as a defense?*

originally contemplated at the time the contract was formed. For instance, a court could discharge a contract because one party would have to pay ten times more than the original estimate to perform the contract.

For someone to invoke the doctrine of **commercial impracticability** successfully, however, the anticipated performance must become *significantly* more difficult or costly. In addition, the added burden of performing *must not have been foreseeable by the parties when the contract was made.*

Frustration of Purpose Closely allied with the doctrine of commercial impracticability is the doctrine of **frustration of purpose.** In principle, a contract will be discharged if unforeseen supervening circumstances make it impossible to attain the purpose both parties had in mind when they made the contract. There are some differences between these doctrines, however. Commercial impracticability usually involves an event that increases the cost or difficulty of performance. In contrast, frustration of purpose typically involves an event that decreases the value of what a party receives under the contract.

13–2e Waiver of Breach

Under certain circumstances, a nonbreaching party may be willing to accept a defective performance of the contract. This knowing relinquishment of a legal right (that is, the right to require satisfactory and full performance) is called a **waiver.**

When a waiver of a breach of contract occurs, the party waiving the breach cannot take any later action on it. In effect, the waiver erases the past breach, and the contract continues as if the breach had never occurred. Of course, the waiver of breach of contract extends only to the matter waived and not to the whole contract. Businesspersons often waive breaches of contract to obtain whatever benefit is still possible out of the contract.

Ordinarily, a waiver by a contracting party will not operate to waive subsequent, additional, or future breaches of contract. This is always true when the subsequent breaches are unrelated to the first breach.

A waiver can extend to subsequent defective performance if a reasonable person would conclude that similar defective performance in the future will be acceptable. Therefore, a *pattern of conduct* that waives a number of successive breaches will operate as a continued waiver. To change this result, the nonbreaching party should give notice to the breaching party that full performance will be required in the future.

The party who has rendered defective or less-than-full performance remains liable for the damages caused by the breach of contract. In effect, the waiver operates to keep the contract going. The waiver prevents the nonbreaching party from declaring the contract at an end or rescinding the contract. The contract continues, but the nonbreaching party can recover damages caused by the defective or less-than-full performance.

See Exhibit 13–3 for a summary of the ways in which a contract can be discharged.

Exhibit 13–3   Contract Discharge

By Operation of Law	By Performance	By Agreement
• Material alteration • Statutes of limitations • Bankruptcy • Impossibility or impracticability of performance • Frustration of purpose	• Complete • Substantial	• Mutual rescission • Novation • Settlement agreement • Accord and satisfaction

By Failure of a Condition	By Breach
If performance is conditional, duty to perform does not become absolute until that condition occurs.	• Material breach • Anticipatory repudiation • Waiver of breach

13-3 Damages

A breach of contract entitles the nonbreaching party to sue for monetary damages. In contract law, damages compensate the nonbreaching party for the loss of the bargain (whereas tort law damages compensate for harm suffered as a result of another's wrongful act). Often, courts say that innocent parties are to be placed in the position they would have occupied had the contract been fully performed.

Realize at the outset, though, that collecting damages through a court judgment requires litigation, which can be expensive and time consuming. Also keep in mind that court judgments are often difficult to enforce, particularly if the breaching party does not have sufficient assets to pay the damages awarded. For these reasons, most parties settle their lawsuits for damages (or other remedies) prior to trial.

13-3a Types of Damages

There are four broad categories of damages awarded by courts:

1. Compensatory (to cover direct losses and costs).
2. Consequential (to cover indirect and foreseeable losses).
3. Punitive (to punish and deter wrongdoing).
4. Nominal (to recognize wrongdoing when no monetary loss is shown).

Compensatory and punitive damages were discussed in the context of tort law. Here, we look at these types of damages, as well as consequential and nominal damages, in the context of contract law.

Compensatory Damages Damages that compensate the nonbreaching party for the *loss of the bargain* are known as *compensatory damages*. These damages compensate the injured party only for damages actually sustained and proved to have arisen directly from the loss of the bargain caused by the breach of contract. They simply replace what was lost because of the wrong or damage and, for this reason, are often said to "make the person whole."

■ **Case in Point 13.16** Janet Murley was the vice president of marketing at Hallmark Cards, Inc., until Hallmark eliminated her position as part of a corporate restructuring. Murley and Hallmark entered into a separation agreement under which she agreed not to work in the greeting card industry for eighteen months and not to disclose or use any of Hallmark's confidential information. In exchange, Hallmark gave Murley a $735,000 severance payment.

After eighteen months, Murley took a job with Recycled Paper Greetings (RPG) for $125,000 and disclosed confidential Hallmark information to RPG. Hallmark sued for breach of contract and won. The jury awarded $860,000 in damages (the $735,000 severance payment and $125,000 that Murley received from RPG). Murley appealed. The appellate court held that Hallmark was entitled only to the return of the $735,000 severance payment. Hallmark was not entitled to the other $125,000 because that additional award would have left Hallmark better off than if Murley had not breached the contract.[20] ■

The standard measure of compensatory damages is the difference between the value of the breaching party's promised performance under the contract and the value of her or his actual performance. This amount is reduced by any loss that the injured party has avoided.

■ **Example 13.17** Randall contracts to perform certain services exclusively for Hernandez during the month of March for $4,000. Hernandez cancels the contract and is in breach. Randall is able to find another job during March but can earn only $3,000. He can sue Hernandez for breach and recover $1,000 as compensatory damages. Randall can also recover from Hernandez the amount that he spent to find the other job. ■ Expenses that are caused directly by a breach of contract—such as those incurred to obtain performance from another source—are known as **incidental damages.**

Note that the measure of compensatory damages often varies by type of contract. Certain types of contracts deserve special mention.

Sale of Goods. In a contract for the sale of goods, the usual measure of compensatory damages is an amount equal to the difference between the contract price and the market price.[21] ■ **Example 13.18** Medik Laboratories contracts to buy ten model UTS network servers from Cal Industries for $4,000 each. Cal Industries, however, fails to deliver the ten servers to Medik. The market price of the servers at the time Medik learns of the breach is $4,500. Therefore, Medik's measure of damages is $5,000 (10 × $500), plus any incidental damages caused by the breach. ■

Sometimes, the buyer breaches when the seller has not yet produced the goods. In that situation, compensatory damages normally equal lost profits on the sale, not the difference between the contract price and the market price.

---

20. *Hallmark Cards, Inc. v. Murley*, 703 F.3d 456 (8th Cir. 2013).
21. More specifically, the amount is the difference between the contract price and the market price at the time and place at which the goods were to be delivered or tendered. See Sections 2–708 and 2–713 of the UCC.

Sale of Land. Ordinarily, because each parcel of land is unique, the remedy for a seller's breach of a contract for a sale of real estate is specific performance. That is, the buyer is awarded the parcel of property for which she or he bargained. (*Specific performance* will be discussed more fully later in this chapter.) The majority of states follow this rule.

When the *buyer* is the party in breach, the measure of damages is typically the difference between the contract price and the market price of the land. The same measure is used when specific performance is not available (because the seller has sold the property to someone else, for instance).

A minority of states apply a different rule when the seller breaches the contract and the breach is not deliberate (intentional). These states limit the prospective buyer's damages to a refund of any down payment made plus any expenses incurred (such as fees for title searches, attorneys, and escrows). Thus, the minority rule effectively returns purchasers to the positions they occupied prior to the sale, rather than giving them the benefit of the bargain.

Construction Contracts. The measure of compensatory damages in a building or construction contract varies depending on which party breaches and when the breach occurs.

1. *Breach by owner.* The owner may breach at three different stages—before, during, or after performance. If the owner breaches *before performance has begun*, the contractor can recover only the profits that would have been made on the contract. (Profits equal the total contract price less the cost of materials and labor.) If the owner breaches *during performance*, the contractor can recover the profits plus the costs incurred in partially constructing the building. If the owner breaches *after the construction has been completed*, the contractor can recover the entire contract price, plus interest.

2. *Breach by contractor.* When the construction contractor breaches the contract—either by failing to begin construction or by stopping work partway through the project—the measure of damages is the cost of completion. The cost of completion includes reasonable compensation for any delay in performance. If the contractor finishes late, the measure of damages is the loss of use.

   ■ **Case in Point 13.19** To remodel his home in Connecticut, Richard Viola hired J.S. Benson of J.S. Benson Woodworking & Design as his contractor. Over a period of five years, Viola paid Benson more than $500,000 to fabricate and install windows and doors, nearly $50,000 for the purchase of lumber, and $10,000 to ship and store the lumber, as well as $111,000 toward the contract price. Nevertheless, Benson failed to complete the project and would not give Viola the lumber that he had purchased despite repeated requests. Viola eventually sued Benson for breaching the contract. A state court held that Benson had breached the contract and ordered him to pay $848,000 in damages. The damages awarded included additional amounts to reimburse Viola for attorneys' fees, rental costs (because he was unable to live in the home), and property taxes.[22] ■

3. *Breach by both owner and contractor.* When the performance of both parties—the construction contractor and the owner—falls short of what their contract required, the courts attempt to strike a fair balance in awarding damages.

Consequential Damages Foreseeable damages that result from a party's breach of contract are called **consequential damages,** or *special damages*. They differ from compensatory damages in that they are caused by special circumstances beyond the contract itself. They flow from the consequences, or results, of a breach. For the nonbreaching party to recover consequential damages, the breaching party must have known (or had reason to know) that special circumstances would cause the nonbreaching party to suffer an additional loss.

When a seller fails to deliver goods, knowing that the buyer is planning to use or resell those goods immediately, a court may award consequential damages for the loss of profits from the planned resale. ■ **Example 13.20** Marty contracts to buy a certain quantity of Quench, a specialty sports drink, from Nathan. Nathan knows that Marty has contracted with Ruthie to resell and ship the Quench within hours of its receipt. The beverage will then be sold to fans attending the Super Bowl. Nathan fails to deliver the Quench on time. Marty can recover the consequential damages—the loss of profits from the planned resale to Ruthie—caused by the nondelivery. (If Marty instead purchases Quench from another vendor and resells them to Ruthie, he can recover only compensatory damages for any difference between the contract price and the market price.) ■

Punitive Damages Punitive damages are very seldom awarded in lawsuits for breach of contract. Because punitive damages are designed to punish a wrongdoer and set an example to deter similar conduct in the future, they

---

22. *Viola v. J.S. Benson*, 2017 WL 2817404 (Conn.Super.Ct. 2017).

have no legitimate place in contract law. A contract is simply a civil relationship between the parties. The law may compensate one party for the loss of the bargain—no more and no less. When a person's actions cause both a breach of contract and a tort (such as fraud), however, punitive damages may be available.

Nominal Damages When no actual damage or financial loss results from a breach of contract and only a technical injury is involved, the court may award **nominal damages** to the innocent party. Awards of nominal damages are often small, such as one dollar, but they do establish that the defendant acted wrongfully. Most lawsuits for nominal damages are brought as a matter of principle under the theory that a breach has occurred and some damages must be imposed regardless of actual loss.

13–3b Liquidated Damages versus Penalties

A **liquidated damages** provision in a contract specifies that a certain dollar amount is to be paid in the event of a *future* default or breach of contract. (*Liquidated* means determined, settled, or fixed.) Liquidated damages clauses are quite common in construction contracts, sales contracts, and contracts with entertainers and professional athletes.

Liquidated damages differ from penalties. Like liquidated damages, a **penalty** specifies a certain amount to be paid in the event of a default or breach of contract. Unlike liquidated damages, it is designed to penalize the breaching party, not to make the innocent party whole. Liquidated damages provisions usually are enforceable. In contrast, if a court finds that a provision calls for a penalty, the agreement as to the amount will not be enforced. Recovery will be limited to actual damages.

To determine if a particular provision is for liquidated damages or for a penalty, a court must answer two questions:

1. When the contract was entered into, was it apparent that damages would be difficult to estimate in the event of a breach?
2. Was the amount set as damages a reasonable estimate and not excessive?

If the answers to both questions are yes, the provision normally will be enforced. If either answer is no, the provision usually will not be enforced.

In the following *Spotlight Case*, the court had to decide whether a clause in a contract was an enforceable liquidated damages provision or an unenforceable penalty.

Spotlight on Liquidated Damages

Case 13.3 Kent State University v. Ford

Court of Appeals of Ohio, Eleventh District, Portage County, 2015 -Ohio- 41, 26 N.E.3d 868 (2015).

Background and Facts Gene Ford signed a five-year contract with Kent State University in Ohio to work as the head coach for the men's basketball team. The contract provided that if Ford quit before the end of the term, he would pay liquidated damages to the school. The amount was to equal his salary ($300,000) multiplied by the number of years remaining on the contract. Laing Kennedy, Kent State's athletic director, told Ford that the contract would be renegotiated within a few years. Four years before the contract expired, however, Ford left Kent State and began to coach for Bradley University at an annual salary of $700,000. Kent State filed a suit in an Ohio state court against Ford, alleging breach of contract. The court enforced the liquidated damages clause and awarded the university $1.2 million. Ford appealed, arguing that the liquidated damages clause in his employment contract was an unenforceable penalty.

In the Language of the Court
Diane V. *GRENDELL*, J. [Judge]
* * * *

* * * The parties agreed on an amount of damages, stated in clear terms in Ford's * * * employment contract. * * * *It is apparent that such damages were difficult, if not impossible, to determine.* * * * The departure of a university's head basketball coach may result in a decrease in ticket sales, impact the ability to successfully recruit players and community support for the team, and require a search for both a new

coach and additional coaching staff. Many of these damages cannot be easily measured or proven. This is especially true given the nature of how such factors may change over the course of different coaches' tenures with a sports program or team. [Emphasis added.]

* * * *

* * * Kennedy's statements to Ford that the contract would be renegotiated within a few years made it clear that Kent State desired Ford to have long-term employment, which was necessary to establish the stability in the program that would benefit recruitment, retention of assistant coaching staff, and community participation and involvement. The breach of the contract impacted all of these areas.

* * * *

Regarding the alleged unreasonableness of the damages, * * * based on the record, we find that the damages were reasonable. * * * Finding a coach of a similar skill and experience level as Ford, which was gained based partially on the investment of Kent State in his development, would have an increased cost. This is evident from the fact that Ford was able to more than double his yearly salary when hired by Bradley University. The salary Ford earned at Bradley shows the loss of market value in coaching experienced by Kent State, $400,000 per year, for four years. Although this may not have been known at the time the contract was executed, it could have been anticipated, and was presumably why Kent State wanted to renegotiate the contract * * * . There was also an asserted decrease in ticket sales, costs associated with the trips for the coaching search, and additional potential sums that may be expended.

* * * *

*As discussed extensively above, there was justification for seeking liquidated damages to compensate for Kent State's losses, and, thus, there was a valid compensatory purpose for including the clause. * * * Given all of the circumstances and facts in this case, and the consideration of the factors above, we cannot find that the liquidated damages clause was a penalty.* [Emphasis added.]

Decision and Remedy *A state intermediate appellate court affirmed the lower court's award. At the time Ford's contract was entered into, ascertaining the damages resulting from a breach was "difficult, if not impossible." The court found, "based on the record, . . . that the damages were reasonable." Thus, the clause was not a penalty—it had "a valid compensatory purpose."*

Critical Thinking

- **Cultural** *How does a college basketball team's record of wins and losses, and its ranking in its conference, support the court's decision in this case?*

13-4 Equitable Remedies for Contract Breach

Sometimes, damages are an inadequate remedy for a breach of contract. In these situations, the nonbreaching party may ask the court for an equitable remedy. Equitable remedies include rescission and restitution, specific performance, and reformation.

13-4a Rescission and Restitution

Rescission is essentially an action to undo, or terminate, a contract—to return the contracting parties to the positions they occupied prior to the transaction.[23] When fraud, a mistake, duress, undue influence, misrepresentation, or lack of capacity to contract is present, unilateral rescission is available. Rescission may also be available by statute. The failure of one party to perform entitles the other party to rescind the contract. The rescinding party must give prompt notice to the breaching party.

---

23. The rescission discussed here is unilateral rescission, in which only one party wants to undo the contract. In *mutual rescission*, both parties agree to undo the contract. Mutual rescission discharges the contract, whereas unilateral rescission generally is available as a remedy for breach of contract.

Generally, to rescind a contract, both parties must make **restitution** to each other by returning goods, property, or funds previously conveyed. If the property or goods can be returned, they must be. If the goods or property have been consumed, restitution must be made in an equivalent dollar amount.

Essentially, restitution involves the plaintiff's recapture of a benefit conferred on the defendant that has unjustly enriched her or him. ■ **Example 13.21** Katie contracts with Mikhail to design a house for her. Katie pays Mikhail $9,000 and agrees to make two more payments of $9,000 (for a total of $27,000) as the design progresses. The next day, Mikhail calls Katie and tells her that he has taken a position with a large architectural firm in another state and cannot design the house. Katie decides to hire another architect that afternoon. Katie can obtain restitution of the $9,000 from Mikhail. ■

Restitution may be appropriate when a contract is rescinded, but the right to restitution is not limited to rescission cases. Because an award of restitution basically returns something to its rightful owner, a party can seek restitution in actions for breach of contract, tort actions, and other types of actions. Restitution can be obtained, for instance, when funds or property have been transferred by mistake or because of fraud or incapacity.

13–4b Specific Performance

The equitable remedy of **specific performance** calls for the performance of the act promised in the contract. This remedy is attractive to a nonbreaching party because it provides the exact bargain promised in the contract. It also avoids some of the problems inherent in a suit for damages, such as collecting a judgment and arranging another contract. In addition, the actual performance may be more valuable than the monetary damages.

Normally, however, specific performance will not be granted unless the party's legal remedy (monetary damages) is inadequate. For this reason, contracts for the sale of goods rarely qualify for specific performance. The legal remedy—monetary damages—is ordinarily adequate in such situations because substantially identical goods can be bought or sold in the market. Only if the goods are unique will a court grant specific performance. For instance, paintings, sculptures, and rare books or coins are so unique that monetary damages will not enable a buyer to obtain substantially identical substitutes in the market.

Sale of Land A court may grant specific performance to a buyer in an action for a breach of contract involving the sale of land. In this situation, the legal remedy of monetary damages may not compensate the buyer adequately. After all, every parcel of land is unique: the same land in

the same location obviously cannot be obtained elsewhere. Only when specific performance is unavailable (such as when the seller has sold the property to someone else) will monetary damages be awarded instead.

A seller of land can also seek specific performance of the contract. ■ **Case in Point 13.22** Developer Charles Ghidorzi formed Crabtree Ridge, LLC, for the sole purpose of purchasing twenty-three acres of vacant land from Cohan Lipp, LLC. Crabtree signed a contract agreeing to pay $3.1 million for the land, which would be developed and paid for in three phases. When an environmental survey showed that the land might contain some wetlands that could not be developed, Crabtree backed out of the deal. Lipp sued Crabtree for breach of contract, seeking specific performance. The court held that Lipp was entitled to specific performance of the land-sale contract.[24] ■

Contracts for Personal Services Contracts for personal services require one party to work personally for another party. Courts generally refuse to grant specific performance of personal-service contracts. One reason is that to order a party to perform personal services against his or her will amounts to a type of involuntary servitude, or slavery, which is prohibited by the U.S. Constitution. Moreover, the courts do not want to monitor contracts for personal services, which usually require the exercise of personal judgment or talent.

13–4c Reformation

Reformation is an equitable remedy used when the parties have *imperfectly* expressed their agreement in writing. Reformation allows a court to rewrite the contract to reflect the parties' true intentions.

Fraud or Mutual Mistake Is Present Courts order reformation most often when fraud or mutual mistake (for instance, a clerical error) is present. Typically, a party seeks reformation so that some other remedy may then be pursued.

■ **Example 13.23** If Carson contracts to buy a forklift from Yoshie, but their contract mistakenly refers to a crane, a mutual mistake has occurred. Accordingly, a court can reform the contract so that it conforms to the parties' intentions and accurately refers to the forklift being sold. ■

Written Contract Incorrectly States the Parties' Oral Agreement A court will also reform a contract when two parties enter into a binding oral contract

---

24. *Cohan Lipp, LLC v. Crabtree Ridge, LLC,* 358 Wis.2d 711, 856 N.W.2d 346 (Wis.Ct.App. 2014).

Exhibit 13–4 Remedies for Breach of Contract

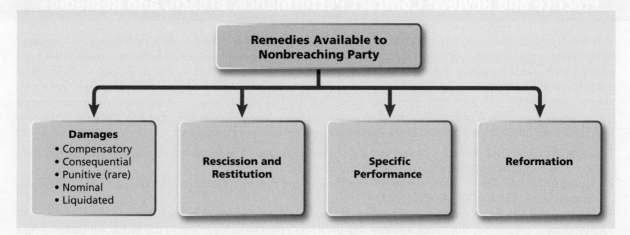

but later make an error when they attempt to put the terms into writing. Normally, a court will allow into evidence the correct terms of the oral contract, thereby reforming the written contract.

Covenants Not to Compete Courts also may reform contracts that contain a written covenant not to compete. Such covenants are often included in contracts for the sale of ongoing businesses and in employment contracts. The agreements restrict the area and time in which one party can directly compete with the other party.

A covenant not to compete may be for a valid and legitimate purpose, but may impose unreasonable area or time restraints. In such instances, some courts will reform the restraints by making them reasonable and will then enforce the entire contract as reformed. Other courts will throw out the entire restrictive covenant as illegal. Thus, when businesspersons create restrictive covenants, they must make sure that the restrictions imposed are reasonable.

■ **Case in Point 13.24** Cardiac Study Center, Inc., a medical practice group, hired Dr. Robert Emerick. Later, Emerick became a shareholder of Cardiac and signed an agreement that included a covenant not to compete. The covenant stated that a physician who left the group promised not to practice competitively in the surrounding area for a period of five years.

After Cardiac began receiving complaints from patients and other physicians about Emerick, it terminated his employment. Emerick sued Cardiac, claiming that the covenant not to compete that he had signed was unreasonable and should be declared illegal. Ultimately, a state appellate court held that the covenant was both reasonable and enforceable. Cardiac had a legitimate

interest in protecting its existing client base and prohibiting Emerick from taking its clients.[25] ■

Exhibit 13–4 graphically summarizes the remedies, including reformation, that are available to the non-breaching party.

13–5 Contract Provisions Limiting Remedies

A contract may include provisions stating that no damages can be recovered for certain types of breaches or that damages will be limited to a maximum amount. A contract may also provide that the only remedy for breach is replacement, repair, or refund of the purchase price. Finally, a contract may provide that one party can seek injunctive relief if the other party breaches the contract.

Provisions stating that no damages can be recovered are called *exculpatory clauses*. Provisions that affect the availability of certain remedies are called *limitation-of-liability clauses*. The Uniform Commercial Code (UCC) provides that in a contract for the sale of goods, remedies can be limited [UCC 2–719(1)].

Whether a limitation-of-liability clause in a contract will be enforced depends on the type of breach that is excused by the provision. Normally, a provision excluding liability for fraudulent or intentional injury will not be enforced. Likewise, a clause excluding liability for illegal acts, acts that are contrary to public policy, or violations of law will not be enforced. A clause that excludes liability for negligence may be enforced in some situations when the parties have roughly equal bargaining positions.

25. *Emerick v. Cardiac Study Center, Inc.*, 166 Wash.App. 1039 (2012).

Practice and Review: Contract Performance, Breach, and Remedies

Val's Foods signs a contract to buy 1,500 pounds of basil from Sun Farms, a small organic herb grower, as long as an independent organization inspects the crop and certifies that it contains no pesticide or herbicide residue. Val's has a contract with several restaurant chains to supply pesto and intends to use Sun Farms' basil in the pesto to fulfill these contracts. While Sun Farms is preparing to harvest the basil, an unexpected hailstorm destroys half the crop. Sun Farms attempts to purchase additional basil from other farms, but it is late in the season, and the price is twice the normal market price. Sun Farms is too small to absorb this cost and immediately notifies Val's that it will not fulfill the contract. Using the information presented in the chapter, answer the following questions.

1. Suppose that the basil does not pass the chemical-residue inspection. Which concept discussed in the chapter might allow Val's to refuse to perform the contract in this situation?
2. Under which legal theory or theories might Sun Farms claim that its obligation under the contract has been discharged by operation of law? Discuss fully.
3. Suppose that Sun Farms contacts every basil grower in the country and buys the last remaining chemical-free basil anywhere. Nevertheless, Sun Farms is able to ship only 1,475 pounds to Val's. Would this fulfill Sun Farms' obligations to Val's? Why or why not?
4. Now suppose that Sun Farms sells its operations to Happy Valley Farms. As a part of the sale, all three parties agree that Happy Valley will provide the basil as stated under the original contract. What is this type of agreement called?

Debate This . . .   *The doctrine of commercial impracticability should be abolished.*

Terms and Concepts

anticipatory repudiation 273	duress 270	performance 270
bilateral mistake 266	frustration of purpose 277	restitution 282
breach of contract 273	impossibility of performance 275	*scienter* 269
commercial impracticability 277	incidental damages 278	specific performance 282
condition 270	liquidated damages 280	tender 270
condition precedent 270	mutual rescission 274	undue influence 269
consequential damages 279	nominal damages 280	unilateral mistake 265
discharge 270	novation 274	voluntary consent 265
discharge in bankruptcy 275	penalty 280	waiver 277

Issue Spotters

1. Ready Foods contracts to buy two hundred carloads of frozen pizzas from Stealth Distributors. Before Ready or Stealth starts performing, can the parties call off the deal? What if Stealth has already shipped the pizzas? Explain your answers. (See *Performance and Discharge.*)
2. Greg contracts to build a storage shed for Haney, who pays Greg in advance, but Greg completes only half the work. Haney pays Ipswich $500 to finish the shed. If Haney sues Greg, what will be the measure of recovery? (See *Damages.*)

- **Check your answers to the Issue Spotters against the answers provided in Appendix B at the end of this text.**

Business Scenarios and Case Problems

13–1. Conditions of Performance. The Caplans contract with Faithful Construction, Inc., to build a house for them for $360,000. The specifications state "all plumbing bowls and fixtures . . . to be Crane brand." The Caplans leave on vacation, and during their absence, Faithful is unable to buy and install Crane plumbing fixtures. Instead, Faithful installs Kohler brand fixtures, an equivalent in the industry. On completion of the building contract, the Caplans inspect the work, discover the substitution, and refuse to accept the house, claiming Faithful has breached the conditions set forth in the specifications. Discuss fully the Caplans' claim. (See *Performance and Discharge*.)

13–2. Undue Influence. Juan is an elderly man who lives with his nephew, Samuel. Juan is totally dependent on Samuel's support. Samuel tells Juan that unless he transfers a tract of land he owns to Samuel for a price 35 percent below its market value, Samuel will no longer support and take care of him. Juan enters into the contract. Discuss fully whether Juan can set aside this contract. (See *Voluntary Consent*.)

13–3. Material Breach. The Northeast Independent School District in Bexar County, Texas, hired STR Constructors, Ltd., to renovate a middle school. STR subcontracted the tile work in the school's kitchen to Newman Tile, Inc. (NTI). The project had already fallen behind schedule. As a result, STR allowed other workers to walk over and damage the newly installed tile before it had cured, forcing NTI to constantly redo its work. Despite NTI's requests for payment, STR remitted only half the amount due under their contract. When the school district refused to accept the kitchen, including the tile work, STR told NTI to quickly make repairs. A week later, STR terminated their contract. Did STR breach the contract with NTI? Explain. [*STR Constructors, Ltd. v. Newman Tile, Inc.*, 395 S.W.3d 383 (Tex.App.—El Paso 2013)] (See *Performance and Discharge*.)

13–4. Discharge by Operation of Law. Dr. Jake Lambert signed an employment agreement with Baptist Health Services, Inc., to provide cardiothoracic surgery services to Baptist Memorial Hospital–North Mississippi, Inc., in Oxford, Mississippi. Complaints about Lambert's behavior arose almost immediately. He was evaluated by a team of doctors and psychologists, who diagnosed him as suffering from obsessive-compulsive personality disorder and concluded that he was unfit to practice medicine. Based on this conclusion, the hospital suspended his staff privileges. Citing the suspension, Baptist Health Services claimed that Lambert had breached his employment contract. What is Lambert's best defense to this claim? Explain. [*Baptist Memorial Hospital–North Mississippi, Inc. v. Lambert*, 157 So.3d 109 (Miss.App. 2015)] (See *Performance and Discharge*.)

13–5. Business Case Problem with Sample Answer— Limitation-of-Liability Clauses. Mia Eriksson was a seventeen-year-old competitor in horseback-riding events. Her riding coach was Kristi Nunnink. Eriksson signed an agreement that released Nunnink from all liability except for damages caused by Nunnink's "direct, willful and wanton negligence." During an event at Galway Downs in Temecula, California, Eriksson's horse struck a hurdle. She fell from the horse and the horse fell on her, causing her death. Her parents, Karan and Stan Eriksson, filed a suit in a California state court against Nunnink for wrongful death. Is the limitation-of-liability agreement that Eriksson signed likely to be enforced in her parents' case? If so, how will it affect their claim? Explain. [*Eriksson v. Nunnink*, 233 Cal.App.4th 708, 183 Cal.Rptr.3d 234 (4 Dist. 2015)] (See *Contract Provisions Limiting Remedies*.)

- **For a sample answer to Problem 13–5, go to Appendix C at the end of this text.**

13–6. Damages. Robert Morris was a licensed insurance agent working for his father's independent insurance agency when he contacted Farmers Insurance Exchange in Alabama about becoming a Farmers agent. According to Farmers' company policy, Morris was an unsuitable candidate due to his relationship with his father's agency. But no Farmers representative told Morris of this policy, and none of the documents that he signed expressed it. Farmers trained Morris and appointed him its agent. About three years later, however, Farmers terminated the appointment for "a conflict of interest because his father was in the insurance business." Morris filed a suit in an Alabama state court against Farmers, claiming that he had been fraudulently induced to leave his father's agency to work for Farmers. If Morris was successful, what type of damages was he most likely awarded? What was the measure of damages? Discuss. [*Farmers Insurance Exchange v. Morris*, 228 So.3d 971 (Ala. 2016)] (See *Damages*.)

13–7. Substantial Performance. Melissa Gallegos bought a used 1996 Saturn automobile for $2,155 from Raul Quintero, doing business as JR's Motors. Their written contract focused primarily on the transfer of physical possession of the vehicle and did not mention who would pay the taxes on the sale. Gallegos paid Quintero $2,200, believing that this amount included the taxes. When she asked him for the title to the vehicle, he told her that only the state could provide the title and only after the taxes were paid. Quintero added that they had orally agreed Gallegos would pay the taxes. Without the title, Gallegos could not obtain license plates and legally operate the vehicle. More than six years later, she filed a suit in a Texas state court against Quintero, alleging breach of contract. Did Quintero substantially perform his obligation under the contract? Explain. [*Gallegos v. Quintero*, 2018 WL

655539 (Tex.App.—Corpus Christi-Edinburg 2018)] (See *Performance and Discharge.*)

13–8. Reformation. Dr. John Holm signed a two-year employment agreement with Gateway Anesthesia Associates, PLLC. During negotiations for the agreement, Gateway's president, Dr. Jon Nottingham, told Holm that on completion of the contract he would become a partner in the firm and that during the term he would be paid "like a partner." The written agreement did not reflect this promise—the contract read that Holm would be paid based on "net collections" for his services and did not state that he would become a partner. Later, Gateway told Holm that it did not intend to make him a partner. Holm filed a complaint in an Arizona state court against Gateway, alleging breach. Before the trial, Holm filed a motion to reform the contract to express what he had been told. Nottingham did not dispute Holm's account. What is the basis for the reformation of a contract? Is it appropriate in this case? Why or why not? [*Holm v. Gateway Anesthesia Associates, PLLC,* 2018 WL 770503 (Ariz.Ct.App. Div. 1 2018)] (See *Equitable Remedies for Contract Breach.*)

13–9. A Question of Ethics—The IDDR Approach and Fraudulent Misrepresentation. *Data Consulting Group contracted with Weston Medsurg Center, PLLC, a health-care facility in Charlotte, North Carolina, to install, maintain, and manage Weston's computers and software. At about the same time, Ginger Blackwood began to work for Weston as a medical billing and coding specialist. Soon, she was submitting false time reports and converting Weston documents and data to her own purposes. At Blackwood's request, Data Consulting manager Nasko Dinev removed evidence of Blackwood's actions from her work computer.* [*Weston Medsurg Center, PLLC v. Blackwood,* 795 S.E.2d 829 (N.C.Ct.App. 2017)] (See Voluntary Consent.)

(a) What should Weston do when it learns of these activities? With respect to this situation, identify and consider the firm's primary ethical dilemma using the IDDR approach.

(b) Suppose that despite Dinev's efforts, Weston is later able to recover the data that was removed from Blackwood's work computer. How might this affect Weston's choices? Discuss.

Time-Limited Group Assignment

13–10. Breach and Remedies. Frances Morelli agreed to sell Judith Bucklin a house in Rhode Island for $177,000. The sale was supposed to be closed by September 1. The contract included a provision that "if Seller is unable to convey good, clear, insurable, and marketable title, Buyer shall have the option to: (a) accept such title as Seller is able to convey without reduction of the Purchase Price, or (b) cancel this Agreement and receive a return of all Deposits."

An examination of the public records revealed that the house did not have marketable title. Bucklin offered Morelli additional time to resolve the problem, and the closing did not occur as scheduled. Morelli decided that "the deal was over" and offered to return the deposit. Bucklin refused and,

in mid-October, decided to exercise her option to accept the house without marketable title. She notified Morelli, who did not respond. She then filed a lawsuit against Morelli in a state court. (See *Performance and Discharge* and *Damages.*)

(a) One group will discuss whether Morelli breached the contract and will decide in whose favor the court should rule.

(b) A second group will assume that Morelli did breach the contract and will determine what the appropriate remedy is in this situation.

(c) A third group will list some possible reasons why Bucklin wanted to go through with the transaction even when faced with not receiving marketable title.

Chapter 14

Sales and Lease Contracts

When we turn to contracts for the sale and lease of goods, we move away from common law principles and into the area of statutory law. State statutory law governing sales and lease transactions is based on the Uniform Commercial Code (UCC), which has been adopted as law by all of the states.[1] Of all the

attempts to produce a uniform body of laws relating to commercial transactions in the United States, none has been as successful as the UCC.

The goal of the UCC is to simplify and to streamline commercial transactions. The UCC allows parties to form sales and lease contracts, including those entered into online, without observing the same degree of formality used in forming other types of contracts.

Today, businesses often engage in sales and lease transactions on a global scale. The United Nations Convention on Contracts for the International Sale of Goods (CISG) governs international sales contracts. The CISG is a model uniform law that applies only when a nation has adopted it, just as the UCC applies only to the extent that it has been adopted by a state.

---

1. Louisiana has not adopted Articles 2 and 2A, however.

14–1 The Scope of Articles 2 (Sales) and 2A (Leases)

Article 2 of the UCC sets forth the requirements for *sales contracts*, as well as the duties and obligations of the parties involved in the sales contract. Article 2A covers similar issues for *lease contracts*. Bear in mind, however, that the parties to sales or lease contracts are free to agree to terms different from those stated in the UCC.

14–1a Article 2—The Sale of Goods

Article 2 of the UCC (as adopted by state statutes) governs **sales contracts,** or contracts for the sale of goods. To facilitate commercial transactions, Article 2 modifies some of the common law contract requirements that were discussed in the previous chapters.

To the extent that it has not been modified by the UCC, however, the common law of contracts also applies to sales contracts. In other words, the common law requirements for a valid contract—agreement, consideration, capacity, and legality—are also applicable to sales contracts.

In general, the rule is that whenever a conflict arises between a common law contract rule and the state

statutory law based on the UCC, the UCC controls. Thus, when a UCC provision addresses a certain issue, the UCC rule governs. When the UCC is silent, the common law governs. The relationship between general contract law and the law governing sales of goods is illustrated in Exhibit 14–1.

In regard to Article 2, keep two points in mind.

1. Article 2 deals with the sale of *goods*. It does not deal with real property (real estate), services, or intangible property such as stocks and bonds. Thus, if the subject matter of a dispute is goods, the UCC governs. If it is real estate or services, the common law applies.
2. In some situations, the rules can vary depending on whether the buyer or the seller is a *merchant*.

We look now at how the UCC defines a *sale, goods,* and *merchant status.*

What Is a Sale? The UCC defines a **sale** as "the passing of title [evidence of ownership rights] from the seller to the buyer for a price" [UCC 2–106(1)]. The price may be payable in cash or in other goods or services. ■ **Case in Point 14.1** Blasini, Inc., contracted to buy the business assets of the Attic Bar & Grill in Omaha, Nebraska, from Cheran Investments, LLC. Blasini obtained insurance and was making monthly payments on the assets, which

Exhibit 14–1 The Law Governing Contracts

This exhibit graphically illustrates the relationship between general contract law and statutory law (UCC Articles 2 and 2A) governing contracts for the sale and lease of goods. Sales contracts are not governed exclusively by Article 2 of the UCC but are also governed by general contract law whenever it is relevant and has not been modified by the UCC.

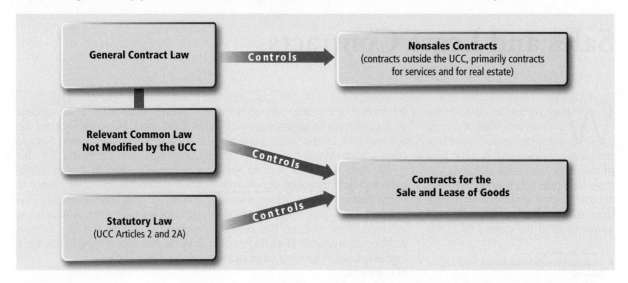

included furniture and equipment. A fire broke out and damaged the assets involved in the sale. Because the purchase price had not yet been fully paid, a dispute arose concerning who was entitled to the insurance proceeds for the damage.

Nautilus Insurance Company asked a Nebraska state court to resolve the matter. Ultimately, a state appellate court held that the sale of the Attic's business assets involved goods, and thus the agreement was governed by the UCC. Under UCC 2–401, title to the goods passed to Blasini at the time of contract formation, regardless of whether the entire purchase price had been paid. Therefore, Blasini was entitled to the insurance proceeds.[2] (For a discussion of how states can impose taxes on online sales, see this chapter's *Digital Update* feature.)

What Are Goods?

To be characterized as a *good*, an item of property must be *tangible*, and it must be *movable*. **Tangible property** has physical existence—it can be touched or seen. **Intangible property**—such as corporate stocks and bonds, patents and copyrights, and ordinary contract rights—has only conceptual existence and thus does not come under Article 2. A *movable* item can be carried from place to place. Hence, real estate is excluded from Article 2.

Goods Associated with Real Estate. Goods *associated* with real estate often do fall within the scope of Article 2 [UCC 2–107]. For instance, a contract for the sale of minerals, oil, or gas is a contract for the sale of goods if *severance, or separation, is to be made by the seller*. Similarly, a contract for the sale of growing crops or timber to be cut is a contract for the sale of goods *regardless of who severs them from the land*.

■ **Case in Point 14.2** Perry Dan Cruse owned a business in Indiana that bought standing timber, cut it, and then resold it. Donald Freyberger had a contract with Cruse under which Cruse was to harvest 120 choice trees from Freyberger's land within six months. As payment, Freyberger would receive a percentage of the net proceeds from the sale of the cut timber. Cruse harvested and cut the trees but then filed for bankruptcy before the timber was sold. Freyberger filed a claim with the bankruptcy court, asserting that he had a "vendor's lien" on the timber because Cruse owed him $15,150 on the contract. (A lien would give Freyberger's claim priority over Cruse's other creditors.)

The bankruptcy court held that the timber was personal property (goods) under the UCC regardless of who cut it. Because no vendor's lien can arise on personal property under Indiana law, Freyberger's claim did not receive any special priority under bankruptcy law, and the debt could be discharged.[3] ■

---

2. *Nautilus Insurance Co. v. Cheran Investments, LLC*, 2014 WL 292809 (Neb.Ct.App. 2014).

3. *In re Cruse*, 2013 WL 323275 (Bankr. S.D.Ind. 2013).

Digital Update

Taxing Web Purchases

In 1992, the United States Supreme Court ruled that an individual state cannot compel an out-of-state business that lacks a substantial physical presence within that state to collect and remit state taxes.[a] Congress has the power to pass legislation requiring out-of-state corporations to collect and remit state sales taxes, but it has not done so. Thus, for some years, online retailers without a physical presence in a state were not required to collect sales taxes from state residents. (State residents are supposed to self-report their purchases and pay use taxes to the state, which they rarely do.)

Redefining Physical Presence

A number of states found a way to circumvent the Supreme Court's 1992 ruling—they simply redefined *physical presence*. New York started the trend when it changed its tax laws in this manner. In New York, an online retailer that pays any party within New York to solicit business for its products is considered to have a physical presence in the state and must collect state taxes. Since then, around half of the states have made similar changes.

These laws, often called "Amazon tax" laws because they are aimed largely at Amazon.com, affect all online sellers, especially retailers that pay affiliates to direct traffic to their websites. The laws have been upheld by several courts.[b]

The Supreme Court Changes Course

In 2018, in *South Dakota v. Wayfair, Inc.,*[c] the United States Supreme Court overruled its earlier decision

and opened the door to state taxation of online sales. The South Dakota legislature had enacted a statute that required certain out-of-state sellers to collect and remit sales tax "as if the seller had a physical presence in the state." The law applied only to sellers that sell more than $100,000 worth of goods or services within the state per year. South Dakota then sued three large retailers, Wayfair, Overstock.com, and Newegg, for failing to collect taxes as required under this law. The lower courts and the state's highest court ruled in favor of the retailers because of the Supreme Court's precedent requiring physical presence.

When the case reached the Supreme Court, however, the justices reexamined the earlier decision, and five out of nine of them chose to overrule it. The majority found that the case's focus on physical presence created an "online sales tax loophole" that gave out-of-state businesses an advantage. The justices concluded that in today's online environment, physical presence in a taxing state is not necessary for the seller to have a substantial connection with the state.

Chief Justice John Roberts wrote the dissenting opinion. He noted, "E-Commerce has grown into a significant and vibrant part of our national economy against the backdrop of established rules, including the physical-presence rule. Any alteration to those rules with the potential to disrupt the development of such a critical segment of the economy should be undertaken by Congress."

----

a. *Quill Corp. v. North Dakota*, 504 U.S. 298, 112 S.Ct. 1904, 119 L.Ed.2d 91 (1992).
b. *Direct Marketing Association v. Brohl*, 814 F.3d 1129 (10th Cir. 2016); *D & H Distributing Co. v. Commissioner of Revenue*, 477 Mass. 538, 79 N.E.3d 409 (2017).
c. ___ U.S. ___, 138 S.Ct. 2080, 201 L.Ed.2d 403 (2018).

Critical Thinking *Does the Supreme Court's decision in* South Dakota v. Wayfair, Inc., *make it more or less likely that Congress will enact legislation that requires out-of-state corporations to collect and pay taxes to states for online sales?*

Goods and Services Combined. When contracts involve a combination of goods and services, courts generally use the **predominant-factor test** to determine whether a contract is primarily for the sale of goods or the sale of services.[4] If a court decides that a mixed contract is primarily a goods contract, *any* dispute, even a dispute over the services portion, will be decided under the UCC.

----

4. UCC 2–314(1) does stipulate that serving food or drinks is a "sale of goods" for purposes of the implied warranty of merchantability, which will be discussed in the context of warranties. The UCC also specifies that selling unborn animals or rare coins qualifies as a "sale of goods."

■ **Case in Point 14.3** Kenneth Sack and N111KJ, LLC, contracted to buy a jet from Cessna Aircraft Company for $7.2 million. As part of the agreement, Cessna promised to manage the jet—that is, rent it out on N111KJ's behalf—for five years to help recoup the purchase price. Three years later, Cessna informed N111KJ that the jet was being dropped from the management program. Because of this decision, N111KJ was forced to sell the jet for less than 80 percent of the purchase price. Later, N111KJ filed a suit in a federal district court against Cessna, claiming breach of contract under the

UCC. The court dismissed the claim, ruling that the contract was not subject to the UCC because managing a jet was a service. N111KJ appealed.

A federal appellate court reversed the lower court's dismissal. The contract involved a sale of goods (the jet) and a sale of services (its management). Under the predominant-factor test, the clear purpose of the agreement was the sale of the jet to N111KJ. Its management was a secondary purpose.[5] ∎

Who Is a Merchant? Article 2 governs the sale of goods in general. It applies to sales transactions between all buyers and sellers. In a limited number of instances, though, the UCC presumes that special business standards ought to be imposed because of merchants' relatively high degree of commercial expertise.[6] Such standards do not apply to the casual or inexperienced seller or buyer (consumer).

Section 2–104 sets forth three ways in which merchant status can arise:

1. A merchant is a person who *deals in goods of the kind* involved in the sales contract. Thus, a retailer, a wholesaler, or a manufacturer is a merchant of the goods sold in his or her business. A merchant for one type of goods is not necessarily a merchant for another type. For instance, a sporting goods retailer is a merchant when selling tennis rackets but not when selling a used computer.
2. A merchant is a person who, by occupation, *holds himself or herself out as having knowledge and skill* unique to the practices or goods involved in the transaction. This broad definition may include banks or universities as merchants.
3. A person who *employs a merchant as a broker, agent, or other intermediary* has the status of merchant in that transaction. Hence, if an art collector hires a broker to purchase or sell art for her, the collector is considered a merchant in the transaction.

In summary, a person is a **merchant** when she or he, acting in a mercantile capacity, possesses or uses an expertise specifically related to the goods being sold. This basic distinction is not always clear-cut. For instance, state courts appear to be split on whether farmers should be considered merchants.

5. *Sack v. Cessna Aircraft Co.*, 676 Fed.Appx. 887 (11th Cir. 2017).
6. The provisions that apply only to merchants deal principally with the Statute of Frauds, firm offers, additional terms in acceptances, warranties, and contract modification. These special rules, which reflect expedient business practices commonly known to merchants in the commercial setting, will be discussed later in this chapter.

14–1b Article 2A—Leases

Leases of personal property (goods such as automobiles and industrial equipment) have become increasingly common. In this context, a lease is a transfer of the right to possess and use goods for a period of time in exchange for payment. Article 2A of the UCC was created to fill the need for uniform guidelines in this area.

Article 2A covers any transaction that creates a lease of goods or a sublease of goods [UCC 2A–102, 2A–103(1)(k)]. Article 2A is essentially a repetition of Article 2, except that it applies to leases of goods rather than sales of goods and thus varies to reflect differences between sales and lease transactions. (Note that Article 2A is not concerned with leases of real property, such as land or buildings.)

14–2 The Formation of Sales and Lease Contracts

In regard to the formation of sales and lease contracts, the UCC modifies the common law in several ways. We look here at how Articles 2 and 2A of the UCC modify common law contract rules. Remember, though, that parties to sales and lease contracts are basically free to establish whatever terms they wish.

The UCC comes into play when the parties either fail to provide certain terms in their contract or wish to change the effect of the UCC's terms in the contract's application. The UCC makes this very clear by its repeated use of such phrases as "unless the parties otherwise agree" and "absent a contrary agreement by the parties."

14–2a Offer

In general contract law, the moment a definite offer is met by an unqualified acceptance, a binding contract is formed. In commercial sales transactions, the verbal exchanges, correspondence, and actions of the parties may not reveal exactly when a binding contractual obligation arises. The UCC states that an agreement sufficient to constitute a contract can exist even if the moment of its making is undetermined [UCC 2–204(2), 2A–204(2)].

Open Terms Under the common law of contracts, an offer must be definite enough for the parties (and the courts) to ascertain its essential terms when it is accepted. In contrast, the UCC states that a sales or lease contract will not fail for indefiniteness even if one or more terms are left open as long as *both* of the following are true:

1. The parties intended to make a contract.
2. There is a reasonably certain basis for the court to grant an appropriate remedy [UCC 2–204(3), 2A–204(3)].

The UCC provides numerous *open-term* provisions that can be used to fill the gaps in a contract. For instance, if the parties have not agreed on a price, the court will determine a "reasonable price at the time for delivery" [UCC 2–305(1)]. When the parties do not specify payment terms, payment is due at the time and place at which the buyer is to receive the goods [UCC 2–310(a)]. When

no delivery terms are specified, the buyer normally takes delivery at the seller's place of business [UCC 2–308(a)].

Keep in mind, though, that if too many terms are left open, a court may find that the parties did not intend to form a contract. Also, the *quantity* of goods involved usually must be expressly stated in the contract. If the quantity term is left open, the courts will have no basis for determining a remedy.

In the following case, one company orally agreed to store another company's goods in anticipation of forming a contract, but they did not agree on how long that arrangement would last. The question was whether the open term in their agreement rendered the contract unenforceable.

Case 14.1

Toll Processing Services, LLC v. Kastalon, Inc.
United States Court of Appeals, Seventh Circuit, 880 F.3d 820 (2018).

Background and Facts Toll Processing Services, LLC, a subsidiary of International Steel Services, Inc., was formed to own and operate a pickle line. A pickle line is used in the steel industry to process hot-rolled steel coil through acid tanks to remove rust and impurities. Toll Processing purchased a used pickle line that had been serviced by Kastalon, Inc., which provides equipment and repairs for the steel industry. The line included fifty-seven pickle-line rolls, some of which were in need of repair.

Toll Processing was planning to reinstall the used pickle line in its own facility but did not yet have a facility. Kastalon agreed to move the pickle rolls to its facility and store them, at no cost, until Toll Processing could issue a purchase order to Kastalon to recondition the rolls. Both parties believed that Toll Processing would complete its plan to reinstall the pickle line within months, but they did not discuss the time frame.

Kastalon moved the pickle rolls to its facility over a period of three months but then had no further contact with Toll Processing for two years. Believing that the pickle rolls were of little value and that Toll Processing had gone out of business, Kastalon eventually scrapped the rolls and received $6,300 from a recycler. The following year, Toll Processing contacted Kastalon and requested a price quote for reconditioning the rolls, at which point Kastalon informed Toll that the rolls had been scrapped.

Toll Processing sued Kastalon for breach of contract (in addition to several other claims). A district court granted summary judgment in favor of Kastalon, finding that the oral agreement between the parties did not have a specific duration and lacked consideration. Toll Processing appealed to a federal appellate court.

In the Language of the Court
PEPPER, District Judge.
* * * *

Under Illinois law, oral agreements are enforceable "so long as there is an offer, an acceptance, and a meeting of the minds as to the terms of the agreement." *To be enforceable, such an oral agreement must be sufficiently definite as to its material terms.* The parties do not dispute that the duration of Kastalon's obligation to store the rolls was a material term of their agreement; their dispute relates to the length of the duration. [Emphasis added.]

* * * Toll Processing argued that Kastalon agreed to store the rolls until Toll Processing issued a purchase order for Kastalon to refurbish the rolls—whenever that might be. Kastalon confirmed that it had agreed to store the rolls until Toll Processing found a location for the pickle line and issued the purchase

Case 14.1 Continues

order for the refurbishment of the rolls, but insisted that this was to be for a short time—a period of three or four months. This discrepancy, the district court found, showed that the parties did not have a mutual understanding as to the duration of the storage agreement.

On appeal, Toll Processing argues that "the parties' conduct established an agreement on the material terms, and the undisputed facts of record established that there was consideration to support the agreement." Toll Processing also argues that the district court erred because the duration of the contract either was tied to the reinstallation of the pickle line, or presented a genuine dispute of material fact regarding the parties' mutual intent.

Kastalon responded that [Toll Processing's in-house attorney] admitted that the parties did not reach an agreement that Kastalon was to hold the rolls indefinitely, and that he admitted that the alleged oral agreement placed no obligations on Toll Processing other than to advise Kastalon that it had received a purchase order for the pickle line and was ready to proceed with work involving the rolls. According to Kastalon, the spare and vague terms of this oral agreement were too indefinite to be enforced under Illinois law.

Kastalon's expectation that Toll Processing would hire it to repair and refurbish the rolls constitutes consideration. But we conclude that the district court correctly entered judgment in Kastalon's favor as to Toll Processing's breach of contract claim, because the evidence shows that the parties did not have a mutual understanding that Kastalon would store the rolls indefinitely.

The duration of the agreement was to be determined by the date on which Toll Processing issued a purchase order to Kastalon to repair and refurbish the rolls for use in the newly installed pickle line. When Kastalon agreed to store the rolls, however, Toll Processing did not know when—or even if—it would issue that purchase order. The parties hoped and anticipated that Toll Processing would issue the purchase order within months, but Toll Processing conceded that it was possible it might never have issued a purchase order.

Decision and Remedy *The appellate court affirmed the judgment of the district court on the breach of contract claim. Although parties may have attempted to form a contract, they did not reach a mutual understanding that Kastalon would store the pickle rolls for any certain period of time. Because there was no meeting of the minds on this term, the agreement was unenforceable. The appellate court reversed and remanded the district court's decision on Toll Processing's other claims, however.*

Critical Thinking
- **What If the Facts Were Different?** *Suppose that the parties admitted that they had agreed Kastalon would store the rolls for up to one year. How would this have affected the court's decision on breach of contract?*
- **Ethical** *Was it unethical for Kastalon to scrap the rolls without attempting to contact Toll Processing? Explain.*

Requirements Contracts. Requirements contracts are common in the business world and normally are enforceable. In a **requirements contract,** the buyer agrees to purchase and the seller agrees to sell all or up to a stated amount of what the buyer requires.

■ **Example 14.4** Newport Cannery forms a contract with Victor Tu. The cannery agrees to purchase from Tu, and Tu agrees to sell to the cannery, all of the green beans that the cannery requires during the following summer. There is implicit consideration in this contract because the buyer (the cannery) gives up the right to buy goods (green beans) from any other seller. This forfeited right creates a legal *detriment*—that is, consideration. ■

If, however, the buyer promises to purchase only if he or she *wishes* to do so, the promise is illusory (without consideration) and unenforceable by either party. Similarly, if the buyer reserves the right to buy the goods from someone other than the seller, the promise is unenforceable (illusory) as a requirements contract.

Output Contracts. In an **output contract,** the seller agrees to sell and the buyer agrees to buy all or up to a stated amount of what the seller produces. ■ **Example 14.5** Ruth Sewell has planted two acres of organic tomatoes. Bella Union, a local restaurant, agrees to buy all of the tomatoes that Sewell produces that year to use at the restaurant. Again, because the seller essentially forfeits the right to sell goods to another buyer, there is implicit consideration in an output contract. ■

The UCC imposes a *good faith limitation* on requirements and output contracts. The quantity under such contracts is the amount of requirements or the amount of output that occurs during a *normal* production period. The actual quantity purchased or sold cannot be unreasonably disproportionate to normal or comparable prior requirements or output [UCC 2–306(1)].

Merchant's Firm Offer Under regular contract principles, an offer can be revoked at any time before acceptance. The major common law exception is an *option contract*, in which the offeree pays consideration for the offeror's irrevocable promise to keep the offer open for a stated period. The UCC creates a second exception for *firm offers* made by a merchant concerning the sale or lease of goods (regardless of whether or not the offeree is a merchant).

A **firm offer** arises when a merchant-offeror gives *assurances in a signed writing* that the offer will remain open. The merchant's firm offer is irrevocable without the necessity of consideration[7] for the stated period or, if no definite period is stated, a reasonable period (neither to exceed three months) [UCC 2–205, 2A–205].

To qualify as a firm offer, the offer must be:

1. *Written* (or electronically recorded, such as in an e-mail).
2. *Signed* by the offeror.

■ **Example 14.6** Osaka, a used-car dealer, e-mails a letter to Gomez on January 1, stating, "I have a used Toyota RAV4 on the lot that I'll sell you for $22,000 any time between now and January 31." This e-mail creates a firm offer, and Osaka will be liable for breach of contract if he sells the RAV4 to another person before January 31. ■

14–2b Acceptance

Acceptance of an offer to buy, sell, or lease goods generally may be made in any reasonable manner and by any reasonable means. The UCC permits acceptance of an offer to buy goods "either by a prompt *promise* to ship or by the prompt or current shipment of conforming or nonconforming goods" [UCC 2–206(1)(b)]. *Conforming goods* accord with the contract's terms, whereas *nonconforming goods* do not.

---

7. If the offeree pays consideration, then an option contract (not a merchant's firm offer) is formed.

The prompt shipment of nonconforming goods constitutes both an acceptance, which creates a contract, and a breach of that contract. This rule does not apply if the seller **seasonably** (within a reasonable amount of time) notifies the buyer that the nonconforming shipment is offered only as an *accommodation*, or as a favor. The notice of accommodation must clearly indicate to the buyer that the shipment does not constitute an acceptance and that, therefore, no contract has been formed.

■ **Example 14.7** Mendez orders one thousand *blue* smart fitness watches from Halderson. Halderson ships one thousand *black* smart fitness watches to Mendez. If Halderson notifies Mendez that it has only black watches in stock, and the black watches are being sent as an accommodation, then the shipment is an offer. A contract will be formed only if Mendez accepts the black watches.

If, however, Halderson ships black watches *without* notifying Mendez that the goods are being sent as an accommodation, the shipment is both an acceptance and a breach of the resulting contract. Mendez can sue Halderson for any appropriate damages. ■

Communication of Acceptance Under the common law, because a unilateral offer invites acceptance by performance, the offeree need not notify the offeror of performance unless the offeror would not otherwise know about it. In other words, a unilateral offer can be accepted by beginning performance.

The UCC is more stringent than the common law in this regard because it requires notification. Under the UCC, if the offeror is not notified within a reasonable time that the offeree has accepted the contract by beginning performance, then the offeror can treat the offer as having lapsed before acceptance [UCC 2–206(2), 2A–206(2)].

Additional Terms Recall that under the common law, the *mirror image rule* requires that the terms of the acceptance exactly match those of the offer. ■ **Example 14.8** Adderson e-mails an offer to sell twenty Samsung Galaxy tablets to Beale. If Beale accepts the offer but changes it to require more powerful tablets, then there is no contract if the mirror image rule applies. ■

To avoid such problems, the UCC dispenses with the mirror image rule. Under the UCC, a contract is formed if the offeree's response indicates a *definite* acceptance of the offer, *even if the acceptance includes terms additional to or different from those contained in the offer* [UCC 2–207(1)]. Whether the additional terms become part of the contract depends, in part, on whether the parties are nonmerchants or merchants.

Rules When One Party or Both Parties Are Nonmerchants. If one (or both) of the parties is a *nonmerchant*, the contract is formed according to the terms of the original offer. The contract does not include any of the additional terms in the acceptance [UCC 2–207(2)].

Rules When Both Parties Are Merchants. The UCC includes a special rule for merchants to avoid the "battle of the forms," which occurs when two merchants exchange separate standard forms containing different contract terms.

Under UCC 2–207(2), in contracts *between merchants*, the additional terms *automatically* become part of the contract *unless* one of the following conditions arises:

1. The original offer expressly limited acceptance to its terms.
2. The new or changed terms materially alter the contract.
3. The offeror objects to the new or changed terms within a reasonable period of time.

When determining whether an alteration is material, courts consider several factors. Generally, if the modification does not involve any unreasonable element of surprise or hardship for the offeror, a court will hold that the modification did not materially alter the contract. Courts also consider the parties' prior dealings.

Conditioned on Offeror's Assent. The offeree's response is not an acceptance if it contains additional or different terms and is expressly *conditioned* on the offeror's assent to those terms [UCC 2–207(1)]. This is true whether or not the parties are merchants.

■ **Example 14.9** Philips offers to sell Hundert 650 pounds of turkey thighs at a specified price and with specified delivery terms. Hundert responds, "I accept your offer for 650 pounds of turkey thighs *on the condition that you agree to give me ninety days to pay for them.*" Hundert's response will be construed *not* as an acceptance but as a counteroffer, which Philips may or may not accept. ■

Additional Terms May Be Stricken. The UCC provides yet another option for dealing with conflicting terms in the parties' writings. Section 2–207(3) states that conduct by both parties that recognizes the existence of a contract is sufficient to establish a sales contract—even if the parties' writings do not otherwise establish a contract. In this situation, "the terms of the particular contract will consist of those terms on which the writings of the parties agree, together with any supplementary terms incorporated under any other provisions of this Act." In a dispute over contract terms, this provision allows a court simply to strike from the contract those terms on which the parties do not agree.

As noted previously, the fact that a merchant's acceptance frequently contains terms that add to or even conflict with those of the offer is often referred to as the "battle of the forms." Although the UCC tries to eliminate this battle, the problem of differing contract terms still arises in commercial settings, particularly when standard forms (for placing and confirming orders) are used.

14–2c Consideration

The common law rule that a contract requires consideration also applies to sales and lease contracts. Unlike the common law, however, the UCC does not require a contract modification to be supported by new consideration. The UCC states that an agreement modifying a contract for the sale or lease of goods "needs no consideration to be binding" [UCC 2–209(1), 2A–208(1)]. Of course, any contract modification must be made in good faith [UCC 1–304].

In some situations, an agreement to modify a sales or lease contract without consideration must be in writing to be enforceable. For instance, if the contract itself specifies that any changes to the contract must be in a signed writing, only those changes agreed to in a signed writing are enforceable.

Sometimes, when a consumer (nonmerchant) is buying goods from a merchant-seller, the merchant supplies a form that contains a prohibition against oral modification. In those situations, the consumer must sign a separate acknowledgment of the clause for it to be enforceable [UCC 2–209(2), 2A–208(2)]. Also, any modification that makes a sales contract come under Article 2's writing requirement (its Statute of Frauds, discussed next) usually requires a writing to be enforceable.

See Concept Summary 14.1 for a review of the UCC's rules on offer, acceptance, and consideration.

14–2d The Statute of Frauds

The UCC contains Statute of Frauds provisions covering sales and lease contracts. Under these provisions, sales contracts for goods priced at $500 or more and lease contracts requiring total payments of $1,000 or more must be in writing to be enforceable [UCC 2–201(1), 2A–201(1)]. (These low threshold amounts may eventually be raised.)

Sufficiency of the Writing A writing, including an e-mail or other electronic record, will be sufficient to satisfy the UCC's Statute of Frauds as long as it:

1. Indicates that the parties intended to form a contract.

Concept Summary 14.1

Offer, Acceptance, and Consideration under the UCC

Offer	• Not all terms (including payment and delivery) have to be included for a contract to be formed. • The price does not have to be included for a contract to be formed. • The contract normally must specify the quantity of goods involved. • An offer by a merchant in a signed writing with assurances that the offer will not be withdrawn is irrevocable without consideration (for up to three months).
Acceptance	• Acceptance may be made by any reasonable means of communication. It is effective when dispatched. • Acceptance of an offer can be made by a promise to ship or by the shipment of conforming goods, or by prompt shipment of nonconforming goods unless accompanied by a notice of accommodation. • Acceptance by performance requires notice within a reasonable time. Otherwise, the offer can be treated as lapsed. • A definite expression of acceptance creates a contract even if the terms of the acceptance differ from those of the offer (unless acceptance is expressly conditioned on consent to the additional or different terms).
Consideration	A *modification* of a contract for the sale or lease of goods does not require consideration as long as it is made in good faith.

---

2. Is signed by the party (or agent of the party) against whom enforcement is sought. (Remember that a typed name can qualify as a signature on an electronic record.)

The contract normally will not be enforceable beyond the quantity of goods shown in the writing, however. All other terms can be proved in court by oral testimony. For leases, the writing must reasonably identify and describe the goods leased and the lease term.

Special Rules for Contracts between Merchants

The UCC provides a special rule for merchants in sales transactions (there is no corresponding rule that applies to leases under Article 2A). Merchants can satisfy the Statute of Frauds if, after the parties have agreed orally, one of the merchants sends a signed written confirmation to the other merchant within a reasonable time.

The communication must indicate the terms of the agreement, and the merchant receiving the confirmation must have reason to know of its contents. Unless the merchant who receives the confirmation gives written notice of objection to its contents within ten days after receipt, the writing is sufficient against the receiving merchant, even though she or he has not signed it [UCC 2–201(2)].

■ **Example 14.10** Alfonso is a merchant-buyer in Cleveland. He contracts over the telephone to purchase $6,000 worth of spare aircraft parts from Goldstein, a merchant-seller in New York City. Two days later, Goldstein e-mails a signed confirmation detailing the terms of the oral contract, and Alfonso subsequently receives it. Alfonso does not notify Goldstein in writing that he objects to the contents of the confirmation within ten days of receipt. Therefore, Alfonso cannot raise the Statute of Frauds as a defense against the enforcement of the oral contract. ■

Exceptions The UCC defines three exceptions to the writing requirements of the Statute of Frauds [UCC 2–201(3), 2A–201(4)].

1. *Specially manufactured goods.* An oral contract for the sale or lease of goods will be enforceable if it is for goods that are specially manufactured for a particular buyer or lessee, the goods are not suitable for selling or leasing to others, and the seller or lessor has substantially started manufacturing the goods.

Exhibit 14–2 Major Differences between Contract Law and Sales Law

Topic	Contract Law	Sales Law
Contract Terms	The contract must contain all material terms.	Open terms are acceptable, if the parties intended to form a contract, but the quantity term normally must be specified, and the contract is not enforceable beyond the quantity term.
Acceptance	Mirror image rule applies. If additional terms are added in acceptance, a counteroffer is created.	Mirror image rule does not apply. Additional terms will not negate acceptance unless acceptance is made expressly conditional on assent to the additional terms.
Contract Modification	Modification requires consideration.	Modification does not require consideration.
Irrevocable Offers	Option contracts (with consideration) are irrevocable.	Merchants' firm offers (without consideration) are irrevocable.
Statute of Frauds Requirements	All material terms must be included in the writing.	Writing is required only for the sale of goods priced at $500 or more, but the contract is not enforceable beyond the quantity specified. Merchants can satisfy the requirement by a written confirmation evidencing their agreement. Exceptions exist for (1) specially manufactured goods, (2) admissions, and (3) partial performance.

2. *Admissions.* An oral contract for the sale or lease of goods is enforceable if the party against whom enforcement is sought admits in pleadings, testimony, or other court proceedings that a sales or lease contract was made.

3. *Partial performance.* An oral contract for the sale or lease of goods is enforceable if payment has been made and accepted or goods have been received and accepted. The oral contract will be enforced at least to the extent that performance actually took place.

The exceptions just discussed and other ways in which sales law differs from general contract law are summarized in Exhibit 14–2.

14–2e Unconscionability

An unconscionable contract is one that is so unfair and one-sided that it would be unreasonable to enforce it. The UCC allows a court to evaluate a contract or any clause in a contract, and if the court deems it to have been unconscionable *at the time it was made*, the court can do any of the following [UCC 2–302, 2A–108]:

1. Refuse to enforce the contract.
2. Enforce the remainder of the contract without the unconscionable part.
3. Limit the application of the unconscionable term to avoid an unconscionable result.

The following classic case illustrates an early application of the UCC's unconscionability provisions.

Classic Case 14.2

Jones v. Star Credit Corp.
Supreme Court of New York, Nassau County, 59 Misc.2d 189, 298 N.Y.S.2d 264 (1969).

Background and Facts The Joneses agreed to purchase a freezer for $900 as the result of a salesperson's visit to their home. Tax and financing charges raised the total price to $1,234.80. Later, the Joneses, who had made payments totaling $619.88, brought a suit in a New York state court to have the purchase contract declared unconscionable under the UCC. At trial, the freezer was found to have a maximum retail value of approximately $300.

In the Language of the Court
Sol M. *WACHTLER*, Justice.
* * * *

* * * [Section 2–302 of the UCC] authorizes the court to find, as a matter of law, that a contract or a clause of a contract was "unconscionable at the time it was made," and upon so finding the court may refuse to enforce the contract, excise the objectionable clause or limit the application of the clause to avoid an unconscionable result.

* * * *

* * * The question which presents itself is whether or not, under the circumstances of this case, the sale of a freezer unit having a retail value of $300 for $900 ($1,439.69 including credit charges and $18 sales tax) is unconscionable as a matter of law.

Concededly, deciding [this case] is substantially easier than explaining it. No doubt, the mathematical disparity between $300, which presumably includes a reasonable profit margin, and $900, which is exorbitant on its face, carries the greatest weight. Credit charges alone exceed by more than $100 the retail value of the freezer. These alone may be sufficient to sustain the decision. Yet, a caveat [warning] is warranted lest we reduce the import of Section 2–302 solely to a mathematical ratio formula. It may, at times, be that; yet it may also be much more. The very limited financial resources of the purchaser, known to the sellers at the time of the sale, is entitled to weight in the balance. Indeed, the value disparity itself leads inevitably to the felt conclusion that knowing advantage was taken of the plaintiffs. In addition, *the meaningfulness of choice essential to the making of a contract can be negated by a gross inequality of bargaining power.* [Emphasis added.]

* * * *

* * * The defendant has already been amply compensated. In accordance with the statute, the application of the payment provision should be limited to amounts already paid by the plaintiffs and the contract be reformed and amended by changing the payments called for therein to equal the amount of payment actually so paid by the plaintiffs.

Decision and Remedy The court held that the contract was not enforceable and reformed the contract so that no further payments were required.

Critical Thinking
- **Social** *Why would the seller's knowledge of the buyers' limited resources support a finding of unconscionability?*
- **Impact of This Case on Today's Law** *This early classic case illustrates the approach that many courts take today when deciding whether a sales contract is unconscionable—an approach that focuses on "excessive" price and unequal bargaining power. Most of the litigants who have used UCC 2–302 successfully could demonstrate both an absence of meaningful choice and contract terms that were unreasonably favorable to the other party.*

14–3 Title, Risk, and Insurable Interest

Before the creation of the UCC, *title*—the right of ownership—controlled all issues of rights and remedies of the parties to a sales contract. It was frequently difficult to determine when title actually passed from the seller to the buyer, however. It was also difficult to predict how a court would decide which party had title at the time of a loss.

Because of such problems, the UCC has separated the question of title as much as possible from the question of the rights and obligations of buyers, sellers, and third parties. In some situations, title is still relevant under the

UCC, and the UCC has special rules for determining when title passes. (These rules do not apply to leased goods, obviously, because title remains with the lessor, or owner, of the goods.) In most situations, however, the UCC has replaced the concept of title with three other concepts: identification, risk of loss, and insurable interest.

14–3a Identification

Before any interest in goods can pass from the seller or lessor to the buyer or lessee, the goods must be (1) in existence and (2) identified to the contract [UCC 2–105(2)]. **Identification** takes place when specific goods are designated as the subject matter of a sales or lease contract.

Title and risk of loss cannot pass to the buyer from the seller unless the goods are identified to the contract. (As mentioned, title to leased goods remains with the lessor.) Identification is significant because it gives the buyer or lessee the right to insure (or to have an insurable interest in) the goods and the right to recover from third parties who damage the goods.

The parties can agree in their contract on when identification will take place. (This type of agreement does not effectively pass title and risk of loss on future goods, such as unborn cattle, however.) If the parties do not so specify, the UCC provisions discussed here determine when identification takes place [UCC 2–501(1), 2A–217].

Existing Goods If the contract calls for the sale or lease of specific and determined goods that are already in existence, identification takes place at the time the contract is made. ■ **Example 14.11** Litco Company contracts to lease a fleet of five cars designated by their vehicle identification numbers (VINs). Because the cars are identified by their VINs, identification has taken place, and Litco acquires an insurable interest in the cars at the time of contracting. ■

Future Goods Any goods that are not in existence at the time of contracting are known as future goods. The following rules apply to identification of future goods:

1. If a sale or lease involves unborn animals to be born within twelve months after contracting, identification takes place when the animals are conceived.
2. If a sale involves crops that are to be harvested within twelve months (or in the next harvest season occurring after contracting, whichever is longer), identification takes place when the crops are planted. If the sales contract does not refer to crops by when they will be harvested, then identification takes place when the crops begin to grow.
3. In a sale or lease of any other future goods, identification occurs when the seller or lessor ships, marks, or otherwise designates the goods as those to which the contract refers. Future goods that fall into this category might include solar panels that are to be designed and manufactured after a contract is signed for their purchase.

Goods That Are Part of a Larger Mass Goods that are part of a larger mass are identified when the goods are marked, shipped, or somehow designated by the seller or lessor as the particular goods to pass under the contract. ■ **Example 14.12** Briggs orders 10,000 pairs of men's jeans from a lot that contains 90,000 articles of clothing for men, women, and children. Until the seller separates the 10,000 pairs of men's jeans from the other items, title and risk of loss remain with the seller. ■

A common exception to this rule involves fungible goods. **Fungible goods** are goods that are alike naturally, by agreement, or by trade usage. Typical examples include specific grades or types of wheat, petroleum, and cooking oil, which usually are stored in large containers. Owners of fungible goods typically hold title as *tenants in common* (owners with undivided shares of the whole), which facilitates further sales. A seller-owner can pass title and risk of loss to the buyer without actually separating the goods. The buyer replaces the seller as an owner in common [UCC 2–105(4)].

■ **Example 14.13** Alvarez, Braudel, and Carpenter are farmers. They deposit, respectively, 5,000 bushels, 3,000 bushels, and 2,000 bushels of grain of the same grade and quality in a grain elevator. The three become owners in common, with Alvarez owning 50 percent of the 10,000 bushels, Braudel 30 percent, and Carpenter 20 percent. Alvarez contracts to sell her 5,000 bushels of grain to Treyton. Because the goods are fungible, she can pass title and risk of loss to Treyton without physically separating the 5,000 bushels. Treyton now becomes an owner in common with Braudel and Carpenter. ■

14–3b When Title Passes

Once goods exist and are identified, the provisions of UCC 2–401 apply to the passage of title. In nearly all subsections of UCC 2–401, the words "unless otherwise explicitly agreed" appear. In other words, the buyer and the seller can reach an explicit agreement as to when title will pass.

Without an explicit agreement to the contrary, *title passes to the buyer at the time and the place the seller performs by delivering the goods* [UCC 2–401(2)]. For instance, if a person buys cattle at a livestock auction, title will pass to the buyer when the cattle are physically delivered to him or her (unless otherwise agreed). (The delivery of goods may sometimes be accomplished by drones, as discussed in this chapter's *Managerial Strategy* feature.)

■ **Case in Point 14.14** Timothy Allen contracted with Indy Route 66 Cycles, Inc., to have a motorcycle custom built for him. Indy built the motorcycle and issued a "Certificate of Origin." Later, federal law enforcement officers arrested Allen on drug charges and seized his property, including the Indy-made cycle, which officers found at the home of Allen's sister, Tena. The government alleged that the motorcycle was subject to forfeiture as the proceeds of drug trafficking.

Managerial Strategy · Commercial Use of Drones

The commercial use of drones—small, pilotless aerial vehicles—has been relatively slow to develop in the United States. Possible commercial uses of drones are numerous—railroad track inspection, oil and gas pipeline review, medical deliveries, real estate videos for use by brokers, discovery for land boundary disputes, and many others. In addition, businesses have begun to develop drones for delivery of goods. Amazon is developing Prime Air, for instance, and Google's parent company is working on Project Wing.

The Federal Aviation Administration Rules

Commercial drone delivery service is widely available in other parts of the world, including Australia and China. The delay in the United States resulted from regulatory lags. The Federal Aviation Administration (FAA), which regulates all unmanned aircraft systems, first proposed rules on commercial drone use in 2015, several years after Congress directed it to do so. These rules were not finalized until 2016.[a]

The FAA's rules require operators to apply for a license to use drones commercially. Drone flights are limited to daylight hours, and drones are not allowed to go above five hundred feet or fly faster than one hundred miles per hour. The rules also require that licensed drone operators maintain a continuous visual line of sight with the drones during operation. In addition, drones cannot be flown over anyone who is not directly participating in the operation.

Court Actions

In the past, the FAA has attempted to fine other-than-recreational users of drones. One case involved

a. 14 C.F.R. Part 107.

Texas EquuSearch, a group that searches for missing persons. The organization requested an emergency injunction after receiving an e-mail from an FAA employee indicating that its drone use was illegal. The U.S. Court of Appeals for the District of Columbia Circuit refused to act on the suit. The court stated that the e-mail from the FAA did not have legal effect and therefore was not subject to judicial review.[b] In a subsequent case, that same federal appellate court also held that the FAA's "registration rule," which requires recreational operators of model aircraft drones to register with the FAA, was valid.[c]

In a case involving an administrative hearing, the FAA assessed a civil penalty against Raphael Pirker for careless and reckless operation of an unmanned aircraft. Pirker flew a drone over the University of Virginia while filming a video advertisement for the medical school. Pirker appealed to the National Transportation Safety Board Office of Administrative Law Judges, and the board ruled in his favor.[d]

Business Questions

1. *What benefits can delivery by commercial drone provide to consumers?*
2. *Why might the United States have been slow to adopt commercial drone delivery in comparison with some other nations?*

b. *Texas EquuSearch Mounted Search and Recovery Team, RP Search Services, Inc., v. Federal Aviation Administration*, 2014 WL 2860332 (D.C.Cir. 2014).
c. *Taylor v. Huerta*, 856 F.3d 1089 (D.C.Cir. 2017).
d. *Huerta v. Pirker*, Decisional Order of National Transportation Safety Board Office of Administrative Law Judges, 2014 WL 3388631 (N.T.S.B. March 6, 2014).

Indy filed a claim against the government, arguing that it owned the cycle because it still possessed the "Certificate of Origin." The court applied UCC Section 2–401(2) and ruled in favor of the government. Testimony by Indy's former vice president was "inconclusive" but implied that Indy had delivered the motorcycle to Allen. Indy had given up possession of the cycle to Allen, and this was sufficient to pass title, even though Indy had kept a "Certificate of Origin."[8] ■

Shipment and Destination Contracts Unless otherwise agreed, delivery arrangements can determine

8. *United States v. 2007 Custom Motorcycle*, 2011 WL 232331 (D.Ariz. 2011).

when title passes from the seller to the buyer. In a **shipment contract,** the seller is required or authorized to ship goods by carrier, such as a trucking company. The seller is required only to deliver the goods into the hands of the carrier, and title passes to the buyer at the time and place of shipment [UCC 2–401(2)(a)]. Generally, *all contracts are assumed to be shipment contracts if nothing to the contrary is stated in the contract.*

In a **destination contract,** the seller is required to deliver the goods to a particular destination, usually directly to the buyer, but sometimes to another party designated by the buyer. Title passes to the buyer when the goods are *tendered* at that destination [UCC 2–401(2)(b)]. *Tender of delivery* occurs when the seller places or hold conforming goods at the buyer's disposal (with any necessary notice), enabling the buyer to take possession [UCC 2–503(1)].

Delivery without Movement of the Goods

Sometimes, a sales contract does not call for the seller to ship or deliver the goods (such as when the buyer is to pick up the goods). In that situation, the passage of title depends on whether the seller must deliver a **document of title,** such as a bill of lading or a warehouse receipt, to the buyer. A *bill of lading*[9] is a receipt for goods that is signed by a carrier and serves as a contract for the transportation of the goods. A *warehouse receipt* is a receipt issued by a warehouser for goods stored in a warehouse.

When a Title Document Is Required. When a title document is required, title passes to the buyer *when and where the document is delivered.* Thus, if the goods are stored in a warehouse, title passes to the buyer when the appropriate documents are delivered to the buyer. The goods never move. In fact, the buyer can choose to leave the goods at the same warehouse for a period of time, and the buyer's title to those goods will be unaffected.

When a Title Document Is Not Required. When no document of title is required and the goods are identified to the contract, title passes at the time and place the sales contract is made. If the goods have not been identified, title does not pass until identification occurs.

■ **Case in Point 14.15** Alaska Air Group, Inc. (AAG), and Horizon Air Industries, Inc., contracted to purchase thirty Embraer 175 (E175) regional jets from the manufacturer. Deliveries began, but Horizon was experiencing a shortage of pilots and did not have enough pilots who were qualified to fly the E175. After ten of the E175s were delivered to Horizon, AAG and Horizon delayed further deliveries until Horizon had more qualified pilots.

The International Brotherhood of Teamsters, Airline Division, and its Airline Professionals Association (the union) filed a lawsuit against AAG and Horizon alleging labor law violations. The union claimed that AAG and Horizon had committed to acquiring no fewer than thirty of the E175s to be flown exclusively by the union's pilots. The union argued that five of the E175s intended for Horizon were subsequently "diverted" to, and acquired by, SkyWest, which violated the rights of union pilots.

The court, however, applied UCC Section 2–401 to the dispute over these five aircraft and ruled that title to goods (when no document of title is required) does not pass until identification occurs. Horizon's purchase contract did not identify the specific aircrafts to be sold, such as by serial or registration numbers, and there was no clear evidence that the SkyWest E175s were ever "earmarked" for Horizon. Thus, the sale of five E175s to SkyWest did not affect Horizon's agreement to purchase thirty E175s and did not violate the rights of the union pilots. The court therefore dismissed the complaint against AAG and Horizon.[10] ■

14–3c Risk of Loss

At the various stages of a sale or lease transaction, the question may arise as to who bears the risk of loss. In other words, who suffers the financial loss if the goods are damaged, destroyed, or lost in transit? Under the UCC, risk of loss does not necessarily pass with title. When risk of loss passes from a seller or lessor to a buyer or lessee is generally determined by the contract between the parties.

Sometimes, the contract states expressly when the risk of loss passes. At other times, it does not, and a court must interpret the existing terms to determine whether the risk has passed. When no provision in the contract indicates when risk passes, the UCC provides special rules, based on delivery terms, to guide the courts.

Delivery with Movement of the Goods— Carrier Cases

When the contract involves movement of the goods via a common carrier but does not specify when risk of loss passes, the courts first look for specific delivery terms in the contract. For instance, the term F.O.B. (free on board) indicates that the selling price of goods includes transportation costs to the specific F.O.B. location named in the contract. The seller pays the expenses and carries the risk of loss to the F.O.B. location named [UCC 2–319(1)]. *Unless the parties agree otherwise,* such terms will determine which party will pay the costs of delivering the goods and who will bear the risk of loss. If the contract does not include delivery terms, then the courts must decide whether the contract is a shipment or a destination contract.

Shipment Contracts. In a shipment contract, the seller or lessor is required or authorized to ship goods by carrier, but is not required to deliver them to a particular destination. The risk of loss in a shipment contract passes to the

9. The term *bill of lading* has been used by international carriers for many years. It derives from *bill,* which historically referred to a schedule of costs for services, and the verb *to lade,* which means to load cargo onto a ship or other carrier.

10. *International Brotherhood of Teamsters, Airline Division v. Alaska Air Group, Inc.,* 2018 WL 3328226 (W.D.Wash. 2018).

buyer or lessee when the goods are delivered to the carrier [UCC 2–509(1)(a), 2A–219(2)(a)].

■ **Example 14.16** Pitman, a seller in Texas, sells five hundred cases of grapefruit to a buyer in New York, F.O.B. Houston. This term authorizes shipment by carrier and indicates that the buyer is to pay the transportation charges. Risk passes to the buyer when conforming goods are properly placed in the possession of the carrier in Houston. If the goods are damaged in transit, the loss is the buyer's. (Actually, buyers have recourse against carriers, subject to certain limitations, and they usually insure the goods from the time the goods leave the seller.) ■

Destination Contracts. In a destination contract, the risk of loss passes to the buyer or lessee when the goods are tendered to the buyer or lessee at the specified destination [UCC 2–509(1)(b), 2A–219(2)(b)]. In *Example 14.16*, if the contract had been a destination contract, F.O.B. New York, risk of loss during transit to New York would have been the seller's. Risk of loss would not have passed to the buyer until the carrier tendered the grapefruit to the buyer in New York.

Whether a contract is a shipment contract or a destination contract can have significant consequences for the parties. When an agreement is ambiguous as to whether it is a shipment or a destination contract, courts normally will presume that it is a shipment contract. Thus, the parties must use clear and explicit language to overcome this presumption and create a destination contract.

Delivery without Movement of the Goods The UCC also addresses situations in which the contract does not require the goods to be shipped or moved. Frequently, the buyer or lessee is to pick up the goods from the seller or lessor, or the goods are to be held by a bailee. A **bailment** is a temporary delivery of personal property, without passage of title, into the care of another, called a *bailee*. Under the UCC, a bailee is a party who—by a bill of lading, warehouse receipt, or other document of title—acknowledges possession of goods and/or contracts to deliver them. For instance, a warehousing company or a trucking company may be a bailee.

Goods Held by the Seller. When the seller keeps the goods for pickup, a document of title usually is not used. If the seller is not a merchant, the risk of loss to goods held by the seller passes to the buyer on *tender of delivery* [UCC 2–509(3)]. Thus, the seller bears the risk of loss until he or she makes the goods available to the buyer and notifies the buyer that the goods are ready to be picked up.

If the seller is a merchant, risk of loss to goods held by the seller passes to the buyer when the buyer *actually takes physical possession of the goods* [UCC 2–509(3)]. In other words, the merchant bears the risk of loss between the time the contract is formed and the time the buyer picks up the goods.

Goods Held by a Bailee. When a bailee is holding goods that are to be delivered under a contract without being moved, the goods are usually represented by a document of title. The title document may be written on paper or evidenced by an electronic record.

A document of title is either *negotiable* or *nonnegotiable*, depending on whether the transferee is a buyer or lessee and on how the title document is transferred. With a negotiable document of title, a party can transfer the rights by signing and delivering, or in some situations simply delivering, the document. The rights to the goods—free of any claims against the party that issued the document—pass with the document to the transferee. With a nonnegotiable document of title, the transferee obtains only the rights that the party transferring the document had, subject to any prior claims.

When goods are held by a bailee, risk of loss passes to the buyer when one of the following occurs:

1. The buyer receives a negotiable document of title for the goods.
2. The bailee acknowledges the buyer's right to possess the goods.
3. The buyer receives a nonnegotiable document of title, *and* the buyer has had a *reasonable time* to present the document to the bailee and demand the goods. If the bailee refuses to honor the document, the risk of loss remains with the seller [UCC 2–503(4)(b), 2–509(2)].

With respect to leases, if goods held by a bailee are to be delivered without being moved, the risk of loss passes to the lessee on acknowledgment by the bailee of the lessee's right to possession of the goods [UCC 2A–219(2)(b)].

Risk of Loss When a Sales or Lease Contract Is Breached When a sales or lease contract is breached, the transfer of risk operates differently depending on which party breaches. Generally, the party in breach bears the risk of loss.

When the seller or lessor breaches and the goods are so nonconforming that the buyer has the right to reject them, the risk of loss does not pass to the buyer until either:

1. The defects are **cured** (that is, the goods are repaired, replaced, or discounted in price by the seller).
2. The buyer accepts the goods in spite of their defects (thus waiving the right to reject).

When the buyer or lessee breaches, the general rule is that the risk of loss *immediately shifts* to the buyer or lessee. This rule has three important limitations [UCC 2–510(3), 2A–220(2)]:

1. The seller or lessor must already have identified the contract goods.
2. The buyer or lessee bears the risk for only a *commercially reasonable* time after the seller or lessor has learned of the breach.
3. The buyer or lessee is liable only to the extent of any deficiency in the seller's or lessor's insurance coverage.

14–3d Insurable Interest

Parties to sales and lease contracts often obtain insurance coverage to protect against damage, loss, or destruction of goods. Any party purchasing insurance, however, must have a sufficient interest in the insured item to obtain a valid policy. Insurance laws—not the UCC—determine sufficiency. The UCC is helpful, though, because it contains certain rules regarding insurable interests in goods.

A buyer or lessee has an **insurable interest** in *identified goods.* The moment the contract goods are identified by the seller or lessor, the buyer or lessee has a property interest in them. That interest allows the buyer or lessee to obtain the necessary insurance coverage for those goods even before the risk of loss has passed [UCC 2–501(1), 2A–218(1)].

A seller has an insurable interest in goods as long as he or she retains title to the goods. Even after title passes to a buyer, a seller who has a *security interest* (a right to secure payment) in the goods still has an insurable interest [UCC 2–501(2)]. Thus, both the buyer and the seller can have an insurable interest in identical goods at the same time. Of course, the buyer or seller must sustain an actual loss to have the right to recover from an insurance company.

In regard to leases, the lessor retains an insurable interest in leased goods unless the lessee exercises an option to buy. In that event, the risk of loss passes to the lessee [UCC 2A–218(3)].

14–4 Performance Obligations in Sales and Lease Contracts

The performance that is required of the parties under a sales or lease contract consists of the duties and obligations each party has under the terms of the contract. The basic obligation of the seller or lessor is to *transfer and deliver conforming goods.* The basic obligation of the buyer or lessee is to *accept and pay for conforming goods* in accordance with the contract [UCC 2–301, 2A–516(1)].

Overall performance of a sales or lease contract is controlled by the agreement between the parties. When the contract is unclear and disputes arise, the courts look to the UCC and impose standards of good faith and commercial reasonableness.

The obligations of good faith and commercial reasonableness underlie every sales and lease contract. The UCC's good faith provision, which can never be disclaimed, reads as follows: "Every contract or duty within this Act imposes an obligation of good faith in its performance or enforcement" [UCC 1–304]. *Good faith* means honesty in fact. For a merchant, it means honesty in fact and the observance of reasonable commercial standards of fair dealing in the trade [UCC 2–103(1)(b)]. In other words, merchants are held to a higher standard of performance or duty than are nonmerchants.

14–4a Obligations of the Seller or Lessor

The basic duty of the seller or lessor is to deliver the goods called for under the contract to the buyer or lessee. Goods that conform to the contract description in every way are called **conforming goods.** To fulfill the contract, the seller or lessor must either deliver or tender delivery of conforming goods to the buyer or lessee.

Tender of Delivery **Tender of delivery** occurs when the seller or lessor makes conforming goods available and gives the buyer or lessee whatever notification is reasonably necessary to enable the buyer or lessee to take delivery [UCC 2–503(1), 2A–508(1)].

Tender must occur at a *reasonable hour* and in a *reasonable manner.* For example, a seller cannot call the buyer at 2:00 A.M. and say, "The goods are ready. I'll give you twenty minutes to get them." Unless the parties have agreed otherwise, the goods must be tendered for delivery at a reasonable hour and kept available for a reasonable time to enable the buyer to take possession [UCC 2–503(1)(a)].

Normally, all goods called for by a contract must be tendered in a single delivery unless the parties have agreed on delivery in several lots or *installments* (discussed shortly) [UCC 2–307, 2–612, 2A–510]. ■ **Example 14.17** An order for 1,000 Under Armour men's shirts cannot be delivered two shirts at a time. The parties may agree, however, that the shirts will be delivered in four orders of 250 each as they are produced (for summer, fall, winter, and spring inventory). Tender of delivery may then occur in this manner. ■

Place of Delivery The buyer and seller (or lessor and lessee) may agree that the goods will be delivered to a particular destination where the buyer or lessee will take possession. If the contract does not indicate where the goods will be delivered, then the place for delivery will be one of the following:

1. The *seller's place of business*.
2. The *seller's residence*, if the seller has no business location [UCC 2–308(a)].
3. The *location of the goods*, if both parties know at the time of contracting that the goods are located somewhere other than the seller's business [UCC 2–308(b)].

■ **Example 14.18** Li Wan and Boyd both live in San Francisco. In San Francisco, Li Wan contracts to sell Boyd five used trucks, which both parties know are located in a Chicago warehouse. If nothing more is specified in the contract, the place of delivery for the trucks is Chicago. Li Wan may tender delivery by giving Boyd either a negotiable or a nonnegotiable document of title. Alternatively, Li Wan may obtain the bailee's (warehouser's) acknowledgment that Boyd is entitled to possession.[11] ■

Delivery via Carrier In many instances, it is clear from the surrounding circumstances or delivery terms in the contract (such as F.O.B. or F.A.S.) that the parties intended the goods to be moved by a carrier. In carrier contracts, the seller fulfills the obligation to deliver the goods through either a shipment contract or a destination contract.

Shipment Contracts. Recall that a *shipment contract* requires or authorizes the seller to ship goods by a carrier, rather than to deliver them at a particular destination [UCC 2–319, 2–509(1)(a)]. Under a shipment contract, unless otherwise agreed, the seller must do the following:

1. Place the goods into the hands of the carrier.
2. Make a contract for their transportation that is reasonable according to the nature of the goods and their value. (For instance, certain types of goods need refrigeration in transit.)
3. Obtain and promptly deliver or tender to the buyer any documents necessary to enable the buyer to obtain possession of the goods from the carrier.
4. Promptly notify the buyer that shipment has been made [UCC 2–504].

If the seller does not make a reasonable contract for transportation or notify the buyer of the shipment, the buyer can reject the goods, but only if a *material loss* or a *significant delay* results. ■ **Example 14.19** Zigi's Organic Fruits sells strawberries to Lozier under a shipment contract. If Zigi's does not arrange for refrigerated transportation and the berries spoil during transport, a material loss to Lozier will likely result. ■

Of course, the parties are free to make agreements that alter the UCC's rules and allow the buyer to reject goods for other reasons.

Destination Contracts. In a *destination contract*, the seller agrees to deliver conforming goods to the buyer at a particular destination. The goods must be tendered at a reasonable hour and held at the buyer's disposal for a reasonable length of time. The seller must also give the buyer appropriate notice and any necessary documents to enable the buyer to obtain delivery from the carrier [UCC 2–503].

The Perfect Tender Rule The seller or lessor has an obligation to ship or tender *conforming goods*. The buyer or lessee is then obligated to accept and pay for the goods according to the contract terms [UCC 2–507].

Under the common law, the seller was obligated to deliver goods that conformed with the terms of the contract in every detail (unless the doctrine of substantial performance applied). This was called the **perfect tender rule.** The UCC preserves the perfect tender rule by providing that if goods or tender of delivery fails *in any respect* to conform to the contract, the buyer or lessee may accept the goods, reject the entire shipment, or accept part and reject part [UCC 2–601, 2A–509].

The corollary to this rule is that if the goods conform in every respect, the buyer or lessee does not have a right to reject the goods. ■ **Case in Point 14.20** U.S. Golf & Tennis Centers, Inc., agreed to buy 96,000 golf balls from Wilson Sporting Goods Company for a total price of $20,000. Wilson represented that U.S. Golf was receiving its lowest price ($5 per two-dozen unit).

Wilson shipped golf balls to U.S. Golf that conformed to the contract in quantity and quality, but it did not receive payment. U.S. Golf claimed that it had learned that Wilson had sold the product for $2 per unit to another buyer. U.S. Golf asked Wilson to reduce the contract price of the balls to $4 per unit. Wilson refused and filed a suit. The court ruled in favor of Wilson. Because it was undisputed that the shipment of golf balls conformed to the contract specifications, U.S. Golf was obligated to accept the goods and pay the agreed-on price.[12] ■

---

11. Unless the buyer objects, the seller may also tender delivery by instructing the bailee in a writing to release the goods to the buyer without the bailee's acknowledgment of the buyer's rights [UCC 2–503(4)]. Risk of loss, however, does not pass until the buyer has had a reasonable amount of time in which to present the document or the instructions.

12. *Wilson Sporting Goods Co. v. U.S. Golf and Tennis Centers, Inc.*, 2012 WL 601804 (Tenn.App. 2012).

Exceptions to the Perfect Tender Rule Because of the rigidity of the perfect tender rule, several exceptions to the rule have been created. For instance, exceptions to the perfect tender rule may be established by agreement. The parties may agree, for instance, that defective goods or parts will not be rejected if the seller or lessor is able to repair or replace them within a reasonable period of time. In this situation, the perfect tender rule does not apply.

Cure. The UCC does not specifically define the term *cure*, but it refers to the right of the seller or lessor to repair, adjust, or replace defective or nonconforming goods [UCC 2–508, 2A–513].

The seller or lessor has a right to attempt to "cure" a defect when the following are true:

1. A delivery is rejected because the goods were nonconforming.
2. The time for performance has not yet expired.
3. The seller or lessor provides timely notice to the buyer or lessee of the intention to cure.
4. The cure can be made within the contract time for performance.

Even if the contract time for performance has expired, the seller or lessor can still cure if he or she had *reasonable grounds to believe that the nonconforming tender would be acceptable to the buyer or lessee* [UCC 2–508(2), 2A–513(2)].

The right to cure substantially restricts the right of the buyer or lessee to reject goods. To reject, the buyer or lessee must inform the seller or lessor of the particular defect. If the defect is not disclosed, the buyer or lessee cannot later assert the defect as a defense if the defect is one that the seller or lessor could have cured.

Substitution of Carriers. Sometimes, an agreed-on manner of delivery (such as the use of a particular carrier) becomes impracticable or unavailable through no fault of either party. In that situation, if a commercially reasonable substitute is available, this substitute performance is sufficient tender to the buyer and must be used [UCC 2–614(1)]. The seller or lessor is required to arrange for a substitute carrier and normally is responsible for any additional shipping costs (unless the contract states otherwise).

Commercial Impracticability. Occurrences unforeseen by either party when a contract was made may make performance commercially impracticable. When this occurs, the perfect tender rule no longer applies. The seller or lessor must, however, notify the buyer or lessee as soon as practicable that there will be a delay or nondelivery [UCC 2–615, 2A–405].

Commercial impracticability arises only when the parties, at the time the contract was made, had no reason to anticipate that the event would occur. It does not extend to problems that could have been foreseen, such as an increase in cost resulting from inflation.

■ **Case in Point 14.21** In a classic 1970s case, Maple Farms, Inc., entered into a contract to supply a school district in New York with milk for one school year. The contract price was the market price of milk in June, but by December, the price of raw milk had increased by 23 percent. Maple Farms stood to lose $7,350 on this contract (and more on similar contracts with other school districts). To avoid performing the contract, Maple Farms filed a suit and claimed that the unanticipated cost increases made performance "impracticable." A New York trial court disagreed. Because inflation and fluctuating prices could have been foreseen, they did not render performance of this contract impracticable. The court granted summary judgment in favor of the school district.[13] ■

Sometimes, the unforeseen event only *partially* affects the capacity of the seller or lessor to perform. Therefore, the seller or lessor can *partially* fulfill the contract but cannot tender total performance. In this event, the seller or lessor is required to distribute any remaining goods or deliveries fairly and reasonably among the parties to whom it is contractually obligated [UCC 2–615(b), 2A–405(b)]. The buyer or lessee must receive notice of the allocation and has the right to accept or reject it [UCC 2–615(c), 2A–405(c)].

Destruction of Identified Goods. Sometimes, an unexpected event, such as a fire, totally destroys goods through no fault of either party before risk passes to the buyer or lessee. In such a situation, *if the goods were identified at the time the contract was formed*, the parties are excused from performance [UCC 2–613, 2A–221]. If the goods are only partially destroyed, the buyer or lessee can inspect them and either treat the contract as void or accept the damaged goods with a reduction in the contract price.

Assurance and Cooperation. If one party has "reasonable grounds" to believe that the other party will not perform, the first party may *in writing* "demand adequate assurance of due performance" from the other party. Until such assurance is received, the first party may "suspend" further performance without liability. What constitutes "reasonable grounds" is determined by commercial

---

13. *Maple Farms, Inc. v. City School District of Elmira, New York*, 76 Misc.2d 1080, 352 N.Y.S.2d 784 (1974).

standards. If the requested assurances are not forthcoming within a reasonable time (not to exceed thirty days), the failure to respond may be treated as a repudiation of the contract [UCC 2–609, 2A–401].

Sometimes, the performance of one party depends on the cooperation of the other. When cooperation is not forthcoming, the first party can either proceed to perform the contract in any reasonable manner or suspend performance without liability and hold the uncooperative party in breach [UCC 2–311(3)].

14–4b Obligations of the Buyer or Lessee

The main obligation of the buyer or lessee under a sales or lease contract is to pay for the goods tendered. Once the seller or lessor has adequately tendered delivery, the buyer or lessee is obligated to accept the goods and pay for them according to the terms of the contract.

Payment In the absence of any specific agreements, the buyer or lessee must make payment at the time and place the goods are *received* [UCC 2–310(a), 2A–516(1)]. When a sale is made on credit, the buyer is obligated to pay according to the specified credit terms (for instance, 60, 90, or 120 days), not when the goods are received. The credit period usually begins on the *date of shipment* [UCC 2–310(d)]. Under a lease contract, a lessee must make the lease payment that was specified in the contract [UCC 2A–516(1)].

Payment can be made by any means agreed on between the parties—cash or any other method generally acceptable in the commercial world. If the seller demands cash, the seller must permit the buyer reasonable time to obtain it [UCC 2–511].

Right of Inspection Unless the parties otherwise agree, or for C.O.D. (collect on delivery) transactions, the buyer or lessee has an absolute right to inspect the goods before making payment. This right allows the buyer or lessee to verify that the goods tendered or delivered conform to the contract. If the goods are not as ordered, the buyer or lessee has no duty to pay. *An opportunity for inspection is therefore a condition precedent to the right of the seller or lessor to enforce payment* [UCC 2–513(1), 2A–515(1)].

Inspection can take place at any reasonable place and time and in any reasonable manner. Generally, what is reasonable is determined by custom of the trade, past practices of the parties, and the like. The buyer bears the costs of inspecting the goods but can recover the costs from the seller if the goods do not conform and are rejected [UCC 2–513(2)].

Acceptance After having had a reasonable opportunity to inspect the goods, the buyer or lessee can demonstrate acceptance in any of the following ways:

1. The buyer or lessee indicates (by words or conduct) to the seller or lessor that the goods are conforming or that he or she will retain them in spite of their nonconformity [UCC 2–606(1)(a), 2A–515(1)(a)].
2. The buyer or lessee fails to reject the goods within a reasonable period of time [UCC 2–602(1), 2–606(1)(b), 2A–515(1)(b)].
3. In sales contracts, the buyer will be deemed to have accepted the goods if he or she performs any act inconsistent with the seller's ownership. For instance, any use or resale of the goods—except for the limited purpose of testing or inspecting the goods—generally constitutes an acceptance [UCC 2–606(1)(c)].

■ **Case in Point 14.22** Hemacare Plus, Inc., ordered more than $660,000 in specialty pharmaceutical products from Cardinal Health 108, LLC. Cardinal supplied the products, which Hemacare used and did not reject or return. Hemacare did not pay the invoices for the goods delivered, however, so Cardinal filed a lawsuit for breach of contract in a federal district court. Because Hemacare had used the pharmaceutical products, the court found that it had accepted the goods. Therefore, the court granted a summary judgment to Cardinal, awarding $688,920 in damages (including interest, attorneys' fees, and costs).[14] ■

Partial Acceptance If some of the goods delivered do not conform to the contract and the seller or lessor has failed to cure, the buyer or lessee can make a *partial* acceptance [UCC 2–601(c), 2A–509(1)]. The same is true if the nonconformity was not reasonably discoverable before acceptance. (In the latter situation, the buyer or lessee may be able to revoke the acceptance, as will be discussed later in this chapter.)

A buyer or lessee cannot accept less than a single commercial unit, however. The UCC defines a *commercial unit* as a unit of goods that, by commercial usage, is viewed as a "single whole" for purposes of sale. A commercial unit cannot be divided without materially impairing the character of the unit, its market value, or its use [UCC 2–105(6), 2A–103(1)(c)]. A commercial unit can be a single article (such as a machine), a set of articles (such as a suite of furniture), a quantity (such as a bale, a gross, or a carload), or any other unit treated in the trade as a single whole.

---

14. *Cardinal Health 108, LLC v. Hemacare Plus, Inc.*, 2017 WL 114405 (S.D.Ala. 2017).

Anticipatory Repudiation What if, before the time for contract performance, one party clearly communicates to the other the intention *not* to perform? Such an action is a breach of the contract by *anticipatory repudiation.* When anticipatory repudiation occurs, the nonbreaching party has a choice of two responses:

1. Treat the repudiation as a final breach by pursuing a remedy.
2. Wait to see if the repudiating party will decide to honor the contract despite the avowed intention to renege [UCC 2–610, 2A–402].

In either situation, the nonbreaching party may suspend performance.

The UCC permits the breaching party to "retract" his or her repudiation (subject to some limitations). This can be done by any method that clearly indicates the party's intent to perform. Once retraction is made, the rights of the repudiating party under the contract are reinstated. There can be no retraction, however, if since the time of the repudiation the other party has canceled or materially changed position or otherwise indicated that the repudiation is final [UCC 2–611, 2A–403].

14–5 Remedies for Breach of Sales and Lease Contracts

Sometimes, circumstances make it difficult for a party to carry out the promised performance, leading to a breach of the contract. When a breach occurs, the aggrieved (wronged) party looks for remedies. Note that in contrast to the common law of contracts, remedies under the UCC are cumulative in nature—meaning that the aggrieved party is not limited to one exclusive remedy.

14–5a Remedies of the Seller or Lessor

When the buyer or lessee is in breach, the remedies available to the seller or lessor depend on the circumstances existing at the time of the breach. The most pertinent considerations are which party has possession of the goods, whether the goods are in transit, and whether the buyer or lessee has rejected or accepted the goods. If the buyer or lessee breaches the contract *before the goods have been delivered*, the seller or lessor has the right to pursue the remedies discussed next.

The Right to Cancel the Contract If the buyer or lessee breaches the contract, the seller or lessor can choose to simply cancel the contract [UCC 2–703(f), 2A–523(1)(a)].

The seller or lessor must notify the buyer or lessee of the cancellation, and at that point all remaining obligations of the seller or lessor are discharged. The buyer or lessee is not discharged from all remaining obligations, however. She or he is in breach, and the seller or lessor can pursue remedies available under the UCC for breach.

The Right to Withhold Delivery In general, sellers and lessors can withhold delivery or discontinue performance of their obligations under sales or lease contracts when the buyers or lessees are in breach [UCC 2–703(a), 2A–523(1)(c)]. This is true whether a buyer or lessee has wrongfully rejected or revoked acceptance of contract goods (discussed later), failed to make a payment, or repudiated the contract. The seller or lessor can also refuse to deliver the goods to a buyer or lessee who is insolvent (unable to pay debts as they become due) unless the buyer or lessee pays in cash [UCC 2–702(1), 2A–525(1)].

The Right to Resell or Dispose of the Goods When a buyer or lessee breaches or repudiates the contract while the seller or lessor is in possession of the goods, the seller or lessor can resell or dispose of the goods. Any resale of the goods must be made in good faith and in a commercially reasonable manner. The seller must give the original buyer reasonable notice of the resale, unless the goods are perishable or will rapidly decline in value [UCC 2–706(2), (3)].

The seller can retain any profits made as a result of the sale and can hold the buyer or lessee liable for any loss [UCC 2–703(d), 2–706(1), 2A–523(1)(e), 2A–527(1)]. (Here, a loss is any deficiency between the resale price and the contract price.) In lease transactions, the lessor can lease the goods to another party and recover damages from the original lessee. Damages include any unpaid lease payments up to the time the new lease begins. The lessor can also recover any deficiency between the lease payments due under the original lease and those due under the new lease, along with incidental damages [UCC 2A–527(2)].

When the goods contracted for are *unfinished at the time of the breach*, the seller or lessor can do either of the following:

1. Cease manufacturing the goods and resell them for scrap or salvage value.
2. Complete the manufacture and resell or dispose of the goods, and hold the buyer or lessee liable for any deficiency.

In choosing between these two alternatives, the seller or lessor must exercise reasonable commercial judgment in order to mitigate the loss and obtain maximum value from the unfinished goods [UCC 2–704(2), 2A–524(2)].

The Right to Recover Damages for the Buyer's Nonacceptance
If a buyer or lessee repudiates a contract or wrongfully refuses to accept the goods, a seller or lessor can bring an action to recover the damages sustained. Ordinarily, the amount of damages equals the difference between the contract price or lease payments and the market price or lease payments at the time and place of tender of the goods, plus incidental damages [UCC 2–708(1), 2A–528(1)].

When the ordinary measure of damages is inadequate to put the seller or lessor in as good a position as the buyer's or lessee's performance would have, the UCC provides an alternative. In that situation, the proper measure of damages is the lost profits of the seller or lessor, including a reasonable allowance for overhead and other expenses [UCC 2–708(2), 2A–528(2)].

The Right to Stop Delivery of Goods in Transit
When the seller or lessor has delivered the goods to a carrier or a bailee but the buyer or lessee has not yet received them, the goods are said to be *in transit*. If the seller or lessor learns that the buyer or lessee is insolvent, the seller or lessor can stop the delivery of the goods still in transit, regardless of the quantity of goods shipped. A different rule applies if the buyer or lessee is in breach but is not insolvent. In this situation, the seller or lessor can stop the goods in transit only if the quantity shipped is at least a carload, a truckload, a planeload, or a larger shipment [UCC 2–705(1), 2A–526(1)].

To stop delivery, the seller or lessor must *timely notify* the carrier or other bailee that the goods are to be returned or held for the seller or lessor. If the carrier has sufficient time to stop delivery, the goods must be held and delivered according to the instructions of the seller or lessor. The seller or lessor is liable to the carrier for any additional costs incurred [UCC 2–705(3), 2A–526(3)].

Once the seller or lessor reclaims the goods in transit, she or he can pursue the remedies allowed to sellers and lessors when the goods are in their possession.

14–5b Remedies of the Buyer or Lessee
Like the remedies available to sellers and lessors, the remedies available to buyers and lessees depend on the circumstances at the time of the breach. Relevant factors include whether the seller has refused to deliver conforming goods or has delivered nonconforming goods. If the seller or lessor refuses to deliver the goods

to the buyer or lessee, the basic remedies available to the buyer or lessee include those discussed next.

The Right to Cancel the Contract
When a seller or lessor fails to make proper delivery or repudiates the contract, the buyer or lessee can cancel, or rescind, the contract. The buyer or lessee is relieved of any further obligations under the contract but retains all rights to other remedies against the seller or lessor [UCC 2–711(1), 2A–508(1)(a)]. (The right to cancel the contract is also available to a buyer or lessee who has rightfully rejected goods or revoked acceptance, as will be discussed shortly.)

The Right to Obtain Goods upon Insolvency
If a buyer or lessee has partially or fully paid for goods that are in the possession of a seller or lessor who becomes insolvent, the buyer or lessee can obtain the goods. The seller or lessor must have become insolvent within ten days after receiving the first payment, and the goods must be identified to the contract. To exercise this right, the buyer or lessee must pay the seller or lessor any unpaid balance of the purchase price or lease payments [UCC 2–502, 2A–522].

The Right to Obtain Specific Performance
A buyer or lessee can obtain specific performance if the goods are unique or the remedy at law (monetary damages) is inadequate [UCC 2–716(1), 2A–521(1)]. Ordinarily, an award of damages is sufficient to place a buyer or lessee in the position she or he would have occupied if the seller or lessor had fully performed. When the contract is for the purchase of a particular work of art or a similarly unique item, however, damages may not be sufficient. Under these circumstances, equity requires that the seller or lessor perform exactly by delivering the particular goods identified to the contract.

The Right of Cover
In certain situations, buyers and lessees can protect themselves by obtaining **cover**—that is, by buying or leasing substitute goods for those that were due under the contract. This option is available when the seller or lessor repudiates the contract or fails to deliver the goods, or when a buyer or lessee has rightfully rejected goods or revoked acceptance. In purchasing or leasing substitute goods, the buyer or lessee must act in good faith and without unreasonable delay [UCC 2–712, 2A–518].

After obtaining substitute goods, the buyer or lessee can recover the following from the seller or lessor:

1. The difference between the cost of cover and the contract price (or lease payments).
2. Incidental damages that resulted from the breach.

3. Consequential damages to compensate for indirect losses (such as lost profits) resulting from the breach that were reasonably foreseeable at the time of contract formation. The amount of consequential damages is reduced by any amount the buyer or lessee saved as a result of the breach. (For instance, the buyer might obtain cover without having to pay delivery charges that were part of the original sales contract.)

Buyers and lessees are not required to cover, and failure to do so will not bar them from using any other remedies available under the UCC. A buyer or lessee who fails to cover, however, risks collecting a lower amount of consequential damages. A court may reduce the consequential damages by the amount of the loss that could have been avoided had the buyer or lessee purchased or leased substitute goods.

The Right to Replevy Goods Buyers and lessees also have the right to replevy goods. **Replevin**[15] is an action to recover identified goods in the hands of a party who is unlawfully withholding them. Under the UCC, a buyer or lessee can replevy goods identified to the contract if the seller or lessor has repudiated or breached the contract. To maintain an action to replevy goods, buyers and lessees must usually show that they were unable to cover for the goods after making a reasonable effort [UCC 2–716(3), 2A–521(3)].

The Right to Recover Damages If a seller or lessor repudiates the contract or fails to deliver the goods, the buyer or lessee can sue for damages. For the buyer, the measure of recovery is the difference between the contract price and the market price of the goods at the time the buyer *learned* of the breach. For the lessee, the measure is the difference between the lease payments and the lease payments that could be obtained for the goods at the time the lessee learned of the breach. The market price or market lease payments are determined at the place where the seller or lessor was supposed to deliver the goods. The buyer or lessee can also recover incidental and consequential damages less the expenses that were saved as a result of the breach [UCC 2–713, 2A–519].

■ **Case in Point 14.23** Les Entreprises Jacques Defour & Fils, Inc., contracted to buy a thirty-thousand-gallon industrial tank from Dinsick Equipment Corporation for $70,000. Les Entreprises hired Xaak Transport, Inc., to pick up the tank, but when Xaak arrived at the pickup

location, there was no tank. Les Entreprises paid Xaak $7,459 for its services and filed a suit against Dinsick. The court awarded compensatory damages of $70,000 for the tank and incidental damages of $7,459 for the transport.

To establish a breach of contract requires an enforceable contract, substantial performance by the nonbreaching party, a breach by the other party, and damages. In this case, Les Entreprises agreed to buy a tank and paid the price. Dinsick failed to tender or deliver the tank, or to refund the price. The shipping costs were a necessary part of performance, so this was a reasonable expense.[16] ■

The Right to Reject the Goods If either the goods or their tender fails to conform to the contract in any respect, the buyer or lessee can reject all of the goods or any commercial unit of the goods [UCC 2–601, 2A–509]. On rejecting the goods, the buyer or lessee may obtain cover or cancel the contract, and may seek damages just as if the seller or lessor had refused to deliver the goods.

The buyer or lessee must reject the goods within a reasonable amount of time after delivery or tender of delivery and must seasonably notify the seller or lessor [UCC 2–602(1), 2A–509(2)]. If the buyer or lessee fails to reject the goods within a reasonable amount of time, acceptance will be presumed.

When rejecting goods, the buyer or lessee must also designate defects that are ascertainable by reasonable inspection. Failure to do so precludes the buyer or lessee from using such defects to justify rejection or to establish breach if the seller or lessor could have cured the defects [UCC 2–605, 2A–514]. A merchant-buyer or lessee has a good faith obligation to follow any reasonable instructions received from the seller or lessor with respect to the goods [UCC 2–603, 2A–511].

The Right to Revoke Acceptance Acceptance of the goods precludes the buyer or lessee from exercising the right of rejection. It does not necessarily prevent the buyer or lessee from pursuing other remedies, however. In certain circumstances, a buyer or lessee is permitted to *revoke* his or her acceptance of the goods.

Acceptance of a lot or a commercial unit can be revoked if the nonconformity *substantially* impairs the value of the lot or unit *and* if one of the following factors is present:

1. Acceptance was based on the reasonable assumption that the nonconformity would be cured, and it has not been cured within a reasonable period of time [UCC 2–608(1)(a), 2A–517(1)(a)].

---

15. Pronounced ruh-*pleh*-vun, derived from the Old French word *plevir*, meaning "to pledge."

16. *Les Entreprises Jacques Defour & Fils, Inc. v. Dinsick Equipment Corp.*, 2011 WL 307501 (N.D.Ill. 2011).

2. The failure of the buyer or lessee to discover the nonconformity was reasonably induced either by the difficulty of discovery before acceptance or by assurances made by the seller or lessor [UCC 2–608(1)(b), 2A–517(1)(b)].

■ **Case in Point 14.24**   Armadillo Distribution Enterprises, Inc., is a major distributor of musical instruments. Armadillo contracted with a Chinese corporation, Hai Yun Musical Instruments Manufacture Company, Ltd., to manufacture one thousand drum kits. Hai Yun had made drums for Armadillo in the past. Hai Yun furnished samples for Armadillo's approval prior to manufacturing the kits. After Armadillo inspected and approved the samples, Hai Yun delivered five shipping containers of drum kits and Armadillo began distribution.

Armadillo soon started receiving complaints from its retail outlet customers concerning product returns due to cosmetic and structural defects in the drum kits. Armadillo immediately inspected the remaining four shipment containers and discovered that a high percentage of the drum kits were defective and unfit for commercial distribution. Armadillo revoked its acceptance of the kits and filed a suit in federal court for breach of contract. The district court ruled that Hai Yun had breached the contract by delivering nonconforming goods. The court awarded Armadillo nearly $90,000 in direct and incidental damages.[17] ■

Revocation of acceptance is not effective until notice is given to the seller or lessor. Notice must occur within a reasonable time after the buyer or lessee either discovers or *should have discovered* the grounds for revocation. Additionally, revocation must occur before the goods

---

17. *Armadillo Distribution Enterprises, Inc. v. Hai Yun Musical Instruments Manufacture Co., Ltd.*, 142 F.Supp.3d 1245 (M.D.Fla. 2015).

have undergone any substantial change (such as spoilage) not caused by their own defects [UCC 2–608(2), 2A–517(4)]. Once acceptance is revoked, the buyer or lessee can pursue remedies, just as if the goods had been rejected.

The Right to Recover Damages for Accepted Goods   A buyer or lessee who has accepted nonconforming goods may also keep the goods and recover damages [UCC 2–714(1), 2A–519(3)]. To do so, the buyer or lessee must notify the seller or lessor of the breach within a reasonable time after the defect was or should have been discovered. Failure to give notice of the defects (breach) to the seller or lessor normally bars the buyer or lessee from pursuing any remedy [UCC 2–607(3), 2A–516(3)]. In addition, the parties to a sales or lease contract can insert into the contract a provision requiring the buyer or lessee to give notice of any defects in the goods within a prescribed period.

When the goods delivered are not as promised, the measure of damages generally equals the difference between the value of the goods as accepted and their value if they had been delivered as warranted. An exception occurs if special circumstances show proximately caused damages of a different amount [UCC 2–714(2), 2A–519(4)]. The buyer or lessee is also entitled to incidental and consequential damages when appropriate [UCC 2–714(3), 2A–519]. With proper notice to the seller or lessor, the buyer or lessee can also deduct all or any part of the damages from the price or lease payments still due under the contract [UCC 2–717, 2A–516(1)].

Is two years after a sale of goods a reasonable time in which to discover a defect in those goods and notify the seller of a breach? That was the question in the following case.

Spotlight on Baseball Cards

Case 14.3 Fitl v. Strek

Supreme Court of Nebraska, 269 Neb. 51, 690 N.W.2d 605 (2005).

Background and Facts   In 1995, James Fitl attended a sports-card show in San Francisco, California, where he met Mark Strek, doing business as Star Cards of San Francisco, an exhibitor at the show. Later, on Strek's representation that a certain 1952 Mickey Mantle Topps baseball card was in near-mint condition, Fitl bought the card from Strek for $17,750. Strek delivered it to Fitl in Omaha, Nebraska, and Fitl placed it in a safe-deposit box.

In May 1997, Fitl sent the card to Professional Sports Authenticators (PSA), a sports-card grading service. PSA told Fitl that the card was ungradable because it had been discolored and doctored. Fitl complained to Strek, who replied that Fitl should have initiated a return of the card sooner.

Case 14.3 Continues

Case 14.3 Continued

According to Strek, "a typical grace period for the unconditional return of a card [was within] 7 days to 1 month" of its receipt. In August, Fitl sent the card to ASA Accugrade, Inc. (ASA), another grading service, for a second opinion of the value. ASA also concluded that the card had been refinished and trimmed. Fitl filed a suit in a Nebraska state court against Strek, seeking damages. The court awarded Fitl $17,750, plus his court costs. Strek appealed to the Nebraska Supreme Court.

In the Language of the Court
WRIGHT, J. [Judge]
* * * *

Strek claims that the [trial] court erred in determining that notification of the defective condition of the baseball card 2 years after the date of purchase was timely pursuant to [UCC] 2–607(3)(a).

* * * The [trial] court found that Fitl had notified Strek within a reasonable time after discovery of the breach. Therefore, our review is whether the [trial] court's finding as to the reasonableness of the notice was clearly erroneous.

Section 2–607(3)(a) states: "Where a tender has been accepted * * * the buyer must within a reasonable time after he discovers or should have discovered any breach notify the seller of breach or be barred from any remedy." [Under UCC 1–204(2),] *"what is a reasonable time for taking any action depends on the nature, purpose and circumstances of such action."* [Emphasis added.]

The notice requirement set forth in Section 2–607(3)(a) serves three purposes.

* * * The most important one is to enable the seller to make efforts to cure the breach by making adjustments or replacements in order to minimize the buyer's damages and the seller's liability. A second policy is to provide the seller a reasonable opportunity to learn the facts so that he may adequately prepare for negotiation and defend himself in a suit. A third policy * * * is the same as the policy behind statutes of limitation: to provide a seller with a terminal point in time for liability.

* * * *A party is justified in relying upon a representation made to the party as a positive statement of fact when an investigation would be required to ascertain its falsity.* In order for Fitl to have determined that the baseball card had been altered, he would have been required to conduct an investigation. We find that he was not required to do so. Once Fitl learned that the baseball card had been altered, he gave notice to Strek. [Emphasis added.]

* * * One of the most important policies behind the notice requirement * * * is to allow the seller to cure the breach by making adjustments or replacements to minimize the buyer's damages and the seller's liability. However, even if Fitl had learned immediately upon taking possession of the baseball card that it was not authentic and had notified Strek at that time, there is no evidence that Strek could have made any adjustment or taken any action that would have minimized his liability. In its altered condition, the baseball card was worthless.

* * * Earlier notification would not have helped Strek prepare for negotiation or defend himself in a suit because the damage to Fitl could not be repaired. Thus, the policies behind the notice requirement, to allow the seller to correct a defect, to prepare for negotiation and litigation, and to protect against stale claims at a time beyond which an investigation can be completed, were not unfairly prejudiced by the lack of an earlier notice to Strek. Any problem Strek may have had with the party from whom he obtained the baseball card was a separate matter from his transaction with Fitl, and an investigation into the source of the altered card would not have minimized Fitl's damages.

Decision and Remedy *The state supreme court affirmed the decision of the lower court. Under the circumstances, notice of a defect in the card two years after its purchase was reasonable. The buyer had reasonably relied on the seller's representation that the card was "authentic" (which it was not), and when the defects were discovered, the buyer had given timely notice.*

Critical Thinking

- **Legal Environment** *What might a court award to a buyer who prevails in a dispute such as the one in this case?*
- **What If the Facts Were Different?** *Suppose that Fitl and Strek had included in their deal a written clause requiring Fitl to give notice of any defect in the card within "7 days to 1 month" of its receipt. Would the result have been different? Why or why not?*

14–6 Warranties

In sales and lease law, a warranty is an assurance or guarantee by the seller or lessor about the quality and features of the goods being sold or leased. The Uniform Commercial Code (UCC) has numerous rules governing product warranties. Articles 2 (on sales) and 2A (on leases) designate several types of warranties that can arise in a sales or lease contract, including warranties of title, express warranties, and implied warranties.

Because a warranty imposes a duty on the seller or lessor, a breach of warranty is a breach of the seller's or lessor's promise. Assuming that the parties have not agreed to limit or modify the remedies available, if the seller or lessor breaches a warranty, the buyer or lessee can sue to recover damages. Under some circumstances, a breach of warranty can allow the buyer or lessee to rescind (cancel) the agreement.

14–6a Warranties of Title

Under the UCC, three types of title warranties—*good title*, *no liens*, and *no infringements*—can automatically arise in sales and lease contracts [UCC 2–312, 2A–211]. Normally, a seller or lessor can disclaim or modify these title warranties only by including *specific language* in the contract. For instance, sellers may assert that they are transferring only such rights, title, and interest as they have in the goods.

In most sales, sellers warrant that they have good and valid title to the goods sold and that the transfer of the title is rightful [UCC 2–312(1)(a)]. A second warranty of title protects buyers and lessees who are *unaware* of any encumbrances (claims or liabilities—usually called *liens*[18]) against goods at the time the contract is made [UCC 2–312(1)(b), 2A–211(1)]. This warranty protects buyers who, for instance, unknowingly purchase goods that are subject to a creditor's security interest. (A *security interest* in this context is an interest in the goods that secures payment or performance of an obligation.) If a creditor legally repossesses the goods from a buyer *who had no actual knowledge of the security interest*, the buyer can recover from the seller for breach of warranty. (In contrast, a buyer who has *actual knowledge of a security interest* has no recourse against a seller.) Article 2A affords similar protection for lessees [UCC 2A–211(1)].

A third type of warranty of title arises automatically when the seller or lessor is a merchant. A merchant-seller or lessor warrants that the buyer or lessee takes the goods

---

18. Pronounced *leens.*

free of infringements from any copyright, trademark, or patent claims of a third person [UCC 2–312(3), 2A–211(2)].

14–6b Express Warranties

A seller or lessor can create an **express warranty** by making representations concerning the quality, condition, description, or performance potential of the goods.

Under UCC 2–313 and 2A–210, express warranties arise when a seller or lessor indicates any of the following:

1. That the goods conform to any *affirmation* (declaration that something is true) *of fact or promise* that the seller or lessor makes to the buyer or lessee about the goods. Such affirmations or promises are usually made during the bargaining process when a seller or lessor makes representations about a product.
2. That the goods conform to any *description* of them.
3. That the goods conform to any *sample or model* of the goods shown to the buyer or lessee.

Express warranties can be found in a seller's or lessor's advertisement, brochure, or promotional materials, in addition to being made orally or in an express warranty provision in a sales or lease contract.

Basis of the Bargain To create an express warranty, a seller or lessor does not have to use formal words, such as *warrant* or *guarantee*. It is only necessary that a reasonable buyer or lessee would regard the representation as being part of the basis of the bargain [UCC 2–313(2), 2A–210(2)].

The UCC does not explicitly define the phrase "basis of the bargain." Generally, it means that the buyer or lessee must have relied on the representation at the time of entering into the agreement. Therefore, a court must determine whether each representation was made at such a time and in such a way that it induced the buyer or lessee to enter into the contract.

Statements of Opinion and Value Only statements of fact create express warranties. A seller or lessor who states an opinion about or recommends the goods thus does not create an express warranty [UCC 2–313(2), 2A–210(2)].

■ **Case in Point 14.25** Kathleen Arthur underwent a surgical procedure for neck pain. Her surgeon implanted an Infuse Bone Graft device made by Medtronic, Inc. Although the device was not approved for this use, a sales representative for Medtronic allegedly had told the surgeon that the Infuse device could be appropriate for this surgery.

The surgery did not resolve Arthur's neck pain, and she developed numbness in her arm and fingers. She filed a breach-of-warranty claim against Medtronic, alleging that the salesperson's statements had created an express warranty. The court dismissed Arthur's case, however. The sales representative's alleged statements concerning the appropriateness of the Infuse device for Arthur's surgery represented an opinion and did not create an express warranty.[19] ■

Similarly, a seller or lessor who makes a statement about the value or worth of the goods (such as "this is worth a fortune") does not create an express warranty. If the seller or lessor is an expert, however, and gives an opinion as an expert to a layperson, then a warranty may be created.

14–6c Implied Warranties

An **implied warranty** is one that *the law derives* by inference from the nature of the transaction or the relative situations or circumstances of the parties. Under the UCC, merchants impliedly warrant that the goods they sell or lease are merchantable and, in certain circumstances, fit for a particular purpose.

Implied Warranty of Merchantability Every sale or lease of goods made by a merchant who deals in goods of the kind sold or leased automatically gives rise to an **implied warranty of merchantability** [UCC 2–314, 2A–212]. Thus, a merchant who is in the business of selling ski equipment makes an implied warranty of merchantability every time he sells a pair of skis. A neighbor selling her skis at a garage sale does not (because she is not in the business of selling goods of this type).

To be *merchantable*, goods must be "reasonably fit for the ordinary purposes for which such goods are used." They must be of at least average, fair, or medium-grade quality. "Merchantable" food, for instance, is food that is fit to eat on the basis of consumer expectations. The goods must also be adequately packaged and labeled. In addition, they must conform to the promises or affirmations of fact made on the container or label, if any.

When goods are nonmerchantable, or defective, the buyer can sue for breach of the implied warranty of merchantability. ■ **Case in Point 14.26** Joy Pipe, USA, L.P., is in the business of selling steel couplings for use in oil field drilling operations. Joy Pipe entered into a contract with Fremak Industries (a broker) to purchase grade P-110 steel made in India by ISMT Limited. When the steel arrived, Joy Pipe machined it into couplings, which it then sold to its customers. Two companies that used these couplings in oil wells had well failures and notified Joy Pipe.

Joy Pipe then discovered that the ISMT steel it had purchased was of a much lower grade than P-110. It was the lower quality that had caused the couplings to fail. After Joy Pipe paid another company to locate and replace the nonconforming steel, it sued ISMT, in part for breach of the implied warranty of merchantability. A jury awarded Joy Pipe nearly $3 million in damages, and an appellate court affirmed the jury's award.[20] ■

Implied Warranty of Fitness for a Particular Purpose The **implied warranty of fitness for a particular purpose** arises in the sale or lease of goods when a seller or lessor (merchant or nonmerchant) knows *both* of the following:

1. The particular purpose for which a buyer or lessee will use the goods.
2. That the buyer or lessee is relying on the skill and judgment of the seller or lessor to select suitable goods [UCC 2–315, 2A–213].

A "particular purpose" of the buyer or lessee differs from the "ordinary purpose for which goods are used" (merchantability). Goods can be merchantable but unfit for a particular purpose.

■ **Example 14.27** Sheryl needs a gallon of paint to match the color of her living room walls—a light shade somewhere between coral and peach. She takes a sample to Sherwin-Williams and requests a gallon of paint of that color. Instead, the salesperson gives her a gallon of bright blue paint. Here, the salesperson has not breached any warranty of implied merchantability—the bright blue paint is of high quality and suitable for interior walls. The salesperson has breached an implied warranty of fitness for a particular purpose, though, because the paint is not the right color for Sheryl's purpose (to match her living room walls). ■

A seller or lessor need not have actual knowledge of the buyer's or lessee's particular purpose. It is sufficient if a seller or lessor "has reason to know" the purpose and that the buyer or lessee is relying on her or his judgment or skill in selecting or furnishing suitable goods.

Warranties Implied from Prior Dealings or Trade Custom Implied warranties can also arise (or be excluded or modified) as a result of course of dealing or usage of trade [UCC 2–314(3), 2A–212(3)]. Without evidence to the contrary, when both parties to a sales or lease contract have knowledge of a well-recognized trade custom, the courts will infer that both parties intended for that custom to apply to their contract.

19. *Arthur v. Medtronic, Inc.*, 123 F.Supp.3d 1145 (E.D.Mo. 2015).

20. *Joy Pipe, USA, L.P. v. ISMT Limited*, 703 Fed.Appx. 253 (5th Cir. 2017).

■ **Example 14.28** Industry-wide custom is to lubricate a new car before it is delivered. If a dealer fails to lubricate a car, the dealer can be held liable to a buyer for damages resulting from the breach of an implied warranty. (This would also be negligence on the part of the dealer.) ■

14–6d Warranty Disclaimers

The UCC generally permits warranties to be disclaimed or limited by specific and unambiguous language, provided that this is done in a manner that protects the buyer or lessee from surprise. The manner in which a seller or lessor can disclaim warranties varies with the type of warranty. A seller or lessor can disclaim all oral express warranties by including in the contract a written disclaimer. The disclaimer must be in language that is clear and conspicuous and must be called to a buyer's or lessee's attention [UCC 2–316(1), 2A–214(1)]. This allows the seller or lessor to avoid false allegations that oral warranties were made. Note that a buyer or lessee must be made aware of any warranty disclaimers or modifications *at the time the contract is formed.*

Normally, unless circumstances indicate otherwise, the implied warranties of merchantability and fitness are disclaimed by an expression such as "as is" or "with all faults." Both parties must be able to clearly understand from the language used that there are no implied warranties [UCC 2–316(3)(a), 2A–214(3)(a)]. (Note, however, that some states have passed consumer protection statutes that forbid "as is" sales or make it illegal to disclaim warranties of merchantability on consumer goods.)

To specifically disclaim an implied warranty of merchantability, a seller or lessor must mention the word *merchantability.* The disclaimer need not be written, but if it is, the writing must be conspicuous or displayed in such a way that a reasonable person would notice it [UCC 2–316(2), 2A–214(4)]. To disclaim an implied warranty of fitness for a particular purpose, the disclaimer must be in a writing and must be conspicuous. The writing does not have to mention the word *fitness.* It is sufficient if, for instance, the disclaimer states, "There are no warranties that extend beyond the description on the face hereof."

14–7 Contracts for the International Sale of Goods

International sales contracts between firms or individuals located in different countries may be governed by the 1980 United Nations Convention on Contracts for the International Sale of Goods (CISG). The CISG governs international contracts only if the countries of the parties to the contract have ratified the CISG and if the parties have not agreed that some other law will govern their contract.

The CISG has been adopted by more than eighty-four countries, including the United States, Canada, some Central and South American countries, China, most European nations, Japan, and Mexico. That means that the CISG is the uniform international sales law of countries that account for more than two-thirds of all global trade. (The appendix at the end of this chapter shows an actual international sales contract used by the Starbucks Coffee Company.)

14–7a Applicability of the CISG

Essentially, the CISG is to international sales contracts what Article 2 of the UCC is to domestic sales contracts. In domestic transactions, the UCC applies when the parties to a contract for a sale of goods have failed to specify in writing some important term, such as price or delivery. Similarly, whenever the parties to international transactions have failed to specify in writing the precise terms of a contract, the CISG will be applied.

Unlike the UCC, *the CISG does not apply to consumer sales.* Neither the UCC nor the CISG applies to contracts for services.

14–7b A Comparison of CISG and UCC Provisions

The provisions of the CISG, although similar for the most part to those of the UCC, differ from them in some respects. Major differences exist between the CISG and the UCC in regard to the mirror image rule and irrevocable offers, for instance. If the CISG and the UCC conflict, the CISG applies (because it is a treaty of the U.S. national government and therefore is supreme).

The Mirror Image Rule Under the UCC, a definite expression of acceptance that contains additional terms can still result in the formation of a contract, unless the additional terms are conditioned on the assent of the offeror. In other words, as we have explained, the UCC does away with the mirror image rule in domestic sales contracts.

Under the CISG, however, a contract can be formed even though the acceptance contains additional terms, unless the additional terms materially alter the contract. If an additional term relates to payment, quality, quantity, price, time and place of delivery, extent of one party's liability to the other, or the settlement of disputes, the CISG considers the added term a material alteration.

In effect, then, the CISG requires that the terms of the acceptance mirror those of the offer.

■ **Case in Point 14.29** VLM Food Trading International, Inc., a Canadian agricultural supplier, sold frozen potatoes to Illinois Trading Company, an American buyer and seller of produce. For each of their transactions, Illinois Trading sent a purchase order setting out the terms, and VLM responded with a confirming e-mail. VLM then shipped the order, Illinois Trading accepted it, and VLM followed up with a "trailing" invoice. Only the trailing invoices included a provision that the buyer would be liable for attorneys' fees if it breached the contract.

Nine transactions occurred without incident. Illinois Trading ran into financial difficulties, however, and did not pay for the next nine shipments. VLM filed a suit in a federal district court against the buyer, seeking to recover the unpaid amount plus attorneys' fees. Illinois Trading admitted that it owed the price for the potatoes but contested liability for the attorneys' fees. A federal appellate court agreed with Illinois Trading that under the CISG, the attorneys' fee provision in the trailing invoice did not become part of the parties' contract. The attorneys' fee provision was a material alteration to the contract terms, and Illinois Trading had not agreed to the additional term.[21] ■

Irrevocable Offers UCC 2–205 provides that a merchant's firm offer is irrevocable, even without consideration, if the merchant gives assurances in a signed writing. In contrast, under the CISG, an offer can become irrevocable without a signed writing. Article 16(2) of the CISG provides that an offer will be irrevocable if:

1. The offeror states orally that the offer is irrevocable.
2. The offeree reasonably relies on the offer as being irrevocable.

In both of these situations, the offer will be irrevocable even without a writing and without consideration.

---

21. *VLM Food Trading International, Inc. v. Illinois Trading Co.*, 811 F.3d 247 (7th Cir. 2016).

Practice and Review: Sales and Lease Contracts

Guy Holcomb owns and operates Oasis Goodtime Emporium, an adult entertainment establishment. Holcomb wanted to create an adult Internet system for Oasis that would offer customers adult-theme videos and "live" chat room programs using performers at the club. On May 10, Holcomb signed a work order authorizing Thomas Consulting Group (TCG) "to deliver a working prototype of a customer chat system, demonstrating the integration of live video and chatting in a Web browser." In exchange for creating the prototype, Holcomb agreed to pay TCG $64,697. On May 20, Holcomb signed an additional work order in the amount of $12,943 for TCG to install a customized firewall system. The work orders stated that Holcomb would make monthly installment payments to TCG, and both parties expected the work would be finished by September.

Due to unforeseen problems largely attributable to system configuration and software incompatibility, the project required more time than anticipated. By the end of the summer, the website was still not ready, and Holcomb had fallen behind in his payments to TCG. TCG threatened to cease work and file a suit for breach of contract unless the bill was paid. Rather than make further payments, Holcomb wanted to abandon the project. Using the information presented in the chapter, answer the following questions.

1. Would a court be likely to decide that the transaction between Holcomb and TCG was covered by the Uniform Commercial Code (UCC)? Why or why not?
2. Would a court be likely to consider Holcomb a merchant under the UCC? Why or why not?
3. Did the parties have a valid contract under the UCC? Were any terms left open in the contract? If so, which terms? How would a court deal with open terms?
4. Suppose that Holcomb and TCG meet in October in an attempt to resolve their problems. At that time, the parties reach an oral agreement that TCG will continue to work without demanding full payment of the past due amounts and Holcomb will pay TCG $5,000 per week. Assuming the contract falls under the UCC, is the oral agreement enforceable? Why or why not?

Debate This . . . *The UCC should require the same degree of definiteness of terms, especially with respect to price and quantity, as contract law does.*

Terms and Concepts

Issue Spotters

1. E-Design, Inc., orders 150 computer desks. Fav-O-Rite Supplies, Inc., ships 150 printer stands. Is this an acceptance of the offer or a counteroffer? If it is an acceptance, is it a breach of the contract? Why or why not? What if Fav-O-Rite told E-Design it was sending the printer stands as "an accommodation"? (See *The Formation of Sales and Lease Contracts*.)

2. Country Fruit Stand orders eighty cases of peaches from Downey Farms. Without stating a reason, Downey delivers thirty cases instead of eighty and delivers at the wrong time. Does Country have the right to reject the shipment? Explain. (See *Performance Obligations in Sales and Lease Contracts*.)

• Check your answers to the Issue Spotters against the answers provided in Appendix B at the end of this text.

Business Scenarios and Case Problems

14–1. Merchant's Firm Offer. On May 1, Jennings, a car dealer, e-mails Wheeler and says, "I have a 1955 Thunderbird convertible in mint condition that I will sell you for $13,500 at any time before June 9. [Signed] Peter Jennings." By May 15, having heard nothing from Wheeler, Jennings sells the car to another. On May 29, Wheeler accepts Jennings's offer and tenders $13,500. When told Jennings has sold the car to another, Wheeler claims Jennings has breached their contract. Is Jennings in breach? Explain. (See *The Formation of Sales and Lease Contracts*.)

14–2. Additional Terms. Strike offers to sell Bailey one thousand shirts for a stated price. The offer declares that shipment will be made by Dependable truck line. Bailey replies, "I accept your offer for one thousand shirts at the price quoted. Delivery to be by Yellow Express truck line." Both Strike and Bailey are merchants. Three weeks later, Strike ships the shirts by Dependable truck line, and Bailey refuses to accept delivery. Strike sues for breach of contract. Bailey claims that there never was a contract because his reply, which included a modification of carriers, did not constitute an acceptance. Bailey further claims that even if there had been a contract, Strike would have been in breach because Strike shipped the shirts by Dependable, contrary to the contract terms. Discuss fully Bailey's claims. (See *The Formation of Sales and Lease Contracts*.)

14–3. Goods and Services Combined. Allied Shelving and Equipment, Inc., sells and installs shelving systems. National

Deli, LLC, contracted with Allied to provide and install a parallel rack system (a series of large shelves) in National's warehouse. Both parties were dissatisfied with the result. National filed a suit in a Florida state court against Allied, which filed a counterclaim. Each contended that the other had materially breached the contract. The court applied common law contract principles to rule in National's favor on both claims. Allied appealed, arguing that the court should have applied the UCC. When does a court apply common law principles to a contract that involves both goods and services? In this case, why might an appellate court rule that the UCC should be applied instead? Explain. [*Allied Shelving & Equipment, Inc. v. National Deli, LLC*, 40 Fla. L. Weekly D145, 154 So.3d 482 (Dist.Ct.App. 2015)] (See *The Scope of Articles 2 (Sales) and 2A (Leases)*.)

14–4. Express Warranties. Charity Bell bought a used Toyota Avalon from Awny Gobran of Gobran Auto Sales, Inc. The odometer showed that the car had been driven 147,000 miles. Bell asked whether it had been in any accidents. Gobran replied that it was in good condition. The parties signed a warranty disclaimer that the vehicle was sold "as is." Problems with the car arose the same day as the purchase. Gobran made a few ineffectual attempts to repair it before refusing to do more. Meanwhile, Bell obtained a vehicle history report from Carfax, which showed that the Avalon had been damaged in an accident and that its last reported odometer reading was 237,271.

Was the "as is" disclaimer sufficient to put Bell on notice that the odometer reading could be false and that the car might have been in an accident? Can Gobran avoid any liability that might otherwise be imposed because Bell did not obtain the Carfax report until *after* she bought the car? Discuss. [*Gobran Auto Sales, Inc. v. Bell*, 335 Ga.App. 873, 783 S.E.2d 389 (2016)] (See *Warranties*.)

14–5. Acceptance. New England Precision Grinding, Inc. (NEPG), sells precision medical parts in Massachusetts. NEPG agreed to supply Kyphon, Inc., with stylets and nozzles. NEPG contracted with Simply Surgical, LLC, to obtain the parts from Iscon Surgicals, Ltd. The contract did not mention Kyphon or require Kyphon's acceptance of the parts. Before shipping, Iscon would certify that the parts conformed to NEPG's specifications. On receiving the parts, NEPG would certify that they conformed to Kyphon's specifications. On delivery, Kyphon would also inspect the parts.

After about half a dozen transactions, NEPG's payments to Simply Surgical lagged, and the seller refused to make further deliveries. NEPG filed a suit in a Massachusetts state court against Simply Surgical, alleging breach of contract. NEPG claimed that Kyphon had rejected some of the parts, which gave NEPG the right not to pay for them. Do the UCC's rules with respect to acceptance support or undercut the parties' actions? Discuss. [*New England Precision Grinding, Inc. v. Simply Surgical, LLC*, 89 Mass.App.Ct. 176, 46 N.E.3d 590 (2016)] (See *The Formation of Sales and Lease Contracts*.)

14–6. Business Case Problem with Sample Answer— Remedies of the Buyer or Lessee. M.C. and Linda Morris own a home in Gulfport, Mississippi, that was extensively damaged in Hurricane Katrina. The Morrises contracted with Inside Outside, Inc. (IO), to rebuild their kitchen. When the new kitchen cabinets were delivered, some defects were apparent, and as installation progressed, others were revealed. IO ordered replacement parts to cure the defects. Before the parts arrived, however, the parties' relationship deteriorated, and IO offered to remove the cabinets and refund the price. The Morrises also asked to be repaid for the installation fee. IO refused but emphasized that it was willing to fulfill its contractual obligations. At this point, are the Morrises entitled to revoke their acceptance of the cabinets? Why or why not? [*Morris v. Inside Outside, Inc.*, 185 So.3d 413 (Miss.Ct.App. 2016)] (See *Remedies for Breach of Sales and Lease Contracts*.)

• For a sample answer for Problem 14–6, go to Appendix C at the end of this text.

14–7. Requirements Contracts. Medalist Golf, Inc., a high-end golf course builder, was working on a new golf course project in Missouri. Chris Williams, doing business as Cane Creek Sod, submitted a bid with Medalist to provide Meyer Zoysia grass sod for the project. Williams and Medalist executed a "grass supplier agreement" that specified the type and quality of grass to be used, as well as the price, and gave Medalist a right to inspect and reject the sod. The parties estimated the quantity of sod needed for the project to be twenty-one acres. Williams had approximately sixty-five acres of Meyer Zoysia grass sod growing at the time. The agreement

did not specify the amount of sod that Medalist would purchase from Williams, nor did it say that Medalist would buy Williams's sod exclusively. Later, when Medalist had an expert inspect Williams's sod (before it was harvested), the expert concluded that it did not meet the quality standards required for the project. Medalist therefore rejected the sod. Williams sued for breach of contract. Was the "grass supplier agreement" enforceable as a requirements contract? Why or why not? [*Williams v. Medalist Golf, Inc.*, 910 F.3d 1041 (8th Cir. 2018)] (See *The Formation of Sales and Lease Contracts*.)

14–8. Implied Warranties. Harold Moore bought a barrel-racing horse named Clear Boggy for $100,000 for his daughter. The seller was Betty Roper, who appraises barrel-racing horses. (Barrel racing is a rodeo event in which a horse and rider attempt to complete a cloverleaf pattern around preset barrels in the fastest time.) Clear Boggy was promoted for sale as a competitive barrel-racing horse. On inquiry, Roper represented that Clear Boggy did not have any performance issues or medical problems, and that the only medications the horse had been given were hock injections, a common treatment.

Shortly after the purchase, Clear Boggy began exhibiting significant performance problems, including nervousness, unwillingness to practice, and stalling during runs. Roper then disclosed that the horse had been given shoulder injections prior to the sale and had previously stalled in competition. Moore took the horse to a veterinarian and discovered that it suffered from arthritis, impinged vertebrae, front-left-foot problems, and a right-hind-leg fracture. The vet recommended, and Moore paid for, surgery to repair the leg fracture, but Clear Boggy remained unfit for competition. Moore also discovered that the horse had been scratched from a competition prior to the sale because it was injured. Can Moore prevail in a lawsuit against Roper for breach of the implied warranty of fitness for a particular purpose? Why or why not? [*Moore v. Roper*, 2018 WL 1123868 (E.D.Okla. 2018)] (See *Warranties*.)

14–9. A Question of Ethics—The IDDR Approach and Buyer's Remedies. *Samsung Telecommunications America, LLC, makes Galaxy phones. Daniel Norcia bought a Galaxy S4 in a Verizon store in San Francisco, California. A Verizon employee opened the box, unpacked the phone, and helped Norcia transfer his contacts to the new phone. Norcia took the phone, and its charger and headphones, and left the store. Less than a year later, he filed an action on behalf of himself and other Galaxy S4 buyers in a federal district court against Samsung, alleging that the manufacturer misrepresented the phone's storage capacity and rigged it to operate at a higher speed when it was being tested. [Norcia v. Samsung Telecommunications America, LLC, 845 F.3d 1279 (9th Cir. 2017)] (See* Remedies for Breach of Sales and Lease Contracts*.)*

(a) Samsung included an arbitration provision in a brochure in the Galaxy S4 box. Would it be ethical of Samsung to assert the arbitration clause?

(b) Why would corporate decision makers choose to misrepresent their product? Explain, using the *Discussion* and *Review* steps of the IDDR approach.

Time-Limited Group Assignment

14–10. Warranties. Milan purchased saffron extract, marketed as "America's Hottest New Way to a Flat Belly," online from Dr. Chen. The website stated that recently published studies showed a significant weight loss (more than 25 percent) for people who used pure saffron extract as a supplement *without diet or exercise*. Dr. Chen said that the saffron suppresses appetite by increasing levels of serotonin, which reduces emotional eating. Milan took the extract as directed without any resulting weight loss. (See *Warranties*.)

(a) The first group will determine whether Dr. Chen's website made any express warranty on the saffron extract or its effectiveness in causing weight loss.

(b) The second group will discuss whether the implied warranty of merchantability applies to the purchase of weight-loss supplements.

(c) The third group will decide if Dr. Chen's sale of saffron extract breached the implied warranty of fitness for a particular purpose.

(d) The fourth group will evaluate the possible success of a suit against a company that offers weight-loss products requiring no diet or exercise given that, according to current common knowledge, people must burn more calories than they consume to lose weight.

① OVERLAND COFFEE IMPORT CONTRACT
OF THE
② GREEN COFFEE ASSOCIATION
OF
NEW YORK CITY, INC.*

Contract Seller's No.: **504617**
Buyer's No.: **P9264**
Date: **10/11/26**

SOLD BY: **XYZ Co.**
TO: **Starbucks**

③ QUANTITY: **Five Hundred** (**500**) Tons of (Bags) **Mexican** coffee
weighing about **152.117 lbs.** per bag.

PACKAGING: Coffee must be packed in clean sound bags of uniform size made of sisal, henequen, jute, burlap, or similar
woven material, without inner lining or outer covering of any material properly sewn by hand and/or machine.
④ Bulk shipments are allowed if agreed by mutual consent of Buyer and Seller.

DESCRIPTION: **High grown Mexican Altura**
⑤

PRICE: At **Ten/$10.00 dollars** U.S. Currency, per **lb.** net, (U.S. Funds)
Upon delivery in Bonded Public Warehouse at **Laredo, TX**
(City and State)

⑥ PAYMENT: **Cash against warehouse receipts**

Bill and tender to DATE when all import requirements and governmental regulations have been satisfied, and
coffee delivered or discharged (as per contract terms). Seller is obliged to give the Buyer two (2) calendar
days free time in Bonded Public Warehouse following but not including date of tender.

⑦ ARRIVAL: During **December** via **truck**
(Period)   (Method of Transportation)
from **Mexico** for arrival at **Laredo, TX, USA**
(Country of Exportation)   (Country of Importation)
Partial shipments permitted.

⑧ ADVICE OF Advice of arrival with warehouse name and location, together with the quantity, description, marks and place of
ARRIVAL: entry, must be transmitted directly, or through Seller's Agent/Broker, to the Buyer or his Agent/ Broker. Advice
will be given as soon as known but not later than the fifth business day following arrival at the named warehouse.
Such advice may be given verbally with written confirmation to be sent the same day.

⑨ WEIGHTS: (1) DELIVERED WEIGHTS: Coffee covered by this contract is to be weighed at location named in tender.
Actual tare to be allowed.
(2) SHIPPING WEIGHTS: Coffee covered by this contract is sold on shipping weights. Any loss in
weight exceeding **1/2** percent at location named in tender is for account of Seller at contract price.
(3) Coffee is to be weighed within fifteen (15) calendar days after tender. Weighing expenses, if any, for
account of **Seller** (Seller or Buyer)

⑩ MARKINGS: Bags to be branded in English with the name of Country of Origin and otherwise to comply with laws
and regulations of the Country of Importation, in effect at the time of entry, governing marking of import
merchandise. Any expense incurred by failure to comply with these regulations to be borne by
Exporter/Seller.

RULINGS: The "Rulings on Coffee Contracts" of the Green Coffee Association of New York City, Inc., in effect on the
date this contract is made, is incorporated for all purposes as a part of this agreement, and together herewith,
constitute the entire contract. No variation or addition hereto shall be valid unless signed by the parties to
the contract.
⑪ Seller guarantees that the terms printed on the reverse hereof, which by reference are made a part hereof, are
identical with the terms as printed in By-Laws and Rules of the Green Coffee Association of New
York City, Inc., heretofore adopted.
Exceptions to this guarantee are:
ACCEPTED: COMMISSION TO BE PAID BY:
XYZ Co. **Seller**
Seller
BY _**DM**_
Agent
Starbucks
Buyer
BY _✓_ **ABC Brokerage**
⑫ Agent Broker(s)
⑬ When this contract is executed by a person acting for another, such person hereby represents that he is
fully authorized to commit his principal.

Source: The Green Coffee Association of New York City, Inc.

1 This is a contract for a sale of coffee to be *imported* internationally. If the parties have their principal places of business located in different countries, the contract may be subject to the United Nations Convention on Contracts for the International Sale of Goods (CISG). If the parties' principal places of business are located in the United States, the contract may be subject to the Uniform Commercial Code (UCC).

2 Quantity is one of the most important terms to include in a contract. Without it, a court may not be able to enforce the contract.

3 Weight per unit (bag) can be exactly stated or approximately stated. If it is not so stated, usage of trade in international contracts determines standards of weight.

4 Packaging requirements can be conditions for acceptance and payment. Bulk shipments are not permitted without the consent of the buyer.

5 A description of the coffee and the "Markings" constitute express warranties. International contracts rely more heavily on descriptions and models or samples than do warranties in contracts for the domestic sales of goods.

6 Under the UCC, parties may enter into a valid contract even though the price is not set. Under the CISG, a contract must provide for an exact determination of the price.

7 The terms of payment may take one of two forms: credit or cash. Credit terms can be complicated. A cash term can be simple, and payment can be made by any means acceptable in the ordinary course of business (for example, a personal check or a letter of credit). If the seller insists on actual cash, the buyer must be given a reasonable time to get it.

8 *Tender* means the seller has placed goods that conform to the contract at the buyer's disposition. This contract requires that the coffee meet all import regulations and that it be ready for pickup by the buyer at a "Bonded Public Warehouse." (A bonded *warehouse* is a place in which goods can be stored without payment of taxes until the goods are removed.)

9 The delivery date is significant because, if it is not met, the buyer may hold the seller in breach of the contract. Under this contract, the seller is given a "period" within which to deliver the goods, instead of a specific day. The seller is also given some time to rectify goods that do not pass inspection (see the "Guarantee" clause on page two of the contract).

10 As part of a proper tender, the seller (or its agent) must inform the buyer (or its agent) when the goods have arrived at their destination.

11 In some contracts, delivered and shipping weights can be important. During shipping, some loss can be attributed to the type of goods (spoilage of fresh produce, for example) or to the transportation itself. A seller and buyer can agree on the extent to which either of them will bear such losses.

12 Documents are often incorporated in a contract by reference, because including them word for word can make a contract difficult to read. If the document is later revised, the entire contract might have to be reworked. Documents that are typically incorporated by reference include detailed payment and delivery terms, special provisions, and sets of rules, codes, and standards.

13 In international sales transactions, and for domestic deals involving certain products, brokers are used to form the contracts. When so used, the brokers are entitled to a commission.

(Continued)

An Example of a Contract for the International Sale of Coffee — Continued

TERMS AND CONDITIONS

14 ARBITRATION: All controversies relating to, in connection with, or arising out of this contract, its modification, making or the authority or obligations of the signatories hereto, and whether involving the principals, agents, brokers, or others who actually subscribe hereto, shall be settled by arbitration in accordance with the "Rules of Arbitration" of the Green Coffee Association of New York City, Inc., as they exist at the time of the arbitration (including provisions as to payment of fees and expenses). Arbitration is the sole remedy hereunder, and it shall be held in accordance with the law of New York State, and judgment of any award may be entered in the courts of that State, or in any other court of competent jurisdiction. All notices or judicial service in reference to arbitration or enforcement shall be deemed given if transmitted as required by the aforesaid rules.

15 GUARANTEE: (a) If all or any of the coffee is refused admission into the country of importation by reason of any violation of governmental laws or acts, which violation existed at the time the coffee arrived at Bonded Public Warehouse, seller is required, as to the amount not admitted and as soon as possible, to deliver replacement coffee in conformity to all terms and conditions of this contract, excepting only the Arrival terms, but not later than thirty (30) days after the date of the violation notice. Any payment made and expenses incurred for any coffee denied entry shall be refunded within ten (10) calendar days of denial of entry, and payment shall be made for the replacement delivery in accordance with the terms of this contract. Consequently, if Buyer removes the coffee from the Bonded Public Warehouse, Seller's responsibility as to such portion hereunder ceases.
(b) Contracts containing the overstamp "No Pass–No Sale" on the face of the contract shall be interpreted to mean: If any or all of the coffee is not admitted into the country of Importation in its original condition by reason of failure to meet requirements of the government's laws or Acts, the contract shall be deemed null and void as to that portion of the coffee which is not admitted in its original condition. Any payment made and expenses incurred for any coffee denied entry shall be refunded within ten (10) calendar days of denial of entry.

16 CONTINGENCY: This contract is not contingent upon any other contract.

CLAIMS: Coffee shall be considered accepted as to quality unless within *fifteen* (15) calendar days after delivery at Bonded Public Warehouse or within *fifteen* (15) calendar days after all Government clearances have been received, whichever is later, either:
(a) Claims are settled by the parties hereto, or,
(b) Arbitration proceedings have been filed by one of the parties in accordance with the provisions hereof.
17 (c) If neither (a) nor (b) has been done in the stated period or if any portion of the coffee has been removed from the Bonded Public Warehouse before representative sealed samples have been drawn by the Green Coffee Association of New York City, Inc., in accordance with its rules, Seller's responsibility for quality claims ceases for that portion so removed.
(d) Any question of quality submitted to arbitration shall be a matter of allowance only, unless otherwise provided in the contract.

18 DELIVERY: (a) No more than three (3) chops may be tendered for each lot of 250 bags.
(b) Each chop of coffee tendered is to be uniform in grade and appearance. All expense necessary to make coffee uniform shall be for account of seller.
(c) Notice of arrival and/or sampling order constitutes a tender, and must be given not later than the fifth business day following arrival at Bonded Public Warehouse stated on the contract.

INSURANCE: Seller is responsible for any loss or damage, or both, until Delivery and Discharge of coffee at the Bonded Public Warehouse in the Country of Importation.

All Insurance Risks, costs and responsibility are for Seller's Account until Delivery and Discharge of coffee at the Bonded Public Warehouse in the Country of Importation.

Buyer's insurance responsibility begins from the day of importation or from the day of tender, whichever is later.

19 FREIGHT: Seller to provide and pay for all transportation and related expenses to the Bonded Public Warehouse in the Country of Importation.

20 EXPORT DUTIES/TAXES: Exporter is to pay all Export taxes, duties or other fees or charges, if any, levied because of exportation.

IMPORT DUTIES/TAXES: Any Duty or Tax whatsoever, imposed by the government or any authority of the Country of Importation, shall be borne by the Importer/Buyer.

21 INSOLVENCY OR FINANCIAL FAILURE OF BUYER OR SELLER: If, at any time before the contract is fully executed, either party hereto shall meet with creditors because of inability generally to make payment of obligations when due, or shall suspend such payments, fail to meet his general trade obligations in the regular course of business, shall file a petition in bankruptcy or, for an arrangement, shall become insolvent, or commit an act of bankruptcy, then the other party may at his option, expressed in writing, declare the aforesaid to constitute a breach and default of this contract, and may, in addition to other remedies, decline to deliver further or make payment or may sell or purchase for the defaulter's account, and may collect damage for any injury or loss, or shall account for the profit, if any, occasioned by such sale or purchase.

This clause is subject to the provisions of (11 USC 365 (e) 1) if invoked.

22 BREACH OR DEFAULT OF CONTRACT: In the event either party hereto fails to perform, or breaches or repudiates this agreement, the other party shall subject to the specific provisions of this contract be entitled to the remedies and relief provided for by the Uniform Commercial Code of the State of New York. The computation and ascertainment of damages, or the determination of any other dispute as to relief, shall be made by the arbitrators in accordance with the Arbitration Clause herein.

Consequential damages shall not, however, be allowed.

23

© S.F/Shutterstock.com

14 Arbitration is the settling of a dispute by submitting it to a disinterested party (other than a court), which renders a decision. The procedures and costs can be provided for in an arbitration clause or incorporated through other documents. To enforce an award rendered in an arbitration, the winning party can "enter" (submit) the award in a court "of competent jurisdiction."

15 When goods are imported internationally, they must meet certain import requirements before being released to the buyer. Because of this, buyers frequently want a guaranty clause that covers the goods not admitted into the country. The clause may either require the seller to replace the goods within a stated time or allow the contract for those goods not admitted to be void.

16 In the "Claims" clause, the parties agree that the buyer has a certain time within which to reject the goods. The right to reject is a right by law and does not need to be stated in a contract. If the buyer does not exercise the right within the time specified in the contract, the goods will be considered accepted.

17 Many international contracts include definitions of terms so that the parties understand what they mean. Some terms are used in a particular industry in a specific way. Here, the word *chop* refers to a unit of like-grade coffee beans. The buyer has a right to inspect ("sample") the coffee. If the coffee does not conform to the contract, the seller must correct the nonconformity.

18 The "Delivery," "Insurance," and "Freight" clauses, with the "Arrival" clause on page one of the contract, indicate that this is a destination contract. The seller has the obligation to deliver the goods to the destination, not simply deliver them into the hands of a carrier. Under this contract, the destination is a "Bonded Public Warehouse" in a specific location. The seller bears the risk of loss until the goods are delivered at their destination. Typically, the seller will have bought insurance to cover the risk.

19 Delivery terms are commonly placed in all sales contracts. Such terms determine who pays freight and other costs and, in the absence of an agreement specifying otherwise, who bears the risk of loss. International contracts may use these delivery terms, or they may use INCOTERMS, which are published by the International Chamber of Commerce. For example, the INCOTERM DDP (delivered duty paid) requires the seller to arrange shipment, obtain and pay for import or export permits, and get the goods through customs to a named destination.

20 Exported and imported goods are subject to duties, taxes, and other charges imposed by the governments of the countries involved. International contracts spell out who is responsible for these charges.

21 This clause protects a party if the other party should become financially unable to fulfill the obligations under the contract. Thus, if the seller cannot afford to deliver, or the buyer cannot afford to pay, for the stated reasons, the other party can consider the contract breached. This right is subject to "11 USC 365(e)(1)," which refers to a specific provision of the U.S. Bankruptcy Code dealing with executory contracts.

22 In the "Breach or Default of Contract" clause, the parties agree that the remedies under this contract are the remedies (except for consequential damages) provided by the UCC, as in effect in the state of New York. The amount and "ascertainment" of damages, as well as other disputes about relief, are to be determined by arbitration.

23 Three clauses frequently included in international contracts are omitted here. There is no choice-of-language clause designating the official language to be used in interpreting the contract terms. There is no choice-of-forum clause designating the place in which disputes will be litigated, except for arbitration (law of New York State). Finally, there is no *force majeure* clause relieving the sellers or buyers from nonperformance due to events beyond their control.

Chapter 15

Creditor-Debtor Relations and Bankruptcy

Many people struggle to pay their debts. Although in the old days, debtors were punished and sometimes even sent to prison for failing to pay what they owed, debtors today rarely go to jail. They have many other options, including *bankruptcy*, which is the last resort in resolving creditor-debtor problems.

The right to petition for bankruptcy relief under federal law is an essential aspect of our capitalistic society, in which we have great opportunities for financial success but may also encounter financial difficulties. For instance, many retail chains (including Radio Shack, Sears, and Toys R Us) have filed for bankruptcy in the last decade, in part due to increased online shopping.

Shopping malls throughout America are struggling to keep their anchor stores (such as Nordstrom and Macy's) open and profitable, given the prevalence of Amazon and other Internet sellers. Brick-and-mortar retailers are expected to continue filing for bankruptcy for years to come. Therefore, every businessperson should have some understanding of this topic.

15-1 Laws Assisting Creditors

Normally, creditors have no problem collecting the debts owed to them. When disputes arise over the amount owed, however, or when a debtor simply cannot or will not pay, what happens? What remedies are available to creditors when a debtor **defaults** (fails to pay as promised)? Here, we examine some basic laws that assist the creditor and debtor in resolving their dispute before the debtor resorts to bankruptcy.

The remedies we discuss next are available regardless of whether a creditor is secured or unsecured. *Secured creditors* are those whose loans are backed by *collateral*, which is specific property (such as a car or a house) pledged by a borrower to ensure repayment. The loans made by *unsecured creditors*, such as companies that provide credit cards, are not backed by collateral.

15-1a Liens

A **lien** is an encumbrance on (claim against) property to satisfy a debt or protect a claim for the payment of a debt. Liens may arise under the common law (usually by possession of the property) or under statutory law. *Mechanic's liens* are statutory liens, whereas *artisan's liens* were recognized at common law. *Judicial liens* may be used by a creditor to collect on a debt before or after a

judgment is entered by a court. Liens are a very important tool for creditors because they generally take priority over other claims against the same property.

Mechanic's Liens Sometimes, a person who has contracted for labor, services, or materials to be furnished for making improvements on real property does not immediately pay for the improvements. When that happens, the creditor can place a **mechanic's lien** on the property.

Real Property Secures the Debt. A mechanic's lien creates a special type of debtor-creditor relationship in which the real estate itself becomes security for the debt. ■ **Example 15.1** Kirk contracts to paint Tanya's house for an agreed-on price to cover labor and materials. If Tanya refuses to pay or pays only a portion of the charges after the work is completed, a mechanic's lien against the property can be created. Kirk is then a lienholder, and the real property is encumbered (burdened) with the mechanic's lien for the amount owed. ■

If the property owner fails to pay the debt, the lienholder is technically entitled to foreclose on the real estate and sell it. (As will be discussed, *foreclosure* is the process by which a creditor legally takes a debtor's property to satisfy a debt.) The sale proceeds are then used to pay the debt and the costs of the legal proceedings. The surplus, if any, is paid to the former owner.

In the real world, however, small-amount mechanic's liens are rarely the basis of foreclosure. Rather, these liens simply remain on the books of the state until the house is sold. At closing (when the sale is finalized), the seller agrees to pay any mechanic's liens out of the proceeds of the sale before the seller receives any of the funds.

Governed by State Law. State law governs the procedures that must be followed to create a mechanic's lien (or other statutory lien). Generally, the lienholder must file a written notice of lien within a specific time period (usually 60 to 120 days) from the last date on which material or labor was provided.

Artisan's Liens When a debtor fails to pay for labor and materials furnished for the repair or improvement of *personal* property, a creditor can recover payment through an **artisan's lien.** Artisan's liens usually take priority over other creditors' claims to the same property.[1]

Lienholder Must Retain Possession. In contrast to a mechanic's lien, an artisan's lien is *possessory.* That is, the lienholder ordinarily must have retained possession of the property and have expressly or impliedly agreed to provide the services on a cash, not a credit, basis. The lien remains in existence as long as the lienholder maintains possession, and the lien is terminated once possession is *voluntarily* surrendered, unless the surrender is only temporary.[2]

■ **Case in Point 15.2** Carrollton Exempted Village School District (in Ohio) hired Clean Vehicle Solutions America, LLC (CVSA, based in New York), to convert ten school buses from diesel to compressed natural gas. The contract price was $660,000. The district paid a $400,000 deposit and agreed to pay installments of $26,000 to CVSA after the delivery of each converted bus. After the first two buses were delivered, the district refused to continue the contract, claiming that the conversion made the two buses unsafe to drive.

Both parties filed breach-of-contract lawsuits. CVSA also asserted an artisan's lien over two other buses that it still had in its possession because it had started converting them to natural gas and spent $65,000 doing so. Regardless of the outcome in the parties' lawsuits, CVSA has an artisan's lien that gives it a priority claim to those two buses as long as they remain in its possession. The

buses will act as security for the district's payment of at least the amount CVSA has spent converting them to natural gas.[3] ■

Foreclosure on Personal Property. Modern statutes permit the holder of an artisan's lien to foreclose and sell the property subject to the lien to satisfy the debt. As with a mechanic's lien, the lienholder is required to give notice to the owner of the property before the foreclosure and sale. The sale proceeds are used to pay the debt and the costs of the legal proceedings, and the surplus, if any, is paid to the former owner.

Judicial Liens When a debt is past due, a creditor can bring a legal action against the debtor to collect the debt. If the action is successful, the court awards the creditor a judgment against the debtor (usually for the amount of the debt plus any interest and legal costs incurred). Frequently, however, the creditor is unable to collect the awarded amount.

To ensure that a judgment in the creditor's favor will be collectible, the creditor may request that certain property of the debtor be seized to satisfy the debt. A court's order to seize the debtor's property is known as a *writ of attachment* if it is issued before a judgment. If the order is issued after a judgment, it is referred to as a *writ of execution.*

Writ of Attachment. In the context of judicial liens, **attachment** refers to a court-ordered seizure and the taking into custody of property before a judgment is obtained on a past-due debt. Because attachment is a *prejudgment* remedy, it occurs either at the time a lawsuit is filed or immediately afterward.

A creditor must comply with the specific state's statutory restrictions and requirements. The due process clause of the Fourteenth Amendment to the U.S. Constitution requires that the debtor be given notice and an opportunity to be heard. The creditor must have an enforceable right to payment of the debt under law and must follow certain procedures. Otherwise, the creditor can be liable for damages for wrongful attachment.

The typical procedure for attachment is as follows:

1. The creditor files with the court an *affidavit* (a written statement, made under oath). The affidavit states that the debtor has failed to pay and indicates the statutory grounds under which attachment is sought.
2. The creditor must post a bond to cover at least the court costs, the value of the property attached, and the value of the loss of use of that property suffered by the debtor.

---

1. An artisan's lien has priority over a filed statutory lien (such as a title lien on an automobile or a lien filed under Article 9 of the UCC) and a bailee's lien (such as a storage lien).

2. Involuntary surrender of possession by a lienholder, such as when a police officer seizes goods from a lienholder, does not terminate the lien.

3. *Clean Vehicle Solutions America, LLC v. Carrollton Exempted Village School District Board of Education,* 2015 WL 5459852 (S.D.N.Y. 2015).

3. When the court is satisfied that all the requirements have been met, it issues a **writ of attachment.** The writ directs the sheriff or other officer to seize the debtor's nonexempt property. If the creditor prevails at trial, the seized property can be sold to satisfy the judgment.

Writ of Execution. If a creditor wins a judgment against a debtor and the debtor will not or cannot pay the amount due, the creditor can request a **writ of execution** from the court. A writ of execution is an order that directs the sheriff to seize (levy) and sell any of the debtor's nonexempt real or personal property. The writ applies only to property that is within the court's geographic jurisdiction (usually the county in which the courthouse is located).

The proceeds of the sale are used to pay the judgment, accrued interest, and costs of the sale. Any excess is paid to the debtor. The debtor can pay the judgment and redeem the nonexempt property at any time before the sale takes place. (Because of exemption laws and bankruptcy laws, however, many judgments are practically uncollectible.)

15–1b Garnishment

An order for **garnishment** permits a creditor to collect a debt by seizing property of the debtor that is being held by a third party. As a result of a garnishment proceeding, for instance, the debtor's employer may be ordered by the court to turn over a portion of the debtor's wages to pay the debt. Many other types of property can be garnished as well, including funds in a bank account, tax refunds, pensions, and trust funds. It is only necessary that the property is not exempt from garnishment and is in the possession of a third party.

■ **Case in Point 15.3** When Edward G. Tinsley divorced Michelle Townsend, they entered into a marital settlement contract. They agreed to sell the marital home and split the proceeds evenly. But Tinsley refused to cooperate with the sale. A court therefore appointed a trustee to sell the house for them and ordered the sheriff to evict Tinsley. Tinsley then conveyed the house to a trust established in his name. Even after the sheriff evicted Tinsley from the house and changed the locks, Tinsley managed to move back in and change the locks again.

Tinsley was arrested for trespassing and charged with contempt of court (for disobeying court orders). In the meantime, Tinsley secretly sold the home for $150,000 and deposited the proceeds into a bank account held in the name of Edward G. Tinsley Living Trust at SunTrust Bank. After learning of the sale, the court-appointed trustee obtained a writ of garnishment on all of Tinsley's and his trust's bank accounts at SunTrust Bank. Despite numerous objections from Tinsley (and a trial and appeal), SunTrust Bank eventually complied with the garnishment order and sent all the funds to the trustee.[4] ■

Procedures Garnishment can be a prejudgment remedy, requiring a hearing before a court, but it is most often a postjudgment remedy. State law governs garnishment actions, so the specific procedures vary from state to state.

In some states, the judgment creditor needs to obtain only one order of garnishment, which will then apply continuously to the judgment debtor's wages until the entire debt is paid. In other states, the judgment creditor must go back to court for a separate order of garnishment for each pay period.

Laws Limiting the Amount of Wages Subject to Garnishment Both federal and state laws limit the amount that can be taken from a debtor's weekly take-home pay through garnishment proceedings.[5] Federal law provides a minimal framework to protect debtors from losing all their income to pay judgment debts.[6] State laws also provide dollar exemptions, and these amounts are often larger than those provided by federal law. Under federal law, an employer cannot dismiss an employee because his or her wages are being garnished.

15–1c Creditors' Composition Agreements

Creditors may contract with the debtor for discharge of the debtor's liquidated debts (debts that are definite, or fixed, in amount) on payment of a sum less than that owed. These agreements are referred to as **creditors' composition agreements** (or *composition agreements*) and usually are held to be enforceable unless they are formed under duress.

15–1d Suretyship and Guaranty

When a third person promises to pay a debt owed by another in the event that the debtor does not pay, either a *suretyship* or a *guaranty* relationship is created. Exhibit 15–1 illustrates these relationships. The third person's creditworthiness becomes the security for the debt owed.

---

4. *Tinsley v. SunTrust Bank*, 2016 WL 687545 (Md.App. 2016).
5. Some states (such as Texas) do not permit garnishment of wages by private parties except under a child-support order.
6. For instance, the federal Consumer Credit Protection Act, 15 U.S.C. Sections 1601 *et seq.,* provides that a debtor can retain either 75 percent of his or her disposable earnings per week or an amount equivalent to thirty hours of work paid at federal minimum wage rates, whichever is greater.

Exhibit 15–1   Suretyship and Guaranty Parties

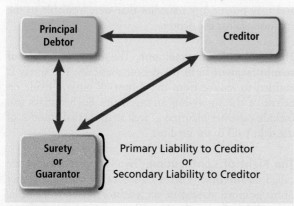

Suretyship and guaranty provide creditors with the right to seek payment from the third party if the primary debtor, or *principal*, defaults on her or his obligations. Normally, a guaranty must be in writing to be enforceable under the Statute of Frauds, unless its main purpose is to benefit the guarantor. Traditionally, a suretyship agreement did not require a writing to be enforceable, and oral surety agreements were sufficient. But now some states require a writing to enforce a suretyship.

At common law, there were significant differences in the liability of a surety and a guarantor. Today, however, the distinctions outlined here have been abolished in some states.

Suretyship   A contract of strict **suretyship** is a promise made by a third person to be responsible for the debtor's obligation. It is an express contract between the **surety** (the third party) and the creditor.

In the strictest sense, the surety is primarily liable for the debt of the principal. The creditor can demand payment from the surety from the moment the debt is due. The creditor need not exhaust all legal remedies against the principal debtor before holding the surety responsible for payment.

■ **Example 15.4**   Roberto Delmar wants to borrow from the bank to buy a used car. Because Roberto is still in college, the bank will not lend him the funds without a cosigner. Roberto's father, José Delmar, who has dealt with the bank before, agrees to cosign the note, thereby becoming a surety who is jointly liable for payment of the debt. When José Delmar cosigns the note, he becomes primarily liable to the bank. On the note's due date, the bank can seek payment from either Roberto or José Delmar, or both jointly. ■

Guaranty   With a suretyship arrangement, the surety is *primarily* liable for the debtor's obligation. With a guaranty

arrangement, the **guarantor**—the third person making the guaranty—is *secondarily* liable.

The guarantor can be required to pay the obligation *only after the principal debtor defaults*, and usually only after the creditor has made an attempt to collect from the debtor. The guaranty contract terms determine the extent and time of the guarantor's liability.

■ **Case in Point 15.5**   To finance a development project in Delaware, Brandywine Partners, LLC, borrowed $15.9 million from HSBC Realty Credit Corp. (USA). As part of the deal, Brian O'Neill, principal for Brandywine, signed a guaranty that designated him the "primary obligor" for $8.1 million of the loan. Brandywine defaulted, and HSBC filed a suit in a federal district court against O'Neill to recover on the guaranty. O'Neill filed a counterclaim, alleging that HSBC had fraudulently induced him to sign the guaranty.

O'Neill argued that the loan agreement valued the property at $26.5 million and that HSBC knew this was not the property's real value. O'Neill also claimed that the parties had agreed that if Brandywine defaulted, HSBC could recover its loan by selling the property—before trying to collect from the guaranty.

The court ruled in favor of HSBC and dismissed O'Neill's counterclaim. A federal appellate court affirmed. The guaranty stated that O'Neill was familiar with the value of the property, that he was not relying on it as an inducement to sign the guaranty, and that HSBC made no representations to induce him to sign. The guaranty also provided that HSBC could enforce its rights against him without trying to recover on the property first.[7] ■

Actions That Release the Surety and the Guarantor   Basically, the same actions will release either a surety or a guarantor from an obligation. For simplicity, this subsection and the following subsections will refer just to sureties, but remember that the same rules generally apply to guarantors.

1. *Material modification.* Making any material modification to the terms of the original contract without the surety's consent will discharge the surety's obligation. (The extent to which the surety is discharged depends on whether he or she was compensated and the amount of loss suffered from the modification. For instance, a father who receives no consideration for acting as a surety on his daughter's loan will be completely discharged if the loan contract is modified without his consent.)

7. *HSBC Realty Credit Corp. (USA) v. O'Neill*, 745 F.3d 564 (1st Cir. 2014).

2. *Surrender of property.* If a creditor surrenders the collateral to the debtor or impairs the collateral without the surety's consent, these acts can reduce the obligation of the surety. If the creditor's actions reduce the value of the property used as collateral, the surety is released to the extent of any loss suffered.

3. *Payment or tender of payment.* Naturally, any payment of the principal obligation by the debtor or by another person on the debtor's behalf will discharge the surety from the obligation. Even if the creditor refused to accept the payment when it was tendered, if the creditor knew about the suretyship, the obligation of the surety can be discharged.

Defenses of the Surety and the Guarantor

Generally, the surety or guarantor can also assert any of the defenses available to the principal debtor to avoid liability on the obligation to the creditor. A few exceptions do exist, however. They apply to both sureties and guarantors, but again, for simplicity, we refer just to sureties.

1. *Incapacity and bankruptcy.* Incapacity and bankruptcy are personal defenses, which can be asserted only by the person who is affected. Therefore, the surety cannot assert the principal debtor's incapacity or bankruptcy as a defense. (A surety may assert his or her own incapacity or bankruptcy as a defense, of course.)

2. *Statute of limitations.* The surety cannot assert the statute of limitations as a defense. (In contrast, the principal debtor can claim the statute of limitations as a defense to payment.)

3. *Fraud.* If the creditor fraudulently induced the person to act as a surety on the debt, the surety or guarantor can assert fraud as a defense. In most states, the creditor must inform the surety, before the formation of the suretyship contract, of material facts known by the creditor that would substantially increase the surety's risk. Failure to so inform may constitute fraud and render the suretyship obligation voidable.

Rights of the Surety and the Guarantor

When the surety or guarantor pays the debt owed to the creditor, he or she acquires certain rights, as discussed next. Again, for simplicity, the discussion refers just to sureties.

The Right of Subrogation. The surety has the legal **right of subrogation.** Simply stated, this means that any right that the creditor had against the debtor now becomes the right of the surety. Included are creditor rights in bankruptcy, rights to collateral possessed by the creditor, and rights to judgments obtained by the creditor.

In short, the surety now stands in the shoes of the creditor and may pursue any remedies that were available to the creditor against the debtor.

The Right of Reimbursement. The surety has a **right of reimbursement** from the debtor. Basically, the surety is entitled to receive from the debtor all outlays made on behalf of the suretyship arrangement. Such outlays can include expenses incurred as well as the actual amount of the debt paid to the creditor.

The Right of Contribution. Two or more sureties are called **co-sureties.** When a co-surety pays more than her or his proportionate share on a debtor's default, she or he has a **right of contribution.** That means the co-surety is entitled to recover from the other co-sureties the amount paid above the surety's obligation. Generally, a co-surety's liability either is determined by agreement or, in the absence of agreement, is set at the maximum liability under the suretyship contract.

■ **Example 15.6** Yasser and Stuart, two co-sureties, are obligated under a suretyship contract to guarantee Jules's debt. Stuart's maximum liability is $15,000, and Yasser's is $10,000. Jules owes $10,000 and is in default. Stuart pays the creditor the entire $10,000.

In the absence of an agreement to the contrary, Stuart can recover $4,000 from Yasser. The amount of the debt that Yasser agreed to cover ($10,000) is divided by the total amount that he and Stuart together agreed to cover ($25,000). The result is multiplied by the amount of the default, yielding the amount that Yasser owes—($10,000 ÷ $25,000) × $10,000 = $4,000. ■

15–2 Mortgages

When individuals purchase real property, they typically make a **down payment** in cash and borrow the remaining funds from a financial institution. The borrowed funds are secured by a **mortgage**—a written instrument that gives the creditor a lien on the debtor's real property as security for payment of a debt. The creditor is the *mortgagee,* and the debtor is the *mortgagor.*

15–2a Fixed-Rate versus Adjustable-Rate Mortgages

Lenders offer various types of mortgages to meet the needs of different borrowers, but a basic distinction is whether the interest rate is fixed or variable. A *fixed-rate mortgage* has a fixed, or unchanging, rate of interest, so the payments remain the same for the duration of the loan. Lenders determine the interest rate for a standard fixed-rate mortgage loan based on a variety of factors, including the borrower's credit history, credit score, income, and debts.

With an *adjustable-rate mortgage (ARM)*, the rate of interest paid by the borrower changes periodically. Typically, the initial interest rate for an ARM is set at a relatively low fixed rate for a specified period, such as a year or three years. After that time, the interest rate adjusts periodically—often, annually. The interest rate adjustment is calculated by adding a certain number of percentage points (called the margin) to an index rate (one of various government interest rates).

ARMs contractually shift the risk that the interest rate will change from the lender to the borrower. Borrowers will have lower initial payments if they are willing to assume the risk of all future interest rate increases.

15–2b Mortgage Provisions

Because a mortgage involves a transfer of real property, it must be in writing to comply with the Statute of Frauds. Mortgages normally are lengthy and formal documents containing many provisions, including the following:

1. *The terms of the underlying loan.* These include the loan amount, the interest rate, the period of repayment, and other important financial terms, such as the margin and index rate for an ARM.
2. *A prepayment penalty clause.* A **prepayment penalty clause** requires the borrower to pay a penalty if the mortgage is repaid in full within a certain period. A prepayment penalty helps to protect the lender should the borrower refinance within a short time after obtaining a mortgage.
3. *Provisions relating to the maintenance of the property.* Because the mortgage conveys an interest in the property to the lender, the lender often requires the borrower to maintain the property to protect the lender's investment.
4. *A statement obligating the borrower to maintain homeowner's insurance on the property.* **Homeowner's insurance** protects the lender's interest in the event of a loss due to certain hazards, such as fire or storm damage.
5. *A list of the non-loan financial obligations to be borne by the borrower.* For instance, the borrower typically is required to pay all property taxes, assessments, and other claims against the property.
6. *Creditor protections.* When creditors extend mortgages, they are advancing a significant amount of funds for a number of years. Consequently, creditors usually require debtors to obtain **mortgage insurance** if they

do not make a down payment of at least 20 percent of the purchase price.

Creditors record the mortgage with the appropriate office in the county where the property is located so that their interest in the property is officially on record.

15–2c Mortgage Foreclosure

If the homeowner *defaults*, or fails to make the mortgage payments, the lender has the right to foreclose on the mortgaged property. **Foreclosure** is the legal process by which the lender repossesses and auctions off the property that has secured the loan.

Foreclosure is expensive and time consuming. It generally benefits neither the borrowers, who lose their homes, nor the lenders, which face the prospect of losses on their loans. Therefore, both lenders and borrowers are motivated to avoid foreclosure proceedings if possible.

Ways to Avoid Foreclosure Possible methods of avoiding foreclosure include a forbearance, workout agreement, and short sale.

A **forbearance** is a postponement of part or all of the payments on a loan for a limited time. This option works well when the debtor can solve the problem by securing a new job, selling the property, or finding another acceptable solution.

A **workout agreement** is a contract that describes the respective rights and responsibilities of the borrower and the lender as they try to resolve the default. Usually, the lender agrees to delay seeking foreclosure. In exchange, the borrower provides additional financial information that might be used to modify the mortgage.

A lender may sometimes agree to a **short sale,** which is a sale of the property for less than the balance due on the mortgage loan. Typically, the borrower has to show some hardship, such as the loss of a job, a decline in the value of the home, a divorce, or a death in the household. The lender often has approval rights in a short sale, so the sale process may take much longer than an ordinary real estate transaction.

Foreclosure Procedure If all efforts to find another solution fail, the lender will proceed to foreclosure. The lender must strictly comply with the state statute governing foreclosures.

In the following case, a property owner defaulted on her mortgage, and the lender obtained a writ of execution for a sheriff's sale of the property. After the sale, the former owner asked the court that had issued the writ to set aside the sale, and the court refused. In doing so, did the court abuse its discretion?

Banc of California, N.A.[a] v. Madhok

Superior Court of New Jersey, Appellate Division, 2019 WL 149660 (2019).

Background and Facts   Ritu Madhok borrowed $213,069 from Banc of California, N.A., to buy a house in Iselin, New Jersey. She executed a note for the amount and a mortgage to secure payment of the note. Ten months later, she stopped making payments. Banc of California filed an action in a New Jersey state court to foreclose on the mortgage. The court granted the bank's request for a sheriff's sale of the property.

The sale was postponed for three months to give Madhok an opportunity to submit a loss mitigation package—which is an application to avoid foreclosure that includes a statement of personal financial difficulties, along with pay stubs, tax returns, bank statements, and other information to support the statement. Madhok provided a partial, incomplete package the day before the sale, and the sale went ahead as scheduled. More than a month later, Madhok filed a motion to vacate the sale. The court denied the motion. She appealed, arguing that the court's denial of the motion was an abuse of discretion.

In the Language of the Court

PER CURIAM [By the Whole Court].

* * * *

Foreclosure proceedings seek primary or principal relief which is equitable in nature. An application to open, vacate or otherwise set aside a foreclosure judgment or proceeding * * * is subject to an abuse of discretion standard. Accordingly, a trial judge's application or denial of equitable remedies should not be disturbed unless it can be shown that the trial court palpably abused its discretion, that is, that its finding was so wide off the mark that a manifest denial of justice resulted.

A motion to vacate a sheriff's sale is governed by [New Jersey] Rule [of Court] 4:65-5, which states that any objection to the sale must be served "within ten days after the sale or at any time thereafter before the delivery of the conveyance." Examples of valid grounds for objection include fraud, accident, surprise, irregularity, or impropriety in the sheriff's sale. None of these grounds are applicable here. Under Rule 4:65-5, the trial court has discretion to set aside a sale if the defendant alleges a valid independent ground for equitable relief. * * * However, despite the court's broad discretion to employ equitable remedies, this power should be sparingly exercised and a sale [should] be vacated only when necessary to correct a plain injustice.

*Here, [after the default] defendant procrastinated until the eve of the sheriff's sale to pursue loss mitigation options, coupled with the submission of an incomplete loss mitigation application. * * * Under these circumstances, we cannot find that the trial court abused its discretion in denying defendant's motion, made one month after the sheriff's sale.* [Emphasis added.]

Decision and Remedy   *A state intermediate appellate court affirmed the lower court's order denying Madhok's motion to vacate the sheriff's sale. The lower court did not abuse its discretion by refusing Madhok's request. She delayed until the day before the sale to apply for a loan modification and then provided only a partial loss mitigation application.*

Critical Thinking

- **Economic**   *The bank was willing to process a loan modification based on the debtor's loss mitigation application while simultaneously pursuing foreclosure on her property. Is the bank's dual tracking an abusive practice? Explain.*
- **What If the Facts Were Different?**   *Suppose that before the sale, Madhok had filed a motion for more time to file a complete loss mitigation application. Would the result have been different? Discuss.*

---

a. The initials *N.A.* stands for "National Association."

15–3 Protection for Debtors

The law protects debtors as well as creditors. Consumer protection statutes protect debtors' rights, for instance, and bankruptcy laws are designed specifically to assist debtors in need of help. In addition, in most states, certain types of real and personal property are exempt from execution or attachment. State exemption statutes usually include both real and personal property.

15–3a Exempted Real Property

Probably the most familiar exemption is the **homestead exemption.** The purpose of the homestead exemption is to ensure that the debtor will retain some form of shelter.

The General Rule Each state permits the debtor to retain the value of the family home up to a specified dollar amount free from the claims of unsecured creditors or trustees in bankruptcy. (Note that federal bankruptcy law places a cap on the amount that debtors filing bankruptcy can claim as exempt under their states' homestead exemption.)

■ **Example 15.7** Vince Beere owes Chris Veltman $40,000. The debt is the subject of a lawsuit, and the court awards Veltman a judgment of $40,000 against Beere. Beere's homestead (property and house) is valued at $50,000, and the homestead exemption is $25,000. There are no outstanding mortgages or other liens on his homestead. To satisfy the judgment debt, Beere's family home is sold at public auction for $45,000. The proceeds of the sale are distributed as follows:

1. Beere is given $25,000 as his homestead exemption.
2. Veltman is paid $20,000 toward the judgment debt, leaving a $20,000 *deficiency judgment* (that is, "left-over debt"). The deficiency judgment can be satisfied from any other nonexempt property (personal or real) that Beere may own, if permitted by state law. ■

Limitations In a few states, statutes allow the homestead exemption only if the judgment debtor has a family. If a judgment debtor does not have a family, a creditor may be entitled to collect the full amount realized from the sale of the debtor's home. In addition, the homestead exemption interacts with other areas of law and can sometimes operate to cancel out a portion of a lien on a debtor's real property.

15–3b Exempted Personal Property

Personal property that is most often exempt from satisfaction of judgment debts includes the following:

1. Household furniture, up to a specified dollar amount.
2. Clothing and certain personal possessions, such as family pictures or a Bible.
3. A vehicle (or vehicles) for transportation, up to a specified dollar amount.
4. Certain classified animals, usually livestock but including pets.
5. Equipment that the debtor uses in a business or trade, such as tools or professional instruments, up to a specified dollar amount.

15–4 The Bankruptcy Code

Bankruptcy relief is provided under federal law. Although state laws may play a role in bankruptcy proceedings, particularly state property laws, the governing law is based on federal legislation.

Article I, Section 8, of the U.S. Constitution gave Congress the power to establish "uniform laws on the subject of bankruptcies throughout the United States." Federal bankruptcy legislation was first enacted in 1898 and since then has undergone several modifications, including the 2005 Bankruptcy Reform Act.[8] Federal bankruptcy laws (as amended) are called the Bankruptcy Code or, more simply, the Code.

Bankruptcy law in the United States has two main goals:

1. To protect a debtor by giving him or her a fresh start without creditors' claims.
2. To ensure equitable treatment of creditors who are competing for a debtor's assets.

Thus, the law attempts to balance the rights of the debtor and of the creditors.

15–4a Bankruptcy Courts

Bankruptcy proceedings are held in federal bankruptcy courts, which are under the authority of U.S. district courts. Rulings from bankruptcy courts can be appealed to the district courts.

A bankruptcy court can conduct a jury trial if the appropriate district court has authorized it and the parties to the bankruptcy consent. Bankruptcy courts follow the Federal Rules of Bankruptcy Procedure rather than the Federal Rules of Civil Procedure. Bankruptcy court judges are appointed for terms of fourteen years.

---

8. The full title of the act was the Bankruptcy Abuse Prevention and Consumer Protection Act, Pub. L. No. 109-8, 119 Stat. 23 (2005), 11 U.S.C. Sections 101 *et seq.*

15–4b Types of Bankruptcy Relief

The Bankruptcy Code is contained in Title 11 of the *United States Code* and has eight chapters. Chapters 1, 3, and 5 of the Code contain general definitional provisions, as well as provisions governing case administration, creditors, the debtor, and the estate. These three chapters normally apply to all kinds of bankruptcies.

Four chapters of the Code set forth the most important types of relief that debtors can seek:

1. Chapter 7 provides for **liquidation** proceedings (the selling of all nonexempt assets and the distribution of the proceeds to the debtor's creditors).
2. Chapter 11 governs reorganizations.
3. Chapter 12 (for family farmers and family fishermen) and Chapter 13 (for individuals) provide for the adjustment of debts by persons with regular incomes.[9]

Note that a debtor (except for a municipality) need not be insolvent (unable to pay debts as they come due) to file for bankruptcy relief under the Bankruptcy Code. Anyone obligated to a creditor can declare bankruptcy.

15–4c Special Requirements for Consumer-Debtors

A **consumer-debtor** is a debtor whose debts result primarily from the purchase of goods for personal, family, or household use. The Bankruptcy Code requires that the clerk of the court give all consumer-debtors written notice of the general purpose, benefits, and costs of each chapter under which they might proceed. In addition, the clerk must provide consumer-debtors with information on the types of services available from credit counseling agencies.

15–5 Liquidation Proceedings

Liquidation under Chapter 7 of the Bankruptcy Code is probably the most familiar type of bankruptcy proceeding and is often referred to as an *ordinary*, or *straight, bankruptcy.* Put simply, a debtor in a liquidation bankruptcy turns all assets over to a **bankruptcy trustee,** a person appointed by the court to manage the debtor's funds. The trustee sells the nonexempt assets and distributes the proceeds to creditors. With certain exceptions, the debtor is then granted a **discharge** (or termination) of the remaining debts and is no longer obligated to pay.

Any "person"—defined as including individuals, partnerships, and corporations[10]—may be a debtor in a liquidation proceeding. A husband and wife may file jointly for bankruptcy under a single petition. Railroads, insurance companies, banks, savings and loan associations, investment companies licensed by the Small Business Administration, and credit unions *cannot* be debtors in a liquidation bankruptcy. Other chapters of the Bankruptcy Code or other federal or state statutes apply to them.

A straight bankruptcy can be commenced by the filing of either a voluntary or an involuntary **petition in bankruptcy**—the document that is filed with a bankruptcy court to initiate bankruptcy proceedings. If a debtor files the petition, the bankruptcy is voluntary. If one or more creditors file a petition to force the debtor into bankruptcy, the bankruptcy is involuntary.

15–5a Voluntary Bankruptcy

To bring a voluntary petition in bankruptcy, the debtor files official forms designated for that purpose in the bankruptcy court. The law now requires that *before* debtors can file a petition, they must receive credit counseling from an approved nonprofit agency within the 180-day period preceding the date of filing. Debtors filing a Chapter 7 petition must include a certificate proving that they have received individual or group counseling from an approved agency within the last 180 days.

A consumer-debtor who is filing for liquidation bankruptcy must confirm the accuracy of the petition's contents. The debtor must also state in the petition, at the time of filing, that he or she understands the relief available under other chapters of the Code and has chosen to proceed under Chapter 7.

Attorneys representing consumer-debtors must file an affidavit stating that they have informed the debtors of the relief available under each chapter of the Bankruptcy Code. In addition, the attorneys must reasonably attempt to verify the accuracy of the consumer-debtors' petitions and schedules (described next). Failure to do so is considered perjury.

Chapter 7 Schedules The voluntary petition must contain the following schedules:

1. A list of both secured and unsecured creditors, their addresses, and the amount of debt owed to each.
2. A statement of the financial affairs of the debtor.

---

9. There are no Chapters 2, 4, 6, 8, or 10 in Title 11. Such "gaps" are not uncommon in the *United States Code.* They occur because chapter numbers (or other subdivisional unit numbers) are sometimes reserved for future use when a statute is enacted. (A gap may also appear if a law has been repealed.)

10. The definition of *corporation* includes unincorporated companies and associations. It also covers labor unions.

3. A list of all property owned by the debtor, including property that the debtor claims is exempt.
4. A list of current income and expenses.
5. A certificate of credit counseling.
6. Proof of payments received from employers within sixty days prior to the filing of the petition.
7. A statement of the amount of monthly income, itemized to show how the amount is calculated.
8. A copy of the debtor's federal income tax return for the most recent year ending immediately before the filing of the petition.

The official forms must be completed accurately, sworn to under oath, and signed by the debtor. To conceal assets or knowingly supply false information on these schedules is a crime under the bankruptcy laws.

With the exception of tax returns, failure to file the required schedules within forty-five days after the filing of the petition will result in an automatic dismissal of the petition. (An extension may be granted, however.) The debtor has up to seven days before the date of the first creditors' meeting to provide a copy of the most recent tax returns to the trustee.

In addition, a debtor may be required to file a tax return at the end of each tax year while the case is pending and to provide a copy to the court. This may be done at the request of the court, a creditor, or the **U.S. trustee**—a government official who performs administrative tasks that a bankruptcy judge would otherwise have to perform.

Substantial Abuse—Means Test

A bankruptcy court can dismiss a Chapter 7 petition if the use of Chapter 7 constitutes a "substantial abuse" of bankruptcy law. The revised Code provides a *means test* to determine a debtor's eligibility for Chapter 7. The purpose of the test is to keep upper-income people from abusing the bankruptcy process by filing for Chapter 7, as was thought to have happened in the past. The test forces more people to file for Chapter 13 bankruptcy rather than have their debts discharged under Chapter 7.

The Basic Formula. A debtor wishing to file for bankruptcy must complete the means test to determine whether she or he qualifies for Chapter 7. The debtor's average monthly income in recent months is compared with the median income in the geographic area in which the person lives. (The U.S. Trustee Program provides these data at its website, www.justice.gov/ust.) If the debtor's income is below the median income, the debtor usually is allowed to file for Chapter 7 bankruptcy, as there is no presumption of bankruptcy abuse.

Applying the Means Test to Future Disposable Income. If the debtor's income is above the median income, then further calculations must be made to determine the debtor's future disposable income. As a basis for the calculations, it is presumed that the debtor's recent monthly income will continue for the next sixty months. *Disposable income* is then calculated by subtracting living expenses and secured debt payments, such as mortgage payments, from monthly income. *Living expenses* are amounts allowed under formulas used by the Internal Revenue Service for necessary items (such as food, clothing, housing, and transportation).

Can the Debtor Afford to Pay Unsecured Debts? Once future disposable income has been estimated, that amount is used to determine whether the debtor will have income that could be applied to unsecured debts. The courts may also consider the debtor's bad faith or other circumstances indicating substantial abuse.

■ **Case in Point 15.8** John and Sarah Buoy filed for Chapter 7 bankruptcy. For the past three months, John's gross monthly income had been $4,900, and Sarah's had been $6,761. They had five children. They owed secured debts of $34,321 on a Subaru Impreza and a BMW 328i, on which they intended to continue making loan payments (this is called *reaffirmation*, as will be discussed later). They owed $123,000 on a mortgage and $19,000 in student loans, and their unsecured debts were $4,900.

An auditor for the U.S. Trustee Program reviewed the Buoys' Chapter 7 schedule and concluded that the family's gross income figures were understated. Because of a mistake in the math, the Buoys had miscalculated their income by approximately $800 a month (or nearly $650 after taxes). The debtors claimed that they had incurred additional expenses after filing the petition, including orthodontic braces and another car. Even with those expenses, however, the court found that they would have an additional $400 a month in future disposable income and would receive sizeable tax refunds. The court concluded that the Buoys could afford to pay their debts and dismissed the Chapter 7 petition for substantial abuse.[11] ■

Additional Grounds for Dismissal

As already noted, a court can dismiss a debtor's voluntary petition for Chapter 7 relief for substantial abuse or for failure to provide the necessary documents within the specified time.

In addition, a court might dismiss a Chapter 7 in two other situations. First, if the debtor has been convicted of a violent crime or a drug-trafficking offense, the victim

---

11. *In re Buoy*, 2017 WL 3194755 (Bankr. N.D. Ohio 2017).

can file a motion to dismiss the voluntary petition.[12] Second, if the debtor fails to pay postpetition domestic-support obligations (which include child and spousal support), the court may dismiss the debtor's petition.

Order for Relief If the voluntary petition for bankruptcy is found to be proper, the filing of the petition will itself constitute an **order for relief.** (An order for relief is a court's grant of assistance to a petitioner.) Once a consumer-debtor's voluntary petition has been filed, the trustee and creditors must be given notice of the order for relief by mail not more than twenty days after entry of the order.

15–5b Involuntary Bankruptcy

An involuntary bankruptcy occurs when the debtor's creditors force the debtor into bankruptcy proceedings. An involuntary case cannot be filed against a charitable institution or a farmer (an individual or business that receives more than 50 percent of gross income from farming operations).

An involuntary petition should not be used as an everyday debt-collection device, and the Code provides penalties for the filing of frivolous petitions against debtors. If the court dismisses an involuntary petition, the petitioning creditors may be required to pay the costs and attorneys' fees incurred by the debtor in defending against the petition. If the petition was filed in bad faith, damages can be awarded for injury to the debtor's reputation. Punitive damages may also be awarded.

Requirements For an involuntary action to be filed, the following requirements must be met:

1. If the debtor has twelve or more creditors, three or more of these creditors having unsecured claims totaling at least $16,750 must join in the petition.
2. If a debtor has fewer than twelve creditors, one or more creditors having a claim totaling $16,750 or more may file.[13]

Order for Relief If the debtor challenges the involuntary petition, a hearing will be held, and the bankruptcy court will enter an order for relief if it finds either of the following:

1. The debtor is not paying debts as they come due.
2. A general receiver, assignee, or custodian took possession of, or was appointed to take charge of, substantially all of the debtor's property within 120 days before the filing of the petition.

If the court grants an order for relief, the debtor will be required to supply the same information in the bankruptcy schedules as in a voluntary bankruptcy.

15–5c Automatic Stay

The moment a petition, either voluntary or involuntary, is filed, an **automatic stay,** or suspension, of all actions by creditors against the debtor or the debtor's property normally goes into effect. The automatic stay prohibits creditors from taking any act to collect, assess, or recover a claim against the debtor that arose before the filing of the petition. The stay normally continues until the bankruptcy proceeding is closed or dismissed. (In some circumstances, it is possible to petition the bankruptcy court for relief from the automatic stay, as will be discussed shortly.)

If a creditor *knowingly* violates the automatic stay (a willful violation), any injured party, including the debtor, is entitled to recover actual damages, costs, and attorneys' fees. Punitive damages may be awarded as well. ■ **Case in Point 15.9** Stefanie Kuehn filed for bankruptcy. When she requested a transcript from the university at which she had obtained her master's degree, the university refused because she still owed more than $6,000 in tuition. Kuehn complained to the bankruptcy court, which ruled that the university had violated the automatic stay by refusing to provide a transcript in an attempt to collect an unpaid tuition debt. The decision was affirmed on appeal.[14] ■

The Adequate Protection Doctrine Underlying the Code's automatic-stay provision for a secured creditor is a concept known as *adequate protection.* The **adequate protection doctrine,** among other things, protects secured creditors from losing their security as a result of the automatic stay.

The bankruptcy court can provide adequate protection by requiring the debtor or trustee to make periodic cash payments or a one-time cash payment. The court can also require the debtor or trustee to provide additional collateral or replacement liens to the extent that the stay may actually cause the value of the property to decrease.

---

12. Note that the court may not dismiss a case on this ground if the debtor's bankruptcy is necessary to satisfy a claim for a domestic-support obligation.

13. 11 U.S.C. Section 303. The amounts stated in this chapter are in accordance with those computed on April 1, 2019. The dollar amounts are adjusted every three years on April 1.

14. *In re Kuehn,* 563 F.3d 289 (7th Cir. 2009).

Exceptions to the Automatic Stay The Code provides the following exceptions to the automatic stay:

1. Domestic-support obligations, including any debt owed to or recoverable by a spouse, a former spouse, a child of the debtor, that child's parent or guardian, or a governmental unit.
2. Proceedings against the debtor related to divorce, child custody or visitation, domestic violence, and support enforcement.
3. Investigations by a securities regulatory agency (such as an investigation into insider trading).
4. Certain statutory liens for property taxes.

Requests for Relief from the Automatic Stay
A secured creditor or other party in interest can petition the bankruptcy court for relief from the automatic stay. If a creditor or other party requests relief from the stay, the stay will automatically terminate sixty days after the request, unless the court grants an extension or the parties agree otherwise.

Secured Property The automatic stay on secured property terminates forty-five days after the creditors' meeting unless the debtor redeems or reaffirms certain debts. (Creditors' meetings and reaffirmation will be discussed later in this chapter.) In other words, the debtor cannot keep the secured property (such as a financed automobile), even if she or he continues to make payments on it, without reinstating the rights of the secured party to collect on the debt.

Bad Faith If the debtor had two or more bankruptcy petitions dismissed during the prior year, the Code presumes bad faith. In such a situation, the automatic stay does *not* go into effect until the court determines that the petition was filed in good faith.

In addition, the automatic stay on secured debts will terminate thirty days after the petition is filed if the debtor filed a bankruptcy petition that was dismissed within the prior year. Any party in interest can request that the court extend the stay by showing that the filing is in good faith.

15–5d Estate in Bankruptcy

Once a bankruptcy petition is filed, an *estate in bankruptcy* (or an *estate in property*) is created. The estate consists of all the debtor's interests in property, wherever located, including all of the following:

1. *Community property*—that is, property jointly owned by married persons in certain states.
2. Property transferred in a transaction voidable by the trustee.
3. Proceeds and profits from the property of the estate.

Certain after-acquired property to which the debtor becomes entitled *within 180 days after filing* may also become part of the estate. Such after-acquired property includes gifts, inheritances, property settlements (from divorce), and life insurance death proceeds.

Generally, though, the filing of a bankruptcy petition fixes a dividing line. Property acquired prior to the filing of the petition becomes property of the estate, and property acquired after the filing of the petition, except as just noted, remains the debtor's.

15–5e The Bankruptcy Trustee

Promptly after the order for relief in the liquidation proceeding has been entered, a trustee is appointed. The basic duty of the trustee is to collect the debtor's available estate and reduce it to cash for distribution, preserving the interests of both the debtor and the unsecured creditors. The trustee is held accountable for administering the debtor's estate.

To enable the trustee to accomplish this duty, the Code gives the trustee certain powers. These powers must be exercised within two years of the order for relief.

The Trustee's Powers The trustee has the power to require persons holding the debtor's property at the time the petition is filed to deliver the property to the trustee.[15] To enable the trustee to implement this power, the Code provides that the trustee has rights *equivalent* to those of certain other parties, such as a creditor who has a judicial lien. This power of a trustee, which is equivalent to that of a lien creditor, is known as *strong-arm power*.

In addition, the trustee has specific *powers of avoidance*. They enable the trustee to set aside (avoid) a sale or other transfer of the debtor's property and take the property back for the debtor's estate. These powers apply to voidable rights available to the debtor, preferences, and fraudulent transfers by the debtor. Each power is discussed in more detail next. A trustee can also avoid certain statutory liens.

The debtor shares most of the trustee's avoidance powers. Thus, if the trustee does not take action to enforce one of the rights just mentioned, the debtor in a liquidation bankruptcy can enforce that right.[16]

---

15. Usually, the trustee takes constructive, rather than actual, possession of the debtor's property. For instance, to obtain control of a debtor's business inventory, a trustee might change the locks on the doors to the business and hire a security guard.

16. Under a Chapter 11 bankruptcy, for which no trustee other than the debtor generally exists, the debtor has the same avoidance powers as a trustee under Chapter 7. Under Chapters 12 and 13, a trustee must be appointed.

Voidable Rights A trustee steps into the shoes of the debtor. Thus, any reason that a debtor can use to obtain the return of her or his property can be used by the trustee as well. These grounds include fraud, duress, incapacity, and mutual mistake.

■ **Example 15.10** Ben sells his boat to Tara. Tara gives Ben a check, knowing that she has insufficient funds in her bank account to cover the check. Tara has committed fraud. Ben has the right to avoid that transfer and recover the boat from Tara. If Ben files for bankruptcy relief under Chapter 7, the trustee can exercise the same right to recover the boat from Tara, and the boat becomes a part of the debtor's estate. ■

Preferences A debtor is not permitted to transfer property or to make a payment that favors—or gives a **preference** to—one creditor over others. The trustee is allowed to recover payments made both voluntarily and involuntarily to one creditor in preference over another.

To have made a recoverable preferential payment, an *insolvent* debtor must have transferred property, for a *pre-existing* debt, within *ninety days* before the filing of the bankruptcy petition. The transfer must have given the creditor more than the creditor would have received as a result of the bankruptcy proceedings. The Code presumes that a debtor is insolvent during the ninety-day period before filing a petition.

If a **preferred creditor** (one who has received a preferential transfer) has sold the property to an innocent third party, the trustee cannot recover the property from the innocent party. The preferred creditor, however, generally can be held liable for the value of the property.

Preferences to Insiders. Sometimes, the creditor receiving the preference is an insider. An **insider** is an individual, partner, partnership, corporation, or officer or director of a corporation (or a relative of one of these) who has a close relationship with the debtor. In this situation, the avoidance power of the trustee extends to transfers made within *one year* before filing. (If the transfer was fraudulent, as will be discussed shortly, the trustee can avoid transfers made within *two years* before filing.) The trustee must, however, prove that the debtor was insolvent when the transfer occurred and that the transfer was made to or for the benefit of an insider.

Transfers That Do Not Constitute Preferences. Not all transfers are preferences. Most courts generally assume that payment for services rendered *within fifteen days* before the payment is not a preference. In addition, if a creditor receives payment in the ordinary course of business from a debtor, such as payment of last month's cell phone bill, the bankruptcy trustee cannot recover the payment.

■ **Case in Point 15.11** David Tidd operated a business performing small home repairs as well as house-building projects. Tidd and his son regularly purchased supplies for the business on credit from S. W. Collins. Eventually, Tidd filed for Chapter 7 bankruptcy. Within ninety days preceding his filing, Tidd had made four payments for materials to S. W. Collins, totaling $46,000. The trustee filed a motion seeking to avoid this transfer as a preference. The court, however, concluded that the transfer was a substantially contemporaneous exchange of value (current consideration) and not a preference. The payments were made in the ordinary course of business. Therefore, the court found in Tidd's favor and denied the trustee's motion.[17] ■

The Code also permits a consumer-debtor to transfer any property to a creditor up to a specified total value ($6,825 in 2021) without the transfer's constituting a preference. Payment of domestic-support debts does not constitute a preference.

Fraudulent Transfers A trustee may avoid fraudulent transfers or obligations if they (1) were made within two years prior to the filing of the petition or (2) were made with actual intent to hinder, delay, or defraud a creditor. ■ **Case in Point 15.12** David Dearmond owned interests in several companies, including Briartowne, LLC, Hillside, LLC, and Bluffs of Sevier County, LLC. When Briartowne defaulted on a $623,499 promissory note, SmartBank filed an action against Briartowne, Dearmond, and others.

Five months later, Dearmond sold a property to his fiancée, Patricia Harper, for $90,000, after having recently bought it for $400,000. Two days after that, Dearmond created two irrevocable trust agreements and transferred all of his interest in Hillside and Bluffs of Sevier County to those trusts. The trusts named Harper as the primary beneficiary. Although SmartBank obtained a judgment against Dearmond (and the other owners of Briartowne), it was unable to collect from these assets.

A year and a half later, Dearmond filed a petition for bankruptcy. The trustee filed a motion seeking to avoid the fraudulent transfers made to benefit Harper. The court concluded that the transfers should be set aside because they were made with actual intent to hinder, delay, or defraud a creditor. The court entered a judgment for the trustee in an amount equivalent to the value of the fraudulent transfers.[18] ■

---

17. *In re Tidd*, 2017 WL 4011014 (Bankr. D.Me. 2017).
18. *In re Dearmond*, 2017 WL 4220396 (Bankr. E.D.Tenn. 2017).

Transfers made for less than reasonably equivalent consideration are also vulnerable if the debtor thereby became insolvent or was left engaged in business with an unreasonably small amount of capital. When a fraudulent transfer is made outside the Code's two-year limit, creditors may seek alternative relief under state laws. Some state laws may allow creditors to recover transfers made up to three years before the filing of a petition.

15–5f Exemptions

An individual debtor is entitled to exempt (exclude) certain property from a Chapter 7 bankruptcy. The Bankruptcy Code exempts the following property, up to a specified dollar amount that changes every three years:[19]

1. A portion of equity in the debtor's home (the homestead exemption).
2. Motor vehicles, up to a certain value (usually just one vehicle).
3. Reasonably necessary clothing, household goods and furnishings, and household appliances (the aggregate value not to exceed a certain amount).
4. Jewelry, up to a certain value.
5. Tools of the debtor's trade or profession, up to a certain value.
6. A portion of unpaid but earned wages.
7. Pensions.
8. Public benefits, including public assistance (welfare), Social Security, and unemployment compensation, accumulated in a bank account.
9. Damages awarded for personal injury, up to a certain amount.

Property that is *not* exempt under federal law includes bank accounts, cash, family heirlooms, collections of stamps and coins, second cars, and vacation homes.

Individual states have the power to pass legislation precluding debtors from using the federal exemptions within the state. A majority of the states have done this. In those states, debtors may use only state, not federal, exemptions. In the rest of the states, debtors may choose either the exemptions provided under state law or the federal exemptions.

Note that the Bankruptcy Code limits the amount of equity that can be claimed under the homestead exemption. In general, if the debtor acquired the homestead

within three and a half years preceding the date of filing for bankruptcy, the maximum equity exempted is $170,350, even if state law would permit a higher amount. In addition, the state homestead exemption is available only if the debtor has lived in a state for two years before filing the bankruptcy petition.

15–5g Creditors' Meeting

Within a reasonable time after the order for relief has been granted (not more than forty days), the trustee must call a meeting of the creditors listed in the schedules filed by the debtor. The bankruptcy judge does not attend this meeting. The debtor is required to attend (unless excused by the court) and to submit to examination under oath by the creditors and the trustee. At the meeting, the trustee ensures that the debtor is aware of the potential consequences of bankruptcy and of the possibility of filing under a different chapter of the Code.

15–5h Creditors' Claims

To be entitled to receive a portion of the debtor's estate, each creditor normally files a *proof of claim* with the bankruptcy court within ninety days of the creditors' meeting. A proof of claim is necessary if there is any dispute concerning the claim. The proof of claim lists the creditor's name and address, as well as the amount that the creditor asserts is owed to the creditor by the debtor.

When the debtor has no assets—called a "no-asset case"—creditors are notified of the debtor's petition for bankruptcy but are instructed not to file a claim. In no-asset cases, the unsecured creditors will receive no payment, and most, if not all, of these debts will be discharged.

15–5i Distribution of Property

The Code provides specific rules for the distribution of the debtor's property to secured and unsecured creditors. If any amount remains after the priority classes of creditors have been satisfied, it is turned over to the debtor.

Distribution to Secured Creditors The Code requires that consumer-debtors file a statement of intention with respect to secured collateral. They can choose to pay off the debt and redeem the collateral, claim it is exempt, reaffirm the debt and continue making payments, or surrender the property to the secured party.

---

19. The dollar amounts stated in the Bankruptcy Code are adjusted automatically every three years on April 1 based on changes in the Consumer Price Index. The adjusted amounts are rounded to the nearest $25.

If the collateral is surrendered to the secured party, the secured party can either (1) accept it in full satisfaction of the debt or (2) sell it and use the proceeds to pay off the debt. Thus, the secured party has priority over unsecured parties as to the proceeds from the disposition of the collateral. Should the collateral be insufficient to cover the secured debt owed, the secured creditor becomes an unsecured creditor for the difference (deficiency).

There are limited exceptions to these rules. For instance, certain unsecured creditors can sometimes step into the shoes of secured tax creditors in Chapter 7 liquidation proceedings. In such situations, when the collateral securing the tax claims is sold, the unsecured creditors are paid first. This exception does not include holders of unsecured claims for administrative expenses incurred in Chapter 11 cases that are converted to Chapter 7 liquidations. In the following case, the plaintiff argued that it should.

Case 15.2

In re Anderson

United States Court of Appeals, Fourth Circuit, 811 F.3d 166 (2016).

Background and Facts   Henry Anderson filed a voluntary petition in a federal bankruptcy court for relief under Chapter 11 of the Bankruptcy Code. The U.S. Department of the Treasury, through the Internal Revenue Service (IRS), filed a proof of claim against the bankruptcy estate for $997,551, of which $987,082 was secured by the debtor's property. Stubbs & Perdue, P.A., served as Anderson's legal counsel. During the proceedings, the court approved compensation of $200,000 to Stubbs for its services. These fees constituted an unsecured claim against the estate for administrative expenses.

Later, Anderson's case was converted to a Chapter 7 liquidation. The trustee accumulated $702,630 for distribution to the estate's creditors—not enough to pay the claims of both the IRS and Stubbs. The trustee excluded Stubbs's claim. Stubbs objected, but the court dismissed Stubbs's objection. A federal district court upheld the dismissal. Stubbs appealed, arguing that the IRS's claim should be subordinated to its claim for legal fees.

In the Language of the Court

Pamela *HARRIS*, Circuit Judge:

* * * *

* * * Before any of the events at issue here, Section 724(b)(2) * * * provided all holders of administrative expense claims, like Stubbs, with the right to subordinate secured tax creditors in Chapter 7 liquidations. But that statutory scheme was criticized on the ground that it created perverse incentives, encouraging Chapter 11 debtors and their representatives to incur administrative expenses even where there was no real hope for a successful reorganization, to the detriment of secured tax creditors when Chapter 7 liquidation ultimately proved necessary.

* * * Congress responded with a fix * * * to limit the class of administrative expenses covered by Section 724(b)(2) * * *. *In order to provide greater protection for holders of tax liens * * *, unsecured Chapter 11 administrative expense claims would no longer take priority over secured tax claims in Chapter 7 liquidations.* [Emphasis added.]

* * * *

* * * The Bankruptcy Technical Corrections Act [BTCA] * * * clarified that Chapter 11 administrative expense claimants do not hold subordination rights under Section 724(b)(2).

* * * Eleven months later, the Debtor's bankruptcy case converted from Chapter 11 to Chapter 7, implicating Section 724(b)(2) for the first time.

* * * *

* * * *As a general rule, a court is to apply the law in effect at the time it renders its decision.* [Emphasis added.]

* * * *

Stubbs argues, however, that it would be unjust to apply the BTCA version of Section 724(b)(2) * * * to disallow payment on its unsecured claim for Chapter 11 fees. Prior to the BTCA, Stubbs contends, it was entitled to subordinate the IRS's secured claim.

The problem with Stubbs's argument is its premise: that Stubbs held subordination rights under Section 724(b)(2) before the BTCA was enacted * * * . Before the BTCA was enacted, Section 724(b)(2) had no application to the Debtor's case at all. It afforded Stubbs no entitlement to subordinate the IRS's secured tax claim for the threshold reason that it simply did not apply in the Chapter 11 proceedings that began in this case * * * and did not end until * * * eleven months *after* the BTCA's passage. The pre-BTCA version of Section 724(b)(2) that Stubbs invokes, in other words, never controlled this case.

Decision and Remedy *The U.S. Court of Appeals for the Fourth Circuit affirmed the dismissal of Stubbs's claim. Under Section 724(b)(2), "it is clear that Stubbs is not entitled to subordinate the IRS's secured tax claim in favor of its unsecured claim to Chapter 11 administrative expenses."*

Critical Thinking
- **Legal Environment** *Why, as a general rule, should a court apply the law that is in effect at the time the court renders its decision?*
- **What If the Facts Were Different?** *Suppose that Anderson had filed his initial bankruptcy petition under Chapter 7, not under Chapter 11. Would the result have been different? Discuss.*

Distribution to Unsecured Creditors Bankruptcy law establishes an order of priority for debts owed to *unsecured* creditors, and they are paid in the order of their priority. Claims for domestic-support obligations, such as child support and alimony, have the highest priority among unsecured creditors, so these claims must be paid first. Each class, or group, must be fully paid before the next class is entitled to any of the remaining proceeds.

If there are insufficient proceeds to fully pay all the creditors in a class, the proceeds are distributed *proportionately* to the creditors in that class. Classes lower in priority receive nothing. In almost all Chapter 7 bankruptcies, the funds will be insufficient to pay all creditors.

Exhibit 15–2 illustrates the collection and distribution of property in most voluntary bankruptcies. The exhibit includes a listing of the classes of unsecured creditors.

Exhibit 15–2 Collection and Distribution of Property in Most Voluntary Bankruptcies

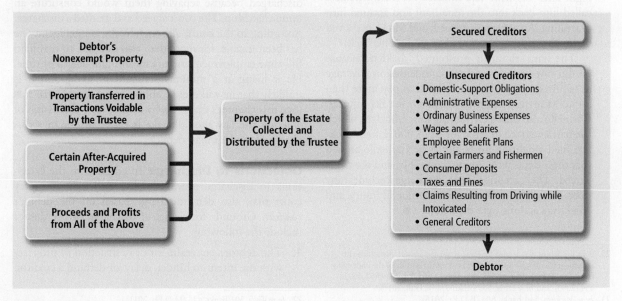

15–5j Discharge

From the debtor's point of view, the primary purpose of liquidation is to obtain a fresh start through a discharge of debts. A discharge voids, or sets aside, any judgment on a discharged debt and prevents any action to collect it. Certain debts, however, are not dischargeable in bankruptcy. Also, certain debtors may not qualify to have all debts discharged in bankruptcy. These situations are discussed next.

Exceptions to Discharge Claims that are not dischargeable in bankruptcy include the following:

1. Claims for back taxes accruing within two years prior to bankruptcy.
2. Claims for amounts borrowed by the debtor to pay federal taxes or any nondischargeable taxes.
3. Claims against property or funds obtained by the debtor under false pretenses or by false representations.
4. Claims by creditors who were not notified of the bankruptcy. These claims did not appear on the schedules the debtor was required to file.
5. Claims based on fraud[20] or misuse of funds by the debtor while acting in a fiduciary capacity or claims involving the debtor's embezzlement or larceny.
6. Domestic-support obligations and property settlements as provided for in a separation agreement or divorce decree.
7. Claims for amounts due on a retirement account loan.
8. Claims based on willful or malicious conduct by the debtor toward another or the property of another.

■ **Case in Point 15.13** Anthony Mickletz owned a pizza restaurant that employed John Carmello. One night after Carmello had finished his shift, Mickletz called him back into the restaurant and accused him of stealing. An argument ensued, and Mickletz shoved Carmello, causing him to fall and injure his back.

The state criminally prosecuted Mickletz because he did not provide workers' compensation coverage as required by law. He was ordered to pay more than $45,000 in restitution to Carmello for his injuries. Carmello also filed a civil suit against Mickletz, which the parties agreed to settle for $175,000. Later, Mickletz filed a petition for bankruptcy. Carmello argued that these debts were nondischargeable, and the court agreed. The exception from discharge includes any debts for willful (deliberate or intentional) injury, and Mickletz's actions were deliberate.[21] ■

9. Certain government fines and penalties.
10. Student loans, unless payment of the loans imposes an undue hardship on the debtor and the debtor's dependents (when paying the loan would leave the debtor unable to maintain a minimum standard of living, for instance).
11. Consumer debts of more than a specified amount ($725 in 2021) for luxury goods or services owed to a single creditor incurred within ninety days of the order for relief.
12. Cash advances totaling more than a threshold amount ($1,000 in 2021) that are extensions of open-end consumer credit obtained by the debtor within seventy days of the order for relief.
13. Judgments against a debtor as a result of the debtor's operation of a motor vehicle while intoxicated.
14. Fees or assessments arising from property in a homeowners' association, as long as the debtor retained an interest in the property.
15. Taxes with respect to which the debtor failed to provide required or requested tax documents.

■ **Case in Point 15.14** At the time he filed for Chapter 7 bankruptcy, Terence Wolfe had not been consistently employed for twenty years. He had been fired from numerous positions for behavioral issues and had difficulty finding and holding a job. Wolfe had been diagnosed with personality disorders and ultimately was granted disability status by the U.S. government. He was living on disability payments of $1,126 per month at the time he filed for Chapter 7 bankruptcy.

Among Wolfe's debts were more than $131,000 in student loan debts. Wolfe sought to have these debts discharged because repaying them would constitute an undue hardship. The court agreed and granted a discharge. According to the court, although Wolfe is intelligent, "he has been unable, for more than two decades, to maintain full-time employment for any meaningful length of time. He is living at a minimal standard of living and it is unlikely that he will ever be able to repay these loans."[22] ■ (See this chapter's *Ethics Today* feature for a discussion of whether the law should make it easier to obtain a discharge of student loan debts.)

Objections to Discharge In addition to the exceptions to discharge previously discussed, a bankruptcy court may also deny discharge based on the debtor's *conduct*. Grounds for denial of discharge of the debtor include the following:

1. The debtor's concealment or destruction of property with the intent to hinder, delay, or defraud a creditor.

---

20. Even if a debtor who is sued for fraud settles the lawsuit, the settlement agreement may not be discharged in bankruptcy because of the underlying fraud. See *Archer v. Warner*, 538 U.S. 314, 123 S.Ct. 1462, 155 L.Ed.2d 454 (2003); and *In re Pierce*, 563 Bankr. 698 (C.D.Ill. 2017).
21. *In re Mickletz*, 544 Bankr. 804 (E.D.Pa. 2016).

22. *In re Wolfe*, 501 Bankr. 426 (M.D.Fla. 2011).

Should There Be More Relief for Student Loan Defaults?

According to many observers, student loan debt has reached crisis levels in the United States. Outstanding student loan balances total more than $1.5 *trillion* nationally and are growing by around $3,000 *per second*. About 20 percent are ninety or more days' delinquent or are in default. That is the highest delinquency rate among all forms of debt, including credit cards, automobile loans, and mortgages. The average student loan debt is more than $35,000.

Consequences of Default

Any student borrower who has not made regular payments for nine months is in default. If you are in default on a student loan, the U.S. Department of Education can do any of the following to collect:

1. Keep your tax refund if you were supposed to receive one.
2. Garnish your paycheck without obtaining a court judgment.
3. Take your federal benefits, such as Social Security retirement payments or disability payments.

In addition, in some states any professional license that you have can be revoked. The Department of Education can also bring a lawsuit against you. If it wins, it can collect the judgment from your bank accounts or place a lien on any real property that you own.

Political Impetus

Politicians and society are increasingly discussing student loan debt and the costs of higher education. Some are asking Congress to allow federal student loans to be discharged in most bankruptcy proceedings. Others advocate making college education free or at least reducing the costs charged to certain students. One plan calls for reducing the interest rates that can be charged. Another proposal is to prohibit the federal government from profiting from student loan debt (the government brings in more than $42 billion a year from student loans).

Critical Thinking *Why does the Bankruptcy Code provide that student loans should not be dischargeable unless there is undue hardship? What argument can be made in favor of allowing student loans to be dischargeable?*

2. The debtor's fraudulent concealment or destruction of financial records.
3. The grant of a discharge to the debtor within eight years before the petition was filed.
4. The debtor's failure to complete the required consumer education course.
5. The debtor's involvement in proceedings in which the debtor could be found guilty of a felony. (Basically, a court may not discharge any debt until the completion of felony proceedings against the debtor.)

When a discharge is denied under any of these circumstances, the debtor's assets are still distributed to the creditors. After the bankruptcy proceeding, however, the debtor remains liable for the unpaid portion of all claims.

In addition, a discharge may be revoked within one year if it is discovered that the debtor acted fraudulently or dishonestly during the bankruptcy proceeding. If that occurs, a creditor whose claim was not satisfied in the distribution of the debtor's property can proceed with his or her claim against the debtor.

15–5k Reaffirmation of Debt

An agreement to pay a debt dischargeable in bankruptcy is called a **reaffirmation agreement.** A debtor may wish

to pay a debt—such as a debt owed to a family member, physician, bank, or some other creditor—even though the debt could be discharged in bankruptcy. Also, as noted previously, a debtor cannot retain secured property while continuing to pay without entering into a reaffirmation agreement.

Procedures To be enforceable, reaffirmation agreements must be made before the debtor is granted a discharge. The agreement must be signed and filed with the court. Court approval is required unless the debtor is represented by an attorney during the negotiation of the reaffirmation and submits the proper documents and certifications. Even when the debtor is represented by an attorney, court approval may be required if it appears that the reaffirmation will result in undue hardship to the debtor.

When court approval is required, a separate hearing will take place. The court will approve the reaffirmation only if it finds that the agreement will not result in undue hardship to the debtor and that the reaffirmation is consistent with the debtor's best interests.

Required Disclosures To discourage creditors from engaging in abusive reaffirmation practices, the law provides specific language for disclosures that must be given to debtors entering into reaffirmation agreements. Among other things, these disclosures explain that the debtor is not required to reaffirm any debt. They also inform the debtor that liens on secured property, such as mortgages and cars, will remain in effect even if the debt is not reaffirmed.

The reaffirmation agreement must disclose the amount of the debt reaffirmed, the rate of interest, the date payments begin, and the right to rescind. The disclosures also caution the debtor: "Only agree to reaffirm a debt if it is in your best interest. Be sure you can afford the payments you agree to make."

The original disclosure documents must be signed by the debtor, certified by the debtor's attorney, and filed with the court at the same time as the reaffirmation agreement. A reaffirmation agreement that is not accompanied by the original signed disclosures will not be effective.

■ **Case in Point 15.15** The owner of a seafood import business, Howard Lapides, signed a secured promissory note for $400,000 with Venture Bank for a revolving line-of-credit loan. Part of the collateral for that loan was a third mortgage on the Lapideses' home (two other banks held prior mortgages). Eventually, Howard and his wife filed for Chapter 7 bankruptcy protection, and their personal debts were discharged. Afterward, Venture Bank convinced the Lapideses to sign a reaffirmation agreement by telling them that it would refinance all three mortgages so that they could keep their house.

The Lapideses made twelve $3,500 payments to Venture Bank, but when the bank did not refinance the other mortgages, they stopped making payments. Venture Bank filed a suit, but a court refused to enforce the reaffirmation agreement because it violated the Bankruptcy Code. The agreement had never been signed by the Lapideses' attorney or filed with the bankruptcy court.[23] ■

15–6 Reorganizations

The type of bankruptcy proceeding most commonly used by corporate debtors is the Chapter 11 *reorganization.* In a reorganization, the creditors and the debtor formulate a plan under which the debtor pays a portion of the debts and is discharged of the remainder. The debtor is allowed to continue in business.

As noted, this type of bankruptcy generally involves a corporate reorganization. Nevertheless, any debtor (except a stockbroker or a commodities broker) who is

eligible for Chapter 7 relief is eligible for relief under Chapter 11. Railroads are also eligible.

Congress has established a "fast-track" Chapter 11 procedure for small-business debtors whose liabilities do not exceed a specified amount (about $2.7 million) and who do not own or manage real estate. The fast-track procedure enables a debtor to avoid the appointment of a creditors' committee and also shortens the filing periods and relaxes certain other requirements. Because the process is shorter and simpler, it is less costly.

The same principles that govern the filing of a liquidation (Chapter 7) petition apply to reorganization (Chapter 11) proceedings. The case may be brought either voluntarily or involuntarily. The automatic-stay provision and its exceptions (such as substantial abuse), as well as the adequate protection doctrine, apply in reorganizations.

15–6a Best Interests of the Creditors

Once a Chapter 11 petition has been filed, a bankruptcy court can dismiss or suspend proceedings at any time if dismissal or suspension would better serve the interests of the creditors. Before taking such an action, the court must give notice and conduct a hearing. The Code also allows a court, after notice and a hearing, to dismiss a case under reorganization "for cause" when there is no reasonable likelihood of rehabilitation. Similarly, a court can dismiss when there is an inability to effect a plan or an unreasonable delay by the debtor that may harm the interests of creditors. A debtor whose petition is dismissed for these reasons can file a subsequent Chapter 11 petition in the future.

15–6b Debtor in Possession

On entry of the order for relief, the debtor generally continues to operate the business as a **debtor in possession (DIP).** The court, however, may appoint a trustee (often referred to as a *receiver*) to operate the debtor's business. The court will choose this action if gross mismanagement of the business is shown or if appointing a trustee is in the best interests of the estate.

The DIP's role is similar to that of a trustee in a liquidation bankruptcy.[24] The DIP is entitled to avoid preferential payments made to creditors and fraudulent transfers of assets. The DIP can also exercise a trustee's strong-arm powers. The DIP has the power to decide whether to cancel or assume prepetition executory contracts (contracts that are not yet performed) or unexpired leases.

23. *Venture Bank v. Lapides,* 800 F.3d 442 (8th Cir. 2015).

24. 11 U.S.C. Section 544(a).

Cancellation of executory contracts or unexpired leases can be of substantial benefit to a Chapter 11 debtor. ■ **Example 15.16** Five years ago, APT Corporation leased an office building for a twenty-year term. Now, APT can no longer pay the rent due under the lease and has filed for Chapter 11 reorganization. In this situation, the debtor in possession can cancel the lease, and APT will not be required to continue paying the substantial rent due for fifteen more years. ■

15–6c Creditors' Committees

As soon as practicable after the entry of the order for relief, a creditors' committee of unsecured creditors is appointed.[25] The business's suppliers may serve on the committee. The committee can consult with the trustee or the DIP concerning the administration of the case or the formulation of the plan. Additional creditors' committees may be appointed to represent special interest creditors.

Generally, no orders affecting the estate will be entered without the consent of the committee or after a hearing in which the judge is informed of the committee's position. As mentioned earlier, businesses with debts of less than a specified amount that do not own or manage real estate can avoid creditors' committees. In these fast-track proceedings, orders can be entered without a committee's consent.

15–6d The Reorganization Plan

A reorganization plan to rehabilitate the debtor is a plan to conserve and administer the debtor's assets in the hope of an eventual return to successful operation and solvency. The plan must be fair and equitable and must do the following:

1. Designate classes of claims and interests.
2. Specify the treatment to be afforded to the classes of creditors. (The plan must provide the same treatment for all claims in a particular class.)
3. Provide an adequate means for the plan's execution. (Individual debtors are required to utilize postpetition assets as necessary to execute the plan.)
4. Provide for payment of tax claims over a five-year period.

The plan need not provide for full repayment to unsecured creditors. Instead, creditors receive a percentage of each dollar owed to them by the debtor.

Acceptance of the Plan Once the plan has been developed, it is submitted to each class of creditors for acceptance. For the plan to be adopted, each class must accept it. A class has accepted the plan when a majority of the creditors in the class, representing two-thirds of the amount of the total claim, vote to approve it. If the debtor fails to procure creditor consent of the plan within 180 days, any party may propose a plan.

Confirmation of the Plan Confirmation is conditioned on the debtor's certifying that all postpetition domestic-support obligations have been paid in full. In addition, even when all classes of creditors accept the plan, the court may refuse to confirm it if it is not "in the best interests of the creditors." For small-business debtors, if the plan meets the listed requirements, the court must confirm the plan within forty-five days (unless this period is extended).

The plan can be modified on the request of the debtor, the DIP, the trustee, the U.S. trustee, or a holder of an unsecured claim. If an unsecured creditor objects to the plan, specific rules apply to the value of property to be distributed under the plan. Tax claims must be paid over a five-year period.

Even if only one class of creditors has accepted the plan, the court may still confirm the plan under the Code's so-called **cram-down provision.** In other words, the court may confirm the plan over the objections of a class of creditors. Before the court can exercise the right of cram-down confirmation, it must be demonstrated that the plan does not discriminate unfairly against any creditors and is fair and equitable.

Discharge The plan is binding on confirmation. Nevertheless, the law provides that confirmation of a plan does not discharge an individual debtor. *For individual debtors, the plan must be completed before discharge will be granted,* unless the court orders otherwise. For all other debtors, the court may order discharge at any time after the plan is confirmed.

On discharge, the debtor is given a reorganization discharge from all claims not protected under the plan. This discharge does not apply to any claims that would be denied discharge under liquidation.

15–7 Bankruptcy Relief under Chapter 12 and Chapter 13

In addition to bankruptcy relief through liquidation and reorganization, the Code also provides for family-farmer and family-fisherman debt adjustments (Chapter 12)

---

25. If the debtor has filed a reorganization plan accepted by the creditors, the trustee (receiver) may decide *not* to call a meeting of the creditors.

and individuals' repayment plans (Chapter 13). The procedures for filing Chapter 12 and Chapter 13 plans are very similar. Because Chapter 13 plans are the more commonly used of the two types, we discuss Chapter 13 first.

15–7a Individuals' Repayment Plans— Chapter 13

Chapter 13 of the Bankruptcy Code provides for "Adjustment of Debts of an Individual with Regular Income." Individuals with regular income who owe debts not exceeding specified amounts may take advantage of bankruptcy repayment plans. (The limit for fixed unsecured debts is around $420,000, and the limit for fixed secured debts is about $1.3 million.) Partnerships and corporations are excluded.

Among those eligible are salaried employees and sole proprietors, as well as individuals who live on welfare, Social Security, fixed pensions, or investment income. Many small-business debtors have a choice of filing under either Chapter 11 or Chapter 13. Repayment plans offer some advantages because they are less expensive and less complicated than reorganization or liquidation proceedings.

Filing the Petition A Chapter 13 repayment plan case can be initiated only by the debtor's filing of a voluntary petition or by court conversion of a Chapter 7 petition. Recall that a court may convert a Chapter 7 petition because of a finding of substantial abuse under the means test. In addition, certain liquidation and reorganization cases may be converted to repayment plan cases with the consent of the debtor.[26]

A trustee, who will make payments under the plan, must be appointed. On the filing of a repayment plan petition, the automatic stay previously discussed takes effect. Although the stay applies to all or part of the debtor's consumer debt, it does not apply to any business debt incurred by the debtor or to any domestic-support obligations.

Good Faith Requirement The Bankruptcy Code imposes the requirement of good faith on a debtor at both the time of the filing of the petition and the time of the filing of the plan. The Code does not define good faith, but if the circumstances on the whole indicate bad faith, a court can dismiss a debtor's Chapter 13 petition.

The Repayment Plan A plan of rehabilitation by repayment must provide for the following:

1. The turning over to the trustee of such future earnings or income of the debtor as is necessary for execution of the plan.
2. Full payment through deferred cash payments of all claims entitled to priority, such as taxes.[27]
3. Identical treatment of all claims within a particular class. (The Code permits the debtor to list co-debtors, such as guarantors or sureties, as a separate class.)

The repayment plan may provide either for payment of all obligations in full or for payment of a lesser amount. A debtor must apply the means test to identify the amount of disposable income that will be available to repay creditors. The debtor must begin making payments under the proposed plan within thirty days after the plan has been filed and must continue to make "timely" payments.[28] If the debtor fails to make timely payments or to commence payments within the thirty-day period, the court can convert the case to a Chapter 7 bankruptcy or dismiss the petition.

Length of the Plan. The length of the payment plan can be three or five years, depending on the debtor's family income. If the family income is greater than the median family income in the relevant geographic area under the means test, the term of the proposed plan must be three years.[29] The term may not exceed five years.

Confirmation of the Plan. After the plan is filed, the court holds a confirmation hearing, at which interested parties (such as creditors) may object to the plan. The hearing must be held at least twenty days, but no more than forty-five days, after the meeting of the creditors. The debtor must have filed all prepetition tax returns and paid all postpetition domestic-support obligations before a court will confirm any plan.

The court will confirm a plan with respect to each claim of a secured creditor under any of the following circumstances:

1. If the secured creditors have accepted the plan.
2. If the plan provides that secured creditors retain their liens until there is payment in full or until the debtor receives a discharge.

---

26. A Chapter 13 repayment plan may be converted to a Chapter 7 liquidation at the request of the debtor or, under certain circumstances, by a creditor "for cause." A Chapter 13 case may be converted to a Chapter 11 case after a hearing.

27. As with a Chapter 11 reorganization plan, full repayment of all claims is not always required.

28. The bankruptcy trustee holds on to these payments until the court either confirms or denies the debtor's plan. If the court confirms the plan, the trustee distributes the funds to creditors as stated in the plan. If the court denies the debtor's plan, the trustee returns the funds, minus administrative expenses, to the debtor.

29. See 11 U.S.C. Section 1322(d) for details on when the court will find that the Chapter 13 plan should extend to a five-year period.

3. If the debtor surrenders the property securing the claims to the creditors.

In addition, for a motor vehicle purchased within 910 days before the petition is filed, the plan must provide that a creditor with a purchase-money security interest (PMSI) retains its lien until the entire debt is paid. For PMSIs on other personal property, the payment plan must cover debts incurred within a one-year period preceding the filing.

Discharge After the debtor has completed all payments, the court grants a discharge of all debts provided for by the repayment plan. Generally, all debts are dischargeable except the following:

1. Allowed claims not provided for by the plan.
2. Certain long-term debts provided for by the plan.
3. Certain tax claims and payments on retirement accounts.
4. Claims for domestic-support obligations.
5. Debts related to injury or property damage caused while driving under the influence of alcohol or drugs.

In the following case, a Chapter 13 debtor's domestic-support obligations were at issue. Under the Bankruptcy Code, a debt constitutes a domestic-support obligation if it is "in the nature of alimony, maintenance, or support." The question before the court was whether a parent's promise to pay his children's college expenses met this requirement.

Case 15.3

In re Chamberlain
United States Court of Appeals, Tenth Circuit, 721 Fed.Appx. 826 (2018).

Background and Facts When Stephen and Judith Chamberlain were divorced, their marital settlement agreement included a "College Education" provision. In this provision, Stephen promised to "pay the costs of tuition, room and board, books, registration fees, and reasonable application fees incident to . . . an undergraduate college education" for each of their three children: Sarah, Kate, and John. Stephen failed to meet this obligation. Judith obtained an order in a Maryland state court to enforce the agreement and initiated an effort to collect. Stephen filed a petition for bankruptcy under Chapter 13. Judith filed a creditor's claim with the bankruptcy court, contending that the college expenses were domestic-support obligations and thus created priority claims that had to be fully paid. The court agreed, and Stephen appealed.

In the Language of the Court
Robert E. *BACHARACH*, Circuit Judge.
* * * *

* * * Stephen argued that his obligation to pay his children's college expenses did not constitute a domestic support obligation because it was not "in the nature of * * * support."
* * * *

* * * The court properly conducted a dual inquiry to determine whether these obligations involved support, looking first to the intent of the parties at the time they entered into their agreement, and then to the substance of the obligation.

* * * With respect to the initial issue of intent, the court appropriately considered

- the language and structure of the college expense obligation in the marital settlement agreement and
- the parties' testimony regarding surrounding circumstances, including the disparity in Stephen and Judith's financial circumstances at the time of the divorce.

The bankruptcy court found that the parties had intended Stephen's college expense obligation to constitute support because * * *

- the evidence established that Stephen and Judith had viewed a college education as an important part of their children's upbringing,
- the couple had long intended to provide for the children's education, and
- this intent could not be carried out at the time of the divorce, given the couple's relative financial capabilities, without Stephen assuming this obligation.

* * * *

* * * In determining whether Stephen's obligation involved support, the bankruptcy court also considered the substance of Stephen's obligation. The critical question in determining whether the obligation is, in substance, support is the function served by the obligation at the time of the divorce.

Case 15.3 Continues

In turn, *the function of the obligation is affected by the parties' relative financial circumstances at the time of the divorce.* [Emphasis added.]

Here, the bankruptcy court reasonably determined that Stephen was the only parent financially able to pay for the children's college education. Thus, the court was justified in regarding Stephen's obligation, in substance, as support.

Decision and Remedy *The U.S. Court of Appeals for the Tenth Circuit affirmed the judgment of the bankruptcy court. "Stephen's college expense obligation was 'in the nature of support' as required for a domestic support obligation under the Bankruptcy Code."*

Critical Thinking

- **Legal Environment** *Maryland law arguably does not include postsecondary education expenses in the definition of "child support." Should this state law have governed the court's conclusion in the* Chamberlain *case? Why or why not?*
- **What If the Facts Were Different?** *Suppose that the marital settlement agreement had obligated Stephen to assume the mortgage debt on the family home. If all other facts were the same, would the result have been different?*

15–7b Family Farmers and Fishermen— Chapter 12

Congress created Chapter 12 of the Bankruptcy Code to help relieve economic pressure on small farmers. In 2005, Congress extended this protection to family fishermen, modified its provisions somewhat, and made it a permanent chapter in the Bankruptcy Code. (Previously, the statutes authorizing Chapter 12 had to be periodically renewed by Congress.)

Concept Summary 15.1 compares bankruptcy procedures under Chapters 7, 11, 12, and 13.

Definitions For purposes of Chapter 12, a *family farmer* is one whose gross income is at least 50 percent farm dependent and whose debts are at least 50 percent farm related. The total debt for a family farmer must not exceed a specified amount (around $4.2 million in 2019). A partnership or close corporation that is at least 50 percent owned by the farm family can also qualify as a family farmer.[30]

A *family fisherman* is one whose gross income is at least 50 percent dependent on commercial fishing operations[31] and whose debts are at least 80 percent related to commercial fishing. The total debt for a family fisherman must not exceed a certain amount (about $2 million in 2021). As with family farmers, a partnership or close corporation can also qualify.

Filing the Petition The procedure for filing a family-farmer or family-fisherman bankruptcy plan is similar to the procedure for filing a repayment plan under Chapter 13. The debtor must file a plan not later than ninety days after the order for relief has been entered. The filing of the petition creates an automatic stay prohibiting creditors' actions against the estate.

A farmer or fisherman who has already filed a reorganization or repayment plan may convert it to a Chapter 12 plan. The debtor may also convert a Chapter 12 plan to a liquidation plan.

Content and Confirmation of the Plan The content of a plan under Chapter 12 is basically the same as that of a Chapter 13 repayment plan. Generally, the plan must be confirmed or denied within forty-five days of filing.

The plan must provide for payment of secured debts at the value of the collateral. If the secured debt exceeds the value of the collateral, the remaining debt is unsecured.

For unsecured debtors, the plan must be confirmed in either of the following circumstances: (1) the value of the property to be distributed under the plan equals the amount of the claim, or (2) the plan provides that all of the debtor's disposable income to be received in a three-year period (or longer, by court approval) will be applied to making payments. Disposable income is all income received less amounts needed to support the farmer or fisherman and his or her family and to continue the farming or commercial fishing operation. Completion of payments under the plan discharges all debts provided for by the plan.

---

30. Note that for a corporation or partnership to qualify under Chapter 12, at least 80 percent of the value of the firm's assets must consist of assets related to the farming operation.
31. Commercial fishing operations include catching, harvesting, or raising fish, shrimp, lobsters, urchins, seaweed, shellfish, or other aquatic species or products.

Concept Summary 15.1

Forms of Bankruptcy Relief Compared

Form	Chapter 7	Chapter 11	Chapters 12 and 13
Purpose	Liquidation.	Reorganization.	Adjustment.
Who Can Petition	Debtor (voluntary) or creditors (involuntary).	Debtor (voluntary) or creditors (involuntary).	Debtor (voluntary) only.
Who Can Be a Debtor	Any "person" (including partnerships, corporations, and municipalities) except railroads, insurance companies, banks, savings and loan institutions, investment companies licensed by the Small Business Administration, and credit unions. Farmers and charitable institutions cannot be involuntarily petitioned. If the court finds the petition to be a substantial abuse of the use of Chapter 7, the debtor may be required to convert to a Chapter 13 repayment plan.	Any debtor eligible for Chapter 7 relief. Railroads are also eligible. Individuals have specific rules and limitations.	**Chapter 12**—Any family farmer (one whose gross income is at least 50 percent farm dependent and whose debts are at least 50 percent farm related) or family fisherman (one whose gross income is at least 50 percent dependent on commercial fishing operations and whose debts are at least 80 percent related to commercial fishing) or any partnership or close corporation at least 50 percent owned by a family farmer or fisherman, when total debt does not exceed a specified amount. **Chapter 13**—Any individual (not partnerships or corporations) with regular income who owes fixed (liquidated) unsecured debts of less than a specified amount or fixed secured debts of less than a specified amount.
Procedure Leading to Discharge	Nonexempt property is sold, and the proceeds are distributed (in order) to priority groups. Dischargeable debts are terminated.	Plan is submitted. If the plan is approved and followed, debts are discharged.	Plan is submitted and must be approved if the value of the property to be distributed equals the amount of the claims or if the debtor turns over disposable income for a three-year or five-year period. If the plan is followed, debts are discharged.
Advantages	On liquidation and distribution, most or all debts are discharged, and the debtor has an opportunity for a fresh start.	Debtor continues in business. Creditors can either accept the plan, or it can be "crammed down" on them. The plan allows for the reorganization and liquidation of debts over the plan period.	Debtor continues in business or possession of assets. If the plan is approved, most debts are discharged after the plan period.

Practice and Review: Creditor-Debtor Relations and Bankruptcy

Three months ago, Janet Hart's husband of twenty years died of cancer. Although he had medical insurance, he left Janet with outstanding medical bills of more than $50,000. Janet has two teenage daughters to support. She has worked at the local library for the past ten years, earning $1,500 per month. Since her husband's death, she has also received $1,500 in Social Security benefits and $1,100 in life insurance proceeds every month, for a total monthly income of $4,100. After making the mortgage payment of $1,500 and paying the amounts due on other debts, Janet has barely enough left to buy groceries for her family. She decides to file for Chapter 7 bankruptcy, hoping for a fresh start. Using the information presented in the chapter, answer the following questions.

1. What must Janet do before filing a petition for relief under Chapter 7?
2. How much time does Janet have after filing the bankruptcy petition to submit the required schedules? What happens if Janet does not meet the deadline?
3. Assume that Janet files a petition under Chapter 7. Further assume that the median family income in the geographic area in which Janet lives is $49,300. What steps would a court take to determine whether Janet's petition is presumed to be "substantial abuse" using the means test?
4. Suppose that the court determines that no *presumption* of substantial abuse applies in Janet's case. Nevertheless, the court finds that Janet does have the ability to pay at least a portion of the medical bills out of her disposable income. What would the court likely order in that situation?

Debate This ...   *Rather than being allowed to file Chapter 7 bankruptcy petitions, individuals and couples should always be forced to make an effort to pay off their debts through Chapter 13.*

Terms and Concepts

adequate protection doctrine 332	forbearance 327	preference 334
artisan's lien 323	foreclosure 327	preferred creditor 334
attachment 323	garnishment 324	prepayment penalty clause 327
automatic stay 332	guarantor 325	reaffirmation agreement 339
bankruptcy trustee 330	homeowner's insurance 327	right of contribution 326
consumer-debtor 330	homestead exemption 329	right of reimbursement 326
co-surety 326	insider 334	right of subrogation 326
cram-down provision 341	lien 322	short sale 327
creditors' composition	liquidation 330	surety 325
agreement 324	mechanic's lien 322	suretyship 325
debtor in possession (DIP) 340	mortgage 326	U.S. trustee 331
default 322	mortgage insurance 327	workout agreement 327
discharge 330	order for relief 332	writ of attachment 324
down payment 326	petition in bankruptcy 330	writ of execution 324

Issue Spotters

1. Alyssa owes Don $5,000 and refuses to pay. Don obtains a garnishment order and serves it on Alyssa's employer. If the employer complies with the order and Alyssa stays on the job, is one order enough to garnish Alyssa's wages for each pay period until the debt is paid? Explain. (See *Laws Assisting Creditors*.)

2. After graduating from college, Tina works briefly as a salesperson before filing for bankruptcy. Tina's petition states that her only debts are student loans, taxes accruing within the last year, and a claim against her based on her misuse of customers' funds during her employment. Are these debts dischargeable in bankruptcy? Explain. (See *Liquidation Proceedings*.)

• **Check your answers to the Issue Spotters against the answers provided in Appendix B at the end of this text.**

Business Scenarios and Case Problems

15–1. Liens. Nabil is the owner of a relatively old home valued at $105,000. The home's electrical system is failing, and the wiring needs to be replaced. Nabil contracts with Kandhari Electrical to replace the electrical system. Kandhari performs the repairs, and on June 1 submits a bill of $10,000 to Nabil. Because of financial difficulties, Nabil does not pay the bill. Nabil's only asset is his home, but his state's homestead exemption is $60,000. Discuss fully Kandhari's remedies in this situation. (See *Laws Assisting Creditors*.)

15–2. Voluntary versus Involuntary Bankruptcy. Burke has been a rancher all her life, raising cattle and crops. Her ranch is valued at $500,000, almost all of which is exempt under state law. Burke has eight creditors and a total indebtedness of $70,000. Two of her largest creditors are Oman ($30,000 owed) and Sneed ($25,000 owed). The other six creditors have claims of less than $5,000 each. A drought has ruined all of Burke's crops and forced her to sell many of her cattle at a loss. She cannot pay off her creditors. (See *Liquidation Proceedings*.)

(a) Under the Bankruptcy Code, can Burke, with a $500,000 ranch, voluntarily petition herself into bankruptcy? Explain.

(b) Could either Oman or Sneed force Burke into involuntary bankruptcy? Explain.

15–3. Business Case Problem with Sample Answer— Discharge in Bankruptcy. Like many students, Barbara Hann financed her education partially through loans. These loans included three federally insured Stafford Loans of $7,500 each ($22,500 in total). Hann believed that she had repaid the loans, but when she filed a Chapter 13 petition, Educational Credit Management Corp. (ECMC) filed an unsecured proof of claim based on the loans. Hann objected. At a hearing at which ECMC failed to appear, Hann submitted correspondence from the lender that indicated the loans had been paid. The court entered an order sustaining Hann's objection. Despite the order, can ECMC resume its effort to collect on Hann's loans? Explain. [*In re Hann*, 711 F.3d 235 (1st Cir. 2013)] (See *Liquidation Proceedings*.)

- **For a sample answer to Problem 15–3, go to Appendix C at the end of this text.**

15–4. Discharge. Michael and Dianne Shankle divorced. An Arkansas state court ordered Michael to pay Dianne alimony and child support, as well as half of the $184,000 in their investment accounts. Instead, Michael withdrew more than half of the investment funds and spent them. Over the next several years, the court repeatedly held Michael in contempt for failing to pay Dianne. Six years later, Michael filed for Chapter 7 bankruptcy, including in the petition's schedule the debt to Dianne of unpaid alimony, child support, and investment funds. Is Michael entitled to a discharge of this debt, or does it qualify as an exception? Explain. [*In re Shankle*, 554 Fed.Appx. 264 (5th Cir. 2014)] (See *Liquidation Proceedings*.)

15–5. Discharge under Chapter 13. James Thomas and Jennifer Clark married and had two children. They bought a home in Ironton, Ohio, with a loan secured by a mortgage. Later, they took out a second mortgage. On their divorce, the court gave Clark custody of the children and required Clark to pay the first mortgage. The divorce decree also required Thomas and Clark to make equal payments on the second mortgage and provided that Clark would receive all proceeds on the sale of the home. Thomas failed to make any payments, and Clark sold the home. At that point, she learned that Auto Now had a lien on the home because Thomas had not made payments on his car. Clark used all the sale proceeds to pay off the lien and the mortgages. When Thomas filed a petition for a Chapter 13 bankruptcy in a federal bankruptcy court, Clark filed a proof of claim for the mortgage and lien debts. Clark claimed that Thomas should not be able to discharge these debts because they were part of his domestic-support obligations. Are these debts dischargeable? Explain. [*In re Thomas*, 591 Fed.Appx. 443 (6th Cir. 2015)] (See *Bankruptcy Relief under Chapter 12 and Chapter 13*.)

15–6. Liquidation Proceedings. Jeffrey Krueger and Michael Torres, shareholders of Cru Energy, Inc., were embroiled in litigation in a Texas state court. Both claimed to act on Cru's behalf, and each charged the other with attempting to obtain control of Cru through fraud and other misconduct. Temporarily prohibited from participating in Cru's business, Krueger formed Kru, a company with the same business plan and many of the same shareholders as Cru. Meanwhile, to delay the state court proceedings, Krueger filed a petition for a Chapter 7 liquidation in a federal bankruptcy court. He did not reveal his interest in Kru to the bankruptcy court. Ownership of Krueger's Cru shares passed to the bankruptcy trustee, but Krueger ignored this. He called a meeting of Cru's shareholders—except Torres—and voted those shares to remove Torres from the board and elect himself chairman, president, chief executive officer, and treasurer. The Cru board then dismissed all of Cru's claims against Krueger in his suit with Torres. Are there sufficient grounds for the bankruptcy court to dismiss Krueger's bankruptcy petition? Discuss. [*In re Krueger*, 812 F.3d 365 (5th Cir. 2016)] (See *Liquidation Proceedings*.)

15–7. Garnishment. Grand Harbour Condominium Owners Association, Inc., obtained a judgment in an Ohio state court against Gene and Nancy Grogg for $45,458. To satisfy the judgment, Grand Harbour filed a notice of garnishment with the court, seeking funds held by the Groggs in various banks. The Groggs disputed Grand Harbour's right to garnish the funds. They claimed that the funds were exempt Social Security and pension proceeds, but they offered no proof of this claim. The banks responded by depositing $23,911 with the court. These funds were delivered to Grand Harbour. Later, the Groggs filed a petition for bankruptcy in a federal bankruptcy court and were granted a discharge of debts. The

Groggs then filed a "motion to return funds to debtors" but provided no evidence that their debt to Grand Harbour had been included in the bankruptcy discharge. What is Grand Harbour's best argument in response to the Groggs' motion? [*Grand Harbour Condominium Owners Association, Inc. v. Grogg*, 2016 -Ohio- 1386 (Ohio Ct.App. 2016)] (See *Laws Assisting Creditors*.)

15–8. The Reorganization Plan. Under the "plain language" of the Bankruptcy Code, at least one class of creditors must accept a Chapter 11 plan for it to be confirmed. Transwest Resort Properties, Inc., and four related companies filed a petition for bankruptcy under Chapter 11. The five debtors filed a joint reorganization plan. Several classes of their creditors approved the plan. Grasslawn Lodging, LLC, filed a claim based on its loan to two of the companies and objected to the plan. Grasslawn further asserted that the Code's confirmation requirement applied on a "per debtor," not a "per plan," basis, and because Grasslawn was the only class member for two of the debtors, the plan in this case did not meet the test. Can the court order a "cram-down"? Why or why not? [*In the Matter of Transwest Resort Properties, Inc.*, 881 F.3d 724 (9th Cir. 2018)] (See *Reorganizations*.)

15–9. A Question of Ethics—The IDDR Approach and Reorganization. *Jevic Transportation Corporation filed a petition in a federal bankruptcy court for a Chapter 11 reorganization. A group of former Jevic truck drivers, including Casimir Czyzewski, filed a suit and won a judgment against the firm for unpaid wages. This judgment entitled the workers to payment from Jevic's estate ahead of its unsecured creditors. Later, some of Jevic's unsecured creditors filed a suit against some of its other unsecured creditors. The plaintiffs won a judgment on the ground that the firm's payments to the defendants constituted fraudulent transfers and preferences. These parties then negotiated, without the truck drivers' consent, a settlement agreement that called for the workers to receive nothing on their claims while the creditors were to be paid proportionately. [Czyzewski v. Jevic Holding Corp., __ U.S. __, 137 S.Ct. 973, 197 L.Ed.2d 398 (2017)] (See Reorganizations.)*

(a) Was it ethical of the truck drivers to obtain a judgment entitling them to payment ahead of the unsecured creditors? Why or why not?

(b) Was it ethical of the unsecured creditors to agree that the workers would receive nothing on their claims? Use the IDDR approach to decide.

Time-Limited Group Assignment

15–10. Student Loan Debt. Cathy Coleman took out loans to complete her college education. After graduation, Coleman was irregularly employed as a teacher before filing a petition in a federal bankruptcy court under Chapter 13. The court confirmed a five-year plan under which Coleman was required to commit all of her disposable income to paying the student loans. Less than a year later, when Coleman was laid off, she still owed more than $100,000 to Educational Credit Management Corporation. Coleman asked the court to discharge the debt on the ground that it would be an undue hardship for her to pay it. (See *Liquidation Proceedings*.)

(a) The first group will determine when a debtor normally is entitled to a discharge under Chapter 13.

(b) The second group will discuss whether student loans are dischargeable and when "undue hardship" is a legitimate ground for an exception to the general rule.

(c) The third group will outline the goals of bankruptcy law and make an argument, based on these facts and principles, in support of Coleman's request.

Alberto Corelli offers to pay $2,500 to purchase a painting titled *Moonrise* from Tara Shelley, an artist whose works have been causing a stir in the art world. Shelley accepts Corelli's offer. Assuming that the contract has met all of the requirements for a valid contract, answer the following questions.

1. **Minors.** Corelli is a minor when he purchases the painting. Is the contract void? Is it voidable? What is the difference between these two conditions? A month after his eighteenth birthday, Corelli decides that he would rather have the $2,500 than the painting. He informs Shelley that he is disaffirming the contract and requests that Shelley return the $2,500 to him. When she refuses to do so, Corelli brings a court action to recover the $2,500. What will the court likely decide in this situation? Why?

2. **Capacity.** Both parties are adults, and the contract, which is in writing, states that Corelli will pay Shelley the $2,500 the following day. In the meantime, Shelley allows Corelli to take the painting home with him. The next day, Corelli's son returns the painting to Shelley, stating that he is canceling the contract. He explains that lately his father has been behaving strangely, that he seems to be mentally incompetent at times, and that he clearly was not acting rationally when he bought the painting, which he could not afford. Is the contract enforceable? Discuss fully.

3. **Agreement in E-Contracts.** Both parties are adults. Shelley, on her website, offers to sell the painting for $2,500. Corelli accepts the offer by clicking on an "I accept" box on the computer screen displaying the offer. Among other terms, the online offer includes a forum-selection clause stating that any disputes under the contract are to be resolved by a court in California, the state in which Shelley lives. After Corelli receives the painting, he notices a smear of paint across the lower corner that was not visible in the digitized image that appeared on Shelley's website. Corelli calls Shelley, tells her about the smear, and says that he wants to cancel the contract and return the painting.

   When Shelley refuses to cooperate, Corelli sues her in a Texas state court, seeking to rescind the contract. Shelley claims that any suit against her must be filed in a California court in accordance with the forum-selection clause. Corelli maintains that the forum-selection clause is unconscionable and should not be enforced. What factors will the court consider in deciding this case? What will the court likely decide? Would it matter whether Corelli read the terms of the online offer before clicking on "I accept"?

4. **Impossibility of Performance.** Both parties are adults, and the contract is in writing. The contract calls for Shelley to deliver the painting to Corelli's gallery in two weeks. Corelli has already arranged to sell the painting to a third party for $4,000 (a $1,500 profit), but it must be available for the third party in two weeks, or the sale will not go through. Shelley knows this but does not deliver the painting at the time promised. Corelli sues Shelley for $1,500 in damages. Shelley claims that performance was impossible because her mother became seriously ill and required Shelley's care. Who will win this lawsuit, and why?

Nondisclosure Agreements

Nondisclosure agreements (NDAs), or confidentiality agreements, are contracts that require one or more parties to keep quiet about a stated piece of information, whether it is a company's trade secrets or a politician's extramarital affairs. NDAs are quite common and can be used in a variety of business settings to prevent a party from disclosing information deemed to be confidential.

Types of Nondisclosure Agreements

Nondisclosure agreements can be classified in several ways, including the following:

- Bilateral (mutual) NDAs involve two parties and restrict both parties from disclosing the confidential information.
- Multilateral NDAs involve three or more parties.
- Unilateral NDAs prevent only one party from divulging the confidential information.

Bilateral NDAs are common when businesses are considering some kind of joint venture or merger, or when the parties anticipate sharing intellectual property with business partners and contractors. Unilateral NDAs are commonly used in settlement agreements, to prevent a party from discussing the terms of settlement. They are also often used with employees, to prohibit them from disclosing a firm's proprietary information and secrets.

Consider an example: Emergency Medical Training Solutions (EMTS) provides courses and training for emergency medical service providers. One of its courses qualifies students to take the national emergency medical technician (EMT) exam and become a licensed EMT. To fulfill its accreditation requirement, EMTS entered into a consortium agreement with Arlington [Texas] Career Institute (ACI).

EMTS hired Sheila Elliott to be the program director of the consortium and required her to sign NDAs with EMTS and ACI. The NDAs specified that Elliott would not use or disclose processes, information, records, or specifications of the consortium except in the course of her employment and for the benefit of the consortium. Several years later, Elliott wrote a letter to the chief executive officer of EMTS requesting a raise, in which she took credit for keeping EMTS "running smooth and profitable."

The day after she sent the letter, Elliott resigned and filed a complaint against EMTS with the Texas Department of State Health Services. She also began making public allegations that EMTS engaged in unlawful business practices, communicating these claims to ACI, to former EMTS students, and on the Internet. Because of Elliott's allegations, ACI withdrew from the consortium agreement with EMTS, and EMTS lost profits.

EMTS sued Elliott for breaching the NDAs. Elliott, though, argued that she had a right to free speech related to the training of EMTs, which was a matter of public concern. A Texas trial court held in favor of EMTS, but the finding was reversed on appeal. Ultimately, the Texas Supreme Court overturned the state appellate court and held that EMTS had established by clear and convincing evidence that Elliott had violated the NDAs. The state's highest court remanded the case to the trial court to determine the proper relief.[1]

---

1. *S&S Emergency Training Services, Inc. v. Elliott*, 62 Tex.Sup.J. 289, 564 S.W.3d 843 (2018).

Enforceability of Nondisclosure Agreements

Most state courts enforce NDAs that are reasonable and that do not require parties to keep silent about illegal activities. The common law of contracts applies to NDAs, of course. Thus, if there is a problem with contractual capacity, mistake, or undue influence, the NDA will not be enforceable. In addition, some courts will refuse to enforce an NDA that is overly burdensome in its restrictions—such as when there is no time or geographical limitation[2]—much as they would refuse to enforce an unreasonable noncompete clause.

Ethical Connection

The use of NDAs has been on the rise for decades, and a significant proportion of the U.S. workforce are bound to their companies by NDAs. But the tide may be turning. After a number of high-profile sexual assault and sexual harassment cases in Hollywood—and media reports of how many female victims were silenced by NDAs—the #MeToo movement gained momentum.

Nearly every state now restricts NDAs in settlements of claims involving sexual harassment and sexual assault. California started the trend when it banned NDAs in cases involving sexual assault, sexual harassment, and sex discrimination. New York's law permits the use of such confidentiality agreements only if requested by the *victim* of sexual assault or harassment. Washington state's statute allows victims of sexual assault or harassment to testify and provide discovery about the incident regardless of any nondisclosure or arbitration agreement.[3]

The #MeToo movement has also used social media to pressure large companies and law firms—such as Munger, Tolles & Olson, a large California law firm—to stop requiring employees to sign NDAs.

Ethics Question *Is sexual assault or sexual harassment more unethical than other types of misconduct, such as mishandling company finances, lying to clients, or stealing? Explain.*

Critical Thinking *Why would the women who were sexually assaulted or harassed have signed the NDA?*

---

2. See, for example, *Foster Cable Services, Inc. v. Deville*, 368 F.Supp.3d 1265 (W.D.Ark. 2019).
3. Washington Revised Code Section 4.24.840.

The Business and Employment Environment

LEGAL ENVIRONMENT

CROSS · MILLER

Chapter 16

Small Businesses and Franchises

A goal of many business students is to become an **entrepreneur,** one who initiates and assumes the financial risk of a new business enterprise and undertakes to provide or control its management. Many of today's biggest corporations, such as Apple, Alphabet (Google), and Amazon, were originally very small companies started by entrepreneurs. Jeff Bezos, founder of Amazon, and Steve Jobs, founder of Apple, started their companies in their garages.

One of the first decisions an entrepreneur must make is which form of business organization will be most appropriate for the new endeavor. In selecting an organizational form, the entrepreneur will consider a number of factors. These include (1) ease of creation, (2) the liability of the owners, (3) tax considerations, and (4) the ability to raise capital. Keep these factors in mind as you read this unit and learn about the various forms of business organization. Remember, too, in

considering these business forms that the primary motive of an entrepreneur is to make profits.

Traditionally, entrepreneurs have used three major business forms—the sole proprietorship, the partnership, and the corporation. In this chapter, we examine sole proprietorships and partnerships. We also look at franchises. Although the franchise is not, strictly speaking, a business organizational form, it is widely used today by entrepreneurs to start a business.

16–1 General Considerations for Small Businesses

Most small businesses begin as sole proprietorships. Once the business is under way, the owner discovers several disadvantages with being a sole proprietorship, including unlimited personal liability and difficulty raising capital. The owner and any additional investors may then want to establish a more formal organization, such as a limited partnership (LP), a limited liability partnership (LLP), a limited liability company (LLC), or a corporation. These forms of business limit the owner's personal liability, or legal responsibility, for business debts and obligations. Each business form has its own advantages and disadvantages, but legal limited liability generally is necessary for those who wish to raise outside capital.

16–1a Requirements for All Business Forms

Any business, whatever its form, has to meet a variety of legal requirements, which typically relate to the following:

1. Business name registration.
2. Occupational licensing.

3. State tax registration (for instance, to obtain permits for collecting and remitting sales taxes).
4. Health and environmental permits.
5. Zoning and building codes.
6. Import/export regulations.

If the business has employees, the owner must also comply with a host of laws governing the workplace.

16–1b Protecting Intellectual Property

Protecting rights in intellectual property is a central concern for many small businesses. For instance, software companies and app developers depend on their copyrights and patents to protect their investments in the research and development required to create new programs. Without copyright or patent protection, a competitor or a customer could simply copy the software or app.

Trademarks Choosing a trademark or service mark and making sure that it is protected under trademark law can be crucial to the success of a new business venture. Indeed, a factor to consider in choosing a name for a business entity is whether the business name will be used as a trademark. The general rule is that a trademark cannot be the same as another's mark or so similar that confusion might result.

For the most protection, trademarks should be registered with the U.S. Patent and Trademark Office (PTO). If a mark is federally registered, the owner may use the symbol ® with the mark. This well-known symbol puts others on notice of the registration and helps to prevent trademark infringement. An owner who has not registered can use the symbol ™. Registration with the PTO should be renewed five years after the initial registration and at ten-year intervals thereafter.

Trade Secrets Much of the value of a small business may lie in its trade secrets, such as information about product development, production processes and techniques, and customer lists. Preserving the secrecy of the information is necessary for legal protection.

As a practical matter, trade secrets must be divulged to key employees. Thus, any business runs the risk that those employees might disclose the secrets to competitors—or even set up competing businesses themselves.

To protect their trade secrets, companies may require employees who have access to trade secrets to agree in their employment contracts never to divulge those secrets. A small business may also choose to include a covenant not to compete in an employment contract. A noncompete clause will help to protect against the possibility that a key employee will go to work for a competitor or set up a competing business.

16–1c Obtaining Loans

Raising capital is critical to the growth of most small businesses. In the early days of a business, the sole proprietor may be able to contribute sufficient capital, but as the business becomes successful, more funds may be needed. The owner may want to raise capital from external sources to expand the business. One way to do this is to borrow funds.

Obtaining a bank loan is beneficial for small businesses because it allows the owner to retain full ownership and control of the business. Note, though, that the bank may place some restrictions on future business decisions as a condition of granting the loan. In addition, bank loans may not be available for some businesses. Banks are usually reluctant to lend significant sums to businesses that are not yet established. Even if a bank is willing to make such a loan, the bank may require personal guaranty contracts from the owner, putting the owner's personal assets at risk.

Loans with desirable terms may be available from the U.S. Small Business Administration (SBA). One SBA program provides loans of up to $25,000 to businesspersons who are women, low-income individuals, or members of minority groups. Be aware that the SBA requires business owners to put some of their own funds at risk in the business. In addition, many states offer small-business grants to individuals starting a business.

16–2 Sole Proprietorships

In the earliest stages, as mentioned, a small business may operate as a **sole proprietorship,** which is the simplest form of business. In this form, the owner is the business. Thus, anyone who does business without creating a separate business organization has a sole proprietorship. The law considers all new, single-owner businesses to be sole proprietorships unless the owner affirmatively adopts some other form.

More than two-thirds of all U.S. businesses are sole proprietorships. Sole proprietors can own and manage any type of business from an informal home-office or Web-based undertaking to a large restaurant or construction firm. Most sole proprietorships are small enterprises, however. About 99 percent of the sole proprietorships in the United States have revenues of less than $1 million per year.

16–2a Advantages of the Sole Proprietorship

A major advantage of the sole proprietorship is that the proprietor owns the entire business and receives all of the profits (because she or he assumes all of the risk). In addition, starting a sole proprietorship is easier and less costly than starting any other kind of business because few legal formalities are required. Generally, no documents need to be filed with the government to start a sole proprietorship.[1]

Taxes A sole proprietor pays only personal income taxes (including Social Security and Medicare taxes) on the business's profits. The profits are reported as personal income on the proprietor's personal income tax return. In other words, the business itself need not file an income tax return. Sole proprietors are allowed to establish retirement accounts that are tax-exempt until the funds are withdrawn.

---

1. Small sole proprietorships may, however, need to comply with zoning requirements, obtain appropriate licenses from the state, and the like.

Like any form of business enterprise, a sole proprietorship can be liable for other taxes, such as those collected and applied to the disbursement of unemployment compensation. Whether liability for

the unpaid unemployment compensation taxes of a sole proprietorship remains with the seller or must be assumed by the buyer was at issue in the following case.

A. Gadley Enterprises, Inc. v. Department of Labor and Industry, Office of Unemployment Compensation Tax Services

Commonwealth Court of Pennsylvania, 2016 WL 55591 (2016).

In the Language of the Court
SIMPSON, Judge.
* * * *

[Julianne Gresh (Predecessor)] operated [Romper Room Day Care (Romper Room)], a childcare center, as a sole proprietorship for 12 years. Predecessor owed the [Pennsylvania Department of Labor and Industry, Office of Unemployment Compensation Tax Services (Department)] substantial unpaid UC [unemployment compensation] contributions, interest and penalties. She admitted liability and entered payment plans with the Department * * * . Pursuant to these payment plans, she made monthly payments in the minimal amount of $50. Predecessor was on the verge of losing her license to operate, and sought another entity to operate the location as a childcare facility.

[A. Gadley Enterprises, Inc. (Purchaser)] operated a childcare center, Young Environment Learning Center, in Erie, Pennsylvania. Purchaser decided to purchase assets from Predecessor in order to open a satellite location of Young Environmental Learning Center at the prior location of Romper Room. Purchaser and Predecessor executed an asset purchase agreement (Agreement).

Through the Agreement, Purchaser paid a total of $37,000 for Predecessor's tangible and intangible assets. This total was comprised of $10,000 for the use of the name "Romper Room," $10,790 for a covenant not to compete, and $17,210 for tangible assets listed on [an attached] Inventory List.

* * * The Inventory List did not include any of Predecessor's personal assets other than those used in the operation of Romper Room.

* * * Four days *after* executing the Agreement, * * * Predecessor notified the Department of the sale.

* * * The Department issued Purchaser a Notice of Assessment (Notice) in the amount of $43,370.49 for UC contributions, interest and penalties owed by Predecessor. The Notice stated Purchaser was liable because it purchased 51% or more of Predecessor's assets.

In response, Purchaser filed a petition [with the Department] for reassessment.
* * * *

Based on the evidence presented at the hearing [held on the petition], the Department issued its decision and order denying the petition for reassessment.
* * * *

Purchaser then filed a petition to review to this Court.
* * * *

[43 Pennsylvania Statutes Section 788.3(a), part of the state's Unemployment Compensation Law] provides:

(a) Every employer * * * , who shall sell in bulk fifty-one percent or more of his assets, including but not limited to, any stock of goods, wares or merchandise of any kind, fixtures, machinery, equipment, building or real estate, shall give the department ten (10) days' notice of the sale prior to completion of the transfer * * * . The employer shall present to the purchaser of such property, a certificate * * * showing that all reports have been filed and contributions, interest and penalties paid to the date of the proposed transfer. The failure of the purchaser to require such certificate shall render such purchaser liable to the department for the unpaid contributions, interest and penalties.

* * * *

There is no dispute that Purchaser did not obtain a clearance certificate reflecting Predecessor's payment of UC liability. There is also no dispute that Predecessor owed the Department for outstanding UC contributions, interest and penalties in the amount of $43,370.49 at the time of the sale.
* * * *

Purchaser argues substantial evidence does not support the Department's finding that it purchased more than 51% of the [Predecessor's] assets.
* * * *

The Agreement establishes that the Inventory List sets forth all business assets of Predecessor. Gresh confirmed the Inventory List was a complete list of assets used in the operation of her business.

The Inventory List reflects a total value of assets equaling $19,210. * * * The parties reduced the purchase price by $2,000 to account for the reduced value of the assets when Purchaser removed certain assets from the complete Inventory List. Purchaser acquired all the assets included in the Inventory List, other than those removed, for $17,210. The amount constitutes approximately 90% of the value of the complete list of assets ($19,210 × .9 = $17,289).

The Agreement, supplemented by corroborating [supporting] testimony, constitutes substantial evidence to support the Department's finding that the sale qualified as a bulk sale of more than 51% of Predecessor's assets.
* * * *

Purchaser also argues the Department erred in construing the term "assets" in the bulk sales provision to include only business assets when determining whether a sale met the 51% threshold. Purchaser asserts the provision does not differentiate between business and personal assets of an employer and there is no legal distinction when the employer is a sole proprietor.

* * * *

* * * The definition of "employer" [in the UC Law] includes a sole proprietor like Predecessor.

The word "assets" is not defined in the [UC] Law.

[In Section 788.3(a)] the term "assets" precedes a list of examples, followed by the phrase "including but not limited to."

* * * *

* * * The examples * * * indicate that the term "assets" refers to business assets. This conclusion is buttressed [reinforced] by the context of the statute as a whole, which pertains to employers operating businesses and paying employees as part of their business operations.

The factual circumstances surrounding the sale also indicate the term "assets" means "business assets." Here, the context is the sale of a business, in the childcare industry, to another business engaged in the same industry that intends to operate a childcare facility at the location of the former business. The Agreement reflects the intention of the parties that Purchaser would operate the childcare facility as a satellite location. [Emphasis added.]

* * * *

* * * The provision does not treat sole proprietors differently than other employers. The provision contains no exemption of liability for a purchaser when an employer operates as a sole proprietorship. Nor does it contain an exemption from liability when the former employer entered a repayment plan with the Department.

Moreover, Purchaser's interpretation does not consider *the purpose of the bulk*

sales provision. That purpose is to ensure an employer does not divest itself of assets without satisfying outstanding liabilities, either itself or by the purchaser. This Court agrees with the Department that Gresh's repayment agreement in the minimal amount of $50 per month does not satisfy the UC liability. [Emphasis added.]

* * * *

In sum, the Department's construction of assets as business assets is reasonable and consistent with the context and purpose of [the] bulk sales provision. Purchaser's failure to obtain a clearance certificate rendered it liable for Predecessor's unpaid UC contributions, interest and penalties, regardless of Predecessor's repayment agreement. Therefore, this Court upholds the Department's interpretation of the bulk sales provision.

* * * *

* * * For the foregoing reasons, we affirm the Department.

Legal Reasoning Questions

1. As is clear from the law applied in this case, and the result, the liability of a business for unpaid taxes "follows the assets." Why?

2. What action can Gadley take now to avoid suffering the loss of the funds required to cover Gresh's unpaid taxes?

3. What action should a buyer take *before* purchasing the assets of a business to avoid liability for the seller's unpaid taxes?

Flexibility A sole proprietorship offers more flexibility than does a partnership or a corporation. The sole proprietor is free to make any decision she or he wishes concerning the business—including what kind of business to pursue, whom to hire, and when to take a vacation. The sole proprietor can sell or transfer all or part of the business to another party at any time without seeking approval from anyone else. In contrast, approval is typically required from partners in a partnership and from shareholders in a corporation.

16–2b Disadvantages of the Sole Proprietorship

The major disadvantage of the sole proprietorship is that the proprietor alone bears the burden of any losses or liabilities incurred by the business enterprise. In other words, the sole proprietor has unlimited liability for all obligations that arise in doing business. Any lawsuit against the business or its employees can lead to unlimited personal liability for the owner of a sole proprietorship.

■ **Case in Point 16.1** Michael Sark operated a logging business as a sole proprietorship. To acquire equipment for the business, Sark and his wife, Paula, borrowed funds from Quality Car & Truck Leasing, Inc. Eventually, the logging business failed, and Sark was unable to pay his creditors, including Quality. The Sarks filed a bankruptcy petition and sold their house (valued at $203,500) to their son, Michael, Jr., for one dollar but continued to live in it.

Three months later, Quality obtained a judgment in an Ohio state court against the Sarks for $150,480. Quality also filed a claim to set aside the transfer of the house to Michael, Jr., as a fraudulent conveyance. The trial court ruled in Quality's favor, and the Sarks appealed. A state intermediate appellate court affirmed. The Sarks were personally liable for the debts of the sole proprietorship and could not protect assets from creditors by fraudulently conveying their home to a relative.[2] ■

---

2. *Quality Car & Truck Leasing, Inc. v. Sark*, 2013 -Ohio- 44 (Ct.App. 2013)

Personal Assets at Risk Creditors can pursue the owner's personal assets to satisfy any business debts. Although sole proprietors may obtain insurance to protect the business, liability can easily exceed policy limits. This unlimited liability is a major factor to be considered in choosing a business form.

■ **Example 16.2** Sheila Fowler operates a golf shop near a world-class golf course as a sole proprietorship. One of Fowler's employees fails to secure a display of golf clubs. They fall on Dean Maheesh, a professional golfer, and seriously injure him. If Maheesh sues Fowler's shop and wins, Fowler's personal liability could easily exceed the limits of her insurance policy. Fowler could lose not only her business, but also her house, car, and any other personal assets that can be attached to pay the judgment. ■

Lack of Continuity and Limited Ability to Raise Capital The sole proprietorship also has the disadvantage of lacking continuity after the death of the proprietor. When the owner dies, so does the business—it is automatically dissolved.

Another disadvantage is that in raising capital, the proprietor is limited to his or her personal funds and any loans that he or she can obtain for the business. Lenders may be unwilling to make loans to sole proprietorships, particularly start-ups, because the sole proprietor risks unlimited personal liability and may not be able to pay. (See this chapter's *Digital Update* feature for a discussion of one court's refusal to discharge a loan made to a sole proprietor who had declared bankruptcy.)

Digital Update — A Sole Proprietorship, Facebook Poker, and Bankruptcy

One major downside of a sole proprietorship is that it is more difficult for a sole proprietor to obtain funding for start-up and expansion. Moreover, if funding is obtained through loans, the sole proprietor is exposed to personal liability.

Personal Liability Exposure for an Online Start-up

Consider a case that came before the United States bankruptcy court in Massachusetts.[a] Michael Dewhurst, living in Raynham, Massachusetts, sometimes did computer work for Gerald Knappik. Dewhurst decided to start a new business venture—the commercial development of an online poker-playing application. Dewhurst envisioned an application that would enable multiple individuals to play poker together over the Internet through Facebook. Dewhurst informed Knappik of his business plan and predicted that his Facebook poker application "was going to be something very big."

Knappik initially loaned $50,000 to Dewhurst for the project. The loan agreement stated, "The sole purpose of this loan agreement is to provide funds on a personal level for the startup of said business project, in conjunction with borrower's personal funds, not limited to startup costs, operating expenses, advertising costs."

That was the first of a series of personal loans that totaled $220,000.

Dewhurst had repaid only $9,000 on the total outstanding debt when he filed for bankruptcy. Ultimately, the bankruptcy court ascertained that at least $120,000 of the loans that were supposed to be used exclusively for the Facebook poker project had been used for other activities. Furthermore, Dewhurst kept "no contemporaneous records of his disbursements and uses of this cash, no cash journal, ledger, or disbursement slips of any kind."

The Lender Objects to a Bankruptcy Discharge of Monies Owed

During bankruptcy proceedings, Knappik requested that the bankruptcy court deny discharge of Dewhurst's debts to him. Upon review, the court stated that "Dewhurst's failure to keep and preserve adequate records makes it impossible to reconstruct an accurate and complete account of financial affairs and business transactions." The bankruptcy judge ultimately denied discharge of $120,000 of the debt owed to Knappik. Thus, a sole proprietor's failed attempt to create an online poker-playing application led to personal liability even after he had filed for bankruptcy.

Critical Thinking *Sole proprietorships, as well as other businesses, routinely seek funding for online projects. How can the individuals involved avoid personal liability?*

a. *In re Dewhurst*, 528 Bankr. 211 (D.Mass. 2015). See also, *In re Zutrau*, 563 Bankr. 431 (1st Cir. 2017).

16-3 Partnerships

A *partnership* arises from an agreement, express or implied, between two or more persons to carry on a business for a profit. Partners are co-owners of the business and have joint control over its operation and the right to share in its profits. The traditional form of partnership discussed in this chapter is commonly referred to as a *general partnership* to distinguish it from existing limited liability forms of partnership.

16-3a Basic Partnership Concepts

Partnerships are governed both by common law concepts—in particular, those relating to agency—and by statutory law. As in so many other areas of business law, the National Conference of Commissioners on Uniform State Laws has drafted uniform laws for partnerships, and these have been widely adopted by the states.

Agency Concepts and Partnership Law When two or more persons agree to do business as partners, they enter into a special relationship with one another. To an extent, their relationship is similar to an *agency relationship* (to be discussed in a later chapter), because each partner is deemed to be the agent of the other partners and of the partnership. Thus, concepts of agency law apply—specifically, the individuals (agents) are charged with knowledge of, and responsibility for, acts carried out within the scope of the partnership relationship. In their relationships with one another, partners, like agents, are bound by *fiduciary duties*, meaning they are required to act primarily in the best interests of one another.

In one important way, however, partnership law differs from agency law. The partners in a partnership agree to commit funds or other assets, labor, and skills to the business with the understanding that profits and losses will be shared. Thus, each partner has an *ownership interest* in the firm. In a nonpartnership agency relationship, the agent usually does not have an ownership interest in the business and is not obligated to bear a portion of ordinary business losses.

The Uniform Partnership Act The Uniform Partnership Act (UPA) governs the operation of partnerships *in the absence of express agreement* and has done much to reduce controversies in the law relating to partnerships. A majority of the states have enacted the amended version of the UPA.

Definition of a Partnership The UPA defines a **partnership** as "an association of two or more persons to carry on as co-owners a business for profit" [UPA 101(6)]. Note that the UPA's definition of *person* includes corporations, so a corporation can be a partner in a partnership [UPA 101(10)]. The *intent* to associate is a key element of a partnership, and one cannot join a partnership unless all other partners consent [UPA 401(i)].

Essential Elements of a Partnership Questions may sometimes arise as to whether a business enterprise is a legal partnership, especially when there is no formal, written partnership agreement. To determine whether a partnership exists, courts usually look for the following three essential elements, which are implicit in the UPA's definition:

1. A sharing of profits or losses.
2. A joint ownership of the business.
3. An equal right to be involved in the management of the business.

If the evidence in a particular case is insufficient to establish all three factors, the UPA provides a set of guidelines to be used.

The court in the following case considered these and other factors to determine whether a partnership existed between two participants in a new restaurant venture.

Case 16.2

Harun v. Rashid

Court of Appeals of Texas, Dallas, 2018 WL 329292 (2018).

Background and Facts Mohammed Harun was interested in opening a new restaurant, Spice-N-Rice, in Irving, Texas, but he lacked the financial resources to do so. He asked Sharif Rashid if Rashid was interested in financing the venture. Rashid was interested and provided about $60,000 in funding. In addition, he helped negotiate a lease for the restaurant, was a signatory on its bank account, paid for advertising, and bought furniture, equipment, and supplies.

Case 16.2 Continues

Case 16.2 Continued

Rashid also hired a bookkeeper to handle the restaurant's accounting. The bookkeeper later expressed concern about Harun's reporting of Spice-N-Rice's income on his personal tax return. Shortly thereafter, Harun removed Rashid from the bank account and locked him out of the restaurant's premises. Rashid filed a suit in a Texas state court against Harun and Spice-N-Rice, alleging the existence of a partnership and a breach of fiduciary duty. Harun denied that he and Rashid had ever been partners. The court ruled that a partnership existed and awarded damages to Rashid. The defendants appealed.

In the Language of the Court

Opinion by Justice *SCHENCK*.

 * * * *

In determining whether a partnership was created, we consider several factors, including (1) the parties' receipt or right to receive a share of profits of the business; (2) any expression of an intent to be partners in the business; (3) participation or right to participate in control of the business; (4) any agreement to share or sharing losses of the business or liability for claims by third parties against the business; and (5) any agreement to contribute or contributing money or property to the business. *Proof of each of these factors is not necessary to establish a partnership.* [Emphasis added.]

 * * * *

At trial, Rashid presented evidence through his testimony that: (a) Harun approached him indicating he had found a good location to open a restaurant and needed a partner to finance the operation; (b) Harun asked him to be his partner; (c) he and Harun were equal business partners in the restaurant; (d) he and Harun agreed to share equally in the profits and losses; (e) he and Harun met with the leasing agents to negotiate the lease of the restaurant space; (f) he and Harun had equal access to the restaurant's bank account; (g) he hired and communicated with the bookkeeper; (h) he was very involved in preparing paperwork for the restaurant; (i) he paid restaurant-related bills, and purchased furniture and equipment for the restaurant; (j) he was not an employee of the restaurant or Harun, nor did he receive any pay for the work he performed on behalf of the restaurant; and (k) he invested approximately $60,000 in the business. We conclude the trial court's finding a partnership existed between Harun and Rashid is supported by more than a scintilla [speck] of evidence.

Finally, * * * appellants [Harun and Spice-N-Rice] argue Rashid was not entitled to an award of damages because there was no partnership and thus there could be no breach of fiduciary duty. As we have concluded there is sufficient evidence Harun and Rashid were partners in Spice-N-Rice, we overrule appellants' * * * issue.

Decision and Remedy   *A state intermediate appellate court affirmed the lower court's award to Rashid of actual damages of $36,000 (the difference between his initial investment of $60,000 and the amount repaid by Huran), punitive damages of $36,000, and attorneys' fees of $79,768.64, plus interest and costs.*

Critical Thinking

* **Legal Environment**   *Harun's income tax return and other documents prepared by the bookkeeper on behalf of Spice-N-Rice identified the business as a sole proprietorship. Should the appellate court have reversed the finding of a partnership on this basis? Explain.*
* **What If the Facts Were Different?**   *Suppose that Huran had complained that there was no evidence of an agreement between himself and Rashid to share losses. Would the result have been different? Why or why not?*

The Sharing of Profits and Losses. The sharing of both profits and losses from a business creates a presumption that a partnership exists. ■ **Case in Point 16.3** David Tubb, representing Superior Shooting Systems, Inc., entered into an agreement with Aspect International, Inc., to create a business that would make and sell ammunition to the public. Their contract stated that both companies would participate in the business and split the profits equally, but it did not say explicitly that they would share the losses. It also did not specify what type of entity the business would be.

A dispute arose between the two companies, and the matter ended up in court. A Texas appellate court held that the two corporations had created a partnership even though there was no express agreement to share in losses. Because they had agreed to share control and ownership of the business and to split the profits equally, they would also have to share the losses equally.[3] ∎

A court will not presume that a partnership exists if shared profits were received as payment of any of the following [UPA 202(c)(3)]:

1. A debt by installments or interest on a loan.
2. Wages of an employee or payment for the services of an independent contractor.
3. Rent to a landlord.
4. An annuity to a surviving spouse or representative of a deceased partner.
5. A sale of the **goodwill** (the valuable reputation of a business viewed as an intangible asset) of a business or property.

∎ **Example 16.4** A debtor, Mason Snopel, owes a creditor, Alice Burns, $5,000 on an unsecured debt. They agree that Snopel will pay 10 percent of his monthly business profits to Burns until the loan with interest has been repaid. Although Snopel and Burns are sharing profits from the business, they are not presumed to be partners. ∎

Joint Property Ownership. Joint ownership of property does not in and of itself create a partnership [UPA 202(c)(1) and (2)]. The parties' intentions are key. ∎ **Example 16.5** Chiang and Burke jointly own farmland and lease it to a farmer for a share of the profits from the farming operation in lieu of fixed rental payments. This arrangement normally would not make Chiang, Burke, and the farmer partners. ∎

Entity versus Aggregate At common law, a partnership was treated only as an aggregate of individuals and never as a separate legal entity. Thus, at common law a lawsuit could never be brought by or against the firm in its own name. Each individual partner had to sue or be sued.

Today, in contrast, a majority of the states follow the UPA and treat a partnership as an entity for most purposes. For instance, a partnership usually can sue or be sued, collect judgments, and have all accounting performed in the name of the partnership entity [UPA 201, 307(a)].

As an entity, a partnership may hold the title to real or personal property in its name rather than in the names of the individual partners. Additionally, federal procedural laws permit the partnership to be treated as an entity in suits in federal courts and bankruptcy proceedings.

Tax Treatment of Partnerships Modern law does treat a partnership as an aggregate of the individual partners rather than a separate legal entity in one situation—for federal income tax purposes. The partnership is a pass-through entity and not a tax-paying entity. A **pass-through entity** is a business entity that has no tax liability. The entity's income is passed through to the owners, who pay income taxes on it.

Thus, the income or losses the partnership incurs are "passed through" the entity framework and attributed to the partners on their individual tax returns. The partnership itself pays no taxes and is responsible only for filing an **information return** with the Internal Revenue Service.

A partner's profit from the partnership (whether distributed or not) is taxed as individual income to the individual partner. Similarly, partners can deduct a share of the partnership's losses on their individual tax returns (in proportion to their partnership interests).

16–3b Formation and Operation

A partnership is a voluntary association of individuals. As such, it is formed by the agreement of the partners. As a general rule, agreements to form a partnership can be *oral, written,* or *implied by conduct.* Some partnership agreements, however, such as one authorizing partners to transfer interests in real property, must be in writing to be legally enforceable.

A partnership agreement, also known as **articles of partnership,** can include almost any terms that the parties wish, unless they are illegal or contrary to public policy or statute [UPA 103]. The provisions commonly specify the amount of capital that each partner is contributing and the percentage of profits and losses of the business that each partner will receive.

The rights and duties of partners are governed largely by the specific terms of their partnership agreement. In the absence of provisions to the contrary in the partnership agreement, the law imposes certain rights and duties, as discussed in the following subsections. The character and nature of the partnership business generally influence the application of these rights and duties.

Duration of the Partnership The partnership agreement can specify the duration of the partnership by stating that it will continue until a designated date or until the

---

3. *Tubb v. Aspect International, Inc.,* 2017 WL 192919 (Tex.App.—Tyler 2017).

completion of a particular project. This is called a *partnership for a term*. Generally, withdrawing from a partnership for a term prematurely (before the expiration date) constitutes a breach of the agreement, and the responsible partner can be held liable for any resulting losses [UPA 602(b)(2)]. If no fixed duration is specified, the partnership is a *partnership at will*. A partnership at will can be dissolved at any time without liability.

Partnership by Estoppel When a third person has reasonably and detrimentally relied on the representation that a nonpartner was part of a partnership, a court may conclude that a **partnership by estoppel** exists.

Liability Imposed. A partnership by estoppel may arise when a person who is not a partner holds himself or herself out as a partner and makes representations that third parties rely on. In this situation, a court may impose liability—but not partnership rights—on the alleged partner.

Nonpartner as an Agent. A partnership by estoppel may also be imposed when a partner represents, expressly or impliedly, that a nonpartner is a member of the firm. In this situation, the nonpartner may be regarded as an agent whose acts are binding on the partnership [UPA 308].

■ **Case in Point 16.6** Jackson Paper Manufacturing Company made paper used by Stonewall Packaging, LLC. Jackson and Stonewall had officers and directors in common, and they shared employees, property, and equipment. In reliance on Jackson's business reputation, Best Cartage, Inc., agreed to provide transportation services for Stonewall and bought thirty-seven tractor-trailers to use in fulfilling the contract. Best provided the services until Stonewall terminated the agreement.

Best filed a suit for breach of contract against Stonewall and Jackson, seeking $500,678 in unpaid invoices and consequential damages of $1,315,336 for the tractor-trailers it had purchased. Best argued that Stonewall and Jackson had a partnership by estoppel. The court agreed, finding that the "defendants combined labor, skills, and property to advance their alleged business partnership." Jackson had negotiated the agreement on Stonewall's behalf. Jackson also had bought real estate, equipment, and general supplies for Stonewall with no expectation that Stonewall would repay these expenditures. This was sufficient to prove a partnership by estoppel.[4] ■

Rights of Partners The rights of partners in a partnership relate to the following areas: management, interest

---

4. *Best Cartage, Inc. v. Stonewall Packaging, LLC*, 219 N.C.App. 429, 727 S.E.2d 291 (2012).

in the partnership, compensation, inspection of books, accounting, and property.

Management Rights. In a general partnership, all partners have equal rights in managing the partnership [UPA 401(f)]. Unless the partners agree otherwise, each partner has one vote in management matters *regardless of the proportional size of his or her interest in the firm.* In a large partnership, partners often agree to delegate daily management responsibilities to a management committee made up of one or more of the partners.

A majority vote controls decisions on ordinary matters connected with partnership business, unless otherwise specified in the agreement. Decisions that significantly change the nature of the partnership or that are outside the ordinary course of the partnership business, however, require the *unanimous* consent of the partners [UPA 301(2), 401(i), 401(j)]. For instance, unanimous consent is likely required for a partnership to admit new partners, to amend the partnership agreement, or to enter a new line of business.

Interest in the Partnership. Each partner is entitled to the proportion of business profits and losses that is specified in the partnership agreement. If the agreement does not apportion profits (indicate how the profits will be shared), the UPA provides that profits will be shared equally. If the agreement does not apportion losses, losses will be shared in the same ratio as profits [UPA 401(b)].

■ **Example 16.7** The partnership agreement between Rick and Brett provides for capital contributions of $60,000 from Rick and $40,000 from Brett. If the agreement is silent as to how Rick and Brett will share profits or losses, they will share both profits and losses equally.

In contrast, if the agreement provides for profits to be shared in the same ratio as capital contributions, 60 percent of the profits will go to Rick, and 40 percent will go to Brett. Unless the agreement provides otherwise, losses will be shared in the same ratio as profits. ■

Compensation. Devoting time, skill, and energy to partnership business is a partner's duty and generally is not a compensable service. Rather, as mentioned, a partner's income from the partnership takes the form of a distribution of profits according to the partner's share in the business.

Partners can, of course, agree otherwise. For instance, the managing partner of a law firm often receives a salary—in addition to her or his share of profits—for performing special administrative or managerial duties.

Inspection of the Books. Partnership books and records must be kept accessible to all partners. Each partner has the right to receive full and complete information concerning the conduct of all aspects of partnership business [UPA 403]. Partners have a duty to provide the information to the firm, which has a duty to preserve it and to keep accurate records.

The partnership books must be kept at the firm's principal business office (unless the partners agree otherwise). Every partner is entitled to inspect all books and records on demand and can make copies of the materials. The personal representative of a deceased partner's estate has the same right of access to partnership books and records that the decedent would have had [UPA 403].

Accounting of Partnership Assets or Profits. An accounting of partnership assets or profits is required to determine the value of each partner's share in the partnership. An accounting can be performed voluntarily, or it can be compelled by court order. Under UPA 405(b), a partner has the right to bring an action for an accounting during the term of the partnership, as well as on the partnership's dissolution.

Property Rights. Property acquired by a partnership is the property of the partnership and not of the partners individually [UPA 203]. Partnership property includes all property that was originally contributed to the partnership and anything later purchased by the partnership or in the partnership's name (except in rare circumstances) [UPA 204].

A partner may use or possess partnership property only on behalf of the partnership [UPA 401(g)]. A partner is not a co-owner of partnership property and has no right to sell, mortgage, or transfer partnership property to another [UPA 501].

Because partnership property is owned by the partnership and not by the individual partners, the property cannot be used to satisfy the personal debts of individual partners. A partner's creditor, however, can petition a court for a **charging order** to attach the partner's *interest* in the partnership to satisfy the partner's obligation [UPA 502]. A partner's interest in the partnership includes her or his proportionate share of any profits that are distributed. A partner can also assign her or his right to receive a share of the partnership profits to another to satisfy a debt.

16–3c Duties and Liabilities of Partners

The duties and liabilities of partners are derived from agency law. Each partner is an agent of every other partner and acts as both a principal and an agent in any business transaction within the scope of the partnership agreement.

Each partner is also a general agent of the partnership in carrying out the usual business of the firm "or business of the kind carried on by the partnership" [UPA 301(1)]. Thus, every act of a partner concerning partnership business and "business of the kind" and every contract signed in the partnership's name bind the firm.

Fiduciary Duties The fiduciary duties that a partner owes to the partnership and to the other partners are the duty of care and the duty of loyalty [UPA 404(a)]. Under the UPA, a partner's *duty of care* is limited to refraining from "grossly negligent or reckless conduct, intentional misconduct, or a knowing violation of law" [UPA 404(c)]. A partner is not liable to the partnership for simple negligence or honest errors in judgment in conducting partnership business.

The *duty of loyalty* requires a partner to account to the partnership for "any property, profit, or benefit" derived by the partner in the conduct of the partnership's business or from the use of its property. A partner must also refrain from competing with the partnership in business or dealing with the firm as an adverse party [UPA 404(b)]. The duty of loyalty can be breached by self-dealing, misusing partnership property, disclosing trade secrets, or usurping a partnership business opportunity.

A partner's fiduciary duties may not be waived or eliminated in the partnership agreement. In fulfilling them, each partner must act consistently with the obligation of good faith and fair dealing [UPA 103(b), 404(d)]. The agreement can specify acts that the partners agree will violate a fiduciary duty.

Note that a partner may pursue his or her own interests without automatically violating these duties [UPA 404(e)]. The key is whether the partner has disclosed the interest to the other partners. ■ **Example 16.8** Jayne Trell, a partner at Jacoby & Meyers, owns a shopping mall. Trell may vote against a partnership proposal to open a competing mall, provided that she fully discloses her interest in the existing shopping mall to the other partners at the firm. ■

Authority of Partners The UPA affirms general principles of agency law that pertain to a partner's authority to bind a partnership in contract. If a partner acts within the scope of her or his authority, the partnership is legally bound to honor the partner's commitments to third parties.

A partner may also subject the partnership to tort liability under agency principles. When a partner is carrying on partnership business with third parties in the usual way, apparent authority exists, and both the partner and the firm share liability. The partnership will not be liable, however, if the third parties *know* that the partner has no such authority.

Limitations on Authority. A partnership may limit a partner's capacity to act as the firm's agent or transfer property on its behalf by filing a "statement of partnership authority" in a designated state office [UPA 105, 303]. Such limits on a partner's authority normally are effective only with respect to third parties who are notified of the limitation. (An exception is made in real estate transactions when the statement of authority has been recorded with the appropriate state office.)

The Scope of Implied Powers. The extent of implied authority generally is broader for partners than for ordinary agents. In an ordinary partnership, the partners can exercise all implied powers reasonably necessary and customary to carry on that particular business. Some customarily implied powers include the authority to make warranties on goods in the sales business and the power to enter into contracts consistent with the firm's regular course of business.

Liability of Partners One significant disadvantage associated with a general partnership is that the partners are *personally* liable for the debts of the partnership. In most states, the liability is essentially unlimited, because the acts of one partner in the ordinary course of business subject the other partners to personal liability [UPA 305]. Note that normally the partnership's assets must be exhausted before creditors can reach the partners' individual assets.

Joint Liability. Each partner in a partnership generally is jointly liable for the partnership's obligations. **Joint liability** means that a third party must sue all of the partners as a group, but each partner can be held liable for the full amount. If, for instance, a third party sues one partner on a partnership contract, that partner has the right to demand that the other partners be sued with her or him. In fact, if all of the partners are not named as defendants in a lawsuit, then the assets of the partnership cannot be used to satisfy any judgment in that case.

Joint and Several Liability. In the majority of the states, under UPA 306(a), partners are both jointly and severally (separately, or individually) liable for all partnership obligations. **Joint and several liability** means that a third party has the option of suing all of the partners together (jointly) or one or more of the partners separately (severally). All partners in a partnership can be held liable even

if a particular partner did not participate in, know about, or ratify the conduct that gave rise to the lawsuit.

A judgment against one partner severally does not extinguish the others' liability. (Similarly, a release of one partner does not discharge the partners' several liability.) Those not sued in the first action normally may be sued subsequently, unless the court in the first action held that the partnership was in no way liable. If a plaintiff is successful in a suit against a partner or partners, he or she may collect on the judgment only against the assets of those partners named as defendants.

Indemnification. With joint and several liability, a partner who commits a tort can be required to indemnify (reimburse) the partnership for any damages it pays. Indemnification will typically be granted *unless* the tort was committed in the ordinary course of the partnership's business.

■ **Example 16.9** Nicole Martin, a partner at Patti's Café, is working in the café's kitchen one day when her young son suffers serious injuries to his hands from a dough press. Her son, through his father, files a negligence lawsuit against the partnership. Even if the suit is successful and the partnership pays damages to Martin's son, the firm, Patti's Café, is not entitled to indemnification. Martin would not be required to indemnify the partnership because her negligence occurred in the ordinary course of the partnership's business (making food for customers). ■

Liability of Incoming Partners. A partner newly admitted to an existing partnership is not personally liable for any partnership obligations incurred *before* the person became a partner [UPA 306(b)]. The new partner's liability to the partnership's existing creditors is limited to her or his capital contribution to the firm.

■ **Example 16.10** Smartclub, an existing partnership with four members, admits a new partner, Alex Jaff. He contributes $100,000 to the partnership. Smartclub has debts amounting to $600,000 at the time Jaff joins the firm. Although Jaff's capital contribution of $100,000 can be used to satisfy Smartclub's obligations, Jaff is not personally liable for partnership debts incurred before he became a partner. If, however, the partnership incurs additional debts after Jaff becomes a partner, he will be personally liable for those amounts, along with all the other partners. ■

16–3d Dissociation and Termination

Dissociation occurs when a partner ceases to be associated in the carrying on of the partnership business. Dissociation normally entitles the partner to have his or her interest purchased by the partnership. It also terminates the partner's actual authority to act for the partnership and to participate in running its business.

Once dissociation occurs, the partnership may continue to do business without the dissociated partner. If the partners no longer wish to (or are unable to) continue the business, the partnership may be terminated (dissolved).

Events That Cause Dissociation Under UPA 601, a partner can be dissociated from a partnership in any of the following ways:

1. By the partner's voluntarily giving notice of an "express will to withdraw." (When a partner gives notice of intent to withdraw, the remaining partners must decide whether to continue the partnership business. If they decide not to continue, the voluntary dissociation of a partner will dissolve the firm [UPA 801(1)].)
2. By the occurrence of an event specified in the partnership agreement.
3. By a unanimous vote of the other partners under certain circumstances, such as when a partner transfers substantially all of her or his interest in the partnership.
4. By order of a court or arbitrator if the partner has engaged in wrongful conduct that affects the partnership business. The court can order dissociation if a partner breached the partnership agreement or violated a duty owed to the partnership or to the other partners. Dissociation may also be ordered if the partner engaged in conduct that makes it "not reasonably practicable to carry on the business in partnership with the partner" [UPA 601(5)].
5. By the partner's declaring bankruptcy, assigning his or her interest in the partnership for the benefit of creditors, becoming physically or mentally incapacitated, or dying.

Wrongful Dissociation A partner has the *power* to dissociate from a partnership at any time, but she or he may not have the *right* to do so. If the partner lacks the right to dissociate, then the dissociation is considered wrongful under the law [UPA 602]. When a partner's dissociation breaches a partnership agreement, for instance, it is wrongful.

■ **Example 16.11** Jenkins & Whalen's partnership agreement states that it is a breach of the agreement for any partner to assign partnership property to a creditor without the consent of the other partners. If Kenzie, a partner, makes such an assignment, she has not only breached the agreement but has also wrongfully dissociated from the partnership. ■

A partner who wrongfully dissociates is liable to the partnership and to the other partners for damages caused by the dissociation. This liability is in addition to any other obligation of the partner to the partnership or to the other partners.

Effects of Dissociation Dissociation (rightful or wrongful) terminates some of the rights of the dissociated partner and requires that the partnership purchase his or her interest. It also alters the liability of the partners to third parties.

On a partner's dissociation, his or her right to participate in the management and conduct of the partnership business terminates [UPA 603]. The partner's duty of loyalty also ends. A partner's duty of care continues only with respect to events that occurred before dissociation, unless the partner participates in winding up the partnership's business (discussed shortly).

■ **Example 16.12** Debbie Pearson is a partner at the accounting firm Bubb & Flint. If she leaves the partnership, she can immediately compete with the firm for new clients. She must exercise care in completing ongoing client transactions that involved the partnership, however. She must also account to Bubb & Flint for any fees received from the former clients based on those transactions. ■

Buyouts. After a partner's dissociation, his or her interest in the partnership must be purchased according to the rules in UPA 701. The **buyout price** is based on the amount that would have been distributed to the partner if the partnership had been wound up on the date of dissociation. Offset against the price are amounts owed by the partner to the partnership, including damages for wrongful dissociation, if applicable.

Liability to Third Parties. For two years after a partner dissociates from a continuing partnership, the partnership may be bound by the acts of the dissociated partner based on apparent authority [UPA 702]. In other words, if a third party reasonably believed at the time of a transaction that the dissociated partner was still a partner, the partnership may be liable. Similarly, a dissociated partner may be liable for partnership obligations entered into during the two-year period following dissociation [UPA 703].

To avoid this possible liability, a partnership should notify its creditors, customers, and clients of a partner's dissociation. In addition, either the partnership or the dissociated partner can file a statement of dissociation in the appropriate state office to limit the dissociated partner's authority to ninety days after the filing [UPA 704]. Filing this statement helps to minimize the firm's potential liability for the former partner and vice versa.

Partnership Termination The same events that cause dissociation can result in the end of the partnership if the remaining partners no longer wish to (or are unable to) continue the partnership business. A partner's departure will not necessarily end the partnership, though. Generally, the partnership can continue if the remaining partners consent [UPA 801].

The termination of a partnership is referred to as **dissolution,** which essentially means the commencement of the winding up process. **Winding up** is the actual process of collecting, liquidating, and distributing the partnership assets.

Dissolution. Dissolution of a partnership generally can be brought about by acts of the partners, by operation of law, or by judicial decree [UPA 801]. Any partnership (including one for a fixed term) can be dissolved by the partners' agreement. If the partnership agreement states that it will dissolve on a certain event, such as a partner's death or bankruptcy, then the occurrence of that event will dissolve the partnership. A partnership for a fixed term or a particular undertaking is dissolved by operation of law at the expiration of the term or on the completion of the undertaking.

■ **Case in Point 16.13** Clyde Webster, James Theis, and Larry Thomas formed T&T Agri-Partners Company to own and farm 180 acres in Illinois for a fixed term. Under the partnership agreement, the death of any partner would dissolve the partnership. Nevertheless, when Webster died, Theis and Thomas did not liquidate T&T and distribute its assets. Webster's estate filed a complaint in state court seeking to dissolve the partnership. The court ordered the defendants to dissolve the partnership and distribute its assets in accord with the provisions of the partnership agreement. A reviewing court affirmed on appeal. A partnership business cannot continue after one partner dies when the partnership agreement specified that the death of one partner would terminate the business.[5] ■

Any event that makes it unlawful for the partnership to continue its business will result in dissolution [UPA 801(4)]. Under the UPA, a court may order dissolution when it becomes obviously impractical for the firm to continue—for instance, if the business can only be operated at a loss [UPA 801(5)].

---

5. *Estate of Webster v. Thomas,* 2013 Ill.App.5th 120121-U, 2013 WL 164041 (2013).

Winding Up and Distribution of Assets. After dissolution, the partnership continues for the limited purpose of winding up the business. Each partner must exercise good faith when dissolving a partnership. The partners cannot create new obligations on behalf of the partnership. They have authority only to complete transactions begun but not finished at the time of dissolution and to wind up the business of the partnership [UPA 803, 804(1)].

Winding up includes collecting and preserving partnership assets, discharging liabilities (paying debts), and accounting to each partner for the value of his or her interest in the partnership. Partners continue to have fiduciary duties to one another and to the firm during this process. UPA 401(h) provides that a partner is entitled to compensation for services in winding up partnership affairs above and apart from his or her share in the partnership profits. A partner may also receive reimbursement for expenses incurred in the process.

Both creditors of the partnership and creditors of the individual partners can make claims on the partnership's assets. In general, partnership creditors share proportionately with the partners' individual creditors in the partners' assets, which include their interests in the partnership.

A partnership's assets are distributed according to the following priorities [UPA 807]:

1. Payment of debts, including those owed to partner and nonpartner creditors.
2. Return of capital contributions and distribution of profits to partners.

If the partnership's liabilities are greater than its assets, the partners bear the losses in the same proportion in which they shared the profits unless they have agreed otherwise.

Partnership Buy-Sell Agreements. Before entering into a partnership, partners may agree on how the assets will be valued and divided in the event that the partnership dissolves. Such an agreement may eliminate costly negotiations or litigation later.

The agreement may provide for one or more partners to buy out the other or others, should the situation warrant. This is called a **buy-sell agreement,** or simply a *buyout agreement.* Alternatively, the agreement may specify that one or more partners will determine the value of the interest being sold and that the other or others will decide whether to buy or sell.

Under UPA 701(a), if a partner's dissociation does not result in a dissolution of the partnership, a buyout of the partner's interest is mandatory. The UPA contains an extensive set of buyout rules that apply when the partners do not have a buyout agreement. Basically, a withdrawing partner receives the same amount through a buyout that he or she would receive if the business were winding up [UPA 701(b)].

16–4 Franchises

Instead of setting up a sole proprietorship to market their own products or services, many entrepreneurs opt to purchase a franchise. A **franchise** is an arrangement in which the owner of intellectual property—such as a trademark, a trade name, or a copyright—licenses others to use it in the selling of goods or services. A **franchisee** (a purchaser of a franchise) is generally legally independent of the **franchisor** (the seller of the franchise). At the same time, the franchisee is economically dependent on the franchisor's integrated business system. In other words, a franchisee can operate as an independent businessperson but still obtain the advantages of a regional or national organization.

Today, franchising companies and their franchisees account for a significant portion of all retail sales in this country. Well-known franchises include McDonald's, 7-Eleven, and Holiday Inn. Franchising has also become a popular way for businesses to expand their operations internationally without violating the legal restrictions that many nations impose on foreign ownership of businesses.

16–4a Types of Franchises

Many different kinds of businesses sell franchises, and numerous types of franchises are available. Generally, though, franchises fall into one of three classifications: distributorships, chain-style business operations, and manufacturing arrangements.

Distributorship In a *distributorship*, a manufacturer (the franchisor) licenses a dealer (the franchisee) to sell its product. Often, a distributorship covers an exclusive territory. Automobile dealerships and beer distributorships are common examples.

■ **Example 16.14** Black Bear Beer Company distributes its brands of beer through a network of authorized wholesale distributors, each with an assigned territory. Marik signs a distributorship contract for the area from Gainesville to Ocala, Florida. If the contract states that Marik is the exclusive distributor in that area, then no other franchisee may distribute Black Bear beer in that region. ■

Chain-Style Business Operation In a *chain-style business operation*, a franchise operates under a franchisor's trade name and is identified as a member of a select group of dealers that engage in the franchisor's business. The franchisee is generally required to follow standardized or prescribed methods of operation. Often, the franchisor insists that the franchisee maintain certain standards of performance.

In addition, the franchisee may be required to obtain materials and supplies exclusively from the franchisor. Chipotle Mexican Grill and most other fast-food chains are examples of this type of franchise. Chain-style franchises are also common in service-related businesses, including real estate brokerage firms, such as Century 21, and tax-preparing services, such as H&R Block, Inc.

Manufacturing Arrangement In a *manufacturing*, or *processing-plant, arrangement*, the franchisor transmits to the franchisee the essential ingredients or formula to make a particular product. The franchisee then markets the product either at wholesale or at retail in accordance with the franchisor's standards. Examples of this type of franchise include Pepsi-Cola and other soft-drink bottling companies.

16–4b Laws Governing Franchising

Because a franchise relationship is primarily a contractual relationship, it is governed by contract law. If the franchise exists primarily for the sale of products manufactured by the franchisor, the law governing sales contracts as expressed in Article 2 of the Uniform Commercial Code applies.

Additionally, the federal government and most states have enacted laws governing certain aspects of franchising. Generally, these laws are designed to protect prospective franchisees from dishonest franchisors and to prevent franchisors from terminating franchises without good cause.

Federal Regulation of Franchises The federal government regulates franchising through laws that apply to specific industries and through the Franchise Rule, created by the Federal Trade Commission (FTC).

Industry-Specific Standards. Congress has enacted laws that protect franchisees in certain industries, such as automobile dealerships and service stations. These laws protect the franchisee from unreasonable demands and bad faith terminations of the franchise by the franchisor.

In the automobile industry, a manufacturer-franchisor cannot make unreasonable demands of dealer-franchisees or set unrealistically high sales quotas. If a manufacturer-franchisor terminates a franchise because of a dealer-franchisee's failure to comply with unreasonable demands, the manufacturer may be liable for damages.[6]

---

6. Automobile Dealers' Day in Court Act, 15 U.S.C. Sections 1221 *et seq.*

Similarly, federal law prescribes the conditions under which a franchisor of service stations can terminate the franchise.[7] In addition, federal antitrust laws sometimes apply in specified circumstances to prohibit certain types of anticompetitive agreements.

The Franchise Rule. The FTC's Franchise Rule requires franchisors to disclose certain material facts that a prospective franchisee needs in order to make an informed decision concerning the purchase of a franchise.[8] Those who violate the Franchise Rule are subject to substantial civil penalties, and the FTC can sue on behalf of injured parties to recover damages.

The rule requires the franchisor to make numerous written disclosures to prospective franchisees (see Exhibit 16–1). All representations made to a prospective franchisee must have a reasonable basis. For instance, if a franchisor provides projected earnings figures, the franchisor must indicate whether the figures are based on actual data or hypothetical examples. If a franchisor makes sales or earnings projections based on actual data for a specific franchise location, the franchisor must disclose the number and percentage of its existing franchises that have achieved this result.

State Regulation of Franchising State legislation varies but often is aimed at protecting franchisees from unfair practices and bad faith terminations by franchisors. A number of states have laws similar to the federal rules that require franchisors to provide presale disclosures to prospective franchisees.[9] Many state laws require that a disclosure document (known as the Franchise Disclosure Document, or FDD) be registered or filed with a state official. State laws may also require that a franchisor submit advertising aimed at prospective franchisees to the state for approval.

To protect franchisees, a state law might require the disclosure of information such as the actual costs of operation, recurring expenses, and profits earned, along with evidence substantiating these figures. State laws related to deceptive trade practices may also apply and prohibit certain types of actions by franchisors. To prevent arbitrary or bad faith terminations, a state law may prohibit termination without "good cause" or require that certain procedures be followed in terminating a franchise.

---

7. Petroleum Marketing Practices Act (PMPA), 15 U.S.C. Sections 2801 *et seq.*
8. 16 C.F.R. Parts 436 and 437.

9. These states include California, Florida, Hawaii, Illinois, Indiana, Maryland, Michigan, Minnesota, New York, North Dakota, Oregon, Rhode Island, South Dakota, Texas, Utah, Virginia, Washington, and Wisconsin.

Exhibit 16–1 The FTC's Franchise Rule Requirements

Requirement	Explanation
Written (or Electronic) Disclosures	The franchisor must make numerous disclosures, such as the range of goods and services included and the value and estimated profitability of the franchise. Disclosures can be delivered on paper or electronically. Prospective franchisees must be able to download and save any electronic disclosure documents.
Reasonable Basis for Any Representations	To prevent deception, all representations made to a prospective franchisee must have a reasonable basis at the time they are made.
Projected Earnings Figures	If a franchisor provides projected earnings figures, the franchisor must indicate whether the figures are based on actual data or hypothetical examples. The Franchise Rule does not require franchisors to provide potential earnings figures, however.
Actual Data	If a franchisor makes sales or earnings projections based on actual data for a specific franchise location, the franchisor must disclose the number and percentage of its existing franchises that have achieved this result.
Explanation of Terms	Franchisors are required to explain termination, cancellation, and renewal provisions of the franchise contract to potential franchisees before the agreement is signed.

16–4c The Franchise Contract

The franchise relationship is defined by the contract between the franchisor and the franchisee. The franchise contract specifies the terms and conditions of the franchise and spells out the rights and duties of the franchisor and the franchisee. If either party fails to perform its contractual duties, that party may be subject to a lawsuit for breach of contract. Furthermore, if a franchisee is induced to enter into a franchise contract by the franchisor's fraudulent misrepresentation, the franchisor may be liable for damages. Generally, statutes and the case law governing franchising tend to emphasize the importance of good faith and fair dealing in franchise relationships.

Because each type of franchise relationship has its own characteristics, franchise contracts tend to differ. Nonetheless, certain major issues typically are addressed in a franchise contract. We look at some of them next.

Payment for the Franchise

The franchisee ordinarily pays an initial fee or lump-sum price for the franchise license (the privilege of being granted a franchise). This fee is separate from the various products that the franchisee purchases from or through the franchisor. The franchise agreement may also require the franchisee to pay a percentage of the franchisor's advertising costs and certain administrative expenses.

In some industries, the franchisor relies heavily on the initial sale of the franchise for realizing a profit. In other industries, the continued dealing between the parties brings profit to both. Generally, the franchisor receives a stated percentage of the annual (or monthly) sales or volume of business done by the franchisee.

Business Premises

The franchise agreement may specify whether the premises for the business must be leased or purchased outright. Sometimes, a building must be constructed to meet the terms of the agreement. The agreement will specify whether the franchisor or the franchisee is responsible for supplying equipment and furnishings for the premises.

Location of the Franchise

Typically, the franchisor determines the territory to be served. Some franchise contracts give the franchisee exclusive rights, or "territorial rights," to a certain geographic area. Other franchise contracts, while defining the territory allotted to a particular franchise, either specifically state that the franchise is nonexclusive or are silent on the issue of territorial rights.

Many franchise disputes arise over territorial rights, and the implied covenant of good faith and fair dealing often comes into play in this area of franchising. If the contract does not grant exclusive territorial rights to the franchisee and the franchisor allows a competing franchise to be established nearby, the franchisee may suffer significant lost profits. In this situation, a court may hold that the franchisor breached an implied covenant of good faith and fair dealing.

Business Organization

The franchisor may require that the business use a particular organizational form and capital structure. The franchise agreement may also set out standards such as sales quotas and record-keeping requirements. Additionally, a franchisor may retain stringent control over the training of personnel involved in the operation and over administrative aspects of the business.

Quality Control by the Franchisor

The day-to-day operation of the franchise business normally is left up to the franchisee. Nonetheless, the franchise agreement may specify that the franchisor will provide some degree of supervision and control so that it can protect the franchise's name and reputation.

Means of Control. When the franchise prepares a product, such as food, or provides a service, such as motel accommodations, the contract often states that the franchisor will establish certain standards for the facility. Typically, the contract will state that the franchisor is permitted to make periodic inspections to ensure that the standards are being maintained.

As a means of controlling quality, franchise agreements also typically limit the franchisee's ability to sell the franchise to another party. ■ **Example 16.15** Mark Keller, Inc., an authorized Jaguar franchise, contracts to sell its dealership to Henrique Autos West. A Jaguar franchise generally cannot be sold without Jaguar Cars' permission. Prospective franchisees must meet Jaguar's customer satisfaction standards. If Henrique Autos fails to meet those standards, Jaguar can refuse to allow the sale and can terminate the franchise. ■

Degree of Control. As a general rule, the validity of a provision permitting the franchisor to establish and enforce certain quality standards is unquestioned. The franchisor has a legitimate interest in maintaining the quality of the product or service to protect its name and reputation.

If a franchisor exercises too much control over the operations of its franchisees, however, the franchisor risks potential liability. A franchisor may occasionally be held liable—under the doctrine of *respondeat superior*—for the tortious acts of the franchisees' employees.

■ **Example 16.16** The National Labor Relations Board (NLRB) received 180 employee complaints that certain McDonald's restaurants had engaged in unfair labor practices. Employees alleged that the restaurants had fired or penalized workers for participating in protests over wages and working conditions. Investigators found that at least some of the complaints had merit. The NLRB ruled that McDonald's USA, LLC, could be held jointly liable along with several of its franchisees for labor and wage violations. The NLRB reasoned that McDonald's exerts sufficient control over its franchisees to be found liable for the franchisees' employment law violations. ■

Pricing Arrangements Franchises provide the franchisor with an outlet for the firm's goods and services. Depending on the nature of the business, the franchisor may require the franchisee to purchase certain supplies from the franchisor at an established price.[10] A franchisor cannot, however, set the prices at which the franchisee

---

10. Although a franchisor can require franchisees to purchase supplies from it, requiring a franchisee to purchase exclusively from the franchisor may violate federal antitrust laws.

will resell the goods. Such price setting may be a violation of state or federal antitrust laws, or both. A franchisor can suggest retail prices but cannot mandate them.

16–4d Franchise Termination

The duration of the franchise is a matter to be determined between the parties. Sometimes, a franchise relationship starts with a short trial period, such as a year, so that the franchisee and the franchisor can determine whether they want to stay in business with one another. At other times, the duration of the franchise contract correlates with the term of the lease for the business premises, and both are renewable at the end of that period.

Grounds for Termination Set by the Franchise Contract
Usually, the franchise agreement specifies that termination must be "for cause" and then defines the grounds for termination. Cause might include, for instance, the death or disability of the franchisee, insolvency of the franchisee, breach of the franchise agreement, or failure to meet specified sales quotas.

In the following case, a franchisee contended that the franchisor did not have good cause for termination.

Case 16.3

S&P Brake Supply, Inc. v. Daimler Trucks North America, LLC
Supreme Court of Montana, 2018 MT 25, 390 Mont. 243, 411 P.3d 1264 (2018).

Background and Facts S&P Brake Supply, Inc., was the sole authorized dealer for Western Star Trucks in Yellowstone County, Montana. S&P operated its franchise under an agreement with Daimler Trucks North America, LLC. The agreement required that S&P sell a certain number of trucks in its area of responsibility (Yellowstone County). Over a three-year period, S&P sold only two trucks. Daimler advised its franchisee to use more effective marketing strategies and to hire more sales staff, among other things.

The next year, primarily because of S&P's failure to meet its sales goals, Daimler notified S&P that the franchise was being terminated. S&P objected, but the Montana Department of Justice, Motor Vehicle Division, ruled in Daimler's favor, and a state court upheld the department's decision. S&P appealed to the Montana Supreme Court.

In the Language of the Court
Justice Jim *RICE* delivered the Opinion of the Court.
* * * *

S&P argues * * * the [lower] court erred in its assessment of the [Montana Department of Justice, Motor Vehicle Division's] determination.
* * * *

S&P argues that an analysis of its sales performance [should have been] restricted to evidence related to Yellowstone County. Daimler established that S&P had failed to meet new truck sales objectives * * *, which are set for all Western Star dealers using an algorithm that considers market factors and the population of a dealer's area of responsibility. * * * Daimler offered its analysis of S&P's "dealer market share," which compared how many trucks S&P sold in its AOR [area of responsibility] to how many Western Star trucks were annually registered in Yellowstone County, to measure how well S&P was reaching and serving local customers. Of the seven Western Star trucks registered in Yellowstone County [during the last four years of S&P's franchise,] only two had been sold by S&P, an indicator to Daimler that S&P was not well serving its market, as the majority of customers were purchasing their Western Star trucks elsewhere. This evidence was premised upon S&P's performance in Yellowstone County.

Daimler also argued S&P's "dealer market share" was low compared to Western Star's "regional market share," a factor which is compiled from national truck registration data to compare S&P's sales performance in its AOR with Western Star's regional performance. While this assessment included evidence from outside the Yellowstone County franchise location, the [lower] court properly noted that *limiting the evidence to only Yellowstone County would not allow a comparison to other dealers where there is only one dealer in a county,* reasoning that *"when only one franchisee exists in a market, expanded data must be considered. Otherwise, a lone franchisee could never be terminated."* [Emphasis added.]

* * * The Department found, "The bottom line is that S&P's sales were deficient no matter which way one analyzed the data," and this determination was supported by substantial evidence.

Decision and Remedy *The Montana Supreme Court affirmed the judgment of the lower court. The court concluded, "The evidence focused on S&P's performance in Yellowstone County and was properly considered." Thus, Daimler had the grounds to terminate S&P's franchise.*

Critical Thinking
- **Legal Environment** *Considering that S&P was the only Western Star truck dealer in Yellowstone County, did discontinuing the franchise injure the public interest? Explain.*
- **Economic** *The department concluded that S&P's failure to use more effective marketing strategies and to hire more sales staff had breached the franchise agreement. S&P argued that these were not material breaches because the agreement's fundamental purpose was to sell trucks. Is S&P correct? Discuss.*

Notice Requirements. Most franchise contracts provide that notice of termination must be given. If no set time for termination is specified, then a reasonable time, with notice, is implied. A franchisee must be given reasonable time to wind up the business—that is, to do the accounting and return the copyright or trademark or any other property of the franchisor.

Opportunity to Cure a Breach. A franchise agreement may allow the franchisee to attempt to cure an ordinary, curable breach within a certain time after notice so as to postpone, or even avoid, termination. Even when a contract contains a notice-and-cure provision, however, a franchisee's breach of the duty of honesty and fidelity may be enough to allow the franchisor to terminate the franchise.

■ **Case in Point 16.17** Milind and Minaxi Upadhyaya entered into a franchise contract with 7-Eleven, Inc., to operate a store in Pennsylvania. The contract included a notice-and-cure provision. Under 7-Eleven's usual contract, franchisees lease the store and equipment, and receive a license to use 7-Eleven's trademarks and other

intellectual property. 7-Eleven receives a percentage of the store's gross profit (net sales less the cost of goods sold).

A 7-Eleven manager noticed a high rate of certain questionable transactions at the Upadhyayas' store and began investigating. The investigation continued for nearly two years and revealed that the store had been misreporting its sales so as to conceal sales proceeds from 7-Eleven. Evidence indicated that nearly one-third of the store's sales transactions had not been properly recorded. 7-Eleven sent a "non-curable" notice of material breach and termination of the franchise to the Upadhyayas. The franchisees argued that they had not been given an opportunity to cure the breach. The court found there was sufficient evidence of fraud to warrant immediate termination without an opportunity to cure.[11] ■

Wrongful Termination Because a franchisor's termination of a franchise often has adverse consequences for the franchisee, much franchise litigation involves

11. *7-Eleven, Inc. v. Upadhyaya*, 926 F.Supp.2d 614 (E.D.Pa. 2013).

claims of wrongful termination. Generally, the termination provisions of contracts are more favorable to the franchisor than to the franchisee. This means that the franchisee, who normally invests substantial time and financial resources in making the franchise operation successful, may receive little or nothing for the business on termination. The franchisor owns the trademark and hence the business.

It is in this area that statutory and case law become important. The federal and state laws discussed earlier attempt, among other things, to protect franchisees from the arbitrary or unfair termination of their franchises by the franchisors.

The Importance of Good Faith and Fair Dealing Generally, both statutory law and case law emphasize the importance of good faith and fair dealing in terminating a franchise relationship. In determining whether a franchisor has acted in good faith when terminating a franchise agreement, the courts usually try to balance the rights of both parties.

If a court perceives that a franchisor has arbitrarily or unfairly terminated a franchise, the franchisee will be provided with a remedy for wrongful termination. A court will be less likely to consider a termination wrongful if the franchisor's decision was made in the normal course of business and reasonable notice was given.

Practice and Review: Small Businesses and Franchises

Carlos Del Rey decided to open a Mexican fast-food restaurant and signed a franchise contract with a national chain called La Grande Enchilada. The contract required the franchisee to strictly follow the franchisor's operating manual and stated that failure to do so would be grounds for terminating the franchise contract. The manual set forth detailed operating procedures and safety standards, and provided that a La Grande Enchilada representative would inspect the restaurant monthly to ensure compliance.

Nine months after Del Rey began operating his restaurant, a spark from the grill ignited an oily towel in the kitchen. No one was injured, but by the time firefighters were able to put out the fire, the kitchen had sustained extensive damage. The cook told the fire department that the towel was "about two feet from the grill" when it caught fire. This was in compliance with the franchisor's manual that required towels be placed at least one foot from the grills. Nevertheless, the next day La Grande Enchilada notified Del Rey that his franchise would terminate in thirty days for failure to follow the prescribed safety procedures. Using the information presented in the chapter, answer the following questions.

1. What type of franchise was Del Rey's La Grande Enchilada restaurant?
2. If Del Rey operated the restaurant as a sole proprietorship, who bore the loss for the damaged kitchen? Explain.
3. Assume that Del Rey filed a lawsuit against La Grande Enchilada, claiming that his franchise was wrongfully terminated. What is the main factor that a court would consider in determining whether the franchise was wrongfully terminated?
4. Would a court be likely to rule that La Grande Enchilada had good cause to terminate Del Rey's franchise in this situation? Why or why not?

Debate This . . . *A partnership should automatically end when one partner dissociates from the firm.*

Terms and Concepts

articles of partnership 361	franchise 367	partnership 359
buyout price 365	franchisee 367	partnership by estoppel 362
buy-sell agreement 366	franchisor 367	pass-through entity 361
charging order 363	goodwill 361	sole proprietorship 355
dissociation 364	information return 361	winding up 366
dissolution 366	joint and several liability 364	
entrepreneur 354	joint liability 364	

Issue Spotters

1. Darnell and Eliana are partners in D&E Designs, an architectural firm. When Darnell dies, his widow claims that as Darnell's heir, she is entitled to take his place as Eliana's partner or to receive a share of the firm's assets. Is she right? Why or why not? (See *Partnerships*.)

2. Anchor Bottling Company and U.S. Beverages, Inc. (USB), enter into a franchise agreement that states the franchise may be terminated at any time "for cause." Anchor fails to meet USB's specified sales quota. Does this constitute "cause" for termination? Why or why not? (See *Franchises*.)

• Check your answers to the Issue Spotters against the answers provided in Appendix B at the end of this text.

Business Scenarios and Case Problems

16–1. Franchising. Maria, Pablo, and Vicky are recent college graduates who would like to go into business for themselves. They are considering purchasing a franchise. If they enter into a franchising arrangement, they would have the support of a large company that could answer any questions they might have. Also, a firm that has been in business for many years would be experienced in dealing with some of the problems that novice businesspersons might encounter. These and other attributes of franchises can lessen some of the risks of the marketplace. What other aspects of franchising—positive and negative—should Maria, Pablo, and Vicky consider before committing themselves to a particular franchise? (See *Franchises*.)

16–2. Partnership Formation. Daniel is the owner of a chain of shoe stores. He hires Rubya to be the manager of a new store, which is to open in Grand Rapids, Michigan. Daniel, by written contract, agrees to pay Rubya a monthly salary and 20 percent of the profits. Without Daniel's knowledge, Rubya represents himself to Classen as Daniel's partner and shows Classen the agreement to share profits. Classen extends credit to Rubya. Rubya defaults. Discuss whether Classen can hold Daniel liable as a partner. (See *Partnerships*.)

16–3. Control of a Franchise. National Foods, Inc., sells franchises to its fast-food restaurants, known as Chicky-D's. Under the franchise agreement, franchisees agree to hire and train employees strictly according to Chicky-D's standards. Chicky-D's regional supervisors are required to approve all job candidates before they are hired and all general policies affecting those employees. Chicky-D's reserves the right to terminate a franchise for violating the franchisor's rules. In practice, however, Chicky-D's regional supervisors routinely approve new employees and individual franchisees' policies. After several incidents of racist comments and conduct by Tim, a recently hired assistant manager at a Chicky-D's, Sharon, a counterperson at the restaurant, resigns. Sharon files a suit in a federal district court against National. National files a motion for summary judgment, arguing that it is not liable for harassment by franchise employees. Will the court grant National's motion? Why or why not? (See *Franchises*.)

16–4. Winding Up. Dan and Lori Cole operated a Curves franchise exercise facility in Angola, Indiana, as a partnership. The firm leased commercial space from Flying Cat, LLC, for a renewable three-year term and renewed the lease for a second three-year term. But two years after the renewal, the Coles divorced. By the end of the second term, Flying Cat was owed more than $21,000 on the lease. Without telling the landlord about the divorce, Lori signed another extension. More rent went unpaid. Flying Cat obtained a judgment in an Indiana state court against the partnership for almost $50,000. Can Dan be held liable? Why or why not? [*Curves for Women Angola v. Flying Cat*, LLC, 983 N.E.2d 629 (Ind.App. 2013)] (See *Partnerships*.)

16–5. Spotlight on Liberty Tax Service—Quality Control. JTH Tax, Inc., doing business as Liberty Tax Service, provides tax preparation and related loan services through company-owned and franchised stores. Liberty's agreement with its franchisees reserved the right to control their ads. In operations manuals, Liberty provided step-by-step instructions, directions, and limitations regarding the franchisees' ads and retained the right to unilaterally modify the steps at any time. The California attorney general filed a suit in a California state court against Liberty, alleging that its franchisees had used misleading or deceptive ads regarding refund anticipation loans and e-refund checks. Can Liberty be held liable? Discuss. [*People v. JTH Tax, Inc.*, 212 Cal.App.4th 1219, 151 Cal.Rptr.3d 728 (1 Dist. 2013)] (See *Franchises*.)

16–6. Quality Control. The franchise agreement of Domino's Pizza, LLC, sets out operational standards, including safety requirements, for a franchisee to follow but provides that the franchisee is an independent contractor. Each franchisee is free to use its own means and methods. For example, Domino's does not know whether a franchisee's delivery drivers are complying with vehicle safety requirements. MAC Pizza Management, Inc., operates a Domino's franchise. A vehicle driven by Joshua Balka, a MAC delivery driver, hydroplaned due to a bald tire and wet pavement. It struck the vehicle of Devavaram and Ruth Christopher, killing Ruth and injuring Devavaram. Is Domino's liable for negligence? Explain. [*Domino's Pizza, LLC v. Reddy*, 2015 WL 1247349 (Tex.App.—Beaumont 2015)] (See *Franchises*.)

16–7. Business Case Problem with Sample Answer—Franchise Termination. Executive Home Care Franchising, LLC, sells in-home health-care franchises. Clint, Massare, and Greer Marshall entered into a franchise agreement with

Executive Home Care. The agreement provided that the franchisees' failure to comply with the agreement's terms would likely cause irreparable harm to the franchisor, entitling it to an injunction. About two years later, the Marshalls gave up their franchise. They returned thirteen boxes of documents, stationery, operating manuals, marketing materials, and other items—everything in their possession that featured Executive Home Care trademarks. They quit operating out of the franchised location. They transferred the phone number back to the franchisor and informed their clients that they were no longer associated with Executive Home Care. They continued to engage in the home health-care business, however, under the name "Well-Being Home Care Corp." Is Executive Home Care entitled to an injunction against the Marshalls and their new company? Discuss. [*Executive Home Care Franchising, LLC v. Marshall Health Corp.*, 642 Fed.Appx. 181 (3d Cir. 2016)] (See *Franchises*.)

- For a sample answer to Problem 16–7, go to Appendix C at the end of this text.

16–8. Dissociation and Dissolution. Marc Malfitano and seven others formed Poughkeepsie Galleria as a partnership to own and manage a shopping mall in New York. The partnership agreement stated that "all decisions to be made by the Partners shall be made by the casting of votes" with "no less than fifty-one percent" of the partners "required to approve any matter." The agreement also provided that the partnership would dissolve on "the election of the Partners" or "the happening of any event which makes it unlawful for the business . . . to be carried on." Later, Malfitano decided

to dissociate from the firm and wrote to the other partners, "I hereby elect to dissolve the Partnership." Did Malfitano have the power and the right to dissociate from Poughkeepsie Galleria? Could he unilaterally dissolve the partnership? Can the other partners continue the business? Which, if any, of these actions violate the partnership agreement? Discuss. [*Congel v. Malfitano*, 31 N.Y.3d 272, 76 N.Y.S.3d 873, 101 N.E.3d 341 (2018)] (See *Partnerships*.)

16–9. A Question of Ethics—The IDDR Approach and Sole Proprietorships. *Tom George was the sole owner of Turbine Component Super Market, LLC (TCSM), when its existence was terminated by the state of Texas. A TCSM creditor, Turbine Resources Unlimited, filed and won a suit in a Texas state court against George for breach of contract. The plaintiff sought to collect the amount of the judgment through a sale of George's property. Instead of turning his assets over to the court, however, George tried to hide them by reforming TCSM. Without telling the court, he paid an unrelated debt with $100,000 of TCSM's funds. George claimed that the funds were a loan and that he was merely an employee of TCSM. [*Mitchell v. Turbine Resources Unlimited, Inc.*, 523 S.W.3d 189 (Tex.App.—Houston 2017)] (See* Sole Proprietorships.)

(a) Is it more likely that the court will recognize TCSM as an LLC or a sole proprietorship? Why?

(b) Using the *Discussion* step of the IDDR approach, consider whether the owner of a business has an ethical obligation to represent the character and purpose of the organization truthfully.

Time-Limited Group Assignment

16–10. Liability of Partners. At least six months before the Summer Olympic Games in Atlanta, Georgia, Stafford Fontenot and four others agreed to sell Cajun food at the games and began making preparations. On May 19, the group (calling themselves "Prairie Cajun Seafood Catering of Louisiana") applied for a business license from the county health department. Later, Ted Norris sold a mobile kitchen to them for $40,000. They gave Norris an $8,000 check drawn on the "Prairie Cajun Seafood Catering of Louisiana" account and two promissory notes, one for $12,000 and the other for $20,000. The notes, which were dated June 12, listed only Fontenot "d/b/a Prairie Cajun Seafood" as the maker (*d/b/a* is an abbreviation for "doing business as").

On July 31, Fontenot and his friends signed a partnership agreement, which listed specific percentages of profits and

losses. They drove the mobile kitchen to Atlanta, but business was disastrous. When the notes were not paid, Norris filed a suit in a Louisiana state court against Fontenot, seeking payment. (See *Partnerships*.)

(a) The first group will discuss the elements of a partnership and determine whether a partnership exists among Fontenot and the others.

(b) The second group will determine who can be held liable on the notes and why.

(c) The third group will discuss the concept of "d/b/a," or "doing business as." Does a person who uses this designation when signing checks or promissory notes avoid liability on the checks or notes?

Chapter 17

Limited Liability Business Forms

Our government allows entrepreneurs to choose from a variety of business organizational forms. In selecting among them, businesspersons are motivated to choose organizational forms that limit their liability. Limited liability may allow them to take more business risk, which is associated with the potential for higher profits.

An increasingly common form of business organization is the *limited liability company (LLC)*. LLCs have become the organizational form of choice among many small businesses. Other limited liability business forms include the *limited liability partnership (LLP)*, the *limited partnership (LP)*, and the *limited liability limited partnership (LLLP)*.

17–1 The Limited Liability Company

A **limited liability company (LLC)** is a hybrid that combines the limited liability aspects of a corporation and the tax advantages of a partnership. The LLC has been available for only a few decades, but it has become the preferred structure for many small businesses.

LLCs are governed by state statutes, which vary from state to state. In an attempt to create more uniformity, the National Conference of Commissioners on Uniform State Laws issued the Uniform Limited Liability Company Act (ULLCA). Less than one-fifth of the states have adopted it, however. Thus, the law governing LLCs remains far from uniform.

Nevertheless, some provisions are common to most state statutes. We base our discussion of LLCs on these common elements.

17–1a The Nature of the LLC

LLCs share many characteristics with corporations. Like corporations, LLCs must be formed and operated in compliance with state law. Like the shareholders of a corporation, the owners of an LLC, who are called **members,** enjoy limited liability [ULLCA 303].[1]

Limited Liability of Members Members of LLCs are shielded from personal liability in most situations. In other words, the liability of members normally is limited to the amount of their investments.

An exception arises when a member has significantly contributed to the LLC's tortious conduct. ■ **Case in Point 17.1** Randy Coley, the sole member and manager of East Coast Cablevision, LLC, installed cable television systems for many hotels and resorts. Coley established a DIRECTV Satellite Master Antenna Television (SMATV) account in the name of Massanutten Resort. The system provided programming to 168 timeshare units, as well as to the resort's bar, golf shop, lobbies, and waterpark. The bill for the resort's account was sent to (and paid by) East Coast Cablevision, which in turn billed the customers.

Over time, East Coast Cablevision began providing cable services to additional customers using the resort's SMATV account but did not pay DIRECTV for these other customers. Ultimately, another cable dealer affiliated with DIRECTV sued Coley for not paying for all of the DIRECTV programming transmissions that East Coast's customers had received. The court held that because Coley had played a direct role in the unauthorized transmissions, he could be held personally liable for them.[2] ■

When Liability May Be Imposed The members of an LLC, like the shareholders in a corporation, can lose their limited personal liability in certain circumstances. For instance, when an individual guarantees payment of

---

1. Members of an LLC can also bring derivative actions, which you will read about in regard to corporations, on behalf of the LLC [ULLCA 101]. As with a corporate *shareholder's derivative suit*, any damages recovered go to the LLC, not to the members personally.

2. *Sky Cable, LLC v. Coley*, 2013 WL 3517337 (W.D.Va. 2013). See also, *DIRECTV, LLC v. OLCR, Inc.*, 2016 WL 4679037 (E.D.Pa. 2016).

a business loan to the LLC, that individual is personally liable for the business's obligation. In addition, if an LLC member fails to comply with certain formalities, such as by commingling personal and business funds, a court can impose personal liability.

Under various principles of corporate law, courts may hold the owners of a business liable for its debts. On rare occasions, for instance, courts ignore the corporate structure ("pierce the corporate veil") to expose the shareholders to personal liability when it is required to achieve justice.

Similarly, courts will sometimes pierce the veil of an LLC to hold its members personally liable. Note, however, that courts have reserved piercing the veil of an LLC for circumstances that are clearly extraordinary. There must normally be some flagrant disregard of the LLC formalities, as well as fraud or malfeasance on the part of the LLC member.

■ **Case in Point 17.2** Tom and Shannon Brown purchased a new home in Hattiesburg, Mississippi, from Ray Richard and Nick Welch. Richard had hired Waldron Properties, LLC (WP), to build the home. Several years later, cracks began to develop in the walls of the Browns' home as a result of defects in the construction of the foundation. The Browns sued Murray Waldron, the sole member of WP, for breach of warranty under the state's New Home Warranty Act (NHWA). Because the required NHWA notice they had received when they bought the home was signed by Waldron personally, they claimed that Waldron was personally liable.

The trial court found that WP, not Waldron individually, was the builder of the Browns' home. The Browns appealed. They contended that even if WP was the builder, the court should pierce the veil of the LLC and hold Waldron personally liable. The state appellate court disagreed and affirmed the lower court's ruling. The Browns had not entered into a contract with either Waldron or WP. There was not sufficient evidence that Waldron had disregarded LLC formalities or had engaged in fraud or other misconduct to justify piercing the LLC's veil to hold him personally liable.[3] ■

Other Similarities to Corporations Another similarity between corporations and LLCs is that LLCs are legal entities apart from their owners. As a legal person, the LLC can sue or be sued, enter into contracts, and hold title to property [ULLCA 201]. The terminology used to describe LLCs formed in other states or nations is also similar to that used in corporate law. For instance, an LLC formed in one state but doing business in another state is referred to in the second state as a *foreign LLC*.

17–1b The Formation of the LLC

LLCs are creatures of statute and thus must follow state statutory requirements.

Articles of Organization To form an LLC, **articles of organization** must be filed with a central state agency—usually the secretary of state's office [ULLCA 202]. Typically, the articles must include the name of the business, its principal address, the name and address of a registered agent, the members' names, and how the LLC will be managed [ULLCA 203]. The business's name must include the words *Limited Liability Company* or the initials *LLC* [ULLCA 105(a)]. Although a majority of the states permit one-member LLCs, some states require at least two members.

Preformation Contracts Businesspersons sometimes enter into contracts on behalf of a business organization that is not yet formed. Persons who are forming a corporation, for instance, may enter into contracts during the process of incorporation but before the corporation becomes a legal entity. These contracts are referred to as *preincorporation contracts*. The individual promoters who sign the contracts are bound to their terms. Once the corporation is formed and adopts the preincorporation contracts (by means of a *novation*, which substitutes a new contract for the old contract), it can enforce the contract terms.

In dealing with the preorganization contracts of LLCs, courts may apply the well-established principles of corporate law relating to preincorporation contracts. That is to say, when the promoters of an LLC enter preformation contracts, the LLC, once formed, can adopt the contracts by a novation and then enforce them.

■ **Case in Point 17.3** 607 South Park, LLC, entered into an agreement to sell a hotel to 607 Park View Associates, Ltd., which then assigned the rights to the purchase to another company, 02 Development, LLC. At the time, 02 Development did not yet exist—it was legally created several months later. 607 South Park subsequently refused to sell the hotel to 02 Development, and 02 Development sued for breach of the purchase agreement.

A California appellate court ruled that LLCs should be treated the same as corporations with respect to preorganization contracts. Although 02 Development did not exist when the agreement was executed, once it came into existence, it could enforce any preorganization contract made on its behalf.[4] ■

---

3. *Brown v. Waldron*, 186 So.3d 955 (Miss.Ct.App. 2016).

4. *02 Development, LLC v. 607 South Park, LLC*, 159 Cal.App.4th 609, 71 Cal.Rptr.3d 608 (2008). See also, *Davis Wine Co. v. Vina Y Bodega Estampa, S.A.*, 823 F.Supp.2d 1159 (D.Or. 2011).

17–1c Jurisdictional Requirements

As we have seen, LLCs and corporations share several characteristics, but a significant difference between these organizational forms involves federal jurisdictional requirements. Under the federal jurisdiction statute, a corporation is deemed to be a citizen of the state where it is incorporated and maintains its principal place of business. The statute does not mention the state citizenship of partnerships, LLCs, and other unincorporated associations. The courts, however, have tended to regard these entities as citizens of every state of which their members are citizens.

The state citizenship of an LLC may come into play when a party sues the LLC based on diversity of citizenship. Remember that when parties to a lawsuit are from different states and the amount in controversy exceeds $75,000, a federal court can exercise diversity jurisdiction. *Total* diversity of citizenship must exist, however.

■ **Example 17.4** Jen Fong, a citizen of New York, wishes to bring a suit against Skycel, an LLC formed under the laws of Connecticut. One of Skycel's members also lives in New York. Fong will not be able to bring a suit against Skycel in federal court on the basis of diversity jurisdiction because the defendant LLC is also a citizen of New York. The same would be true if Fong was bringing a suit against multiple defendants and one of the defendants lived in New York. ■

17–1d Advantages of the LLC

The LLC offers many advantages to businesspersons, which is why this form of business organization has become increasingly popular.

Limited Liability A key advantage of the LLC is the limited liability of its members. The LLC as an entity can be held liable for any loss or injury caused by the wrongful acts or omissions of its members. As we have seen, however, members themselves generally are not personally liable.

In the following case, a consumer died as a result of using an allegedly defective product made and sold by an LLC. The consumer's children sought to hold the LLC's sole member and manager personally liable for the firm's actions.

Case **17.1**

Hodge v. Strong Built International, LLC

Court of Appeal of Louisiana, Third Circuit, 159 So.3d 1159 (2015).

Background and Facts Donald Hodge was hunting in a deer stand when its straps—which held Hodge high up in a tree—failed. When the straps failed, Hodge and the deer stand fell to the ground, killing Hodge. Louisiana-based Strong Built International, LLC, was the maker and seller of the deer stand, and Ken Killen was Strong Built's sole member and manager.

Hodge's children, Donald and Rachel Hodge, filed a lawsuit in a Louisiana state court against Strong Built and Killen. They sought damages on a theory of product liability for the injury and death of their father caused by the allegedly defective deer stand. Killen filed a motion for summary judgment, asserting that he was not personally liable to the Hodges. The court granted the motion and issued a summary judgment in Killen's favor, dismissing the claims against him. The Hodges appealed.

In the Language of the Court

AMY, Judge.

* * * *

* * * An LLC member or manager's liability to third parties is delineated in [Louisiana Revised Statute (La.R.S.)] 12:1320, which states:

* * * *

* * * no member, manager, employee, or agent of a limited liability company is liable in such capacity for a debt, obligation, or liability of the limited liability company.

* * * *

* * * That protection is not unlimited. Pursuant to La.R.S. 12:1320(D), *a member or manager may be subjected to personal liability for claims involving * * * breach of a professional duty or other negligent or wrongful act.* [Emphasis added.]

Case 17.1 Continues

Case 17.1 Continued

* * * In an affidavit, Mr. Killen asserted that he is "not an engineer, nor a licensed professional in any profession in Louisiana or any other state." Mr. Killen also asserts that he:

> was a participant in the creation of the deer stand which * * * Strong Built International, L.L.C. manufactured and sold, but [he] never personally dictated or participated in the design, selection of materials used in the manufacture, or the manufacture of, or the selection of any warnings to any deer stand for the use or consumption by any consumer beyond my input and work as a manager * * * and member of * * * Strong Built International, L.L.C.

The plaintiffs offered no evidence to contradict Mr. Killen's affidavit in this regard. Accordingly, we find no basis for Mr. Killen's personal liability under the "breach of professional duty" exception.

Neither do we find sufficient evidence in the record to create a genuine issue of material fact with regard to the "other negligent or wrongful act" exception.

* * * With regard to [this exception], the member (or manager) must have a duty of care to the plaintiff. * * * That duty must be "something more" than the duties arising out of the LLC's contract with the plaintiff.

* * * *

* * * Mr. Killen states in his affidavit that not only was he not personally responsible for the design and manufacture of the deer stands while involved with Strong Built International * * * but that any involvement that he may have had was in his capacity as a member and manager. *The plaintiffs have submitted nothing to show that Mr. Killen's actions are "something more" than his duties as a member/ manager of the LLC.* [Emphasis added.]

Decision and Remedy *A state intermediate appellate court affirmed the judgment in Killen's favor. Under the applicable Louisiana state LLC statute, no member or manager of an LLC is liable in that capacity for the liability of the company. There are exceptions, but the Hodges failed to show that Killen's actions went beyond his duties as a member and manager of Strong Built.*

Critical Thinking

- **Economic** *Why does the law allow—and even encourage—limits to the liability of a business organization's owners and managers for the firm's actions? Discuss.*

Flexibility in Taxation Another advantage of the LLC is its flexibility in regard to taxation. An LLC that has *two or more members* can choose to be taxed as either a partnership or a corporation. A corporate entity normally must pay income taxes on its profits, and the shareholders must then pay personal income taxes on any of those profits that are distributed as dividends. An LLC that wants to distribute profits to its members almost always prefers to be taxed as a partnership to avoid the "double taxation" that is characteristic of the corporate entity.

Unless an LLC indicates that it wishes to be taxed as a corporation, the Internal Revenue Service (IRS) automatically taxes it as a partnership. This means that the LLC, as an entity, pays no taxes. Rather, as in a partnership, profits are "passed through" the LLC to the members, who then personally pay taxes on the profits. If an LLC's members want to reinvest profits in the business rather than distribute the profits to members, however, they may prefer to be taxed as a corporation. Corporate income tax rates may be lower than personal tax rates. Part of the attractiveness of the LLC is this flexibility with respect to taxation.

An LLC that has only *one member* cannot be taxed as a partnership. For federal income tax purposes, one-member LLCs are automatically taxed as sole proprietorships unless they indicate that they wish to be taxed as corporations. With respect to state taxes, most states follow the IRS rules.

Management and Foreign Investors Another advantage of the LLC for businesspersons is the flexibility it offers in terms of business operations and management, as will be discussed shortly. Foreign investors are allowed to become LLC members, so organizing as an LLC can enable a business to attract investors from other countries. (Many other nations—including France, Germany, Ireland, Japan, the United Kingdom, and most countries in Latin America—have business forms that provide for limited liability much like an LLC.)

17–1e Disadvantages of the LLC

The main disadvantage of the LLC is that state LLC statutes are not uniform. Therefore, businesses that operate in more than one state may not receive consistent treatment in these states.

Generally, most states apply to a foreign LLC (an LLC formed in another state) the law of the state where the LLC was formed. Difficulties can arise, though, when one state's court must interpret and apply another state's laws.

17–2 LLC Management and Operation

The members of an LLC have considerable flexibility in managing and operating the business. Here, we discuss management options, fiduciary duties owed, and the operating agreement and general operating procedures of LLCs.

17–2a Management of an LLC

Basically, LLC members have two options for managing the firm, as shown in Exhibit 17–1. The firm can be either a "member-managed" LLC or a "manager-managed" LLC. Most state LLC statutes and the ULLCA provide

Exhibit 17–1 Management of an LLC

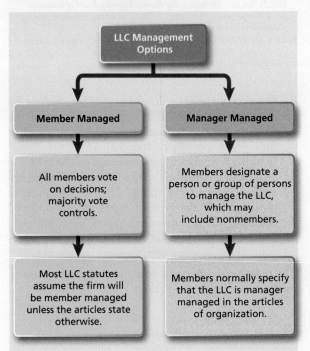

that unless the articles of organization specify otherwise, an LLC is assumed to be member managed [ULLCA 203(a)(6)].

In a *member-managed* LLC, all of the members participate in management, and decisions are made by majority vote [ULLCA 404(a)]. In a *manager-managed* LLC, the members designate a group of persons to manage the firm. The management group may consist of only members, both members and nonmembers, or only nonmembers.

However an LLC is managed, its managers need to be aware of the firm's potential liability under employment-discrimination laws. Those laws may sometimes extend to individuals who are not members of a protected class, as discussed in this chapter's *Managerial Strategy* feature.

17–2b Fiduciary Duties

Under the ULLCA, managers in a manager-managed LLC owe fiduciary duties (the duty of loyalty and the duty of care) to the LLC and its members [ULLCA 409(a), 409(h)]. (This same rule applies in corporate law—corporate directors and officers owe fiduciary duties to the corporation and its shareholders.) Because not all states have adopted the ULLCA, some state statutes provide that managers owe fiduciary duties only to the LLC and not to the LLC's members.

To whom the fiduciary duties are owed can affect the outcome of litigation. ■ **Case in Point 17.5** Leslie Polk and his children, Yurii and Dusty Polk and Lezanne Proctor, formed Polk Plumbing, LLC, in Alabama. Dusty and Lezanne were managers of the LLC. Eventually, Yurii quit the firm. A year and a half later, Leslie "fired" Dusty and Lezanne and denied them access to the LLC's books and offices, but continued to operate the business.

Dusty and Lezanne filed a suit in an Alabama state court against Leslie, claiming breach of fiduciary duty. The trial court instructed the jury that it could not consider the plaintiffs' "firing" as part of their claim. Thus, although the jury found in their favor, it awarded only one dollar to each in damages. The plaintiffs appealed, and a state intermediate appellate court reversed and remanded the case for a new trial. Leslie did not have the authority under the terms of the LLC's operating agreement to fire two managers. The trial court had erred in not allowing the jury to consider the circumstances of Dusty and Lezanne's "firing" as part of their breach-of-fiduciary-duty claim.[5] ■

---

5. *Polk v. Polk*, 70 So.3d 363 (Ala.Civ.App. 2011).

Managerial Strategy — **Can a Person Who Is Not a Member of a Protected Class Sue for Discrimination?**

Under federal law and the laws of most states, discrimination in employment based on race, color, religion, national origin, gender, age, or disability is prohibited. Persons who are members of these protected classes can sue if they are subjected to discrimination. But can a person subjected to discrimination bring a lawsuit if he is not a member of a protected class, even though managers and other employees believe that he is? This somewhat unusual situation occurred in New Jersey.

Courts in New Jersey

Myron Cowher worked at Carson & Roberts Site Construction & Engineering, Inc. For more than a year, at least two of his supervisors directed almost daily barrages of anti-Semitic remarks at him. They believed that he was Jewish, although his actual background was German-Irish and Lutheran.

Cowher brought a suit against the supervisors and the construction company, claiming a hostile work environment. The trial court, however, ruled that he did not have standing to sue under New Jersey law because he was not Jewish and, thus, was not a member of a protected class. Cowher appealed.

The appellate court disagreed with the trial court. The court ruled that if Cowher could prove that the discrimination "would not have occurred but for the perception that he was Jewish," his claim was covered

by New Jersey's antidiscrimination law.[a] Thus, in the appellate court's view, the nature of the discriminatory remarks—and not the actual characteristics of the plaintiff—determines whether the remarks are actionable.

Another New Jersey court followed the precedent set by the *Cowher* case to allow Shi-Juan Lin, a Chinese worker whose fiancé and child were black, to recover for racial discrimination. The employer created a hostile work environment by allowing Lin's supervisor to constantly use the "n" word at work. The employer knew that even though Lin was not black, she was hurt by the supervisor's remarks. Therefore, the court affirmed an administrative law judge's award of damages for pain and suffering, plus attorneys' fees.[b]

Business Questions

1. *Should a manager for an LLC respond to employee complaints of discrimination any differently than a manager at a corporation, a partnership, or a sole proprietorship? Why or why not?*

2. *How can a company, whether an LLC or some other business form, reduce the chances of discrimination lawsuits?*

---
a. *Cowher v. Carson & Roberts*, 425 N.J.Super. 285, 40 A.3d 1171 (2012). See also, *Sheridan v. Egg Harbor Township Board of Education*, 2015 WL 9694404 (N.J.Super.Ct. 2016), involving a plaintiff who alleged discrimination based on obesity.
b. *Lin v. Dane Construction Co.*, 2014 WL 8131876 (N.J.Super.Ct. 2015).

17–2c The LLC Operating Agreement

The members of an LLC can decide how to operate the various aspects of the business by forming an **operating agreement** [ULLCA 103(a)]. In many states, an operating agreement is not required for an LLC to exist, and if there is one, it need not be in writing. Generally, though, LLC members should protect their interests by creating a written operating agreement.

Operating agreements typically contain provisions relating to the following areas:

1. Management and how future managers will be chosen or removed. (Although most LLC statutes are silent on this issue, the ULLCA provides that members may choose and remove managers by majority vote [ULLCA 404(b)(3)].)
2. How profits will be divided.
3. How membership interests may be transferred.

4. Whether the dissociation of a member, such as by death or departure, will trigger dissolution of the LLC, and how a buyout price will be calculated in the event of a member's dissociation.
5. Whether formal members' meetings will be held.
6. How voting rights will be apportioned. (If the agreement does not cover voting, LLC statutes in most states provide that voting rights are apportioned according to each member's capital contributions.[6] Some states provide that, in the absence of an agreement to the contrary, each member has one vote.)

The provisions commonly included in operating agreements are also shown in Exhibit 17–2.

---
6. In contrast, partners in a general partnership typically have equal rights in management and equal voting rights unless they specify otherwise in their partnership agreement.

Exhibit 17–2 Provisions Commonly Included in an LLC Operating Agreement

Management	Sets forth who will manage the LLC and how future managers will be chosen or removed. (The ULLCA provides that members may choose and remove managers by majority vote.)
Profits	Establishes how profits will be divided among members.
Membership	Specifies how membership interests may be transferred.
Dissociation and Dissolution	Clarifies which events cause the dissociation of a member—such as by death or retirement—and trigger the LLC's dissolution. Provides a method of calculating a buyout price for a member's dissociation.
Member Meetings	Determines whether or not formal members' meetings will be held.
Voting Rights	Details how voting rights will be apportioned, such as according to each member's capital contribution or by allowing one vote for each member.

If a dispute arises and there is no agreement covering the topic under dispute, the state LLC statute will govern the outcome. For instance, most LLC statutes provide that if the members have not specified how profits will be divided, they will be divided equally among the members. When an issue is not covered by an operating agreement or by an LLC statute, the courts often apply principles of partnership law.

Sometimes, as in the following case, an operating agreement and the state's LLC statutes are applied together to determine the outcome of a dispute between the members of an LLC.

Case 17.2

Schaefer v. Orth

Court of Appeals of Wisconsin, 2018 WI App 35, 382 Wis.2d 271, 915 N.W.2d 730 (2018).

Background and Facts Jason Schaefer and Randy Orth created Grilled Cheese, LLC, to own and operate a "Tom and Chee" franchise, a casual restaurant specializing in grilled cheese sandwiches and soups. The operating agreement provided that Schaefer would be responsible for the restaurant's day-to-day operations, for which the LLC would pay him a monthly salary and bonuses. Orth would be responsible for the LLC's business and financial decisions and would not receive any compensation.

The restaurant reported a profit only in its first full month of operations. Five months later, when Schaefer was not paid his salary and bonuses, he quit. Later, Orth closed the restaurant and worked to wind up the business. Both parties lost the entire amounts they had invested in the LLC. Schaefer filed

Case 17.2 Continues

a suit in a Wisconsin state court against Orth, claiming Orth had breached their contract by failing to pay Schaefer's salary. The court directed a verdict in Orth's favor. Schaefer appealed.

In the Language of the Court

PER CURIAM [By the Whole Court].

* * * *

* * * The [lower] court granted Orth's motion for a directed verdict because it determined there was no credible evidence to support a conclusion that Orth was personally liable to Schaefer for the unpaid wages and bonuses to which Schaefer was entitled under the operating agreement.

At trial, both Orth and Schaefer testified it was the LLC's responsibility to pay Schaefer the wages and bonuses set forth in the operating agreement, and Orth was not personally required to pay Schaefer those amounts.

The operating agreement's unambiguous language confirms that the LLC, not Orth, was responsible for paying Schaefer's wages and bonuses. The section of the agreement pertaining to "Distributions" specifically lists Schaefer's wages and bonuses as distributions to be paid to Schaefer before other distributions to the LLC's members. The agreement specifies that distributions are made from *the LLC's* available funds. The section of the agreement pertaining to "Profits" similarly states that, in the case of any profit resulting from the LLC's operations, "the LLC shall, as the first priority, allocate Profit to Schaefer to the extent, if any, that (A) all service compensation accruing in his favor through the date of the relevant allocation, exceeds (B) all prior allocations under this Clause." The agreement defines the term profit as the *LLC's* profit.

The language cited above plainly demonstrates that the LLC was responsible for paying Schaefer's wages and bonuses. Wisconsin's LLC statutes provide that "the debts, obligations and liabilities of a limited liability company, whether arising in contract, tort or otherwise, shall be solely the debts, obligations and liabilities of the limited liability company." With certain exceptions not applicable here, *"a member or manager of a limited liability company is not personally liable for any debt, obligation or liability of the limited liability company, except that a member or manager may become personally liable by his or her acts or conduct other than as a member or manager."* There is no evidence Orth was acting outside his capacity as a member or manager of the LLC when he failed to pay Schaefer's wages and bonuses. As a result, Orth is not personally liable to Schaefer for the payment of those amounts. [Emphasis added.]

Decision and Remedy *A state intermediate appellate court affirmed the lower court's judgment. "The evidence presented at trial does not permit a legal conclusion that Orth was personally liable to Schaefer for" his unpaid salary and bonuses.*

Critical Thinking

- **Economic** *The operating agreement stated that an "aggrieved party may pursue all redress permitted by law," including attorneys' fees. Under this provision, is Schaefer entitled to an award of attorneys' fees even though the trial court granted Orth's motion for a directed verdict? Discuss.*
- **Legal Environment** *Could Schaefer have sued the LLC to recover his unpaid salary and bonuses? Explain.*

17–3 Dissociation and Dissolution of an LLC

Recall that in a partnership, *dissociation* occurs when a partner ceases to be associated in the carrying on of the partnership business. The same concept applies to LLCs. And like a partner in a partnership, a member of an LLC has the *power* to dissociate at any time but may not have the *right* to dissociate.

Under the ULLCA, the events that trigger a member's dissociation from an LLC are similar to the events causing a partner to be dissociated under the Uniform Partnership Act (UPA). These include voluntary withdrawal, expulsion by other members, court order, incompetence, bankruptcy, and death. Generally, if a member dies or otherwise dissociates from an LLC, the other members may continue to carry on the LLC business unless the operating agreement provides otherwise.

17–3a Effects of Dissociation from an LLC

When a member dissociates from an LLC, he or she loses the right to participate in management and the right to act as an agent for the LLC. The member's duty of loyalty to the LLC also terminates, and the duty of care continues only with respect to events that occurred before dissociation.

Generally, the dissociated member also has a right to have his or her interest in the LLC bought out by the other members. The LLC's operating agreement may contain provisions establishing a buyout price. If it does not, the member's interest usually is purchased at fair value. In states that have adopted the ULLCA, the LLC must purchase the interest at fair value within 120 days after the dissociation.

If the member's dissociation violates the LLC's operating agreement, it is considered legally wrongful, and the dissociated member can be held liable for damages caused by the dissociation. ■ **Example 17.6** Chadwick and Barrow are members in an LLC. Chadwick manages the accounts, and Barrow, who has many connections in the community and is a skilled investor, brings in the business. If Barrow wrongfully dissociates from the LLC, the LLC's business will suffer, and Chadwick can hold Barrow liable for the loss of business resulting from her withdrawal. ■

17–3b Dissolution of an LLC

Regardless of whether a member's dissociation was wrongful or rightful, normally the dissociated member has no right to force the LLC to dissolve. The remaining members can opt either to continue or to dissolve the business.

Members can also stipulate in their operating agreement that certain events will cause dissolution, or they can agree that they have the power to dissolve the LLC by vote. As with partnerships, a court can order an LLC to be dissolved in certain circumstances. For instance, a court might order dissolution when the members have engaged in illegal or oppressive conduct, or when it is no longer feasible to carry on the business.

■ **Case in Point 17.7** Three men—Walter Perkins, Gary Fordham, and David Thompson—formed Venture Sales, LLC, to develop a subdivision in Petal, Mississippi. Each contributed land and funds, resulting in total holdings of 466 acres of land and about $158,000 in cash. Perkins was busy as an assistant coach for the Cleveland Browns, so he trusted Fordham and Thompson to develop the property. More than ten years later, however, they still had not done so, although they had formed two other LLCs and developed two other subdivisions in the area.

Fordham and Thompson claimed that they did not know when they could develop Venture's property and suggested selling it at a discounted price, but Perkins disagreed. Perkins then sought a judicial dissolution of Venture Sales. The court ordered the dissolution. Because Venture Sales was not meeting the economic purpose for which it was established (developing a subdivision), continuing the business was impracticable.[7] ■

A judge's exercise of discretion to order the dissolution of an LLC was disputed in the following case.

7. *Venture Sales, LLC v. Perkins*, 86 So.3d 910 (Miss. 2012).

Case Analysis 17.3

Reese v. Newman
District of Columbia Court of Appeals, 131 A.3d 880 (2016).

In the Language of the Court
KING, Senior Judge:

* * * Allison Reese and * * * Nicole Newman were co-owners of ANR Construction Management, LLC * * *. Following disputes over management of the company, Newman notified Reese in writing that she intended to * * * dissolve and wind-up the LLC. Reese did not want to dissolve the LLC but preferred that Newman simply be dissociated so that Reese could continue the business herself. Newman filed

an action for judicial dissolution in [a District of Columbia court against Reese]. Reese filed a counterclaim for Newman's dissociation * * *. Following a jury trial, the jury * * * found grounds for both judicial dissolution and forced dissociation of Newman; the court, thereafter, ordered judicial dissolution of the LLC. * * * Reese appeals.

* * * *

Reese argues that the trial court erred when it purported to use discretion in choosing between dissolution of the

LLC, as proposed by Newman, and forcing dissociation of Newman from the LLC, as proposed by Reese. Reese argues that the [District of Columbia (D.C.)] statute [governing dissociation from an LLC] does not allow for any discretion by the court, and that, in fact, the statute mandates that the court order dissociation of Newman based on the jury's findings.

In matters of statutory interpretation, we review the trial court's decision *de novo*. Our analysis starts with the plain

Case 17.3 Continues

Case 17.3 Continued

language of the statute, as the general rule of statutory interpretation is that the intent of the lawmaker is to be found in the language that he has used. To that end, *the words of the statute should be construed according to their ordinary sense and with the meaning commonly attributed to them.* [Emphasis added.]

Reese argues that the court was required to dissociate Newman from the LLC under [D.C. Code] Section 29–806.02(5) which reads:

A person *shall* be dissociated as a member from a limited liability company when:
* * * *
(5) On application by the company, the person is expelled as a member by judicial order because the person has:
(A) Engaged, or is engaging, in wrongful conduct that has adversely and materially affected, or will adversely and materially affect, the company's activities and affairs;
(B) Willfully or persistently committed, or is willfully and persistently committing, a material breach of the operating agreement or the person's duties or obligations under Section 29–804.09; or
(C) Engaged, or is engaging, in conduct relating to the company's activities which makes it not reasonably practicable to carry on the activities with the person as a member.

Reese's interpretation of the statute is that, upon application to the court by a company, a judge shall dissociate a member of an LLC, when that member commits any one of the actions described in subsections (5)(A)-(C).

* * * While the introductory language of Section 29–806.02 does use the word "shall"—that command is in no way directed at the trial judge. It

reads, "a person shall be dissociated * * * when," and then goes on to recite fifteen separate circumstances describing different occasions when a person shall be dissociated from an LLC. That is to say, when one of the events described in subparagraphs (1) through (15) occurs, the member shall be dissociated. Subparagraph (5), however, is merely one instance for which a person shall be dissociated; that is, when and if a judge has ordered a member expelled because she finds that any conditions under (5)(A)-(C) have been established. In other words, the command in the introductory language is not directed at the trial judge, it is directed at all the circumstances set forth in subparagraphs (1) through (15) * * *. There is nothing in the language of Section 29–806.02(5) that strips a judge of her discretion because it does not require the judge to expel the member if any of the enumerated conditions are established. In short, Section 29–806.02(5) means: *when a judge has used her discretion to expel a member of an LLC by judicial order, under any of the enumerated circumstances in (5)(A)-(C), that member shall be dissociated.* [Emphasis added.]

* * * Although Reese argues that the language of the "dissociation" section of the District's code should be read as forcing the hand of a trial judge who finds grounds for dissociation, Reese attempts to read the "dissolution" section differently.

Reese differentiates the sections by pointing to the dissolution section's express authorization to order a remedy other than dissolution in Section 29-807.01(b) which provides: "in a proceeding brought under subsection (a) (5) of this section, the * * * Court may order a remedy other than dissolution."

While we are satisfied that judicial dissolution of an LLC is discretionary under this statute, Reese's attempt to buttress [reinforce] her argument that Section 29–806.02(5) is compulsory by pointing to this express provision in the dissolution section and the absence of a similar express provision in the dissociation section is unavailing. First, * * * the only "shall" in the dissociation section is in the introductory language, and the same "shall" can be found in the same place, in the dissolution section: "a limited liability company is dissolved, and its activities and affairs *shall be wound up*, upon the occurrence of any of the following." If that language does not make the rest of the section mandatory in the dissolution section, and we are persuaded that it does not, it cannot be said that the "shall" in the introduction of the dissociation section does the opposite.
* * * *

In sum, we hold that Section 29–806.02(5) can only be interpreted to mean: when a judge finds that any of the events in (5)(A)-(C) have taken place, she may (*i.e.*, has discretion to) expel by judicial order a member of an LLC, and when a judge has done so the member shall be dissociated. *Moreover, when both grounds for dissociation of a member and dissolution of the LLC exist, the trial judge has discretion to choose either alternative.* [Emphasis added.]

Here, the jury * * * found that grounds were present for either outcome. The trial judge acknowledged that both options were on the table and then exercised her discretion in ordering that dissolution take place. We find no reason to disturb that order.
* * * *

Accordingly, the judgment in this appeal is therefore affirmed.

Legal Reasoning Questions

1. What dispute gave rise to the action filed in the court in this case? How did that dispute lead to the issue on appeal?

2. What is the role of an appellate court when reviewing the exercise of discretion by a trial court?

3. Newman alleged that after she delivered her notice to dissolve ANR Construction, Reese locked her out of the LLC's bank accounts, blocked her access to the LLC's files and e-mail, and ended her salary and health benefits. Did any of the jury's findings support these allegations? Explain.

17–3c Winding Up of an LLC

When an LLC is dissolved, any members who did not wrongfully dissociate may participate in the winding up process. To wind up the business, members must collect, liquidate, and distribute the LLC's assets.

Members may preserve the assets for a reasonable time to optimize their return, and they continue to have the authority to perform reasonable acts in conjunction with winding up. In other words, the LLC will be bound by the reasonable acts of its members during the winding up process. Once all of the LLC's assets have been sold, the proceeds are distributed. Debts to creditors are paid first (including debts owed to members who are creditors of the LLC). The members' capital contributions are returned next, and any remaining amounts are then distributed to members in equal shares or according to their operating agreement.

17–4 Limited Liability Partnerships

The **limited liability partnership (LLP)** is a hybrid form of business designed mostly for professionals who normally do business as partners in a partnership. Almost all of the states have enacted LLP statutes. The major advantage of the LLP is that it allows a partnership to continue as a pass-through entity for tax purposes but limits the personal liability of the partners. The LLP is especially attractive for professional service firms and family businesses. All of the "Big Four" accounting firms—the four largest international accountancy and professional services firms—are organized as LLPs, including Ernst & Young, LLP, and PricewaterhouseCoopers, LLP.

17–4a Formation of an LLP

LLPs must be formed and operated in compliance with state statutes, which may include provisions of the UPA. The appropriate form must be filed with a central state agency, usually the secretary of state's office, and the business's name must include either "Limited Liability Partnership" or "LLP" [UPA 1001, 1002]. An LLP must file an annual report with the state to remain qualified as an LLP in that state [UPA 1003]. In most states, it is relatively easy to convert a general partnership into an LLP because the firm's basic organizational structure remains the same. Additionally, all of the statutory and common law rules governing partnerships still apply, apart from those modified by the LLP statute. Normally, LLP statutes are simply amendments to a state's already existing partnership law.

17–4b Liability in an LLP

An LLP allows professionals, such as attorneys and accountants, to avoid personal liability for the malpractice of other partners. Of course, a partner in an LLP is still liable for her or his own wrongful acts, such as negligence. Also liable is the partner who supervised the individual who committed a wrongful act. (This generally is true for all types of partners and partnerships, not just LLPs.)

■ **Example 17.8** Five lawyers operate a law firm as an LLP. One of the attorneys, Dan Kolcher, is sued for malpractice and loses. The firm's malpractice insurance is insufficient to pay the judgment. If the firm had been organized as a general partnership, the personal assets of the other attorneys could be used to satisfy the obligation. Because the firm is organized as an LLP, however, no other partner at the firm can be held *personally* liable for Kolcher's malpractice, unless she or he acted as Kolcher's supervisor. In the absence of a supervisor, only Kolcher's personal assets can be used to satisfy the judgment. ■

Although LLP statutes vary from state to state, generally each state statute limits the liability of partners in some way. For instance, Delaware law protects each innocent partner from the "debts and obligations of the partnership arising from negligence, wrongful acts, or misconduct." The UPA more broadly exempts partners in an LLP from personal liability for any partnership obligation, "whether arising in contract, tort, or otherwise" [UPA 306(c)].

Liability outside the State of Formation When an LLP formed in one state wants to do business in another state, it may be required to file a statement of foreign qualification in the second state [UPA 1102]. Because state LLP statutes are not uniform, a question sometimes arises as to which law applies if the LLP statutes in the two states provide different liability protection. Most states apply the law of the state in which the LLP was formed, even when the firm does business in another state, which is also the rule under UPA 1101.

Sharing Liability among Partners When more than one partner in an LLP commits malpractice, there is a question as to how liability should be shared. Is each partner jointly and severally liable for the entire result, as a general partner would be in most states? Recall that *joint and several liability* means that a plaintiff may collect a judgment from all of the partners together (jointly) or one or more of the partners separately (severally).

Some states provide instead for proportionate liability—that is, for separate determinations of the negligence of the partners. ■ **Example 17.9** Accountants Zach and Lyla are partners in an LLP, with Zach supervising Lyla. Lyla negligently fails to file a tax return for a client, Centaur Tools. Centaur files a suit against Zach and Lyla. Under a proportionate liability statute, Zach will be liable for no more than his portion of the responsibility for the missed tax deadline. In a state that does not allow for proportionate liability, Zach can be held liable for the entire loss. ■

17–4c Family Limited Liability Partnerships

A **family limited liability partnership (FLLP)** is a limited liability partnership in which the partners are related to each other—for instance, as spouses, parents and children, siblings, or cousins. A person acting in a fiduciary capacity for persons so related can also be a partner. All of the partners must be natural persons or be acting in a fiduciary capacity for the benefit of natural persons.

Probably the most significant use of the FLLP is in agriculture. Family-owned farms sometimes find this form of business organization beneficial. The FLLP offers the same advantages as other LLPs with certain additional advantages. For instance, in Iowa, FLLPs are exempt from real estate transfer taxes when partnership real estate is transferred among partners.[8]

17–5 Limited Partnerships

We now look at a business organizational form that limits the liability of *some* of its owners—the **limited partnership (LP).** Limited partnerships originated in medieval Europe and have been in existence in the United States since the early 1800s. Today, most states and the District of Columbia have adopted laws based on the Revised Uniform Limited Partnership Act (RULPA).

Limited partnerships differ from general partnerships in several ways. Exhibit 17–3 compares the characteristics of general and limited partnerships.[9]

A limited partnership consists of at least one **general partner** and one or more **limited partners.** A general partner assumes management responsibility for the partnership and has full responsibility for the

partnership and for all its debts. A limited partner contributes cash or other property and owns an interest in the firm but is not involved in management responsibilities. A limited partner is not personally liable for partnership debts beyond the amount of his or her investment. If a limited partner takes part in the management of the business, however, she or he may forfeit that limited liability.

■ **Case in Point 17.10** Valley View Enterprises, Inc., built Pine Lakes Golf Club and Estates in Trumbull County, Ohio, in two phases. Valley View Properties, Ltd., a limited partnership, cut out the roadways and constructed sewer, water, and stormwater lines with inlets. Joseph Ferrara was the owner and the president of Valley View Enterprises and the sole general partner of Valley View Properties.

Ferrara failed to obtain the proper permits for the development work in a timely manner and failed to comply with their requirements once they had been obtained. As a result, the state's attorney general, Michael DeWine, sued the Valley View entities and Ferrara for violating Ohio's water pollution-control laws. Ultimately, a state appellate court held that Ferrara was liable because he was the sole general partner of Valley View Properties (even though he was not subject to liability as an officer of the corporation).[10] ■

17–5a Formation of an LP

In contrast to the private and informal agreement that usually suffices to form a general partnership, the formation of a limited partnership is a public and formal proceeding. The partners must strictly follow statutory requirements. Not only must a limited partnership have at least one general partner and one limited partner, but the partners must also sign a **certificate of limited partnership.**

The certificate of limited partnership must include certain information, including the name, mailing address, and capital contribution of each general and limited partner. The certificate must be filed with the designated state official—under the RULPA, the secretary of state. The certificate usually is open to public inspection.

17–5b Liabilities of Partners in an LP

General partners are personally liable to the partnership's creditors. Thus, at least one general partner is necessary in a limited partnership so that someone has personal liability. This policy can be circumvented in states that allow a corporation to be the general partner in a partnership. Because the corporation has limited liability

---

8. Iowa Code Section 428A.2.
9. Under the UPA, a general partnership can be converted into a limited partnership and vice versa [UPA 902, 903]. The UPA also provides for the merger of a general partnership with one or more general or limited partnerships [UPA 905].

10. *DeWine v. Valley View Enterprises, Inc.*, 2015 -Ohio- 1222 (Ohio Ct.App. 2015).

Exhibit 17–3 A Comparison of General Partnerships and Limited Partnerships

	General Partnership (UPA)	Limited Partnership (RULPA)
Creation	By agreement of two or more persons to carry on a business as co-owners for profit.	By agreement of two or more persons to carry on a business as co-owners for profit. Must include one or more general partners and one or more limited partners. Filing of a certificate with the secretary of state is required.
Sharing of Profits and Losses	By agreement. In the absence of agreement, profits are shared equally by the partners, and losses are shared in the same ratio as profits.	Profits are shared as required in the certificate of limited partnership agreement, and losses are shared likewise, up to the amount of the limited partners' capital contributions. In the absence of a provision in the certificate of limited partnership, profits and losses are shared on the basis of percentages of capital contributions.
Liability	Unlimited personal liability of all partners.	Unlimited personal liability of all general partners; limited partners liable only to the extent of their capital contributions.
Capital Contribution	No minimum or mandatory amount; set by agreement.	Set by agreement.
Management	By agreement. In the absence of agreement, all partners have an equal voice.	Only the general partner (or general partners) make management decisions. Limited partners have no voice. Limited partners who participate in management are subject to liability as general partners if a third party has reason to believe that they are general partners. Safe harbors exist that allow a limited partner to perform work as a contractor, an employee, or and to perform certain other activities for the partnership without incurring personal liability for participating in management.
Duration	Terminated by agreement of the partners, but can continue to do business even when a partner dissociates from the partnership.	Terminated by agreement as in the certificate of limited partnership or by retirement, death, or mental incompetence of a general partner in the absence of the right of the other general partners to continue the partnership. Death of a limited partner does not terminate the partnership, unless he or she is the only remaining limited partner.
Distribution of Assets on Liquidation— Order of Priorities	1. Payment of debts, including those owed to partner and nonpartner creditors. 2. Return of capital contributions and distribution of profit to partners.	1. Outside creditors and partner creditors. 2. Partners and former partners entitled to distributions of partnership assets. 3. Unless otherwise agreed, return of capital contributions and distribution of profit to partners.

by virtue of corporation statutes, if a corporation is the general partner, no one in the limited partnership has personal liability.

The liability of a limited partner, as mentioned, is limited to the capital that she or he contributes or agrees to contribute to the partnership [RULPA 502]. Limited partners enjoy this limited liability only so long as they do not participate in management [RULPA 303].

A limited partner who participates in management and control of the business will be just as liable as a general partner to any creditor who transacts business with the limited partnership. Liability arises when the creditor believes, based on the limited partner's conduct, that the limited partner is a general partner [RULPA 303]. Such conduct includes acting as a general partner, knowingly allowing her or his name to be used in partnership business, or contributing services to the partnership. The extent to which a limited partner can engage in management before being exposed to liability is not always clear, however.

A number of "safe harbors" protect a limited partner from liability for acting as a general partner [RULPA 303(a)]. For instance, safe harbors allow a limited partner to consult with the general partner regarding partnership business, act as a contractor or employee of the partnership, and participate in winding up the business. A limited partner who engages in only one of the safe-harbor activities normally is *not* exposed to personal liability for participating in the management and control of the business.

17–5c Rights and Duties of Partners in an LP

With the exception of the right to participate in management, limited partners have essentially the same rights as general partners. Limited partners have a right of access to the partnership's books and to information regarding partnership business. On dissolution of the partnership, limited partners are entitled to a return of their contributions in accordance with the partnership certificate [RULPA 201(a)(10)]. They can also assign their interests subject to the certificate [RULPA 702, 704]. In addition, they can sue an outside party on behalf of the firm if the general partners with authority to do so have refused to file suit [RULPA 1001].

17–5d Dissociation and Dissolution of an LP

A general partner has the power to voluntarily dissociate, or withdraw, from a limited partnership unless the partnership agreement specifies otherwise. Under the RULPA, a limited partner can withdraw from the partnership by giving six months' notice, unless the partnership agreement specifies a term. In reality, though, most limited partnership agreements do specify a term, which eliminates the limited partner's right to withdraw. Also, some states have passed laws prohibiting the withdrawal of limited partners.

Events That Cause Dissociation In a limited partnership, a general partner's voluntary dissociation from the firm normally will lead to dissolution *unless* all partners agree to continue the business. Similarly, the bankruptcy, retirement, death, or mental incompetence of a general partner will cause the dissociation of that partner and the dissolution of the limited partnership unless the other members agree to continue the firm [RULPA 801]. Bankruptcy of a limited partner, however, does not dissolve the partnership unless it causes the bankruptcy of the firm. In addition, death or an assignment of the

interest (right to receive distributions) of a limited partner does not dissolve a limited partnership [RULPA 702, 704, 705]. A limited partnership can be dissolved by court decree [RULPA 802].

Distribution of Assets On dissolution, creditors' claims, including those of partners who are creditors, take first priority. After that, partners and former partners receive unpaid distributions of partnership assets. Unless otherwise agreed, they are also entitled to a return of their contributions in the proportions in which they share in distributions [RULPA 804].

Valuation of Assets Disputes commonly arise about how the partnership's assets should be valued and distributed and whether the business should be sold. ■ **Case in Point 17.11** Actor Kevin Costner was a limited partner in Midnight Star Enterprises, LP, which runs a casino, bar, and restaurant in South Dakota. There were two other limited partners, Carla and Francis Caneva, who owned a small percentage of the partnership (3.25 units each) and received salaries for managing its operations. Another company owned by Costner, Midnight Star Enterprises, Limited (MSEL), was the general partner. Costner thus controlled a majority of the partnership (93.5 units).

When communications broke down between the partners, MSEL asked a court to dissolve the partnership. MSEL's accountant determined that the firm's fair market value was $3.1 million. The Canevas presented evidence that a competitor would buy the business for $6.2 million. The Canevas wanted the court to force Costner to either buy the business for that price within ten days or sell it on the open market to the highest bidder. Ultimately, the state's highest court held in favor of Costner. A partner cannot force the sale of a limited partnership when the other partners want to continue the business. The court also accepted the $3.1 million buyout price of MSEL's accountant and ordered Costner to pay the Canevas the value of their 6.5 partnership units.[11] ■

Buy-Sell Agreements As mentioned earlier, partners can agree ahead of time on how the partnership's assets will be valued and divided if the partnership dissolves. This is true for limited partnerships as well as for general partnerships. Buy-sell agreements can help the partners avoid disputes. Nonetheless, buy-sell agreements do not eliminate all potential for litigation, especially if the terms are subject to more than one interpretation.

---

11. *In re Dissolution of Midnight Star Enterprises, LP*, 2006 SD 98, 724 N.W.2d 334 (2006).

■ **Case in Point 17.12** Natural Pork Production II, LLP (NPP), an Iowa limited liability partnership, raises hogs. Under a partnership buy-sell agreement, NPP was obligated to buy a dissociating partner's interests but could defer the purchase if it would negatively affect (impair) the firm's capital or cash flow. Under the contract terms, after the "impairment circumstance" changed, NPP was to make the purchase within thirty days. Two of NPP's limited partners, Craton Capital, LP, and Kruse Investment Company, notified NPP of their dissociation. A wave of similar notices from other limited partners followed.

NPP declared an impairment circumstance and refused to buy out the limited partners because of it. Craton and Kruse filed a suit asking a state court to order NPP to buy their units. The court ruled in the plaintiffs' favor. The wording of the buyout provision stated the firm "shall" buy out the partners, which meant it was mandatory. The impairment circumstance only deferred the purchase, and thus NPP was required to buy out the limited partners.[12] ■

17–5e Limited Liability Limited Partnerships

A **limited liability limited partnership (LLLP)** is a type of limited partnership. An LLLP differs from a limited partnership in that a general partner in an LLLP has the same liability as a limited partner in a limited partnership. In other words, the liability of all partners is limited to the amount of their investments in the firm.

A few states provide expressly for LLLPs. In states that do not provide for LLLPs but do allow for limited partnerships and limited liability partnerships, a limited partnership should probably still be able to register with the state as an LLLP.

---

12. *Craton Capital, LP v. Natural Pork Production II, LLP*, 797 N.W.2d 623 (Iowa Ct.App. 2011).

Practice and Review: Limited Liability Business Forms

The city of Papagos, Arizona, had a deteriorating bridge in need of repair on a prominent public roadway. The city posted notices seeking proposals for an artistic bridge design and reconstruction. Davidson Masonry, LLC, which was owned and managed by Carl Davidson and his wife, Marilyn Rowe, decided to submit a bid to create a decorative concrete structure that incorporated artistic metalwork. They contacted Shana Lafayette, a local sculptor who specialized in large-scale metal creations, to help them design the bridge. The city selected their bridge design and awarded them the contract for a commission of $184,000.

Davidson Masonry and Lafayette then entered into an agreement to work together on the bridge project. Davidson Masonry agreed to install and pay for concrete and structural work, and Lafayette agreed to install the metalwork at her expense. They agreed that overall profits would be split, with 25 percent going to Lafayette and 75 percent going to Davidson Masonry. Lafayette designed numerous metal sculptures of trout that were incorporated into colorful decorative concrete forms designed by Rowe. Davidson performed the structural engineering. The group worked together successfully until the completion of the project. Using the information presented in the chapter, answer the following questions.

1. Would Davidson Masonry automatically be taxed as a partnership or a corporation?
2. Is Davidson Masonry member managed or manager managed?
3. Suppose that during construction, Lafayette asked Carl Davidson to rent space in a warehouse that was close to the bridge so that she could work on her sculptures near the site where they would eventually be installed. Carl Davidson signed the rental contract in his own name rather than the name of the LLC. The other members of Davidson Masonry were not aware of the rental agreement. In this situation, would a court likely hold that Davidson Masonry was liable on the contract that Carl Davidson had entered? Why or why not?
4. Now suppose that Rowe has an argument with her husband and wants to withdraw from being a member of Davidson Masonry. What is the term for such a withdrawal, and what effect would it have on the LLC?

Debate This . . .   *Because LLCs are essentially just partnerships with limited liability for members, all partnership laws should apply.*

Terms and Concepts

articles of organization 376
certificate of limited partnership 386
family limited liability partnership
   (FLLP) 386
general partner 386

limited liability company (LLC) 375
limited liability limited partnership
   (LLLP) 389
limited liability partnership (LLP) 385
limited partner 386

limited partnership (LP) 386
member 375
operating agreement 380

Issue Spotters

1. Gabriel, Harris, and Ida are members of Jeweled Watches, LLC. What are their options with respect to the management of their firm? (See *LLC Management and Operation*.)

2. Dorinda, Luis, and Elizabeth form a limited partnership. Dorinda is a general partner, and Luis and Elizabeth are limited partners. If Elizabeth is petitioned into involuntary bankruptcy, will that cause a dissolution of the limited partnership? (See *Limited Partnerships*.)

• **Check your answers to the Issue Spotters against the answers provided in Appendix B at the end of this text.**

Business Scenarios and Case Problems

17–1. Limited Liability Companies. John, Lesa, and Tabir form a limited liability company. John contributes 60 percent of the capital, and Lesa and Tabir each contribute 20 percent. Nothing is decided about how profits will be divided. John assumes that he will be entitled to 60 percent of the profits, in accordance with his contribution. Lesa and Tabir, however, assume that the profits will be divided equally. A dispute over the profits arises, and ultimately a court has to decide the issue. What law will the court apply? In most states, what will result? How could this dispute have been avoided in the first place? Discuss fully. (See *The Limited Liability Company*.)

17–2. Diversity Jurisdiction and Limited Liability Companies. Joe, a resident of New Jersey, wants to open a restaurant. He asks Kay, his friend, an experienced attorney and a New Yorker, for her business and legal advice in exchange for a 20 percent ownership interest in the restaurant. Kay helps Joe negotiate a lease for the restaurant premises and advises Joe to organize the business as a limited liability company (LLC).

Joe forms Café Olé, LLC, and with Kay's help, obtains financing. Then, the night before the restaurant opens, Joe tells Kay that he is "cutting her out of the deal." The restaurant proves to be a success. Kay wants to file a suit in a federal district court against Joe and the LLC. Can a federal court exercise jurisdiction over the parties based on diversity of citizenship? Explain. (See *The Limited Liability Company*.)

17–3. LLC Dissolution. Walter Van Houten and John King formed 1545 Ocean Avenue, LLC, with each managing 50 percent of the business. Its purpose was to renovate an existing building and construct a new commercial building. Van Houten and King quarreled over many aspects of the work on the properties. King claimed that Van Houten paid the contractors too much for the work performed.

As the projects neared completion, King demanded that the LLC be dissolved and that Van Houten agree to a buyout. Because the parties could not agree on a buyout, King sued for dissolution. The trial court enjoined (prevented) further work on the projects until the dispute was settled. As the ground for dissolution, King cited the fights over management decisions. There was no claim of fraud or frustration of purpose. The trial court ordered that the LLC be dissolved, and Van Houten appealed. Should either of the owners be forced to dissolve the LLC before the completion of its purpose—that is, before the building projects are finished? Explain. [*In re 1545 Ocean Avenue, LLC*, 72 A.D.3d 121, 893 N.Y.S.2d 590 (2010)] (See *Dissociation and Dissolution of an LLC*.)

17–4. Business Case Problem with Sample Answer—LLC Operation. After Hurricane Katrina struck the Gulf Coast, James Williford, Patricia Mosser, Marquetta Smith, and Michael Floyd formed Bluewater Logistics, LLC, to bid on construction contracts. Under Mississippi law, every member of a member-managed LLC is entitled to participate in managing the business. The operating agreement provided for a "super majority" 75 percent vote to remove a member who "has either committed a felony or under any other circumstances that would jeopardize the company status" as a contractor. After Bluewater had completed more than $5 million in contracts, Smith told Williford that she, Mosser, and Floyd were exercising their "super majority" vote to fire him. No reason was provided. Williford sued Bluewater and the other members. Did Smith, Mosser, and Floyd breach the state LLC statute, their fiduciary duties, or the Bluewater operating agreements? Discuss. [*Bluewater Logistics, LLC v. Williford*, 55 So.3d 148 (Miss. 2011)] (See *LLC Management and Operation*.)

• **For a sample answer to Problem 17–4, go to Appendix C at the end of this text.**

17–5. Jurisdictional Requirements. Fadal Machining Centers, LLC, and MAG Industrial Automation Centers, LLC, sued a New Jersey–based corporation, Mid-Atlantic CNC, Inc., in federal district court. Ten percent of MAG was owned by SP MAG Holdings, a Delaware LLC. SP MAG had six members, including a Delaware limited partnership called Silver Point Capital Fund and a Delaware LLC called SPCP Group III. In turn, Silver Point and SPCP Group had a common member, Robert O'Shea, who was a New Jersey citizen. Assuming that the amount in controversy exceeds $75,000, does the district court have diversity jurisdiction? Why or why not? [*Fadal Machining Centers, LLC v. Mid-Atlantic CNC, Inc.*, 464 Fed.Appx. 672 (9th Cir. 2012)] (See *The Limited Liability Company*.)

17–6. Jurisdictional Requirements. Siloam Springs Hotel, LLC, operates a Hampton Inn in Siloam Springs, Arkansas. Siloam bought insurance from Century Surety Company to cover the hotel. When guests suffered injuries due to a leak of carbon monoxide from the heating element of an indoor swimming pool, Siloam filed a claim with Century. Century denied coverage, which Siloam disputed. Century asked a federal district court to resolve the dispute. In asserting that the federal court had jurisdiction, Century noted that the amount in controversy exceeded $75,000 and that the parties had complete diversity of citizenship. Century is "a corporation organized under the laws of Ohio, with its principal place of business in Michigan," and Siloam is "a corporation organized under the laws of Oklahoma, with its principal place of business in Arkansas." Can the court exercise diversity jurisdiction in this case? Discuss. [*Siloam Springs Hotel, LLC v. Century Surety Co.*, 781 F.3d 1233 (10th Cir. 2015)] (See *The Limited Liability Company*.)

17–7. Limited Liability. Vision Metals, Inc., owned and operated a pipe manufacturing facility that caused groundwater contamination. The Texas Commission on Environmental Quality (TCEQ) issued a plan that obligated Vision to treat the water and monitor the treatment. Later, Vision sold the property to White Lion Holdings, LLC. Bernard Morello, the sole member of White Lion, knew of the environmental obligations accompanying the property. When White Lion failed to comply with the TCEQ plan, the agency filed a suit in a Texas state court against Morello, asserting violations of the state's environmental rules. Morello was charged with personally removing the facility's treatment plant and monitoring system. Considering the nature of an LLC, what is Morello's best argument that he is not liable? Is this argument likely to succeed? Explain. [*State of Texas v. Morello*, 61 Tex.Sup. Ct.J. 381, 547 S.W.3d 881 (2018)] (See *The Limited Liability Company*.)

17–8. A Question of Ethics—The IDDR Approach and LLC Operation and Management. Q Restaurant Group Holdings, LLC, owns and operates Q-BBQ restaurants. Michael Lapidus managed the restaurants and conducted the day-to-day operations. This included bargaining with the restaurants' vendors, buying the supplies, keeping the books and records of account, and handling the company's money. Lapidus also dealt with the staff and made the hiring and firing decisions. He was expected to use his best efforts to grow the profitability of the restaurants. The LLC discovered, however, that Lapidus was misappropriating and converting company funds to his own use. He was also exposing the LLC to liability by mistreating female employees and vendors. When the members voted to terminate Lapidus, he changed the passwords on the Q-BBQ social media accounts, interfered with the employees during their work hours, and refused to return company property in his possession. [*Q Restaurant Group Holdings, LLC v. Lapidus*, 2017 IL App (2d) 170804-U (2017)] (See *LLC Management and Operation*.)

(a) What action should the LLC take against Lapidus? Consider the ethics of each of the options, using the IDDR approach.

(b) Suppose that Lapidus was in the midst of a contentious divorce, experiencing severe financial problems, and undergoing psychological distress as a consequence. Could these issues excuse his conduct at work? Discuss.

Time-Limited Group Assignment

17–9. Fiduciary Duties in LLCs. Newbury Properties Group owns, manages, and develops real property. Jerry Stoker and the Stoker Group, Inc. (the Stokers), also develop real property. Newbury entered into agreements with the Stokers concerning a large tract of property in Georgia. The parties formed Bellemare, LLC, to develop various parcels of the tract for residential purposes. The operating agreement of Bellemare indicated that "no Member shall be accountable to the LLC or to any other Member with respect to any other business or activity even if the business or activity competes with the LLC's business." Later, when Newbury contracted with other parties to develop parcels within the tract in competition with Bellemare, LLC, the Stokers sued, alleging breach of fiduciary duty. (See *LLC Management and Operation*.)

(a) The first group will discuss and outline the fiduciary duties that the members of an LLC owe to each other.

(b) The second group will determine whether the terms of an operating agreement can alter these fiduciary duties.

(c) The third group will decide in whose favor the court should rule in this situation.

Chapter 18

Corporations

The *corporation* is a creature of statute. A corporation is an artificial being, existing only in law and being neither tangible nor visible. Its existence generally depends on state law, although some corporations, especially public organizations, are created under federal law. Each state has its own body of corporate law, and these laws are not entirely uniform.

The Model Business Corporation Act (MBCA) is a codification of modern corporation law that has been influential in shaping state corporation statutes. Today, the majority of state statutes are guided by the most recent version of the MBCA, often referred to as the Revised Model Business Corporation Act (RMBCA).

Keep in mind, however, that there is considerable variation among the laws of states that have used the MBCA or the RMBCA as a basis for their statutes. In addition, several states do not follow either act. Consequently, individual state corporation laws should be relied on to determine corporate law rather than the MBCA or RMBCA.

18–1 Nature and Classification

A **corporation** is a legal entity created and recognized by state law. This business entity can have one or more owners (called *shareholders*), and it operates under a name distinct from the names of its owners. Both individuals and other businesses can be shareholders. The corporation substitutes itself for its shareholders when conducting corporate business and incurring liability. Its authority to act and the liability for its actions, however, are separate and apart from the shareholders who own it.

A corporation is recognized under U.S. law as a person—an artificial *legal person*, as opposed to a *natural person*. As a "person," it enjoys many of the same rights and privileges under state and federal law that U.S. citizens enjoy. For instance, corporations possess the same right of access to the courts as citizens and can sue or be sued. The constitutional guarantees of due process, free speech, and freedom from unreasonable searches and seizures also apply to corporations.

18–1a Corporate Personnel

In a corporation, the responsibility for the overall management of the firm is entrusted to a *board of directors*, whose members are elected by the shareholders. The board of directors makes the policy decisions and hires *corporate officers* and other employees to run the daily business operations.

When an individual purchases a share of stock in a corporation, that person becomes a shareholder and an owner of the corporation. Unlike the partners in a partnership, the body of shareholders can change constantly without affecting the continued existence of the corporation. A shareholder can sue the corporation, and the corporation can sue a shareholder. Additionally, under certain circumstances, a shareholder can sue on behalf of a corporation.

18–1b The Limited Liability of Shareholders

One of the key advantages of the corporate form is the limited liability of its owners. Normally, corporate shareholders are not personally liable for the obligations of the corporation beyond the extent of their investments.

In certain limited situations, however, a court can *pierce the corporate veil* and impose liability on shareholders for the corporation's obligations. Additionally, creditors often will not extend credit to small companies unless the shareholders assume personal liability, as guarantors, for corporate obligations.

18–1c Corporate Earnings and Taxation

When a corporation earns profits, it can either pass them on to shareholders in the form of **dividends** or retain them as profits. These **retained earnings,** if invested properly, will yield higher corporate profits in the future. In theory, higher profits will cause the price of the company's stock to rise. Individual shareholders can then reap the benefits in the capital gains they receive when they sell their stock.

Corporate Taxation Whether a corporation retains its profits or passes them on to the shareholders as dividends, those profits are subject to income taxation by various levels of government. Failure to pay taxes can lead to severe consequences. The state can suspend the organization's corporate status until the taxes are paid and can even dissolve the corporation for failing to pay taxes.

Another important aspect of corporate taxation is that corporate profits can be subject to double taxation. The company pays tax on its profits. Then, if the profits are passed on to the shareholders as dividends, the shareholders must also pay income tax on them. (This is true unless the dividends represent distributions of capital, which are returns of holders' investments in the stock of the company.) The corporation normally does not receive a tax deduction for dividends it distributes. This double-taxation feature is one of the major disadvantages of the corporate form.

Holding Companies Some U.S. corporations use holding companies to reduce or defer their U.S. income taxes. At its simplest, a **holding company** (sometimes referred to as a *parent company*) is a company whose business activity consists of holding shares in another company. Typically, the holding company is established in a low-tax or no-tax offshore jurisdiction, such as the Cayman Islands, Dubai, Hong Kong, Luxembourg, Monaco, or Panama.

Sometimes, a U.S. corporation sets up a holding company in a low-tax offshore environment and then transfers its cash, bonds, stocks, and other investments to the holding company. In general, any profits received by the holding company on these investments are taxed at the rate of the offshore jurisdiction where the company is registered. Once the profits are brought "onshore," though, they are taxed at the federal corporate income tax rate. Any payments received by the shareholders are also taxable at the full U.S. rates.

18–1d Criminal Acts

Under modern criminal law, a corporation may be held liable for the criminal acts of its agents and employees. Although corporations cannot be imprisoned, they can be fined. (Of course, corporate directors and officers can be imprisoned, and many have been.) In addition, under sentencing guidelines for crimes committed by corporate employees (white-collar crimes), corporations can face fines amounting to hundreds of millions of dollars.

18–1e Tort Liability

A corporation is liable for the torts committed by its agents (including most employees who deal with third parties) or officers within the course and scope of their employment. The doctrine of *respondeat superior*, which will be discussed in the next chapter, applies to corporations in the same way as it does to other agency relationships.

■ **Case in Point 18.1** Mark Bloom was an officer and a director of MB Investment Partners, Inc. (MB), at the time that he formed North Hills, LP, a stock investment fund. Bloom and other MB employees used MB's offices and equipment to administer investments in North Hills.

Later, investors in North Hills requested a full redemption of their investments. By that time, however, most of the funds that had been invested were gone. North Hills had, in fact, been a Ponzi scheme that Bloom had used to finance his lavish personal lifestyle, taking at least $20 million from North Hills for his personal use.

Barry Belmont and other North Hills investors filed a suit in a federal district court against MB, alleging fraud. The court held that MB was liable for Bloom's fraud. MB appealed, and the appellate court affirmed. Tort liability can be attributed to a corporation for the acts of its agent that were committed within the scope of the agent's employment.[1] ■

Because corporations can be liable for their employees' fraud and other misconduct, companies need to be careful about whom they hire and how much they monitor or supervise their employees. Some companies are using special software designed to predict employee misconduct before it occurs, as discussed in this chapter's *Digital Update* feature.

18–1f Classification of Corporations

Corporations can be classified in several ways. The classification of a corporation normally depends on its location, purpose, and ownership characteristics, as described in the following subsections.

Domestic, Foreign, and Alien Corporations A corporation is referred to as a **domestic corporation** by its home state (the state in which it incorporates). A corporation formed in one state but doing business in another is referred to in the second state as a **foreign corporation.**

---

1. *Belmont v. MB Investment Partners, Inc.*, 708 F.3d 470 (3d Cir. 2013).

Digital Update — Programs That Predict Employee Misconduct

Monitoring employees' e-mails and phone conversations at work is generally legal.[a] But what about using software to analyze employee behavior with the goal of predicting, rather than observing, wrongdoing? Now we are entering into the digital realm of *predictive analytics*.

Spy agencies around the world today use analytic software to predict who will engage in a terrorist act, where it will happen, and when. Software applied to data mining of employee behavior (usually just online) actually has been around for several years as well. For example, Amazon started using employee-monitoring programs to predict who might quit. But later, such programs started being used to predict misconduct.

JPMorgan Chase Attempts to Reduce Its Legal Bills

JPMorgan Chase & Company, the world's largest private financial institution, also is perhaps the world's largest purchaser of legal services in that sector. Its legal bills have exceeded $36 billion. The company's management found that employees had engaged in dubious

mortgage bond sales and rigged foreign exchange and energy markets, among many other transgressions. The company hired an extra 2,500 compliance officers and spent almost $750 million on compliance operations during one three-year period.

As a result, JPMorgan now uses software to identify—in advance of any wrongdoing—"rogue" employees. The software analyzes a wide range of inputs on employees' behavior in an attempt to identify patterns that point to future misconduct. If successful, the program will certainly be implemented by other financial institutions.

An Ethical Problem?

A former Federal Reserve Bank examiner, Mark Williams, raised an important issue with respect to predictive analytics: "Policing intentions can be a slippery slope. Do people get a scarlet letter for something they have yet to do?" In other words, will employees be labeled as wrongdoers before they have actually done anything wrong?

....

Critical Thinking *Is thinking about committing a crime illegal?*

a. Electronic Communications Privacy Act, 18 U.S.C.A. Section 2511(2)(d).

A corporation formed in another country (say, Mexico) but doing business in the United States is referred to in the United States as an **alien corporation.**

A corporation does not have an automatic right to do business in a state other than its state of incorporation. In some instances, it must obtain a *certificate of authority* in any state in which it plans to do business. Once the certificate has been issued, the corporation generally can exercise in that state all of the powers conferred on it by its home state. If a foreign corporation does business in a state without obtaining a certificate of authority, the state can impose substantial fines and sanctions on that corporation.

Note that most state statutes specify certain activities, such as soliciting orders via the Internet, that are not considered "doing business" within the state. For instance, a foreign corporation normally does not need a certificate of authority to sell goods or services via the Internet or by mail.

What constitutes doing business within a state? In the following case, the court answered that question.

Case 18.1

Drake Manufacturing Co. v. Polyflow, Inc.

Superior Court of Pennsylvania, 2015 PA Super 16, 109 A.3d 250 (2015).

Background and Facts Drake Manufacturing Company, a Delaware corporation, entered into a contract to sell certain products to Polyflow, Inc., headquartered in Pennsylvania. Drake promised to ship the goods from Drake's plant in Sheffield, Pennsylvania, to Polyflow's place of business in Oaks, Pennsylvania, as well as to addresses in California, Canada, and Holland.

When Polyflow withheld payment of about $300,000 for some of the goods, Drake filed a breach-of-contract suit in a Pennsylvania state court against Polyflow seeking to collect the unpaid amount.

But Drake had failed to obtain a certificate of authority to do business in Pennsylvania as a foreign corporation. Polyflow asserted that this failure to register with the state deprived Drake of the capacity to bring an action against Polyflow in the state's courts. The court issued a judgment in Drake's favor. Polyflow appealed.

In the Language of the Court
Opinion by *JENKINS*, J. [Judge]:
* * * *

[15 Pennsylvania Consolidated Statutes (Pa.C.S.)] Section 4121 provides: "A foreign business corporation, before doing business in this Commonwealth, shall procure a certificate of authority to do so from the Department of State."

* * * Typical conduct requiring a certificate of authority includes maintaining an office to conduct local intrastate business [and] entering into contracts relating to local business or sales.

A corporation is not "doing business" solely because it resorts to the courts of this Commonwealth to recover an indebtedness. [Emphasis added.]
* * * *

[15 Pa.C.S.] Section 4141(a) provides in relevant part that "a nonqualified foreign business corporation doing business in this Commonwealth * * * shall not be permitted to maintain any action or proceeding in any court of this Commonwealth until the corporation has obtained a certificate of authority."
* * * *

* * * The evidence demonstrates that Drake failed to submit a certificate of authority into evidence prior to the verdict in violation of 15 Pa.C.S. Section 4121. Therefore, the trial court should not have permitted Drake to prosecute its action.

The trial court contends that Drake is exempt from the certificate of authority requirement because it merely commenced suit in Pennsylvania to collect a debt * * *. Drake did much more, however, than file suit or attempt to collect a debt. Drake maintains an office in Pennsylvania to conduct local business, conduct which typically requires a certificate of authority. Drake also entered into a contract with Polyflow, and * * * shipped couplings and portable swaging machines to Polyflow's place of business in Pennsylvania * * *. In short, *Drake's conduct was * * * regular, systematic, and extensive, * * * thus constituting the transaction of business and requiring Drake to obtain a certificate of authority.* [Emphasis added.]

We also hold that Drake needed a certificate of authority to sue Polyflow in Pennsylvania for Polyflow's failure to pay for out-of-state shipments in California, Canada and Holland. A foreign corporation that "does business" in Pennsylvania * * * must obtain a certificate in order to prosecute a lawsuit in this Commonwealth, regardless of whether the lawsuit itself concerns in-state conduct or out-of-state conduct.

Decision and Remedy *A state intermediate appellate court reversed the judgment in Drake's favor. Under Pennsylvania state statutes, Drake was required to obtain a certificate of authority to do business in that state. Drake failed to do so. The court should not have allowed Drake to prosecute its action against Polyflow.*

Critical Thinking
• **Legal Environment** *Why would the appellate court permit Polyflow to get away with not paying for delivered and presumably merchantable goods?*

Public and Private Corporations A **public corporation** is a corporation formed by the government to meet some political or governmental purpose. Cities and towns that incorporate are common examples. In addition, many federal government organizations, such as the U.S. Postal Service, the Tennessee Valley Authority, and AMTRAK, are public corporations.

Note that a public corporation is not the same as a **publicly held corporation.** A publicly held corporation (often called a *public company*) is any corporation whose shares are publicly traded in a securities market, such as the New York Stock Exchange or the NASDAQ. (The NASDAQ is an electronic stock exchange founded by the National Association of Securities Dealers.)

Private corporations, in contrast, are created either wholly or in part for private benefit—that is, for profit. Most corporations are private. Although they may serve a public purpose, as a public electric or gas utility does, they are owned by private persons rather than by a government.[2]

Nonprofit Corporations Corporations formed for purposes other than making a profit are called *nonprofit* or *not-for-profit* corporations. Private hospitals, educational institutions, charities, and religious organizations, for instance, are frequently organized as nonprofit corporations. The nonprofit corporation is a convenient form of organization that allows various groups to own property and to form contracts without exposing the individual members to personal liability.

Close Corporations Most corporate enterprises in the United States fall into the category of close corporations. A **close corporation** is one whose shares are held by relatively few persons, often members of a family. Close corporations are also referred to as *closely held, family,* or *privately held* corporations.

Usually, the members of the small group constituting the shareholders of a close corporation are personally known to each other. Because the number of shareholders is so small, there is no trading market for the shares. In practice, a close corporation is often operated like a partnership.

The statutes in many states allow close corporations to depart significantly from certain formalities required by traditional corporation law.[3] Under the RMBCA, close corporations have considerable flexibility in determining their operating rules [RMBCA 7.32]. If all of a corporation's shareholders agree in writing, the corporation can operate without directors and bylaws. In addition, the corporation can operate without annual or special shareholders' or directors' meetings, stock certificates, or formal records of shareholders' or directors' decisions.[4]

Management of Close Corporations. Management of a close corporation resembles that of a sole proprietorship or a partnership, in that control is held by a single shareholder or a tightly knit group of shareholders. As a corporation, however, the firm must meet all specific legal requirements set forth in state statutes.

To prevent a majority shareholder from dominating the company, a close corporation may require that more than a simple majority of the directors approve any action taken by the board. In a larger corporation, such a requirement would typically apply only to extraordinary actions (such as selling all the corporate assets) and not to ordinary business decisions.

Transfer of Shares in Close Corporations. By definition, a close corporation has a small number of shareholders. Thus, the transfer of one shareholder's shares to someone else can cause serious management problems. The other shareholders may find themselves required to share control with someone they do not know or like. ■ **Example 18.2** Three siblings, Sherry, Karen, and Henry Johnson, are the only shareholders of Johnson's Car Wash, Inc. Henry wants to sell his shares, but Sherry and Karen do not want him to sell the shares to a third person unknown to them. ■

To avoid this situation, a close corporation can restrict the transferability of shares to outside persons. Shareholders can be required to offer their shares to the corporation or to the other shareholders before selling them to an outside purchaser. In fact, in a few states close corporations must transfer shares in this manner under state statutes.

One way the close corporation can effect restrictions on transferability is by spelling them out in a **shareholder agreement.** A shareholder agreement can also provide for proportional control when one of the original shareholders dies. The decedent's shares of stock in the corporation can be divided in such a way that the proportionate holdings of the survivors, and thus their proportionate control, will be maintained.

Misappropriation of Close Corporation Funds. Sometimes, a majority shareholder in a close corporation takes advantage of his or her position and misappropriates company funds. In such situations, the normal remedy for the injured minority shareholders is to have their shares appraised and to be paid the fair market value for them.

■ **Case in Point 18.3** John Murray, Stephen Hopkins, and Paul Ryan were officers, directors, employees, and majority shareholders of Olympic Adhesives, Inc. Merek Rubin was a minority shareholder. Murray, Hopkins, and Ryan were paid salaries. Twice a year, they paid themselves additional compensation—between 75 and

---

2. The United States Supreme Court first recognized the property rights of private corporations and clarified the distinction between public and private corporations in the landmark case *Trustees of Dartmouth College v. Woodward*, 17 U.S. (4 Wheaton) 518, 4 L.Ed. 629 (1819).
3. In some states, such as Maryland, a close corporation need not have a board of directors.
4. Shareholders cannot agree, however, to eliminate certain rights of shareholders, such as the right to inspect corporate records or the right to bring *shareholder's derivative suits* (lawsuits on behalf of the corporation).

98 percent of Olympic's net profits, allocated according to their stock ownership. Rubin filed a suit against the majority shareholders, alleging that their compensation deprived him of his share of Olympic's profits.

The court explained that a salary should reasonably relate to a corporate officer's ability and the quantity and quality of his or her services. The court found that a reasonable amount of compensation would have been 10 percent of Olympic's average annual net sales. Therefore, the additional compensation the majority shareholders paid themselves—based on stock ownership and not on performance—was excessive. The court ordered the defendants to repay Olympic nearly $6 million to be distributed among its shareholders. On appeal, the reviewing court affirmed this decision.[5] ∎

S Corporations A close corporation that meets the qualifying requirements specified in Subchapter S of the Internal Revenue Code can choose to operate as an **S corporation.** (A corporation will automatically be taxed under Subchapter C unless it elects S corporation status.) If a corporation has S corporation status, it can avoid the imposition of income taxes at the corporate level while retaining many of the advantages of a corporation, particularly limited liability. Among the numerous requirements for S corporation status, the following are the most important:

1. The corporation must be a domestic corporation.
2. The corporation must not be a member of an affiliated group of corporations.
3. The shareholders must be individuals, estates, or certain trusts and tax-exempt organizations. Partnerships and nonqualifying trusts cannot be shareholders. Corporations can be shareholders under certain circumstances.
4. The corporation must have no more than one hundred shareholders.
5. The corporation must have only one class of stock, although it is not necessary that all shareholders have the same voting rights.
6. No shareholder of the corporation may be a nonresident alien.

An S corporation is treated differently than a regular corporation for tax purposes. An S corporation is taxed like a partnership, so the corporate income passes through to the shareholders, who pay personal income tax on it. This treatment enables the S corporation to avoid the double taxation imposed on regular corporations. In addition, the shareholders' tax brackets may be lower than the tax bracket that the corporation would have been in if the tax had been imposed at the corporate level.

In spite of these tax benefits, the S corporation has lost much of its appeal. The newer limited liability business forms (such as LLCs, LPs, and LLPs) offer similar tax advantages and greater flexibility.

Professional Corporations Professionals such as physicians, lawyers, dentists, and accountants can incorporate. A professional corporation typically is identified by the letters *P.C.* (professional corporation), *S.C.* (service corporation), or *P.A.* (professional association).

In general, the laws governing the formation and operation of professional corporations are similar to those governing ordinary business corporations. There are some differences in terms of liability, however, because the shareholder-owners are professionals who are held to a higher standard of conduct. For liability purposes, some courts treat professional corporations somewhat like partnerships and hold each professional liable for malpractice committed within the scope of the business by others in the firm.

Benefit Corporations A growing number of states have enacted legislation that creates a relatively new corporate form called a *benefit corporation.* A **benefit corporation** is a for-profit corporation that seeks to have a material positive impact on society and the environment. Benefit corporations differ from traditional corporations in the following ways:

1. *Purpose.* Although a benefit corporation is designed to make a profit, its purpose is to benefit the public as a whole. (In contrast, the purpose of an ordinary business corporation is to provide long-term shareholder value.) The directors of a benefit corporation must, during the decision-making process, consider the impact of their decisions on society and the environment.
2. *Accountability.* Shareholders of a benefit corporation determine whether the company has achieved a material positive impact. Shareholders also have a right of private action, called a *benefit enforcement proceeding*, enabling them to sue the corporation if it fails to pursue or create public benefit.
3. *Transparency.* A benefit corporation must issue an annual benefit report on its overall social and environmental performance that uses a recognized third-party standard to assess its performance. The report must be delivered to the shareholders and posted on a public website.

5. *Rubin v. Murray*, 79 Mass.App.Ct. 64, 943 N.E.2d 949 (2011).

In the following case, a benefit corporation took an action that it believed would have a positive impact on the persons it was established to serve. Two of those affected by the action disagreed and filed a suit to challenge the action.

Greenfield v. Mandalay Shores Community Association

California Court of Appeal, Second District, Division 6, 21 Cal.App.5th 896, 230 Cal.Rptr.3d 827 (2018).

Background and Facts Mandalay Shores is a beach community in California's Oxnard Coastal Zone where nonresidents have vacationed for decades, renting homes on a short-term basis. Robert and Demetra Greenfield own a single-family residence at Mandalay Shores that they rent to families for periods of less than thirty days.

Mandalay Shores Community Association is a mutual benefit corporation established for the development of the community. The association adopted a resolution banning short-term rentals (STRs), claiming that it was necessary to reduce parking, noise, and trash problems. Homeowners who rented their homes "for less than 30 consecutive days" were subject to fines of up to $5,000 per offense.

The Greenfields filed a suit in a California state court against the association, contending that the STR ban violated the California Coastal Act. The court denied the plaintiffs' request for a preliminary injunction to prohibit the enforcement of the resolution. The Greenfields appealed.

In the Language of the Court

YEGAN, Acting P.J. [Presiding Judge]

* * * *

* * * The California Coastal Act is intended to, among other things, "maximize public access to and along the coast and maximize public recreational opportunities to the coastal zone consistent with sound resources conservation principles and constitutionally protected right of private property owners." The Coastal Act requires that any person who seeks to undertake a "development" in the coastal zone to obtain a coastal development permit. "Development" is broadly defined to include, among other things, any "change in the density or intensity of use of land." * * * * *"Development" under the Coastal Act is not restricted to activities that physically alter the land or water.* [Emphasis added.]

* * * *

* * * The STR ban changes the intensity of use and access to single-family residences in the Oxnard Coastal Zone. STRs were common in [Mandalay Shores] before the STR ban; now they are prohibited.

Respondent asserts that the STR ban is necessary to curtail the increasing problem of short-term rentals which cause parking, noise, and trash problems. *STR bans, however, are a matter for the City and Coastal Commission to address.* STRs may not be regulated by private actors where it affects the intensity of use or access to single-family residences in a coastal zone. The question of whether a seven-day house rental is more of a neighborhood problem than a 31-day rental must be decided by the City and the Coastal Commission, not a homeowner's association. [Emphasis added.]

* * * Respondent's STR ban affects 1,400 [housing] units and cuts across a wide swath of beach properties that have historically been used as short-term rentals. A *prima facie* showing has been made to issue a preliminary injunction staying [prohibiting] enforcement of the STR ban until trial.

Decision and Remedy *A state intermediate appellate court reversed the lower court's denial of the Greenfields' motion and ordered the issuance of a preliminary injunction. "Mandalay Shores Community Association . . . has erected a monetary barrier to the beach. It has no right to do so."*

Critical Thinking

- **Legal Environment** *Did the STR ban adopted by the association comport with or contravene its status as a benefit corporation? Discuss.*
- **What If the Facts Were Different?** *Suppose that instead of adopting an STR ban on its own, the association had petitioned the city and the Coastal Commission to impose one. Would the result have been different? Explain.*

18–2 Corporate Formation and Powers

Incorporating a business is much simpler today than it was twenty years ago, and many states allow businesses to incorporate via the Internet. Here, we examine the process by which a corporation comes into existence.

18–2a Promotional Activities

In the past, preliminary steps were taken to organize and promote a business prior to incorporating. Contracts were made with investors and others on behalf of the future corporation. Today, due to the relative ease of forming a corporation in most states, persons incorporating their business rarely, if ever, engage in preliminary promotional activities.

Nevertheless, businesspersons should understand that they are personally liable for any preincorporation contracts made with investors, accountants, or others on behalf of the future corporation. Personal liability continues until the newly formed corporation assumes liability for the preincorporation contracts through a novation.

18–2b Incorporation Procedures

Each state has its own set of incorporation procedures. Most often, they are listed on the secretary of state's website. Generally, however, all incorporators follow several basic steps, discussed next.

Select the State of Incorporation Because state corporate laws differ, individuals seeking to incorporate a business may look for the states that offer the most advantageous tax or other provisions. Many corporations, for instance, have chosen to incorporate in Delaware because it has historically had the least restrictive laws, along with provisions that favor corporate management. For reasons of convenience and cost, though, businesses often choose to incorporate in the state in which the corporation's business will primarily be conducted.

Secure an Appropriate Corporate Name The choice of a corporate name is subject to state approval to ensure against duplication or deception. Most state statutes require a search to confirm that the chosen corporate name is available. A new corporation's name cannot be the same as, or deceptively similar to, the name of an existing corporation doing business within the state. All states require the corporation's name to include the word *Corporation (Corp.)*, *Incorporated (Inc.)*, *Company (Co.)*, or *Limited (Ltd.)*.[6]

---

6. Failure to use one of these terms to disclose corporate status may be grounds for holding an individual incorporator liable for corporate contracts under agency law.

Prepare the Articles of Incorporation The primary document needed to incorporate a business is the **articles of incorporation.** The articles include basic information about the corporation and serve as a primary source of authority for its future organization and business functions. The person or persons who execute (sign) the articles are the *incorporators.* Generally, the articles must include the following information [RMBCA 2.02]:

1. The name of the corporation.
2. The number of shares of stock the corporation is authorized to issue [RMBCA 2.02(a)]. (Large corporations often also state a par value for each share, such as $0.20 per share, and specify the various types or classes of stock authorized for issuance.)
3. The name and street address of the corporation's initial registered agent and registered office. The registered agent is the person who can receive legal documents (such as orders to appear in court) on behalf of the corporation. The registered office often is the main corporate office.
4. The name and address of each incorporator.

In addition, the articles *may* set forth other information, such as the names and addresses of the initial members of the board of directors and the duration and purpose of the corporation. A corporation has perpetual existence unless the articles state otherwise. As to the corporation's purpose, a corporation can be formed for any lawful purpose, and the RMBCA does not require the articles to include a specific statement of purpose. Consequently, the articles often include only a general statement of purpose. By not mentioning specifics, the corporation avoids the need for future amendments to the corporate articles [RMBCA 2.02(b)(2)(i), 3.01]. Similarly, the articles do not provide much detail about the firm's operations, which are spelled out in the company's *bylaws* (discussed shortly).

File the Articles with the State Once the articles of incorporation have been prepared and signed, they are sent to the appropriate state official, usually the secretary of state, along with the required filing fee. In most states, the secretary of state then stamps the articles "Filed" and returns a copy of the articles to the incorporators. Once this occurs, the corporation officially exists.

18–2c First Organizational Meeting to Adopt Bylaws

After incorporation, the first organizational meeting must be held. If the articles of incorporation named the initial board of directors, then the directors, by majority vote, call the meeting. If the articles did not name the directors (as is typical), then the incorporators hold the meeting to elect the directors and complete any other business necessary.

Usually, the most important function of this meeting is the adoption of **bylaws,** which are the internal rules of management for the corporation. The bylaws cannot conflict with the state corporation statute or the articles of incorporation [RMBCA 2.06]. Under the RMBCA, the shareholders may amend or repeal the bylaws. The board of directors may also amend or repeal the bylaws, unless the articles of incorporation or provisions of the state corporation statute reserve this power to the shareholders [RMBCA 10.20].

The bylaws typically describe such matters as voting requirements for shareholders, the election of the board of directors, and the methods of replacing directors. Bylaws also frequently outline the manner and time of holding shareholders' and board meetings.

18–2d Improper Incorporation

The procedures for incorporation are very specific. If they are not followed precisely, others may be able to challenge the existence of the corporation. Errors in incorporation procedures can become important when, for instance, a third party who is attempting to enforce a contract or bring a suit for a tort injury learns of them.

De Jure Corporations If a corporation has substantially complied with all conditions precedent to incorporation, the corporation is said to have *de jure* (rightful and lawful) existence. In most states and under RMBCA 2.03(b), the secretary of state's filing of the articles of incorporation is conclusive proof that all mandatory statutory provisions have been met [RMBCA 2.03(b)].

Sometimes, the incorporators fail to comply with all statutory mandates. If the defect is minor, such as an incorrect address listed on the articles of incorporation, most courts will overlook the defect and find that a *de jure* corporation exists.

De Facto Corporations If the defect in formation is substantial, such as a corporation's failure to hold an organizational meeting to adopt bylaws, the outcome will vary depending on the jurisdiction. Some states, including Mississippi, New York, Ohio, and Oklahoma, recognize the common law doctrine of *de facto* corporation.[7]

In those states, the courts will treat a corporation as a legal corporation despite a defect in its formation if the following three requirements are met:

1. A state statute exists under which the corporation can be validly incorporated.
2. The parties have made a good faith attempt to comply with the statute.
3. The parties have already undertaken to do business as a corporation.

Many state courts, however, have interpreted their states' version of the RMBCA as abolishing the common law doctrine of *de facto* corporations. These states include Alaska, Arizona, Minnesota, New Mexico, Oregon, South Dakota, Tennessee, Utah, and Washington, as well as the District of Columbia. In those jurisdictions, if there is a substantial defect in complying with the incorporation statute, the corporation does not legally exist, and the incorporators are personally liable.

Corporation by Estoppel Sometimes, a business association holds itself out to others as being a corporation when it has made no attempt to incorporate. In those situations, the firm normally will be estopped (prevented) from denying corporate status in a lawsuit by a third party. The estoppel doctrine most commonly applies when a third party contracts with an entity that claims to be a corporation but has not filed articles of incorporation. It may also apply when a third party contracts with a person claiming to be an agent of a corporation that does not in fact exist.

When justice requires, courts in some states will treat an alleged corporation as if it were an actual corporation for the purpose of determining rights and liabilities in particular circumstances.[8] Recognition of corporate status does not extend beyond the resolution of the problem at hand.

■ **Case in Point 18.4** Dale Ross formed Big Little Farms, Inc. (BLF), in Trumbull County, Ohio, to breed and train racehorses. Dale failed to pay BLF's taxes, and the state cancelled its corporate status. Dale continued operating the farm business, however. Over a number of years, Dale's brother, Gene, loaned him funds to make improvements to BLF. At one point, Dale signed—as president of BLF Corporation—a promissory note to Gene and a mortgage on the farm. A few months later, Gene died. Gene's wife filed a claim against Dale and his wife seeking, in part, to foreclose on the mortgage. Then Dale died. Dale's wife claimed that the mortgage note her husband had signed was void because the corporation did not legally exist at the time he had signed it.

---

7. See, for example, *In re Hausman*, 13 N.Y.3d 408, 893 N.Y.S.2d 499, 921 N.E.2d 191 (2009).

8. Some states have expressly rejected the common law theory of corporation by estoppel, finding that it is inconsistent with their statutory law.

Gene's wife argued that Dale's estate should not be able to avoid paying a note that Dale had knowingly signed as president of a corporation whose legal status had been revoked. Ultimately, a state appellate court ruled that the mortgage note was valid. BLF was estopped from denying its corporate status for the purpose of invalidating the loan contract.[9] ■

18–2e Corporate Financing

Part of the process of corporate formation involves financing. Corporations normally are financed by the issuance and sale of corporate securities. **Securities**—stocks and bonds—evidence an ownership interest in a corporation or a promise of repayment of debt by a corporation. Some corporations may also seek alternative financing through *venture capital*, *private equity capital*, and *crowdfunding*.

Bonds Bonds are *debt securities*, which represent the borrowing of funds. Bonds are issued by business firms and by governments at all levels as evidence of funds they are borrowing from investors.

Bonds normally have a designated *maturity date*—the date when the principal, or face amount, of the bond is returned to the bondholder. Bondholders also receive fixed-dollar interest payments, usually semiannually, during the period of time prior to maturity. For that reason, they are sometimes referred to as *fixed-income securities*. Because debt financing represents a legal obligation of the corporation, various features and terms of a particular bond issue are specified in a lending agreement.

Of course, not all debt is in the form of bonds. For instance, some debt is in the form of accounts payable and notes payable, which typically are short-term debts. Bonds are simply a way for the corporation to split up its long-term debt so that it can be more easily marketed.

Stocks Issuing stocks is another way for corporations to obtain financing [RMBCA 6.01]. **Stocks,** or *equity securities*, represent the purchase of ownership in the business firm. The true ownership of a corporation is represented by **common stock.** Common stock provides an interest in the corporation with regard to (1) control, (2) earnings, and (3) net assets. A shareholder's interest is generally proportionate to the number of shares he or she owns out of the total number of shares issued. Any person who purchases common stock acquires voting rights— one vote per share held.

An issuing firm is not obligated to return a principal amount per share to each holder of its common stock, nor does the firm have to guarantee a dividend. Indeed, some corporations never pay dividends. Holders of common stock are investors who assume a *residual* position in the overall financial structure of a business. They benefit when the market price of the stock increases. In terms of receiving payment for their investments, they are last in line.

Preferred stock is an equity security with *preferences*. Usually, this means that holders of preferred stock have priority over holders of common stock as to dividends and payment on dissolution of the corporation. The preferences must be stated in the articles of incorporation. Holders of preferred stock may or may not have the right to vote. Although holders of preferred stock have a stronger position than common shareholders with respect to dividends and claims on assets, they will not share in the full prosperity of the firm if it grows successfully over time.

Venture Capital Start-up businesses and high-risk enterprises often obtain venture capital financing. **Venture capital** is capital provided to new businesses by professional, outside investors (*venture capitalists*, typically groups of wealthy investors and securities firms). Venture capital investments are high risk—the investors must be willing to lose all of their invested funds—but offer the potential for well-above-average returns in the future.

To obtain venture capital financing, the start-up business typically gives up a share of its ownership to the venture capitalists. In addition to funding, venture capitalists may provide managerial and technical expertise, and they nearly always are given some control over the new company's decisions. Many Internet-based companies, such as Google and Amazon, were initially financed by venture capital.

Private Equity Capital Private equity firms pool funds from wealthy investors and use this **private equity capital** to invest in existing corporations. Usually, a private equity firm buys an entire corporation and then reorganizes it. Sometimes, divisions of the purchased company are sold off to pay down debt.

Ultimately, the private equity firm may sell shares in the reorganized (and perhaps more profitable) company to the public in an *initial public offering (IPO)*. Then the private equity firm can make profits by selling its shares in the company to the public.

Crowdfunding Start-up businesses can also attempt to obtain financing through *crowdfunding*. **Crowdfunding** is a cooperative activity in which people network and pool funds and other resources via the Internet to assist a

9. *Lamancusa v. Big Little Farms, Inc.*, 2013 -Ohio- 5815, 5 N.E.3d 1080 (Ohio App. 2013).

cause or invest in a venture. Sometimes, crowdfunding is used to raise funds for charitable purposes, such as disaster relief, but increasingly it is being used to finance budding entrepreneurs.

Starting in 2016, Securities and Exchange Commission (SEC) rules allow companies to offer and sell securities through crowdfunding—removing a decades-old ban on public solicitation for private investments. As a result, companies can advertise investment opportunities to the general public. According to the SEC, the rules are intended to help smaller companies raise capital while providing investors with additional protections. Companies are required to make specific disclosures and are limited to raising $1 million a year through crowdfunding.

18–2f Corporate Powers

When a corporation is created, the express and implied powers necessary to achieve its purpose also come into existence.

Express Powers The express powers of a corporation are found in its articles of incorporation, in the law of the state of incorporation, and in the state and federal constitutions. Corporate bylaws and the resolutions of the corporation's board of directors also establish express powers.

The following order of priority is used if a conflict arises among the various documents involving a corporation:

1. The U.S. Constitution.
2. State constitutions.
3. State statutes.
4. The articles of incorporation.
5. Bylaws.
6. Resolutions of the board of directors.

It is important that the bylaws set forth the specific operating rules of the corporation. State corporation statutes frequently provide default rules that apply if the company's bylaws are silent on an issue.

On occasion, the U.S. government steps in to challenge what a corporation may consider one of its express powers. This chapter's *Global Insight* feature discusses a dispute between the U.S. government and Microsoft Corporation over a demand that the company provide the government with access to e-mail stored in servers on foreign soil.

Implied Powers When a corporation is created, it acquires certain implied powers. Barring express constitutional, statutory, or other prohibitions, the corporation has the implied power to perform all acts reasonably necessary to accomplish its corporate purposes. For this reason, a corporation has the implied power to borrow and

lend funds within certain limits and to extend credit to parties with whom it has contracts.

Most often, the president or chief executive officer of the corporation signs the necessary documents on behalf of the corporation. Such corporate officers have the implied power to bind the corporation in matters directly connected with the *ordinary* business affairs of the enterprise.

There are limits to what a corporate officer can do. For instance, a corporate officer does not have the authority to bind the corporation to an action that will greatly affect the corporate purpose or undertaking, such as the sale of substantial corporate assets.

Ultra Vires Doctrine The term *ultra vires* means "beyond the power." In corporate law, acts of a corporation that are beyond its express or implied powers are *ultra vires* acts. In the past, most cases dealing with *ultra vires* acts involved contracts made for unauthorized purposes. Now, because the articles of incorporation of most private corporations do not state a specific purpose, the *ultra vires* doctrine has declined in importance.

Nevertheless, cases involving *ultra vires* acts are sometimes brought against nonprofit corporations or municipal (public) corporations. ■ **Case in Point 18.5** Four men formed a nonprofit corporation to create the Armenian Genocide Museum & Memorial (AGM&M). The bylaws appointed them as trustees (similar to corporate directors) for life. One of the trustees, Gerard Cafesjian, became the chair and president of AGM&M. Eventually, the relationship among the trustees deteriorated, and Cafesjian resigned.

The corporation then brought a suit claiming that Cafesjian had engaged in numerous *ultra vires* acts, self-dealing, and mismanagement. Although the bylaws required an 80 percent affirmative vote of the trustees to take action, Cafesjian had taken many actions without the board's approval. He had also entered into contracts for real estate transactions in which he had a personal interest. Because Cafesjian had taken actions that exceeded his authority and had failed to follow rules set forth in the bylaws, the court ruled that the corporation could go forward with its suit.[10] ■

Remedies for *Ultra Vires* Acts Under Section 3.04 of the RMBCA, shareholders can seek an injunction from a court to prevent (or stop) the corporation from engaging in *ultra vires* acts. The attorney general in the state of incorporation can also bring an action to obtain an injunction against the *ultra vires* transactions or to

---

10. *Armenian Assembly of America, Inc. v. Cafesjian,* 692 F.Supp.2d 20 (D.C. Cir. 2010).

Global Insight   Does Cloud Computing Have a Nationality?

Most people use "the cloud" for the storage of their digital data—photos, e-mails, music, documents, and just about anything else. Not surprisingly, major global digital players like Apple, Amazon, Google, and Microsoft have spent billions to create "clouds" of servers all over the world. In the clouds are stored confidential, organized, and secure data.

Microsoft and Google Battle Federal Warrants

The U.S. government issued a warrant to Microsoft Corporation to produce e-mails related to a narcotics case from a Hotmail account. That account was hosted in a Microsoft cloud location in Ireland. Microsoft refused, arguing that the U.S. government did not have the power to issue a warrant for information stored in a foreign country and that doing so would threaten the privacy of U.S. citizens. A federal district court in New York confirmed the government's right to the Ireland-located e-mails, but that decision was reversed on appeal. Ultimately, the United States Supreme Court granted *certiorari* to resolve the dispute.[a]

In a subsequent case related to a criminal investigation, the government issued a warrant to access e-mails that Google had stored outside the United States. Google made the same arguments that Microsoft had, but a federal district court ruled in the government's favor. The court reasoned that there were differences in how the two corporations stored the cloud data overseas. Microsoft had stored the data exclusively in Ireland, so it "resided" in that location.

Google had separated its cloud data into components and constantly moved it around the globe to improve network efficiency.[b]

The CLOUD Act

In 2018, Congress enacted the Clarifying Lawful Overseas Use of Data Act (CLOUD Act), which amended existing law.[c] The CLOUD Act requires service providers to preserve, back up, or disclose the contents of wire or electronic communications, as well as any record pertaining to a customer or subscriber within the provider's possession, custody, or control. Under the act, service providers have a duty to preserve this information, regardless of whether it is located inside or outside the United States.

After the CLOUD Act was passed, the government in the *Microsoft* case obtained a new warrant pursuant to the act. By the time the case reached the United States Supreme Court, there was no longer any dispute to resolve. The Court found that the government had the authority under the CLOUD Act to issue warrants to access information extraterritorially (and vacated the appellate court's decision).[d]

Critical Thinking *How might the CLOUD Act affect the privacy of U.S. citizens who store their information in the cloud?*

a. *United States v. Microsoft Corp.*, __ U.S. __, 138 S.Ct. 356, 199 L.Ed.2d 261 (2017).

b. *In the Matter of the Search of Content Stored at Premises Controlled by Google, Inc.*, 2017 WL 1487625 (N.D.Cal. 2017).

c. 18 U.S.C. Section 2703.

d. *United States v. Microsoft Corp.*, __ U.S. __ 138 S.Ct. 1186, 200 L.Ed.2d 610 (2018).

---

seek dissolution of the corporation. The corporation or its shareholders (on behalf of the corporation) can seek damages from the officers and directors who were responsible for the *ultra vires* acts.

18-3 Piercing the Corporate Veil

Occasionally, the owners use a corporate entity to perpetrate a fraud, circumvent the law, or in some other way accomplish an illegitimate objective. In these situations, the courts will ignore the corporate structure by **piercing the corporate veil** and exposing the shareholders to personal liability [RMBCA 2.04].

Generally, courts pierce the veil when the corporate privilege is abused for personal benefit or when

the corporate business is treated so carelessly that it is indistinguishable from that of a controlling shareholder. When the facts show that great injustice would result from a shareholder's use of a corporation to avoid individual responsibility, a court will look behind the corporate structure to the individual shareholders.

18-3a Factors That Lead Courts to Pierce the Corporate Veil

The following are some of the factors that frequently cause the courts to pierce the corporate veil:

1. A party is tricked or misled into dealing with the corporation rather than the individual.

2. The corporation is set up never to make a profit or always to be insolvent. Alternatively, it is too thinly

capitalized—that is, it has insufficient capital at the time it is formed to meet its prospective debts or potential liabilities.

3. The corporation is formed to evade an existing legal obligation.

4. Statutory corporate formalities, such as holding required corporation meetings, are not followed.

5. Personal and corporate interests are mixed together, or **commingled,** to such an extent that the corporation has no separate identity.

■ **Case in Point 18.6** Dog House Investments, LLC, operated a dog "camp" in Nashville, Tennessee. Dog House leased the property from Teal Properties, Inc., which was owned by Jerry Teal, its sole shareholder. Under the lease, the landlord promised to repair damage that rendered the property "untenantable" (unusable). Following a flood, Dog House notified Jerry that the property was untenantable. Jerry assured Dog House that the flood damage was covered by insurance but took no steps to restore the property. The parties then agreed that Dog House would undertake the repairs and be reimbursed by Teal Properties.

Dog House spent $39,000 to repair the damage and submitted invoices for reimbursement. Teal Properties recovered $40,000 from its insurance company but did not pay Dog House. Close to bankruptcy, Dog House sued Teal Properties and Jerry. The court pierced the corporate veil and held Jerry personally liable for the repair costs. An appellate court affirmed. Teal Properties owned no property and had no assets. It received rent but paid it immediately to Jerry. The court concluded that the company was not operated as an entity separate from its sole shareholder.[11] ■

18–3b A Potential Problem for Close Corporations

The potential for corporate assets to be used for personal benefit is especially great in a close corporation. In such a corporation, the separate status of the corporate entity and the shareholders (often family members) must be carefully preserved. Practices that invite trouble for a close corporation include the commingling of corporate and personal funds and the shareholders' continuous personal use of corporate property (for instance, vehicles).

Typically, courts are reluctant to hold shareholders in close corporations personally liable for corporate obligations unless there is some evidence of fraud or wrongdoing. ■ **Case in Point 18.7** Pip, Jimmy, and Theodore Brennan are brothers and shareholders of Brennan's, Inc.,

which owns and operates New Orleans's famous Brennan's Restaurant. As a close corporation, Brennan's, Inc., did not hold formal corporate meetings with agendas and minutes, but it did maintain corporate books, hold corporate bank accounts, and file corporate tax returns.

The Brennan brothers retained attorney Edward Colbert to represent them in a family matter, and the attorney's bills were sent to the restaurant and paid from the corporate account. Later, when Brennan's, Inc., sued Colbert for malpractice, Colbert argued that the court should pierce the corporate veil because the Brennan brothers did not observe corporate formalities. The court refused to do so, however, because there was no evidence of fraud, malfeasance, or other wrongdoing by the Brennan brothers. There is no requirement for small, close corporations to operate with the formality usually expected of larger corporations.[12] ■

18–3c The Alter-Ego Theory

Sometimes, courts pierce the corporate veil under the theory that the corporation was not operated as a separate entity. Rather, it was just another side (the *alter ego*) of the individual or group that actually controlled the corporation. This is called the alter-ego theory.

The alter-ego theory is applied when a corporation is so dominated and controlled by an individual (or group) that the separate identities of the person (or group) and the corporation are no longer distinct. Courts use the alter-ego theory to avoid injustice or fraud that would result if wrongdoers were allowed to hide behind the protection of limited liability.

■ **Case in Point 18.8** Steiner Electric Company (Steiner) is an Illinois corporation that sells electrical products. Steiner sold goods to Delta Equipment Company and Sackett Systems, Inc., on credit. Both Delta and Sackett were owned and controlled by a single shareholder—Leonard Maniscalco. Steiner was not fully paid for the products it sold on credit to Delta and Sackett. Eventually, Steiner sued Delta and won a default judgment, but by that time, Delta had been dissolved. Steiner then asked a state court to pierce the corporate veil and hold Maniscalco liable for the debts of the two companies, claiming the companies were merely Maniscalco's alter egos.

The court agreed and held Maniscalco liable. Delta and Sackett were inadequately capitalized, transactions were not properly documented, funds were commingled, and corporate formalities were not observed. Maniscalco

---

11. *Dog House Investments, LLC v. Teal Properties, Inc.*, 448 S.W.3d 905 (Tenn.App. 2014).

12. *Brennan's, Inc. v. Colbert*, 85 So.3d 787 (La.App.4th Cir. 2012).

had consistently treated both companies in such a manner that they were, in practice, his alter egos.[13] ∎

18–4 Corporate Directors and Officers

Corporate directors, officers, and shareholders all play different roles within the corporate entity. Sometimes, actions that may benefit the corporation as a whole do not coincide with the separate interests of the individuals making up the corporation. In such situations, it is important to know the rights and duties of all participants in the corporate enterprise.

18–4a Role of Directors and Officers

The board of directors is the ultimate authority in every corporation. Directors have responsibility for all policy-making decisions necessary to the management of all corporate affairs. Additionally, the directors must act as a body in carrying out routine corporate business. The board selects and removes the corporate officers, determines the capital structure of the corporation, and declares dividends. Each director has one vote, and customarily the majority rules.

Directors are sometimes inappropriately characterized as *agents* because they act on behalf of the corporation. No *individual* director, however, can act as an agent to bind the corporation. As a group, directors collectively control the corporation in a way that no agent is able to control a principal. In addition, although directors occupy positions of trust and control over the corporation, they are not *trustees*, because they do not hold title to property for the use and benefit of others.

Few qualifications are required for directors. Only a handful of states impose minimum age and residency requirements. A director may be a shareholder, but that is not necessary (unless the articles of incorporation or bylaws require ownership interest).

Election of Directors Subject to statutory limitations, the number of directors is set forth in the corporation's articles or bylaws. Historically, the minimum number of directors has been three, but today many states permit fewer. Normally, the incorporators may appoint the first board of directors in the articles of incorporation. If not, then the incorporators hold a meeting after incorporation to elect the directors and complete any other

business necessary (such as adopting bylaws). The initial board serves until the first annual shareholders' meeting. Subsequent directors are elected by a majority vote of the shareholders.

A director usually serves for a term of one year—from annual meeting to annual meeting. Most state statutes permit longer and staggered terms. A common practice is to elect one-third of the board members each year for a three-year term. In this way, there is greater management continuity.

A director can be removed *for cause*—that is, for failing to perform a required duty—either as specified in the articles or bylaws or by shareholder action. The board of directors may also have the power to remove a director for cause, subject to shareholder review. In most states, a director cannot be removed without cause unless the shareholders reserved the right to do so at the time of election. When a vacancy on the board occurs, such as if a director dies or resigns, either the shareholders or the board itself can fill the vacant position, depending on state law or on the provisions of the bylaws. Often, for instance, an election is held, and shareholders vote to fill the vacancy. Note that even when an election is authorized, a court can invalidate the results if the directors have attempted to manipulate the election in order to reduce the shareholders' influence.

Compensation of Directors In the past, corporate directors were rarely compensated. Today, directors are often paid at least nominal sums. In large corporations, they may receive more substantial compensation because of the time, work, effort, and especially risk involved.

Most states permit the corporate articles or bylaws to authorize compensation for directors. In fact, the Revised Model Business Corporation Act (RMBCA) states that unless the articles or bylaws provide otherwise, the board itself may set the directors' compensation [RMBCA 8.11]. Directors also receive indirect benefits, such as business contacts and prestige, and other rewards, such as stock options.

In many corporations, directors are also chief corporate officers (such as president or chief executive officer) and receive compensation in their managerial positions. A director who is also an officer of the corporation is referred to as an **inside director,** whereas a director who does not hold a management position is an **outside director.** Typically, a corporation's board of directors includes both inside and outside directors.

Board of Directors' Meetings The board of directors conducts business by holding formal meetings with recorded minutes. The dates of regular meetings are usually established in the articles or bylaws or by board resolution, and ordinarily no further notice is required. Special meetings can be called as well, with notice sent to all directors.

13. *Steiner Electric Co. v. Maniscalco*, 51 N.E.3d 45 (2016).

Most states allow directors to participate in board of directors' meetings from remote locations. Directors can participate via telephone, Web conferencing, or Skype, provided that all the directors can simultaneously hear each other during the meeting [RMBCA 8.20].

Normally, a majority of the board of directors constitutes a *quorum* [RMBCA 8.24]. A **quorum** is the minimum number of members of a body of officials or other group who must be present for business to be validly transacted. Some state statutes specifically allow corporations to set a quorum at less than a majority but not less than one-third of the directors.[14]

Once a quorum is present, the directors transact business and vote on issues affecting the corporation Each director present at the meeting has one vote.[15] Ordinary matters generally require a simple majority vote, but certain extraordinary issues may require a greater-than-majority vote.

Committees of the Board of Directors

When a board of directors has a large number of members and must deal with myriad complex business issues, meetings can become unwieldy. Therefore, the boards of large, publicly held corporations typically create committees of directors and delegate certain tasks to these committees. By focusing on specific subjects, committees can increase the efficiency of the board.

Two common types of committees are the *executive committee* and the *audit committee*. An executive committee handles interim management decisions between board meetings. It is limited to dealing with ordinary business matters and does not have the power to declare dividends, amend the bylaws, or authorize the issuance of stock. The audit committee is responsible for the selection, compensation, and oversight of the independent public accountants that audit the firm's financial records. The Sarbanes-Oxley Act requires all publicly held corporations to have an audit committee.

Rights of Directors

A corporate director must have certain rights to function properly in that position, including the rights to participation, inspection, and indemnification.

Right to Participation. The *right to participation* means that directors are entitled to participate in all board of directors' meetings and have a right to be notified of these meetings. Because the dates of regular board meetings are usually specified in the bylaws, no notice of these meetings is required. If special meetings are called,

however, notice is required unless waived by the director [RMBCA 8.23].

Right of Inspection. A director also has a *right of inspection*, which means that each director can access the corporation's books and records, facilities, and premises. Inspection rights are essential for directors to make informed decisions and to exercise the necessary supervision over corporate officers and employees. This right of inspection is almost absolute and cannot be restricted by the articles, bylaws, or any act of the board of directors.

■ **Case in Point 18.9** NavLink, Inc., a Delaware corporation, provides high-end data management for customers and governments in Saudi Arabia, Qatar, Lebanon, and the United Arab Emirates. NavLink's co-founders, George Chammas and Laurent Delifer, served on its board of directors.

Chammas and Delifer were concerned about the company's 2015 annual budget and three-year operating plan. Despite repeated requests, Chammas was never given the meeting minutes from several board meetings in 2015. Chammas and Delifer believed that the other directors were withholding information and holding secret "pre-board meetings" at which plans and decisions were being made without them. They filed a suit in a Delaware state court seeking inspection rights.

The court ordered NavLink to provide the plaintiffs with board meeting minutes and with communications from NavLink's secretary regarding the minutes. The plaintiffs were also entitled to inspect corporate documents and communications concerning NavLink's budget and three-year plan.[16] ■

Right to Indemnification. When a director becomes involved in litigation by virtue of her or his position, the director may have a *right to indemnification* (reimbursement) for the legal costs, fees, and damages incurred. Most states allow corporations to indemnify and purchase liability insurance for corporate directors [RMBCA 8.51].

Corporate Officers and Executives

Corporate officers and other executive employees are hired by the board of directors. At a minimum, most corporations have a president, one or more vice presidents, a secretary, and a treasurer. In most states, an individual can hold more than one office, such as president and secretary, and can be both an officer and a director of the corporation.

In addition to carrying out the duties articulated in the bylaws, corporate and managerial officers act as

---

14. See, for instance, Delaware Code Annotated Title 8, Section 141(b); and New York Business Corporation Law Section 707.

15. Except in Louisiana, which allows a director to vote by proxy under certain circumstances.

16. *Chammas v. NavLink, Inc.*, 2016 WL 767714 (Del.Ch. 2016).

agents of the corporation. Therefore, the ordinary rules of agency generally apply to their employment.

Corporate officers and other high-level managers are employees of the company, so their rights are defined by employment contracts. Nevertheless, the board of directors normally can remove a corporate officer at any time with or without cause. If the directors remove an officer in violation of the terms of an employment contract, however, the corporation may be liable for breach of contract.

18–4b Duties and Liabilities of Directors and Officers

The duties of corporate directors and officers are similar because both groups are involved in decision making and are in positions of control. Directors and officers are considered to be fiduciaries of the corporation because their relationship with the corporation and its shareholders is one of trust and confidence. As fiduciaries, directors and officers owe ethical—and legal—duties to the corporation and to the shareholders as a group. These fiduciary duties include the duty of care and the duty of loyalty.

Duty of Care Directors and officers must exercise due care in performing their duties. The standard of *due care* has been variously described in judicial decisions and codified in many state corporation codes. Generally, it requires a director or officer to:

1. Act in good faith (honestly).
2. Exercise the care that an ordinarily prudent (careful) person would exercise in similar circumstances.
3. Do what she or he believes is in the best interests of the corporation [RMBCA 8.30(a), 8.42(a)].

If directors or officers fail to exercise due care and the corporation or its shareholders suffer harm as a result, the directors or officers can be held liable for negligence. (An exception is made if the *business judgment rule* applies, as discussed shortly.)

Duty to Make Informed Decisions. Directors and officers are expected to be informed on corporate matters and to conduct a reasonable investigation of the situation before making a decision. They must, for instance, attend meetings and presentations, ask for information from those who have it, read reports, and review other written materials. In other words, directors and officers must investigate, study, and discuss matters and evaluate alternatives before making a decision. They cannot decide on the spur of the moment without adequate research.

Although directors and officers are expected to act in accordance with their own knowledge and training, they are also normally entitled to rely on information given to them by certain other persons. Under the laws of most states and Section 8.30(b) of the RMBCA, such persons include competent officers or employees, professionals such as attorneys and accountants, and committees of the board of directors. (The committee must be one on which the director does not serve, however.) The reliance must be in good faith to insulate a director from liability if the information later proves to be inaccurate or unreliable.

Duty to Exercise Reasonable Supervision. Directors are also expected to exercise a reasonable amount of supervision when they delegate work to corporate officers and employees. ■ **Example 18.10** Dana, a corporate bank director, fails to attend any board of directors' meetings for five years. In addition, Dana never inspects any of the corporate books or records and generally fails to supervise the activities of the bank president and the loan committee. Meanwhile, Fulton, the bank president, who is a corporate officer, makes various improper loans and permits large overdrafts. In this situation, Dana (the corporate director) can be held liable to the corporation for losses resulting from the unsupervised actions of the bank president and the loan committee. ■

Dissenting Directors. Directors' votes at board of directors' meetings should be entered into the minutes. Sometimes, an individual director disagrees with the majority's vote (which becomes an act of the board of directors). Unless a dissent is entered in the minutes, the director is presumed to have assented. If the directors are later held liable for mismanagement as a result of a decision, dissenting directors are rarely held individually liable to the corporation. For this reason, a director who is absent from a given meeting sometimes registers a dissent with the secretary of the board regarding actions taken at the meeting.

The Business Judgment Rule Directors and officers are expected to exercise due care and to use their best judgment in guiding corporate management, but they are not insurers of business success. Under the **business judgment rule,** a corporate director or officer will not be liable to the corporation or to its shareholders for honest mistakes of judgment and bad business decisions.

Courts give significant deference to the decisions of corporate directors and officers, and consider the reasonableness of a decision at the time it was made, without the benefit of hindsight. Thus, corporate decision makers are not subjected to second-guessing by shareholders or others in the corporation. The business judgment rule will apply as long as the director or officer:

1. Took reasonable steps to become informed about the matter.
2. Had a rational basis for her or his decision.

3. Did not have a conflict between her or his personal interest and the interest of the corporation.

The business judgment rule provides broad protections to corporate decision makers. In fact, most courts will apply the rule unless there is evidence of bad faith, fraud, or a clear breach of fiduciary duties.

Duty of Loyalty *Loyalty* can be defined as faithfulness to one's obligations and duties. In the corporate context, the duty of loyalty requires directors and officers to subordinate their personal interests to the welfare of the corporation. For instance, a director should not oppose a transaction that is in the corporation's best interest simply because pursuing it may cost the director his or her position. Directors cannot use corporate funds or confidential corporate information for personal advantage and must refrain from self-dealing.

Cases dealing with the duty of loyalty typically involve one or more of the following:

1. Competing with the corporation.
2. Usurping (taking personal advantage of) a corporate opportunity.
3. Pursuing an interest that conflicts with that of the corporation.
4. Using information that is not available to the public to make a profit trading securities (insider trading).
5. Authorizing a corporate transaction that is detrimental to minority shareholders.
6. Selling control over the corporation.

The following *Classic Case* illustrates the conflict that can arise between a corporate officer's personal interest and his or her duty of loyalty.

Classic Case 18.3

Guth v. Loft, Inc.

Supreme Court of Delaware, 23 Del.Ch. 255, 5 A.2d 503 (1939).

Background and Facts In 1930, Charles Guth became the president of Loft, Inc., a candy-and-restaurant chain. Guth and his family also owned Grace Company, which made syrups for soft drinks. Coca-Cola Company supplied Loft with cola syrup. Unhappy with what he felt was Coca-Cola's high price, Guth entered into an agreement with Roy Megargel to acquire the trademark and formula for Pepsi-Cola and form Pepsi-Cola Corporation. Neither Guth nor Megargel could finance the new venture, however, and Grace Company was insolvent.

Without the knowledge of Loft's board, Guth used Loft's capital, credit, facilities, and employees to further the Pepsi enterprise. At Guth's direction, a Loft employee made the concentrate for the syrup, which was sent to Grace to add sugar and water. Loft charged Grace for the concentrate but allowed forty months' credit. Grace charged Pepsi for the syrup but also granted substantial credit. Grace sold the syrup to Pepsi's customers, including Loft, which paid on delivery or within thirty days. Loft also paid for Pepsi's advertising. Finally, with profits declining as a result of switching from Coca-Cola, Loft filed a suit in a Delaware state court against Guth, Grace, and Pepsi, seeking their Pepsi stock and an accounting. The court entered a judgment in the plaintiff's favor. The defendants appealed to the Delaware Supreme Court.

In the Language of the Court

LAYTON, Chief Justice, delivering the opinion of the court:
* * * *

Corporate officers and directors are not permitted to use their position of trust and confidence to further their private interests. * * * They stand in a fiduciary relation to the corporation and its stockholders.

A public policy, existing through the years, and derived from a profound knowledge of human characteristics and motives, has established *a rule that demands of a corporate officer or director, peremptorily [not open for debate] and inexorably [unavoidably], the most scrupulous observance of his duty, not only affirmatively to protect the interests of the corporation committed to his charge, but also to refrain from doing anything that would work injury to the corporation* * * *. The rule that requires an undivided and unselfish loyalty to the corporation demands that there shall be no conflict between duty and self-interest. [Emphasis added.]
* * * *

*** *If there is presented to a corporate officer or director a business opportunity which the corporation is financially able to undertake [that] is *** in the line of the corporation's business and is of practical advantage to it *** and, by embracing the opportunity, the self-interest of the officer or director will be brought into conflict with that of his corporation, the law will not permit him to seize the opportunity for himself.* *** In such circumstances, *** the corporation may elect to claim all of the benefits of the transaction for itself, and the law will impress a trust in favor of the corporation upon the property, interests and profits so acquired.* [Emphasis added.]

* * * *

*** *The appellants contend that no conflict of interest between Guth and Loft resulted from his acquirement and exploitation of the Pepsi-Cola opportunity [and] that the acquisition did not place Guth in competition with Loft ***. [In this case, however,] Guth was Loft, and Guth was Pepsi. He absolutely controlled Loft. His authority over Pepsi was supreme. As Pepsi, he created and controlled the supply of Pepsi-Cola syrup, and he determined the price and the terms. What he offered, as Pepsi, he had the power, as Loft, to accept. Upon any consideration of human characteristics and motives, he created a conflict between self-interest and duty. He made himself the judge in his own cause. *** Moreover, a reasonable probability of injury to Loft resulted from the situation forced upon it. Guth was in the same position to impose his terms upon Loft as had been the Coca-Cola Company.*

*** *The facts and circumstances demonstrate that Guth's appropriation of the Pepsi-Cola opportunity to himself placed him in a competitive position with Loft with respect to a commodity essential to it, thereby rendering his personal interests incompatible with the superior interests of his corporation; and this situation was accomplished, not openly and with his own resources, but secretly and with the money and facilities of the corporation which was committed to his protection.*

Decision and Remedy *The Delaware Supreme Court upheld the judgment of the lower court. The state supreme court was "convinced that the opportunity to acquire the Pepsi-Cola trademark and formula, goodwill and business belonged to [Loft], and that Guth, as its President, had no right to appropriate the opportunity to himself."*

Critical Thinking
- **What If the Facts Were Different?** *Suppose that Loft's board of directors had approved Pepsi-Cola's use of its personnel and equipment. Would the court's decision have been different? Discuss.*
- **Impact of This Case on Today's Law** *This early Delaware decision was one of the first to set forth a test for determining when a corporate officer or director has breached the duty of loyalty. The test has two basic parts: Was the opportunity reasonably related to the corporation's line of business, and was the corporation financially able to undertake the opportunity? The court also considered whether the corporation had an interest or expectancy in the opportunity. It recognized that when the corporation had "no interest or expectancy, the officer or director is entitled to treat the opportunity as his own."*

Conflicts of Interest Corporate directors often have many business affiliations, and a director may sit on the board of more than one corporation. Of course, directors are precluded from entering into or supporting businesses that operate in direct competition with corporations on whose boards they serve. Their fiduciary duty requires them to make a full disclosure of any potential conflicts of interest that might arise in any corporate transaction [RMBCA 8.60].

Sometimes, a corporation enters into a contract or engages in a transaction in which an officer or director has a personal interest. The director or officer must make a *full disclosure* of the nature of the conflicting interest and all facts pertinent to the transaction. He or she must

also abstain from voting on the proposed transaction. When these rules are followed, the transaction can proceed. Otherwise, directors would be prevented from ever having financial dealings with the corporations they serve.

■ **Example 18.11** Ballo Corporation needs office space. Stephanie Colson, one of its five directors, owns the building adjoining the corporation's headquarters. Colson can negotiate a lease for the space to Ballo if she fully discloses her conflicting interest and any facts known to her about the proposed transaction to Ballo and the other four directors. If the lease arrangement is fair and reasonable, Colson abstains from voting on it, and the other members of the corporation's board of directors unanimously approve it, the contract is valid. ■

Liability of Directors and Officers Directors and officers are exposed to liability on many fronts. They can be held liable for negligence in certain circumstances, as previously discussed. They may also be held liable for the crimes and torts committed by themselves or by employees under their supervision.

Additionally, if shareholders perceive that the corporate directors are not acting in the best interests of the corporation, they may sue the directors on behalf of the corporation. (This is known as a *shareholder's derivative suit*, which will be discussed later in this chapter.) Directors and officers can also be held personally liable under a number of statutes, such as statutes enacted to protect consumers or the environment.

18–5 Shareholders

The acquisition of a share of stock makes a person an owner and a shareholder in a corporation. Shareholders thus own the corporation. Although they have no legal title to corporate property, such as buildings and equipment, they do have an equitable (ownership) interest in the firm.

As a general rule, shareholders have no responsibility for the daily management of the corporation, although they are ultimately responsible for choosing the board of directors, which does have such control. Ordinarily, corporate officers and other employees owe no direct duty to individual shareholders (unless some contract or special relationship exists between them in addition to the corporate relationship).

The duty of officers and directors is to act in the best interests of the corporation and its shareholder-owners *as a whole.* In turn, as you will read later in this chapter, controlling shareholders owe a fiduciary duty to minority shareholders.

18–5a Shareholders' Powers

Shareholders must approve fundamental changes affecting the corporation before the changes can be implemented. Hence, shareholder approval normally is required to amend the articles of incorporation or bylaws, to conduct a merger or dissolve the corporation, and to sell all or substantially all of the corporation's assets. Some of these powers are subject to prior board approval. Shareholder approval may also be requested (though it is not required) for certain other actions, such as to approve an independent auditor.

Shareholders also have the power to vote to elect or remove members of the board of directors. As described earlier, the first board of directors is either named in the articles of incorporation or chosen by the incorporators to serve until the first shareholders' meeting. From that time

on, selection and retention of directors are exclusively shareholder functions.

Directors usually serve their full terms. If the shareholders judge them unsatisfactory, they are simply not reelected. Shareholders have the inherent power, however, to remove a director from office *for cause* (breach of duty or misconduct) by a majority vote. Some state statutes (and some articles of incorporation) permit removal of directors without cause by the vote of a majority of the shareholders entitled to vote.[17]

18–5b Shareholders' Meetings

Shareholders' meetings must occur at least annually. In addition, special meetings can be called to deal with urgent matters. A corporation must notify its shareholders of the date, time, and place of an annual or special shareholders' meeting at least ten days, but not more than sixty days, before the meeting date [RMBCA 7.05].[18] (The date and time of the annual meeting can be specified in the bylaws.) Notice of a special meeting must include a statement of the purpose of the meeting, and business transacted at the meeting is limited to that purpose.

The RMBCA does not specify how the notice must be given. Most corporations do specify in their bylaws the acceptable methods of notifying shareholders about meetings. Also, some states' incorporation statutes outline the means of notice that a corporation can use in that jurisdiction. For instance, in Alaska, notice may be given in person, by mail, or by fax, e-mail, blog, or Web post—as long as the shareholder has agreed to that electronic method.[19]

Proxies It usually is not practical for owners of only a few shares of stock of publicly traded corporations to attend a shareholders' meeting. Therefore, the law allows stockholders to appoint another person as their agent to vote their shares at the meeting. The agent's formal authorization to vote the shares is called a **proxy** (from the Latin *procurare*, meaning "to manage or take care of"). Proxy materials are sent to all shareholders before shareholders' meetings.

Management often solicits proxies, but any person can solicit proxies to concentrate voting power. Proxies have been used by groups of shareholders as a device for taking over a corporation. Proxies normally are revocable (can be withdrawn), unless they are specifically designated as irrevocable

17. Most states allow *cumulative voting* for directors (described shortly). If cumulative voting is authorized, a director may not be removed if the number of votes against removal would be sufficient to elect a director under cumulative voting. See, for instance, California Corporations Code Section 303A. See also Section 8.08(c) of the RMBCA.
18. The shareholder can waive the requirement of notice by signing a waiver form [RMBCA 7.06]. A shareholder who does not receive notice but who learns of the meeting and attends without protesting the lack of notice is said to have waived notice by such conduct.
19. Alaska Statutes Section 10.06.410, Notice of Shareholders' Meetings.

and coupled with an interest. A proxy is coupled with an interest when, for instance, the person receiving the proxies from shareholders has agreed to buy their shares. Under RMBCA 7.22(c), proxies are valid for eleven months, unless the proxy agreement mandates a longer period.

Shareholder Proposals

When shareholders want to change a company policy, they can put their ideas up for a shareholder vote. They do this by submitting a shareholder proposal to the board of directors and asking the board to include the proposal in the proxy materials that are sent to all shareholders before meetings.

Rules for Proxies and Shareholder Proposals

The Securities and Exchange Commission (SEC) regulates the purchase and sale of securities. The SEC has special provisions relating to proxies and shareholder proposals. SEC Rule 14a-8 provides that all shareholders who own stock worth at least $1,000 are eligible to submit proposals for inclusion in corporate proxy materials. The corporation is required to include information on whatever proposals will be considered at the shareholders' meeting along with proxy materials. Only those proposals that relate to significant policy considerations, not ordinary business operations, must be included.

Under the SEC's e-proxy rules,[20] all public companies must post their proxy materials on the Internet and notify shareholders how to find that information. Although the law requires proxy materials to be posted online, public companies may also send the materials to shareholders by other means, including paper documents and DVDs sent by mail.

18–5c Shareholder Voting

Shareholders exercise ownership control through the power of their votes. Corporate business matters are presented in the form of *resolutions*, which shareholders vote to approve or disapprove. Each common shareholder normally is entitled to one vote per share.

The articles of incorporation can exclude or limit voting rights, particularly for certain classes of shares. For instance, owners of preferred shares are usually denied the right to vote [RMBCA 7.21]. If a state statute requires specific voting procedures, the corporation's articles or bylaws must be consistent with the statute.

Quorum Requirements

For shareholders to act during a meeting, a quorum must be present. Generally, a quorum exists when shareholders holding more than 50 percent of the outstanding shares are present. State laws often permit the articles of incorporation to set higher or lower quorum requirements, however. In some states, obtaining the unanimous written consent of shareholders is a permissible alternative to holding a shareholders' meeting [RMBCA 7.25].

Once a quorum is present, voting can proceed. If a state statute requires specific voting procedures, the corporation's articles or bylaws must be consistent with the statute. A majority vote of the shares represented at the meeting usually is required to pass resolutions. At times, more than a simple majority vote is required, either by a state statute or by the corporate articles. Extraordinary corporate matters, such as a merger, consolidation, or dissolution of the corporation, require approval by a higher percentage of all corporate shares entitled to vote [RMBCA 7.27].

Voting Lists

The corporation prepares a voting list before each shareholders' meeting. Ordinarily, only persons whose names appear on the corporation's stockholder records as owners are entitled to vote.

The voting list contains the name and address of each shareholder as shown on the corporate records on a given cutoff date, or *record date.* (Under RMBCA 7.07, the bylaws or board of directors may fix a record date that is as much as seventy days before the meeting.) The voting list also includes the number of voting shares held by each owner. The list is usually kept at the corporate headquarters and must be made available for shareholder inspection [RMBCA 7.20].

Cumulative Voting

Most states permit, and many require, shareholders to elect directors by *cumulative voting*, a voting method designed to allow minority shareholders to be represented on the board of directors. When cumulative voting is not required, the entire board can be elected by a majority of shares.

Formula. With cumulative voting, each shareholder is entitled to a total number of votes equal to the number of board members to be elected multiplied by the number of voting shares that the shareholder owns. The shareholder can cast all of these votes for one candidate or split them among several nominees for director. All candidates stand for election at the same time.

How Cumulative Voting Works. Cumulative voting can best be understood by example. ■ **Example 18.12** A corporation has 10,000 shares issued and outstanding. The minority shareholders hold 3,000 shares, and the majority shareholders hold the other 7,000 shares. Three members of the board are to be elected. The majority shareholders' nominees are Alvarez, Beasley, and Caravel. The minority shareholders' nominee is Dovrik. Can Dovrik be elected to the board by the minority shareholders?

---

20. 17 C.F.R. Parts 240, 249, and 274.

If cumulative voting is allowed, the answer is yes. The minority shareholders have 9,000 votes among them (the number of directors to be elected times the number of shares, or 3 × 3,000 = 9,000 votes). All of these votes can be cast to elect Dovrik. The majority shareholders have 21,000 votes (3 × 7,000 = 21,000 votes), but these votes must be distributed among their three nominees.

The principle of cumulative voting is that no matter how the majority shareholders cast their 21,000 votes, they will not be able to elect all three directors if the minority shareholders cast all of their 9,000 votes for Dovrik, as illustrated in Exhibit 18–1. ∎

Other Voting Techniques Before a shareholders' meeting, a group of shareholders can agree in writing to vote their shares together in a specified manner. Such agreements, called *shareholder voting agreements*, usually are held to be valid and enforceable. A shareholder can also vote by proxy, as noted earlier.

Another technique is for shareholders to enter into a *voting trust*. A **voting trust** is an agreement (a trust contract) under which a shareholder assigns the right to vote his or her shares to a trustee, usually for a specified period of time. The trustee is then responsible for voting the shares on behalf of all the shareholders in the trust. The shareholder retains all rights of ownership (for instance, the right to receive dividend payments) except the power to vote the shares [RMBCA 7.30].

18–5d Rights of Shareholders

Shareholders possess numerous rights in addition to the right to vote their shares, and we examine several here.

Stock Certificates In the past, corporations commonly issued **stock certificates** that evidenced ownership of a specified number of shares in the corporation. Only a few jurisdictions still require physical stock certificates, and shareholders there have the right to demand that the corporation issue certificates (or replace those that were lost or destroyed). Stock is intangible personal property, however, and the ownership right exists independently of the certificate itself.

In most states and under RMBCA 6.26, a board of directors may provide that shares of stock will be uncertificated, or "paperless"—that is, no actual, physical stock certificates will be issued. Notice of shareholders' meetings, dividends, and operational and financial reports are distributed according to the ownership lists recorded in the corporation's books.

Preemptive Rights Sometimes, the articles of incorporation grant preemptive rights to shareholders [RMBCA 6.30]. With **preemptive rights,** a shareholder receives a preference over all other purchasers to subscribe to or purchase a prorated share of a new issue of stock. Generally, preemptive rights must be exercised within a specific time period (usually thirty days).

A shareholder who is given preemptive rights can purchase a percentage of the new shares being issued that is equal to the percentage of shares she or he already holds in the company. This allows each shareholder to maintain her or his proportionate control, voting power, and financial interest in the corporation. ∎ **Example 18.13** Katlin is a shareholder who owns 10 percent of a company. Because she also has preemptive rights, she can buy 10 percent of

Exhibit 18–1 Results of Cumulative Voting

Ballot	Majority Shareholder Votes			Minority Shareholder Votes	Directors Elected
	Alvarez	*Beasley*	*Caravel*	*Dovrik*	
1	10,000	10,000	1,000	9,000	Alvarez, Beasley, Dovrik
2	9,001	9,000	2,999	9,000	Alvarez, Beasley, Dovrik
3	6,000	7,000	8,000	9,000	Beasley, Caravel, Dovrik

any new issue (to maintain her 10 percent position). Thus, if the corporation issues 1,000 more shares, Katlin can buy 100 of the new shares. ■

Preemptive rights are most important in close corporations because each shareholder owns a relatively small number of shares but controls a substantial interest in the corporation. Without preemptive rights, it would be possible for a shareholder to lose his or her proportionate control over the firm. Nevertheless, preemptive rights do not exist unless provided for in the articles of incorporation.

Stock Warrants Stock warrants are rights given by a company to buy stock at a stated price by a specified date. Usually, when preemptive rights exist and a corporation is issuing additional shares, it gives its shareholders stock warrants. Warrants are often publicly traded on securities exchanges.

Dividends As mentioned, a *dividend* is a distribution of corporate profits or income *ordered by the directors* and paid to the shareholders in proportion to their shares in the corporation. Dividends can be paid in cash, property, stock of the corporation that is paying the dividends, or stock of other corporations.[21]

State laws vary, but each state determines the general circumstances and legal requirements under which dividends are paid. State laws also control the sources of revenue to be used. All states allow dividends to be paid from the undistributed net profits earned by the corporation, for instance. A number of states allow dividends to be paid out of any surplus.

Illegal Dividends. Dividends are illegal if they are improperly paid from an unauthorized account or if their payment causes the corporation to become insolvent (unable to pay its debts as they come due). Generally, shareholders must return illegal dividends only if they knew that the dividends were illegal when the payment was received (or if the dividends were paid when the corporation was insolvent). Whenever dividends are illegal or improper, the board of directors can be held personally liable for the amount of the payment.

The Directors' Failure to Declare a Dividend. When directors fail to declare a dividend, shareholders can ask a court to compel the directors to do so. To succeed, the shareholders must show that the directors have acted so unreasonably in withholding the dividend that their conduct is an abuse of their discretion.

Often, a corporation accumulates large cash reserves for a legitimate corporate purpose, such as expansion or research. The mere fact that the firm has sufficient earnings or surplus available to pay a dividend normally is not enough to compel the directors to declare a dividend. The courts are reluctant to interfere with corporate operations and will not compel directors to declare dividends unless abuse of discretion is clearly shown.

Inspection Rights Shareholders in a corporation enjoy both common law and statutory inspection rights. The RMBCA provides that every shareholder is entitled to examine specified corporate records, including voting lists [RMBCA 7.20, 16.02]. The shareholder may inspect in person, or an attorney, accountant, or other authorized individual can do so as the shareholder's agent. In some states, a shareholder must have held her or his shares for a minimum period of time immediately preceding the demand to inspect or must hold a certain percentage of outstanding shares.

A shareholder has a right to inspect and copy corporate books and records only for a *proper purpose*, and the request to inspect must be made in advance. A shareholder who is denied the right of inspection can seek a court order to compel the inspection.

■ **Case in Point 18.14** Carlia Cichon is president of Advent Home Medical, Inc. Her daughter, Amanda Hammoud, owned 400 shares (40 percent) of Advent stock. Hammoud submitted a written request to Cichon to review Advent's financial records "to monitor the financial health of the corporation." When Advent did not respond, Hammoud filed a complaint in a state court seeking an order to compel the corporation to permit an inspection. The court granted Hammoud's motion to compel the inspection. Advent appealed. A Michigan state appellate court affirmed. Hammoud was a shareholder and had stated a proper purpose for inspecting the records she requested.[22] ■

The power of inspection is fraught with potential abuses, and the corporation is allowed to protect itself from them. For instance, a shareholder can properly be denied access to corporate records to prevent harassment or to protect trade secrets or other confidential corporate information.

Transfer of Shares Corporate stock represents an ownership right in intangible personal property. The law generally recognizes the owner's right to transfer stock to another person unless there are valid restrictions on its transferability, such as frequently occur with close corporation stock.

When shares are transferred, a new entry is made in the corporate stock book to indicate the new owner. Until

---

21. On one occasion, a distillery declared and paid a dividend in bonded whiskey.

22. *Hammoud v. Advent Home Medical, Inc.,* 2018 WL 1072988 (Mich.Ct.App. 2018).

the corporation is notified and the entry is complete, all rights—including voting rights, notice of shareholders' meetings, and the right to dividend distributions—remain with the current record owner.

The Shareholder's Derivative Suit   When the corporation is harmed by the actions of a third party, the directors can bring a lawsuit in the name of the corporation against that party. If the corporate directors fail to bring a lawsuit, shareholders can do so "derivatively" in what is known as a **shareholder's derivative suit.**

The right of shareholders to bring a derivative action is especially important when the wrong suffered by the corporation results from the actions of the corporate directors and officers. For obvious reasons, the directors and officers would probably be unwilling to take any action against themselves.

Before shareholders can bring a derivative suit, they must submit a written demand to the corporation, asking the board of directors to take appropriate action [RMBCA 7.40]. The directors then have ninety days in which to act. Only if they refuse to do so can the derivative suit go forward. In addition, a court will dismiss a derivative suit if a majority of the directors or an independent panel determines in good faith that the lawsuit is not in the best interests of the corporation [RMBCA 7.44].

When shareholders bring a derivative suit, they are not pursuing rights or benefits for themselves personally but are acting as guardians of the corporate entity. Therefore, if the suit is successful, any damages recovered normally go into the corporation's treasury, not to the shareholders personally.

18–5e Duties and Liabilities of Shareholders

One of the hallmarks of the corporate form of organization is that shareholders are not personally liable for the debts of the corporation. If the corporation fails, the shareholders can lose their investments, but that generally is the limit of their liability. As discussed previously, in certain instances, a court will pierce the corporate veil (disregard the corporate entity) and hold the shareholders individually liable. But these situations are the exception, not the rule.

A shareholder can also be personally liable in certain other rare instances. One relates to illegal dividends, which were mentioned previously. Another relates to *watered stock.* Finally, in certain instances, a majority shareholder who engages in oppressive conduct or attempts to exclude minority shareholders from receiving certain benefits can be held personally liable.

Watered Stock   When a corporation issues shares for less than their fair market value, the shares are referred to

as **watered stock.**[23] Usually, the shareholder who receives watered stock must pay the difference to the corporation (the shareholder is personally liable). In some states, the shareholder who receives watered stock may be liable to creditors of the corporation for unpaid corporate debts.

■ **Example 18.15**   During the formation of a corporation, Gomez, one of the incorporators, transfers his property, Sunset Beach, to the corporation for 10,000 shares of stock at a par value of $100 per share for a total price of $1 million. After the property is transferred and the shares are issued, Sunset Beach is carried on the corporate books at a value of $1 million.

On appraisal, it is discovered that the market value of the property at the time of transfer was only $500,000. The shares issued to Gomez are therefore watered stock, and he is liable to the corporation for the difference between the value of the shares and the value of the property. ■

Duties of Majority Shareholders   In some instances, a majority shareholder is regarded as having a fiduciary duty to the corporation and to the minority shareholders. This duty arises when a single shareholder (or a few shareholders acting in concert) owns a sufficient number of shares to exercise *de facto* control over the corporation. In these situations, the majority shareholder owes a fiduciary duty to the minority shareholders.

When a majority shareholder breaches her or his fiduciary duty to a minority shareholder, the minority shareholder can sue for damages. A breach of fiduciary duties by those who control a close corporation normally constitutes what is known as *oppressive conduct.* A common example of a breach of fiduciary duty occurs when the majority shareholders "freeze out" the minority shareholders and exclude them from certain benefits of participating in the firm.

■ **Example 18.16**   Brodie, Jordan, and Barbara form a close corporation to operate a machine shop. Brodie and Jordan own 75 percent of the shares in the company, but all three are directors. After disagreements arise, Brodie asks the company to purchase his shares, but his requests are refused. A few years later, Brodie dies, and his wife, Ella, inherits his shares. Jordan and Barbara refuse to perform a valuation of the company, deny Ella access to corporate information, do not declare any dividends, and refuse to elect Ella as a director. In this situation, the majority shareholders have violated their fiduciary duty to Ella. ■

---

23. The phrase *watered stock* was originally used to describe cattle that were kept thirsty during a long drive and then were allowed to drink large quantities of water just before their sale. The increased weight of the "watered stock" allowed the seller to reap a higher profit.

18–6 Major Business Forms Compared

When deciding which form of business organization to choose, businesspersons normally consider several factors, including ease of creation, the liability of the owners, tax considerations, and the ability to raise capital. Each major form of business organization offers distinct advantages and disadvantages with respect to these and other factors.

Exhibit 18–2 summarizes the essential advantages and disadvantages of each of the forms of business organization discussed in this text.

Exhibit 18–2 Major Forms of Business Compared

	Sole Proprietorship	Partnership	Corporation
Method of Creation	Created at will by owner.	Created by agreement of the parties.	Authorized by the state under the state's corporation law.
Legal Position	Not a separate entity; owner is the business.	A general partnership is a separate legal entity in most states.	Always a legal entity separate and distinct from its owners—a legal fiction for the purposes of owning property and being a party to litigation.
Liability	Unlimited liability.	Unlimited liability.	Limited liability of shareholders—shareholders are not liable for the debts of the corporation.
Duration	Determined by owner; automatically dissolved on owner's death.	Terminated by agreement of the partners, but can continue to do business even when a partner dissociates from the partnership.	Can have perpetual existence.
Transferability of Interest	Interest can be transferred, but individual's proprietorship then ends.	Although partnership interest can be assigned, assignee does not have full rights of a partner.	Shares of stock can be transferred.
Management	Completely at owner's discretion.	Each partner has a direct and equal voice in management unless expressly agreed otherwise in the partnership agreement.	Shareholders elect directors, who set policy and appoint officers.
Taxation	Owner pays personal taxes on business income.	Each partner pays pro rata share of income taxes on net profits, whether or not they are distributed.	Double taxation—corporation pays income tax on net profits, with no deduction for dividends, and shareholders pay income tax on disbursed dividends they receive.
Organizational Fees, Annual License Fees, and Annual Reports	None or minimal.	None or minimal.	All required.
Transaction of Business in Other States	Generally no limitation.	Generally no limitation.[a]	Normally must qualify to do business and obtain certificate of authority.

a. A few states have enacted statutes requiring that foreign partnerships qualify to do business there.

Continues

Exhibit 18–2 Major Forms of Business Compared—Continued

	Limited Partnership	Limited Liability Company	Limited Liability Partnership
Method of Creation	Created by agreement to carry on a business for profit. At least one party must be a general partner and the other(s) limited partner(s). Certificate of limited partnership is filed.	Created by an agreement of the member-owners of the company. Articles of organization are filed. Charter must be issued by the state.	Created by agreement of the partners. A statement of qualification for the limited liability partnership is filed.
Legal Position	Treated as a legal entity.	Treated as a legal entity.	Generally, treated same as a general partnership.
Liability	Unlimited liability of all general partners. Limited partners are liable only to the extent of capital contributions.	Member-owners' liability is limited to the amount of capital contributions or investments.	Varies, but under the Uniform Partnership Act, liability of a partner for acts committed by other partners is limited.
Duration	By agreement in certificate, or by termination of the last general partner (retirement, death, or the like) or last limited partner.	Unless a single-member LLC, can have perpetual existence (same as a corporation).	Remains in existence until cancellation or revocation.
Transferability of Interest	Interest can be assigned, but if assignee becomes a member with consent of other partners, certificate must be amended.	Member interests are freely transferable.	Interest can be assigned same as in a general partnership.
Management	General partners have equal voice or by agreement. Limited partners may not retain limited liability if they actively participate in management.	Member-owners can fully participate in management or can designate a group of persons to manage on behalf of the members.	Same as a general partnership.
Taxation	Generally taxed as a partnership.	LLC is not taxed, and members are taxed personally on profits "passed through" the LLC.	Same as a general partnership.
Organizational Fees, Annual License Fees, and Annual Reports	Organizational fee required; usually not others.	Organizational fee required. Others vary with states.	Fees are set by each state for filing statements of qualification, statements of foreign qualification, and annual reports.
Transaction of Business in Other States	Generally no limitations.	Generally no limitations, but may vary depending on state.	Must file a statement of foreign qualification before doing business in another state.

Practice and Review: Corporations

William Sharp was the sole shareholder and manager of Chickasaw Club, Inc., an S corporation that operated a popular nightclub of the same name in Columbus, Georgia. Sharp maintained a corporate checking account but paid the club's employees, suppliers, and entertainers in cash out of the club's proceeds. Sharp owned the property on which the club was located. He rented it to the club but made mortgage payments out of the club's proceeds and often paid other personal expenses with Chickasaw corporate funds.

At 12:45 A.M. on July 31, eighteen-year-old Aubrey Lynn Pursley, who was already intoxicated, entered the Chickasaw Club. A city ordinance prohibited individuals under the age of twenty-one from entering nightclubs, but Chickasaw employees did not check Pursley's identification to verify her age. Pursley drank more alcohol at Chickasaw and was visibly intoxicated when she left the club at 3:00 A.M. with a beer in her hand. Shortly afterward, Pursley lost control of her car, struck a tree, and was killed. Joseph Dancause, Pursley's stepfather, filed a tort lawsuit in a Georgia state court against Chickasaw Club, Inc., and William Sharp, seeking damages. Using the information presented in the chapter, answer the following questions.

1. Under what theory might the court in this case make an exception to the limited liability of shareholders and hold Sharp personally liable for the damages? What factors would be relevant to the court's decision?
2. Suppose that Chickasaw's articles of incorporation failed to describe the corporation's purpose or management structure, as required by state law. Would the court be likely to rule that Sharp is personally liable to Dancause on that basis? Why or why not?
3. Suppose that the club extended credit to its regular patrons, although neither the articles of incorporation nor the corporate bylaws authorized this practice. Would the corporation likely have the power to engage in this activity? Explain.
4. How would the court classify the Chickasaw Club corporation—domestic or foreign, public or private? Why?

Debate This . . .   *The sole shareholder of an S corporation should not be able to avoid liability for the torts of her or his employees.*

Terms and Concepts

alien corporation 394	foreign corporation 393	S corporation 397
articles of incorporation 399	holding company 393	securities 401
benefit corporation 397	inside director 405	shareholder agreement 396
bond 401	outside director 405	shareholder's derivative suit 414
business judgment rule 407	piercing the corporate veil 403	stock 401
bylaws 400	preemptive rights 412	stock certificate 412
close corporation 396	preferred stock 401	stock warrant 413
commingled 404	private equity capital 401	*ultra vires* 402
common stock 401	proxy 410	venture capital 401
corporation 392	public corporation 395	voting trust 412
crowdfunding 401	publicly held corporation 395	watered stock 414
dividend 392	quorum 406	
domestic corporation 393	retained earnings 392	

Issue Spotters

1. Northwest Brands, Inc., is a small business incorporated in Minnesota. Its one class of stock is owned by twelve members of a single family. Ordinarily, corporate income is taxed at the corporate and shareholder levels. Is there a way for Northwest Brands to avoid this double taxation? Explain your answer. (See *Nature and Classification*.)

2. Wonder Corporation has an opportunity to buy stock in XL, Inc. The directors decide that instead of having Wonder buying the stock, the directors will buy it. Yvon, a Wonder shareholder, learns of the purchase and wants to sue the directors on Wonder's behalf. Can she do it? Explain. (See *Shareholders*.)

- **Check your answers to the Issue Spotters against the answers provided in Appendix B at the end of this text.**

Business Scenarios and Case Problems

18–1. Preincorporation. Cummings, Okawa, and Taft are recent college graduates who want to form a corporation to manufacture and sell digital tablets. Peterson tells them he will set in motion the formation of their corporation. First, Peterson makes a contract with Owens for the purchase of a piece of land for $200,000. Owens does not know of the prospective corporate formation at the time the contract is signed. Second, Peterson makes a contract with Babcock to build a small plant on the property being purchased. Babcock's contract is conditional on the corporation's formation. Peterson secures all necessary capitalization and files the articles of incorporation. (See *Corporate Formation and Powers*.)

(a) Discuss whether the newly formed corporation, Peterson, or both are liable on the contracts with Owens and Babcock.

(b) Discuss whether the corporation is automatically liable to Babcock on formation.

18–2. Conflicts of Interest. Oxy Corp. is negotiating with Wick Construction Co. for the renovation of Oxy's corporate headquarters. Wick, the owner of Wick Construction Co., is also one of the five members of Oxy's board of directors. The contract terms are standard for this type of contract. Wick has previously informed two of the other directors of his interest in the construction company. Oxy's board approves the contract by a three-to-two vote, with Wick voting with the majority. Discuss whether this contract is binding on the corporation. (See *Corporate Directors and Officers*.)

18–3. Duty of Loyalty. Kids International Corporation produced children's wear for Walmart and other retailers. Gila Dweck was a Kids director and its chief executive officer. Because she felt that she was not paid enough, she started Success Apparel to compete with Kids. Success operated out of Kids' premises, used its employees, borrowed on its credit, took advantage of its business opportunities, and capitalized on its customer relationships. As an "administrative fee," Dweck paid Kids 1 percent of Success's total sales. Did Dweck breach any fiduciary duties? Explain. [*Dweck v. Nasser*, 2012 WL 3194069 (Del.Ch. 2012)] (See *Corporate Directors and Officers*.)

18–4. Tort Liability. Jennifer Hoffman took her cell phone to a store owned by R&K Trading, Inc., for repairs. Later, Hoffman filed a suit in a New York state court against R&K, Verizon Wireless, Inc., and others. Hoffman sought to recover damages for a variety of torts, including infliction of emotional distress and negligent hiring and supervision. She alleged that an R&K employee, Keith Press, had examined her phone in a back room, accessed private photos of her stored on her phone, and disseminated the photos to the public. Hoffman testified that "after the incident, she learned from another R&K employee that personal information and pictures had been removed from the phones of other customers." Can R&K be held liable for the torts of its employees? Explain. [*Hoffman v. Verizon Wireless, Inc.*, 125 A.D.3d 806, 5 N.Y.S.3d 123 (2 Dept. 2015)] (See *Nature and Classification*.)

18–5. Piercing the Corporate Veil. In New York City, 2406-12 Amsterdam Associates, LLC, brought an action in a New York state court against Alianza Dominicana and Alianza, LLC, to recover unpaid rent. The plaintiff asserted cause to pierce the corporate veil, alleging that Alianza Dominicana had made promises to pay its rent while discreetly forming Alianza, LLC, to avoid liability for it. According to 2406-12, Alianza, LLC, was 90 percent owned by Alianza Dominicana, had no employees, and had no function but to hold Alianza Dominicana's assets away from its creditors. The defendants filed a motion to dismiss the plaintiff's claim. Assuming that 2406-12's allegations are true, are there sufficient grounds to pierce the corporate veil of Alianza, LLC? Discuss. [*2406-12 Amsterdam Associates, LLC v. Alianza, LLC*, 136 A.D.3d 512, 25 N.Y.S.3d 167 (1 Dept. 2016)] (See *Piercing the Corporate Veil*.)

18–6. Business Case Problem with Sample Answer— Rights of Shareholders. FCR Realty, LLC, and Clifford B. Green & Sons, Inc., were co-owned by three brothers— Frederick, Clifford Jr., and Richard Green. Each brother was a shareholder of the corporation. Frederick was a controlling shareholder, as well as president. Each brother owned a one-third interest in the LLC. Clifford believed that Frederick had misused LLC and corporate funds to pay nonexistent debts and liabilities and had diverted LLC assets to the corporation. He also contended that Frederick had disbursed about $1.8 million in corporate funds to Frederick's own separate business. Clifford hired an attorney and filed an action on behalf of the two companies against Frederick for breach of fiduciary duty. Frederick argued that Clifford lacked the knowledge necessary to adequately represent the companies' interests because he did not understand financial statements. Can Clifford maintain the action against Frederick? If so, and if the suit is successful, who would recover any damages? Explain. [*FCR Realty, LLC v. Green*, 2016 WL 571449 (Conn.Super.Ct. 2016)] (See *Shareholders*.)

- **For a sample answer to Problem 18–6, go to Appendix C at the end of this text.**

18–7. Duties and Liabilities of Directors and Officers.
M&M Country Store, Inc., operated a gas station and convenience store. Debra Kelly bought M&M from Mary Millett. Under the purchase agreement, Millett was to remain as the corporation's sole shareholder until the price was fully paid. A default on any payment would result in the return of M&M to Millett. During Kelly's management of M&M, taxes were not remitted, vendors were not paid, repairs were not made, and the store's gas tanks and shelves were often empty. Kelly commingled company and personal funds, kept inaccurate records, and allowed M&M's business licenses and insurance policies to lapse. After she defaulted on her payments to Millett and surrendered M&M, the company incurred significant expenses to pay outstanding bills and replenish the inventory. Can M&M recover these costs from Kelly? Explain. [*M&M Country Store, Inc. v. Kelly*, 159 A.D.3d 1102, 71 N.Y.S.3d 707 (3 Dept. 2018)] (See *Corporate Directors and Officers*.)

18–8. Certificate of Authority. Armour Pipe Line Company assigned leases to its existing oil wells in Texas to Sandel Energy, Inc. The assignment included royalties for the oil produced from the wells. Armour specified that the assignment "does not pertain to production attributable to these leases from any new wells," reserving for itself an interest in those royalties. Later, Armour—a foreign corporation in Texas—forfeited its certificate of authority to do business in the state. More than three years later, the certificate was reissued. Meanwhile, new wells were drilled on the leases. Sandel filed a suit in a Texas state court against Armour, claiming that the reservation of a royalty interest in those wells was "ineffective" because of the temporary forfeiture. When and why does a corporation need a certificate of authority? Is Armour entitled to the royalties from the new wells? Discuss. [*Armour Pipeline Co. v. Sandel Energy, Inc.*, 546 S.W.3d 455 (Tex.App.—Houston (14th Dist.) 2018)] (See *Nature and Classification*.)

18–9. A Question of Ethics—The IDDR Approach and Piercing the Corporate Veil. *The University of Missouri requires employees to disclose inventions developed during their employment so that the university can choose whether to exercise the right to ownership. Galen Suppes was an associate professor at the university, and the university provided the lab he used for his work. In the lab, he developed the technology to transform glycerol, a byproduct of biodiesel production, into propylene glycol, a compound used to make antifreeze. Without informing the university, Suppes formed Renewable Alternatives (RA) to patent the invention and license the ownership rights. On learning of these actions, the university filed a suit in a Missouri state court against Suppes for breach of the duty of loyalty. The court ordered him to assign his invention to the university. On appeal, Suppes alleged that he had improperly been held liable for the actions of RA. He argued that the university had failed to make a case for piercing the corporate veil on the alter-ego theory. A state intermediate appellate court affirmed the lower court's order. "The University was not required to show that Suppes was the alter ego of RA . . . . The University brought a breach of loyalty claim directly against Suppes for Suppes's own actions." [Curators of University of Missouri v. Suppes, __ S.W.3d __, 2019 WL 121983 (Mo.App. W.D. 2019)] (See Piercing the Corporate Veil.)*

(a) Apply the IDDR approach to evaluate the ethics of Suppes's decision to profit from his research without informing his employer.

(b) What might a university do to encourage innovation by its employees and avoid disputes over the ownership rights to the results? Discuss.

Time-Limited Group Assignment

18–10. Corporate versus LLC Form of Business. The limited liability company (LLC) may be the best organizational form for most businesses. For a significant number of firms, however, the corporate form or some other form of organization may be better. (See *Nature and Classification*.)

(a) The first group will outline several reasons why a firm might be better off as a corporation than as an LLC.

(b) The second group will discuss the differences between corporations and LLCs in terms of their management structures.

Chapter 19

Agency Relationships

One of the most common, important, and pervasive legal relationships is that of **agency.** In an agency relationship involving two parties, one of the parties, called the *agent*, agrees to represent or act for the other, called the *principal*. The principal has the right to control the agent's conduct in matters entrusted to the agent.

Agency relationships are crucial in the business world. By using agents, a principal can conduct multiple business operations at the same time in different locations. Indeed, the only way that certain business entities can function is through their agents. For instance, a corporate officer is an agent who serves in a representative capacity for the corporation. The officer has the authority to bind the corporation to a contract. Only through its officers can corporations enter into contracts.

Most employees are also considered to be agents of their employers.

Today, however, the United States is experiencing a trend toward a so-called *gig economy*, which centers on short-term, independent workers who are not employees. Companies like Uber and Lyft provide evidence of this trend. This type of on-demand employment raises questions related to agency, making agency an increasingly important topic for students of business law and the legal environment to understand.

19–1 Agency Law

Section 1(1) of the *Restatement (Third) of Agency*[1] defines *agency* as "the fiduciary relation [that] results from the manifestation of consent by one person to another that the other shall act in his [or her] behalf and subject to his [or her] control, and consent by the other so to act." In other words, in a principal-agent relationship, the parties have agreed that the agent will act *on behalf and instead of* the principal in negotiating and transacting business with third parties.

The term **fiduciary** is at the heart of agency law. This term can be used both as a noun and as an adjective. When used as a noun, it refers to a person having a duty created by his or her undertaking to act primarily for another's benefit in matters connected with the undertaking. When used as an adjective, as in the phrase *fiduciary relationship*, it means that the relationship involves trust and confidence.

Agency relationships commonly exist between employers and employees. Agency relationships may sometimes also exist between employers and independent contractors who are hired to perform special tasks or services.

19–1a Employer-Employee Relationships

Normally, all employees who deal with third parties are deemed to be agents. A salesperson in a department store, for instance, is an agent of the store's owner (the principal) and acts on the owner's behalf. Any sale of goods made by the salesperson to a customer is binding on the principal. Similarly, most representations of fact made by the salesperson with respect to the goods sold are binding on the principal.

Because employees who deal with third parties generally are deemed to be agents of their employers, agency law and employment law overlap considerably. Agency relationships, however, can exist outside an employer-employee relationship, so agency law has a broader reach than employment law. Additionally, agency law is based on the common law, whereas much employment law is statutory law.

Employment laws (state and federal) apply only to the employer-employee relationship. Statutes governing Social Security, withholding taxes, workers' compensation, unemployment compensation, workplace safety, and employment discrimination apply only if an employer-employee relationship exists. *These laws do not apply to independent contractors.*

---

1. The *Restatement (Third) of Agency* is an authoritative summary of the law of agency and is often referred to by judges in their decisions and opinions.

19–1b Employer–Independent Contractor Relationships

Independent contractors are not employees because, by definition, those who hire them have no control over the details of their work performance. Section 2 of the *Restatement (Third) of Agency* defines an **independent contractor** as follows:

> [An independent contractor is] a person who contracts with another to do something for him [or her] but who is not controlled by the other nor subject to the other's right to control with respect to his [or her] physical conduct in the performance of the undertaking. He [or she] may or may not be an agent.

Building contractors and subcontractors are independent contractors. A property owner who hires a contractor and subcontractors to complete a project does not control the details of the way they perform their work. Truck drivers who own their vehicles and hire out on a per-job basis are independent contractors, but truck drivers who drive company trucks on a regular basis usually are employees. See this chapter's *Ethics Today* feature for a discussion of disputes involving the classification of drivers working for Uber and Lyft.

The relationship between a principal and an independent contractor may or may not involve an agency relationship. To illustrate: A homeowner who hires a real estate broker to sell her house has contracted with an independent contractor (the broker). The homeowner has also established an agency relationship with the broker for the specific purpose of selling the property. Another example is an insurance agent, who is both an independent contractor and an agent of the insurance company for which he sells policies. (Note that an insurance *broker*, in contrast, normally is an agent of the person obtaining insurance and not of the insurance company.)

19–1c Determination of Employee Status

The courts are frequently asked to determine whether a particular worker is an employee or an independent contractor. How a court decides this issue can have a significant effect on the rights and liabilities of the parties.

Criteria Used by the Courts In deciding whether a worker is categorized as an employee or an independent contractor, courts often consider the following questions:

1. *How much control does the employer exercise over the details of the work?* If the employer exercises considerable control over the details of the work and the day-to-day activities of the worker, this indicates employee status. This is perhaps the most important factor weighed by the courts in determining employee status.
2. *Is the worker engaged in an occupation or business distinct from that of the employer?* If so, this points to independent-contractor, not employee, status.
3. *Is the work usually done under the employer's direction or by a specialist without supervision?* If the work is normally done under the employer's direction, this indicates employee status.
4. *Does the employer supply the tools at the place of work?* If so, this indicates employee status.
5. *For how long is the person employed?* If the person is employed for a long period of time, this indicates employee status.
6. *What is the method of payment—by time period or at the completion of the job?* Payment by time period, such as once every two weeks or once a month, indicates employee status.
7. *What degree of skill is required of the worker?* If a great degree of skill is required, this may indicate that the person is an independent contractor hired for a specialized job and not an employee.

Workers sometimes benefit from having employee status. For instance, employers are required to pay certain taxes, such as Social Security and unemployment taxes, for employees but not for independent contractors. In addition, federal statutes governing employment discrimination apply only in employer-employee relationships.

For the same reasons, employers may benefit from identifying those working for them as independent contractors. In addition, an employer normally is not liable for the actions of an independent contractor. ■ **Case in Point 19.1** AAA North Jersey, Inc., contracted with Five Star Auto Service to perform towing and auto repair services for AAA. One night, Terence Pershad, a Five Star tow-truck driver, responded to an AAA call for assistance by the driver of a car involved in an accident. While at the scene, Pershad got into a fight with Nicholas Coker, a passenger in the disabled car, and assaulted him with a knife.

Coker filed a suit against Pershad, Five Star, and AAA, alleging that AAA was responsible for Pershad's tortious conduct. The court ruled that Pershad was Five Star's employee and that Five Star was an independent

<table>
</table>

Ethics Today — Is It Fair to Classify Uber and Lyft Drivers as Independent Contractors?

The transportation-for-hire world has changed dramatically since Uber, Lyft, and other transportation-sharing companies came onto the scene. Uber started in San Francisco in 2009, and now its services are available in over 80 countries and around 700 cities worldwide. Its main competitor, Lyft, was launched in 2012 and operates in more than 350 cities in the United States and Canada.

The growth in transportation sharing has not been without its setbacks. Most of them involve laws that have prohibited Uber and Lyft from operating in certain cities, as well as lawsuits by drivers claiming that they were misclassified.

Classification of Workers

Workers in the United States generally fall into two categories: employees and independent contractors. Employment laws, including minimum wage and antidiscrimination statutes, cover employees. Such laws do not cover most independent contractors. Enter the digital age of on-demand workers who obtain job assignments via apps.

Workers for Lyft, Uber, and similar companies choose when and where they will perform their duties. They do not choose how much they will be paid, however. For them, employment is a take-it-or-leave-it proposition. They electronically accept the platform terms of the apps, or they obtain no work assignments.

Some critics of this contractual system argue that there should be a new category of workers with "dependent-contractor" status who receive some of the protections traditionally given only to employees. Certain aspects of current labor law would be attached to the relationships between dependent contractors and their employers.

Worker Misclassification Lawsuits

A number of former or current Uber and Lyft drivers have pursued legal remedies to change their job classification and to obtain better benefits. In California, for instance, two federal court judges allowed separate lawsuits to go before juries on the question of whether

on-demand drivers should be considered employees rather than independent contractors.[a]

In a similar case, rather than go to court, Lyft settled a worker misclassification lawsuit for $12.25 million. The suit, which was settled in 2016, had been brought in 2013. The settlement did not achieve a reclassification of Lyft drivers as employees, however. Instead, Lyft agreed to change its terms of service to conform with California's independent contractor status regulations. For instance, the company can no longer deactivate drivers' accounts without reason and without warning the drivers. Drivers have to be given a fair hearing first. Even though the lawsuit and the agreement were California based, the new terms of service apply to all Lyft's drivers nationwide.[b]

Competitors Sue Uber

In many cities, competitors, especially taxi drivers, have sued Uber. These lawsuits have involved claims of unfair competition, lack of minimum wages, and unsafe vehicles. A taxi driver sued Uber in northern California, for instance, but a federal district court ruled in favor of Uber's request for summary judgment.[c]

Another suit was brought in Pennsylvania. In this one, Checker Cab of Philadelphia claimed that Uber was violating Pennsylvania's unfair competition law. Checker Cab sought a preliminary injunction to prevent Uber from taking away its customers. The federal district court refused to grant an injunction, however, because Checker Cab failed to show irreparable harm. That decision was upheld on appeal.[d]

Critical Thinking *What choices do disgruntled Uber and Lyft drivers have?*

a. *Cotter v. Lyft, Inc.*, 60 F.Supp.3d 1067 (N.D.Cal. 2015); *O'Connor v. Uber Technologies, Inc., et al.*, Case No. C-13-3826 EMC (N.D.Cal. 2015), and 201 F.Supp.3d 1110 (2016).
b. *Cotter v. Lyft, Inc.*, 193 F.Supp.3d 1030 (N.D.Cal. 2016); and *Cotter v. Lyft, Inc.*, 2017 WL 1033527 (N.D.Cal. 2017).
c. *Rosen v. Uber Technologies, Inc.*, 164 F.Supp.3d 1165 (N.D.Cal. 2016).
d. *Checker Cab of Philadelphia, Inc. v. Uber Technologies, Inc.*, 643 Fed. Appx. 229 (3d Cir. 2016).

contractor, not AAA's employee. An appellate court affirmed the ruling. Because AAA did not control Five Star's work, it was not liable for a tort committed by Five Star's employee.[2] ■

2. *Coker v. Pershad*, 2013 WL 1296271 (N.J.App. 2013).

Criteria Used by the IRS The Internal Revenue Service (IRS) has established its own criteria for determining whether a worker is an independent contractor or an employee. The most important factor is the degree of control the business exercises over the worker.

The IRS tends to closely scrutinize a firm's classification of its workers because, as mentioned, employers can avoid certain tax liabilities by hiring independent contractors instead of employees. Even when a firm has classified a worker as an independent contractor, the IRS may decide that the worker is actually an employee. If the IRS decides that an employee is misclassified, the employer will be responsible for paying any applicable Social Security, withholding, and unemployment taxes due for that employee.

Employee Status and "Works for Hire" Ordinarily, a person who creates a copyrighted work is the owner of it—unless it is a "work for hire." Under the Copyright Act, any copyrighted work created by an employee within the scope of her or his employment at the request of the employer is a "work for hire." The employer owns the copyright to the work.

In contrast, when an employer hires an independent contractor—such as a freelance artist, writer, or computer programmer—the independent contractor normally owns the copyright. An exception is made if the parties agree in writing that the work is a "work for hire" and the work falls into one of nine specific categories, including audiovisual works, collective works (such as magazines), motion pictures, textbooks, tests, and translations.

■ **Case in Point 19.2** As a freelance contractor, Brian Cooley created two sculptures of dinosaur eggs for the National Geographic Society for use in connection with an article in its magazine, *National Geographic*. Cooley spent hundreds of hours researching, designing, and constructing the sculptures. National Geographic hired Louis Psihoyos to photograph Cooley's sculptures for the article. Cooley and Psihoyos had separate contracts with National Geographic in which each transferred the copyrights in their works to National Geographic for a limited time.

The rights to the works were returned to the artists at different times after publication. Psihoyos then began licensing his photographs of Cooley's sculptures to third parties in return for royalties. He digitized the photographs and licensed them to various online stock photography companies, and they appeared in several books published by Penguin Group. Cooley sued Psihoyos for copyright infringement.

Psihoyos argued that he owned the photos and could license them however he saw fit, but a federal district court disagreed. The court found that Psihoyos did not have an unrestricted right to use and license the photos. When Psihoyos reproduced an image of a Cooley sculpture, he reproduced the sculpture, which infringed on Cooley's copyright. Therefore, the court granted a summary judgment to Cooley.[3] ■

19–2 Formation of the Agency Relationship

Agency relationships normally are consensual. They come about by voluntary consent and agreement between the parties. Normally, the agreement need not be in writing, and consideration is not required.

A person must have contractual capacity to be a principal.[4] The idea is that those who cannot legally enter into contracts directly should not be allowed to do so indirectly through an agent. Any person can be an agent, however, regardless of whether he or she has the capacity to contract (including minors).

An agency relationship can be created for any legal purpose. An agency relationship created for a purpose that is illegal or contrary to public policy is unenforceable. ■ **Example 19.3** Archer (as principal) contracts with Burke (as agent) to sell illegal narcotics. The agency relationship is unenforceable because selling illegal narcotics is a felony and is contrary to public policy. If Burke sells the narcotics and keeps the profits, Archer cannot sue to enforce the agency agreement. ■

An agency relationship can arise in four ways: by agreement of the parties, by ratification, by estoppel, and by operation of law.

19–2a Agency by Agreement

Most agency relationships are based on an express or implied agreement that the agent will act for the principal and that the principal agrees to have the agent so act. An agency agreement can take the form of an express written contract or be created by an oral agreement, such as when a person hires a neighbor to mow his lawn on a regular basis.

An agency agreement can also be implied by conduct. ■ **Case in Point 19.4** Gilbert Bishop was admitted to a nursing home, Laurel Creek Health Care Center, suffering from various physical ailments. He was not able to use his hands well enough to write but was otherwise mentally competent. Bishop's sister offered to sign the admission papers for him, but it was Laurel Creek's policy to have the patient's spouse sign the forms if the patient could not.

Bishop's sister then brought his wife, Anna, to the hospital to sign the paperwork, which included a mandatory arbitration clause. Later, when the family filed a lawsuit against Laurel Creek, the nursing home sought to enforce the arbitration clause. Ultimately, a Kentucky appellate court held that Bishop was bound by the contract and the arbitration clause his wife had signed. Bishop's conduct

---

3. *Cooley v. Penguin Group (USA), Inc.*, 31 F.Supp.3d 599 (S.D.N.Y. 2014).

4. Note that some states allow a minor to be a principal. When a minor is permitted to be a principal, any resulting contracts will be voidable by the minor-principal but *not* by the adult third party.

had indicated that he was giving his wife authority to act as his agent in signing the admission papers.[5] ∎

19–2b Agency by Ratification

On occasion, a person who is in fact not an agent (or who is an agent acting outside the scope of her or his authority) makes a contract on behalf of another (a principal). If the principal approves or affirms that contract by word or by action, an agency relationship is created by *ratification*. Ratification involves a question of intent, and intent can be expressed by either words or conduct.

19–2c Agency by Estoppel

Sometimes, a principal causes a third person to believe that another person is the principal's agent, and the third person acts to his or her detriment in reasonable reliance on that belief. When this occurs, the principal is "estopped to deny" (prevented from denying) the agency relationship. The principal's actions have created the *appearance* of an agency that does not in fact exist, creating an agency by estoppel.

The Third Party's Reliance Must Be Reasonable
The third person must prove that he or she *reasonably* believed that an agency relationship existed.[6] Facts and

circumstances must show that an ordinary, prudent person familiar with business practice and custom would have been justified in concluding that the agent had authority.

Created by the Principal's Conduct Note that the acts or declarations of a purported *agent* in and of themselves do not create an agency by estoppel. Rather, it is the deeds or statements of the *principal* that create an agency by estoppel. ∎ **Case in Point 19.5** Francis Azur was president and chief executive officer of ATM Corporation of America. Michelle Vanek was Azur's personal assistant. Among other duties, she reviewed his credit-card statements. For seven years, Vanek took unauthorized cash advances from Azur's credit-card account with Chase Bank. The charges appeared on at least sixty-five monthly statements.

When Azur discovered Vanek's fraud, he fired her and closed the account. He filed a suit against Chase, arguing that the bank should not have allowed Vanek to take cash advances. The court concluded that Azur (the principal) had given the bank reason to believe that Vanek (the agent) had authority. Therefore, Azur was estopped (prevented) from denying Vanek's authority.[7] ∎

The question in the following case was whether the doctrine of agency by estoppel applied to a hospital whose emergency room physician was an independent contractor.

---

5. *Laurel Creek Health Care Center v. Bishop,* 2010 WL 985299 (Ky.App. 2010).

6. These concepts also apply when a person who is, in fact, an agent undertakes an action that is beyond the scope of her or his authority.

7. *Azur v. Chase Bank, USA, N.A.,* 601 F.3d 212 (3d Cir. 2010).

Case 19.1

Riedel v. Akron General Health System

Court of Appeals of Ohio, Eighth District, 2018 -Ohio- 840, 97 N.E.3d 508 (2018).

Background and Facts Akron General Health System owns and operates health-care centers, including Lodi Community Hospital, in Ohio. Aaron Riedel was experiencing severe back pain when he visited the emergency room at Lodi. Attending physician Chris Kalapodis failed to timely diagnose the problem—a spinal epidural abscess. Riedel filed a suit in an Ohio state court against the hospital, alleging that the physician's negligence was the proximate cause of Riedel's subsequent paraplegia and seeking to recover medical expenses and the cost of future care. Lodi argued that it was not liable because Kalapodis was not its employee or agent. The jury issued a verdict in Riedel's favor and found that he was entitled to $5.2 million in damages, which the court awarded. Lodi appealed.

In the Language of the Court
Anita Laster *MAYS*, J. [Judge]:
* * * *

* * * A hospital may be held liable under the doctrine of agency by estoppel for the negligence of independent medical practitioners practicing in the hospital if it holds itself out to the public as a provider of medical services and in the absence of notice or knowledge to the contrary, the patient looks to the hospital, as opposed to the individual practitioner, to provide competent medical care.

Lodi argues that both prongs of the requirements must be met and that the evidence was insufficient to meet the second prong of the test because Riedel did not testify that he "looked to the hospital, as opposed to the individual practitioner, to provide competent medical care" and that he admitted that he was "going to be treated by a doctor" upon his arrival at the hospital.

The emergency room has become the community medical center, serving as the portal of entry to the myriad of services available at the hospital. As an industry, hospitals spend enormous amounts of money advertising in an effort to compete with each other for the health care dollar, thereby inducing the public to rely on them in their time of medical need. The public, in looking to the hospital to provide such care, is unaware of and unconcerned with the technical complexities and nuances surrounding the contractual and employment arrangements between the hospital and the various medical personnel operating therein. Indeed, often the very nature of a medical emergency precludes choice. *Public policy dictates that the public has every right to assume and expect that the hospital is the medical provider it purports to be.* [Emphasis added.]

* * * *

Unless the patient merely viewed the hospital as the *situs* [the physical location where his] physician would treat [him], [he] had the right to assume and expect that the treatment was being rendered through hospital employees and that any negligence associated therewith would render the hospital liable.

There is no evidence in the record that Riedel had a doctor-patient relationship with Dr. Kalapodis prior to the Lodi emergency room encounter. Riedel testified that Lodi was close to his daughters' home and he was seeking emergency medical care. Riedel had no information that Dr. Kalapodis was not directly employed by Lodi. We agree with [Riedel] that it is hardly unusual for a person seeking emergency medical care to expect to be treated by a physician employed by a hospital.

Decision and Remedy *A state intermediate appellate court affirmed the order of the trial court. The court stated, "The record contains substantial competent evidence to support the jury's finding of liability by estoppel." As for the remedy, the amount of the damages fell within the range of estimates in expert analyses submitted by the parties supporting the cost of the life-care plan for Riedel's permanent disability.*

Critical Thinking

- **Legal Environment** *An unconscious individual transported to a hospital would be unable to demonstrate that he or she was seeking care from the hospital and not a particular physician. Would the public policy considerations stated in the* Riedel *case apply? Why or why not?*
- **What If the Facts Were Different?** *Suppose that a sign had been posted in the Lodi emergency room spelling out the legal relationship between the hospital and the attending physician. Would the result have been different? Explain.*

19–2d Agency by Operation of Law

The courts may find an agency relationship in the absence of a formal agreement in other situations as well. This may occur in family relationships, such as when one spouse purchases certain basic necessaries and charges them to the other spouse's account. The courts often rule that a spouse is liable for payment for the necessaries because of either a social policy or a legal duty to supply necessaries to family members.

Agency by operation of law may also occur in emergency situations. If an agent cannot contact the principal and failure to act would cause the principal substantial loss, the agent may take steps beyond the scope of her or his authority. For instance, a railroad engineer may contract on behalf of his or her employer for medical care for an injured motorist hit by the train.

19–3 Duties, Rights, and Remedies of Agents and Principals

Once the principal-agent relationship has been created, both parties have duties that govern their conduct. As discussed previously, the principal-agent relationship is *fiduciary*—based on trust. In a fiduciary relationship, each party owes the other the duty to act with the utmost good faith.

19–3a Agent's Duties to the Principal

Generally, the agent owes the principal five duties—performance, notification, loyalty, obedience, and accounting (see Exhibit 19–1).

Performance An implied condition in every agency contract is the agent's agreement to use reasonable diligence and skill in performing the work. When an agent fails to perform his or her duties, liability for breach of contract may result.

The degree of skill or care required of an agent usually is that expected of a reasonable person under similar circumstances. Generally, this is interpreted to mean ordinary care. If an agent has represented herself or himself as possessing special skills, however, the agent is expected to exercise the degree of skill claimed. Failure to do so constitutes a breach of the agent's duty.

Not all agency relationships are based on contract. In some situations, an agent acts gratuitously—that is, without payment. A gratuitous agent cannot be liable for breach of contract because there is no contract. He or she is subject only to tort liability. Once a gratuitous agent has begun to act in an agency capacity, he or she has the duty to continue to perform in that capacity. A gratuitous agent must perform in an acceptable manner and is subject to the same standards of care and duty to perform as other agents.

■ **Example 19.6** Bower's friend Alcott is a real estate broker. Alcott offers to sell Bower's vacation home at no charge. If Alcott never attempts to sell the home, Bower has no legal cause of action to force her to do so. If Alcott does attempt to sell the home to Friedman, but then performs so negligently that the sale falls through, Bower can sue Alcott for negligence. ■

Notification An agent is required to notify the principal of all matters that come to her or his attention concerning the subject matter of the agency. This is the *duty of notification*, or the duty to inform.

■ **Example 19.7** Perez, an artist, is about to negotiate a contract to sell a series of paintings to Barber's Art Gallery for $25,000. Perez's agent learns that Barber is insolvent and will be unable to pay for the paintings. The agent has a duty to inform Perez of Barber's insolvency because it is relevant to the subject matter of the agency, which is the sale of Perez's paintings. ■

Generally, the law assumes that the principal is aware of any information acquired by the agent that is relevant to the agency—regardless of whether the agent actually passes on this information to the principal. It is a basic tenet of agency law that notice to the agent is notice to the principal.

Loyalty Loyalty is one of the most fundamental duties in a fiduciary relationship. Basically, the agent has the duty to act *solely for the benefit of his or her principal* and not in the interest of the agent or a third party. For instance, an agent cannot represent two principals in the same transaction unless both know of the dual capacity and consent to it.

The duty of loyalty also means that any information or knowledge acquired through the agency relationship is confidential. It is a breach of loyalty to disclose such information either during the agency relationship or after

Exhibit 19–1 Duties of the Agent

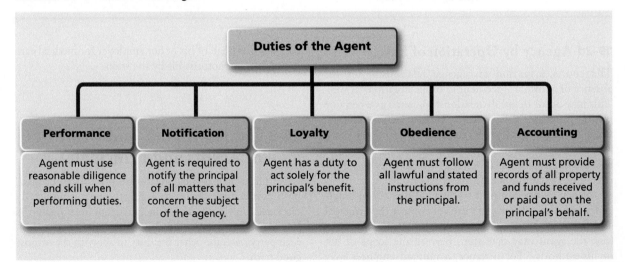

Duties of the Agent				
Performance	**Notification**	**Loyalty**	**Obedience**	**Accounting**
Agent must use reasonable diligence and skill when performing duties.	Agent is required to notify the principal of all matters that concern the subject of the agency.	Agent has a duty to act solely for the principal's benefit.	Agent must follow all lawful and stated instructions from the principal.	Agent must provide records of all property and funds received or paid out on the principal's behalf.

its termination. Typical examples of confidential information are trade secrets and customer lists compiled by the principal.

The agent's loyalty must be undivided. The agent's actions must be strictly for the benefit of the principal and must not result in any secret profit for the agent.

■ **Example 19.8** Don contracts with Leo, a real estate agent, to negotiate the purchase of an office building. Leo discovers that the property owner will sell the building only as a package deal with another parcel. Leo buys the two properties, intending to resell the building to Don. Leo has breached his fiduciary duty. As a real estate agent, Leo has a duty to communicate all offers to Don, his principal, and not to purchase the property secretly and then resell it to Don. Leo is required to act in Don's best interests and can become the purchaser in this situation only with Don's knowledge and approval. ■

Obedience When acting on behalf of the principal, an agent has a duty to follow all lawful and clearly stated instructions of the principal. Any deviation from such instructions is a violation of this duty.

During emergency situations, however, when the principal cannot be consulted, the agent may deviate from the instructions without violating this duty. Whenever instructions are not clearly stated, the agent can fulfill the duty of obedience by acting in good faith and in a manner reasonable under the circumstances.

Accounting Unless the agent and principal agree otherwise, the agent must keep and make available to the principal an account of all property and funds received and paid out on the principal's behalf. This includes gifts from third parties in connection with the agency.

■ **Example 19.9** Marla is a salesperson for Roadway Supplies. Knife River Construction gives Marla a new tablet as a gift for prompt deliveries of Roadway's paving materials. The tablet belongs to Roadway. ■

The agent has a duty to maintain a separate account for the principal's funds and must not intermingle these funds with the agent's personal funds. If a licensed professional (such as an attorney) violates this duty, he or she may be subject to disciplinary action by the licensing authority (such as the state bar association). Of course, the professional will also be liable to his or her client (the principal) for failure to account.

19–3b Principal's Duties to the Agent

The principal also has certain duties to the agent (as shown in Exhibit 19–2). These duties relate to compensation, reimbursement and indemnification, cooperation, and safe working conditions.

Compensation In general, when a principal requests certain services from an agent, the agent reasonably expects payment. For instance, when an accountant or an attorney is asked to act as an agent, an agreement to compensate the agent for this service is implied. The principal therefore has a duty to pay the agent for services rendered.

Unless the agency relationship is gratuitous and the agent does not act in exchange for payment, the principal must pay the agreed-on value for the agent's services. If no amount has been expressly agreed on, then the

Exhibit 19–2 Duties of the Principal

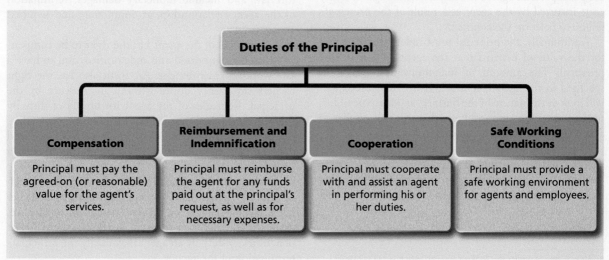

Duties of the Principal			
Compensation	**Reimbursement and Indemnification**	**Cooperation**	**Safe Working Conditions**
Principal must pay the agreed-on (or reasonable) value for the agent's services.	Principal must reimburse the agent for any funds paid out at the principal's request, as well as for necessary expenses.	Principal must cooperate with and assist an agent in performing his or her duties.	Principal must provide a safe working environment for agents and employees.

principal owes the agent the customary compensation for such services. The principal also has a duty to pay that compensation in a timely manner.

■ **Case in Point 19.10** Keith Miller worked as a sales representative for Paul M. Wolff Company, a subcontractor specializing in concrete-finishing services. Sales representatives at Wolff were paid a 15 percent commission on projects that met a 35 percent gross profit threshold. The commission was paid after the projects were completed. When Miller resigned, he asked for commissions on fourteen projects for which he had secured contracts but which had not yet been completed. Wolff refused, so Miller sued.

The court found that "an agent is entitled to receive commissions on sales that result from the agent's efforts," even after the employment or agency relationship ends. Miller had met the gross profit threshold on ten of the unfinished projects, and therefore, he was entitled to more than $21,000 in commissions.[8] ■

Reimbursement and Indemnification

Whenever an agent disburses funds at the request of the principal, the principal has a duty to reimburse the agent. The principal must also reimburse the agent (even a gratuitous agent) for any necessary expenses incurred in the course of the reasonable performance of her or his agency duties. Agents cannot recover for expenses incurred as a result of their own misconduct or negligence.

Subject to the terms of the agency agreement, the principal has the duty to *indemnify* (compensate) an agent for liabilities incurred because of authorized and lawful acts and transactions. For instance, if the agent, on the principal's behalf, forms a contract with a third party, and the principal fails to perform the contract, the third party may sue the agent for damages. In this situation, the principal is obligated to compensate the agent for any costs incurred by the agent as a result of the principal's failure to perform the contract.

Additionally, the principal must indemnify the agent for the value of benefits that the agent confers on the principal. The amount of indemnification usually is specified in the agency contract. If it is not, the courts will look to the nature of the business and the type of loss to determine the amount. Note that this rule applies to acts by gratuitous agents as well.

Cooperation

A principal has a duty to cooperate with the agent and to assist the agent in performing his or her duties. The principal must do nothing to prevent that performance.

For instance, when a principal grants an agent an exclusive territory, the principal creates an **exclusive agency,** in which the principal cannot compete with the agent or appoint or allow another agent to compete. If the principal does so, he or she violates the exclusive agency and is exposed to liability for the agent's lost profits.

■ **Example 19.11** Penny (the principal) creates an exclusive agency by granting Andrew (the agent) a territory within which only Andrew may sell Penny's organic skin care products. If Penny starts to sell the products herself within Andrew's territory—or permits another agent to do so—Penny has failed to cooperate with the agent. Because she has violated the exclusive agency, Penny can be held liable for Andrew's lost sales or profits. ■

Safe Working Conditions

The common law requires the principal to provide safe working premises, equipment, and conditions for all agents and employees. The principal has a duty to inspect working areas and to warn agents and employees about any unsafe situations. When the agent is an employee, the employer's liability is frequently covered by state workers' compensation insurance. In addition, federal and state statutes often require the employer to meet certain safety standards.

19–3c Rights and Remedies of Agents and Principals

In general, for every duty of the principal, the agent has a corresponding right, and vice versa. When one party to the agency relationship violates his or her duty to the other party, the nonbreaching party is entitled to a remedy. The remedies available arise out of contract and tort law and include monetary damages, termination of the agency relationship, an injunction, and required accountings.

As mentioned, the agent has the right to be compensated, to be reimbursed and indemnified, and to have a safe working environment. An agent also has the right to perform agency duties without interference by the principal. Remedies of the agent for breach of duty by the principal follow normal contract and tort remedies. An agent can also withhold further performance and demand that the principal give an accounting in certain situations.

A principal has contract remedies for an agent's breach of fiduciary duties. The principal also has tort remedies if the agent engages in misrepresentation, negligence, deceit, libel, slander, or trespass. In addition, any breach of a fiduciary duty by an agent may justify the principal's termination of the agency.

---

8. *Miller v. Paul M. Wolff Co.*, 178 Wash.App. 957, 316 P.3d 1113 (2014).

19–4 Agent's Authority

The liability of a principal to third parties with whom an agent contracts depends on whether the agent had the authority to enter into legally binding contracts on the principal's behalf. An agent's authority can be either *actual* (express or implied) or *apparent*. If an agent contracts outside the scope of his or her authority, the principal may still become liable by ratifying the contract.

19–4a Express Authority

Express authority is authority declared in clear, direct, and definite terms. Express authority can be given orally or in writing.

The Equal Dignity Rule In most states, the **equal dignity rule** requires that if the contract being executed is or must be in writing, then the agent's authority must also be in writing. (Recall that a writing includes an electronic record.) Failure to comply with the equal dignity rule can make a contract voidable *at the option of the principal*. The law regards the contract at that point as a mere offer. If the principal decides to accept the offer, the acceptance must be ratified, or affirmed, in writing.

■ **Example 19.12** Paloma (the principal) orally asks Austin (the agent) to sell a ranch that Paloma owns. Austin finds a buyer and signs a sales contract on behalf of Paloma to sell the ranch. Because a contract for an interest in real property must be in writing, the equal dignity rule applies. The buyer cannot enforce the contract unless Paloma subsequently ratifies Austin's agency status *in a writing*. Once the sales contract is ratified, either party can enforce rights under the contract. ■

Modern business practice allows several exceptions to the equal dignity rule:

1. An executive officer of a corporation normally can conduct *ordinary* business transactions without obtaining written authority from the corporation.
2. When the agent acts in the presence of the principal, the rule does not apply.
3. When the agent's act of signing is merely a formality, then the agent does not need written authority to sign. ■ **Example 19.13** Sandra Healy (the principal) negotiates a contract but is called out of town the day it is to be signed. If Healy orally authorizes Derek Santini to sign, the oral authorization is sufficient. ■

Power of Attorney Giving an agent a **power of attorney** confers express authority.[9] The power of

attorney is a written document and usually is notarized. (A document is notarized when a **notary public**—a person authorized to attest to the authenticity of signatures—signs, dates, and imprints the document with her or his seal of authority.) Most states have statutory provisions for creating a power of attorney.

A power of attorney can be *special* (permitting the agent to perform specified acts only), or it can be *general* (permitting the agent to transact all business for the principal). Because a general power of attorney grants extensive authority to the agent, it should be used with great caution and usually only in exceptional circumstances. Ordinarily, a power of attorney terminates on the incapacity or death of the person giving the power.[10]

19–4b Implied Authority

An agent has the **implied authority** to do what is reasonably necessary to carry out express authority and accomplish the objectives of the agency. Authority can also be implied by custom or inferred from the position the agent occupies.

■ **Example 19.14** Archer is employed by Packard Grocery to manage one of its stores. Packard has not expressly stated that Archer has authority to contract with third persons. Nevertheless, authority to manage a business implies authority to do what is reasonably required (as is customary or can be inferred from a manager's position) to operate the business. This includes forming contracts to hire employees, buying merchandise and equipment, and advertising the products sold in the store. ■

Note, however, that an agent's implied authority cannot contradict his or her express authority. Thus, if a principal has limited an agent's express authority, then the fact that the agent customarily would have such authority is irrelevant. ■ **Example 19.15** Juanita Alvarez is the owner of six Baja Tacos restaurants. Alvarez (the principal) strictly forbids the managers (agents) of her taco shops from entering into contracts to hire additional workers. Therefore, the fact that managers customarily would have authority to hire employees is immaterial. ■

19–4c Apparent Authority

Actual authority (express or implied) arises from what the principal makes clear *to the agent*. Apparent authority, in

---

9. An agent who holds a power of attorney is called an *attorney-in-fact* for the principal. The holder does not have to be an attorney-at-law (and often is not).

10. A *durable* power of attorney, however, continues to be effective despite the principal's incapacity or death. An elderly person, for instance, might grant a durable power of attorney to provide for the handling of property and investments or specific health-care needs should he or she become incompetent.

contrast, arises from what the principal causes a *third party* to believe. An agent has **apparent authority** when the principal, by either word or action, causes a third party reasonably to believe that the agent has authority to act, even though the agent has no express or implied authority.

A Pattern of Conduct Apparent authority usually comes into existence through a principal's pattern of conduct over time. ■ **Case in Point 19.16** Gilbert Church owned a horse breeding farm managed by Herb Bagley. Advertisements for the breeding rights to one of Church Farm's stallions, Imperial Guard, directed all inquiries to "Herb Bagley, Manager." Vern and Gail Lundberg bred Thoroughbred horses. The Lundbergs contacted Bagley and executed a preprinted contract giving them breeding rights to Imperial Guard "at Imperial Guard's location," subject to approval of the mares by Church. Bagley handwrote a statement on the contract that guaranteed the Lundbergs "six live foals in the first two years." He then signed it "Gilbert G. Church by H. Bagley."

The Lundbergs bred four mares, which resulted in one live foal. Church then moved Imperial Guard from Illinois to Oklahoma. The Lundbergs sued Church for breaching the contract by moving the horse. Church claimed that Bagley was not authorized to sign contracts for Church or to change or add terms, but only to present preprinted contracts to potential buyers. Church testified that although Bagley was his farm manager and the contact person for breeding rights, Bagley had never before modified the preprinted forms or signed Church's name on them. The jury found in favor of the Lundbergs and awarded $147,000 in damages. Church appealed, but the state appellate court affirmed the judgment. The court reasoned that because Church allowed circumstances to lead the Lundbergs to believe Bagley had the authority, Church was bound by Bagley's actions.[11] ■

Apparent Authority and Estoppel A court can apply the doctrine of agency by estoppel when a principal has given a third party reason to believe that an agent has authority to act. If the third party honestly relies on the principal's representations to his or her detriment, the principal may be *estopped* (prevented) from denying that the agent had authority.

In the following case, a condominium owner argued that the Condominium Association that managed the units could not enforce bylaws that some of the Association's board members had themselves violated. The owner argued, in essence, that the board members were agents acting with the authority of the Association.

---

11. *Lundberg v. Church Farm, Inc.*, 151 Ill.App.3d 452, 502 N.E.2d 806 (1986).

Case 19.2

Dearborn West Village Condominium Association v. Makki
Court of Appeals of Michigan, 2019 WL 97152 (2019).

Background and Facts Dearborn West Village Condominium Association manages the Dearborn West Village Condominium complex in Dearborn, Michigan. The complex's bylaws permit a condominium owner to lease his or her unit for single-family residential use, but only if the owner is transferred out of the state and first provides a lease to the Association for its review.

Mohamed Makki bought five units and, without meeting the conditions of the bylaws, rented all of the units to third parties. The Association filed a complaint in a Michigan state court against Makki to enforce the bylaws and terminate the rentals. The court issued a judgment in favor of the Association.

Makki appealed, asserting that individual board members who had offered to sell him units they were using as rental properties were acting with apparent authority on behalf of the Association. Thereby, he argued, the Association had waived its right to enforce the leasing restrictions in the bylaws.

In the Language of the Court
PER CURIAM. [By the Whole Court]
* * * *

Defendant contends that former board members leased, and approved of co-owners' leasing, condominium units to third parties in violation of plaintiff's bylaws, approved the leases he used with his third-party lessees, and provided assurances that the board would not enforce the bylaws' relevant leasing provisions. He argues that these actions of the board members * * * bound plaintiff, such that plaintiff cannot now enforce the bylaws at issue * * * . We disagree.
* * * *

Defendant has failed to cite any authority for his underlying premise that the *ultra vires* actions of a board member(s) [actions beyond the person's legal authority] bind plaintiff. *Generally, an agent's actions that are outside the scope of the agent's authority do not bind a principal. Dealings or engagements of the agent beyond the scope of his authority do not bind the principal.* Pursuant to the [Michigan] Condominium Act, the administration of a condominium project is governed by the condominium bylaws. According to plaintiff's bylaws, the board of directors may not do things prohibited by the bylaws, and the board has a duty to enforce the bylaws. Thus, board members who leased their units to third parties in violation of the leasing restrictions and who failed to enforce the leasing restrictions violated the bylaws. The actions defendant alleges of board members were clearly outside the scope of the board's authority as delineated by the bylaws and, therefore, cannot bind plaintiff. Further, * * * the fact that the * * * board may not have enforced the restrictions on leasing units does not prohibit plaintiff from doing so now. Thus, defendant's argument that plaintiff waived strict enforcement of the bylaws fails. [Emphasis added.]

* * * *

In sum, it is undisputed that defendant did not comply with the leasing restrictions in the association's bylaws. The fact that one or more board members did not comply with the provision does not obligate plaintiff to accept or approve the leasing of condominium units in violation of its bylaws.

Decision and Remedy *A state intermediate appellate court affirmed the lower court's judgment. Estoppel does not apply to bind a principal when an agent's actions are outside the scope of the agent's authority. The board members who leased their units to third parties in violation of the bylaws were themselves in violation of the restrictions. Their actions were outside the scope of their authority and did not bind the association.*

Critical Thinking
- **Legal Environment** *Normally, modification of the Association's bylaws requires the approval of two-thirds of the unit owners. Could Makki have successfully argued that the actions of the board members who violated the bylaws modified them in accord with the principles of freedom to contract? Explain.*
- **Economic** *Why might a condominium complex's bylaws impose restrictions on individual owners' leasing of their units? Why might some of those owners opt to violate the restrictions? Discuss.*

19–4d Emergency Powers

When an unforeseen emergency demands action by the agent to protect or preserve the property and rights of the principal, but the agent is unable to communicate with the principal, the agent has emergency power.
■ **Example 19.17** Rob Fulsom is an engineer for Pacific Drilling Company. While Fulsom is acting within the scope of his employment, he is severely injured in an accident on an oil rig many miles from home. Acosta, the rig supervisor, directs Thompson, a physician, to give medical aid to Fulsom and to charge Pacific for the medical services.

Acosta, an agent, has no express or implied authority to bind the principal, Pacific Drilling, for Thompson's medical services. Because of the emergency situation, however, the law recognizes Acosta as having authority to act appropriately under the circumstances. ■

19–4e Ratification

Ratification occurs when the principal affirms, or accepts responsibility for, an agent's *unauthorized* act.

When ratification occurs, the principal is bound to the agent's act, and the act is treated as if it had been authorized by the principal *from the outset.* Ratification can be either express or implied.

If the principal does not ratify the contract, the principal is not bound, and the third party's agreement with the agent is viewed as merely an unaccepted offer. The third party can revoke it at any time, without liability, before the principal ratifies the contract. The agent, however, may be liable to the third party for misrepresenting her or his authority.

The requirements for ratification can be summarized as follows:

1. The agent must have acted on behalf of an identified principal who subsequently ratifies the action.
2. The principal must know all of the material facts involved in the transaction. If a principal ratifies a contract without knowing all of the facts, the principal can rescind (cancel) the contract.
3. The principal must affirm the agent's act in its entirety.

4. The principal must have the legal capacity to authorize the transaction at the time the agent engages in the act and at the time the principal ratifies. The third party must also have the legal capacity to engage in the transaction.
5. The principal's affirmation (ratification) must occur before the third party withdraws from the transaction.
6. The principal must observe the same formalities when ratifying the act as would have been required to authorize it initially.

19–5 Liability in Agency Relationships

Frequently, a question arises as to which party, the principal or the agent, should be held liable for contracts formed by the agency or for torts and crimes committed by the agent.

19–5a Liability for Contracts

Liability for contracts formed by an agent depends on how the principal is classified and on whether the actions of the agent were authorized or unauthorized. Principals are classified as disclosed, partially disclosed, or undisclosed.[12]

1. A **disclosed principal** is a principal whose identity is known by the third party at the time the contract is made by the agent.
2. A **partially disclosed principal** is a principal whose identity is not known by the third party. Nevertheless, the third party knows that the agent is or *may be* acting for a principal at the time the contract is made. ■ **Example 19.18** Eileen has contracted with a real estate agent to sell certain property. She wishes to keep her identity a secret, but the agent makes it clear to potential buyers of the property that he is acting in an agency capacity. In this situation, Eileen is a partially disclosed principal. ■
3. An **undisclosed principal** is a principal whose identity is totally unknown by the third party. In addition, the third party has no knowledge that the agent is acting in an agency capacity at the time the contract is made.

Authorized Acts If an agent acts within the scope of her or his authority, normally the principal is obligated to perform the contract regardless of whether the principal

was disclosed, partially disclosed, or undisclosed. Whether *the agent may also be held liable* under the contract, however, depends on the disclosed, partially disclosed, or undisclosed status of the principal.

Disclosed or Partially Disclosed Principal. A disclosed or partially disclosed principal is liable to a third party for a contract made by the agent. If the principal is disclosed, the agent has no contractual liability for the nonperformance of the principal or the third party. If the principal is partially disclosed, in most states the agent is also treated as a party to the contract. Thus, the third party can hold the agent liable for contractual nonperformance.

■ **Case in Point 19.19** Stonhard, Inc., makes epoxy and urethane flooring and installs it in industrial and commercial buildings. Marvin Sussman contracted with Stonhard to install flooring at a Blue Ridge Farms food-manufacturing facility in Brooklyn, New York. Sussman did not disclose that he was acting as an agent for the facility's owner, Blue Ridge Foods, LLC, at the time of contract formation.

When Stonhard was not paid for the flooring it installed, it filed a suit against the facility, its owner, and Sussman to recover damages for breach of contract. The lower court dismissed the complaint against Sussman personally, but on appeal a reviewing court reversed that decision. The contract had been signed by Sussman "of Blue Ridge Farms." That evidence indicated that Sussman was acting as an agent for a partially disclosed principal, in that the agency relationship was known, but not the principal's identity. "As an agent for an undisclosed [or partially disclosed] principal, Sussman became personally liable under the contract."[13] ■

Undisclosed Principal. When neither the fact of an agency relationship nor the identity of the principal is disclosed, the undisclosed principal is bound to perform just as if the principal had been fully disclosed at the time the contract was made.

When a principal's identity is undisclosed and the agent is forced to pay the third party, the agent is entitled to be *indemnified* (compensated) by the principal. The principal had a duty to perform, even though his or her identity was undisclosed, and failure to do so will make the principal ultimately liable.

Once the undisclosed principal's identity is revealed, the third party generally can elect to hold either the principal or the agent liable on the contract. Conversely, the

---

12. *Restatement (Third) of Agency*, Section 1.04(2).

13. *Stonhard, Inc. v. Blue Ridge Farms, LLC*, 114 A.D.3d 757, 980 N.Y.S.2d 507 (2 Dept. 2014).

undisclosed principal can require the third party to fulfill the contract, *unless* one of the following is true:

1. The undisclosed principal was expressly excluded as a party in the written contract.
2. The contract is a negotiable instrument signed by the agent with no indication of signing in a representative capacity.[14]
3. The performance of the agent is personal to the contract, thus allowing the third party to refuse the principal's performance.

Unauthorized Acts If an agent has no authority but nevertheless contracts with a third party, the *principal* cannot be held liable on the contract. It does not matter whether the principal was disclosed, partially disclosed, or undisclosed. The *agent* is liable.

■ **Example 19.20** Chu signs a contract for the purchase of a truck, purportedly acting as an agent under authority granted by Navarro. In fact, Navarro has not given Chu any such authority. Navarro refuses to pay for the truck, claiming that Chu had no authority to purchase it. The seller of the truck is entitled to hold Chu liable for payment. ■

If the principal is disclosed or partially disclosed, and the agent contracts with a third party without authorization, the agent is liable to the third party. The agent's liability here is based on his or her breach of the *implied warranty of authority*, not on the breach of the contract itself.[15] An agent impliedly warrants that he or she has the authority to enter into a contract on behalf of the principal. If the third party knows at the time the contract is made that the agent does not have authority, then the agent is not personally liable.

Actions by E-Agents Although in the past standard agency principles applied only to *human* agents, today these same agency principles also apply to e-agents. An electronic agent, or **e-agent,** is a semiautonomous software program that is capable of executing specific tasks, such as searching through many databases and retrieving relevant information for the user.

E-agents can enter into binding agreements on behalf of their principals. Thus, if consumers place an order over the Internet, and the company (principal) takes the order via an e-agent, the company cannot later claim that it did not receive the order.

19–5b Liability for Torts and Crimes

Obviously, any person, including an agent, is liable for his or her own torts and crimes. Whether a principal can also be held liable for an agent's torts and crimes depends on several factors, which we examine here.

Principal's Tortious Conduct A principal who acts through an agent may be liable for harm resulting from the principal's own negligence or recklessness. Thus, a principal may be liable if he or she gives improper instructions, authorizes the use of improper materials or tools, or establishes improper rules that result in the agent's committing a tort.

Similarly, a principal who authorizes an agent to commit a tort may be liable to persons or property injured thereby, because the act is considered to be the principal's. ■ **Example 19.21** Pedro directs his agent, Andy, to cut the corn on specific acreage, which neither of them has the right to do. The harvest is therefore a trespass (a tort), and Pedro is liable to the owner of the corn. ■

Note that an agent acting at the principal's direction can be liable, along with the principal, for committing the tortious act even if the agent was unaware that the act was wrong. Assume in *Example 19.21* that Andy, the agent, did not know that Pedro lacked the right to harvest the corn. Andy can nonetheless be held liable to the owner of the field for damages, along with Pedro, the principal.

Liability for Agent's Misrepresentation A principal is exposed to tort liability whenever a third person sustains a loss due to the agent's misrepresentation. The principal's liability depends on whether the agent was actually or apparently authorized to make representations and whether the representations were made within the scope of the agency. The principal is always directly responsible for an agent's misrepresentation made within the scope of the agent's authority.

■ **Example 19.22** Ainsley is a demonstrator for Pavlovich's products. Pavlovich sends Ainsley to a home show to demonstrate the products and to answer questions from consumers. Pavlovich has given Ainsley authority to make statements about the products. If Ainsley makes only true representations, all is fine. But if he makes false claims, Pavlovich will be liable for any injuries or damages sustained by third parties in reliance on Ainsley's false representations. ■

When a principal has placed an agent in a position of apparent authority—making it possible for the agent to defraud a third party—the principal may also be liable for the agent's fraudulent acts. For instance, partners

---

14. Under the Uniform Commercial Code (UCC), only the agent is liable if the instrument neither names the principal nor shows that the agent signed in a representative capacity [UCC 3–402(b)(2)].
15. The agent is not liable on the contract because the agent was never intended personally to be a party to the contract.

in a partnership generally have the apparent implied authority to act as agents of the firm. Thus, if one of the partners commits a tort or a crime, the partnership itself—and often the other partners personally—can be held liable for the loss.

Liability for Agent's Negligence An agent is liable for his or her own torts. A principal may also be liable for harm an agent causes to a third party under the doctrine of **respondeat superior,**[16] a Latin term meaning "let the master respond." Under the doctrine of *respondeat superior*, the principal-employer is liable for any harm caused to a third party by an agent-employee in the course or scope of employment. The doctrine imposes **vicarious liability,** or indirect liability, because the principal-employer is being held liable for torts committed by an agent-employee.

When an agent commits a negligent act in such a situation, *both* the agent and the principal are liable. ■ **Example 19.23** Aegis hires SDI to provide landscaping services for its property. An herbicide sprayed by SDI employee David Hoggatt enters the Aegis building through the air-conditioning system and causes Catherine Warner, an Aegis employee, to suffer a heart attack. If Warner sues, both SDI (principal) and Hoggatt (agent) can be held liable for negligence. ■

---

16. Pronounced ree-*spahn*-dee-uht soo-*peer*-ee-your. The doctrine of *respondeat superior* applies not only to employer-employee relationships but also to other principal-agent relationships in which the principal has the right of control over the agent.

The doctrine of *respondeat superior* is similar to the theory of strict liability in that liability is imposed regardless of fault. Every person has a duty to manage his or her affairs so as not to injure another. This duty applies even when a person acts through an agent (controls the conduct of another). This chapter's *Global Insight* feature discusses whether nations that follow Islamic law recognize the doctrine of *respondeat superior*.

Determining the Scope of Employment. The key to determining whether a principal may be liable for the torts of an agent under the doctrine of *respondeat superior* is whether the torts are committed within the scope of the agency. Courts may consider the following factors in determining whether a particular act occurred within the course and scope of employment:

1. Whether the employee's act was authorized by the employer.
2. The time, place, and purpose of the act.
3. Whether the act was one commonly performed by employees on behalf of their employers.
4. The extent to which the employer's interest was advanced by the act.
5. The extent to which the private interests of the employee were involved.
6. Whether the employer furnished the means or instrumentality (such as a truck or a machine) by which an injury was inflicted.

Global Insight | **Islamic Law and *Respondeat Superior***

The doctrine of *respondeat superior* is well established in the legal systems of the United States and most Western countries. As you have already read, under this doctrine, employers can be held liable for the acts of their employees. The doctrine of *respondeat superior* is not universal, however. Most Middle Eastern countries, for example, do not follow this doctrine.

Codification of Islamic Law

Islamic law, as codified in the *sharia*, holds to a strict belief that responsibility for human actions lies with the individual and cannot be vicariously (indirectly) extended to others. This belief and other concepts of Islamic law are based on the writings of Muhammad, the seventh-century prophet whose revelations form the basis of the Islamic religion and, by extension, the *sharia*.

Muhammad's prophecies are documented in the Koran (Qur'an), which is the principal source of the *sharia*.

An Exception

Islamic law does allow for an employer to be responsible for an employee's actions when the actions result from a direct order given by the employer to the employee. This principle also applies to contractual obligations. Note that the master is responsible *only* if direct orders were given. Otherwise stated, unless an employee is obeying a direct order of the employer, liability for the employee's actions does not extend to the employer.

Critical Thinking *How would U.S. society be affected if employers could not be held vicariously liable for their employees' torts?*

7. Whether the employer had reason to know that the employee would perform the act in question and whether the employee had done it before.
8. Whether the act involved the commission of a serious crime.

The Distinction between a "Detour" and a "Frolic." A useful insight into the concept of "scope of employment" can be gained from Judge Baron Parke's classic distinction between a "detour" and a "frolic" in the case of *Joel v. Morison* (1834).[17] In this case, the English court held that if a servant merely took a detour from his master's business, the master will be responsible. If, however, the servant was on a "frolic of his own" and not in any way "on his master's business," the master will not be liable.

■ **Example 19.24** While driving his employer's vehicle to call on a customer, Mandel decides to stop at a store—which is three blocks off his route—to take care of a personal matter. As Mandel approaches the store, he negligently runs into a parked vehicle owned by Chan. In this situation, because Mandel's detour from the employer's business is not substantial, he is still acting within the scope of employment, and the employer is liable.

But suppose instead that Mandel decides to pick up a few friends in another city for cocktails and in the process negligently runs his vehicle into Chan's. In this situation, the departure from the employer's business is substantial—Mandel is on a "frolic" of his own. Thus, the employer normally will not be liable to Chan for damages. ■

17. 6 Car. & P. 501, 172 Eng.Rep. 1338 (1834).

An employee going to and from work or to and from meals usually is considered to be outside the scope of employment. If travel is part of a person's position, however, as it is for a traveling salesperson, then travel time is normally considered within the scope of employment.

Liability for Agent's Intentional Torts Most intentional torts that individuals commit have no relation to their employment, and their employers will not be held liable. Nevertheless, under the doctrine of *respondeat superior*, the employer can be liable for intentional torts that an employee commits within the course and scope of employment. For instance, a department store owner is liable when a security guard who is a store employee commits the tort of false imprisonment while acting within the scope of employment.

In addition, an employer who knows or should know that an employee has a propensity for committing tortious acts is liable for the employee's acts even if they would not ordinarily be considered within the scope of employment. ■ **Example 19.25** Chaz, the owner of the Comedy Club, hires Alec as a bouncer even though he knows that Alec has a history of arrests for criminal assault and battery. In this situation, Chaz may be liable if Alec viciously attacks a customer in the parking lot after hours. ■ An employer is also liable for permitting an employee to engage in reckless actions that can injure others. Needless to say, most employers purchase liability insurance to cover their potential liability for employee conduct.

Whether an agent's allegedly tortious conduct fell within the scope of the agent's employment, making the principal vicariously liable, was at the heart of the dispute in the following case.

Case Analysis 19.3

M.J. v. Wisan
Utah Supreme Court, 2016 UT 13, 371 P.3d 21 (2016).

In the Language of the Court
Associate Chief Justice LEE * * *:
* * * *

[Members of the Fundamentalist Church of Jesus Christ of Latter-Day Saints ("FLDS Church") in Utah formed the United Effort Plan Trust ("UEP Trust" or the "Trust"). The Trust] members deeded their property to the UEP Trust to be managed by Church

leaders. Church leaders, who were also trustees, then used this property to minister to the needs of the members.
* * * *

[At the time of the events leading up to this case,] the Trust was operated for the express purpose of furthering the doctrines of the FLDS Church, including the practice of * * * marriage involving underage girls.

* * * *
[Later, as a result of unrelated litigation, a state court reformed the Trust] by excising the purpose of advancing the religious doctrines and goals of the FLDS Church to the degree that any of these were illegal, including * * * sexual activity between adults and minors. [The court appointed Bruce Wisan to head the Trust.]

Case 19.3 Continues

* * * *

[Later,] M.J., a former member of the FLDS Church and beneficiary of the UEP Trust, [filed this suit in a Utah state court against Wisan, as head of the Trust, alleging that] when she was fourteen years old, she was forced to marry Allen Steed, her first cousin. The wedding was performed by Warren Jeffs, who at the time was acting president of both the FLDS Church and * * * the Trust. * * * M.J. claims that Steed repeatedly sexually assaulted and raped her * * * . She requested a divorce from Steed on multiple occasions, but Jeffs refused to allow it. He also refused to let M.J. live * * * separately from her husband.

* * * She seeks to hold * * * the Trust vicariously liable for intentional infliction of emotional distress.

* * * M.J. * * * claims that Jeffs and other trustees were acting "in furtherance of the trust administration and within the scope of their authority," and thus contends that the Trust should be liable under the doctrine of *respondeat superior*.

* * * *

The Trust filed a series of motions for summary judgment. All of those motions were denied. The Trust then filed [this] petition for review.

* * * *

* * * Under [Utah Code Section 75–7–1010, Utah's version of Section 1010 of the Uniform Trust Code,] a trust is liable for the trustee's acts performed "in the course of administering the trust."

* * * The terms of the statute, in context, are quite clear. "In the course of" *is the traditional formulation of the standard for vicarious liability under the doctrine of* respondeat superior. *We accordingly interpret the Uniform Trust Act as incorporating the established standard of* respondeat superior *liability.* Thus, under [Section 75–7–1010] a trust is liable for the acts of a trustee when the trustee was acting within the scope of his responsibility as a trustee. [Emphasis added.]

* * * *

The difficult question for the law in this field has been to define the line between a course of conduct subject to the employer's control and an independent course of conduct not connected to the principal. *An independent course of conduct is a matter so removed from the agent's duties that the law, in fairness, eliminates the principal's vicarious liability.* Such a course of conduct is one that represents a departure from, not an escalation of, conduct involved in performing assigned work or other conduct that an employer permits or controls. [Emphasis added.]

Our cases have identified three factors of relevance to this inquiry: (1) whether the agent's conduct is of the general kind the agent is employed to perform; (2) whether the agent is acting within the hours of the agent's work and the ordinary spatial boundaries of the employment; and (3) whether the agent's acts were motivated, at least in part, by the purpose of serving the principal's interest.

* * * In the case law of a number of states, spatial and time boundaries are no longer essential hallmarks of an agency relationship. Instead, the law now recognizes that agents may interact on an employer's behalf with third parties although the employee is neither situated on the employer's premises nor continuously or exclusively engaged in performing assigned work.

A number of courts have also questioned the viability of the requirement that an agent's acts be motivated in some part by an intention to serve the principal's purposes.

* * * In [some] jurisdictions, * * * courts avoid the use of motive or intention to determine whether an employee's tortious conduct falls within the scope of employment and adopt a different standard for identifying the tie between the tortfeasor's employment and the tort. One such standard is whether the tort is a generally foreseeable consequence of the enterprise

undertaken by the employer or is incident to it—in other words, whether the agent's conduct is not so unusual or startling that it seems unfair to include the loss resulting from it in the employer's business costs, or whether the tort was engendered by the employment or an outgrowth of it. Another considers whether the employment furnished the specific impetus for a tort or increased the general risk that the tort would occur. These tests leave to the finder of fact the challenge of determining whether a tortfeasor's employment did more than create a happenstance opportunity to commit the tort.

* * * To resolve this case we need not choose * * * between the purpose or motive test * * * and the alternative formulations * * * because we find that the Trust's attempts to defeat its liability on summary judgment fail under any of the * * * formulations.

We do openly endorse one particular aspect of * * * the doctrine of *respondeat superior*, however. Specifically * * * we hold that an agent need not be acting within the hours of the employee's work and the ordinary spatial boundaries of the employment in order to be acting within the course of his employment. * * * We acknowledge that in today's business world much work is performed for an employer away from a defined work space and outside of a limited work shift. And we accordingly reject the Trust's attempt to escape liability on the ground that Jeffs's acts as a trustee were not performed while he was on the Trust's clock or at a work space designated for his work for the Trust. Instead we hold that the key question is whether Jeffs was acting within the scope of employment when performing work assigned by the employer or engaging in a course of conduct subject to the employer's control.

[The Trust argues] that settled case-law establishes "as a matter of law that the sexual misconduct of an employee is outside the scope of employment."

Granted, there are many cases that so conclude * * * and some of those cases * * * turn principally on the ground that * * * an agent who commits a sexual assault * * * cannot be viewed as advancing, even in part, the purposes of his principal. Yet some of the cases in this field (particularly more recent ones) * * * adopt * * * a standard that turns not on motive or purpose but on foreseeability, or on whether the employee's acts were engendered by or an outgrowth of the employment, or the employment furnished the impetus for the tort.

* * * *

And we conclude that this is one of those cases. Given Jeffs's unique role as leader of the FLDS Church, and in light of the unusual, troubling function of * * * marriage involving young brides in the FLDS culture, we hold that a reasonable factfinder could conclude that Jeffs was acting within the scope of his role as a trustee in directing Steed to engage in sexual activity with M.J.

* * * *

* * * We affirm the denial of the Trust's motions for summary judgment on that basis.

Legal Reasoning Questions

1. Why do some courts apply a standard for imposing vicarious liability that does not rely on motive or purpose to determine whether an agent's tortious conduct falls within the scope of employment?

2. Why, in some states, are the boundaries of work time and space no longer essential factors in determining the scope of employment in an agency relationship?

3. Whom does the result in this case benefit? Why?

Liability for Independent Contractor's Torts
Generally, an employer is not liable for physical harm caused to a third person by the negligent act of an independent contractor in the performance of the contract. This is because the employer does not have *the right to control* the details of an independent contractor's performance.

Courts make an exception to this rule when the contract involves unusually hazardous activities, such as blasting operations, the transportation of highly volatile chemicals, or the use of poisonous gases. In these situations, strict liability is imposed, and an employer cannot be shielded from liability merely by using an independent contractor.

Liability for Agent's Crimes
An agent is liable for his or her own crimes. A principal or employer normally is *not* liable for an agent's crime even if the crime was committed within the scope of authority or employment. An exception to this rule is made when the principal or employer participated in the crime by conspiracy or other action.

In addition, in some jurisdictions, a principal may be liable under specific statutes if an agent, in the course and scope of employment, violates certain regulations. For instance, a principal might be liable for an agent's violation of sanitation rules or regulations governing prices, weights, or the sale of liquor.

19–6 Termination of an Agency

Agency law is similar to contract law in that both an agency and a contract may be terminated by an act of the parties or by operation of law. Once the relationship between the principal and the agent has ended, the agent no longer has the right (*actual* authority) to bind the principal. For an agent's *apparent* authority to be terminated, though, third persons may also need to be notified that the agency has been terminated.

19–6a Termination by Act of the Parties

An agency may be terminated by certain acts of the parties, which include lapse of time, achievement of purpose, occurrence of a specific event, mutual agreement, and at the option of one party.

When an agency agreement specifies the time period during which the agency relationship will exist, the agency ends when that time period expires. If no definite time is stated, then the agency continues for a reasonable time and can be terminated at will by either party. What constitutes a reasonable time depends on the circumstances and the nature of the agency relationship.

The parties can, of course, mutually agree to end their agency relationship. In addition, as a general rule, either party can terminate the agency relationship without the agreement of the other. The act of termination is called *revocation* if done by the principal and *renunciation* if done by the agent.

Wrongful Termination Although both parties have the *power* to terminate the agency, they may not always possess the *right* to do so. Wrongful termination can subject the canceling party to a lawsuit for breach of contract. ■ **Case in Point 19.26** Smart Trike, Ltd., a Singapore manufacturing company based in Israel, contracted with a New Jersey firm, Piermont Products, LLC, to distribute its products in the United States and Canada. The parties' contract required six months' notice of termination, during which time Smart Trike was to continue paying commissions to Piermont for products that were sold. When Smart Trike terminated the agreement without providing the required notice, Piermont sued for breach of contract. The court held in favor of Piermont. Under the terms of the agreement, Piermont was entitled to receive commissions for Smart Trike products that it had sold during the six months after the notice of termination.[18] ■

Even in an agency at will—in which either party may terminate at any time—the principal who wishes to terminate must give the agent *reasonable* notice. The notice must be at least sufficient to allow the agent to recoup his or her expenses and, in some situations, to make a normal profit.

Notice of Termination When the parties terminate an agency, it is the principal's duty to inform any third parties who know of the existence of the agency that it has been terminated. No particular form is required for notice of termination to be effective. The principal can personally notify the agent, or the agent can learn of the termination through some other means. Although an agent's actual authority ends when the agency is terminated, an agent's *apparent authority* continues until the third party receives notice (from any source) that such authority has been terminated.

---

18. *Smart Trike, MNF, PTE, Ltd. v. Piermont Products, LLC,* 147 A.D.3d 477, 48 N.Y.S.3d 23 (2017).

19–6b Termination by Operation of Law

Certain events terminate agency authority automatically because their occurrence makes it impossible for the agent to perform or improbable that the principal would continue to want performance. We look at these events here. Note that when an agency terminates by operation of law, normally there is no duty to notify third persons.

1. *Death or insanity.* The general rule is that the death or insanity of either the principal or the agent automatically and immediately terminates an ordinary agency relationship. Knowledge of the death or insanity is not required. Some states, however, have enacted statutes that change the common law rule to require an agent's knowledge of the principal's death before termination.
2. *Impossibility.* When the specific subject matter of an agency is destroyed or lost, the agency terminates. Similarly, when it is impossible for the agent to perform the agency lawfully because of a change in the law, the agency terminates.
3. *Changed circumstances.* Sometimes, an event occurs that has such an unusual effect on the subject matter of the agency that the agent can reasonably infer that the principal will not want the agency to continue. In such situations, the agency terminates. ■ **Example 19.27** Baird hires Joslen to sell a tract of land for $40,000. Subsequently, Joslen learns that there is oil under the land and that the land is worth $1 million. The agency and Joslen's authority to sell the land for $40,000 are terminated. ■
4. *Bankruptcy.* If either the principal or the agent petitions for bankruptcy, the agency *usually* is terminated. In certain circumstances, such as when the agent's financial status is irrelevant to the purpose of the agency, the agency relationship may continue. Insolvency, as distinct from bankruptcy, does not necessarily terminate the relationship. (An *insolvent* person is one who cannot pay debts as they come due or whose liabilities exceed his or her assets.)
5. *War.* When the principal's country and the agent's country are at war with each other, the agency is terminated. In this situation, the agency is automatically suspended or terminated because there is no way to enforce the legal rights and obligations of the parties.

Practice and Review: Agency Relationships

Lynne Meyer, on her way to a business meeting and in a hurry, stopped at a Buy-Mart store for a new car charger for her smartphone. There was a long line at one of the checkout counters, but a cashier, Valerie Watts, opened another counter and began loading the cash drawer. Meyer told Watts that she was in a hurry and asked Watts to work faster. Instead, Watts slowed her pace. At this point, Meyer hit Watts. It is not clear whether Meyer hit Watts intentionally or, in an attempt to retrieve the car charger, hit her inadvertently.

In response, Watts grabbed Meyer by the hair and hit her repeatedly in the back of the head, while Meyer screamed for help. Management personnel separated the two women and questioned them about the incident. Watts was immediately fired for violating the store's no-fighting policy. Meyer subsequently sued Buy-Mart, alleging that the store was liable for the tort (assault and battery) committed by its employee. Using the information presented in the chapter, answer the following questions.

1. Under what doctrine discussed in this chapter might Buy-Mart be held liable for the tort committed by Watts?
2. What is the key factor in determining whether Buy-Mart is liable under this doctrine?
3. How is Buy-Mart's potential liability affected by whether Watts's behavior constituted an intentional tort or a tort of negligence?
4. Suppose that when Watts applied for the job at Buy-Mart, she disclosed in her application that she had previously been convicted of felony assault and battery. Nevertheless, Buy-Mart hired Watts as a cashier. How might this fact affect Buy-Mart's liability for Watts's actions?

Debate This ...   *The doctrine of* respondeat superior *should be modified to make agents solely liable for their tortious (wrongful) acts committed within the scope of employment.*

Terms and Concepts

agency 420
apparent authority 430
disclosed principal 432
e-agent 433
equal dignity rule 429
exclusive agency 428

express authority 429
fiduciary 420
implied authority 429
independent contractor 421
notary public 429
partially disclosed principal 432

power of attorney 429
ratification 431
respondeat superior 434
undisclosed principal 432
vicarious liability 434

Issue Spotters

1. Winona contracted with XtremeCast, a broadcast media firm, to cohost an Internet-streaming sports program. Winona and XtremeCast signed a new contract for each episode. In each contract, Winona agreed to work a certain number of days for a certain salary. During each broadcast, Winona was free to improvise her performance. She had no other obligation to work for XtremeCast. Was Winona an independent contractor? (See *Agency Law*.)

2. Davis contracts with Estee to buy a certain horse on her behalf. Estee asks Davis not to reveal her identity. Davis

makes a deal with Farmland Stables, the owner of the horse, and makes a down payment. Estee does not pay the rest of the price. Farmland Stables sues Davis for breach of contract. Can Davis hold Estee liable for whatever damages he has to pay? Why or why not? (See *Liability in Agency Relationships*.)

• **Check your answers to the Issue Spotters against the answers provided in Appendix B at the end of this text.**

Business Scenarios and Case Problems

19–1. *Respondeat Superior.* ABC Tire Corp. hires Arnez as a traveling salesperson and assigns him a geographic area and time schedule in which to solicit orders and service customers. Arnez is given a company car to use in covering the territory. One day, Arnez decides to take his personal car to cover part of his territory. It is 11:00 A.M., and Arnez has just finished calling on all customers in the city of Tarrytown. His next appointment is at 2:00 P.M. in the city of Austex, twenty miles down the road. Arnez starts out for Austex, but halfway there he decides to visit a former college roommate who runs a farm ten miles off the main highway. Arnez is enjoying his visit with his former roommate when he realizes that it is 1:45 P.M. and that he will be late for the appointment in Austex. Driving at a high speed down the country road to reach the main highway, Arnez crashes his car into a tractor, severely injuring Thomas, the driver of the tractor. Thomas claims that he can hold ABC Tire Corp. liable for his injuries. Discuss fully ABC's liability in this situation. (See *Liability in Agency Relationships.*)

19–2. Duty of Loyalty. Peter hires Alice as an agent to sell a piece of property he owns. The price is to be at least $30,000. Alice discovers that the fair market value of Peter's property is actually at least $45,000 and could be higher because a shopping mall is going to be built nearby. Alice forms a real estate partnership with her cousin Carl. Then she prepares for Peter's signature a contract for the sale of the property to Carl for $32,000. Peter signs the contract. Just before closing and passage of title, Peter learns about the shopping mall and the increased fair market value of his property. Peter refuses to deed the property to Carl. Carl claims that Alice, as Peter's agent, solicited a price above that agreed on when the agency was created and that the contract is therefore binding and enforceable. Discuss fully whether Peter is bound to this contract. (See *Duties, Rights, and Remedies of Agents and Principals.*)

19–3. Employee versus Independent Contractor. Stephen Hemmerling was a driver for the Happy Cab Company. Hemmerling paid certain fixed expenses and followed various rules relating to the use of the cab, the hours that could be worked, and the solicitation of fares, among other things. Rates were set by the state. Happy Cab did not withhold taxes from Hemmerling's pay. While driving the cab, Hemmerling was injured in an accident and filed a claim for workers' compensation benefits in a state court. Such benefits are not available to independent contractors. On what basis might the court hold that Hemmerling was an employee? Explain. (See *Agency Law.*)

19–4. Business Case Problem with Sample Answer— Determining Employee Status. Nelson Ovalles worked as a cable installer for Cox Rhode Island Telecom, LLC, under an agreement with a third party, M&M Communications, Inc. The agreement stated that no employer-employee

relationship existed between Cox and M&M's technicians, including Ovalles. Ovalles was required to designate his affiliation with Cox on his work van, clothing, and identification badge. Cox had minimal contact with him, however, and had limited power to control how he performed his duties. Cox supplied cable wire and similar items, but the equipment was delivered to M&M, not to Ovalles. On a workday, while Ovalles was fulfilling a work order, his van rear-ended a car driven by Barbara Cayer. Is Cox liable to Cayer? Explain. [*Cayer v. Cox Rhode Island Telecom, LLC,* 85 A.3d 1140 (R.I. 2014)] (See *Agency Law.*)

• **For a sample answer to Problem 19–4, go to Appendix C at the end of this text.**

19–5. Agency Relationships. Standard Oil of Connecticut, Inc., sells home heating, cooling, and security systems. Standard schedules installation and service appointments with its customers and then contracts with installers and technicians to do the work. The company requires an installer or technician to complete a project by a certain time but to otherwise "exercise independent judgment and control in the execution of any work." The installers and technicians are licensed and certified by the state. Standard does not train them, provide instruction manuals, supervise them at customers' homes, or inspect their work. The installers and technicians use their own equipment and tools, and they can choose which days they work. Standard pays a set rate per project. According to criteria used by the courts, are these installers and technicians independent contractors or employees? Why? [*Standard Oil of Connecticut, Inc. v. Administrator, Unemployment Compensation Act,* 320 Conn. 611, 134 A.3d 581 (2016)] (See *Agency Law.*)

19–6. Agent's Authority. Kindred Nursing Centers East, LLC, owns and operates Whitesburg Gardens, a long-term care and rehabilitation facility, in Huntsville, Alabama. Lorene Jones was admitted to the facility following knee-replacement surgery. Jones's daughter, Yvonne Barbour, signed the admission forms required by Whitesburg Gardens as her mother's representative in her presence. Jones did not object. The forms included an "Alternative Dispute Resolution Agreement," which provided for binding arbitration in the event of a dispute between "the Resident" (Jones) and "the Facility" (Whitesburg Gardens). Six days later, Jones was transferred to a different facility. After recovering from the surgery, she filed a suit in an Alabama state court against Kindred, alleging substandard care on a claim of negligence. Can Jones be compelled to submit her claim to arbitration? Explain. [*Kindred Nursing Centers East, LLC v. Jones,* 201 So.3d 1146 (Ala. 2016)] (See *Agent's Authority.*)

19–7. Agent's Authority. Devin Fink was the manager of Precision Tune Auto Care in Charlotte, North Carolina. Randall Stywall brought her car to the shop to have the rear shocks replaced. Fink filled out the service order with an estimate of the cost. Later, Stywall returned to pick up her car, and Fink collected payment for the work. When Stywall started to drive away, however, the car bounced as if the shocks had not been replaced. A complaint to Precision's corporate office resulted in the discovery that, in fact, the work had not been done and Fink had kept the payment. He was charged with larceny against his employer. He argued that he had not committed this crime because the victim was Stywall, not Precision. Which agency principles support the charge against Fink? Explain. [*State of North Carolina v. Fink*, 798 S.E.2d 537 (2017)] (See *Agent's Authority*.)

19–8. Agency Relationships. Jane Westmas was killed when a tree branch cut by Creekside Tree Service, Inc., fell on her. At the time, Jane was walking on a public path through the private property of Conference Point Center on the shore of Lake Geneva in Wisconsin. Conference Point had contracted with Creekside to trim and remove trees from its property, but the owner had no control of the details of Creekside's work. Jane's husband, John, and her son, Jason, filed a suit in a Wisconsin state court against Creekside, alleging that the service's negligence caused her death. Creekside contended that it was immune from the suit under a state statute providing that "no . . . agent of an owner is liable for the death of . . . a person engaging in a recreational activity on the owner's property." Could Creekside be held liable for Jane's death? Why or why not? [*Westmas v. Creekside Tree Service, Inc.*, 2018 WI 12, 379 Wis.2d 471, 907 N.W.2d 68 (2018)] (See *Agency Law*.)

19–9. A Question of Ethics—The IDDR Approach and Agency Relationships. *The sale of insurance is a highly specialized field that requires considerable training, education, and skill. American Family Insurance Company sells its products through a network of insurance agents. At the start of their tenure, the agents sign an agreement stating that they are independent contractors. They work out of their own offices, set their own hours, provide the resources to run their offices, and hire and pay their own staff members. The agents file their taxes as independent contractors and deduct their expenses as self-employed business owners. American Family requires the agents to file daily activity reports, prioritize the sale of certain policies, and engage in specific sales tactics. The company approves the agents' office locations and imposes qualifications on their staff members. The agents are paid in commissions. Walid Jammal and other agents filed a suit in a federal district court against American Family, claiming that the company classified them as independent contractors to deprive them of employee benefits. [Jammal v. American Family Insurance Co., 914 F.3d 449 (6th Cir. 2019)] (See* Agency Law.*)*

(a) Use the IDDR approach to consider the ethics of American Family's decision not to provide its agents with employee benefits.

(b) Apply the criteria used by the courts to decide whether the agents in this case should be categorized as employees or independent contractors.

Time-Limited Group Assignment

19–10. Liability for Independent Contractor's Torts. Dean Brothers Corp. owns and operates a steel drum manufacturing plant. Lowell Wyden, the plant superintendent, hired Best Security Patrol, Inc. (BSP), a security company, to guard Dean property and "deter thieves and vandals." Some BSP security guards, as Wyden knew, carried firearms. Pete Sidell, a BSP security guard, was not certified as an armed guard but nevertheless came to work with his gun (in a briefcase).

While working at the Dean plant on October 31, Sidell fired his gun at Tyrone Gaines, in the belief that Gaines was an intruder. The bullet struck and killed Gaines. Gaines's mother filed a lawsuit claiming that her son's death was the result of BSP's negligence, for which Dean was responsible. (See *Liability in Agency Relationships*.)

(a) The first group will determine what the plaintiff's best argument is to establish that Dean is responsible for BSP's actions.

(b) The second group will discuss Dean's best defense and formulate arguments to support it.

(c) The third group will consider slightly different facts. Suppose that Dean Brothers had an express policy prohibiting all security guards from carrying firearms on its property and that Wyden had told BSP about this policy. Nevertheless, Sidell had brought his weapon to work and then fired it, killing Gaines. Could Dean be held responsible for negligence in that situation? Explain.

Chapter 20

Employment Law

Until the early 1900s, most employer-employee relationships were governed by the common law. Even today, under the common law *employment-at-will doctrine,* private employers have considerable freedom to hire and fire workers at will, regardless of the employees' performance.

Numerous statutes and administrative agency regulations now also govern the workplace. Thus, to a large extent, statutory law has displaced common law doctrines. In the next few chapters, we look at the most significant laws regulating employment relationships.

Note that the distinction made under agency law between employee status and independent-contractor status is important here. The employment laws that will be discussed apply only to the employer-employee relationship. They do not apply to independent contractors.

Suppose that Gary Randall works as an activities director for Valley Manor, a retirement community that offers several independent- and assisted-living options. As director, Randall normally spends his days at the Manor, where he hires and supervises other employees. One day, though, when another employee calls in sick, Randall accompanies residents on an excursion to a local art museum.

During the trip, Randall falls down some cement stairs and breaks his pelvis. He is taken by ambulance to a hospital, where he is told that he will need surgery and likely have a long recovery time. Does Randall qualify for workers' compensation coverage, or did this injury occur outside the scope of his employment? What about the time he will need to take off from work—is Randall entitled to take unpaid medical leave under federal law? If he takes unpaid leave, can he return to his original position afterward? These are some of the employment issues that will be discussed in this chapter.

20–1 Employment at Will

Employment relationships have traditionally been governed by the common law doctrine of **employment at will.** Under this doctrine, either party may terminate the employment relationship at any time and for any reason, unless doing so violates an employee's statutory or contractual rights.

Today, the majority of U.S. workers continue to have the legal status of "employees at will." In other words, this common law doctrine is still in widespread use, and only one state (Montana) does not apply it.

Nonetheless, federal and state statutes governing employment relationships prevent the doctrine from being applied in a number of circumstances. An employer may not fire an employee if doing so would violate a federal or state statute, such as a law prohibiting employment discrimination.

20–1a Common Law Exceptions to the Employment-at-Will Doctrine

As noted, statutory law has affected the application of the employment-at-will doctrine. In addition, the courts have carved out various exceptions to the doctrine based on contract theory, tort theory, and public policy.

Exceptions Based on Contract Theory Some courts have held that an *implied* employment contract exists between the employer and the employee. If the employee is fired outside the terms of the implied contract, he or she may succeed in an action for breach of contract even though no written employment contract exists.

■ **Example 20.1** BDI Enterprises' employment manual and personnel bulletin both state that, as a matter of policy, workers will be dismissed only for good cause. Julie Chin is an employee at BDI. If Chin reasonably expects BDI to follow this policy, a court may find that there is an implied contract based on the terms stated in the manual and bulletin. ■ Generally, the key consideration in determining whether an employment manual creates an implied contractual obligation is the employee's reasonable expectations.

An employer's oral promises to employees regarding discharge policy may also be considered part of an implied contract. If the employer fires a worker in a manner contrary to what was promised, a court may hold that the employer has violated the implied contract and is liable for damages.

Exceptions Based on Tort Theory In some situations, the discharge of an employee may give rise to an action for wrongful discharge (discussed shortly) under tort theories. Abusive discharge procedures may result in a lawsuit for intentional infliction of emotional distress or defamation. In addition, some courts have permitted workers to sue their employers under the tort theory of fraud. Fraud might be alleged when an employer made false promises to a prospective employee.

■ **Example 20.2** Goldfinch Consulting, Inc., induces Brianna to leave a lucrative job and move to another state by offering her "a long-term job with a thriving business." In fact, Goldfinch is not only having significant financial problems but is also planning a merger that will result in the elimination of the position offered to Brianna. If she takes the job in reliance on Goldfinch's representations and is fired shortly thereafter, Brianna may be able to bring an action against the employer for fraud. ■

Exceptions Based on Public Policy The most common exception to the employment-at-will doctrine is made on the basis that the employer's reason for firing the employee violates a fundamental public policy of the jurisdiction. Generally, the courts require that the public policy involved be expressed clearly in the statutory law governing the jurisdiction.

The public-policy exception may apply to an employee discharged for **whistleblowing**—that is, telling government authorities, upper-level managers, or the media that the employer is engaged in some unsafe or illegal activity. Normally, however, whistleblowers seek protection from retaliatory discharge under federal and state statutes, such as the Whistleblower Protection Act.[1]

■ **Case in Point 20.3** Dale Yurk was employed at Application Software Technology (AST) Corporation. He discovered that AST was planning to reuse and resell software that it had developed for the city of Detroit. Yurk contacted his superiors—including the company's chief executive officer—and told them that he believed the resale infringed on the city's intellectual property rights. Shortly afterward, AST terminated Yurk's employment.

Yurk sued AST, alleging that the company had violated both the Whistleblower Protection Act and public policy. A federal district court held that Yurk had stated a claim under the Whistleblower Protection Act but dismissed the claim alleging that the company had violated public policy.[2] ■

The issue in the following case was whether the employment-at-will doctrine could be applied to support the discharge of an employee who brought a handgun to work but left it locked in his vehicle—in plain sight. The employee who was fired claimed that a public-policy exception prevented the employer from discharging him under the circumstances.

1. 5 U.S.C. Sections 1201 *et seq.*, and 2302(b)(8)–(9).
2. *Yurk v. Application Software Technology Corp.*, 2017 WL 661014 (E.D.Mich. 2017).

Case 20.1

Caterpillar, Inc. v. Sudlow
Court of Appeals of Indiana, 52 N.E.3d 19 (2016).

Background and Facts The firearms policy at a Caterpillar, Inc., facility in Indiana allowed employees who were legally permitted to possess firearms to store the weapons in their vehicles "in line with state law." The state firearms statute required firearms stored in vehicles to be locked in a trunk, kept in the glove compartment, or otherwise placed out of sight.

William Sudlow, an employee at Caterpillar, drove to work one day with a loaded Ruger .357 Magnum handgun—for which he had a permit—stuffed between the center console and the driver's seat. Sudlow left the gun there when he parked and entered the building to begin his workday. Another Caterpillar employee was walking through the parking lot, noticed the handgun in Sudlow's vehicle, and reported it to the head of security.

Case 20.1 Continues

Two days later, Sudlow was fired for violating the company's firearms policy. The same day, Caterpillar posted a new firearms policy that explicitly stated that firearms in employees' vehicles must be kept "secured and out of sight." Sudlow filed a complaint in an Indiana state court against Caterpillar, alleging wrongful discharge. The trial court found in Sudlow's favor, and a jury awarded him $85,000 in damages. Caterpillar appealed, arguing that the public-policy exception did not apply to Sudlow's firing.

In the Language of the Court
BAKER, Judge.
* * * *

Here, Caterpillar's Firearms Policy did not prohibit conduct that is protected by the [Indiana's] Firearms Statute. * * * Indeed, * * * Caterpillar could have enacted a more restrictive policy * * * but it chose not to do so. It is readily apparent that neither the Firearms Policy nor Caterpillar's interpretation thereof violated the Firearms Statute. *As a cause of action under the Firearms Statute is authorized only when an employer violates the statute, Sudlow has no right to recover on this basis.* [Emphasis added.]
* * * *

If Sudlow does not have a cause of action under the Firearms Statute, his only recourse would be something akin to a wrongful termination claim. It is undisputed that he was an at-will employee, meaning that his employment could have been terminated by either party at will, with or without a reason. There are three exceptions to the employment-at-will doctrine, but the parties discuss only the public policy exception: we have recognized a public policy exception to the employment-at-will doctrine if a clear statutory expression of a right or duty is contravened [violated].

The Firearms Statute is the best expression of Indiana's public policy regarding the right to transport and store firearms at work. And while this statute does confer a right to store a weapon in a trunk, glove compartment, or out of sight in a locked vehicle, it simply does not confer a right to store a weapon in a vehicle in plain sight. It is apparent, therefore, that in this case, *there was no contravention of a clear statutory expression of a right*. As a result, the public policy exception to the employment-at-will doctrine does not apply [to Sudlow's claim of wrongful discharge], and Sudlow is not entitled to relief under the common law. [Emphasis added.]

Decision and Remedy *The state appellate court found in favor of Caterpillar and reversed and remanded the case to the trial court. Caterpillar had not violated a "clear statutory expression of a right," because Indiana's firearms statute did not grant a right to store a gun in a vehicle in plain sight.*

Critical Thinking
- **Ethical** *Is the employment-at-will doctrine fair to employees? Why or why not?*

20–1b Wrongful Discharge

Whenever an employer discharges an employee in violation of an employment contract or a statutory law protecting employees, the employee may bring an action for **wrongful discharge.** For instance, an employee who is terminated in retaliation for some protected activity, such as whistleblowing or participating in an employment-discrimination investigation, can sue for wrongful discharge.

Even if an employer's actions do not violate any provisions in an employment contract or statute, the employer may still be subject to liability. An employee can sue for wrongful discharge under a common law doctrine, such as a tort theory or agency. For instance, if while firing a female employee, an employer publicly discloses private facts about her sex life, that employee could sue for wrongful discharge based on an invasion of privacy. Similarly, if a salesperson is fired because she refuses to participate in falsifying consumers' credit applications as instructed by her employer, she can sue for wrongful discharge as a matter of public policy.[3]

---

3. See *Anderson v. Reeds Jewelers, Inc.*, 2017 WL 1987249 (E.D.Va. 2017).

20–2 Wages, Hours, and Layoffs

In the 1930s, Congress enacted several laws to regulate the wages and working hours of employees, including the following:

1. The Davis-Bacon Act[4] requires contractors and subcontractors working on federal government construction projects to pay "prevailing wages" to their employees.
2. The Walsh-Healey Act[5] applies to U.S. government contracts. It requires that a minimum wage, as well as overtime pay at 1.5 times regular pay rates, be paid to employees of manufacturers or suppliers entering into contracts with agencies of the federal government.
3. The Fair Labor Standards Act (FLSA)[6] extended wage-hour requirements to cover all employers engaged in interstate commerce or in producing goods for interstate commerce. Certain other types of businesses were included as well. The FLSA, as amended, provides the most comprehensive federal regulation of wages and hours today.

20–2a Child Labor

The FLSA prohibits oppressive child labor. Restrictions on child labor differ by age group.

Children under fourteen years of age are allowed to do only certain types of work. They can deliver newspapers, work for their parents, and be employed in entertainment and (with some exceptions) agriculture. Children aged fourteen and fifteen are allowed to work, but not in hazardous occupations. There are also restrictions on how many hours per day and per week children in these age groups can work.

Working times and hours are not restricted for persons between the ages of sixteen and eighteen, but they cannot be employed in hazardous jobs. None of these restrictions apply to persons over the age of eighteen.

20–2b Minimum Wages

The FLSA provides that a **minimum wage** must be paid to covered nonexempt employees. Most states also have minimum wages. More than half of the states have set their minimum wages above the federal minimum wage. When the state minimum wage is greater than the federal minimum wage, the employee is entitled to the higher wage.

---

4. 40 U.S.C. Sections 276a–276a-5.
5. 41 U.S.C. Sections 35–45.
6. 29 U.S.C. Sections 201 *et seq.*

■ **Example 20.4** The Oakland Raiders paid $1.25 million to settle wage claims made by the team's cheerleading squad (the Raiderettes) as a class action. The cheerleaders had complained that they were not being paid for hours that they spent attending other events and performing other tasks required of them by contract. After the time spent performing these other tasks was factored in, the cheerleaders were receiving wages that were well below California's minimum wage, persuading the Raiders to settle the dispute. ■

Are employees entitled to receive wages for all the time they spend at work, including times when they are taking a personal break? See this chapter's *Ethics Today* feature for a discussion of this issue.

20–2c Tipped Workers

When an employee receives tips while on the job, the FLSA gives employers a tip credit toward the minimum wage amount. The employer is required to pay only $2.13 an hour in direct wages—if that amount, plus the tips received, equals at least the federal minimum wage. If an employee's tips and direct wages do not equal the federal minimum wage, the employer must make up the difference. Note that some states have enacted laws to prevent employers from including tips in the minimum wage. In these states, tipped workers receive the regular minimum wage.

20–2d Overtime Provisions and Exemptions

Under the FLSA, any employee who works more than forty hours per week must be paid no less than 1.5 times her or his regular pay for all hours worked over forty. The FLSA overtime provisions apply only after an employee has worked more than forty hours per *week*. Therefore, employees who work ten hours a day, four days per week, are not entitled to overtime pay.

Certain employees are exempt from the FLSA's overtime provisions. These employees generally include executive, administrative, and professional employees, as well as outside salespersons and those who create computer code. Executive and administrative employees are those whose primary duty is management and who exercise discretion and independent judgment.

■ **Case in Point 20.5** Patty Lee Smith was a pharmaceutical sales representative for Johnson and Johnson (J&J). She traveled to ten physicians' offices a day to promote the benefits of J&J's drug Concerta. Smith's work was unsupervised, she controlled her own schedule, and she received an annual salary of $66,000. When she filed a claim for overtime pay, the court held that she was an

Ethics Today — Is It Fair to Dock Employees' Pay for Bathroom Breaks?

For some employees, "punching a time clock" means accounting for *all* of the time that they are not working. These employees must "punch in" when they arrive and "punch out" when they leave for the day, of course, but they also must clock out when they take personal breaks, including bathroom breaks, coffee breaks, and smoking breaks.

What the Law Says

The Fair Labor Standards Act[a] does not require that an employer offer its employees personal breaks. If an employer does offer them, though, employees must be compensated during those breaks. Otherwise, the employer may effectively be in violation of federal minimum wage laws.

A Pennsylvania Publisher Faces Fines for Unpaid Bathroom Breaks

The issue of unpaid bathroom breaks came to the fore when the U.S. Department of Labor (DOL) filed a lawsuit against American Future Systems, Inc. (doing business as Progressive Business Publications). The DOL alleged that American Future Systems had created a compensation system in which none of its six thousand employees were compensated for bathroom breaks.

The DOL argued that all workday breaks of twenty minutes or less are compensable time.[b] Because American Future Systems did not compensate its employees for such breaks, those employees were not properly credited for all compensable time. The result was that they had "been paid below the minimum wage established by the Fair Labor Standards Act (FLSA).[c] A federal district court agreed and ordered the company to pay past and current employees almost $2 million to compensate for the lost break time. A federal appellate court affirmed the decision.[d]

The Ethical Issue

Irrespective of the illegality of not paying for personal breaks, there is an ethical issue. Should workers have to face the choice of taking a bathroom break or getting paid? Adam Welsh, a senior trial attorney for the Department of Labor, argued that the answer is no. "I think it's the rare employer who doesn't allow its employees to go to the bathroom," Welsh said.

Critical Thinking *Consider a company whose employees include both smokers and nonsmokers. The smokers take numerous paid smoking breaks, while the nonsmokers do not. Is there an ethical issue here? Discuss.*

a. 29 U.S.C. Sections 201 *et seq.*
b. 29 C.F.R. Part 785.18.
c. 29 U.S.C. Section 206(a)(1)(c).
d. *U.S. Department of Labor v. American Future Systems, Inc.*, 873 F.3d 420 (3d Cir. 2017).

administrative employee and therefore exempt from the FLSA's overtime provisions.[7] ∎

Along with exempt employees, workers who make more than a specified amount are not eligible for overtime

7. *Smith v. Johnson and Johnson*, 593 F.3d 280 (3d Cir. 2010).

pay under the FLSA. An employer can voluntarily pay overtime to ineligible employees but cannot waive or reduce the overtime requirements of the FLSA.

The question in the following case was whether an auto dealer's service advisors fit within the FLSA overtime-pay exemption.

Case 20.2

Encino Motorcars, LLC v. Navarro
Supreme Court of the United States, __ U.S. __, 138 S.Ct. 1134, 200 L.Ed.2d 433 (2018).

Background and Facts Encino Motorcars, LLC, owned a Mercedes-Benz dealership in California. Encino employed service advisors whose duties included suggesting repair and maintenance services, recording service orders, following up with customers as the services are performed, and explaining all the work performed, among other functions.

Case 20.2 Continued
Some of Encino's service advisors, including Hector Navarro, filed a suit against Encino in a federal district court, alleging that the dealership had violated the Fair Labor Standards Act (FLSA) by failing to pay them overtime. Encino argued that the FLSA's exemption from the overtime-pay requirement applied to Navarro and its other service advisors. The court agreed and dismissed the complaint. The U.S. Court of Appeals for the Ninth Circuit reversed the dismissal. Encino appealed to the United States Supreme Court.

In the Language of the Court
Justice *THOMAS* delivered the opinion of the Court.
* * * *

The FLSA exempts from its overtime-pay requirement "any salesman, partsman, or mechanic primarily engaged in selling or servicing automobiles, trucks, or farm implements, if he is employed by a nonmanufacturing establishment primarily engaged in the business of selling such vehicles or implements to ultimate purchasers." The parties agree that [Encino] is a "nonmanufacturing establishment primarily engaged in the business of selling [automobiles] to ultimate purchasers." The parties also agree that a service advisor is not a "partsman" or "mechanic," and that a service advisor is not "primarily engaged * * * in selling automobiles." The question, then, is whether service advisors are "salesmen * * * primarily engaged in * * * servicing automobiles." We conclude that they are.
* * * *

A service advisor is obviously a "salesman." The term "salesman" is not defined in the statute, so we give the term its ordinary meaning. *The ordinary meaning of "salesman" is someone who sells goods or services. Service advisors do precisely that. * * * Service advisors sell customers services for their vehicles.* [Emphasis added.]
* * * *

Service advisors are also "primarily engaged in * * * servicing automobiles." The word "servicing" in this context can mean either the action of maintaining or repairing a motor vehicle, or the action of providing a service. Service advisors satisfy both definitions. Service advisors are integral to the servicing process. * * * If you ask the average customer who services his car, the primary, and perhaps only, person he is likely to identify is his service advisor.

True, service advisors do not spend most of their time physically repairing automobiles. But the statutory language is not so constrained. All agree that partsmen, for example, are "primarily engaged in * * * servicing automobiles." But partsmen, like service advisors, do not spend most of their time under the hood. Instead, they obtain the vehicle parts * * * and provide those parts to the mechanics. In other words, the phrase "primarily engaged in * * * servicing automobiles" must include some individuals who do not physically repair automobiles themselves but who are integrally involved in the servicing process. That description applies to partsmen and service advisors alike.

Decision and Remedy *The United States Supreme Court reversed the federal appellate court's decision and remanded the case. Navarro and the other service advisors were exempt from the overtime-pay requirement of the FLSA and thus not entitled to overtime pay.*

Critical Thinking
- **Legal Environment** *The salesmen, mechanics, and partsmen identified in the FLSA exemption work irregular hours, sometimes away from their principal work site. Service advisors typically work ordinary, fixed schedules on site. Should the Court have considered these attributes in making its decision in the* Encino *case? Discuss.*
- **What If the Facts Were Different?** *Suppose that the FLSA exemption covered "any salesman or mechanic primarily engaged in selling or servicing automobiles" but not "any partsman." Would the result have been different? Explain.*

20–2e Interaction of State and Federal Wage and Overtime Laws

State legislation may include rules that impact federal wage and overtime laws. For instance, if a state requires employers to give employees one day off per week, an employee who works that day may be entitled to over-time wages.

■ **Case in Point 20.6** Christopher Mendoza and Meagan Gordon were Nordstrom employees in California. Nord-strom had asked both Mendoza and Gordon to fill in for other employees. As a result, both had worked more than six consecutive days without receiving a day off. California state law prohibits employers from causing employees "to work more than six days in seven." The employees filed suit against Nordstrom, Inc., and the case ultimately came before the California Supreme Court.

At issue was whether the law applies on a calendar basis, with each workweek considered a fixed unit, or on a rolling basis. If the rolling basis was used, as Nordstrom argued that it should be, employees could work more than six consecutive days if on average they had one day off per seven. The state's highest court held that Nordstrom had violated California's law. Employees are entitled to one day off each workweek, not one day in seven on a rolling basis. Employees could choose to work the seventh day, but employers could not encourage or force them to do so, the court said.[8] ■

20–2f Layoffs

The Worker Adjustment and Retraining Notification (WARN) Act[9] applies to employers with at least one hundred full-time employees. The act requires these employers to provide sixty days' notice before implemen-ting a mass layoff or closing a plant that employs more than fifty full-time workers. A mass layoff is a layoff of at least one-third of the full-time employees at a particular job site.

The WARN Act is intended to give workers advance notice so that they can start looking for new jobs while they are still employed. It is also intended to alert state agencies so that they can provide training and other resources for displaced workers. Employers thus must provide advance notice of the layoff both to the affected workers and to state and local government authorities. (An employer may notify the workers' union representa-tive, if the workers are members of a labor union.) Even companies that anticipate filing for bankruptcy normally must provide notice under the WARN Act.

An employer that violates the WARN Act can be fined up to $500 for each day of the violation. Employees can recover back pay for each day of the violation (up to sixty days), plus reasonable attorneys' fees.

20–3 Family and Medical Leave

The Family and Medical Leave Act (FMLA)[10] allows employees to take time off work for family or medical reasons or in certain situations that arise from military service. A majority of the states have similar legislation. The FMLA does not supersede any state or local law that provides more generous protection.

20–3a Coverage and Applicability

The FMLA requires employers that have fifty or more employees to provide *unpaid* leave for specified reasons. (Some employers voluntarily offer paid family leave, but this is not a requirement of the FMLA.) The FMLA expressly covers private and public (government) employees who have worked for their employers for at least a year.

An eligible employee may take up to *twelve weeks of leave* within a twelve-month period for any of the follow-ing reasons:

1. To care for a newborn baby within one year of birth.
2. To care for an adopted or foster child within one year of the time the child is placed with the employee.
3. To care for the employee's spouse, child, or parent who has a serious health condition.
4. If the employee suffers from a serious health condi-tion and is unable to perform the essential functions of her or his job.
5. For any qualifying exigency (nonmedical emergency) arising out of the fact that the employee's spouse, son, daughter, or parent is a covered military member on active duty.[11] For instance, an employee can take leave to arrange for child care or to deal with financial or legal matters when a spouse is being deployed overseas.

In addition, an employee may take up to *twenty-six weeks of military caregiver leave* within a twelve-month period to care for a family member with a serious injury or ill-ness incurred as a result of military duty.[12]

In the following case, an employee asked for medi-cal leave to care for her mother on a trip to Las Vegas, Nevada.

---

8. *Mendoza v. Nordstrom, Inc.*, 2 Cal.5th 1074, 216 Cal.Rptr.3d 889, 393 P.3d 375 (2017).
9. 29 U.S.C. Sections 2101 *et seq.*
10. 29 U.S.C. Sections 2601, 2611–2619, 2651–2654.
11. 29 C.F.R. Part 825.126.
12. 29 C.F.R. Part 825.200.

Ballard v. Chicago Park District

United States Court of Appeals, Seventh Circuit, 741 F.3d 838 (2014).

Background and Facts Beverly Ballard worked for the Chicago Park District. She lived with her mother, Sarah, who suffered from end-stage congestive heart failure. Beverly served as Sarah's primary caregiver with support from Horizon Hospice & Palliative Care. The hospice helped Sarah plan and secure funds for an end-of-life goal, a "family trip" to Las Vegas. To accompany Sarah as her caretaker, Beverly asked the Park District for unpaid time off under the Family and Medical Leave Act (FMLA). The employer refused, but Beverly and Sarah took the trip as planned.

Later, the Park District terminated Beverly for "unauthorized absences." She filed a suit in a federal district court against the employer. The court issued a decision in Beverly's favor. The Park District appealed, arguing that Beverly had been absent from work on a "recreational trip."

In the Language of the Court

FLAUM, Circuit Judge.

* * * *

We begin with the text of the [FMLA]: an eligible employee is entitled to leave "in order to care for" a family member with a "serious health condition."

* * * *

* * * *The FMLA's text does not restrict care to a particular place or geographic location.* For instance, it does not say that an employee is entitled to time off "to care *at home* for" a family member. *The only limitation it places on care is that the family member must have a serious health condition.* We are reluctant, without good reason, to read in another limitation that Congress has not provided. [Emphasis added.]

* * * *

Sarah's basic medical, hygienic, and nutritional needs did not change while she was in Las Vegas, and Beverly continued to assist her with those needs during the trip. In fact, * * * Beverly's presence proved quite important indeed when a fire at the hotel made it impossible to reach their room, requiring Beverly to find another source of insulin and pain medicine. Thus, at the very least, [Beverly] requested leave in order to provide physical care.

* * * *

* * * The Park District describes [Beverly's] travel as a "recreational trip" or a "non-medically related pleasure trip." It also raises the specter that employees will help themselves to unpaid FMLA leave in order to take personal vacations, simply by bringing seriously ill family members along. So perhaps what the Park District means to argue is that the real reason Beverly requested leave was in order to take a free pleasure trip, and not in order to care for her mother. * * * However, * * * an employer concerned about the risk that employees will abuse the FMLA's leave provisions may of course require that requests be certified by the family member's health care provider. And any worries about opportunistic leave-taking in this case should be tempered by the fact that this dispute arises out of the hospice and palliative care context.

If Beverly had sought leave to care for her mother in Chicago, her request would have fallen within the scope of the FMLA. So too if Sarah had lived in Las Vegas instead of with her daughter, and Beverly had requested leave to care for her mother there. Ultimately, other than a concern that our straightforward reading will "open the door to increased FMLA requests," the Park District gives us no reason to treat the current scenario any differently.

Decision and Remedy *The U.S. Court of Appeals for the Seventh Circuit affirmed the lower court's judgment. Under the FMLA, an eligible employee is entitled to take leave from work to care for a family member with a serious health condition. The care is not restricted to a particular place (such as "at home").*

Critical Thinking

- **What If the Facts Were Different?** *Suppose that Beverly had requested leave to make arrangements for a change in Sarah's care, such as a transfer to a nursing home. Is it likely that the result would have been different? Explain.*
- **Legal Environment** *Under the FMLA, an employee is eligible for leave when he or she is needed to care for a family member. Should "needed to care for" be interpreted to cover only ongoing physical care? Discuss.*

20–3b Benefits and Protections

When an employee takes FMLA leave, the employer must continue the worker's health-care coverage on the same terms as if the employee had continued to work. On returning from FMLA leave, most employees must be restored to their original position or to a comparable position (with nearly equivalent pay and benefits, for instance). An important exception allows the employer to avoid reinstating a *key employee*—defined as an employee whose pay falls within the top 10 percent of the firm's workforce.

20–3c Violations

An employer that violates the FMLA can be required to provide various remedies, including the following:

1. Damages to compensate the employee for lost wages and benefits, denied compensation, and actual monetary losses (such as the cost of providing care for a family member). Compensatory damages are available up to an amount equivalent to the employee's wages for twelve weeks.
2. Job reinstatement.
3. Promotion, if a promotion has been denied.

A successful plaintiff is also entitled to court costs and attorneys' fees. In addition, if the plaintiff shows that the employer acted in bad faith, the plaintiff can receive two times the amount of damages awarded by a judge or jury. Supervisors can also be held personally liable, as employers, for violations of the act.

Employers generally are required to notify employees when an absence will be counted against FMLA leave. If an employer fails to provide such notice, and that failure to notify causes harm to the employee, the employer can be sanctioned.[13]

20–4 Health, Safety, and Income Security

Under the common law, employees who were injured on the job had to file lawsuits against their employers to obtain recovery. Today, numerous state and federal statutes protect employees from the risk of accidental injury, death, or disease resulting from their employment. In addition, the government protects employees' income through Social Security, Medicare, unemployment insurance, and the regulation of pensions and health insurance plans.

20–4a The Occupational Safety and Health Act

At the federal level, the primary legislation protecting employees' health and safety is the Occupational Safety and Health Act,[14] which is administered by the Occupational Safety and Health Administration (OSHA). The act imposes on employers a general duty to keep the workplace safe.

To this end, OSHA has established specific safety standards that employers must follow, depending on the industry. For instance, OSHA regulations require the use of safety guards on certain mechanical equipment. It also sets maximum levels of exposure to substances in the workplace that may be harmful to workers' health.

■ **Case in Point 20.7** James Bobo worked at the Tennessee Valley Authority (TVA) nuclear power plant for more than twenty-two years. He eventually contracted asbestos-induced lung cancer. After his death, his wife, Barbara, was diagnosed with malignant mesothelioma. She sued the TVA in federal court, alleging that its negligence had resulted in her being exposed to "take-home" asbestos when she washed her husband's work clothes over the years. Although she died prior to trial, her children continued the suit.

At trial, the plaintiffs proved that the TVA knew about OSHA regulations—adopted during the time of James's employment—to protect not only workers but also their families. These rules were aimed at preventing asbestos fibers from clinging to an employee's street clothes, skin, or hair and being taken off the TVA property. The court held in favor of the plaintiffs and awarded $3.3 million. The TVA appealed. A federal appellate court affirmed that the TVA was liable for failing to follow OSHA regulations but remanded the case for a recalculation of the damages awarded.[15] ■

Notices, Records, and Reports The Occupational Safety and Health Act requires that employers post certain notices in the workplace, maintain specific records, and submit reports. Employers with eleven or more employees are required to keep occupational injury and illness records for each employee. Each record must be made

---

13. This was the United States Supreme Court's holding in *Ragsdale v. Wolverine World Wide, Inc.*, 535 U.S. 81, 122 S.Ct. 1155, 152 L.Ed.2d 167 (2002).

14. 29 U.S.C. Sections 651 *et seq.*
15. *Bobo v. Tennessee Valley Authority*, 855 F.3d 1294 (11th Cir. 2017).

available for inspection when requested by an OSHA compliance officer.

Whenever a work-related fatality or serious injury requiring hospitalization occurs, employers must report directly to OSHA. The employer must notify OSHA within eight hours if an employee dies and submit a report within twenty-four hours for any inpatient hospitalization, amputation, or loss of an eye. A company that fails to do so will be fined. Following the incident, a complete inspection of the premises is mandatory.

Inspections OSHA compliance officers may enter and inspect the facilities of any establishment covered by the Occupational Safety and Health Act. Employees may also file complaints of violations. Under the act, an employer cannot discharge an employee who files a complaint or who, in good faith, refuses to work in a high-risk area if bodily harm or death might result.

20–4b State Workers' Compensation Laws

State **workers' compensation laws** establish an administrative procedure for compensating workers injured on the job. Instead of suing, an injured worker files a claim with the state agency or board that administers local workers' compensation claims.

All states require employers to provide workers' compensation insurance, but the specific rules vary by state. Most states have a state fund that employers pay into for workers' compensation coverage. Usually, employers can purchase insurance from a private insurer as an alternative to paying into the state fund. Most states also allow certain employers to be *self-insured*—that is, employers that show an ability to pay claims do not need to buy insurance.

No state covers all employees under its workers' compensation statute. Typically, domestic workers, agricultural workers, temporary employees, and employees of common carriers (companies that provide transportation services to the public) are excluded. Minors are covered.

Requirements for Receiving Workers' Compensation In general, the only requirements to recover benefits under state workers' compensation laws are:

1. The existence of an employment relationship.
2. An *accidental* injury that *occurred on the job or in the course of employment,* regardless of fault. (An injury that occurs while an employee is commuting to or from work usually is not covered.)

■**Example 20.8** Dynea USA, Inc., requires its employees to wear steel-toed boots for safety. The boots cause employee Tony Schrader to develop a sore on his leg.

The skin over Schrader's sore breaks, and within a week, he is hospitalized with a methicillin-resistant staphylococcus aureus (MRSA) infection. He files a workers' compensation claim. Dynea argues that Schrader's injury did not occur on the job because the MRSA bacteria that caused the infection was on Schrader's skin before he came to work. Nevertheless, Schrader is entitled to workers' compensation benefits. Dynea required its employees to wear the boots that caused the sore on Schrader's leg, which subsequently became infected with MRSA. Even if the bacteria was on Schrader's skin before he came to work, it was the rubbing of the boot at work that caused the sore through which the bacteria entered his body. Therefore, the injury occurred on the job, and Schrader qualifies for workers' compensation. ■

An injured employee must notify her or his employer promptly (usually within thirty days of the accident). Generally, an employee must also file a workers' compensation claim within a certain period (sixty days to two years) from the time the injury is first noticed, rather than from the time of the accident.

Workers' Compensation versus Litigation If an employee accepts workers' compensation benefits, he or she may not sue for injuries caused by the employer's negligence. By barring lawsuits for negligence, workers' compensation laws also prevent employers from avoiding liability by using defenses such as contributory negligence or assumption of risk. A worker may sue an employer who *intentionally* injures the worker, however.

20–4c Income Security

Federal and state governments participate in insurance programs designed to protect employees and their families from the financial impact of retirement, disability, death, hospitalization, and unemployment. The key federal law in this area is the Social Security Act.[16]

Social Security The Social Security Act provides for old-age (retirement), survivors', and disability insurance. The act is therefore often referred to as OASDI. Retired workers who are covered by Social Security receive monthly payments from the Social Security Administration, which administers the Social Security Act. Social Security benefits are fixed by statute but increase automatically with increases in the cost of living.

Medicare Medicare is a federal government health-insurance program administered by the Social Security

---

16. 42 U.S.C. Sections 301 *et seq.*

Administration for people sixty-five years of age and older and for some under age sixty-five who are disabled. It originally had two parts, one pertaining to hospital costs and the other to nonhospital medical costs, such as visits to physicians' offices. It now offers additional coverage options and a prescription-drug plan. People who have Medicare hospital insurance can obtain additional federal medical insurance if they pay monthly premiums.

Tax Contributions Under the Federal Insurance Contributions Act (FICA),[17] both employers and employees contribute to Social Security and Medicare, although the contributions are determined differently. The employer withholds the employee's FICA contributions from the employee's wages and ordinarily matches the contributions.

For Social Security, the basis for the contributions is the employee's annual wage base—the maximum amount of the employee's wages that is subject to the tax. The wage threshold changes annually. The Social Security tax rate is currently 12.4 percent, but the rate changes periodically.

The Medicare tax rate is 2.9 percent. Unlike Social Security, Medicare has no cap on the amount of wages subject to the tax. So even if an employee's salary is well above the cap for Social Security, he or she will still owe Medicare tax on the total earned income.

For Social Security and Medicare together, typically the employer and the employee each pay 7.65 percent. This is equivalent to 6.2 percent (half of 12.4 percent) for Social Security plus 1.45 percent (half of 2.9 percent) for Medicare up to the maximum wage base. Any earned income above that threshold is taxed only for Medicare. Self-employed persons pay both the employer's and the employee's portions of the Social Security and Medicare taxes. Additionally, under the Affordable Care Act, high-income earners are subject to an additional Medicare tax of 0.9 percent (for a total rate of 3.8 percent).

Private Retirement Plans The major federal statute that regulates employee retirement plans is the Employee Retirement Income Security Act (ERISA).[18] This act empowers a branch of the U.S. Department of Labor to enforce its provisions governing employers that have private pension funds for their employees. ERISA does *not* require an employer to establish a pension plan. When a plan exists, however, ERISA provides standards for its management.

ERISA created the Pension Benefit Guaranty Corporation (PBGC), an independent federal agency, to provide timely and uninterrupted payment of voluntary private pension benefits. The pension plans pay annual insurance premiums (at set rates adjusted for inflation) to the PBGC, which then pays benefits to participants in the event that a plan is unable to do so.

A key provision of ERISA concerns vesting. **Vesting** gives an employee a legal right to receive pension benefits when she or he stops working. Before ERISA was enacted, some employees who had worked for companies for many years received no pension benefits when their employment terminated, because those benefits had not vested. Under ERISA, generally all employee contributions to pension plans vest immediately. Employee rights to employer contributions vest after five years of employment.

Unemployment Insurance The Federal Unemployment Tax Act (FUTA)[19] created a state-administered system that provides unemployment compensation to eligible individuals who have lost their jobs. The FUTA and state laws require employers that fall under the provisions of the act to pay unemployment taxes at regular intervals. The proceeds from these taxes are then paid out to qualified unemployed workers.

To be eligible for unemployment compensation, a worker must be willing and able to work. Workers who have been fired for misconduct or who have voluntarily left their jobs are not eligible for benefits. Normally, workers must be actively seeking employment to continue receiving benefits.

■ **Example 20.9** Martha works for Baily Snowboards in Vermont. One day at work, Martha receives a text from her son saying that he has been taken to the hospital. Martha rushes to the hospital and does not return to work for several days. Bailey hires someone else for Martha's position, and Martha files for unemployment benefits. Martha's claim will be denied because she left her job voluntarily and made no effort to maintain contact with her employer. ■

COBRA The Consolidated Omnibus Budget Reconciliation Act (COBRA)[20] enables employees to continue, for a limited time, their health-care coverage after they are no longer eligible for group health-insurance plans. The workers—not the employers—pay the premiums for the continued coverage.

COBRA prohibits an employer from eliminating a worker's medical, vision, or dental insurance when the worker's employment is terminated or when a reduction in the worker's hours would affect coverage. Termination of employment may be voluntary or involuntary.

---

17. 26 U.S.C. Sections 3101 *et seq.*
18. 29 U.S.C. Sections 1001 *et seq.*
19. 26 U.S.C. Sections 3301 *et seq.*
20. 29 U.S.C. Sections 1161–1169.

Only workers fired for gross misconduct are excluded from protection. Employers, with some exceptions, must inform employees of COBRA's provisions before the termination or reduction of work hours.

A worker has sixty days from the date on which the group coverage would stop to decide whether to continue with the employer's group insurance plan. If the worker chooses to continue coverage, the employer is obligated to keep the policy active for up to eighteen months (twenty-nine months if the worker is disabled). The coverage must be the same as that provided to the worker (and his or her family members) prior to the termination or reduction of work. An employer that does not comply with COBRA risks substantial penalties, including a tax of up to 10 percent of the annual cost of the group plan or $500,000, whichever is less.

Employer-Sponsored Group Health Plans The Health Insurance Portability and Accountability Act (HIPAA)[21] contains provisions that affect employer-sponsored group health plans. For instance, HIPAA restricts the manner in which employers collect, use, and disclose the health information of employees and their families. Employers must designate privacy officials, distribute privacy notices, and train employees to ensure that employees' health information is not disclosed to unauthorized parties.

Failure to comply with HIPAA regulations can result in civil penalties of up to $100 per person per violation (with a cap of $25,000 per year). Employers are also subject to criminal prosecution for certain types of HIPAA violations. An employer can face up to $250,000 in criminal fines and imprisonment for up to ten years if convicted.

Affordable Care Act The Affordable Care Act[22] (commonly referred to as Obamacare) requires most employers with fifty or more full-time employees to offer health-insurance benefits. Under the act, any business offering health benefits to its employees (even if not legally required to do so) may be eligible for tax credits of up to 35 percent to offset the costs.

An employer who fails to provide health benefits as required under the statute can be fined up to $2,000 for each employee after the first thirty people. (This is known as the 50/30 rule: employers with fifty employees must provide insurance, and those failing to do so will be fined for each employee after the first thirty.) An employer who offers a plan that costs an employee more than 9.5 percent of the employee's income may be assessed a penalty.

---

21. 29 U.S.C. Sections 1181 *et seq.*
22. Pub. L. No. 111-148, 124 Stat. 119 (2010), codified in various sections of 42 U.S.C.

20–5 Employee Privacy Rights

Concerns about the privacy rights of employees have arisen as employers have purportedly used invasive tactics to monitor and screen workers. Perhaps the greatest privacy concern in employment today involves electronic monitoring of employees' activities.

20–5a Electronic Monitoring

More than half of employers engage in some form of electronic monitoring of their employees. Many employers review employees' e-mail, as well as their social media posts and other Internet messages. Employers may also make video recordings of their employees at work, record their telephone conversations, and listen to their voice mail.

Employee Privacy Protection Employees of private (nongovernment) employers have some privacy protection under tort law and state constitutions. In addition, state and federal statutes may limit an employer's conduct in certain respects. For instance, the Electronic Communications Privacy Act prohibits employers from intercepting an employee's personal electronic communications unless they are made on devices and systems furnished by the employer.

Nonetheless, employers do have considerable leeway to monitor employees in the workplace. In addition, private employers generally are free to use filtering software to block access to certain websites, such as sites containing sexually explicit images. The First Amendment's protection of free speech prevents only *government employers* from restraining speech by blocking websites.

Reasonable Expectation of Privacy When determining whether an employer should be held liable for violating an employee's privacy rights, the courts generally weigh the employer's interests against the employee's reasonable expectation of privacy. Normally, if employees have been informed that their communications are being monitored, they cannot reasonably expect those interactions to be private. In addition, a court will typically hold that employees do not have a reasonable expectation of privacy when using a system (such as an e-mail system) provided by the employer.

If employees are *not* informed that certain communications are being monitored, the employer may be held liable for invading their privacy. Most employers that engage in electronic monitoring notify their employees about the monitoring. Nevertheless, a general policy may not sufficiently protect an employer monitoring forms of communications that the policy fails to mention. For instance, notifying employees that their e-mails and phone calls may be monitored does not necessarily protect an employer who monitors social media posts or text messages.

20–5b Other Types of Monitoring

In addition to monitoring their employees' online activities, employers also engage in other types of employee screening and monitoring. The practices discussed next have often been challenged as violations of employee privacy rights.

Lie-Detector Tests At one time, many employers required employees or job applicants to take polygraph examinations (lie-detector tests). Today, the Employee Polygraph Protection Act[23] generally prohibits employers from requiring employees or job applicants to take lie-detector tests or suggesting or requesting that they do so. The act also restricts employers' ability to use or ask about the results of any lie-detector test or to take any negative employment action based on the results.

Certain employers are exempt from these prohibitions. Federal, state, and local government employers, and certain security service firms, may conduct polygraph tests. In addition, companies that manufacture and distribute controlled substances may perform lie-detector tests. Other employers may use polygraph tests when investigating losses attributable to theft, including embezzlement and the theft of trade secrets.

Drug Testing In the interests of public safety and to reduce unnecessary costs, many employers, including the government, require their employees to submit to drug testing.

---

23. 29 U.S.C. Sections 2001 *et seq.*

Public Employers. Government (public) employers are constrained in drug testing by the Fourth Amendment to the U.S. Constitution, which prohibits unreasonable searches and seizures. Drug testing of public employees is allowed by statute for transportation workers, however. Courts normally uphold drug testing of certain employees when drug use in a particular job may threaten public safety. Also, when there is a reasonable basis for suspecting public employees of drug use, courts often find that drug testing does not violate the Fourth Amendment.

Private Employers. The Fourth Amendment does not apply to drug testing conducted by private employers. Hence, the privacy rights and drug testing of private-sector employees are governed by state law. Many states have statutes that allow drug testing by private employers but restrict when and how the testing may be performed. A collective bargaining agreement negotiated by a labor union may also provide protection against drug testing (or may authorize drug testing in certain conditions).

The permissibility of testing a private employee for drugs often hinges on whether the employer's testing was reasonable. Random drug tests and even "zero-tolerance" policies (which deny a "second chance" to employees who test positive for drugs) have been held to be reasonable. It is also reasonable to require employees of private employers who are under contract with the federal government to undergo standard background investigations to disclose possible drug use.

Practice and Review: Employment Law

Rick Saldona worked as a traveling salesperson for Aimer Winery. Sales constituted 90 percent of Saldona's work time. Saldona worked an average of fifty hours per week but received no overtime pay. Saldona had worked for Aimer for ten years when his new supervisor, Caesar Braxton, claimed that he had been inflating his reported sales calls and required him to submit to a polygraph test. Saldona reported Braxton to the U.S. Department of Labor, which prohibited Aimer from requiring Saldona to take a polygraph test for this purpose.

Shortly after that, Saldona's wife, Venita, fell from a ladder and sustained a head injury while employed as a full-time agricultural harvester. Saldona presented Aimer's human resources department with a letter from his wife's physician indicating that she would need daily care for several months, and Saldona took leave for three months. Aimer had sixty-three employees at that time. When Saldona returned to Aimer, he was informed that his position had been eliminated because his sales territory had been combined with an adjacent territory. Using the information presented in the chapter, answer the following questions.

1. Would Saldona have been legally entitled to receive overtime pay at a higher rate? Why or why not?
2. What is the maximum length of time Saldona would have been allowed to take leave to care for his injured spouse?
3. Under what circumstances would Aimer have been allowed to require an employee to take a polygraph test?
4. Would Aimer likely be able to avoid reinstating Saldona under the *key employee* exception? Why or why not?

Debate This ... *The U.S. labor market is highly competitive, so state and federal laws that require overtime pay are unnecessary and should be abolished.*

Terms and Concepts

employment at will 442	vesting 452	workers' compensation laws 451
minimum wage 445	whistleblowing 443	wrongful discharge 444

Issue Spotters

1. American Manufacturing Company (AMC) issues an employee handbook that states that employees will be discharged only for good cause. One day, Greg, an AMC supervisor, says to Larry, "I don't like your looks. You're fired." Can AMC be held liable for breach of contract? If so, why? If not, why? (See *Employment at Will.*)

2. Erin, an employee of Fine Print Shop, is injured on the job. For Erin to obtain workers' compensation, must her injury have been caused by Fine Print's negligence? Does it matter whether the action causing the injury was intentional? Explain. (See *Health, Safety, and Income Security.*)

- **Check your answers to the Issue Spotters against the answers provided in Appendix B at the end of this text.**

Business Scenarios and Case Problems

20–1. Family and Medical Leave Act. Serge worked for Service Attendant Corporation (SAC). He requested time off under the Family and Medical Leave Act (FMLA) from April 29 through May 31 to undergo treatment for alcoholism. For the month of May, he was hospitalized as part of the treatment. When he did not return to work on June 1, SAC fired him. Did SAC violate Serge's rights under the FMLA? Explain your answer. (See *Family and Medical Leave.*)

20–2. Wrongful Discharge. Denton and Carlo were employed at an appliance plant. Their job required them to perform occasional maintenance work while standing on a wire mesh twenty feet above the plant floor. Other employees had fallen through the mesh, and one of them had been killed by the fall. When their supervisor told them to perform tasks that would likely involve walking on the mesh, Denton and Carlo refused because they feared they might suffer bodily injury or death. Because they refused to do the requested work, the two employees were fired from their jobs. Was their discharge wrongful? If so, under what federal employment law? To what federal agency or department should they turn for assistance? (See *Employment at Will.*)

20–3. Spotlight on Coca Cola—Family and Medical Leave Act. Jennifer Willis worked for Coca Cola Enterprises, Inc. (CCE), in Louisiana as a senior account manager. On a Monday in May 2003, Willis called her supervisor to tell him that she was sick and would not be able to work that day. She also said that she was pregnant, but she did not say she was sick because of the pregnancy. On Tuesday, she called to ask where to report to work and was told that she could not return without a doctor's release. She said that she had a doctor's appointment on "Wednesday," which her supervisor understood to be the next day. Willis meant the following Wednesday.

For more than a week, Willis did not contact CCE. When she returned to work, she was told that she had violated CCE's "No Call/No Show" policy. Under this policy "an employee absent from work for three consecutive days without notifying the supervisor during that period will be considered to have voluntarily resigned." She was fired.

Willis filed a suit in a federal district court against CCE under the Family and Medical Leave Act (FMLA). To be eligible for FMLA leave, an employee must inform an employer of the reason for the leave. Did Willis meet this requirement? Did CCE's response to Willis's absence violate the FMLA? Explain. [*Willis v. Coca Cola Enterprises, Inc.,* 445 F.3d 413 (5th Cir. 2006)] (See *Family and Medical Leave.*)

20–4. Exceptions to the Employment-at-Will Doctrine. Li Li worked for Packard Bioscience, and Mark Schmeizl was her supervisor. Schmeizl told Li to call Packard's competitors, pretend to be a potential customer, and request "pricing information and literature." Li refused to perform the assignment. She told Schmeizl that she thought the work was illegal and recommended that he contact Packard's legal department. Although a lawyer recommended against the practice, Schmeizl insisted that Li perform the calls. Moreover, he later wrote negative performance reviews because she was unable to get the requested information when she called competitors and identified herself as a Packard employee. Several months later, Li was terminated on Schmeizl's recommendation. Can Li bring a claim for wrongful discharge? Why or why not? [*Li Li v. Canberra Industries,* 134 Conn.App. 448, 39 A.3d 789 (2012)] (See *Employment at Will.*)

20–5. Business Case Problem with Sample Answer—Unemployment Compensation. Fior Ramirez worked as a housekeeper for Remington Lodging & Hospitality, a hotel in Atlantic Beach, Florida. After her father in the Dominican Republic suffered a stroke, she asked her employer for time off to be with him. Ramirez's manager, Katie Berkowski, refused the request. Two days later, Berkowski received a call from Ramirez to say that she was with her father. He died about a week later, and Ramirez returned to work, but Berkowski told her that she had abandoned her position. Ramirez applied for unemployment compensation. Under the applicable state statute, "an employee is disqualified from receiving benefits if he or she voluntarily left work without good cause." Does Ramirez qualify for benefits? Explain. [*Ramirez v. Reemployment Assistance Appeals Commission*, 39 Fla.L.Weekly D317, 135 So.3d 408 (1 Dist. 2014)] (See *Health, Safety, and Income Security*.)

- For a sample answer to Problem 20–5, go to Appendix C at the end of this text.

20–6. Unemployment Compensation. Jefferson Partners, LP, entered into a contract (known as a collective bargaining agreement) with the Amalgamated Transit Union. Under the contract, drivers had to either join the union or pay a fair share—85 percent—of union dues, which were used to pay for administrative costs incurred by the union. An employee who refused to pay was subject to discharge. Jefferson hired Tiffany Thompson to work as a bus driver. When told about the requirement, Thompson said that she thought it was unfair and illegal. She refused either to join the union or to pay the dues. More than two years later, she was fired on the ground that her continued refusal constituted misconduct. Is Thompson eligible for unemployment compensation? Explain. [*Thompson v. Jefferson Partners, LP*, 2016 WL 953038 (Minn. Ct.App. 2016)] (See *Health, Safety, and Income Security*.)

20–7. Family and Medical Leave. To qualify for leave under the Family and Medical Leave Act (FMLA), an employee must comply with his or her employer's usual and customary notice requirements, including call-in policies. Robert Stein, an employee of Atlas Industries, Inc., tore his meniscus (a knee injury) at work. Stein took medical leave to have surgery on the knee. Ten weeks into his recovery, Stein's doctor notified Atlas that Stein could return to work with light-duty restrictions in two days. Stein, however, thought he was on leave for several more weeks. Atlas company policy provided that employees who missed three workdays without notification were subject to automatic termination. Stein did not return to work or call in as Atlas expected. Four days later, he was fired. Did Stein's discharge violate the FMLA? Discuss. [*Stein v. Atlas Industries, Inc.*, 730 Fed.Appx. 313 (6th Cir. 2018)] (See *Family and Medical Leave*.)

20–8. A Question of Ethics—The IDDR Approach and Employee Privacy Rights. *Scherer Design Group, LLC (SDG), provides telecommunications services. Chad Schwartz, an SDG employee, sought to obtain an ownership stake in the firm. When this proved unsuccessful, Schwartz quit to start a competing firm, Ahead Engineering, LLC, and recruited Daniel Hernandez, an SDG colleague, to join him. Hernandez used an SDG computer to transmit his employer's client information to Schwartz's firm via Facebook. One of SDG's largest clients, ExteNet, left SDG to become Schwartz's client. After Hernandez resigned, SDG used his company laptop to surreptitiously (secretively) access his Facebook account, which revealed the actions Hernandez had taken to secure SDG's client information and trade secrets. SDG filed a suit in a federal district court against Schwartz's firm and Hernandez, claiming a breach of the duty of loyalty and seeking an injunction to stop their solicitation of SDG's clients. The defendants argued that SDG's "hacking" of Hernandez's Facebook account barred the plaintiff's right to injunctive relief (under the equitable doctrine of unclean hands).* [Scherer Design Group, LLC v. Ahead Engineering, LLC, *764 Fed.Appx. 147 (3d Cir. 2019)*] (See Employee Privacy Rights.)

(a) Use the IDDR approach to evaluate the ethics of SDG's decision to access Hernandez's Facebook account.

(b) Should SDG's use of a company laptop to access Hernandez's Facebook account bar SDG's right to an injunction? Explain.

Time-Limited Group Assignment

20–9. Wrongful Discharge. Stefan Sorril, a health teacher at Madison Middle School and a triathlete, appeared shirtless and showed off his "ripped" body as an extra on an episode of a new reality TV show. A week after the show aired, school officials called him into the district office and asked for his resignation. Sorril later claimed that he was pressured and coerced into resigning. He said the school officials had informed him that—as a result of his appearance on the show—he would no longer be offered tenure (a senior academic's contractual right not to be terminated without just cause). Sorril subsequently sued for wrongful discharge. (See *Employment at Will*.)

(a) The first group will discuss whether Sorril was an employee at will and how that status would affect his claim.

(b) The second group will determine if Sorril can assert any of the exceptions to the employment-at-will doctrine.

(c) The third group will decide whether the school district should be held liable for wrongful discharge and explain its reasoning.

Chapter 21

Employment Discrimination

Out of the 1960s civil rights movement to end racial and other forms of discrimination grew a body of law protecting employees against discrimination in the workplace. Legislation, judicial decisions, and administrative agency actions restrict employers from discriminating against workers on the basis of race, color, religion, national origin, gender, age, and disability. A class of persons defined by one or more of these criteria is known as a **protected class.**

Several federal statutes prohibit **employment discrimination** against members of protected classes. The most important is Title VII of the Civil Rights Act.[1] Title VII prohibits employment discrimination on the basis of race, color, religion, national origin, and gender. The Age Discrimination in Employment Act[2] and the Americans with Disabilities Act[3] prohibit discrimination on the basis of age and disability, respectively. The protections afforded under these laws also extend to U.S. citizens who are working abroad for U.S. firms or for companies that are controlled by U.S. firms.

Suppose that Marta Brown had been a medical assistant for a group of physicians for five years before she married a Turkish man and became a Muslim. She began wearing a hijab (head scarf) and taking several breaks each day to pray. The physicians, who had given Brown positive job evaluations in the past, began treating her differently. They forbade her from wearing the hijab at work and told her that she could perform prayers during her lunch break only if she left the building. The physicians also started finding problems with her work performance and gave her a poor evaluation.

Eventually, Brown was dismissed from her position. Can she sue for employment discrimination? What evidence would she need to prove her case? Do private employers have to accommodate their employees' religious practices even if they are inconsistent with the employers' beliefs? These are some of the questions that will be answered in this chapter.

---

1. 42 U.S.C. Sections 2000e *et seq.*

2. 29 U.S.C. Sections 621–634.
3. 42 U.S.C. Sections 12102–12118.

21–1 Title VII of the Civil Rights Act

Title VII of the Civil Rights Act prohibits job discrimination against employees, applicants, and union members on the basis of race, color, national origin, religion, and gender at any stage of employment. Title VII bans discrimination in the hiring process, discipline procedures, discharge, promotion, and benefits.

Title VII applies to employers with fifteen or more employees and labor unions with fifteen or more members. It also applies to labor unions that operate hiring halls (where members go regularly to be assigned jobs), employment agencies, and state and local governing units or agencies. The United States Supreme Court has ruled that an employer with fewer than fifteen employees is not automatically shielded from a lawsuit filed under Title VII.[4] In addition, the act prohibits discrimination in most federal government employment. When Title VII applies to the employer, any employee—including an undocumented worker—can bring an action for employment discrimination.

21–1a The Equal Employment Opportunity Commission

The Equal Employment Opportunity Commission (EEOC) monitors compliance with Title VII. An employee alleging discrimination must file a claim with the EEOC before a lawsuit can be brought against the employer. The EEOC may investigate the dispute and

---

4. *Arbaugh v. Y&H Corp.*, 546 U.S. 500, 126 S.Ct. 1235, 163 L.Ed.2d 1097 (2006).

attempt to obtain the parties' voluntary consent to an out-of-court settlement. If a voluntary agreement cannot be reached, the EEOC may file a suit against the employer on the employee's behalf.

■ **Case in Point 21.1** Jacqueline Cote met her wife, Diana Smithson, in Maine while they were both employees at Wal-Mart. They moved to Massachusetts and were married a few days after the state legalized same-sex marriage, and they continued working at a Wal-Mart there. Smithson eventually quit work to take care of Cote's elderly mother. Cote tried to enroll her partner in Wal-Mart's health plan but coverage was denied. Five years later, Smithson was diagnosed with cancer.

Cote filed a claim with the EEOC arguing that Wal-Mart had intentionally discriminated against her on the basis of sex by denying her same-sex partner insurance benefits. The EEOC agreed that Cote was treated differently and wrongly denied benefits and ordered Wal-Mart to work with Cote to help pay Smithson's medical bills. Cote also filed a class-action lawsuit against Wal-Mart, which was later settled for $7.5 million.[5] ■

The EEOC does not investigate every claim of employment discrimination. Generally, it takes only "priority cases," such as cases involving retaliatory discharge (firing an employee in retaliation for submitting a claim to the EEOC) and cases involving types of discrimination that are of particular concern to the EEOC. If the EEOC decides not to investigate a claim, the EEOC issues a "right to sue" that allows the employee to bring his or her own lawsuit against the employer.

21–1b Limitations on Class Actions

The United States Supreme Court issued an important decision that limited the rights of employees to bring discrimination claims against their employer as a group, or class. The Court held that to bring a class action, employees must prove a company-wide policy of discrimination that had a common effect on all the plaintiffs covered by the action.[6]

21–1c Intentional and Unintentional Discrimination

Title VII of the Civil Rights Act prohibits both intentional and unintentional discrimination.

Intentional Discrimination Intentional discrimination by an employer against an employee is known as **disparate-treatment discrimination.** Because intent may sometimes be difficult to prove, courts have established certain procedures for resolving disparate-treatment cases.

A plaintiff who sues on the basis of disparate-treatment discrimination must first make out a **prima facie case.** *Prima facie* is Latin for "at first sight" or "on its face." Legally, it refers to a fact that is presumed to be true unless contradicted by evidence.

Establishing a *Prima Facie* Case. To establish a *prima facie* case of disparate-treatment discrimination in hiring, a plaintiff must show all of the following:

1. The plaintiff is a member of a protected class.
2. The plaintiff applied and was qualified for the job in question.
3. The plaintiff was rejected by the employer.
4. The employer continued to seek applicants for the position or filled the position with a person not in a protected class.

A plaintiff who can meet these relatively easy requirements has made out a *prima facie* case of illegal discrimination in hiring and will win in the absence of a legally acceptable employer defense.

Sometimes, current and former employees make a claim of discrimination. When the plaintiff alleges that the employer fired or took some other adverse employment action against him or her, the same basic requirements apply. To establish a *prima facie* case, the plaintiff must show that he or she was fired or treated adversely for discriminatory reasons.

Burden-Shifting Procedure. Once the *prima facie* case is established, the burden then shifts to the employer-defendant, who must articulate a legal reason for not hiring the plaintiff. (Again, this also applies to firing and other adverse employment actions.) If the employer did not have a legal reason for taking the adverse employment action, the plaintiff wins.

If the employer can articulate a legitimate reason for the action, the burden shifts back to the plaintiff. To prevail, the plaintiff must then show that the employer's reason is a *pretext* (not the true reason) and that the employer's decision was actually motivated by discriminatory intent.

Unintentional Discrimination Employers often use interviews and tests to choose from among a large number of applicants for job openings. Minimum educational requirements are also common. These practices and procedures may have an unintended discriminatory impact on a protected class. **Disparate-impact discrimination**

---

5. *Cote v. Wal-Mart Stores, Inc.*, Civil Action No. 15-CV-12945-WGY, a federal district court judge approved the class-action settlement on May 16, 2017.
6. *Wal-Mart Stores, Inc. v. Dukes*, 564 U.S. 338, 131 S.Ct. 2541, 180 L.Ed.2d 374 (2011).

occurs when a protected group of people is adversely affected by an employer's practices, procedures, or tests, even though they do not appear to be discriminatory.

In a disparate-impact discrimination case, the complaining party must first show that the employer's practices, procedures, or tests are effectively discriminatory. Once the plaintiff has made out a *prima facie* case, the burden of proof shifts to the employer to show that the practices or procedures in question were justified.

There are two ways of showing that an employer's practices, procedures, or tests are effectively discriminatory—that is, that disparate-impact discrimination exists.

Pool of Applicants. A plaintiff can prove a disparate impact by comparing the employer's workforce to the pool of qualified individuals available in the local labor market. The plaintiff must show that (1) as a result of educational or other job requirements or hiring procedures, (2) the percentage of nonwhites, women, or members of other protected classes in the employer's workforce (3) does not reflect the percentage of that group in the pool of qualified applicants. If the plaintiff can show a connection between the practice and the disparity, he or she has made out a *prima facie* case and need not provide evidence of discriminatory intent.

Rate of Hiring. A plaintiff can also prove disparate-impact discrimination by comparing the employer's *selection rates* of members and nonmembers of a protected class (nonwhites and whites, for instance, or women and men). When an educational or other job requirement or hiring procedure excludes members of a protected class from an employer's workforce at a substantially higher rate than nonmembers, discrimination occurs.

Under EEOC guidelines, a selection rate for a protected class that is less than four-fifths, or 80 percent, of the rate for the group with the highest rate of hiring generally is regarded as evidence of disparate impact. ■ **Example 21.2** Shady Cove District Fire Department administers an exam to applicants for the position of firefighter. At the exam session, one hundred white applicants take the test, and fifty pass and are hired—a selection rate of 50 percent. At the same exam session, sixty minority applicants take the test, but only twelve pass and are hired—a selection rate of 20 percent. Because 20 percent is less than four-fifths (80 percent) of 50 percent, the test will be considered discriminatory under EEOC guidelines. ■

21–1d Discrimination Based on Race, Color, and National Origin

Title VII prohibits employers from discriminating against employees or job applicants on the basis of race, color, and national origin. Race is interpreted broadly to apply to the ancestry or ethnic characteristics of a group of persons, such as Native Americans. National origin refers to discrimination based on a person's birth in another country or his or her ancestry or culture, such as Hispanic.

If an employer's standards or policies for selecting or promoting employees have a discriminatory effect on employees or job applicants in these protected classes, then a presumption of illegal discrimination arises. To avoid liability, the employer must show that its standards or policies have a substantial, demonstrable relationship to realistic qualifications for the job in question.

■ **Case in Point 21.3** Jiann Min Chang was an instructor at Alabama Agricultural and Mechanical University (AAMU). When AAMU terminated his employment, Chang filed a lawsuit claiming discrimination based on national origin. Chang established a *prima facie* case because he (1) was a member of a protected class, (2) was qualified for the job, (3) suffered an adverse employment action, and (4) was replaced by someone outside his protected class (a non-Asian instructor).

When the burden of proof shifted to the employer, however, AAMU showed that Chang had argued with a vice president and refused to comply with her instructions. The court ruled that AAMU had not renewed Chang's contract for a legitimate reason—insubordination—and therefore was not liable for unlawful discrimination.[7] ■

Reverse Discrimination Title VII also protects against *reverse discrimination*—that is, discrimination against members of a majority group, such as white males. ■ **Case in Point 21.4** Montana's Department of Transportation receives federal funds for transportation projects. As a condition of receiving the funds, Montana was required to set up a program to avoid discrimination and promote awarding contracts to disadvantaged business enterprises (DBEs). DBEs are businesses owned by members of socially and economically disadvantaged groups, such as minority groups. Mountain West Holding Company, Inc., installs signs, guardrails, and concrete barriers on highways in Montana and competes against DBEs for contracts.

Mountain West sued the state in federal court for violating Title VII by giving preference to DBEs. At trial, the

---

7. *Jiann Min Chang v. Alabama Agricultural and Mechanical University*, 355 Fed.Appx. 250 (11th Cir. 2009).

court pointed out that any classifications based on race are permissible "only if they are narrowly tailored measures that further compelling governmental interests." Montana thus had the burden of showing that its DBE program met this requirement. To show that the DBE program addressed actual discrimination, the state presented a study that reported disparities in state-awarded contracts and provided anecdotal evidence of a "good ol' boys'" network within the state's contracting industry. The district court accepted this evidence and concluded that Montana had satisfied its burden. A federal appellate court reversed, though, finding that the evidence was insufficient to prove a history of discrimination that would justify the preferences given to DBEs.[8] ■

Potential Section 1981 Claims Victims of racial or ethnic discrimination may also have a cause of action under 42 U.S.C. Section 1981. This section, which was enacted in 1866 to protect the rights of freed slaves, prohibits discrimination on the basis of race or ethnicity in the formation or enforcement of contracts. Because employment is often a contractual relationship, Section 1981 can provide an alternative basis for a plaintiff's action and is potentially advantageous because there is no limit on the damages that can be awarded. (There are some caps on damages under Title VII, as will be discussed later in this chapter.)

21–1e Discrimination Based on Religion

Title VII of the Civil Rights Act also prohibits government employers, private employers, and unions from discriminating against persons because of their religion. (This chapter's *Digital Update* feature discusses how employers who examine prospective employees' social media posts, including posts concerning religion, might engage in unlawful discrimination.)

Employers cannot treat their employees more or less favorably based on their religious beliefs or practices. They also cannot require employees to participate in any religious activity or forbid them from participating in one.

■ **Example 21.5** After Jason Sewell, a salesperson for JC Chevy, fails to attend the weekly prayer meetings of dealership employees for several months, he is discharged. If he can show that the dealership requires its employees to attend prayer gatherings and that he was fired for not attending, he has a valid claim of religious discrimination. ■

Reasonable Accommodation An employer must "reasonably accommodate" the religious practices and

sincerely held religious beliefs of its employees, unless to do so would cause undue hardship to the employer's business. An employee's religion might prohibit her or him from working on a certain day of the week, for instance, or at a certain type of job. Reasonable accommodation is required even if the belief is not based on the doctrines of a traditionally recognized religion, such as Christianity or Judaism, or of a denomination, such as Baptist.

Undue Hardship A reasonable attempt to accommodate does not necessarily require the employer to make every change an employee requests or to make a permanent change for an employee's benefit. An employer is not required to make an accommodation that would cause the employer undue hardship.

■ **Case in Point 21.6** Leontine Robinson worked as an administrative assistant in the emergency department at Children's Hospital Boston. The hospital started requiring all employees who worked in or had access to patient-care areas to receive the influenza (flu) vaccine. When Robinson, who had taken a tetanus vaccine, refused to get the flu vaccine based on her religious beliefs, the hospital terminated her employment. Robinson filed a lawsuit alleging religious discrimination. The hospital argued that allowing Robinson to keep her patient-care position without receiving the vaccine would create an undue hardship. The court agreed and granted a summary judgment for the hospital.[9] ■

21–1f Discrimination Based on Gender

Under Title VII and other federal acts, employers are forbidden from discriminating against employees on the basis of sex, or gender. Employers are prohibited from classifying or advertising jobs as male or female unless they can prove that the gender of the applicant is essential to the job. In addition, employers cannot have separate male and female seniority lists and cannot refuse to promote employees based on their gender.

Gender Must Be a Determining Factor Generally, to succeed in a suit for sex discrimination, a plaintiff must demonstrate that gender was a determining factor in the employer's decision to hire, fire, or promote him or her. Typically, this involves looking at all of the surrounding circumstances.

■ **Case in Point 21.7** Wanda Collier worked for Turner Industries Group, LLC, in the maintenance department. She complained to her supervisor that Jack

8. *Mountain West Holding Co., Inc. v. State of Montana,* 691 Fed.Appx. 326 (9th Cir. 2017).

9. *Robinson v. Children's Hospital Boston,* 2016 WL 1337255 (D.Mass. 2016).

Digital Update

Hiring Discrimination Based on Social Media Posts

Human resource officers in most companies routinely check job candidates' social media posts when deciding whom to hire. Certainly, every young person is warned not to post photos that she or he might later regret having made available to potential employers. But a more serious issue involves standard reviewing of job candidates' social media information. Specifically, do employers discriminate based on such information?

An Experiment in Hiring Discrimination via Online Social Networks

Two researchers at Carnegie-Mellon University conducted an experiment to determine whether social media information posted by prospective employees influences employers' hiring decisions.[a] The researchers created false résumés and social media profiles. They submitted job applications on behalf of the fictional "candidates" to about four thousand U.S. employers. They then compared employers' responses to different groups—for example, to Muslim candidates versus Christian candidates.

The researchers found that candidates whose public profiles indicated that they were Muslim were less likely to be called for interviews than Christian applicants. The difference was particularly pronounced in parts of the country with more conservative residents. In those locations, Muslims received callbacks only 2 percent of the time, compared with 17 percent for Christian applicants. According to the authors of the study, "Hiring discrimination via online searches of candidates may not be widespread, but online disclosures of personal traits can significantly influence the hiring decisions of a self-selected set of employers."

Job Candidates' Perception of the Hiring Process

Job candidates frequently view the hiring process as unfair when they know that their social media profiles have been used in the selection process. This perception may make litigation more likely. Nevertheless, 84 percent of employers report that they use social media in recruiting job applicants. One-third of those admit that they have disqualified applicants based on content found in their social media accounts.[b]

The EEOC Speaks Up

The Equal Employment Opportunity Commission (EEOC) has investigated how prospective employers can use social media to engage in discrimination in the hiring process. Given that the Society for Human Resource Management estimates that more than three-fourths of its members use social media in employment screening, the EEOC is interested in regulating this procedure.

Social media sites, examined closely, can provide information to a prospective employer on the applicant's race, color, national origin, disability, religion, and other protected characteristics. The EEOC reminds employers that such information—whether it comes from social media postings or other sources—may not legally be used to make employment decisions on prohibited bases, such as race, gender, and religion.

Critical Thinking *Can you think of a way a company could use information from an applicant's social media posts without running the risk of being accused of hiring discrimination?*

a. A. Acquisti and C. N. Fong, "An Experiment in Hiring Discrimination via Online Social Networks," *Social Service Research Network*, October 26, 2014.

b. Alexia Elejalde-Ruiz, "Using Social Media to Disqualify Job Candidates Is Risky," *Chicago Tribune*, January 11, 2016.

Daniell, the head of the department, treated her unfairly. Collier's supervisor told her that Daniell had a problem with her gender and was harder on women. The supervisor talked to Daniell about Collier's complaint but did not take any disciplinary action.

A month later, Daniell confronted Collier, pushing her up against a wall and berating her. After this incident, Collier filed a formal complaint and kept a male co-worker with her at all times. Soon after, Collier was fired. She subsequently filed a lawsuit alleging gender discrimination. The court allowed Collier's claim to go to a jury

because there was sufficient evidence that gender was a determining factor in Daniell's conduct.[10] ■

The Federal Bureau of Investigation (FBI) requires that its applicants meet certain physical fitness standards. For women, the standards include the ability to complete a minimum of fourteen push-ups. Men must be able to complete at least thirty. Whether this difference constituted discrimination on the basis of gender was at issue in the following case.

---

10. *Collier v. Turner Industries Group, LLC*, 797 F.Supp.2d 1029 (D. Idaho 2011).

Bauer v. Lynch

United States Court of Appeals, Fourth Circuit, 812 F.3d 340 (2016).

In the Language of the Court
KING, Circuit Judge.
* * * *

The FBI [Federal Bureau of Investigation] trains its Special Agent recruits at the FBI Academy in Quantico, Virginia. * * * All Trainees must pass a physical fitness test (the "PFT").

* * * The FBI requires every Special Agent recruit to pass the PFT twice: once to gain admission to the Academy, and a second time to graduate.
* * * *

* * * Trainees * * * need to satisfy the following standards * * *:

Event	Men	Women
Sit-ups	38	35
300-meter sprint	52.4s	64.9s
Push-ups	30	14
1.5-mile run	12m, 42s	13m, 5s

* * * *

After the attacks of September 11, 2001, * * * Jay Bauer resolved to contribute to the defense of our country by becoming a Special Agent in the FBI. [At the time,] he * * * served as an assistant professor at the University of Wisconsin–Milwaukee.

* * * Bauer took the PFT for the first time and failed. Although he achieved sixteen points on the test, Bauer completed only twenty-five push-ups * * *. The FBI allowed Bauer to retest [three months later] and he passed, that time completing thirty-two push-ups. With his fitness screening complete, the FBI invited Bauer to report to the Academy.

Bauer's time at the Academy largely showed great potential for a career as a Special Agent. He passed all academic tests, demonstrated proficiency in his firearms and defensive tactics training, and met all expectations for the practical applications and skills components of the Academy. Bauer's classmates also selected him as the class leader

and spokesperson for the Academy graduation. Unfortunately, Bauer faced a dilemma: he was unable to pass the PFT at Quantico.

During his twenty-two weeks at the Academy, Bauer took the PFT five times. On each occasion, he would have passed but for his failure to achieve the minimum standard for push-ups. Bauer's results, and his corresponding point scores for each event, were as follows:

Week	Sit-ups	300-meter sprint (sec.)	Push-ups	1.5-mile run (min.)	Total Points
1	40 (2)	42.6 (8)	26 (0)	10:49 (4)	14
7	47 (4)	43.4 (7)	25 (0)	10:24 (5)	16
14	50 (6)	43.7 (7)	28 (0)	10:45 (4)	17
18	51 (6)	43.8 (7)	27 (0)	11:09 (4)	17
22	49 (5)	44.1 (6)	29 (0)	10:57 (4)	15

Following his final failure of the PFT, Bauer * * * was [allowed to] resign with the possibility of future employment with the FBI * * *. Bauer * * * immediately signed a resignation letter. Two weeks later, the FBI offered Bauer a position as an Intelligence Analyst in its Chicago Field Office. He accepted and has been employed in that position since.
* * * *

* * * Bauer filed this Title VII action in [a federal district court] against [Loretta Lynch,] the Attorney General. According to the claims in Bauer's complaint, the FBI's use of the gender-normed PFT standards contravened * * * Title VII * * * which prohibits sex discrimination by federal employers.
* * * *

In his summary judgment motion, Bauer maintained that the FBI's use of the gender-normed PFT standards was facially discriminatory [involving explicit categorization, such as by sex or race].
* * * *

* * * The district court agreed with Bauer, granting his motion for summary judgment.
* * * *

The Attorney General * * * filed a timely * * * appeal.
* * * *

Title VII requires that any "personnel actions affecting employees or applicants for employment" taken by federal employers "shall be made free from any discrimination based on * * * sex." * * * *A plaintiff is entitled to demonstrate discrimination by showing that the employer uses a facially discriminatory employment practice. [The Supreme Court has outlined] a "simple test" for identifying facial sex discrimination: such discrimination appears "where the evidence shows treatment of a person in a manner which but for that person's sex would be different."* [Emphasis added.]

* * * The district court applied [this] test and concluded that, because Bauer would have been held to a lower minimum number of push-ups had he been a woman, the gender-normed PFT standards constitute facial sex discrimination. The Attorney General maintains on appeal, however, that because the PFT assesses an overall level of physical fitness, and equally fit men and women possess innate physiological differences that lead to different performance outcomes, the PFT's gender-normed standards actually require the same level of fitness for all Trainees. In that way, the Attorney General contends, the PFT standards do not treat the sexes differently and therefore do not contravene Title VII.
* * * *

* * * The Attorney General * * * maintains that * * * some differential treatment of men and women based upon inherent physiological differences is not only lawful but also potentially required.
* * * *

Men and women simply are not physiologically the same for the purposes of physical fitness programs.

* * * Physical fitness standards suitable for men may not always be suitable for women, and accommodations addressing physiological differences between the sexes are not necessarily unlawful.

* * * The physiological differences between men and women impact their relative abilities to demonstrate the same levels of physical fitness. In other words, equally fit men and women demonstrate their fitness differently. Whether physical fitness standards discriminate based on sex, therefore, depends on whether they require men and women to demonstrate different levels of fitness.

Put succinctly, *an employer does not contravene [violate] Title VII when it utilizes physical fitness standards that distinguish between the sexes on the basis of their physiological differences but impose an equal burden of compliance on both men and women, requiring the same level of physical fitness of each.* Because the FBI purports to assess physical fitness by imposing the same burden on both men and women, this rule applies to Bauer's Title VII claims. Accordingly, the district court erred in failing to apply the rule in its disposition of Bauer's motion for summary judgment. [Emphasis added.]
* * * *

Pursuant to the foregoing, we vacate the judgment of the district court and remand for * * * further proceedings.

Legal Reasoning Questions

1. According to the reasoning of the court in the *Bauer* case, when do different employment standards for men and women satisfy Title VII's requirement of equality?

2. In what other circumstances might the rule in this case apply?

3. If Bauer had ultimately succeeded in his claim, what might the remedy have been? What else might have resulted?

Pregnancy Discrimination The Pregnancy Discrimination Act[11] expanded Title VII's definition of sex discrimination to include discrimination based on pregnancy. Women affected by pregnancy, childbirth, or related medical conditions must be treated the same as other persons not so affected but similar in ability to work. For instance, an employer cannot discriminate against a pregnant woman by withholding benefits available to others under employee benefit programs.

In the following case, an employer accommodated many employees who had lifting restrictions due to disabilities but refused to accommodate a pregnant employee with a similar restriction. Did this refusal constitute a violation of the Pregnancy Discrimination Act?

11. 42 U.S.C. Section 2000e(k).

Case 21.2

Young v. United Parcel Service, Inc.
Supreme Court of the United States, ___ U.S. ___, 135 S.Ct. 1338, 191 L.Ed.2d 279 (2015).

Background and Facts Peggy Young was a driver for United Parcel Service, Inc. (UPS). When she became pregnant, her doctor advised her not to lift more than twenty pounds. UPS required drivers to lift up to seventy pounds and told Young that she could not work under a lifting restriction. She filed a suit in a federal district court against UPS, claiming an unlawful refusal to accommodate her pregnancy-related lifting restriction. She alleged that UPS had multiple light-duty-for-injury categories to accommodate individuals whose nonpregnancy-related disabilities created work restrictions similar to hers.

UPS responded that, because Young did not fall into any of those categories, it had not discriminated against her. The court issued a summary judgment in UPS's favor. The U.S. Court of Appeals of the Fourth Circuit affirmed the judgment. Young appealed to the United States Supreme Court.

In the Language of the Court
Justice *BREYER* delivered the opinion of the Court.
* * * *

* * * A plaintiff alleging that the denial of an accommodation constituted disparate treatment under the Pregnancy Discrimination Act * * * may make out a *prima facie* case by showing that she belongs to

Case 21.2 Continues

Case 21.2 Continued

the protected class, that she sought accommodation, that the employer did not accommodate her, and that the employer did accommodate others similar in their ability or inability to work.

The employer may then seek to justify its refusal to accommodate the plaintiff by relying on legitimate, nondiscriminatory reasons for denying her accommodation. [Emphasis added.]

If the employer offers an apparently legitimate, nondiscriminatory reason for its actions, the plaintiff may in turn show that the employer's proffered reasons are in fact pretextual [contrived]. We believe that the plaintiff may reach a jury on this issue by providing sufficient evidence that the employer's policies impose a significant burden on pregnant workers, and that the employer's legitimate, nondiscriminatory reasons are not sufficiently strong to justify the burden, but rather—when considered along with the burden imposed—give rise to an inference of intentional discrimination.

The plaintiff can create a genuine issue of material fact as to whether a significant burden exists by providing evidence that the employer accommodates a large percentage of nonpregnant workers while failing to accommodate a large percentage of pregnant workers. Here, for example, if the facts are as Young says they are, she can show that UPS accommodates most nonpregnant employees with lifting limitations while categorically failing to accommodate pregnant employees with lifting limitations. Young might also add that the fact that UPS has multiple policies that accommodate nonpregnant employees with lifting restrictions suggests that its reasons for failing to accommodate pregnant employees with lifting restrictions are not sufficiently strong—to the point that a jury could find that its reasons for failing to accommodate pregnant employees give rise to an inference of intentional discrimination.

* * * *

* * * A party is entitled to summary judgment if there is no genuine dispute as to any material fact and the movant [that is, a person who applies to a court for a ruling in his or her favor] is entitled to judgment as a matter of law. * * * *Viewing the record in the light most favorable to Young, there is a genuine dispute as to whether UPS provided more favorable treatment to at least some employees whose situation cannot reasonably be distinguished from Young's.* [Emphasis added.]

Decision and Remedy *The United States Supreme Court vacated the judgment of the U.S. Court of Appeals for the Fourth Circuit and remanded the case for further proceedings. Young created a genuine dispute as to whether UPS had provided more favorable treatment to employees whose situation could not reasonably be distinguished from hers. On remand, the court must determine whether Young also created a genuine issue of material fact as to whether UPS's reasons for treating Young less favorably were a pretext.*

Critical Thinking

• **Legal Environment** *Could UPS have succeeded in this case if it had claimed simply that it would be more expensive or less convenient to include pregnant women among those whom it accommodates? Explain.*

Post-Pregnancy Discrimination An employer must continue to reasonably accommodate an employee's medical conditions related to pregnancy and childbirth, even after the pregnancy has ended. ■ **Case in Point 21.8** Professional Ambulance, LLC, hired Allison Mayer as an emergency medical technician (EMT) while she was still breastfeeding an infant. She was supposed to work three twelve-hour shifts a week, but Professional did not provide her with a schedule so that she could arrange child care. Mayer informed Professional that she needed to take short breaks to use a pump to express breast milk. At first, her supervisor told her to take these breaks in the restroom, but Mayer objected because the conditions were unsanitary. Then she was told to take the

breaks in an office that was not private or secure, which made her uncomfortable because the male EMTs could hear her pumping.

A few weeks later, Professional fired Mayer, claiming that it was because other employees had complained that she was rude and abusive. The employer refused to provide her with further explanation and replaced her with a male EMT with fewer qualifications. Mayer sued. A federal district court found that Mayer had established a *prima facie* case of discrimination on the basis of pregnancy, childbirth, or related medical conditions.[12] ■

---

12. *Mayer v. Professional Ambulance, LLC*, 211 F.Supp.3d 408 (D.R.I. 2016).

Wage Discrimination The Equal Pay Act[13] requires equal pay for male and female employees working at the same establishment doing similar work. To determine whether the Equal Pay Act has been violated, a court looks to the primary duties of the two jobs—the job content rather than the job description controls. If a court finds that the wage differential is due to "any factor other than gender," such as a seniority or merit system, then it does not violate the Equal Pay Act.

The Lilly Ledbetter Fair Pay Act made discriminatory wages actionable under federal law regardless of when the discrimination began.[14] Previously, plaintiffs had to file a complaint within a limited time period. Today, if a plaintiff continues to work for the employer while receiving discriminatory wages, the time period for filing a complaint is practically unlimited.

Discrimination against Transgender Persons
In the past, most courts held that Title VII does not protect transgender persons from discrimination. The situation may be changing, however. A growing number of federal courts are interpreting Title VII's protections against gender discrimination to apply to transsexuals.
■ **Case in Point 21.9** Deborah Fabian, an orthopedic surgeon, applied for an on-call position at the Hospital of Central Connecticut. The hospital apparently declined to hire Fabian because she disclosed her identity as a transgender woman. Fabian sued the hospital alleging violations of Title VII of the Civil Rights Act and the Connecticut Fair Employment Practices Act (CFEPA).

The hospital filed a summary judgment motion, arguing that neither Title VII nor the Connecticut statute prohibits discrimination on the basis of transgender identity. The federal district court rejected this argument, however, finding that discrimination on the basis of transgender identity is discrimination on the basis of sex for Title VII purposes. Fabian was entitled to take her case to a jury and argue violations of Title VII and the CFEPA.[15] ■

21–1g Constructive Discharge

The majority of Title VII complaints involve unlawful discrimination in decisions to hire or fire employees. In some situations, however, employees who leave their jobs voluntarily can claim that they were "constructively discharged" by the employer. **Constructive discharge** occurs when the employer causes the employee's working

conditions to be so intolerable that a reasonable person in the employee's position would feel compelled to quit.

When constructive discharge is claimed, the employee can pursue damages for loss of income, including back pay. These damages ordinarily are not available to an employee who left a job voluntarily.

Proving Constructive Discharge To prove constructive discharge, an employee must present objective proof of intolerable working conditions. The employee must also show that the employer knew or had reason to know about these conditions yet failed to correct them within a reasonable time period. In addition, courts generally require the employee to show causation—that the employer's unlawful discrimination caused the working conditions to be intolerable. Put in a different way, the employee's resignation must be a foreseeable result of the employer's discriminatory action. Courts weigh the facts on a case-by-case basis.

Employee demotion is one of the most frequently cited reasons for a finding of constructive discharge, particularly when the employee was subjected to humiliation.
■ **Example 21.10** Khalil's employer humiliates him by informing him in front of his co-workers that he is being demoted to an inferior position. Khalil's co-workers then continually insult him, harass him, and make derogatory remarks to him about his national origin (he is from Iran). The employer is aware of this discriminatory treatment but does nothing to remedy the situation, despite Khalil's repeated complaints. After several months, Khalil quits his job and files a Title VII claim. In this situation, Khalil will likely have sufficient evidence to maintain an action for constructive discharge in violation of Title VII. ■

Applies to All Title VII Discrimination Plaintiffs can use constructive discharge to establish any type of discrimination claim under Title VII, including race, color, national origin, religion, gender, and pregnancy. It is most commonly asserted in cases involving sexual harassment. Constructive discharge may also be used in cases involving discrimination based on age or disability (discussed later in this chapter).

21–1h Sexual Harassment

Title VII also protects employees against **sexual harassment** in the workplace. Sexual harassment can take two forms:

1. *Quid pro quo* harassment occurs when sexual favors are demanded in return for job opportunities, promotions, salary increases, or other benefits. *Quid pro quo* is a Latin phrase that is often translated as "something in exchange for something else."

---

13. 29 U.S.C. Section 206(d).
14. Pub. L. No. 111-2, 123 Stat. 5 (2009), amending various sections in Titles 29 and 42, especially 42 U.S.C. Section 2000e-5[e].
15. *Fabian v. Hospital of Central Connecticut*, 172 F.Supp.3d 509 (D.Conn. 2016).

2. *Hostile-environment* harassment occurs when a pattern of sexually offensive conduct runs throughout the workplace and the employer has not taken steps to prevent or discourage it. Such harassment exists when the workplace is permeated with discriminatory intimidation, ridicule, and insult, and this harassment is so severe or pervasive that it alters the conditions of employment.

Harassment by Supervisors For an employer to be held liable for a supervisor's sexual harassment, the supervisor normally must have taken a *tangible employment action* against the employee. A **tangible employment action** is a significant change in employment status or benefits. Such an action occurs when an employee is fired, refused a promotion, demoted, or reassigned to a position with significantly different responsibilities, for instance. Only a supervisor, or another person acting with the authority of the employer, can cause this sort of harm. A constructive discharge also qualifies as a tangible employment action.

The United States Supreme Court issued several important rulings in cases alleging sexual harassment by supervisors that established what is known as the "*Ellerth/Faragher* affirmative defense."[16] The defense has two elements:

1. The employer must have taken reasonable care to prevent and promptly correct any sexually harassing behavior (by establishing effective harassment policies and complaint procedures, for instance).
2. The plaintiff-employee must have unreasonably failed to take advantage of preventive or corrective opportunities provided by the employer to avoid harm.

An employer that can prove both elements normally will not be liable for a supervisor's harassment.

Retaliation by Employers Employers sometimes retaliate against employees who complain about sexual harassment or other Title VII violations. Retaliation can take many forms. An employer might demote or fire the person, or otherwise change the terms, conditions, and benefits of employment.

Title VII prohibits retaliation, and employees can sue their employers when it occurs. In a *retaliation claim*, an individual asserts that she or he has suffered harm as a result of making a charge, testifying, or participating in a Title VII investigation or proceeding.

Requirements for Protection. To be protected under Title VII's retaliation provisions, the plaintiff must have opposed a practice prohibited by Title VII and suffered an adverse employment action as a result of that opposition.

■ **Case in Point 21.11** Myrta Morales-Cruz had a tenure-track teaching position at the University of Puerto Rico School of Law. When her probationary period was almost over, Morales-Cruz asked the university's administrative committee to grant a one-year extension for her tenure review. The dean recommended that the extension be granted but also called her "insecure," "immature," and "fragile." Another professor commented that had she shown "poor judgment" and exhibited "personality flaws."

After Morales-Cruz complained about these comments in writing to the chancellor, the dean recommended denying the one-year extension, and the administrative committee did just that. Morales-Cruz later filed a retaliation lawsuit. She claimed that the dean had retaliated against her for complaining to the chancellor about the "discriminatory" comments made in the course of her request for an extension.

The court held that Morales-Cruz had not provided a reasonable foundation for a retaliation action. Under Title VII, an employer may not retaliate against an employee because he or she has opposed a practice prohibited by Title VII. But the court found that Morales-Cruz did not allege any facts that could be construed as gender-based discrimination. Although the comments she complained about were hardly flattering, they were entirely gender-neutral. Thus, she was not engaging in protected conduct when she opposed the remarks.[17] ■

Protection May Extend to Others. Title VII's retaliation protection extends to employees who speak out about discrimination against other employees during an employer's internal investigation. For instance, Title VII may protect an employee who is fired after his wife files a gender discrimination claim against their employer.

Harassment by Co-Workers and Others When harassment by co-workers, rather than supervisors, creates a hostile working environment, an employee may still have a cause of action against the employer. Normally, though, the employer will be held liable only if management knew or should have known about the harassment and failed to take immediate remedial action.

Occasionally, a court may also hold an employer liable for harassment by *nonemployees* if the employer knew about the harassment and failed to take corrective action.

---

16. *Burlington Industries, Inc. v. Ellerth*, 524 U.S. 742, 118 S.Ct. 2257, 141 L.Ed.2d 633 (1998); and *Faragher v. City of Boca Raton*, 524 U.S. 775, 118 S.Ct. 2275, 141 L.Ed.2d 662 (1998).

17. *Morales-Cruz v. University of Puerto Rico*, 676 F.3d 220 (1st Cir. 2012).

■ **Example 21.12** Jordan, who owns and manages a Great Bites restaurant, knows that one of his regular customers, Dean, repeatedly harasses Kaylia, a waitress. If Jordan does nothing and permits the harassment to continue, he may be liable under Title VII even though Dean is not an employee of the restaurant. ■

In the following case, a female firefighter claimed that her male co-workers subjected her to a hostile working environment and that the fire department knew about the harassment but failed to act. The city (the defendant) responded that there was no evidence to support this claim.

Franchina v. City of Providence

United States Court of Appeals, First Circuit, 881 F.3d 32 (2018).

Background and Facts Lori Franchina, a rescue lieutenant with the Providence Fire Department in Rhode Island, was assigned to work a shift with fellow firefighter Andre Ferro. During the shift, Ferro subjected her to unprofessional sexual comments and conduct. Based on Franchina's account of Ferro's actions, fire chief Curt Varone filed an intra-department complaint charging Ferro with sexual harassment. No action was taken, however. Other firefighters then began to treat Franchina with contempt. She was spit on and shoved and was forced to undergo verbal assaults, insubordination, and other kinds of negative treatment. She submitted forty different complaints of harassment to her superiors.

Franchina filed a suit in a federal district court against the city of Providence, asserting that she had been subjected to a hostile work environment as a result of her gender in violation of Title VII. The city argued that Franchina presented no evidence to support her claim. A jury issued a verdict in her favor and awarded damages. The city appealed.

In the Language of the Court

THOMPSON, Circuit Judge.

Sticks and stones may break some bones, but harassment can hurt forever.

* * * *

Here, Franchina presented a plethora [a great deal] of evidence showing that the impetus [motivation] for the discrimination she sustained was based in part on her being a female. *In gender discrimination cases premised on a hostile work environment, Title VII permits a plaintiff to prove unlawful discrimination by demonstrating that the workplace is permeated with discriminatory intimidation, ridicule, and insult that is sufficiently severe or pervasive to alter the conditions of the victim's employment and create an abusive working environment.* Evidence of sexual remarks, innuendos, ridicule, and intimidation may be sufficient to support a jury verdict for a hostile work environment. Here, there was repeated evidence that Franchina was called a "bitch," * * *, and "Frangina" [a combination of her last name and the word "vagina"]. The use of these words is inherently gender-specific and their repeated and hostile use * * * can reasonably be considered evidence of sexual harassment. In fact a raft of case law * * * establishes that the use of sexually degrading, gender-specific epithets, such as "slut," * * *, "whore," and "bitch" * * *, has been consistently held to constitute harassment based upon sex. This case is no different. In fact, there was more. [Emphasis added.]

There was also evidence that [within the fire department] women were treated as less competent; a treatment barred by Title VII. The critical issue, Title VII's text indicates, is whether members of one sex are exposed to disadvantageous terms or conditions of employment to which members of the other sex are not exposed. There was evidence that men treated women better when they were perceived as willing to have sex with them. There was evidence that Franchina was subjected to humiliating sexual remarks and innuendos by Ferro, including asking the plaintiff if she wanted to have babies and if he could help her conceive. This type of sexually based *animus* [hostility] is a hallmark of Title VII.

In sum, the jury heard evidence of repeated hostile, gender-based epithets, ill treatment of women as workers, sexual innuendoes, and preferential treatment for women who were more likely to sleep with the men of the department. This sampling of evidence demonstrates that the accumulated effect * * * taken together constitutes a hostile work environment.

Case 21.3 Continues

Case 21.3 Continued   **Decision and Remedy** *The U.S. Court of Appeals for the First Circuit affirmed the judgment. "The abuse Lori Franchina suffered at the hands of the Providence Fire Department is nothing short of abhorrent . . . . Employers should be cautioned that turning a blind eye to blatant discrimination does not generally fare well under anti-discrimination laws like Title VII."*

Critical Thinking

- **Economic** *Because of the constant harassment, Franchina had to be placed on injured-on-duty status. Later, diagnosed with severe post-traumatic stress disorder and unable to work again as a rescue lieutenant, she "retired." What is the appropriate measure of damages for this result? Discuss.*
- **Legal Environment** *What steps might an employer take to avoid the circumstances that occurred in the* Franchina *case?*

Same-Gender Harassment In *Oncale v. Sundowner Offshore Services, Inc.*,[18] the United States Supreme Court held that Title VII protection extends to individuals who are sexually harassed by members of the same gender. Proving that the harassment in same-gender cases is "based on sex" can be difficult, though. It is easier to establish a case of same-gender harassment when the harasser is homosexual.

Sexual-Orientation Harassment Title VII does not explicitly prohibit discrimination or harassment based on a person's sexual orientation. Nonetheless, federal courts have occasionally ruled that sexual orientation is protected under Title VII.[19] In addition, a growing number of states have enacted laws that prohibit sexual-orientation discrimination in private employment. Some states, such as Michigan, explicitly prohibit discrimination based on a person's gender identity or expression. Many companies and other organizations, such as the National Football League, have also voluntarily established nondiscrimination policies that include sexual orientation.

21–1i Online Harassment

Employees' online activities can create a hostile working environment in many ways. Racial jokes, ethnic slurs, or other comments contained in e-mail, texts, blogs, or social media can lead to claims of hostile-environment harassment or other forms of discrimination. A worker who regularly sees sexually explicit images on a co-worker's computer screen, for instance, may find the images offensive and claim that they create a hostile working environment. Nevertheless, employers may be able to

avoid liability for online harassment by taking prompt remedial action.

21–1j Remedies under Title VII

Employer liability under Title VII can be extensive. If the plaintiff successfully proves that unlawful discrimination occurred, he or she may be awarded reinstatement, back pay, retroactive promotions, and damages.

Several limits apply to damages. Compensatory damages are available only in cases of intentional discrimination. Punitive damages may be recovered against a private employer only if the employer acted with malice or reckless indifference to an individual's rights. The total amount of compensatory and punitive damages that plaintiffs can recover from specific employers depends on the size of the employer. For instance, there is a $50,000 cap on damages from employers with one hundred or fewer employees.

21–2 Discrimination Based on Age

Age discrimination is potentially the most widespread form of discrimination because anyone—regardless of race, color, national origin, or gender—could be a victim at some point in life. The Age Discrimination in Employment Act[20] (ADEA), as amended, prohibits employment discrimination on the basis of age against individuals forty years of age or older. The act also prohibits mandatory retirement for nonmanagerial workers. In addition, the ADEA protects federal and private-sector employees from retaliation based on age-related complaints.[21]

---

18. 523 U.S. 75, 118 S.Ct. 998, 140 L.Ed.2d 201 (1998).
19. See, for instance, *Zarda v. Altitude Express, Inc.*, 883 F.3d 100 (2d Cir. 2018); and *Wittmer v. Phillips 66 Company*, 915 F.3d 328 (5th Cir. 2019).

20. 29 U.S.C. Sections 621 *et seq.*
21. *Gomez-Perez v. Potter*, 553 U.S. 474, 128 S.Ct. 1931, 170 L.Ed.2d 887 (2008).

For the act to apply, an employer must have twenty or more employees, and the employer's business activities must affect interstate commerce. The EEOC administers the ADEA, but the act also permits private causes of action against employers for age discrimination.

21–2a Procedures under the ADEA

The burden-shifting procedure under the ADEA differs from the procedure under Title VII. As explained earlier, if the plaintiff in a Title VII case can show that the employer was motivated, at least in part, by unlawful discrimination, the burden of proof shifts to the employer. Thus, in cases in which the employer has a "mixed motive" for discharging an employee, the employer has the burden of proving that its reason was legitimate.

Under the ADEA, in contrast, a plaintiff must show that the unlawful discrimination was not just *a* reason but *the* reason for the adverse employment action. In other words, the employee has the burden of establishing *but for* causation—that is, "but for" the employee's age, the action would not have been taken.

Prima Facie Age Discrimination To establish a *prima facie* case of age discrimination, the plaintiff must show that she or he was all of the following:

1. A member of the protected age group.
2. Qualified for the position from which she or he was discharged.
3. Discharged because of age discrimination.

Then the burden shifts to the employer to give a legitimate nondiscriminatory reason for the adverse action.

Pretext If the employer offers a legitimate reason for its action, then the plaintiff must show that the stated reason is only a pretext. The plaintiff is required to prove that the plaintiff's age was the real reason for the employer's decision.

■ **Case in Point 21.13** Jerry Stever was a financial adviser at U.S. Bancorp, Inc. He was terminated at age sixty-eight for "deficient performance." Stever sued U.S. Bancorp in federal court alleging age discrimination and claiming that deficient performance was a pretext. The plaintiff proved that he was in the protected age group (over forty) and was qualified for the position, but he lacked proof that he had been discharged because of his age.

Stever argued that two younger financial advisers had received more favorable treatment from the company than he had. Showing that "similarly situated" younger employees were treated more favorably would have given rise to an inference of discrimination. The court found no evidence of preferential treatment, however. One of the men had generated considerably more revenue than Stever, and the other man differed from Stever in terms of seniority and prior performance. Thus, they were not similarly situated to Stever. Stever also claimed that his manager had made the comment, "We old dogs had to learn new tricks." The district court found that this single stray remark was not sufficient to demonstrate age discrimination and granted summary judgment to U.S. Bancorp. A federal appellate court affirmed the decision.[22] ■

21–2b Replacing Older Workers with Younger Workers

Numerous age discrimination cases have been brought against employers who, to cut costs, replaced older, higher-salaried employees with younger, lower-salaried workers. In such situations, whether a firing is discriminatory or simply part of a rational business decision to prune the company's ranks is not always clear.

The plaintiff must prove that the discharge was motivated by age bias. The plaintiff need not prove that she or he was replaced by a person "outside the protected class" (under the age of forty). The replacement worker need only be younger than the plaintiff. Nevertheless, the greater the age gap, the more likely the plaintiff will succeed in showing age discrimination.

21–2c State Employees Not Covered by the ADEA

Generally, the states are immune from lawsuits brought by private individuals in federal court (unless a state consents to such a suit). This immunity stems from the United States Supreme Court's interpretation of the Eleventh Amendment.

State immunity under the Eleventh Amendment is not absolute. When fundamental rights are at stake, Congress has the power to abrogate (abolish) state immunity to private suits through legislation. For instance, Congress has chosen to subject states to private lawsuits under the Family Medical Leave Act.

The Court has found, however, that state employers are generally immune from private suits brought by employees under the ADEA. State employers are also usually immune from suits brought under the Americans with Disabilities Act and the Fair Labor Standards Act.

---

22. *Stever v. U.S. Bancorp, Inc.*, 690 Fed.Appx. 491 (9th Cir. 2017).

21–3 Discrimination Based on Disability

The Americans with Disabilities Act (ADA)[23] prohibits disability-based discrimination in all workplaces with fifteen or more workers. An exception is state government employers, who are generally immune under the Eleventh Amendment, as just mentioned. Basically, the ADA requires that employers "reasonably accommodate" the needs of persons with disabilities unless to do so would cause the employer to suffer an "undue hardship." Amendments to the ADA broadened the coverage of its protections, as will be discussed shortly.

21–3a Procedures under the ADA

To prevail on a claim under the ADA, a plaintiff must show that he or she (1) has a disability, (2) is otherwise qualified for the employment in question, and (3) was excluded from the employment solely because of the disability. As in Title VII cases, the plaintiff must pursue the claim through the EEOC before filing an action in court for a violation of the ADA.

The EEOC may decide to investigate and perhaps sue the employer on behalf of the employee. The EEOC can bring a suit even if the employee previously signed an agreement with the employer to submit job-related disputes to arbitration.[24] If the EEOC decides not to sue, then the employee may do so.

Plaintiffs in lawsuits brought under the ADA may seek many of the same remedies that are available under Title VII. These include reinstatement, back pay, a limited amount of compensatory and punitive damages (for intentional discrimination), and certain other forms of relief. Repeat violators may be ordered to pay fines of up to $100,000.

21–3b What Is a Disability?

The ADA is broadly drafted to cover persons with physical or mental impairments that "substantially limit" their everyday activities. Specifically, the ADA defines a *disability* as including any of the following:

1. A physical or mental impairment that substantially limits one or more of the major life activities of the affected individual.

2. A record of having such an impairment.
3. Being regarded as having such an impairment.

Health conditions that have been considered disabilities under federal law include alcoholism, acquired immune deficiency syndrome (AIDS), blindness, cancer, cerebral palsy, diabetes, heart disease, muscular dystrophy, and paraplegia. Testing positive for the human immunodeficiency virus (HIV) has qualified as a disability, as has morbid obesity. (A morbidly obese person weighs twice the normal weight for his or her height.)

Association with Disabled Persons A separate provision in the ADA prevents employers from taking adverse employment actions based on stereotypes or assumptions about individuals who associate with people who have disabilities.[25] An employer cannot, for instance, refuse to hire the parent of a child with a disability based on the assumption that the person will miss work too often or be unreliable.

■ **Example 21.14** Joan, an employer, refuses to hire Edward, who has a daughter with a physical disability. She consciously bases her decision on the assumption that Edward will have to miss work frequently to care for his daughter. Edward can sue Joan for violating the ADA's provisions. ■

Mitigating Measures At one time, the courts focused on whether a person had a disability *after* the use of corrective devices or medication. Thus, a person with severe myopia (nearsightedness) whose eyesight could be corrected by wearing glasses did not qualify as having a disability. With the corrective lenses, the person's major life activities were not substantially impaired. Then Congress amended the ADA to strengthen its protections and prohibit employers from considering mitigating measures when determining if an individual has a disability.

Disability is now determined on a case-by-case basis. A condition may fit the definition of disability in one set of circumstances, but not in another. ■ **Case in Point 21.15** Larry Rohr, a welding specialist for a power district in Arizona, was diagnosed with type 2 diabetes. To keep his condition under control, Rohr was required to follow a complex regimen of daily insulin injections and blood tests, as well as a strict diet. Therefore, his physician forbade him from taking work assignments that involved overnight, out-of-town travel, which were common in his job.

---

23. 42 U.S.C. Sections 12101 *et seq.*
24. This was the Supreme Court's ruling in *Equal Employment Opportunity Commission v. Waffle House, Inc.*, 534 U.S. 279, 122 S.Ct. 754, 151 L.Ed.2d 755 (2002).

25. 42 U.S.C. Section 12112(b)(4).

Because of these limitations, the power district asked him to transfer, apply for federal disability benefits, or take early retirement. Rohr sued for disability discrimination. The lower court granted summary judgment for the employer. Rohr appealed. A federal appellate court reversed. The court held that under the amended ADA, diabetes is a disability if it significantly restricts an individual's eating (a major life activity), as it did for Rohr. Therefore, Rohr was entitled to a trial on his discrimination claim.[26] ■

Disclosure of Confidential Medical Information
ADA provisions also require employers to keep their employees' medical information confidential.[27] An employee who discovers that an employer has disclosed his or her confidential medical information has a right to sue the employer—even if the employee was not technically disabled. The prohibition against disclosure also applies to other employees acting on behalf of the employer.

■ **Case in Point 21.16** George Shoun was working at his job at Best Formed Plastics, Inc., when he fell and injured his shoulder. Another Best Formed employee, Jane Stewart, prepared an accident report for the incident and processed Shoun's workers' compensation claim. As a result of the injury, Shoun had to take off several months of work and received workers' compensation benefits.

Stewart posted on her Facebook page a statement about how Shoun's shoulder injury "kept him away from work for 11 months and now he is trying to sue us." Shoun sued Best Formed under the ADA for wrongfully disclosing confidential information about his medical condition to other people via Facebook. He claimed that the action resulted in loss of employment and impairment of his earning capacity. The court allowed Shoun's claim to go forward to trial.[28] ■

21–3c Reasonable Accommodation
The ADA does not require that employers accommodate the needs of job applicants or employees with disabilities who are not otherwise qualified for the work. If a job applicant or an employee with a disability, with reasonable accommodation, can perform essential job functions, however, the employer must make the accommodation.

Required modifications may include installing ramps for a wheelchair, establishing flexible working hours, creating or modifying job assignments, and designing or

improving training materials and procedures. Generally, employers should give primary consideration to employees' preferences in deciding what accommodations should be made.

Undue Hardship Employers who do not accommodate the needs of persons with disabilities must demonstrate that the accommodations would cause *undue hardship* in terms of being significantly difficult or expensive for the employer. Usually, the courts decide whether an accommodation constitutes an undue hardship on a case-by-case basis.

■ **Example 21.17** Bryan Lockhart, who uses a wheelchair, works for a cell phone company that provides parking for its employees. Lockhart informs his supervisor that the parking spaces are so narrow that he is unable to extend the ramp on his van that allows him to get in and out of the vehicle. Lockhart therefore requests that the company reasonably accommodate his needs by paying a monthly fee for him to use a larger parking space in an adjacent lot. In this situation, a court will likely find that it is *not* an undue hardship for the employer to pay for additional parking for Lockhart. ■

Job Applications and Physical Exams Employers must modify their job-application and selection process so that those with disabilities can compete for jobs with those who do not have disabilities. For instance, a job announcement might be modified to allow applicants to respond by e-mail as well as by telephone, so that it does not discriminate against potential applicants with hearing impairments.

Employers are restricted in the kinds of questions they may ask on job-application forms and during preemployment interviews. In addition, employers cannot require persons with disabilities to submit to preemployment physicals unless such exams are required of all other applicants. An employer can disqualify the applicant only if the medical problems discovered during a preemployment physical would make it impossible for the applicant to perform the job.

Health-Insurance Plans Workers with disabilities must be given equal access to any health insurance provided to other employees and cannot be excluded from coverage. An employer can put a limit, or cap, on health-care payments under its group health policy, but the cap must apply equally to all insured employees. Any group health-care plan that makes a disability-based distinction in its benefits violates the ADA (unless the employer can justify its actions under the business necessity defense, as will be discussed shortly).

26. *Rohr v. Salt River Project Agricultural Improvement and Power District*, 555 F.3d 850 (9th Cir. 2009).
27. 42 U.S.C. Sections 12112(d)(3)(B), (C), and 12112(d)(4)(C).
28. *Shoun v. Best Formed Plastics, Inc.*, 28 F.Supp.3d 786 (N.D.Ind. 2014).

Substance Abusers Drug addiction is considered a disability under the ADA because it is a substantially limiting impairment. The act does not protect individuals who are actually using illegal drugs, however. Instead, the ADA protects only persons with *former* drug addictions—those who have completed or are now participating in a supervised drug-rehabilitation program. Individuals who have used drugs casually in the past also are not protected under the act. They are not considered addicts and therefore do not have a disability (addiction).

People suffering from alcoholism are also protected by the ADA. Employers cannot legally discriminate against employees simply because they suffer from alcoholism. Of course, employers can prohibit the use of alcohol in the workplace and require that employees not be under the influence of alcohol while working. Employers can also fire or refuse to hire a person who is an alcoholic if (1) the person poses a *substantial risk of harm* to himself or herself or to others, and (2) the risk cannot be reduced by reasonable accommodation.

21–4 Discrimination Based on Military Status

The Uniformed Services Employment and Reemployment Rights Act (USERRA)[29] prohibits discrimination against persons who have served in the military. In effect, the USERRA makes military service and status a protected class and gives members of this class a right to sue an employer for violations.

21–4a Broad Application and Provisions

The USERRA covers *all* employers, public and private, large and small. Even an employer with only one employee is subject to its provisions.[30] The act also applies to U.S. employers operating in foreign countries.

Under the USERRA, military plaintiffs can sue not only the employer but also individual employees who were acting in an official capacity for the employer. In other words, these employees—supervisors, for instance—can be held personally liable for violations. Additionally, there is no statute of limitations for bringing a lawsuit. The cause of action could have arisen ten weeks or ten years before the suit was filed.

The USERRA specifies that veterans can be terminated from their employment only "for cause." The employer is obligated to give employees a list of all the behaviors that would trigger a for-cause termination.

21–4b *Prima Facie* Case of Discrimination under the USERRA

To establish a *prima facie* case of discrimination under the USERRA, the plaintiff must establish that the employer took an adverse employment action based in part on the employee's connection with the military. The connection to the military may be through the plaintiff's membership, service, or application for service, or it may be through providing testimony or statements concerning the military service of another.[31] If another similarly situated person who did not serve in the military or engage in a protected activity was treated more favorably than the plaintiff, the employer has violated the USERRA.

■ **Case in Point 21.18** Baldo Bello, a staff sergeant with the United States Marine Corps Reserve, was employed by the Village of Skokie as a police officer. Police officers in Skokie normally have nine regular days off (RDOs) per month and eight sick days per year. Skokie officers who are in the reserve receive two weeks of paid leave for annual training each summer, but they do not receive pay for the required weekend military training.

During his first four years as an officer at Skokie, Bello always requested RDOs to cover his weekend training. After that, he started requesting military leave for the two to four days of drills per month, in addition to his nine RDOs. Skokie at first granted Bello military leave for monthly drills but later began to deny the requests.

When Skokie officials told Bello that he needed to schedule his RDOs to cover his weekend military training, Bello filed a suit in a federal district court alleging violations of the USERRA. Skokie filed a motion for summary judgment, which the court denied. The court found that Bello was meeting his employer's legitimate expectations. Bello was therefore entitled to a trial on the issue of whether Skokie had treated his leave requests less favorably than requests from other employees.[32] ■

21–4c Plaintiffs May Be Entitled to Promotions

Under the USERRA, returning service members are to be reemployed in the jobs that they would have attained had

---

29. Pub. L. No. 103-353, 108 Stat. 3149 (1994), codified at 38 U.S.C. Sections 4301 *et seq.*
30. 20 C.F.R. Part 1002.34(a).

31. 38 U.S.C. Section 4311(c).
32. *Bello v. Village of Skokie*, 151 F.Supp.3d 849 (N.D.Ill. 2015). For another USERRA violation, see *O'Farrell v. Department of Defense*, 882 F.3d 1080 (Fed. Cir. 2018).

they not been absent for military service. Reinstatement could affect their seniority, status, pay, and other rights and benefits (such as health-care and pension plans). In essence, this means that if a returning service member sues an employer for violations of the USERRA and is successful, she or he could receive not only damages and reinstatement but also a promotion.

Concept Summary 21.1 reviews the coverage of the employment discrimination laws discussed in this chapter.

21–5 Defenses to Employment Discrimination

The first line of defense for an employer charged with employment discrimination is to assert that the plaintiff has failed to meet his or her initial burden of proving that discrimination occurred. As noted, plaintiffs bringing age discrimination claims may find it difficult to meet this initial burden because they must prove that age discrimination was the reason for their employer's decision.

Once a plaintiff succeeds in proving that discrimination occurred, the burden shifts to the employer to justify the discriminatory practice. Possible justifications include that the discrimination resulted from a business necessity, a bona fide occupational qualification, or a seniority system. In some situations, as noted earlier, an effective

antiharassment policy and prompt remedial action when harassment occurs may shield employers from liability for sexual harassment under Title VII.

21–5a Business Necessity

An employer may defend against a claim of disparate-impact (unintentional) discrimination by asserting that a practice that has a discriminatory effect is a **business necessity.** ■ **Example 21.19** EarthFix, Inc., an international consulting agency, requires its applicants to be fluent in at least two languages. If this requirement is shown to have a discriminatory effect, EarthFix can defend it based on business necessity. That is, the company can argue that its workers must speak more than one language to perform their jobs at the required level of competence. If EarthFix can demonstrate a definite connection between this requirement and job performance, it normally will succeed in this business necessity defense. ■

21–5b Bona Fide Occupational Qualification

Another defense applies when discrimination against a protected class is essential to a job—that is, when a particular trait is a **bona fide occupational qualification (BFOQ).**

Concept Summary 21.1

Coverage of Employment Discrimination Laws

Title VII of the Civil Rights Act	• Prohibits discrimination based on race, color, national origin, religion, and gender (including pregnancy); prohibits sexual harassment. • Applies to employers with fifteen or more employees.
Age Discrimination in Employment Act	• Prohibits discrimination against persons over forty years of age. • Applies to employers with twenty or more employees.
Americans with Disabilities Act (as amended)	• Prohibits discrimination against persons with a mental or physical impairment that substantially limits a major life activity, or who have a record of such an impairment or who are regarded as having such an impairment; prohibits discrimination against persons who are associated with a disabled person. • Applies to employers with fifteen or more employees.
Uniformed Services Employment and Reemployment Rights Act	• Prohibits discrimination against persons who have served in the military. • Applies to all employers, even if they have only one employee.

Note that race, color, and national origin can never be BFOQs.

Generally, courts have restricted the BFOQ defense to situations in which the employee's gender or religion is essential to the job. For instance, a women's clothing store might legitimately hire only female sales attendants if part of an attendant's job involves assisting clients in the store's dressing rooms.

21–5c Seniority Systems

An employer with a history of discrimination may have no members of protected classes in upper-level positions. Nevertheless, the employer may have a defense against a discrimination suit if promotions or other job benefits have been distributed according to a fair *seniority system.* In a **seniority system,** workers with more years of service are promoted first or laid off last.

■ **Case in Point 21.20** Cathalene Johnson, an African American woman, was a senior service agent for Federal Express Corporation (FedEx). After working for FedEx for more than seventeen years, she resigned and filed a suit against the company for discrimination based on race and gender, as well as for violation of the Equal Pay Act. Johnson claimed that FedEx had paid a white male co-worker about two dollars more per hour than she had received for basically the same position. FedEx argued that the man had seniority. He had worked for FedEx for seven years longer, was the most senior employee at the station where Johnson worked, and had been a courier in addition to being a service agent. The court ruled that FedEx's seniority system was fair and provided a defense to Johnson's claims.[33] ■

21–5d After-Acquired Evidence of Employee Misconduct

In some situations, employers have attempted to avoid liability for employment discrimination on the basis of "after-acquired evidence" of an employee's misconduct. After-acquired evidence refers to evidence that the employer discovers after a lawsuit has been filed.

■ **Example 21.21** Pratt Legal Services fires Lucy, who then sues Pratt for employment discrimination. During pretrial investigation, Pratt discovers that Lucy made material misrepresentations on her job application. Had Pratt known of these misrepresentations, it would have had grounds to fire Lucy. ■

After-acquired evidence of wrongdoing cannot shield an employer entirely from liability for employment discrimination. It may, however, be used to limit the amount of damages for which the employer is liable.

21–6 Affirmative Action

Federal statutes and regulations providing for equal opportunity in the workplace were designed to reduce or eliminate discriminatory practices with respect to hiring, retaining, and promoting employees. **Affirmative action** programs go a step further and attempt to "make up" for past patterns of discrimination by giving members of protected classes preferential treatment in hiring or promotion. During the 1960s, all federal and state government agencies, private companies that contracted to do business with the federal government, and institutions that received federal funding were required to implement affirmative action policies.

Title VII of the Civil Rights Act neither requires nor prohibits affirmative action. Thus, most private companies and organizations have not been required to implement affirmative action policies, though many have done so voluntarily. Affirmative action programs have been controversial, however, particularly when they have resulted in reverse discrimination against members of a majority group, such as white males.

21–6a Equal Protection Issues

Because of their inherently discriminatory nature, affirmative action programs may violate the equal protection clause of the Fourteenth Amendment to the U.S. Constitution. Any federal, state, or local government affirmative action program that uses racial or ethnic classifications as the basis for making decisions is subject to strict scrutiny by the courts—the highest standard to meet.

Today, an affirmative action program normally is constitutional only if it attempts to remedy past discrimination and does not make use of quotas or preferences. Furthermore, once such a program has succeeded in the goal of remedying past discrimination, it must be changed or eliminated.

21–6b State Laws Prohibiting Affirmative Action Programs

Some states have enacted laws that prohibit affirmative action programs at public institutions (colleges, universities, and state agencies) within their borders. These states

---

33. *Johnson v. Federal Express Corp.*, 996 F.Supp.2d 302 (M.D.Pa. 2014).

include Arizona, California, Florida, Michigan, Nebraska, New Hampshire, Oklahoma, and Washington. The United States Supreme Court has recognized that states have the power to enact such bans.

■ **Case in Point 21.22** Michigan voters passed an initiative to amend the state's constitution to prohibit publicly funded colleges from granting preferential treatment to any group on the basis of race, sex, color, ethnicity, or national origin. The law also prohibited Michigan from considering race and sex in public hiring and contracting decisions.

A group that supports affirmative action programs in education sued the state's attorney general and others,

claiming that the initiative deprived minority groups of equal protection and violated the U.S. Constitution.

A federal appellate court agreed that the law violated the equal protection clause, but the United States Supreme Court reversed. The Court did not rule on the constitutionality of any specific affirmative action program but held that a state has the inherent power to ban affirmative action within that state.[34] ■

---

34. *Schuette v. Coalition to Defend Affirmative Action, Integration and Immigrant Rights*, 572 U.S. 291, 134 S.Ct. 1623, 188 L.Ed.2d 613 (2014).

Practice and Review: Employment Discrimination

Michelle Lyle, an African American woman, was hired by Warner Brothers Television Productions to be a scriptwriters' assistant for the writers of *Friends*, a popular television series. One of her essential job duties was to type detailed notes for the scriptwriters during brainstorming sessions in which they discussed jokes, dialogue, and story lines. The writers then combed through Lyle's notes after the meetings for script material. During these meetings, the three male scriptwriters told lewd and vulgar jokes and made sexually explicit comments and gestures. They often talked about their personal sexual experiences and fantasies, and some of these conversations were then used in episodes of *Friends*.

During the meetings, Lyle never complained that she found the writers' conduct offensive. After four months, Lyle was fired because she could not type fast enough to keep up with the writers' conversations during the meetings. She filed a suit against Warner Brothers, alleging sexual harassment and claiming that her termination was based on racial discrimination. Using the information presented in the chapter, answer the following questions.

1. Would Lyle's claim of racial discrimination be for intentional (disparate-treatment) or unintentional (disparate-impact) discrimination? Explain.
2. Can Lyle establish a *prima facie* case of racial discrimination? Why or why not?
3. When Lyle was hired, she was told that typing speed was extremely important to the position. At the time, she maintained that she could type eighty words per minute, so she was not given a typing test. It later turned out that Lyle could type only fifty words per minute. What impact might typing speed have on Lyle's lawsuit?
4. Lyle's sexual-harassment claim is based on the hostile working environment created by the writers' sexually offensive conduct at meetings that she was required to attend. The writers, however, argue that their behavior was essential to the "creative process" of writing for *Friends*, a show that routinely contained sexual innuendos and adult humor. Which defense discussed in the chapter might Warner Brothers assert using this argument?

Debate This . . .   *Members of minority groups and women no longer need special legislation to protect them from employment discrimination.*

Terms and Concepts

affirmative action 474
bona fide occupational qualification (BFOQ) 473
business necessity 473
constructive discharge 465

disparate-impact discrimination 458
disparate-treatment discrimination 458
employment discrimination 457
prima facie case 458
protected class 457

seniority system 474
sexual harassment 465
tangible employment action 466

Issue Spotters

1. Ruth is a supervisor for a Subs & Suds restaurant. Tim is a Subs & Suds employee. The owner announces that some employees will be discharged. Ruth tells Tim that if he has sex with her, he can keep his job. Is this sexual harassment? Why or why not? (See *Title VII of the Civil Rights Act.*)

2. Koko, a person with a disability, applies for a job at Lively Sales Corporation for which she is well qualified, but she is rejected. Lively continues to seek applicants and eventually fills the position with a person who does not have a disability. Could Koko succeed in a suit against Lively for discrimination? Explain. (See *Discrimination Based on Disability.*)

- **Check your answers to the Issue Spotters against the answers provided in Appendix B at the end of this text.**

Business Scenarios and Case Problems

21–1. Title VII Violations. Discuss fully whether either of the following actions would constitute a violation of Title VII of the Civil Rights Act, as amended. (See *Title VII of the Civil Rights Act.*)

(a) Tennington, Inc., is a consulting firm with ten employees. These employees travel on consulting jobs in seven states. Tennington has an employment record of hiring only white males.

(b) Novo Films is making a movie about Africa and needs to employ approximately one hundred extras for this picture. To hire these extras, Novo advertises in all major newspapers in Southern California. The ad states that only African Americans need apply.

21–2. Religious Discrimination. Gina Gomez, a devout Roman Catholic, worked for Sam's Department Stores, Inc., in Phoenix, Arizona. Sam's considered Gomez a productive employee because her sales exceeded $200,000 per year. At the time, the store gave its managers the discretion to grant unpaid leave to employees but prohibited vacations or leave during the holiday season—October through December. Gomez felt that she had a "calling" to go on a "pilgrimage" in October to a location in Bosnia where some persons claimed to have had visions of the Virgin Mary. The Catholic Church had not designated the site an official pilgrimage site, the visions were not expected to be stronger in October, and tours were available at other times. The store managers denied Gomez's request for leave, but she had a nonrefundable ticket and left anyway. Sam's terminated her employment, and she could not find another job. Can Gomez establish a *prima facie* case of religious discrimination? Explain. (See *Title VII of the Civil Rights Act.*)

21–3. Spotlight on Dress Code Policies—Discrimination Based on Gender. Burlington Coat Factory Warehouse, Inc., had a dress code that required male salesclerks to wear business attire consisting of slacks, shirt, and a necktie. Female salesclerks, by contrast, were required to wear a smock so that customers could readily identify them. Karen O'Donnell and other female employees refused to wear smocks. Instead they reported to work in business attire and were suspended. After numerous suspensions, the female employees were fired for violating Burlington's dress code policy. All other conditions of employment, including salary, hours, and benefits, were the same for female and male employees. Was the dress code policy discriminatory? Why or why not? [*O'Donnell v. Burlington Coat Factory Warehouse, Inc.*, 656 F.Supp. 263 (S.D. Ohio 1987)] (See *Title VII of the Civil Rights Act.*)

21–4. Sexual Harassment by a Co-Worker. Billie Bradford worked for the Kentucky Department of Community Based Services (DCBS). One of Bradford's co-workers, Lisa Stander, routinely engaged in extreme sexual behavior (such as touching herself and making crude comments) in Bradford's presence. Bradford and others regularly complained about Stander's conduct to their supervisor, Angie Taylor. Rather than resolve the problem, Taylor nonchalantly told Stander to stop, encouraged Bradford to talk to Stander, and suggested that Stander was just having fun. Assuming that Bradford was subjected to a hostile work environment, could DCBS be liable? Why or why not? [*Bradford v. Department of Community Based Services*, 2012 WL 360032 (E.D.Ky. 2012)] (See *Title VII of the Civil Rights Act.*)

21–5. Age Discrimination. Paul Rangel was a sales professional for the pharmaceutical company sanofi-aventis U.S. LLC (S-A). For twenty years, Rangel had satisfactory performance reviews until S-A issued new "Expectations" guidelines that included sales call quotas and other standards that he failed to meet. After two years of negative performance reviews, Rangel—who was then more than forty years old—was terminated. The termination was part of a nationwide reduction of all sales professionals who had not met the "Expectations" guidelines, including younger workers. Did S-A engage in age discrimination? Discuss. [*Rangel v. sanofi aventis U.S., LLC*, 507 Fed. Appx. 786 (10th Cir. 2013)] (See *Discrimination Based on Age.*)

21–6. Discrimination Based on Disability. Cynthia Horn worked for Knight Facilities Management–GM, Inc., in Detroit, Michigan, as a janitor. When Horn developed a sensitivity to cleaning products, her physician gave her a "no exposure to cleaning solutions" restriction. Knight discussed possible accommodations with Horn. She suggested that restrooms be eliminated from her cleaning route or that she be provided with a respirator. Knight explained that she would be exposed to cleaning solutions in any situation and concluded that there was no work available within her physician's restriction. Has Knight violated the Americans with Disabilities Act by failing to provide Horn with the requested accommodations? Explain. [*Horn v. Knight Facilities Management–GM, Inc.*, 556 Fed.Appx. 452 (6th Cir. 2014)] (See *Discrimination Based on Disability*.)

21–7. Business Case Problem with Sample Answer—Sexual Harassment. Jamel Blanton was a male employee at a Pizza Hut restaurant operated by Newton Associates, Inc., in San Antonio, Texas. Blanton was subjected to sexual and racial harassment by the general manager, who was female. Newton had a clear, straightforward antidiscrimination policy and complaint procedure. The policy provided that in such a situation, an employee should complain to the harasser's supervisor. Blanton alerted a shift leader and an assistant manager about the harassment, but they were subordinate to the general manager and did not report the harassment to higher-level management. When Blanton finally complained to a manager with authority over the general manager, the employer investigated and fired the general manager within four days. Blanton filed a suit in a federal district court against Newton, seeking to impose liability on the employer for the general manager's actions. What is Newton's best defense? Discuss. [*Blanton v. Newton Associates, Inc.*, 593 Fed.Appx. 389 (5th Cir. 2015)] (See *Title VII of the Civil Rights Act*.)

• **For a sample answer to Problem 21–7, go to Appendix C at the end of this text.**

21–8. Discrimination Based on Disability. Dennis Wallace was a deputy sheriff for Stanislaus County, California, when he injured his left knee. After surgery, he was subject to limits on prolonged standing, walking, and running. The county assigned him to work as a bailiff. The sergeants who supervised him rated his performance above average. Less than a year later, without consulting those supervisors, the county

placed him on an unpaid leave of absence, under the mistaken belief that he could not safely perform the essential functions of the job. Wallace filed an action in a California state court against the county, alleging discrimination based on disability. Under state law, discriminatory intent is shown by evidence that an actual or perceived disability was a "substantial motivating factor or reason" for an employer's adverse employment action. An employee is not required to show that the action was motivated by animosity or ill will. Could Wallace likely prove the "substantial motivating factor or reason" element? Explain. [*Wallace v. County of Stanislaus*, 245 Cal.App.4th 109, 199 Cal.Rptr.3d 462 (5 Dist. 2016)] (See *Discrimination Based on Disability*.)

21–9. A Question of Ethics—The IDDR Approach and Unintentional Discrimination. *McLane Company is a supply-chain services company that distributes goods to retailers. McLane requires employees with physically demanding jobs to have physical evaluations, both when they start work and when they return after medical leave. After working in a physically demanding job for McLane for eight years, Damiana Ochoa took maternity leave. When she returned to work, she failed the physical evaluation and was fired. She filed a discrimination complaint with the Equal Employment Opportunity Commission (EEOC). The agency issued a subpoena—an order to appear in court—seeking the names and contact information of McLane employees who had been asked to have evaluations throughout the company's national operations.* [McLane Co. v. Equal Employment Opportunity Commission, __ U.S. __, 137 S.Ct. 1159, 197 L.Ed.2d 500 (2017)] (See Title VII of the Civil Rights Act.)

(a) On what legal ground might McLane legitimately refuse to comply with the EEOC's subpoena? What practical factors could affect the choice not to comply? Discuss.

(b) Using the IDDR approach, consider whether McLane has an ethical duty to comply with the subpoena.

Time-Limited Group Assignment

21–10. Racial Discrimination. Two African American plaintiffs sued the producers of the reality television series *The Bachelor* and *The Bachelorette* for racial discrimination. The plaintiffs claimed that the shows had never featured persons of color in the lead roles. The plaintiffs also alleged that the producers did not provide people of color who auditioned for the lead roles with the same opportunities to compete as white people who auditioned. (See *Title VII of the Civil Rights Act*.)

(a) The first group will assess whether the plaintiffs can establish a *prima facie* case of disparate-treatment discrimination.

(b) The second group will consider whether the plaintiffs can establish disparate-impact discrimination.

(c) The third group will assume that the plaintiffs established a *prima facie* case and that the burden has shifted to the employer to articulate a legal reason for not hiring the plaintiffs. What legitimate reasons might the employer assert for not hiring the plaintiffs in this situation? Should the law require television producers to hire persons of color for lead roles in reality television shows? Discuss.

Chapter 22

Immigration and Labor Law

Immigration law and policy in the United States are topics of significant national debate. To a substantial degree, the immigration debate concerns the nation's employment environment. For this reason, Congress enacted legislation in the late twentieth century to prohibit employers from hiring illegal immigrants. Today, immigration law has evolved into a myriad of complex rules that employers must follow.

The origin of many of the laws pertaining to the workplace can be traced back to the Industrial Revolution of the nineteenth century. During the Industrial Revolution, fewer Americans were self-employed than ever before, and employers generally set the terms of employment. Moreover, with increasing industrialization, the size of workplaces and the number of on-the-job hazards increased. Workers came to believe that to counter the power and freedom of their employers and to protect themselves, they needed to organize into unions.

Beginning in 1932, Congress enacted a number of statutes that generally increased employees' rights. At the heart of these rights is the right to join unions and engage in *collective bargaining* with management to negotiate working conditions, salaries, and benefits for a group of workers. This chapter also examines strikes, lockouts, and the labor practices that are considered unfair under federal law.

22–1 Immigration Law

The United States did not have any laws restricting immigration until the late nineteenth century. Immigration law has become increasingly important in recent years, however. An estimated 12 million undocumented immigrants now live in the United States, and many of them came to find jobs. Because U.S. employers face serious penalties if they hire undocumented workers, it is necessary for businesspersons to understand immigration laws. The most important laws affecting immigration in the context of employment are the Immigration Reform and Control Act (IRCA)[1] and the Immigration Act.[2]

22–1a The Immigration Reform and Control Act (IRCA)

When the IRCA was enacted in 1986, it provided amnesty to certain groups of aliens living illegally in the United States at the time. It also established a system that sanctions employers that hire immigrants who lack work authorization.

The IRCA makes it illegal to hire, recruit, or refer for a fee someone not authorized to work in this country. Through Immigration and Customs Enforcement officers, the federal government conducts random compliance audits and engages in enforcement actions against employers who hire undocumented workers.

I-9 Employment Verification To comply with IRCA requirements, an employer must perform **I-9 verifications** for new hires, including those hired as "contractors" or "day workers" if they work under the employer's direct supervision. Form I-9, Employment Eligibility Verification, which is available from U.S. Citizenship and Immigration Services,[3] must be completed *within three days* of a worker's commencement of employment. The three-day period allows the employer to check the form's accuracy, and to review and verify documents establishing the prospective worker's identity and eligibility for employment in the United States.

---

1. 29 U.S.C. Section 1802.
2. This act amended various provisions of the Immigration and Nationality Act, 8 U.S.C. Sections 1101 *et seq.*

3. U.S. Citizenship and Immigration Services is a federal agency that is part of the U.S. Department of Homeland Security.

Documentation Requirements The employer must declare, under penalty of perjury, that an employee produced documents establishing his or her identity and legal employability. A U.S. passport establishing the person's citizenship is acceptable documentation. So is a document authorizing a foreign citizen to work in the United States, such as a permanent resident card.

Most legal actions alleging violations of I-9 rules are brought against employees who provide false information or documentation. If the employee enters false information on the I-9 form or presents false documentation, the employer can fire the worker, who then may be subject to deportation. Nevertheless, employers must be honest when verifying an employee's documentation. If an employer "should have known" that the worker was unauthorized, the employer has violated the rules.

Enforcement The largest investigative arm of the U.S. Department of Homeland Security is U.S. Immigration and Customs Enforcement (ICE). ICE has a general inspection program that conducts random compliance audits. Other audits may occur if the agency receives a written complaint alleging that an employer has committed violations. Government inspections include a review of an employer's file of I-9 forms. The government does not need a subpoena or a warrant to conduct such an inspection.

If an investigation reveals a possible violation, ICE will bring an administrative action and issue a Notice of Intent to Fine, which sets out the charges against the employer. The employer has a right to a hearing on the enforcement action if it files a request within thirty days. This hearing is conducted before an administrative law judge, and the employer has a right to counsel and to discovery. The typical defense in such actions is good faith or substantial compliance with the documentation provisions.

Penalties An employer who violates the law by hiring an unauthorized worker is subject to substantial penalties. The employer can be fined up to $2,200 for each unauthorized employee for a first offense, $5,000 per employee for a second offense, and up to $11,000 for subsequent offenses. Employers who have engaged in a "pattern or practice of violations" are subject to criminal penalties, which include additional fines and imprisonment for up to ten years. A company can also be barred from future government contracts.

In determining the penalty, ICE considers the seriousness of the violation and the employer's past compliance. ICE regulations also identify factors that will mitigate (lessen) or aggravate (increase) the penalty under certain circumstances. An employer that cooperates in the investigation, for instance, may receive a lesser penalty than an uncooperative employer.

22–1b The Immigration Act

Often, U.S. businesses find that they cannot hire enough domestic workers with specialized skills. For this reason, U.S. immigration laws have long made provisions for businesses to hire specially qualified foreign workers.

The Immigration Act of 1990 placed caps on the number of visas (entry permits) that can be issued to immigrants each year, including employment-based visas. Employment-based visas may be classified as permanent (immigrant) or temporary (nonimmigrant). Employers who wish to hire workers with either type of visa must comply with detailed government regulations.[4]

I-551 Permanent Resident Card A company seeking to hire a noncitizen worker may do so if the worker is self-authorized. To be self-authorized, a worker must either be a lawful permanent resident or have a valid temporary Employment Authorization Document. A lawful permanent resident can prove his or her status to an employer by presenting an **I-551 Permanent Resident Card,** known as a green card, or a properly stamped foreign passport.

Many immigrant workers are not already self-authorized, and an employer that wishes to hire them can attempt to obtain labor certification, or green cards, for them. A limited number of new green cards are issued each year. A green card can be obtained only for a person who is being hired for a permanent, full-time position. (A separate authorization system provides for the temporary entry and hiring of nonimmigrant visa workers.)

To gain authorization for hiring a foreign worker, an employer must show that no U.S. worker is qualified, willing, and able to take the job. The government has detailed regulations governing the advertising of positions as well as the certification process. Any U.S. applicants who meet the stated job qualifications must be interviewed for the position. The employer must also be able to show that the qualifications required for the job are a business necessity.

The H-1B Visa Program The most common and controversial visa program today is the H-1B visa system. To obtain an H1-B visa, the potential employee must be qualified in a "specialty occupation," meaning that

---

4. The most relevant regulations can be found at 20 C.F.R. Part 655 (for temporary employment) and 20 C.F.R. Part 656 (for permanent employment).

the individual has highly specialized knowledge and has attained a bachelor's or higher degree or its equivalent. Individuals with H-1B visas can stay in the United States for three to six years and can work only for the sponsoring employer.

The recipients of these visas include numerous high-tech workers. A maximum of sixty-five thousand H-1B visas are set aside each year for new immigrants. That limit is typically reached within the first few weeks of the year. Consequently, technology companies often complain that Congress needs to expand the number of H-1B visas available, to encourage the best and the brightest minds to work in the United States. Critics of the H-1B visa program, however, believe that employers are sometimes using it to replace American workers with lower-paid foreign labor.

Labor Certification   An employer who wishes to submit an H-1B application must first file a Labor Condition Application on a form known as ETA 9035. The employer must agree to provide a wage level at least equal to the wages offered to other individuals with similar experience and qualifications. The employer must also show that the hiring will not adversely affect other workers similarly employed. The employer is required to inform U.S. workers of the intent to hire a foreign worker by posting the form. The U.S. Department of Labor reviews the applications and may reject them for omissions or inaccuracies.

H-2, O, L, and E Visas   Other specialty temporary visas are available for other categories of employees. H-2 visas provide for workers performing agricultural labor of a seasonal nature. O visas provide entry for persons who have "extraordinary ability in the sciences, arts, education, business, or athletics," which has been demonstrated by sustained national or international acclaim. L visas allow a company's foreign managers or executives to work inside the United States. E visas permit the entry of certain foreign investors or entrepreneurs.

22–1c State Immigration Legislation

Until 2010, federal law exclusively governed immigration and the treatment of illegal immigrants. Then Arizona enacted a law that required Arizona law enforcement officials to identify and charge immigrants in Arizona who were there illegally, potentially leading to the immigrants' deportation. Among other things, that law required immigrants to carry their papers at all times and allowed police to check a person's immigration status during any law enforcement action.

In *Arizona v. United States*,[5] the United States Supreme Court upheld the controversial "show-me-your-papers" provision, which requires police to check the immigration status of persons stopped for other violations. All other provisions of Arizona's law were struck down as unconstitutional violations of the supremacy clause. The Supreme Court's decision does not prohibit states from enacting laws related to immigration, but it does set some limits.

22–2 Federal Labor Laws

Federal labor laws governing union-employer relations have developed considerably since the first law was enacted in 1932. Initially, the laws were concerned with protecting the rights and interests of workers. Subsequent legislation placed some restraints on unions and granted rights to employers. We look here at four major federal statutes regulating union-employer relations.

22–2a Norris-LaGuardia Act

Congress protected peaceful strikes, picketing, and boycotts in 1932 in the Norris-LaGuardia Act.[6] The statute restricted the power of federal courts to issue injunctions against unions engaged in peaceful strikes. In effect, this act declared a national policy permitting employees to organize.

22–2b National Labor Relations Act

One of the foremost statutes regulating labor is the 1935 National Labor Relations Act (NLRA).[7] This act established the rights of employees to engage in collective bargaining and to strike.

Unfair Labor Practices   The NLRA specifically defined a number of employer practices as unfair to labor:

1. Interference with the efforts of employees to form, join, or assist labor organizations or to engage in concerted activities for their mutual aid or protection.
2. An employer's domination of a labor organization or contribution of financial or other support to it.
3. Discrimination in the hiring of or the awarding of tenure to employees for reason of union affiliation.

---

5. 567 U.S. 387, 132 S.Ct. 2492, 183 L.Ed.2d 351 (2012).
6. 29 U.S.C. Sections 101 *et seq.*
7. 29 U.S.C. Sections 151 *et seq.*

4. Discrimination against employees for filing charges under the act or giving testimony under the act.

5. Refusal to bargain collectively with the duly designated representative of the employees.

The National Labor Relations Board The NLRA created the National Labor Relations Board (NLRB) to oversee union elections and to prevent employers from engaging in unfair and illegal union activities and unfair labor practices.

The NLRB has the authority to investigate employees' charges of unfair labor practices and to file complaints against employers in response to these charges. When violations are found, the NLRB may issue a **cease-and-desist order** compelling the employer to stop engaging in the unfair practices. Cease-and-desist orders can be enforced by a federal appellate court if necessary. After the NLRB rules on claims of unfair labor practices, its decision may be appealed to a federal court.

■ **Case in Point 22.1** Roundy's, Inc., which operates a chain of stores in Wisconsin, became involved in a dispute with a local construction union. When union members started distributing "extremely unflattering" flyers outside the stores, Roundy's ejected them from the property. The NLRB filed a complaint against Roundy's for unfair labor practices. An administrative law judge ruled that Roundy's had violated the law by discriminating against the union, and a federal appellate court affirmed. It is an unfair labor practice for an employer to prohibit union members from distributing flyers outside a store when it allows nonunion members to do so.[8] ■

Good Faith Bargaining Under the NLRA, employers and unions have a duty to bargain in good faith. Bargaining over certain subjects is mandatory, and a party's refusal to bargain over these subjects is an unfair labor practice that can be reported to the NLRB. For instance, bargaining is mandatory for subjects relating to wages or working hours.

Workers Protected by the NLRA To be protected under the NLRA, an individual must be an employee or a job applicant. (If job applicants were not covered, the NLRA's ban on discrimination in regard to hiring would mean little.) Additionally, individuals who are hired by a union to organize a company (union organizers) are to be considered employees of the company for NLRA purposes.[9]

Even a temporary worker hired through an employment agency might qualify for protection under the NLRA. ■ **Case in Point 22.2** Matthew Faush was an African American employee of Labor Ready, which provides temporary employees to businesses. Faush was assigned to a job stocking shelves at a Tuesday Morning store in Pennsylvania. After he was fired by Tuesday Morning, Faush filed a suit alleging discrimination. Tuesday Morning argued that Faush was not its employee. A federal court, however, found that the NLRA's protections may extend to temporary workers and that Faush was entitled to a trial.[10] ■

22–2c Labor-Management Relations Act

The Labor-Management Relations Act (LMRA, or Taft-Hartley Act)[11] was passed in 1947 to prohibit certain unfair union practices. For instance, the act outlawed the **closed shop**—a firm that requires union membership as a condition of employment. The act preserved the legality of the union shop, however. A **union shop** does not require union membership as a prerequisite for employment but can, and usually does, require that workers join the union after a specified time on the job.

The LMRA also prohibited unions from refusing to bargain with employers, engaging in certain types of picketing, and *featherbedding* (causing employers to hire more employees than necessary). In addition, the act allowed individual states to pass **right-to-work laws**—laws making it illegal for union membership to be required for *continued* employment in any establishment. Thus, union shops are technically illegal in the twenty-seven states that have right-to-work laws.

22–2d Labor-Management Reporting and Disclosure Act

The Labor-Management Reporting and Disclosure Act (LMRDA)[12] established an employee bill of rights and reporting requirements for union activities. The act also outlawed **hot-cargo agreements,** in which employers voluntarily agree with unions not to handle, use, or deal in goods of other employers produced by nonunion employees.

The LMRDA strictly regulates unions' internal business procedures, including elections. For instance, it requires unions to hold regularly scheduled elections of

8. *Roundy's, Inc. v. NLRB*, 674 F.3d 638 (7th Cir. 2012).
9. See the United States Supreme Court's landmark decision in *NLRB v. Town & Country Electric, Inc.*, 516 U.S. 85, 116 S.Ct. 450, 133 L.Ed.2d 371 (1995).

10. *Faush v. Tuesday Morning, Inc.*, 808 F.3d 208 (3d Cir. 2015).
11. 29 U.S.C. Sections 141 *et seq.*
12. 29 U.S.C. Sections 401 *et seq.*

officers using secret ballots. Ex-convicts are prohibited from holding union office. Moreover, union officials are accountable for union property and funds. Members have the right to attend and to participate in union meetings, to nominate officers, and to vote in most union proceedings.

22-3 Union Organization

Typically, the first step in organizing a union at a particular firm is to have the workers sign authorization cards. An **authorization card** usually states that the worker desires to have a certain union, such as the United Auto Workers, represent the workforce.

If a majority of the workers sign authorization cards, the union organizers (unionizers) present the cards to the employer and ask for formal recognition of the union. The employer is not required to recognize the union at this point, but it may do so voluntarily on a showing of majority support.

22-3a Union Elections

If the employer does not voluntarily recognize the union—or if less than a majority of the workers sign authorization cards—the union organizers can petition for an election. The organizers present the authorization cards to the NLRB with a petition to hold an election on unionization. For an election to be held, they must demonstrate that at least 30 percent of the workers to be represented support a union or an election.

Appropriate Bargaining Unit Not every group of workers can form a single union. The proposed union must represent an *appropriate bargaining unit*. One key requirement is a *mutuality of interest* among all the workers to be represented by the union. Factors considered in determining whether there is a mutuality of interest include the similarity of the jobs of the workers to be unionized and their physical location.

NLRB Rules Expedite Elections NLRB rules that took effect in 2015 expedite union elections by allowing as little as ten days to pass between the filing of a petition and the ensuing election. In the past, elections were held an average of thirty-eight days after a petition was filed. The shorter timeline favors unions because it gives

employers less time to respond to organizing campaigns, which unions often spend months preparing.

The NLRB requires that a company hold a pre-election hearing within eight days after it receives a petition for an organizing election. On the day before the hearing, the company must also submit a "statement of position" laying out every argument it intends to make against the union. Any argument that the company does not include in its position paper can be excluded from evidence at the hearing. Once the hearing is held, an election can be scheduled right away.

Voting If an election is held, the NLRB supervises the election and ensures secret voting and voter eligibility. If the proposed union receives majority support in a fair election, the NLRB certifies the union as the bargaining representative for the employees.

22-3b Union Election Campaigns

Many disputes between labor and management arise during union election campaigns. Generally, the employer has control over unionizing activities that take place on company property and during working hours. Thus, the employer may limit the campaign activities of union supporters as long as it has a legitimate business reason for doing so. The employer may also reasonably limit when and where union solicitation may occur in the workplace, provided that the employer is not discriminating against the union. (Can union organizers use company e-mail during campaigns? See this chapter's *Managerial Strategy* feature for a discussion of this topic.)

■ **Example 22.3** A union is seeking to organize clerks at a department store owned by Amanti Enterprises. Amanti can prohibit all union solicitation in areas of the store open to the public because the unionizing activities could interfere with the store's business. It can also restrict union-related activities to coffee breaks and lunch hours. If Amanti allows solicitation for charitable causes in the workplace, however, it may not prohibit union solicitation. ■

An employer may campaign among its workers against the union, but the NLRB carefully monitors and regulates the tactics used by management. If the employer issues threats ("If the union wins, you'll all be fired") or engages in other unfair labor practices, the NLRB may certify the union even though the union lost the election. Alternatively, the NLRB may ask a court to order a new election.

Managerial Strategy

Union Organizing Using a Company's E-Mail System

When union organizers start an organizing drive, there are certain restrictions on what they can do, particularly within the workplace. Both employers and employees must comply with Section 7 of the National Labor Relations Act (NLRA).

Protected Concerted Activities

Under Section 7, employees have certain rights to communicate among themselves. Section 7 states, "Employees shall have the right to self-organization, . . . and to engage in other concerted activities for the purpose of collective bargaining or other mutual aid or protection. . . ."

What about communication via e-mail? Can union organizers use a company-operated e-mail system for organizing purposes? Companies typically provide e-mail systems so that employees can communicate with outsiders and among themselves as part of their jobs. Generally, company policies have prohibited the use of company-owned and operated e-mail systems for other than job-related communications. Some union organizers have challenged this prohibition.

The NLRB's Perspective Evolves

The first major case concerning this issue was decided by the National Labor Relations Board (NLRB) in 2007. The NLRB allowed an employer's written policy prohibiting the use of a company-provided e-mail system for solicitations not related to work. Seven years later,

however, the NLRB reversed its position, finding "that employee use of e-mail for statutorily protected communications on non-working time must presumptively be permitted by employers who have chosen to give employees access to their e-mail systems."[a] The NLRB argued that its earlier decision had failed to adequately protect "employees' rights under the NLRA." The board also stated that it had a responsibility "to adapt the Act to the changing patterns of industrial life."

The rules today are clear. Once an organizing election is scheduled, a company must turn over all telephone numbers and home and e-mail addresses of the company's employees to union organizers within two days. The organizers can then communicate with employees via the company's e-mail system.

Business Questions

1. *Employees meeting around the water cooler or coffee machine have always had the right to discuss work-related matters. Is an employer-provided e-mail system or social media outlet simply a digital water cooler? Why or why not?*

2. *If your company instituted a policy stating that employees should "think carefully about 'friending' co-workers," would that policy be lawful? Why or why not?*

a. *Purple Communications, Inc. and Communication Workers of America, AFL-CIO*, Cases 21-CA-095151, 21-RC-091531, and 21-RC-091584, March 16, 2015.

Whether an employer violated its employees' rights under the National Labor Relations Act during a

union election campaign was at issue in the following case.

Case Analysis 22.1

Contemporary Cars, Inc. v. National Labor Relations Board

United States Court of Appeals, Seventh Circuit, 814 F.3d 859 (2016).

In the Language of the Court

HAMILTON, Circuit Judge.

* * * *

* * * Contemporary Cars, Inc., * * * sells and services cars in Maitland, Florida. Bob Berryhill, the dealership's general manager, is responsible for the dealership's overall operations. * * * AutoNation owns the dealership, as well

as over 200 other dealerships throughout the United States.

This case focuses on the dealership's service department [which the dealership had previously split into three teams].

* * * The International Association of Machinists began a campaign * * * to organize the service technicians.

* * * The technicians talked among themselves and held off-site meetings.

* * * *

* * * The union filed its representation petition. The [National Labor Relations Board] approved the proposed bargaining unit, and an election was scheduled.

Case 22.1 Continues

In the weeks before the election, Berryhill and AutoNation vice president * * * Brian Davis held group [and individual] meetings [with the technicians]. * * * One week before the election, * * * Berryhill * * * announced that the dealership was working on fixing problems the technicians had and that he was replacing two team leaders, [Andre] Grobler and Oudit Manbahal, with new team leaders.

* * * Technician Anthony Roberts * * * was then playing a leading role in the union organizing. * * * About a week before the union election, the dealership laid off Roberts, though Roberts had a higher skill rating, more hours, and more seniority than many other technicians.

* * * * The technicians voted in favor of unionizing.

* * * After the election, the dealership challenged the certification of the union as the exclusive representative of a bargaining unit consisting of service technicians. * * * The [National Labor Relations] Board affirmed the certification.

* * * The Board * * * filed a complaint alleging that the dealership and AutoNation had violated * * * the National Labor Relations Act. * * * An administrative law judge found * * * that the dealership and AutoNation had indeed violated the Act by interfering with their employees' protected rights to engage in concerted activity and to organize a union [and] by firing Anthony Roberts due to anti-union animus [hostility]. [The judge ordered the dealership to cease its interference with its employees' rights and to reinstate Roberts. The judge also ordered AutoNation to post a notice at all of its dealerships that it was rescinding the no-solicitation rule.] The Board affirmed the * * * order.

The dealership and AutoNation petitioned [the U.S. Court of Appeals for Seventh Circuit] for judicial review. [The NLRB cross-petitioned for enforcement of the order.]

* * * *

The administrative law judge found, and the Board affirmed, that the

dealership and AutoNation in a number of instances acted unlawfully to frustrate their employees' protected rights to engage in concerted activity and to organize a union.

* * * *

* * * The dealership violated [the Act] in the run-up to the election by coercively creating an impression of surveillance of union activity, interrogating employees about union activity, and soliciting and promising to remedy employee grievances.

* * * *

[Team Leader] Grobler created a coercive impression of surveillance when he commented on technician Juan Cazorla's attendance of union meetings.

* * * Grobler asked [Cazorla] why he was in such a rush to leave work * * *, suggesting that Cazorla had "that meeting" to go to. Cazorla pretended not to know what Grobler was talking about, although he was in fact rushing to get to a union meeting. Again [on a different occasion] Grobler commented to Cazorla that he had "better rush" since he had a meeting * * *. It would have been reasonable for Cazorla to infer from Grobler's comments that his union activities were under management surveillance.

* * * *

* * * Berryhill coercively interrogated employees [when he] called them individually into his office and asked them about union activity. The dealership's service director was also present. * * * The setting of the meetings in Berryhill's office, Berryhill's and the director's positions of authority, and the fact that each technician was alone and outnumbered by managers all support the finding of coercion.

* * * *

* * * At the * * * meetings, Berryhill asked the technicians how the dealership could improve. * * * Berryhill [stated] that he was "working on" the problems and "in progress" on the solutions. * * * The * * * meetings also included inquiries about the union effort. * * * This was an effort to frustrate the union

organizing drive by soliciting and at least implicitly promising to adjust grievances.

* * * *

* * * AutoNation vice president * * * Davis coercively interrogated a * * * technician, Tumeshwar Persaud * * *. Davis * * * asked him how he felt about the union election. * * * The question forced Persaud, who had not previously disclosed his union support, either to disclose his own union sympathies or to report on his perception of his fellow employees' union support.

* * * Davis held a meeting with employees at which he solicited employee complaints and, upon hearing that management had been unresponsive to employee complaints in the past, said that employees could call him or talk to him at any time. This meeting was part of a series of * * * meetings that management held in the run-up to the union election. * * * Davis was implicitly promising to remedy grievances with the goal of frustrating the union effort.

* * * *

* * * AutoNation * * * promulgated [publicized] an overly broad no-solicitation policy in the employee handbook used at all of its facilities. * * * AutoNation's policy prohibited any solicitation on AutoNation property at any time. * * * *The policy * * * amounted to an unfair labor practice because of the likelihood it would chill protected concerted activity.* [Emphasis added.]

* * * *

* * * The dealership's discharge of Anthony Roberts * * * a week before the election was motivated by anti-union animus.

* * * *

* * * Berryhill's identification of Roberts as a troublemaker and instigator of the organizational campaign established that anti-union animus was a substantial factor motivating Roberts's layoff. * * * The dealership's stated reason for firing Roberts—that he lacked sufficient electronic diagnostic skills—failed to establish that Roberts would have been laid off in the absence of anti-union animus. * * * Roberts was

more productive and had a higher skill rating than many technicians who were retained.

* * * *

Substantial evidence and a reasonable basis in law support the Board's order and the administrative law judge's order to the extent affirmed by the Board. We

DENY the dealership and AutoNation's petition for review and ENFORCE the Board's order in its entirety.

Legal Reasoning Questions

1. What might the dealership have asserted in defense to the charge that its actions violated its employees' rights?

2. After the election but before the union was certified, the dealership laid off four technicians and cut others' pay without bargaining with the union, claiming economic hard times. Did these steps constitute an unfair labor practice? Discuss.

3. What could the employer have done to avoid the charge in this case?

22–3c Collective Bargaining

If the NLRB certifies a union, the union becomes the *exclusive bargaining representative* of the workers. The central legal right of a union is to engage in collective bargaining on the members' behalf. **Collective bargaining** is the process by which labor and management negotiate the terms and conditions of employment. Collective bargaining allows the representatives elected by union members to speak on behalf of the members at the bargaining table. Subjects for negotiation may include workplace safety, employee discounts, health-care plans, pension funds, and apprentice and scholarship programs.

Once an employer and a union sit down at the conference table, they must negotiate in good faith and make a reasonable effort to come to an agreement. They are not obligated to reach an agreement. They must, however, approach the negotiations with the idea that an agreement is possible. Both parties may engage in hard bargaining, but the bargaining process itself must be geared to reaching a compromise—not avoiding a compromise.

Although good faith is a matter of subjective intent, a party's actions can be used to evaluate the party's good or bad faith. Exhibit 22–1 illustrates some differences between good faith and bad faith bargaining. If an employer (or a union) refuses to bargain in good faith without justification, it has committed an unfair labor practice.

Exhibit 22–1 Good Faith versus Bad Faith in Collective Bargaining

Good Faith Bargaining	Bad Faith Bargaining
1. Negotiating with the belief that an agreement is possible	1. Excessive delaying tactics
2. Seriously considering the other side's positions	2. Insistence on unreasonable contract terms
3. Making reasonable proposals	3. Rejecting a proposal without offering a counterproposal
4. Being willing to compromise	4. Engaging in a campaign among workers to undermine the union
5. Sending bargainers who have the authority to enter into agreements for the company	5. Constantly shifting positions on disputed contract terms
	6. Sending bargainers who lack the authority to commit the company to a contract

22–4 Strikes and Lockouts

Even when labor and management have bargained in good faith, they may be unable to reach a final agreement. When extensive collective bargaining has been conducted and an impasse results, the union may call a strike against the employer to pressure it into making concessions.

In a **strike,** the unionized employees leave their jobs and refuse to work. The workers also typically picket the workplace, standing outside the facility with signs stating their complaints. A strike is an extreme action. Striking workers lose their rights to be paid, and management loses production and may lose customers when orders cannot be filled.

Most strikes take the form of "economic strikes," which are initiated because the union wants a better contract. ■ **Example 22.4** Teachers in Eagle Point, Oregon, engage in an economic strike after contract negotiations with the school district fail to bring an agreement on pay, working hours, and subcontracting jobs. The unionized teachers picket outside the school building. Classes are canceled for a few weeks until the district can find substitute teachers who will fill in during the strike. ■

22–4a The Right to Strike

The right to strike is guaranteed by the NLRA, within limits. Strike activities, such as picketing, are protected by the free speech guarantee of the First Amendment to the U.S. Constitution. Persons who are not employees have a right to participate in picketing an employer. The NLRA also gives workers the right to refuse to cross a picket line of fellow workers engaged in a lawful strike. Employers are permitted to hire replacement workers to substitute for the striking workers.

22–4b Illegal Strikes

In the following situations, the conduct of the strikers may cause the strikes to be illegal:

1. *Violent strikes.* The use of violence (including the threat of violence) against management employees or substitute workers is illegal.
2. *Massed picketing.* If the strikers form a barrier and deny management or other nonunion workers access to the plant, the strike is illegal.
3. *Sit-down strikes.* Strikes in which employees simply stay in the plant without working are illegal.
4. *No-strike clause.* A strike may be illegal if it contravenes a no-strike clause that was in the previous collective bargaining agreement between the employer and the union.

5. *Secondary boycotts.* A **secondary boycott** is an illegal strike that is directed against someone other than the strikers' employer, such as companies that sell materials to the employer. ■ **Example 22.5** The unionized workers of SemiCo go on strike. To increase their economic leverage, the workers picket the leading suppliers and customers of SemiCo in an attempt to hurt the company's business. SemiCo is considered the primary employer, and its suppliers and customers are considered secondary employers. Picketing of the suppliers or customers is a secondary boycott. ■
6. *Wildcat strikes.* A wildcat strike occurs when a small number of workers, perhaps dissatisfied with a union's representation, call their own strike. The union is the exclusive bargaining representative of a group of workers, and only the union can call a strike. Therefore, a wildcat strike, unauthorized by the certified union, is illegal.

22–4c After a Strike Ends

In a typical strike, the employer has a right to hire permanent replacements during the strike. The employer need not terminate the replacement workers when the economic strikers seek to return to work. In other words, striking workers are not guaranteed the right to return to their jobs after the strike if satisfactory replacement workers have been found.

If the employer has not hired replacement workers to fill the strikers' positions, however, then the employer must rehire the economic strikers to fill any vacancies. Employers may not discriminate against former economic strikers, and those who are rehired retain their seniority rights.

22–4d Lockouts

Lockouts are the employer's counterpart to the workers' right to strike. A **lockout** occurs when the employer shuts down to prevent employees from working. Lockouts usually are used when the employer believes that a strike is imminent or the parties have reached a stalemate in collective bargaining.

■ **Example 22.6** Owners of the teams in the National Football League (NFL) imposed a lockout on the NFL players' union in 2011 after negotiations on a new collective bargaining agreement broke down. The U.S. economy was struggling at the time, and the NFL owners had proposed to reduce players' salaries and extend the season by two games because of decreased profits. A settlement was reached before the start of the football season. The players accepted a somewhat smaller proportion of the revenue generated in exchange for better working conditions and more retirement benefits. The owners agreed to keep the same number of games per season. ∎

Some lockouts are illegal. An employer may not use a lockout as a tool to break the union and pressure employees into decertification, which occurs when union members vote to dissociate from the union. An employer must be able to show some economic justification for the lockout.

22–5 Unfair Labor Practices

The preceding sections have discussed unfair labor practices involved in union elections, collective bargaining, and strikes. Many unfair labor practices may occur within the normal working relationship as well. The most important of these practices are discussed in the following sections and listed in Exhibit 22–2.

22–5a Employer's Unfair Labor Practices

Thousands of complaints are filed each year by employees claiming that their employer has engaged in an unfair labor practice in violation of the NLRA. Charges often arise when an employer coerces, interferes with, or refuses to recognize an employee's protected rights.

Employer's Refusal to Recognize the Union and to Negotiate As discussed, once a union has been certified, an employer must recognize and bargain in good faith with the union. Failure to do so is an unfair labor practice.

Certification places responsibility on the union as well. Because the NLRA embraces a policy of majority rule, certification of the union as the bargaining unit's representative binds all of the employees in that bargaining unit. Thus, the union must fairly represent all the members of the bargaining unit.

Certification does not mean that a union will continue indefinitely as the exclusive representative of the bargaining unit. If the union loses the support of a majority of those it represents, an employer is not obligated to continue to recognize or negotiate with the union.

As a practical matter, a newly elected representative needs time to establish itself among the workers and to begin to formulate and implement its programs. Therefore, a union is immune from attack by employers and from repudiation by the employees for a period of one year after certification.

Employer's Interference in Union Activities The NLRA declares it to be an unfair labor practice for an employer to interfere with, restrain, or coerce employees in the exercise of their rights to form a union and bargain collectively. Unlawful employer interference may take a variety of forms.

Courts have found it an unfair labor practice for an employer to make threats that may interfere with an employee's decision to join a union. Even asking employees about their views on the union may be considered coercive. Employees responding to such questioning must be able to remain anonymous and must receive assurances against employer reprisals.

Employers also may not prohibit certain forms of union activity in the workplace. If an employee has a grievance with the company, the employer cannot prevent the union's participation in support of that employee.

If an employer has unlawfully interfered with the operation of a union, the NLRB or a reviewing court may issue a cease-and-desist order. The company typically is required to post the order on a bulletin board and renounce its past unlawful conduct.

Exhibit 22–2 Basic Unfair Labor Practices

It is unfair for employers to...	It is unfair for unions to...
1. Refuse to recognize a union and refuse to bargain in good faith. 2. Interfere with, restrain, or coerce employees in their efforts to form a union and bargain collectively. 3. Dominate a union. 4. Discriminate against union workers. 5. Punish employees for engaging in concerted activity.	1. Refuse to bargain in good faith. 2. Picket to coerce unionization without the support of a majority of the employees. 3. Demand the hiring of unnecessary excess workers. 4. Discriminate against nonunion workers. 5. Agree to participate in a secondary boycott. 6. Engage in an illegal strike. 7. Charge excessive membership fees.

Protected, concerted activity can take many forms. In the following case, the court had to decide whether an employee's objection to another employee's discharge was "insubordinate behavior" or a protected act.

Staffing Network Holdings, LLC v. National Labor Relations Board
United States Court of Appeals, Seventh Circuit, 815 F.3d 296 (2016).

Background and Facts Staffing Network Holdings, LLC, provides temporary and long-term employees to a variety of employers, including ReaderLink, a company that fills book orders for other businesses. ReaderLink's workers include "pickers," who select books to fill orders and place the books in boxes. Other employees include "stockers," who bring the boxes to the pickers to fill.

One afternoon, Staffing Network's on-site manager at ReaderLink, Andy Vega, fired a stocker for his "attitude." Griselda Barrera, Olga Gutierrez, and other pickers complained that this was not fair. Vega replied that he could send them all home. Barrera told the others to "stand up against all the injustice." Vega told her to leave. She protested but left. Later, she was told not to return.

Barrera filed a claim for unemployment compensation. The state asked Staffing Network to provide the reason for her separation from work, to which Staffing Network responded that Barrera was disrupting production. Barrera also filed an unfair labor practice charge with the National Labor Relations Board (NLRB). The NLRB filed a complaint against Staffing Network for terminating Barrera. An administrative law judge (ALJ) rejected the employer's claim that Barrera's "insubordinate behavior" justified the discharge, and ordered reinstatement and payment of back wages and benefits. Staffing Network petitioned for review. The NLRB petitioned for enforcement of the ALJ's order.

In the Language of the Court
ROVNER, Circuit Judge.
* * * *

Accepting the ALJ's factual findings (which were in turn affirmed by the Board), the only * * * question is whether those facts lend substantial evidence to the Board's finding that the company wrongfully terminated Barrera * * * . *An employer violates [the National Labor Relations Act] when it threatens employees with discipline or discharge for engaging in concerted activity that is protected.* Threats of discharge, discipline, other reprisals against employees for engaging in union activity violate the Act because these acts reasonably tend to coerce employees in the exercise of their rights, regardless of whether they do, in fact, coerce. The tendency to coerce is judged from the viewpoint of the employee. [Emphasis added.]

* * * The company's response to the State's unemployment inquiry provides a veritable smoking gun on the issue of the reason for Barrera's termination. Asked to provide the reason for Barrera's involuntary separation, Staffing Network explained that after a stocker was told to speed up his work, Barrera objected and then began "talking to some of the ladies in the line disrupting the production." According to Vega's own description of events, after he told Barrera to punch out and go home "if she does not want to work," Barrera "ignored the request and continued to get the ladies in the line worked up saying this was going against the law and that they have to stand up against all the injustice we are committing. Due to this, Griselda Barrera cannot return to ReaderLink." With this response to the State, the company essentially admitted the relevant facts supporting the ALJ's conclusion. *It is well settled that a brief, on-the-job work-stoppage is a form of economic pressure entitled to protection under the Act.* That is the type of action that Vega described in his response to the State in justifying Barrera's discharge. Witness testimony also supported the finding that Staffing Network terminated Barrera because of her concerted, protected activity in protesting Vega's treatment of [the stocker] in relation to the terms and conditions of his employment and that of the pickers. Namely, Barrera and Gutierrez both testified that Vega told Barrera to leave because she and the other pickers protested Vega's unfair treatment of [the stocker]. Therefore, substantial evidence supports the Board's finding that the company violated the Act when it discharged Barrera for engaging in protected, concerted activity. [Emphasis added.]

Decision and Remedy *The U.S. Court of Appeals for the Seventh Circuit denied Staffing Network's petition for review and granted the NLRB's petition for enforcement of the ALJ's order. "The pickers' temporary work stoppage and complaints to Vega regarding his treatment of [the fired stocker] constituted protected, concerted activity."*

Critical Thinking
- **Legal Environment** *The NLRB ordered Staffing Network to reinstate Barrera at ReaderLink and to pay her back wages and benefits. What other remedies might be appropriate in this case?*
- **What If the Facts Were Different?** *Suppose that instead of telling Barrera to leave Vega had said, "Get back to work" and had then left the area. Would the result have been different? Discuss.*

Employer's Domination of a Union In the early days of unionization, employers fought back by forming employer-sponsored unions to represent employees. These "company unions" were seldom more than the puppets of management. The NLRA outlawed company unions and any other form of employer domination of workers' unions.

Under the law against employer domination, an employer can have no say in which employees belong to the union or which employees serve as union officers. Nor may supervisors or other management personnel participate in union meetings.

Company actions that support a union may be considered improper potential domination. A company cannot give union workers pay for time spent on union activities, because this is considered undue support for the union. A company may not provide financial aid to a union and may not solicit workers to join a union.

Employer's Discrimination against Union Employees The NLRA prohibits employers from discriminating against workers because they are union officers or are otherwise associated with a union. When workers must be laid off, the company cannot consider union participation as a criterion for deciding whom to fire.

The provisions prohibiting discrimination also apply to hiring decisions. ■ **Example 22.7** Certain employees of SemiCo are represented by a union, but the company is attempting to weaken the union's strength. The company is prohibited from requiring potential new hires to guarantee that they will not join the union. ■

22–5b Union's Unfair Labor Practices

Certain union activities are declared to be unfair labor practices by the Labor-Management Relations Act. Secondary boycotts and illegal strikes, discussed earlier, are examples of such unfair labor practices.

Coercion Another significant unfair labor practice by a union is coercion or restraint to affect an employee's decision to participate in or refrain from participating in union activities. Obviously, it is unlawful for a union to threaten an employee or a family with violence for failure to join the union. The law's prohibition includes economic coercion as well. ■ **Example 22.8** A union official declares, "We have a lot of power here. You had better join the union, or you may lose your job." This threat is an unfair labor practice. ■

The NLRA provides unions with the authority to regulate their own internal affairs, which includes disciplining union members. This discipline cannot be used in an improperly coercive fashion, however. ■ **Example 22.9** Jake Kowalski is a union member who feels that the union is no longer providing proper representation for employees at his workplace. He starts a campaign to decertify the union. The union may expel Kowalski from membership, but it may not fine or otherwise discipline him. ■

Discrimination A union may not discriminate against workers because they refuse to join. In addition, the Labor-Management Relations Act also prohibits a union from using its influence to cause an employer to discriminate against workers who refuse to join the union. A union cannot force an employer to deny promotions to workers who fail to join the union.

Other Unfair Practices Other unfair labor practices by unions include demanding the hiring of unnecessary workers, participating in picketing to coerce unionization without majority employee support, and refusing to engage in good faith bargaining with employer representatives.

Unions are allowed to bargain for certain "union security clauses" in contracts. Although closed shops are illegal, a union can bargain for a provision that requires workers to contribute to the union within thirty days after they are hired. This is typically called a union shop, or agency shop, clause.

The union shop clause can compel workers to begin paying dues to the certified union but cannot require the worker to "join" the union. Dues payment can be required to prevent workers from taking the benefits of union bargaining without contributing to the union's efforts. The clause cannot require workers to contribute their efforts to the union, however, or to go out on strike.

Even a requirement of dues payment has its limits. Excessive initiation fees or dues may be illegal. Unions often use their revenues to contribute to causes or to lobby politicians. A nonunion employee subject to a union shop clause who must pay dues cannot be required to contribute to this sort of union expenditure.

In the following case, a union used picketing as part of a campaign to organize the employees of a hotel in Hawaii. The picketing did not deny management or nonunion employees access to the hotel, but it did block or impede employees and others from entering or exiting the premises for brief periods of time. Was the evidence sufficient to support an order finding that the union's actions restrained or coerced employees in violation of the National Labor Relations Act?

Case 22.3

Unite Here! Local 5 v. National Labor Relations Board

United States Court of Appeals, Ninth Circuit, 768 Fed.Appx. 627 (2019).

Background and Facts Unite Here! Local 5 sponsored pickets at the Aston Waikiki Beach Hotel in Honolulu, Hawaii. For several months, on a regular basis, individuals numbering from twelve to two hundred marched across the hotel's entrance at its *porte cochere*—a one-way, U-shaped, covered driveway. The picketing blocked or impeded hotel employees and others from entering or exiting the hotel for a few minutes at a time. Taxis and other vehicles, including cars driven by guests, were also stopped and delayed.

Aqua-Aston Hospitality, LLC, the Aston's operator, filed charges with the National Labor Relations Board (NLRB) against Unite Here! Local 5. The filing prompted the NLRB to issue two complaints against the union. After hearings, the union was found to have violated the National Labor Relations Act (NLRA). On review, the NLRB affirmed the finding. Unite Here! Local 5 petitioned the U.S. Court of Appeals for the Ninth Circuit for a review of the NLRB's decision.

In the Language of the Court
MEMORANDUM.
* * * *

The NLRB bears primary responsibility for developing and applying national labor policy. *So long as the Board's interpretation of the [National Labor Relations] Act [NLRA] in a case is rational and consistent with the statute, its rulings are afforded considerable deference.* The NLRB's findings of fact are conclusive if they are supported by substantial evidence on the record as a whole. As to a factual finding, the court may not displace the Board's choice between two fairly conflicting views, even though the court would justifiably have made a different choice had the matter been before it *de novo*. Given the NLRB's special expertise in the field of labor relations, we defer to the reasonable derivative inferences drawn by the Board from credited evidence. [Emphasis added.]

Section 7 of the NLRA grants employees "the right to self-organization, to form, join, or assist labor organizations, to bargain collectively through representatives of their own choosing, and to engage in other concerted activities for the purpose of collective bargaining or other mutual aid or protection." It also guarantees employees "the right to refrain from any or all of such activities." Section 8(b)(1)(A) makes it "an unfair labor practice for a labor organization or its agents * * * to restrain or coerce * * * employees in the exercise of the rights guaranteed in section [7 of the Act]." Determining the existence of a restraint or coercion turns on whether the misconduct is such that, under the circumstances existing, it may reasonably tend to coerce or intimidate employees in the exercise of rights protected under the Act.

Substantial evidence supports the NLRB's finding that the Union had deliberately, repeatedly, and persistently blocked numerous vehicles driven by employees for 1–4 minutes at a time, and engaged in similar conduct by temporarily blocking numerous vehicles in the presence or view of the hotel valet and bell employees. The NLRB * * * rejected the Union's argument that its conduct was brief and merely inconvenienced vehicles and was minor or *de minimis* [too minor to be of legal consequence], and distinguished the Union's actions from cases that involved only a few affected employees during months of picketing. Short delays, occurring regularly over the course of months and affecting workers during their performance of work duties, as well as others in the presence of employees, is sufficient to reasonably find that such actions violated the NLRA. The explanations of the NLRB's legal position * * * were therefore not inadequate, irrational or arbitrary.

Decision and Remedy   *The U.S. Court of Appeals for the Ninth Circuit affirmed the decision of the NLRB and the findings of its administrative law judges that the union was in violation of the NLRA.*

Critical Thinking
- **Economic**   *Why are strikers permitted to picket, but not to picket aggressively? Discuss.*
- **Legal Environment**   *What penalty should be imposed on Unite Here! Local 5 for its misconduct? Explain.*

Practice and Review: Immigration and Labor Law

In April, several employees of Javatech, Inc., a computer hardware developer with 250 employees, started organizing the Javatech Employees Union (JEU). When Javatech refused to voluntarily recognize the union, organizers petitioned the National Labor Relations Board (NLRB) for an election. In June, the NLRB conducted an election that showed that a majority of Javatech employees supported the union. JEU was certified and began bargaining with management over wages and benefits.

The following January, Javatech management offered the JEU a 1 percent annual wage increase for all employees with no other changes in employment benefits. The JEU countered by requesting a 3 percent wage increase and an employee health-insurance package. Javatech management responded that the 1 percent wage increase was the company's only offer. The JEU petitioned the NLRB for an order requesting good faith bargaining. After meeting with an NLRB representative, Javatech management still refused to consider modifying its position. JEU leaders then became embroiled in a dispute about whether the JEU should accept this offer or go on strike.

New union leaders were elected in July, and the employer refused to meet with the new JEU representatives, claiming that the union no longer had majority support from employees. In August, a group of seven Javatech engineers began feeling ill while working with a new adhesive used in creating motherboards. The seven engineers discussed going on strike without union support. Before they had reached an agreement, one of the engineers, Rosa Molina, became dizzy while working with the adhesive and walked out of the workplace. Using the information presented in the chapter, answer the following questions.

1. How many of Javatech's 250 employees must have signed authorization cards to allow the JEU to petition the NLRB for an election?
2. What must Javatech change in its collective bargaining negotiations to demonstrate that it is bargaining in good faith with the JEU, as required by labor law?
3. Could the seven engineers legally call a strike? What would such a strike be called?
4. Would Molina's safety walkout be protected under the Labor-Management Relations Act? Explain.

Debate This . . .   *To attract the brightest minds to work in the United States, there should be no limit on the number of H-1B visas available to immigrants with highly specialized knowledge.*

Terms and Concepts

authorization card 482
cease-and-desist order 481
closed shop 481
collective bargaining 485

hot-cargo agreements 481
I-9 verifications 478
I-551 Permanent Resident Card 479
lockout 486

right-to-work laws 481
secondary boycott 486
strike 486
union shop 481

Issue Spotters

1. Aanan Gara is the head of human resources at Skytech, Inc., a firm in Silicon Valley, California. Because Skytech cannot find enough domestic workers with specialized skills, Gara wants to recruit qualified employees from other nations. What must Gara do under the Immigration Act to hire foreign employees for Skytech? (See *Immigration Law.*)

2. Onyx applies for work with Precision Design Company, which requires union membership as a condition

of employment. She also applies for work with Quality Engineering, Inc., which does not require union membership as a condition of employment but requires employees to join a union after six months on the job. Are these conditions legal? Why or why not? (See *Federal Labor Laws.*)

• **Check your answers to the Issue Spotters against the answers provided in Appendix B at the end of this text.**

Business Scenarios and Case Problems

22–1. Unfair Labor Practices. Consolidated Stores is undergoing a unionization campaign. Prior to the union election, management states that the union is unnecessary to protect workers. Management also provides bonuses and wage increases to the workers during this period. The employees reject the union. Union organizers protest that the wage increases during the election campaign unfairly prejudiced the vote. Should these wage increases be regarded as an unfair labor practice? Discuss. (See *Unfair Labor Practices.*)

22–2. Appropriate Bargaining Unit. A group of employees at the Briarwood Furniture Company's manufacturing plant were interested in joining a union. Briarwood employs four hundred unskilled workers and one hundred skilled workers in its plant. The unskilled workers operate the industrial machinery used in processing Briarwood's line of standardized plastic office furniture. The skilled workers, who work in an entirely separate part of the plant, are experienced artisans who craft Briarwood's line of expensive wood furniture products. Do you see any problems with a single union's representing all the workers at the Briarwood plant? Explain. (See *Union Organization.*)

22–3. Spotlight on Verizon—Collective Bargaining. Verizon New York, Inc. (VNY), provides telecommunications services. VNY and the Communications Workers of America (CWA) are parties to collective bargaining agreements covering installation and maintenance employees. At one time, VNY supported annual blood drives. VNY, the CWA, and charitable organizations jointly set dates, arranged appointments, and adjusted work schedules for the drives. For each drive, about a thousand employees, including managers, spent up to four hours traveling to a donor site, giving blood, recovering, and returning to their jobs. Employees received full pay

for the time. In 2001, VNY told the CWA that it would no longer allow employees to participate "on Company time," claiming that it had experienced problems meeting customer requests for service during the drives. The CWA filed a complaint with the National Labor Relations Board (NLRB), asking that VNY be ordered to bargain over the decision. Did VNY commit an unfair labor practice? Should the NLRB grant the CWA's request? Why or why not? [*Verizon New York, Inc. v. National Labor Relations Board*, 360 F.3d 206 (D.C. Cir. 2004)] (See *Union Organization.*)

22–4. Immigration Work Status. Mohammad Hashmi, a citizen of Pakistan, entered the United States on a student visa. Two years later, when he applied for a job at Compu-Credit, he completed an I-9 form and checked the box to indicate that he was "a citizen or national of the United States." Soon after submitting that form, he married a U.S. citizen. Several months later, the federal immigration services claimed that Hashmi had misrepresented himself as a U.S. citizen. Hashmi contended that he had not misrepresented himself. At an administrative hearing, he testified that when he filled out the I-9 form he believed that he was a "national of the United States" because he was legally in the country under a student visa and was going to marry a U.S. citizen. He requested that his immigration status be adjusted to account for the fact that he was employed and married to an American. The immigration judge rejected that request and found that Hashmi had made a false claim on the I-9 form. He ruled that Hashmi was "inadmissible" to the United States and that his legal status in the country could not be amended because of his marriage or employment. Hashmi appealed. Should Hashmi's visa status be changed because of his marriage and employment? Why or why not? How should the appellate court rule in this case? [*Hashmi v. Mukasey,* 533 F.3d 700 (8th Cir. 2008)] (See *Immigration Law.*)

22–5. Business Case Problem with Sample Answer—Unfair Labor Practices. The Laborers' International Union of North America, Local 578, and Shaw Stone & Webster Construction, Inc., agreed on a provision in their collective bargaining agreement that required all employees to pay dues to the union. Sebedeo Lopez went to work for Shaw Stone without paying the union dues. When the union pressed the company to fire him, Lopez agreed to pay. The union continued to demand his discharge, however, and Shaw Stone fired him. Was the union guilty of unfair labor practices? Why or why not? [*Laborers' International Union of North America, Local 578 v. National Labor Relations Board*, 594 F.3d 732 (10th Cir. 2010)] (See *Unfair Labor Practices*.)

- **For a sample answer to Problem 22–5, go to Appendix C at the end of this text.**

22–6. Collective Bargaining. SDBC Holdings, Inc., acquired Stella D'oro Biscuit Company, a bakery in New York City. At the time, a collective bargaining agreement existed between Stella D'oro and Local 50, Bakery, Confectionary, Tobacco Workers and Grain Millers International Union. During negotiations to renew the agreement, Stella D'oro refused to give the union a copy of the company's financial statement. Stella D'oro did allow Local 50 to examine and take notes on the financial statement and offered the union an opportunity to make its own copy. Did Stella D'oro engage in an unfair labor practice? Discuss. [*SDBC Holdings, Inc. v. National Labor Relations Board*, 711 F.3d 281 (2d Cir. 2013)] (See *Union Organization*.)

22–7. Labor Unions. Carol Garcia and Pedro Salgado were bus drivers for Latino Express, Inc., a transportation company. Garcia and Salgado began soliciting signatures from other drivers to certify the Teamsters Local Union No. 777 as the official representative of the employees. Latino Express fired Garcia and Salgado. The two drivers filed a claim with the National Labor Relations Board (NLRB), alleging that the employer had committed an unfair labor practice. Which employer practice defined by the National Labor Relations Act did the plaintiffs most likely charge Latino Express with committing? Is the employer's discharge of Garcia and Salgado likely to be construed as a legitimate act in opposition to union solicitation? If a violation is found, what can the NLRB do? Discuss. [*Ohr v. Latino Express, Inc.*, 776 F.3d 469 (7th Cir. 2015)] (See *Union Organization*.)

22–8. A Question of Ethics—The IDDR Approach and Immigration Law. *Split Rail Fence Company sells and installs fencing materials in Colorado. U.S. Immigration and Customs Enforcement (ICE) sent Split Rail a list of the company's employees whose documentation did not satisfy the Form I-9 employment eligibility verification requirements. The list included long-term workers who had been involved in company activities, parties, and picnics. They had bank accounts, driver's licenses, cars, homes, and mortgages. At Split Rail's request, the employees orally verified that they were eligible to work in the United States. Unwilling to accept the oral verifications, ICE filed a complaint against Split Rail for its continued employment of the individuals.* [*Split Rail Fence Co. v. United States*, 852 F.3d 1228 (10th Cir. 2017)] *(See* Immigration Law.*)*

(a) Using the IDDR approach, identify Split Rail's ethical dilemma. What steps might the company take to resolve it? Explain.

(b) Is penalizing employers the best approach to take in attempting to curb illegal immigration? Discuss.

Time-Limited Group Assignment

22–9. Immigration. Nicole Tipton and Sadik Seferi owned and operated a restaurant in Iowa. Acting on a tip from the local police, agents of Immigration and Customs Enforcement executed search warrants at the restaurant and at an apartment where some restaurant workers lived. The agents discovered six undocumented aliens who worked at the restaurant and lived together. When the I-9 forms for the restaurant's employees were reviewed, none were found for the six aliens. They were paid in cash while other employees were paid by check. Tipton and Seferi were charged with hiring and harboring undocumented aliens. (See *Immigration Law*.)

(a) The first group will develop an argument that Tipton and Seferi were guilty of hiring and harboring illegal aliens.

(b) The second group will assess whether Tipton and Seferi can assert a defense by claiming that they did not know that the workers were unauthorized aliens.

(c) The third group will determine the potential penalties that Tipton and Seferi could face for violating the Immigration Reform and Control Act by hiring six unauthorized workers.

Two brothers, Ray and Paul Ashford, start a business—Ashford Brothers, Inc.—manufacturing a new type of battery system for hybrid automobiles. The batteries hit the market at the perfect time and are in great demand.

1. **Agency.** Loren, one of Ashford's salespersons, anxious to make a sale, intentionally quotes a price to a customer that is $500 lower than Ashford has authorized for the product. The customer purchases the product at the quoted price. When Ashford learns of the deal, it claims that it is not legally bound to the sales contract because it has not authorized Loren to sell the product at that price. Is Ashford bound to the contract? Discuss fully.

2. **Workers' Compensation.** One day, Gina, an Ashford employee, suffers a serious burn when she accidentally spills some acid on her hand. The accident occurs because another employee, who is suspected of using illegal drugs, carelessly bumps into her. Gina's hand requires a series of skin grafts before it heals sufficiently to allow her to return to work. Gina wants to obtain compensation for her lost wages and medical expenses. Can she do that? If so, how?

3. **Drug Testing.** After Gina's injury, Ashford decides to conduct random drug tests on all of its employees. Several employees claim that the testing violates their privacy rights, and they file a lawsuit. What factors will the court consider in deciding whether the random drug testing is legally permissible?

4. **COBRA.** Ashford provides health insurance for its two hundred employees, including Dan. For personal medical reasons, Dan takes twelve weeks' leave. During this period, can Dan continue his coverage under Ashford's health-insurance plan? After Dan returns to work, Ashford closes Dan's division and terminates the employees, including Dan. Can Dan continue his coverage under Ashford's health-insurance plan after the termination? Explain.

5. **Sexual Harassment.** Aretha, another employee at Ashford, is disgusted by the sexually offensive behavior of several male employees. She complains to her supervisor on several occasions about the behavior, but the supervisor merely laughs at her concerns. Aretha decides to bring a legal action against the company for sexual harassment. Does Aretha's complaint concern *quid pro quo* harassment or hostile-environment harassment? What federal statute protects employees from sexual harassment? What remedies are available under that statute? What procedures must Aretha follow in pursuing her legal action?

Health Insurance and Small Business

Small businesses are the foundation of the U.S. economy. Increasing health-care costs and decreasing insurance coverage in the early 2000s forced many small firms to stop offering health-care coverage to their employees. Congress therefore enacted comprehensive health-insurance reforms intended to improve access, affordability, and quality in health care. An especially important law is the Patient Protection and Affordable Care Act (ACA), which is often referred to as Obamacare. The ACA sets forth responsibilities and benefits for businesses determined in part by the size of an employer's workforce.[1]

What Is a Small Business?

The ACA defines a *small business* as a firm with fewer than fifty full-time equivalent (FTE) employees. An FTE employee works thirty or more hours per week. Two half-time employees count as one FTE employee. This definition fits about 96 percent of all businesses (5.8 million out of 6 million firms). In fact, 90 percent of all U.S. firms have fewer than twenty FTE employees.

What Responsibilities Does the ACA Impose on Small Businesses?

Large businesses—those with fifty or more FTE employees—are required to offer health insurance to their employees or pay a penalty.[2] For a small business, however, there is *no* requirement to offer health insurance. For a small firm that chooses to do so, the ACA imposes minimum standards on health plans.

Summary of Benefits and Coverage All employers, including small businesses, are required to provide their employees with a "Summary of Benefits and Coverage" that includes an explanation of the costs. The summary should be in plain language. Employees can use this information to compare their employer's plan with private plans, which the employees may opt to buy instead. An employer is not required to contribute to the premium for an employee's private plan.

Waiting Period Employees who are eligible for employer-sponsored health insurance must not be made to wait more than ninety days for coverage.

Notice of Marketplace Coverage Options Small businesses that do not offer health insurance can provide their employees with a "Notice of Marketplace Coverage Options." The notice can inform employees about their options with respect to the health-insurance marketplace.

---

1. For the complete text of the ACA, see Pub. L. No. 111-148, 124 Stat. 119 (2010). Also significant are the health-care amendments of the Health Care and Education Reconciliation Act, see Pub. L. No. 111-152, 124 Stat. 1029 (2010).
2. Before the ACA, more than 95 percent of these employers already offered health insurance to their employees.

What Benefits Does the ACA Offer Small Businesses?

The ACA provides benefits to small businesses by expanding insurance coverage options, reducing related costs, and giving employers and employees more control over their own health care.

Health-Insurance Marketplace A small business can buy health-insurance coverage for its employees through the ACA's Small Business Health Options Program (SHOP). Coverage can be offered to employees any time during the year.

The SHOP marketplace offers multiple plans from private insurance companies. An employer can choose which plans to make available to its employees, whether to cover the employees' dependents, how much of the premiums the employer will pay, and other options.[3]

Small Business Health-Care Tax Credit Employers with fewer than twenty-five FTE employees, each of whom is paid an average annual wage of less than $50,000, may be eligible for a health-care tax credit. To be eligible, an employer must cover at least 50 percent of the cost of the premiums for its employees' health insurance and buy the coverage through SHOP. Dental and vision care coverage also qualifies. An employer does not need to offer coverage to part-time employees (those working fewer than thirty hours per week) or to employees' dependents to qualify for the credit.

The amount of the credit may be as much as 50 percent of an employer's contribution toward its employees' premium costs. The smaller the business, the higher the credit—the credit is highest for firms with fewer than ten employees who are paid an average of $25,000 or less. Eligible small businesses can claim a business-expense deduction for the premiums in excess of the credit.[4]

Wellness Programs A wellness program requires individuals to meet a specific standard related to health, such as a low blood cholesterol level, to obtain a reward. Employers that promote employee health through workplace wellness programs are eligible for a reward of up to 30 percent of the cost of health coverage. The reward for a program designed to prevent or reduce the use of tobacco can be as much as 50 percent. The cost of health coverage includes employer-paid premiums and benefits.

Rebates The ACA requires insurance companies to spend at least 80 percent of premiums on medical care, not administrative costs. Insurers who do not meet this goal must provide rebates to policyholders.[5] These policyholders include employers that provide group health insurance for their employees.

Standard Operating Rules The ACA accelerated the adoption of standard operating rules for health-insurance plan administration. Operating rules are the business rules and guidelines for health-insurance plans. The ACA requires one format and one set of codes for claims, remittance advice, service authorization, eligibility verification, and claims status inquiry.

---

3. See the SHOP resources available for small businesses at www.healthcare.gov.

4. See Internal Revenue Service, *Small Business Health Care Tax Credit and the SHOP Marketplace*, at www.irs.gov.

5. See Internal Revenue Service, *Medical Loss Ratio (MLR) FAQs*, at www.irs.gov.

Nondiscriminatory Pricing The ACA ended the discriminatory insurance industry practice of increasing premiums because an employee filed a claim or got older or because a business hired a woman. At one time, premiums could increase by up to 200 percent in these circumstances.

Ethical Connection

Many critics have opposed the ACA, and some have attempted to abolish it.[6] In addition, some evidence has suggested that employers have reduced the hours of their employees to avoid the requirements of the ACA. Many argue that the reduction in the percentage of Americans who could work but are choosing to remain out of the labor force is due to the ACA.

Ethics Question *Are small businesses ethically obligated to offer their employees health insurance? Discuss.*

Critical Thinking *Should the mandate to offer employees health insurance be extended to include small businesses? Or should it be repealed altogether? Explain.*

---

6. The United States Supreme Court has upheld key parts of the ACA several times. See *National Federation of Independent Business v. Sebelius*, 567 U.S. 519, 132 S.Ct. 2566, 183 L.Ed.2d 450 (2012); and *King v. Burwell*, __ U.S. __, 135 S.Ct. 2480, 192 L.Ed.2d 483 (2015). The Court has held certain U.S. Department of Health and Human Services regulations issued under the act to be invalid, however. See *Burwell v. Hobby Lobby Stores, Inc.*, 573 U.S. 682, 134 S.Ct. 2751, 189 L.Ed.2d 675 (2014).

The Regulatory Environment

Chapter 23

Administrative Agencies

Government agencies established to administer the law have a great impact on the day-to-day operations of businesses. In its early years, the United States had a simple, nonindustrial economy with little regulation. As the economy has grown and become more complex, the size of government has also increased, and so has the number, size, and power of administrative agencies.

In some circumstances, new agencies have been created in response to a crisis. For instance, Congress enacted the Dodd-Frank Wall Street Reform and Consumer Protection Act after a major financial crisis. Among other things, this statute created the Financial Stability Oversight Council to identify and respond to emerging risks in the financial system. It also created an agency called the Consumer Financial Protection Bureau (CFPB) to protect consumers from alleged abusive practices by financial institutions, mortgage lenders, and credit-card companies.

As the number of agencies has multiplied, so have the rules, orders, and decisions that they issue. Today, there are rules covering almost every aspect of a business's operations. These regulations make up the body of *administrative law*.

23-1 The Practical Significance of Administrative Law

Whereas statutory law is created by legislatures, administrative law is created by administrative agencies. When Congress (or a state legislature) enacts legislation, it typically adopts a rather general statute and leaves its implementation to an **administrative agency.** The agency then creates the detailed rules and regulations necessary to carry out the statute. The administrative agency, with its specialized personnel, has the time, resources, and expertise to make the detailed decisions required for regulation.

23-1a Administrative Agencies Exist at All Levels of Government

Administrative agencies are spread throughout the government. At the federal level, the Securities and Exchange Commission regulates a firm's capital structure and financing, as well as its financial reporting. The National Labor Relations Board oversees relations between a firm and any unions with which it may deal. The Equal Employment Opportunity Commission also regulates employer-employee relationships. The Environmental Protection Agency and the Occupational Safety and Health Administration affect the way a firm manufactures its products, and the Federal Trade Commission influences the way it markets those products.

There are administrative agencies at the state and local levels as well. Commonly, a state agency (such as a state pollution-control agency) is created as a parallel to a federal agency (such as the Environmental Protection Agency). Just as federal statutes take precedence over conflicting state statutes, so do federal agency regulations take precedence over conflicting state regulations. Because the rules of state and local agencies vary widely, we focus here exclusively on federal administrative law.

23-1b Agencies Provide a Comprehensive Regulatory Scheme

Often, administrative agencies at various levels of government work together and share the responsibility of creating and enforcing particular regulations. ■ **Example 23.1** When Congress enacted the Clean Air Act, it provided only general directions for the prevention of air pollution. The specific pollution-control requirements imposed on businesses are almost entirely the product of decisions made by the Environmental Protection Agency (EPA). Moreover, the EPA works with parallel environmental agencies at the state level to analyze existing data and determine the appropriate pollution-control standards. ■

Legislation and regulations have significant benefits—in the example of the Clean Air Act, a cleaner environment than existed in decades past. At the same time, these benefits entail considerable costs for business. The EPA has estimated the costs of compliance with the Clean Air Act at many tens of billions of dollars yearly. Although the agency has calculated that the overall benefits of its regulations often exceed their costs, the burden on business is substantial. Business therefore has a strong incentive to try to influence the regulatory environment through lobbying.

23-2 Agency Creation and Powers

Congress creates federal administrative agencies. By delegating some of its authority to make and implement laws, Congress can indirectly monitor a particular area in which it has passed legislation. Delegation enables Congress to avoid becoming bogged down in the details relating to enforcement—details that are often best left to specialists.

To create an administrative agency, Congress passes **enabling legislation,** which specifies the name, purposes, functions, and powers of the agency being created. Federal administrative agencies can exercise only those powers that Congress has delegated to them in enabling legislation. Through similar enabling acts, state legislatures create state administrative agencies.

An agency's enabling statute defines its legal authority. An agency cannot regulate beyond the powers granted by the statute, and it may be required to take some regulatory action by the terms of that statute. When regulated groups oppose a rule adopted by an agency, they often bring a lawsuit arguing that the rule was not authorized by the enabling statute and is therefore void. Conversely, a group may file a suit claiming that an agency has illegally *failed* to pursue regulation required by the enabling statute.

23-2a Enabling Legislation—An Example

Congress created the Federal Trade Commission (FTC) in the Federal Trade Commission Act.[1] The act prohibits unfair methods of competition and deceptive trade practices. It also describes the procedures that the FTC must follow to charge persons or organizations with violations of the act, and it provides for judicial review of agency

orders. The act grants the FTC the power to do the following:

1. Create "rules and regulations for the purpose of carrying out the Act."
2. Conduct investigations of business practices.
3. Obtain reports from interstate corporations concerning their business practices.
4. Investigate possible violations of federal antitrust statutes. (The FTC shares this task with the Antitrust Division of the U.S. Department of Justice.)
5. Publish findings of its investigations.
6. Recommend new legislation.
7. Hold trial-like hearings to resolve certain trade disputes that involve FTC regulations or federal antitrust laws.

The commission that heads the FTC is composed of five members. The president, with the advice and consent of the Senate, appoints each of the FTC commissioners for a term of seven years. The president also designates one of the commissioners to be the chair.

23-2b Types of Agencies

There are two basic types of administrative agencies: executive agencies and independent regulatory agencies.

Federal *executive agencies* include the cabinet departments of the executive branch, which assist the president in carrying out executive functions, and the subagencies within the cabinet departments. The Occupational Safety and Health Administration, for instance, is a subagency within the U.S. Department of Labor. Executive agencies usually have a single administrator, director, or secretary who is appointed by the president to oversee the agency and can be removed by the president at any time. Exhibit 23–1 lists the cabinet departments and some of their most important subagencies.

Independent regulatory agencies, such as the Federal Trade Commission and the Securities and Exchange Commission (SEC), are outside the federal executive departments (those headed by a cabinet secretary). The president's power is less pronounced in regard to independent agencies, whose officers serve for fixed terms and cannot be removed without just cause. See Exhibit 23–2 for a list of selected independent regulatory agencies and their principal functions.

23-2c Agency Powers and the Constitution

Administrative agencies occupy an unusual niche in the U.S. governmental structure, because they exercise powers that normally are divided among the three branches of government. Agencies' powers include functions

1. 15 U.S.C. Sections 41–58.

Exhibit 23–1 Executive Departments and Important Subagencies

Department	Selected Subagencies
State	Passport Office; Bureau of Diplomatic Security; Foreign Service; Bureau of Intelligence and Research
Treasury	Internal Revenue Service; U.S. Mint
Interior	U.S. Fish and Wildlife Service; National Park Service; Bureau of Indian Affairs; Bureau of Land Management
Justice[a]	Federal Bureau of Investigation; Drug Enforcement Administration; Bureau of Prisons; U.S. Marshals Service
Agriculture	Soil Conservation Service; Agricultural Research Service; Food Safety and Inspection Service
Commerce[b]	Bureau of the Census; Bureau of Economic Analysis; U.S. Patent and Trademark Office; National Oceanic and Atmospheric Administration
Labor[b]	Occupational Safety and Health Administration; Bureau of Labor Statistics; Employment Standards Administration; Office of Labor-Management Standards
Defense[c]	National Security Agency; Joint Chiefs of Staff; Departments of the Air Force, Navy, Army
Housing and Urban Development	Government National Mortgage Association; Office of Fair Housing and Equal Opportunity
Transportation	Federal Aviation Administration; Federal Highway Administration; National Highway Traffic Safety Administration
Energy	Office of Civilian Radioactive Waste Management; Office of Nuclear Energy; Energy Information Administration
Health and Human Services[d]	Food and Drug Administration; Centers for Medicare and Medicaid Services; Centers for Disease Control and Prevention; National Institutes of Health
Education[d]	Office of Elementary and Secondary Education; Office of Postsecondary Education; Office of Vocational and Adult Education
Veterans Affairs	Veterans Health Administration; Veterans Benefits Administration; National Cemetery Administration
Homeland Security	U.S. Citizenship and Immigration Services; Directorate of Border and Transportation Services; U.S. Coast Guard; Federal Emergency Management Agency

a. Formed from the Office of the Attorney General.
b. Formed from the Department of Commerce and Labor.
c. Formed from the Department of War and the Department of the Navy.
d. Formed from the Department of Health, Education, and Welfare.

associated with the legislature *(rulemaking)*, the executive branch *(enforcement)*, and the courts *(adjudication)*.

The constitutional principle of *checks and balances* allows each branch of government to act as a check on the actions of the other two branches. Furthermore, the U.S. Constitution authorizes only the legislative branch to create laws. Yet administrative agencies, to which the Constitution does not specifically refer, can make **legislative rules,** or *substantive rules*, that are as legally binding as laws that Congress passes.

Administrative agencies also issue **interpretive rules,** which simply declare policy and do not affect legal rights or obligations. ■ **Example 23.2** The Equal Employment Opportunity Commission periodically issues interpretive rules indicating how it plans to interpret the provisions of certain statutes, such as the Americans with Disabilities

Exhibit 23-2 Selected Independent Regulatory Agencies

Name of Agency	Principal Duties
Federal Reserve System (the Fed) Board of Governors	Determines policy with respect to interest rates, credit availability, and the money supply (including various "bailouts" in the financial sector).
Federal Trade Commission (FTC)	Prevents businesses from engaging in unfair trade practices; stops the formation of monopolies in the business sector.
Securities and Exchange Commission (SEC)	Regulates the nation's stock exchanges, in which shares of stock are bought and sold; enforces the securities laws.
Federal Communications Commission (FCC)	Regulates communications by telegraph, cable, telephone, radio, satellite, Internet, and television.
National Labor Relations Board (NLRB)	Protects employees' rights to join unions and bargain collectively with employers; attempts to prevent unfair labor practices by both employers and unions.
Equal Employment Opportunity Commission (EEOC)	Works to eliminate discrimination in employment based on religion, gender, race, color, disability, national origin, or age; investigates claims of discrimination.
Environmental Protection Agency (EPA)	Undertakes programs aimed at reducing air and water pollution; works with state and local agencies to help fight environmental hazards.
Nuclear Regulatory Commission (NRC)	Ensures that electricity-generating nuclear reactors in the United States are built and operated safely; regularly inspects operations of such reactors.

Act. These informal rules provide enforcement guidelines for agency officials. ■

The Delegation Doctrine Courts generally hold that Article I of the U.S. Constitution is the basis for all administrative law. Section 1 of that article grants all legislative powers to Congress and requires Congress to oversee the implementation of all laws. Article I, Section 8, gives Congress the power to make all laws necessary for executing its specified powers. Under what is known as the **delegation doctrine,** courts interpret these passages as granting Congress the power to establish administrative agencies and delegate to them the power to create rules for implementing those laws.

The three branches of government exercise certain controls over agency powers and functions, as discussed next, but in many ways administrative agencies function independently. For this reason, administrative agencies, which constitute the **bureaucracy,** are sometimes referred to as the fourth branch of the U.S. government.

Executive Controls The executive branch of government exercises control over agencies both through

the president's power to appoint federal officers and through the president's veto power. The president may veto enabling legislation passed by Congress or congressional attempts to modify an existing agency's authority.

Legislative Controls Congress exercises authority over agency powers through legislation. Congress gives power to an agency through enabling legislation and can take power away—or even abolish an agency altogether—through subsequent legislation. Legislative authority is required to fund an agency, and enabling legislation usually sets certain time and monetary limits on the funding of particular programs. Congress can always revise these limits.

In addition to its power to create and fund agencies, Congress has the authority to investigate the implementation of its laws and the agencies that it has created. Congress also has the power to "freeze" the enforcement of most federal regulations before the regulations take effect. (Another legislative check on agency actions is the Administrative Procedure Act, discussed shortly.)

Judicial Controls The judicial branch exercises control over agency powers through the courts' review of agency actions. As you will read shortly, the Administrative Procedure Act provides for judicial review of most agency decisions. Agency actions are not automatically subject to judicial review, however. The party seeking court review must first exhaust all administrative remedies under what is called the **exhaustion doctrine** before seeking court review.[2]

■ **Example 23.3** The Federal Trade Commission (FTC) claims that Simtek Industries used deceptive advertising and orders it to run new ads correcting the misstatements. Simtek contends that its ads were not deceptive. Under the exhaustion doctrine, Simtek must go through the entire FTC process before it can bring a suit against the FTC in court to challenge the order. ■

23–2d The Administrative Procedure Act

Sometimes, Congress specifies certain procedural requirements in an agency's enabling legislation. In the absence of any directives from Congress concerning a particular agency procedure, the Administrative Procedure Act (APA)[3] applies.

---

2. The plaintiff must also have *standing to sue* the agency.
3. 5 U.S.C. Sections 551 *et seq.*

The Arbitrary and Capricious Test One of Congress's goals in enacting the APA was to provide for more judicial control over administrative agencies. To that end, the APA provides that courts should "hold unlawful and set aside" agency actions found to be "arbitrary, capricious, an abuse of discretion, or otherwise not in accordance with law."[4] Under this standard, parties can challenge regulations as contrary to law or as so irrational that they are arbitrary and capricious.

There is no precise definition of what makes a rule arbitrary and capricious, but the standard includes factors such as whether the agency has done any of the following:

1. Failed to provide a rational explanation for its decision.
2. Changed its prior policy without justification.
3. Considered legally inappropriate factors.
4. Entirely failed to consider a relevant factor.
5. Rendered a decision plainly contrary to the evidence.

The following case involved a challenge to the boundaries of a wild and scenic river established by the National Park Service. The plaintiff—an owner of land that fell within the protected area—claimed that the boundaries were set arbitrarily and capriciously.

---

4. 5 U.S.C. Section 706(2)(A).

Case 23.1

Simmons v. Smith

United States Court of Appeals, Eighth Circuit, 888 F.3d 994 (2018).

Background and Facts The Niobrara River runs through northern Nebraska before flowing into the Missouri River along the border between Nebraska and South Dakota. Pursuant to the Niobrara Scenic River Designation Act, the National Park Service (NPS)—led by Paul Hedren, the NPS superintendent of the Niobrara—established the boundaries of the Niobrara Scenic River Area (NSRA). The process involved public meetings, conversations with local landowners and other stakeholders, and scientific evidence. The statute required the agency to focus on protecting five "outstandingly remarkable values" (ORVs)—scenic, recreational, geologic, fish and wildlife, and paleontological.

Lee Simmons operated a recreational outfitter business on the Niobrara. At least twenty-five acres of his land fell within the NSRA boundaries established by the NPS. Arguing that the agency acted arbitrarily and capriciously in drawing those boundaries, Simmons filed a suit in a federal district court against Paul Smith, the agency's acting director. The court issued a judgment in Smith's favor. Simmons appealed.

In the Language of the Court
KELLY, Circuit Judge.
* * * *

Simmons * * * argues that NPS acted arbitrarily and capriciously in setting the boundary on his property because it did not identify specific ORVs that existed in that area. We agree with Simmons's premise to a certain extent, but, based on the facts of this case, we reach the opposite conclusion.
In crafting the boundaries, NPS is required to use the ORV determinations as a guide to decide which

land should be included within the boundary in order to protect and enhance the ORVs. But * * * *NPS is not required to include only land with outstandingly remarkable values.* * * * NPS explained that [the placement of the] boundary * * * sought to balance the various ORVs "as equitably as possible" * * * . Thus, *as long as the boundary placement was rationally connected to the protection of ORVs, NPS was not required to identify a specific ORV on any specific piece of property.* And Simmons does not allege that NPS acted contrary to its stated objective of protecting these values. [Emphasis added.]

Moreover, the record amply demonstrates that multiple ORVs were identified within the boundary line in question. Specifically, Simmons's land contains a large portion of viewshed [a geographical area that includes all line-of-site property viewable from that location] that is directly downstream from Berry Bridge, which is a common launch point for recreational canoeists on the river. His land also contains a large and particularly impressive stand of ponderosa pine trees and habitats that support bald eagle foraging. Indeed, the final boundary line on Simmons's property tracks quite closely the extent of the viewshed and the ponderosa stand. Simmons does not dispute these facts. Instead, he relies on a statement by Hedren—made during a lengthy deposition—in which he said that he could not identify specific features on Simmons's property. But, read in context, that statement indicates confusion about the location of Simmons's property, not confusion about the existence of ORVs. At various other points in the deposition, Hedren clearly and specifically identified which ORVs motivated his boundary determination on this property.

In sum, we see no flaw—either generally or related specifically to Simmons's property—in the public, thorough, and comprehensive process that NPS undertook to establish the boundaries of the NSRA.

Decision and Remedy *The U.S. Court of Appeals for the Eighth Circuit affirmed the judgment of the lower court. "NPS engaged in a methodical, time-consuming boundary-drawing process. It used the appropriate statutory standard to identify outstandingly remarkable values and it drew a boundary line that sought to protect those values."*

Critical Thinking

- **Economic** *Why would an owner of land that falls within the boundaries of a federally protected wild and scenic river challenge those boundaries?*
- **What If the Facts Were Different?** *Suppose that instead of establishing the boundaries of the NSRA to protect ORVs, the NPS had drawn the boundaries to set the area's size at a certain number of acres. Would the result in this case have been different? Explain.*

Fair Notice The APA also includes many requirements concerning the notice that regulatory agencies must give to those affected by its regulations. For instance, an agency may change the way it applies a certain regulatory principle. Before the change can be carried out, the agency must give fair notice of what conduct will be expected in the future.

■ **Case in Point 23.4** The 1934 Communications Act established a system of limited-term broadcast licenses subject to various conditions. One condition was the indecency ban, which prohibited the uttering of "any obscene, indecent, or profane language by means of radio communication." For nearly thirty years, the Federal Communications Commission (FCC) invoked this ban only when the offensive language had been repeated, or "dwelled on," in the broadcast. It was not applied to "fleeting expletives" (offensive words used only briefly).

Then the FCC changed its policy, declaring that an offensive term, such as the F-word, was actionably indecent even if it was used only once. In 2006, the FCC applied this rule to two Fox Television broadcasts, each of which contained a single use of the F-word. The broadcasts had aired before the FCC's change in policy. The FCC ruled that these two broadcasts were indecent, and Fox appealed the ruling. Ultimately, the case reached the United States Supreme Court, and the Court determined that the FCC's order should be set aside. Because the FCC did not provide fair notice prior to the broadcasts in question that fleeting expletives could constitute actionable indecency, the standards were unconstitutionally vague.[5] ■

5. *Federal Communications Commission v. Fox Television Stations, Inc.*, 567 U.S. 239, 132 S.Ct. 2307, 183 L.Ed.2d 234 (2012).

23–3 The Administrative Process

All federal agencies must follow specific procedural requirements as they go about fulfilling their three basic functions: rulemaking, enforcement, and adjudication. These three functions make up what is known as the **administrative process.** As mentioned, the APA imposes requirements that all federal agencies must follow in the absence of contrary provisions in the enabling legislation. This act is an integral part of the administrative process.

23–3a Rulemaking

The major function of an administrative agency is **rulemaking**—the formulation of new regulations, or rules. The APA defines a *rule* as "an agency statement of general or particular applicability and future effect designed to implement, interpret, or prescribe law and policy."[6]

Regulations are sometimes said to be *legislative* because, like statutes, they have a binding effect. Thus, violators of agency rules may be punished. Because agency rules have such significant legal force, the APA established procedures for agencies to follow in creating (amending, or removing) rules.

Many rules must be adopted using the APA's **notice-and-comment rulemaking,** which involves three basic steps:

1. Notice of the proposed rulemaking.
2. A comment period.
3. The final rule.

The APA recognizes some limited exceptions to its procedural requirements, but they are seldom invoked.

■ **Example 23.5** The Occupational Safety and Health Act authorized the Occupational Safety and Health Administration (OSHA) to develop and issue rules governing safety in the workplace. When OSHA wants to formulate rules regarding safety in the steel industry, it has to follow the specific procedures outlined by the APA. ■

The impetus for rulemaking may come from various sources, including Congress and the agency itself. In addition, private parties may petition an agency to begin a rulemaking (or repeal a rule). For instance, environmental groups have petitioned for stricter air-pollution controls to combat emissions that may contribute to climate change.

Notice of the Proposed Rulemaking When a federal agency decides to create a new rule, the agency publishes a notice of the proposed rulemaking proceedings

6. 5 U.S.C. Section 551(4).

in the *Federal Register.* The *Federal Register* is a daily publication of the executive branch that prints government orders, rules, and regulations.

The notice states where and when the proceedings will be held, the agency's legal authority for making the rule (usually its enabling legislation), and the terms or subject matter of the rule. The agency must also make available to the public certain other information, such as the key scientific data underlying the proposal. The proposed rule is often reported by the news media and published in the trade journals of the industries that will be affected.

Comment Period Following the publication of the notice of the proposed rulemaking proceedings, the agency must allow ample time for persons to comment in writing on the proposed rule. The purpose of this comment period is to give interested parties the opportunity to express their views on the proposed rule in an effort to influence agency policy. The comments can be made in writing or, if a hearing is held, orally. All comments become a public record that others can examine.

■ **Example 23.6** Brown Trucking learns that the U.S. Department of Transportation is considering a new regulation that will have a negative impact on its ability to do business and on its profits. A notice of the rulemaking is published in the *Federal Register.* Later, a public hearing is held so that proponents and opponents can offer evidence and question witnesses. At this hearing, Brown's owner orally expresses his opinion about the pending rule. ■

The agency need not respond to all comments, but it must respond to any significant comments that bear directly on the proposed rule. The agency responds by either modifying its final rule or explaining, in a statement accompanying the final rule, why it did not make any changes. In some circumstances, particularly when less formal procedures are used, an agency may accept comments after the comment period is closed.

The Final Rule After the agency reviews the comments, it drafts the final rule and publishes it in the *Federal Register.* The final rule can include modifications based on the public comments. If substantial changes are made, however, a new proposal and a new opportunity for comment are required. The final rule is later compiled along with the rules and regulations of other federal administrative agencies in the *Code of Federal Regulations.*

Final rules have binding legal effect unless the courts later overturn them. If an agency fails to follow proper rulemaking procedures when it issues a final rule, however, the resulting rule may not be binding.

■ Example 23.7 Members of the Hemp Industries Association (HIA) manufacture and sell food products made from hemp seed and oil. These products may contain trace amounts of THC, a component of marijuana. Without following formal rulemaking procedures, the Drug Enforcement Administration (DEA) publishes rules that effectively ban the possession and sale of HIA's food products, treating them as controlled substances. A court will most likely overturn the rules because the DEA did not follow formal rulemaking procedures. ■

Informal Agency Actions Rather than take the time to conduct notice-and-comment rulemaking, agencies have increasingly been using more informal methods of policymaking, such as issuing interpretive rules and guidance documents. As mentioned earlier, unlike legislative rules, interpretive rules simply declare policy and do not affect legal rights or obligations. Guidance documents advise the public on the agencies' legal and policy positions.

Informal agency actions are exempt from the APA's requirements because they do not establish legal rights. A party cannot be directly prosecuted for violating an interpretive rule or a guidance document. Nevertheless, an informal action can be important because it warns regulated entities that the agency may engage in formal rulemaking if they ignore its informal policymaking.

23–3b Enforcement

Although rulemaking is the most prominent agency activity, rule enforcement is also critical. Often, an agency enforces its own rules. After a final rule is issued, agencies conduct investigations to monitor compliance with the rule or the terms of the enabling statute.

An agency investigation of this kind might begin when the agency receives a report of a possible violation. In addition, many agency rules require compliance reporting from regulated entities, and such a report may trigger an enforcement investigation.

Inspections and Tests In conducting investigations, many agencies gather information through on-site inspections. Sometimes, inspecting an office, a factory, or some other business facility is the only way to obtain the evidence needed to prove a regulatory violation. At other times, an inspection or test is used in place of a formal hearing to show the need to correct or prevent an undesirable condition.

Administrative inspections and tests cover a wide range of activities, including safety inspections of underground coal mines, safety tests of commercial equipment and automobiles, and environmental monitoring of factory emissions. An agency may also ask a firm or individual to submit certain documents or records to the agency for examination.

Normally, business firms comply with agency requests to inspect facilities or business records because it is in any firm's interest to maintain a good relationship with regulatory bodies. In some instances, however, such as when a firm thinks an agency's request is unreasonable and disruptive, the firm may refuse to comply with the request. In such situations, an agency may resort to the use of a subpoena or a search warrant.

Subpoenas There are two basic types of subpoenas. The subpoena *ad testificandum*[7] ("to testify") is an ordinary subpoena. It is a writ, or order, compelling a witness to appear at an agency hearing. The subpoena *duces tecum*[8] ("bring it with you") compels an individual or organization to hand over books, papers, records, or documents to the agency. An administrative agency may use either type of subpoena to obtain testimony or documents.

There are limits on what an agency can demand. To determine whether an agency is abusing its discretion in pursuing information as part of an investigation, a court may consider such factors as the following:

1. *The purpose of the investigation.* An investigation must have a legitimate purpose. An agency may not issue an administrative subpoena to inspect business records if the motive is to harass or pressure the business into settling an unrelated matter, for instance.
2. *The relevance of the information being sought.* Information is relevant if it reveals that the law is being violated or if it assures the agency that the law is not being violated.
3. *The specificity of the demand for testimony or documents.* A subpoena must, for instance, adequately describe the material being sought.
4. *The burden of the demand on the party from whom the information is sought.* For instance, the cost to the company of copying requested documents or providing digital information may become burdensome. (Note that a business generally is protected from revealing information such as trade secrets.)

Search Warrants The Fourth Amendment protects against unreasonable searches and seizures by requiring that in most instances a physical search for evidence must be conducted under the authority of a search warrant.

---

7. Pronounced ad tes-te-fe-*kan*-dum.
8. Pronounced *doo*-suhs *tee*-kum.

An agency's search warrant is an order directing law enforcement officials to search a specific place for a specific item and seize it for the agency.[9]

Agencies can conduct warrantless searches in several situations. Warrants are not required to conduct searches in highly regulated industries. Firms that sell firearms or liquor, for instance, are automatically subject to inspections without warrants. Sometimes, a statute permits warrantless searches of certain types of hazardous operations, such as coal mines. Also, a warrantless inspection in an emergency situation is normally considered reasonable.

23–3c Adjudication

After conducting an investigation of a suspected rule violation, an agency may initiate an administrative action against an individual or organization. Most administrative actions are resolved through negotiated settlements at their initial stages. Sometimes, though, an action ends in formal **adjudication**—the resolution of the dispute through a hearing conducted by the agency.

Negotiated Settlements Depending on the agency, negotiations may involve a simple conversation or a series of informal conferences. Whatever form the negotiations take, their purpose is to rectify the problem to the agency's satisfaction and eliminate the need for additional proceedings.

Settlement is an appealing option to firms for two reasons: to avoid appearing uncooperative and to avoid the expense involved in formal adjudication proceedings and in possible later appeals. Settlement is also an attractive option for agencies. To conserve their resources and avoid formal actions, administrative agencies devote a great deal of effort to giving advice and negotiating solutions to problems.

Formal Complaints If a settlement cannot be reached, the agency may issue a formal complaint against the suspected violator. ■ **Example 23.8** The Environmental Protection Agency (EPA) finds that Acme Manufacturing, Inc., is polluting groundwater in violation of federal pollution laws. The EPA issues a complaint against Acme in an effort to bring the plant into compliance with federal regulations. This complaint is a public document, and a press release may accompany it. Acme will respond by filing an answer to the EPA's allegations. If Acme and the EPA cannot agree on a settlement, the case will be adjudicated. ■

The Hearing Agency adjudication may involve a trial-like arbitration procedure before an **administrative law judge (ALJ).** The Administrative Procedure Act (APA) requires that before the hearing takes place, the agency must issue a notice that includes the facts and law on which the complaint is based, the legal authority for the hearing, and its time and place. The administrative agency adjudication process is described next and illustrated graphically in Exhibit 23–3.

The Role of the Administrative Law Judge An ALJ presides over the hearing and has the power to administer oaths, take testimony, rule on questions of evidence, and make determinations of fact. Technically, the ALJ, who works for the agency prosecuting the case, is not an

Exhibit 23–3 The Formal Administrative Agency Adjudication Process

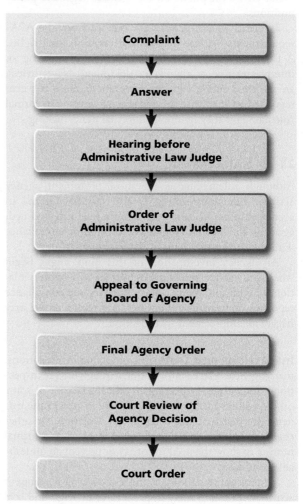

Complaint

Answer

Hearing before Administrative Law Judge

Order of Administrative Law Judge

Appeal to Governing Board of Agency

Final Agency Order

Court Review of Agency Decision

Court Order

---

9. The United States Supreme Court held that the warrant requirement applies to the administrative process in *Marshall v. Barlow's, Inc.*, 436 U.S. 307, 98 S.Ct. 1816, 56 L.Ed.2d 305 (1978).

independent judge. Nevertheless, the law requires an ALJ to be unbiased.

Certain safeguards prevent bias on the part of the ALJ and promote fairness in the proceedings. For instance, the APA requires that the ALJ be separate from an agency's investigative and prosecutorial staff. The APA also prohibits *ex parte* (private) communications between the ALJ and any party to an agency proceeding, including the agency and the company involved. Finally, provisions of the APA protect the ALJ from agency disciplinary actions unless the agency can show good cause for such an action.

Hearing Procedures   Hearing procedures vary widely from agency to agency. Administrative agencies generally exercise substantial discretion over the type of procedure that will be used. Frequently, disputes are resolved through informal adjudication proceedings. ■ **Example 23.9** The Federal Trade Commission (FTC) charges Good Foods, Inc., with deceptive advertising. Representatives of Good Foods and the FTC, their counsel, and the ALJ meet at a table in a conference room to resolve the dispute informally. ■

A formal adjudicatory hearing, in contrast, resembles a trial in many respects. Prior to the hearing, the parties are permitted to undertake discovery—involving depositions, interrogatories, and requests for documents or other information. The discovery process usually is not quite as extensive as it would be in a court proceeding.

The hearing itself must comply with the procedural requirements of the APA and must also meet the constitutional standards of due process. The burden of proof in an enforcement proceeding is placed on the agency. During the hearing, the parties may give testimony, present other evidence, and cross-examine adverse witnesses.

Trials and administrative agency hearings do differ in some respects. A significant difference is that normally much more information, including hearsay (secondhand information), can be introduced as evidence during an administrative hearing.

Agency Orders   Following a hearing, the ALJ renders an **initial order,** or decision, on the case. Either party can appeal the ALJ's decision to the board or commission that governs the agency. If displeased with the result, the party can appeal that decision to a federal appellate court.

■ **Example 23.10** The EPA issues a complaint against Acme Manufacturing, Inc., for polluting groundwater. The complaint results in a hearing before an ALJ, who rules in the EPA's favor. If Acme is dissatisfied with the decision, it can appeal to the EPA commission and then to a federal appellate court. ■

If no party appeals the case, the ALJ's decision becomes the **final order** of the agency. The ALJ's decision also becomes final if a party appeals and the commission and the court decline to review the case. If a party appeals and the case is reviewed, the final order comes from the commission's decision (or, if that decision is appealed, that of the reviewing court).

In the following case, a federal appellate court reviewed the Drug Enforcement Administration's denial of a university professor's application to register to cultivate marijuana.

Case 23.2

Craker v. Drug Enforcement Administration
United States Court of Appeals, First Circuit, 714 F.3d 17 (2013).

Background and Facts   Dr. Lyle Craker, a professor in the University of Massachusetts's Department of Plant, Soil and Insect Sciences, applied to the Drug Enforcement Administration (DEA, a federal law enforcement agency) for permission to register to manufacture marijuana for clinical research. He stated that "a second source of plant material is needed to facilitate privately funded Food and Drug Administration (FDA)-approved research into medical uses of marijuana, ensuring a choice of sources and an adequate supply of quality, research-grade marijuana for medicinal applications."

An administrative law judge recommended that Craker's application be granted, but a DEA deputy administrator issued an order denying his application. Under the DEA's interpretation, the federal Controlled Substances Act (CSA) requires an applicant to prove both that effective controls against diversion of the marijuana for unapproved purposes are in place and that its supply and the competition to supply it are inadequate. The deputy administrator determined that the professor had not proved that effective controls against the marijuana's diversion were in place or that supply and competition were inadequate. Craker petitioned the U.S. Court of Appeals for the First Circuit to review the order.

Case 23.2 Continues

Case 23.2 Continued

In the Language of the Court
HOWARD, Circuit Judge.
* * * *

Since 1968, the National Center for Natural Products Research ("NCNPR") at the University of Mississippi has held the necessary registration and a government contract to grow marijuana for research purposes. The contract is administered by the National Institute on Drug Abuse ("NIDA"), a component of the National Institutes of Health ("NIH"), which, in turn, is a component of the [U.S.] Department of Health and Human Services ("HHS"). The contract is opened for competitive bidding every five years. The NCNPR is the only entity registered by the DEA to manufacture marijuana.
* * * *

Dr. Craker's argument with respect to competition is essentially that there cannot be "adequately competitive conditions" when there is only one manufacturer of marijuana.

The Administrator * * * observed that NIDA had provided marijuana manufactured by the University of Mississippi either at cost or free to researchers, and that Dr. Craker had made no showing of how he could provide it for less * * *. Additionally, the Administrator noted that Dr. Craker is free to bid on the contract when it comes up for renewal.

*We see nothing improper in the Administrator's approach. The [CSA's] term "adequately competitive conditions" is not necessarily as narrow as the petitioner suggests. * * * That the current regime may not be the most competitive situation possible does not render it "inadequate."* [Emphasis added.]
* * * *

In finding that Dr. Craker failed to demonstrate that the current supply of marijuana was not adequate and uninterrupted, the Administrator observed that there were over 1,000 kilograms of marijuana in NIDA possession, an amount which far exceeds present research demands and "any foreseeable" future demand. Dr. Craker does not dispute this finding, or that the current amount is more than ninety times the amount he proposes to supply. Instead, he argues that the adequacy of supply must not be measured against NIDA-approved research, but by whether the supply is adequate to supply projects approved by the FDA. But even if we were to accept his premise—which we don't—Dr. Craker fails to demonstrate that the supply is inadequate for those needs, either. He merely states that certain projects were rejected as "not bona-fide" by NIDA, a claim which does not address the adequacy of supply. The fact that Dr. Craker disagrees with the method by which marijuana research is approved does not undermine the substantial evidence that supports the Administrator's conclusion.

Decision and Remedy *The U.S. Court of Appeals for the First Circuit denied Craker's petition to review the agency's order "because the Administrator's interpretation of the CSA is permissible and her findings are reasonable and supported by the evidence."*

Critical Thinking
- **Economic** *Why should a court wait to review an agency's order until the order has gone through the entire procedural process and can be considered final?*
- **Legal Environment** *Under what standard does a court defer to an agency's interpretation of a statute? Did the court in this case appear to have applied that standard to the DEA's interpretation of the Controlled Substances Act? Discuss.*

23–4 Judicial Deference to Agency Decisions

When asked to review agency decisions, courts historically granted deference to the agency's judgment. In other words, the courts tended to accept the agency's judgment, often citing the agency's great expertise in the subject area of the regulation. This deference seems especially appropriate when applied to an agency's analysis of factual questions, but should it also extend to an agency's interpretation of its own legal authority? In *Chevron U.S.A., Inc. v. Natural Resources Defense Council, Inc.,*[10] the United States Supreme Court held that it should. By so ruling, the Court created a standard of broadened deference to agencies on questions of legal interpretation.

---
10. 467 U.S. 837, 104 S.Ct. 2778, 81 L.Ed.2d 694 (1984).

23–4a The Holding of the *Chevron* Case

At issue in the *Chevron* case was whether the courts should defer to an agency's interpretation of a statute giving it authority to act. The Environmental Protection Agency (EPA) had interpreted the phrase "stationary source" in the Clean Air Act as referring to an entire manufacturing plant, and not to each facility within a plant. The agency's interpretation enabled it to adopt the so-called bubble policy, which allowed companies to offset increases in emissions in part of a plant with decreases elsewhere in the plant. This interpretation reduced pollution-control compliance costs to manufacturers. An environmental group challenged the legality of the EPA's interpretation.

The Supreme Court held that the courts should defer to an agency's interpretation of law as well as fact. The Court found that the agency's interpretation of the statute was reasonable. The Court's decision in the *Chevron* case created a new standard for courts to use when reviewing agency interpretations of law. This standard involves the following two questions:

1. Did Congress directly address the issue in dispute in the statute? If so, the statutory language prevails.

2. If the statute is silent or ambiguous, is the agency's interpretation "reasonable"? If it is, a court should uphold the agency's interpretation even if the court would have interpreted the law differently.

23–4b When Courts Will Give *Chevron* Deference to Agency Interpretation

The notion that courts should defer to agencies on matters of law has been controversial. Under the holding of the *Chevron* case, when the meaning of a particular statute's language is unclear and an agency interprets it, the court must follow the agency's interpretation as long as it is reasonable. This has led to considerable litigation to test the boundaries of the *Chevron* holding, and many agency interpretations continue to be challenged in court. Some commentators believe that conservative justices on the United States Supreme Court will ultimately overturn the deference required under the *Chevron* decision.

The following case involves a federal agency's role in determining whether foreign pilots may be certified to operate large U.S.-registered aircraft.

Case Analysis 23.3

Olivares v. Transportation Security Administration

United States Court of Appeals, District of Columbia Circuit, 819 F.3d 454 (2016).

In the Language of the Court

EDWARDS, Senior Circuit Judge:

* * * *

I. BACKGROUND

In the aftermath of the tragic terrorist attacks on September 11, 2001, Congress created the Transportation Security Administration [TSA] to shore up our nation's civil aviation security. [TSA is part of the U.S.] Department of Homeland Security under the direction of the Secretary of Homeland Security.

* * * No pilot may serve in any capacity as an airman with respect to a civil aircraft * * * without an airman certificate from FAA [Federal Aviation Administration]. For large aircraft, pilots must obtain additional certification known as a Type Rating. [Under the

Aviation and Transportation Security Act of 2001,] aliens [foreign pilots] who seek training and certification to operate large, U.S.-registered aircraft must first secure clearance by TSA. If TSA determines that an alien applicant presents a risk to aviation or national security, then that applicant is ineligible to receive the training necessary to secure a large aircraft Type Rating from FAA.

* * * *

[Alberto Olivares (Petitioner), a citizen of Venezuela,] received [an] opportunity to pilot a large, U.S.-registered aircraft. * * * Petitioner applied to attend an FAA-certified flight school in France, and TSA conducted a background investigation.

* * * *

* * * TSA concluded that Petitioner was a "Threat to Transportation/National Security" [and] sent an email to Petitioner denying his application.

* * * Petitioner filed his petition for review with this court. * * * Andrea Vara executed a sworn declaration explaining TSA's grounds for denying Petitioner's application for training. Ms. Vara is employed by [TSA] as the Alien Flight Student Program Manager. She has been responsible for managing TSA's Alien Flight Student Program, which conducts security threat assessments on individuals who are not U.S. citizens or nationals who seek flight instruction or recurrent training from FAA-certified flight training providers.

The Vara Declaration makes it clear that Ms. Vara was the Government

Case 23.3 Continues

Case 23.3 Continued

official who made the determination that Petitioner's application should be denied * * * . The Vara Declaration states:

> * * * Petitioner submitted Training Request # 565192, seeking to train at FlightSafety International—Paris Learning Center.
>
> * * * Petitioner was subject to an investigation, which revealed the following. In 2007, Petitioner pled guilty to conspiracy to possess with intent to distribute controlled substances and the U.S. District Court for the Northern District of Illinois sentenced him to eighty (80) months imprisonment. Petitioner's conviction made him inadmissible to the United States and led to the revocation of his FAA Airman's Certificate. Petitioner was deported to his home country of Venezuela in March 2010.
>
> A public news article published after Petitioner was deported provided a U.S. address for Petitioner. Further, records indicated that Petitioner was a suspected international trafficker in firearms. There was evidence that Petitioner had previously been involved in the export of weapons and U.S. currency to Venezuela by private aircraft, was the second pilot of an aircraft from which several weapons and $500,000 was seized by local authorities in Aruba, and that one of his associates was arrested in Aruba for smuggling firearms.
>
> This information, viewed as a whole, demonstrated Petitioner's willingness to consistently disregard the law and to use an aircraft for criminal activity, in opposition to U.S. security interests. The information also raised concerns that Petitioner may use his flight training to advance the interests of a criminal enterprise, which could include an enterprise that seeks to do harm to the United States.
>
> Based on all the foregoing information, I concluded Petitioner posed a threat to aviation and national security and * * * denied his training request.
>
> * * * *

II. ANALYSIS
A. THE COURT'S JURISDICTION

* * * An action taken by TSA on behalf of the Secretary of Homeland Security is clearly subject to review.

* * * *

B. STANDARD OF REVIEW

Pursuant to the Administrative Procedure Act, we must uphold TSA's decisions unless they are arbitrary, capricious, an abuse of discretion, or otherwise not in accordance with law.

What is important here is that, because Congress has entrusted TSA with broad authority over civil aviation security, it is TSA's job—not * * * ours—to strike a balance between convenience and security. Therefore, *in cases of this sort, we must defer to TSA actions that reasonably interpret and enforce the safety and security obligations of the agency.* * * * *Courts do not second-guess expert agency judgments on potential risks to national security. Rather, we defer to the informed judgment of agency officials whose obligation it is to assess risks to national security.* [Emphasis added.]

* * * *

D. PETITIONER'S * * * CLAIM

* * * *

* * * Petitioner argues that TSA should not have used his suspected firearms trafficking or his Massachusetts address to support its decision. [TSA had discovered that, even though Olivares had been deported with no right to return to the United States, he maintained a local address in Massachusetts.] Petitioner claims that the Massachusetts address actually belongs to his brother, and Petitioner insists that he has never illegally entered the United States. Petitioner also points out that the firearms incident occurred nearly two decades ago and that he was merely suspected of being involved. In light of the limited standard of review that controls the disposition of this case, these arguments are not persuasive. It was rational for TSA to find it suspicious and thus consider information indicating that a deported individual appeared to maintain a current U.S. address and had been suspected of involvement in firearms trafficking. The agency's weighing of this information, along with the information regarding Petitioner's known criminal history, was not inconsistent with reasoned decision making.

Given TSA's broad authority to assess potential risks to aviation and national security, the agency's clear and reasonable explanation offered in the Vara Declaration, and the limited standard of review [under the holding in the *Chevron* case], we are in no position to second-guess TSA's judgment in denying Petitioner's application. In assessing risks to national security, conclusions must often be based on informed judgment rather than concrete evidence, and that reality affects what we may reasonably insist on from the Government. When it comes to collecting evidence and drawing factual inferences in this area, the lack of competence on the part of the courts is marked, and respect for the Government's conclusions is appropriate. Where no factual certainties exist or where facts alone do not provide the answer * * * we require only that the agency so state and go on to identify the considerations it found persuasive.

It is self-evident that TSA's action against Petitioner was related to the agency's goals of improving the safety of air travel. TSA was not required to show that Petitioner would engage in activities designed to compromise aviation or national security. Rather, the agency was merely required to give a reasonable explanation as to why it believed that Petitioner presented a risk to aviation or national security. The Vara Declaration satisfies this legal obligation. [Emphasis added.]

III. CONCLUSION

For the reasons set forth above, the petition for review is denied.

Legal Reasoning Questions

1. What impact did the Vara Declaration have on the court's ruling in this case?

2. Is a court's evaluation of an agency's assessment of a risk to national security different from a review of other agency determinations? Explain.

3. Should the agency at the center of this case have revealed the reasons for its decision before Olivares filed a suit challenging it? Explain.

23–5 Public Accountability

As a result of public concern over the powers exercised by administrative agencies, Congress passed several laws to make agencies more accountable through public scrutiny. Here, we discuss the most significant of these laws.

23–5a Freedom of Information Act

The Freedom of Information Act (FOIA)[11] requires the federal government to disclose certain records to any person or entity on written request, even if no reason is given for the request. All federal government agencies must make their records available electronically on the Internet and in other electronic formats.

The FOIA exempts certain types of records, such as those pertaining to national security and those containing information that is confidential or personal. ■ **Example 23.11** Juanita, a reporter from an online health magazine, makes an FOIA request to the Centers for Disease Control and Prevention for a list of people who have contracted a highly contagious virus. The Centers for Disease Control and Prevention will not have to comply, because the requested information is confidential and personal. ■

For other records, a request that complies with the FOIA procedures need only contain a reasonable description of the information sought. An agency's failure to comply with an FOIA request can be challenged in a federal district court. The media, industry trade associations, public-interest groups, and even companies seeking information about competitors rely on these FOIA provisions to obtain information from government agencies.

23–5b Government in the Sunshine Act

The Government in the Sunshine Act,[12] or open meeting law, requires that "every portion of every meeting of an agency" be open to "public observation." The act also

requires that the public be provided with adequate advance notice of scheduled meetings and agendas.

Like the FOIA, the Sunshine Act contains certain exceptions. Closed meetings are permitted in the following situations:

1. The subject of the meeting concerns accusing any person of a crime.

2. Open meetings would frustrate implementation of future agency actions.

3. The subject of the meeting involves matters relating to future litigation or rulemaking.

Courts interpret these exceptions to allow open access whenever possible.

23–5c Regulatory Flexibility Act

Concern over the effects of regulation on the efficiency of businesses, particularly smaller ones, led Congress to pass the Regulatory Flexibility Act.[13] in 1980. Under this act, whenever a new regulation will have a "significant impact upon a substantial number of small entities," the agency must conduct a regulatory flexibility analysis. The analysis must measure the cost that the rule would impose on small businesses and consider less burdensome alternatives. The act also contains provisions to alert small businesses about forthcoming regulations. The act relieved small businesses of some record-keeping burdens, especially with regard to hazardous waste management.

23–5d Small Business Regulatory Enforcement Fairness Act

The Small Business Regulatory Enforcement Fairness Act[14] includes various provisions intended to ease the regulatory burden on small businesses:

1. Federal agencies must prepare guides that explain in plain English how small businesses can comply with federal regulations.

---

11. 5 U.S.C. Section 552.
12. 5 U.S.C. Section 552b.
13. 5 U.S.C. Sections 601–612.
14. 5 U.S.C. Sections 801 *et seq.*

2. Congress may review new federal regulations for at least sixty days before they take effect, giving opponents of the rules time to present their arguments.
3. The courts may enforce the Regulatory Flexibility Act. This provision helps to ensure that federal agencies will consider ways to reduce the economic impact of new regulations on small businesses.

4. The Office of the National Ombudsman at the Small Business Administration was set up to receive comments from small businesses about their dealings with federal agencies. Based on these comments, Regional Small Business Regulatory Fairness Boards rate the agencies and publicize their findings.

Practice and Review: Administrative Agencies

Assume that the Securities and Exchange Commission (SEC) has a rule that it will enforce statutory provisions prohibiting insider trading only when the insiders make monetary profits for themselves. Then the SEC makes a new rule, declaring that it will now bring enforcement actions against individuals for insider trading even if the individuals did not personally profit from the transactions. In making the new rule, the SEC does not conduct a rulemaking procedure but simply announces its decision. A stockbrokerage objects that the new rule was unlawfully developed without opportunity for public comment. The brokerage firm challenges the rule in an action that ultimately is reviewed by a federal appellate court. Using the information presented in the chapter, answer the following questions.

1. Is the SEC an executive agency or an independent regulatory agency? Does it matter to the outcome of this dispute? Explain.
2. Suppose that the SEC asserts that it has always had the statutory authority to pursue persons for insider trading regardless of whether they personally profited from the transactions. This is the only argument the SEC makes to justify changing its enforcement rules. Would a court be likely to find that the SEC's action was arbitrary and capricious under the Administrative Procedure Act (APA)? Why or why not?
3. Would a court be likely to give *Chevron* deference to the SEC's interpretation of the law on insider trading? Why or why not?
4. Now assume that a court finds that the new rule is merely "interpretive." What effect would this determination have on whether the SEC had to follow the APA's rulemaking procedures?

Debate This . . . *Because an administrative law judge (ALJ) acts as both judge and jury, there should always be at least three ALJs in each administrative hearing.*

Terms and Concepts

adjudication 508
administrative agency 500
administrative law judge (ALJ) 508
administrative process 506
bureaucracy 503

delegation doctrine 503
enabling legislation 501
exhaustion doctrine 504
final order 509
initial order 509

interpretive rules 502
legislative rules 502
notice-and-comment
  rulemaking 506
rulemaking 506

Issue Spotters

1. The U.S. Department of Transportation (DOT) sometimes hears an appeal from a party whose contract with the DOT has been canceled. An administrative law judge (ALJ) who works for the DOT hears this appeal. What safeguards promote the ALJ's fairness? (See *The Administrative Process*.)

2. Techplate Corporation learns that a federal administrative agency is considering a rule that will have a negative impact on the firm's ability to do business. Does the firm have any opportunity to express its opinion about the pending rule? Explain. (See *The Administrative Process*.)

• Check your answers to the Issue Spotters against the answers provided in Appendix B at the end of this text.

Business Scenarios and Case Problems

23–1. Rulemaking and Adjudication Powers. For decades, the Federal Trade Commission (FTC) resolved fair trade and advertising disputes through individual adjudications. Then the FTC began promulgating rules that defined fair and unfair trade practices. In cases involving violations of these rules, the due process rights of participants were more limited and did not include cross-examination. Although anyone charged with violating a rule would receive a full adjudication, the legitimacy of the rule itself could not be challenged in the adjudication. Furthermore, a party charged with violating a rule was almost certain to lose the adjudication. Affected parties complained to a court, arguing that their rights before the FTC were unduly limited by the new rules. What would the court examine to determine whether to uphold the new rules? (See *The Administrative Process*.)

23–2. Informal Rulemaking. Assume that the Food and Drug Administration (FDA), using proper procedures, adopts a rule describing its future investigations. This new rule covers all future circumstances in which the FDA wants to regulate food additives. Under the new rule, the FDA is not to regulate food additives without giving food companies an opportunity to cross-examine witnesses. Later, the FDA wants to regulate methyl isocyanate, a food additive. The FDA undertakes an informal rulemaking procedure, without cross-examination, and regulates methyl isocyanate. Producers protest, saying that the FDA promised them the opportunity for cross-examination. The FDA responds that the Administrative Procedure Act does not require such cross-examination and that it is free to withdraw the promise made in its new rule. If the producers challenge the FDA in court, on what basis would the court rule in their favor? Explain. (See *The Administrative Process*.)

23–3. Business Case Problem with Sample Answer— Agency Powers. A well-documented rise in global temperatures has coincided with a significant increase in the concentration of carbon dioxide in the atmosphere. Many scientists believe that the two trends are related, because when carbon dioxide is released into the atmosphere, it produces a greenhouse effect, trapping solar heat. Under the Clean Air Act (CAA), the Environmental Protection Agency (EPA) is authorized to regulate "any" air pollutants "emitted into . . . the ambient air" that in its "judgment cause, or contribute to, air pollution."

A group of private organizations asked the EPA to regulate carbon dioxide and other "greenhouse gas" emissions from new motor vehicles. The EPA refused, stating, among other things, that the most recent congressional amendments to the CAA did not authorize any new, binding auto emissions limits. Nineteen states, including Massachusetts, asked a district court to review the EPA's denial. Did the EPA have the authority to regulate greenhouse gas emissions from new motor vehicles? If so, was its stated reason for refusing to do so consistent with that authority? Discuss. [*Commonwealth of Massachusetts v. Environmental Protection Agency*, 549 U.S. 497, 127 S.Ct. 1438, 167 L.Ed.2d 248 (2007)] (See *Agency Creation and Powers*.)

• For a sample answer to Problem 23–3, go to Appendix C at the end of this text.

23–4. Judicial Deference. After Dave Conley died of lung cancer, his widow filed for benefits under the Black Lung Benefits Act. To qualify for benefits under the act, she had to show that exposure to coal dust was a substantial contributing factor in her husband's death. Conley had been a coal miner, but he had also been a longtime smoker. At the benefits hearing, a physician testified that coal dust was a substantial factor in Conley's death. No evidence was presented to support this conclusion, however. The administrative law judge awarded benefits. On appeal, should a court defer to this decision? Discuss. [*Conley v. National Mines Corp.*, 595 F.3d 297 (6th Cir. 2010)] (See *Judicial Deference to Agency Decisions*.)

23–5. Arbitrary and Capricious Test. Michael Manin, an airline pilot, was twice convicted of disorderly conduct, a minor misdemeanor. To renew his flight certification with the National Transportation Safety Board (NTSB), Manin filed an application that asked him about his criminal history. He did not disclose his two convictions. When these came to light more than ten years later, Manin argued that he had not known that he was required to report convictions for minor misdemeanors. The NTSB's policy was to consider an applicant's understanding of what information a question sought before determining whether an answer was false. But without explanation, the agency departed from this policy, refused to consider Manin's argument, and revoked his certification. Was this action arbitrary or capricious? Explain. [*Manin v. National Transportation Safety Board*, 627 F.3d 1239 (D.C. Cir. 2011)] (See *Agency Creation and Powers*.)

23–6. Adjudication. Mechanics replaced a brake assembly on the landing gear of a CRJ–700 plane operated by GoJet Airlines, LLC. The mechanics installed gear pins to lock the assembly in place during the repair but failed to remove one of the pins after they had finished. On the plane's next flight, a warning light alerted the pilots that the landing gear would not retract after takeoff. There was a potential for danger, but the pilots flew the CRJ–700 safely back to the departure airport. No one was injured, and no property was damaged. The Federal Aviation Administration (FAA) cited GoJet for violating FAA regulations by "carelessly or recklessly operating an unairworthy airplane." GoJet objected to the citation. To which court can GoJet appeal for review? On what ground might that court decline to review the case? [*GoJet Airlines, LLC v. Federal Aviation Administration*, 743 F.3d 1168 (8th Cir. 2014)] (See *The Administrative Process*.)

23–7. Judicial Deference to Agency Decisions. Knox Creek Coal Corporation operates coal mines in West Virginia. The U.S. Department of Labor charged Knox's Tiller No. 1 Mine with "significant and substantial" (S&S) violations of the Federal Mine Safety and Health Act. According to the charges, inadequately sealed enclosures of electrical equipment in the mine created the potential for an explosion. The Mine Act designates a violation as S&S when it "*could significantly and substantially contribute to the cause and effect of a coal or other mine safety or health hazard.*" Challenging the S&S determination, Knox filed a suit against the secretary of labor. The secretary argued that the word *could* means "merely possible"—if there is a violation, the existence of a hazard is assumed. This position was consistent with agency and judicial precedent and the Mine Act's history and purpose. Knox argued that *could* requires proof of the likelihood of a hazard. When does a court defer to an agency's interpretation of law? Do those circumstances exist in this case? Discuss. [*Knox Creek Coal Corp. v. Secretary of Labor, Mine Safety and Health Administration* 811 F.3d 148 (4th Cir. 2016)] (See *Judicial Deference to Agency Decisions*.)

23–8. The Arbitrary and Capricious Test. The Sikh Cultural Society, Inc. (SCS), petitioned the United States Citizenship and Immigration Services (USCIS) for a special immigrant religious worker visa for Birender Singh.

The USCIS denied the request for several reasons. Despite certain statutory requirements, there were discrepancies or inadequate evidence as to Singh's compensation, housing, and employment history. The SCS did not provide all of the requested information. In addition, the SCS did not show that Singh had worked continuously for the previous two years. The SCS filed a suit in a federal district court against the USCIS, arguing that the denial was arbitrary and capricious. In applying the arbitrary and capricious standard, what agency actions or omissions does a court typically consider? Does the denial of Singh's visa pass the test? Explain. [*Sikh Cultural Society, Inc. v. United States Citizenship and Immigration Services*, 720 Fed.Appx. 649 (2d Cir. 2018)] (See *Agency Creation and Powers*.)

23–9. A Question of Ethics—The IDDR Approach and the Arbitrary and Capricious Test. *The Delaware River Port Authority (DRPA) solicited bids to repaint the Commodore Barry Bridge, a mile-long structure spanning the Delaware River between New Jersey and Pennsylvania. Alpha Painting & Construction Company, an experienced contractor that had previously worked for the DRPA, submitted the lowest bid. Under DRPA guidelines, a "responsible" contractor has the "capacity" and "capability" to do a certain job. A "responsive" contractor includes all required documents with its bid. Alpha's bid did not include certain required accident and insurance data. For this reason, and without checking further, the DRPA declared that Alpha was "not responsible" and awarded the contract to the second-lowest bidder.* [*Alpha Painting & Construction Co., Inc. v. Delaware River Port Authority, 853 F.3d 671 (3d Cir. 2017)] (See Agency Creation and Powers.)*

(a) Using the *Inquiry* step of the IDDR approach, identify the ethical issue the DRPA faced when deciding whether to accept or reject Alpha's bid.

(b) Using the *Discussion* step of the IDDR approach, consider whether the DRPA's rejection of Alpha was ethical.

Time-Limited Group Assignment

23–10. Investigation. Kathleen Dodge was a flight attendant for United Continental Holdings, Inc. (UCH). After being assigned to work in Paris, France, she became pregnant. Because UCH does not allow its flight attendants to fly during their third trimester of pregnancy, Dodge was placed on involuntary leave. She applied for temporary disability benefits through the French social security system. Her request was denied because UCH does not contribute to the French system on behalf of its U.S.-based flight attendants. Dodge filed a charge of discrimination with the U.S. Equal Employment Opportunity Commission (EEOC), alleging that UCH had discriminated against her and other Americans. The EEOC issued a subpoena, asking UCH to detail all benefits received by all UCH employees living outside the United States. UCH refused to provide

the information on the ground that it was irrelevant and compliance would be unduly burdensome. The EEOC filed a suit in a federal district court against UCH. (See *The Administrative Process*.)

(a) The first group will decide whether the court should enforce the subpoena and explain why or why not.

(b) The second group will discuss whether the EEOC should be able to force a U.S. company operating overseas to provide the same disability benefits to employees located there as it does to employees in the United States.

(c) The third group will determine whether UCH should be required to contribute to the French social security system for employees who reside in France and explain why or why not.

Chapter 24

Consumer Protection

All statutes, agency rules, and common law judicial decisions that serve to protect the interests of consumers are classified as **consumer law.** Traditionally, in disputes involving consumers, it was assumed that the freedom to contract carried with it the obligation to live by the deal made. Over time, this attitude has changed considerably.

Today, countless federal and state laws attempt to protect consumers from unfair trade practices, unsafe products, discriminatory or unreasonable credit requirements, and other problems related to consumer transactions. Nearly every agency and department of the federal government has an office of consumer affairs, and most states have one or more such offices. The state attorney general's office typically assists consumers as well.

In the last decade, there has been a renewed interest in attempting to protect consumers in their dealings with credit-card companies, financial institutions, and insurance companies. Congress has enacted credit-card regulations and financial reforms to regulate the nation's largest banks. It has also enacted health-care reforms and revised food safety laws.

24–1 Advertising, Marketing, and Sales

Numerous federal laws have been passed to define the duties of sellers and the rights of consumers. Exhibit 24–1 shows many of the areas of consumer law that are regulated by federal statutes. We begin our discussion of this legislation by examining some of the laws and regulations relating to advertising, marketing, and sales. Although we focus on federal law, realize that state consumer protection laws in these and other areas often provide more sweeping and significant protections than do federal laws.

24–1a Deceptive Advertising

One of the most important federal consumer protection laws is the Federal Trade Commission Act.[1] The act created the Federal Trade Commission (FTC) to carry out the broadly stated goal of preventing unfair and deceptive trade practices, including deceptive advertising.

Generally, **deceptive advertising** occurs if a reasonable consumer would be misled by the advertising claim. Vague generalities and obvious exaggerations, known as *puffery*, are permissible. ■ **Case in Point 24.1** Sheila Cruz and others sued Anheuser-Busch Companies, LLC, for falsely advertising "Bud Light Lime-A-Rita" beverages as "light." She argued that the word "light" was misleading because the drinks contained more calories than light beer (Bud Light). The court dismissed Cruz's case, and a federal appellate court affirmed. The Lime-A-Rita beverages were advertised as "Margaritas with a Twist," so no reasonable consumer would believe they were the same as light beer. They also contained fewer calories than traditional tequila margaritas. Thus, the court concluded that the label was not misleading.[2] ■ When a claim takes on the appearance of authenticity, however, it may create problems.

Claims That Appear to Be Based on Factual Evidence Advertising that *appears* to be based on factual evidence but, in fact, is not reasonably supported by evidence will be deemed deceptive. ■ **Case in Point 24.2** MedLab, Inc., advertised that its weight-loss supplement ("The New Skinny Pill") would cause users to lose substantial amounts of weight rapidly. The ads claimed that "clinical studies prove" that people who take the pill lose "as much as 15 to 18 pounds per week and as much as 50 percent of all excess weight in just 14 days, without dieting or exercising." The FTC sued MedLab for deceptive advertising.

---

1. 15 U.S.C. Sections 41–58.

2. *Cruz v. Anheuser-Busch Companies, LLC*, 682 Fed.Appx. 583 (9th Cir. 2017).

Exhibit 24–1 Selected Areas of Consumer Law Regulated by Statutes

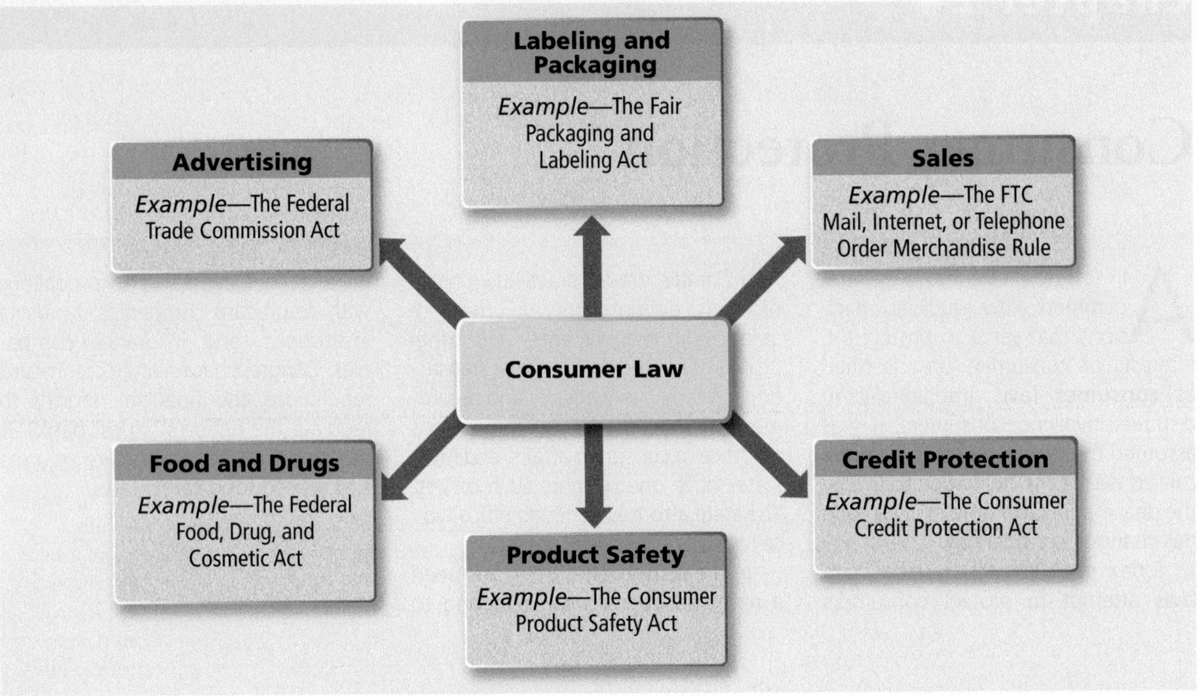

An expert hired by the FTC to evaluate the claim testified that to lose the amount of weight advertised, "a 200-pound individual would need to run between 57 and 68 miles every day"—the equivalent of more than two marathons per day. The court concluded that the advertisement was false and misleading, granted the FTC a summary judgment, and issued a permanent injunction to stop MedLab from running the ads.[3] ■

The following case involved an advertising claim based on limited scientific evidence.

3. *Federal Trade Commission v. MedLab, Inc.*, 615 F.Supp.2d 1068 (N.D.Cal. 2009).

POM Wonderful, LLC v. Federal Trade Commission

United States Court of Appeals, District of Columbia Circuit, 777 F.3d 478 (2015).

Background and Facts POM Wonderful, LLC, makes and sells pomegranate-based products. In ads, POM touted medical studies claiming to show that daily consumption of its products could treat, prevent, or reduce the risk of heart disease, prostate cancer, and erectile dysfunction. These ads mischaracterized the scientific evidence.

The Federal Trade Commission (FTC) charged POM with, and held POM liable for, making false, misleading, and unsubstantiated representations in violation of the Federal Trade Commission Act. POM was barred from running future ads asserting that its products treat or prevent any disease unless "randomized, controlled, human clinical trials" (RCTs, for "randomized controlled trials") demonstrated statistically significant results. POM petitioned the U.S. Court of Appeals for the District of Columbia Circuit to review this injunctive order.

In the Language of the Court
SRINIVASAN, Circuit Judge:
＊＊＊＊

＊＊＊POM's ads ＊＊＊ convey the net impression that clinical studies or trials show that a causal relation has been established between the consumption of the challenged POM products and its efficacy [ability] to treat, prevent or reduce the risk of the serious diseases in question. The Commission found that experts in the relevant fields would require RCTs ＊＊＊ to establish such a causal relationship.

The Commission examined each of the studies invoked by petitioners in their ads, concluding that the referenced studies fail to qualify as RCTs of the kind that could afford adequate substantiation. Petitioners' claims therefore were deceptive.
＊＊＊＊

＊＊＊The Commission's finding is supported by substantial record evidence. That evidence includes written reports and testimony from medical researchers stating that experts in the fields of cardiology and urology require randomized, double-blinded, placebo-controlled clinical trials to substantiate any claim that a product treats, prevents, or reduces the risk of disease.

The Commission drew on that expert testimony to explain why the attributes of well-designed RCTs are necessary to substantiate petitioners' claims. A control group, for example, allows investigators to distinguish between real effects from the intervention, and other changes, including those due to the mere act of being treated (placebo effect) and the passage of time. Random assignment of a study's subjects to treatment and control groups increases the likelihood that the treatment and control groups are similar in relevant characteristics, so that any difference in the outcome between the two groups can be attributed to the treatment. And when a study is double-blinded ([that is,] when neither the study participants nor the investigators know which patients are in the treatment group and which patients are in the control group), it is less likely that participants or investigators will consciously or unconsciously take actions potentially biasing the results.
＊＊＊＊

＊＊＊The need for RCTs is driven by the claims petitioners have chosen to make. ＊＊＊ *An advertiser ＊＊＊ may assert a health-related claim backed by medical evidence falling short of an RCT if it includes an effective disclaimer disclosing the limitations of the supporting research.* Petitioners did not do so. [Emphasis added.]

Decision and Remedy *The U.S. Court of Appeals for the District of Columbia Circuit enforced the FTC's order prohibiting POM from running misleading ads. The court pointed out that "An advertiser who makes express representations about the level of support for a particular claim must possess the level of proof claimed in the ad and must convey that information to consumers in a non-misleading way."*

Critical Thinking
- **Ethical** *POM claimed that it is unethical to require RCTs to substantiate disease-related claims about food products. It argued that, for instance, "doctors cannot . . . ethically deprive a control group of patients of all Vitamin C for a decade to determine whether Vitamin C helps prevent cancer." Is this a valid argument? Why or why not?*

Claims Based on Half-Truths Some advertisements contain "half-truths," meaning that the presented information is true but incomplete and may therefore lead consumers to a false conclusion. ■ **Example 24.3** The maker of Campbell's soups advertised that "most" Campbell's soups are low in fat and cholesterol and thus helpful in fighting heart disease. What the ad did not say was that many Campbell's soups are high in sodium and that high-sodium diets may increase the risk of heart disease. Hence, the FTC ruled that Campbell's claims were deceptive. ■ In addition,

advertising that contains an endorsement by a celebrity may be deemed deceptive if the celebrity does not actually use the product.

Bait-and-Switch Advertising The FTC has issued rules that govern specific advertising techniques. One of the FTC's most important regulations is its "Guides Against Bait Advertising."[4]

4. 16 C.F.R. Part 238.

Some retailers systematically advertise merchandise at low prices to get customers into their stores. But when the customers arrive, they find that the merchandise is not in stock. Salespersons then encourage them to purchase more expensive items instead. This practice, known as **bait-and-switch advertising,** is a form of deceptive advertising. The low price is the "bait" to lure the consumer into the store. The salesperson is instructed to "switch" the consumer to a different, more expensive item.

Under the FTC guidelines, bait-and-switch advertising occurs if the seller does any of the following:

1. Refuses to show the advertised item.
2. Fails to have a reasonable quantity of the item in stock.
3. Fails to promise to deliver the advertised item within a reasonable time.
4. Discourages employees from selling the advertised item.

Online Deceptive Advertising

Deceptive advertising occurs in the online environment as well as offline. The FTC actively monitors online advertising. It has identified hundreds of websites that have made false or deceptive claims for products and services ranging from medical treatments to exercise equipment and weight-loss aids.

The FTC has issued guidelines to help online businesses comply with existing laws prohibiting deceptive advertising. These guidelines include the following requirements:

1. All ads—both online and offline—must be truthful and not misleading.
2. The claims made in an ad must be substantiated—that is, advertisers must have evidence to back up their claims.
3. Ads cannot be unfair, which the FTC defines as "likely to cause substantial consumer injury that consumers could not reasonably avoid and that is not outweighed by the benefit to consumers or competition."
4. Ads must disclose relevant limitations and qualifying information concerning the claims advertisers are making.
5. Required disclosures must be "clear and conspicuous." For instance, because consumers may not read an entire Web page, an online disclosure should be placed as close as possible to the claim being qualified. Generally, hyperlinks to disclosures are recommended only for lengthy disclosures. If a hyperlink is used, it should be obvious and should be placed as close as possible to the information it qualifies.

The FTC creates additional guidelines as needed to respond to new issues that arise with online advertising. One current issue involves so-called native ads, which are discussed in this chapter's *Digital Update* feature.

Federal Trade Commission Actions

The FTC receives complaints from many sources, including competitors of alleged violators, consumers, trade associations, Better Business Bureaus, and government organizations and officials. When the agency receives numerous and widespread complaints about a particular problem, normally it will investigate.

Formal Complaint. If the FTC concludes that a given advertisement is unfair or deceptive, it drafts a formal complaint, which is sent to the alleged offender. The company may agree to settle the complaint without further proceedings. If not, the FTC can conduct a hearing in which the company can present its defense.

FTC Orders and Remedies. If the FTC succeeds in proving that an advertisement is unfair or deceptive, it usually issues a **cease-and-desist order** requiring the company to stop the challenged advertising. In some circumstances, it may also impose a sanction known as **counteradvertising.** This requires the company to advertise anew—in print, on the Internet, on radio, and on television—to inform the public about the earlier misinformation. The FTC sometimes institutes a **multiple product order,** which requires a firm to stop false advertising for all of its products, not just the product involved in the original action.

Damages When Consumers Are Injured. When a company's deceptive ad involves wrongful charges to consumers, the FTC may seek other remedies, including damages. ■ **Case in Point 24.4** The FTC sued Bronson Partners, LLC, for deceptively advertising two products—Chinese Diet Tea and Bio-Slim Patch. Bronson's ads claimed that the diet tea "eliminates 91 percent of absorbed sugars," "prevents 83 percent of fat absorption," and "doubles your metabolic rate to burn calories fast." The Bio-Slim Patch ads promised "lasting weight loss" and claimed that "ugly fatty tissue will disappear at a spectacular rate" as product users wear the patch while carrying on their normal lifestyle.

Eventually, Bronson conceded that it had engaged in deceptive advertising, and the FTC sought damages. The court awarded the FTC $1,942,325, which was the amount of Bronson's revenues from the two products.[5] ■

Possibility of Restitution. When a company's deceptive ad leads to wrongful payments by consumers, the FTC may seek other remedies, including restitution. ■ **Case in Point 24.5** Verity International, Ltd., billed

---

5. *Federal Trade Commission v. Bronson Partners, LLC,* 654 F.3d 359 (2d Cir. 2011).

Digital Update

Regulating "Native" Ads on the Internet

Sponsored content on the Internet—content that someone pays to put there—is everywhere. One particular type of sponsored content is the "native" ad. Here, *native* describes advertisements that follow the natural form and function of the user experience into which they are placed. Thus, such an ad matches the rest of a Web page's content, including the visual design, as if it were "native" to the page.

Native Ad Integration on Desktops and Mobile Devices

Perhaps the most obvious native ads are in search engine results. When you type "native ads" in a Google search box, you will find that the first several "hits" listed in the search results are actually sponsored ads. Yet they have the look and feel of the rest of the search results.

Additionally, native ads are often placed within stories in online publications. Suppose, for instance, that you are reading a story on your smartphone about new fashions. You will likely see a native ad that looks as if it is part of the story but that is actually sponsored and perhaps written by a clothing company.

Some native ads are delivered via "recommendation widgets." Usually, the widgets are integrated into a page but do not mimic the appearance of the page. Rather, they direct you to a different Web page— perhaps telling you that "you might like" that site. Clicking the widget takes you to the site.

Native ads have become increasingly popular because desktop, smartphone, and tablet users have figured out how to block traditional online ads. Moreover, native ads are less intrusive than traditional online ads—important because of the increasing number of consumers who most often access small screens, such as those on smartphones.

The Federal Trade Commission Takes Action

In response to the growth in native advertising, the Federal Trade Commission (FTC) issued guidelines.[a]

The FTC starts out with the basic question "[A]s native advertising evolves, are consumers able to differentiate advertising from other content?" In its guidance document,[b] the FTC suggests the following:

- Disclosures should be placed where consumers will notice them.
- Disclosures should be placed not after the native ad, but before or above it.
- Disclosures should remain with native ads if the ads are republished.
- Once consumers arrive on a click- or tap-into page where the complete native ad appears, disclosures should be placed as close as possible to where consumers will look first.
- Disclosures should stand out and should be understandable.

More Than 33 Percent of Native Ads Are Not Compliant

In spite of the FTC's guidelines for native advertising, more than one-third of publishers of such ads are not compliant. On average, a native advertising campaign runs for two months or longer. Consequently, millions of consumers view noncompliant native ads on the Internet on a regular basis.

The FTC has stepped up its compliance campaign and has brought actions against some retailers. For instance, Lord & Taylor was charged with deceiving consumers after running an extensive native advertising campaign. The campaign included an article in an online fashion publication and numerous Instagram posts—but none of this material was identified as sponsored content. Ultimately, the FTC settled its case against the retailer.

Critical Thinking *What is the equivalent of native advertising in commercially released movies?*

a. Federal Trade Commission, *Native Advertising: A Guide to Business*, available at www.ftc.gov.

b. Federal Trade Commission, *.com Disclosures: How to Make Effective Disclosures in Digital Advertising*, available at www.ftc.gov.

phone-line subscribers who accessed certain online pornography sites at the rate for international calls to Madagascar. When consumers complained about the charges, Verity told them that the charges were valid and had to be paid, or the consumers would face further collection actions. A federal appellate court held that this representation of "uncontestability" was deceptive and a violation of the FTC act. The court ordered Verity to pay nearly $18 million in restitution to consumers.[6] ■

6. *Federal Trade Commission v. Verity International, Ltd.*, 443 F.3d 48 (2d Cir. 2006).

False Advertising Claims under the Lanham Act The Lanham Act[7] protects trademarks, and it also covers false advertising claims. To state a successful claim for false advertising under this act, a business must establish each of the following elements:

1. An injury to a commercial interest in reputation or sales.
2. Direct causation of the injury by false or deceptive advertising.
3. A loss of business from buyers who were deceived by the advertising.

---

7. 15 U.S.C. Sections 1051 *et seq.*

State Laws Concerning False Advertising State consumer-fraud statutes also prohibit false, misleading, and deceptive advertising. Recovery under a state law typically requires proof of the following elements:

1. The defendant committed a deceptive or unfair act.
2. The act was committed in the course of trade or commerce.
3. The defendant intended that others rely on the deception.
4. The plaintiff suffered actual damages proximately caused by the deception.

At issue in the following case was a plaintiff's claim under Illinois's consumer-fraud statute.

Case 24.2

Haywood v. Massage Envy Franchising, LLC

United States Court of Appeals, Seventh Circuit, 887 F.3d 329 (2018).

Background and Facts Massage Envy, LLC, is a franchisor based in Arizona that grants licenses to independently owned and operated entities for the use of its name, trademark, and standardized operations. Massage Envy's website advertises its services, including an "Introductory 1-hour Massage Session." At the bottom of the homepage, a link to "pricing and promotional details" leads to a page with disclaimers. One disclaimer, titled "Session," explains that a "session includes massage or facial and time for consultation and dressing."

Through the website, Kathy Haywood, a resident of Illinois, scheduled an appointment. At the session, for which Haywood paid with a gift card, she received a massage that lasted no more than fifty minutes. Citing Massage Envy's online ad, Haywood filed a suit in a federal district court against the company, alleging unfair and deceptive business practices in violation of the Illinois Consumer Fraud and Deceptive Business Practices Act (ICFA). The court dismissed the claim. Haywood appealed.

In the Language of the Court

BAUER, Circuit Judge.

* * * *

To state a claim under the ICFA * * * Haywood must plausibly allege: (1) a deceptive act or promise by Massage Envy; (2) Massage Envy's intent that she rely on the deceptive act; (3) the deceptive act occurred during a course of conduct involving trade or commerce; and (4) actual damage as a result of the deceptive act. *Actual damage in this context means that Haywood must have suffered actual pecuniary [financial] loss. Additionally, the deceptive act must have been the "but-for" cause of the damage.* [Emphasis added.]

* * * *

* * * [Haywood's] allegations fail to establish the requisite causation. * * * Here, the only reasonable conclusion is that Massage Envy's representations regarding the one-hour massage session were not the but-for cause of any alleged injury. There is no allegation in the complaint that her belief about the length of the massage caused Haywood to make the appointment. To the contrary, the only reasonable and plausible inference is that only the receipt of a gift card caused her to book a massage; the alleged deceptive representations did not influence that decision. * * * She cannot, based on these allegations, establish that Massage Envy's alleged deception was the but-for cause of her injury, and her claims fail as a result.

Decision and Remedy The U.S. Court of Appeals for the Seventh Circuit affirmed the dismissal. "The district court did not abuse its discretion in dismissing the complaint."

Critical Thinking

- **Economic** *A fraud injury can be measured in two ways. As a loss of the benefit of the bargain, damages consist of the difference between the value of what was promised and the value of what was received. Under the out-of-pocket rule, the measure is the difference between the price paid and the market value of what was received. If Haywood had established her claim, which of these methods would have applied? Why?*
- **What If the Facts Were Different?** *Suppose that reliance was not an element of a consumer-fraud claim under the ICFA. Would the result in this case have been different? Explain.*

24–1b Marketing

In addition to regulating advertising practices, Congress has passed several laws to protect consumers against other marketing practices.

Telephone Solicitation The Telephone Consumer Protection Act (TCPA)[8] prohibits telephone solicitation using an automatic telephone dialing system or a prerecorded voice. The TCPA also makes it illegal to transmit unsolicited advertisements without the sender having an established business relationship with the recipient or first obtaining the recipient's permission. (Most states also have laws regulating telephone solicitation.)

The Federal Communications Commission (FCC) enforces the TCPA. The FCC imposes substantial fines ($11,000 each day) on companies that violate the provisions of the act. The TCPA also gives consumers a right to sue for either $500 for each violation of the act or for the actual monetary losses resulting from a violation, whichever is greater. If a court finds that a defendant willfully or knowingly violated the act, the court has the discretion to treble (triple) the amount of damages awarded.

Fraudulent Telemarketing The Telemarketing and Consumer Fraud and Abuse Prevention Act[9] directed the FTC to establish rules governing telemarketing and to bring actions against fraudulent telemarketers.

The FTC's Telemarketing Sales Rule (TSR)[10] requires a telemarketer to identify the seller's name, describe the product being sold, and disclose all material facts related to the sale (such as the total cost). The TSR makes it illegal for telemarketers to misrepresent information or facts about their goods or services. A telemarketer must also remove a consumer's name from its list of potential contacts if the customer so requests.

An amendment to the TSR established the national Do Not Call Registry. Telemarketers must refrain from calling those consumers who have placed their names on the list. The TSR applies to any offer made to consumers in the United States—even if the offer comes from a foreign firm.

■ **Case in Point 24.6** Jason Abraham formed Instant Response Systems, LLC (IRS), to sell medical alert monitoring systems to the elderly. IRS employed telemarketers to make sales calls to people aged sixty-four years and older. Some of these consumers were on the Do Not Call Registry. IRS telemarketers, using company-supplied scripts, falsely told consumers that they were calling in response to a request for information about its medical alert services. Consumers who did not order the IRS system were still billed for it, receiving follow-up letters and calls accusing them of nonpayment. When they objected, IRS employees resorted to threats.

The FTC sued IRS and Abraham in a federal district court for violating the Telemarketing Sales Rule and won. IRS's telemarketers had made false and misleading statements to consumers and had used threats to force them to make payments. IRS had also called individuals on the Do Not Call Registry without permission. The court ordered Abraham to pay more than $3.4 million (the amount of revenues he had received through the company's unlawful scheme). The court also permanently enjoined (prohibited) Abraham from marketing medical alert systems in the future.[11] ■

24–1c Sales

A number of statutes protect consumers by requiring the disclosure of certain terms in sales transactions and providing rules governing unsolicited merchandise. The FTC has regulatory authority in this area, as do some other federal agencies.

8. 47 U.S.C. Sections 227 *et seq.*
9. 15 U.S.C. Sections 6101–6108.
10. 16 C.F.R. Part 310.

11. *Federal Trade Commission v. Instant Response Systems, LLC,* 2015 WL 1650914 (E.D.N.Y. 2015).

Many states and the FTC have **"cooling-off" laws** that permit the buyers of goods sold door-to-door to cancel their contracts within three business days. The FTC rule also requires that consumers be notified in Spanish of this right if the oral negotiations for the sale were in that language.

The contracts that fall under these cancellation rules include trade show sales contracts, contracts for home equity loans, Internet purchase contracts, and home (door-to-door) sales contracts. In addition, certain states have passed laws allowing consumers to cancel contracts for dating services, gym memberships, and weight loss programs.

The FTC Mail, Internet, or Telephone Order Merchandise Rule[12] protects consumers who purchase goods via mail, Internet, phone, or fax. Merchants are required to ship orders within the time promised in their advertisements and to notify consumers when orders cannot be shipped on time. If the seller does not give an estimated shipping time, it must ship within thirty days. Merchants must also issue a refund within a specified period of time when a consumer cancels an order.

24–2 Labeling and Packaging Laws

A number of federal and state laws deal specifically with the information given on labels and packages. In general, labels must be accurate, and they must use words that are easily understood by the ordinary consumer. In some instances, labels must specify the raw materials used in the product, such as the percentage of cotton, nylon, or other fiber used in a garment. In other instances, the product must carry a warning, such as those required on cigarette and e-cigarette packages and advertising.[13]

24–2a Automobile Fuel Economy Labels

The Energy Policy and Conservation Act (EPCA)[14] requires automakers to attach an information label to every new car. The label must include the Environmental Protection Agency's fuel economy estimate for the vehicle. ■ **Case in Point 24.7** Gaetano Paduano bought a new Honda Civic Hybrid in California. The information label on the car included the fuel economy estimate from the Environmental Protection Agency (EPA). Honda's sales brochure added, "Just drive the Hybrid like you would a conventional car and save on fuel bills."

When Paduano discovered that the car's fuel economy was less than half of the EPA's estimate, he sued Honda for deceptive advertising under a California law. The automaker claimed that the federal law (the EPCA) preempted the state's deceptive advertising law. The court held in Paduano's favor, finding that the federal statute did not preempt a claim for deceptive advertising made under state law.[15] ■

24–2b Food Labeling

Because the quality and safety of food are so important to consumers, several statutes deal specifically with food labeling. The Fair Packaging and Labeling Act[16] requires that food product labels identify (1) the product, (2) the net quantity of the contents (and, if the number of servings is stated, the size of a serving), (3) the manufacturer, and (4) the packager or distributor. The act includes additional requirements concerning descriptions on packages, savings claims, components of nonfood products, and standards for the partial filling of packages.

Nutritional Content of Food Products Food products must bear labels detailing the nutritional content, including the number of calories and the amounts of various nutrients that the food contains. The Nutrition Labeling and Education Act[17] requires food labels to provide standard nutrition facts and regulates the use of such terms as *fresh* and *low fat*.

The U.S. Food and Drug Administration (FDA) and the U.S. Department of Agriculture (USDA) are the primary agencies that issue regulations on food labeling. These rules are published in the *Federal Register* and updated annually.

Caloric Content of Restaurant Foods The Affordable Care Act, or Obamacare, includes provisions aimed at combating the problem of obesity in the United States. All restaurant chains with twenty or more locations are required to post the caloric content of the foods on their menus so that customers will know how many calories the foods contain.[18] Foods offered through vending machines must also be labeled so that their caloric content is visible to would-be purchasers.

In addition, restaurants are supposed to post guidelines on the number of calories that an average person requires

---

12. 16 C.F.R. Part 435.
13. 15 U.S.C. Sections 1331–1341.
14. 49 U.S.C. Section 32908(b)(1).
15. *Paduano v. American Honda Motor Co.*, 169 Cal.App.4th 1453, 88 Cal.Rptr.3d 90 (2009).
16. 15 U.S.C. Sections 1451 *et seq.*
17. 21 U.S.C. Section 343-1.
18. See Section 4205 of the Patient Protection and Affordable Care Act, Pub. L. No. 111-148, 124 Stat. 119 (2010).

daily so that customers can determine what portion of a day's calories a particular food will provide. The hope is that consumers, armed with this information, will consider the number of calories when they make their food choices. The federal law on menu labeling supersedes all previous state and local laws in this area.

24–3 Protection of Health and Safety

Although labeling and packaging laws promote consumer health and safety, there is a significant distinction between regulating the information dispensed about a product and regulating the actual content of the product. The classic example is tobacco products. Producers of tobacco products must use labels that warn consumers about the health hazards associated with their use, but the sale of tobacco products has not been subjected to significant restrictions. We now examine various laws that regulate the actual products made available to consumers.

24–3a The Federal Food, Drug, and Cosmetic Act

The most important federal legislation regulating food and drugs is the Federal Food, Drug, and Cosmetic Act (FDCA).[19] The act protects consumers against adulterated (contaminated) and misbranded foods and drugs. The FDCA establishes food standards, specifies safe levels of potentially hazardous food additives, and provides classifications of foods and food advertising. Most of these statutory requirements are monitored and enforced by the FDA.

Interestingly, the European Union and a number of other countries, such as Canada, have banned some foods that the FDA assumes to be safe. These foods include brominated vegetable oil (a common ingredient in sports drinks, such as Gatorade) and Olestra/Olean (a cholesterol-free fat substitute found in certain potato chips). Food products containing such substances may not be sold in the European Union. Similarly, certain food colorings found in processed foods in the United States (in M&Ms and Kraft macaroni and cheese, for instance) are not allowed in foods in some other countries.

Tainted Foods In the last twenty years or so, many people in the United States have contracted food poisoning from eating foods that were contaminated, often with salmonella or *E. coli* bacteria. ■ **Example 24.8** During

a period of several years, hundreds of people across the United States were sickened by eating tainted food at the popular restaurant chain Chipotle Mexican Grill. Other fast food restaurants have had similar problems. Causes of illness in these outbreaks have included *E. coli* and salmonella, as well as the highly contagious norovirus. ■

Congress enacted the Food Safety Modernization Act (FSMA)[20] to provide greater government control over the U.S. food safety system. The act gives the FDA authority to directly recall any food products that it suspects are tainted, rather than relying on the producers to recall items.

The FSMA requires anyone who manufactures, processes, packs, distributes, receives, holds, or imports food products to pay a fee and register with the U.S. Department of Health and Human Services. (There are some exceptions for small farmers.) Owners and operators of such facilities are required to analyze and identify food safety hazards, implement preventive controls, monitor effectiveness, and take corrective actions. The FSMA places additional restrictions on importers of food and requires them to verify that imported foods meet U.S. safety standards.

Drugs and Medical Devices The FDA is also responsible under the FDCA for ensuring that drugs are safe and effective before they are marketed to the public. Because the FDA must ensure the safety of new medications, there is always a delay before drugs are available to the public, and this sometimes leads to controversy.

■ **Case in Point 24.9** A group of citizens petitioned the FDA to allow everyone access to "Plan B"—the morning-after birth control pill—without a prescription. The FDA denied the petition and continued to require women under the age of seventeen to obtain a prescription. The group appealed to a federal district court, claiming that the prescription requirement would delay access to the pill. The pill should be taken as soon as possible after sexual intercourse, preferably within twenty-four hours. The court ruled in favor of the plaintiffs and ordered the FDA to make the morning-after pill available to people of any age without a prescription.[21] ■

24–3b The Consumer Product Safety Act

The Consumer Product Safety Act[22] created a comprehensive regulatory scheme over consumer safety matters and established the Consumer Product Safety Commission (CPSC).

---

19. 21 U.S.C. Sections 301 *et seq.*

20. Pub. L. No. 111-353, 124 Stat. 3885 (2011). This statute affected numerous parts of Title 21 of the U.S.C.
21. *Tummino v. Hamburg*, 936 F.Supp.2d 162 (E.D.N.Y. 2013).
22. 15 U.S.C. Sections 2051 *et seq.*

The CPSC's Authority The CPSC conducts research on the safety of individual consumer products and maintains a clearinghouse on the risks associated with various products. The Consumer Product Safety Act authorizes the CPSC to do the following:

1. Set safety standards for consumer products.
2. Ban the manufacture and sale of any product that the commission believes poses an "unreasonable risk" to consumers. (Products banned by the CPSC have included various types of fireworks, cribs, and toys, as well as many products containing asbestos or vinyl chloride.)
3. Remove from the market any products it believes to be imminently hazardous. The CPSC frequently works in conjunction with manufacturers to conduct voluntary recalls of defective products from stores. ■ **Example 24.10** In cooperation with the CPSC, the Scandinavian company IKEA recalled 3 million baby bed canopies and 30 million wall-mounted children's lamps because they posed a strangulation risk to children. ■
4. Require manufacturers to report on any products already sold or intended for sale if the products have proved to be hazardous.
5. Administer other product-safety legislation, including the Child Protection and Toy Safety Act[23] and the Federal Hazardous Substances Act.[24]

Notification Requirements The Consumer Product Safety Act requires the distributors of consumer products to notify the CPSC immediately if they receive information that a product "contains a defect which . . . creates a substantial risk to the public" or "an unreasonable risk of serious injury or death."

■ **Example 24.11** A company that sells juicers receives twenty-three letters from customers complaining that during operation the juicer suddenly exploded, sending pieces of glass and razor-sharp metal across the room. The company must immediately notify the CPSC because the alleged defect creates a substantial risk to the public. ■

24–3c Health-Care Reforms

Health-care reforms enacted in 2010 (the ACA, or Obamacare) made some changes in Americans' rights and benefits with regard to health care.[25] The legislation also affected certain insurance company practices.

Expanded Coverage for Children and Seniors The reforms enabled more children to obtain health-insurance coverage and allowed young adults (under age twenty-six) to remain on their parents' health insurance policies. The legislation also ended lifetime limits and most annual limits on care, and gave insured persons access to recommended preventive services (such as cancer screening and vaccinations) without cost. Some Medicare drug benefits were also changed.

Controlling Costs of Health Insurance In an attempt to control the rising costs of health insurance, certain restrictions were placed on insurance companies. Insurance companies must spend at least 85 percent of all premium dollars collected from large employers (80 percent of the premiums collected from individuals and small employers) on benefits and quality improvement. If insurance companies do not meet these goals, they must provide rebates to consumers. Additionally, states can require insurance companies to justify any premium increases to be eligible to participate in state-sponsored health-insurance exchanges.

24–4 Credit Protection

Credit protection is one of the more important aspects of consumer protection legislation. Nearly 80 percent of U.S. consumers have credit cards, and most carry a balance on these cards—a total of more than $1 trillion nationwide. The Consumer Financial Protection Bureau (CFPB) is the agency that oversees the credit practices of banks, mortgage lenders, and credit-card companies.

24–4a The Truth-in-Lending Act

A key statute regulating the credit and credit-card industries is the Truth-in-Lending Act (TILA), the name commonly given to Title I of the Consumer Credit Protection Act, as amended.[26] The TILA is basically a *disclosure law*. It is administered by the Federal Reserve Board and requires sellers and lenders to disclose credit terms and loan terms so that individuals can shop around for the best financing arrangements.

Application TILA requirements apply only to those who, in the ordinary course of business, lend funds, sell on credit, or arrange for the extension of credit. Thus, sales or loans made between two consumers do not come

---

23. 15 U.S.C. Section 1262(e).
24. 15 U.S.C. Sections 1261 *et seq.*
25. Patient Protection and Affordable Health Care Act, Pub. L. No. 111-148, 124 Stat. 119 (2010); and the Health Care and Education Reconciliation Act, Pub. L. No. 111-152, 124 Stat. 1029 (2010).

26. 15 U.S.C. Sections 1601 *et seq.*

under the protection of the act. Additionally, this law protects only debtors who are natural persons (as opposed to the artificial "person" of a corporation). It does not extend to other legal entities.

Disclosure Requirements

The TILA's disclosure requirements are contained in **Regulation Z,** issued by the Federal Reserve Board of Governors. If the contracting parties are subject to the TILA, the requirements of Regulation Z apply to any transaction involving an installment sales contract that calls for payment to be made in more than four installments. Transactions subject to Regulation Z typically include installment loans, retail and installment sales, car loans, home-improvement loans, and certain real estate loans if the amount of financing is less than $25,000.

Under the provisions of the TILA, all of the terms of a credit instrument must be clearly and conspicuously disclosed. A lender must disclose the annual percentage rate (APR), finance charge, amount financed, and total payments (the sum of the amount loaned, plus any fees, finance charges, and interest). If a creditor fails to follow the *exact* procedures required by the TILA, the creditor risks contract rescission (cancellation) under the act.

Equal Credit Opportunity

The Equal Credit Opportunity Act (ECOA)[27] amended the TILA. The ECOA prohibits the denial of credit solely on the basis of race, religion, national origin, color, gender, marital status, or age. The act also prohibits credit discrimination on the basis of whether an individual receives certain forms of income, such as public-assistance benefits.

Under the ECOA, a creditor may not require a cosigner on a credit instrument if the applicant qualifies under the creditor's standards of creditworthiness for the amount and terms of the credit request. ■ **Case in Point 24.12** T.R. Hughes, Inc., and Summit Pointe, LLC, obtained financing from Frontenac Bank to construct two real estate developments near St. Louis, Missouri. The bank also required the builder, Thomas R. Hughes, and his wife, Carolyn, to sign personal guaranty agreements for the loans.

When the borrowers failed to make the loan payments, the bank sued the two companies and Thomas and Carolyn Hughes personally, and foreclosed on the properties. Carolyn claimed that the personal guaranty contracts that she signed were obtained in violation of the ECOA. The court held that because the applicant, Thomas R. Hughes, was creditworthy, the personal

guaranties of Carolyn Hughes were obtained in violation of the ECOA and therefore unenforceable.[28] ■

Credit-Card Rules

The TILA also contains provisions regarding credit cards. One provision limits the liability of a cardholder to $50 per card for unauthorized charges made before the creditor is notified that the card has been lost. If a consumer receives an *unsolicited* credit card in the mail that is later stolen, the company that issued the card cannot charge the consumer for any unauthorized charges.

Another provision requires credit-card companies to disclose the balance computation method that is used to determine the outstanding balance and to state when finance charges begin to accrue. Other provisions set forth procedures for resolving billing disputes with the credit-card company. These procedures are used if, for instance, a cardholder thinks that an error has occurred in billing or wishes to withhold payment for a faulty product purchased by credit card.

Amendments to Credit-Card Rules

Amendments to the TILA's credit-card rules added the following protections:

1. A company may not retroactively increase the interest rates on existing card balances unless the account is sixty days delinquent.
2. A company must provide forty-five days' advance notice to consumers before changing its credit-card terms.
3. Monthly bills must be sent to cardholders twenty-one days before the due date.
4. The interest rate charged on a customer's credit-card balance may not be increased except in specific situations, such as when a promotional rate ends.
5. A company may not charge over-limit fees except in specified situations.
6. When the customer has balances at different interest rates, payments in excess of the minimum amount due must be applied first to the balance with the highest rate. (For instance, a higher interest rate is commonly charged for cash advances.)
7. A company may not compute finance charges based on the previous billing cycle (a practice known as double-cycle billing). This practice hurts consumers because they are charged interest for the previous cycle even if they have paid the bill in full.

---

27. 15 U.S.C. Sections 1691 *et seq.*

28. *Frontenac Bank v. T.R. Hughes, Inc.*, 404 S.W.3d 272 (Mo.App. 2012).

24–4b The Fair Credit Reporting Act

The Fair Credit Reporting Act (FCRA)[29] protects consumers against inaccurate credit reporting and requires that lenders and other creditors report correct, relevant, and up-to-date information. The act provides that

29. 15 U.S.C. Sections 1681 *et seq.*

consumer credit reporting agencies may issue credit reports to users only for specified purposes. Legitimate purposes include extending credit, issuing insurance policies, and responding to the consumer's request.

Whether an Internet service provider had a legitimate purpose to pull a customer's credit report was at issue in the following case.

Case Analysis 24.3

Santangelo v. Comcast Corp.

United States District Court, Northern District of Illinois, Eastern Division, 162 F.Supp.3d 691 (2016).

In the Language of the Court
John Z. *LEE*, United States District Judge
      * * * *

I. Factual and Procedural Background
    [Keith Santangelo filed a complaint in a federal district court against Comcast Corporation, alleging a violation of the Fair Credit Reporting Act (FCRA).] Santangelo alleges * * * that he contacted Comcast through the company's online customer service "Chat" function * * * and requested Internet service for his new apartment. During the chat session, a Comcast representative asked Santangelo for permission to run a credit inquiry. Santangelo asked if any option was available to avoid the credit inquiry. The Comcast representative told him that the company would forgo the inquiry if he paid a $50 deposit.
    The option to pay a $50 deposit in order to avoid a credit inquiry was an explicit part of Comcast's official Risk Management Policy * * *. The policy also required a $50 deposit from any prospective customer who agreed to a credit inquiry but whose credit score proved to be unsatisfactory. According to Santangelo, the deposit policy "reflects Comcast's calculated business decision and belief that the collection of a $50 deposit is sufficient to cover the risk presented by a person with bad credit and is sufficient to cover the risk presented by a person who refuses a credit pull."
    Santangelo opted to pay the $50 deposit in lieu of a credit inquiry. * * * Nevertheless, Comcast, without

Santangelo's authorization, pulled his credit report * * *. This credit inquiry depleted [lowered] Santangelo's credit score.
      * * * *
    * * * Comcast now moves to dismiss the * * * complaint.
II. Analysis
      * * * *
    *FCRA prohibits the obtaining of a "consumer report," commonly known as a credit report, except for purposes authorized by that statute. The statute lists specific permissible purposes, such as * * * any * * * "legitimate business need * * * in connection with a business transaction that is initiated by the consumer."* These limitations are intended to produce a balance between consumer privacy and the needs of a modern, credit-driven economy. [Emphasis added.]
    Santangelo contends that Comcast did not have a permissible purpose for obtaining his credit report after he paid the $50 deposit in exchange for the company's promise not to check his credit. If he is correct and the company's violation was willful, he would be entitled to recover attorney's fees and either actual damages or statutory damages between $100 and $1,000. If the company's violation was merely negligent, Santangelo would be permitted to recover only attorney's fees and actual damages.
1. Standing
    Comcast first argues that Santangelo lacks standing to bring his FCRA claim. To establish standing * * * a plaintiff

must show * * * the injury is fairly traceable to the challenged action of the defendant.
    According to Comcast, Santangelo has not alleged an injury-in-fact that is fairly traceable to the FCRA violation he claims. Santangelo responds that he has sustained three injuries-in-fact: the loss of the $50 he paid as a deposit, the violation of his legal right not to have his credit report pulled without a permissible purpose, and the resulting depletion of his credit score.
      * * * *
    * * * It was the very fact that Comcast received the $50 from Santangelo before it performed the credit check that made it illegal. * * * And once Comcast checked Santangelo's credit, it should have refunded the deposit immediately, rather than keeping it. Comcast's receipt and withholding of the $50, therefore, is inextricable [inseparable] from the FCRA violation and can be said to be fairly traceable to the FCRA violation. * * * Even if the $50.00 deposit were fully refundable, Santangelo still has standing based on the lost time-value of the money.
    * * * Santangelo also has sufficiently alleged an injury-in-fact by alleging that Comcast obtained his credit report without a permissible purpose in violation of the FCRA.
    Because the FCRA grants consumers a legally protected interest in limiting access to their credit reports and provides redress for violations, * * * *Santangelo's allegations about Comcast's interference with that legally protected interest are sufficient*

to establish * * * *standing.* [Emphasis added.]

* * * Santangelo also alleges that the FCRA violation in this case depleted his credit score. In response, Comcast contends that a reduced credit score, without resulting damages, does not constitute an injury.

* * * The Court agrees with Santangelo that a depleted credit score is sufficient to constitute an injury * * *. Credit scores are of great importance in our economy, and a depleted credit score could affect a consumer in numerous ways, inflicting harm that often may be difficult to prove or quantify. Congress has the power to discourage the needless depletion of consumers' credit scores even when the depleted score cannot be neatly tied to a financial harm.

2. Sufficiency of Santangelo's allegations

Comcast next argues that Santangelo's allegations do not state an FCRA claim.

* * * *

In his * * * complaint, Santangelo * * * alleges that Comcast's deposit policies demonstrate its lack of a legitimate need to run credit checks with respect to consumers who paid a $50 deposit. According to the * * * complaint, Comcast's established policy is to forgo a credit check in exchange for a $50 deposit. The company also has a policy of accepting a $50 deposit from consumers who opt for a credit check but prove to have poor credit. Santangelo compares this situation to that of a car dealer who accepts a cash payment for the full purchase price of a car. * * * The car dealer * * * does not have a legitimate need to obtain the purchaser's credit report. Similarly, a landlord does not have a legitimate need to obtain a tenant's credit report if the tenant is entitled to a lease renewal without regard to creditworthiness.

In response, Comcast * * * argues that it had a legitimate business need to establish Santangelo's creditworthiness despite his deposit because—unlike in the car dealer example—his $50 deposit would cover less than two months of service in a long-term contract. * * * [Santangelo] contends that, under company policy, his creditworthiness was irrelevant to Comcast's determination of his eligibility for service once the deposit was collected, much like the tenants in [the landlord example].

* * * *

* * * Comcast's mere violation of its alleged agreement not to pull Santangelo's credit report does not support an FCRA claim. But the possibility that the company itself believed that its customers' creditworthiness was irrelevant if they paid a deposit is enough.

Comcast's final argument for dismissing Santangelo's FCRA claim is that he neither explicitly alleges that the company's actions were willful, which is necessary to trigger statutory damages, nor identifies any actual damages that he could recover if Comcast acted only negligently. Although [Santangelo] does not use the word willful in his complaint, he alleges that the company obtained his credit report despite that it "knew that it did not have a legitimate business need." This allegation implies recklessness at the very least, and reckless conduct qualifies as willful conduct under the FCRA.

* * * *

III. Conclusion

* * * The Court denies Comcast's motion to dismiss.

Legal Reasoning Questions

1. Comcast argued that it had refunded Santangelo's $50, plus interest in the amount of $10, four months after pulling his credit report. Does this argument undercut the plaintiff's claim to have standing? Why or why not?

2. What might discovery reveal that would affect the outcome in this case? Explain.

3. What damages might Santangelo be able to prove based on the depletion of his credit score?

Consumer Notification and Inaccurate Information Any time a consumer is denied credit or insurance on the basis of her or his credit report, the consumer must be notified of that fact. The notice must include the name and address of the credit reporting agency that issued the report. The same notice must be sent to consumers who are charged more than others ordinarily would be for credit or insurance because of their credit reports.

Under the FCRA, consumers may request the source of any information used by the credit agency, as well as the identity of anyone who has received an agency's report.

Consumers are also permitted to access the information about them contained in a credit reporting agency's files.

If a consumer discovers that an agency's files contain inaccurate information, he or she should report the problem to the agency. On the consumer's written (or electronic) request, the agency must conduct a systematic examination of its records. Any unverifiable or erroneous information must be deleted within a reasonable period of time.

Remedies for Violations A credit reporting agency that fails to comply with the act is liable for actual damages, plus additional damages not to exceed $1,000 and attorneys' fees.[30] Creditors and other companies that use information from credit reporting agencies may also be liable for violations of the FCRA. The United States Supreme Court has held that an insurance company's failure to notify new customers that they were paying higher insurance rates as a result of their credit scores was a *willful* violation of the FCRA.[31]

■ **Case in Point 24.13** After graduating from college, Richard Williams applied for a job with Rent-A-Center as an account representative. As part of the application process, he agreed to a criminal-background check. Rent-A-Center contracted with First Advantage LNS Screening Solutions, Inc., a credit reporting agency that provides background checks. First Advantage reported to Rent-A-Center that a Richard Williams had a sale-of-cocaine record in another part of the state. Williams disputed the report. When First Advantage investigated, it determined that the criminal record was for a different person with the same name. It removed that criminal record from Williams's report. By then, however, it was too late, as Rent-A-Center had hired someone else.

Williams continued applying for other jobs. Eventually, another prospective employer ran a background check through First Advantage. This time, First Advantage reported to the employer that Williams had been convicted of aggravated battery on a pregnant woman. Again, it turned out to be a different Richard Williams, but by then, the employer had rejected Williams and hired someone else. Williams sued First Advantage in a federal district court for willfully violating the FCRA. After a jury trial, he was awarded $250,000 in compensatory damages and $3.3 million in punitive damages. First Advantage filed a motion for a new trial, which the court denied. Evidence supported the jury's finding that First Advantage willfully violated the FCRA and that the damages awarded were appropriate and not unconstitutionally excessive.[32] ■

24–4c The Fair and Accurate Credit Transactions Act

Congress passed the Fair and Accurate Credit Transactions Act (FACTA) in an effort to combat identity theft.[33] The act amended the TILA and established a national fraud alert system. Consumers who suspect that they have been or may be victimized by identity theft can place an alert on

their credit files. When a consumer establishes that identity theft has occurred, the credit reporting agency must stop reporting allegedly fraudulent account information.

FACTA also requires the major credit reporting agencies to provide consumers with free copies of their own credit reports every twelve months. Another provision requires account numbers on credit-card receipts to be truncated (shortened). Merchants, employees, or others who may have access to the receipts can no longer obtain the consumers' names and full credit-card numbers. Financial institutions must work with the FTC to identify "red flag" indicators of identity theft and to develop rules for the disposal of sensitive credit information.

24–4d The Fair Debt Collection Practices Act

The Fair Debt Collection Practices Act (FDCPA)[34] attempts to curb perceived abuses by collection agencies. The act applies only to specialized debt-collection agencies and attorneys who regularly attempt to collect debts on behalf of someone else, usually for a percentage of the amount owed. Creditors attempting to collect debts are not covered by the act unless, by misrepresenting themselves, they cause debtors to believe they are collection agencies.

Requirements of the Act Under the FDCPA, a collection agency may *not* do any of the following:

1. Contact the debtor at the debtor's place of employment if the debtor's employer objects.
2. Contact the debtor at inconvenient or unusual times (such as three o'clock in the morning), or at any time if the debtor is being represented by an attorney.
3. Contact third parties other than the debtor's parents, spouse, or financial adviser about payment of a debt unless a court authorizes such action.
4. Harass or intimidate the debtor (by using abusive language or threatening violence, for instance) or make false or misleading statements (such as posing as a police officer).
5. Communicate with the debtor at any time after receiving notice that the debtor is refusing to pay the debt, except to advise the debtor of further action to be taken by the collection agency.

The FDCPA also requires a collection agency to include a **validation notice** when it initially contacts a debtor for payment of a debt or within five days of that initial contact. The notice must state that the debtor has

---

30. 15 U.S.C. Section 1681n.
31. *Safeco Insurance. Co. of America v. Burr*, 551 U.S. 47, 127 S.Ct. 2201, 167 L.Ed.2d 1045 (2007).
32. *Williams v. First Advantage LNS Screening Solutions, Inc.*, 238 F.Supp.3d 1333 (N.D.Fla. 2017).
33. Pub. L. No. 108-159, 117 Stat. 1952 (2003).

34. 15 U.S.C. Sections 1692 *et seq.*

thirty days in which to dispute the debt and to request a written verification of the debt from the collection agency.

Enforcement of the Act The Federal Trade Commission is primarily responsible for enforcing the FDCPA. A debt collector who fails to comply with the act is liable for actual damages, plus additional damages not to exceed $1,000 and attorneys' fees.

Debt collectors who violate the act are exempt from liability if they can show that the violation was not

intentional and resulted from a bona fide error. Furthermore, the error must have occurred in spite of procedures the company had already put in place to avoid such errors. The "bona fide error" defense typically has been applied to mistakes of fact or clerical errors. A few courts have gone further and allowed the good faith error defense in other circumstances.[35]

35. See, for instance, *Scheffler v. Altran Financial, LP*, 2018 WL 4126447 (D.Minn. 2018); and *Zortman v. J.C. Christensen & Associates, Inc.*, 870 F.Supp.2d 694 (D.Minn. 2012).

Practice and Review: Consumer Protection

Leota Sage saw a local motorcycle dealer's newspaper advertisement offering a MetroRider EZ electric scooter for $1,699. When she went to the dealership, however, she learned that the EZ model had been sold out. The salesperson told Sage that he still had the higher-end MetroRider FX model in stock for $2,199 and would sell her one for $1,999. Sage was disappointed but decided to purchase the FX model.

When Sage said that she wished to purchase the scooter on credit, she was directed to the dealer's credit department. As she filled out the credit forms, the clerk told Sage, who is an Asian American, that she would need a cosigner to obtain a loan. Sage could not understand why she would need a cosigner and asked to speak to the store manager. The manager apologized, told her that the clerk was mistaken, and said that he would "speak to" the clerk. The manager completed Sage's credit application, and Sage then rode the scooter home. Seven months later, Sage received a letter from the manufacturer informing her that a flaw had been discovered in the scooter's braking system and that the model had been recalled. Using the information presented in the chapter, answer the following questions.

1. Did the dealer engage in deceptive advertising? Why or why not?
2. Suppose that Sage had ordered the scooter through the dealer's website but the dealer had been unable to deliver it by the date promised. What would the FTC have required the merchant to do in that situation?
3. Assuming that the clerk required a cosigner based on Sage's race or gender, what act prohibits such credit discrimination?
4. What organization has the authority to ban the sale of scooters based on safety concerns?

Debate This . . . *Laws against bait-and-switch advertising should be abolished because no consumer is ever forced to buy anything.*

Terms and Concepts

bait-and-switch advertising 520	"cooling-off" laws 524	multiple product order 520
cease-and-desist order 520	counteradvertising 520	Regulation Z 527
consumer law 517	deceptive advertising 517	validation notice 530

Issue Spotters

1. United Pharmaceuticals, Inc., believes that it has developed a new drug that will be effective in the treatment of patients with AIDS. The drug has had only limited testing, but United wants to make the drug widely available as soon as possible. To market the drug, what must United

prove to the U.S. Food and Drug Administration? (See *Protection of Health and Safety*.)
2. Gert buys a notebook computer from EZ Electronics. She pays for it with her credit card. When the computer proves defective, she asks EZ to repair or replace

it, but EZ refuses. What can Gert do? (See *Credit Protection.*)

- Check your answers to the Issue Spotters against the answers provided in Appendix B at the end of this text.

Business Scenarios and Case Problems

24–1. Credit-Card Rules. Maria Ochoa receives two new credit cards on May 1. She has solicited one of them from Midtown Department Store, and the other arrives unsolicited from High-Flying Airlines. During the month of May, Ochoa makes numerous credit-card purchases from Midtown Department Store, but she does not use the High-Flying Airlines card. On May 31, a burglar breaks into Ochoa's home and steals both credit cards, along with other items. Ochoa notifies the Midtown Department Store of the theft on June 2, but she fails to notify High-Flying Airlines. Using the Midtown credit card, the burglar makes a $500 purchase on June 1 and a $200 purchase on June 3. The burglar then charges a vacation flight on the High-Flying Airlines card for $1,000 on June 5. Ochoa receives the bills for these charges and refuses to pay them. Discuss Ochoa's liability for the charges. (See *Credit Protection.*)

24–2. Spotlight on McDonald's—Food Labeling. McDonald's Corp.'s Happy Meal® meal selection consists of an entrée, a small order of french fries, a small drink, and a toy. In the early 1990s, McDonald's began to aim its Happy Meal marketing at children aged one to three. In 1995, McDonald's began making nutritional information for its food products available in documents known as "McDonald's Nutrition Facts." Each document lists the food items that the restaurant serves and provides a nutritional breakdown, but the Happy Meal is not included.

Marc Cohen filed a suit against McDonald's in an Illinois state court. Among other things, Cohen alleged that McDonald's had violated a state law prohibiting consumer fraud and deceptive business practices by failing to adhere to the Nutrition Labeling and Education Act (NLEA). The NLEA sets out different requirements for products specifically intended for children under the age of four—for instance, the products' labels cannot declare the percent of daily value of nutritional components. Does it make sense to have different requirements for children of this age? Why or why not? Should a state court impose such regulations? Explain. [*Cohen v. McDonald's Corp.*, 347 Ill.App.3d 627, 808 N.E.2d 1 (1 Dist. 2004)] (See *Labeling and Packaging Laws.*)

24–3. Deceptive Advertising. Brian Cleary and Rita Burke filed a suit against cigarette maker Philip Morris USA, Inc., seeking class-action status for a claim of deceptive advertising. Cleary and Burke claimed that "light" cigarettes, such as Marlboro Lights, were advertised as safer than regular cigarettes, even though the health effects are the same. They contended that the tobacco companies concealed the true nature of light cigarettes. Philip Morris correctly claimed that it was authorized by the government to advertise cigarettes, including light cigarettes.

Assuming that is true, should the plaintiffs still be able to bring a deceptive advertising claim against the tobacco company? Why or why not? [*Cleary v. Philip Morris USA, Inc.*, 683 F.Supp.2d 730 (N.D.Ill. 2010)] (See *Advertising, Marketing, and Sales.*)

24–4. Business Case Problem with Sample Answer—Fair Debt-Collection Practices. Bank of America hired Atlantic Resource Management, LLC, to collect a debt from Michael E. Engler. Atlantic called Engler's employer and asked his supervisor about the company's policy concerning the execution of warrants. The caller then told the supervisor that, to stop process of the warrant, Engler needed to call Atlantic about "Case Number 37291 NY0969" during the first three hours of his next shift. When Engler's supervisor told him about the call, Engler feared that he might be arrested, and he experienced discomfort, embarrassment, and emotional distress at work. Can Engler recover under the Fair Debt Collection Practices Act? Why or why not? [*Engler v. Atlantic Resource Management, LLC*, 2012 WL 464728 (W.D.N.Y. 2012)] (See *Credit Protection.*)

- For a sample answer to Problem 24–4, go to Appendix C at the end of this text.

24–5. Deceptive Advertising. Innovative Marketing, Inc. (IMI), used a "scareware" scheme to sell computer security software. IMI's Internet ads redirected consumers to sites where they were told that a scan of their computers had detected dangerous files—viruses, spyware, and "illegal" pornography. In fact, no scans were conducted. Kristy Ross, an IMI cofounder and vice president, reviewed and edited the ads, and was aware of the many complaints that consumers had made about them. An individual can be held liable under the Federal Trade Commission Act's prohibition of deceptive practices if the person participated directly in the deceptive practices or had the authority to control them and had or should have had knowledge of them. Were IMI's ads deceptive? If so, can Ross be held liable? Explain. [*Federal Trade Commission v. Ross*, 743 F.3d 886 (4th Cir. 2014)] (See *Advertising, Marketing, and Sales.*)

24–6. Debt Collection. Zakia Mashiri owns a home in San Diego, California. She is a member of the Westwood Club Homeowners' Association (HOA), which charges each member an annual fee. When Mashiri failed to pay the fee, the law firm of Epsten Grinnell & Howell sent her a letter demanding payment. The letter read, "Failure to pay your . . . account in full within thirty-five days from the date of this letter will result in a lien . . . against your property." Mashiri asked for validation of the debt. Within two weeks of receiving it, she sent the HOA a check for the fee. Meanwhile, the law firm filed a lien against her property. Mashiri filed a lawsuit in a federal district court against the law firm, alleging a violation of the Fair Debt Collection Practices Act. On what provision of the act did Mashiri likely base her allegation? Will she succeed in her lawsuit against the law firm? Explain your answer. [*Mashiri v. Epsten Grinnell & Howell*, 845 F.3d 984 (9th Cir. 2017)] (See *Credit Protection*.)

24–7. False Advertising. Rainbow School, Inc., has run a child-care facility in Fayetteville, North Carolina, for more than twenty years. In addition to using the word "rainbow" in its name, the school uses rainbow imagery on its logo. Rainbow Early Education Holding, LLC, operates child-care facilities in several states. Early Education opened a branch in Fayetteville near the Rainbow School under the name "Rainbow Child Care Center," which also used rainbow imagery on its logo. The school filed a suit in a federal district court against Early Education, alleging a violation of the Lanham Act. The parties entered into a settlement agreement that required Early Education to stop using the word "rainbow" in connection with its Fayetteville facility. The court issued an injunction to enforce the agreement. Nevertheless, Early Education continued to use the word "rainbow" in domain names, links, and meta tags associated with its Fayetteville facility's website. Rainbow School imagery was used in a mailer inviting residents to the "nearest Rainbow Child Care Center." Did Early Education violate the Lanham Act? Explain. [*Rainbow School, Inc. v. Rainbow Early Education Holding, LLC*, 887 F.3d 610 (4th Cir. 2018)] (See *Advertising, Marketing, and Sales*.)

24–8. A Question of Ethics—The IDDR Approach and Consumer Protection. In *Richland, Washington, Robert Ingersoll planned his wedding to include about a hundred guests, a photographer, a caterer, a wedding cake, and flowers. Ingersoll had been a customer of Arlene's Flowers and Gifts for more than nine years and had spent several thousand dollars at the shop. When he approached Arlene's owner, Baronelle Stutzman, to buy flowers for his wedding, she refused because Ingersoll and his fiancé, Curt Freed, were a same-sex couple. Deeply offended, Ingersoll and Freed dropped their wedding plans and married in a modest ceremony.* [*Arlene's Flowers, Inc., v. State of Washington*, ___ U.S. ___, 138 S.Ct. 2671, 201 L.Ed.2d 1067 (2018)] (See Advertising, Marketing, and Sales.)

(a) Federal and state laws attempt to protect consumers from unfair trade practices, including discriminatory requirements, related to consumer transactions. Using the *Review* step of the IDDR approach, consider whether it would be ethically fair to hold Stutzman personally liable for a violation of these laws.

(b) Using the *Discussion* step of the IDDR approach, consider actions that Ingersoll and Freed as consumers might take in response to Arlene's—Stutzman's—discriminatory rejection of their offer to do business.

Time-Limited Group Assignment

24–9. Consumer Protections. Many states have enacted laws that go even further than federal law to protect consumers. These laws vary tremendously from state to state. (See *Advertising, Marketing, and Sales*.)

(a) The first group will decide whether having different laws is fair to sellers who may be prohibited from engaging in a practice in one state that is legal in another.

(b) The second group will consider how these different laws might affect a business.

(c) The third group will determine whether it is fair that residents of one state have more protection than residents of another.

Chapter 25

Environmental Law

Concern over the degradation of the environment has increased over time in response to the environmental effects of population growth, urbanization, and industrialization. Environmental protection is not without a price, however. For many businesses, the costs of complying with environmental regulations are high, and for some they may seem too high. A constant tension exists between the desire to increase profits and productivity and the desire to protect the environment. This same tension exists in foreign nations.

China, for instance, has traditionally focused on the growth of its industries. Today, the air in many Chinese cities is so polluted that it causes many premature deaths each year.

After the Chinese government discovered that many of its companies were violating environmental rules, it started a campaign against environmental violations that has penalized more than thirty thousand companies. In addition, legislation was enacted to strengthen the nation's environmental protections and to give government

inspectors broader authority. China's wave of enforcement affects not only Chinese corporations but also foreign corporations doing business there.

In the United States, environmental law consists primarily of statutes passed by federal, state, and local governments and regulations issued by administrative agencies. Before examining statutory and regulatory environmental laws, however, we look at the remedies against environmental pollution that are available under the common law.

25–1 Common Law Actions

Common law remedies against environmental pollution originated centuries ago in England. Those responsible for operations that created dirt, smoke, noxious odors, noise, or toxic substances were sometimes held liable under common law theories of nuisance or negligence. Today, individuals who have suffered a harm from pollution continue to rely on the common law to obtain damages and injunctions against business polluters.

25–1a Nuisance

Under the common law doctrine of **nuisance,** persons may be held liable if they use their property in a manner that unreasonably interferes with others' rights to use or enjoy their own property. Courts typically balance the harm caused by the pollution against the costs of stopping it.

Courts have often denied injunctive relief on the ground that the hardships that would be imposed on the polluter and on the community are greater than the hardships suffered by the plaintiff. ■ **Example 25.1** Hewitt's factory causes neighboring landowners to suffer from smoke, soot, and vibrations. But if the factory is the core of the local

economy, a court may leave it in operation and award monetary damages to the injured parties. Damages can include compensation for any decline in the value of their property caused by Hewitt's operation. ■

To obtain relief from pollution under the nuisance doctrine, a property owner may have to identify a distinct harm separate from that affecting the general public. This harm is referred to as a "private" nuisance. Under the common law, individuals were denied standing (access to the courts) unless they suffered a harm distinct from that suffered by the public at large. Some states still require this. A public authority (such as a state's attorney general), however, can sue to stop a "public" nuisance.

25–1b Negligence and Strict Liability

An injured party may sue a business polluter in tort under negligence and strict liability theories. A negligence action is based on a business's alleged failure to use reasonable care toward a party whose injury was foreseeable and was caused by the lack of reasonable care. For instance, employees might sue an employer whose failure to use proper pollution controls has contaminated the air, causing the employees to suffer respiratory illnesses. Lawsuits for personal injuries caused by exposure to a toxic substance, such as asbestos, radiation, or hazardous waste, have given rise to a growing body of tort law known as **toxic torts.**

Businesses that engage in ultrahazardous activities—such as the transportation of radioactive materials—are strictly liable for any injuries the activities cause. In a strict liability action, the injured party does not have to prove that the business failed to exercise reasonable care.

25–2 Federal, State, and Local Regulations

All levels of government in the United States regulate some aspect of the environment. In this section, we look at some of the ways in which the federal, state, and local governments control business activities and land use in the interests of environmental preservation and protection.

25–2a State and Local Regulations

Many states have enacted laws to protect the environment. State laws may restrict a business's discharge of chemicals into the air or water or regulate its disposal of toxic wastes. States may also regulate the disposal or recycling of other wastes, including glass, metal, plastic containers, and paper. Additionally, states may restrict emissions from motor vehicles.

City, county, and other local governments also regulate some aspects of the environment. For instance, local zoning laws may be designed to inhibit or regulate the growth of cities and suburbs. In the interest of safeguarding the environment, such laws may prohibit certain land uses. Even when zoning laws permit a business's proposed development plan, the plan may have to be altered to lessen the development's environmental impact. In addition, cities and counties may impose rules regulating methods of waste removal, the appearance of buildings, the maximum noise level, and other aspects of the local environment.

State and local regulatory agencies also play a significant role in implementing federal environmental legislation. Typically, the federal government relies on state and local governments to enforce federal environmental statutes and regulations, such as those regulating air quality.

25–2b Federal Regulations

Congress has passed a number of statutes to control the impact of human activities on the environment. Exhibit 25–1 lists and summarizes the major federal environmental statutes discussed in this chapter. Most of these statutes are designed to address pollution in the air, water, or land. Some specifically regulate toxic chemicals, including pesticides, herbicides, and hazardous wastes.

Environmental Regulatory Agencies The primary federal agency regulating environmental law is the Environmental Protection Agency (EPA). Other federal agencies with authority to regulate specific environmental matters include the Department of the Interior, the Department of Defense, the Department of Labor, the Food and Drug Administration, and the Nuclear Regulatory Commission.

Most federal environmental laws provide that citizens can sue to enforce environmental regulations if government agencies fail to do so. Similarly, citizens can sue to limit enforcement actions if agencies go too far in their actions. Typically, a threshold hurdle in such suits is meeting the requirements for standing to sue. (For an interesting variation on standing to sue, see this chapter's *Global Insight* feature.)

In the following case, an animal advocacy organization brought a suit to stop the "taking" (killing) of migratory birds at New York City's John F. Kennedy International Airport (JFK). Birds had been involved in several near-catastrophes at JFK. A collision between herring gulls and a passenger jet, for instance, had caused the jet's engine to explode and the aircraft to catch fire. To reduce the risk, the Port Authority that operates JFK obtained a permit from the U.S. Fish and Wildlife Service to take a quantity of birds. The advocacy group challenged the issuance of this permit.

Case Analysis 25.1

Friends of Animals v. Clay

United States Court of Appeals, Second Circuit, 811 F.3d 94 (2016).

In the Language of the Court
José A. *CABRANES*, Circuit Judge.
* * * *
BACKGROUND
The taking of migratory birds is governed by the Migratory Bird Treaty

Act ("MBTA"). The MBTA, which implements a series of treaties as federal law, prohibits the taking of any bird protected by those treaties unless and except as permitted by regulations promulgated under the statute.

* * * One such regulation is 50 C.F.R. [Code of Federal Regulations] Section 21.41. Under Section 21.41, [the U.S. Fish and Wildlife Service (FWS)] may issue "depredation permits" that authorize the taking (or possession or

Case 25.1 Continues

transport) of migratory birds that are causing injury to certain human interests.

* * * *

[Friends of Animals (FOA) filed a suit in a federal district court against William Clay, Deputy Administrator in the U.S. Department of Agriculture and others, including FWS, challenging the issuance of a permit for the taking of certain birds that threatened to interfere with aircraft at the John F. Kennedy International Airport (JFK) in New York City. The court issued a summary judgment in favor of the defendants. FOA appealed to the U.S. Court of Appeals for the Second Circuit.]

The permit * * * identifies eighteen species of migratory birds that have, in the past, compromised public safety at JFK, and authorizes the Port Authority to take a quota of birds of each species.

In addition to setting out these species-specific quotas, the challenged permit contains an "emergency-take" provision. This provision empowers the Port Authority, "in emergency situations only," to take any migratory bird (except bald eagles, golden eagles, or endangered or threatened species) that poses a "direct threat to human safety"—defined as a "threat of serious bodily injury or a risk to human life"—even if it is of a species not listed on the permit. FWS rarely includes an emergency take provision in its migratory bird permits, but— mindful of the grave risks that arise when birds congregate near aircraft—it makes an exception for airports.

DISCUSSION

FOA directs its challenge at the * * * permit's emergency-take provision. According to FOA, Section 21.41 does not authorize FWS to issue a permit that allows the emergency take of a migratory bird irrespective of its species. Instead, FOA argues, permit applicants like the Port Authority must provide species-specific information to FWS, and

FWS may authorize the taking of only those species specifically listed on the permit. Contending that FWS's alleged failure to abide by the requirements of Section 21.41 has resulted in the Port Authority's unlawful taking of a number of migratory birds, * * * FOA asks us to invalidate the operative permit as the product of agency action that was arbitrary, capricious, an abuse of discretion, or otherwise not in accordance with law.

* * * *

FWS's authority to issue depredation permits under Section 21.41 is limited in certain respects by subsections (c) and (d) of that provision. Subsection (d) provides, for instance, that a permit's duration is limited to one year. Subsection (c) sets forth conditions common to all permits, such as the prohibition of certain hunting practices and mandatory steps for disposing of birds that have been killed; it also states that depredation permits are subject to the general conditions set forth in 50 C.F.R. Part 13. Various provisions in Part 13, in turn, further hem in the agency's permitting authority. *But among the express limitations on FWS's discretion imposed by Section 21.41(c)–(d) and Part 13, we find nothing to indicate that FWS may not issue a permit that contains an emergency-take provision. Accordingly, unless some other feature of the regulatory regime counsels otherwise, we must conclude that FWS has authority to issue permits of the type challenged here.* [Emphasis added.]

FOA argues that this other feature is found in Section 21.41(b). This provision states that an application for a depredation permit must [identify] * * * "the particular species of migratory birds committing [an] injury." According to FOA, that regulation, when read in connection with Section 21.41(c)(1)—which provides that "permittees may not kill migratory birds unless specifically

authorized on the permit"—makes clear that a depredation permit may not authorize the taking of bird species not listed on the permit's face.

We disagree. Section 21.41(b) by its terms governs the conduct of applicants, not FWS, and specifies what information must be included in the permit application, not the permit itself. Indeed, the provision is styled as a direct address to applicants, to whom it gives point-by-point instructions for seeking a permit. FOA identifies no particular reason why we should read this subsection, contrary to its plain language, as a limit on FWS's authority to issue permits rather than as a means to ensure that applicants provide FWS with information germane to the permitting determination. Section 21.41(b) is a hopelessly slender reed on which to rest the argument that FWS is powerless to authorize the Port Authority to take migratory birds that threaten air safety.

Nor does the language of Section 21.41(c)(1) alter this conclusion. True, this subsection provides that permittees must "not kill migratory birds unless specifically authorized on the permit." But this is in no way inconsistent with the * * * permit's emergency-take provision. *The permit authorizes the Port Authority, in emergency situations, to "take * * * any migratory birds * * * when the migratory birds * * * are posing a direct threat to human safety."* The permit thus specifically authorizes the taking of migratory birds if certain conditions are met—and one method of taking a bird is killing it. [Emphasis added.]

* * * *

CONCLUSION

In sum, we hold that FWS did not run afoul of Section 21.41 in issuing to the Port Authority the * * * depredation permit. The * * * order of the District Court is accordingly AFFIRMED.

Legal Reasoning Questions

1. In what circumstance might the Port Authority—or anyone else—take a migratory bird without a permit and *not* be sanctioned?
2. Under the plaintiff's suggested reading of the regulation at issue in this case, what difficult choice would the Port Authority face?
3. Why is the taking of birds, or any wildlife, protected by treaty and federal law? What should be the limit to this protection?

Exhibit 25–1   Major Federal Environmental Statutes

Popular Name	Purpose	Statute Reference
Rivers and Harbors Appropriations Act	To prohibit ships and manufacturers from discharging and depositing refuse in navigable waterways.	33 U.S.C. Sections 401–418.
Federal Insecticide, Fungicide, and Rodenticide Act	To control the use of pesticides and herbicides.	7 U.S.C. Sections 136 *et seq*.
Federal Water Pollution Control Act (Clean Water Act)	To eliminate the discharge of pollutants from major sources into navigable waters.	33 U.S.C. Sections 1251–1387.
Clean Air Act	To control air pollution from mobile and stationary sources.	42 U.S.C. Sections 7401 *et seq*.
National Environmental Policy Act	To limit environmental harm from federal government activities.	42 U.S.C. Sections 4321 *et seq*.
Marine Protection, Research, and Sanctuaries Act (Ocean Dumping Act)	To prohibit the dumping of radiological, chemical, and biological warfare agents and high-level radioactive waste into the ocean.	16 U.S.C. Sections 1401 *et seq*.
Endangered Species Act	To protect species that are threatened with extinction.	16 U.S.C. Sections 1531–1544.
Safe Drinking Water Act	To regulate pollutants in public drinking water systems.	42 U.S.C. Sections 300f–300j-27.
Toxic Substances Control Act	To regulate toxic chemicals and chemical compounds.	15 U.S.C. Sections 2601–2692.
The Resource Conservation and Recovery Act	To determine which forms of solid waste should be considered hazardous and to establish regulations to monitor and control hazardous waste disposal.	42 U.S.C. Sections 6901 *et seq*.
Comprehensive Environmental Response, Compensation, and Liability Act (CERCLA, or Superfund)	To regulate the clean-up of hazardous-waste disposal sites.	42 U.S.C. Sections 9601–9675.
Small Business Liability Relief and Brownfields Revitalization Act	To allow developers who comply with state voluntary clean-up programs to avoid federal liability for the properties that they decontaminate and develop.	42 U.S.C. Section 9628.

Global Insight   Can a River Be a Legal Person?

Years ago, a famous law journal article entitled, "Should Trees Have Standing?" addressed the issue of who has the legal right to bring a lawsuit when nature is involved.[a] That issue remains with us today. To have standing, a party wishing to sue must have a stake in the outcome. If the courts did not impose fairly strict requirements on who has standing, they would be flooded with many more lawsuits than are filed today.

A New Zealand River Is Now a Legal Person

So, can a river have standing? In New Zealand, apparently so. New Zealand has enacted a law that declares that the Whanganui River is a legal person, meaning that it can own property, incur debts, and petition the courts. Those in favor of this law point out that throughout the world, certain organizations have legal rights and responsibilities that do not depend on the individuals who staff those organizations. So why can't a river have legal rights as well?

"I Am the River, and the River Is Me."

New Zealand's law is the outcome of a dispute between the country's indigenous Maori tribes, who consider the Whanganui River sacred, and others who use the river. The Maori tribes contend that there is a deep spiritual connection between themselves and the river by stating, "I am the river, and the river is me." The law acknowledges that the river is a "living whole." In principle, this law ended an ownership dispute dating back more than 140 years. Today, the river has two guardians: the New Zealand government and the Maori tribes.

Critical Thinking *Soon after passage of the New Zealand law, a court in India ruled that two of its biggest rivers, the Yamuna and the Ganges, are legal persons. What is the purpose of such laws?*

a. Stone, Christopher D., "Should Trees Have Standing? Toward Legal Rights for Natural Objects," *Southern California Law Review*, Vol. 45 (1972): pp. 450–501.

Environmental Impact Statements All agencies of the federal government must take environmental factors into consideration when making significant decisions. The National Environmental Policy Act[1] requires that an **environmental impact statement (EIS)** be prepared for every major federal action that significantly affects the quality of the environment. An EIS must analyze the following:

1. The impact that the action will have on the environment.
2. Any adverse effects on the environment and alternative actions that might be taken.
3. Any irreversible effects the action might generate.

An action qualifies as "major" if it involves a substantial commitment of resources (monetary or otherwise). An action is "federal" if a federal agency has the power to control it. ■ **Example 25.2** Development of a ski resort by a private developer on federal land may require an EIS. Construction or operation of a nuclear plant, which requires a federal permit, necessitates an EIS, as does creation of a dam as part of a federal project. ■

If an agency decides that an EIS is unnecessary, it must issue a statement supporting this conclusion. Private individuals, consumer interest groups, businesses, and others who believe that a federal agency's activities threaten the environment often use EISs as a means to challenge those activities. (See Exhibit 25–2 for a summary of when an EIS is required.)

25–3 Air Pollution

Federal involvement with air pollution goes back to the 1950s and 1960s, when Congress authorized funds for air-pollution research and enacted the Clean Air Act.[2] The Clean Air Act provides the basis for issuing regulations to control multistate air pollution. It covers both mobile sources (such as automobiles and other vehicles) and stationary sources (such as electric utilities and industrial plants) of pollution.

---

1. 42 U.S.C. Sections 4321 *et seq.*

2. 42 U.S.C. Sections 7401 *et seq.*

Exhibit 25-2 Environmental Impact Statements

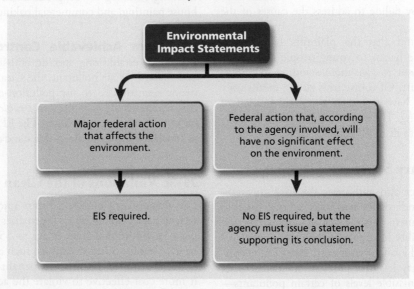

25-3a Mobile Sources

Regulations governing air pollution from automobiles and other mobile sources specify pollution standards and establish time schedules for meeting the standards. The EPA periodically updates the pollution standards in light of new developments and data, usually reducing the amount of emissions allowed.

Authority to Regulate Greenhouse Gases Many scientists and others around the world maintain that greenhouse gases, such as carbon dioxide (CO_2), contribute to climate change. The Clean Air Act, as amended, however, does not specifically mention CO_2 emissions. Therefore, the EPA did not regulate CO_2 emissions from motor vehicles until after the Supreme Court ruled that it had the authority to do so.

■ **Case in Point 25.3** Environmental groups and several states, including Massachusetts, sued the EPA in an effort to force the agency to regulate CO_2 emissions from motor vehicles. The case eventually reached the United States Supreme Court. The EPA argued that the plaintiffs lacked standing because global climate change has widespread effects, so the individual plaintiffs could not show particularized harm. Furthermore, the agency claimed that it did not have authority under the Clean Air Act to address global climate change and regulate CO_2 emissions.

The Court, however, ruled that Massachusetts had standing because its coastline, including state-owned lands, faced an imminent threat from rising sea levels purportedly caused by climate change. The Court also held that the Clean Air Act's broad definition of "air pollutant" gives the EPA authority to regulate CO_2. The Clean Air Act requires the EPA to regulate any air pollutants that might "endanger public health or welfare." Accordingly, the Court ordered the EPA to determine whether CO_2 was a pollutant that endangered public health.[3] ■

The EPA later concluded that greenhouse gases, including CO_2 emissions, *do* constitute a public danger. In fact, the EPA now also regulates greenhouse gas emissions from airplanes.

Controlling Climate Change In 2016, a federal district court in Oregon allowed an unprecedented lawsuit to go forward against the U.S. government for doing too little to control climate change. ■ **Case in Point 25.4** A group of young people (aged eight to nineteen) filed a suit against the federal government, as well as the fossil fuel industry. The plaintiffs argued that the government has known for years that excessive CO_2 emissions cause climate change and threaten catastrophic consequences.

---

3. *Commonwealth of Massachusetts v. Environmental Protection Agency*, 549 U.S. 497, 127 S.Ct. 1438, 167 L.Ed.2d 248 (2007).

They claimed that the government had violated their constitutional rights by failing to address the causes of the CO_2 emissions.

The court found that the plaintiffs had alleged particular, concrete harms to young people and future generations sufficient to give them standing to pursue their claims in court. Of course, this ruling means only that the plaintiffs have met their threshold burden of establishing standing. The court simply denied the government's motion to dismiss.[4] ■

25–3b Stationary Sources

The Clean Air Act also authorizes the EPA to establish air-quality standards for stationary sources (such as manufacturing plants). But the act recognizes that the primary responsibility for implementing these standards rests with state and local governments. The EPA sets primary and secondary levels of ambient standards—that is, maximum permissible levels of certain pollutants—and the states formulate plans to achieve those standards. Different standards apply depending on whether the sources of pollution are located in clean areas or polluted areas and whether they are existing sources or major new sources.

Hazardous Air Pollutants The Clean Air Act focuses on controlling hazardous air pollutants (HAPs)—those likely to cause death or a serious irreversible or incapacitating condition, such as cancer or neurological or reproductive damage. The act requires the EPA to list all HAPs on a prioritized schedule. In all, nearly two hundred substances—including asbestos, benzene, beryllium, cadmium, mercury, and vinyl chloride—have been classified as hazardous. They are emitted from stationary sources by a variety of business activities, including

smelting (melting ore to produce metal), dry cleaning, house painting, and commercial baking.

Maximum Achievable Control Technology
Instead of establishing specific emissions standards for each hazardous air pollutant, the Clean Air Act requires major *new* sources[5] to use pollution-control equipment that represents the *maximum achievable control technology*, or MACT, to reduce emissions. The EPA issues guidelines as to what equipment meets this standard.[6]

25–3c Violations of the Clean Air Act

For violations of emission limits under the Clean Air Act, the EPA can assess civil penalties of up to $25,000 per day. Additional fines of up to $5,000 per day can be assessed for other violations, such as failure to maintain the required records. To penalize those who find it more cost-effective to violate the act than to comply with it, the EPA is authorized to impose a penalty equal to the violator's economic benefits from noncompliance. Persons who provide information about violators may be paid up to $10,000. Private citizens can also sue violators.

Those who knowingly violate the act, including corporate officers, may be subject to criminal penalties. For instance, knowingly making false statements or failing to report violations may be punishable by fines of up to $1 million and imprisonment for up to two years.

In the following case, the phrase "knowingly violate" was at the center of the dispute in an individual's appeal of his conviction for Clean Air Act violations.

---

4. *Juliana v. United States*, 217 F.Supp.3d 1224 (D.Or. 2016); 339 F.Supp.3d 1062 (D.Or. 2018).

5. The term *major new sources* includes existing sources modified by a change in a method of operation that increases emissions.
6. The EPA has also issued rules to regulate hazardous air pollutants emitted by landfills. See 40 C.F.R. Part 60.

Case 25.2

United States v. O'Malley
United States Court of Appeals, Seventh Circuit, 739 F.3d 1001 (2014).

Background and Facts Duane O'Malley owned and operated Origin Fire Protection. Michael Pinski hired Origin to remove and dispose of 2,200 feet of insulation from a building Pinski owned in Kankakee, Illinois. The insulation contained asbestos, which Pinski, O'Malley, and O'Malley's employees recognized. O'Malley did not have a license to remove asbestos, and none of his employees were trained in complying with federal asbestos regulations. Nevertheless, Origin removed the debris and disposed of it at various sites, including a vacant lot where it spilled onto the soil, resulting in clean-up costs of nearly $50,000.

In a federal district court, a jury convicted O'Malley of removing, transporting, and dumping asbestos in violation of the Clean Air Act. The court sentenced him to 120 months of imprisonment, three years of supervised release, a fine of $15,000, and $47,085.70 in restitution to the Environmental Protection Agency (EPA). O'Malley appealed.

In the Language of the Court
TINDER, Circuit Judge.
* * * *

On appeal to this court, O'Malley * * * claims that because the [EPA's regulations] define "asbestos-containing material" as only six types of regulated asbestos, the government was required to prove that O'Malley knew that the asbestos in the building was one of the six forms of regulated asbestos. He asserts that the government did not present evidence to demonstrate O'Malley's knowledge of the type of asbestos in the building.
* * * *

O'Malley is correct that not all forms of asbestos are subject to regulation. The Clean Air Act [under Section 7412] authorizes the regulation of hazardous air pollutants, one of which is asbestos. "Because asbestos is not typically emitted through a conveyance designed and constructed to emit or capture it, such as a pipe or smokestack, but rather escapes from more diffuse sources such as open construction or demolition sites, EPA adopted a work-practice standard for the handling of asbestos in building demolition and renovation." * * * The work practice standard promulgated for the handling of asbestos applies only to the six types of "regulated asbestos-containing material (RACM)," [which includes "friable asbestos material"]. "Friable asbestos material" is defined as "any material containing more than 1 percent asbestos * * * that, when dry, can be crumbled, pulverized, or reduced to powder by hand pressure." Thus, there is no question that the material in [this case]—which was both friable and contained asbestos at concentrations ranging from four percent to forty-eight percent—was indeed "regulated asbestos-containing material."
* * * *

*The Clean Air Act makes it a crime for any person to "knowingly violate any * * * requirement or prohibition of * * * Section 7412, * * * including a requirement of any rule" promulgated under Section 7412. * * * The* district court instructed the jury on the knowledge elements as follows: "The government must prove * * * the defendant knew that asbestos-containing material was in the building." [Emphasis added.]

O'Malley argues that the knowledge element instruction should have required the government to prove that the defendant knew that regulated asbestos-containing material, not simply asbestos-containing material, was in the building. But this cannot be correct. * * * The phrase "knowingly violates" does not "carv[e] out an exception to the general rule that ignorance of the law is no excuse." The *mens rea* [criminal intent] required by the phrase is one that is higher than strict liability * * *. But it is certainly much lower than specific intent, especially when, as here, "dangerous * * * materials are involved," because "the probability of regulation is so great that anyone who is aware that he is in possession of them or dealing with them must be presumed to be aware of the regulation." The very fact that O'Malley was knowingly working with asbestos-containing material met the *mens rea* requirement.

Decision and Remedy *The U.S. Court of Appeals for the Seventh Circuit affirmed the lower court's judgment. The federal appellate court disagreed with O'Malley's claim that the government was required to prove that he knew the asbestos was one of the six types of regulated asbestos. "The very fact that O'Malley was knowingly working with asbestos-containing material met the* mens rea *requirement."*

Critical Thinking
- **What If the Facts Were Different?** *Suppose that O'Malley had been licensed to remove the asbestos. Would the result have been different? Why or why not?*

25–4 Water Pollution

Water pollution stems mostly from industrial, municipal, and agricultural sources. Pollutants entering streams, lakes, and oceans include organic wastes, heated water, sediments from soil runoff, nutrients (including fertilizers and human and animal wastes), and toxic chemicals and other hazardous substances.

Federal regulations governing water pollution can be traced back to the 1899 Rivers and Harbors Appropriation Act.[7] These regulations prohibited ships and manufacturers from discharging or depositing refuse in navigable waterways without a permit.[8] In 1948, Congress passed the Federal Water Pollution Control Act (FWPCA),[9] but its regulatory system and enforcement powers proved to be inadequate.

25–4a The Clean Water Act

In 1972, Congress passed amendments to the FWPCA, and the amended act became known as the Clean Water Act (CWA). The CWA established the following goals: (1) make waters safe for swimming, (2) protect fish and wildlife, and (3) eliminate the discharge of pollutants into the water. The CWA also set specific schedules, which were later extended by amendment and by the Water Quality Act.[10] Under these schedules, the EPA limits the discharge of various types of pollutants based on the technology available for controlling them.

Permit System for Point-Source Emissions The CWA established a permit system for regulating discharges from "point sources" of pollution, which include industrial, municipal, and agricultural facilities.[11] Under this system, called the National Pollutant Discharge Elimination System (NPDES), any point source emitting pollutants into water must have a permit. Pollution not from point sources, such as runoff from small farms, is not subject to much regulation.

NPDES permits can be issued by the EPA and authorized state agencies and Indian tribes, but only if the discharge will not violate water-quality standards. Permits must be reissued every five years. Although initially the NPDES system focused mainly on industrial wastewater, it was later expanded to cover stormwater discharges.

In practice, the NPDES system under the CWA includes the following elements:

1. National effluent (pollution) standards set by the EPA for each industry.
2. Water-quality standards set by the states under EPA supervision.
3. A discharge permit program that sets water-quality standards to limit pollution.
4. Special provisions for toxic chemicals and for oil spills.
5. Construction grants and loans from the federal government for publicly owned treatment works, primarily sewage treatment plants.

Standards for Equipment Regulations generally specify that the *best available control technology*, or BACT, be installed. The EPA issues guidelines as to what equipment meets this standard. Essentially, the guidelines require the most effective pollution-control equipment available.

New sources must install BACT equipment before beginning operations. Existing sources are subject to timetables for the installation of BACT equipment and must immediately install equipment that utilizes the *best practical control technology*, or BPCT. The EPA also issues guidelines as to what equipment meets this standard.

Exhibit 25–3 reviews the pollution-control equipment standards required under the Clean Air Act and the Clean Water Act.

Wetlands The CWA prohibits the filling or dredging of **wetlands** unless a permit is obtained from the Army Corps of Engineers. The EPA defines *wetlands* as "those areas that are inundated or saturated by surface or ground water at a frequency and duration sufficient to support . . . vegetation typically adapted for life in saturated soil conditions." Wetlands are thought to be vital to the ecosystem because they filter streams and rivers and provide habitat for wildlife.

■ **Case in Point 25.5** To build a home in Idaho, Michael and Chantell Sackett filled part of their residential lot with dirt and rock. A few months later, they received a compliance order from the EPA that required them to restore their property immediately or face fines of $75,000 a day. The EPA order claimed that, because their property was near a major lake, the Sacketts had polluted wetlands in violation of the Clean Water Act.

The Sacketts requested a hearing with the EPA, but it was denied. They then sued the EPA in federal district court, asserting, among other things, that the compliance order was "arbitrary and capricious" under the Administrative Procedure Act. The district court held that it could not review the EPA's compliance order because it was not

7. 33 U.S.C. Sections 401 *et seq.*
8. The term *navigable waters* is interpreted today as including intrastate lakes and streams used by interstate travelers and industries, as well as coastal and freshwater wetlands.
9. 33 U.S.C. Sections 1251–1387.
10. This act amended 33 U.S.C. Section 1251.
11. 33 U.S.C. Section 1342.

Exhibit 25–3 Pollution-Control Equipment Standards under the Clean Air Act and the Clean Water Act

The Clean Air Act	The Clean Water Act
• Major sources of pollution must use pollution-control equipment that represents the *maximum achievable control technology*, or MACT, to reduce emissions.	• New sources of pollution must install the *best available control technology*, or BACT, before beginning operations. • Existing sources must immediately install equipment that utilizes the *best practical control technology*, or BPCT, and meet a timetable for installing BACT equipment.

a final agency action. An appellate court affirmed, but the United States Supreme Court reversed. The Court held that the Sacketts could challenge the EPA's compliance order in federal court. The government could not force them to comply with the EPA order without providing an opportunity for judicial review.[12] ∎

Violations of the Clean Water Act Because point-source water pollution control is based on a permit system, the permits are the key to enforcement. States have primary responsibility for enforcing the permit system, subject to EPA monitoring.

Discharging emissions into navigable waters without a permit, or in violation of pollution limits under a permit, violates the CWA. Violators are subject to a

variety of civil and criminal penalties. Depending on the violation, civil penalties range from $10,000 to $25,000 per day, but not more than $25,000 per violation. Lying about a violation is more serious than admitting the truth about improper discharges.

Criminal penalties apply only if a violation was intentional. Criminal penalties range from a fine of $2,500 per day and imprisonment for up to one year to a fine of $1 million and fifteen years' imprisonment. Injunctive relief and damages can also be imposed. The polluting party can be required to clean up the pollution or pay for the cost of doing so.

In the following case, a fishing boat had pumped overboard oil-contaminated water from the inside of the boat. The issue before the court was whether the evidence related to this discharge was sufficient to support a conviction of the vessel's owner for violating the Clean Water Act.

12. *Sackett v. Environmental Protection Agency*, 566 U.S. 120, 132 S.Ct. 1367, 182 L.Ed.2d 367 (2012).

Case 25.3

United States v. Fox
United States Court of Appeals, Ninth Circuit, 761 Fed.Appx. 765 (2019).

Background and Facts Bingham Fox owned and operated the fishing boat/vessel *Native Sun*. According to the vessel's log, Fox was aware of continuous problems with leaking oil in the engine room and of the crew's unsuccessful efforts to mop it up. The oil contaminated the bilge water, which is water from inside the lower part of a boat. Fox knew about the contamination and bought enzymes for the crew to treat the oily bilge water. This bilge water was then sucked through a submersible pump that lacked an oil-water separator and discharged overboard.

Following an inspection of the *Native Sun* by the U.S. Coast Guard, Fox was charged in a federal district court with knowingly discharging oil into navigable waters in potentially harmful quantities in violation of the Clean Water Act. The defendant argued that he told the crew to pump from the bottom of the bilge so as to capture only water and that he did not actually know oil was being pumped overboard along with the water. A jury convicted him of the charge. Fox appealed the conviction to the U.S. Court of Appeals for the Ninth Circuit.

Case 25.3 Continues

In the Language of the Court

MEMORANDUM.

* * * *

* * * Fox argues that the Government's evidence was insufficient to establish that Fox knew, during the time periods alleged in the indictment, that the *Native Sun* crew members discharged oil in quantities that may have been harmful.

Viewing the evidence in the light most favorable to the prosecution, a rational trier of fact could have found the essential elements of the crime beyond a reasonable doubt. The jury heard testimony that after Fox purchased the vessel and had it sailed to its new harbor in Blaine, Fox was "fully aware" of the leakage problems with the *Native Sun*. Fox's employee testified that the bilge levels were so high on the trip to Blaine that the *Native Sun* had to pump the bilge "straight into the ocean." The employee also testified about one oil discharge incident where Fox was present and provided dish soap to squirt on the sheen to "make the oil immediately drop to the bottom," instead of reporting the discharge.

Fox knew that the vessel needed to keep replenishing its oil to replace the amount being leaked. For example, on the *Native Sun*'s trip to Alaska, the testimony established that more than two gallons of oil leaked to the engine room bilge every 24 hours, and the crew had to pump the oily bilge water at least once every five days to keep the vessel afloat. Various crew members testified that Fox provided them with oil-absorbent pads to try to mop up the oil in the engine room and bilge, and he also purchased enzymes to try to treat the oily bilge water. The evidence would allow a fact-finder to determine that Fox directed the *Native Sun* crew to pump the bilge with the knowledge that the pumping system relied on "skimming" the top layer of oily bilge water and mopping up the oil with oil-absorbent pads. *A rational jury could conclude that Fox, knowing that there was excessive oil in the bilge and that regular pumping of the bilge was occurring without an oil-water-separator, knowingly directed his crew to discharge oily bilge water.* [Emphasis added.]

Decision and Remedy *The U.S. Court of Appeals for the Ninth Circuit affirmed Fox's conviction for violation of the Clean Water Act. The court reasoned that the jury was "rational" to conclude that Fox knew his vessel's bilge was contaminated with oil, which was being pumped overboard along with the water from the bilge.*

Critical Thinking

- **Legal Environment** *Fox introduced into evidence two receipts showing that he had properly disposed of oily water on shore and indicated that he had more. Should Fox have been exonerated on the basis of these receipts? Why or why not?*
- **Ethical** *Was it ethical for Fox to attempt to avoid responsibility for the violation of the Clean Water Act by blaming his crew? Discuss.*

25–4b Drinking Water

The Safe Drinking Water Act[13] requires the EPA to set maximum levels for pollutants in public water systems. The operators of public water systems must come as close as possible to meeting the EPA's standards by using the best available technology that is economically and technologically feasible.

Under the act, each supplier of drinking water is required to send an annual statement describing the source of its water to every household it supplies. The statement must also disclose the level of any contaminants in the water and any possible health concerns associated with the contaminants.

■ **Example 25.6** The city of Flint, Michigan, changed its source of drinking water from the Detroit water system to the Flint River. Detroit's water was treated to prevent lead from leaching into the water from aging lead pipes. The Flint River water was not treated, however, allowing lead to leach into the water from the aging pipes. Flint's drinking water became contaminated with lead—a serious public health hazard. By the time Flint sent out the required EPA notices, thousands of children had been exposed to drinking water with high lead levels.

---

13. 42 U.S.C. Sections 300f–300j-27.

Numerous civil and criminal actions were filed as a result of the incident. In addition, fixing the water system cost the city millions of dollars. ■

25–4c Ocean Dumping

The Marine Protection, Research, and Sanctuaries Act[14] (popularly known as the Ocean Dumping Act) regulates the transportation and dumping of pollutants into ocean waters. It prohibits the ocean dumping of any radiological, chemical, and biological warfare agents and high-level radioactive waste.

The act also established a permit program for transporting and dumping other materials, and designated certain areas as marine sanctuaries. Each violation of any provision or permit requirement in the Ocean Dumping Act may result in a civil penalty of up to $50,000. A knowing violation is a criminal offense that may result in a $50,000 fine, imprisonment for not more than a year, or both. A court may also grant an injunction to prevent an imminent or continuing violation.

25–4d Oil Pollution

When more than 10 million gallons of oil leaked into Alaska's Prince William Sound from the *Exxon Valdez* supertanker in 1989, Congress responded by passing the Oil Pollution Act.[15] (At that time, the *Exxon Valdez* disaster was the worst oil spill in U.S. history, but the British Petroleum oil spill in the Gulf of Mexico in 2010 surpassed it.)

Under the Oil Pollution Act, any oil facility, oil shipper, vessel owner, or vessel operator that discharges oil into navigable waters or onto an adjoining shore may be liable for clean-up costs and damages. The polluter can also be ordered to pay for damage to natural resources, private property, and the local economy, including the increased cost of providing public services.

25–5 Toxic Chemicals and Hazardous Waste

Control of toxic chemicals and hazardous waste has become increasingly important. If not properly disposed of, these substances may seriously endanger human health and the environment—for instance, by contaminating public drinking water.

25–5a Pesticides and Herbicides

The Federal Insecticide, Fungicide, and Rodenticide Act (FIFRA)[16] regulates the use of pesticides and herbicides. These substances must be (1) registered before they can be sold, (2) certified and used only for approved applications, and (3) used in limited quantities when applied to food crops.

EPA Actions The EPA can cancel or suspend registration of substances that it has identified as harmful and can inspect the factories where the chemicals are made. A substance is deemed harmful if human exposure to the substance, including exposure through eating food, results in a risk of one in a million (or higher) of developing cancer.[17]

Violations and Penalties It is a violation of FIFRA to sell a pesticide or herbicide that is either unregistered or has had its registration canceled or suspended. It is also a violation to sell a pesticide or herbicide with a false or misleading label. For instance, it is an offense to sell a substance that has a chemical strength that is different from the concentration described on the label. It is also a violation to destroy or deface any labeling required under the act.

Penalties for commercial dealers include imprisonment for up to one year and a fine of up to $25,000 (producers can be fined up to $50,000). Farmers and other private users of pesticides or herbicides who violate the act are subject to a $1,000 fine and incarceration for up to thirty days.

Note that a state can also regulate the sale and use of federally registered pesticides. ■ **Case in Point 25.7** The EPA conditionally registered Strongarm, a weed-killing pesticide made by Dow Agrosciences, LLC. When Texas peanut farmers applied Strongarm to their crops, it damaged the crops and failed to control the growth of weeds. The farmers sued Dow for violations of Texas law, but the lower courts ruled that FIFRA preempted their claims. The farmers appealed to the United States Supreme Court. The Court held that under a specific provision of FIFRA, a state can regulate the sale and use of federally registered pesticides so long as the regulation does not permit anything that FIFRA prohibits.[18] ■

14. 16 U.S.C. Sections 1401 *et seq.*
15. 33 U.S.C. Sections 2701 *et seq.*
16. 7 U.S.C. Sections 136 *et seq.*
17. 21 U.S.C. Section 346a.
18. *Bates v. Dow Agrosciences, LLC,* 544 U.S. 431, 125 S.Ct. 1788, 161 L.Ed.2d 687 (2005).

25–5b Toxic Substances

The Toxic Substances Control Act[19] regulates chemicals and chemical compounds that are known to be toxic, such as asbestos and polychlorinated biphenyls. The act also controls the introduction of new chemical compounds by requiring investigation of any possible harmful effects from these substances.

Under the act, the EPA can require that manufacturers, processors, and other entities planning to use chemicals first determine their effects on human health and the environment. The EPA can regulate substances that could pose an imminent hazard or an unreasonable risk of injury to health or the environment. The EPA can also require special labeling, limit the use of a substance, set production quotas, or prohibit the use of a substance altogether.

25–5c The Resource Conservation and Recovery Act

The Resource Conservation and Recovery Act (RCRA)[20] was Congress's response to growing concerns about the effects of hazardous waste materials on the environment. The RCRA required the EPA to determine which forms of solid waste should be considered hazardous and to establish regulations to monitor and control hazardous waste disposal.

Among other things, the act requires all producers of hazardous waste materials to properly label and package any hazardous waste to be transported. Amendments to the RCRA decrease the use of land containment in the disposal of hazardous waste and require smaller generators of hazardous waste to comply with the act.

Under the RCRA, a company may be assessed a civil penalty of up to $25,000 for each violation.[21] The penalty is based on the seriousness of the violation, the probability of harm, and the extent to which the violation deviates from RCRA requirements. Criminal penalties include fines of up to $50,000 for each day of violation, imprisonment for up to two years (in most instances), or both. Criminal fines and the time of imprisonment can be doubled for certain repeat offenders.

25–5d Superfund

The Comprehensive Environmental Response, Compensation, and Liability Act (CERCLA),[22] commonly known as Superfund, regulates the clean up of disposal sites in which hazardous waste is leaking into the environment. CERCLA, as amended, has four primary elements:

1. It established an information-gathering and analysis system that enables the government to identify chemical dump sites and determine the appropriate action.
2. It authorized the EPA to respond to emergencies and to arrange for the clean-up of a leaking site directly if the persons responsible fail to clean up the site within a reasonable time.
3. It created a Hazardous Substance Response Trust Fund (also called *Superfund*) to pay for the clean-up of hazardous sites using funds obtained through taxes on certain businesses.
4. It allowed the government to recover the clean-up costs from persons who were (even remotely) responsible for hazardous substance releases.

Potentially Responsible Parties Superfund provides that when a release or a potential release of hazardous chemicals from a site occurs, the following persons may be held responsible for cleaning up the site:

1. The person who generated the wastes disposed of at the site.
2. The person who transported the wastes to the site.
3. The person who owned or operated the site at the time of the disposal.
4. The current owner or operator of the site.

A person falling within one of these categories is referred to as a **potentially responsible party (PRP)**. If the PRPs do not clean up the site, the EPA can clean up the site and recover the clean-up costs from the PRPs.

Strict Liability of PRPs. Superfund imposes strict liability on PRPs, and that liability cannot be avoided through transfer of ownership. Thus, selling a site where hazardous wastes were disposed of does not relieve the seller of liability, and the buyer also becomes liable for the clean-up.

Liability also extends to businesses that merge with or buy corporations that have violated CERCLA. A parent corporation is not automatically liable for the violations of its subsidiary. It can be held liable, however, if the subsidiary was merely a shell company or if the parent corporation participated in or controlled the facility.[23]

---

19. 15 U.S.C. Sections 2601–2692.
20. 42 U.S.C. Sections 6901 *et seq*.
21. 42 U.S.C. Section 6928(a).
22. 42 U.S.C. Sections 9601–9675.

23. The landmark case establishing the liability of a parent corporation under CERCLA is *United States v. Bestfoods*, 524 U.S. 51, 118 S.Ct. 1876, 141 L.Ed.2d 43 (1998).

Joint and Several Liability of PRPs. Liability under Superfund is usually joint and several. In other words, a PRP who generated *only a fraction of the hazardous waste* disposed of at a site may nevertheless be liable for *all* of the clean-up costs. CERCLA authorizes a party who has incurred clean-up costs to bring a "contribution action" against any other person who is liable or potentially liable for a percentage of the costs.

Minimizing Liability One way for a business to minimize its potential liability under Superfund is to conduct environmental compliance audits of its own operations regularly. That is, the business can investigate its own operations and property to determine whether any environmental hazards exist.

The EPA encourages companies to conduct self-audits and promptly detect, disclose, and correct wrongdoing. Companies that do so are subject to lighter penalties for violations of environmental laws. (Fines may be reduced as much as 75 percent.)

In addition, under EPA guidelines, the EPA will waive all fines if a small company corrects environmental violations within 180 days after being notified of the violations (or 360 days if pollution-prevention techniques are involved). The policy does not apply to criminal violations of environmental laws or to violations that pose a significant threat to public health, safety, or the environment.

Defenses There are a few defenses to liability under CERCLA. The most important is the *innocent landowner defense*,[24] which may protect a landowner who acquired the property after it was used for hazardous waste disposal.

To succeed in this defense, the landowner must show, among other things, that at the time the property was acquired, she or he had no reason to know that it had been used for hazardous waste disposal. The landowner must also show that at the time of the purchase, she or he undertook "all appropriate inquiries." That is, he or she investigated the previous ownership and uses of the property to determine whether there was reason for concern about hazardous substances. In effect, then, this defense protects only property owners who took precautions and investigated the possibility of environmental hazards before buying the property.

24. 42 U.S.C. Section 9601(35)(B).

Practice and Review: Environmental Law

Residents of Lake Caliopa, Minnesota, began noticing an unusually high number of lung ailments among the local population. Several concerned citizens pooled their resources and commissioned a study to compare the frequency of these health conditions in Lake Caliopa with national averages. The study concluded that residents of Lake Caliopa experienced four to seven times the rate of frequency of asthma, bronchitis, and emphysema as the population nationwide.

During the study period, citizens began expressing concerns about the large volume of smog emitted by the Cotton Design apparel manufacturing plant on the outskirts of town. The plant had a production facility two miles east of town beside the Tawakoni River and employed seventy full-time workers. Just downstream on the Tawakoni River, the city of Lake Caliopa operated a public water works facility, which supplied all city residents with water.

The Minnesota Pollution Control Agency required Cotton Design to install new equipment to control air and water pollution. Later, citizens sued Cotton Design for various respiratory ailments allegedly caused or compounded by smog from Cotton Design's factory. Using the information presented in the chapter, answer the following questions.

1. Under the common law, what would each plaintiff be required to identify in order to be given relief by the court?
2. What standard for limiting emissions into the air does Cotton Design's pollution-control equipment have to meet?
3. If Cotton Design's emissions violated the Clean Air Act, how much can the EPA assess in fines per day?
4. What information must the city send to every household that it supplies with water?

Debate This . . . *The courts should reject all cases in which the wetlands in question do not consist of bodies of water that exist during the entire year.*

Terms and Concepts

environmental impact
  statement (EIS) 538
nuisance 534

potentially responsible
  party (PRP) 546
toxic torts 535

wetlands 542

Issue Spotters

1. Resource Refining Company's plant emits smoke and fumes. Resource's operation includes a short railway system, and trucks enter and exit the grounds continuously. Constant vibrations from the trains and trucks rattle nearby residential neighborhoods. The residents sue Resource. Are there any reasons why the court might refuse to issue an injunction against Resource's operation? Explain. (See *Common Law Actions*.)

2. ChemCorp generates hazardous wastes from its operations. Disposal Trucking Company transports those

wastes to Eliminators, Inc., which owns a site for hazardous waste disposal. Eliminators sells the property on which the disposal site is located to Fluid Properties, Inc. If the Environmental Protection Agency cleans up the site, from whom can it recover the cost? (See *Toxic Chemicals and Hazardous Waste*.)

- **Check your answers to the Issue Spotters against the answers provided in Appendix B at the end of this text.**

Business Scenarios and Case Problems

25–1. The Clean Water Act. Fruitade, Inc., is a processor of a soft drink called Freshen Up. Fruitade uses returnable bottles, which it cleans with a special acid to allow for further beverage processing. The acid is diluted with water and then allowed to pass into a navigable stream. Fruitade crushes its broken bottles and throws the crushed glass into the stream. Discuss fully any environmental laws that Fruitade has violated. (See *Water Pollution*.)

25–2. Environmental Protection. Moonbay is a home-building corporation that primarily develops retirement communities. Farmtex owns a number of feedlots in Sunny Valley. Moonbay purchases 20,000 acres of farmland in the same area and begins building and selling homes on this acreage. In the meantime, Farmtex continues to expand its feedlot business, and eventually only 500 feet separate the two operations. Because of the odor and flies from the feedlots, Moonbay finds it difficult to sell the homes in its development. Moonbay wants to enjoin (prevent) Farmtex from operating its feedlot in the vicinity of the retirement home development. Under what common law theory would Moonbay file this action? Has Farmtex violated any federal environmental laws? Discuss. (See *Common Law Actions*.)

25–3. Spotlight on the Grand Canyon—Environmental Impact Statement. The U.S. National Park Service (NPS) manages the Grand Canyon National Park in Arizona under a management plan that is subject to periodic review. After nine years of background work and the completion of a comprehensive environmental impact statement, the NPS issued a new management plan for the park. The plan allowed for the continued use of rafts on the Colorado River, which runs

through the Grand Canyon. The number of rafts was limited, however. Several environmental groups criticized the plan because they felt that it still allowed too many rafts on the river. The groups asked a federal appellate court to overturn the plan, claiming that it violated the wilderness status of the national park. When can a federal court overturn a determination by an agency such as the NPS? Explain. [*River Runners for Wilderness v. Martin*, 593 F.3d 1064 (9th Cir. 2010)] (See *Federal, State, and Local Regulations*.)

25–4. Superfund. A by-product of phosphate fertilizer production is pyrite waste, which contains arsenic and lead. From 1884 to 1906, seven phosphate fertilizer plants operated on a forty-three-acre site in Charleston, South Carolina. Planters Fertilizer & Phosphate Company bought the site in 1906 and continued to make fertilizer. In 1966, Planters sold the site to Columbia Nitrogen Corp. (CNC), which also operated the fertilizer plants. In 1985, CNC sold the site to James Holcombe and J. Henry Fair. After the site was sold, CNC was acquired by another company, PCS Nitrogen, Inc., which never owned or operated the fertilizer plants. Holcombe and Fair subdivided and sold the site to Allwaste Tank Cleaning Inc., Robin Hood Container Express, the city of Charleston, and Ashley II of Charleston, Inc. Ashley spent almost $200,000 cleaning up the contaminated soil. Who can be held liable for the cost? Why? [*PCS Nitrogen, Inc. v. Ashley II of Charleston LLC*, 714 F.3d 161 (4th Cir. 2013)] (See *Toxic Chemicals and Hazardous Waste*.)

25–5. Business Case Problem with Sample Answer— Environmental Impact Statements. The U.S. Forest Service (USFS) proposed a travel management plan (TMP) for the Beartooth Ranger District in the Pryor and Absaroka Mountains in the Custer National Forest of southern Montana. The TMP would convert unauthorized user-created routes within the wilderness to routes authorized for motor vehicle use. It would also permit off-road "dispersed vehicle camping" within 300 feet of the routes, with some seasonal restrictions. The TMP would ban cross-country motorized travel outside the designated routes. Is an environmental impact statement required before the USFS implements the TMP? If so, what aspects of the environment should the USFS consider in preparing it? Discuss. [*Pryors Coalition v. Weldon*, 551 Fed.Appx. 426 (9th Cir. 2014)] (See *Federal, State, and Local Regulations.*)

• **For a sample answer to Problem 25–5, go to Appendix C at the end of this text.**

25–6. The Clean Water Act. ICG Hazard, LLC, operates the Thunder Ridge surface coal mine in Leslie County, Kentucky, under a National Pollutant Discharge Elimination System permit issued by the Kentucky Division of Water (KDOW). As part of the operation, ICG discharges selenium into the surrounding water. Selenium is a naturally occurring element that endangers aquatic life once it reaches a certain concentration. KDOW knew when it issued the permit that mines in the area could produce selenium but did not specify discharge limits for the element in ICG's permit. Instead, the agency imposed a one-time monitoring requirement, which ICG met. Does ICG's discharge of selenium violate the Clean Water Act? Explain. [*Sierra Club v. ICG Hazard, LLC*, 781 F.3d 281 (6th Cir. 2015)] (See *Water Pollution.*)

25–7. State Regulations. Olivia Chernaik and other Oregon residents filed a suit in an Oregon state court against Governor Kate Brown and other government officials. According to the plaintiffs, the state holds "vital natural resources," including water, air, land, and wildlife, in trust for the benefit of its citizens. The plaintiffs alleged that "Oregon has the ability to curtail greenhouse gas emissions, increase carbon sequestration, and take the steps necessary to protect the [state's resources] from the adverse effects of climate change." The plaintiffs claimed, however, that the state had failed to uphold its "fiduciary obligation to protect and preserve those resources." The plaintiffs asked the court to order the defendants to "develop and implement a carbon reduction plan that will protect [resources] by the best available science." The basis of the plaintiffs' claim was the common law public-trust doctrine. Under this doctrine, a state holds certain resources in trust for the public's use and cannot convey or otherwise dispose of them in a manner that would interfere with this right. Is the court likely to grant the plaintiffs' request? Explain. [*Chernaik v. Brown*, 295 Or.App. 584, 436 P.3d 26 (2019)] (See *Federal, State, and Local Regulations.*)

25–8. A Question of Ethics—The IDDR Approach and Superfund. *Sevenson Environmental Services was hired to clean up a Superfund site in Manville, New Jersey, where the soil was contaminated with creosote. (Creosote is a flammable, oily mixture of chemical compounds often used for preserving wood or as a pesticide.) The Environmental Protection Agency (EPA) funded the effort. Sevenson's project manager was Gordon McDonald, whose responsibilities included hiring subcontractors through a bidding process. McDonald made the contamination look as severe as possible to pressure rival bidders to bid higher. He showed the bids to one of the competitors, John Bennett, and permitted him to submit a new "lowest" bid in exchange for a kickback of $13.50 per ton of cleaned soil. Bennett won the contract, which (because of McDonald's manipulation of the bidding process) covered the amount of the kickback. The scheme was eventually discovered, and Bennett was charged with criminal fraud. [*United States v. Bennett*, 688 Fed.Appx. 169 (3d Cir. 2017)] (See Toxic Chemicals and Hazardous Waste.)*

(a) What was Bennett's ethical dilemma in this case? Using the IDDR approach, discuss and evaluate the actions he chose to resolve it.

(b) Suppose that Bennett had refused the kickback scheme, had won the contract with an honest low bid, and had been paid for the work, but had not actually performed his part of the deal. Would this situation have been ethically distinct from the true facts? Explain.

Time-Limited Group Activity

25–9. Clean-Up Costs. It has been estimated that for every dollar spent cleaning up hazardous-waste sites, administrative agencies spend seven dollars in overhead. (See *Toxic Chemicals and Hazardous Waste.*)

(a) The first group will list and explain possible ways to trim these administrative costs.

(b) The second group will evaluate whether the laws pertaining to hazardous waste clean-up can or should be changed to reduce the costs to government.

Chapter 26

Real Property and Land-Use Control

From the earliest times, property has provided a means for survival. Primitive peoples lived off the fruits of the land, eating the vegetation and wildlife. Later, as the wildlife was domesticated and the vegetation cultivated, people used their property for pastures and farmland. Throughout history, property has continued to be an indicator of family wealth and social position.

In the Western world, the protection of an individual's right to his or her property has become one of our most important rights.

In this chapter, we look at the nature of real property and the ways in which it can be owned. We examine the legal requirements involved in the transfer of real property. We even consider, in this chapter's *Spotlight Case*, whether the buyer of a haunted house can rescind the sale.

Realize that real property rights are never absolute. There is a higher right—that of the government to take, for compensation, private land for public use. Later in the chapter, we discuss this right, as well as other restrictions on the ownership or use of property. We conclude the chapter with a discussion of land-use control and zoning laws.

26-1 The Nature of Real Property

Real property (or realty) consists of land and everything permanently attached to it, including structures and other fixtures. Real property encompasses airspace and subsurface rights, as well as rights to plants and vegetation. In essence, real property is immovable.

26-1a Land and Structures

Land includes the soil on the surface of the earth and the natural products or artificial structures that are attached to it. Land further includes all the waters contained on or under its surface and much, but not necessarily all, of the airspace above it. The exterior boundaries of land extend down to the center of the earth and up to the farthest reaches of the atmosphere (subject to certain qualifications).

26-1b Airspace and Subsurface Rights

The owner of real property has rights to both the airspace above the land and the soil and minerals underneath it. Any limitations on either airspace rights or subsurface rights, called *encumbrances*, normally must be indicated on the document that transfers title at the time of purchase.

The ways in which ownership rights in real property can be limited will be examined later in this chapter.

Airspace Rights Disputes concerning airspace rights may involve the right of commercial and private planes to fly over property and the right of individuals and governments to seed clouds and produce artificial rain. Flights over private land normally do not violate property rights unless the flights are so low and so frequent that they directly interfere with the owner's enjoyment and use of the land. Leaning walls or projecting eave spouts or roofs may also violate the airspace rights of an adjoining property owner.

Subsurface Rights In many states, ownership of land can be separated from ownership of its subsurface. In other words, the owner of the surface may sell subsurface rights to another person. When ownership is separated into surface and subsurface rights, each owner can pass title to what she or he owns without the consent of the other owner.

Subsurface rights can be extremely valuable, as these rights include the ownership of minerals, oil, or natural gas. But a subsurface owner's rights would be of little value if he or she could not use the surface to exercise those rights. Hence, a subsurface owner has a right (called a *profit*, discussed later in this chapter) to go onto the surface of the land to, for instance, find and remove minerals.

Of course, conflicts can arise between the surface owner's use of the property and the subsurface owner's need to extract minerals, oil, or natural gas. In that situation, one party's interest may become subservient (secondary) to the other party's interest either by statute or by case law.

If the owners of the subsurface rights excavate, they are absolutely (strictly) liable if their excavation causes the surface to collapse. Many states have statutes that also make the excavators liable for any damage to structures on the land. Typically, these statutes set out precise requirements for excavations of various depths.

26–1c Plant Life and Vegetation

Plant life, both natural and cultivated, is also considered to be real property. In many instances, the natural vegetation, such as trees, adds greatly to the value of realty. When a parcel of land is sold and the land has growing crops on it, the sale includes the crops, unless otherwise specified in the sales contract. When crops are sold by themselves, however, they are considered to be personal property, or goods. Consequently, the sale of crops is a sale of goods and is governed by the Uniform Commercial Code (UCC) rather than by real property law.

26–1d Fixtures

Certain personal property can become so closely associated with the real property to which it is attached that the law views it as real property. Such property is known as a **fixture**—an item affixed to realty, meaning that it is attached to the real property in a permanent way. The item may be embedded in the land or permanently attached to the property or to another fixture on the property by means of cement, plaster, bolts, nails, or screws. An item, such as a statue, may even sit on the land without being attached, as long as the owner *intends* it to be a fixture.

Fixtures are included in the sale of land unless the sales contract specifies otherwise. The issue of whether an item is a fixture (and thus real estate) or not a fixture (and thus personal property) often arises with respect to land sales, real property taxation, insurance coverage, and divorces. How the issue is resolved can have important consequences for the parties involved.

Typical Fixtures Some items can only be attached to property permanently—such as tile floors, cabinets, and recessed lighting. Because such items are attached

permanently, it is assumed that the owner intended them to be fixtures. Also, when an item of property is custom-made for installation on real property, as storm windows are, the item usually is classified as a fixture.

In addition, an item that is firmly attached to the land and integral to its use may be deemed a fixture. For instance, a mobile home or a complex irrigation system bolted to a cement slab on a farm can be a fixture. The courts assume that owners, in making such installations, intend the objects to become part of their real property.

The Role of Intent Generally, when the courts need to determine whether a certain item is a fixture, they examine the intention of the party who placed the object on the real property. When the intent of that party is in dispute, the courts usually will deem that the item is a fixture if either or both of the following are true:

- The property attached cannot be removed without causing substantial damage to the remaining realty.
- The property attached is so adapted to the rest of the realty as to have become a part of it.

■ **Case in Point 26.1** Terminal 5, a facility owned by the Port of Seattle (Port), was used in loading and unloading the shipping containers used to transport goods by ship. APL Limited entered into a long-term lease with the Port for use of Terminal 5 and for use of Port-owned container cranes. Terminal 5 was substantially rebuilt, and steel cranes were constructed and installed. The cranes were 100 feet apart, 198 feet tall, and 85 feet wide, and were mounted on rails embedded in concrete. They were hard-wired to a dedicated high-voltage electrical system built specifically for Terminal 5 and were attached to the power substation by cables.

APL later filed a lawsuit against the state of Washington for a refund of sales tax it had paid on the lease of the cranes. The state argued that the cranes were personal property and, as such, subject to sales tax. The trial court ruled in favor of the state, but a Washington appellate court reversed. The reviewing court found that the trial court had not sufficiently taken the Port's intent into account in determining that the cranes were personal property, not fixtures. "When the owner and the person that [attaches property to realty] are one and the same, a rebuttable presumption arises that the owner's intention was for the [property] to become part of the realty." The reviewing court remanded the case so the lower court could examine evidence of the Port's intent.[1] ■

1. *APL Limited v. Washington State Department of Revenue*, 154 Wash.App. 1020 (2010).

Trade Fixtures Are Personal Property Trade fixtures are an exception to the rule that fixtures are a part of the real property to which they are attached. A **trade fixture** is personal property that is installed for a commercial purpose *by a tenant* (one who rents real property from the owner, or landlord).

Trade fixtures remain the property of the tenant unless removal would irreparably damage the building or realty. A walk-in cooler, for instance, purchased and installed by a tenant who uses the premises for a restaurant, is a trade fixture. The tenant can remove the cooler from the premises when the lease terminates but ordinarily must repair any damage that the removal causes or compensate the landlord for the damage.

26–2 Ownership and Other Interests in Real Property

Ownership of property is an abstract concept that cannot exist independently of the legal system. No one can actually possess, or *hold*, a piece of land, the air above it, the earth below it, and all the water contained on it. One can only possess *rights* in real property.

Numerous rights are involved in real property ownership, which is why property ownership is often viewed as a bundle of rights. One who possesses the entire bundle of rights is said to hold the property in *fee simple*, which is the most complete form of ownership. When only some of the rights in the bundle are transferred to another person, the effect is to limit the ownership rights of both the transferor of the rights and the recipient.

Ownership interests in real property have traditionally been referred to as *estates in land*, which include fee simple estates, life estates, and leasehold estates. We examine these types of estates in this section, and we also discuss several forms of concurrent ownership of property. Finally, we describe certain interests in real property that is owned by others.

26–2a Ownership in Fee Simple

In a **fee simple absolute,** the owner has the greatest aggregation of rights, privileges, and power possible. The owner can give the property away or dispose of the property by *deed* or by *will*. When there is no will, the fee simple passes to the owner's legal heirs on her or his death. A fee simple absolute is potentially infinite in duration and is assigned forever to a person and her or his

heirs without limitation or condition.[2] The owner has the rights of *exclusive* possession and use of the property.

The rights that accompany a fee simple absolute include the right to use the land for whatever purpose the owner sees fit. Of course, other laws, including applicable zoning, noise, and environmental laws, may limit the owner's ability to use the property in certain ways. A person who uses his or her property in a manner that unreasonably interferes with others' right to use or enjoy their own property can be liable for the tort of *nuisance*.

■ **Case in Point 26.2** Nancy and James Biglane owned and lived in a building next door to the Under the Hill Saloon, a popular bar that featured live music. During the summer, the Saloon, which had no air-conditioning, opened its windows and doors, and live music echoed up and down the street.

The Biglanes installed extra insulation, thicker windows, and air-conditioning units in their building. Nevertheless, the noise from the Saloon kept the Biglanes awake at night. Eventually, they sued the owners of the Saloon for nuisance. The court held that the noise from the bar unreasonably interfered with the Biglanes' right to enjoy their property and prohibited the Saloon from opening its windows and doors while playing music.[3] ■

26–2b Life Estates

A **life estate** is an estate that lasts for the life of some specified individual. A **conveyance,** or transfer of real property, "to A for his life" creates a life estate.[4] The life tenant's ownership rights cease to exist on the life tenant's death.

The life tenant has the right to use the land, provided that he or she commits no **waste** (injury to the land). In other words, the life tenant cannot use the land in a manner that would adversely affect its value. The life tenant can use the land to harvest crops or, if mines and oil wells are already on the land, can extract minerals and oil from it, but the life tenant cannot establish new wells or mines. The life tenant can also create liens, *easements* (discussed shortly), and leases, but none can extend beyond the life

---

2. In another type of estate, the *fee simple defeasible*, ownership in fee simple automatically terminates if a stated event occurs. For instance, property might be conveyed (transferred) to a school only as long as it is used for school purposes. In addition, the fee simple may be subject to a *condition subsequent*. This means that if a stated event occurs, the prior owner of the property can bring an action to regain possession of the property.
3. *Biglane v. Under the Hill Corp.*, 949 So.2d 9 (Miss. 2007).
4. A less common type of life estate is created by the conveyance "to A for the life of B." This is known as an estate *pur autre vie*—that is, an estate for the duration of the life of another.

of the tenant. In addition, with few exceptions, the life tenant has an exclusive right to possession during his or her lifetime.

Along with these rights, the life tenant also has some duties—to keep the property in repair and to pay property taxes. In short, the owner of the life estate has the same rights as a fee simple owner except that she or he must maintain the value of the property during her or his tenancy.

The distinction between a life estate and a fee simple determined the result in the following case.

Case 26.1

In the Matter of the Estate of Nelson

Supreme Court of North Dakota, 2018 ND 118, 910 N.W.2d 856 (2018).

Background and Facts When Sidney Solberg died, 100 mineral acres—that is, the right to all of the minerals under a certain 100 acres—and other real property in his estate were distributed to his widow, Lillian, for her life. The remainder interest (the right of ownership after Lillian's interest ended) was conveyed to their four children, including Glenn Solberg.

Later, Lillian married Lyle Nelson. When Lillian passed away, a codicil (addition) to her will allegedly gave the 100 mineral acres to Glenn. The codicil also purported to create for Glenn an option to buy the other real property she had inherited from Sidney. When Nelson died, Glenn filed a claim in a North Dakota state court against Nelson's estate. Glenn asserted that under the terms of the codicil to Lillian's will, he was entitled to the ownership of the 100 mineral acres and the right to buy the other property. The court dismissed Glenn's claim. He appealed to the state supreme court.

In the Language of the Court

JENSEN, Justice.

* * * *

Our law regarding the rights of someone who holds a life interest in property is * * * well established. It is well-settled [that] a life estate holder is entitled to both the possession and the use of the property, * * * including the right to rents, issues, and profits generated by the parcel * * * . *A life tenant is entitled to possession and enjoyment of the property as long as the estate endures; he or she may convey or lease his or her interest, but may not disregard the rights of those who take when the life estate ends.* * * * No future interest can be defeated or barred by any alienation [voluntary transfer of real property] or other act of the owner of the [life] interest. [Emphasis added.]

In this case, Lillian Nelson obtained a life estate interest in the 100 mineral acres and in the option property * * * from Sidney Solberg's estate. The codicil relied upon by Glenn Solberg itself identifies Lillian Nelson's interest as being limited to a life estate. As a life tenant she was limited to conveying an interest in her property only to the extent of her life and she could not make any transfers that would disregard the rights of those who would take the property when her life ended. As such, Lillian Nelson's attempt to provide an interest in the 100 mineral acres to Glenn Solberg in her * * * will is invalid because it disregards the rights of those who would take the property when her life ended. Similarly, her attempt to convey a right of first refusal to the option property * * * is also invalid because it disregards the rights of those who would take the property when her life ended.

Upon Lillian Nelson's death * * * her life interest ended and the 100 mineral acres and the option property became the property of her four children as the holders of the remainder interest. * * * The Lyle Nelson Estate did not hold, and Lyle Nelson never held, an interest in the 100 mineral acres or the option property. * * * Glenn Solberg could not recover property from the Lyle Nelson Estate if Lyle Nelson never held an interest in the property.

Decision and Remedy *The Supreme Court of North Dakota affirmed the dismissal of Glenn's claim. "The [lower] court properly concluded that, with certainty, it would be impossible for Glenn Solberg to obtain the relief he requested from the Lyle Nelson Estate."*

Case 26.1 Continues

Case 26.1 Continued

Critical Thinking

- **Legal Environment** *Lillian could not divest (deprive) her children of their remainder interest in the property of her life estate. Are there any actions that the owner of a life estate could take legitimately that would divest the holder of a remainder interest in the property of this interest?*
- **What If the Facts Were Different?** *Suppose that Sidney Solberg had disposed of his entire estate in fee simple before his death. Would the result have been different? Discuss.*

26–2c Concurrent Ownership

Persons who share ownership rights simultaneously in particular property (including real property and personal property) are said to have **concurrent ownership.** There are two principal types of concurrent ownership: *tenancy in common* and *joint tenancy.* Concurrent ownership rights can also be held in a *tenancy by the entirety* or as *community property,* but these types of concurrent ownership are less common.

Tenancy in Common The term **tenancy in common** refers to a form of co-ownership in which each of two or more persons owns an undivided interest in the property. The interest is undivided because each tenant shares rights in the whole property. On the death of a tenant in common, that tenant's interest in the property passes to her or his heirs. ■ **Example 26.3** Four friends purchase a condominium unit in Hawaii together as tenants in common. This means that each of them has a one-fourth ownership interest in the whole. If one of the four owners dies a year after the purchase, his ownership interest passes to his heirs (his wife and children, for instance) rather than to the other tenants in common. ■

Unless the co-tenants have agreed otherwise, a tenant in common can transfer her or his interest in the property to another without the consent of the remaining co-owners. In most states, it is presumed that a co-tenancy is a tenancy in common unless there is specific language indicating the intent to establish a joint tenancy.

Joint Tenancy In a **joint tenancy,** each of two or more persons owns an undivided interest in the property, but a deceased joint tenant's interest passes to the surviving joint tenant or tenants.

Right of Survivorship. The right of a surviving joint tenant to inherit a deceased joint tenant's ownership interest—referred to as a *right of survivorship*—distinguishes a joint tenancy from a tenancy in common. ■ **Example 26.4** Jerrold and Eva are married and purchase a house as joint tenants. The title to the house clearly expresses the intent to create a joint tenancy because it refers to Jerrold and Eva as "joint tenants with right of survivorship." Jerrold has three children from a prior marriage. If Jerrold dies, his interest in the house automatically passes to Eva rather than to his children from the prior marriage. ■

Termination of a Joint Tenancy. A joint tenant can transfer her or his rights by sale or gift to another without the consent of the other joint tenants. Doing so terminates the joint tenancy, however. The person who purchases the property or receives it as a gift becomes a tenant in common, not a joint tenant. ■ **Example 26.5** Three brothers, Brody, Saul, and Jacob, own a parcel of land as joint tenants. Brody is experiencing financial difficulties and sells his interest in the real property to Beth. The sale terminates the joint tenancy, and now Beth, Saul, and Jacob hold the property as tenants in common. ■

A joint tenant's interest can also be levied against (seized by court order) to satisfy the tenant's *judgment creditors*—creditors entitled to payment after a court proceeding. If this occurs, the joint tenancy terminates, and the remaining owners hold the property as tenants in common. (Judgment creditors can also seize the interests of tenants in a tenancy in common.)

Tenancy by the Entirety A less common form of shared ownership of real property by married persons is a **tenancy by the entirety.** It differs from a joint tenancy in that neither spouse may separately transfer his or her interest during his or her lifetime unless the other spouse consents. In some states in which statutes give the wife the right to convey her property, this form of concurrent ownership has effectively been abolished. A divorce, either spouse's death, or mutual agreement will terminate a tenancy by the entirety.

Community Property A limited number of states[5] allow married couples to own property as **community property.** If property is held as community property, each spouse technically owns an undivided one-half

---

5. These states include Alaska, Arizona, California, Idaho, Louisiana, Nevada, New Mexico, Texas, Washington, and Wisconsin. Puerto Rico allows property to be owned as community property as well.

interest in the property. This type of ownership applies to most property acquired by the husband or the wife during the course of the marriage. It generally does *not* apply to property acquired prior to the marriage or to property acquired by gift or inheritance as separate property during the marriage. After a divorce, community property is divided equally in some states and according to the discretion of the court in other states.

26–2d Leasehold Estates

A **leasehold estate** is created when a real property owner or lessor (landlord) agrees to convey the right to possess and use the property to a lessee (tenant) for a certain period of time. The tenant's right to possession is *temporary*, which is what distinguishes a tenant from a purchaser, who acquires title to the property.

In every leasehold estate, the tenant has a *qualified* right to exclusive possession. It is qualified because the landlord has a right to enter onto the premises to ensure that no waste is being committed. In addition, the tenant can use the land—for instance, by harvesting crops—but cannot injure it by such activities as cutting down timber to sell or extracting oil.

Fixed-Term Tenancy A **fixed-term tenancy,** also called a *tenancy for years*, is created by an express contract stating that the property is leased for a specified period of time, such as a month, a year, or a period of years. Signing a one-year lease to occupy an apartment, for instance, creates a fixed-term tenancy. Note that the term need not be specified by date and can be conditioned on the occurrence of an event, such as leasing a cabin for the summer or an apartment during Mardi Gras.

At the end of the period specified in the lease, the lease ends (without notice), and possession of the property returns to the lessor. If the tenant dies during the period of the lease, the lease interest passes to the tenant's heirs as personal property. Often, leases include renewal or extension provisions.

Periodic Tenancy A **periodic tenancy** is created by a lease that does not specify a term but does specify that rent is to be paid at certain intervals, such as weekly, monthly, or yearly. The tenancy is automatically renewed for another rental period unless properly terminated. ■ **Example 26.6** Jewel, LLC, enters into a lease with Capital Properties. The lease states, "Rent is due on the tenth day of every month." This provision creates a periodic tenancy from month to month. ■ A periodic tenancy sometimes arises after a fixed-term tenancy ends when the landlord allows the tenant to retain possession and continue paying monthly or weekly rent.

Under the common law, to terminate a periodic tenancy, the landlord or tenant must give at least one period's notice to the other party. If the tenancy is month to month, for instance, one month's notice must be given prior to the last month's rent payment. Today, however, state statutes often require a different period of notice before the termination of a tenancy.

Tenancy at Will With a **tenancy at will,** either party can terminate the tenancy without notice. This type of tenancy can arise if a landlord rents property to a tenant "for as long as both agree" or allows a person to live on the premises without paying rent. Tenancy at will is rare today because most state statutes require a landlord to provide some period of notice to terminate a tenancy. States may also require a landowner to have sufficient cause (a legitimate reason) to end a residential tenancy.

Tenancy at Sufferance The mere possession of land without right is called a **tenancy at sufferance.** A tenancy at sufferance is not a true tenancy because it is created when a tenant *wrongfully* retains possession of property. Whenever a fixed-term tenancy or a periodic tenancy ends and the tenant continues to retain possession of the premises without the owner's permission, a tenancy at sufferance is created.

26–2e Nonpossessory Interests

In contrast to the types of property interests just described, some interests in land do not include any rights to possess the property. These interests are therefore known as **nonpossessory interests.** They include *easements, profits*, and *licenses*.

An **easement** is the right of a person to make limited use of another person's real property without taking anything from the property. The right to walk across another's property, for instance, is an easement. In contrast, a **profit** is the right to go onto land owned by another and take away some part of the land itself or some product of the land. ■ **Example 26.7** Shawn owns real property known as the Dunes. Shawn gives Carmen the right to go there and remove all of the sand and gravel that she needs for her cement business. Carmen has a profit. ■

Easements and profits can be classified as either *appurtenant* or *in gross*. Because easements and profits are similar and the same rules apply to both, we discuss them together.

Easement or Profit Appurtenant An easement (or profit) *appurtenant* arises when the owner of one piece of land has a right to go onto (or remove something from) an adjacent piece of land owned by another. The land that is benefited by the easement is called the *dominant estate*, and the land that is burdened is called the *servient estate*.

Because easements appurtenant are intended to *benefit the land*, they run (are conveyed) with the land when it is transferred. ■ **Example 26.8** Owen has a right to drive his car across Gary's land, which is adjacent to Owen's property. This right-of-way over Gary's property is an easement appurtenant to Owen's land. If Owen sells his land, the easement runs with the land to benefit the new owner. ■

Easement or Profit in Gross In an easement or profit *in gross*, the right to use or take things from another's land is given to one who does not own an adjacent tract of land. These easements are intended to *benefit a particular person or business*, not a particular piece of land, and cannot be transferred.

■ **Example 26.9** Avery owns a parcel of land with a marble quarry. Avery conveys to Classic Stone Corporation the right to come onto her land and remove up to five hundred pounds of marble per day. Classic Stone owns a profit in gross and cannot transfer this right to another. ■ Similarly, when a utility company is granted an easement to run its power lines across another's property, it obtains an easement in gross.

Creation of an Easement or Profit Most easements and profits are created by an express grant in a contract, deed, or will. This allows the parties to include terms defining the extent and length of time of use. In some situations, however, an easement or profit can be created without an express agreement.

An easement or profit may arise by **implication** when the circumstances surrounding the division of a parcel of property imply its creation. ■ **Example 26.10** Barrow divides a parcel of land that has only one well for drinking water. If Barrow conveys the half without a well to Dean, a profit by implication arises because Dean needs drinking water. ■

An easement may also be created by **necessity.** An easement by necessity does not require division of property for its existence. A person who rents an apartment, for instance, has an easement by necessity in the private road leading up to it.

An easement arises by **prescription** when one person exercises an easement, such as a right-of-way, on another person's land without the landowner's consent. The use must be apparent and continue for the length of time required by the applicable statute of limitations. (In much the same way, title to property may be obtained by *adverse possession*, as will be discussed later in this chapter.)

■ **Case in Point 26.11** Junior and Wilma Thompson sold twenty-one of their fifty acres of land in Missouri to Walnut Bowls, Inc. The deed expressly reserved an easement to the Thompsons' remaining twenty-nine acres, but it did not fix a precise location for the easement.

James and Linda Baker subsequently bought the remaining acreage of the Thompsons' land.

Many years later—on learning of the easement to the Bakers' property—a potential buyer of Walnut Bowls' property refused to go through with the sale. Walnut Bowls then put steel cables across its driveway entrances, installed a lock and chain on an access gate, and bolted a "No Trespassing" sign facing the Bakers' property. The Bakers filed a suit in a Missouri state court to determine the location of the easement. Citing the lack of an express location, the court held that there was no easement.

The Bakers appealed, and a state intermediate appellate court reversed that decision. The reviewing court held that an easement existed and instructed the trial court to determine its location. An easement can be created by deed even though its specific location is not identified. The location can later be fixed by agreement between the parties or inferred from use. If the easement is not identified in either of these ways, a court must determine the location.[6] ■

Termination of an Easement or Profit An easement or profit can be terminated or extinguished in several ways. The simplest way is to deed it back to the owner of the land that is burdened by it. Similarly, if the owner of an easement or profit acquires the property burdened by it, then it is merged into the property.

Another way to terminate an easement or profit is to abandon it and provide evidence of the intent to relinquish the right to use it. Mere nonuse will not extinguish an easement or profit, however, *unless the nonuse is accompanied by an overt act showing the intent to abandon.* An overt act might be, for instance, installing and using a different access road to one's property and discontinuing using an easement across the neighboring property. In any case, a court must be convinced that there was an intent to abandon the easement or profit.

License In the context of real property, a **license** is the revocable right of a person to come onto another person's land. It is a personal privilege that arises from the consent of the owner of the land and can be revoked by the owner. A ticket to attend a movie at a theater or a concert is an example of a license.

In essence, a license grants a person the authority to enter the land of another and perform a specified act or series of acts without obtaining any permanent interest in the land. When a person with a license exceeds the authority granted and undertakes some action on the property that is not permitted, the property owner can sue that person for the tort of trespass.

■ **Case in Point 26.12** Richard and Mary Orman purchased real property owned at one time by Sandra Curtis.

---

6. *Baker v. Walnut Bowls, Inc.*, 423 S.W.3d 293 (Mo.Ct.App. 2014).

Part of the garage extended nine feet onto Curtis's neighboring property. In an agreement on file with the deed, Curtis had given the Ormans permission to use the garage as long as it continued to be used as a garage. After the Ormans moved in, they converted the garage's workshop into guest quarters but continued to use the garage as a garage.

A dispute arose over the driveway shared by Curtis and the Ormans, which straddled the property line. The Ormans filed a suit claiming that Curtis left "junk objects" near the driveway that impeded their access. Curtis countered that the permission she had given the buyers to use the garage was a license. She claimed that the Ormans, by converting the workshop into living quarters, had exceeded their authority under the license, which she could therefore revoke. The court looked at the agreement's wording, which clearly gave the Ormans the right to use the garage but did not mention the workshop. The court concluded that because the Ormans were continuing to use the garage as a garage, Curtis could not revoke their right to do so.[7] ∎

Exhibit 26–1 illustrates the various interests in real property discussed in this chapter.

26–3 Transfer of Ownership

Ownership interests in real property are frequently transferred by sale, and the terms of the transfer are specified in a real estate sales contract. When real property is sold, the type of interest being transferred and the conditions

---
7. *Orman v. Curtis*, 54 Misc.3d 1206(A), 50 N.Y.S.3d 27 (2017).

of the transfer normally are set forth in a *deed* executed by the person who is conveying the property. Real property ownership can also be transferred by gift, by will or inheritance, by adverse possession, or by eminent domain.

26–3a Real Estate Sales Contracts

In some ways, a sale of real estate is similar to a sale of goods because it involves a transfer of ownership, often with specific warranties. A sale of real estate, however, is a more complicated transaction that involves certain formalities that are not required in a sale of goods. In part because of these complications, real estate brokers or agents who are licensed by the state assist the buyers and sellers during the sales transaction.

Usually, after some negotiation (offers, counteroffers, and responses), the parties enter into a detailed contract setting forth their agreement. A contract for a sale of land includes such terms as the purchase price, the type of deed the buyer will receive, the condition of the premises, and any items that will be included.

Unless the buyer pays cash for the property, the buyer must obtain financing through a mortgage loan. Real estate sales contracts are often contingent on the buyer's ability to obtain financing at or below a specified rate of interest. The contract may also be contingent on certain events, such as the completion of a land survey or the property's passing one or more inspections. Normally, the buyer is responsible for having the premises inspected for physical or mechanical defects and for insect infestation.

Exhibit 26–1 Interests in Real Property

Type of Interest	Description
Ownership Interests	1. *Fee simple*—The most complete form of ownership. 2. *Life estate*—An estate that lasts for the life of a specified individual. 3. *Concurrent ownership*—When two or more persons hold title to property together, concurrent ownership exists. Examples of concurrent ownership include: a. Tenancy in common b. Joint tenancy c. Tenancy by the entirety d. Community property
Leasehold Estates	1. Fixed-term tenancy (tenancy for years) 2. Periodic tenancy 3. Tenancy at will 4. Tenancy at sufferance
Nonpossessory Interests	1. Easements 2. Profits 3. Licenses

Closing Date and Escrow The contract usually fixes a date for performance, or **closing,** that frequently is four to twelve weeks after the contract is signed. On this day, the seller conveys the property to the buyer by delivering the deed to the buyer in exchange for payment of the purchase price.

Deposits toward the purchase price normally are held in a special account, called an **escrow account,** until all of the conditions of sale have been met. Once the closing takes place, the funds in the escrow account are transferred to the seller.

Marketable Title The title to the property is especially important to the buyer. A grantor (seller) is obligated to transfer **marketable title,** or good title, to the grantee (buyer). Marketable title means that the grantor's ownership is free from encumbrances (except those disclosed by the grantor) and free of defects.

If the buyer signs a purchase contract and then discovers that the seller does not have a marketable title, the buyer can withdraw from the contract. ■ **Example 26.13** Chan enters into an agreement to buy Fortuna Ranch from Hal. Chan then discovers that Hal has given Pearl an option to purchase the ranch and the option has not expired. In this situation, the title is not marketable, because Pearl could exercise the option and Hal would be compelled to sell the ranch to her. Therefore, Chan can withdraw from the contract to buy the property. ■

The most common way of ensuring title is through **title insurance,** which insures the buyer against loss from defects in title to real property. When financing the purchase of real property, almost all lenders require title insurance to protect their interests in the collateral for the loan.

Implied Warranties in the Sale of New Homes
The common law rule of *caveat emptor* ("let the buyer beware") held that the seller of a home made no warranty as to its soundness or fitness (unless the contract or deed stated otherwise). Today, however, most states consider a warranty—the **implied warranty of habitability**—to be implied by the seller in the sale of *new* homes.

Under this warranty, the seller of a new house warrants that it will be fit for human habitation even if the deed or contract of sale does not include such a warranty. Essentially, the seller is warranting that the house is in reasonable working order and is of reasonably sound construction. The seller can be liable if the home is defective. In some states, the warranty protects not only the first purchaser but any subsequent purchaser as well.

Seller's Duty to Disclose Hidden Defects In most jurisdictions, courts impose on sellers a duty to disclose any known defect that materially affects the value of the property and that the buyer could not reasonably discover. Failure to disclose such a defect gives the buyer a right to rescind the contract and to sue for damages based on fraud or misrepresentation.

There normally is a limit to the time within which the buyer can bring a suit against the seller based on the defect. Time limits run from either the date of the sale or the day that the buyer discovered (or should have discovered) the defect. ■ **Example 26.14** Ian Newson partially renovates a house in Louisiana and sells it to Jerry and Tabitha Moreland for $170,000. Two months after the Morelands move in, they discover rotten wood behind the tile in the bathroom and experience problems with the plumbing. The state statute specifies that the Morelands have one year from the date of the sale or the discovery of the defect to file a lawsuit. Therefore, the Morelands must file a suit within twelve months of discovering the defects (which would be fourteen months from the date of the sale). ■

In the following *Spotlight Case,* the court had to decide whether the buyer of a house had the right to rescind the sales contract because he was not told that the house was allegedly haunted.

Spotlight on Sales of Haunted Houses

Case 26.2 Stambovsky v. Ackley

Supreme Court, Appellate Division, New York, 169 A.D.2d 254, 572 N.Y.S.2d 672 (1991).

Background and Facts Jeffrey Stambovsky signed a contract to buy Helen Ackley's home in Nyack, New York. After the contract was signed, Stambovsky discovered that the house was widely reputed to be haunted. The Ackley family claimed to have seen poltergeists on numerous occasions over the prior nine years. The Ackleys had been interviewed and quoted in both a national publication (*Reader's Digest*) and the local newspaper. The house was described as "a riverfront Victorian (with ghost)" when it was part of a walking tour of Nyack. When Stambovsky discovered the house's reputation, he sued to rescind the contract and recover his down payment. He alleged that Ackley and her real estate agent made material misrepresentations when they failed to disclose Ackley's belief that the home was haunted. Ackley argued that, under the doctrine of *caveat emptor*, she was under no duty to disclose to the buyer the home's haunted reputation. The trial court dismissed Stambovsky's case. Stambovsky appealed.

In the Language of the Court

Justice *RUBIN* delivered the opinion of the court.

* * * *

While I agree with [the trial court] that the real estate broker, as agent for the seller, is under no duty to disclose to a potential buyer the phantasmal reputation of the premises and that, in his pursuit of a legal remedy for fraudulent misrepresentation against the seller, plaintiff hasn't a ghost of a chance, I am nevertheless moved by the spirit of equity to allow the buyer to seek rescission of the contract of sale and recovery of his down payment. New York law fails to recognize any remedy for damages incurred as a result of the seller's mere silence, applying instead the strict rule of *caveat emptor*. Therefore, the theoretical basis for granting relief, even under the extraordinary facts of this case, is elusive if not ephemeral [short-lived].

* * * *

The doctrine of caveat emptor *requires that a buyer act prudently to assess the fitness and value of his purchase and operates to bar the purchaser who fails to exercise due care from seeking the equitable remedy of rescission.* * * * Applying the strict rule of *caveat emptor* to a contract involving a house possessed by poltergeists conjures up visions of a psychic or medium routinely accompanying the structural engineer and Terminix man on an inspection of every home subject to a contract of sale. It portends [warns] that the prudent attorney will establish an escrow account lest the subject of the transaction come back to haunt him and his client—or pray that his malpractice insurance coverage extends to supernatural disasters. In the interest of avoiding such untenable consequences, the notion that a haunting is a condition which can and should be ascertained upon reasonable inspection of the premises is a hobgoblin which should be exorcised from the body of legal precedent and laid quietly to rest. [Emphasis added.]

* * * *

In the case at bar [under consideration], defendant seller deliberately fostered the public belief that her home was possessed. Having undertaken to inform the public at large, to whom she has no legal relationship, about the supernatural occurrences on her property, she may be said to owe no less a duty to her contract vendee. It has been remarked that the occasional modern cases, which permit a seller to take unfair advantage of a buyer's ignorance so long as he is not actively misled are "singularly unappetizing." Where, as here, the seller not only takes unfair advantage of the buyer's ignorance but has created and perpetuated a condition about which he is unlikely to even inquire, enforcement of the contract (in whole or in part) is offensive to the court's sense of equity. Application of the remedy of rescission, within the bounds of the narrow exception to the doctrine of *caveat emptor* set forth herein, is entirely appropriate to relieve the unwitting purchaser from the consequences of a most unnatural bargain.

Decision and Remedy *The New York appellate court found that the doctrine of* caveat emptor *did not apply in this case. The court allowed Stambovsky to rescind the purchase contract and recover the down payment.*

Critical Thinking

- **Ethical** *In not disclosing the house's reputation to Stambovsky, was Ackley's behavior unethical? If so, was it unethical because she knew something he did not, or was it unethical because of the nature of the information she omitted? What if Ackley had failed to mention that the roof leaked or that the well was dry—conditions that a buyer would normally investigate? Explain your answer.*

- **Legal Environment** *Why did the court decide that applying the strict rule of* caveat emptor *was inappropriate in this case? How would applying this doctrine increase costs for the purchaser?*

26–3b Deeds

Possession and title to land are passed from person to person by means of a **deed**—the instrument used to transfer real property. Deeds must meet certain requirements, but unlike a contract, a deed does not have to be supported by legally sufficient consideration. Gifts of real property are common, and they require deeds even though there is no consideration for the gift.

To be valid, a deed must include the following:

1. The names of the grantor (the giver or seller) and the grantee (the donee or buyer).
2. Words evidencing the intent to convey (for instance, "I hereby bargain, sell, grant, or give"). No specific words are necessary. If the deed does not specify the type of estate being transferred, it presumptively transfers the property in fee simple absolute.
3. A legally sufficient description of the land. The description must include enough detail to distinguish the property being conveyed from every other parcel of land. The property can be identified by reference to an official survey or recorded plat map, or each boundary can be described by metes and bounds. **Metes and bounds** is a system of measuring boundary lines by the distance between two points, often using physical features of the local geography. A property description might say, for instance, "beginning at the southwesterly intersection of Court and Main Streets, then West 40 feet to the fence, then South 100 feet, then Northeast approximately 120 feet back to the beginning."
4. The grantor's (and frequently his or her spouse's) signature.
5. Delivery of the deed.

Different types of deeds provide different degrees of protection against defects of title. A defect of title exists, for instance, if an undisclosed third person has an ownership interest in the property.

Warranty Deeds A **warranty deed** contains the greatest number of warranties and thus provides the most extensive protection against defects of title. In most states, special language is required to create a general warranty deed. Warranty deeds commonly include the following covenants:

1. A covenant that the grantor has the title to, and the power to convey, the property.
2. A covenant of quiet enjoyment (a warranty that the buyer will not be disturbed in her or his possession of the land).
3. A covenant that transfer of the property is made without knowledge of adverse claims of third parties.

Generally, the warranty deed makes the grantor liable for all defects of title during the time that the property was held by the grantor and previous titleholders. ■ **Example 26.15** Sanchez sells a two-acre lot and office building by warranty deed to Fast Tech, LLC. Subsequently, Amy shows that she has better title than Sanchez had and evicts Fast Tech. Here, Fast Tech can sue Sanchez for breaching the covenant of quiet enjoyment. Fast Tech can recover the purchase price of the land, plus any other damages incurred as a result. ■

Special Warranty Deed A **special warranty deed,** or *limited warranty deed*, in contrast, warrants only that the grantor or seller held good title during his or her ownership of the property. In other words, the seller does not guarantee that there are no adverse claims by third parties against any previous owners of the property.

If the special warranty deed discloses all liens or other encumbrances, the seller will not be liable to the buyer if a third person subsequently interferes with the buyer's ownership. If the third person's claim arises out of, or is related to, some act of the seller, however, the seller will be liable to the buyer for damages.

Quitclaim Deed A **quitclaim deed** offers the least protection against defects in the title. Basically, a quitclaim deed conveys to the grantee whatever interest the grantor had. If the grantor had no interest, then the grantee receives no interest. (Naturally, if the grantor had a defective title or no title at all, a conveyance by warranty deed or special warranty deed would not cure the defect. Such a deed, however, would give the buyer a cause of action to sue the seller.)

Quitclaim deeds are often used when the seller, or grantor, is uncertain as to the extent of his or her rights in the property. They may also be used to release a party's interest in a particular parcel of property. This may be necessary, for instance, in divorce settlements or business dissolutions when the grantors are dividing up their interests in real property.

Grant Deed With a **grant deed,** the grantor simply states, "I grant the property to you" or "I convey, or bargain and sell, the property to you." By state statute, grant deeds carry with them an implied warranty that the grantor owns the property and has not previously transferred it to someone else or encumbered it, except as set out in the deed.

26–3c Recording Statutes

Once the seller delivers the deed to the buyer (at closing), legal title to the property is conveyed. Nevertheless, the buyer should promptly record the deed with the state records office. Every state has a **recording statute,** which allows deeds to be recorded in the public record for a fee. Deeds generally are recorded in the county in which the property is located. Many state statutes require that the grantor sign the deed in the presence of two witnesses before it can be recorded.

Recording a deed gives notice to the public that a certain person is now the owner of a particular parcel of real estate. By putting everyone on notice as to the true owner, recording a deed prevents the previous owners from fraudulently conveying the land to other purchasers.

26–3d Adverse Possession

A person who wrongfully possesses the real property of another (by occupying or using the property) may eventually acquire title to it through adverse possession. **Adverse possession** is a means of obtaining title to land without delivery of a deed and without the consent of— or payment to—the true owner. Thus, adverse possession is a method of *involuntarily* transferring title to the property from the true owner to the adverse possessor.

Essentially, when one person possesses the real property of another for a certain statutory period of time, that person acquires title to the land. The statutory period varies from three to thirty years, depending on the state, with ten years being most common.

Requirements for Adverse Possession For property to be held adversely, four elements must be satisfied:

1. *Possession must be actual and exclusive.* The possessor must physically occupy the property. This requirement is clearly met if the possessor lives on the property, but it may also be met if the possessor builds fences, erects structures, plants crops, or even grazes animals on the land.

2. *Possession must be open, visible, and notorious, not secret or clandestine.* The possessor must occupy the land for all the world to see. This requirement ensures that the true owner is on notice that someone is possessing the owner's property wrongfully.

3. *Possession must be continuous and peaceable for the required period of time.* This requirement means that the possessor must not be interrupted in the occupancy by the true owner or by the courts. Continuous does not mean constant. It simply means that the possessor has continuously occupied the property in some fashion for the statutory time. Peaceable means that no force was used to possess the land.

4. *Possession must be hostile and adverse.* In other words, the possessor cannot be living on the property with the owner's permission and must claim the property as against the whole world.

■ **Case in Point 26.16** Leslie and Ethel Cline owned a 141-acre property to the south of State Route 316 in Ohio. Rogers Farm Enterprises, LLC, owned 399 acres to the north of State Route 316. When the Clines originally bought their farm, they believed that State Route 316 was the dividing line between their property and Rogers Farm. Later, a survey showed that a 3.95-acre strip of land on the Clines' side of the road, which the Clines had been farming, actually belonged to Rogers Farm.

After twenty-one years, the Clines filed a suit claiming that they had acquired title to the property through adverse possession. The court granted title to the Clines. Rogers Farm appealed. An Ohio state appellate court affirmed. The Clines had been openly and continuously farming on the disputed strip of land for the requisite period of time under Ohio's statute (twenty-one years) and legally owned it.[8] ■

The following case raised the question of whether a landowner next to a rail line could acquire a portion of the right-of-way by adverse possession.

8. *Cline v. Rogers Farm Enterprises, LLC,* 2017 -Ohio- 1379, 87 N.E.3d 637 (Ohio Ct.App. 2017).

Case Analysis 26.3

Montgomery County v. Bhatt
Court of Appeals of Maryland, 446 Md. 79, 130 A.3d. 424 (2016).

In the Language of the Court
Glenn T. HARRELL, Jr., J. [Judge]

Driving that train, high on cocaine, Casey Jones you better watch your speed. Trouble ahead, trouble behind,

And you know that notion just crossed my mind.

—The Grateful Dead, *Casey Jones,* on Workingman's Dead (Warner Bros. Records 1970).

Although the record of the present case does not reflect a comparable level of drama as captured by the refrain of "Casey Jones," it hints at plenty of potential trouble, both ahead and

Case 26.3 Continues

behind, for a pair of public works projects (one in place and the other incipient [in development]) cherished by the government and some citizens of Montgomery County.

The Capital Crescent Trail is a well-known hiker/biker route that runs between Georgetown in the District of Columbia and Silver Spring, Maryland. Its path was used formerly as the Georgetown Branch of the Baltimore & Ohio (B&O) Railroad. After the trains stopped running in 1985, the property was transferred in 1988 to the government of Montgomery County, Maryland, via a quitclaim deed for a consideration of $10 million. It is planned that the Maryland portion of the former rail line (and current interim hiker/biker trail) will become the proposed Purple Line, a commuter light rail project.

BACKGROUND

* * * Ajay Bhatt owns 3313 Coquelin Terrace (a subdivided, single-family residential lot—"Lot 8"—improved by a dwelling) in Chevy Chase, Montgomery County, Maryland. He purchased this property in 2006 from his aunt, who owned the property since at least the 1970s. The lot abuts the Georgetown Branch of the B&O Railroad/Capital Crescent Trail. In 1890, the right-of-way that was the rail line (and is today the hiker/biker trail) was conveyed in a fee-simple deed from George Dunlop, grantor, to the Metropolitan Southern Railroad Company ("the Railroad"), grantee.

The right-of-way was obtained by the County * * * from the Railroad pursuant to the federal Rails-to-Trails Act. [Federal regulations] allow the County to preserve the land as a hiker/biker trail until the County chooses whether and when to restore a form of rail service within the right-of-way.

On 18 October 2013, Montgomery County issued to Bhatt a civil citation asserting a violation of Section 49-10(b) of the Montgomery County Code, which prohibits a property owner from erecting or placing "any structure, fence,

post, rock, or other object in a public right-of-way." The * * * claimed violation was the placement and maintenance by Bhatt's predecessors-in-interest of Lot 8 of a fence and shed within the former rail line (and current hiker/biker trail) right-of-way, without a permit. * * * The District Court of Maryland, sitting in Montgomery County, * * * found Bhatt guilty * * * and ordered him to remove the fence and shed encroaching upon the County's right-of-way.

The appeal was heard *de novo* by the [Maryland] Circuit Court. [When a court hears a case *de novo*, it decides the issues without reference to the legal conclusions or assumptions made by the previous court.]

* * * *

Bhatt's defense to the charged violation of Section 49–10(b) was that he owned the encroached-upon land by adverse possession.

Bhatt argued that, because the fence had been located beyond the property line of Lot 8 since at least 1963, the Railroad was obliged to take action to remove it prior to the maturation of the twenty-year period for adverse possession.

* * * The Circuit Court vacated the District Court's judgment and dismissed the violation citation. * * * The Circuit Court concluded ultimately that Bhatt had a creditable claim for adverse possession.

The County petitioned this Court for a writ of *certiorari*. * * * We granted the Petition.

* * * *

DISCUSSION

I. Contentions

* * * The County contends * * * that, because this Court has considered previously a railroad line to be analogous to a public highway for most purposes, the land in question is not subject to an adverse possession claim.

* * * Bhatt rejects the public highway-railroad line analogy because the land was in private, not public, use during its operation as a rail line.

II. Analysis

a. Railroads as Public Highways

A railroad is in many essential respects a public highway, and the rules of law applicable to one are generally applicable to the other. Railroads are owned frequently by private corporations, but this has never been considered a matter of any importance * * * because the function performed is that of the State. Railroad companies operate as a public use and are not viewed strictly as private corporations since they are publicly regulated common carriers. *Essentially, a railroad is a highway dedicated to the public use.* [Emphasis added.]

* * * *

b. May a public highway (or any portion of its right-of-way, no matter the type of real property interest by which it is held) be possessed adversely by an abutting private citizen?

* * * *Nothing is more solidly established than the rule that title to property held by a municipal corporation in its governmental capacity, for a public use, cannot be acquired by adverse possession.* [Emphasis added.]

* * * *

* * * Because time does not run against the state, or the public, * * * public highways are not subject to a claim for adverse possession, except in the limited circumstances of a clear abandonment by the State. By parity [equivalence] of reasoning applied to the present case, railway lines [are] also not * * * subject to a claim for adverse possession, without evidence of clear abandonment or a clear shift away from public use.

c. Use of the right-of-way

* * * We do not find in this record, however, that there is any evidence of abandonment by the rail line operator (or Montgomery County) or that the right-of-way was taken out of public use such that a claim for adverse possession could ripen within this right-of-way.

* * * *

The 1890 Dunlop Deed shows that the purchase made by the Railroad was from a private landowner. There was no evidence adduced [offered] by Bhatt supporting a conclusion that the right-of-way was abandoned and was not being used by the public, even during the period from 1985 when the freight service ended and 1988 when the property was conveyed to the County and became a hiker/biker trail as an interim public use.

＊＊＊＊

Because no evidence was presented by Bhatt to show that the current use of the right-of-way by Montgomery County is unreasonable or that the Railroad or the County abandoned the right-of-way, no claim for adverse possession will lie. Accordingly, we shall reverse the judgment of the Circuit Court. Bhatt's fence and shed encroached upon the right-of-way in violation of Montgomery

County Code Section 49–10(b). The District Court got it right.

JUDGMENT OF THE CIRCUIT COURT FOR MONTGOMERY COUNTY REVERSED. CASE REMANDED TO THAT COURT WITH INSTRUCTIONS TO AFFIRM THE JUDGMENT OF THE DISTRICT COURT OF MARYLAND, SITTING IN MONTGOMERY COUNTY.

Legal Reasoning Questions

1. Bhatt claimed to have met all of the requirements to acquire a strip of public land through adverse possession. Which element did the court find had *not* been met? Why?

2. What is the "potential trouble, both ahead and behind, for a pair of public works projects" hinted at in this case? In whose favor is that "trouble" likely to be resolved?

3. Should a private party, by encroaching on a public right-of-way, be able to acquire title adverse to the public rights? Discuss.

Purpose of the Doctrine There are a number of public-policy reasons for the adverse possession doctrine. These include society's interest in resolving boundary disputes, determining title when title is in question, and assuring that real property remains in the stream of commerce. More fundamentally, the doctrine punishes owners who do not take action when they see adverse possession and rewards possessors for putting land to productive use.

26–4 Limitations on the Rights of Property Owners

No ownership rights in real property can ever really be absolute—that is, an owner of real property cannot always do whatever she or he wishes on or with the property. Nuisance and environmental laws, for instance, restrict certain types of activities. Property ownership is also conditional on the payment of property taxes. Zoning laws and building permits frequently restrict the use of realty. In addition, if a property owner fails to pay debts, the property may be seized to satisfy judgment creditors. In short, the rights of every property owner are subject to certain conditions and limitations.

26–4a Eminent Domain

Even ownership in fee simple absolute is limited by a superior ownership. Just as the king was the ultimate landowner in medieval England, today the government has an ultimate ownership right in all land in the United States. This right, known as **eminent domain,** is sometimes referred to as the *condemnation power* of government or as a **taking.** It gives the government the right to acquire possession of real property in the manner directed by the *takings clause* of the U.S. Constitution and the laws of the state whenever the public interest requires it.

The power of eminent domain generally is invoked through **condemnation** proceedings. ■ **Example 26.17** When a new public highway is to be built, the government decides where to build it and how much land to condemn. After the government determines that a particular parcel of land is necessary for the highway, it will first offer to buy the property. If the owner refuses the offer, the government brings a judicial (condemnation) proceeding to obtain title to the land. ■

Condemnation proceedings usually involve two distinct phases. The first seeks to establish the government's right to take the property, and the second determines the fair value of the property.

Right to Take the Property In the first phase of condemnation proceedings, the government must prove that it needs to acquire privately owned property for a public use. ■ **Example 26.18** Franklin County, Iowa, engages Bosque Systems to build a liquefied natural gas pipeline that crosses the property of more than two hundred landowners. Some property owners consent to this use and accept the Bosque's offer of compensation. Others refuse the offer. A court will likely deem the pipeline to be a public use. Therefore, the government can exert its eminent domain power to "take" the land, provided that it pays just compensation to the property owners. ■

Just Compensation The U.S. Constitution and state constitutions require that the government pay just compensation to the landowner when invoking its condemnation power. Just compensation means fair value. In the second phase of the condemnation proceeding, the court determines the fair value of the land, which usually is approximately equal to its market value.

Property may be taken by the government only for public use, not for private benefit. But can eminent domain be used to promote private development when the development is deemed to be in the public interest? See this chapter's *Ethics Today* feature for a discussion of this issue.

26–4b Inverse Condemnation

Typically, a government agency exercises the power of eminent domain in the manner just discussed. **Inverse condemnation,** in contrast, occurs when a government simply takes private property from a landowner without paying any compensation, thereby forcing the landowner to sue the government for compensation.

The taking can be physical, as when a government agency uses or occupies the land, or it may be constructive, as when an agency regulation results in loss of property value. The United States Supreme Court has held that even temporary flooding of land by the government may result in liability under the takings clause.[9]

■ **Case in Point 26.19** In Walton County, Florida, water flows through a ditch from Oyster Lake to the Gulf of Mexico. When Hurricane Opal caused the water to rise in Oyster Lake, Walton County reconfigured the drainage to divert the overflow onto the nearby property of William and Patricia Hemby. The flow was eventually restored to pre-hurricane conditions, but during a later emergency, water was diverted onto the Hembys' property again. This diversion was not restored.

The Hembys filed a suit against the county. After their deaths, their daughter Cozette Drake pursued the claim. The court found that by allowing the water diversion to remain on Drake's property long after the emergency had passed, the county had engaged in a permanent or continuous physical invasion. This invasion rendered Drake's property useless and deprived her of

---

9. *Arkansas Game and Fish Commission v. United States*, 568 U.S. 23, 133 S.Ct. 511, 184 L.Ed.2d 417 (2012).

Ethics Today

Should Eminent Domain Be Used to Promote Private Development?

Issues of fairness often arise when the government takes private property for public use. One issue is whether it is fair for a government to take property by eminent domain and then convey it to private developers.

For instance, suppose a city government decides that it is in the public interest to have a larger parking lot for a local, privately owned sports stadium. Or suppose it decides that its citizens would benefit from having a manufacturing plant locate in the city to create more jobs. The government may condemn certain tracts of existing housing or business property and then convey the land to the privately owned stadium or manufacturing plant.

Such actions may bring in private developers and businesses that provide jobs and increase tax revenues, thus revitalizing communities. But is the land really being taken for "public use," as required by the Fifth Amendment to the U.S. Constitution?

The Supreme Court's Ruling

In 2005, the United States Supreme Court ruled that the power of eminent domain may be used to further

economic development.[a] At the same time, the Court recognized that individual states have the right to pass laws that prohibit takings for economic development.

The States' Responses

Since the Court's ruling, the vast majority of the states have passed laws to curb the government's ability to take private property and subsequently give it to private developers. Nevertheless, loopholes in some state legislation still allow takings for redevelopment of slum areas. Thus, the debate over whether (and when) it is fair for the government to take citizens' property for economic development continues.

Critical Thinking *At what point might the predicted benefits of a new private commercial endeavor outweigh the constitutional requirement of a taking only for public use?*

---

a. *Kelo v. City of New London, Connecticut*, 545 U.S. 469, 125 S.Ct. 2655, 162 L.Ed.2d 439 (2005).

its beneficial enjoyment. Drake was therefore entitled to receive compensation from the county.[10] ■

26–4c Restrictive Covenants

A private restriction on the use of land is known as a **restrictive covenant.** If the restriction is binding on the party who initially purchases the property and on subsequent purchasers as well, it is said to "run with the land." A covenant running with the land must be in writing (usually it is in the deed), and subsequent purchasers must have reason to know about it.

■ **Example 26.20** In the course of developing a fifty-lot suburban subdivision, Levitt records a declaration of restrictions effectively limiting construction on each lot to one single-family house. Each lot's deed includes a reference to the declaration with a provision that the purchaser and her or his successors are bound to those restrictions. Thus, each purchaser assumes ownership with notice of the restrictions. If an owner attempts to build a duplex (or any noncompliant structure) on a lot, the other owners may obtain a court order to prevent the construction.

Alternatively, Levitt might simply have included the restrictions on the subdivision's map, filed the map in the appropriate public office, and included a reference to the map in each deed. Under these circumstances, each owner would still have been held to have constructive notice of the restrictions. ■

26–5 Land-Use Control and Zoning

The rules and regulations that collectively manage the development and use of land are known as **zoning laws.** Zoning laws were first used in the United States to segregate slaughterhouses, distilleries, kilns, and other businesses that might pose a nuisance to nearby residences. The growth of modern urban areas led to an increased need to organize uses of land. Today, zoning laws enable municipalities to control the speed and type of development within their borders by creating different zones and regulating the use of property allowed in each zone.

The United States Supreme Court has held that zoning is a constitutional exercise of a government's police powers.[11] Therefore, as long as zoning ordinances are rationally related to the health, safety, or welfare of the community, a municipal government has broad discretion to carry out zoning as it sees fit.

26–5a Purpose and Scope of Zoning Laws

The purpose of zoning laws is to manage the land within a community in a way that encourages sustainable and organized development while controlling growth in a manner that serves the interests of the community. One of the basic elements of zoning is the classification of land by permissible use, but zoning extends to other aspects of land use as well.

Permissible Uses of Land Municipalities generally divide their available land into districts according to the land's present and potential future uses. Typically, land is classified into the following types of permissible uses:

1. *Residential.* In areas that a municipality has designated for **residential use,** landowners can construct buildings for human habitation.
2. *Commercial.* Land assigned for business activities is designated as being for **commercial use,** sometimes called business use. An area with a number of retail stores, offices, supermarkets, and hotels might be designated as a commercial or business district. Land used for entertainment purposes, such as movie theaters and sports stadiums, also falls into this category, as does land used for government activities.
3. *Industrial.* Areas that are designated for **industrial use** typically encompass light and heavy manufacturing, shipping, and heavy transportation. For instance, undeveloped land with easy access to highways and railroads might be classified as suitable for future use by industry. Although industrial uses can be profitable for a city seeking to raise tax revenue, such uses can also result in noise, smoke, or vibrations that interfere with others' enjoyment of their property. Consequently, areas zoned for industrial use generally are kept as far as possible from residential districts and some commercial districts.
4. *Conservation districts.* Sometimes, state governments require municipalities to establish certain areas that are dedicated to carrying out local soil and water conservation efforts. For instance, wetlands might be designated as a conservation district.

A city's residential, commercial, and industrial districts may be divided, in turn, into subdistricts. For instance, zoning ordinances may regulate the type, density, size, and approved uses of structures within a given district. Thus, a residential district may be divided into low-density (single-family homes with large lots), high-density (single- and multiple-family homes with small lots), and planned-unit (condominiums or apartments) subdistricts.

---

10. *Drake v. Walton County*, 34 Fla.L.Weekly D745, 6 So.3d 717 (1 Dist. 2009).
11. *Village of Euclid, Ohio v. Ambler Realty Co.*, 272 U.S. 365, 47 S.Ct. 114, 71 L.Ed. 303 (1926).

Other Zoning Restrictions Zoning rules extend to much more than the permissible use of land. In residential districts, for instance, an ordinance may require a house or garage to be set back a specific number of feet from a neighbor's property line.

In commercial districts, zoning rules may attempt to maintain a certain visual aesthetic. Therefore, businesses may be required to construct buildings of a certain height and width so that they conform to the style of other commercial buildings in the area.

Businesses may also be required to provide parking for patrons or take other measures to manage traffic. Sometimes, municipalities limit construction of new businesses to prevent traffic congestion.

Zoning laws may even attempt to regulate the public morals of the community. For instance, cities commonly impose severe restrictions on the location and operation of adult businesses and medical (or recreational) marijuana dispensaries.

26–5b Exceptions to Zoning Laws

Zoning restrictions are not absolute. It is impossible for zoning laws to account for every contingency. The purpose of zoning is to control development, not to prevent it altogether or to limit the government's ability to adapt to changing circumstances or unforeseen needs. Hence, legal processes have been developed to allow for exceptions to zoning laws, such as *variances* and *special-use permits*.

Variances A property owner who wants to use his or her land in a manner not permitted by zoning rules can request a **variance,** which allows an exception to the rules. The property owner making the request must demonstrate that the requested variance:

1. Is necessary for reasonable development.
2. Is the least intrusive solution to the problem.
3. Will not alter the essential character of the neighborhood.

Hardship Situations. Property owners normally request variances in *hardship situations*—that is, when complying with the zoning rules would be too difficult or costly due to existing property conditions. ■ **Example 26.21** Lin, a homeowner, wants to replace her single-car garage with a two-car garage. If she does so, however, the garage will be closer to her neighbor's property than is permitted by the zoning rules. In this situation, she may ask for a variance. She can claim that the configuration of her property would make it difficult and costly to comply with the zoning code, so compliance would create a hardship for her. ■

Similarly, a church might request a variance from height restrictions in order to erect a new steeple. Or a furniture store might ask for a variance from *footprint* limitations so that it can expand its showroom. (A building's footprint is the area of ground that it covers.)

Note that the hardship may not be self-created. In other words, a person who buys property with zoning restrictions in effect usually cannot then argue that he or she needs a variance in order to use the property as intended.

Public Hearing. In almost all instances, before a variance is granted, there must be a public hearing with adequate notice to neighbors who may object to the exception. After the public hearing, a hearing examiner appointed by the municipality (or the local zoning board or commission) determines whether to grant the exception. When a variance is granted, it applies only to the specific parcel of land for which it was requested and does not create a regulation-free zone.

Special-Use Permits Sometimes, zoning laws permit a certain use only if the property owner complies with specific requirements to ensure that the proposed use does not harm the immediate neighborhood. In such instances, the zoning board can issue **special-use permits,** also called *conditional-use permits*.

■ **Example 26.22** An area is designated as a residential district, but small businesses are permitted to operate there so long as they do not affect the characteristics of the neighborhood. A bank asks the zoning board for a special-use permit to open a branch in the area. At the public hearing, the bank demonstrates that the branch will be housed in a building that conforms to the style of other structures in the area. The bank also shows that adequate parking will be available and that landscaping will shield the parking lot from public view. Unless there are strong objections from the branch's prospective neighbors, the board will likely grant the permit. ■

Special Incentives In addition to granting exceptions to zoning regulations, municipalities may also wish to encourage certain kinds of development. To do so, they offer incentives, often in the form of lower tax rates or tax credits. For instance, to attract new businesses that will provide jobs and increase the tax base, a city may offer lower property tax rates for a period of years. Similarly, homeowners may receive tax credits for historic preservation if they renovate and maintain older homes.

Practice and Review: Real Property and Land-Use Control

Vern Shoepke purchased a two-story home from Walter and Eliza Bruster in the town of Roche, Maine. The warranty deed did not specify what covenants would be included in the conveyance. The property was adjacent to a public park that included a popular Frisbee golf course. (Frisbee golf is a sport similar to golf but using Frisbees.) Wayakichi Creek ran along the north end of the park and along Shoepke's property. The deed allowed Roche citizens the right to walk across a five-foot-wide section of the lot beside Wayakichi Creek as part of a two-mile public trail system. Teenagers regularly threw Frisbee golf discs from the walking path behind Shoepke's property over his yard to the adjacent park. Shoepke habitually shouted and cursed at the teenagers, demanding that they not throw objects over his yard. Two months after moving into his Roche home, Shoepke leased the second floor to Lauren Slater for nine months. After three months of tenancy, Slater sublet the second floor to a local artist, Javier Indalecio. (The lease agreement did not specify that Shoepke's consent would be required to sublease the second floor.) Over the remaining six months, Indalecio's use of oil paints damaged the carpeting in Shoepke's home. Using the information presented in the chapter, answer the following questions.

1. What is the term for the right of Roche citizens to walk across Shoepke's land on the trail?
2. What covenants would most courts infer were included in the warranty deed that was used in the property transfer from the Brusters to Shoepke?
3. Suppose that Shoepke wants to file a trespass lawsuit against some teenagers who continually throw Frisbees over his land. Shoepke discovers, however, that when the city put in the Frisbee golf course, the neighborhood homeowners signed an agreement that limited their right to complain about errant Frisbees. What is this type of promise or agreement called in real property law?
4. Can Shoepke hold Slater financially responsible for the damage to the carpeting caused by Indalecio? Why or why not?

Debate This . . .   *Under no circumstances should a local government be able to condemn property in order to sell it later to real estate developers for private use.*

Terms and Concepts

adverse possession 561
closing 558
commercial use 565
community property 554
concurrent ownership 554
condemnation 563
conveyance 552
deed 560
easement 555
eminent domain 563
escrow account 558
fee simple absolute 552
fixed-term tenancy 555
fixture 551
grant deed 560
implication 556

implied warranty of
  habitability 558
industrial use 565
inverse condemnation 564
joint tenancy 554
leasehold estate 555
license 556
life estate 552
marketable title 558
metes and bounds 560
necessity 556
nonpossessory interests 555
periodic tenancy 555
prescription 556
profit 555
quitclaim deed 560

recording statute 561
residential use 565
restrictive covenant 565
special-use permits 566
special warranty deed 560
taking 563
tenancy at sufferance 555
tenancy at will 555
tenancy by the entirety 554
tenancy in common 554
title insurance 558
trade fixture 552
variance 566
warranty deed 560
waste 552
zoning laws 565

Issue Spotters

1. Bernie sells his house to Consuela under a warranty deed. Later, Delmira appears, holding a better title to the house than Consuela has. Delmira wants to have Consuela evicted from the property. What can Consuela do? (See *Transfer of Ownership*.)

2. Grey owns a commercial building in fee simple. Grey transfers temporary possession of the building to Haven Corporation. Can Haven transfer possession for even less time to Idyll Company? Explain. (See *Ownership and Other Interests in Real Property*.)

- **Check your answers to the Issue Spotters against the answers provided in Appendix B at the end of this text.**

Business Scenarios and Case Problems

26–1. Property Ownership. Madison owned a tract of land, but he was not sure that he had full title to the property. When Rafael expressed an interest in buying the land, Madison sold it to Rafael and executed a quitclaim deed. Rafael properly recorded the deed immediately. Several months later, Madison learned that he had had full title to the tract of land. He then sold the land to Linda by warranty deed. Linda knew of the earlier purchase by Rafael but took the deed anyway and later sued to have Rafael evicted from the land. Linda claimed that because she had a warranty deed, her title to the land was better than that conferred by Rafael's quitclaim deed. Will Linda succeed in claiming title to the land? Explain. (See *Transfer of Ownership*.)

26–2. Zoning. The county intends to rezone an area from industrial use to residential use. Land within the affected area is largely undeveloped, but nonetheless it is expected that the proposed action will reduce the market value of the affected land by as much as 50 percent. Will the landowners be successful in suing to have the action declared a taking of their property, entitling them to just compensation? Why or why not? (See *Land-Use Control and Zoning*.)

26–3. Zoning and Variances. Joseph and Lois Ryan hired a contractor to build a home in Weston, Connecticut. The contractor submitted plans to the town that included a roof height of thirty-eight feet for the proposed dwelling. This exceeded the town's roof-height restriction of thirty-five feet. The contractor and the architect revised the plans to meet the restriction, and the town approved the plans and issued a zoning permit and a building permit. After the roof was constructed, a code enforcement officer discovered that it measured thirty-seven feet, seven inches high.

The officer issued a cease-and-desist order requiring the Ryans to "remove the height violation and bring the structure into compliance." The Ryans appealed to the zoning board, claiming that the error was not theirs but that of their general contractor and architect. The zoning board upheld the cease-and-desist order but later granted the Ryans a variance because "the roof height was out of compliance by approximately two feet, . . . the home [was] perched high on the land and [was] not a detriment to the neighborhood, and . . . the hardship was created by the contractor's error."

Neighbors (including Curtis Morikawa) appealed to a court. They argued that the hardship claimed was solely economic. In addition, they argued that even though it was unintended, the hardship was self-created. The trial court ruled in favor of the neighbors, and the Ryans appealed. How should the reviewing court rule? Were there legitimate grounds for granting a variance? Discuss. [*Morikawa v. Zoning Board of Appeals of Town of Weston*, 126 Conn.App. 400, 11 A.3d 735 (2011)] (See *Land-Use Control and Zoning*.)

26–4. Adverse Possession. The McKeag family operated a marina on their lakefront property in Bolton, New York. For more than forty years, the McKeags used a section of property belonging to their neighbors, the Finleys, as a beach for the marina's customers. The McKeags also stored a large float on the beach during the winter months, built their own retaining wall, and planted bushes and flowers there. The McKeags prevented others from using the property, including the Finleys. Nevertheless, the families always had a friendly relationship, and at one point a member of the Finley family gave the McKeags permission to continue using the beach. He also reminded them of his ownership several times, to which they said nothing. The McKeags also asked for permission to mow grass on the property and once apologized for leaving a jet ski there. Can the McKeags establish adverse possession over the statutory period of ten years? Why or why not? [*McKeag v. Finley*, 93 A.D.3d 925, 939 N.Y.S.2d 644 (3 Dept. 2012)] (See *Transfer of Ownership*.)

26–5. Real Estate Sales Contracts. A California state statute requires sellers to provide a real estate "Transfer Disclosure Statement" (TDS) to buyers of residential property consisting of one to four dwelling units. Required disclosures include information about significant defects, including hazardous materials, encroachments, easements, fill, settling, flooding, drainage problems, neighborhood noise, damage from natural disasters, and lawsuits. Mark Hartley contracted with Randall Richman to buy Richman's property in Ventura, California. The property included a commercial building and a residential duplex with two dwelling units. Richman did not provide a TDS, claiming that it was not required because the property was "mixed use"—that is, it included both a commercial building and a residential building. Hartley refused to go through with the deal. Did Hartley breach their contract, or did Richman's failure to provide a TDS excuse Hartley's non-performance? Discuss. [*Richman v. Hartley*, 224 Cal.App.4th 1182, 169 Cal. Rptr.3d 475 (2 Dist. 2014)] (See *Transfer of Ownership*.)

26–6. Business Case Problem with Sample Answer—Joint Tenancies.
Arthur and Diana Ebanks owned three properties in the Cayman Islands in joint tenancy. With respect to joint tenancies, Cayman law is the same as U.S. law. When the Ebankses divorced, the decree did not change the tenancy in which the properties were held. On the same day as the divorce filing, Arthur executed a will providing that "any property in my name and that of another as joint tenants . . . will pass to the survivor, and I instruct my Personal Representative to make no claim thereto." Four years later, Arthur died. His brother Curtis, the personal representative of his estate, asserted that Arthur's interest in the Cayman properties was part of the estate. Diana said that the sole interest in the properties was hers. To whom do the Cayman properties belong? Why? [*Ebanks v. Ebanks*, 41 Fla.L.Weekly D291, 198 So.3d 712 (2 Dist. 2016)] (See *Ownership and Other Interests in Real Property*.)

- For a sample answer to Problem 26–6, go to Appendix C at the end of this text.

26–7. Eminent Domain.
In the city of Tarrytown, New York, Citibank operated a branch that included a building and a parking lot with thirty-six spaces. Tarrytown leased twenty-one of the spaces from Citibank for use as public parking. When Citibank closed the branch and decided to sell the building, the public was denied access to the parking lot. After a public hearing, the city concluded that it should exercise its power of eminent domain to acquire the twenty-one spaces to provide public parking. Is this an appropriate use of the power of eminent domain? Suppose that Citibank opposes the plan and alternative sites are available. Should Tarrytown be required to acquire those sites instead of Citibank's property? In any event, what is Tarrytown's next step? Explain. [*Matter of Citibank, N.A. v. Village of Tarrytown*, 149 A.D.3d 931, 52 N.Y.S.3d 398 (2 Dept. 2017)] (See *Transfer of Ownership*.)

26–8. Transfer of Ownership.
Craig and Sue Shaffer divided their real property into two lots. They enclosed one lot with a fence and sold it to the Murdocks. The other lot was sold to the Cromwells. All of the parties orally agreed that the fence marked the property line. Over the next three decades, each lot was sold three more times. Houses were built, and the lots were landscaped, including lilac bushes planted against the fence. Later, one of the owners removed the fence, and another built a shed next to where it had been. On the lot with the shed, the Talbots erected a carport abutting the lilac bushes, which all previous owners believed was planted on the property line. Then, the Nielsons bought the adjacent lot and measured it according to the legal description in the deed. The Nielsons discovered that the Talbots' carport encroached on their property by about thirteen feet. Are the Nielsons entitled to damages for their "lost" property from any party? Explain. [*Nielson v. Talbot*, 163 Idaho 480, 415 P.3d 348 (2018)] (See *Transfer of Ownership*.)

26–9. A Question of Ethics—The IDDR Approach and Easements.
Two organizations, Class A Investors Post Oak, LP, and Cosmopolitan Condominium VP, LP, owned adjacent pieces of property in Houston, Texas. Each owner-organization planned to build a high-rise tower on its lot. The organizations signed an agreement that granted each of them an easement in the other's property to "facilitate the development." Cosmopolitan built its residential high-rise first. Later, Class A began moving forward with its plan for a mixed-use high-rise. Cosmopolitan objected that the proposed tower would "be vastly oversized for its proposed location; situated perilously close to [Cosmopolitan's] building; create extraordinary traffic hazards; impede fire protection and other emergency vehicles in the area; and substantially interfere with the use and enjoyment of [Cosmopolitan's] property." [Cosmopolitan Condominium Owners Association v. Class A Investors Post Oak, LP, 2017 WL 1520448 (Tex.App.—Houston 2017)] (See Ownership and Other Interests in Real Property.)

(a) On what basis can Class A proceed with its plan? Explain, using the IDDR approach.

(b) On what ethical ground might Cosmopolitan continue to oppose its neighbor's project? Discuss.

Time-Limited Group Assignment

26–10. Adverse Possession.
The Wallen family owned a cabin on Lummi Island in the state of Washington. A driveway ran from the cabin across their property to South Nugent Road. Floyd Massey bought the adjacent lot and built a cabin on it in 1980. To gain access to his property, Massey used a bulldozer to extend the driveway, without the Wallens' permission but also without their objection. Twenty-five years later, the Wallens sold their property to Wright Fish Company. Massey continued to use and maintain the driveway without permission or objection. Later, Massey sold his property to Robert Drake. Drake and his employees continued to use and maintain the driveway without permission or objection, although Drake knew it was located largely on Wright's property. Still later, Wright sold its lot to Robert Smersh. The next year, Smersh told Drake to stop using the driveway. Drake filed a suit against Smersh, claiming adverse possession. (See *Transfer of Ownership*.)

(a) The first group will decide whether Drake's use of the driveway meets all of the requirements for adverse possession.

(b) The second group will determine how the court should rule in this case and why. Does it matter that Drake knew the driveway was located largely on Wright's (and then Smersh's) property? Should it matter? Why or why not?

(c) The third group will evaluate the underlying policy and fairness of adverse possession laws. Should the law reward persons who take possession of someone else's land for their own use? Does it make sense to punish owners who allow someone else to use their land without complaint? Explain.

(d) The fourth group will consider how the laws governing adverse possession vary from state to state. To acquire title through adverse possession, a person might be required to possess the property for five years in one state, for instance, and for twenty years in another. Are there any legitimate reasons for such regional differences? Would it be better if all states had the same requirements? Explain your answers.

Chapter 27

Antitrust Law

After the Civil War (1861–1865), the American public became increasingly concerned about declining competition in the marketplace. Large corporate enterprises at that time were attempting to reduce or eliminate competition by legally tying themselves together in *business trusts*.

The most famous trust was the Standard Oil trust of the late 1800s. Participants in the trust transferred their stock to a trustee. The trustee then fixed prices, controlled production, and established exclusive geographic markets for all of the oil companies that were members of the trust. Some observers began to argue that the trust wielded so much economic power that corporations outside the trust could not compete effectively.

Eventually, legislators at both the state and the federal level began to enact laws to rein in the trusts. Hence, the laws regulating economic competition in the United States today are referred to as **antitrust laws.** At the national level, important antitrust legislation includes the Sherman Antitrust Act[1] passed in 1890, and the Clayton Act[2] and the Federal Trade Commission Act[3] passed in 1914. We examine these major federal antitrust statutes in this chapter.

The purpose of antitrust legislation was—and still is—to foster competition. Behind these laws lies our society's belief that competition leads to lower prices, better products, a wider selection of goods, and more product information.

---

1. 15 U.S.C. Sections 1–7.
2. 15 U.S.C. Sections 12–27.
3. 15 U.S.C. Sections 41–58.

27-1 The Sherman Antitrust Act

The author of the Sherman Antitrust Act, Senator John Sherman, was the brother of the famed Civil War general William Tecumseh Sherman. He was also a recognized financial authority. He had been concerned for years about what he saw as diminishing competition within U.S. industry and the emergence of monopolies. He told Congress that the Sherman Act "does not announce a new principle of law, but applies old and well-recognized principles of the common law."[4]

Indeed, today's antitrust laws are the direct descendants of common law actions intended to limit **restraints of trade** (agreements between or among firms that have the effect of reducing competition in the marketplace). Such actions date to the fifteenth century in England. The common law was not always consistent, however, and had not been effective in curbing the trusts. That is why Sherman proposed the Sherman Antitrust Act, often simply called the Sherman Act.

---

4. 21 *Congressional Record* 2456 (1890).

27-1a Major Provisions of the Sherman Act

Sections 1 and 2 contain the main provisions of the Sherman Act:

1. Every contract, combination in the form of trust or otherwise, or conspiracy, in restraint of trade or commerce among the several States, or with foreign nations, is hereby declared to be illegal [and is a felony punishable by fine and/or imprisonment].

2. Every person who shall monopolize, or attempt to monopolize, or combine or conspire with any other person or persons, to monopolize any part of the trade or commerce among the several States, or with foreign nations, shall be deemed guilty of a felony [and is similarly punishable].

27-1b Differences between Section 1 and Section 2

The two sections of the Sherman Act are quite different. Section 1 requires two or more persons, because a person cannot contract, combine, or conspire alone. Thus, the essence of the illegal activity is *the act of joining together.* Section 2, though, can apply either to one person or to two

571

or more persons because it refers to "every person." Thus, unilateral conduct can result in a violation of Section 2.

It follows that the cases brought to the courts under Section 1 of the Sherman Act differ from those brought under Section 2. Section 1 cases are often concerned with whether an agreement (written or oral) leads to a restraint of trade. Section 2 cases deal with the structure of a monopoly that exists in the marketplace.

The term **monopoly** generally is used to describe a market in which there is a single seller or a very limited number of sellers. Whereas Section 1 focuses on agreements that are restrictive—that is, agreements that have a wrongful purpose—Section 2 looks at the so-called misuse of **monopoly power** in the marketplace. Monopoly power exists when a firm has an extreme amount of **market power**—the power to affect the market price of its product.

Both Section 1 and Section 2 seek to curtail market practices that result in undesired monopoly pricing and output behavior. For a case to be brought under Section 2, however, the "threshold" or "necessary" amount of monopoly power must already exist. We illustrate the different requirements for violating these two sections of the Sherman Act in Exhibit 27–1.

27–1c Jurisdictional Requirements

The Sherman Act applies only to restraints that have a significant impact on interstate commerce. Courts have generally held that any activity that substantially affects interstate commerce falls within the scope of the Sherman Act. As will be discussed later in this chapter, the Sherman Act also extends to parties outside the U.S. who are engaged in activities that affect U.S. foreign commerce.

Federal courts have exclusive jurisdiction over antitrust cases brought under the Sherman Act. State laws regulate local restraints on competition, and state courts decide claims brought under those laws.

27–2 Section 1 of the Sherman Act

The underlying assumption of Section 1 of the Sherman Act is that society's welfare is harmed if rival firms are permitted to join in an agreement that consolidates their market power or otherwise restrains competition. The types of trade restraints that Section 1 of the Sherman Act prohibits generally fall into two broad categories: *horizontal restraints* and *vertical restraints*, both of which will be discussed shortly. First, we look at the rules that the courts may apply when assessing the anticompetitive impact of alleged restraints of trade.

27–2a *Per Se* Violations versus the Rule of Reason

Some restraints are so substantially anticompetitive that they are deemed ***per se* violations**—illegal *per se* (inherently)—under Section 1. Other agreements, even though they result in enhanced market power, do not *unreasonably* restrain trade and are therefore lawful. Using the **rule of reason,** the courts analyze anticompetitive agreements that allegedly violate Section 1 of the Sherman Act to determine whether they actually constitute reasonable restraints of trade.

Rationale for the Rule of Reason The need for a rule-of-reason analysis of some agreements in restraint of trade is obvious. If the rule of reason had not been developed, almost any business agreement could conceivably be held to violate the Sherman Act. United States Supreme Court Justice Louis Brandeis effectively phrased this sentiment in *Chicago Board of Trade v. United States*, a case decided in 1918:

> Every agreement concerning trade, every regulation of trade, restrains. To bind, to restrain, is of their very essence. The true test of legality is whether the restraint

Exhibit 27–1 Required Elements of a Sherman Act Violation

Section 1 Violation Requirements	Section 2 Violation Requirements
1. An agreement between two or more parties, 2. That unreasonably restrains competition, and 3. Affects interstate commerce.	1. The possession of monopoly power in the relevant market, and 2. The willful acquisition or maintenance of that power as distinguished from its growth or development as a consequence of a superior product, business acumen, or historic accident.

imposed is such as merely regulates and perhaps thereby promotes competition or whether it is such as may suppress or even destroy competition.[5]

Factors That Courts Consider When analyzing an alleged Section 1 violation under the rule of reason, a court will consider the following factors:

1. The purpose of the agreement.
2. The parties' ability to implement the agreement to achieve that purpose.
3. The effect or potential effect of the agreement on competition.
4. Whether the parties could have relied on less restrictive means to achieve their purpose.

■ **Case in Point 27.1** A group of consumers sued NBC Universal, Inc., the Walt Disney Company, and other broadcasters, as well as cable and satellite distributors. The consumers claimed that the bundling together of high-demand and low-demand television channels in cable and satellite programming packages violates the Sherman Act. Bundling forces consumers to pay for channels that they do not watch to have access to channels they watch regularly.

The consumers argued that the defendants—through their control of high-demand programming—exercised market power that made it impossible for any distributor to offer unbundled programs. A federal appellate court ruled in favor of the defendants and dismissed the case. The court reasoned that the Sherman Act applies to actions that diminish competition and that the bundling of channels does not injure competition.[6] ■

27–2b Horizontal Restraints

The term **horizontal restraint** is encountered frequently in antitrust law. A horizontal restraint is any agreement that in some way restrains competition between rival firms competing in the same market. Horizontal restraints may include price-fixing agreements, group boycotts, market divisions, trade associations, and joint ventures.

Price Fixing Any **price-fixing agreement**—an agreement among competitors to fix prices—constitutes a *per se* violation of Section 1. The agreement on price need not be explicit. As long as it restricts output or artificially fixes price, it violates the law.

The Reason Behind the Agreement Is Not a Defense. A price-fixing agreement is always a violation of Section 1, even if there are good reasons behind it. ■ **Case in Point 27.2** In a classic price-fixing case, independent oil producers in Texas and Louisiana were caught between falling demand due to the Great Depression of the 1930s and increasing supply from newly discovered oil fields. A group of the major refining companies agreed to buy "distress" gasoline (excess supplies) from the independents so as to dispose of it in an "orderly manner." Although there was no explicit agreement as to price, it was clear that the purpose of the agreement was to limit the supply of gasoline on the market and thereby raise prices.

There may have been good reasons for the agreement. Nonetheless, the United States Supreme Court recognized the potentially adverse effects that such an agreement could have on open and free competition. The Court held that the reasonableness of a price-fixing agreement is never a defense. Any agreement that restricts output or artificially fixes price is a *per se* violation of Section 1.[7] ■

Price-Fixing Cartels Today. Price-fixing cartels (groups) are still commonplace in today's business world, particularly among global companies. International price-fixing cartels have been alleged in numerous industries, including air freight, auto parts, computer monitors, digital commerce, and drug manufacturing.

■ **Case in Point 27.3** After Amazon.com released the Kindle e-book reader, it began selling e-book downloads at $9.99 (lower than the actual cost) and made up the difference by selling more Kindles. When the iPad entered the e-book scene, Apple and some book publishers agreed to use Apple's "agency" model, which Apple was already using for games and apps. The agency model allowed the book publishers to set their own prices while Apple kept 30 percent as a commission.

The U.S. government sued Apple and the publishers for price fixing. Because the publishers involved in the arrangement chose prices that were relatively similar, the government argued that price fixing was evident and "would not have occurred without the conspiracy among the defendants." Ultimately, a federal appellate court held that Apple's agreement with publishers to raise e-book prices was a *per se* illegal price-fixing conspiracy. As a result, Apple was ordered to pay $400 million to consumers and $50 million in attorneys' fees.[8] ■

---

5. 246 U.S. 231, 38 S.Ct. 242, 62 L.Ed. 683 (1918).
6. *Brantley v. NBC Universal, Inc.*, 675 F.3d 1192 (9th Cir. 2012).

7. *United States v. Socony-Vacuum Oil Co.*, 310 U.S. 150, 60 S.Ct. 811, 84 L.Ed. 1129 (1940).
8. *United States v. Apple, Inc.*, 791 F.3d 290 (2d Cir. 2015). Apple had previously agreed to settle the case for these amounts if its appeal was unsuccessful.

Group Boycotts A **group boycott** is an agreement by two or more sellers to refuse to deal with (that is, to boycott) a particular person or firm. Because they involve concerted action, group boycotts have been held to constitute *per se* violations of Section 1 of the Sherman Act.

To prove a violation of Section 1, the plaintiff must demonstrate that the boycott or joint refusal to deal was undertaken with the intention of eliminating competition or preventing entry into a given market. Although most boycotts are illegal, a few, such as group boycotts against a supplier for political reasons, may be protected under the First Amendment right to freedom of expression.

Horizontal Market Division It is a *per se* violation of Section 1 of the Sherman Act for competitors to divide up territories or customers. ■ **Example 27.4** AXM Electronics Basics, Halprin Servo Supplies, and Aicarus Prime Electronics compete against each other in the states of Kansas, Nebraska, and Oklahoma. The three firms agree that AXM will sell products only in Kansas, Halprin will sell only in Nebraska, and Aicarus will sell only in Oklahoma.

This concerted action violates Section 1 of the Sherman Act. It reduces marketing costs and allows all three firms (assuming there is no other competition) to raise the price of the goods sold in their respective states. The same violation would take place if the three firms divided up their customers by class rather than region. They might agree that AXM would sell only to institutional purchasers (such as governments and schools) in all three states, Halprin only to wholesalers, and Aicarus only to retailers. The result would be the same. ■

Trade Associations Businesses in the same general industry or profession frequently organize trade associations to pursue common interests. A trade association may engage in various joint activities, such as exchanging information, representing the members' business interests before governmental bodies, and conducting advertising campaigns. Trade associations also frequently are involved in setting regulatory standards to govern the industry or profession.

Generally, the rule of reason is applied to many of these horizontal actions. If a court finds that a trade association practice or agreement that restrains trade is sufficiently beneficial both to the association and to the public, it may deem the restraint reasonable.

In *concentrated industries*, however, trade associations can be, and have been, used as a means to facilitate anticompetitive actions, such as fixing prices or allocating markets. A **concentrated industry** is one in which either a single firm or a small number of firms control a large percentage of market sales. When trade association agreements have substantially anticompetitive effects, a court

will consider them to be in violation of Section 1 of the Sherman Act.

Joint Ventures When two or more individuals or business entities join together in a particular commercial enterprise, it is called a *joint venture*. Joint ventures undertaken by competitors are also subject to antitrust laws. If a joint venture does not involve price fixing or market divisions, the agreement will be analyzed under the rule of reason. Whether the joint undertaking violates Section 1 will then depend on the factors stated earlier in this chapter. A court will look at the venture's purpose, the potential benefits relative to the likely harms, and whether there are less restrictive alternatives for achieving the same goals.

27–2c Vertical Restraints

A **vertical restraint** of trade results from an agreement between firms at different levels in the manufacturing and distribution process. In contrast to horizontal relationships, which occur at the same level of operation, vertical relationships encompass the entire chain of production.

The chain of production normally includes the purchase of inventory, basic manufacturing, distribution to wholesalers, and eventual sale of a product at the retail level. For some products, these distinct phases are carried on by different firms. In other instances, a single firm carries out two or more of the separate functional phases. Such enterprises are said to be **vertically integrated firms**.

Even though firms operating at different functional levels are not in direct competition with one another, they are in competition with other firms. Thus, agreements between firms standing in a vertical relationship may affect competition. Some vertical restraints are *per se* violations of Section 1. Others are judged under the rule of reason.

Territorial or Customer Restrictions In arranging for the distribution of its products, a manufacturing firm often wishes to insulate dealers from direct competition with other dealers selling its products. To do so, the manufacturer may institute territorial restrictions or attempt to prohibit wholesalers or retailers from reselling the products to certain classes of buyers, such as competing retailers.

May Have Legitimate Purpose. A firm may have legitimate reasons for imposing territorial or customer restrictions. For instance, an electronics manufacturer may wish to prevent a dealer from reducing costs and undercutting rivals by offering its products without promotion or customer service. In this situation, the cost-cutting dealer reaps the benefits (sales of the product) paid for by other dealers who undertake promotion and arrange for customer service. By not providing customer service (and relying on a nearby dealer to provide these services), the cost-cutting dealer may also harm the manufacturer's reputation.

Judged under the Rule of Reason. Territorial and customer restrictions were once considered *per se* violations of Section 1.[9] In 1977, the United States Supreme Court held that they should be judged under the rule of reason. ■ **Case in Point 27.5** The Supreme Court case involved GTE Sylvania, Inc., a manufacturer of television sets. Sylvania limited the number of retail franchises that it granted in any given geographic area. It also required each franchisee to sell only Sylvania products from the location at which it was franchised. Sylvania retained sole discretion to increase the number of retailers in an area.

When Sylvania decided to open a new franchise, it terminated the franchise of Continental T.V., Inc., an existing franchisee in the area that would have been in competition with the new franchise. Continental filed a lawsuit claiming that Sylvania's vertically restrictive franchise system violated Section 1 of the Sherman Act. The Supreme Court found that "vertical restrictions promote interbrand competition by allowing the manufacturer to achieve certain efficiencies in the distribution of his products." Therefore, Sylvania's vertical system, which was not price restrictive, did not constitute a *per se* violation of Section 1 of the Sherman Act.[10] ■

The decision in the *Continental* case marked a definite shift from rigid characterization of territorial and customer restrictions to a more flexible, economic analysis of these vertical restraints under the rule of reason. This rule is still applied in most vertical restraint cases.

Resale Price Maintenance Agreements An agreement between a manufacturer and a distributor or retailer in which the manufacturer specifies what the retail prices of its products must be is known as a **resale price maintenance agreement.** Such agreements were once considered to be *per se* violations of Section 1 of the Sherman Act.

Today, however, both *maximum* resale price maintenance agreements and *minimum* resale price maintenance agreements are judged under the rule of reason.[11]

The setting of a maximum price that retailers and distributors can charge for a manufacturer's products may sometimes increase competition and benefit consumers.

27–3 Section 2 of the Sherman Act

Section 1 of the Sherman Act proscribes certain concerted, or joint, activities that restrain trade. In contrast, Section 2 condemns "every person who shall monopolize, or attempt to monopolize." Thus, two distinct types of behavior are subject to sanction under Section 2: *monopolization* and *attempts to monopolize.*

One tactic that may be involved in either offense is predatory pricing. **Predatory pricing** occurs when one firm (the predator) attempts to drive its competitors from the market by selling its product at prices substantially *below* the normal costs of production. Once the competitors are eliminated, the predator presumably will raise its prices far above their competitive levels to recapture its losses and earn higher profits.

27–3a Monopolization

The United States Supreme Court has defined **monopolization** as involving the following two elements:

1. The possession of monopoly power in the relevant market.
2. "The willful acquisition or maintenance of the power as distinguished from growth or development as a consequence of a superior product, business acumen, or historic accident."[12]

To establish a violation of Section 2, a plaintiff must prove both of these elements—monopoly power and an *intent* to monopolize.

Defining Monopoly Power The Sherman Act does not define *monopoly.* In economic theory, monopoly refers to control of a specific market by a single entity. It is well established in antitrust law, however, that a firm may be a monopolist even though it is not the sole seller in a market.

Additionally, size alone does not determine whether a firm is a monopoly. ■ **Example 27.6** A "mom and pop" grocery store located in the isolated town of Happy Camp, Idaho, is a monopolist if it is the only grocery store serving that particular market. Size in relation to the market is what matters, because monopoly involves the power to affect prices. ■

9. See *United States v. Arnold, Schwinn & Co.*, 388 U.S. 365, 87 S.Ct. 1856, 18 L.Ed.2d 1249 (1967).
10. *Continental T.V., Inc. v. GTE Sylvania, Inc.*, 433 U.S. 36, 97 S.Ct. 2549, 53 L.Ed.2d 568 (1977).
11. The United States Supreme Court ruled that maximum resale price agreements should be judged under the rule of reason in *State Oil Co. v. Khan*, 522 U.S. 3, 118 S.Ct. 275, 139 L.Ed.2d 199 (1997). In *Leegin Creative Leather Products, Inc. v. PSKS, Inc.*, 551 U.S. 877, 127 S.Ct. 2705, 168 L.Ed.2d 623 (2007), the Supreme Court found that the rule of reason also applies to minimum resale price agreements.
12. *United States v. Grinnell Corp.*, 384 U.S. 563, 86 S.Ct. 1698, 16 L.Ed.2d 778 (1966).

Proving Monopoly Power Monopoly power can be proved by direct evidence that the firm used its power to control prices and restrict output.[13] Usually, though, there is not enough evidence to show that the firm intentionally controlled prices, so the plaintiff has to offer indirect, or circumstantial, evidence of monopoly power.

To prove monopoly power indirectly, the plaintiff must show that the firm has a dominant share of the relevant market and that new competitors entering that market face significant barriers. ■ **Case in Point 27.7** DuPont manufactures and sells para-aramid fiber, a synthetic fiber used to make body armor, fiber-optic cables, and tires, among other things. Although several companies around the world manufacture this fiber, only three sold it in the U.S. market—DuPont (based in the United States), Teijin (based in the Netherlands), and Kolon Industries, Inc. (based in Korea). DuPont, the industry leader, at times has produced 60 percent of all para-aramid fibers purchased in the United States.

After DuPont brought a suit against Kolon for theft and misappropriation of trade secrets, Kolon counterclaimed that DuPont had illegally monopolized and attempted to monopolize the U.S. para-aramid market in violation of Section 2. Kolon claimed that, to deter competition, DuPont had illegally used multiyear supply agreements for all of its high-volume para-aramid customers. A federal appellate court, however, found that there was insufficient proof that DuPont had possessed monopoly power in the U.S. market during the relevant time period. Additionally, the court concluded that Kolon had not shown that the supply agreements foreclosed competition. Therefore, the court held in favor of DuPont on the antitrust claims.[14] ■

Relevant Market Before a court can determine whether a firm has a dominant market share, it must define the relevant market. The relevant market consists of two elements: (1) a relevant product market and (2) a relevant geographic market.

Relevant Product Market. The relevant product market includes all products that have identical attributes (all brands of tea, for instance), as well as products that are reasonably interchangeable with them. Products are considered reasonably interchangeable if consumers treat them as acceptable substitutes. For instance, tea and coffee are reasonably interchangeable, so they may be included in the same relevant product market.

Establishing the relevant product market is often the key issue in monopolization cases because the way the market is defined may determine whether a firm has monopoly power. When the product market is defined narrowly, the degree of a firm's market power appears greater.

■ **Example 27.8** White Whale Apps acquires Springleaf Apps, its main competitor in nationwide Android-based mobile phone apps. White Whale maintains that the relevant product market consists of all online retailers of mobile phone apps. The Federal Trade Commission (FTC), however, argues that the relevant product market consists of retailers that sell only apps for Android mobile phones. Under the FTC's narrower definition, White Whale can be seen to have a dominant share of the relevant product market. Thus, the FTC can take appropriate actions against White Whale. ■

In the following case, the FTC alleged that the leading U.S. producer of domestic iron pipe fittings sought to maintain monopoly power in violation of antitrust law. The FTC filed this action under Section 5 of the Federal Trade Commission Act. Section 5, like Section 2 of the Sherman Act, requires proof of both the possession of monopoly power in the relevant market and the willful acquisition or maintenance of that power.

---

13. See, for example, *Broadcom Corp. v. Qualcomm, Inc.*, 501 F.3d 297 (3d Cir. 2007).
14. *Kolon Industries, Inc. v. E.I. DuPont de Nemours & Co.*, 748 F.3d 160 (4th Cir. 2014).

Case Analysis 27.1

McWane, Inc. v. Federal Trade Commission
United States Court of Appeals, Eleventh Circuit, 783 F.3d 814 (2015).

In the Language of the Court
MARCUS, Circuit Judge:

* * * *

* * * Pipe fittings join together pipes and help direct the flow of pressurized water in pipeline systems. They are sold primarily to municipal water authorities and their contractors. Although there are several thousand unique configurations of fittings (different shapes, sizes, coatings, etc.), approximately 80% of the demand is for about 100 commonly used fittings.

Fittings are commodity products produced to American Water Works Association ("AWWA") standards, and any fitting that meets AWWA specifications is interchangeable, regardless of the country of origin.

* * * Certain municipal, state, and federal laws require [government] waterworks projects to use domestic-only fittings. Domestic fittings sold for use in projects with domestic-only specifications command higher prices than imported fittings.

* * * *

* * * In late 2009, McWane [Inc., headquartered in Birmingham, Alabama,] was the only supplier of domestic fittings.

* * * Looking to take advantage of the increased demand for domestic fittings prompted by [the passage of the American Recovery and Reinvestment Act of 2009 (ARRA), which provided a large infusion of money for waterworks projects that required domestic pipe fittings, Star Pipe Products] decided to enter the market for domestic [fittings].

In response to Star's forthcoming entry into the * * * market, McWane implemented its "Full Support Program" in order "to protect its domestic brands and market position." * * * McWane informed customers that if they did not "fully support McWane branded products for their domestic fitting and accessory requirements," they "may forgo participation in any unpaid rebates they had accrued for domestic fittings and accessories or shipment of their domestic fitting and accessory orders of McWane products for up to 12 weeks."

* * * *

* * * The FTC issued a * * * complaint charging * * * that McWane's * * * Full Support Program constituted unlawful maintenance of a monopoly over the domestic fittings market.

* * * *

* * * The Commission found that the relevant market was the supply of domestically manufactured fittings for use in domestic-only waterworks projects, because imported fittings are not a substitute for domestic fittings for such projects. The Commission noted that this conclusion was bolstered by the higher prices charged for domestic fittings used in domestic-only projects. The Commission also found that McWane had monopoly power in that market, with 90–95% market share * * * and [that there were] substantial barriers to entry in the form of major capital outlays required to produce domestic fittings.

The Commission [also found] that McWane's Full Support Program * * * foreclosed Star's access to distributors for domestic fittings and harmed competition, thereby contributing significantly to the maintenance of McWane's monopoly power in the market. It noted that * * * the country's two largest waterworks distributors (with a combined 60% market share), prohibited their branches from purchasing domestic fittings from Star after the Full Support Program was announced * * *. Unable to attract [customers], Star was prevented from generating the revenue needed to acquire its own foundry, a more efficient means of producing domestic fittings; thus, its growth into a rival that could challenge McWane's monopoly power was artificially stunted.

Moreover, the Commission found that * * * McWane's * * * conduct had an impact on price: after the Full Support Program was implemented, McWane raised domestic fittings prices and increased its gross profits despite flat production costs, and it did so across states, regardless of whether Star had entered the market as a competitor.

* * * *

[The Commission issued an order directing McWane to stop requiring exclusivity from its customers.] McWane filed a timely petition in this Court seeking review of the Commissioner's order.

* * * *

* * * *Given the identification of persistent price differences between domestic fittings and imported fittings, the distinct customers, and the lack of reasonable substitutes in this case, there was sufficient evidence to support the Commission's market definition.* [Emphasis added.]

* * * *

* * * The evidence of McWane's overwhelming market share (90%), the large capital outlays required to enter the domestic fittings market, and McWane's undeniable continued power over domestic fittings prices amount to sufficient evidence that a reasonable mind might accept as adequate to support the Commission's conclusion [that McWane possessed monopoly power in the relevant market].

* * * *

* * * We agree that [McWane's] conduct amounts to a violation of Section 5 of the Federal Trade Commission Act.

Accordingly, we AFFIRM.

Legal Reasoning Questions

1. How did McWane's Full Support Program harm competition? Explain.

2. What did the Federal Trade Commission conclude? What "factual and economic" evidence supported this conclusion?

3. Instead of imposing an exclusivity policy, what action might McWane have taken to benefit its customers and compete with Star?

Relevant Geographic Market. The second component of the relevant market is the geographic extent of the market in which the firm and its competitors sell the product or services. For products that are sold nationwide, the geographic boundaries of the market can encompass the entire United States.

If transportation costs are significant or a producer and its competitors sell in only a limited area (one in which customers have no access to other sources of the product), then the geographic market is limited to that area. A national firm may thus compete in several distinct areas and have monopoly power in one geographic area but not in another.

Generally, the geographic market is that section of the country within which a firm can increase its price a bit without attracting new sellers or losing many customers to alternative suppliers outside that area. Of course, the Internet is changing perceptions of the size and limits of a geographic market. It may become difficult to perceive any geographic market as local, except for products that are not easily transported, such as concrete.

The Intent Requirement Monopoly power, in and of itself, does not constitute the offense of monopolization under Section 2 of the Sherman Act. The offense also requires an *intent* to monopolize.

A dominant market share may be the result of good business judgment or the development of a superior product. It may simply be the result of a historical accident. In these situations, the acquisition of monopoly power is not an antitrust violation. Indeed, it would be contrary to society's interest to condemn every firm that acquired a position of power because it was well managed and efficient and marketed a product desired by consumers.

If a firm possesses market power as a result of carrying out some purposeful act to acquire or maintain that power through anticompetitive means, however, then it is in violation of Section 2. In most monopolization cases, intent may be inferred from evidence that the firm had monopoly power and engaged in anticompetitive behavior.

Unilateral Refusals to Deal As discussed previously, joint refusals to deal (group boycotts) are subject to close scrutiny under Section 1 of the Sherman Act. A single manufacturer acting unilaterally, though, normally is free to deal, or not to deal, with whomever it wishes.[15]

Nevertheless, in some instances, a unilateral refusal to deal will violate Section 2 of the Sherman Act. These instances occur only if (1) the firm refusing to deal has— or is likely to acquire—monopoly power and (2) the refusal is likely to have an anticompetitive effect on a particular market.

■ **Example 27.9** Clark Industries owns three of the four major downhill ski areas in Blue Hills, Idaho. Clark refuses to continue participating in a jointly offered six-day "all Blue Hills" lift ticket. Clark's refusal to cooperate with its smaller competitor is a violation of Section 2 of the Sherman Act. Because Clark owns three-fourths of the local ski areas, it has monopoly power. Thus, its unilateral refusal to deal has an anticompetitive effect on the market. ■

---

15. For a classic case in this area, see *United States v. Colgate & Co.*, 250 U.S. 300, 39 S.Ct. 465, 63 L.Ed. 992 (1919). See also, *Pacific Bell Telephone Co. v. Linkline Communications, Inc.*, 555 U.S. 438, 129 S.Ct. 1109, 172 L.Ed.2d 836 (2009).

27–3b Attempts to Monopolize

Section 2 also prohibits **attempted monopolization** of a market, which requires proof of the following three elements:

1. Anticompetitive conduct.
2. The specific intent to exclude competitors and garner monopoly power.
3. A "dangerous" probability of success in achieving monopoly power. The probability cannot be dangerous unless the alleged offender possesses some degree of market power. Only serious threats of monopolization are condemned as violations.

27–4 The Clayton Act

Congress enacted the Clayton Act to strengthen federal antitrust laws. The act was aimed at specific anticompetitive or monopolistic practices that the Sherman Act did not cover. The substantive provisions of the act—set out in Sections 2, 3, 7, and 8—deal with four distinct forms of business behavior, which are declared illegal but not criminal. For each provision, the act states that the behavior is *illegal only if it tends to substantially lessen competition or to create monopoly power.*

27–4a Section 2—Price Discrimination

Section 2 of the Clayton Act prohibits **price discrimination,** which occurs when a seller charges different prices to competing buyers for identical goods or services. Congress strengthened this section by amending it with the passage of the Robinson-Patman Act in 1936. As amended, Section 2 prohibits price discrimination that cannot be justified by differences in production costs, transportation costs, or cost differences due to other reasons. In short, a seller cannot charge one buyer a lower price than it charges that buyer's competitor.

Requirements To violate Section 2, the seller must be engaged in interstate commerce, the goods must be of like grade and quality, and the goods must have been sold to two or more purchasers. In addition, the effect of the price discrimination must be to substantially lessen competition, tend to create a monopoly, or otherwise injure competition. Without proof of an actual injury resulting from the price discrimination, the plaintiff cannot recover damages.

Note that price discrimination claims can arise from discounts, offsets, rebates, or allowances given to one buyer over another. Moreover, giving favorable credit terms, delivery, or freight charges to some buyers, but not others, can also lead to allegations of price discrimination. For instance, when a seller offers goods to different customers at the same price but includes free delivery for certain buyers, it may violate Section 2 in some circumstances.

Defenses There are several statutory defenses to liability for price discrimination, including the following:

1. *Cost justification.* If the seller can justify the price reduction by demonstrating that a particular buyer's purchases saved the seller costs in producing and selling the goods, the seller will not be liable for price discrimination.

2. *Meeting a competitor's prices.* If the seller charged the lower price in a good faith attempt to meet an equally low price of a competitor, the seller will not be liable for price discrimination. ■ **Example 27.10** Rogue, Inc., is a retail dealer of Mercury Marine outboard motors in Shady Cove, Oregon. Mercury Marine also sells its motors to other dealers in the Shady Cove area. When Rogue discovers that Mercury is selling its outboard motors at a substantial discount to Rogue's largest competitor, it files a price discrimination lawsuit. Mercury Marine can defend itself by showing that the discounts given to Rogue's competitor were made in good faith to meet the low price charged by another manufacturer of marine motors. ■

3. *Changing market conditions.* A seller may lower its price on an item in response to changing conditions affecting the market or the marketability of the goods concerned. Sellers are allowed to readjust their prices to meet the realities of the market without liability for price discrimination. Thus, if an advance in technology makes a particular product less marketable than it was previously, a seller can lower the product's price.

State Laws Concerning Price Discrimination

Some states have enacted statutes that prohibit price discrimination. A state statute may apply when a business sells goods or services at different prices to buyers in different locations within the state. Some such laws protect specific businesses, such as auto dealerships, from discriminatory wholesale or incentive pricing.

Other state laws, including unfair competition statutes, also protect businesses and consumers from economic injuries caused by wrongful business practices. In the following case, a state court considered whether an allegation of age-based price discrimination in violation of the state's civil rights statute could support a claim for a violation of the state's unfair competition statute.

Case 27.2

Candelore v. Tinder, Inc.

California Court of Appeal, Second District, Division 3, 19 Cal.App.5th 1138, 228 Cal.Rptr.3d 336 (2018).

Background and Facts Tinder, Inc., owns and operates the dating app, Tinder. The free version of the app presents users with photos of potential people to date. When a photo appears on the device's screen, the user can swipe right to express approval or swipe left to express disapproval. The premium service, Tinder Plus, allows users to access additional features of the app for a monthly fee. Tinder charges consumers who are age thirty and older $19.99 per month for Tinder Plus, while it charges consumers under the age of thirty only $9.99 or $14.99 per month.

On behalf of consumers who were over age thirty when they subscribed to Tinder Plus, Allan Candelore filed a suit in a California state court against Tinder, Inc. Candelore alleged age-based price discrimination in violation of California's civil rights statute—which prohibits arbitrary discrimination by businesses on the basis of personal characteristics—and the state's unfair competition law (UCL). The court concluded that the company's age-based pricing model was justified by public policies that promote "profit maximization by the vendor, a legitimate goal in our capitalistic economy." Candelore appealed.

In the Language of the Court

CURREY, J. [Judge]

* * * *

* * * Whatever interest society may have—if any—in increasing patronage among those under the age of thirty who may be interested in the premium features of an online dating app, that interest is not sufficiently compelling to justify discriminatory age-based pricing that may well exclude less economically advantaged individuals over the age of thirty from enjoying the same premium features.

Case 27.2 Continues

As for profit maximization, we have no quarrel with the trial court's conclusion that it can be an acceptable business objective and can be advanced by price discrimination. As anyone who has attended an auction can attest, individuals may and often do value goods and services differently. Some are willing and able to pay a higher price than others for the same product. And, as any student of elementary microeconomics knows, sellers of goods and services could (at least theoretically) maximize profits if they could engage in price discrimination by charging higher prices to those consumers willing to pay them, and lower prices to the rest. For example, a seller might offer several versions of its product, with different features, trim, branding, etc., each at a different price, in an effort to increase overall profits. Or a seller might seek to attract bargain hunters by offering temporary price reductions during a sale or other promotion. *But the quest for profit maximization can never serve as an excuse for prohibited discrimination among potential customers.* [Emphasis added.]
* * * *

As alleged, Tinder's pricing model discriminates against users age thirty and over * * * . While we make no judgment about the true character of Tinder's pricing model, or whether evidence exists to establish a sufficient justification for charging older users more than younger users, we conclude the complaint's allegations are sufficient to state a claim for age discrimination in violation of the [state's civil rights statute].
* * * *

The UCL prohibits, and provides civil remedies for, unfair competition, which includes any unlawful, unfair or fraudulent business act or practice. Its purpose is to protect both consumers and competitors by promoting fair competition in commercial markets for goods and services.
* * * *Any law or regulation—federal or state, statutory or common law—can serve as a predicate [ground] for a * * * violation.* Because we conclude the complaint adequately states a claim for violation of the [civil rights statute], we also conclude the allegations are sufficient to state a claim under * * * the UCL. [Emphasis added.]

Decision and Remedy *A state intermediate appellate court reversed the judgment of the lower court. "Tinder's alleged discriminatory pricing model violates the public policy embodied in the [state's civil rights statute, and] the UCL . . . provides an independent basis for relief on the facts alleged."*

Critical Thinking
- **Legal Environment** *A California statute provides for the waiver of fees at state university campuses for senior citizens. What distinguishes this differential treatment from the discriminatory practice at issue in the* Candelore *case?*
- **Economic** *Instead of personal characteristics such as age, could a business like Tinder use economic distinctions to broaden its user base and increase profits? Discuss.*

27–4b Section 3—Exclusionary Practices

Under Section 3 of the Clayton Act, sellers or lessors cannot condition the sale or lease of goods on the buyer's or lessee's promise not to use or deal in the goods of the seller's competitor. In effect, this section prohibits two types of vertical agreements involving exclusionary practices—exclusive-dealing contracts and tying arrangements.

Exclusive-Dealing Contracts A contract under which a seller forbids a buyer to purchase products from the seller's competitors is called an **exclusive-dealing contract.** A seller is prohibited from making an exclusive-dealing contract under Section 3 if the effect of the contract is "to substantially lessen competition or tend to create a monopoly."

In the past, courts were more inclined to find that exclusive-dealing contracts substantially lessened competition. ■ **Case in Point 27.11** In one classic case, Standard Oil Company, the largest gasoline seller in the nation in the late 1940s, made exclusive-dealing contracts with independent stations in seven western states. The contracts involved 16 percent of all retail outlets, whose sales were approximately 7 percent of all retail sales in that market. The United States Supreme Court ruled that the market was substantially concentrated because the seven largest gasoline suppliers all used exclusive-dealing contracts with their independent retailers and together controlled 65 percent of the market.

Looking at market conditions after the arrangements were instituted, the Court found that market shares were extremely stable and that entry into the market was apparently restricted. Thus, the Court held that the Clayton Act had been violated because competition was "foreclosed in a substantial share" of the relevant market.[16] ■ Note that since the Supreme Court's decision in the *Standard Oil* case, a number of subsequent decisions have called the holding into question.[17]

Today, it is clear that to violate antitrust law, an exclusive-dealing agreement (or a tying arrangement, discussed next) must qualitatively and substantially harm competition. To prevail, a plaintiff must present affirmative evidence that the performance of the agreement will foreclose competition and harm consumers.

Tying Arrangements When a seller conditions the sale of a product (the tying product) on the buyer's agreement to purchase another product (the tied product) produced or distributed by the same seller, a **tying arrangement** results. The legality of a tying arrangement (or *tie-in sales agreement*) depends on several factors, such as the purpose of the agreement. Courts also focus on the agreement's likely effect on competition in the relevant markets (the market for the tying product and the market for the tied product).

Section 3 of the Clayton Act has been held to apply only to commodities, not to services. Tying arrangements, however, can also be considered agreements that restrain trade in violation of Section 1 of the Sherman Act. Thus, cases involving tying arrangements of services have been brought under Section 1 of the Sherman Act. Although earlier cases condemned tying arrangements as illegal *per se*, courts now evaluate tying agreements under the rule of reason.[18]

■ **Case in Point 27.12** James Batson bought a nonrefundable ticket from Live Nation Entertainment, Inc., to attend a rock concert at the Charter One Pavilion in Chicago. The front of the ticket noted that the price included a nine-dollar parking fee. Batson did not have a car to park, however. In fact, he had walked to the concert venue and had bought the ticket just before the performance.

Frustrated at being charged for parking that he did not need, Batson filed a suit in a federal district court against Live Nation. He argued that the bundled parking fee was a tying arrangement in violation of Section 1 of the Sherman Act. The court dismissed the suit, and a federal appellate court affirmed. The court was unable to identify a product market in which Live Nation had sufficient power to force consumers who wanted to attend a concert (the tying product) to buy "useless parking rights" (the tied product). While it may have been annoying, there was no evidence that Live Nation's parking tie-in restrained competition for parking in Chicago.[19] ■

27–4c Section 7—Mergers

Under Section 7 of the Clayton Act, a person or business organization cannot hold stock or assets in more than one business when "the effect . . . may be to substantially lessen competition." Section 7 is the statutory authority for preventing mergers or acquisitions that could result in monopoly power or a substantial lessening of competition in the marketplace. Section 7 applies to both horizontal and vertical mergers, as discussed shortly.

A crucial consideration in most merger cases is **market concentration.** Determining market concentration involves allocating percentage market shares among the various companies in the relevant market. When a small number of companies share a large part of the market, the market is concentrated. ■ **Example 27.13** If the four largest grocery stores in Miami account for 80 percent of all retail food sales, the market is concentrated in those four firms. If one of these stores absorbs the assets and liabilities of another, so that the other ceases to exist, the result is a merger that further concentrates the market and possibly diminishes competition. ■

Competition is not necessarily diminished solely as a result of market concentration. Courts will consider other factors in determining if a merger violates Section 7. One factor of particular importance is whether the merger will make it more difficult for *potential* competitors to enter the relevant market.

---

16. *Standard Oil Co. of California v. United States*, 337 U.S. 293, 69 S.Ct. 1051, 93 L.Ed. 1371 (1949).

17. See, for example, *In re Cox Enterprises, Inc.*, 835 F.3d 1195 (10th Cir. 2016; and *Stop & Shop Supermarket Co. v. Blue Cross & Blue Shield of Rhode Island*, 373 F.3d 57 (1st Cir. 2004).

18. *Illinois Tool Works, Inc. v. Independent Ink, Inc.*, 547 U.S. 28, 126 S.Ct. 1281, 164 L.Ed.2d 26 (2006). This decision was the first time the United States Supreme Court recognized that tying arrangements can have legitimate business justifications.

19. *Batson v. Live Nation Entertainment, Inc.*, 746 F.3d 827 (7th Cir. 2014).

Horizontal Mergers A merger between firms that compete with each other in the same market is called a **horizontal merger.** If a horizontal merger creates an entity with a significant market share, the merger may be considered illegal because it increases market concentration. The Federal Trade Commission (FTC) and the U.S. Department of Justice (DOJ) have established guidelines for determining which mergers will be challenged.[20]

When analyzing the legality of a horizontal merger, the courts consider three additional factors. The first factor is the overall concentration of the relevant market. The second is the relevant market's history of tending toward concentration. The final factor is whether the merger is apparently designed to establish market power or restrict competition.

Vertical Mergers A **vertical merger** occurs when a company at one stage of production acquires a company at a higher or lower stage of production. An example of a vertical merger is a company merging with one of its suppliers or retailers.

Whether a vertical merger will be deemed illegal generally depends on several factors, such as whether the merger creates a single firm that controls an undue percentage share of the relevant market. The courts also analyze the concentration of firms in the market, barriers to entry into the market, and the apparent intent of the merging parties. If a merger does not prevent competitors of either of the merging firms from competing in a segment of the market, the merger will not be condemned as foreclosing competition and thus will be deemed legal.

27-4d Section 8—Interlocking Directorates

Section 8 of the Clayton Act deals with *interlocking directorates*—that is, the practice whereby individuals serve as directors on the boards of two or more competing companies simultaneously. Specifically, no person may be a director for two or more competing corporations at the same time if either of the corporations has capital, surplus, undivided profits, or competitive sales that exceed a specified threshold amount. The Federal Trade Commission adjusts the threshold amounts each year.

---

20. These guidelines include a formula for assessing the degree of concentration in the relevant market called the Herfindahl-Hirschman Index (HHI), which is available at www.justice.gov/atr/herfindahl-hirschman-index. The HHI is calculated by squaring the market share of each firm competing in the market and then summing the resulting numbers.

27-5 Enforcement and Exemptions

The federal agencies that enforce the federal antitrust laws are the U.S. Department of Justice (DOJ) and the Federal Trade Commission (FTC), which was established by the Federal Trade Commission Act. Section 5 of that act condemns all forms of anticompetitive behavior that are not covered under other federal antitrust laws.

27-5a Agency Actions

Only the DOJ can prosecute violations of the Sherman Act, which can be either criminal or civil offenses. Violations of the Clayton Act are not crimes, but the act can be enforced by either the DOJ or the FTC through civil proceedings.

The DOJ or the FTC may ask the courts to impose various remedies, including dissolution or **divestiture** (making a company give up one or more of its operations). A meatpacking firm, for instance, might be forced to divest itself of control or ownership of butcher shops.

The FTC has sole authority to enforce violations of Section 5 of the Federal Trade Commission Act. FTC actions are effected through administrative orders, but if a firm violates an FTC order, the FTC can seek court sanctions for the violation.

27-5b Private Actions

A private party who has been injured as a result of a violation of the Sherman Act or the Clayton Act can sue for **treble damages** (three times the actual damages suffered) and attorneys' fees. In some instances, private parties may also seek injunctive relief to prevent antitrust violations. A party wishing to sue under the Sherman Act must prove that:

1. The antitrust violation either caused or was a substantial factor in causing the injury that was suffered.
2. The unlawful actions of the accused party affected business activities of the plaintiff that were protected by the antitrust laws.

Additionally, the United States Supreme Court has held that to pursue antitrust lawsuits, private parties must present some evidence suggesting that an illegal agreement was made.[21]

---

21. *Bell Atlantic Corp. v. Twombly,* 550 U.S. 544, 127 S.Ct. 1955, 167 L.Ed.2d 929 (2007).

A private party can bring an action under Section 2 of the Sherman Act based on the attempted enforcement of a fraudulently obtained patent. This is called a *Walker Process* claim.[22] To prevail, the plaintiff must first show that the defendant obtained the patent by committing fraud on the U.S. Patent and Trademark Office and enforced the patent with knowledge of the fraud. The

---

22. The name of the claim comes from the title of the case in which the claim originated—*Walker Process Equipment v. Food Machine and Chemical Corp.*, 382 U.S. 172, 86 S.Ct. 347, 15 L.Ed.2d 247 (1965).

plaintiff must then establish all the other elements of a Sherman Act monopolization claim—anticompetitive conduct, an intent to monopolize, and a dangerous probability of achieving monopoly power.

In the following case, a respiratory filter manufacturer was accused of patent infringement. The manufacturer sought a declaratory judgment of noninfringement and asserted a *Walker Process* claim. One of the primary issues was whether a court could award treble damages based on the amount of attorneys' fees that the plaintiff incurred.

Case 27.3

TransWeb, LLC v. 3M Innovative Properties Co.
United States Court of Appeals, Federal Circuit, 812 F.3d 1295 (2016).

Background and Facts TransWeb, LLC, manufactures respirator filters made of nonwoven fibrous material to be worn by workers at contaminated worksites. At a filtration industry exposition, TransWeb's founder, Kumar Ogale, handed out samples of TransWeb's filter material. At the time, 3M Innovative Properties Company was experimenting with filter materials. At the expo, 3M employees obtained the TransWeb samples. More than a year later, 3M obtained patents for its filter products and filed a suit against TransWeb, claiming infringement. 3M asserted that it had not received the TransWeb samples until after its patent application had been filed. The suit was dismissed.

TransWeb then filed a suit in a federal district court, seeking a declaratory judgment of non-infringement and asserting a *Walker Process* claim. A jury found that 3M had obtained its patents through fraud, that its assertion of the patents against TransWeb violated antitrust law, and that TransWeb was entitled to attorneys' fees as damages. TransWeb had incurred $7.7 million defending against 3M's infringement suit. The court trebled this to $23 million. 3M appealed.

In the Language of the Court
HUGHES, Circuit Judge.
* * * *

3M argues that the district court erred in awarding the $23 million of attorney-fees damages, because TransWeb failed to show any link between those attorney fees and an impact on competition. 3M argues that those attorney fees had no effect on competition because they did not force TransWeb out of the market or otherwise affect prices in the market.
* * * *

3M's argument focuses on the fact that the harmful effect on competition proven by TransWeb at trial never actually came about. TransWeb proved at trial that increased prices for fluorinated filter * * * respirators would have resulted had 3M succeeded in its suit.
* * * *

* * * 3M's unlawful act was * * * aimed at reducing competition and would have done so had the suit been successful. 3M's unlawful act was the bringing of suit based on a patent known to be fraudulently obtained. What made this act unlawful under the antitrust laws was its attempt to gain a monopoly based on this fraudulently obtained patent. TransWeb's attorney fees flow directly from this unlawful aspect of 3M's act. * * * The attorney fees are precisely the type of loss that the claimed violations would be likely to cause.
* * * *

* * * *It is the abuse of the legal process by the antitrust-defendant that makes the attorney fees incurred by the antitrust-plaintiff during that legal process a relevant antitrust injury.* [Emphasis added.]

Case 27.3 Continues

No assertion of a patent known to be fraudulently obtained can be a proper use of legal process. No successful outcome of that litigation, regardless of how much the patentee subjectively desires it, would save that suit from being improper due to its tainted origin.

* * * The antitrust laws exist to protect competition. If we were to hold that TransWeb can seek antitrust damages only [by] forfeiture of competition, but not [by] defending the anticompetitive suit, then we would be incentivizing the former over the latter. * * * This is not in accord with the purpose of those very same antitrust laws.

Furthermore, it furthers the purpose of the antitrust laws to encourage TransWeb to bring its antitrust suit * * * instead of waiting to be excluded from the market * * *. If TransWeb proceeds only after being excluded from the market * * *, then the [injury] will no longer be borne by TransWeb alone, but rather would be shared by all consumers in the relevant markets.

Decision and Remedy *The U.S. Court of Appeals for the Federal Circuit affirmed the lower court's judgment and award of trebled attorneys' fees. "TransWeb's attorney fees appropriately flow from the unlawful aspect of 3M's antitrust violation and thus are an antitrust injury that can properly serve as the basis for antitrust damages."*

Critical Thinking
- **Legal Environment** *How would TransWeb's injury have been "shared by all consumers in the relevant markets" if TransWeb had not sued until after it had been driven out of those markets by 3M's actions?*
- **Ethical** *What does 3M's conduct suggest about its corporate ethics?*

27–5c Exemptions from Antitrust Laws

There are many legislative and constitutional limitations on antitrust enforcement. Most of the statutory and judicially created exemptions to the antitrust laws apply only in certain areas (see Exhibit 27–2). One of the most significant exemptions covers joint efforts by businesspersons to obtain legislative, judicial, or executive action. Under this exemption, for instance, movie producers can jointly lobby Congress to change the copyright laws without being held liable for attempting to restrain trade. Another exemption covers professional baseball teams.

27–6 U.S. Antitrust Laws in the Global Context

U.S. antitrust laws have a broad application. Not only may persons in foreign nations be subject to their provisions, but the laws may also be applied to protect foreign consumers and competitors from violations committed by U.S. business firms. Consequently, *foreign persons*, a term that by definition includes foreign governments, may sue under U.S. antitrust laws in U.S. courts.

27–6a The Extraterritorial Application of U.S. Antitrust Laws

Section 1 of the Sherman Act provides for the extraterritorial effect of the U.S. antitrust laws. Any conspiracy that has a *substantial effect* on U.S. commerce is within the reach of the Sherman Act. The violation may even occur outside the United States, and foreign governments as well as individuals can be sued for violation of U.S. antitrust laws.

Before U.S. courts will exercise jurisdiction and apply antitrust laws, it must be shown that the alleged violation had a substantial effect on U.S. commerce. U.S. jurisdiction is automatically invoked, however, when a *per se* violation occurs.

If a domestic firm, for instance, joins a foreign cartel to control the production, price, or distribution of goods, and this cartel has a *substantial effect* on U.S. commerce, a *per se* violation may arise. Hence, both the domestic firm and the foreign cartel can be sued for violation of the U.S. antitrust laws.

Likewise, if a foreign firm doing business in the United States enters into a price-fixing or other anticompetitive agreement to control a portion of U.S. markets, a *per se* violation may exist. ■ **Case in Point 27.14** Carrier Corporation is a U.S. firm that manufactures air-conditioning and refrigeration (ACR) equipment. To make these products, Carrier uses ACR copper tubing it buys from Outokumpu Oyj, a Finnish company. Carrier is one of the world's largest purchasers of ACR copper tubing.

After the Commission of the European Communities found that Outokumpu had conspired with other companies to fix ACR tubing prices in Europe, Carrier filed a suit in a U.S. court. Carrier alleged that the cartel had

Exhibit 27–2 Exemptions to Antitrust Enforcement

Exemption	Source and Scope
Labor	The Clayton Act—Permits unions to organize and bargain without violating antitrust laws and specifies that strikes and other labor activities normally do not violate any federal law.
Agricultural Associations	The Clayton Act and the Capper-Volstead Act—Allow agricultural cooperatives to set prices.
Fisheries	The Fishermen's Cooperative Marketing Act—Allows the fishing industry to set prices.
Insurance Companies	The McCarran-Ferguson Act—Exempts the insurance business in states in which the industry is regulated.
Exporters	The Webb-Pomerene Act—Allows U.S. exporters to engage in cooperative activity to compete with similar foreign associations. The Export Trading Company Act—Permits the U.S. Department of Justice to exempt certain exporters.
Professional Baseball	The United States Supreme Court—Has held that professional baseball is exempt because it is not "interstate commerce."[a]
Oil Marketing	The Interstate Oil Compact—Allows states to set quotas on oil to be marketed in interstate commerce.
Defense Activities	The Defense Production Act—Allows the president to approve, and thereby exempt, certain activities to further the military defense of the United States.
Small Businesses' Cooperative Research	The Small Business Administration Act—Allows small firms to undertake cooperative research.
State Actions	The United States Supreme Court—Has held that actions by a state are exempt if the state clearly articulates and actively supervises the policy behind its action.[b]
Regulated Industries	Federal Agencies—Industries (such as airlines) are exempt when a federal administrative agency (such as the Federal Aviation Administration) has primary regulatory authority.
Businesspersons' Joint Efforts to Seek Government Action	The United States Supreme Court—Cooperative efforts by businesspersons to obtain legislative, judicial, or executive action are exempt unless it is clear that an effort is "objectively baseless" and is an attempt to make anticompetitive use of government processes.[c]

a. *Federal Baseball Club of Baltimore, Inc. v. National League of Professional Baseball Clubs,* 259 U.S. 200, 42 S.Ct. 465, 66 L.Ed. 898 (1922). See also *Right Field Rooftops, LLC v. Chicago Cubs Baseball Club, LLC,* 870 F.3d 682 (7th Cir. 2017).
b. See *Parker v. Brown,* 317 U.S. 341, 63 S.Ct. 307, 87 L.Ed. 315 (1943).
c. *Eastern Railroad Presidents Conference v. Noerr Motor Freight, Inc.,* 365 U.S. 127, 81 S.Ct. 523, 5 L.Ed.2d 464 (1961); and *United Mine Workers of America v. Pennington,* 381 U.S. 657, 89 S.Ct. 1585, 14 L.Ed.2d 626 (1965). These two cases established the exception often referred to as the *Noerr-Pennington* doctrine.

also conspired to fix prices in the United States by agreeing that only Outokumpu would sell ACR tubing in the U.S. market. The district court dismissed the case for lack of jurisdiction, but a federal appellate court reversed. The reviewing court found that the alleged anticompetitive conspiracy had a substantial effect on U.S. commerce. Therefore, the U.S. courts had jurisdiction over the Finnish defendant.[23] ■

23. *Carrier Corp. v. Outokumpu Oyj,* 673 F.3d 430 (6th Cir. 2012).

27–6b The Application of Foreign Antitrust Laws

Large U.S. companies increasingly need to be concerned about the application of foreign antitrust laws. The European Union (EU), in particular, has stepped up its enforcement actions against antitrust violators.

European Union Enforcement The EU's laws promoting competition are stricter in many respects than those of the United States and define more conduct a anticompetitive. The EU actively pursues antitrust violators, especially individual companies and cartels that allegedly engage in monopolistic conduct. EU investigations of possible antitrust violations often take years. See this chapter's *Digital Update* feature for a discussion of how the EU has been pursuing Google, Inc., for antitrust violations.

Increased Enforcement in Asia and Latin America Many other nations also have laws that promote competition and prohibit trade restraints. Japanese antitrust laws forbid unfair trade practices, monopolization, and restrictions that unreasonably restrain trade. China's antitrust rules restrict monopolization and price

fixing (except that the Chinese government can set prices on exported goods). Indonesia, Malaysia, South Korea, and Vietnam all have statutes protecting competition. Argentina, Brazil, Chile, Peru, and several other Latin American countries have adopted modern antitrust laws as well.

Most of the antitrust laws apply extraterritorially, as U.S. antitrust laws do. This means that a U.S. company may be subject to another nation's antitrust laws if the company's conduct has a substantial effect on that nation's commerce. For instance, China once fined the U.S. chipmaker Qualcomm, Inc., $975 million for violating antitrust laws. China has also targeted Microsoft, Inc., in its antitrust investigations and has searched Microsoft's company servers in China for evidence of violations.

Digital Update
The European Union Issues Record Fines against Google in Antitrust Case

"Just google it." Google's search engine is so dominant that the company name has become a verb synonymous with conducting an Internet search. According to the European Commissioner for Competition, Margrethe Vestager, Google is too dominant, at least with respect to comparison shopping and product searches. For that reason, the European Union (EU) formally charged Google with an antitrust violation. The investigation culminated in a fine of $2.7 billion and a ruling that Google had breached EU antitrust regulations by abusing its dominant position in the search engine market. (At the time, this was a record amount, but the EU later fined Google $5 billion on antitrust charges stemming from its use of its Android mobile operating system to block rivals.)

Google Put Its Shopping Results above Other Search Results

The EU claimed that for nearly ten years, Google had promoted its own comparison shopping service at the expense of competitors. It did this by "positioning and prominently displaying its comparison shopping service in its general search result pages, irrespective of its merits." As a result, "users [did] not necessarily see the most relevant results in response to queries—to the detriment of consumers and rival comparison shopping services."

Google contended that it could not change its core software and that the results in its search algorithms were based on relevance. In addition, Google argued that it had actually boosted traffic to its Web competitors. Indeed, search engines have proliferated on the Web, suggesting that Google's success has not eliminated competition.

Nevertheless, the EU's decision ordered Google to change the way it displays search results in the EU—or face more fines. When Google shows comparison

shopping services in response to a user's query, the search results should show the most relevant services first. Google appealed the EU's order, and experts predict that the dispute may continue for years.

The Compartmentalization of Search on the Web

More and more frequently, Internet users do not engage in general searches. Rather, they know exactly where to go to obtain product information. When they want information on movies, for instance, they go to the Internet Movie Data Base (IMDB) rather than Google. When they want information on music, they go to iTunes. When they want to search for the cheapest airfares, they go to Kayak or similar sites. When they want to find the best rates on hotels, they go to sites such as hotels.com, tripadvisor.com, and trivago.com. And when they are interested in buying a product, they frequently go to Amazon or eBay. Amazon, in particular, has fine-tuned its ability to generate advertising revenues through its Amazon-sponsored links.

And, of course, social media must be considered. More people are on social media sites than ever before, particularly on their mobile devices. These users spend far more time on Instagram and Facebook than they do on Google, and they often "crowdsource"—that is, look for answers from friends on social media rather than search on Google. Social media sites are also becoming increasingly competitive with Google in the services they offer, including mobile payments and instant messaging.

Critical Thinking *How does the increasing popularity of specialized search engines weaken the EU's argument that Google has harmed consumers?*

Practice and Review: Antitrust Law

The Internet Corporation for Assigned Names and Numbers (ICANN) is a nonprofit entity that organizes Internet domain names. It is governed by a board of directors elected by various groups with commercial interests in the Internet. One of ICANN's functions is to authorize an entity to serve as a registry for certain "Top Level Domains" (TLDs). ICANN and VeriSign entered into an agreement that authorized VeriSign to serve as a registry for the ".com" TLD and provide registry services in accordance with ICANN's specifications. VeriSign complained that ICANN was restricting the services that it could make available as a registrar, blocking new services, imposing unnecessary conditions on those services, and setting the prices at which the services were offered. VeriSign claimed that ICANN's control of the registry services for domain names violated Section 1 of the Sherman Act. Using the information presented in the chapter, answer the following questions.

1. Should ICANN's actions be judged under the rule of reason or be deemed *per se* violations of Section 1 of the Sherman Act? Why?
2. Should ICANN's actions be viewed as a horizontal or a vertical restraint of trade? Why?
3. Does it matter that ICANN's directors are chosen by groups with a commercial interest in the Internet? Explain.
4. If the dispute is judged under the rule of reason, what might be ICANN's defense for having a standardized set of registry services that must be used?

Debate This ...   *The Internet and the rise of e-commerce have rendered our current antitrust concepts and laws obsolete.*

Terms and Concepts

antitrust laws 571	monopolization 575	rule of reason 572
attempted monopolization 578	monopoly 572	treble damages 582
concentrated industry 574	monopoly power 572	tying arrangement 581
divestiture 582	*per se* violations 572	vertically integrated firms 574
exclusive-dealing contract 580	predatory pricing 575	vertical merger 582
group boycott 574	price discrimination 578	vertical restraint 574
horizontal merger 582	price-fixing agreement 573	
horizontal restraint 573	resale price maintenance	
market concentration 581	agreement 575	
market power 572	restraints of trade 571	

Issue Spotters

1. Under what circumstances would Pop's Market, a small store in a small, isolated town, be considered a monopolist? If Pop's is a monopolist, is it in violation of Section 2 of the Sherman Act? Why or why not? (See *Section 2 of the Sherman Act.*)
2. Maple Corporation conditions the sale of its syrup on the buyer's agreement to buy Maple's pancake mix. What

factors would a court consider to decide whether this arrangement violates the Clayton Act? (See *The Clayton Act.*)

- **Check your answers to the Issue Spotters against the answers provided in Appendix B at the end of this text.**

Business Scenarios and Case Problems

27–1. Group Boycott. Jorge's Appliance Corp. was a new retail seller of appliances in Sunrise City. Because of its innovative sales techniques and financing, Jorge's attracted many customers. As a result, the appliance department of No-Glow Department Store, a large chain store with a great deal of buying power, lost a substantial number of sales. No-Glow told a number of appliance manufacturers from whom it made large-volume purchases that if they continued to sell to Jorge's, No-Glow would stop buying from them. The manufacturers immediately stopped selling appliances to Jorge's. Jorge's filed a suit against No-Glow and the manufacturers, claiming that their actions constituted an antitrust violation. No-Glow and the manufacturers were able to prove that Jorge's was a small retailer with a small market share. They claimed that because the relevant market was not substantially affected, they were not guilty of restraint of trade. Discuss fully whether there was an antitrust violation. (See *Section 1 of the Sherman Act.*)

27–2. Antitrust Laws. Allitron, Inc., and Donovan, Ltd., are interstate competitors selling similar appliances, principally in the states of Illinois, Indiana, Kentucky, and Ohio. Allitron and Donovan agree that Allitron will no longer sell in Indiana and Ohio and that Donovan will no longer sell in Illinois and Kentucky. Have Allitron and Donovan violated any antitrust laws? If so, which law? Explain. (See *Section 1 of the Sherman Act.*)

27–3. Price Fixing. Together, EMI, Sony BMG Music Entertainment, Universal Music Group Recordings, Inc., and Warner Music Group Corporation produced, licensed, and distributed 80 percent of the digital music sold in the United States. The companies formed MusicNet to sell music to online services that sold the songs to consumers. MusicNet required all of the services to sell the songs at the same price and subject to the same restrictions. Digitization of music became cheaper, but MusicNet did not change its prices. Did MusicNet violate the antitrust laws? Explain. [*Starr v. Sony BMG Music Entertainment*, 592 F.3d 314 (2d Cir. 2010)] (See *Section 1 of the Sherman Act.*)

27–4. Business Case Problem with Sample Answer— Price Discrimination. Dayton Superior Corporation sells its products in interstate commerce to several companies, including Spa Steel Products, Inc. The purchasers often compete directly with each other for customers. For three years, one of Spa Steel's customers purchased Dayton Superior's products from two of Spa Steel's competitors. According to the customer, Spa Steel's prices were always 10 to 15 percent higher for the same products. As a result, Spa Steel lost sales to at least that customer and perhaps others. Spa Steel wants to sue Dayton Superior for price discrimination. Which requirements for such a claim under Section 2 of the Clayton Act does Spa Steel satisfy? What additional facts will it need to prove? [*Dayton Superior Corp. v. Spa Steel Products, Inc.*, 2012 WL 113663 (N.D.N.Y. 2012)] (See *The Clayton Act.*)

- **For a sample answer to Problem 27–4, go to Appendix C at the end of this text.**

27–5. Section 1 of the Sherman Act. The National Collegiate Athletic Association (NCAA) and the National Federation of State High School Associations (NFHS) set a new standard for non-wood baseball bats. Their goal was to ensure that aluminum and composite bats performed like wood bats in order to enhance player safety and reduce technology-driven home runs and other big hits. Marucci Sports, LLC, makes non-wood bats. Under the new standard, four of Marucci's eleven products were decertified for use in high school and collegiate games. Marucci filed suit against the NCAA and the

NFHS under Section 1 of the Sherman Act. At trial, Marucci's evidence focused on injury to its own business. Did the NCAA and NFHS's standard restrain trade in violation of the Sherman Act? Explain. [*Marucci Sports, LLC v. National Collegiate Athletic Association*, 751 F.3d 368 (5th Cir. 2014)] (See *Section 1 of the Sherman Act.*)

27–6. Mergers. St. Luke's Health Systems, Ltd., operated an emergency clinic in Nampa, Idaho. Saltzer Medical Group, P.A., had thirty-four physicians practicing at its offices in Nampa. Saint Alphonsus Medical Center operated the only hospital in Nampa. St. Luke's acquired Saltzer's assets and entered into a five-year professional service agreement with the Saltzer physicians. This affiliation resulted in a combined share of two-thirds of the Nampa adult primary care provider market. Together, the two entities could impose a significant increase in the prices charged to patients and insurers, and correspondence between the parties indicated that they would. Saint Alphonsus filed a suit against St. Luke's to block the merger. Did this affiliation violate antitrust law? Explain. [*Saint Alphonsus Medical Center-Nampa, Inc. v. St. Luke's Health System, Ltd.*, 778 F.3d 775 (9th Cir. 2015)] (See *The Clayton Act.*)

27–7. Section 1 of the Sherman Act. Manitou North America, Inc., makes and distributes telehandlers (forklifts with extendable telescopic booms) to dealers throughout the United States. Manitou agreed to make McCormick International, LLC, its exclusive dealer in the state of Michigan. Later, Manitou entered into an agreement with Gehi Company, which also makes and sells telehandlers. The companies agreed to allocate territories within Michigan among certain dealers for each manufacturer, limiting the dealers' selection of competitive products to certain models. Under this agreement, McCormick was precluded from buying or selling Gehi telehandlers. What type of trade restraint did the agreement between Manitou and Gehi represent? Is this a violation of antitrust law? If so, who was injured, and how were they injured? Explain. [*Manitou North America, Inc. v. McCormick International, LLC*, 2016 WL 439354 (Mich.Ct.App. 2016)] (See *Section 1 of the Sherman Act.*)

27–8. Tying Arrangements. PRC-Desoto International, Inc., makes and distributes more than 90 percent of the aerospace sealant used in military and commercial aircraft. Packaging Systems, Inc., buys the sealant in wholesale quantities, repackages it into special injection kits, and sells the kits on the retail market to aircraft maintenance companies. PRC-Desoto bought one of the two main manufacturing companies of injection kits and announced a new policy to prohibit the repackaging of its sealant for resale. Packaging Systems was forced to buy both the sealant and the kits from PRC-Desoto. Due to the anti-repackaging constraint, the reseller could no longer meet its buyers' needs for pre-filled injection kits. Does this policy represent an unlawful tying arrangement? Explain. [*Packaging Systems, Inc. v. PRC-Desoto International, Inc.*, 2018 WL 735978 (C.D.Cal. 2018)] (See *The Clayton Act.*)

27–9. A Question of Ethics—The IDDR Approach and Section 2 of the Sherman Act. *Apple, Inc., controls which apps can run on its iPhone software. Apple's App Store is a website where iPhone users can find, buy, and download the apps. Apple prohibits third-party developers from selling iPhone apps through channels other than the App Store, threatening to cut off sales by any developer who violates this prohibition. Apple also discourages iPhone owners from downloading unapproved apps, threatening to void iPhone warranties if they do. Seven iPhone app buyers filed a complaint in a federal district court against Apple.*

The plaintiffs alleged that the firm monopolized the market for iPhone apps. [In re Apple iPhone Antitrust Litigation, 846 F.3d 313 (9th Cir. 2017)] (See Section 2 of the Sherman Act.)

(a) Using the *Decision* step of the IDDR approach, provide reasons why Apple might attempt to protect iPhone software by setting narrow boundaries on the sales of related apps and aggressively enforcing them.

(b) Explain why Apple's actions in this case might be considered unethical.

Time-Limited Group Assignment

27–10. Antitrust Violations. Residents of the city of Madison, Wisconsin, became concerned about overconsumption of liquor near the campus of the University of Wisconsin (UW). The city initiated a new policy, imposing conditions on area bars to discourage reduced-price "specials" that were believed to encourage high-volume and dangerous drinking. Later, the city began to draft an ordinance to ban all drink specials. Bar owners responded by announcing that they had "voluntarily" agreed to discontinue drink specials on Friday and Saturday nights after 8:00 P.M. The city put its ordinance on hold. Several UW students

filed a lawsuit against the local bar owners' association, alleging violations of antitrust law. (See *Section 1 of the Sherman Act.*)

(a) The first group will identify the grounds on which the plaintiffs might base their claim for relief and formulate an argument on behalf of the plaintiffs.

(b) The second group will determine whether the defendants are exempt from the antitrust laws.

(c) The third group will decide how the court should rule in this dispute and provide reasons for the ruling.

Chapter 28

Investor Protection and Corporate Governance

After the stock market crash of October 29, 1929, and the ensuing economic depression, Congress enacted legislation to regulate securities markets. The result was the Securities Act of 1933[1] and the Securities Exchange Act of 1934.[2] Both acts were designed to provide investors with more information to help them make buying and selling decisions about securities and to prohibit deceptive, unfair, and manipulative practices. *Securities* generally include any instruments evidencing corporate ownership (stock) or debt (bonds).

Today, the sale and transfer of securities are heavily regulated by federal and state statutes and by government agencies. The Securities and Exchange Commission (SEC) is the main independent regulatory agency that administers the 1933 and 1934 securities acts. The SEC also plays a key role in interpreting the provisions of these acts (and their amendments) and in creating regulations governing the purchase and sale of securities. The agency continually updates regulations in response to legislation, such as the Dodd-Frank Wall Street Reform and Consumer Protection Act[3] and the Economic Growth, Regulatory Relief, and Consumer Protection Act.[4]

1. 15 U.S.C. Sections 77a-77aa.
2. 15 U.S.C. Sections 78a *et seq.*
3. Pub. L. No. 111-203, 124 Stat. 1376 (2010), codified at 12 U.S.C. Sections 5301 *et seq.*
4. Pub. L. No. 115-174, 132 Stat. 1296 (2018).

28–1 The Securities Act of 1933

The Securities Act of 1933 governs initial sales of stock by businesses. The act was designed to prohibit various forms of fraud and to stabilize the securities industry by requiring that investors receive financial and other significant information concerning the securities being offered for public sale. Basically, the purpose of this act is to require disclosure. The 1933 act provides that all securities transactions must be registered with the SEC unless they are specifically exempt from the registration requirements.

28–1a What Is a Security?

Section 2(1) of the Securities Act contains a broad definition of **securities,** which generally include the following:[5]

1. Instruments and interests commonly known as securities, such as preferred and common stocks, bonds, debentures, and stock warrants.

2. Interests commonly known as securities, such as stock options, puts, and calls, that involve the right to purchase a security or a group of securities on a national security exchange.

3. Notes, instruments, or other evidence of indebtedness, including certificates of interest in a profit-sharing agreement and certificates of deposit.

4. Any fractional undivided interest in oil, gas, or other mineral rights.

5. Investment contracts, which include interests in limited partnerships and other investment schemes.

The *Howey* Test In interpreting the act, the United States Supreme Court has held that an **investment contract** is any transaction in which a person (1) invests (2) in a common enterprise (3) reasonably expecting profits (4) derived *primarily* or *substantially* from others' managerial or entrepreneurial efforts. Known as the *Howey* test, this definition continues to guide the determination of what types of contracts can be considered securities.[6]

5. 15 U.S.C. Section 77b(1).

6. *Securities and Exchange Commission v. W. J. Howey Co.*, 328 U.S. 293, 66 S.Ct. 1100, 90 L.Ed. 1244 (1946).

■ **Case in Point 28.1** James Nistler and his wife bought undeveloped land in Jackson County, Oregon, and created an LLC to develop it. The property, called Tennessee Acres, was divided into six lots. Nistler obtained investors for the development by telling them that they would earn 12 to 15 percent interest on their investment and be repaid in full within a specified time. The property was never developed, the investors were never paid, and a substantial part of the funds provided by the investors were used to pay Nistler and his wife.

Nistler was convicted of securities fraud. He appealed, claiming that the investments at issue did not involve "securities," but a state appellate court affirmed his conviction. The court found that there had been a pooling of funds from a group of investors whose interests had been secured by the same land. The value of that land had been highly dependent on Nistler's use of the investors' funds to develop the land. In other words, the investors had engaged in a common enterprise from which they reasonably expected to profit, and that profit would be derived from the development efforts of Nistler.[7] ■

Many Types of Securities For our purposes, it is convenient to think of securities in their most common form—stocks and bonds issued by corporations. Bear in mind, though, that securities can take many forms, including interests in whiskey, cosmetics, worms, beavers, boats, vacuum cleaners, muskrats, and cemetery lots. Almost any stake in the ownership or debt of a company can be considered a security. Investment contracts in condominiums, franchises, limited partnerships in real estate, and oil or gas or other mineral rights have qualified as securities.

28–1b Registration Statement

Section 5 of the Securities Act broadly provides that if a security does not qualify for an exemption, that security must be *registered* before it is offered to the public. Issuing corporations must file a *registration statement* with the SEC and must provide all investors with a *prospectus*.

A **prospectus** is a disclosure document that describes the security being sold, the financial operations of the issuing corporation, and the investment or risk attaching to the security. The prospectus also serves as a selling tool for the issuing corporation. The SEC allows an issuer to deliver its prospectus to investors electronically via the Internet.[8]

In principle, the registration statement and the prospectus supply sufficient information to enable unsophisticated investors to evaluate the financial risk involved.

Contents of the Registration Statement The registration statement must be written in plain English and fully describe the following:

1. The securities being offered for sale, including their relationship to the registrant's other securities.
2. The corporation's properties and business (including a financial statement certified by an independent public accounting firm).
3. The management of the corporation, including managerial compensation, stock options, pensions, and other benefits. (See this chapter's *Managerial Strategy* feature for a discussion of an SEC rule that imposes additional requirements on the disclosure of management compensation.) Any interests of directors or officers in any material transactions with the corporation must also be disclosed.
4. How the corporation intends to use the proceeds of the sale.
5. Any pending lawsuits or special risk factors.

All companies, both domestic and foreign, must file their registration statements electronically so that they can be posted on the SEC's online EDGAR (Electronic Data Gathering, Analysis, and Retrieval) database. Investors can then access the statements via the Internet. The EDGAR database includes material on initial public offerings (IPOs), proxy statements (concerning voting authority), annual reports, registration statements, and other documents that have been filed with the SEC.

Registration Process The registration statement does not become effective until it has been reviewed and approved by the SEC (unless it is filed by a *well-known seasoned issuer*, as discussed shortly). The 1933 act restricts the types of activities that an issuer can engage in at each stage of the registration process. If an issuer violates these restrictions, investors can rescind their contracts to purchase the securities.

Prefiling Period. During the *prefiling period* (before the registration statement is filed), the issuer normally cannot sell or offer to sell the securities. Once the registration statement has been filed, a waiting period begins while the SEC reviews the registration statement for completeness.[9]

---

7. *State of Oregon v. Nistler*, 268 Or.App. 470, 342 P.3d 1035 (2015).
8. Basically, an electronic prospectus must meet the same requirements as a printed prospectus. The SEC rules address situations in which the graphics, images, or audio files in or accompanying a printed prospectus cannot be reproduced in an electronic form. 17 C.F.R. Section 232.304.

9. The waiting period must last at least twenty days but nearly always extends much longer because the SEC inevitably requires numerous changes and additions to the registration statement.

Managerial Strategy

The SEC's Pay-Ratio Disclosure Rule

Congress passed the Dodd-Frank Wall Street Reform and Consumer Protection Act in 2010 following a worldwide financial crisis.[a] One of the goals of the act was to improve accountability and transparency in the financial system. A brief section in the lengthy bill requires a publicly held company to disclose the ratio of the total compensation of its chief executive officer (CEO) to the median compensation of its workers. For instance, if the annual pay of the median employee is $45,790 and the total compensation of the CEO is $12,260,000, then the pay ratio is 1 to 268. Otherwise stated, the CEO makes 268 times more than the median income for employees.

Five Years in the Making

For five years, the Securities and Exchange Commission (SEC) hesitated to adopt a disclosure rule as mandated by the Dodd-Frank act. The SEC received almost 300,000 comments and issued its own comments on the proposed rule.[b] The commissioners also indicated that they were unsure what potential economic benefits, "if any," would be realized from making this information public. The SEC estimated that the pay-ratio disclosure rule would cause companies to perform almost 550,000 hours in annual paperwork, plus cost them roughly $75 million per year to hire outside professionals.

---

a. Pub. L. No. 111-203, 124 Stat. 1376 (2010), codified at 12 U.S.C. Sections 5301 *et seq.*
b. 2013 WL 6503197 (2013, S.E.C. Release Nos. 33-9452 and 34-70443). See also https://www.sec.gov/news/statement/additional-dissenting-statement-on-pay-ratio-disclosure.html.

Dealing with the Rule

The final rule was 1,800 words long, and managers initially may find it difficult to implement. Fortunately for them, the SEC realizes that it can only ask for "reasonable estimates" of the CEO-worker pay ratio.

The CEO's measured compensation includes salary, bonuses, stocks and options, incentive plans, and other financial rewards. In theory, calculating this amount is fairly straightforward.

Calculating the median income of the company's labor force is more difficult. Note that the median income is not the average income of employees. Rather, the rule requires the company to identify a "median" employee as the basis for comparison.

The rule does give companies flexibility in determining how to identify this median employee. Statistical sampling can be used, for instance. And the rule states, "Since identifying the median involves finding the employee in the middle, it may not be necessary to determine the exact compensation amounts for every employee paid more or less than that employee in the middle." The rule also permits companies to make the median employee determination only once every three years.

Business Questions

1. *Why might the SEC pay-ratio disclosure rule cause certain businesses to eliminate low-wage workers?*
2. *How might the SEC pay-ratio disclosure rule help shareholders?*

Waiting Period. During the waiting period, the securities can be offered for sale but cannot be sold by the issuing corporation. Only certain types of offers are allowed at this time. All issuers can distribute a *preliminary prospectus*,[10] which contains most of the information that will be included in the final prospectus but often does not include a price.

Most issuers can distribute a *free-writing prospectus* during this period (although some inexperienced issuers will need to file a preliminary prospectus first).[11] A **free-writing prospectus** is any type of written, electronic, or graphic offer that describes the issuer or its securities and includes a legend indicating that the investor may obtain the prospectus at the SEC's website.

---

10. A preliminary prospectus may also be called a *red herring prospectus*. The name comes from the legend printed in red across the prospectus stating that the registration has been filed but has not become effective.
11. See SEC Rules 164 and 433.

Posteffective Period. Once the SEC has reviewed and approved the registration statement and the waiting period is over, the registration is effective, and the *posteffective period* begins. The issuer can now offer and sell the securities without restrictions.

If the company issued a preliminary or free-writing prospectus to investors, it must provide those investors with a final prospectus either before or at the time they purchase the securities. The issuer can make the final prospectus available to investors to download from a website if it notifies them of the appropriate Internet address.

28–1c Well-Known Seasoned Issuers

A *well-known seasoned issuer* (WKSI) is a firm that has issued at least $1 billion in securities in the last three years or has outstanding stock valued at $700 million or more in the hands of the public. WKSIs have greater flexibility than other issuers. They can file registration statements the day they announce a new offering and are not required to wait for SEC review and approval. They can also use a free-writing prospectus at any time, even during the prefiling period.

28–1d Exempt Securities

Certain types of securities are exempt from the registration requirements of the Securities Act because they are low-risk investments or are regulated by other statutes.[12] Exempt securities maintain their exempt status forever and can also be resold without being registered. Exempt securities include the following:

- Government-issued securities.
- Bank and financial institution securities.
- Short-term notes and drafts (negotiable instruments that have a maturity date that does not extend beyond nine months).
- Securities of nonprofit, educational, and charitable organizations.
- Securities issued by common carriers (railroads and trucking companies).
- Insurance policies, endowments, and annuity contracts.
- Securities issued in a corporate reorganization in which one security is exchanged for another or in a bankruptcy proceeding.
- Securities issued in stock dividends and stock splits.

28–1e Exempt Transactions

The Securities Act also exempts certain transactions from registration requirements (see Exhibit 28–1 for a summary of these exemptions). The transaction exemptions are very broad and can enable an issuer to avoid the high cost and complicated procedures associated with registration. For instance, private (nonpublic) offerings that involve a small number of investors generally are exempt. Securities offered and sold only to residents of the state in which the issuing firm is incorporated and does business are also exempt. In addition, crowdfunding is allowed without SEC registration, as discussed in this chapter's *Digital Update* feature.

Note, however, that even when a transaction is exempt from registration requirements, the offering is still subject to the antifraud provisions of the 1933 act (and the 1934 act).

Exhibit 28–1 Exempt Transactions under the 1933 Securities Act

Exempt Transactions

Regulation A

Securities issued by an issuer that has offered less than $50 million in securities during any twelve-month period if the issuer meets specific requirements:

- Tier 1—For offerings of up to $20 million in a twelve-month period. (Unlimited number of investors, both accredited and unaccredited.)

- Tier 2—For offerings of up to $50 million with additional review requirements in a twelve-month period. (Unlimited number of investors, but unaccredited investors may not invest more than 10 percent of their annual income or net worth.)

Regulation D

- **Rule 504:** Noninvestment company offerings up to $5 million in any twelve-month period.

- **Rule 506:** Private noninvestment company offerings in unlimited amounts that are not generally advertised or solicited. (Unlimited number of accredited investors and thirty-five unaccredited investors.)

- **Rule 147:** Offerings restricted to residents of the state in which the issuing company is organized and doing business.

Unregistered Restricted Securities

Restricted securities must be registered before a resale *unless* they qualify for a safe harbor under Rule 144 or 144A.

Regulation A Offerings An exemption from registration is available for an issuer's security offerings that do not exceed a specified amount during any twelve-month period.[13] Under Regulation A,[14] the issuer must file with

---

12. Securities Offering Reform, codified at 17 C.F.R. Parts 200, 228, 229, 230, 239, 240, 243, 249, and 274.

13. 15 U.S.C. Section 77c(b).
14. 17 C.F.R. Sections 230.251–230.263.

Digital Update

Investment Crowdfunding—Regulations and Restrictions

Small entrepreneurs today can gain access to public funds through crowdfunding without filing a registration statement with the Securities and Exchange Commission (SEC). Generally, crowdfunding refers to raising small sums of money from a large number of individuals via the Internet. Crowdfunding as a way for businesses to raise equity capital was made possible by the Jumpstart Our Business Startups Act, or JOBS Act—specifically, by Title III of the statute, also known as the "Crowdfund Act."[a]

Restrictions on Those Who Invest

The Crowdfund Act imposes certain restrictions on investors. The aggregate amount sold to any investor cannot exceed the greater of $2,000 or 5 percent of the investor's annual income or net worth if that net worth is less than $100,000. For investors with higher incomes or net worth, the limit is 10 percent.

Other Restrictions

Companies seeking investment funds through crowdfunding cannot offer shares directly to investors. They must go through an online fundraising platform registered with the SEC. Some companies that provide such platforms, such as Venture.com, take an active role in the crowdfunding process, drafting paperwork and soliciting investors. Others, such as NextSeed and StartEngine, take a more hands-off approach. An increasing number of approved crowdfunding portals are available. They usually impose a fee of 5 to 9 percent of the funds raised.

---

a. 17 C.F.R. Parts 200, 227, 232, 239, 240, and 249.

Of course, a potential start-up entrepreneur does not simply create a video and ask people to send money via the Internet. Paperwork must be filed prior to the start of a crowdfunding campaign, and detailed financial statements must be available for potential investors. Indiegogo, Inc., an international crowdfunding website, has estimated that companies spend at least $7,000 on compliance and other regulatory matters before starting a crowdfunding campaign.

The Success Rate

Investors who provide funds to crowdfunded start-ups naturally expect a return on their investment. Consider, though, that half of all new companies are not in business five years after start-up. Consider further that many companies offering investment opportunities via crowdfunding have already been rejected by professional investors. Otherwise stated, these investors did not believe that the companies' products, services, or management warranted investment.

Thus, the fact that you have shares in a company because you invested in its crowdfunding campaign does not mean that you can do much with them. Those shares are not publicly traded. It may be difficult, if not impossible, to cash out the shares unless the new firm is acquired by a larger company or goes public through an initial public offering.

Critical Thinking *What alternatives are there to crowdfunding for a start-up business?*

---

the SEC a notice of the issue and an offering circular, which must also be provided to investors before the sale. Regulation A provides a much less expensive process than the procedures associated with full registration.

There are two types of public offerings under this regulation:

- Tier 1—For securities offerings of up to $20 million in a twelve-month period.
- Tier 2—For securities offerings of up to $50 million in a twelve-month period.

An issuer of $20 million or less of securities can elect to proceed under either Tier 1 or Tier 2. Both tiers are subject to certain basic requirements, and Tier 2 offerings are subject to additional requirements. Purchasers under Tier 2 who are not *accredited investors* cannot purchase shares that cost more than 10 percent of their annual income

or net worth. (An **accredited investor** is a sophisticated investor, such as a bank, an insurance company, or a person whose income or net worth exceeds a certain amount.)

Changes Made by Regulation A+. The cap for Regulation A was originally $5 million. In 2015, the SEC adopted final rules (Regulation A+, or Reg A+) to increase the amount to $50 million and make it easier for small and mid-sized businesses to raise capital. These changes were made in connection with the Jumpstart Our Business Startups, or JOBS Act.[15] Expanding the issuers that qualify for exemption under Regulation A has decreased the significance of the other exemptions listed in Exhibit 28–1. In addition, Reg A+ has allowed for an increase in online crowdfunding.

---

15. Pub. L. No. 112-106, 126 Stat. 306 (2012).

■ **Example 28.2** Myomo, Inc., is a company based in Massachusetts that makes robotic medical devices for people with upper-body paralysis. The company relied on venture capital funding for a number of years but decided to take advantage of the amended Regulation A when it became available. Seeking to raise $15 million, Myomo became the first company to issue an initial public offering under Regulation A+. ■

Testing the Waters. Before preparing a Regulation A offering circular, companies are allowed to "test the waters" for potential interest. To *test the waters* means to determine potential interest without actually selling any securities or requiring any commitment from those who express interest.

Small Offerings—Regulation D The SEC's Regulation D contains several exemptions from registration requirements (Rules 504 and 506) for offers that either involve a small dollar amount or are made in a limited manner.

Rule 504. Rule 504 is an exemption used by many small businesses. It provides that noninvestment company offerings up to $5 million in any twelve-month period are exempt.[16] Noninvestment companies are firms that are not engaged primarily in the business of investing or trading in securities. (In contrast, an **investment company** is a firm that buys a large portfolio of securities and professionally manages it on behalf of many smaller shareholders/owners. A **mutual fund** is a well-known type of investment company.)

■ **Example 28.3** Zeta Enterprises is a limited partnership that develops commercial property. Zeta intends to offer $600,000 of its limited partnership interests for sale between June 1 and next May 31. The buyers will become limited partners in Zeta. Because an interest in a limited partnership meets the definition of a security (discussed earlier), this offering would be subject to the registration and prospectus requirements of the Securities Act of 1933.

Under Rule 504, however, the sales of Zeta's interests are exempt from these requirements because Zeta is a noninvestment company making an offering of less than $5 million in a given twelve-month period. Therefore, Zeta can sell its interests without filing a registration statement with the SEC or issuing a prospectus to any investor. ■

Rule 506—Private Placement Exemption. Rule 506 exempts private, noninvestment company offerings that are not generally solicited or advertised. This exemption is often referred to as the *private placement exemption* because it exempts "transactions not involving any public offering."[17] There are no limits on the amounts offered. In addition, there can be an unlimited number of accredited investors and up to thirty-five unaccredited investors. To qualify for the exemption, the issuer must believe that each unaccredited investor has sufficient knowledge or experience in financial matters to be capable of evaluating the investment's merits and risks.[18]

The private placement exemption has been an important exemption for firms that want to raise funds through the sale of securities without registering them. ■ **Example 28.4** Citco Corporation needs to raise capital to expand its operations. Citco decides to make a private $10 million offering of its common stock directly to two hundred accredited investors and a group of thirty highly sophisticated, but unaccredited, investors. Citco provides all of these investors with a prospectus and material information about the firm, including its most recent financial statements.

As long as Citco notifies the SEC of the sale, this offering will likely qualify as an exempt transaction under Rule 506. The offering is nonpublic and generally not advertised. There are fewer than thirty-five unaccredited investors, and each of them possesses sufficient knowledge and experience to evaluate the risks involved. The issuer has provided all purchasers with the material information. Thus, Citco likely will *not* be required to comply with the registration requirements of the Securities Act of 1933. ■

Intrastate Offerings—Rule 147 Also exempt are intrastate transactions involving purely local offerings.[19] This exemption applies to most offerings that are restricted to residents of the state in which the issuing company is organized and doing business. For nine months after the last sale, virtually no resales may be made to nonresidents, and precautions must be taken against this possibility. These offerings remain subject to applicable laws in the state of issue.

Resales and Safe Harbor Rules Most securities can be resold without registration. The Securities Act provides exemptions for resales by most persons other

---

16. 17 C.F.R. Section 230.504. Small businesses in California may also be exempt under 17 C.F.R. Section 230.1001 and Cal. Corporations Code Section 25102(n).1001. California's rule permits limited offerings of up to $5 million *per transaction*, if they satisfy certain conditions.

17. 15 U.S.C. Section 77d.
18. 17 C.F.R. Section 230.506.
19. 15 U.S.C. Section 77c(a)(11); 17 C.F.R. Section 230.147.

than issuers or underwriters. The average investor who sells shares of stock need not file a registration statement with the SEC.

Resales of restricted securities acquired under Rule 506, however, trigger the registration requirements *unless the party selling them complies with Rule 144 or Rule 144A.* These rules are sometimes referred to as safe harbors.

Rule 144. Rule 144 exempts restricted securities from registration on resale if all of the following conditions are met:

1. There is adequate current public information about the issuer. ("Adequate current public information" refers to the reports that certain companies are required to file under the 1934 Securities Exchange Act.)
2. The person selling the securities has owned them for at least six months if the issuer is subject to the reporting requirements of the 1934 act. If the issuer is not subject to the 1934 act's reporting requirements, the seller must have owned the securities for at least one year.
3. The securities are sold in certain limited amounts in unsolicited brokers' transactions.
4. The SEC is notified of the resale.[20]

---

20. 17 C.F.R. Section 230.144.

Rule 144A. Securities that at the time of issue were not of the same class as securities listed on a national securities exchange or quoted in a U.S. automated interdealer quotation system may be resold under Rule 144A.[21] They may be sold only to a qualified institutional buyer (an institution, such as an insurance company or a bank, that owns and invests at least $100 million in securities). The seller must take reasonable steps to ensure that the buyer knows that the seller is relying on the exemption under Rule 144A.

28–1f Violations of the 1933 Act

It is a violation of the Securities Act to intentionally defraud investors by misrepresenting or omitting facts in a registration statement or prospectus. Liability may also be imposed on those who are negligent with respect to the preparation of these publications. Selling securities before the effective date of the registration statement or under an exemption for which the securities do not qualify also results in liability.

Can the omission of a material fact make a statement of opinion misleading to an ordinary investor? That was the question before the United States Supreme Court in the following case.

---

21. 17 C.F.R. Section 230.144A.

Case 28.1

Omnicare, Inc. v. Laborers District Council Construction Industry Pension Fund

Supreme Court of the United States__ U.S. __, 135 S.Ct. 1318, 191 L.Ed.2d 253 (2015).

Background and Facts Omnicare, Inc., a pharmacy services company, filed a registration statement in connection with a public offering. The statement expressed the company's opinion that it was in compliance with federal and state laws. Later, the federal government accused Omnicare of receiving kickbacks from pharmaceutical manufacturers. Some purchasers of the stock, including Laborers District Council Construction Industry Pension Fund, filed a suit in a federal district court against Omnicare.

The plaintiffs alleged that Omnicare's legal-compliance opinion was "untrue" and that Omnicare had, in violation of the Securities Act, "omitted to state [material] facts necessary" to make that opinion not misleading. Omnicare argued that "no reasonable person, in any context, can understand a pure statement of opinion to convey anything more than the speaker's own mindset." The district court dismissed the pension funds' suit, but the U.S. Court of Appeals for the Sixth Circuit reversed the dismissal. Omnicare appealed to the United States Supreme Court.

In the Language of the Court
Justice *KAGAN* delivered the opinion of the Court.
    * * * *
    * * * Whether a statement is "misleading" depends on the perspective of a reasonable investor: The inquiry * * * is objective.

* * * *

* * * A reasonable person understands, and takes into account, the difference * * * between a statement of fact and one of opinion. She recognizes the import of words like "I think" or "I believe," and grasps that they convey some lack of certainty as to the statement's content.

But Omnicare takes its point too far, because a reasonable investor may, depending on the circumstances, understand an opinion statement to convey facts about how the speaker has formed the opinion—or, otherwise put, about the speaker's basis for holding that view. And if the real facts are otherwise, but not provided, the opinion statement will mislead its audience. Consider an unadorned statement of opinion about legal compliance: "We believe our conduct is lawful." * * * If the issuer made the statement in the face of its lawyers' contrary advice, or with knowledge that the Federal Government was taking the opposite view, the investor * * * has cause to complain: He expects not just that the issuer believes the opinion (however irrationally), but that it fairly aligns with the information in the issuer's possession at the time. Thus, *if a registration statement omits material facts about the issuer's inquiry into or knowledge concerning a statement of opinion, and if those facts conflict with what a reasonable investor would take from the statement itself, then [the Securities Act] creates liability.* [Emphasis added.]

An opinion statement, however, is not necessarily misleading when an issuer knows, but fails to disclose, some fact cutting the other way. * * * A reasonable investor does not expect that *every* fact known to an issuer supports its opinion statement. [Emphasis in the original.]

Moreover, *whether an omission makes an expression of opinion misleading always depends on context.* Registration statements as a class are formal documents, filed with the SEC as a legal prerequisite for selling securities to the public. Investors do not, and are right not to, expect opinions contained in those statements to reflect baseless, off-the-cuff judgments, of the kind that an individual might communicate in daily life. At the same time, an investor reads each statement within such a document, whether of fact or opinion, in light of all its surrounding text, including hedges, disclaimers, and apparently conflicting information. And the investor takes into account the customs and practices of the relevant industry. * * * The reasonable investor understands a statement of opinion in its full context, and [the Securities Act] creates liability only for the omission of material facts that cannot be squared with such a fair reading. [Emphasis added.]

Decision and Remedy *The United States Supreme Court concluded that "neither [of the lower courts] considered the Funds' omissions theory with the right standard in mind." The Court therefore vacated the decision of the appellate court and remanded the case "for a determination of whether the Funds have stated a viable omissions claim (or, if not, whether they should have a chance to replead)."*

Critical Thinking
- **Legal Environment** *Would a reasonable investor have cause to complain if an issuer, without having consulted a lawyer, states, "We believe our conduct is lawful"? Explain.*

Remedies Criminal violations of the 1933 act are prosecuted by the U.S. Department of Justice. Violators may be fined up to $10,000, imprisoned for up to five years, or both.

The SEC is authorized to impose civil sanctions against those who willfully violate the act. It can request an injunction to prevent further sales of the securities involved or ask a court to grant other relief, such as ordering a violator to refund profits. Private parties who purchase securities and suffer harm as a result of false or omitted statements or other violations may bring a suit in a federal court to recover their losses and additional damages.

Defenses There are three basic defenses to charges of violations under the 1933 act. A defendant can avoid liability by proving any of the following:

1. The statement or omission was not material.
2. The plaintiff knew about the misrepresentation at the time the stock was purchased.
3. The defendant exercised *due diligence* in preparing or reviewing the registration and reasonably believed at the time that the statements were true. This important defense is available to an underwriter or subsequent seller but not to the issuer.

■ **Case in Point 28.5** In preparation for an initial public offering (IPO), Blackstone Group, LP, filed a registration statement with the SEC. At the time, Blackstone's corporate private equity investments included FGIC Corporation (which insured investments in subprime mortgages) and Freescale Semiconductor, Inc. Before the IPO, FGIC's customers began to suffer large losses, and Freescale lost an exclusive contract to make wireless 3G chipsets for Motorola, Inc. (its largest customer). The losses suffered by these two companies would affect Blackstone. Nevertheless, Blackstone's registration statement did not mention the impact on its revenues of the investments in FGIC and Freescale.

Martin Litwin and others who had invested in Blackstone's IPO filed a suit in a federal district court against Blackstone and its officers, alleging material omissions from the statement. Blackstone argued as a defense that the omissions were not material, and the lower court dismissed the case. The plaintiffs appealed. A federal appellate court ruled that the alleged omissions were reasonably likely to be material and remanded the case. The plaintiffs were entitled to the opportunity to prove at a trial that Blackstone had omitted material information that it was required to disclose.[22] ■

28–2 The Securities Exchange Act of 1934

The 1934 Securities Exchange Act provides for the regulation and registration of securities exchanges, brokers, dealers, and national securities associations, such as the National Association of Securities Dealers (NASD). Unlike the 1933 act, which is a one-time disclosure law, the 1934 act provides for continuous periodic disclosures by publicly held corporations to enable the SEC to regulate subsequent trading.

The Securities Exchange Act applies to companies that have assets in excess of $10 million and five hundred or more shareholders. These corporations are referred to as *Section 12 companies* because they are required to register their securities under Section 12 of the 1934 act. Section 12 companies must file reports with the SEC annually and quarterly, and sometimes even monthly if specified events occur (such as a merger).

The act also authorizes the SEC to engage in market surveillance to deter undesirable market practices such as fraud, market manipulation, and misrepresentation. In addition, the act provides for the SEC's regulation of proxy solicitations for voting.

28–2a Section 10(b), SEC Rule 10b-5, and Insider Trading

Section 10(b) is one of the more important sections of the Securities Exchange Act. This section prohibits the use of any manipulative or deceptive mechanism in violation of SEC rules and regulations. Among the rules that the SEC has promulgated pursuant to the 1934 act is **SEC Rule 10b-5,** which prohibits the commission of fraud in connection with the purchase or sale of any security.

SEC Rule 10b-5 applies to almost all cases concerning the trading of securities, whether on organized exchanges, in over-the-counter markets, or in private transactions. Generally, the rule covers just about any form of security. The securities need not be registered under the 1933 act for the 1934 act to apply.

Private parties can sue for securities fraud under Rule 10b-5. The basic elements of a securities fraud action are as follows:

1. A *material misrepresentation* (or omission) in connection with the purchase and sale of securities.
2. *Scienter* (a wrongful state of mind).
3. *Reliance* by the plaintiff on the material misrepresentation.
4. An *economic loss.*
5. *Causation,* meaning that there is a causal connection between the misrepresentation and the loss.

Insider Trading One of the major goals of Section 10(b) and SEC Rule 10b-5 is to prevent **insider trading,** which occurs when persons buy or sell securities on the basis of information that is not available to the public. Corporate directors, officers, and majority shareholders, among others, often have advance inside information that can affect the future market value of the corporate stock. Obviously, if they act on this information, their positions give them a trading advantage over the general public and other shareholders.

The 1934 act defines inside information. It also extends liability to those who take advantage of such information in their personal transactions when they know that the information is unavailable to those with whom they are dealing. Section 10(b) of the 1934 act and SEC Rule 10b-5 apply to anyone who has access to

---

22. *Litwin v. Blackstone Group, LP,* 634 F.3d 706 (2d Cir. 2011).

or receives information of a nonpublic nature on which trading is based—not just to corporate "insiders."

Disclosure under SEC Rule 10b-5

Any material omission or misrepresentation of material facts in connection with the purchase or sale of a security may violate Section 10(b) of the 1934 act and SEC Rule 10b-5. The key to liability (which can be civil or criminal) is whether the information omitted or misrepresented is *material*.

The following are some examples of material facts calling for disclosure under SEC Rule 10b-5:

1. Fraudulent trading in the company stock by a broker-dealer.
2. A dividend change (whether up or down).
3. A contract for the sale of corporate assets.
4. A new discovery, a new process, or a new product.
5. A significant change in the firm's financial condition.
6. Potential litigation against the company.

Note that any one of these facts, by itself, is not automatically considered material. It will be regarded as a material fact only if it is significant enough that it would likely affect an investor's decision as to whether to purchase or sell the company's securities.

■ **Example 28.6**   Zilotek, Inc., is the defendant in a class-action product liability suit that its attorney, Paula Frasier, believes the company will lose. Frasier has advised Zilotek's directors, officers, and accountants that the company will likely have to pay a substantial damages award. Zilotek plans to make a $5 million offering of newly issued stock before the date when the trial is expected to end. Zilotek's potential liability and the financial consequences to the firm are material facts that must be disclosed, because they are significant enough to affect an investor's decision to purchase the stock. ■

The decision that follows is from a *Classic Case* interpreting materiality under SEC Rule 10b-5.

Classic Case 28.2

SEC v. Texas Gulf Sulphur Co.
United States Court of Appeals, Second Circuit, 401 F.2d 833 (1968).

Background and Facts   Texas Gulf Sulphur Company (TGS) conducted aerial geophysical surveys over more than 15,000 square miles of eastern Canada. The operations indicated concentrations of commercially exploitable minerals. At one site near Timmins, Ontario, TGS drilled a hole that appeared to yield a core with an exceedingly high mineral content. The company did not disclose the results of the core sample to the public.

After learning of the sample, TGS officers and employees made substantial purchases of TGS's stock or accepted stock options (rights to purchase stock). On April 11, 1964, an unauthorized report of the mineral find appeared in the newspapers. On the following day, TGS issued a press release that played down the discovery and stated that it was too early to tell whether the ore find would be significant.

Several months later, TGS announced that the strike was expected to yield at least 25 million tons of ore. Subsequently, the price of TGS stock rose substantially. The Securities and Exchange Commission (SEC) brought a suit against the officers and employees of TGS for violating SEC Rule 10b-5. The officers and employees argued that the information on which they had traded had not been material at the time of their trades because the mine had not then been commercially proved. The trial court held that most of the defendants had not violated SEC Rule 10b-5, and the SEC appealed.

In the Language of the Court
WATERMAN, Circuit Judge.
* * * *

* * * Whether facts are material within Rule 10b-5 when the facts relate to a particular event and are undisclosed by those persons who are knowledgeable thereof *will depend at any given time upon a balancing of both the indicated probability that the event will occur and the anticipated magnitude of the event in light of the totality of the company activity.* Here, * * * knowledge of the possibility, which surely was more than marginal, of the existence of a mine of the vast magnitude indicated by the remarkably rich drill core located rather close to the surface (suggesting mineability by the less expensive openpit method) within the confines of a large anomaly (suggesting an extensive region of mineralization) might well

Case 28.2 Continues

have affected the price of TGS stock and would certainly have been an important fact to a reasonable, if speculative, investor in deciding whether he should buy, sell, or hold. [Emphasis added.]

* * * *

* * * A major factor in determining whether the * * * discovery was a material fact is the importance attached to the drilling results by those who knew about it. * * * The timing by those who knew of it of their stock purchases * * *—purchases in some cases by individuals who had never before purchased * * * TGS stock—virtually compels the inference that the insiders were influenced by the drilling results.

Decision and Remedy *The appellate court ruled in favor of the SEC. All of the trading by insiders who knew of the mineral find before its true extent had been publicly announced had violated SEC Rule 10b-5.*

Critical Thinking

- **Impact of This Case on Today's Law** *This landmark case affirmed the principle that the test of whether information is "material," for SEC Rule 10b-5 purposes, is whether it would affect the judgment of reasonable investors. The corporate insiders' purchases of stock and stock options indicated that they were influenced by the drilling results and that the information about the drilling results was material. The courts continue to cite this case when applying SEC Rule 10b-5 to cases of alleged insider trading.*
- **What If the Facts Were Different?** *Suppose that further drilling had revealed that there was not enough ore at this site for it to be mined commercially. Would the defendants still have been liable for violating SEC Rule 10b-5? Why or why not?*

Outsiders and SEC Rule 10b-5 The traditional insider-trading case involves true insiders—corporate officers, directors, and majority shareholders who have access to (and trade on) inside information. Increasingly, however, liability under Section 10(b) of the 1934 act and SEC Rule 10b-5 has been extended to include certain "outsiders"—those who trade on inside information acquired indirectly. Two theories have been developed under which outsiders may be held liable for insider trading: the *tipper/tippee theory* and the *misappropriation theory.*

Tipper/Tippee Theory. Anyone who acquires inside information as a result of a corporate insider's breach of his or her fiduciary duty can be liable under SEC Rule 10b-5. This liability extends to **tippees** (those who receive "tips" from insiders) and even *remote tippees* (tippees of tippees).

The key to liability under this theory is that the inside information must have been obtained as a result of someone's breach of a fiduciary duty to the corporation whose shares were traded. The tippee is liable only if the following requirements are met:

1. There is a breach of a duty not to disclose inside information.
2. The disclosure is made in exchange for personal benefit.
3. The tippee knows (or should know) of this breach and benefits from it.

■ **Case in Point 28.7** Eric McPhail was a member of the same country club as an executive at American Superconductor. While they were golfing, the executive shared information with McPhail about the company's expected earnings, contracts, and other major developments, trusting that McPhail would keep the information confidential. Instead, McPhail tipped six of his other golfing buddies at the country club, and they all used the nonpublic information to their advantage in trading. In this situation, the executive breached his duty not to disclose the information, which McPhail knew. McPhail (the tippee) is liable under SEC Rule 10b-5, and so are his other golfing buddies (remote tippees). All of the tippees traded on inside information to their benefit.[23] ■

Misappropriation Theory. Liability for insider trading may also be established under the misappropriation theory. This theory holds liable an individual who wrongfully obtains (misappropriates) inside information and trades on it for her or his personal gain. Basically, this individual has stolen information rightfully belonging to another.

The misappropriation theory has been controversial because it significantly extends the reach of SEC Rule 10b-5 to outsiders who ordinarily would *not* be deemed fiduciaries of the corporations in whose stock they trade. It is not always wrong to disclose material, nonpublic information about a company to a person who would not otherwise be privy to it. Nevertheless, a person who obtains the information and trades securities on it can be held liable.

■ **Case in Point 28.8** Robert Bray, a real estate developer, first met Patrick O'Neill, an executive at Eastern

---

23. *United States v. McPhail*, 831 F.3d 1 (1st Cir. 2016). Three other defendants agreed to settle with the SEC and return the trading profits. See SEC press release 2014-134, "SEC Charges Group of Amateur Golfers in Insider Trading Ring."

Bank, at the Oakley Country Club, and the two men became good friends. One day, Bray told O'Neill that he needed cash to fund a project and asked O'Neill if he had any "bank stock tips" for him. O'Neill rattled off a few names of local banks. Then Bray wrote the word "Wainwright" on a napkin and slid it across the bar to O'Neill.

O'Neill, who knew that Eastern Bank was in the process of buying Wainwright Bank, told Bray, "This could be a good one." The next day, Bray bought 25,000 shares of Wainwright stock, and he bought another 31,000 shares a few weeks later. Eastern then publicly announced that it was buying Wainwright, and the stock price doubled. Bray eventually sold the stock at a profit of $300,000.

The SEC prosecuted Bray for insider trading using the misappropriation theory. He was convicted after a jury trial. On appeal, the conviction was affirmed. Bray and O'Neill had been good friends for years. The jury could reasonably have concluded that Bray not only knew that he had traded on material, nonpublic information, but also knew that O'Neill owed Eastern a duty of loyalty and confidentiality.[24] ■

Insider Reporting and Trading—Section 16(b)

Section 16(b) of the 1934 act provides for the recapture by the corporation of all profits realized by an insider on a

purchase and sale, or sale and purchase, of the corporation's stock within any six-month period.[25] It is irrelevant whether the insider actually uses inside information—all such **short-swing profits** must be returned to the corporation.

In the context of Section 16(b), insiders means officers, directors, and large stockholders of Section 12 corporations. (Large stockholders are those owning 10 percent of the class of equity securities registered under Section 12 of the 1934 act.) To discourage such insiders from using nonpublic information about their companies to their personal benefit in the stock market, the SEC requires them to file reports concerning their ownership and trading of the corporation's securities.

Section 16(b) applies not only to stock but also to warrants, options, and securities convertible into stock. In addition, the courts have fashioned complex rules for determining profits. Note, though, that the SEC exempts a number of transactions under Rule 16b-3.[26]

Exhibit 28–2 compares the effects of SEC Rule 10b-5 and Section 16(b). Because of the various ways in which

---

24. *United States v. Bray*, 853 F.3d 18 (1st Cir. 2017).

25. A person who expects the price of a particular stock to decline can realize profits by "selling short"—selling at a high price and repurchasing later at a lower price to cover the "short sale."

26. 17 C.F.R. Section 240.16b-3.

Exhibit 28–2 Comparison of Coverage, Application, and Liability under SEC Rule 10b-5 and Section 16(b)

Area of Comparison	SEC Rule 10b-5	Section 16(b)
What is the subject matter of the transaction?	Any security (does not have to be registered).	Any security (does not have to be registered).
What transactions are covered?	Purchase or sale.	Short-swing purchase and sale or short-swing sale and purchase.
Who is subject to liability?	Almost anyone with inside information under a duty not to disclose—including officers, directors, controlling shareholders, and tippees.	Officers, directors, and certain shareholders who own 10 percent or more.
Is omission or misrepresentation necessary for liability?	Yes.	No.
Are there any exempt transactions?	No.	Yes, there are a number of exemptions.
Who may bring an action?	A person transacting with an insider, the SEC, or a purchaser or seller damaged by a wrongful act.	A corporation or a shareholder by derivative action.

insiders can incur liability under these provisions, corporate insiders should seek the advice of competent counsel before trading in the corporation's stock.

The Private Securities Litigation Reform Act

The disclosure requirements of SEC Rule 10b-5 had the unintended effect of deterring the disclosure of forward-looking information, such as financial forecasts. To understand why, consider the following situation. ■ **Example 28.9** XT Company announces that its projected earnings for a future time period will be a certain amount, but its forecast turns out to be wrong. The earnings are, in fact, much lower, and the price of XT's stock is affected negatively. The shareholders bring a class-action suit against XT, alleging that its directors violated SEC Rule 10b-5 by disclosing misleading financial information. ■

In an attempt to solve the problem and promote full disclosure, Congress passed the Private Securities Litigation Reform Act (PSLRA).[27] The PSLRA provides a "safe harbor" for publicly held companies that make forward-looking statements. Those who make such statements are protected against liability for securities fraud if they include "meaningful cautionary statements identifying important factors that could cause actual results to differ materially from those in the forward-looking statement."[28]

The PSLRA also affects the level of detail required in securities fraud complaints. Plaintiffs must specify each misleading statement and say how it led them to a mistaken belief.

28–2b Regulation of Proxy Statements

Section 14(a) of the Securities Exchange Act regulates the solicitation of proxies from shareholders of Section 12 companies. The SEC regulates the content of proxy statements. Whoever solicits a proxy must fully and accurately disclose in the proxy statement all of the facts that are pertinent to the matter on which the shareholders are to vote. SEC Rule 14a-9 is similar to the antifraud provisions of SEC Rule 10b-5. Remedies for violations range from injunctions to prevent a vote from being taken to monetary damages.

28–2c Violations of the 1934 Act

As mentioned earlier, violations of Section 10(b) of the Securities Exchange Act and SEC Rule 10b-5, including insider trading, may lead to both criminal and civil liability.

***Scienter* Requirement** For either criminal or civil sanctions to be imposed, *scienter* must exist—that is, the violator must have had an intent to defraud or knowledge of his or her misconduct. *Scienter* can be proved by showing that the defendant made false statements or wrongfully failed to disclose material facts. In some situations, it can even be proved by showing that the defendant was consciously reckless as to the truth or falsity of his or her statements.

■ **Case in Point 28.10** Etsy, Inc., a Brooklyn-based company, operates a website that connects buyers and sellers of handmade and vintage goods. When Etsy went public, it filed a prospectus and registration statement that set forth its commitment to working solely with "responsible, small-batch manufacturing partners" that adhere to Etsy's ethical expectations. Further, it described the company as "a mindful, transparent, and humane business." The statement also explained the company's methods for safeguarding against counterfeit goods and goods that infringe on another's copyright or trademark rights.

Saleh Altayyar and several other investors sued Etsy, alleging that it had misrepresented or omitted material facts in its registration statement. The plaintiffs claimed that Etsy had made false and misleading statements about its values and that nearly 5 percent of its goods were counterfeit or infringing. Etsy argued that it had exercised due diligence and reasonably believed that the statements were true and contained no omissions of material facts. A federal district court in New York ruled in Etsy's favor and dismissed the case. The court found that the plaintiffs had not established *scienter*. "The plaintiffs may disagree with the defendants' opinions [statements about the company], but disagreement does not render the opinions false."[29] ■

In a complaint alleging a violation, the plaintiff must state facts giving rise to an inference of *scienter*. The dispute in the following case was whether, as part of an allegation of securities fraud under Section 10(b) of the 1934 act, the plaintiffs adequately alleged required elements of the claim.

---

27. Pub. L. No. 104-67, 109 Stat. 737 (1995), codified in various sections of Title 15 of the *United States Code*.

28. 15 U.S.C. Sections 77z-2 and 78u-5.

29. *Altayyar v. Etsy, Inc.*, 242 F.Supp.3d 161 (E.D.N.Y. 2017).

Singer v. Reali

United States Court of Appeals, Fourth Circuit, 883 F.3d 425 (2018).

Background and Facts TranS1, Inc., a medical device company, sold the "System," a spinal surgical procedure. TranS1's financial success hinged on whether health insurers and government health-care programs would reimburse the claims of surgeons who used the System. When the American Medical Association designated the System to be "experimental," surgeons could no longer count on being reimbursed for its use. TranS1 then coached surgeons to file fraudulent claims that would allow for full reimbursement. The company's officers publicly stated that they were "assisting surgeons in obtaining appropriate reimbursement" but did not reveal the fraudulent scheme.

When TranS1 disclosed that the government was investigating the firm, the value of its stock dropped. Phillip Singer and other shareholders filed a suit in a federal district court against Kenneth Reali and other officers, alleging a violation of Section 10(b). The court dismissed the complaint. The plaintiffs appealed.

In the Language of the Court

KING, Circuit Judge:

* * * *

* * * *The material misrepresentation element* * * *of a Section 10(b) claim requires an allegation that the defendant acted deceptively, i.e., that the defendant engaged in deceptive acts such as misstatements and omissions by those with a duty to disclose. Furthermore, the deceptive act must concern a material fact.* [Emphasis added.]

* * * *

* * * The Complaint is sufficient to establish that, by choosing to speak about its reimbursement practices, the Company possessed a duty to disclose its alleged illegal conduct. The Company violated that duty and acted deceptively by way of false statements and statements that were misleading because they omitted the fraudulent reimbursement scheme. Furthermore, the facts of that scheme were material, in that a reasonable investor would have considered the scheme important in deciding whether to buy or sell TranS1 stock.

* * * *

* * * To allege the *scienter* element, a plaintiff must demonstrate that the defendant acted with a mental state embracing intent to deceive, manipulate, or defraud.

* * * *

By alleging that the fraudulent reimbursement scheme was known to the Officers, clearly illegal, and fundamental to TranS1's financial success, the Complaint * * * gives rise to a strong inference that TranS1 and the Officers intended to deceive the market, or at the very least acted recklessly, when they made false and misleading statements about the Company's reimbursement practices that omitted the fraudulent reimbursement scheme.

* * * *

* * * The * * * causation element requires the pleading of a sufficiently direct relationship between the plaintiff's economic loss and the defendant's fraudulent conduct, which may be accomplished by alleging facts establishing that the defendant's misrepresentation or omission was one substantial cause of the investment's decline in value.

* * * *

[After the government began its investigation, TranS1] revealed enough facts for the market to finally recognize what the Officers' previous statements had materially omitted: the existence of the Company's fraudulent reimbursement scheme.

* * * According to the Complaint, the revelations * * * caused the value of TranS1's stock to plummet more than 40 percent * * * . Such an allegation is wholly adequate to demonstrate that the exposure of the Company's fraud was at least one substantial cause of the investment's decline in value.

Case 28.3 Continues

Case 28.3 Continued **Decision and Remedy** *The U.S. Court of Appeals for the Fourth Circuit vacated the judgment of the district court and remanded the case. "The Complaint sufficiently pleads the material misrepresentation, scienter, and loss causation elements of the Section 10(b) claim."*

Critical Thinking

- **Legal Environment** *In documents available to the public, Trans1 included general warnings about "the risks of regulatory scrutiny and litigation." Did this satisfy the company's duty to disclose its allegedly fraudulent scheme? Why or why not?*
- **Economic** *If the plaintiffs can prove the elements of their claim, what should be the measure of their damages? Explain.*

***Scienter* Not Required for Section 16(b) Violations** Violations of Section 16(b) include the sale by insiders of stock acquired less than six months before the sale. When a person is selling securities that he or she does not yet own at a higher price and is planning to purchase them later at a lower price, it is called a *short sale*. It is a violation of Section 16(b) for insiders involved in a short sale to sell the acquired stock less than six months *after* the sale. These violations are subject to civil sanctions. Liability under Section 16(b) is strict liability. Neither *scienter* nor negligence is required.

Criminal Penalties For violations of Section 10(b) and Rule 10b-5, an individual may be fined up to $5 million, imprisoned for up to twenty years, or both. A partnership or a corporation may be fined up to $25 million. Under Section 807 of the Sarbanes-Oxley Act, for a *willful* violation of the 1934 act the violator can be imprisoned for up to twenty-five years (in addition to being subject to a fine).

For a defendant to be convicted in a criminal prosecution under the securities laws, there can be no reasonable doubt that the defendant knew he or she was acting wrongfully. In other words, a jury is not allowed merely to speculate that the defendant may have acted willfully.

■ **Case in Point 28.11** Douglas Newton was the president and sole director of Real American Brands, Inc. (RLAB). RLAB owned the Billy Martin's USA brand and operated a Billy Martin's retail boutique at the Trump Plaza in New York City. (Billy Martin's, a Western wear store, was co-founded by Billy Martin, the one-time manager of the New York Yankees.)

Newton agreed to pay kickbacks to Chris Russo, whom he believed to be the manager of a pension fund, to induce the fund to buy shares of RLAB stock. Newton later arranged for his friend Yan Skwara to pay similar kickbacks for the fund's purchase of stock in U.S.

Farms, Inc. In reality, the pension fund was fictitious, and Newton and Skwara had been dealing with agents of the Federal Bureau of Investigation (FBI). Newton was charged with securities fraud and convicted by a jury (Skwara pled guilty). Newton appealed, but a federal appellate court upheld his conviction.

According to the court, the evidence established that in each transaction, the amount of the kickback was added to the price of the stock, which artificially increased the stock price. The evidence sufficiently proved that Newton had engaged in a scheme to defraud the supposed pension fund. His words and conduct, which were revealed on video at the trial, showed his intent to defraud the pension fund investors.[30] ■

Civil Sanctions The SEC can also bring a civil action against anyone who purchases or sells a security while in possession of material nonpublic information in violation of the 1934 act or SEC rules.[31] The violation must occur through the use of a national securities exchange or a broker or dealer.[32] A court can assess a penalty amounting to as much as triple the profits gained or the loss avoided by the guilty party.[33]

The Insider Trading and Securities Fraud Enforcement Act enlarged the class of persons who may be subject to civil liability for insider trading. In addition, this act gave the SEC authority to offer monetary rewards to informants.[34]

Private parties may also sue violators of Section 10(b) and Rule 10b-5. A private party can obtain rescission (cancellation) of a contract to buy securities or damages to the extent of the violator's illegal profits. Those found

---

30. *United States v. Newton,* 559 Fed.Appx. 902 (11th Cir. 2014).
31. 15 U.S.C. Section 78u(d)(3)(A).
32. Transactions pursuant to a public offering by an issuer of securities are exempted.
33. 15 U.S.C. Section 78u(d)(3)(B).
34. 15 U.S.C. Section 78u-1.

liable have a right to seek contribution from those who share responsibility for the violations, including accountants, attorneys, and corporations. For violations of Section 16(b), a corporation can bring an action to recover the short-swing profits.

28–2d Securities Fraud Online and Ponzi Schemes

A problem that the SEC faces is how to enforce the antifraud provisions of the securities laws in the online environment. Internet-related forms of securities fraud include many types of investment scams. Spam, online newsletters and bulletin boards, chat rooms, blogs, social media, and tweets can all be used to spread false information and perpetrate fraud. For a relatively small cost, fraudsters can even build sophisticated Web pages to facilitate their investment scams.

Investment Newsletters Hundreds of online investment newsletters provide information on stocks. Legitimate online newsletters can help investors gather valuable information, but some e-newsletters are used for fraud. The law allows companies to pay these newsletters to tout their securities. The newsletters are required to disclose who paid for the advertising, but many newsletters do not follow that law. Thus, an investor reading an online newsletter may believe that the information is unbiased, when in fact the fraudsters will directly profit by convincing investors to buy or sell particular stocks.

Ponzi Schemes Although much securities fraud occurs online, schemes conducted primarily offline have not disappeared. The SEC files numerous enforcement actions against perpetrators of *Ponzi schemes*. (Ponzi schemes are fraudulent investment operations that pay returns to investors from new capital paid to the fraudsters rather than from a legitimate investment.) Such schemes sometimes target U.S. residents and convince them to invest in offshore companies or banks.

28–3 State Securities Laws

Today, every state has its own corporate securities laws, or **blue sky laws,** that regulate the offer and sale of securities within its borders. (The phrase *blue sky laws* comes from a United States Supreme Court decision in 1917. The Court stated that the purpose of such laws was to prevent "speculative schemes which have no more basis

than so many feet of 'blue sky.'")[35] Article 8 of the Uniform Commercial Code, which has been adopted by all of the states, also imposes various requirements relating to the purchase and sale of securities.

28–3a Requirements under State Securities Laws

State securities laws apply mainly to intrastate transactions (transactions within one state). Typically, state laws have disclosure requirements and antifraud provisions, many of which are patterned after Section 10(b) of the Securities Exchange Act of 1934 and SEC Rule 10b-5. State laws also provide for the registration of securities offered or issued for sale within the state and impose disclosure requirements.

■ **Case in Point 28.12** Randall Fincke was the founder, director, and officer of Access Cardiosystems, Inc., a small start-up company that sold portable automated external heart defibrillators. Fincke prepared a business plan stating that Access's "patent counsel" had advised the firm that "its product does not infringe any patents." This statement was false—patent counsel had never offered Access any opinion on the question of infringement.

Fincke gave this plan to potential investors, including Joseph Zimmel, who bought $1.5 million in Access shares. When the company later filed for Chapter 11 bankruptcy protection, Zimmel filed a complaint with the federal bankruptcy court, alleging that Fincke had violated the Massachusetts blue sky law. The court awarded Zimmel $1.5 million in damages, and the award was affirmed on appeal. Fincke had solicited investors "by means of" a false statement of material fact, in violation of the fraud provisions in the state's securities laws.[36] ■

Methods of registration, required disclosures, and exemptions from registration vary among states. Unless an exemption from registration is applicable, issuers must register or qualify their stock with the appropriate state official, often called a *corporations commissioner*. Additionally, most state securities laws regulate securities brokers and dealers.

28–3b Concurrent Regulation

Since the adoption of the 1933 and 1934 federal securities acts, the state and federal governments have regulated securities concurrently. Issuers must comply with both federal and state securities laws, and exemptions from federal law are not exemptions from state laws.

---

35. *Hall v. Geiger-Jones Co.*, 242 U.S. 539, 37 S.Ct. 217, 61 L.Ed. 480 (1917).
36. *In re Access Cardiosystems, Inc.*, 776 F.3d 30 (1st Cir. 2015).

The dual federal and state system has not always worked well. Today, many of the duplicate regulations have been eliminated, and the SEC has exclusive power to regulate most national securities activities.

The National Conference of Commissioners on Uniform State Laws substantially revised the Uniform Securities Act to coordinate state and federal securities regulation and enforcement efforts. Nearly half of the states have adopted the most recent version of the Uniform Securities Act.

28–4 Corporate Governance

Corporate governance can be narrowly defined as the relationship between a corporation and its shareholders. Some argue for a broader definition—that corporate governance specifies the rights and responsibilities among different participants in the corporation, such as the board of directors, managers, shareholders, and other stakeholders, and spells out the rules and procedures for making decisions on corporate affairs. Regardless of the way it is defined, effective corporate governance requires more than just compliance with laws and regulations.

Effective corporate governance is essential in large corporations because corporate ownership (by shareholders) is separated from corporate control (by officers and managers). Under these circumstances, officers and managers may attempt to advance their own interests at the expense of the shareholders. Well-publicized corporate scandals have clearly illustrated how the misconduct of corporate managers can cause harm to companies and to society. Indeed, with the globalization of business, corporate governance has become even more important because a corporation's bad acts (or lack of control systems) can have far-reaching consequences.

28–4a Aligning the Interests of Officers and Shareholders

Some corporations have sought to align the financial interests of their officers with those of the company's shareholders by providing the officers with **stock options.** These options enable holders to purchase shares of the corporation's stock at a set price. When the market price rises above that level, the officers can sell their shares for a profit. Because a stock's market price generally increases as the corporation prospers, the options give the officers a financial stake in the corporation's well-being and supposedly encourage them to work hard for the benefit of the shareholders.

Problems with Stock Options Options have turned out to be an imperfect device for encouraging effective governance. Executives in some companies have been tempted to "cook" the company's books in order to keep share prices higher so that they can sell their stock for a profit. Executives in other corporations have experienced no losses when share prices dropped because their options were "repriced" so that they did not suffer from the price decline. Thus, although stock options theoretically can motivate officers to protect shareholder interests, stock option plans have sometimes become a way for officers to take advantage of shareholders.

Outside Directors With stock options generally failing to work as planned, there has been an outcry for more outside directors (those with no formal employment affiliation with the company). The theory is that independent directors will more closely monitor the actions of corporate officers. Hence, today we see more boards with outside directors. Note, though, that outside directors may not be truly independent of corporate officers. They may be friends or business associates of the leading officers.

28–4b Promoting Accountability

Effective corporate governance standards are designed to address problems such as those mentioned earlier and to motivate officers to make decisions that promote the financial interests of the company's shareholders. Generally, corporate governance entails corporate decision-making structures that monitor employees (particularly officers) to ensure that they are acting for the benefit of the shareholders. Thus, corporate governance involves, at a minimum:

1. The audited reporting of financial conditions at the corporation so that managers can be evaluated.
2. Legal protections for shareholders so that violators of the law who attempt to take advantage of shareholders can be punished for misbehavior and victims can recover damages for any associated losses.

Governance and Corporate Law State corporation statutes set up the legal framework for corporate governance. Under the corporate law of Delaware, where most major companies incorporate, all corporations must have certain structures of corporate governance in place. The most important structure, of course, is the board of directors, because the board makes the major decisions about the future of the corporation.

The Board of Directors Under corporate law, a corporation must have a board of directors elected by the shareholders. Directors are responsible for ensuring that the corporation's officers are operating wisely and in the exclusive interest of shareholders. Directors receive reports from the officers and give them managerial direction. In reality, though, corporate directors devote a relatively small amount of time to monitoring officers.

Ideally, shareholders would monitor the directors' supervision of the officers. In practice, however, it can be difficult for shareholders to monitor directors and hold them responsible for corporate failings. Although the directors can be sued if they fail to do their jobs effectively, directors are rarely held personally liable.

The Audit Committee. A crucial committee of the board of directors is the *audit committee*, which oversees the corporation's accounting and financial reporting processes, including both internal and outside auditors. Unless the committee members have sufficient expertise and are willing to spend the time to carefully examine the corporation's bookkeeping methods, however, the audit committee may be ineffective.

The audit committee also oversees the corporation's "internal controls." These controls, carried out largely by the company's internal auditing staff, are measures taken to ensure that reported results are accurate. For instance, internal controls help to determine whether a corporation's debts are collectible. If the debts are not collectible, it is up to the audit committee to make sure that the corporation's financial officers do not simply pretend that payment will eventually be made.

The Compensation Committee. Another important committee of the board of directors is the *compensation committee*, which determines the compensation of the company's officers. As part of this process, the committee must assess the officers' performance and attempt to design a compensation system that will align the officers' interests with those of the shareholders.

28–4c The Sarbanes-Oxley Act

In 2002, following a series of corporate scandals, Congress passed the Sarbanes-Oxley Act,[37] which addresses certain issues relating to corporate governance. Generally, the act attempts to increase corporate accountability by imposing strict disclosure requirements and harsh penalties for violations of securities laws. Among other things, the act requires chief corporate executives to take personal responsibility for the accuracy of financial statements and reports that are filed with the SEC.

Additionally, the act requires that certain financial and stock-transaction reports be filed with the SEC

---

37. 15 U.S.C. Sections 7201 *et seq.*

earlier than was required under the previous rules. The act also created a new entity, called the Public Company Accounting Oversight Board, to regulate and oversee public accounting firms. Other provisions of the act established private civil actions and expanded the SEC's remedies in administrative and civil actions.

Because of the importance of this act for corporate leaders and for those dealing with securities transactions, we highlight some of its key provisions relating to corporate accountability in Exhibit 28–3.

More Internal Controls and Accountability
The Sarbanes-Oxley Act introduced direct *federal* corporate governance requirements for publicly traded companies. The law addressed many of the corporate governance procedures just discussed and created new requirements in an attempt to make the system work more effectively. The requirements deal with independent monitoring of company officers by both the board of directors and auditors.

Sections 302 and 404 of the Sarbanes-Oxley Act require high-level managers (the most senior officers) to establish and maintain an effective system of internal controls. The system must include "disclosure controls and procedures" to ensure that company financial reports are accurate and timely and to document financial results prior to reporting.

Senior management must reassess the system's effectiveness annually. Some companies have had to take expensive steps to bring their internal controls up to the federal standards. Hundreds of companies have reported that they identified and corrected shortcomings in their internal control systems as a result.

Exemptions for Smaller Companies
The act initially required all public companies to have an independent auditor file a report with the SEC on management's assessment of internal controls. Congress, however, later enacted an exemption for smaller companies in an effort to reduce compliance costs. Public companies with a market capitalization, or public float, of less than $75 million no longer need to have an auditor report on management's assessment of internal controls.

Certification and Monitoring Requirements
Section 906 of the Sarbanes-Oxley Act requires that chief executive officers and chief financial officers certify the accuracy of the information in the corporate financial statements. The statements must "fairly represent in all material respects, the financial conditions and results of operations of the issuer." This requirement makes the officers directly accountable for the accuracy of their financial reporting and precludes any "ignorance defense" if shortcomings are later discovered.

Exhibit 28–3 Some Key Provisions of the Sarbanes-Oxley Act Relating to Corporate Accountability

Certification Requirements

Under *Section 906* of the Sarbanes-Oxley Act, the chief executive officers (CEOs) and chief financial officers (CFOs) of most major companies listed on public stock exchanges must certify financial statements that are filed with the SEC. CEOs and CFOs have to certify that filed financial reports "fully comply" with SEC requirements and that all of the information reported "fairly represents in all material respects, the financial conditions and results of operations of the issuer."

Under *Section 302* of the act, CEOs and CFOs of reporting companies are required to certify that a signing officer reviewed each quarterly and annual filing with the SEC and that none contained untrue statements of material fact. Also, the signing officer or officers must certify that they have established an internal control system to identify all material information and that any deficiencies in the system were disclosed to the auditors.

Internal Controls

Financial Controls—*Section 404(a)* requires all public companies to assess the effectiveness of their internal controls over financial reporting. *Section 404(b)* requires independent auditors to report on management's assessment of internal controls, but certain companies are exempted.

Loans to Directors and Officers—*Section 402* prohibits any reporting company—as well as any private company that is filing an initial public offering—from making personal loans to directors and executive officers.

Protection for Whistleblowers—*Section 806* protects "whistleblowers"—employees who "blow the whistle" on securities violations by their employers—from being fired or in any way discriminated against by their employers.

Blackout Periods—*Section 306* prohibits certain types of securities transactions during "blackout periods"— periods during which the issuer's ability to purchase, sell, or otherwise transfer funds in individual account plans (such as pension funds) is suspended.

Enhanced Penalties

- *Violations of Section 906 Certification Requirements*—A CEO or CFO who certifies a financial report or statement filed with the SEC knowing that the report or statement does not fulfill all of the requirements of *Section 906* will be subject to criminal penalties of up to $1 million in fines, ten years in prison, or both. *Willful* violators of the certification requirements may be subject to $5 million in fines, twenty years in prison, or both.

- *Violations of the Securities Exchange Act of 1934*—Penalties for securities fraud under the 1934 act were also increased. Individual violators may be fined up to $5 million, imprisoned for up to twenty years, or both. *Willful* violators may be imprisoned for up to twenty-five years in addition to being fined.

- *Destruction or Alteration of Documents*—Anyone who alters, destroys, or conceals documents or otherwise obstructs any official proceeding will be subject to fines, imprisonment for up to twenty years, or both.

- *Other Forms of White-Collar Crime*—The act stiffened the penalties for certain criminal violations, such as federal mail and wire fraud, and ordered the U.S. Sentencing Commission to revise the sentencing guidelines for white-collar crimes.

Statute of Limitations for Securities Fraud

Section 804 provides that a private right of action for securities fraud may be brought no later than two years after the discovery of the violation or five years after the violation, whichever is earlier.

The act also includes requirements to improve directors' monitoring of officers' activities. All members of a publicly traded corporation's audit committee, which oversees the corporation's accounting and financial reporting processes, must be outside directors. The audit committee must have a written charter that sets out its duties and provides for performance appraisal. At least one "financial expert" must serve on the audit committee, which must hold executive meetings without company officers present. In addition to reviewing the internal controls, the committee also monitors the actions of the outside auditor.

Practice and Review: Investor Protection and Corporate Governance

Dale Emerson served as the chief financial officer for Reliant Electric Company, a distributor of electricity serving portions of Montana and North Dakota. Reliant was in the final stages of planning a takeover of Dakota Gasworks, Inc., a natural gas distributor that operated solely within North Dakota. Emerson went on a weekend fishing trip with his uncle, Ernest Wallace. Emerson mentioned to Wallace that he had been putting in a lot of extra hours at the office planning a takeover of Dakota Gasworks. When he returned from the fishing trip, Wallace purchased $20,000 worth of Reliant stock. Three weeks later, Reliant made a tender offer to Dakota Gasworks stockholders and purchased 57 percent of Dakota Gasworks stock. Over the next two weeks, the price of Reliant stock rose 72 percent before leveling out. Wallace then sold his Reliant stock for a gross profit of $14,400. Using the information presented in the chapter, answer the following questions.

1. Would registration with the SEC be required for Dakota Gasworks securities? Why or why not?
2. Did Emerson violate Section 10(b) of the Securities Exchange Act of 1934 and SEC Rule 10b-5? Why or why not?
3. What theory or theories might a court use to hold Wallace liable for insider trading?
4. Under the Sarbanes-Oxley Act, who would be required to certify the accuracy of the financial statements Reliant filed with the SEC?

Debate This . . . *Insider trading should be legalized.*

Terms and Concepts

accredited investor 594
blue sky laws 605
corporate governance 606
free-writing prospectus 592
insider trading 598

investment company 595
investment contract 590
mutual fund 595
prospectus 591
SEC Rule 10b-5 598

securities 590
short-swing profits 601
stock options 606
tippees 600

Issue Spotters

1. When a corporation wishes to issue certain securities, it must provide sufficient information for an unsophisticated investor to evaluate the financial risk involved. Specifically, the law imposes liability for making a false statement or omission that is "material." What sort of information would an investor consider material? (See *The Securities Exchange Act of 1934*.)

2. Lee is an officer of Magma Oil, Inc. Lee knows that a Magma geologist has just discovered a new deposit of oil. Can Lee take advantage of this information to buy and sell Magma stock? Why or why not? (See *The Securities Exchange Act of 1934*.)

• **Check your answers to the Issue Spotters against the answers provided in Appendix B at the end of this text.**

Business Scenarios and Case Problems

28–1. Registration Requirements. Estrada Hermanos, Inc., a corporation incorporated and doing business in Florida, decides to sell $1 million worth of its common stock to the public. The stock will be sold only within the state of Florida. José Estrada, the chair of the board, says the offering need not be registered with the Securities and Exchange Commission. His brother, Gustavo, disagrees. Who is right? Explain. (See *The Securities Act of 1933.*)

28–2. Registration Requirements. Huron Corporation has 300,000 common shares outstanding. The owners of these outstanding shares live in several different states. Huron has decided to split the 300,000 shares two for one. Will Huron have to file a registration statement and prospectus on the 300,000 new shares to be issued as a result of the split? Explain. (See *The Securities Act of 1933.*)

28–3. Insider Trading. David Gain was the chief executive officer (CEO) of Forest Media Corporation, which became interested in acquiring RS Communications, Inc. To initiate negotiations, Gain met with RS's CEO, Gill Raz, on Friday, July 12. Two days later, Gain phoned his brother Mark, who bought 3,800 shares of RS stock on the following Monday. Mark discussed the deal with their father, Jordan, who bought 20,000 RS shares on Thursday. On July 25, the day before the RS bid was due, Gain phoned his parents' home, and Mark bought another 3,200 RS shares. The same routine was followed over the next few days, with Gain periodically phoning Mark or Jordan, both of whom continued to buy RS shares. Forest's bid was refused, but on August 5, RS announced its merger with another company. The price of RS stock rose 30 percent, increasing the value of Mark's and Jordan's shares by $664,024 and $412,875, respectively. Did Gain engage in insider trading? What is required to impose sanctions for this offense? Could a court hold Gain liable? Why or why not? (See *The Securities Exchange Act of 1934.*)

28–4. Business Case Problem with Sample Answer— Violations of the 1934 Act. Matrixx Initiatives, Inc., makes and sells over-the-counter pharmaceutical products. Its core brand is Zicam, which accounts for 70 percent of its sales. Matrixx received reports that some consumers had lost their sense of smell (a condition called anosmia) after using Zicam. Four product liability suits were filed against Matrixx, seeking damages for anosmia. In public statements relating to revenues and product safety, however, Matrixx did not reveal this information.

James Siracusano and other Matrixx investors filed a suit in a federal district court against the company and its executives under Section 10(b) of the Securities Exchange Act of 1934 and SEC Rule 10b-5, claiming that the statements were misleading because they did not disclose information regarding the product liability suits. Matrixx argued that to be material, information must consist of a statistically significant number of adverse events that require disclosure. Because Siracusano's claim did not allege that Matrixx knew of a statistically

significant number of adverse events, the company contended that the claim should be dismissed. What is the standard for materiality in this context? Should Siracusano's claim be dismissed? Explain. [*Matrixx Initiatives, Inc. v. Siracusano*, 563 U.S. 27, 131 S.Ct. 1309, 179 L.Ed.2d 398 (2011)] (See *The Securities Exchange Act of 1934.*)

- **For a sample answer to Problem 28–4, go to Appendix C at the end of this text.**

28–5. Disclosure under SEC Rule 10b-5. Dodona I, LLC, invested $4 million in two securities offerings from Goldman, Sachs & Company. The investments were in collateralized debt obligations (CDOs). Their value depended on residential mortgage-backed securities (RMBS), whose value in turn depended on the performance of subprime residential mortgages.

Before marketing the CDOs, Goldman had noticed several "red flags" relating to investments in the subprime market, in which it had invested heavily. To limit its risk, Goldman began betting against subprime mortgages, RMBS, and CDOs, including the CDOs it had sold to Dodona. In other words, Goldman made investments based on the assumption that subprime mortgages and the securities instruments built upon them would decrease in value. In an internal e-mail, one Goldman official commented that the company had managed to "make some lemonade from some big old lemons." Nevertheless, Goldman's marketing materials provided only boilerplate statements about the risks of investing in the securities.

The CDOs were later downgraded to junk status, and Dodona suffered a major loss while Goldman profited. Assuming that Goldman did not affirmatively misrepresent any facts about the CDOs, can Dodona still recover under SEC Rule 10b-5? If so, how? [*Dodona I, LLC v. Goldman, Sachs & Co.*, 847 F.Supp.2d 624 (S.D.N.Y. 2012)] (See *The Securities Exchange Act of 1934.*)

28–6. Violations of the 1933 Act. Three shareholders of iStorage sought to sell their stock through World Trade Financial Corporation. The shares were *restricted securities*—that is, securities acquired in an unregistered, private sale. Restricted securities typically bear a "restrictive" legend clearly stating that they cannot be resold in the public marketplace. This legend had been wrongly removed from the iStorage shares, however. Information about the company that was publicly available included the fact that, despite a ten-year life, it had no operating history or earnings. In addition, it had net losses of about $200,000, and its stock was thinly traded. Without investigating the company or the status of its stock, World Trade sold more than 2.3 million shares to the public on behalf of the three customers. Did World Trade violate the Securities Act of 1933? Discuss. [*World Trade Financial Corp. U.S. v. Securities and Exchange Commission*, 739 F.3d 1243 (9th Cir. 2014)] (See *The Securities Act of 1933.*)

28–7. Securities Act of 1933. Big Apple Consulting USA, Inc., provided small publicly traded companies with a variety of services, including marketing, business planning, and website development and maintenance. CyberKey Corp. sold customizable USB drives. CyberKey falsely informed Big Apple that CyberKey had been awarded a $25 million contract with the Department of Homeland Security. Big Apple used this information in aggressively promoting CyberKey's stock and was compensated for the effort in the form of CyberKey shares. When the Securities and Exchange Commission (SEC) began to investigate, Big Apple sold its shares for $7.8 million. The SEC filed an action in a federal district court against Big Apple, alleging a violation of the Securities Act of 1933. Can liability be imposed on a seller for a false statement that was made by someone else? Explain. [*Securities and Exchange Commission v. Big Apple Consulting USA, Inc.*, 783 F.3d 786 (11th Cir. 2015)] (See *The Securities Act of 1933.*)

28–8. The Securities Exchange Act of 1934. Dilean Reyes-Rivera was the president of Global Reach Trading (GRT), a corporation registered in Puerto Rico. His brother, Jeffrey, was the firm's accountant. Along with GRT sales agents and other promoters, the brothers solicited funds from individuals by promising to invest the funds in low-risk, short-term, high-yield securities. The investors were guaranteed a rate of return of up to 20 percent. Through this arrangement, more than 230 persons provided the brothers with about $22 million. This money was not actually invested, however. Instead, the funds received from later investors were used to pay "returns" to earlier investors. The Reyes-Riveras spent $4.6 million of the proceeds to buy luxury vehicles, houses, furniture, jewelry, and trips for themselves. What is this type of scheme called? What are the potential consequences? Discuss. [*United States v. Reyes-Rivera*, 812 F.3d 79 (1st Cir. 2016)] (See *The Securities Exchange Act of 1934.*)

28–9. Securities Fraud. First Solar, Inc., is one of the world's largest producers of photovoltaic solar panel modules.

When First Solar revealed to the market that the company had discovered defects in its products, the price of the company's stock fell, causing the shareholders to suffer an economic loss. Mineworkers' Pension Scheme and other First Solar shareholders filed a suit in a federal district court against the firm and its officers, alleging a violation of Section 10(b). The plaintiffs contended that for more than two years, First Solar had wrongfully concealed its discovery, misrepresented the cost and scope of the defects, and reported false information on financial statements. On these facts, can the plaintiffs successfully plead the causation element of a securities fraud action under Section 10(b)? Explain. [*Mineworkers' Pension Scheme. v. First Solar, Inc.*, 881 F.3d 750 (9th Cir. 2018)] (See *The Securities Exchange Act of 1934.*)

27–10. A Question of Ethics—The IDDR Approach and Insider Trading. *Nan Huang was a senior data analyst for Capital One Financial Corporation. In violation of the company's confidentiality policies, Huang downloaded and analyzed confidential information regarding purchases made with Capital One credit cards at more than two hundred consumer retail companies and used that information to conduct more than two thousand trades in the securities of those companies. Capital One terminated Huang due to his violation of the company's policies. The next day, Huang boarded a flight to his home country of China. Four days later, the Securities and Exchange Commission filed a complaint against Huang, alleging violations of Section 10(b) and Rule 10b-5. [Securities and Exchange Commission v. Bonan Huang, 684 Fed.Appx. 167 (3d Cir. 2017)] (See The Securities Exchange Act of 1934.)*

(a) Evaluate the ethics of Huang's actions as an employee of Capital One, using the IDDR approach.

(b) When Capital One learned what Huang had done, was the company ethically obligated to terminate him? Explain.

Time-Limited Group Assignment

28–11. Securities Fraud. Karel Svoboda, a credit officer for Rogue Bank, evaluated and approved his employer's extensions of credit to clients. These responsibilities gave Svoboda access to nonpublic information about the clients' earnings, performance, acquisitions, and business plans from confidential memos, e-mail, and other sources. Svoboda devised a scheme with Alena Robles, an independent accountant, to use this information to trade securities. Pursuant to their scheme, Robles traded in the securities of more than twenty different companies and profited by more than $2 million. Svoboda also executed trades for his own profit of more than $800,000, despite their agreement that Robles would do all of the trading. Aware that their scheme violated Rogue Bank's

policy, they attempted to conduct their trades in such a way as to avoid suspicion. When the bank questioned Svoboda about his actions, he lied, refused to cooperate, and was fired. (See *The Securities Exchange Act of 1934.*)

(a) The first group will determine whether Svoboda or Robles committed any crimes.

(b) The second group will decide whether Svoboda or Robles is subject to civil liability. If so, who could file a suit, and on what ground? What are the possible sanctions?

(c) A third group will identify any defenses that Svoboda or Robles could raise and determine their likelihood of success.

Alpha Software, Inc., and Beta Products Corporation—both small firms—are competitors in the business of software research, development, and production.

1. **Consumer Law.** To market its products profitably, Beta considers a number of advertising and labeling proposals. One proposal is that Beta suggest in its advertising that one of its software products has a certain function, even though the product does not actually have that capability. Another suggestion is that Beta sell half of a certain program in packaging that misleads the buyer into believing the entire program is included. To obtain the entire program, customers would need to buy a second product. Can Beta implement these suggestions or otherwise market its products in any way it likes? If not, why not?

2. **Environmental Law.** The production part of Beta's operations generates hazardous waste. Gamma Transport Company transports the waste to Omega Waste Corporation, which owns and operates a hazardous waste disposal site. At the site, some containers leak hazardous waste, and the Environmental Protection Agency (EPA) cleans it up. From whom can the EPA recover the cost of the clean-up?

3. **Antitrust Law.** Alpha and Beta form a joint venture to research, develop, and produce new software for a particular line of computers. Does this business combination violate the antitrust laws? If so, is it a *per se* violation, or is it subject to the rule of reason?

Climate Change

Our planet's average temperature has risen by 1.5 degrees Fahrenheit over the last hundred years. It is predicted that it will rise another 0.5 to 4.5 degrees over the next century. These seemingly small increases in the average temperature can result in significant change to our climate.

What Are the Causes?

Over the last century, our atmosphere experienced a large increase in carbon dioxide and other *greenhouse gases (GHGs)*. GHGs act like a blanket around our planet, absorbing radiation from the surface, trapping it as heat in the atmosphere, and reflecting it back to the surface.

This process, known as the *greenhouse effect*, is necessary to support life. The recent increase in GHGs, however, may be changing our climate. Deforestation, industrial processes, and agricultural practices emit these gases, but the majority of GHGs come from burning fossil fuels to produce energy.[1]

What Are the Effects?

The warmer it gets, the greater the risk for more change to the climate. Ultimately, the climate that we are used to may no longer be a guide for what to expect in the future.

Changes in Weather Rising global temperatures have sometimes coincided with changes in weather. Some locations have seen altered rainfall, resulting in heavier rains and more floods, or more frequent and intense heat waves and droughts. The rising temperatures may also be making our planet's oceans warmer and more acidic. Some glaciers and ice caps are melting, which may cause sea levels to rise.

Impacts on Society The warmer temperatures and changes in weather can affect society in many ways. Agricultural yields, human health, and the supply of energy are affected. More severe weather can lead to higher food and energy prices and increasing insurance costs. (Note, though, that higher average temperatures could lead to more agricultural output and hence lower food prices.) Of course, any impact in one area of human activity can have widespread and unforeseen effects throughout society.

What Can We Do about It?

The effects of climate change may be lessened by choices that reduce GHGs. About half of the states have set statewide GHG emission goals.[2] In the areas of transportation and power generation, two of the options for reducing emissions are the use of low-emission fuels and increased energy efficiency.

Reduce Emissions at the Pump and the Plant Motor vehicles and transportation fuels are sources for nearly a third of GHG emissions in the United States. To reduce these emissions, the

Continues

---

1. Fossil-fuel-burning power plants are the largest single source of GHG emissions in the United States.
2. California established the first statewide goals in 2006 in the Global Warming Solutions Act.

federal government and the states impose emissions standards on cars and trucks, and encourage the use of fuel-efficient vehicles and alternative fuels.

The federal Environmental Protection Agency (EPA) and National Highway Transportation Safety Administration have established standards for GHG emissions and fuel economy for new light-duty cars and trucks through the model year 2025.[3] The standards are projected to save about 4 billion barrels of oil and avoid 2 billion metric tons of GHG emissions per year.

Some states have set low-emission fuel standards. More than a dozen states have set renewable fuel standards to encourage the use of low-emission fuels. Incentives to use alternative fuels include tax exemptions, tax credits, and grants.

To reduce GHG emissions from coal- and gas-fired power plants, the EPA issued the Clean Power Plan (CPP).[4] It is projected that, by the time that the CPP is fully in place in 2030, carbon pollution from the power sector will be 32 percent below 2005 levels. Emissions of sulfur dioxide from power plants will be 90 percent lower than 2005 levels, and emissions of nitrogen oxides will be 72 percent lower. The Trump administration issued a proposal to replace the CPP.

About two-thirds of the states will require power companies to generate a certain percentage or amount of power from renewable energy sources by a specific date, which varies by state. These targets aim to reduce emissions and to improve air quality, diversify energy sources, and create jobs in the renewable energy industry.

Become More Energy Efficient More than half of the states have set standards requiring power companies to save specified amounts of energy. To attain these goals, the utilities must adopt more efficient technology in their operations and encourage their customers to become more energy efficient.

About half of the states dedicate funds to the support of renewable energy projects. More than a dozen of these states formed the Clean Energy States Alliance to coordinate their investments. Nearly all states permit utility customers to sell electricity back to the grid. In most states, utilities offer their customers the opportunity to have a portion of their power provided from renewable sources.

Many states participate in regional climate initiatives. For example, nine states in the northeastern United States formed the Regional Greenhouse Gas Initiative to implement a market-based program to reduce GHG emissions from power plants. The initiative sets an emissions budget, or cap, for each member state. Credits that exceed the actual emissions can be sold. The proceeds generally are invested in energy-efficient renewable energy programs.

Adapt to the Changes The EPA's State and Local Climate and Energy Program provides technical assistance, analytical tools, and outreach support on climate change issues to state, local, and tribal governments.[5] The program directs resource managers to set priorities and to design and implement climate and energy policies tailored to the particular circumstances of their locations.

---

3. 40 C.F.R. Parts 85, 86, and 600, and 49 C.F.R. Parts 523, 531, 533, 600 *et al.* The United States Supreme Court has made clear that the Environmental Protection Agency can regulate GHGs under the Clean Air Act. See *Commonwealth of Massachusetts v. Environmental Protection Agency*, 549 U.S. 497, 127 S.Ct. 1438, 167 L.Ed.2d 248 (2007).

4. 40 C.F.R. Part 60.

5. See Environmental Protection Agency, *State and Local Climate and Energy Program*, available at www.epa.gov.

Part of the process is to assess an area's vulnerability to the effects of climate change and to consider approaches for adapting to the effects. For example, a coastal estuary that is subject to salt-water inundation as a consequence of rising sea levels might benefit from a coastal restoration project.

The U.S. Interagency Climate Change Adaptation Task Force coordinates the efforts for adaptation across government agencies.[6] The task force recommends actions that the federal government can take to respond to the needs of states and local communities. The top priority is to enhance the resilience of natural resources to absorb the impacts of climate change.

Agree to More Limits on Emissions The European Union and 195 nations, including the United States, participated in the 2015 United Nations Climate Change Conference in Paris, France. The parties negotiated the Paris Agreement to encourage the reduction of GHG emissions.[7] The agreement sets a goal of limiting the global temperature increase to less than 2 degrees Celsius. The parties agreed to make "nationally determined contributions" (NDCs) to this goal and to pursue domestic measures designed to achieve the NDCs.[8] None of these agreements are binding, however, and therefore rely on voluntary actions by governments throughout the world. The Trump administration later announced that the United States would withdraw from the Paris Agreement.

Ethical Connection

Have all these efforts had an effect? It seems that they have. The transition to clean energy is happening faster than anticipated, and GHG emissions and air pollution have decreased somewhat.

Furthermore, climate change could have some positive effects. For example, the goals to lessen the impact and adapt to the changes create economic opportunities. There are new markets for alternative sources of power and sales of GHG emission credits, for instance. Climate change also represents a political opportunity to improve air quality and develop domestic sources of clean energy.

A business that takes advantage of these opportunities is not acting unethically. Such a business is, in fact, acting in the best interest of all of us.

Ethics Question *Is it ethical to continue to use fossil fuels? Explain.*

Critical Thinking *What are the advantages of fossil fuels? What are the disadvantages? Discuss.*

---

6. Executive Order, *Preparing the United States for the Impacts of Climate Change*, available at https://obamawww.whitehouse.archives.gov.
7. United Nations Framework Convention on Climate Change, Conference of the Parties, *Adoption of the Paris Agreement. Proposal by the President*, available at http://unfccc.int/resource/docs/2015/cop21/eng/l09r01.pdf.
8. There are, however, no binding emission targets or financial commitments. And the agreement itself will not become binding until fifty-five of the participants who produce more than 55 percent of global GHGs have ratified it.

Appendix A

How to Brief Cases and Analyze Case Problems

How to Brief Cases

To fully understand the law with respect to business, you need to be able to read and understand court decisions. To make this task easier, you can use a method of case analysis that is called *briefing*. There is a fairly standard procedure to follow when you "brief" any court case. You must first read the case opinion carefully. When you feel you understand the case, you can prepare a brief of it.

Although the format of the brief may vary, typically it will present the essentials of the case under headings such as the following:

1. **Citation.** Give the full citation for the case, including the name of the case, the date it was decided, and the court that decided it.
2. **Facts.** Briefly indicate (a) the reasons for the lawsuit; (b) the identity and arguments of the plaintiff(s) and defendant(s), respectively; and (c) the lower court's decision—if appropriate.
3. **Issue.** Concisely phrase, in the form of a question, the essential issue before the court. (If more than one issue is involved, you may have two—or even more—questions here.)
4. **Decision.** Indicate here—with a "yes" or "no," if possible—the court's answer to the question (or questions) in the *Issue* section.
5. **Reason.** Summarize as briefly as possible the reasons given by the court for its decision (or decisions) and the case or statutory law relied on by the court in arriving at its decision.

An Example of a Briefed Sample Court Case

As an example of the format used in briefing cases, we present next a briefed version of the sample court case that was presented in Chapter 1 in Exhibit 1–6.

Yeasin v. Durham
United States Court of Appeals, Tenth Circuit,
719 Fed.Appx. 844 (2018).

Facts Navid Yeasin and A.W. were students at the University of Kansas (KU). They dated for about nine months. When A.W. tried to end the relationship, Yeasin restrained her in his car, took her phone, and threatened to make the "campus environment so hostile that she would not attend any university in the state of Kansas." He repeatedly tweeted disparaging comments about her. Tammara Durham, the university's vice provost for student affairs, found that Yeasin's conduct and tweets violated the school's student code of conduct and sexual-harassment policy. She expelled him. Yeasin filed a suit in a Kansas state court against Durham, and the court determined that he should be reinstated. He then filed a suit in a federal district court against Durham, claiming that she had violated his First Amendment rights by expelling him for the content of his off-campus speech. The court dismissed the claim. Yeasin appealed to the U.S. Court of Appeals for the Tenth Circuit.

Issue Did Durham violate Yeasin's First Amendment rights by expelling him for his online, off-campus speech?

Decision No. The U.S. Court of Appeals for the Tenth Circuit affirmed the lower court's dismissal of Yeasin's suit. "Yeasin can't establish that Dr. Durham violated clearly established law when she expelled him."

Reason Taken together, court decisions show that "at the intersection of university speech and social media, First Amendment doctrine is unsettled." The courts permit schools to circumscribe students' free-speech rights in certain contexts. Yeasin argued, however, that three cases decided by the United States Supreme Court clearly established his right to tweet about A.W. without the university's being able to place restrictions on, or discipline him for, his tweets. In response, the court in the *Yeasin* case pointed out that those cases did not involve circumstances similar to Yeasin's situation. In those cases, no student had been charged with a crime against another student and had then made sexually harassing comments affecting that student's ability to feel safe while attending classes. The court concluded that in this case Durham could reasonably have believed, based on Yeasin's conduct and his tweets, that his presence at the university would disrupt A.W.'s education and interfere with her rights.

A Review of the Briefed Sample Court Case

Here, we provide a review of the briefed sample case that indicates the kind of information contained in each section.

Citation The name of the case is *Yeasin v. Durham*. Navid Yeasin is the plaintiff. Tammara Durham is the defendant. The U.S. Court of Appeals for the Tenth Circuit issued its opinion in this case in 2018. The citation states that this case can be found in Volume 719 of the *Federal Appendix* on page 844.

Facts The *Facts* section identifies the plaintiff and the defendant, describes the events leading up to the suit, and states the allegations made by the plaintiff in the suit. Because this case is a decision of one of the U.S. Courts of Appeals, the lower court's ruling and the *appellant* (the party appealing) are also included.

Issue The *Issue* section presents the central issue (or issues) decided by the court. In this case, the federal appellate court considers whether Durham, the university's vice provost for student affairs, violated clearly established law when she expelled Yeasin, in part, for his off-campus tweets about another KU student.

Decision The *Decision* section includes the court's decision on the issues before it. The decision reflects the opinion of the judge or justice hearing the case. Here, the court affirmed the lower court's dismissal of Yeasin's suit, concluding that he could not show that his expulsion violated clearly established law. Decisions by appellate courts are frequently phrased in reference to the lower court's decision. That is, the appellate court may "affirm" the lower court's ruling or "reverse" it. A case may also be remanded, or sent back, to the lower court for further proceedings.

Reason The *Reason* section includes references to the relevant laws and legal principles that were applied or distinguished in coming to the conclusion arrived at in the case before the court. The relevant law here included court decisions on whether, and in what circumstances, schools can circumscribe students' free-speech rights. This section also explains the court's application of the law to the facts in this case.

Analyzing Case Problems

In addition to learning how to brief cases, students also find it helpful to know how to analyze case problems. Part of the study of business law and the legal environment usually involves analyzing case problems, such as those included in this text at the end of each chapter.

For each case problem in this book, we provide the relevant background and facts of the lawsuit and the issue before the court. When you are assigned one of these problems, your job will be to determine how the court should decide the issue, and why. In other words, you will need to engage in legal analysis and reasoning. Here, we offer some suggestions on how to make this task less daunting. We begin by presenting the following SAMPLE PROBLEM:

> While Janet Lawson, a famous pianist, was shopping in Quality Market, she slipped and fell on a wet floor in one of the aisles. The floor had recently been mopped by one of the store's employees, but there were no signs warning customers that the floor in that area was wet. As a result of the fall, Lawson injured her right arm and was unable to perform piano concerts for the next six months. Had she been able to perform the scheduled

concerts, she would have earned approximately $60,000 over that period of time. Lawson sued Quality Market for this amount, plus another $10,000 in medical expenses. She claimed that the store's failure to warn customers of the wet floor constituted negligence and therefore the market was liable for her injuries. Will the court agree with Lawson? Discuss.

Understand the Facts

This may sound obvious, but before you can analyze or apply the relevant law to a specific set of facts, you must clearly understand those facts. In other words, you should read through the case problem carefully—more than once, if necessary—to make sure you understand the identity of the plaintiff(s) and defendant(s) in the case and the progression of events that led to the lawsuit.

In the sample case problem just given, the identity of the parties is fairly clear. Janet Lawson is the one bringing the suit; therefore, she is the plaintiff. Quality Market, against whom she is bringing the suit, is the defendant. Some of the case problems you may work on have multiple plaintiffs or defendants. Often, it is helpful to use abbreviations for the parties. To indicate a reference to a plaintiff, for example, the *pi* symbol—π—is often used, and a defendant is denoted by a *delta*—Δ.

The events leading to the lawsuit are also fairly straightforward. Lawson slipped and fell on a wet floor, and she contends that Quality Market should be liable for her injuries because it was negligent in not posting a sign warning customers of the wet floor.

When you are working on case problems, realize that the facts should be accepted as they are given. For example, in our sample problem, it should be accepted that the floor was wet and that there was no sign. In other words, avoid making conjectures, such as "Maybe the floor wasn't too wet," or "Maybe an employee was getting a sign to put up," or "Maybe someone stole the sign." Questioning the facts as they are presented only adds confusion to your analysis.

Legal Analysis and Reasoning

Once you understand the facts given in the case problem, you can begin to analyze the case. The IRAC method is a helpful tool to use in the legal analysis and reasoning process. **IRAC** is an acronym for **Issue, Rule, Application, Conclusion.** Applying this method to our sample problem would involve the following steps:

1. First, you need to decide what legal **issue** is involved in the case. In our sample case, the basic issue is whether Quality Market's failure to warn customers of the wet floor constituted negligence. As discussed in the text, negligence is a *tort*—a civil wrong. In a tort lawsuit, the plaintiff seeks to be

compensated for another's wrongful act. A defendant will be deemed negligent if he or she breached a duty of care owed to the plaintiff and the breach of that duty caused the plaintiff to suffer harm.

2. Once you have identified the issue, the next step is to determine what **rule of law** applies to the issue. To make this determination, you will want to review carefully the text of the chapter in which the relevant rule of law for the problem appears. Our sample case problem involves the tort of negligence. The applicable rule of law is the tort law principle that business owners owe a duty to exercise reasonable care to protect their customers ("business invitees"). Reasonable care, in this context, includes either removing—or warning customers of—*foreseeable* risks about which the owner *knew* or *should have known.* (Business owners need not warn customers of "open and obvious" risks.) If a business owner breaches this duty of care (fails to exercise the appropriate degree of care toward customers), and the breach of duty causes a customer to be injured, the business owner will be liable to the customer for the customer's injuries.

3. The next—and usually the most difficult—step in analyzing case problems is the **application** of the relevant rule of law to the specific facts of the case you are studying. In the sample problem, applying the tort law principle just discussed presents few difficulties. An employee of the store had mopped the floor in the aisle where Lawson slipped and fell, but no sign was present indicating that the floor was wet. That a customer might fall on a wet floor is clearly a foreseeable risk. Therefore, the failure to warn customers about the wet floor was a breach of the duty of care owed by the business owner to the store's customers.

4. Once you have completed Step 3, you should be ready to draw your **conclusion.** In our sample problem, Quality Market is liable to Lawson for her injuries, because the market's breach of its duty of care caused Lawson's injuries.

The fact patterns in the business scenarios and case problems presented in this text are not always as simple as those presented in our sample problem. Often, for example, a case has more than one plaintiff or defendant. A case may also involve more than one issue and have more than one applicable rule of law. Furthermore, in some case problems the facts may indicate that the general rule of law should not apply.

For example, suppose that a store employee advised Lawson not to walk on the floor in the aisle because it was wet, but Lawson decided to walk on it anyway. This fact could alter the outcome of the case because the store could then raise the defense of assumption of risk. Nonetheless, a careful review of the chapter text should always provide you with the knowledge you need to analyze the problem thoroughly and arrive at accurate conclusions.

Appendix B
Answers to the *Issue Spotters*

Chapter 1

1. *Under what circumstances might a judge rely on case law to determine the intent and purpose of a statute?* Case law includes courts' interpretations of statutes, as well as constitutional provisions and administrative rules. Statutes often codify common law rules. For these reasons, a judge might rely on the common law as a guide to the intent and purpose of a statute.

2. *Assuming that these convicted war criminals had not disobeyed any law of their country and had merely been following their government's orders, what law had they violated? Explain.* At the time of the Nuremberg trials, "crimes against humanity" were new international crimes. The laws criminalized such acts as murder, extermination, enslavement, deportation, and other inhumane acts committed against any civilian population. These international laws derived their legitimacy from "natural law."

Natural law, which is the oldest and one of the most significant schools of jurisprudence, holds that governments and legal systems should reflect the moral and ethical ideals that are inherent in human nature. Because natural law is universal and discoverable by reason, its adherents believe that all other law is derived from natural law. Natural law therefore supersedes laws created by humans (national, or "positive," law), and in a conflict between the two, national or positive law loses its legitimacy.

The Nuremberg defendants asserted that they had been acting in accordance with German law. The judges dismissed these claims, reasoning that the defendants' acts were commonly regarded as crimes and that the accused must have known that the acts would be considered criminal. The judges clearly believed the tenets of natural law and expected that the defendants, too, should have been able to realize that their acts ran afoul of it. The fact that the "positivist law" of Germany at the time required them to commit these acts was irrelevant. Under natural law theory, the international court was justified in finding the defendants guilty of crimes against humanity.

Chapter 2

1. *What argument could the power utilities use as a defense to the enforcement of this state law?* Even if commercial speech is neither related to illegal activities nor misleading, it may be restricted if a state has a substantial interest that cannot be achieved by less restrictive means. In this situation, the state's interest in energy conservation is substantial, but it could be achieved by less restrictive means. That would be the utilities' defense against the enforcement of this state law.

2. *Is this a violation of equal protection if the only reason for the tax is to protect the local firms from out-of-state competition? Explain.* Yes. The tax would limit the liberty of some persons (out-of-state businesses), so it is subject to a review under the equal protection clause. Protecting local businesses from out-of-state competition is not a legitimate government objective. Thus, such a tax would violate the equal protection clause.

Chapter 3

1. *Does this raise an ethical conflict between Acme and its employees? Between Acme and its shareholders? Explain your answers.* When a corporation decides to respond to what it sees as a moral obligation to correct for past discrimination by adjusting pay differences among its employees, an ethical conflict is raised between the firm and its employees and between the firm and its shareholders. This dilemma arises directly out of the effect such a decision has on the firm's profits. If satisfying this obligation increases profitability, then the dilemma is easily resolved in favor of "doing the right thing."

2. *Does Delta have an ethical duty to remove this product from the market, even if the injuries result only from misuse? Why or why not?* Maybe. On the one hand, it is not the company's "fault" when a product is misused. Also, keeping the product on the market is not a violation of the law, and stopping sales would hurt profits. On the other hand, suspending sales could reduce suffering and could stop potential negative publicity.

Chapter 4

1. *Does the court in Sue's state have jurisdiction over Tipton? What factors will the court consider in determining jurisdiction?* Yes. The court in Sue's state has jurisdiction over Tipton on the basis of the company's minimum contacts with the state.

Courts look at the following factors in determining whether minimum contacts exist: (1) the quantity of the contacts, (2) the nature and quality of the contacts, (3) the source and connection of the cause of action to the contacts, (4) the interest of the forum state, and (5) the convenience of the parties. Attempting to exercise jurisdiction without sufficient minimum contacts would violate the due process clause. Generally, courts have found that jurisdiction is proper when there is substantial business conducted online (with contracts, sales, and so on). Even when there is only some interactivity through a website, courts have sometimes held that jurisdiction is proper. Jurisdiction is not proper when there is merely passive advertising.

Here, all of these factors suggest that the defendant had sufficient minimum contacts with the state to justify the exercise of jurisdiction over the defendant. Two especially important factors were that the plaintiff sold the security system to a resident of the state and that litigating in the defendant's state would be relatively inconvenient for the plaintiff.

2. *If the dispute is not resolved, or if either party disagrees with the decision of the mediator or arbitrator, will a court hear the case? Explain.* Yes. If the dispute is not resolved, or if either party disagrees with the decision of the mediator or arbitrator, a court will hear the case. It is required that the dispute be submitted to mediation or arbitration, but this outcome is not binding.

Chapter 5

1. *Tom can call his first witness. What else might he do?* Tom could file a motion for a directed verdict. This motion asks the judge to direct a verdict for Tom on the ground that Sue presented no evidence that would justify granting her relief. The judge grants the motion if there is insufficient evidence to raise an issue of fact.

2. *Who can appeal to a higher court?* Either a plaintiff or a defendant, or both, can appeal a judgment to a higher court. An appellate court can affirm, reverse, or remand a case, or take any of these actions in combination. To appeal successfully, it is best to appeal on the basis of an error of law, because appellate courts do not usually reverse on findings of fact.

Chapter 6

1. *Can Lou recover from Jana? Why or why not?* Probably. To recover on the basis of negligence, the injured party as a plaintiff must show that the truck's owner owed the plaintiff a duty of care, that the owner breached that duty, that the plaintiff was injured, and that the breach caused the injury.

In this situation, the owner's actions breached the duty of reasonable care. The billboard falling on the plaintiff was the direct cause of the injury, not the plaintiff's own negligence. Thus, liability turns on whether the plaintiff can connect the breach of duty to the injury. This involves the test of proximate cause—the question of foreseeability. The consequences to the injured party must have been a foreseeable result of the owner's carelessness.

2. *What might the firm successfully claim in defense?* The company might defend against the electrician's wife's claim by asserting that the electrician should have known of the risk and, therefore, the company had no duty to warn. According to the problem, the danger is common knowledge in the electrician's field and should have been apparent to this electrician, given his years of training and experience. In other words, the company most likely had no need to warn the electrician of the risk.

The firm could also raise comparative negligence. Both parties' negligence, if any, could be weighed and the liability distributed proportionally. The defendant could also assert assumption of risk, claiming that the electrician voluntarily entered into a dangerous situation, knowing the risk involved.

Chapter 7

1. *Is Superior Vehicles liable? Explain your answer.* Yes. Those who make, sell, or lease goods are liable for the harm or damages caused by those goods to a consumer, user, or bystander. Thus, Superior Vehicles, which installed defective rims on the vehicle, is liable for the injuries proximately caused to the buyer (Uri). A manufacturer is liable for its failure to exercise due care to any person who sustains an injury proximately caused by a negligently made (defective) product. By not inspecting and testing the rims and tires it had installed, Superior Vehicles failed to exercise due care.

2. *What defense might Bensing assert to avoid liability under state law?* Bensing can assert the defense of preemption. An injured party may not be able to sue the manufacturer of defective products that are subject to comprehensive federal regulatory schemes. If the federal government has a comprehensive regulatory scheme (such as it does with medical devices and vaccines), then it is assumed that the rules were designed to ensure a product's safety, and the federal rules will preempt any state regulations. Therefore, Bensing could not be held liable to Rothfus under state law if it complied with the federal drug-labeling requirements.

Chapter 8

1. *Has Roslyn violated any of the intellectual property rights discussed in this chapter? Explain.* Yes. Roslyn has committed theft of trade secrets. Lists of suppliers and customers cannot be patented, copyrighted, or trademarked, but the information they contain is protected against appropriation by others as trade secrets. Most likely, Roslyn signed a contract agreeing not to use this information outside her employment by Organic. But even without such a contract, Organic could make a convincing case against its ex-employee for a theft of trade secrets.

2. *Is this patent infringement? If so, how might Global save the cost of suing World for infringement and at the same time profit from World's sales?* Yes. This is patent infringement. A software maker in this situation might best protect its product, save litigation costs, and profit from its patent by the use of a license. In the context of this problem, a license would grant permission to sell a patented item. (A license can be limited to certain purposes and to the licensee only.)

Chapter 9

1. *Has Karl done anything wrong? Explain.* Karl may have committed trademark infringement. A website that appropriates the key words of other sites with more frequent hits will appear in the same search engine results as the more popular sites. But using another's trademark as a key word without the owner's permission normally constitutes trademark infringement. Of course, some uses of another's trademark as a meta tag may be permissible if the use is reasonably necessary and does not suggest that the owner authorized or sponsored the use.

2. *Can Eagle Corporation stop this use of* eagle*? If so, what must the company show? Explain.* Yes. This may be an instance of trademark dilution. Dilution occurs when a trademark is used, without permission, in a way that diminishes the distinctive quality of the mark. Dilution does not require proof that consumers are likely to be confused by the use of the unauthorized mark. The products involved do not have to be similar. Dilution does require, however, that a mark be famous when the dilution occurs.

Chapter 10

1. *With respect to the gas station, has she committed a crime? If so, what is it?* Yes. With respect to the gas station, she has obtained goods by false pretenses. She might also be charged with larceny and forgery, and most states have special statutes covering illegal use of credit cards.

2. *Has Ben committed a crime? If so, what is it?* Yes. The Counterfeit Access Device and Computer Fraud and Abuse Act provides that a person who accesses a computer online, without permission, to obtain classified data—such as consumer credit files in a credit agency's database—is subject to criminal prosecution. The crime has two elements: accessing the computer without permission and taking data. It is a felony if done for private financial gain. Penalties include fines and imprisonment for up to twenty years. The victim of the theft can also bring a civil suit against the criminal to obtain damages and other relief.

Chapter 11

1. *Under what circumstances would a U.S. court enforce the judgment of the Ecuadoran court?* Under the principle of comity, a U.S. court would defer and give effect to foreign laws and judicial decrees that are consistent with U.S. law and public policy.

2. *How can this attempt to undersell U.S. businesses be defeated?* The practice described in this problem is known as dumping, which is regarded as an unfair international trade practice. Dumping is the sale of imported goods at "less than fair value." Based on the price of those goods in the exporting country, an extra tariff—known as an antidumping duty—can be imposed on the imports.

Chapter 12

1. *Under the Uniform Electronic Transactions Act, what determines the effect of the electronic documents evidencing the parties' deal? Is a party's "signature" necessary? Explain.* First, it might be noted that the Uniform Electronic Transactions Act (UETA) does not apply unless the parties to a contract agree to use e-commerce in their transaction. In this deal, of course, the parties used e-commerce. The UETA removes barriers to e-commerce by giving the same legal effect to e-records and e-signatures as to paper documents and signatures. The UETA does not include rules for those transactions, however.

2. *Is Fred's promise binding? Explain.* Yes. Under the doctrine of detrimental reliance, or promissory estoppel, the promisee is entitled to payment of $5,000 from the promisor on graduation. There was a promise on which the promisee relied, the reliance was substantial and definite (the promisee went to college for the full term, incurring considerable expenses, and will likely graduate). It would only be fair to enforce the promise.

Chapter 13

1. *Before Ready or Stealth starts performing, can the parties call off the deal? What if Stealth has already shipped the pizzas? Explain your answers.* Contracts that are executory on both sides—that is, contracts on which neither party has performed—can be rescinded solely by agreement of the parties. Contracts that are executed on one side—contracts on which one party has performed—can be rescinded only if the party who has performed receives consideration for the promise to call off the deal.

2. *If Haney sues Greg, what will be the measure of recovery?* A nonbreaching party is entitled to his or her benefit of the bargain under the contract. Here, the innocent party is entitled to be put in the position she would have been in if the contract had been fully performed. The measure of the benefit is the cost to complete the work ($500). These are compensatory damages.

Chapter 14

1. *Is this an acceptance of the offer or a counteroffer? If it is an acceptance, is it a breach of the contract? Why or why not? What if Fav-O-Rite told E-Design it was sending the printer stands as "an accommodation"?* A shipment of nonconforming goods constitutes an acceptance of the offer and a breach, unless the seller seasonably notifies the buyer that the nonconforming shipment does not constitute an acceptance and is offered only as an accommodation. Thus, since there was no notification here, the shipment was both an acceptance and a breach. If, however, Fav-O-Rite had notified E-Design that it was sending the printer stands as an accommodation, the shipment would not constitute an acceptance, and Fav-O-Rite would not be in breach.

2. *Does Country have the right to reject the shipment? Explain.* Yes. A seller is obligated to deliver goods that conform to a contract in every detail. This is the perfect tender rule. The exception of the seller's right to cure does not apply here, because the seller delivered too little too late to take advantage of this exception.

Chapter 15

1. *If the employer complies with the order and Alyssa stays on the job, is one order enough to garnish all of Alyssa's wages for each pay period until the debt is paid? Explain.* No. In some states, a creditor must go back to court for a separate order of garnishment for each pay period. Also, federal and state laws limit the amount of money that can be garnished from a debtor's pay.

2. *Are these debts dischargeable in bankruptcy? Explain.* No. Besides the claims listed in this problem, the debts that cannot be discharged in bankruptcy include amounts borrowed to pay back taxes, goods obtained by fraud, debts that were not listed in the petition, domestic-support obligations, certain cash advances, and others.

Chapter 16

1. *When Darnell dies, his widow claims that as Darnell's heir, she is entitled to take his place as Eliana's partner or to receive a share of the firm's assets. Is she right? Why or why not?* No. A widow (or widower) has no right to take a dead partner's place. A partner's death causes dissociation, after which the partnership must purchase the dissociated partner's partnership interest. Therefore, the surviving partners must pay Darnell's widow the value of his interest in the partnership.

2. *Does this constitute "cause" for termination? Why or why not?* Yes. Failing to meet a specified sales quota can constitute a breach of a franchise agreement. If the franchisor is acting in good faith, "cause" may also include the death or disability of the franchisee, the insolvency of the franchisee, and a breach of another term of the franchise agreement.

Chapter 17

1. *What are their options with respect to the management of their firm?* The members of a limited liability company (LLC) may designate a group to run their firm, in which situation the firm would be considered a manager-managed LLC. The group may include only members, only nonmembers, or members and nonmembers. If, instead, all members participate in management, the firm would be a member-managed LLC. In fact, unless the members agree otherwise, all members are considered to participate in the management of the firm.

2. *If Elizabeth is petitioned into involuntary bankruptcy, will that cause a dissolution of the limited partnership?* Bankruptcy of the limited partnership itself causes dissolution, but bankruptcy of one of the limited partners does not dissolve the partnership unless it causes the bankruptcy of the firm.

Chapter 18

1. *Is there a way for Northwest Brands to avoid this double taxation? Explain your answer.* Yes. Small businesses that meet certain requirements can qualify as S corporations, created specifically to permit small businesses to avoid double taxation. The six requirements of an S corporation are (1) the firm must be a domestic corporation, (2) the firm must not be a member of an affiliated group of corporations, (3) the firm must have fewer than a certain number of shareholders, (4) the shareholders must be individuals, estates, or qualified trusts (or corporations in some cases), (5) there can be only one class of stock, and (6) no shareholder can be a nonresident alien.

2. *Yvon, a Wonder shareholder, learns of the purchase and wants to sue the directors on Wonder's behalf. Can she do it? Explain.* Yes. A shareholder can bring a derivative suit on behalf of a corporation if some wrong is done to the corporation. Normally, any damages recovered go into the corporate treasury.

Chapter 19

1. *Was Winona an independent contractor?* Yes. An independent contractor is a person who contracts with another—the principal—to do something but who is neither controlled by the other nor subject to the principal's right to control with respect to the performance. Independent contractors are not employees, because those who hire them have no control over the details of their performance.

2. *Can Davis hold Estee liable for whatever damages he has to pay? Why or why not?* Yes. A principal has a duty to indemnify (reimburse) an agent for liabilities incurred because of authorized and lawful acts and transactions, and for losses suffered because of the principal's failure to perform his or her duties.

Chapter 20

1. *Can AMC be held liable for breach of contract? If so, why? If not, why not?* Yes. Some courts have held that an implied employment contract exists between employer and employee under an employee handbook that states employees will be dismissed only for good cause. An employer who fires a worker contrary to this promise can be held liable for breach of contract.

2. *For Erin to obtain workers' compensation, must her injury have been caused by Fine Print's negligence? Does it matter whether the action causing the injury was intentional? Explain.* Workers' compensation laws establish a procedure for compensating workers who are injured on the job. Instead of suing to collect benefits, an injured worker notifies the employer of an injury and files a claim with the appropriate state agency. The right to recover normally is determined without regard to negligence or fault, but intentionally inflicted injuries are not covered. Unlike the potential for recovery in a lawsuit based on negligence or fault, recovery under a workers' compensation statute is limited to the specific amount designated in the statute for the employee's injury.

Chapter 21

1. *Is this sexual harassment? Why or why not?* Yes. One type of sexual harassment occurs when a request for sexual favors is a condition of employment, and the person making the request is a supervisor or acts with the authority of the employer. A tangible employment action, such as threatening to fire an employee who rejects sexual advances, may also lead to the employer's liability for the supervisor's conduct. That the injured employee is a male and the supervisor a female, instead of the other way around, does not affect the outcome. Same-gender harassment is also actionable.

2. *Could Koko succeed in a suit against Lively for discrimination? Explain.* Yes, if she can show that Lively failed to hire her solely because of her disability. The other elements for a discrimination suit based on a disability are that the plaintiff (1) has a disability and (2) is otherwise qualified for the job. Both of these elements appear to be satisfied in this situation.

Chapter 22

1. What must Gara do under the Immigration Act to hire foreign employees for Skytech? To hire a foreign individual to work in the United States, an employer must submit a petition to the U.S. Citizenship and Immigration Services, which determines whether the job candidate meets the legal standards. Each visa is for a specific job. In this situation, because Gara is looking for persons with specialized skills, he needs to show the individual qualifies for an H-1B visa. To qualify, the person must have highly specialized knowledge and a bachelor's degree or higher. Because only sixty-five thousand H-1B visas are set aside each year for immigrants, Gara must be prepared and file the application within the first few weeks of the year.

2. Are these conditions legal? Why or why not? No. A *closed shop*—a company that requires union membership as a condition of employment—is illegal. A *union shop*—a company that does not require union membership as a condition of employment but requires workers to join the union after a certain time on the job—is illegal in a state with a right-to-work law, which makes it illegal to require union membership for continued employment.

Chapter 23

1. What safeguards promote the ALJ's fairness? Under the Administrative Procedure Act (APA), the administrative law judge (ALJ) must be separate from the agency's investigative and prosecutorial staff. *Ex parte* (private) communications between the ALJ and a party to a proceeding are prohibited. Under the APA, an ALJ is exempt from agency discipline except on a showing of good cause.

2. Does the firm have any opportunity to express its opinion about the pending rule? Explain. Yes. Administrative rulemaking starts with the publication of a notice of the rulemaking in the *Federal Register*. A public hearing is held at which proponents and opponents can offer evidence and question witnesses. After the hearing, the agency considers what was presented at the hearing and drafts the final rule.

Chapter 24

1. To market the drug, what must United prove to the U.S. Food and Drug Administration? Under an extensive set of procedures established by the U.S. Food and Drug Administration, which administers the Federal Food, Drug, and Cosmetic Act, drugs must be shown to be effective as well as safe before they may be marketed to the public. In general, manufacturers are responsible for ensuring that the drugs they offer for sale are free of any substances that could injure consumers.

2. What can Gert do? Under the Truth-in-Lending Act, a buyer who wishes to withhold payment for a faulty product purchased with a credit card must follow specific procedures to settle the dispute. The credit-card issuer then must intervene and attempt to settle the dispute.

Chapter 25

1. Are there any reasons why the court might refuse to issue an injunction against Resource's operation? Explain. Yes. On the ground that the hardships that would be imposed on the polluter and on the community are greater than the hardships suffered by the residents, the court might deny an injunction. If the plant is the core of the local economy, for instance, the residents may be awarded only damages.

2. If the Environmental Protection Agency cleans up the site, from whom can it recover the cost? The Comprehensive Environmental Response, Compensation, and Liability Act regulates the clean-up of hazardous-waste disposal sites. Any potentially responsible party can be charged with the entire cost of cleaning up a site. Potentially responsible parties include the party that generated the waste (ChemCorp), the party that transported the waste to the site (Disposal), the party that owned or operated the site at the time of the disposal (Eliminators), and the current owner or operator of the site (Fluid). A party held responsible for the entire cost may be able to recoup some of it in a lawsuit against other potentially responsible parties.

Chapter 26

1. What can Consuela do? This is a breach of the warranty deed's covenant of quiet enjoyment. The buyer (Consuela) can sue the seller (Bernie) and recover the purchase price of the house, plus any damages.

2. Can Haven transfer possession for even less time to Idyll Company? Explain. Yes. An owner of a fee simple has the most rights possible—he or she can give the property away, sell it, transfer it by will, use it for almost any purpose, possess it to the exclusion of all the world, or as in this situation, transfer possession for any period of time. The party to whom possession is transferred can also transfer his or her interest (usually only with the owner's permission) for any lesser period of time.

Chapter 27

1. Under what circumstances would Pop's Market, a small store in a small, isolated town, be considered a monopolist? If Pop's is a monopolist, is it in violation of Section 2 of the Sherman Act? Why or why not? Size alone does not determine whether a firm is a monopoly—size in relation to the market is what matters. A small store in a small, isolated town is a monopolist if it is the only store serving that market. Monopoly involves the power to affect prices and output. If a firm has sufficient market power to control prices and exclude competition, that firm has monopoly power. Monopoly power in itself is not a violation of Section 2 of the Sherman Act. The offense also requires that the defendant intended to acquire or maintain that power through anticompetitive means.

2. What factors would a court consider to decide whether this arrangement violates the Clayton Act? This agreement is a tying arrangement. The legality of a tying arrangement depends on the purpose of the agreement, the agreement's likely effect on competition in the relevant markets (the market for the tying product and the market for the tied product), and other factors. Tying arrangements for commodities are subject to Section 3 of the Clayton Act. Tying arrangements for services can be agreements in restraint of trade in violation of Section 1 of the Sherman Act.

Chapter 28

1. *What sort of information would an investor consider material?* Under the 1934 Securities Exchange Act and SEC Rule 10b-5, a corporation can be held liable for any material omissions or misrepresentations of material facts to investors. Minor omissions and inaccuracies do not lead to liability. A fact will be considered material to an investor only if it is significant enough that it would likely affect the investor's decision to purchase or sell the company's securities. This would include facts that have an important bearing on the condition of the issuer and its business—liabilities, loans to officers and directors, customer delinquencies, contracts for the sale of corporate assets, new discoveries or products, and pending lawsuits.

2. *Can Lee take advantage of this information to buy and sell Magma stock? Why or why not?* No. The Securities Exchange Act of 1934 extends liability to officers and directors in their personal transactions for taking advantage of inside information when they know it is unavailable to the persons with whom they are dealing.

Appendix C

Sample Answers for
Business Case Problems with Sample Answer

Problem 1–5. *Reading Citations.* The court's opinion in this case—*Ryan Data Exchange, Ltd. v. Graco, Inc.*, 913 F.3d 726 (8th Cir. 2019)—can be found in Volume 913 of the *Federal Reporter, Third Series*, on page 726. The U.S. Court of Appeals for the Eighth Circuit issued this opinion in 2019.

Problem 2–3. *Freedom of Speech.* No. Wooden's conviction was not unconstitutional. Certain speech is not protected under the First Amendment. Speech that violates criminal laws—threatening speech, for example—is not constitutionally protected. Other unprotected speech includes fighting words, or words that are likely to incite others to respond violently. Speech that harms the good reputation of another, or defamatory speech, is also unprotected.

In his e-mail and audio notes to the alderwoman, Wooden referred to a sawed-off shotgun, domestic terrorism, and the assassination and murder of various politicians. He compared the alderwoman to the biblical character Jezebel, referring to her as a "bitch in the Sixth Ward." These references caused the alderwoman to feel threatened. The First Amendment does not protect such threats, which in this case violated a state criminal statute. There was nothing unconstitutional about punishing Wooden for this unprotected speech.

In the actual case on which this problem is based, Wooden appealed his conviction, arguing that it violated his right to freedom of speech. Under the principles set out above, the Missouri Supreme Court affirmed the conviction.

Problem 3–6. *Business Ethics.* It seems obvious from the facts stated in this problem that Hratch Ilanjian behaved unethically. Ethics, of course, involves questions relating to the fairness, justness, rightness, or wrongness of an action. Business ethics focuses on how businesspersons apply moral and ethical principles in making their decisions and whether those decisions are right or wrong.

In this problem, Ilanjian misrepresented himself to Vicken Setrakian, the president of Kenset Corporation, leading Setrakian to believe that Ilanjian was an international businessman who could help turn around Kenset's business in the Middle East. Ilanjian insisted that Setrakian provide him with confidential business documents. Then, claiming that they had an agreement, Ilanjian demanded full and immediate payment. He threatened to disclose the confidential information to a Kenset supplier if payment was not forthcoming. Kenset denied that they had a contract. In the ensuing litigation, during discovery, Ilanjian was uncooperative. Each of these acts was unethical.

In the actual case on which this problem is based, a trial court concluded that there was no contract, ordered the return of the confidential documents, and enjoined (prevented) Ilanjian from using the information. The U.S. Court of Appeals for the Third Circuit affirmed.

Problem 4–7. *Corporate Contacts.* No. The defendants' motion to dismiss the suit for lack of personal jurisdiction should not be granted. A corporation normally is subject to jurisdiction in a state in which it is doing business. A court applies the minimum-contacts test to determine whether it can exercise jurisdiction over an out-of-state corporation. This requirement is met if the corporation sells its products within the state or places its goods in the "stream of commerce" with the intent that the goods be sold in the state.

In this problem, the state of Washington filed a suit in a Washington state court against LG Electronics, Inc., and nineteen other foreign companies that participated in the global market for cathode ray tube (CRT) products. The state alleged a conspiracy to raise prices and set production levels in the market for CRTs in violation of a state consumer protection statute. The defendants filed a motion to dismiss the suit for lack of personal jurisdiction. These goods were sold for many years in high volume in the United States, including the state of Washington. In other words, the corporations purposefully established minimum contacts in the state of Washington. This is a sufficient basis for a Washington state court to assert personal jurisdiction over the defendants.

In the actual case on which this problem is based, the court dismissed the suit for lack of personal jurisdiction. On appeal, a state intermediate appellate court reversed on the reasoning stated above.

Problem 5–6. *Discovery.* Yes. The items that were deleted from a Facebook page can be recovered. Normally, a party must hire an expert to recover material in an electronic format, and this can be time consuming and expensive.

Electronic evidence, or e-evidence, consists of all computer-generated or electronically recorded information, such as posts on Facebook and other social media sites. The effect that e-evidence can have in a case depends on its relevance and what it reveals. In the facts presented in this problem, Isaiah should be sanctioned for deleting items that were subject to a discovery request. He should be required to cover Allied's cost to hire the recovery expert and attorneys' fees to confront the misconduct. In a jury trial, the court might also instruct the jury to presume that any missing items are harmful to Isaiah's case. If all of the material is retrieved and presented at the trial, any prejudice to Allied's case might thereby be mitigated. If not, the court might go so far as to order a new trial.

In the actual case on which this problem is based, Allied hired an expert, who determined that Isaiah had in fact removed some photos and other items from his Facebook page. After the expert testified about the missing material, Isaiah provided Allied with all of it, including the photos that he had deleted. Allied sought a retrial, but the court instead reduced the amount of Isaiah's damages by the amount that it cost Allied to address his "misconduct."

Problem 6–4. *Negligence.* Negligence requires proof that (1) the defendant owed a duty of care to the plaintiff, (2) the defendant breached that duty, (3) the defendant's breach caused the plaintiff's injury, and (4) the plaintiff suffered a legally recognizable injury. With respect to the duty of care, a business owner has a duty to use reasonable care to protect business invitees. This duty includes an obligation to discover and correct or warn of unreasonably dangerous conditions that the owner of the premises should reasonably foresee might endanger an invitee. Some risks are so obvious that an owner need not warn of them. But even if a risk is obvious, a business owner may not be excused from the duty to protect its customers from foreseeable harm.

Because Lucario was the Weatherford's business invitee, the hotel owed her a duty of reasonable care to make its premises safe for her use. The balcony ran nearly the entire width of the window in Lucario's room. She could have reasonably believed that the window was a means of access to the balcony. The window/balcony configuration was dangerous, however, because the window opened wide enough for an adult to climb out, but the twelve-inch gap between one side of the window and the balcony was unprotected. This unprotected gap opened to a drop of more than three stories to a concrete surface below.

Should the hotel have anticipated the potential harm to a guest who opened the window in Room 59 and attempted to access the balcony? The hotel encouraged guests to "step out onto the balcony" to smoke. The dangerous condition of the window/balcony configuration could have been remedied at a minimal cost. These circumstances could be perceived as creating an "unreasonably dangerous" condition. And it could be concluded that the hotel created or knew of the condition and failed to take reasonable steps to warn of it or correct it. Of course, the Weatherford might argue that the window/balcony configuration was so obvious that the hotel was not liable for Lucario's fall.

In the actual case on which this problem is based, the court concluded that the Weatherford did not breach its duty of care to Lucario. On McMurtry's appeal—Lucario's estate's personal representative—a state intermediate appellate court held that this conclusion was in error, vacated the lower court's judgment in favor of the hotel on this issue, and remanded the case.

Problem 7–5. *Product Liability.* Here, the accident was caused by Jett's inattention, not by the texting device in the cab of his truck. In a product liability case based on a design defect, the plaintiff has to prove that the product was defective at the time it left the hands of the seller or lessor. The plaintiff must also show that this defective condition made it "unreasonably dangerous" to the user or consumer. If the product was delivered in a safe condition and subsequent mishandling made it harmful to the user, the seller or lessor normally is not liable. To successfully assert a design defect, a plaintiff has to show that a reasonable alternative design was available and that the defendant failed to use it.

The plaintiffs could contend that the defendant manufacturer of the texting device owed them a duty of care because injuries to vehicle drivers and passengers, and others on the roads, were reasonably foreseeable due to the product's design, which (1) required the driver to divert his eyes from the road to view an incoming text from the dispatcher, and (2) permitted the receipt of texts while the vehicle was moving. But manufacturers are not required to design a product incapable of distracting a driver. The duty owed by a manufacturer to the user or consumer of a product does not require guarding against hazards that are commonly known or obvious or protecting against injuries that result from a user's careless conduct. That is what happened here.

In the actual case on which this problem is based, the court reached the same conclusion, based on the reasoning stated above, and an intermediate appellate court affirmed the judgment.

Problem 8–6. *Patents.* One ground on which the denial of the patent application in this problem could be reversed on appeal is that the design of Raymond Gianelli's "Rowing Machine" is *not obvious* in light of the design of the "Chest Press Apparatus for Exercising Regions of the Upper Body."

To obtain a patent, an applicant must demonstrate to the satisfaction of the U.S. Patent and Trademark Office (PTO) that the invention, discovery, process, or design is novel, useful, and not obvious in light of current technology. In this problem, the PTO denied Gianelli's application for a patent for his "Rowing Machine"—an exercise machine on which a user *pulls* on handles to perform a rowing motion against a selected resistance. The PTO considered the device obvious in light of a patented "Chest Press Apparatus for Exercising Regions of the Upper Body"—a chest press exercise machine on which a user *pushes* on handles to overcome a selected resistance. But it can be easily argued that it is not obvious to modify a machine with handles designed to be *pushed* into one with handles designed to be *pulled*. In fact, anyone who has used exercise machines knows that a way to cause injury is to use a machine in a manner not intended by the manufacturer.

In the actual case on which this problem is based, the U.S. Court of Appeals for the Federal Circuit reversed the PTO's denial of Gianelli's application for a patent, based on the reasoning stated above.

Problem 9–5. *Social Media.* Law enforcement can use social media to detect and prosecute suspected criminals. But there must be an authenticated connection between the suspects and the posts. To make this connection, law enforcement officials can present the testimony or certification of authoritative representatives of the social media site or other experts. The posts can be traced through Internet Protocol (IP) addresses. An IP address can reveal the e-mail address, and even the mailing address, of an otherwise anonymous poster. The custodians of Facebook, for example, can verify Facebook pages and posts because they maintain those items as business records in the course of regularly conducted business activities. From those sources, the prosecution in Hassan's case could have tracked the IP address to discover his identity.

In the actual case on which this problem is based, on Hassan's appeal of his conviction, the U.S. Court of Appeals for the Fourth Circuit affirmed.

Problem 10–4. *White-Collar Crime.* Yes. The acts committed by Matthew Simpson and the others constituted wire and mail fraud. Federal law makes it a crime to devise any scheme that uses the U.S. mail, commercial carriers (such as FedEx or UPS), or wire (such as telegraph, telephone, television, the Internet, or e-mail) with the intent to defraud the public.

Here, as stated in the facts, Simpson and his cohorts created and operated a series of corporate entities to defraud telecommunications companies, creditors, credit reporting agencies, and others. Through these entities, Simpson and the others used routing codes and spoofing services to make long-distance calls appear to be local. They stole other firms' network capacity and diverted payments to themselves. They leased goods and services without paying for them. In addition, they assumed false identities, addresses, and credit histories, and they issued false bills, invoices, financial statements, and credit references, in order to hide their association with their entities and with each other. Through the use of this "scheme," the perpetrators defrauded telecommunications companies and other members of the public in order to gain goods and services for themselves. They used wire services—the Internet and, presumably, phones and other qualifying services—to further the scheme.

In the actual case on which this problem is based, a federal district court convicted Simpson of participating in a wire and mail fraud conspiracy (and other crimes). On appeal, the U.S. Court of Appeals for the Fifth Circuit affirmed the conviction.

Problem 11–5. *Import Controls.* Yes. An antidumping duty can be assessed retrospectively (retroactively). But it does not seem likely that such a duty should be assessed here.

In this problem, the Wind Tower Trade Coalition (an association of domestic manufacturers of utility-scale wind towers) filed a suit in the U.S. Court of International Trade against the U.S. Department of Commerce, challenging its decision to impose only *prospective* antidumping duties on imports of utility-scale wind towers from China and Vietnam. The Commerce Department had found that the domestic industry had not suffered any "material injury" or "threat of material injury," and that it would be protected by a prospective assessment. Without a previously cognizable injury—and given the fact that any retrospective duties collected would not be payable to the members of the domestic industry in any event—it does not seem likely that retroactive duties should be imposed.

In the actual case on which this problem is based, the court denied the plaintiff's request for an injunction. On appeal, the

U.S. Court of Appeals for the Federal Circuit affirmed the denial, holding that the lower court had acted within its discretion in determining that retrospective duties were not appropriate.

Problem 12–3. *Requirements of the Offer.* No. TCP is not correct—the bonus plan was not too indefinite to be an offer. One of the requirements for an effective offer is that its terms must be reasonably definite. This enables a court to determine whether a breach has occurred and award an appropriate remedy. Generally, the offer's terms include an identification of the parties and the object or subject of the contract, the consideration to be paid, and the time of performance.

In this problem, TCP provided its employees, including Bahr, with the details of a bonus plan. A district sales manager such as Bahr who achieved 100 percent year-over-year sales growth and a 42 percent gross margin would earn 200 percent of his or her base salary. TCP added that it retained absolute discretion to modify the plan. Bahr exceeded the goal and expected a bonus commensurate with her performance. TCP paid her less than half what its plan promised, however. In the ensuing litigation, TCP claimed that the bonus plan was too indefinite to constitute an offer, but this was not, in fact, the case. The plan provided clear criteria to determine an employee's eligibility for a certain amount within a specific time. A court asked to apply the plan would have little or no doubt as to the amount an employee would be entitled to. The term that reserved discretion to TCP to modify the plan did not sufficiently undercut the clarity of the offer to prevent the formation of a contract.

In the actual case on which this problem is based, the trial court concluded that the reservation of discretion to revoke a plan makes an offer too indefinite and issued a judgment in TCP's favor. A state intermediate appellate court reversed this judgment, holding that TCP's plan was a sufficiently definite offer.

Problem 13–5. *Limitation-of-Liability Clauses.* Yes. The limitation-of-liability agreement that Eriksson signed is likely to be enforced in her parents' suit against Nunnink, their daughter's riding coach. This will likely result in a judgment against them unless they can establish "direct, willful and wanton negligence" on Nunnink's part. A limitation-of-liability clause affects the availability of certain remedies. Under basic contract principles, to be enforceable, these clauses must be clear and unambiguous.

In this problem, Eriksson, a young horseback-riding competitor, signed an agreement that released Nunnink from all liability except for damages caused by Nunnink's "direct, willful and wanton negligence." During an event, Eriksson's horse struck a hurdle, causing her to fall from the horse. The horse fell on her, resulting in her death. Her parents filed a suit against Nunnink for wrongful death. The limitation-of-liability clause signed by Eriksson, however, was straightforward, clear, and unambiguous, and therefore enforceable. Nunnink would be liable only if Eriksson's death was caused by Nunnink's gross negligence. The facts do not state that Eriksson's parents proved that Nunnink was grossly negligent.

In the actual case on which this problem is based, the trial court issued a judgment in Nunnink's favor. A state intermediate appellate court affirmed the judgment on the basis explained here.

Problem 14–6. *Remedies of the Buyer or Lessee.* No. At this point, the Morrises are not entitled to revoke their acceptance of the cabinets that IO delivered. Under the Uniform Commercial Code, acceptance of a lot or a commercial unit can be revoked if a nonconformity substantially impairs the value of the lot or unit and acceptance was based on the reasonable assumption that the nonconformity would be cured, and it has not been cured within a reasonable period of time. One of the corollaries to this rule is, of course, that the seller must be given a reasonable time within which to effect a cure.

Here, the Morrises contracted with IO to rebuild the kitchen in their home on the Gulf Coast of Mississippi after it was extensively damaged in a hurricane. As part of the deal, IO delivered new cabinets. Some defects were apparent, and as installation progressed, others emerged. IO ordered replacement parts to cure the defects and later offered to remove the cabinets and refund the price. The Morrises asked to be reimbursed for the installation fee as well. IO refused this request, but at all times, the seller emphasized that it was willing to fulfill its contractual obligations. The buyers then attempted to revoke their acceptance of the cabinets—before the replacement parts arrived and without attempting to negotiate any other accommodation.

In the actual case on which this problem is based, the Morrises filed a suit in a Mississippi state court against IO. The court dismissed the complaint and entered a judgment in the defendant's favor. A state intermediate appellate court affirmed. "The Morrises were not entitled to recovery because they revoked acceptance of the cabinets before giving IO a reasonable opportunity to cure the defects."

Problem 15–3. *Discharge in Bankruptcy.* No. Educational Credit Management Corporation (ECMC) cannot resume its effort to collect on Hann's loans. After the debtor has completed all payments, the court grants a discharge of all debts provided for by the repayment plan. All debts generally are dischargeable, especially those for which the court either declared that there was no obligation or disallowed on the ground that the underlying debt was satisfied.

In this problem, Hann financed her education partially through loans. When she filed a Chapter 13 petition, ECMC filed an unsecured proof of claim based on the loans. Hann believed that she had repaid the loans in full and objected. The court held a hearing at which ECMC failed to appear, and Hann submitted correspondence from the lender indicating the loans had been paid. The court then entered an order sustaining Hann's objection to ECMC's claim, in effect declaring that there was no obligation and the underlying debt was satisfied. By later attempting to renew efforts to collect on the loans, ECMC would violate the court's order.

In the actual case on which this problem is based, ECMC resumed collection efforts after the bankruptcy. Hann reopened her case and filed a complaint against ECMC, alleging that it

had violated the order sustaining her objection. The court ruled in Hann's favor and sanctioned ECMC for attempting to collect on the debt. On ECMC's appeal, the U.S. Court of Appeals for the First Circuit affirmed.

Problem 16–7. *Franchise Termination.* No. Executive Care is not entitled to an injunction against the Marshals and their new company. An injunction is an extraordinary remedy. To obtain an injunction before a suit is resolved, or arbitration or other alternative dispute resolution procedure is undertaken and completed, a party must establish that he or she will suffer irreparable harm if the injunction is denied.

In the facts of this problem, the Marshalls entered into a franchise agreement with Executive Care to operate a home health-care franchise. The agreement provided that the franchisees' failure to comply with the terms would likely cause irreparable harm to the franchisor, thereby entitling it to an injunction. When the Marshalls gave up their franchise, presumably before the end of its term under the franchise agreement, they returned everything in their possession with Executive Care trademarks. They quit operating out of the franchised location. They transferred the phone number back to Executive Care and informed their clients that they were no longer associated with that firm. Although the Marshalls continued to operate a home health-care business, they did so under the name "Well-Being Home Care Corp." There is nothing in these facts to establish that Executive Care is entitled to a preliminary injunction on the basis of irreparable harm. There appears to be little else the Marshalls might have done to prevent such harm to the franchisor.

In the actual case on which this problem is based, Executive Care filed a suit in a federal district court against the Marshalls and asked the court to issue a preliminary injunction. The court denied the request. On the reasoning stated here, the U.S. Court of Appeals for the Third Circuit affirmed.

Problem 17–4. *LLC Operation.* Part of the attractiveness of a limited liability company (LLC) as a form of business enterprise is its flexibility. The members can decide how to operate the business through an operating agreement. For example, the agreement can set forth procedures for choosing or removing members or managers.

Here, the Bluewater operating agreement provided for a "super majority" vote to remove a member who has committed a felony or under other circumstances that would jeopardize the firm's contractor status. Thus, Smith could not unilaterally "fire" another member without providing a reason. In fact, even a super majority of the members (Smith, Mosser, and Floyd) could not terminate Williford's interest in the firm without providing an acceptable reason—a felony conviction or a circumstance that undercut the firm's status as a contractor. Therefore, Smith, Mosser, and Floyd breached their operating agreement by attempting to remove Williford as a member. They may also have violated their fiduciary duties to Williford (depending on whether Mississippi has adopted the ULLCA), but it is not clear from the facts provided whether they violated the state LLC statute.

In the actual case on which this problem is based, Smith attempted to "fire" Williford without providing a reason. In Williford's suit, the court issued a judgment in his favor. On appeal, the court of appeals reversed, but the Supreme Court of Mississippi reversed the appellate court's decision and reinstated the lower court's holding in favor of Williford. The evidence was sufficient to find that the defendants had breached the LLC's operating agreement.

Problem 18–6. *Rights of Shareholders.* Clifford can pursue his action on the companies' behalf against Frederick. When a corporation is harmed by the actions of a director or officer, the other directors can bring a suit in the name of the company against that party. If the directors do not bring a suit, the shareholders can do so filing what is known as a shareholder's derivative suit. When shareholders bring a derivative suit, they are not pursuing rights or benefits for themselves personally but are acting as guardians of the corporate entity. Thus, if the suit is successful, any damages recovered go into the corporate treasury, not to the shareholders personally.

Here, two firms—one a limited liability company (LLC) and the other a corporation—are owned by three brothers, including Frederick and Clifford. Frederick is a controlling shareholder, and the president, of the corporation. Clifford believed that Frederick had been misusing the companies' funds to pay non-existent debts, divert LLC assets to the corporation, and disburse about $1.8 million in corporate funds to his separate business. Clifford hired an attorney and filed an action on behalf of the two companies against Frederick. This action qualifies as a shareholder's derivative suit. Under these facts, any damages recovered should be paid to the companies.

Frederick's contention that a shareholder who lacks the knowledge necessary to adequately represent a corporation's interest because he or she does not understand financial statements may be a factor that helps defeat a frivolous suit or an action driven by an outside party. But in this case, Clifford demonstrated the requisite knowledge required to represent the firms' interests even if he did not know the details of the companies' financial documents—the action was filed on his instigation, he clearly understood the allegations, and he hired an attorney on whom he could rely to represent the companies' interests.

In the actual case on which this problem is based, Frederick filed a motion to dismiss based on the argument that Clifford lacked standing to bring the suit because he was the wrong party to represent the companies. The court denied the motion, in part, on the reasoning stated above.

Problem 19–4. *Determining Employee Status.* No. Cox is not liable to Cayer for any injuries or damage that she sustained in the accident with Ovalles. Generally, an employer is not liable for physical harm caused to a third person by the negligent act of an independent contractor in the performance of a contract. This is because the employer does not have the right to control the details of the performance. In determining whether a worker has the status of an independent contractor, how much control the employer can exercise over the details of the work is the most important factor weighed by the courts.

In this problem, Ovalles worked as a cable installer for Cox under an agreement with M&M. The agreement disavowed any employer-employee relationship between Cox and M&M's installers. Ovalles was required to designate his affiliation with Cox on his van, clothing, and an ID badge. But Cox had minimal contact with Ovalles and limited power to control the manner in which he performed his work. Cox supplied cable wire and other equipment, but these items were delivered to M&M, not Ovalles. These facts indicate that Ovalles was an independent contractor, not an employee. Thus, Cox was not liable to Cayer for the harm caused to her by Ovalles when his van rear-ended Cayer's car.

In the actual case on which this problem is based, the court issued a judgment in Cox's favor. The Rhode Island Supreme Court affirmed, applying the principles stated above to arrive at the same conclusion.

Problem 20–5. *Unemployment Compensation.* Yes. Ramirez qualifies for unemployment compensation. Generally, to be eligible for unemployment compensation, a worker must be willing and able to work. Workers who have been fired for misconduct or who have voluntarily left their jobs are not eligible for benefits. In the facts of this problem, the applicable state statute disqualifies an employee from receiving benefits if he or she voluntarily leaves work without "good cause."

The issue is whether Ramirez left her job for "good cause." When her father in the Dominican Republic had a stroke, she asked her employer for time off to be with him. Her employer refused the request. But Ramirez left to be with her father and called to inform her employer. It seems likely that this family emergency would constitute "good cause," and Ramirez's call and return to work after her father's death indicated that she did not disregard her employer's interests.

In the actual case on which this problem is based, the state of Florida denied Ramirez unemployment compensation. On Ramirez's appeal, a state intermediate appellate court reversed, on the reasoning stated above.

Problem 21–7. *Sexual Harassment.* Newton's best defense to Blanton's assertion of liability against the employer for its general manager's actions is the "*Ellerth/Faragher* affirmative defense." To establish this defense, an employer must show that it has taken reasonable care to prevent and promptly correct any sexually harassing behavior and that the plaintiff unreasonably failed to take advantage of any opportunity provided by the employer to avoid the harm.

In this problem, Blanton was subjected to sexual harassment by the general manager at their place of employment, a Pizza Hut restaurant operated by Newton. Blanton alerted low-level supervisors about the harassment, but they, like Blanton, were subordinate to the general manager and had no authority over her. Newton had a clear, straightforward antidiscrimination policy and complaint procedure under which an employee was to complain to the harasser's supervisor in such a situation. Once

Blanton finally complained to a manager with authority over the general manager, Newton promptly and effectively responded to Blanton's complaint. His delay in reporting the harassment to the appropriate authority can be construed as an unreasonable failure to take advantage of the opportunity provided by the employer to avoid the harm.

In the actual case on which this problem is based, in Blanton's suit against Newton, a jury found that the plaintiff was harassed as he claimed, but also that the defendant proved the *Ellerth/Faragher* affirmative defense, and the court issued a judgment in the employer's favor. The U.S. Court of Appeals for the Fifth Circuit affirmed.

Problem 22–5. *Unfair Labor Practices.* Before invoking a union-security clause against an employee, the union has an obligation, under the National Labor Relations Act (NLRA), to deal fairly with the employee. The NLRA requires the union to (1) provide the employee with actual notice of the precise amount due, including the months for which dues are owed, (2) explain how it computed the amount due, (3) give the employee a reasonable deadline for payment, and (4) explain to the employee that failure to pay will result in discharge.

Here, substantial evidence supported the NLRB's decision that the union's conduct in arranging to have the employee fired because of outstanding union dues under a union-security agreement—without first having discharged its fiduciary duties—violated the NLRA's prohibition against coercing employees. Such action also violated the prohibition against causing an employer to fire an employee, because the record indicated that the union had not explained to the employee how it had calculated his dues or provided him a reasonable time period in which to make payment. In fact, there was evidence suggesting that the union did just the opposite, first agreeing to a payment schedule with the employee and then having him fired the next day, before he could complete the agreed schedule and while he was on track to do so.

Problem 23–3. *Agency Powers.* The United States Supreme Court held that greenhouse gases fit within the Clean Air Act's (CAA's) definition of *air pollutant*. Thus, the Environmental Protection Agency (EPA) has the authority under that statute to regulate the emissions of such gases from new motor vehicles. According to the Court, the definition, which includes "any" air pollutant, embraces all airborne compounds "of whatever stripe." The EPA's focus on congressional amendments to the act did not address the original intent behind the statute. Nothing in the statute suggests that Congress meant to curtail the agency's power to treat greenhouse gases as air pollutants. In other words, the agency has a preexisting mandate to regulate "any air pollutant" that may endanger the public welfare.

The EPA also argued that, even if it had the authority to regulate greenhouse gas emissions, the agency would not exercise that authority because any regulation would conflict with other administration priorities. The Court acknowledged that the CAA conditions EPA action on the agency's formation of a "judgment" but explained that judgment must relate to whether a pollutant "cause[s], or contribute[s] to, air pollution which

may reasonably be anticipated to endanger public health or welfare." Thus, the EPA can avoid issuing regulations only if the agency determines that greenhouse gases do not contribute to climate change (or if the agency reasonably explains why it cannot or will not determine whether they do). The EPA's refusal to regulate was thus "arbitrary, capricious, or otherwise not in accordance with law." The Court remanded the case for the EPA to "ground its reasons for action or inaction in the statute."

Problem 24–4. *Fair Debt-Collection Practices.* Engler may recover under the Fair Debt Collection Practices Act (FDCPA). Atlantic is subject to the FDCPA because it is a debt-collection agency and was attempting to collect a debt on behalf of Bank of America. Atlantic used offensive collection tactics when it gave Engler's employer the false impression that Engler was a criminal, had a pending case, and was about to be arrested. Engler suffered harm because he experienced discomfort, embarrassment, and distress as a result of Atlantic's abusive conduct. Engler may recover actual damages, statutory damages, and attorneys' fees from Atlantic.

Problem 25–5. *Environmental Impact Statements.* Yes. An environmental impact statement (EIS) is required before the U.S. Forest Service (USFS) implements its proposed travel management plan (TMP). An EIS must be prepared for every major federal action that significantly affects the quality of the environment. An action is "major" if it involves a substantial commitment of resources. An action is "federal" if a federal agency has the power to control it. An EIS must analyze (1) the impact on the environment that the action will have, (2) any adverse effects on the environment and alternative actions that might be taken, and (3) irreversible effects that the action might generate.

Here, the resources committed to the implementation of the USFS's TMP could include the resources within the wilderness and the time and effort dedicated by the agency. The wilderness resources would include the soil, the vegetation, the wildlife, the wildlife habitat, any threatened or endangered species, and other natural assets impacted by the TMP. The agency's resources would include the funds and staff necessary to design, map, maintain, and enforce the TMP. These resources seem substantial. Of course, the implementation of the TMP is federal because the USFS has the power to control it.

As for the aspects of the environment that the agency might consider in preparing the EIS, some of the important factors were just listed—the soil, vegetation, wildlife, wildlife habitat, and threatened or endangered species. Other aspects of the environment impacted by the TMP might include cultural resources, historical resources, wilderness suitability, and other authorized uses of the wilderness. There is a potential for impact by every route that is designed to be part of the system, as well as the "dispersed vehicle camping" to be permitted on the terrain.

In the actual case on which this problem is based, the USFS considered all of the factors listed above. The agency then issued an EIS and a decision implementing the TMP. On a challenge to the EIS, a federal district court issued a judgment in the USFS's favor. The U.S. Court of Appeals for the Ninth Circuit affirmed, stating, "The Forest Service took the requisite hard look at the environmental impacts."

Problem 26–6. *Joint Tenancies.* Under the law of the Cayman Islands, and according to Arthur's will, the disputed property became Diana's sole property when Arthur died. In a joint tenancy, each of two or more persons owns an undivided interest in the property. A deceased joint tenant's interest passes to the surviving joint tenant or tenants. The right of a surviving joint tenant to inherit a deceased joint tenant's ownership interest is referred to as a right of survivorship.

In this problem, Arthur and Diana owned three properties in the Cayman Islands in joint tenancy. (For this purpose, Cayman law is the same as U.S. law.) When the couple divorced, the decree did not change the tenancy. Later, Arthur died. His will provided that any property he held in joint tenancy "will pass to the survivor, and I instruct my Personal Representative to make no claim thereto." Despite this provision, the personal representative of Arthur's estate (his brother, Curtis) asserted that Arthur's interest in the properties was part of the estate. Diana said that the properties were entirely hers. Clearly, Diana is correct. Under the applicable principles of ownership of property by joint tenancy, as the sole surviving joint tenant, Arthur's interest in the properties passed to her. And under the terms of Arthur's will, his interest passed to her (and Curtis was "to make no claim thereto").

In the actual case on which this problem is based, Curtis asked the Florida state court that issued the couple's divorce to declare that Arthur's interest in the Cayman properties was part of his estate. The court ruled in the estate's favor and ordered Diana to sell the properties or buy Arthur's interest in them. A state intermediate appellate court reversed the order.

Problem 27–4. *Price Discrimination.* Spa Steel satisfies most of the requirements for a price discrimination claim under Section 2 of the Clayton Act. Dayton Superior is engaged in interstate commerce, and it sells goods of like grade and quality to several purchasers. Moreover, Spa Steel can show that, because it sells Dayton Superior's products at a higher price than competitors, it lost business and thus suffered an injury. To recover, however, Spa Steel will also need to prove that Dayton Superior charged Spa Steel's competitors a lower price for the same product. Spa Steel cannot recover if its prices were higher for reasons related to its own business, such as having higher overhead expenses or seeking a larger profit.

Problem 28–4. *Violations of the 1934 Act.* An omission or misrepresentation of a material fact in connection with the purchase or sale of a security may violate Section 10(b) of the Securities Exchange Act of 1934 and SEC Rule 10b-5. The key question is whether the omitted or misrepresented information is material. A fact, by itself, is not automatically material. A fact will be regarded as material only if it is significant enough that it would likely affect an investor's decision as to whether to buy or sell the company's securities. For example, a company's potential liability in a product liability suit and the financial consequences to the firm are material facts that must be disclosed because they are significant enough to affect an investor's decision as to whether to buy stock in the company.

In this case, the plaintiffs' claim should not be dismissed. To prevail on their claim that the defendants made material omissions in violation of Section 10(b) and SEC Rule 10b-5, the plaintiffs must prove that the omission was material. Their complaint alleged the omission of information linking Zicam and anosmia (a loss of the sense of smell) and plausibly suggested that reasonable investors would have viewed this information as material. After all, Zicam products account for 70 percent of Matrixx's sales.

Matrixx received reports of consumers who suffered anosmia after using Zicam Cold Remedy. In public statements discussing revenues and product safety, Matrixx did not disclose this information. But the information was significant enough to likely affect a consumer's decision to use the product, and this would affect revenue and ultimately the commercial viability of the product. The information was therefore significant enough to likely affect an investor's decision whether to buy or sell Matrixx's stock, and this would affect the stock price. Thus, the plaintiffs' allegations were sufficient. Contrary to the defendants' assertion, statistical sampling is not required to show materiality—reasonable investors could view reports of adverse events as material even if the reports did not provide statistically significant evidence.

Glossary

A

acceptance In contract law, the offeree's indication to the offeror that the offeree agrees to be bound by the terms of the offeror's proposal.

accord and satisfaction An agreement for payment (or other performance) between two parties, one of whom has a right of action against the other. After the payment has been accepted or other performance has been made, the "accord and satisfaction" is complete, and the obligation is discharged.

accredited investor In the context of securities offerings, sophisticated investors, such as banks, insurance companies, investment companies, the issuer's executive officers and directors, and persons whose income or net worth exceeds certain limits.

actionable Capable of serving as the basis of a lawsuit.

act of state doctrine A doctrine that provides that the judicial branch of one country will not examine the validity of public acts committed by a recognized foreign government within its own territory.

actual malice A condition that exists when a person makes a statement with either knowledge of its falsity or reckless disregard for the truth. In a defamation suit, a statement made about a public figure normally must be made with actual malice for liability to be incurred.

actus reus (pronounced *ak*-tus *ray*-uhs) A guilty (prohibited) act. The commission of a prohibited act and the intent to commit a crime are the two essential elements required for criminal liability.

adequate protection doctrine In bankruptcy law, a doctrine that protects secured creditors from losing their security as a result of an automatic stay. In certain circumstances, the bankruptcy court may provide adequate protection by requiring the debtor or trustee to pay the creditor or provide additional guaranties to protect the creditor against the losses suffered by the creditor as a result of the stay.

adjudication The process of resolving a dispute by presenting evidence and arguments before a neutral third party decision maker in a court or an administrative law proceeding.

administrative agency A federal or state government agency created by the legislature to perform a specific function, such as to make and enforce rules pertaining to the environment.

administrative law judge (ALJ) One who presides over an administrative agency hearing and has the power to administer oaths, take testimony, rule on questions of evidence, and make determinations of fact.

administrative process The procedure used by administrative agencies in fulfilling their three basic functions: rulemaking, enforcement, and adjudication.

adverse possession The acquisition of title to real property through open occupation, without the consent of the owner, for a period of time specified by a state statute. The occupation must be actual, exclusive, open, continuous, and in opposition to all others, including the owner.

affidavit A written voluntary statement of facts, confirmed by the oath or affirmation of the party making it and made before a person having the authority to administer the oath or affirmation.

affirmative action Job-hiring (and school admission) policies that give special consideration to members of protected classes in an effort to overcome present effects of past discrimination.

affirmative defense A response to a plaintiff's claim that does not deny the plaintiff's facts but attacks the plaintiff's legal right to bring an action. An example is the running of the statute of limitations.

agency A relationship between two parties in which one party (the agent) agrees to represent or act for the other (the principal).

agreement A meeting of two or more minds in regard to the terms of a contract; usually broken down into two events—an offer by one party to form a contract, and an acceptance of the offer by the person to whom the offer is made.

alien corporation A corporation formed in another country but doing business in the United States.

allege To state, recite, assert, or charge.

alternative dispute resolution (ADR) The resolution of disputes in ways other than those involved in the traditional judicial process. Negotiation, mediation, and arbitration are forms of ADR.

answer Procedurally, a defendant's response to the plaintiff's complaint.

anticipatory repudiation An assertion or action by a party indicating that he or she will not perform an obligation that he or she is contractually obligated to perform at a future time.

antitrust law Laws protecting commerce from unlawful restraints and anticompetitive practices.

apparent authority Authority that is only apparent, not real. An agent's apparent authority arises when the principal causes a third party to believe that the agent has authority, even though she or he does not.

appellant The party who takes an appeal from one court to another.

appellee The party against whom an appeal is taken—that is, the party who opposes setting aside or reversing the judgment.

arbitration The settling of a dispute by submitting it to a disinterested third party (other than a court), who renders a decision. The decision may or may not be legally binding.

arbitration clause A clause in a contract that provides that, in the event of a dispute, the parties will submit the dispute to arbitration rather than litigate the dispute in court.

arson The malicious burning of another's dwelling. Some statutes have expanded arson to include any real property, regardless of ownership, and the destruction of property by other means—for example, by explosion.

articles of incorporation The document that is filed with the appropriate state official, usually the secretary of state, when a business is incorporated and that contains basic information about the corporation.

articles of organization The document that is filed with the appropriate state official, usually the secretary of state, when a limited liability company is formed.

articles of partnership A written agreement that sets forth each partner's rights and obligations with respect to the partnership.

artisan's lien A possessory lien given to a person who has made improvements and added value to another person's personal property as security for payment for services performed.

assault Any word or action intended to make another person fearful of immediate physical harm; a reasonably believable threat.

assignment The act of transferring to another all or part of one's rights arising under a contract.

assumption of risk A defense against negligence that can be used when the plaintiff was aware of a danger and voluntarily assumed the risk of injury from that danger.

attachment In the context of judicial liens, a court-ordered seizure and taking into custody of property prior to the securing of a judgment for a past-due debt.

attempted monopolization An action by a firm that involves anticompetitive conduct, the intent to gain monopoly power, and a "dangerous probability" of success in achieving monopoly power.

authorization card A card signed by an employee that gives a union permission to act on his or her behalf in negotiations with management.

automatic stay In bankruptcy proceedings, the suspension of almost all litigation and other action by creditors against the debtor or the debtor's property. The stay is effective the moment the debtor files a petition in bankruptcy.

award In the context of litigation, the amount of money awarded to a plaintiff in a civil lawsuit as damages. In the context of arbitration, the arbitrator's decision.

B

bailment A situation in which the personal property of one person (a bailor) is entrusted to another (a bailee), who is obligated to return the bailed property to the bailor or dispose of it as directed.

bait-and-switch advertising Advertising a product at an attractive price and then telling the consumer that the advertised product is not available or is of poor quality and encouraging her or him to purchase a more expensive item.

bankruptcy court A federal court of limited jurisdiction that handles only bankruptcy proceedings.

bankruptcy trustee A person appointed by the court to manage the debtor's funds in a bankruptcy proceeding.

battery The unprivileged, intentional touching of another.

benefit corporation A type of for-profit corporation, available by statute in a number of states, that seeks to have a material positive impact on society and the environment.

beyond a reasonable doubt The standard used to determine the guilt or innocence of a person criminally charged. To be guilty of a crime, one must be proved guilty "beyond and to the exclusion of every reasonable doubt." A reasonable doubt is one that would cause a prudent person to hesitate before acting in matters important to him or her.

bilateral contract A type of contract that arises when a promise is given in exchange for a promise.

bilateral mistake A mistake that occurs when both parties to a contract are mistaken about the same material fact.

Bill of Rights The first ten amendments to the U.S. Constitution.

binding authority Any source of law that a court must follow when deciding a case.

blue sky laws State laws that regulate the offer and sale of securities.

bona fide occupational qualification (BFOQ) An identifiable characteristic reasonably necessary to the normal operation of a particular business. Such characteristics can include gender, national origin, and religion, but not race.

bond A security that evidences a corporate (or government) debt.

botnet Short for robot network—a group of computers that run an application controlled and manipulated only by the software source. Usually, the term is reserved for computers that have been infected by malicious robot software.

breach To violate a law, by an act or an omission, or to break a legal obligation that one owes to another person or to society.

breach of contract The failure, without legal excuse, of a promisor to perform the obligations of a contract.

brief A formal legal document submitted to an appellate court when a case is appealed. The appellant's brief outlines the facts and issues of the case, the judge's rulings or jury's findings that should be reversed or modified, the applicable law, and the arguments on the client's behalf. The appellee usually files an answering brief.

browse-wrap terms Terms and conditions of use that are presented to an Internet user at the time a product, such as software, is downloaded but that need not be agreed to before the product is installed or used.

bureaucracy A large organization that is structured hierarchically to carry out specific functions.

burglary The unlawful entry into a building with the intent to commit a felony. Some state statutes have expanded burglary to include the intent to commit any crime.

business ethics Ethics in a business context; a consensus of what constitutes right or wrong behavior in the world of business and the application of moral principles to situations that arise in a business setting.

business invitees Those people, such as customers or clients, who are invited onto business premises by the owner of those premises for business purposes.

business judgment rule A rule under which courts will not hold corporate officers and directors liable for honest mistakes of judgment and bad business decisions that were made in good faith.

business necessity A defense to an allegation of employment discrimination in which the employer demonstrates that an employment practice that discriminates against members of a protected class is related to job performance.

buyout price The amount payable to a partner on his or her dissociation from a partnership, based on the amount distributable to that partner if the firm were wound up on that date, and offset by any damages for wrongful dissociation.

buy-sell agreement In the context of partnerships, an express agreement made at the time of partnership formation for one or more of the partners to buy out the other or others should the situation warrant.

bylaws The internal rules of management adopted by a corporation at its first organizational meeting.

C

case law The rules of law announced in court decisions. Case law interprets statutes, regulations, constitutional provisions, and other case law.

case on point A previous case involving factual circumstances and issues that are similar to those in the case before the court.

categorical imperative A concept developed by the philosopher Immanuel Kant as an ethical guideline for behavior. In deciding whether an action is right or wrong, or desirable or undesirable, a person should evaluate the action in terms of what would happen if everybody else in the same situation, or category, acted the same way.

causation in fact An act or omission without ("but for") which an event would not have occurred.

cease-and-desist order An administrative or judicial order prohibiting a person or business firm from conducting activities that an agency or court has deemed illegal.

certificate of limited partnership The document that must be filed with a designated state official to form a limited partnership.

certification mark A mark used by one or more persons, other than the owner, to certify the region, materials, mode of manufacture, quality, or accuracy of the owner's goods or services. Examples of certification marks include the "Good Housekeeping Seal of Approval" and "UL Tested."

charging order In partnership law, an order granted by a court to a judgment creditor that entitles the creditor to attach a partner's interest in the partnership.

checks and balances The system by which each of the three branches of the U.S. national government (executive, legislative, and judicial) exercises checks on the powers of the other branches.

citation A reference to a publication in which a legal authority—such as a statute or a court decision—or other source can be found.

civil law The branch of law dealing with the definition and enforcement of all private or public rights, as opposed to criminal matters.

civil law system A system of law derived from that of the Roman Empire and based on a code rather than case law; the predominant system of law in the nations of continental Europe and the nations that were once their colonies. In the United States, Louisiana is the only state that has a civil law system.

click-on agreement An agreement that arises when a buyer, engaging in a transaction on a computer, indicates his or her assent to be bound by the terms of an offer by clicking on a button that says, for example, "I agree"; sometimes referred to as a *click-on license* or a *click-wrap agreement*.

close corporation A corporation whose shareholders are limited to a small group of persons, often family members.

closed shop A firm that requires union membership on the part of its workers as a condition of employment.

closing   The final step in the sale of real estate, in which ownership is transferred to the buyer in exchange for payment of the purchase price.

closing argument   An argument made at a trial after the plaintiff and defendant have finished presenting their cases. Closing arguments are made prior to the jury charges.

cloud computing   The delivery to users of on-demand services from third party servers over a network.

collective bargaining   The process by which labor and management negotiate the terms and conditions of employment, including working hours and workplace conditions.

collective mark   A mark used by members of a cooperative, association, or other organization to certify the region, materials, mode of manufacture, quality, or accuracy of the specific goods or services. Examples of collective marks include the labor union marks found on tags of certain products and the credits of movies, which indicate the various associations and organizations that participated in the making of the movies.

comity   A deference by which one nation gives effect to the laws and judicial decrees of another nation.

commerce clause   The provision in Article I, Section 8, of the U.S. Constitution that gives Congress the power to regulate interstate commerce.

commercial impracticability   A doctrine under which a seller may be excused from performing a contract when (1) a contingency occurs, (2) the contingency's occurrence makes performance impracticable, and (3) the nonoccurrence of the contingency was a basic assumption on which the contract was made.

commercial use   Use of land for business activities only; sometimes called *business use.*

commingle   To put funds or goods together into one mass so that they are mixed to such a degree that they no longer have separate identities.

common law   The body of law developed from custom or judicial decisions in English and U.S. courts, not attributable to a legislature.

common stock   A security that evidences ownership in a corporation. A share of common stock gives the owner a proportionate interest in the corporation with regard to control, earnings, and net assets. Common stock is lowest in priority with respect to payment of dividends and distribution of the corporation's assets on dissolution.

community property   A form of concurrent property ownership in which each spouse owns an undivided one-half interest in property acquired during the marriage.

comparative negligence   A theory in tort law under which the liability for injuries resulting from negligent acts is shared by all parties who were negligent (including the injured party) on the basis of each person's proportionate negligence.

compelling government interest   A test of constitutionality that requires the government to have compelling reasons for passing any law that restricts fundamental rights, such as free speech, or distinguishes between people based on a suspect trait.

compensatory damages   A money award equivalent to the actual value of injuries or damages sustained by the aggrieved party.

complaint   The pleading made by a plaintiff alleging wrongdoing on the part of the defendant; the document that, when filed with a court, initiates a lawsuit.

computer crime   Any violation of criminal law that involves knowledge of computer technology for its perpetration, investigation, or prosecution.

concentrated industry   An industry in which a single firm or a small number of firms control a large percentage of market sales.

concurrent jurisdiction   Jurisdiction that exists when two different courts have the power to hear a case. For example, some cases can be heard in either a federal or a state court.

concurrent ownership   Joint ownership of property (including tenancies in common and joint tenancies).

concurring opinion   A court opinion by one or more judges or justices who agree with the majority but want to make or emphasize a point that was not made or emphasized in the majority's opinion.

condemnation   The judicial procedure by which the government exercises its power of eminent domain. It generally involves two phases: a taking and a determination of fair value.

condition   A possible future event, the occurrence or nonoccurrence of which will trigger the performance of a legal obligation or terminate an existing obligation under a contract.

condition precedent   A condition in a contract that must be met before a party's promise becomes absolute.

confiscation   A government's taking of a privately owned business or personal property without a proper public purpose or an award of just compensation.

conforming goods   Goods that conform to contract specifications.

consequential damages   Special damages that compensate for a loss that is not direct or immediate (for example, lost profits). The special damages must have been reasonably foreseeable at the time the breach or injury occurred in order for the plaintiff to collect them.

consideration   Generally, the value given in return for a promise or a performance. The consideration, which must be present to make the contract legally binding, must be something of legally sufficient value and must be bargained for.

constitutional law   Law that is based on the U.S. Constitution and the constitutions of the various states.

constructive discharge   A termination of employment brought about by making the employee's working conditions so intolerable that the employee reasonably feels compelled to leave.

consumer-debtor   One whose debts result primarily from the purchase of goods for personal, family, or household use.

consumer law   The body of statutes, agency rules, and judicial decisions protecting consumers of goods and services from dangerous manufacturing techniques, mislabeling, unfair credit practices, deceptive advertising, and other such practices.

contract   An agreement that can be enforced in court, formed by two or more parties, each of whom agrees to perform or to refrain from performing some act now or in the future.

contractual capacity   The legal ability to enter into contracts; the threshold mental capacity required by law for a party who enters into a contract to be bound by that contract.

contributory negligence   A theory in tort law under which a complaining party's own negligence contributed to or caused his or her injuries. Contributory negligence is an absolute bar to recovery in a minority of jurisdictions.

conversion   The wrongful taking, using, or retaining possession of personal property that belongs to another.

conveyance   The transfer of title to real property from one person to another by deed or other document.

cookie   A small file sent from a website and stored in a user's Web browser to track the user's Web-browsing activities.

"cooling-off" laws   Laws that allow buyers of goods sold in certain transactions to cancel their contracts within three business days.

copyright   The exclusive right of authors to publish, print, or sell an intellectual production for a statutory period of time. A copyright has the same monopolistic nature as a patent or trademark, but it differs in that it applies exclusively to works of art, literature, and other works of authorship, including computer programs.

corporate governance   A set of policies specifying the rights and responsibilities of the various participants in a corporation and spelling out the rules and procedures for making corporate decisions.

corporate social responsibility   The concept that corporations can and should act ethically and be accountable to society for their actions.

corporation   A corporation is a firm that is authorized by statute to act as legal entity separate and distinct from its owners (shareholders).

cost-benefit analysis   A decision-making technique that involves weighing the costs of a given action against the benefits of the action.

co-surety   A joint surety; one who assumes liability jointly with another surety for the payment of an obligation.

counteradvertising   New advertising that is undertaken to correct earlier false claims that were made about a product.

counterclaim   A claim made by a defendant in a civil lawsuit that, in effect, sues the plaintiff.

counteroffer   An offeree's response to an offer in which the offeree rejects the original offer and at the same time makes a new offer.

court of equity   A court that decides controversies and administers justice according to the rules, principles, and precedents of equity.

court of law   A court in which the only remedies that can be granted are things of value, such as money damages. In the early English king's courts, courts of law were distinct from courts of equity.

covenant not to compete   A contractual promise to refrain from competing with another party for a certain period of time and within a certain geographic area. Although covenants not to compete restrain trade, they are commonly found in partnership agreements, business sale agreements, and employment contracts. If they are ancillary to such agreements, covenants not to compete will normally be enforced by the courts unless the time period or geographic area is deemed unreasonable.

covenant not to sue   An agreement to substitute a contractual obligation for some other type of legal action based on a valid claim.

cover   A buyer's or lessee's purchase on the open market of goods to substitute for those promised but never delivered by the seller or lessor. Under the Uniform Commercial Code, if the cost of cover exceeds the cost of the contract goods, the buyer or lessee can recover the difference, plus incidental and consequential damages.

cram-down provision   A provision of the Bankruptcy Code that allows a court to confirm a debtor's Chapter 11 reorganization plan even though only one class of creditors has accepted it.

creditors' composition agreement   An agreement formed between a debtor and his or her creditors in which the creditors agree to accept a lesser sum than that owed by the debtor in full satisfaction of the debt.

crime   A wrong against society proclaimed in a statute and punishable by society through fines and/or imprisonment— or, in some cases, death.

criminal law   The branch of law that defines and punishes wrongful actions committed against the public.

cross-examination   The questioning of an opposing witness during a trial.

crowdfunding   A cooperative activity in which people network and pool funds and other resources via the Internet to assist a cause (such as disaster relief) or invest in a business venture (such as a startup).

cure   Under the Uniform Commercial Code, the right of a party who tenders nonconforming performance to correct his or her performance within the contract period.

cyber crime   A crime that occurs online, in the virtual community of the Internet, as opposed to the physical world.

cyber fraud   Fraud that involves the online theft of credit-card information, banking details, and other information for criminal use.

cyberlaw   An informal term used to refer to all laws governing electronic communications and transactions, particularly those conducted via the Internet.

cybersquatting   Registering a domain name that is the same as, or confusingly similar to, the trademark of another and then offering to sell that domain name back to the trademark owner.

cyber tort   A tort committed via the Internet.

D

damages   A monetary award sought as a remedy for a breach of contract or a tortious act.

debtor in possession (DIP)   In Chapter 11 bankruptcy proceedings, a debtor who is allowed to continue in possession of the estate in property (the business) and to continue business operations.

deceptive advertising   Advertising that misleads consumers, either by making unjustified claims about a product's performance or by omitting a material fact concerning the product's composition or performance.

deed   A document by which title to real property is passed.

defamation   Any published or publicly spoken false statement that causes injury to another's good name, reputation, or character.

default   Failure to pay a debt when it is due.

default judgment   A judgment entered by a court against a defendant who has failed to appear in court to answer or defend against the plaintiff's claim.

defendant   One against whom a lawsuit is brought, or the accused person in a criminal proceeding.

defense   Reasons that a defendant offers in an action or suit as to why the plaintiff should not obtain what he or she is seeking.

delegation   The transfer of a contractual duty to a third party. The party delegating the duty (the delegator) to the third party (the delegatee) is still obliged to perform on the contract should the delegatee fail to perform.

delegation doctrine   A doctrine based on Article I, Section 8, of the U.S. Constitution, which has been construed to allow Congress to delegate some of its power to make and implement laws to administrative agencies. The delegation is considered to be proper as long as Congress sets standards outlining the scope of the agency's authority.

deposition   The testimony of a party to a lawsuit or of a witness taken under oath before a trial.

destination contract   A contract in which the seller is required to ship the goods by carrier and deliver them at a particular destination. The seller assumes liability for any losses or damage to the goods until they are tendered at the destination specified in the contract.

dilution   With respect to trademarks, a doctrine under which distinctive or famous trademarks are protected from certain unauthorized uses regardless of a showing of competition or a likelihood of confusion. Congress created a federal cause of action for dilution in 1995 with the passage of the Federal Trademark Dilution Act.

direct examination   The examination of a witness by the attorney who calls the witness to the stand at trial to testify on behalf of the attorney's client.

disaffirmance   The legal avoidance, or setting aside, of a contractual obligation.

discharge   (1) The termination of an obligation, such as occurs when the parties to a contract have fully performed their contractual obligations. (2) The termination of a bankruptcy debtor's obligation to pay debts.

discharge in bankruptcy   The release of a debtor from all debts that are provable, except those specifically excepted from discharge by statute.

disclosed principal   A principal whose identity is known to a third party at the time the agent makes a contract with the third party.

discovery   A phase in the litigation process during which the opposing parties may obtain information from each other and from third parties prior to trial.

disparagement of property   An economically injurious false statement made about another's product or property. A general term for torts that are more specifically referred to as *slander of quality* or *slander of title*.

disparate-impact discrimination   Discrimination that results from certain employer practices or procedures that, although not discriminatory on their face, have a discriminatory effect.

disparate-treatment discrimination   A form of employment discrimination that results when an employer intentionally discriminates against employees who are members of protected classes.

dissenting opinion   A court opinion that presents the views of one or more judges or justices who disagree with the majority's decision.

dissociation   The severance of the relationship between a partner and a partnership or between a member and a limited liability company.

dissolution   The formal disbanding of a partnership, corporation, or other business entity. For instance, partnerships can be dissolved by acts of the partners, by operation of law, or by judicial decree.

distributed network   A network that can be used by persons located (distributed) around the country or the globe to share computer files.

distribution agreement   A contract between a seller and a distributor of the seller's products setting out the terms and conditions of the distributorship.

diversity of citizenship   Under Article III, Section 2, of the Constitution, a basis for federal court jurisdiction over a lawsuit between (1) citizens of different states, (2) a foreign country and citizens of a state or of different states, or (3) citizens of a state and citizens or subjects of a foreign country. The amount in controversy must be more than $75,000 before a federal court can take jurisdiction in such cases.

divestiture   A company's sale of one or more of its divisions' operating functions under court order as part of the enforcement of antitrust laws.

dividend   A distribution of corporate profits to the corporation's shareholders in proportion to the number of shares held.

document of title   A writing exchanged in the regular course of business that evidences the right to possession of goods (for example, a bill of lading or a warehouse receipt).

domain name   The series of letters and symbols used to identify a site operator on the Internet; part of an Internet "address."

domestic corporation   In a given state, a corporation that is organized under the law of that state.

double jeopardy   A situation occurring when a person is tried twice for the same criminal offense; prohibited by the Fifth Amendment to the Constitution.

down payment   The part of the purchase price of real property that is paid in cash up front, reducing the amount of the loan or mortgage.

dram shop act   A state statute that imposes liability on the owners of bars and taverns, as well as those who serve alcoholic drinks to the public, for injuries resulting from accidents caused by intoxicated persons when the sellers or servers of alcoholic drinks contributed to the intoxication.

due process clause   The provisions of the Fifth and Fourteenth Amendments to the U.S. Constitution that guarantee that no person shall be deprived of life, liberty, or property without due process of law. Similar clauses are found in most state constitutions.

dumping   The selling of goods in a foreign country at a price below the price charged for the same goods in the domestic market.

duress   Unlawful pressure brought to bear on a person, causing the person to perform an act that he or she would not otherwise perform (or refrain from doing something that he or she would otherwise do).

duty-based ethics   An ethical philosophy rooted in the idea that every person has certain duties to others, including both humans and the planet. Those duties may be derived from religious principles or from other philosophical reasoning.

duty of care   The duty of all persons, as established by tort law, to exercise a reasonable amount of care in their dealings with others. Failure to exercise due care, which is normally determined by the "reasonable person standard," constitutes the tort of negligence.

E

e-agent   A semiautonomous computer program that is capable of executing specific tasks.

early neutral case evaluation   A form of alternative dispute resolution in which a neutral third party evaluates the strengths and weakness of the disputing parties' positions. The evaluator's opinion forms the basis for negotiating a settlement.

easement   A nonpossessory right, established by express or implied agreement, to make limited use of another's property without removing anything from the property.

e-contract   A contract that is entered into in cyberspace and is evidenced only by electronic impulses (such as those that make up a computer's memory), rather than, for example, a typewritten form.

e-evidence   A type of evidence that consists of computer-generated or electronically recorded information, including e-mail, voice mail, spreadsheets, word-processing documents, and other data.

embezzlement   The fraudulent appropriation of money or other property by a person to whom the money or property has been entrusted.

eminent domain   The power of a government to take land from private citizens for public use on the payment of just compensation.

employment at will   A common law doctrine under which either party may terminate an employment relationship at any time for any reason, unless a contract specifies otherwise.

employment discrimination   Unequal treatment of employees or job applicants on the basis of race, color, national origin, religion, gender, age, or disability; prohibited by federal statutes.

enabling legislation   A statute enacted by Congress that authorizes the creation of an administrative agency and specifies the name, composition, purpose, and powers of the agency.

entrapment   In criminal law, a defense in which the defendant claims that he or she was induced by a public official—usually an undercover agent or police officer—to commit a crime that he or she would otherwise not have committed.

entrepreneur   One who initiates and assumes the financial risk of a new business enterprise and undertakes to provide or control its management.

environmental impact statement (EIS)   A formal analysis required for any major federal action that will significantly affect the quality of the environment to determine the action's impact and explore alternatives.

equal dignity rule   A rule requiring that an agent's authority be in writing if the contract to be made on behalf of the principal must be in writing.

equal protection clause   The provision in the Fourteenth Amendment to the U.S. Constitution that guarantees that no state will "deny to any person within its jurisdiction the equal protection of the laws." This clause mandates that state governments treat similarly situated individuals in a similar manner.

equitable maxims   General propositions or principles of law that have to do with fairness (equity).

escrow account   An account generally held in the name of the depositor and the escrow agent. The funds in the account are paid to a third person on fulfillment of the escrow condition.

e-signature   As defined by the Uniform Electronic Transactions Act, "an electronic sound, symbol, or process attached to or logically associated with a record and executed or adopted by a person with the intent to sign the record."

establishment clause   The provision in the First Amendment to the U.S. Constitution that prohibits Congress from establishing a state-sponsored religion, as well as from passing laws that promote religion or show a preference for one religion over another.

estopped   Barred, impeded, or precluded.

ethical reasoning   A reasoning process in which an individual links his or her moral convictions or ethical standards to the particular situation at hand.

ethics   Moral principles and values applied to social behavior.

exclusionary rule   In criminal procedure, a rule under which any evidence that is obtained in violation of the accused's constitutional rights guaranteed by the Fourth, Fifth, and Sixth Amendments, as well as any evidence derived from illegally obtained evidence, will not be admissible in court.

exclusive agency   An agency in which a principal grants an agent an exclusive territory and does not allow another agent to compete in that territory.

exclusive-dealing contract   An agreement under which a seller forbids a buyer to purchase products from the seller's competitors.

exclusive jurisdiction   Jurisdiction that exists when a case can be heard only in a particular court or type of court, such as a federal court or a state court.

exculpatory clause   A clause that releases a contractual party from liability in the event of monetary or physical injury, no matter who is at fault.

executed contract   A contract that has been completely performed by both parties.

executive agency   An administrative agency within the executive branch of government. At the federal level, executive agencies are those within the cabinet departments.

executory contract   A contract that has not yet been fully performed.

exhaustion doctrine   In administrative law, the principle that a complaining party normally must have exhausted all available administrative remedies before seeking judicial review.

export   To sell products to buyers located in other countries.

express authority   Authority expressly given by one party to another. In agency law, an agent has express authority to act for a principal if both parties agree, orally or in writing, that an agency relationship exists in which the agent has the power (authority) to act in the place of, and on behalf of, the principal.

express contract   A contract in which the terms of the agreement are fully and explicitly stated in words, oral or written.

express warranty   A seller's or lessor's oral or written promise, ancillary to an underlying sales or lease agreement, as to the quality, description, or performance of the goods being sold or leased.

expropriation   The seizure by a government of privately owned business or personal property for a proper public purpose and with just compensation.

F

family limited liability partnership (FLLP)   A limited liability partnership (LLP) in which the majority of the partners are members of a family.

federal form of government   A system of government in which the states form a union and the sovereign power is divided between a central government and the member states.

federal question   A question that pertains to the U.S. Constitution, acts of Congress, or treaties. A federal question provides a basis for federal jurisdiction.

Federal Rules of Civil Procedure (FRCP)   The rules controlling procedural matters in civil trials brought before the federal district courts.

fee simple absolute   An ownership interest in land in which the owner has the greatest possible aggregation of rights, privileges, and power. The owner can use, possess, or dispose of the property as he or she chooses during his or her lifetime. On death, the interest in the property passes to the owner's heirs.

felony   A crime—such as arson, murder, rape, or robbery—that carries the most severe sanctions, usually ranging from one year in a state or federal prison to the forfeiture of one's life.

fiduciary   As a noun, a person having a duty created by his or her undertaking to act primarily for another's benefit in matters connected with the undertaking. As an adjective, a relationship founded on trust and confidence.

filtering software   A computer program that screens incoming data according to rules built into the software and controls access to websites with content not consistent with these rules.

final order   The final decision of an administrative agency on an issue. If no appeal is taken, or if the case is not reviewed or considered anew by the agency commission, the administrative law judge's initial order becomes the final order of the agency.

firm offer   An offer (by a merchant) that is irrevocable without consideration for a period of time (not longer than three months). A firm offer by a merchant must be in writing and must be signed by the offeror.

fixed-term tenancy   A type of tenancy under which property is leased for a specified period of time, such as a month, a year, or a period of years; also called a *tenancy for years*.

fixture   An item of personal property that has become so closely associated with real property that it is legally regarded as part of that real property.

forbearance   (1) The act of refraining from exercising a legal right. (2) An agreement between a lender and a borrower in which the lender agrees to temporarily cease requiring mortgage payments, to delay foreclosure, or to accept smaller payments than previously scheduled.

foreclosure   A proceeding in which a mortgagee either takes title to or forces the sale of the mortgagor's property in satisfaction of a debt.

foreign corporation   In a given state, a corporation that does business in that state but is not incorporated there.

forgery   The fraudulent making or altering of any writing in a way that changes the legal rights and liabilities of another.

formal contract   A contract that by law requires a specific form, such as being executed under seal, to be valid.

franchise   Any arrangement in which the owner of a trademark, trade name, or copyright licenses another to use that trademark, trade name, or copyright in the selling of goods or services.

franchisee   One receiving a license to use another's (the franchisor's) trademark, trade name, or copyright in the sale of goods and services.

franchisor   One licensing another (the franchisee) to use the owner's trademark, trade name, or copyright in the selling of goods or services.

fraudulent misrepresentation (fraud)   Any misrepresentation, either by misstatement or by omission of a material fact, knowingly made with the intention of deceiving another and on which a reasonable person would and does rely to his or her detriment.

free exercise clause   The provision in the First Amendment to the U.S. Constitution that prohibits Congress from making any law "prohibiting the free exercise" of religion.

free-writing prospectus   A written, electronic, or graphic communication associated with the offer to sell a security and used during the waiting period to supplement other information about the security.

frustration of purpose   A court-created doctrine under which a party to a contract will be relieved of his or her duty to perform when the objective purpose for performance no longer exists (due to reasons beyond that party's control).

full faith and credit clause   A clause in Article IV, Section 1, of the U.S. Constitution that provides that "Full Faith and Credit shall be given in each State to the public Acts, Records, and Judicial Proceedings of every other State." The clause ensures that rights established under deeds, wills, contracts, and the like in one state will be honored by the other states and that any judicial decision with respect to such property rights will be honored and enforced in all states.

fungible goods   Goods that are alike by physical nature, by agreement, or by trade usage. Examples are wheat, oil, and wine that are identical in type and quality.

G

garnishment   A legal process used by a creditor to collect a debt by seizing property of the debtor (such as wages) that is being held by a third party (such as the debtor's employer).

general damages   In a tort case, an amount awarded to compensate individuals for the nonmonetary aspects of the harm suffered, such as pain and suffering; not available to companies.

general partner   In a limited partnership, a partner who assumes responsibility for the management of the partnership and has full liability for all partnership debts.

Good Samaritan statute   A state statute that provides that persons who rescue or provide emergency services to others in peril—unless they do so recklessly, thus causing further harm—cannot be sued for negligence.

goodwill   In the business context, the valuable reputation of a business viewed as an intangible asset.

grand jury   A group of citizens called to decide, after hearing the state's evidence, whether a reasonable basis (probable cause) exists for believing that a crime has been committed and whether a trial ought to be held.

grant deed   A deed that simply states that property is being conveyed from the grantor to another. Under statute, a grant deed may impliedly warrant that the grantor has at least not conveyed the property's title to someone else.

group boycott   An agreement by two or more sellers to refuse to deal with a particular person or firm.

guarantor   A person who agrees to satisfy the debt of another (the debtor) only after the principal debtor defaults. A guarantor's liability is thus secondary.

H

hacker   A person who uses one computer to break into another.

hearsay   An oral or written statement made out of court that is later offered in court by a witness (not the person who made the statement) to prove the truth of the matter asserted in the statement. Hearsay is generally inadmissible as evidence.

historical school   A school of legal thought that looks to the past to determine what the principles of contemporary law should be.

holding company   A company whose business activity is holding shares in another company.

homeowner's insurance   A form of property insurance that protects the home of the insured person and its contents against losses.

homestead exemption   A law permitting a debtor to retain the family home, either in its entirety or up to a specified dollar amount, free from the claims of unsecured creditors or trustees in bankruptcy.

horizontal merger   A merger between two firms that are competing in the same market.

horizontal restraint   Any agreement that restrains competition between rival firms competing in the same market.

hot-cargo agreement   An illegal agreement in which employers voluntarily agree with unions not to handle, use, or deal in the nonunion-produced goods of other employers.

I

I-551 Alien Registration Receipt   A document, known as a "green card," that shows that a foreign-born individual can legally work in the United States.

I-9 verification   The process of verifying the employment eligibility and identity of a new immigrant worker. It must be completed within three days after the worker commences employment.

identification   In a sale of goods, the express designation of the specific goods provided for in the contract.

identity theft   The act of stealing another's identifying information—such as a name, date of birth, or Social Security number—and using that information to access the victim's financial resources.

impeach   To challenge the credibility of a person's testimony or attempt to discredit a party or witness.

implication   A way of creating an easement or profit in real property when it is reasonable to imply its existence from the circumstances surrounding the division of the property.

implied authority   Authority that is created not by an explicit oral or written agreement but by implication or inference. In agency law, implied authority of the agent can arise from custom, from the position the agent occupies, or from being reasonably necessary to carry out express authority.

implied contract   A contract formed in whole or in part from the conduct of the parties (as opposed to an express contract).

implied warranty   A warranty that the law derives by implication or inference from the nature of the transaction or the relative situation or circumstances of the parties.

implied warranty of fitness for a particular purpose   A warranty that goods sold or leased are fit for a particular purpose. The warranty arises when any seller or lessor knows the particular purpose for which a buyer or lessee will use the goods and knows that the buyer or lessee is relying on the skill and judgment of the seller or lessor to select suitable goods.

implied warranty of habitability   An implied promise by a seller of a new house that the house is fit for human habitation. Also, the implied promise by a landlord that rented residential premises are habitable.

implied warranty of merchantability   A warranty that goods being sold or leased are reasonably fit for the ordinary purpose for which they are sold or leased, are properly packaged and labeled, and are of fair quality. The warranty automatically arises in every sale or lease of goods made by a merchant who deals in goods of the kind sold or leased.

impossibility of performance   A doctrine under which a party to a contract is relieved of his or her duty to perform when performance becomes impossible or totally impracticable (through no fault of either party).

incidental damages Damages that compensate for expenses directly incurred because of a breach of contract, such as those incurred to obtain performance from another source.

independent contractor One who works for, and receives payment from, an employer but whose working conditions and methods are not controlled by the employer. An independent contractor is not an employee but may be an agent.

independent regulatory agency An administrative agency that is not considered part of the government's executive branch and is not subject to the authority of the president. Independent agency officials cannot be removed without cause.

indictment (pronounced in-*dyte*-ment) A charge by a grand jury that a reasonable basis (probable cause) exists for believing that a crime has been committed and that a trial should be held.

industrial use Land use for light or heavy manufacturing, shipping, or heavy transportation.

informal contract A contract that does not require a specified form or formality in order to be valid.

information A formal accusation or complaint (without an indictment) issued in certain types of actions (usually criminal actions involving lesser crimes) by a law officer, such as a magistrate.

information return A tax return submitted by a partnership that reports the business's income and losses. The partnership itself does not pay taxes on the income, but each partner's share of the profit (whether distributed or not) is taxed as individual income to that partner.

initial order In the context of administrative law, an agency's disposition in a matter other than a rulemaking. An administrative law judge's initial order becomes final unless it is appealed.

***in personam* jurisdiction** Court jurisdiction over the "person" involved in a legal action; personal jurisdiction.

***in rem* jurisdiction** Court jurisdiction over a defendant's property.

inside director A person on a corporation's board of directors who is also an officer of the corporation.

insider (1) A corporate director or officer, or other employee or agent, with access to confidential information and a duty not to disclose that information in violation of insider-trading laws. (2) In bankruptcy proceedings, an individual, partner, partnership, corporation, or officer or director of a corporation (or a relative of one of these) who has a close relationship with the debtor.

insider trading The purchase or sale of securities on the basis of information that has not been made available to the public.

insurable interest A property interest in goods being sold or leased that is sufficiently substantial to permit a party to insure against damage to the goods.

intangible property Property that is incapable of being apprehended by the senses (such as by sight or touch). Intellectual property is an example of intangible property.

intellectual property Property resulting from intellectual, creative processes. Patents, trademarks, and copyrights are examples of intellectual property.

intended beneficiary A third party for whose benefit a contract is formed; an intended beneficiary can sue the promisor if such a contract is breached.

intentional tort A wrongful act knowingly committed.

international law The law that governs relations among nations. International customs and treaties are generally considered to be two of the most important sources of international law.

international organization In international law, a term that generally refers to an organization composed mainly of nations and usually established by treaty. The United States is a member of more than one hundred multilateral and bilateral organizations, including at least twenty through the United Nations.

Internet service provider (ISP) A business or organization that offers users access to the Internet and related services.

interpretive rule A nonbinding rule or policy statement issued by an administrative agency that explains how it interprets and intends to apply the statutes it enforces.

interrogatories A series of written questions for which written answers are prepared and then signed under oath by a party to a lawsuit, usually with the assistance of the party's attorney.

inverse condemnation The taking of private property by the government without payment of just compensation as required by the U.S. Constitution. The owner must sue the government to recover just compensation.

investment company A company that acts on the behalf of many smaller shareholders/owners by buying a large portfolio of securities and professionally managing that portfolio.

investment contract In securities law, a transaction in which a person invests in a common enterprise reasonably expecting profits that are derived primarily from the efforts of others.

J

joint and several liability In partnership law, a doctrine under which a plaintiff may sue all of the partners together (jointly) or one or more of the partners separately (severally, or individually).

joint liability In partnership law, a doctrine under which a plaintiff must sue all of the partners as a group, but each partner can be held liable for the full amount.

joint tenancy Joint ownership of property by two or more co-owners in which each co-owner owns an undivided portion of the property. On the death of one of the joint tenants, his or her interest automatically passes to the surviving joint tenant(s).

judicial review The process by which courts decide on the constitutionality of legislative enactments and actions of the executive branch.

jurisdiction The authority of a court to hear a case and decide a specific action.

jurisprudence The science or philosophy of law.

L

laches The equitable doctrine that bars a party's right to legal action if the party has neglected for an unreasonable length of time to act on his or her rights.

larceny The wrongful taking and carrying away of another person's personal property with the intent to permanently deprive the owner of the property. Some states classify larceny as either grand or petit, depending on the property's value.

law A body of enforceable rules governing relationships among individuals and between individuals and their society.

leasehold estate An interest in real property that gives a tenant a qualified right to possess and/or use the property for a limited time under a lease.

legal positivism A school of legal thought centered on the assumption that there is no law higher than the laws created by a national government. Laws must be obeyed, even if they are unjust, to prevent anarchy.

legal realism A school of legal thought that holds that the law is only one factor to be considered when deciding cases and that social and economic circumstances should also be taken into account.

legal reasoning (1) The process of evaluating how various laws apply to a given situation. (2) The process by which a judge harmonizes his or her opinion with the judicial decisions in previous cases.

legislative rule An administrative agency rule that carries the same weight as a congressionally enacted statute.

liability The state of being legally responsible (liable) for something, such as a debt or obligation.

libel Defamation in writing or in some other form (such as a digital recording) having the quality of permanence.

license (1) In the context of intellectual property, a contract permitting the use of a trademark, copyright, patent, or trade secret for certain purposes. (2) In the context of real property, a revocable right or privilege of a person to come on another person's land.

licensee One who receives a license to use, or enter onto, another's property.

lien (pronounced *leen*) A claim against specific property to satisfy a debt.

life estate An interest in land that exists only for the duration of the life of a specified individual, usually the holder of the estate.

limited liability company (LLC) A hybrid form of business enterprise that offers the limited liability of a corporation and the tax advantages of a partnership.

limited liability limited partnership (LLLP) A type of limited partnership in which the liability of the general partner is the same as the liability of the limited partners—that is, the liability of all partners is limited to the amount of their investments in the firm.

limited liability partnership (LLP) A hybrid form of business organization that is used mainly by professionals who normally do business in a partnership. An LLP is a pass-through entity for tax purposes, but a partner's personal liability for the malpractice of other partners is limited.

limited partner In a limited partnership, a partner who contributes capital to the partnership but has no right to participate in its management and has no liability for partnership debts beyond the amount of her or his investment.

limited partnership (LP) A partnership consisting of one or more general partners and one or more limited partners.

liquidated damages An amount, stipulated in the contract, that the parties to a contract believe to be a reasonable estimation of the damages that will occur in the event of a breach.

liquidated debt A debt that is due and certain in amount.

liquidation The sale of the nonexempt assets of a debtor and the distribution of the funds received to creditors.

litigation The process of resolving a dispute through the court system.

lockout An action in which an employer shuts down to prevent employees from working, typically because it cannot reach a collective bargaining agreement with the employees' union.

long arm statute A state statute that permits a state to obtain personal jurisdiction over nonresident defendants. A defendant must have "minimum contacts" with that state for the statute to apply.

M

mailbox rule A rule providing that an acceptance of an offer becomes effective on dispatch.

majority opinion A court opinion that represents the views of the majority (more than half) of the judges or justices deciding the case.

malpractice Professional misconduct or the failure to exercise the requisite degree of skill as a professional. Negligence—the failure to exercise due care—on the part of a professional, such as a physician or an attorney, is commonly referred to as malpractice.

malware Malicious software programs designed to disrupt or harm a computer, network, smartphone, or other device.

marketable title Title to real estate that is reasonably free from encumbrances, defects in the chain of title, and other matters that affect title, such as adverse possession.

market concentration The degree to which a small number of firms control a large percentage of a relevant market.

market power The power of a firm to control the market price of its product. A monopoly has the greatest degree of market power.

market-share liability A theory under which liability is shared among all firms that manufactured and distributed a particular product during a certain period of time. This theory of liability is used only when the specific source of the harmful product is unidentifiable.

mechanic's lien A statutory lien on the real property of another, created to ensure payment for work performed and materials furnished in the repair or improvement of real property, such as a building.

mediation A method of settling disputes outside of court by using the services of a neutral third party, called a mediator. The mediator acts as a communicating agent between the parties and suggests ways in which the parties can resolve their dispute.

member A person who has an ownership interest in a limited liability company.

mens rea (pronounced *mehns ray*-uh) Criminal intent. The commission of a prohibited act and the intent to commit a crime are the two essential elements required for criminal liability.

merchant A person who is engaged in the purchase and sale of goods. Under the Uniform Commercial Code, a person who deals in goods of the kind involved in the sales contract; for further definitions, see UCC 2–104.

metadata Data that are automatically recorded by electronic devices on their hard drives and that provide information about who created a file and when, and who accessed, modified, or transmitted it. Metadata can be described as "data about data."

meta tag Word inserted into a website's key-words field to increase the site's appearance in search engine results.

metes and bounds A way of describing the boundary lines of land according to the distance between two points, often using physical features of the local geography.

minimum wage The lowest wage, either by government regulation or by union contract, that an employer may pay an hourly worker.

mini-trial A private proceeding in which each party to a dispute argues its position before the other side. A neutral third party may be present and act as an adviser if the parties fail to reach an agreement.

mirror image rule A common law rule that requires, for a valid contractual agreement, that the terms of the offeree's acceptance adhere exactly to the terms of the offeror's offer.

misdemeanor A lesser crime than a felony, punishable by a fine or imprisonment for up to one year in other than a state or federal penitentiary.

money laundering Falsely reporting income that has been obtained through criminal activity as income obtained through a legitimate business enterprise—in effect, "laundering" the "dirty money."

monopolization The possession of monopoly power in the relevant market and the willful acquisition or maintenance of that power, as distinguished from growth or development as a consequence of a superior product, business acumen, or historic accident.

monopoly A market in which there is a single seller or a very limited number of sellers.

monopoly power The ability of a monopoly to dictate what takes place in a given market.

moral minimum The minimum degree of ethical behavior expected of a business firm, which is usually defined as compliance with the law.

mortgage A written instrument that gives a creditor (the mortgagee) an interest in, or lien on, the debtor's (mortgagor's) real property as security for a debt. If the debt is not paid, the property can be sold by the creditor and the proceeds used to pay the debt.

mortgage insurance Insurance that compensates a lender for losses due to a borrower's default on a mortgage loan.

motion A procedural request or application presented by an attorney to the court on behalf of a client.

motion for a directed verdict In a state court, a party's request that the judge enter a judgment in her or his favor before the case is submitted to a jury because the other party has not presented sufficient evidence to support the claim. The federal courts refer to this request as a *motion for judgment as a matter of law.*

motion for a judgment as a matter of law In a federal court, a party's request that the judge enter a judgment in her or his favor before the case is submitted to a jury because the other party has not presented sufficient evidence to support the claim. The state courts refer to this request as a *motion for a directed verdict.*

motion for a new trial   A motion asserting that the trial was so fundamentally flawed (because of error, newly discovered evidence, prejudice, or other reason) that a new trial is necessary to prevent a miscarriage of justice.

motion for judgment *n.o.v.*   A motion requesting the court to grant judgment in favor of the party making the motion on the ground that the jury verdict against him or her was unreasonable and erroneous.

motion for judgment on the pleadings   A motion by either party to a lawsuit at the close of the pleadings requesting the court to decide the issue solely on the pleadings without proceeding to trial. The motion will be granted only if no facts are in dispute.

motion for summary judgment   A motion requesting the court to enter a judgment without proceeding to trial. The motion can be based on evidence outside the pleadings and will be granted only if no facts are in dispute.

motion to dismiss   A pleading in which a defendant asserts that the plaintiff's claim fails to state a cause of action (that is, has no basis in law) or that there are other grounds on which a suit should be dismissed.

multiple product order   An order requiring a firm that has engaged in deceptive advertising to cease and desist from false advertising in regard to all the firm's products.

mutual fund   A specific type of investment company that continually buys or sells to investors shares of ownership in a portfolio.

mutual rescission   An agreement between the parties to cancel their contract, releasing the parties from further obligations under the contract. The object of the agreement is to restore the parties to the positions they would have occupied had no contract ever been formed.

N

national law   Law that pertains to a particular nation (as opposed to international law).

natural law   The oldest school of legal thought, based on the belief that the legal system should reflect universal ("higher") moral and ethical principles that are inherent in human nature.

necessity   In criminal law, a defense against liability. Under Section 3.02 of the Model Penal Code, this defense is justifiable if "the harm or evil sought to be avoided" by a given action "is greater than that sought to be prevented by the law defining the offense charged." In real property law, a way of creating an easement when one party must have the easement in order to have access to his or her property.

negligence   The failure to exercise the standard of care that a reasonable person would exercise in similar circumstances.

negotiation   In regard to dispute settlement, a process in which parties attempt to settle their dispute without going to court, with or without attorneys to represent them.

nominal damages   A small monetary award (often one dollar) granted to a plaintiff when no actual damage was suffered or when the plaintiff is unable to show such loss with sufficient certainty.

nonpossessory interest   In the context of real property, an interest that involves the right to use land but not the right to possess it.

normal trade relations (NTR) status   A status granted through an international treaty by which each member nation must treat other members at least as well as it treats the country that receives its most favorable treatment. This status was formerly known as most-favored-nation status.

notary public   A public official authorized to attest to the authenticity of signatures.

notice-and-comment rulemaking   An administrative rulemaking procedure that involves the publication of a notice of a proposed rulemaking in the *Federal Register*, a comment period for interested parties to express their views on the proposed rule, and the publication of the agency's final rule in the *Federal Register*.

novation   The substitution, by agreement, of a new contract for an old one, with the rights under the old one being terminated. Typically, there is a substitution of a new party who is responsible for the contract and the removal of an original party's rights and duties under the contract.

nuisance   A common law doctrine under which persons may be held liable for using their property in a manner that unreasonably interferes with others' rights to use or enjoy their own property.

O

objective theory of contracts   A theory under which the intent to form a contract will be judged by outward, objective facts as interpreted by a reasonable person, rather than by the party's own secret, subjective intentions. Objective facts might include what a party said when entering into the contract, how a party acted or appeared, and the circumstances surrounding the transaction.

offer   A promise or commitment to perform or refrain from performing some specified act in the future.

offeree   A person to whom an offer is made.

offeror   A person who makes an offer.

online dispute resolution (ODR)   The resolution of disputes with the assistance of organizations that offer dispute-resolution services via the Internet.

opening statement   A statement made to the jury at the beginning of a trial by a party's attorney, prior to the presentation of evidence. The attorney briefly outlines the evidence that will be offered and the legal theory that will be pursued.

operating agreement   An agreement in which the members of a limited liability company set forth the details of how the business will be managed and operated.

opinion   A statement by a court expressing the reasons for its decision in a case.

option contract   A contract under which the offeror cannot revoke his or her offer for a stipulated time period and the offeree can accept or reject the offer at any time during this period. The offeree must give consideration for the option to be enforceable.

order for relief   A court's grant of assistance to a complainant. In bankruptcy proceedings, the order relieves the debtor of the immediate obligation to pay the debts listed in the bankruptcy petition.

ordinance   A law passed by a local governing unit, such as a city or a county.

outcome-based ethics   An ethical philosophy that focuses on the impacts of a decision on society or on key stakeholders.

output contract   An agreement in which a seller agrees to sell and a buyer agrees to buy all or up to a stated amount of what the seller produces.

outside director   A person on a corporation's board of directors who does not hold a management position in the corporation.

outsourcing   The practice by which a company hires an outside firm or individual to perform work rather than hiring employees.

P

partially disclosed principal   A principal whose identity is unknown by a third party, but the third party knows that the agent is or may be acting for a principal at the time the agent and the third party form a contract.

partnership   An agreement by two or more persons to carry on, as co-owners, a business for profit.

partnership by estoppel   A partnership imposed by a court when nonpartners have held themselves out to be partners, or have allowed themselves to be held out as partners, and others have detrimentally relied on their misrepresentations.

pass-through entity   A business entity that has no tax liability. The entity's income is passed through to the owners, and they pay taxes on the income.

past consideration   Something given or some act done in the past, which cannot ordinarily be consideration for a later bargain.

patent   A government grant that gives an inventor the exclusive right or privilege to make, use, or sell his or her invention for a limited time period.

peer-to-peer (P2P) networking   The sharing of resources (such as files, hard drives, and processing styles) among multiple computers without the requirement of a central network server.

penalty   A sum inserted into a contract not as a measure of compensation for its breach but rather as punishment for a default. The agreement as to the amount will not be enforced, and recovery will be limited to actual damages.

***per curiam* opinion**   By the whole court; a court opinion written by the court as a whole instead of being authored by a judge or justice.

perfect tender rule   A common law rule under which a seller was required to deliver to the buyer goods that conformed perfectly to the requirements stipulated in the sales contract. A tender of nonconforming goods would automatically constitute a breach of contract. Under the Uniform Commercial Code, the rule has been greatly modified.

performance   In contract law, the fulfillment of one's duties arising under a contract; the normal way of discharging one's contractual obligations.

periodic tenancy   A lease interest in land for an indefinite period involving payment of rent at fixed intervals, such as week to week, month to month, or year to year.

***per se* violation**   A restraint of trade that is so anticompetitive that it is deemed inherently *(per se)* illegal.

persuasive authority   Any legal authority or source of law that a court may look to for guidance but need not follow when making its decision.

petitioner   In equity practice, a party that initiates a lawsuit.

petition in bankruptcy   The document that is filed with a bankruptcy court to initiate bankruptcy proceedings.

petty offense   In criminal law, the least serious kind of criminal offense, such as a traffic or building-code violation.

phishing   Online fraud in which criminals pretend to be legitimate companies by using e-mails or malicious websites that trick individuals and companies into providing useful information, such as bank account numbers, Social Security numbers, and credit-card numbers.

piercing the corporate veil   The action of a court to disregard the corporate entity and hold the shareholders personally liable for corporate debts and obligations.

plaintiff   A party that initiates a lawsuit.

plea bargaining   The process by which a criminal defendant and the prosecutor in a criminal case work out a mutually satisfactory disposition of the case, subject to court approval; usually involves the defendant's pleading guilty to a lesser offense and receiving a lighter sentence.

pleadings   Formal statements made by the plaintiff and the defendant in a lawsuit that detail the facts, allegations, and defenses involved in the litigation; the complaint and answer are part of the pleadings.

plurality opinion   A court opinion that is joined by the largest number of the judges or justices hearing the case, but fewer than half of the total number.

police powers   Powers possessed by states as part of their inherent sovereignty. These powers may be exercised to protect or promote the public order, health, safety, morals, and general welfare.

potentially responsible party (PRP)   A party liable for the costs of cleaning up a hazardous-waste disposal site under the Comprehensive Environmental Response, Compensation, and Liability Act.

power of attorney   Authorization to act as another's agent either in specified circumstances (special) or in all situations (general).

precedent   A court decision that furnishes an example or authority for deciding subsequent cases involving identical or similar facts.

predatory pricing   The pricing of a product below cost with the intent to drive competitors out of the market.

predominant-factor test   A test that courts use to determine whether a contract is primarily for the sale of goods or for the sale of services.

preemption   A doctrine under which certain federal laws preempt, or take precedence over, conflicting state or local laws.

preemptive rights   The right of a shareholder in a corporation to have the first opportunity to purchase a new issue of that corporation's stock in proportion to the amount of stock already owned by the shareholder.

preference   In bankruptcy proceedings, a property transfer or payment made by the debtor that favors one creditor over others.

preferred creditor   In the context of bankruptcy, a creditor who has received a preferential transfer from a debtor.

preferred stock   A security that entitles the holder to payment of fixed dividends and that has priority over common stock in the distribution of assets on the corporation's dissolution.

prepayment penalty clause   A provision in a mortgage loan contract that requires the borrower to pay a penalty if the mortgage is repaid in full within a certain period.

prescription   A way of creating an easement or profit in real property by openly using the property, without the owner's consent, for the required period of time (similar to adverse possession).

pretrial motion   A written or oral application to a court for a ruling or order, made before trial.

price discrimination   A seller's act of charging competing buyers different prices for identical products or services.

price-fixing agreement   An agreement between competitors to fix the prices of products or services at a certain level.

***prima facie* case**   A case in which the plaintiff has produced sufficient evidence of his or her claim that the case will be decided for the plaintiff unless the defendant produces evidence to rebut it.

principle of rights   The principle that human beings have certain fundamental rights (to life, freedom, and the pursuit of happiness, for example). A key factor in determining whether a business decision is ethical under this theory is how that decision affects the rights of others, such as employees, consumers, suppliers, and the community.

private equity capital   Capital funds invested by a private equity firm in an existing corporation, usually to purchase and reorganize it.

privilege   In tort law, the ability to act contrary to another person's right without that person's having legal redress for such acts. Privilege may be raised as a defense to defamation.

privileges and immunities clause   A clause in Article IV, Section 2, of the U.S. Constitution that requires states not to discriminate against one another's citizens. A resident of one state cannot be treated as an alien when in another state; he or she may not be denied such privileges and immunities as legal protection, access to courts, travel rights, and property rights.

privity of contract   The relationship that exists between the promisor and the promisee of a contract.

probable cause   Reasonable grounds for believing that a search should be conducted or that a person should be arrested.

probate court   A state court of limited jurisdiction that conducts proceedings relating to the settlement of a deceased person's estate.

procedural law   Law that establishes the methods of enforcing the rights established by substantive law.

product liability   The legal liability of manufacturers, sellers, and lessors of goods to consumers, users, and bystanders for injuries or damages that are caused by the goods.

product misuse   A defense against product liability that may be raised when the plaintiff used a product in a manner not intended by the manufacturer. If the misuse is reasonably foreseeable, the seller will not escape liability unless measures were taken to guard against the harm that could result from the misuse.

profit   In the context of real property, the right to enter onto another's property and remove something of value from that property.

promise A person's assurance that he or she will or will not do something.

promissory estoppel A doctrine that applies when a promisor makes a clear and definite promise on which the promisee justifiably relies. Such a promise is binding if justice will be better served by the enforcement of the promise.

prospectus A written document required by securities laws when a security is being sold. The prospectus describes the security, the financial operations of the issuing corporation, and the risk attaching to the security.

protected class A group of persons protected by specific laws because of the group's defining characteristics, including race, color, religion, national origin, gender, age, and disability.

proximate cause Legal cause; exists when the connection between an act and an injury is strong enough to justify imposing liability.

proxy Authorization to represent a corporate shareholder to serve as his or her agent and vote his or her shares in a certain manner.

public corporation A corporation owned by a federal, state, or municipal government—not to be confused with a publicly held corporation.

public figure An individual in the public limelight. Public figures include government officials and politicians, movie stars, well-known businesspersons, and generally anybody who becomes known to the public because of his or her position or activities.

publicly held corporation A corporation whose shares are publicly traded in securities markets, such as the New York Stock Exchange or the NASDAQ.

puffery A salesperson's exaggerated claims concerning the quality of goods offered for sale. Such claims involve opinions rather than facts and are not considered to be legally binding promises or warranties.

punitive damages Money damages that may be awarded to a plaintiff to punish the defendant and deter future similar conduct.

Q

question of fact In a lawsuit, an issue involving a factual dispute. A question of fact can be decided by a judge or a jury.

question of law In a lawsuit, an issue involving the application or interpretation of a law. Only a judge, and not a jury, can decide a question of law.

quitclaim deed A deed that conveys only whatever interest the grantor had in the property and therefore offers the least amount of protection against defects of title.

quorum The number of members of a decision-making body that must be present before business may be transacted.

quota A government-imposed trade restriction that limits the number, or sometimes the value, of goods and services that can be imported or exported during a particular time period.

R

ratification The act of accepting and giving legal force to an obligation that previously was not enforceable.

reaffirmation agreement An agreement between a debtor and a creditor in which the debtor voluntarily agrees to pay a debt dischargeable in bankruptcy.

reasonable person standard The standard of behavior expected of a hypothetical "reasonable person." The standard against which negligence is measured and that must be observed to avoid liability for negligence.

rebuttal The refutation of evidence introduced by an adverse party's attorney.

record According to the Uniform Electronic Transactions Act, information that is either inscribed on a tangible medium or stored in an electronic or other medium, and that is retrievable.

recording statute A statute that allow deeds, mortgages, and other real property transactions to be recorded so as to provide notice to future purchasers or creditors of an existing claim on the property.

reformation A court-ordered correction of a written contract so that it reflects the true intentions of the parties.

Regulation Z A set of rules issued by the Federal Reserve Board of Governors to implement the provisions of the Truth-in-Lending Act.

rejoinder The defendant's answer to the plaintiff's rebuttal.

release A contract in which one party forfeits the right to pursue a legal claim against the other party.

relevant evidence Evidence tending to make a fact at issue in the case more or less probable than it would be without the evidence. Only relevant evidence is admissible in court.

remedy The relief given to an innocent party to enforce a right or compensate for the violation of a right.

remedy at law A remedy available in a court of law. Money damages are awarded as a remedy at law.

remedy in equity A remedy allowed by courts in situations where remedies at law are not appropriate. Remedies in equity include injunction, specific performance, rescission and restitution, and reformation.

replevin (pronounced rih-*pleh*-vin) An action to recover specific goods in the hands of a party who is wrongfully withholding them from the other party.

reporter A publication in which court cases are published, or reported.

requirements contract   An agreement in which a buyer agrees to purchase and the seller agrees to sell all or up to a stated amount of what the buyer needs or requires.

resale price maintenance agreement   An agreement between a manufacturer and a retailer in which the manufacturer specifies what the retail prices of its products must be.

rescission   (pronounced rih-*sih*-zhen) A remedy whereby a contract is canceled and the parties are returned to the positions they occupied before the contract was made; may be effected through the mutual consent of the parties, by their conduct, or by court decree.

residential use   Use of land for construction of buildings for human habitation only.

respondeat superior   A doctrine under which a principal-employer is liable for any harm caused to a third party by an agent-employee in the course or scope of employment.

respondent   In equity practice, the party who answers a complaint or other proceeding.

restitution   An equitable remedy under which a person is restored to his or her original position prior to loss or injury, or placed in the position he or she would have been in had the breach not occurred.

restraint of trade   Any contract or combination that tends to eliminate or reduce competition, effect a monopoly, artificially maintain prices, or otherwise hamper the course of trade and commerce as it would be carried on if left to the control of natural economic forces.

restrictive covenant   A private restriction on the use of land. If its benefit or obligation passes with the land's ownership, it is said to "run with the land."

retained earnings   The portion of a corporation's profits that has not been paid out as dividends to shareholders.

revocation   In contract law, the withdrawal of an offer by an offeror. Unless an offer is irrevocable, it can be revoked at any time prior to acceptance without liability.

right of contribution   The right of a co-surety who pays more than his or her proportionate share on a debtor's default to recover the excess paid from other co-sureties.

right of reimbursement   The legal right of a person to be restored, repaid, or indemnified for costs, expenses, or losses incurred or expended on behalf of another.

right of subrogation   The right of a person to stand in the place of (be substituted for) another, giving the substituted party the same legal rights that the original party had.

right-to-work law   A state law providing that employees may not be required to join a union as a condition of retaining employment.

robbery   The act of forcefully and unlawfully taking personal property of any value from another; force or intimidation is usually necessary for an act of theft to be considered a robbery.

rulemaking   The process by which an administrative agency formally adopts a new regulation or amends an old one.

rule of four   A rule of the United States Supreme Court under which the Court will not issue a writ of *certiorari* unless at least four justices agree to do so.

rule of reason   A test used to determine whether an anticompetitive agreement constitutes a reasonable restraint on trade. Courts consider such factors as the purpose of the agreement, its effect on competition, and whether less restrictive means could have been used.

rules of evidence   Rules governing the admissibility of evidence in trial courts.

S

sale   The passing of title (evidence of ownership rights) from a seller to a buyer for a price.

sales contract   A contract for the sale of goods under which the ownership of goods is transferred from a seller to a buyer for a price.

scienter   (pronounced sy-*en*-ter) Knowledge by the misrepresenting party that material facts have been falsely represented or omitted with an intent to deceive.

S corporation   A close business corporation that has most of the attributes of a corporation, including limited liability, but qualifies under the Internal Revenue Code to be taxed as a partnership.

search warrant   An order granted by a public authority, such as a judge, that authorizes law enforcement personnel to search particular premises or property.

seasonably   Within a specified time period. If no period is specified, within a reasonable time.

secondary boycott   A union's refusal to work for, purchase from, or handle the products of a secondary employer, with whom the union has no dispute, for the purpose of forcing that employer to stop doing business with the primary employer, with whom the union has a labor dispute.

SEC Rule 10b-5   A rule of the Securities and Exchange Commission that prohibits the commission of fraud in connection with the purchase or sale of any security.

securities   Generally, stocks, bonds, or other items that represent an ownership interest in a corporation or a promise of repayment of debt by a corporation.

self-defense   The legally recognized privilege to protect one's self or property against injury by another. The privilege of self-defense protects only acts that are reasonably necessary to protect one's self or property.

self-incrimination   Giving testimony in a trial or other legal proceeding that could expose the person testifying to criminal prosecution.

seniority system   A system in which those who have worked longest for an employer are first in line for promotions, salary increases, and other benefits, and are last to be laid off if the workforce must be reduced.

service mark   A mark used in the sale or the advertising of services, such as to distinguish the services of one person from the services of others. Titles, character names, and other distinctive features of radio and television programs may be registered as service marks.

service of process   The delivery of the complaint and summons to a defendant.

sexual harassment   The demanding of sexual favors in return for job promotions or other benefits, or language or conduct that is so sexually offensive that it creates a hostile working environment.

shareholder agreement   An agreement between shareholders that restricts the transferability of shares, often entered into for the purpose of maintaining proportionate control of a close corporation.

shareholder's derivative suit   A suit brought by a shareholder to enforce a corporate cause of action against a third person.

shipment contract   A contract in which the seller is required to ship the goods by carrier. The buyer assumes liability for any losses or damage to the goods after they are delivered to the carrier. Generally, a contract is assumed to be a shipment contract if nothing to the contrary is stated in the contract.

short sale   A sale of real property for an amount that is less than the balance owed on the mortgage loan, usually due to financial hardship.

short-swing profits   Profits earned by a purchase and sale, or sale and purchase, of the same security within a six-month period.

shrink-wrap agreement   An agreement whose terms are expressed in a document located inside a box in which goods (usually software) are packaged; sometimes called a *shrinkwrap license.*

slander   Defamation in oral form.

slander of quality   The publication of false information about another's product, alleging that it is not what its seller claims; also called *trade libel.*

slander of title   The publication of a statement that falsely denies or casts doubt on another's legal ownership of property, causing financial loss to that property's owner.

small claims court   Special courts in which parties may litigate small claims (usually, claims involving $2,500 or less). Attorneys are not required in small claims courts and in many states are not allowed to represent the parties.

social media   Forms of communication through which users create and share information, ideas, messages, and other content via the Internet.

sociological school   A school of legal thought that views the law as a tool for promoting justice in society.

sole proprietorship   The simplest form of business organization, in which the owner is the business. The owner reports business income on his or her personal income tax return and is legally responsible for all debts and obligations incurred by the business.

sovereign immunity   A doctrine that immunizes foreign nations from the jurisdiction of U.S. courts when certain conditions are satisfied.

sovereignty   The quality of having independent authority over a geographic area. For instance, state governments have the authority to regulate affairs within their borders.

space law   Law consisting of the international and national laws that govern activities in outer space.

spam   Bulk, unsolicited (junk) e-mail.

special damages   In a tort case, an amount awarded to compensate the plaintiff for quantifiable monetary losses, such as medical expenses, property damage, and lost wages and benefits (now and in the future).

special-use permit   A permit granted by local zoning authorities that allows for a specific exemption to zoning regulations for a particular piece of land.

special warranty deed   A deed that warrants only that the grantor held good title during his or her ownership of the property and does not warrant that there were no defects of title when the property was held by previous owners.

specific performance   An equitable remedy requiring the breaching party to perform as promised under the contract; usually granted only when money damages would be an inadequate remedy and the subject matter of the contract is unique (for example, real property).

stakeholders   Groups, other than the company's shareholders, that are affected by corporate decisions. Stakeholders include employees, customers, creditors, suppliers, and the community in which the corporation operates.

standing to sue   The requirement that an individual must have a sufficient stake in a controversy before he or she can bring a lawsuit. The plaintiff must demonstrate that he or she has been either injured or threatened with injury.

stare decisis   (pronounced *stahr*-ee dih-*si*-sis) A common law doctrine under which judges are obligated to follow the precedents established in prior decisions within their jurisdictions.

Statute of Frauds   A state statute under which certain types of contracts must be in writing to be enforceable.

statute of limitations   A federal or state statute setting the maximum time period during which a certain action can be brought or certain rights enforced.

statute of repose Basically, a statute of limitations that is not dependent on the happening of a cause of action. Statutes of repose generally begin to run at an earlier date and run for a longer period of time than statutes of limitations.

statutory law The body of law enacted by legislative bodies (as opposed to constitutional law, administrative law, or case law).

stock An ownership (equity) interest in a corporation, measured in units of shares.

stock certificate A certificate issued by a corporation evidencing the ownership of a specified number of shares in the corporation.

stock option A right to buy a given number of shares of stock at a set price, usually within a specified time period.

stock warrant A certificate that grants the owner the option to buy a given number of shares of stock, usually within a set time period.

strict liability Liability regardless of fault. In tort law, strict liability may be imposed on defendants in cases involving abnormally dangerous activities, dangerous animals, or defective products.

strike An action undertaken by unionized workers when collective bargaining fails. The workers leave their jobs, refuse to work, and (typically) picket the employer's workplace.

substantive law Law that defines, describes, regulates, and creates legal rights and obligations.

summary jury trial A method of settling disputes in which a trial is held, but the jury's verdict is not binding. The verdict acts only as a guide to both sides in reaching an agreement during the mandatory negotiations that immediately follow.

summons A document informing a defendant that a legal action has been commenced against him or her and that the defendant must appear in court on a certain date to answer the plaintiff's complaint. The document is delivered by a sheriff or any other person so authorized.

superseding cause An intervening force or event that breaks the connection between a wrongful act and an injury to another; in negligence law, a defense to liability.

supremacy clause The provision in Article VI of the U.S. Constitution that provides that the Constitution, laws, and treaties of the United States are "the supreme Law of the Land." Under this clause, state and local laws that directly conflict with federal law will be rendered invalid.

surety A person, such as a cosigner on a note, who agrees to be primarily responsible for the debt of another.

suretyship An express contract in which a third party to a debtor-creditor relationship (the surety) promises to be primarily responsible for the debtor's obligation.

symbolic speech Nonverbal conduct that expresses opinions or thoughts about a subject. Symbolic speech is protected under the First Amendment's guarantee of freedom of speech.

T

taking The government's taking of private property for public use through the power of eminent domain.

tangible employment action A significant change in employment status or benefits, such as occurs when an employee is fired, refused a promotion, or reassigned to a lesser position.

tangible property Property that has physical existence and can be distinguished by the senses of touch, sight, and so on. A car is tangible property.

tariff A tax on imported goods.

tenancy at sufferance A tenancy that arises when a tenant wrongfully continues to occupy leased property after the lease has terminated.

tenancy at will A type of tenancy that either the landlord or the tenant can terminate without notice.

tenancy by the entirety Joint ownership of property by a married couple in which neither spouse can transfer his or her interest in the property without the consent of the other.

tenancy in common Joint ownership of property in which each party owns an undivided interest that passes to his or her heirs at death.

tender An unconditional offer to perform an obligation by a person who is ready, willing, and able to do so.

tender of delivery Under the Uniform Commercial Code, a seller's or lessor's act of placing conforming goods at the disposal of the buyer or lessee and giving the buyer or lessee whatever notification is reasonably necessary to enable the buyer or lessee to take delivery.

third party beneficiary One for whose benefit a promise is made in a contract but who is not a party to the contract.

tippee A person who receives inside information.

title insurance Insurance commonly purchased by a purchaser of real property to protect against loss in the event that the title to the property is not free from liens or superior ownership claims.

tolled The temporary suspension of the running of a prescribed period (such as a statute of limitations). For instance, a statute of limitations may be tolled until the party suffering an injury has discovered it or should have discovered it.

tort A civil wrong not arising from a breach of contract. A breach of a legal duty that proximately causes harm or injury to another.

tortfeasor One who commits a tort.

toxic tort A civil wrong arising from exposure to a toxic substance, such as asbestos, radiation, or hazardous waste.

trade dress The image and overall appearance of a product—for example, the distinctive decor, menu, layout, and style of service of a particular restaurant. Basically, trade dress is subject to the same protection as trademarks.

trade fixture The personal property of a commercial tenant that has been installed or affixed to real property for a business purpose. When the lease ends, the tenant can remove the fixture but must repair any damage to the real property caused by the fixture's removal.

trade libel The publication of false information about another's product, alleging that it is not what its seller claims; also referred to as *slander of quality*.

trademark A distinctive mark, motto, device, or implement that a manufacturer stamps, prints, or otherwise affixes to the goods it produces so that they may be identified on the market and their origins made known. Once a trademark is established (under the common law or through registration), the owner is entitled to its exclusive use.

trade name A term that is used to indicate part or all of a business's name and that is directly related to the business's reputation and goodwill. Trade names are protected under the common law (and under trademark law, if the name is the same as the firm's trademark).

trade secret Information or a process that gives a business an advantage over competitors who do not know the information or process.

transferred intent A legal principle under which a person who intends to harm one individual, but unintentionally harms a different individual, can be liable to the second victim for an intentional tort.

treaty An agreement formed between two or more independent nations.

treble damages Damages that, by statute, are three times the amount of actual damages suffered.

trespass to land The entry onto, above, or below the surface of land owned by another without the owner's permission or legal authorization.

trespass to personal property The unlawful taking or harming of another's personal property; interference with another's right to the exclusive possession of his or her personal property.

triple bottom line The idea that investors and others should consider not only corporate profits, but also the corporation's impact on people and on the planet when assessing the firm. (The triple bottom line is people, planet, and profits.)

tying arrangement A seller's act of conditioning the sale of a product or service on the buyer's agreement to purchase another product or service from the seller.

typosquatting A form of cybersquatting that relies on mistakes, such as typographical errors, made by Internet users when inputting information into a Web browser.

U

unconscionable (pronounced un-*kon*-shun-uh-bul) Describes a contract or clause that is void on the basis of public policy because one party is forced to accept terms that are unfairly burdensome and that unfairly benefit the dominating party.

undisclosed principal A principal whose identity is unknown by a third party, and that party has no knowledge that the agent is acting for a principal at the time the agent and the third party form a contract.

undue influence Persuasion that is less than actual force but more than advice and that induces a person to act according to the will or purposes of the dominating party.

unenforceable contract A valid contract rendered unenforceable by some statute or law.

uniform law A model law created by the National Conference of Commissioners on Uniform State Laws and/or the American Law Institute for the states to consider adopting. If a state adopts the law, it becomes statutory law in that state. Each state has the option of adopting or rejecting all or part of a uniform law.

unilateral contract A contract that results when an offer can be accepted only by the offeree's performance.

unilateral mistake A mistake that occurs when one party to a contract is mistaken as to a material fact.

union shop A firm that requires all workers, once employed, to become union members within a specified period of time as a condition of their continued employment.

unliquidated debt A debt that is uncertain in amount.

unreasonably dangerous product In product liability, a product that is defective to the point of threatening a consumer's health and safety. A product will be considered unreasonably dangerous if it is dangerous beyond the expectation of the ordinary consumer or if a less dangerous alternative was economically feasible for the manufacturer, but the manufacturer failed to produce it.

U.S. trustee A government official who performs certain administrative tasks that a bankruptcy judge would otherwise have to perform.

usury Charging an illegal rate of interest.

utilitarianism An approach to ethical reasoning in which ethically correct behavior is related to an evaluation of the consequences of a given action on those who will be affected by it. In utilitarian reasoning, a "good" decision is one that results in the greatest good for the greatest number of people affected by the decision.

V

validation notice An initial notice to a debtor from a collection agency informing the debtor that he or she has thirty days to challenge the debt and request verification.

valid contract A contract that results when the elements necessary for contract formation (agreement, consideration, contractual capacity, and legality) are present.

variance An exception from zoning rules granted to a property owner by local zoning authorities.

venture capital Financing provided to new business ventures by professional, outside investors—that is, *venture capitalists*, usually groups of wealthy investors and securities firms.

venue (pronounced *ven*-yoo) The geographical district in which an action is tried and from which the jury is selected.

verdict A formal decision made by a jury.

vertically integrated firm A firm that carries out two or more functional phases (manufacturing, distribution, and retailing, for example) of the chain of production.

vertical merger The acquisition by a company at one stage of production of a company at a higher or lower stage of production (as when a company merges with one of its suppliers or retailers).

vertical restraint A restraint of trade created by an agreement between firms at different levels in the manufacturing and distribution process.

vesting The creation of an absolute or unconditional right or power.

vicarious liability Indirect liability imposed on a supervisory party (such as an employer) for the actions of a subordinate (such as an employee) because of the relationship between the two parties.

virus A type of malware that is transmitted between computers and attempts to do deliberate damage to systems and data.

voidable contract A contract that may be legally avoided (canceled) at the option of one of the parties.

void contract A contract having no legal force or binding effect.

voir dire (pronounced *vwahr deehr*) A French phrase meaning, literally, "to see, to speak" that refers to the jury-selection process. In *voir dire*, the attorneys question prospective jurors to determine whether they are biased or have any connection with a party to the action or with a prospective witness.

voluntary consent Knowing and voluntary agreement to the terms of a contract. If voluntary consent is lacking, the contract will be voidable.

voting trust An agreement (trust contract) under which legal title to shares of corporate stock is transferred to a trustee who is authorized by the shareholders to vote the shares on their behalf.

W

waiver An intentional, knowing relinquishment of a legal right.

warranty deed A deed in which the grantor promises that she or he has title to the property conveyed in the deed, that there are no undisclosed encumbrances on the property, and that the grantee will enjoy quiet possession of the property; provides the greatest amount of protection for the grantee.

waste The use of real property in a manner that damages or destroys its value.

watered stock Shares of stock issued by a corporation for which the corporation receives, as payment, less than the fair market value of the shares.

wetlands Areas of land designated by government agencies as protected areas that support wildlife and that therefore cannot be filled in or dredged by private parties.

whistleblowing An employee's disclosure to government authorities, upper-level managers, or the media that the employer is engaged in unsafe or illegal activities.

white-collar crime Nonviolent crime committed by individuals or corporations to obtain a personal or business advantage.

winding up The second of two stages in the termination of a partnership or corporation, in which the firm's assets are collected, liquidated, and distributed, and liabilities are discharged.

workers' compensation law A state statute establishing an administrative procedure for compensating workers for injuries that arise out of, or in the course of, their employment, regardless of fault. Instead of suing the employer, an injured worker files a claim with the state agency or board that administers local workers' compensation claims.

workout agreement A formal contract between a debtor and his or her creditors in which the parties agree to negotiate a payment plan for the amount due on the loan instead of proceeding to foreclosure.

worm A type of malware that is designed to copy itself from one computer to another without human interaction. A worm can copy itself automatically and can replicate in great volume and with great speed.

writ of attachment A court's order, prior to a trial to collect a debt, directing the sheriff or other officer to seize nonexempt property of the debtor. If the creditor prevails at trial, the seized property can be sold to satisfy the judgment.

writ of *certiorari* (pronounced sur-shee-uh-*rah*-ree) A writ from a higher court asking the lower court for the record of the case for review.

writ of execution A court's order, after a judgment has been entered against the debtor, directing the sheriff to seize (levy) and sell any of the debtor's nonexempt real or personal property. The proceeds of the sale are used to pay off the judgment, accrued interest, and costs of the sale. Any surplus is paid to the debtor.

wrongful discharge An employer's termination of an employee's employment in violation of the law or an employment contract.

Z

zoning laws Rules and regulations that collectively manage the development and use of land.

Table of Cases

Following is a list of all the cases mentioned in this text, including those within the footnotes, features, and case problems. Any case that was an excerpted case for a chapter is given special emphasis by having its title **boldfaced**.

Index